Also by Andrew Burstein

The Original Knickerbocker:
The Life of Washington Irving

Jefferson's Secrets:
Death and Desire at Monticello

The Passions of Andrew Jackson

Letters from the Head and Heart:
Writings of Thomas Jefferson

America's Jubilee: How in 1826 a Generation
Remembered Fifty Years of Independence

Sentimental Democracy:
The Evolution of America's Romantic Self-Image

The Inner Jefferson:
Portrait of a Grieving Optimist

Also by Nancy Isenberg

Fallen Founder: The Life of Aaron Burr

Sex and Citizenship in Antebellum America

Co-edited by Nancy Isenberg and Andrew Burstein

Mortal Remains: Death in Early America

MADISON

and

JEFFERSON

MADISON

and

JEFFERSON

ANDREW BURSTEIN

AND NANCY ISENBERG

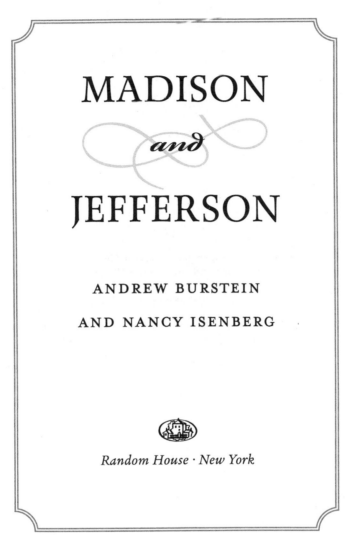

Random House · New York

Published in the United States by Random House, an imprint of The Random House
Publishing Group, a division of Random House, Inc., New York.

RANDOM HOUSE and colophon are registered trademarks of Random House, Inc.

ISBN 978-1-4000-6728-2

Printed in the United States of America

Book design by Virginia Norey

To Jeannie. To David.
And to all who appreciate the true complexity of the past.

There is very little difference in that superstition which leads us to believe in what the world calls "great men" and in that which leads us to believe in witches and conjurors.

—DR. BENJAMIN RUSH TO JOHN ADAMS, 1808

Contents

SIGNS OF A RESTLESS FUTURE

LEGACY

Preface

THOMAS JEFFERSON (1743–1826) AND JAMES MADISON (1751–1836) were country gentlemen who practiced hardball politics in a time of intolerance. As agents of the American Enlightenment, they took premeditated action to overturn ingrained ideas they saw as insidious and unrepublican. As keen political operatives, they fought to humble some equally determined individuals whom they considered misguided or simply threatening. Like all politicians, Madison and Jefferson walked a fine line in condemning corruption while exercising power. They risked their personal prestige because they saw imminent danger. They were watchful. They were guarded. Their times did not allow for complacency.

We need a better understanding than we currently possess of the strong-willed politicians who helped mold the United States. Our modern leaders quote the founders in magnificent tones, hoping to obtain insights into their minds. But they know them mainly as indefatigable characters in an oft-told and problematic story—they tend to see the founders as they were on their best days. The discipline of history exists to reexamine time-honored treatments of people and events, and to separate myth from reality. Historians are concerned, above all, with accuracy in interpretation. As researchers, they are expected to navigate competing explanations and sort out ideological biases. That is how this book came about.

Previous biographers are not in all ways to blame for common effusions and misconceptions. Present beliefs about the early years of the American republic derive to a considerable extent from falsehoods the participants themselves planted, their filial offspring nurtured, and commemorative ritual compounded. Each generation gets to weigh in anew.

One might expect this book to be titled *Jefferson and Madison* rather than *Madison and Jefferson*. Its closest relative, *Jefferson and Madison: The Great*

Collaboration (1950), by Adrienne Koch, remains a serviceable piece of scholarship. The ever-quotable author of the Declaration of Independence took precedence in Koch's title for the same reason that a beautiful monument was erected to his memory in the Tidal Basin of Washington, D.C., in 1943. Madison, the dry, distant "Father of the Constitution," generated little posthumous sentiment.

Textbooks highlight the "Age of Jefferson." Madison's high point as a public figure is generally associated with the one banner year of 1787, when the Constitutional Convention met; his low point was an unheroic flight from the President's House during the British invasion of 1814. His manner and moods remain obscure, his long congressional career understudied. What could be a better invitation to learn more?

Our title is not meant to be cute or ironic. It is not to degrade Jefferson as a force in politics—not one iota—but rather to suggest that it is time to reevaluate their relationship and their distinct individual contributions. Popular historians have done precious little with Madison. And while political scientists have boiled him down to his noteworthy contributions to *The Federalist Papers,* the historians who place him within the larger context of party formation have presented Madison as a man unaffected by an emotional life, a man eclipsed by the more magnetic, more affecting Jefferson.

People have long been tempted to compare the third and fourth presidents. In 1824 an itinerant bookseller called on the Virginia neighbors. Jefferson was a man of "more imagination and passion," he said; Madison, "more natural, candid and profound." What exactly does this distinction mean? Did Madison lack imagination and passion? Was Jefferson less profound? The bookseller had spent too little time with his potential customers to know them at all well, and he was speaking in relative terms anyway.[1]

As a persuasive stylist, Jefferson described the idea of America in ways that students of history have long admired. Investing his words with lyrical power, he indulged often in a sentimental idiom. So yes, he possessed imagination and passion. Madison had a literary faculty too, and a rich wit. But he succeeded foremost as a deliberative, direct, and usually (though not always) tactful legislator. Stepping before the public, he was not concerned with style in the way Jefferson was. Madison preferred to supply information that enlivened an intellectual atmosphere. So yes, he was both candid and profound.

Even though Madison was unsentimental, he was every bit as intense as his more inspirational friend. Those who write about the American founding are dead wrong when they make Madison stiff and stilted. And some historians have rendered Jefferson so placid and elegant as to deprive him of spontaneous moments. Men and women who observed them at their most relaxed, in close quarters, remarked that Madison's facility for conversational humor sometimes led him to make Jefferson the butt of a joke, and Jefferson to laugh so well that he nearly cried. The chapter headings alone instruct the reader that ours is a book about the ruthlessness of politics, aimed at demonstrating what is missing from the genre of Revolutionary heroics. Yet we do not lose sight of the power of personality, without which the annals of time would be cold, linear histories featuring absurdly rational actors.

The founders did not resist when the national creation story was brilliantly painted and sculpted in marble and their personal exploits made into something nobler than they were. We should not expect them to have done otherwise. The truth, however, is that Madison, Jefferson, and their peers loathed as well as they loved. As they chased self-serving objectives, they got bogged down in banking arrangements and caught up in obstacles associated with seductive land deals. To a far greater extent than most realize, their public lives were conditioned by matters of personal health and vital impulses not usually part of the historical record. The giants of politics past immersed themselves in mundane matters that, taken together, measured social status. They juggled responsibilities and were dismayed by unexpected outcomes in many areas of their lives.

To celebrate blindly those who were long ago given poetic protection as "founding fathers," and who remain in the national spotlight today as *our* protectors, invites massive self-deception. In this book we do not denigrate, but historicize, the patriotic impulse. We do all we can to reconstitute the gritty world in which Madison and Jefferson operated. We guide the reader through nuances in eighteenth-century American English—a foreign language in many respects—to help make better historical sense of the emotional range within individual experience. Compared to our own time, the eighteenth and nineteenth centuries were primal and suggestible when it came to people's expectations from life. Yet they were decidedly flamboyant times too, with more ill feeling than studied consensus. This alien culture, which eventually became ours, is more interesting when we strip away the loving haze.

Let us set aside for a moment America's early heroes and speak about the materials of history. It was not a comprehensive mind that brought forth the republic's critical texts. It was, to a large degree, the "tribal" identities of men like Madison and Jefferson, who were Virginians first and keenly aware of the clannish objections that one part of the continent had to the positions and attitudes of another. Though we associate their rich organizing talents with their commanding national legacies, they did nothing without first asking, *How will this play in Virginia?*

If this book has one overriding purpose, it is to bring back overlooked elements in a panicky political culture that dangerously provoked as often as it positively motivated Madison and Jefferson and those who fell into their circle. What reassurance Madison and Jefferson obtained, as they fought for what they believed in, derived in a very real way from the trust they eventually came to lodge in each other. Their partnership was one of the few constants either of them knew over his long political life. Yet it is wrong to suppose that they thought alike, as we will show at length.

They were insatiable readers. They both read extensively in the law. But they were not powerful courtroom pleaders of the sort that swayed juries with oratorical flourishes. That was their close acquaintance and formidable opponent Patrick Henry. Madison never argued a case in court, and Jefferson defended his clients' interests with minimum verbiage. They were concerned with the law in bookish ways; it helped them think of how to improve civil society. This may sound uninviting at first, but their common immersion in dry treatises sheds light on their popular political agendas and cannot be divorced from a history of their long collaboration. If we are to be thorough, we must recover the unromantic elements that produced moments of real excitement.

For a six-foot-two-and-a-half-inch-tall man, Jefferson was not particularly imposing. His eyes were small, his skin tone fair. A delicate pallor shed about him. In later years his grandson remarked on how the sun caused his face to peel. His manner was almost retiring. Though his voice did not carry, he paid attention to acoustic power in all he wrote. He claimed he did not wish to draw attention to himself. He obviously failed in this.

Madison is a bit harder to sum up. Known principally as a political *thinker,* he was surprisingly multifaceted, and as a political *actor* contentious without being divisive. Even so, he was always thought of as "Little Madison" and, to his worst detractors when he was president, "Little Jemmy." The consensus is that he stood about five foot four; his private secretary insisted, years after his death, that he was five foot six. His voice was never described as impressive nor his style as flashy, yet he was frequently (perhaps out of politeness?) praised for his able oratory. He might have been the sort to get lost in a crowd, but he weighed in on every public issue that mattered to Americans for more than half a century. And no one ignored what he had to say.

Both men were excellent dinner-table companions, affable and unhurried. This was the one social function they were bred for and excelled at. The greatest difference between them lay in their approaches to political disputation: Madison thrived in politicized settings of which Jefferson despaired. As the more easily irritated, Jefferson held a deep-seated desire to impose his will and crush his political enemies. Madison's opinions were well defined and forcefully drawn, and he could certainly exhibit cold-heartedness; but he did not carry around the same degree of spite or the same need for historical vindication.

Neither Madison nor Jefferson was truly a "man of the people," in spite of their press. Jefferson, shy by nature, idealized yeoman farmers more than he identified with their grubby lives; the physically unimposing Madison closely observed people and manners, though he was not warm or hearty with strangers. In political councils, he was prepared for anything; no one who has served in Congress can claim to have shown greater determination to shape policy than James Madison. We know more about Jefferson's doggedness, but Madison was no less assertive.

They grew up on plantations in the Virginia countryside as privileged eldest sons. Their country seats, Madison's Montpelier in Orange County and Jefferson's Monticello, to the southwest, in Albemarle County, are about twenty-five miles apart. The world they shared was that of the Piedmont gentry. Jefferson enjoyed his book-lined, mountaintop retreat, which he started building in his twenties and which, for most of his adult life, was a domeless, and simpler, version of what exists today. Jefferson was only fourteen when he came into his patrimony upon the death of his pioneering father; his mother died in 1776.

Except for when he traveled, or sat in legislative bodies in Virginia and Philadelphia, Madison lived with his parents at the mansion built in 1731, twenty years before he was born. Until his death in 1801, Madison's father subsidized his son's education and political career. It is important to point out that although James Madison, Jr., was the eldest son, his political inclination led him to cede day-to-day management of the family estate to his brother Ambrose, four years younger; the politician became squire of

Montpelier as a result of Ambrose's unexpected death in 1793. And it is rarely noted that Eleanor (Nelly) Conway Madison, Madison's mother, was born the same year as George Washington and lived ninety-seven years, until 1829, twelve years *after* her famous son had retired from the presidency. She bore ten children, only three of whom survived her.

Reared for leadership, Madison and Jefferson made connections with similarly inspired scholars at home and abroad. Jefferson remained in Virginia for higher education, but Madison went north to Princeton, where he became comfortable in the culture of the middle colonies. Jefferson escaped Virginia's provincialism by going to France; Madison did not travel abroad but spent many years in Philadelphia and even sought to buy land in New York State.

Theirs was a time when print culture was dominant, when ostensibly personal letters were widely reprinted for the "news" they contained, when weeks and even months passed before information could be acted upon. Political gossip traveled across a rutted, bumpy, and often muddy landscape, or aboard unsteady sailing ships; interior communities struggled to keep pace with the more active and concentrated populations of America's commercial ports. Life revolved around slow, arduous, meaningful communications.

The real story of Madison and Jefferson and their political ascendancy comes alive in this rich cultural terrain. Jefferson, the elder of the pair, took the first step, producing two Revolutionary texts: *A Summary View of the Rights of British America* (1774) and, of course, the Declaration of Independence (1776). Combined, these writings addressed the nature of society and the psychological poverty of British colonialism. He put his political imagination to the test, arriving at a lively and quotable manner of presentation as he made the embrace of liberty a daring proposition. Less well known is his pique: severe and judgmental in private communications, Jefferson spoke his mind to his friends but refused to debate his adversaries in public.

Madison's career in national politics effectively began in 1780. From that year forward, he was known among his peers for a bold legislative agenda. In the 1790s he contributed incisive political pieces to the newspapers—often prompted by Jefferson. Jefferson *appeared* withdrawn, but allies inside Virginia and beyond its borders rarely misunderstood his and Madison's policy preferences.

In constitutional matters, Jefferson opposed a strong executive; yet he became one. He served in executive positions for most of his political career: as Virginia governor, as George Washington's secretary of state, as John Adams's vice president, and as a two-term president. He was in the Continental Congress and Confederation Congress for relatively short periods and, though respected for his mind, voiced few opinions while there. At the Constitutional Convention, Madison worked to establish a strong executive, yet he was a relatively cautious president (though not a weak one, as some have said) who watched as a more aggressive Congress extended its influence. He was a legislator for longer than he was an executive, a leader both in Virginia and in national bodies.

From the above, the story of Madison and Jefferson would appear to be as much about unintended consequences as about straightforward political ambition. As is often true in American politics, not everything is what it seems.

We have written this book to establish what sustained a fifty-year-long personal bond that guided the course of American history. It turns out that beyond the relatively superficial differences outlined above, the Madison-Jefferson relationship was not always as smooth and effortless as history (and the actors themselves) want us to believe. Remarkably, after the Constitutional Convention, Jefferson sought to undermine the ratification process—to Madison's severe embarrassment.

We have to question familiar assumptions if we are to achieve greater clarity in our appreciation of the past. Sometimes we find that what history calls triumphs were, in fact, less than billed. Madison was not particularly successful at the Constitutional Convention, certainly not in the way Americans have been taught and certainly not enough to warrant the title "Father of the Constitution." Nor did *The Federalist Papers* that he collaborated on with Alexander Hamilton and John Jay carry the weight at the state ratifying conventions that our collective memory imagines. Their real value applies to a later time. Jefferson's pseudo-scientific racism, iconoclastic statements about religious practices in America, and other philosophical musings were criticized as part of a larger political game—scare tactics, partisan politics—and did not always mean that the driving moral concerns of his critics were joined to practical solutions.

During much of his public career, Jefferson was steeped in bitter and lasting controversies created by his sometimes careless pen. As the less closely studied of the two, Madison has been grossly oversimplified as a brainy man whose vivacious wife ran his social schedule. Perhaps the most astonishing of ignored facts is Madison's orchestration of Jefferson's career. Jefferson might otherwise have retired from public service after the Revolution, in 1782, and again in 1789, after his five years as a diplomat in France. Madison was the driving force behind Jefferson's reemergence in 1796, when Jefferson was urging Madison, then at the height of his congressional career, to seek the presidency. Rejecting the idea, Madison lured Jefferson away from the quiet of his mountaintop, where he was experimenting with new farming measures, and set him up to battle John Adams. Madison, in short, was Jefferson's campaign manager, long before the term was coined.

It has become customary to refer to Madison as Jefferson's "faithful lieutenant," and at times he certainly was that. But we should remember that the lieutenancy was constructed in the early years of the republic by a politically charged press. Madison was Jefferson's secretary of state and successor; to those of their contemporaries who sought a simple calculus, the dutiful lieutenant sounded right—a convenient shorthand—whether or not it properly described their association. Most of what they said to each other remained between themselves, though we have deduced that Madison periodically exercised veto power over Jefferson's policy decisions.

It has been too easy for history to tag Madison as "modest." This was the very word Jefferson used to explain why Madison did not come to the fore in debate during his first three years on the political stage in Virginia, 1776–79, before he and Jefferson became close. To extrapolate from this statement and define Madison's character as modest is dangerous: "modesty" retrospectively helped to explain, for example, why he was a bachelor until he was past forty. By the same token, contemporaries who identified with the Democratic-Republican Party associated Jefferson's soft, almost feminine voice with his much vaunted harmony-seeking political style— a dubious designation, to say the least.

All historians are answerable for their shortcomings. Even the best resort to synecdoche: they seize on one attribute of an individual's behavior and enlarge it to explain, in the broadest terms, his or her impulses. In the interest of a flowing narrative, much conscientious history is sacrificed. It happens often. The more intensively one researches, the hardier a book's organizing themes are, and the easier it is to become attached to the book's trajectory. For this reason, the research process is both a gold mine and a land mine. Contentment is the researcher's enemy. All of us know what the stakes are when we attempt to overturn received wisdom. We know that readers will judge how scrupulous we have been.

Of the coauthors, Andrew Burstein has previously concentrated on Jefferson as a citizen of the republic of letters, a political writer, and an ex-president contemplating his own mortality. Nancy Isenberg has tackled Jefferson's political instincts insofar as they explain the troubled relationship he had as president with his controversial first-term vice president, Aaron Burr. In refocusing on the founding era, our purpose is not to privilege Madison but merely to restore balance where the historical record is skewed.

Perhaps the bookseller was on to something when he called Madison "more profound," though genius, especially political genius, cannot be defined in rational terms. If Jefferson occasionally used language as camouflage, he charged his words with feeling. That is why his popular appeal is unmatched by any in his time. Madison was appreciated for his candor, but candor usually comes in second place behind imagination in the business of constructing a national memory.

This is a history of two men operating in a world whose cultural and intellectual boundaries Americans are still trying to draw accurately. In that world, the pursuit of happiness was a matter of grave uncertainty. Although it is hard to find agreement among scholars, all are likely to grant that together Madison and Jefferson introduced a mode of persuasion that changed political discourse and moved the country in directions it probably would not otherwise have gone. If history must be a story, then that is the story we tell in this book.

Chronology

1743 April 13	Thomas Jefferson born at Shadwell (Albemarle County), Virginia
1751 March 16	James Madison, Jr., born on the plantation of his maternal relations, raised at Montpelier (Orange County), Virginia
1760–62	Jefferson attends the College of William and Mary
1769–72	Madison attends the College of New Jersey (Princeton)
1772 January	Jefferson marries the widow Martha (Patty) Wayles Skelton
1774 July	Jefferson writes *A Summary View of the Rights of British America*
1774 August	First Virginia Convention meets in Williamsburg
1774 September	First Continental Congress meets in Philadelphia
1775 March	Second Virginia Convention meets; Patrick Henry delivers "Give me liberty" speech; Jefferson elected to the Second Continental Congress
1775 April	Battles of Lexington and Concord
1775 May	Second Continental Congress holds opening meeting
1775 July	Third Virginia Convention establishes Committee of Safety
1776 May	Madison joins Virginia Convention, which instructs its delegation in Philadelphia to move for independence
1776 June	Virginia Declaration of Rights, George Mason its principal author; Richard Henry Lee moves for independence; Jefferson assigned responsibility for drafting Declaration of Independence

1776 October	Madison and Jefferson meet for the first time
1777	Reverend James Madison becomes president of William and Mary
1778	Madison boards with Reverend Madison, as he serves on Governor Patrick Henry's Council of Advisors; Jefferson in Williamsburg during Assembly sessions
1779 June	Jefferson elected governor of Virginia; Madison remains on Council of Advisors
1780 March	Madison enters Congress (Philadelphia)
1781 January	Benedict Arnold invades Virginia, marches on Richmond
1781 June	Jefferson's governorship ends, as British attempt his capture
1781 October	Battle of Yorktown
1782 September	Patty Jefferson dies
1782 December	Believing he is heading to Europe as a peace negotiator, Jefferson arrives in Philadelphia and lodges with Madison, who is courting young "Kitty" Floyd
1783 April	Jefferson returns to Virginia
1783 October	Jefferson travels north again, joining Congress (which has moved to Annapolis), as Madison completes his term
1783 December	Madison leaves Philadelphia for the first time in more than three years, returns to Montpelier
1784 April	Madison elected to Virginia House of Delegates
1784 July	Jefferson sails for France (from Boston)
1785 May	First, limited printing of *Notes on Virginia*
1786 September	Madison attends Annapolis Convention
1787 January	Shays's Rebellion takes place in western Massachusetts
1787 May	Madison attends Constitutional Convention in Philadelphia
1788 June	Madison attends Virginia Ratifying Convention
1789 April	Madison defeats Monroe to win a seat in the first Congress of the United States; inauguration of George Washington
1789 July	French Revolution begins
1789 October	Jefferson departs France for home

1790 January	Hamilton's *Report on Public Credit* proposes assumption of state debts, infuriating Madison
1790 March	Jefferson arrives in New York, assumes duties as secretary of state
1791	First signs of coming revolution in St. Domingue (Haiti)
1791 May	Madison tells Jefferson he considers the national bank conclusive proof of Hamilton's usurpation of power
1791 May–June	Madison and Jefferson tour New York and western New England
1791 October	Philip Freneau's *National Gazette* begins operation
1792 April	Madison writes scathing article, "The Union: Who Are Its Real Friends?"
1792 May	Hamilton writes Virginian Edward Carrington, offering an interpretation of Madison's defection and Jefferson's lust for power
1792 July	Hamilton reopens newspaper attacks aimed principally at Jefferson
1792 September	Madison authors "A Candid State of Parties"
1793 April	America learns England and France are at war; Genet arrives in the United States
1793 June	Hamilton begins publishing "Pacificus" letters
1793 August	Madison responds with his first "Helvidius" letter
1794 January	Jefferson resigns from cabinet and retires to Monticello
1794 September	Madison marries the widow Dolley Payne Todd; Hamilton and Washington overreact to Whiskey Rebellion
1795 June	Senate approves Jay Treaty
1795 August	Edmund Randolph resigns from cabinet, authors self-vindication
1796 April	Madison gives up protesting House exclusion from treaty-making, and Jay Treaty is implemented
1797 March	John Adams inaugurated as second president, Jefferson becomes vice president
1797 May	Jefferson's Mazzei letter of April 1796 translated and published, angering Washington
1798 April	News of XYZ Affair widely disseminated, war fever develops

1798 July	Alien and Sedition Acts passed
1798 September	Jefferson covertly authors Kentucky Resolutions
1798 December	Madison's Virginia Resolutions approved by state assembly
1799 December	Washington dies
1800 September	Gabriel's Rebellion (in vicinity of Richmond) foiled
1800 December	Jefferson and Aaron Burr tied, election moved to House of Representatives
1801 February	James Madison, Sr., dies
1801 March	Jefferson inaugurated as third president
1802 September	Callender publishes articles linking Jefferson and Sally Hemings
1803	Louisiana Purchase
1804 April	Death of Maria Jefferson Eppes
1804 May	Lewis and Clark expedition gets under way (from St. Louis)
1804 July	Burr kills Hamilton in duel
1804	Jefferson easily reelected, George Clinton of New York as vice president
1805 March	Impeachment trial of Justice Samuel Chase ends in acquittal
1807 May	Treason trial of Aaron Burr begins in Richmond
1807 June	*Chesapeake* incident, Royal Navy fires on U.S. ship near Norfolk
1807 December	Embargo approved by Congress
1808 January	Further importation of slaves prohibited by U.S. Constitution
1809 March	Madison inaugurated as fourth president
1810 October	West Florida throws off Spanish rule, is annexed to United States
1811 April	Madison prods Secretary of State Robert Smith to resign
1812 June	Congress declares war on Great Britain
1812 Fall	Madison reelected, defeating DeWitt Clinton
1813	United States achieves naval supremacy on Great Lakes
1814 August	British burn government buildings in Washington, D.C.

1814 September	Madison proclaims British actions "deliberate disregard of the principles of humanity"
1814 December	Treaty of Ghent signed, ending War of 1812
1815 January	Battle of New Orleans
1817 March	James Monroe inaugurated as fifth president; Madison retires to Montpelier
1820	Missouri Compromise
1821	Madison drafts parable based on Missouri question, "Jonathan Bull and Mary Bull" (not published until 1835)
1824 November	Lafayette visits with Madison and Jefferson
1826 July 4	Jefferson and John Adams die
1829 February	Nelly Conway Madison (mother of president) dies at age ninety-seven
1829 March	Andrew Jackson becomes president
1829 December	Madison and Monroe attend Virginia Constitutional Convention
1831 July 4	Monroe dies
1831–32	Nullification controversy
1836 June 28	Madison dies

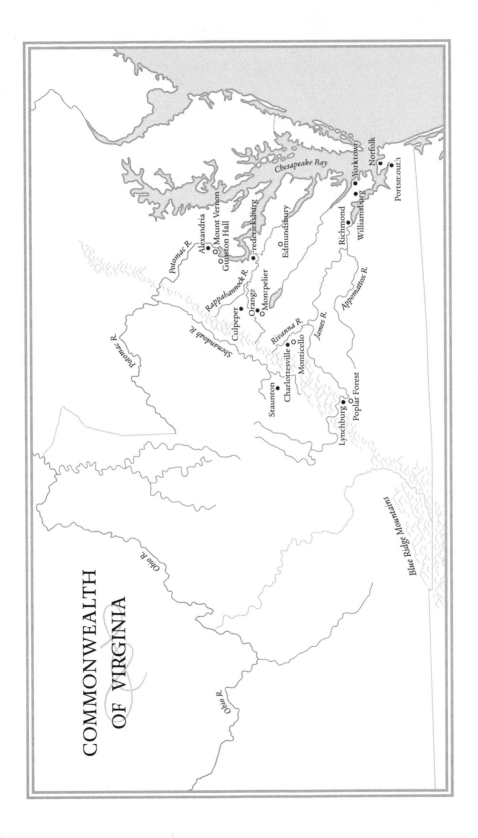

COMMONWEALTH
OF VIRGINIA

Ohio R.

Potomac R.

Potomac R.

Rappahannock R.

Shenandoah R.

Alexandria
Mount Vernon
Gunston Hall
Fredericksburg
Edmundsbury

Culpeper
Orange
Montpelier

Rivanna R.
Charlottesville
Monticello

Staunton

Lynchburg
Poplar Forest

James R.

Appomattox R.

Richmond

Williamsburg
Yorktown
Norfolk
Portsmouth

Chesapeake Bay

Blue Ridge Mountains

Ohio R.

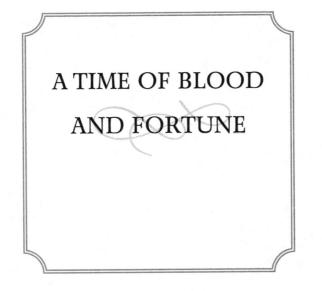

A TIME OF BLOOD
AND FORTUNE

The Virginians
1774–1776

*This morning I received a letter from Mr. Maddison who is a member
of the Virginia Convention, informing me of the declaration
of Independency made by that body.*

—FROM THE MEMORANDUM BOOK OF
PHILADELPHIAN WILLIAM BRADFORD, CA. MAY 21, 1776

*You'l have seen your Instructions to propose Independance and our resolutions
to form a Government . . . The Political Cooks are busy in preparing the dish.*

—EDMUND PENDLETON, IN VIRGINIA, TO THOMAS JEFFERSON,
IN PHILADELPHIA, MAY 24, 1776

IN MAY 1776, AT THE AGE OF TWENTY-FIVE, THE SLIGHTLY FORMED
James Madison, Jr., was party to a critical conversation taking place among
Virginia's leaders in the colonial capital of Williamsburg. Across the middle colonies, some still believed that negotiation with Great Britain could
have its desired effect. But in Virginia active debate had already ended, and
a formal break was to take place. Instructions to that effect were being forwarded to the Virginia delegation at the Second Continental Congress in
Philadelphia—a precise directive from the "Political Cooks" in Virginia.
Without this, thirty-three-year-old Thomas Jefferson would have had priorities other than writing the Declaration of Independence. And that is
where we begin.

Before there was a United States of America, its colonists belonged to
separate competing units within a sprawling empire. Cultures were as diverse as currencies were dissimilar. For most of its existence, Virginia cared

more about its own vital interests, and securing its own expanse, than it cared about forging a common continental bond. The Old Dominion, in total square miles, was the largest of the thirteen colonies. This fact bred satisfaction among its landed elite and a distinctive sensibility as well. Mannered country gentlemen oversaw broad estates that enjoyed commanding views. They had names such as Lee, Randolph, Carter, Harrison, Taylor, and Byrd. They counted their herds, their hogsheads of tobacco, their silver, and the luxuries of the dining table. They calculated provisions for the slave families who shared their land but little else. They sat for portraits; they rode in coaches.

The Virginians were substantially different in temperament from New England's elite. The latter, it was said, were solemn, critical, and intense, trained for the bustle of business. Harsh seasons and a rocky coastline conditioned them. Along with good, plain common sense, the northern environment appeared to have produced a severity of manners and a tautness of disposition that stood in contrast to southerners' relative laxness and fondness for amusement. One can debate whether these traits—exuberance and extravagance versus cunning and conceit—were any better than stereotypes. Nevertheless they prevailed in the literature for quite some time and adhered most to those who guided the political direction of the country.[1]

Only a series of extraordinary events could induce the otherwise divergent colonies to imagine a cooperative future. Once provoked, the states found common ground and eventually united. Before they could, however, the constituent parts of British America had to acknowledge on some level the Virginians' sense of their own importance—their special place on the continent.

We all know that North and South, fourscore and five years after celebrating their initial union, entered into a ruinous civil war. While its origins are debated by scholars, its general contours are well established. Historical memory is hazier as we retreat in time and ask what triggered the French and Indian War, and why it matters. That war eventually extended into Canada and established collective purposes among otherwise disobliging colonies. Hostilities, begun in 1753, were not settled until the French were expelled from all of North America ten years later.

The war was instigated by Virginia. And not just by Virginia, but in a very real way by twenty-one-year-old Major George Washington, at the behest of Virginia's lieutenant governor, Robert Dinwiddie, an intense man with an intense desire to protect and expand the colony's frontier settlements. In November 1753 Washington journeyed west and declared to an encroaching French force that the Ohio Country belonged to Virginia. The British government did not in fact know whether the Ohio Valley lay within Virginia's boundaries; but Dinwiddie forged ahead regardless, unconcerned with the claims of other colonies and aware that he had the support of his colony's leading men. To put it simply, Virginians thought big. Their vast land stood for autonomy and permanence.[2]

If any of the Virginians doubted the propriety of what they wished for, the French and Indian War erased that uncertainty. The conflict aroused a kind of pathos among colonial Americans that, before mid-century, they had experienced only in sermonic messages and declared days of fast. The long and barbarous war created a more powerful literature and a more heated vocabulary of human atrocity. Up to now dramatic poetry had tended to feature individual soldiers' cruelty; now images of a "bleeding country"—stark depictions of communal suffering and redemptive courage—predominated. The political propagandists of the 1770s would paint pictures of an abused and terrorized people striving for justice, happiness, and peace of mind. An enlarged discourse of responsibility drew a deep and dark distinction between heroic values and an unsympathetic and merciless enemy.[3]

In the prelude to the Revolution, two decades after Major Washington's first foray to the west, Virginia had a very different royal governor in Lord Dunmore, who was, compared to the engaging Dinwiddie, hard, spiteful, and suspicious. Patriot planters who met to decide the future of the country felt pressure coming from multiple directions, and yet they were giving up none of their claims to western territory. By 1775 Virginia was part of a defensive union—what was called, for a time, the United Colonies. And George Washington, no longer the young, uncertain emissary of a royal appointee, was a general, the persevering commander of a rebel armed force, and the confident owner of some twenty thousand acres of quite valuable land in western Virginia, awarded to him by Dinwiddie for his service in the 1750s.[4]

Washington took a risk when he agreed to lead the Continental Army. He was doubtful about his inexperienced junior officers and utterly shocked by the lack of discipline among their disrespectful troops. Vulnerable to attack, the newly designated United States of America learned in 1776, one year after he assumed his command, that it was unlikely to win independence from England without considerable aid from the former French enemy. In short, the country frantically struggled to sustain itself as it was striving to establish a collective identity.

Enter James Madison, Jr., and Thomas Jefferson. Theirs were prominent but not heralded names in Virginia—not yet. They are best described as members of the steering committee that directed the patriot effort in 1775–76. Madison made his contributions from Williamsburg, Virginia, and Jefferson made his from Congress in Philadelphia. Both were in the thick of things, but neither had any expectation of increased visibility after completing his present duties.

Their lives were shaped by the Revolution. Their life *visions* were shaped by it too. Yet the Revolutionary experience was not a uniform one across the United Colonies. To write about Madison and Jefferson, we must first see the American Revolution through the eyes of their people, the Virginians.

But we cannot stop there. For the next half-century or more, both in and out of government, Madison and Jefferson devoted themselves to the elusive ideal of a nation possessed of multiple cultures—multiple power centers—and still, somehow, a working Union. Wherever they were employed, they never set aside their provincial identities for long. Even in Williamsburg, on the Atlantic side of their state, they retained their local prejudice in favor of the river-fed interior or Piedmont section. The pair were not simply Virginians; they were Virginians of a particular breed.

"The Ablest Man in Debate"

The year America declared its independence from Great Britain was the year in which James Madison and Thomas Jefferson met. There is anecdotal evidence that as a student, Madison once watched Jefferson argue a court case, but they were never introduced.[5] Neither could have foreseen how essential the other would become to his public career and individual legacy. At that time, in fact, the relationship each had with Edmund Pendleton was far more important than the relationship these two future allies had with each other.

Pendleton should not be lost to history. He was Virginia's preeminent politician at the time of independence, a moderating voice amid turbulence, known for his decisiveness and praised for his diligence. Fifty-five years old in 1776, he was instrumental in Virginia's declaring *its* independence from Great Britain. It was Pendleton who gave Jefferson advance warning that the leaders of the colony were hammering out a text, urging Congress to terminate the relationship with Britain.

Unlike Madison and Jefferson, Pendleton was one of the few leaders not born to wealth. Because his father died before he was born, and his mother, caring for six older children, bore two more by a second husband, Edmund received little attention as a child. First apprenticed to a tailor, he knew nothing of the classics—that measure of wisdom and key to social respect that the children of privilege acquired from their private tutors. But he had a facility for the law, and over the years this studious "son of nobody" acquired a reputation for ethical practice. As an attorney, he wrote up deeds for land purchases. Among his many clients over the years, George Washington and James Madison, Sr., regularly engaged his services.

Beginning in 1745, Edmund Pendleton was one of a small number of attorneys authorized to bring cases before Virginia's most prestigious tribunal, the General Court. From within his legal circle would emerge the leaders of the Revolutionary resistance. As he invested in land—the path to upward mobility since the colony's founding—he became their advocate on more than one front. Though he was not born to privilege, Pendleton's personal genealogy still helped him along. He came into the world the same year as James Madison, Sr., and was the grandson of a seventeenth-century settler, James Taylor, by his second wife. The elder Madison was the great-grandson of the same Taylor, by his first wife.

And so the "son of nobody" became a member of the Virginia House of Burgesses in 1752. It was an association of men united by their strong family and social networks—and not inconsequentially, by their common indebtedness to British merchants—who tended to get on well with one another and with royal appointees as well. Pendleton remained in that body up to its dissolution at the time of the Revolution and expressed opposition to the imposition of taxes even before outspoken younger patriots such as Patrick Henry did. As much a lover of liberty as any of the more memorable founders, Pendleton was no firebrand, no troublemaker. Rather, he was a detail man, cautious, deliberative. Elected as a delegate to the First Continental Congress in 1774, he was joined by George Washington, Patrick Henry, and four others. To take the phrase "cooler heads prevailed" and apply it to Virginia on the eve of the Revolution, his was that cooler head.

The worst one could say of Pendleton he said of himself: that he was a substandard writer. But he had an encyclopedic knowledge of the law and was an easy man for a younger political aspirant to approach. In his 1821 autobiography, Jefferson recalled Pendleton in glowing terms: "one of the most virtuous & benevolent of men, the kindest friend." Both in the General Court and in the House of Burgesses, he had symbolized competency for the young lawyer from Albemarle. He was, Jefferson acknowledged, "the ablest man in debate I ever met with." Madison too completely trusted in his integrity.[6]

Ordinarily, revolutions are long in brewing. Not so America's. Though joint operations of British regulars and colonial American fighters had brought victory in the French and Indian War, the decade 1765–75 proved the undoing of their transatlantic bond. Britain had debts after the war, and Americans were told they had to pay their fair share. No American sat in any governing body in Britain, yet Parliament claimed it could tax the colonies without their consent. The colonists did not like being dictated to from across the sea. They especially resented the loss of local autonomy.

The Stamp Act of 1765 was the opening salvo and provoked everything from angry taunts to street theater. All paper documents across the colonies (newspapers, pamphlets, contracts, and licenses) were to be imprinted with a special stamp, which had to be paid for in hard currency. As a new member of Virginia's House of Burgesses, Patrick Henry introduced a series of resolutions, among which was one insisting that people could be taxed only by their elected representatives. Northern newspapers carried the Virginia Resolves, and Henry acquired a wide reputation. The crisis over taxation was everybody's problem, not a single colony's.

Although the hated Stamp Act was repealed in 1766, Parliament did not retreat. It passed the Declaratory Act, defending its power to impose laws on the colonies "in all cases whatsoever." New taxes followed, including one on tea, the Americans' favorite drink. The drama enlarged in December 1773, as a band of protesters appeared at Boston Harbor dressed in "the Indian manner" and, in defiance of the tax on tea, boarded ships and dumped 342 chests into the deep. The Boston Tea Party has long stood as a symbol of American determination, but at the time even the most uncompromising Virginia patriots thought this form of resistance unwarranted. All awaited Parliament's response. When it came, it was unexpectedly severe.

The Coercive Acts shut down Boston Harbor and curtailed Massachusetts self-government. The Quartering Act placed soldiers in Bostonians' homes. The Quebec Act lowered the Canadian border to the Ohio River and threatened the western land interests of the colonies south of New England, including Virginia. The king, his ministers, and a majority in Parliament all believed that aggressive restrictions were needed to force the wayward Americans into submission, but the new acts only goaded the various colonies to cooperate more closely.[7]

The opposing sides in this face-off regarded each other as obstinate. In 1774 they grew increasingly adamant. For their part, proud Virginians refused to stand idly by as the Bostonians faced hardships. In May of that year the Virginia House of Burgesses called for a day of fasting and prayer as a show of support. Their royal governor, Lord Dunmore, countered by calling a halt to the session. Jefferson, a burgess, had a hand in the fasting resolution; he issued a plea for the colonies to be of "one Heart and one Mind" in answering "every injury to *American* rights." It was in the same year that Jefferson, soft-spoken in person, proved himself a staunch critic on paper with *A Summary View of the Rights of British America*, printed in Williamsburg and subsequently reprinted in Philadelphia and London.

The House of Burgesses, through its Committee of Correspondence, remained in contact with the Massachusetts political organizers. Meeting in rump session at the Raleigh Tavern in Williamsburg, Jefferson and his peers took the decisive step of calling for a "general congress" of the beleaguered colonies. They called as well for a gathering of the best political minds in Virginia. Thus the same men who had previously sat in the House of Burgesses now represented Virginia at an extralegal convention—a shadow government bypassing royal authority. The Virginia Convention met for the first time in August 1774. A few weeks later, when the First Continental Congress convened in Philadelphia, Virginians were given prominence. Peyton Randolph, Speaker of the House of Burgesses, was promptly elected the first president of Congress.[8]

Patriot sentiment disseminated through newspapers. The delegates to Congress were described in supernatural terms as "assembled gods" and "Oracles of our Country." A Marylander claimed that Congress was not only the American equivalent of Parliament but excelled it "in honor, honesty, and public spirit." James Madison, Jr., agreed, writing from his Orange County, Virginia, home to his Philadelphia friend William Bradford: "Proceedings of Congress are universally approved of in this Province & I am persuaded will be faithfully adhered to." Virginia's leaders accomplished much in a few short months. They created a viable opposition government in their colony and authorized their delegation in Philadelphia to voice "the united wisdom of North America" in the intercolonial congress.[9]

Yet the First Continental Congress was not particularly radical. It may have pronounced an embargo on British goods, but it also adopted a conciliatory posture toward King George III. Then over the winter of 1774–75, British forces stationed in Boston marched on towns where weapons and gunpowder were stored. In April 1775 the redcoats, or "lobsterbacks" as the locals derisively called them, raided Lexington and Concord in a renewed attempt to capture stores of ammunition. The ensuing fight brought out thousands of villagers, who took deadly aim from inside their homes and behind trees, routing the redcoats. The provincials gained in confidence. If any doubt remained as to the colonies' future, the Battle of Bunker Hill, in a sweltering June heat, let men and women up and down the coast know that a hot war had begun, one not likely to be confined to the Northeast.

A second Virginia Convention had been held in March 1775. Patrick Henry made an impassioned speech that was remembered but not recorded. Even before Lexington and Concord, he saw where the struggle was heading, and he appealed to Virginia's leaders to remain committed to the cause of liberty at all costs. Whether he actually uttered the immortal "Give me liberty or give me death!" or his clever contemporaries edited their own memories in later years, William Wirt's 1817 biography of Henry made history come alive with the attribution. The words, in fact, are less important than the perception they convey: Virginia, no less than Massachusetts, called the shots. Without Virginia's commitment, colonial resistance would have been tepid, if not impossible.[10]

"American Ardor"

In August 1775 General Washington, a Virginian, was in command of American troops outside Boston. The town itself was occupied territory, with British forces poised to break out and march into the interior. On a smaller scale, Virginians were repelling advances from the last royal governor, who had sought refuge among a group of armed British vessels anchored offshore.

At this critical juncture Edmund Pendleton assumed leadership of the Committee of Safety, his rebellious colony's department of defense. There was no more crucial piece of work than to coordinate resistance, and that was Pendleton's job. When Peyton Randolph died suddenly at the age of fifty-four, Pendleton succeeded him as president of the all-important Virginia Convention, which would meet twice more to map out the future of a self-governing Virginia and weigh its role in the United Colonies.

Virginia had been Britain's first commercial settlement in North America. By mid-1775 it was independent in all but name. Pendleton was, in this way, the state's first executive and remained so through the murky period preceding the legal establishment of a government. During the war years he would be a clearinghouse for political information and an essential sounding board for both Madison and Jefferson.

In early May 1776, in his role as president of the Virginia Convention, meeting again in Williamsburg, Pendleton received the thoughtful twenty-five-year-old James Madison, Jr. The new representative hailed from Orange, and Pendleton well knew that the family's landholdings were the largest in that interior county. He may not yet have known Madison as well as he knew his influential father, Colonel James Madison, but he had certain expectations of this firstborn son of the Virginia gentry.

Madison had not been a real player in provincial politics until this moment. Since his return from the College of New Jersey (Princeton) in 1771, he had been living 125 miles from the colonial capital, at the family estate of Montpelier. Jefferson had already established himself on a larger stage, with finely crafted writings protesting injustice—in particular, his hard-hitting *Summary View of the Rights of British America*, which contended that America was settled by free individuals at the cost of their own blood and their own fortunes. For most of the colonial era, according to Jefferson, they had avoided asking for even a shilling from the British treasury. Jefferson insisted on sizing up political events "with that freedom of language and sentiment which becomes a free people."[11]

Despite his youth, Madison plunged immediately into Revolutionary politics. He was well versed on matters of natural rights and social contract theory. He believed that Great Britain was in the process of defaulting on an agreement based on economic fairness. Though we have no record to suggest a reaction from Madison to Jefferson's *Summary View*, he too was steeped in the vocabulary of those pamphleteers who framed their appeals around such loaded words as *sovereignty, freedom, humanity,* and *happiness*. For several years now, American writers north and south had employed psychologically powerful metaphors to convince themselves that the parent country was betraying a union based on affectionate concern.[12]

Although life on his father's plantation often felt isolating, Madison was more than just theoretically attached to the patriot cause. In 1776 he was as familiar with the political hub of America, Philadelphia, as Jefferson was, and his letters show an eagerness to stay abreast of news from the North. Jefferson was writing from Philadelphia with a minimum of self-censoring to John Page, his close companion from their days at the College of William and Mary and now, along with Pendleton, a member of Virginia's Committee of Safety; Madison had the equivalent outlet in Princeton classmate William Bradford, the son of a prominent Philadelphia printer.

The Bradford firm was the official printer to the Continental Congress, which first met a short time after Madison had concluded a visit to Philadelphia and sampled the political spirit there. He and Bradford exchanged animated, occasionally extravagant letters, each prompting the other with patriot logic. Bradford railed against the "corrupt, ambitious & determined" British ministry. Madison elaborated on "the Characteristics of a free people," attested to the warm sentiments his fellow Virginians felt for Boston's patriots, and praised "American ardor" in opposing the "secret enemies" of good and generous government. He saw little chance that the Crown would deliver justice and was opting for a continental defense against possible attack.[13]

What had shaped his mind? At Princeton, Madison was exposed to a wide variety of subjects, and though he never had any intention of becoming an attorney, he began the study of law in late 1773. His real intellectual passion lay with arguments in favor of religious and civil liberty. Here Reverend John Witherspoon, the president of Princeton, was his guide. A stout man with a Scottish accent as pronounced as his satirical bent, Witherspoon exposed Madison to the Scottish philosophes as well as the powerful Presbyterian critique of religious oppression. The Scots' contribution to the Enlightenment was their particular emphasis on sympathy and sociability—how to nourish manners on a national scale and improve the human condition.

Revolutionary ideas were already in the air at Princeton during Witherspoon's presidency, and he was subsequently elected to the Continental Congress. He would, in fact, be the only ordained minister to sign the Declaration of Independence. The great majority of those who took his classes became avid supporters of the patriot cause.

Passionate about liberty, Witherspoon believed that every human being had a natural inclination to behave morally in pursuit of temporal and eternal happiness alike. But he also believed in sin and human depravity: the moral sense was blunted whenever selfishness—an unjust authority, within or without—took over. Resistance to that authority through acts of virtue preserved liberty of conscience. In Witherspoon's words, conscience set bounds to authority by saying: "Hitherto shalt thou go, but no further."

Believing that liberty of conscience was uniquely a Protestant endowment, he reviled the Catholic Church. "Unjust authority is the very essence of popery," he wrote. The Church of Rome was distant, hierarchical, and oppressive, "making laws to bind the conscience" and punishing those who called its authority into question. Yet he held Protestants responsible for similar abuses, because all human institutions, religious and political, were prone to corruption, bias, and human error. The Church of England itself had an embarrassing history of persecuting Quakers, Presbyterians, and other dissenting sects on English soil.

As tensions built between America and England, Witherspoon saw in the British ministry a replication of these abuses. If the pope was fallible, then so were the British king, his council, and the members of Parliament. In short, London had become another Rome. Its distance from America had generated error, persecution, and the faulty claim that it could make laws "to bind us in all cases whatsoever." In 1776, in one of his best-known published sermons (dedicated to John Hancock, who was then president of the Continental Congress), Witherspoon said that the central aim of American independence was to protect civil and religious liberties. His logic was formidable, and his robust language a strong stimulus for Madison.[14]

Writing to his friend Bradford early in 1774, Madison noted that while the recently engineered Boston Tea Party may have involved too much "boldness," it was ultimately right because of the *"ministerialism"* of the royal governor. His choice of words was not accidental. Madison saw a direct connection between Britain's ministers—the king's chief political advisers—and the established church. Referring to the primacy of the Congregational Church in New England, he wrote: "If the Church of England had been the established and general Religion in all the Northern Colonies as it has been among us here [in Virginia], and uninterrupted tranquility had prevailed throughout the Continent, it is clear to me that slavery and subjection might and would have been gradually insinuated among us."

A state of "tranquility" was nothing desirable—it meant surrender of the will. Madison was saying that the Bostonians' love of liberty flourished in a dissenting religious environment, for Anglicans were without power there. If the Anglican Church had held sway in Massachusetts as it did in Virginia, a general passivity—"slavery and subjection"—would have sunk the colonies into a political grave. Virginia could learn from Boston's example.

Madison possessed the fire of a young activist. Thinking of the contest between freedom and servitude, he was livid that religious persecution should continue in Virginia. In a county near Orange, a half dozen Baptists had been thrown into jail for publishing their beliefs. Madison expressed his disgust with "knavery among the Priesthood," and the "Hell conceived principle of persecution" that raged among the Anglican clergy. Though the House of Burgesses was then considering petitions on behalf of dissenters, he doubted much would change. The self-interested clergy were "numerous and powerful" due to their connection to the "Bishops and the Crown"; they would do all they could to retain control.

Just as he admired the Boston patriots, Madison told Bradford that he wished Virginia could be more like Pennsylvania, where the "air is free" and free people evinced a "liberal and equitable way of thinking as to the rights of conscience." Pennsylvania had long been a haven for religious dissenters; its original charter protected liberty of conscience from state interference. Madison said that Pennsylvania "bore the good effects" of its history. If only, he mused, liberty of conscience might be revived among Virginians.[15]

His 1774 visit to Philadelphia further convinced Madison of the need for change in Virginia. After he returned south, he became a member of the local committee of safety in Orange, where he took part in the confiscation of Tory pamphlets being distributed by an Anglican minister, recommending that the offensive literature be reduced to ashes. Nor did he have qualms about applying tar and feathers to another minister who denied the authority of the Virginia Convention. By January 1775 Madison was reporting to Bradford that Virginians were "procuring the necessaries for defending ourselves." Within a short time, he predicted, there would be "some thousands of well trained High Spirited men ready to meet danger whenever it appears." Between then and early May 1776, when he presented himself to Pendleton, Madison had become a passionate proponent of revolutionary change. The interior counties of Virginia, where he had grown up, were in general more radical than the vulnerable coastal, or Tidewater, region, where the threat to life and property felt more immediate and made men more tentative in their questioning of royal authority.[16]

It is especially interesting that Madison in his early twenties should have sounded so combative and should have so eagerly assumed a leading role in Virginia politics. He had a preoccupation with his physical infirmities, a history of convulsive outbursts attributed to a combination of "feebleness" in constitution and "epileptoid hysteria," or hypochondria. These were believed to be diseases of the learned (those who sap their own strength with too much study). Now generally used to refer to an imaginary medical complaint, *hypochondria* was defined in Madison's day as a weakness in the nervous system producing low spiritedness, fearfulness, and distrust. "I am too dull and infirm now to look out for any extraordinary things in this world," he wrote to Bradford at one point. "My sensations for many months past have intimated to me not to expect a long or healthy life." It may be that he suffered from a form of depression.[17]

"Dull and infirm," Madison, who also had gastrointestinal complaints, was an unlikely candidate for the army. So was the unmartial Jefferson, who though a competent hunter in his youth was too mild and bookish now to partake in acts of physical aggression, even at the moment of revolution. Yet in the expectant autumn months of 1775, Madison was named a colonel and Jefferson a lieutenant (and commander in chief) in their respective county militias. The lead signature on both commissions was that of Edmund Pendleton. Neither would ever put on a uniform. But they were, on paper at least, officers.[18]

"Most of Them Glowing Patriots"

Of those Virginians who preceded Jefferson and Madison in attaining political eminence, Edmund Pendleton was one of the few who did not need to justify his position within the governing elite. Having risen gradually over several decades, he was respected in all corners of the Old Dominion. After Pendleton came the militant Patrick Henry. Forty years old in 1776, Henry was still not content with where he stood among the powerful, though his reputation for soaring oratory held steady and his rustic appeal to ordinary men was making him appear more and more heroic.

Pendleton warmed to the younger patriots Madison and Jefferson, partly because of the quality of their minds and partly because of who their parents were. But he was decidedly unimpressed with Henry, for reasons that had nothing to do with his pedigree—his father, born in Scotland, had achieved respectability in Virginia—and everything to do with his pose.

Patrick Henry was Virginia's darling who became, as time passed, leader of the knee-jerk opposition to every reform that the Madison-Jefferson partnership stood for. Jefferson's account of Henry's career, written in later years to William Wirt, Henry's first biographer, tells how Jefferson disparaged (and no doubt also envied) the talents of the sensation-causing oracle, who was seven years his elder. Jefferson's prejudices may also help to explain Pendleton's discomfort with Henry's ambition.

Jefferson told Wirt that he first met Patrick Henry at the end of 1759, when, just shy of seventeen, he left Albemarle County and rode off to college. At a holiday party, he witnessed the vaunted sociability of Henry, then twenty-four, and came to know of his passion for deer hunting. Should his reference to rusticity be read as neutral in tone, Jefferson added for Wirt that Henry lived for weeks in the wilderness without changing his dirty shirt. In Jefferson's eyes, Henry was a man of hunger and passion and little else, one who resisted gentrification and was a lazy thinker.

A few months after their first meeting, Henry was in Williamsburg to be licensed as an attorney. According to Jefferson, "he told me he had been reading law only 6. weeks." Two of Henry's examiners, brothers Peyton and John Randolph, "signed his license with as much reluctance as their dispositions would permit them to shew." But Jefferson's own law tutor, the virtuous George Wythe, "absolutely refused." The Randolph brothers subsequently acknowledged to Jefferson that they considered Henry "very ignorant of law."

As far as Jefferson was concerned, the facts proved Henry's intellectual weakness. Yet he saw Henry as an ally in the years leading up to the Revolution. "The exact conformity of our political opinions strengthened our friendship," he wrote. What that friendship consisted in, Jefferson did not say. But he did say that as his reputation built, Henry capitalized on every opportunity: "His powers over a jury were so irresistible that he received great fees for his services, & had the reputation of being insatiable in money." Jefferson repeatedly damned Henry with faint praise.

Henry specialized in criminal law, where his obvious passion swayed juries. If we take Jefferson at his word, Henry only preferred jury trials because he sensed that well-educated judges would be able to see through him and expose his limited knowledge of the law. Jefferson dated his break with Henry to 1780, but his extant notes of 1773 (when he observed Henry argue for one side in a marital dispute) already suggest friction: "Henry for the plaintiff avoided, as was his custom, entering the lists of the law . . . running wild in the field of fact." Jefferson's phrasing was colorful but dismissive. A gifted student never celebrated for his public performances, Jefferson disliked Henry's unorthodox manner and was frustrated by the success of style over substance. In this case Henry bested the opposing attorney—none other than Edmund Pendleton, whom Jefferson lavishly praised for his legal erudition.

To the vast majority of Virginians, Henry was a champion. Even an old and begrudging Jefferson was to admit that it was Henry "who gave the first impulse to the ball of revolution." His strength lay in his prophetic power. He sensed what the royal court was up to and made certain that America understood the inevitability of war. He prepared his countrymen for it, risking treason in justifying rebellion.[19]

All recollect Jefferson's role in the Second Continental Congress, in 1776, but he was also among fourteen notables considered in 1774 for inclusion in the seven-member Virginia delegation to the First Continental Congress. In the balloting, Henry tied for third with George Washington. Jefferson came in a distant ninth. He was, at this point, a leader of the second tier only. Whether he expected something more, or felt the slightest bit hurt by the vote that excluded him from the First Continental Congress, is pure conjecture.[20]

Nor can we know precisely who James Madison was referring to when he wrote to his friend Bradford: "This Colony has appointed seven delegates to represent it on this grand occasion, most of them glowing patriots & men of Learning & penetration. It is however the opinion of some good Judges that one or two might be exchanged for the better." The unanimous first-place finisher, Peyton Randolph, and the graceful, classically trained Richard Henry Lee (whom Jefferson later described as "frothy") are unlikely to have struck Madison as lesser lights; nor Pendleton, of course. Richard Bland was advanced in years, and suggestions in Madison's later correspondence point to him as one he considered expendable. The relatively conservative Benjamin Harrison, a man of known veracity noted more for his wide girth and his dark humor than for his scholarly credentials, may have been the other.

Then there was George Washington, who possessed an intellect no better than average. He did not protest the Tea Act at the time it passed Parliament, and he focused his frustration with London on an issue where he stood to lose personally: the military's refusal to award five thousand acres to American officers of the French and Indian War. (He had already paid another Virginia officer for his share and anticipated receiving ten thousand acres.) Beyond this evidence of self-interested behavior, Washington expressed his open concern over Britain's divide-and-conquer approach, its punishing Massachusetts first while hoping to minimize dissent in other, unaffected colonies. It is hard to imagine that Madison meant for Washington to be exchanged.

So how was it that Patrick Henry was able to endear himself to so many of his fellow Virginians? Jefferson again: "I think he was the best humoured man in society I almost ever knew, and the greatest orator that ever lived. He had a consummate knoledge [sic] of the human heart." The original editor of the Madison papers has speculated that Patrick Henry might have been too "fiery" for Madison's tastes. But Henry, at this juncture, seems rather to have *embodied* Madison's Revolutionary spirit.

The personalities of Henry and Washington were rather different: the one gregarious, the other grave. But they received the same number of votes and held similar views while members of the Virginia delegation to the First Continental Congress. Perhaps the most formidable combination of mind and voice in that delegation belonged to Richard Henry Lee, who was born the same year as Washington. Lee had grown up nearby on the estate of Stratford (whose best known occupant, yet unborn, would be his grand-nephew, Confederate general Robert E. Lee). The Lees were already an influential Virginia clan, and Richard Henry was English-educated. The Virginia delegation may not have been quite as intimidating as Madison wished it were, but in their secret proceedings the Virginians were animated and decisive. The southern group worked closely with a Massachusetts delegation that included cousins John and Samuel Adams; combined, they challenged the conservative elements in other colonies point by point.[21]

"We Shall Fall Like Achilles"

Virginia was not fully committed to independence until it tasted British tyranny directly in the form of the royal governor, John Murray, the fourth Lord Dunmore. Appointed in 1770, Dunmore was a passionate Scotsman trained in the military and prone to explosive outbursts. At least one newspaper described him as a "devil more damned in evil." He was berated for his sexual indulgences with "black ladies" and mocked for convening a "promiscuous ball." In 1775–76, Lord Dunmore was the most hated man in the colony. Madison to Bradford: "We defy his power as much as we detest his villainy."[22]

On April 21, 1775, following instructions from the British ministry, Dunmore had removed gunpowder from the public magazine in Williamsburg. He did so clandestinely, ordering a few of his men to slip into town before dawn and carry off fifteen barrels. They loaded them onto a war vessel docked nearby. An alarm was sounded, which drew a crowd, angry and armed, to the town green. A group of the colony's leading men addressed the royal governor at the palace, with reasoned arguments to counteract the energy of the masses. The gunpowder belonged to the colony and not to the king, they claimed. It should be returned because of rumors that a slave revolt was imminent.

Pleased with their mild response, Dunmore offered assurances that the powder would be returned if needed for defense. But the next day the governor abruptly changed his mind. Finding himself accosted by one angry alderman, he lashed out at the entire colony, threatening to free all slaves and reduce the colonial capital to ashes. Dunmore is alleged to have snarled: "I have once fought for the Virginians, and by God I will let them see that I can fight against them."[23]

Within a week, six hundred men had mustered in Fredericksburg, ready to march on Williamsburg. Urged by Pendleton and others to disband, the majority took their leaders' advice. But a few volatile companies thought otherwise. One was an independent company from Jefferson's Albemarle County, and another was from Madison's Orange County. They joined forces with Patrick Henry's Hanover County band and marched east. When news of Henry's troop movement reached the governor, Dunmore fumed that if the marchers did not stop, he would free untold numbers of slaves and spread "devastation where I can reach." He reminded the colonists that they were vulnerable to Indian uprisings too.

Henry never made it to Williamsburg. The leaders of the Virginia Convention convinced him not to proceed, having arranged a truce of sorts in which the governor agreed to compensate the colonists for the gunpowder. Still bent on retribution, Dunmore declared Henry an outlaw, which only made Henry more of a hero; county after county rallied to his defense. When he set out for Philadelphia to resume his seat in the Continental Congress, three companies decked out in full military dress escorted him to the Maryland border. Through one intemperate act, the colonial governor had ensured that his chief rival became Virginia's champion.

Having watched these events unfold, Madison wrote William Bradford a detailed account. Fully aware that most of Virginia's leadership disapproved of Henry's action, he wholeheartedly sided with Henry for his resolute effort "to procure redress." In "the most spirited parts of the country," Madison said, Henry's boldness had "gained him much honor" among the citizenry.

He himself was one of those citizens, drafting an address to express thanks to Henry, which he and his father both signed as ranking members of the Orange County Committee of Safety. In this message to the public, published in the *Virginia Gazette,* Madison contended that Henry had the right to use "violence and reprisal" even if vengeance was his sole motivation. Conditions had changed with the "blow struck" at Lexington and Concord. The time for reconciliation was past.[24]

At this historic moment, then, Madison's thinking was closest to Henry's, setting him apart from Jefferson and Pendleton, who saw Henry as a man of impulse unable to resist responding to Dunmore's provocations. Sizing up the magazine incident, Pendleton concluded that "the Sanguine are for rash measures without consideration, the Flegmatic to avoid that extreme are afraid to move at all, while a third Class take the middle way" toward a "Steddy tho Active Point of defense." Henry's boldness had shifted the balance of power away from the middle ground. Jefferson echoed this view in a letter to William Small, his college mathematics professor, now living in England. He worried that Dunmore had unleashed the "almost ungovernable fury of the people," which no one but the "more intelligent people" of Virginia could temper. In Jefferson's mind, Henry deserved no thanks.[25]

Young Madison had no fear of popular passions and no wish to restrain Henry. He was so deep in the marchers' column and so uncomfortable with Jefferson and the moderates that he bought into a rumor that the half-blind sixty-five-year-old Richard Bland, in Congress at Philadelphia, had "turned traitor" after having been offered a lucrative job by the British. "We all know age is no stranger to avarice," Madison charged, willing even to believe that the venerable Benjamin Franklin had returned from fruitless negotiations in London no longer worthy of the patriots' trust. "Indeed it appears to me that the bare suspicion of his guilt amounts very nearly to a proof of its reality," Madison stated, jumping to conclusions well at odds with his later reputation for reasoned analysis.[26]

Dunmore's real transgression—his most inflammatory act—was the undisguised "malice," as Madison termed it, of threatening to incite a slave uprising. Virginians were not taken by surprise, however. Rumors had been circulating that the design of the British administration all along was to pass an act freeing slaves and servants so that they could then take arms against the Americans. Congressional delegate Richard Henry Lee believed that Americans should free their slaves before the British did. Months before Dunmore revealed his plans, Madison had written to Bradford that he feared an insurrection. There had been a meeting of slaves ("a few...unhappy wretches") who intended to seek out the invaders once British troops landed on Virginia soil. Bradford was no less appalled at the prospect, finding it incomprehensible that "the Spirit of the English" would countenance "so slavish a way of Conquering."[27]

Madison was prepared to admit that its slave population was Virginia's greatest vulnerability, its Achilles' heel: "If we should be subdued," he said in June 1775, "we shall fall like Achilles by the hand of one that knows that secret." Madison knew that free, white Virginians had created an unstable society, and that all their bravado, all their talk of liberty, could not hide this fact. When his paternal grandfather, Ambrose Madison, had died at the age of thirty-six, in 1732, a court determined that he had been poisoned by at least one of his slaves; three were tried, one hanged.[28]

To be literal, using real slaves might be called a "slavish" way of conquering, but that is not precisely what Bradford meant. In 1775 the idea of slaves fighting their masters under sanction of the British military was an insult to the inherited sense of honor claimed by the king's freeborn British subjects in Virginia. London had long maintained that plantation slavery could be safely managed and hitherto had done nothing to reverse or undo the arrangement. A new, "slavish" way of conquering meant setting up British Americans for destruction. Whether one looked at "slavish" conquering as race war or mere indecency, the situation was grim.

In June 1775, once Dunmore fled the governor's palace, fearing for his life, his detractors assumed that his departure was part of a larger plan to invade Virginia. He had already kept the burgesses from meeting for over a year when the Virginia leadership finally felt compelled to establish its substitute government, the Virginia Convention. Fairfax County patriarch George Mason proceeded to devise the first serious plan for an organized military, and Patrick Henry made known his ambition to lead the First Regiment. After Henry won his colonelcy and the title of commander in chief of the Virginia militia, George Washington remarked caustically: "I think my countrymen made a Capitol mistake, when they took Henry out of the Senate to place him in the field; and pity it is, that he does not see this." Washington believed that Henry, energetic though he was, did not reason (or strategize) as a military man should.

Meanwhile Dunmore made good on his threats, initiating raids along the coastline, harassing planters, and recruiting slaves. In November 1775 he did battle with the Princess Anne County militia, seizing its captain and securing a hold on the oceanside town of Norfolk. Victory so emboldened Dunmore that he issued the most infamous of his proclamations, charging rebellious Virginians with treason while promising freedom to all slaves and servants who flocked to his standard.

In simple terms, he had declared war on the Virginia planter class. Arming former slaves turned their great white world upside down. Dunmore's so-called Ethiopian regiment, which helped defeat the Norfolk area militiamen, were musket-bearing slaves led by white officers, eager troops who wore the words *Liberty to Slaves* on their chests. There appeared to be more than one revolution in the offing.[29]

Jefferson recognized Dunmore's new army as a menace. Writing from Philadelphia to his college chum John Page, he concluded his letter by reprising Cato the Elder's call in the Roman Senate, substituting Norfolk for Carthage: *"Delenda est Norfolk"*—Dunmore's stronghold must be destroyed. A prominent planter reported to Jefferson and the Virginia delegation in Congress that Dunmore's ships were "plying up the Rivers, plundering Plantations and using every Art to seduce the Negroes. The Person of no Man in the Colony is safe." Pendleton likewise expressed indignation over Dunmore's "Piratical War," telling Jefferson that all Dunmore really had in mind was to lure slaves on board his ship and then sell them for profit to plantations in the West Indies. This was not true, but it served Pendleton's purposes.

General Washington, stationed outside a besieged Boston, shared in the moral confusion and outright indignation. Dunmore was the "Arch Traitor to the Rights of Humanity," he charged, and if his movement was not quickly crushed, it would have a "snow Ball" effect; for Dunmore knew how to grow his army through a combination of "fear" and "promises," most notably among the "Negros," who otherwise had no reason to be tempted. He too understood that race relations constituted Virginia's Achilles' heel.[30]

Just a few weeks earlier Washington had appealed for a discontinuation of black enlistments in New England. He was uncomfortable with the number of blacks under arms and their easy camaraderie with white soldiers. But the slow pace of recruitment caused him to acquiesce at least to the reenlistment of free blacks. The commander of Continental forces was not alone: in Congress, John Adams echoed Washington's concern, empathizing with the white southern troops who arrived in Massachusetts only to encounter this strange situation.

Lord Dunmore's words and actions ensured that slavery remained central to how Virginians thought about their future prospects. The members of the Virginia gentry felt that their backs were to the wall. Whether or not the Continental Congress acted en masse, the colony's elite was getting closer to declaring Virginia's complete independence from Great Britain.[31]

"The General Inconvenience of Living Here"

Americanness had been forced upon the Virginians. Despite their good educations and their country seats, the English persistently portrayed them as clumsy provincials. In 1770 less than one-tenth of Virginia's white males owned one-half of the colony's land, while their slaves—human beings designated as property—accounted for nearly 40 percent of the population. Under such circumstances, late colonial Virginia would hardly seem to possess the building blocks of a healthy republic.

Madison and Jefferson were passive beneficiaries of a severely hierarchical system. Virginia's landowners had overborrowed to maintain their opulent lifestyle. There is no better proof of the Virginians' rank among the colonies than the fact that their most important product, tobacco, represented some 40 percent of the thirteen colonies' combined exports to Great Britain. And it was declining in value. Financial worries intensified feelings of mistreatment by a Parliament that insisted on taxing the colonies. In short, the Virginians who exercised power at home felt dangerously exposed abroad.[32]

Slavery could not but define them. North of Maryland most slaves were house servants, playing a far less decisive role in the economy. To feed the commercial engine of the South, slavery had been made cruelly efficient. It had to be energetically maintained, policed by communities, and encoded in laws; otherwise it would not thrive. As a result, the Virginia gentry upheld inherently contradictory ideologies in the 1770s. They proclaimed their love of liberty, appealed to philosophy and literature, and exhibited a genteel and increasingly sentimental appreciation for the human potential. Admitting slavery's corruption of whites' morals, they did not, however, abandon the old compulsion to mix kindness with violence in dealing with their human property.

Were they helpless, born wrapped in an economic straightjacket? Or were they spineless? That is history's problem to solve. In 1773 Patrick Henry, writing in a style that belies both Jefferson's and Wirt's descriptions of his intellectual limitations, told a Quaker who had educated and then freed his own slaves what Jefferson, Madison, and their compeers all felt in varying degrees: "Is it not amazing," wrote Henry, "that at a time when the rights of humanity are defined and understood with precision, in a country above all others fond of liberty ... we find men professing religion the most humane, mild, gentle, and generous, adopting a principle as repugnant to humanity as it is inconsistent with the Bible and destructive to liberty?" Henry did not speak in the abstract: "Would anyone believe I am the master of slaves of my own purchase! I am drawn along by the general inconvenience of living here without them. I will not, I cannot justify it."[33]

His words embodied the paradox facing Virginians. Since 1765 white

Americans had repeatedly and dramatically termed their suffering at the hands of Parliament "enslavement." Yet all soon realized that their poignant metaphor invited comparisons to the slavery they practiced. In the famous case of *Somerset v. Steuart* (1772), British jurist Lord Mansfield ruled that slavery could not be sanctioned by the common law. It was, as the trial transcript reads, incompatible with the "natural rights of mankind" and the "mild and humane precepts of Christianity." Once a slave stood on British soil, the very air he breathed gave him legal protection and made him free. A writer in the *New-York Journal* assumed that this ruling would produce "greater ferment" than had the Stamp Act protests, for it placed the regulation of American slavery within the jurisdiction of British courts.

Mansfield had no intention of freeing British slaves or of undermining the British slave trade. But he did imply that Parliament could, if it chose, pass legislation affecting slavery in the colonies. A successful attorney in the case went so far as to declare that the laws of Virginia were as repugnant to the British constitution as the customs found in the "barbarous nations" of Africa. Another contended that recognizing Virginia law in England was no different than permitting a Muslim to bring his fair-skinned slaves to London and rape them at will.[34]

Benjamin Franklin, in England at the time, saw the case as a perfect example of the hypocrisy of Englishmen. The state could congratulate itself on the "Virtue, Love of Liberty, and Equity of its Courts, in setting free a single Negro" named Somerset, while at the same time protecting what Franklin called a "detestable" slave trade on the high seas.

The British did not stop taking potshots at America after *Somerset*. In 1775 the conservative wit Samuel Johnson, essayist and lexicographer, wrote a heckling pamphlet, *Taxation, No Tyranny*, in which he mocked the colonists' use of the slavery metaphor. Johnson famously asked readers: "If slavery be thus fatally contagious, how is it we hear the loudest yelps for liberty among the drivers of slaves?" The American slave poet Phillis Wheatley came to a similar conclusion in a 1774 letter published widely in New England newspapers, pointing out the "strange absurdity" of American slaveholders "whose Words and Actions are so diametrically opposed."[35]

The great contradiction could not be ignored. Only weeks before the First Continental Congress assembled in Philadelphia, the *Pennsylvania Packet* boldly inquired: "Can we suppose the people of England will grant the force of our reasoning, when they are told, that *every colony* in the continent, is deeply involved in the inconsistent practice of keeping *their fellow creatures, in perpetual bondage?*" Cognizant of the *Somerset* ruling, the same patriot writer reasoned that if slaves were instantly free on British soil, then the only way Americans could contend for genuine liberty was to drive an "inhumane practice" from their borders. He urged Congress to outlaw the slave trade. And so it did: in calling for a general boycott of British goods, the colonies' delegates all agreed to a ban on the importation of slaves, which was kept in force even after the other import restrictions were lifted.[36]

The contest with Lord Dunmore obviously tested Virginians' discomfort with the institution of slavery. When it became clear that the *Somerset* precedent was not going to lead to the emancipation of slaves, Dunmore's innovative approach to war—arming slaves—raised new and disquieting prospects. Slave owners now suspected that London was going to issue an "act of Grace," thereby setting all slaves free. The *Virginia Gazette* reacted to the panic by giving a distorted picture of the slaves who sided with Dunmore, putting them in two broad categories: they were either stolen property or wayward men, easily tricked. The writer laughed nervously at the military pretensions of the slave conscripts, supposing that they performed their drills to the absurd tune of "Hungry Niger, parch'd Corn!" The *New-York Gazette* dismissively labeled Dunmore's recruits as the "scum of the country." Depicting slaves and indentured servants as hapless pawns, if not mindless creatures, enabled the Virginia militiaman to conclude that he had nothing to fear from them.[37]

As one can imagine, not all white Virginians believed the stereotype that their slaves were inferior beings. A good many were forced to concede that if given a taste of freedom, slaves were fully capable of pursuing private interests with a will of their own. As slaves began to desert their masters to join up with Dunmore, an unnamed writer in the *Virginia Gazette* promised those who chose to stay with their current masters that slavery would be abolished by the rebellious colony in due course. At the same time, members of the Virginia Committee of Safety executed two liberty-loving slaves who had shown an inclination to serve with Dunmore. Their deaths were meant to serve as an example to others. To judge by the variety of what appeared in the *Virginia Gazette* in 1775–76, there was no universally agreed-upon policy in response to Dunmore's arming of the slaves.[38]

One of the most intriguing reactions comes from the private journal of Robert Carter, a prominent forty-eight-year-old planter who lived sixty miles north of Williamsburg. He owned seventy thousand acres and more than five hundred slaves. On July 13, 1776, he gathered his slaves together and carefully explained the logic behind the Declaration of Independence. He told them that Dunmore had "called upon black People of North America to join him" and enter the king's service. And then, without apparent guile, he asked whether they disliked their "present condition of life" enough to join Dunmore. They replied that they had no wish to fight against the "white people of the 13 united colonies" and proffered their allegiance to Carter, vowing "to use our whole might & force to execute your commands." (This is as his diary reads.) Continuing to treat slaves as rational beings, Carter demanded on the spot that they take an oath of allegiance—which free whites would have to do shortly, when General Washington and the Continental Congress required them to pledge their loyalty to the new government. Carter may have been unusual in his approach, but his history reminds us of the complex psychology involved in relationships between masters and slaves. Both had aspirations. Both constantly reckoned with the meaning and extent of power.[39]

We must be careful not to conflate the eighteenth century with the nineteenth. Once the American Revolution began, the cause of liberty was everywhere shouted, and responsibility for the slave trade was laid at England's door. In later decades, as more North American land was released from foreign dominion and the British brought slavery in their colonies to an end, a new defense of southern slavery was constructed. Tender masters were turned into philanthropists, somehow the holy victims of a northern conspiracy against them, and slavery became "a necessary evil." It was different in 1776, when Virginians would have preferred to wish slavery away. A simple logic told them that differences in physical appearance did not dictate that one person should own another. It was a Boston preacher who pronounced in 1774 that "a dark complexion may cover a fair and beautiful mind," but Virginians too knew that something was terribly wrong.[40]

Madison, schooled at Princeton where he was one of only a handful of Virginians, identified as easily with his northern peers as with his southern. Yet he evidenced no greater discomfort with slavery than Jefferson did. The "junior" James Madison was a dutiful son whose long-lived father bore chief responsibility for the Montpelier plantation. Madison acquiesced to the slavery system his father administered. His letters home show that he had no interest in questioning the man who sent him funds and provided him every opportunity for personal and intellectual growth.

Jefferson, on the other hand, came into his full patrimony with the death of his mother in the spring of 1776. His father, Peter, had died in 1757, when Thomas was only fourteen. Sometime afterward he spied the nearby mountaintop and resolved that he would design a classical villa and place it there. He began to level the ground in 1768 or 1769 and moved there permanently in 1770, the same year that he began courting the young widow Martha (Patty) Wayles Skelton. As war approached, Jefferson continued to direct his slaves to bake bricks on the site and build his splendid Monticello. His father had left him at least 7,500 acres and perhaps fifty slaves; in 1773, upon the death of his father-in-law, John Wayles, a ready participant in the transatlantic slave trade, Jefferson inherited 135 more slaves and, with them, crippling debts to English bankers. It was infinitely harder for Jefferson than for Madison to separate his fortunes from land worked by slaves.[41]

"Adventurers"

To understand *what* Madison and Jefferson represented, we need to better understand *who* they represented. The circle they moved in contained a good number of privileged and determined men, planters and lawyers steeped in Enlightenment doctrine. We see them today in contradictory roles: self-controlled letter writers with strength of will who, as heavy borrowers, remained prisoners of a slave economy.

As noted, the sprawling Virginia economy centered on the production of tobacco. Because that crop destroyed soil, the lure of western lands—rich and fertile Indian lands—was irresistible. Nearly all the leaders of Revolutionary Virginia were invested in one or more western land companies. Peyton Randolph, first president of the Continental Congress, was among the earliest. George Washington and his neighbor George Mason were principal backers of the Ohio Company, which laid claim to 200,000 acres. Richard Henry Lee lobbied the British ministry for a grant of comparable size to promote his Mississippi Company. Both Jefferson and Patrick Henry lent their names to a petition directed to the Governor's Council in 1769, requesting 45,000 acres along the Ohio River.

The speculators from the verdant hills and fertile valleys of Virginia's river-fed Piedmont section deserve our special consideration. Longtime Jefferson family friend and Albemarle neighbor Dr. Thomas Walker was the lead player in the Loyal Land Company over two decades leading to the Revolution. The Loyal Company had an interest in nearly a million acres, primarily in what would become Kentucky. James Madison, Sr., known as Colonel Madison, was a part of this enterprise, and so was Thomas Jefferson's father, who traveled almost as widely as Dr. Walker and whose pioneering map of Virginia hangs at Monticello today. When Peter Jefferson died, his shares in the Loyal Company were divided among his eight surviving children, and Walker was named the guardian of his son. In the late 1760s, Edmund Pendleton became an outspoken advocate for the Loyal Company, when he contested the claims of a rival company in Pennsylvania and lobbied the British government for titles to this desirable territory.

Here was a direct link between the fathers of James Madison and Thomas Jefferson. In one respect, then, the "glue" that held their interests together was Edmund Pendleton. And until he became their enemy, Lord Dunmore was another eager participant in the Loyal Company investment plan. Powerful Virginians were all somehow connected. So it stands to reason that Pendleton's eagerness to declare Virginia independent in May 1776, and to instruct its delegates in the Continental Congress to vote for national independence, was related to the landed gentry's urge for western land. If more evidence is needed of the planters' expansionist ambitions, note that 1776 Virginia's claim to the territory of Kentucky was finally recognized.[42]

These tensions existed because the Proclamation of 1763, issued by the British Parliament, expressly prohibited western migration. London did not wish to be saddled with costly Indian wars merely to support the colonists' desire to spread out. True, American speculators were frustrated by the Proclamation line, but legal restrictions actually did nothing to dissuade all species of squatters from moving into Indian Territory.

Their appetite for land and their hatred for Indians made war inevitable. In 1774, using Indian attacks as an excuse for a full-scale invasion, Lord Dunmore waged war against the Shawnee people of the Ohio Valley. The defeated Indians ceded their land, and Virginians secured through conquest what had been denied through treaties. It was the last action Dunmore authorized (ignoring London's opposition) before giving up on cooperation with the colonists.

Not every Virginian turned a blind eye. As James Madison, Jr., read of these events, he expressed the uncommon view that a war against the Indians had been provoked by Dunmore and others out of self-interest. He did not, however, relate his own father's involvement in western speculation to the seizure of Indian land. Writing to Bradford, Madison conventionally blamed the "unhappy condition of our Frontiers" on the "cruelty of the savages," before acknowledging that the Indians had been provoked and their "mischiefs...grossly magnified & misrepresented" to rationalize expansion.[43]

Though by our standards he displayed little empathy toward Indians, Madison did send Bradford what he called a "specimen of Indian Eloquence and mistaken valour." It was "The Speech of Logan a Shawanese Chief, to Lord Dunmore." Logan was an Ohio Valley Mingo with extremely friendly ties to white settlers—he had taken a white man's name in tribute to a Pennsylvania friend. He accused a Maryland militiaman named Michael Cresap of having murdered the women and children in his family. In his speech, Logan admitted to performing acts of bloodshed to avenge his loved ones' deaths. The speech evoked an image, already familiar to white readers, of the honorable Indian warrior, careless of his own fate, seeking a just retribution and nothing more. "There runs not a drop of my blood in the Veins of any human creature," the Mingo explained, posing and answering a single question: "Who is there to mourn for Logan? No one."[44]

Bradford was so taken by Logan's sublime speech that he saw to its publication in his father's newspaper. Jefferson would read the same lamentation in the *Virginia Gazette* and never forgot it. Yet Madison conveyed a mixed message when he offered only faint praise for Logan's "mistaken valour."

Madison did not elaborate on the Indian problem to the extent that Jefferson did. Like many of the delegates in Congress, Jefferson believed that the British in Canada would be able to "excite" more tribes to ally with them against the rebellious Americans. His words to John Page reveal a deep anger as well as anxiety: "Nothing will reduce those [Indian] wretches so soon as pushing war into the heart of their country. But I would not stop there. I would never cease pursuing them while one of them remained on this side of the Misisippi." He could scarcely see any point in trying to sway Indians to abandon their alliance with the British, for they could only be, he said, "a useless, expensive, ungovernable ally."

This was why the Quebec Act, passed by Parliament in 1774, did more than simply thwart the interests of land speculators. It declared that the border separating Virginia's claims from Canada was to be drawn at the Ohio River. Since the early seventeenth century, based on their original charter, Virginians had held that there was, in effect, no legal barrier to their land claims to the west—the province extended as far west as their imaginations could encompass and their surveyors could range. And so, seen together, Dunmore's willingness to turn slaves against their masters and Parliament's decision to redraw borders led Virginians to see an exponential threat: they were not safe anywhere. The British could easily and unexpectedly send armed parties of Indians across frontiers, while continuing to appeal to the Virginia-born underclass, white and black. From the perspective of the Virginia gentry, 1776 was the culmination of years of intimidation.[45]

Jefferson, like Madison, had little use for real Indians. He was pleased, however, to romanticize the North American continent in ways that suited the ambitions of the upwardly mobile Virginians of his generation. Those who inhabited the lands of Virginia, exclusive of Indians, were, for Jefferson, the descendants of hardy English adventurers. They were the heroes of a fantasy frontier, justifying Anglo-American claims to autonomy, to self-determination. In *A Summary View of the Rights of British America*, Jefferson advertised himself as a discoverer of historical meanings.

As a strategic document, the *Summary View* was a forerunner to the Declaration of Independence, a kind of "test" to determine how his patriot colleagues, as well as the king and Parliament, might react to an assertive picture of American power, Virginia-led. Here, as in his Declaration, Jefferson's argument was dazzlingly drawn, celebrating "the lives, the labors and the fortunes of individual adventurers," who provided a rationale for the right of conquest. Indians commuted from place to place and used the land in the manner of primitive tribes. Lacking the skill of enterprising white adventurers, they could be supplanted for the sake of productivity and progress.[46]

Jefferson relied on a straightforward logic. Early British settlers freely migrated to America, exercising their natural right to explore for "new habitations." Without any help from the British government, "America was conquered, and her settlements made, and firmly established, at the expense of individuals." Emphatically he added: "For themselves they fought, for themselves they conquered, and for themselves alone they have the right to hold." He criticized the British government for discouraging westward settlement, and he rejected what he called the "fictitious principle that all lands belong originally to the king." America was blood-soaked soil, a conquered land, whose conquerors retained the incontrovertible right of ownership. That right superseded their former ties to Britain.[47]

For Jefferson the legal philosopher, British Americans had created for themselves a parallel country to their distant motherland. England's offspring were, in effect, a new race of people—a new lineage, a new bloodline—possessing a real but somewhat thinned blood connection to their transatlantic kinsmen. In reasoning thus, Jefferson transformed the entire continent into a frontier nation formed by a righteous, independent, conquering people—more than a century before the historian Frederick Jackson Turner espoused his famous "frontier thesis," associating Americans' distinctiveness in the world with their desire to conquer frontier.

Jefferson was not the only Virginian to glamorize the frontier for purposes of political argument. His ode to "adventurers" was matched by Madison's evocation of the rifleman, an American original who left his permanent imprint on the land. Writing to his friend Bradford in July 1775, Madison sang the praises of the Virginia sharpshooter, reasoning that the "strength of this Colony will lie chiefly in the rifle-men of the Upland Counties, of whom we shall have great numbers." Who were these heroes? "Brave hearty men," said Madison, men who had rallied against Dunmore and would continue to make their mark on the land. They were known for their rustic appearance, wearing hunting shirts and carrying a tomahawk or scalping knife in their belts. They could repeatedly hit a handheld target at 250 yards. These men were hardly figments of Madison's imagination: he had seen them up close while he drilled with the Orange County militia, honing his own shooting skills.[48]

We have already seen the name of one such frontiersman, the Maryland militia officer Michael Cresap, blamed for the deaths of Indian women and children; his reputed acts had led to the heartrending speech of the Mingo Logan. Incredibly, the same Michael Cresap was heralded in 1775 as a symbol of the rifleman's virtues. Numerous newspapers recounted his exploits. This transformation from murderer to war hero occurred for reasons of patriotism: as news of the battles of Lexington and Concord reached the Ohio frontier, Cresap had organized his own company of riflemen. They attracted attention as they marched all the way to Massachusetts to join the Continental Army, staging shooting exhibitions, even war dances, en route. One paper reported that the riflemen were stripped "naked to the waist and painted like savages." The traveling rifleman-adventurer was an early version of the "Wild West show."[49]

At a time when the British ministry was prepared to use slaves and frontier Indians to carry out acts of violence, Cresap's raw display of masculinity set the new American militiaman apart. Was he the answer to British arrogance? That was the idea. The proud rifleman who appealed to his fellow colonists' pride could be made to symbolize the idea of liberty.

The frontier fighter had great resonance because Americans were otherwise being disparaged. Lord North had announced in Parliament that the mere presence of British redcoats would at once reduce the "cowardly sons of America" to an "unreserved submission." A Pennsylvania paper reported that the colonists had been described in England as "rank dunghill cowards." He would never fire a shot in anger, yet Thomas Jefferson wrote to his Albemarle friend George Gilmer: "As our enemies have found we can reason like men, so now let us show them we can fight like men."[50]

Though they had yet to meet, Madison and Jefferson shared a high opinion of the heroic, arms-bearing Virginian. Around the time of independence, Jefferson was moved to incorporate such a figure into the design of Virginia's state seal. On one side of the escutcheon, or heraldic shield, is the erect figure of a "Virginia rifle man of the present times completely accoutred"; on the other side of the shield stands a seventeenth-century adventurer, dressed in the Elizabethan style. Pierre Eugène Du Simitière, a Swiss illustrator living in Philadelphia, was engaged to produce the design. The penciled description is in Du Simitière's hand, but it reads as if Jefferson had written it.

More than the Declaration of Independence was under consideration in Congress on July 4, 1776. That day Jefferson was appointed to another committee, teamed again with Benjamin Franklin and John Adams. They were to devise a Great Seal for the new republic. It was probably Jefferson, thinking of his native state, who recommended the frontiersman for the national device, this time describing him as "an American soldier completely accoutred in his hunting shirt and trousers, with his tomahawk, powder horn, pouch, &c." Once again Du Simitière was to be responsible for the design.

When Congress finally adopted the Great Seal of the United States ten years later, the American bald eagle was substituted for the soldier. The only part of the seal Franklin, Adams, and Jefferson conceived that remained in 1786 was the unifying motto in Latin: *E Pluribus Unum* or "Out of many, one." By then the nation was at peace, and the winged predator understood to symbolize a burgeoning empire.[51]

"A Declaration of Rights"

Lord Dunmore was strenuously urging an invasion of Virginia in the spring of 1776, but his superiors were bent on a middle colonies strategy, eyeing New York, New Jersey, and Pennsylvania. This did not alter to any great degree the Virginians' campaign of readiness. The state's Committee of Safety removed Patrick Henry, who had no military training or experience, from his role as commander in chief, while allowing him to retain the rank of colonel. Hearing of his demotion, Henry did not think twice before resigning. He blamed Pendleton and never forgot the slight.

Down but not out, the radical retained his base of support. He had inspired younger members of the Virginia gentry with his stirring speeches, and he appealed to the rank and file as well. After the insult to their favorite, many of these raw recruits suddenly questioned whether they should continue in the militia. Even if Henry's military credentials were questionable, the crisis in morale was real. Revolutionary Virginia needed him.[52]

None of this deterred Pendleton, who had a good sense of timing as well as judgment. When the Virginia Convention met for the third time, in May 1776, he capitalized on the prevailing mood and introduced a dramatic resolution calling for the Continental Congress to declare national independence. The vote in Williamsburg was unanimous, and though it was not an official statement of Virginia's independence, it was just that—unambiguous—a de facto denunciation of any political dependency. Britain's flag was pulled down from the top of the capitol, and the flag of Washington's fledgling army rose in its place.[53]

At Pendleton's direction, committees formed for the purpose of establishing a new Virginia government. Madison was assigned to the most significant one, where he was teamed with the state's ablest and most outspoken: the brilliant, testy, and intensely private George Mason; the crusading, charismatic Patrick Henry; and a promising twenty-one-year-old, Edmund Randolph, the amiable son of the colony's most prominent attorney, a Loyalist who had abandoned Virginia for England. Edmund was, no less significantly, nephew of the late Peyton Randolph, the only Virginian of Pendleton's generation whose stature can be said to have exceeded his. In the decades to follow, Randolph would be virtually everywhere Madison and Jefferson were, always holding key posts in the heat of political battle alongside his better-remembered Virginia associates.

Complications have to be expected in the midst of a revolution. The gouty George Mason, a legal scholar who was never actually licensed to practice, lost his wife of twenty-three years in 1773 and was so devastated that he expected to depart public life. George Washington, his longtime Potomac neighbor, was among those routinely urging him to reconsider. The irrepressible Henry needed no such prodding. Edmund Randolph, full of impatient energy and eager to contribute to the cause, was intent on proving how far he stood from his father's Tory principles. He had already done a brief stint in the Continental Army by the spring of 1776, functioning as an aide at Washington's Cambridge, Massachusetts, headquarters. To obtain that posting, he secured letters of recommendation from both Thomas Jefferson and Patrick Henry. Madison and Randolph had much in common: as sons of the Virginia elite, they were expected to come forward and lead—in government, if not in the army.

All Williamsburg was astir on May 24, 1776, as the leading figures gathered. Pendleton wrote to Jefferson, in Philadelphia, about what was going on. "The Political Cooks are busy in preparing the dish," he said, "and as Colo. Mason seems to have the Ascendancy in the great work, I have Sanguine hopes it will be framed to answer its end, Prosperity to the Community and Security to Individuals." While Pendleton made no mention of the young delegate from Orange, James Madison, Jr., had already become a witness to history.[54]

The greatest weight rested on Pendleton's shoulders, but Mason had his hands full and so did Madison. They were all "political cooks" at this moment, and the dish was the Virginia Declaration of Rights. With its exalted language, this impressive document became a guide for future declarations. Jefferson likely had a copy in his hands as he was laboring over his own better-remembered declaration. The tone—the very wording—is unmistakable:

> A Declaration of Rights, made by the Representatives of the good people of Virginia, assembled in full Convention; and recommended to Posterity as the Basis and Foundation of Government.
>
> That all Men are born equally free and independant, and have certain inherent natural Rights, of which they can not by any Compact, deprive or divest their Posterity; among which are the Enjoyment of Life and Liberty, with the Means of acquiring and possessing Property, and pursueing and obtaining Happiness and Safety.[55]

A protracted debate broke out. The Tidewater planter Robert Carter Nicholas protested its all-inclusive language: that "all Men are born equally free and independant" could reasonably be interpreted as justification for the emancipation of Virginia's slaves. Pendleton came up with compromise language, adding after "certain inherent natural Rights" the phrase "of which, *when they enter into a state of society,* they cannot, by any Compact deprive or divest their Posterity" (italics added). Those few words quieted

Nicholas and any others who needed to convince themselves that slaves, as property, had not entered into any compact or joined civil society. The original version was prepared on May 24, and the amended version presented and accepted on June 12.[56]

As the Virginia Declaration proceeds, it addresses qualities of life that are contained in the eighteenth-century meaning of "pursuit of happiness" and that include "Justice, Moderation, Temperance, Frugality," and freedom of the press. Madison was perfectly happy with this language, but he wished it openly advocated the free exercise of religion.

Here, the young legislator made his first decisive attempt to recast republican society. Dissatisfied with the old, unadventurous language of religious *toleration,* Madison wanted something much stronger: "the full and free exercise of [religion], according to the dictates of conscience," which no force could tamper with; religion could not be the basis for social privileges of any kind. Here was the influence of Princeton's John Witherspoon on the rights of conscience.

Toleration was not the same as complete freedom. Toleration meant that the state had the power to grant or limit freedom of conscience. Pendleton and the majority did not wish the disestablishment of the Anglican Church, which Madison's language would have implied; so the young reformer twice redrafted his amendment in order to forge a compromise, and *toleration* was replaced with "all men are equally entitled to the free exercise of religion, according to the dictates of conscience." It would take a whole decade for Madison and Jefferson, combined, to chip away at the establishment. Madison's substitution in the Virginia Declaration of Rights was small but significant, a harbinger of things to come.[57]

"We Must Endeavor to Forget Our Former Love"

In Congress, on July 1, Jefferson wrote to Will Fleming, who like John Page had been an intimate since their college days: "My country," by which he meant Virginia, "will have my political creed in the form of a 'Declaration &c' which I was lately directed to draw." He could not predict that a single paper in his handwriting would attain an iconic quality, and these few words are the only indication of the pride he felt at this historic moment.[58]

Jefferson was, by all accounts, itching to return to his "country," where he knew important work needed to be done, work he expected to influence.

More than he wanted to occupy a seat in Congress, he wanted to claim principal authorship of the state constitution. Pendleton understood this and commiserated. Instead, Jefferson's colleague Richard Henry Lee returned to Virginia first—called home, it was said, because his wife was ill. The real reason may have been the same as Jefferson's: a desire to influence Virginia politics.

Lee had been as provocative in Philadelphia as Henry had been in their home state, proposing, well before any shots were fired at Lexington and Concord, that Congress organize and arm militias. On June 7, 1776, before leaving town, Lee (not Jefferson) introduced the fateful resolution calling for America's national independence. It was owing to his absence (and, some have said, his contentiousness) that Jefferson was given the task of putting on paper the collective reasoning of Congress.[59]

Jefferson thoughtfully composed several drafts of the Declaration in mid-June, which he then passed to Benjamin Franklin and John Adams for review. On one of those days, he learned that Virginia had decided on the new slate of delegates to Congress. His own term would expire in a month, and two of his colleagues were being called home. Although Jefferson had been reelected to Congress, his name was near the bottom of the list of successful candidates. Thinking his popularity in Virginia was waning, he wrote to Will Fleming: "It is a painful situation to be 300. miles from one's country, and thereby open to secret assassination without a possibility of self-defence." As he learned of the vote count in Virginia, Jefferson felt he had to tell Fleming what his role was in declaring national independence. It was as if to say, *Don't my fellow Virginians know how productive I'm being up here?*

As it turned out, Jefferson's concern was unwarranted. His narrow reelection to Congress was strictly a response to his protest to Pendleton that he needed to be with his sickly wife, Patty. This was the rationale Lee had used. But Jefferson was not making excuses: tormented letters to Lee and to John Page, and Patty Jefferson's subsequent medical history, are ample evidence that Jefferson was not scheming to return to Williamsburg. What his correspondence does show, though, is strong concern for his reputation as a statesman and a pronounced suspicion that secret enemies were out to defeat him, or "assassinate" his character.[60]

Hidden angst and sensitivity to personal honor induced Jefferson to take sharp aim at Great Britain in his highly polemical Declaration of Independence. As he and his colleagues had to build a common case on a series of justifications, Jefferson appealed to the "candid world" whose attention—and financial and military support—the Continental Congress wished to attract. The "candid world" encompassed Britain's colonial competitors France, Spain, and the Dutch Republic, plus potential benefactors Prussia and Russia. America wanted to be counted "among the Powers of the earth," to quote from the preamble.

Jefferson of Virginia was doing more than cribbing from Virginia's Declaration of Rights, of course, just as he was expressing more than the collective reasoning of Congress.[61] The animated tone of his Declaration meant that it could be read theatrically. Governments are not changed for "light and transient causes," he says, then segues to a more sentimental form of persuasion by making pain personal and justice nonnegotiable: "All experience hath shown that mankind are more disposed to suffer while evils are sufferable . . . But when a long train of abuses and usurpations . . . evinces a design to reduce them under absolute despotism . . ." Even the sound of his "long train" of words is seductive.

Jefferson knew when to raise the pitch for effect. First, he indicted King George III for having "refused his assent to laws the most wholesome and necessary for the public good." The ensuing verbs increased the severity of the king's alleged crimes: "He has dissolved"; "He has combined with others"; "He has plundered our seas, ravaged our coasts, burnt our towns"; "He has constrained our fellow citizens." "He has"—and here Jefferson associated the tyrant king's official appointments with a predatory, wasting disease—"sent hither swarms of new officers to harass our people and eat out their substance." Jefferson's voice varied subtly across the page: determined, reproachful, confrontational, and at all times principled.

The author of the Declaration did not always get his way. Congress edited out what was possibly Jefferson's most theatrical line of all, his protest of the king's "unfeeling" act in sending mercenary armies to invade America: "These facts," wrote Jefferson most vividly, "have given the last stab to agonizing affection." What could be more unbearable, more unspeakable, than for those who profess to love their fellow countrymen to hire foreigners to commit wanton acts of violence against them? Jefferson presents his conclusion almost as though it had come to him as an epiphany: "Manly spirit bids us to renounce forever these unfeeling brethren." And then his resolve: "We must endeavor to forget our former love for them." It is, indeed, great theater.[62]

But Patrick Henry could provide theater; Jefferson had to do more. And so he carefully constructed a legal brief, justifying the causes for separation. Both British royalists and American patriots habitually referred to the king as a father figure, but Jefferson consciously avoided this metaphor. The text of the Declaration mentions the "present king of Great Britain" once, the "*Christian* king of Great Britain" once, elsewhere dismissing him as a mere "prince" or "chief magistrate." By stripping the king of his royal aura, Jefferson enumerated his crimes as though the "He" that is the subject of the list of crimes was an unexceptional individual, an ordinary political official. If Jefferson did not ritually "kill" the king in his prose, he certainly demoted him. This flawed official, having committed "injuries and usurpations," warranted public censure and justified an act of permanent separation by his colonies.

Jefferson's organizing metaphor was not paternal and filial but marital. His choice of words suggested the breakup of a husband and wife, not a father and child. In the opening paragraph, he announced that a disconnection was occurring between two equal parties: "it becomes necessary for one people to dissolve the bands which have connected them with another." Echoing language usually applied by jurists and philosophers to regulate (and minimize) divorce, Jefferson asserted that governments (like marriage) should not be changed for "light & transient causes." When he described the "patient sufferance of the colonies," he was invoking the image of the long-suffering wife, so often described in the literature of his generation as one "born to suffer and obey."[63]

As Jefferson's argument progressed, allusions to the king as a bad husband became clearer. One passage describing the king's character called him a prince "unfit to be the ruler," who, in the "short compass of twelve years," dominated in a union (read: a twelve-year marriage) marked by cruelty and misadventure. In "future ages," few would believe the "hardiness of one man adventured"—that is, how one man could have been so greedy and rapacious as to commit the "long train of abuses" to which Americans have reacted with understandable outrage. The abusive husband George III was a reckless, and therefore unfit, head of the British household; as an unresponsive spouse, he answered "repeated petitions" with "repeated injuries."

Jefferson wished to make the king's crimes personally felt, so the marriage analogy made perfect sense. The legal bonds that America needed to sever were the bonds of affection, evoked in the Declaration's highly emotive line: "we must endeavor to forget our former love." The marital union collapsed, Jefferson concluded, when the king dispatched to America "disturbers of our harmony"—the military equivalent of a home wrecker— heartless soldiers and "foreign mercenaries" who "invade and destroy us." In 1776 the word *mercenary* stood for acts of rape and pillage committed by the "unfeeling." It was the large number of Hessians hired by the British government to fight in America that provoked this strong reaction.

In line with the stereotype of the cold-blooded mercenary, newspapers that year were to report with pathos the story of a Pennsylvania farmer who surprised a Hessian officer in the act of raping his daughter; he killed the mercenary "in an agony of rage and resentment," only to be killed in turn by a comrade of the offending officer. In labeling the king's appendages "unfeeling," Jefferson was accusing George III of condoning rape and violating the most sacred trust of marriage and family honor.[64]

Influenced by John Locke's concept of the social contract, Jefferson naturally understood that marriage was the first social compact formed in the state of nature, the act that created civil society. Marriage was a voluntary agreement based on consent, whereas absolute monarchy predicated its rule on a combination of descent and brute power. In "constituting . . . government," Jefferson wrote, the American colonies had, sometime past, "adopted one common king." Having done so voluntarily, they could therefore discard the monarchy voluntarily too. Having "abdicated government" in America, "declaring us out of his allegiance & protection," the king could be divorced, just as a husband who ceased caring for his wife could. Here Jefferson drew on one of the Jewish justifications of divorce, the act of repudiation, in which the husband ends the marriage by putting his wife outside his house.[65]

As a practicing attorney, Jefferson was well versed in the arguments for and against divorce. In 1772 he prepared a detailed series of notes for a client who intended to divorce his wife, notes that bear a marked resemblance to Jefferson's world-famous manifesto of 1776. Jotting down his thoughts in two columns, he listed reasons in favor of divorce on one side, and reasons opposed to divorce on the other. His first entry in favor cites the Scottish philosophe David Hume: "Cruel to continue by violence a union made at first by mutual love, but now dissolved by hatred." It is a perfect rendering of his logic in the Declaration. His additional notes in defense of the divorce principle include "Liberty of affection" as a "natural right" and "happiness" as the reason why marriage exists at all. This might help explain, as many over the years have wondered, why Jefferson revised Locke's triad, "life, liberty, and property," by substituting "happiness" for "property." Happiness conjured feelings of "tranquil permanent felicity," another of Jefferson's fine-sounding phrases, which was as integral to his deeply sentimental view of marriage as to his idyllic mountaintop home.[66]

In listing the arguments against divorce, he observed that "frivolous quarrels" must be avoided—this accords with his reference in the Declaration to "light and transient causes." He quoted the eighteenth-century French political philosopher Montesquieu in contending that it was "cruel to confine divorce or repudiation to the husband" without granting the wife the same power. Divorce thus "restores to women their natural right of equality." This is what is conveyed in the opening lines of the Declaration, as America, depicted in Revolution-era cartoons as a passive female, dissolved its "political bands" by necessity, in order to "assume among the powers of the earth a separate & equal station." It was the law of nature and of nature's god.[67]

Reconciliation, like separation, had marital overtones. Politicized people were painfully aware of what it meant when the king repudiated his colonies in an October 1775 speech before Parliament, openly rejecting the colonists' professions of loyalty and affection. He considered these assurances as mere subterfuge. Even so, in the early months of 1776, rumors circulated that the king's ministers were coming up with a plan of reconciliation, and moderate members of the Continental Congress clung to the hope that commissioners would be sent to negotiate favorable terms of reunion.[68]

In March 1776 a particularly lurid piece in the *Virginia Gazette* argued passionately against the possibility of "reconciliation and reunion with your butchers." The writer was echoing Thomas Paine's wildly popular pamphlet *Common Sense,* just published in January. Paine had declared that the only feelings American hearts should harbor toward the British were those of pride and contempt. Whoever could "shake the hands" of "murderers" was no longer worthy of "the name of husband, father, friend, or love," possessing instead the "heart of a coward and the spirit of the sycophant."[69]

Language gives enormous clues to one's emotional state; it is true for communities as well as individuals. In the Revolutionary lexicon, "manly spirit" (which in the Declaration commanded Americans "to renounce forever" their "unfeeling brethren") went hand in hand with honorable behavior, a code first defined by face-to-face gentlemanly contact. Yet on New Year's Day 1776 the *Virginia Gazette* made clear that Great Britain had abandoned the key components of honor: courage, candor, and generosity. Enlisting understood social inferiors (slaves, Indians, and Canadian Catholics) to fight in America was, according to the newspaper, a "base and inhuman stratagem." William Bradford had early protested Britain's "so slavish a way of Conquering," and Jefferson's Declaration weighed in here too: the king's deadly accomplices were savages and mercenaries. By the standards of civilized behavior, George III had unmanned himself. In Jefferson's words, he had turned a "deaf" ear and waged a "cruel" war.[70]

In divorcing their king, Americans had to replace their shadow state governments with legitimate assemblies and new state constitutions. They could now proceed to make alliances with other nations on equal terms. As the stand-in for a king who had abandoned his people, the Continental Congress symbolized a new voluntary covenant, which meant that the Declaration of Independence was simultaneously a public disavowal and a new exchange of vows. When the signatories of the Declaration agreed to "pledge to each other our lives, our fortunes, and our sacred honor," they brought a formal end to the "unfeeling" union by declaring an oath to a new, "feeling" one.[71]

"Consanguinity"

Virginia was on Jefferson's mind as much as the "united States of America" when he composed the Declaration of Independence.[72] The most outstanding proof is his awkward-sounding section on slavery. In describing the slave trade as "piratical warfare" engineered by George III, he was quoting from a letter Pendleton had written to him seven months earlier concerning Dunmore's so-called slave scheme. More to the point, in damning George III for the insidious crime of perpetuating the slave trade (asking how "the Christian king of Great Britain" could have "determined to keep open a market where MEN should be bought & sold"), Jefferson was principally condemning Lord Dunmore. The king stood as proxy for Virginia's last royal governor, who continued to represent the most immediate threat to Virginia's political integrity.

According to Jefferson's rendering of the slave trade, the British kidnapped men from Africa and brought them to America; at this late date they had opted to recruit them for their own convenient, ad hoc use. "He"—the king, Jefferson writes, but he means Dunmore—"is now exciting those very people to rise in arms among us, and to purchase that liberty of which *he* has deprived them, by murdering the people upon whom *he* also obtruded them ["obtrude" meant "to insert by force"]: thus paying off former crimes committed against the *liberties* of one people, with crimes which he urges them to commit against the *lives* of another." This was to turn justice on its head.

The Declaration of Independence had to have unanimous support to be effective, and the delegates from South Carolina and Georgia refused to accept any antislavery language in its text. Thus, Congress took Jefferson's carefully wrought protest against an "execrable commerce" in slaves and deleted it in its entirety.

To be clear, it was not owing to moral outrage, but for purely economic reasons that Virginians had been calling for an end to the slave trade since the 1750s. Jefferson's Declaration referred to slavery as a "cruel war against human nature," an assault on "a distant people who never offended." This was tragedy, but even at this stage, the Virginia slave owner stopped short of calling for emancipation for the enslaved, whose value as property stood to increase with the abolition of the international slave trade. Owners of property who joined the Revolutionary cause had their rights and interests upheld; despite the *Somerset* ruling, unfree human beings, as property, had no claim to the pursuit of happiness. Therefore Jefferson was using the occasion of his writing the Declaration merely to absolve his "country" of Virginia of complicity in the promotion of slavery.[73]

Race mattered in another crucial way: It was an integral part of the mid-eighteenth-century view of nationhood. Dunmore had sparked a race war, and Hessian mercenaries had further cut the cords of an imagined racial kinship that bound Great Britain to her colonies. Transatlantic blood ties, diluted over time, reminded the Revolutionaries of a "consanguinity" that had, in some very significant way, been abandoned. Consanguinity united a people and preserved social harmony. Its loss was catastrophic. Near the end of the text of the final Declaration, just before it voted to "acquiesce in the necessity [of] separation," Congress claimed that America's "British brethren" were "deaf to the voice of justice and of consanguinity." Because of the dissolution of blood ties, England was now a foreign country.

Jefferson had taken Congress in this direction. He simply could not let go of the theory of bloodlines that he had previously incorporated into the steadfast *Summary View*. Repeating his perspective on the history of settlement, he reinserted in his original rough draft of the Declaration the structure of America's unique genealogy: "We have reminded [the British] of the circumstances of our emigration & settlement, . . . that these were effected at the expense of our own blood & treasure, unassisted by the wealth or the strength of Great Britain." Land was marked by the investment of blood.[74]

It all fit with the Virginians' grand vision of a frontier cleared of Indians. The British had deliberately left white settlers vulnerable to "the merciless Indian savages whose known rule of warfare is an undistinguished destruction of all ages, sexes & conditions of existence," according to Jefferson's draft. In this instance, members of the Continental Congress retained Jefferson's language, word for word, proving that they were as sensitive to Virginia's grievance about its land companies' access to western ground as they were responsive to the Deep South's unholy desire to protect the institution of slavery. There was Indian blood yet to spill, because land hunger entailed a certain amount of violence. But Virginians were used to that.

In more than trivial ways, then, the rest of America was following Virginia's lead when, on July 4, 1776, the people of the former British colonies united.

"Virginia Alone Stands Up"

In the summer of 1776 it was called variously "the Declaration of Independency," "the Declaration for Independency," "Declaration of Independence of the United Colonies," and "the Congress's Declaration of the Independence of the United States of America"—sometimes several variants were used in a single newspaper article.[75] All such wordings, however, were accompanied by some form of mass congratulation, to wit: The Declaration "was everywhere received with the utmost Demonstrations of Joy." Yet as Charles Thomson, the secretary of the Continental Congress, observed in the *Pennsylvania Packet* (by invocation of a biblical metaphor) one week before Congress acted: "Should an immediate declaration of Independence take place, we shall only have crossed the Red Sea of our difficulties—A wilderness will still be before us."[76]

Had a new era truly dawned? When word of the Declaration reached Manhattan, which was under impending threat of a British invasion, the *New-York Journal* termed its appearance "a grand Aera in the history of the American states" and "an event which will doubtless be celebrated through a long succession of future ages." In Williamsburg, the Declaration was printed in the newspaper on July 20 and "proclaimed" in public five days later; the news was received in Richmond with "universal shouts of joy," as a thousand citizens gathered for an evening celebration at which toasts were drunk—"the whole conducted with the utmost decorum," the editor found it necessary to add.[77]

While Massachusetts bore the brunt of the initial British onslaught, and New York would next suffer, Virginia's preeminent place in the Revolution seemed secure. As yet unaware of what had just taken place in Philadelphia, a writer in the *Freeman's Journal* of Portsmouth, New Hampshire, spoke to the colonies at large on July 6: "Brothers, The grand, the alarming, tho' necessary crisis, is at length arrived, for a publick declaration of independency . . . Virginia alone stands up, & gives the great example, with positive orders to their delegates to vote for independency at all events." This New Englander was awed by Virginia's longtime role in the union of states: "She has ever been the foremost in our publick measures, and the wisdom of her councils acknowledged by all parties." Would union preserve such memories? Would the exigencies of war remove jealousies, or ultimately sharpen them?[78]

The Virginia gentry was composed of men of power and influence who relished union but prized their own culture above all else. As a distinctive group of people, they cared about marriage and bloodlines and legitimacy, carrying names from one generation to the next and recording their genealogies as they amassed fortunes in land. They moralized generally, paying close attention to the drinking and gambling habits that could and did squander inheritances, ruin marriages, and sink reputations. With Dunmore's challenge in the foreground of their thoughts, it is no accident that both the Virginia Declaration of Rights and the Declaration of Independence repeat the phrase "safety and security" in the context of pursuing happiness.[79]

Not knowing what his Declaration would soon come to mean, or how he would personally benefit from his association with it, Thomas Jefferson sought state honors more than national position. Though his mind was highly regarded by his colleagues and his writing seriously valued, that was all the public posturing he wished to do. James Madison, Jr., was more comfortable speaking up in a deliberative body, and he too was seeing his long political career begin momentously. These two Virginians maintained their independent connections to Edmund Pendleton, Patrick Henry, Edmund Randolph, and other prominent Virginians. But they were not yet interacting with each other directly.

"Your Original Declaration of Independance"

Jefferson possessed a contagious quality of mind. He knew how to write for effect. When Congress met in general session, he scarcely spoke, but he studied the temper of his colleagues and calibrated the wit of those who were on the receiving end of his letters. His economy of words and their sonorous appeal was impressive. From the Declaration alone we can see how he drew attention to himself.

But he was not prepared for either editors or critics. It is hard to say whether the intercession of his congressional colleagues made the Declaration of Independence a stronger or a weaker document.[80] Jefferson certainly had an opinion. Writing to Will Fleming, he distinguished what he had written from what Congress adopted. He let Edmund Pendleton know too, giving the most important of the Virginians his original draft so that it might be placed beside the final form and compared. "I am also obliged by your Original Declaration of Independance," Pendleton cooed. "Your brethren have...altered it much for the worse." He was telling Jefferson just what Jefferson wanted to hear.[81]

Theirs was a typographical culture, one that reveled in great oratory but venerated the written and published word. The blank page was the medium most congenial to Jefferson's talent; but Patrick Henry was the spark that lit the fire that was the Revolution in Virginia. It was his stirring speeches that caused jaws to drop. It was he who played Pied Piper to the common men of the colony, as they marched on the royal governor's mansion. Henry's "Give me liberty or give me death" echoed in 1775. A call to sacrifice was something Thomas Jefferson could never quite pull off. Historian Carl L. Becker argued mischievously many years ago that one could hardly picture Jefferson uttering the seven conspicuous words Henry did; instead, it would have been: "Manly spirit bids us choose to die freemen rather than to live as slaves." Credible, but not inspirational. On July 6, 1776, Patrick Henry became Virginia's first elected governor. When Jefferson succeeded him three years later, and Virginia came under direct attack by British forces, it was inevitable that the two would be compared.[82]

Was Jefferson's prose evidence of genius? Was Patrick Henry's forensic skill evidence of genius? We know that they became rivals, and that Jefferson, who belittled Henry's intellect, resented his pretensions. He would eventually find Madison siding with him in wishing Henry dead. But before we arrive at that toxic moment, a question no one has asked before needs to be spoken: As future-directed politicians, were they both more fascinating than they were perceptive? Jefferson was bewilderingly beautiful on the page; Henry was bewilderingly beautiful before the bar. But bewilderment remains. Both of them were carried away by language.

Another question: Why did Jefferson need Madison to temper his effusions? Though no less radical in the substance of his political doctrine, Madison already comes across in 1776 as unmysterious. In time, he would acquire a reputation for being nonconfrontational. Some might assume that his story lacks the controversial quality of Jefferson's. But that too remains to be seen.

CHAPTER TWO

On the Defensive
1776–1781

We hear from Virginia, that on Monday the 4th inst, at 12 o'clock,
M. a detachment from Earl Cornwallis's army, consisting of 300 cavalry,
and 100 infantry, entered Charlottesville, in Albemarle county. They had been
detached by his Lordship, for the express purpose of seizing the members of the
General Assembly of Virginia . . . His Excellency Gov. Jefferson, and two
other gentlemen (members of the Legislature) it is feared were taken.

—*PENNSYLVANIA PACKET*, JUNE 19, 1781

Governor Jefferson had a very narrow escape.

—JAMES MADISON TO PHILIP MAZZEI, JULY 7, 1781

AS A "JUNIOR," JAMES MADISON HAD TO LIVE UP TO THE REPUTA-
tion of his well-connected father. But during the American Revolution another James Madison was better known than either the one we nowadays
remember as the "Father of the Constitution" or his father. Indeed, before
he met James Madison, Jr., Thomas Jefferson had befriended this other
Madison and helped to advance his career.

The Reverend James Madison of Augusta County was born in 1749, two
years before his Orange County namesake. He was the future U.S. president's second cousin. Growing up in frontier Virginia, to the west of Jefferson's Albemarle, he crossed the Blue Ridge Mountains in the mid-1760s to
study with Jefferson's early teacher, the Reverend James Maury. In 1768 he
enrolled at the College of William and Mary, attaching himself to Jefferson's law professor, the famously gentle and generous George Wythe.

Graduating in 1771, and aided by the strong recommendation of his friend Jefferson, he became, within two years, a professor of natural philosophy and mathematics at the college.

The new professor came into his position with righteous purposes, establishing the Williamsburg Society for the Advancement of Useful Knowledge with the support of Wythe, John Page, and other like-minded men. Though a critic of British policies before the Revolution, he nonetheless set sail for England in 1775, to "enlist under the Banners" of the Anglican Church, as he put it in a letter home. He recrossed the Atlantic the following year, just as Jefferson was contemplating his Declaration in Philadelphia, returning to Virginia by way of New York. As it happened, Madison docked in Manhattan in late July, when the British were preparing to come ashore with a force of ten thousand men. If doubt existed as to Reverend Madison's political identity, he quashed it by spying on the British headquarters in advance of the Battle of Long Island, conveying the intelligence directly to General Washington. Thereafter the American Anglican resumed his professorial duties in Williamsburg. In 1777, at the age of twenty-eight, he was named president of the College of William and Mary, a position he would retain until his death in 1812, at a grave moment in his cousin's presidency.[1]

As a man of Enlightenment science and an Anglican clergyman at the same time, Reverend Madison represented a unique combination of the old and new worlds in Virginia. He was an educator, and education was at the heart of Jefferson's Revolutionary vision of reform for the Old Dominion; but so was disestablishment of the Church of England. Jefferson did not want the church to continue in charge of the College of William and Mary, but he did want his friend Reverend Madison to manage its curriculum. He evidently believed this Madison to be a man of science first, whose mind was open, and who was not a tool of the church.

The James Madison who is our primary concern understood the pecking order. In the late spring and summer of 1776, as his cousin rose in the estimation of Virginia's patriot elite, he continued to occupy a secondary role in Revolutionary politics. Yet he was privy to all serious discussions concerning Virginia's future within the new union of states. He remained in Williamsburg from May through July, when the Virginia Convention went into recess. He returned in the fall, because in establishing a government, the convention men became automatically the first members of the new House of Delegates.

Though Edmund Pendleton was the arranger of most political activities, the leading light in Williamsburg at this time was George Mason, the self-sufficient scholar-aristocrat who, like Jefferson, tended to confine his activism to the printed page. Mason had taken the lead in drafting the Virginia Declaration of Rights in May and now oversaw production of the state's constitution in June. Passed just days before the Declaration of Independence was approved by Congress, Virginia's constitution established a bicameral legislature composed of the House of Delegates (the real lawmakers), whose members were to be popularly elected for single-year terms, and a Senate, whose members were also popularly elected, but for a four-year term. The Senate did not introduce bills, but only put its stamp on those the House of Delegates initiated.

The governor, lacking veto power, was a weak executive by modern standards, voted into office by the Assembly and responsive to a revolving, eight-man council, his official advisers. A strong governor would have stirred fears of executive tyranny in these times. Patrick Henry fought unsuccessfully for the governor's veto right, once he realized that he was likely to be elected governor.

Madison witnessed a fair bit of disputation over how to create constitutional government at the state level. His concern in 1776 was the same as it would be in Philadelphia in 1787: how to build political institutions without making them susceptible to corruption. It was hard to say whether Virginia even had a popular government in 1776. In later years, looking back at the Revolutionary era, Madison tended to emphasize the Virginia constitution's flaws over its laws. Early in their collaboration, he and Jefferson would find common cause in urging improvements to that constitution, only to find that their colleagues did not care to tamper with it. Civil and criminal codes, yes, but not the state constitution.

"Unnatural Distinctions"

Jefferson was noticeably frustrated over the summer months. He hoped to make his mark on the Virginia constitution, but mail between Philadelphia and Williamsburg traveled too slowly for his opinion to count. His proposed plan of government arrived only after debate had ceased. An innocuous preamble was all that the convention adopted that reflected his language.

He wanted the constitution to issue a strong statement about religious freedom, and to be subject to popular review. He also wanted it to give greater voice to the western counties. As things stood, Williamsburg and the eastern Tidewater, areas embracing the most privileged of Virginians, continued to dominate the government. Jefferson would eventually succeed in moving the capital inland to Richmond, but as yet his impact was slight. He wanted to expand suffrage to smaller landowners by awarding fifty acres to any white man who had attained the age of twenty-one. This would have enfranchised thousands in the western part of the state. He also proposed an end to the importation of slaves.

Madison and Jefferson appear to have had no direct knowledge of each other's opinions as yet, though they felt similarly on these subjects. Separately, they weighed the question of who should elect the governor: the legislature, or property holders at large? As the Virginia Convention finalized the constitution and recessed for the summer, Jefferson waited uneasily for news from home. Pendleton wrote, likening the new constitution to a plant whose friends would have to "prune exuberances" from it.[2]

Finally, Jefferson was freed from his duties in Philadelphia. He left the city on September 3, 1776, and six days later rode up his "little mountain" to Monticello, laden with gifts for his wife, Patty. She was a capable manager of the property in her husband's absence, said within the family to possess "a lively play of fancy," a talent for singing and playing the harpsichord, and an "impulsive disposition." For the rest of September, her politician husband tended to household affairs, hiring a bricklayer and paying two of his slaves to clean the chimney. Then, so that he and his wife could comfortably set out together for Williamsburg, Jefferson called in a doctor to tend to her concerns.

Married at seventeen and widowed at nineteen, Patty was pregnant for the fourth time. She had delivered a son who did not long survive her first husband, though the boy lived long enough that Jefferson was prepared to become his stepfather. Six years younger than Jefferson, whom she married at twenty-two, on January 1, 1772, Patty had since given birth to two daughters, only one of whom survived infancy. Little Patsy Jefferson had just celebrated her fourth birthday when the family of three arrived in Williamsburg on October 7, 1776, and took up quarters at George Wythe's house.[3]

Jefferson immediately assumed his seat in the House of Delegates. Madison arrived one week later. Pendleton, who knew Jefferson's temperament, had earlier appealed to him in dramatic terms: "Having the Pleasure of Mrs. Jefferson's Company, I hope you'l get cured of your wish to retire so early in life from the memory of man, and exercise Your talents for the nurture of Our new Constitution." The warhorse of legislatures past knew that Jefferson missed Patty, and he knew enough to expect Jefferson to ride into town charged up, armed with a plan to republicanize government.[4]

That is precisely what occurred. On October 12 Jefferson the Virginian sprang into action, introducing a motion to consider a general revision of the laws of the state. The comprehensive plan he envisioned would restructure the system of criminal laws, liberalize religious life, and expand education beyond the gentry. The state constitution had passed him by, but there were other things he could do to empower the rising generation and satisfy his personal need to institute reform. On October 26 the bill passed, and a special committee was created to rethink the legal system. It consisted of Jefferson, Pendleton, Wythe, Mason, and Thomas Ludwell Lee (Richard Henry's older brother).

When he joined with senior lawmakers Wythe and Pendleton, Jefferson did not consider their effort a piecemeal project to treat distinct laws. He had a far-reaching formula in mind, linked to the theories of manners and mores that had influenced both the *Summary View* and the Declaration of Independence. Jefferson thought big. He saw the law as a record of national character and believed that by changing its laws, Virginia would transform itself into a modern, more enlightened republic. His particular conceit was the belief that Virginia's experiment—Virginia's gain—should become nothing less than a blueprint for the rest of America.

The mid-eighteenth century relied on the law to moderate human passions. Madison, Jefferson, and those like them who pioneered progressive legislation deliberately supplemented their formal legal educations with the philosophical works of John Locke, David Hume, and their French counterparts—writers whose ideas on human understanding, social behavior, and natural rights excited the hopes of the Western world. When he wrote of "life, liberty and the pursuit of happiness," or claimed in his encyclopedic *Notes on Virginia* a few years later that it was "the manners and spirit of a people which preserve a republic in vigour," Jefferson was under the spell of the law.

Attempting to find a set of universal principles for human nature, Madison and Jefferson and Enlightenment thinkers like them were in the process of developing what Hume called a "science of man." Politics was a moral science, the laws an indicator of the health of society. In composing the most famous of his *Federalist* essays, seeking constitutional remedies for the natural appearance of factions, Madison postulated that nations were nothing more than collections of individuals, and national boundaries more moral than physical. If similar manners served to unite, free communication created tension too and made the existence of faction inevitable. The science of man was about finding practical solutions to natural impulses.[5]

As Jefferson embarked on his revisal of the laws, he imagined himself a social engineer. His laboratory, at this point, was Virginia alone. The government's first duty, as he saw it in the fall of 1776, was to remove disabling customs—those that deprived people of their liberty. Rich and poor, powerful and powerless, all lived in an artificial society where smoldering passions corrupted manners. New laws would not only cleanse the statute books but also encourage the exercise of conscience. The best way to triumph over antiquated ideas, Jefferson believed, was to diffuse knowledge among the free population. This would be Virginia's contribution to the Enlightenment.

He saw Virginia as a distinct country whose citizens were imbued with that liberty-loving Saxon heritage he had extolled in *A Summary View.* They, like their forefathers, aimed to acquire land, civilize wilderness, and take advantage of self-government. But Virginia was not without its glaring defects and degenerative tendencies. After generations of colonial rule, an entrenched slaveholding oligarchy (what he later called a "pseudo-aristocracy") had left a large segment of the white population landless and disenfranchised. Liberation from colonial constraints was not enough: the state had to return Virginia to first principles and create a pastoral order that would recover Saxon values and nurture the virtues Jefferson believed most attainable in an agrarian republic.

His classical understanding of a republic involved a majority of independent freeholders having a real stake in society and a real voice in their government. Toward this end, he came up with four principal reforms: first, a more equitable distribution of land, especially with a view to the rights of future generations; second, the gradual abolition of slavery; third, universal public education and a reorganized court system, meant, in combination, to promote a knowledgeable leadership class; and fourth, disestablishment of the Anglican Church, which would free up its lands and substitute for a flawed model of moral supervision (suited, in Jefferson's mind, only to a monarchy) a more enlightened system of tolerance and benevolence.

The first reform Jefferson introduced came under the heading of property law: elimination of entail, which maintained a landed elite from generation to generation. Entail created "unnatural distinctions," he said, and doing away with it would rid Virginia of "every fibre... of an ancient or future aristocracy." Along with the feudal form of entail, Jefferson called for an end to primogeniture, which consolidated land in the hands of the few by passing it from fathers to firstborn sons only.[6]

The practice of entail in Revolution-era Virginia made it impossible for the heirs of a wealthy landowner to sell or bequeath his land. An heir could farm the land and build on it, but he did not own the property outright and could not freely dispose of it. The land belonged to his heirs, in succession, which usually meant each firstborn son.[7]

Jefferson considered this practice dangerous to the life of a republic. The dead hand of long-lost relatives still reached from the grave to control the distribution of property among successive generations. Distribution of property became more and more inequitable over time, as larger chunks of land were concentrated in fewer and fewer hands. If so few families monopolized so much land, Virginians would grow ever more dependent on slavery as slaves were entailed with the land—much as peasants were in feudal Europe.

Entail lay at the heart of Virginia's slaveholding oligarchy. Its overthrow may have been Jefferson's most radical reform. As a resident of the Piedmont, an area of Virginia that was settled relatively late, he was taking on the wealthy planters of the eastern Tidewater. For decades they had controlled the House of Burgesses, their power enhanced by an antiquated system of inheritance. By the Revolution, most Virginia real estate was entailed. Jefferson's initiative would release as much as three-quarters of entailed land, democratizing the distribution of property for future generations.[8]

He had personal reasons for disliking entail. In 1774 he had persuaded the House of Burgesses to allow him to dispose of twelve hundred acres entailed by his wife's father. Governor Dunmore never signed off on it, and he was unable to sell the property. To make matters worse, when Jefferson introduced the bill to abolish entail in the fall of 1776, his chief opponent was his chief ally, Edmund Pendleton. The bill had no problem passing the legislature, but a few aristocratic gentlemen took offense at this imposition on their preeminence. Pendleton wished to make the elimination of entail voluntary in order to maintain harmony within the circle of leadership. But the more conservative of large landowners were outraged by Jefferson's audacity. Tidewater planter Carter Braxton called his land reforms

"Chimerical Schemes," "wild flights of these fanciful Genius's." It was probably the first time that a political opponent dismissed Jefferson as a dangerous visionary. It would not be the last.[9]

The second component of Jefferson's revisal of the laws, slavery, would take a long time to resolve. He fully expected it. Aside from any humanitarian considerations he might have had, Jefferson recognized that the institution of slavery was a deterrent to the improvement of manners, morals, and laws. Weakening the slaveholding oligarchy involved more than instituting land reform; it required undertaking a most proactive kind of social engineering. To be clear, no one on the Virginia political scene was advocating mass emancipation. Freedom for blacks and biracial Virginians might have been seen by some whites as a desirable consequence of Revolutionary action, but a broad liberation plan was not going to be approved, certainly not in the wake of Dunmore's arming of escaped slaves. In Jefferson's circle, and Madison's as well, there was no call for freed slaves to remain in the state and acquire the rights of citizens.[10]

Jefferson's goal was to reduce the slave population and put slavery on the path to extinction. Ending the importation of slaves, which the Assembly would agree to in 1778, was one way to move in this direction. And Jefferson was pragmatic enough to understand that there would have to be certain exceptions to any emancipation plan. He could not expect to abolish inheritance of slaves; or to free those obtained through marriage, or those brought into the state by new residents. He did, however, believe that newly arrived slaves should be granted freedom after five years.[11]

He was an advocate of voluntary manumissions as long as the process helped decrease the slave population. His larger agenda, consistent with the majority view in slave-owning America, was to whiten the population. Free blacks would be compelled to leave the state, as would white women who bore the children of black men. Racial homogeneity was thought essential to the integrity of society.

Jefferson routinely theorized about generational change. He was concerned with memories of mistreatment, the long oppression and resentment that could not be erased. In *Notes on Virginia*, he would contend that each slave inherited the "entail" of "his own miserable condition" from those who preceded. Once again, the dead hand of past generations was reaching into the future, corrupting and disfiguring society by creating factions permanently at war with one another.

Enlightenment doctrine held that slavery destroyed the natural inclination of human beings to become one people and one nation. It was an inherited disease, a social contagion. But abolition was an unreliable cure. Only by exiling free blacks from Virginia, only by establishing a racial quarantine, could Jefferson feel certain that his state would be safe from future degeneration.

In his grand plan, education would suture the separate wounds inflicted by slavery and aristocracy. That way a morally tarnished, property-based master class could evolve into one based on liberal principles and intellectual merit. Of the 126 bills that Jefferson proposed in Williamsburg, Bill no. 79, for "the More General Diffusion of Knowledge," may be said to have crowned his reforms. Bill no. 79 provided for the establishment of primary schools for all free children, grammar schools for the more capable among them, and college for those most gifted, "whom nature hath endowed with genius and virtue."

He wanted good guardians appointed to ensure that physical structures were built and that the tuition of the truly talented would be subsidized by the state. This way education would not be the exclusive province of the wealthy, those whom Jefferson had in mind when he alluded to the "weak and wicked" in Virginia. He found it convenient to see men with aristocratic pretensions as damaged goods in republican society, and to label these effete types as demoralized—literally deprived of morals. He believed that moral laxity had a medical origin, a deficiency in the operation of nerve fibers.

Sensibility, the natural human susceptibility to nervous feeling, would, if properly exploited, engage positive passions, and animate and improve society. If the "weak and sickly" adoration of monarchy and aristocracy (the insensate surrender of power to an artificial elite) was an infirmity, then its temperamental opposite, "firm and bold" compassion (a well-adjusted sensibility), attached to the healthy republican. In later years Jefferson would apply the same theory of political anatomy to Federalists, the privileged class of men he opposed on the national scene. Fitness to rule was visceral.[12]

He was convinced that individual self-cultivation went hand in hand with the new nation's bright and deserving prospects. The law was one tool for him, the infectious vocabulary of heart-enriched sensibility another. He believed that the culture war between active patriots and scornful, idle Tories would determine the personality of the future American.

The same imperative that directed Jefferson's education program informed his court reform bill. Those with a hardy physical constitution, with sound and prudent judgment, were the ones fit for guardianship in a Jeffersonian republic. The social engineer believed that only "men of science"—men of knowledge and discernment—should practice law in the highest court of the state, the General Court of Virginia. He wanted to weed out the poorly trained lawyers from the county courts, whom he coldly dismissed as "insects." Jefferson's programs were not democratic, as we understand the term; in all respects, he had in mind to create a cognitive elite, an all-male intellectual guardian class to fill the ranks in the courts and in government. They would be the architects of future reform.[13]

Religious freedom was another prominent part of Jefferson's reform agenda, though his bitterest battles on this front were to come later. In the fall of 1776 both he and Madison sat on the Committee of Religion, two of its seventeen members meant to consider "all matters and things relating to religion and morality." Old English laws remained on the books: a prison term was still technically possible for one who denied the Trinity and the divine authority of the Scriptures. But when Jefferson proposed getting rid of what he called "spiritual tyranny," once more Pendleton argued against him. Even with Madison and the influential George Mason on his side, the younger liberals could not muster the votes to defeat Pendleton: "cool, smooth, and persuasive," Jefferson categorized the Pendleton of this debate. The Madison-Jefferson side won but a single concession: an agreement that dissenting sects—Quakers, Baptists, Methodists, and Presbyterians—were to be exempt in future from paying taxes in support of the established church. Madison and Jefferson believed that no person of *any* sect should be obliged to support a religious establishment. But the separation of church and state would have to wait, as would many of the 126 bills that the manic reformer Jefferson drafted during the war years in his mission to remake Virginia.[14]

"Lethargick and Insensible"

When they met in Williamsburg that fall, Madison and Jefferson did not become close. But they did associate. By November, Jefferson the bibliophile had purchased books on Madison's behalf. As yet the future allies were probably attuned to their common social connections more than they knew in any depth what positions they held in common. The open-minded Reverend Madison was the most obvious example of the friends they shared, though as members of the Virginia gentry, they would have had numerous human connections of varying importance. For instance, the Italian musician and dancing master who gave violin lessons to Jefferson in the late 1760s also gave dancing lessons to a teenage Madison.[15]

Patrick Henry, governor since July 6, responded to his election by the Virginia Convention with words of hesitancy and caution: "When I reflect that the tyranny of the British king and parliament has kindled a formidable war, now raging throughout this wide-extended continent..., in order to preserve this commonwealth from anarchy and its attendant ruin... I feel my mind filled with anxiety and uneasiness." Given his well-known activism, the choice of Henry was symbolic of the break with England.[16]

The convention also chose twenty-three-year-old Edmund Randolph as the state's attorney general. It was another symbolic, if ironic, choice, as his father, now removed to England, held the very same post under the royal governor. In the Virginia manner, young Randolph was expected to carry on traditions. He would soon be elected to the board of governors of the College of William and Mary and supervise an investigation into the activities of three faculty members accused of harboring Loyalist sympathies. He soon became as regular a correspondent of Madison's and Jefferson's as Pendleton was, and their ally for the next twenty years.[17]

Governor Henry began his term bedridden with malarial fever and unable to take charge of state affairs. One of his colleagues thought that he had, in fact, died during his first week in office. There was, at least, some good news in the neighborhood: the hated Dunmore had fled and no longer posed a real threat. But to the north General Washington's disastrous defeat in the Battle of Long Island delivered New York City into British hands, launching a season of worry and restlessness.

In mid-December Brigadier General Adam Stephen, a fifty-five-year-old Scottish-born Virginian, wrote to Jefferson from the Continental Army's camp on the Delaware River. He was not sanguine. "The Enemy like locusts Sweep the Jerseys," he grumbled, as he reported on the cruelty inflicted on innocents. "They to the disgrace of a Civilisd Nation Ravish the fair Sex, from the Age of Ten to Seventy." Secret Tories were selling out American interests with apparent impunity; a prominent American general, Charles Lee, was just taken prisoner. General Stephen knew George Washington well, having fought by his side in the French and Indian War, but his confidence in Washington at this point was limited. "The Enemy have made greater progress than they themselves expected," he told Jefferson.

A few days would change conditions on the ground and lift Washington's prospects. Indeed, by the time Jefferson read Adam Stephen's letter, the commander of American forces had crossed the Delaware and redeemed himself with surprise attacks on British and Hessian troops at Trenton and Princeton. As hopeful and timely as this news was, Washington made it clear to Congress and his home state alike that his army was in desperate need of supplies. Negligence, incompetence, and bickering among officers over rank made his job doubly trying. He would have no complaint from a new recruit who had sailed from France on a vessel called *La Victoire* and who would put himself, his men, and his money at Washington's disposal. The idealistic, nineteen-year-old Marquis de Lafayette was hungry for battle. Washington made the teenager a major general and put him in charge of a division of Virginia militia. He would have no regrets for having done so.[18]

Congress had issued a request to the states for troops. After an initial surge, it was clear by mid-1777 that enlistments had plummeted. Two years into the war, recruiters, including the twenty-year-old Captain James Monroe, admitted that they would have to turn to unethical means of conscription if they were to meet quotas. Madison's younger brother Ambrose was an officer who had first joined the Revolution as a member of the Culpeper Minutemen. While Ambrose remained in the war, James Madison, Sr., raised troops and supplies in Orange.[19]

War exposed the fragility of the Union. Sectional divisions temporarily suppressed in Congress reemerged in the ranks of the military. Though Washington, a Virginian, had been named commander of the Continental Army in 1775, it did not take New Englanders long to hear that he had rudely smeared their officers for exhibiting the same "unaccountable stupidity" as their lower-class privates. In the autumn of 1776 John Adams, never known for humility himself, mocked the arrogant Virginians for believing that everyone from their state acted heroically; he had heard that they were calling the troops of the North "poltroons"—gutless. Mutual distrust and jealousy lingered, surfacing at crucial moments in the war.[20]

Communication of war news was often sketchy and unreliable. In the midst of this uncertainty, George Mason proposed "for the Preservation of the State, that the usual forms of government shou'd be suspended" and "additional powers be given to the Governour and Council." He wanted Patrick Henry to be granted the power to exercise the legislative as well as executive functions of the state, to be a dictator "during the present imminent Danger of America & the Ruin & Misery which threatens the good People of this Common-Wealth." The general anxiety over America's military prospects was making cautious men amenable to extraordinary quick fixes. Even so, the idea of a Henry dictatorship quickly fizzled. It is not clear whether Henry himself was complicit in the proposal; he likely was not, though Jefferson later insisted that the first American-born governor of Virginia had in fact solicited unwarranted powers.

In May 1777, in a letter from Williamsburg, Jefferson elaborated on his concerns to his former congressional ally John Adams, who was still in Philadelphia. While all was quiet where Adams was, the people of Virginia were becoming, said Jefferson, "lethargick and insensible of the state they are in." The phrase "lethargick and insensible" belonged to that unmistakable eighteenth-century vocabulary that bridged medicine and politics. Jefferson meant that by being dulled to reason, Virginians were no longer able to perceive their own best interests. He wanted more done to secure the Union without compromising its republican character and without investing power in any one individual. Soon afterward Patrick Henry was reelected without opposition to another one-year term. Jefferson had no comment—at least none that was recorded.[21]

Madison was unable to contribute to state-level politics during this period, because in April 1777 he lost reelection to the House of Delegates. As he and his allies subsequently explained, the candidate had not made himself personally available to his Orange neighbors or treated the voters to free food and drink, as his opponent had done. While gentlemen often derided the practice, "treating" had roots deep in colonial life and was by no means confined to the South. In Benjamin Franklin's Philadelphia, for instance, assembly candidates campaigned openly and sometimes took out newspaper ads. When Franklin himself lost in a 1764 reelection bid, one of his devotees quipped that he had "died like a philosopher," or, lost without cheapening his principles. There is nothing to suggest that Madison "died" any less a "philosopher" in the spring of 1777.[22]

He was gone from Williamsburg but not forgotten. The Princeton-educated delegate from Orange had made enough of a mark on the minds of his colleagues that after some months away (presumably at home with his parents), he was called back by a clear majority of the legislature and made a member of the select Council of Advisors to Governor Henry. Given that the new state constitution prevented the governor from acting without the cooperation of his eight advisers, Madison described the situation not as it literally was, a governor and eight councilors, but as "eight governors and a councilor." He would be working closely with the lieutenant governor—the leader of the council—who in this case was John Page, Jefferson's committed friend. If Madison and Jefferson were drawing closer, it was still by indirect means. Jefferson was in Williamsburg when Madison arrived, but once again they appear not to have interacted.[23]

In updating Virginia's legal code, Jefferson collaborated with three elders. One was George Mason, once hesitant to remain in politics, now suddenly ubiquitous; the second was Pendleton; and the third, his college law professor, George Wythe, whom Jefferson called "one of the greatest men of the age." The bills they drafted to cover immediate needs included a wartime measure to indemnify the governor and his Council of Advisors from any decision to forcibly remove from areas where they could easily communicate with the enemy "persons whose affections to the American Cause were suspected." A "Bill concerning Inoculation for Smallpox" was designed to encourage and regulate vaccination, ordering those who had been inoculated (i.e., mildly infected) to stay out of the public until their "distemper" passed. Anyone intentionally spreading smallpox would be punished with a stiff fine or a prison term. Another bill Jefferson was integrally involved in established a land office. This gave the state the right to determine settlement patterns in "unappropriated" lands, the idea being to promote population growth and ensure settlers' loyalty while adding revenue.[24]

As Madison and Jefferson focused on the future of Virginia, the Continental Congress in Philadelphia began debate on the Articles of Confederation, a blueprint for national government. Though the states had united, the closest thing to a common government was the Continental Congress— with its constantly rotating personnel, hardly a central government.

The thirteen articles presented in 1777 declared a "firm league of friendship" and a "perpetual union," yet the Union remained, for all intents and purposes, a collection of independent republics. Congress under the Articles of Confederation would control coinage but would not have the right to levy taxes or regulate overseas trade; its central government lacked executive and judicial branches. Regardless of size or population, the states were to have equal power—one state, one vote. That equality was not to be altered whether a state sent as few as two or as many as seven delegates to Congress; and a two-thirds majority of the states was needed to pass legislation.

Only Virginia was prepared to sign the Articles right away. Several of the states without claims to western territory wanted states like Virginia, whose claims extended all the way to the Mississippi, to cede their questionable lands to the general government. The most resistant was neighboring Maryland. Given Virginians' pride in size, debates over land were destined to delay ratification of the Articles of Confederation for four more years.[25]

"Every Nerve Should Be Strained"

Reverend Madison resumed his professorial duties at the College of William and Mary. He resumed, as well, communication with his patron Jefferson. Unfortunately, their extant letters mainly show a shared concern with astronomical observations, but they were surely comparing ideas about education too. In the spring of 1777 the elder of Williamsburg's two James Madisons became president of the college. His agreeable cousin, as a member of the governor's Council of Advisors, came to board with him the following January; and in appreciation for his kinsman's hospitality, James Madison, Jr., asked his father to send from the country "dried fruits &tc which Mr. Madison [the college president] is very fond of." It was the least he could do, he said, to compensate for the "culinary favours" he daily received.

Although the identically named cousins disagreed on the thorny issue of disestablishment of the Anglican Church in Virginia, their friendship unquestionably deepened in these years. Meanwhile Jefferson took steps to convince the state government to provide public support to the college—his alma mater—by enlarging its faculty and adding "useful sciences" to the curriculum. He did not succeed, but knowing what Jefferson was up to, Reverend Madison did his utmost to preserve the integrity of the college that he had rescued from Tory hands.[26]

A short walk from the college, Governor Henry adapted to the routine of government. The man whom Jefferson considered an ill-educated opportunist had but little opportunity to improvise or even to sound eloquent. Virginia may not have been under direct attack, but these were nonetheless the darkest years of the war. Financial concerns were overwhelming. Hard money was hard to find across America, except among the British forces; as a result Pennsylvania farmers succumbed to temptation, feeding the enemy. Philadelphia fell to the British in the autumn of 1777, prompting Congress to move for a time to York, Pennsylvania. As the enemy enjoyed Philadelphia's relative comfort, Washington's men faced a severe winter and endured privation at Valley Forge.

Madison was one of four councilors who signed on to an official communication from the Executive Council, advising the governor to ship "good rum," wine, sugar, and other food stores to "the exhausted part of America" where Washington's army was situated. That was about all Virginia could to do. The state did not, at this or any other time, draft the numbers of troops Washington requested.[27]

In the spring of 1778 news from abroad improved America's prospects. Veteran diplomat Benjamin Franklin had succeeded in securing French recognition of American independence. The two nations signed a treaty of amity and commerce, and French military aid would shortly follow. At this expectant moment James Madison was returned to the House of Delegates, voted back in by the same men of Orange County who had turned him out the year before. But ineligible to serve simultaneously on the Governor's Council and in the legislature, he opted for the former and remained dutifully at Henry's side another year.[28]

Eight years apart in age, Madison and Jefferson lived very different lives at this time. One was single, the other married with one daughter and a second on the way. Madison went where he was wanted; Jefferson wrestled with his own ambition and stubbornly pressed on. Since the fall of 1776 he more or less commuted between Monticello and Williamsburg. His wife, Patty, did not stay long in the capital, returning to Albemarle for her two pregnancies in 1777 and 1778. The first produced a son who lived but a few weeks, the only son Jefferson had with his wife. Then in August 1778 Mary (Maria) was born. She and her older sister Patsy would be the only two of the Jeffersons' six children to reach adulthood.

Though there was a war on, it was centered elsewhere, so the squire of Monticello kept to his dreams as a builder. He devoted himself to the enlargement of his mountaintop plantation, producing tens of thousands of bricks and planting fruit trees—an enterprise he had begun almost a decade before. In 1769, when his building plans were just ripening, he had called his home "The Hermitage." Soon afterward, the idiosyncratic Italianesque name "Monticello" came to him. Thinking broadly, he sketched out the design for attractive two- and five-room cottages for his white workforce and for the select slave families he wished to settle on Mulberry Row, just below the stylish house where he resided. By the time he actually got around to building along Mulberry Row, however, the slave cabins were humbler than what he had first imagined.

In 1778 Jefferson owned a total of 13,700 acres in six Virginia counties. The Monticello property amounted to 1,000 acres, and he held another 3,225 acres in several sites around Albemarle. From his father-in-law he inherited 7,661 acres in Bedford County, two days' ride south; there he would eventually build the octagonal Poplar Forest house, where as an ex-president he would escape when Monticello was overrun with adoring pilgrims and curious strangers. For now, though, Jefferson was a man of business trained in the law, a wheat and tobacco farmer, a gentleman architect, and a man of taste. His stature as a lawgiver was constantly growing.[29]

In 1778 Virginia's political leaders were prepared to believe that the alliance with France would result in British recognition of their "independency." Richard Henry Lee wrote to Jefferson from Congress that May: "Our enemies are sore pressed." But at the same time, Lee was desperate for the Virginia Assembly to raise more troops and urged: "For God's sake, for the love of our Country, my dear friend, let more vigorous measures be quickly adopted for re-enforcing the Army." Members of the Assembly tried, but they continued to have only limited success in recruitment.

Always a numbers man, Jefferson maintained a tally of enemy killed, wounded, and taken prisoner in the first two years of fighting. He estimated that the American side had lost half as many as the British. He was a member of the legislative committee that raised a new battalion to defend Virginia's port cities. Each man who enlisted was to be paid ten dollars and bear no obligation to fight outside the state.

Jefferson kept coming up with ideas. He proposed conscription of a cavalry regiment in place of more foot soldiers. To continue previously unsuccessful methods of finding volunteers assured more failure. Besides, he figured he knew the sort of man who would serve in the cavalry. As he wrote to Lee, this "new fund" of recruits would be "those whose indolence or education, has unfitted them for foot-service." Just as he thought he had found the source of a "weak and sickly" adoration of monarchy and aristocracy in impaired nerves, he now felt that "indolence" among young men denoted a preference for one form of military service over another. It was his habit to identify fundamental defects of character and intricate moral explanations for human behavior, a prejudice and a conceit he would never outgrow.

He had a sense of purpose beyond the political, of course. At thirty-five, he saw himself as unfulfilled unless he could devote his mind to philosophical musings and scientific observation. Associating the study of Virginia's climate with its people's prospects for happiness, he addressed the Italian Giovanni Fabbroni, the friend of a friend, and suggested that they share temperature measurements—he already compared weather conditions in Williamsburg and Monticello with Reverend Madison, John Page, and others. "Tho' much of my time is employed in the councils of America," Jefferson wrote Fabbroni, "I have yet a little leisure to indulge my fondness for philosophical studies." At the heart of this particular communication was an appeal to Fabbroni to convince Italian musicians and singers to come to America, where, Jefferson promised, they would always find useful employment. Music was, he pronounced, "the favorite passion of my soul, and fortune has cast my lot in a country where it is in a state of deplorable barbarism." He reached for cultural expression in the interest of improvement.[30]

Jefferson's close friend Philip (Filippo) Mazzei, who had put him in touch with fellow Florentine Fabbroni, had lived literally around the corner from Monticello since 1773. Mazzei had been passing through central Virginia looking for a place to settle and experiment with viticulture. Jefferson, whose love of wine would later become legend, convinced him that he should purchase the nearby property; he boarded Mazzei at Monticello until his house was ready for occupancy. In this way, by the outbreak of the Revolution, Jefferson learned to speak the Tuscan strain of Italian and helped to mold his neighbor into an American patriot. They would exchange plants and seeds for years to come.[31]

Through his personal connection with the enterprising Italian, Jefferson came up with an idea of political cunning and advanced it to John Hancock in Congress. Mazzei was interested in soliciting financial support for America's cause in Europe, and Jefferson thought it possible for the commercial Italians, with "immense sums" in London banks, to create financial chaos for Britain by demanding a return of their money all at once. It may have been unrealistic—a magical solution to a complex problem—but Jefferson could not resist speculating on a covert Italian operation. He imagined money flowing across the Atlantic and money drying up in London. "We might do something clever with them," he wrote Hancock of the Italians, "supplying our wants, and perhaps rendering our Enemies bankrupt."[32]

In the first months of 1779, as Governor Henry neared the end of his third one-year term and was constitutionally ineligible for a fourth, he married into the socially prominent Dandridge family. His bride brought twelve slaves to their marriage: Henry now owned forty-two slaves, approximately half as many as Jefferson. The new husband improved his lot by purchasing a ten-thousand-acre plantation in a county that bore his name, near the Virginia–North Carolina border. Henry County had come into being in the first year of his governorship.[33]

Despite a widening war, Virginia was still not directly threatened. Some were quite positive about the future. Alert to the fact that Great Britain was unlikely to receive practical encouragement from the other European powers, Richard Henry Lee repeated his aggressive optimism in a letter to Jefferson: "With our present prospects every nerve should be strained to make the Army strong. By being prepared we shall have a moral certainty of defeating the designs of our enemies the next campaign, which will in my opinion put a glorious period to the war." Even in anticipating the enemy's southern campaign, Lee maintained his confidence: "If we can baffle the Southern invasion...they will be compelled by inevitable necessity to be content with the loss of thirteen flourishing states." Jefferson's old friend Will Fleming, from the same vantage point in Philadelphia, was less sanguine than Lee: "I am apprehensive the enemy will commit great ravages before an effectual check can be given to their progress," he wrote. Morale would be hard to sustain with the invaders' numbers holding steady.[34]

National unity was by no means assured. Fleming said it as well as any better-known patriot of the Revolutionary era: "I have heard much, but seen very little of patriotism and public virtue: If there is any remains of it in America, this is the season for calling it forth, and for its utmost exertions."[35] Evincing his primary concern for Virginia's political foundation, Jefferson continued to advance ideas on the revisal of laws to Mason, Wythe, and Pendleton. Madison would much later observe that, after the Declaration of Independence, Jefferson's work on the revisal was "the most severe" of his labors as a statesman. Mason, suffering from gout and barely able to stand for five minutes at a time, recognized how invaluable Jefferson was. This was why his legislative colleagues were pleased to make Thomas Jefferson governor. As the Albemarle representative left the House of Delegates to take on executive responsibilities, Mason realized that it would be left to him to pick up the slack, despite his aches and pains.[36]

Madison remained in Williamsburg as a member of the Governor's Council. His proximity to power had made him one of Virginia's leading men. As yet neither Madison nor Jefferson could have predicted that their intimacy, which we can date to this moment, would have long-lasting implications. Indeed, Virginia as a whole was unprepared for all that was to come during the administration of Governor Jefferson—when the acrimony accompanying an invasion gave rise to new friendships and gave evidence of incompetence to Jefferson's sworn enemies.

"Quixotism"

During the final six months of 1779 Madison and Jefferson grew to respect each other and work in partnership. One might say that the constitutional requirement that Virginia's governor act in concert with the members of his Council of Advisors was the impetus behind a historic collaboration.

Jefferson rarely plunged ahead in politics, or accepted any new public role, without deliberating at length. Though he would spend upward of forty years in colonial, Revolutionary, and federal government, he had a habit of protesting his public service and periodically announcing to friends his intention to retire to family life. Edward Rutledge of South Carolina had no doubt heard such reluctance to serve from Jefferson's lips while they were in Philadelphia; in a letter of February 1779 he made light of the Virginian's resolve to remove to Monticello permanently and devote himself to study: "When you have condescended to come down from above and interest yourself in Human Affairs . . . ," he prefaced an appeal to Jefferson on a matter of political import.[37]

Jefferson had first intimated to Pendleton in the summer of 1776 that he craved the quiet of private life. As Pendleton had done then, he did once again in May 1779, urging Jefferson not to quit politics. In 1777 Pendleton had suffered a debilitating fall from his horse, broke his hip, and for the remainder of his life was forced to walk with crutches. Though most would have retired after such a calamity, he stayed active in state government. Jefferson, in his prime, had no such excuse, and two weeks before his election as governor, he heard from Virginia's senior statesman, then resting at his Caroline County plantation of Edmundsbury: "You are too young to Ask that happy quietus from the Public, and should at least postpone it 'til you have taught the rising Generation, the forms as well as the Substantial principles of legislation." To which Pendleton added, "A Correspondence with you will give me much pleasure."[38]

Jefferson assumed the governorship at the beginning of June 1779. It was painfully ironic to him that he should have become governor by defeating his dear friend John Page. The candidates' "respective friends" had made them competitors in a close contest neither had invited. "It was their competition, not ours," Jefferson wrote sensitively, reflecting on a friendship that extended to the two men's wives.[39]

He now resided in the governor's palace, where Lord Dunmore had lived in splendor a few short, tumultuous years earlier. Patty and their two little girls were away at her relatives' and would not arrive in Williamsburg for many weeks, while the new state executive reconciled himself to his situation by attaching himself to three of the members of his Council of Advisors: Page, Madison, and another boyhood friend and Albemarle neighbor, John Walker. Most of the papers relating to Jefferson's formal meetings with his councilors are missing, making it difficult to detail the moment when Madison's advice first appealed to him. All we have to judge from are the words Madison recorded in a letter four years after Jefferson's death, in which he said of 1779 that "a friendship was formed, which was for life, and which was never interrupted in the slightest degree for a single moment."[40]

Some of Jefferson's legislative initiatives came before the Assembly in his first year as governor. Clearly unfazed by their differences over church establishment, Pendleton wrote to him: "I am impatient to se [sic] what you call your Quixotism for the diffusion of knowledge." This was when Bill no. 79, on education policy, was presented for debate. Its opening paragraph stated that the best way to prevent tyranny was to "illuminate, as far as practicable, the minds of the people at large." Jefferson's plan would have had the Assembly choose three "honest and able" men each year to serve in each county as aldermen, charged with establishing schools; the aldermen in turn would name an "overseer" to appoint and evaluate teachers. All children, boys and girls, were to be entitled to three years of free elementary education, and to learn reading, writing, and arithmetic, as well as Greek, Roman, English, and American history. Poor but promising boys would go on to free grammar school, studying Latin and Greek languages, geography, and higher math.

The "quixotic" aspect of Jefferson's proposal was its assertion that impoverished circumstances should not be a barrier to social advancement. It was axiomatic for him that native talent should be rewarded and the republic's leaders drawn from a wide pool. Assemblyman Jefferson was wholeheartedly invested in Bill no. 79, but Governor Jefferson seems to have recognized that, in the midst of a costly war, his liberal plan stood little chance of being funded by the state.

Bill no. 80, which directly followed, detailed the nearly hundred-year history of the College of William and Mary and proposed legislation that would expand the number of professorships and guarantee the state's financial commitment to an institution that educated "the future guardians of the rights and liberties of their country." Its Revolutionary language proved to be window dressing, and Bill no. 80, like Bill no. 79, had fantasy written all over it. It soon became clear that Jefferson's painstaking labor on the laws of Virginia had been done prematurely. It would fall to Madison to reintroduce Jefferson's agenda to the Virginia Assembly after the war, when Jefferson himself was abroad and unable to exert any direct influence.[41]

"Retaliation Becomes an Act of Benevolence"

Naturally the war was of paramount importance to all of the nation's governors. But because of the extent of Virginia's land claims, the matter of British and Indian positions in remote areas of the West consumed Jefferson's time as soon as he entered office. In mid-1776 he had prepared a series of recommendations for Pendleton, which he humbly called "undigested stuff," advocating the sale of western lands to people who had little to invest and everything to lose. This plan made more sense to Jefferson than permitting vast tracts of land to be gobbled up by the very rich.[42]

Now in 1779 his chief contact in the distant reaches of the known West was the Virginian with the greatest experience there, Albemarle's George Rogers Clark. (Clark's much younger brother William would later team with Meriwether Lewis, the scion of another Albemarle family, to explore the trans-Mississippi during Jefferson's presidency.) Clark, a redhead like Jefferson and a year younger than Madison, was well known to both future presidents. He had on many occasions visited the Jefferson property. In his teens, he had studied at the school of Scotsman Donald Robertson, where Madison boarded prior to attending Princeton. Though records are scant, Madison and Clark must have overlapped at Robertson's.[43]

Clark was not a scholar but a surveyor and frontier fighter, an "adventurer" who captured the Virginian imagination. Like the similarly formed George Washington, he identified with the cause of land speculators before going on to distinguish himself in war. At the time of the massacre of Chief Logan's family in 1774, he was traveling along the Ohio River with the Indian's antagonist, Michael Cresap. Surveying the Kentucky River on behalf of the Ohio Company in 1775, Clark wrote home that he intended to settle near Frankfort, "ingrossing all ye Land I possibly Can." He urged his father to join him.

Whether by accident or by habit, George Rogers Clark ended up in the middle of multiple conflicts: Dunmore's war with the Indians and then disagreements among the land companies of several states. When the backcountry became a theater in the war with Great Britain, Clark became a principal player. Learning of Jefferson's Declaration, the Virginia constitution, and Patrick Henry's governorship, he returned to Virginia, met with Henry, and secured the legislature's agreement to furnish his frontier forces with five hundred pounds of gunpowder. Clark sent agents to collect intelligence around the Kaskaskia River in Illinois county and, in the second half of 1777, visited Williamsburg again, where Jefferson, as a proponent of western settlement, attended to his needs. From the beginning, Madison, Jefferson, and Henry all pushed for a strong presence along the Mississippi, which they aimed to keep out of foreign hands.

Promoted to colonel, Clark embarked on a momentous expedition, hoping to secure for Virginia and the new United States a string of outposts under British control, including some along the Mississippi. A few in Virginia—Patrick Henry, George Mason, George Wythe, and Jefferson—knew the full character of the secret mission; the rest of the Assembly was informed only of Clark's role in defending Virginia's claim to Kentucky. In 1778 Mason, Wythe, and Jefferson signed a letter to Colonel Clark, authorizing him to make war on any Indian tribes responsible for massacres. The British were enlisting Indians to fight for them, and Jefferson, before his governorship began, called for their expulsion to areas beyond the Mississippi—"the invariable consequence of their beginning a war," he wrote. This may sound extreme, but it was not an unpopular policy. As long as he was judicious and did not interfere with the claims of friendly Indians, Clark was able to guarantee his men that they would receive, in addition to their pay, three hundred acres each.[44]

Knowing Clark was aiming to remove British power from the Mississippi, Jefferson spearheaded bills through the Virginia Assembly designed to invite settlement. He wanted Virginia to stand behind cheap, easily obtainable land and small-scale agriculture. Then, along with George Mason, he helped to keep a dialogue going with states that continued to look askance at Virginia's growth. This strengthened Virginia's position: once the Loyal and other land companies embraced, in principle, *state* sovereignty over all *private* claims, their sister states would show a spirit of compromise by confirming a substantial portion of the companies' claims.[45]

George Rogers Clark took the offensive. From June 1778 he had led his forces into what the Virginia Assembly was calling "Illinois County," capturing the French town of Kaskaskia, below St. Louis. When residents were apprised that the king of France had joined America's cause, the local French militia accepted Clark's offer of American citizenship. This helped him secure the peaceful surrender of nearby Cahokia and later the strategic post at Vincennes, on the Wabash River, at the modern boundary of Illinois and Indiana. As word of mouth spread, a number of Indian tribes got wind that the Virginians were expecting reinforcements—a deception on the part of Clark, because none were coming—and they too abandoned their British allies. It seemed possible that the British position in Detroit would become vulnerable. Over several months Clark persistently harassed the enemy. His relatively small army was stretched thin, though, allowing the British to re-take Vincennes. But then, Clark pulled off a daring and unlikely raid, tak-ing advantage of an unexpected thaw in the middle of February 1779, returning across muddy prairie to Vincennes and capturing the infamous lieutenant governor of Detroit, Henry Hamilton.

Hamilton was known as the "scalp-buyer," or "Hair-Buyer General," owing to his rumored order of indiscriminate Indian attacks on Ameri-cans, including women and children. Hamilton regularly reported back to British headquarters in Quebec the numbers of prisoners taken and the number of scalps received—the latter figure was always much larger. After he was taken prisoner, the explanation Hamilton gave Clark was a familiar one: that he was merely carrying out orders from his superiors. Clark, in turn, allowed those of his men whose relatives had been slain to butcher a number of Hamilton's Indians taken at Vincennes. There was little gentle-manly honor on display and no parole given; when, in the Declaration of Independence, Jefferson referred to savagery and the "known rule of war-fare" on the frontier, this was what he meant.

Patrick Henry had been governor when Clark's expedition was first au-thorized. By the time Hamilton and his officers were led back to Williams-burg, it was June 1779, and they became prisoners of the new governor. A rather different scenario had presented itself when British and Hessian officers were taken prisoner after General John Burgoyne's large army surrendered at Saratoga, New York. All were well treated during their seven-hundred-mile march south to an honorable captivity in Albemarle County, Virginia. Major General von Riedesel and his wife rented Philip Mazzei's estate next to Monticello and received hospitality from the gover-nor and his family.

Such was the contrast between rule-bound European-style combat and the chaos Colonel Clark knew. As one who adhered to principles of reprisal and retribution, Jefferson, who talked music with the German officers, re-fused to show any consideration toward the scalp-buyer. His Council of Advisors agreed that Henry Hamilton and his officers deserved to be kept in irons and confined to the public jail. Thus the symbol of British barbar-ity remained in an unsanitary ten-foot cell for nearly all of Jefferson's two years as governor. Jefferson resisted all pleas for compassion. Just as he had previously listed the evidence that King George III had, without cause, behaved cruelly toward the American people, Jefferson now defended his position with respect to the scalp-buyer by invoking known examples of mistreatment of American prisoners.

There was always the other side. Major General William Phillips was Burgoyne's second in command at Saratoga and one of the captured British officers whom Jefferson treated with respect during his confinement in Albemarle. Phillips invoked the rules of war to appeal on the basis of civilized compassion and reciprocity, asking Jefferson to show clemency toward the prisoner from Detroit. The reply officially came from Jefferson, Madison, and the Council of Advisors, but the style and cadence smacks of Jefferson—certainly the moralizing does: "We think ourselves justified in Governor Hamilton's strict confinement on the general principle of National retaliation," it read. "When a uniform exercise of kindness to prisoners on our part has been returned by as uniform severity on the part of our enemies, you must excuse me for saying it is high time...to teach respect to the dictates of humanity; in such a case, retaliation becomes an act of benevolence." Paraphrasing the passage on Indian treachery in the Declaration of Independence, the letter tacked on these words: "The known rule of warfare with the Indian Savages is an indiscriminate butchery of men women and children." In hiring wild assassins, Hamilton was as guilty of murder as he would be if he had committed the acts with his own hand.[46]

"A Bustling Time"

The third week of July, just as the letter to Major General Phillips was sent, Madison left Williamsburg and returned home to Orange. He wished to escape the malarial conditions that the low-lying capital was known for in the middle months of the year. There are indications in fragments of his surviving correspondence that Madison was ill for at least a part of the time when he served as a member of Governor Jefferson's council. He seems to have been close by in June, when Jefferson was new at his job and Henry Hamilton was on the agenda, and he was there again in November-December, as rampant inflation played havoc with the state's economy.

Then at the end of 1779 Madison agreed to serve Virginia, as Jefferson had four years before, as a delegate to the Continental Congress. He returned to Orange to prepare for the trip to Philadelphia. We have his and

Jefferson's testimony that their "intimacy" had formed by now, but that is all they tell us. What matters is that as Jefferson's time in office grew stressful, Madison was far from the scene.

The one connection that hints at their cooperation involves Madison's role in Mazzei's mission to raise funds on the continent of Europe. Talkative and opinionated, Mazzei had been Jefferson's friend and neighbor for several years, shared his interest in agricultural experimentation, and did much to kindle his interest in wine. Obviously Jefferson was a prime mover in Mazzei's mission, and while Madison, protective of his delicate frame and fearful for his health, declined the offer to sail with the Italian, he did help to orchestrate his voyage and communicated with him on matters of compensation and security.[47]

The Mazzei mission was part of a larger effort to cultivate potential benefactors. While Madison was still in Williamsburg, Jefferson wrote to the governor of Spanish-held Louisiana, Don Bernardo de Gálvez. As part of an official appeal to a "powerfull and wealthy Empire," he apprised the Spaniard of George Rogers Clark's activities on behalf of Virginia. Clark's success in establishing a presence on the Mississippi led Jefferson to propose a regular channel of commerce and communication with the gulf port. Announcing Virginia's entry into Louisiana's general neighborhood, Jefferson presumed that "the nature of those Commodities with which we can reciprocally furnish each other, point out the advantages which may result from a close Connection, and correspondence."

So even at this early moment in the nation's existence, Jefferson had his eye on Louisiana and on the strategic position of the port of New Orleans. He looked for any opportunity to gain an advantage there. When Henry was governor, Don Bernardo had conveyed to Spain Virginia's request for a loan. Jefferson now renewed the application, acknowledging that his state was "encompassed...with Difficulties" and might not be able to repay Spain as readily as "our Gratitude would prompt us to." As an adviser to Governor Henry, Madison had been a party to discussions regarding a Spanish-U.S. military alliance and free use of the port of New Orleans. When he arrived at Congress in Philadelphia, he would be the one to guide debate on relations with Spain and navigation of the Mississippi.[48]

Madison took his seat in March 1780. Snow had kept him in Virginia longer than planned, and the two-wheeled carriage, driven by his slave Billey Gardner, required twelve days, twice as long as usual, to reach Pennsylvania.[49] He commented on the persistent rains he encountered and the "extreme badness of the roads" heading north. Not a single one of the Virginians who had been present in Congress during Jefferson's tenure was still there when Madison joined the delegation. Among his colleagues were Jefferson's neighbor John Walker and Joseph Jones, the uncle of James Monroe, until recently a judge of the Virginia General Court. Fifty-three years old and a past member of Congress (1777–78), Jones was knowledgeable. He would be a sounding board for the new congressman.

Madison had passed the winter studying government finance: he hoped to stop the depreciation of both the Continental currency and the paper currency in Virginia. By the time he took his seat in Congress, he had concluded that the crisis was less a result of the excess printing of money than a matter of the perceived creditworthiness of Virginia and the nation at large. The public had to trust that a note could be redeemed at face value at a specified time.

In his first letter home, Madison reconfirmed for his father that the depreciation of paper currency had introduced "disorder and perplexity" into public affairs. Congress was acting to coordinate exchange rates. It had devalued the dollar, was ceasing to issue Continentals, and was dictating a single, standard paper currency rate to the states. Each state would now be printing new money, backed by the United States and redeemable in six years. Even so, Madison believed that "perplexity" ("anxiety; distraction of mind," according to Dr. Johnson's *Dictionary*) would continue to plague the currency issue.[50]

Madison wrote two letters to Governor Jefferson at this time, the first of which has been lost. Thus, the second, dated March 27–28, 1780, marks the beginning—an inauspicious one—to their surviving correspondence. Madison minced no words as he reported on probable consequences if the currency crisis was not resolved: "An old system of finance discarded as incompetent to our necessities, an untried and precarious one substituted," he warned. "I leave it to your own imagination."

War news was hardly more promising. "Gen. Washington writes that a failure of bread has already commenced in the army," Madison told Jefferson. By May, when he brought Jefferson up to date on currency and credit, Madison expressed equal concern that the national legislature had erred in ceasing to print money (when it passed that responsibility on to the individual states). With reference to Congress, he wrote: "They are now as dependent on the States as the King of England is on parliament."

The updates continued, but information was flowing in one direction only, and Madison grew concerned. He prodded Jefferson to give him an indication that his several "private" letters had arrived safely in the governor's hands. "If your Excellency has written any acknowledgements of them," he said, "they have never reached me." Then, knowing of Jefferson's particular apprehension with regard to Indian attacks, he conveyed ominous war news from upstate New York: "The Savages are making the most distressing incursions, under the direction of the British agents... It is probable the Enemy will be but too successful this campaign in exciting their vindictive spirit against us throughout the whole frontier of the United States." The Continental Army was not helping: "General Washington has found it of the utmost difficulty to repress the mutinous spirit engendered by hunger and want of pay." And then there were the actions of Pennsylvania to reflect on: the governor there had just been given the power to seize supplies from any source whatsoever and deliver them to Washington's army. It was a move that Madison viewed as a dangerous experiment in executive dictatorship. In all, the congressman had nothing to cheer about.[51]

The first of Jefferson's letters to Madison (that we possess) is dated July 26, 1780, from Richmond, the new state capital. While Madison fretted about currency issues, the hamstrung governor was mainly concerned with regional developments. The enemy had devised a new strategy for the dismemberment of the United States. The "Southern war," as Jefferson called it, was under way and centered, for the moment, in South Carolina. He could not decide how best to divide Virginia's contribution of troops and horses among the beleaguered armies of the North and South. Dwindling tobacco profits did not help the situation. At least Jefferson could cap his letter with an optimistic report on Reverend Madison's administration of the College of William and Mary and George Wythe's establishment of a law school there, where "the young men dispute with elegance, method and learning." The governor's sign-off was agreeably unceremonial: "I wish you every felicity."[52]

Within days Madison heard from his cousin directly. "We are here in perfect Repose," the college president wrote, meaning it as a critique of the passivity of the young men who should have been thinking of the war. "The Arrival of ye. French Fleet has dissipated our apprehensions, and I doubt not, but ye lethargic Spirit of Virginia will enjoy her Slumbers." Even the arrival of South Carolina refugees in Williamsburg had had little effect.[53]

Like his cousin, the Reverend Madison was enjoying national prestige. At the end of January 1780, he was granted membership in the American Philosophical Society, the institution founded by Benjamin Franklin in 1743 to showcase the talents of American scholars and scientific experimenters. Alongside Reverend Madison's name in press reports were those of other new members of the society: George Washington (for reasons other than academic), Thomas Jefferson, John Adams, John Jay, and Washington's young aide-de-camp Colonel Alexander Hamilton, who was in his mid-twenties. The curious mingling of names at this uninspired moment amid war makes the society's announcement a sign, if not a portent. With the exception of the college president, who possessed no greater ambition, these were all gentlemen with critical roles to play in the development of a sense of nationhood. Congressman Madison was not on the list.[54]

Edmund Pendleton was starved for information. He wrote to Madison, in his usual happy style, from the seclusion of his estate in Caroline County. "Placed as I am in a Forest, occurrences will not enable me to give you much entertainment," he submitted. The benefits accrued by a continuing correspondence would be far greater for him than for Madison, he said, but he bade the young congressman to keep him abreast of news nonetheless. The reply he received a few weeks later was the first of dozens of informative letters that the two would exchange during Madison's time in Philadelphia. Picking up on Pendleton's natural enthusiasm, Madison wrote to the squire of Edmundsbury with more verve than he showed when he addressed letters to the squire of Monticello.[55]

In May 1780 Charleston fell into enemy hands, and the whole American southern army, more than three thousand men, was taken. Many of them were Virginians. Lord Charles Cornwallis, in charge of the southern strategy, quickly capitalized on a demoralized people by sending raiders into the backcountry. One name stood out: Colonel Banastre Tarleton, a twenty-six-year-old merchant's son from Liverpool. Relentless (some said possessed), Tarleton was flamboyant and hard-charging and coordinated his activities with Tory cavalrymen. Horatio Gates, the American general who had earned fame as the victor at Saratoga, took over the U.S. southern effort and was disastrously defeated at the Battle of Camden after Tarleton broke through his lines.

That autumn another hero of the Battle of Saratoga, Benedict Arnold, was exposed as a traitor as he attempted to turn over the strategic fortification at West Point to the British. As Arnold's defection became known, British and Tory elements moved their increasingly successful campaign from South to North Carolina. As Jefferson mourned the situation, Madison and the Virginia congressional delegation in Philadelphia wrote to him, with more loathing than fear, on the subject of Major General Arnold and his shocking move. "Every Mark of horror and resentment has been expressed by the Army at such atrocious and Complicated Vilainy," they reported jointly. "The Mob in this city have burnt the traitor in Effigy."

When he should have been focused on military strategy, Jefferson was presiding over an impoverished treasury and wishing release from his duties. "Extremely mortifyed" by setbacks in the Carolinas, and doing his best to contribute supplies and reinforcements in "our present moneyless situation," he admitted to Richard Henry Lee in mid-September 1780 that he felt himself no longer up to the job: "The application requisite to the duties of the office I hold is so excessive, and the execution of them after all so imperfect, that I have determined to retire from it at the close of the present campaign."[56]

Adding to the demands of official business, Governor Jefferson was cultivating a young protégé: he had agreed to serve as law tutor to Congressman Joseph Jones's nephew, the twenty-two-year-old James Monroe. After two years of soldiering, Monroe was back in Virginia. He had taken part in several engagements as a Continental Army officer. He had fought Cornwallis at the Battle of Monmouth (New Jersey) in June 1778, where, during a lull in the fighting, the young major led a scouting party to spy on the enemy's movements. Discovering British intentions, he alerted General Washington directly and helped to ensure a positive outcome. After his return south, Monroe began a course of study with George Wythe, in Williamsburg, before exchanging the old capital for the new and taking instruction from the sitting governor in Richmond.[57]

Jefferson felt sympathy for the emotionally demanding Monroe, fifteen years his junior and seven years younger than Madison. As a rule, Jefferson was patient with those who had trouble holding their passions in check, so long as they were loyal and receptive. That was Monroe, who in 1780 assisted the governor by traveling to North Carolina and setting up a network of military communications; his work linking Richmond to points south was of real value to the war effort. In September of that year Monroe wrote fawningly to Jefferson: "I feel that whatever I am at present in the opinion of others or whatever I may be in future has greatly arose from your friendship." It was a prophetic statement. He went on to bemoan the modesty of his "private fortune," a comment he would repeat many times over the years. Monroe's courage could not be doubted, but his saccharine correspondence foretold the different ways in which Jefferson would come to deal with his two closest allies and successors as president.[58]

In Philadelphia, the emotionally restrained Congressman Madison boarded at the home of Mary House and her married daughter, Eliza House Trist, establishing a close bond with his landladies. Other boarders were Virginians Joseph Jones and John Walker and a New York delegate from Suffolk County, Long Island. William Floyd was a signer of the Declaration of Independence, and his daughter Kitty, just thirteen, would soon draw the attention of the bachelor from Orange County, Virginia.

Although the course of the war was in doubt, Madison's ambition was being satisfied. He expressed no inclination to learn at the feet of his father how to manage the plantation economy. At twenty-nine, Madison appears to have been the youngest member of Congress. A Delaware delegate wrote dismissively in his private journal that the slight Virginian "possesses all the self conceit that is common to youth and inexperience." The harshness of the comment may represent an impulsive first impression, the diarist's own defective ego, or the ever-present jealousies that afflicted the politicians of Revolutionary America; but it also suggests that Madison, so often called shy by his biographers, was not a silent member of the national body for long.[59]

Affairs of state looked increasingly bleak, especially the nation's finances. The "13 separate popular bodies" did not function well together, Madison wrote, and it looked like Congress would only see more "uncertainty & delay" and respond with "dilatory & undigested expedients." The enemy remained well provisioned and was on the move. Madison advised his regular correspondents back in Virginia, Edmund Pendleton and Joseph Jones (who had left Congress after only a short stay), that British warships had sailed from New York. Their destination was unknown.

It was clear that Virginia should prepare for an invasion by sea. At the end of October 1780, Madison informed Pendleton that their common fear was well founded. It was Virginia, indeed, that the invaders had selected as their target. "I am sensible of the great difficulties you will have to contend with" was all he could say. He tried to take comfort in the expectation that the state legislature would "arm" the governor and his council with sufficient authority to "call forth the military resources of the Country." Showing the confusion that really governed, Joseph Jones wrote to Madison from Richmond that he was waiting for confirmation of "flattering accounts from the South" that Cornwallis and his entire army had been captured. His nephew Monroe, now a colonel in the Virginia militia, was, Jones noted, a part of the most recently organized detachment of light infantry. But Jones shied from predicting what was to happen next, acknowledging "imperfections" in intelligence reports. Pendleton was more prone to believing good news and told Madison that "loose Accounts" of three thousand British surrendering struck him as "not improbable."

The true picture was not what anyone wanted to hear. The British high command had assessed Virginia's vulnerability. Pendleton realized that the House of Delegates lacked a quorum and would not meet until three weeks after originally scheduled. Virginia's government was on vacation at the worst possible time. Several leading legislators, plus Governor Jefferson, all intended to resign. "It is a little cowardly to quit our Posts in a bustling time," Pendleton contended. He meant Jefferson and others as well. But he certainly meant Jefferson.[60]

"British Horse Came to Monticello"

From the moment British warships were sighted off the coast in October 1780, Jefferson understood that many of the troops he intended to send south to join Gates and engage with Cornwallis in the Carolinas would now have to remain in Virginia. An invasion force of 2,200 men under Major General Alexander Leslie came ashore at Portsmouth and Newport News. The British boasted a mighty cavalry; the Virginia militia was short of weapons. Slaves, hearing of the landings, ran off to join the British. Yet Leslie stopped short, when he might have pushed inland with devastating effect.

Through the mails, Madison and Joseph Jones ran through the options available to slave owners. Jones was interested in a scheme that would raise white recruits by instituting a kind of property tax: "those wealthy in Negroes" would have to part with one, who would be transferred, as property, to a white soldier as a bounty for enlistment. Madison reacted against the idea of a "Negro bounty," suggesting instead that loyal slaves could earn their freedom by enlisting in the fight against the British. Agreeing with Jones that troops were needed quickly, he argued: "Would it not be as well to liberate and make soldiers at once of the blacks themselves as to make them instruments for enlisting white Soldiers? It wd. certainly be more consonant to the principles of liberty which ought never to be lost sight of." Madison tried to frame his proposal logically. Slave recruits would promptly identify with their free comrades, he surmised, "experience having shown that a freeman immediately loses all attachment & sympathy with his former fellow slaves." Though Madison's emphasis lay with practical measures and the psychology of war, he did take the moral high ground, showing that he had no fear in the arming of slaves. He wanted to beat the British at their own game.

Jones figured that Madison's idea of organizing black regiments stood little chance of helping the American cause and might just inspire the British to redouble their own efforts to coax southern slaves into serving the Crown. This, he said, would "bring on the Southern States probably inevitable ruin." Gradual emancipation was "a great and desireable object," Jones went on. But it would be a shame to lose a critical source of labor, all the while risking a "sudden revolution" if Madison's well-meaning experiment were tried.[61]

In November 1780 the unsuccessful General Gates was replaced by a greater general, the Rhode Islander Nathanael Greene, who adopted aggressive tactics in the Carolinas and forced Cornwallis to rethink. But before General Greene could have much effect, the despised Benedict Arnold came ashore near Jamestown just after New Year's Day 1781, marching on Richmond with fifteen hundred men and taking the capital without opposition. Jefferson could not have done much at this moment, though he can be faulted for not mobilizing the militia in time. Sending shock waves through the region, the faithless Arnold quickly left Richmond and returned to the coast. The capital of Virginia was so new, it had no significant public construction worth destroying.

In the midst of upheaval, there was at least one bright spot. At the time of the invasion, George Rogers Clark happened to be in Richmond to meet with Jefferson, and he dealt a punishing blow to one British contingent before being forced to get out of the way of Arnold's superior numbers. A few days later, at the Battle of Cowpens, in South Carolina, Virginian Daniel Morgan orchestrated a resounding defeat of Tarleton's cavalry, claiming more than one hundred British lives while taking more than seven hundred prisoners. It was the first impediment Tarleton's raiders had faced.[62]

Cornwallis ranged over inhospitable country in North Carolina, far from his supply base, chasing after General Greene. In mid-April 1781 he announced that he was "quite tired of marching about the country in quest of adventures" and brought his troops to Yorktown, on Virginia's coast, from where, he predicted, "a successful battle may give us America." The combination of impatience and overconfidence in a general tends to yield quotable lines such as these—in several months Cornwallis's words would come back to haunt him.

Washington dispatched the youngest of his generals, the Marquis de

Lafayette, to Maryland and Virginia. Jefferson notified the French volunteer that Virginians were as yet unprepared for a larger-scale war, blaming four years of a deceptive calm, while fighting raged hundreds of miles north and hundreds of miles south. Virginians had not acquired, he said, the "habits" of those who lived in the face of danger.

Jefferson himself continued to feel ill equipped to direct a war, and he wrote to Madison in March 1781 of his resolve to step down when his term expired at the beginning of June. Madison's wooden and protracted reply is revealing in its lack of assertiveness: "Notwithstanding the personal advantages which you have a right to expect from an emancipation from your present labours,...I cannot forbear lamenting that the State is in the present crisis to lose the benefit of your administration. But as you seem to have made up your final determination in the matter and have I doubt not weighed well the reasons on which it is grounded I shall lament it in silence." At this early stage in their association, Madison seems to have known that he could not change Jefferson's mind, and so he politely gave the governor the benefit of all doubts.[63]

As spring arrived, Arnold's forces were on the move again. Jefferson estimated the enemy at over four thousand strong, poised to come back in his direction from the Norfolk-Portsmouth area. Meanwhile the militia was short of lead. With mordant wit and understatement, Jefferson wrote to the Virginia delegation in Philadelphia of Arnold's intent: "Should this Army from Portsmouth come forth and become active (as we have no reason to believe they came here to Sleep) our Affairs will assume a very disagreeable Aspect." The loss of Chesapeake Bay as a commercial outlet was damaging to public and private shipping. The currency crisis had not relaxed either.[64]

As Arnold pushed inland, Jefferson relocated the state government from Richmond to Charlottesville, in the shadow of Monticello. The Governor's Council was absent from the scene, and he was left to his own devices. He is supposed to have met at this time with Lafayette, who was awaiting reinforcements from Pennsylvania. Acknowledging his impotence, Jefferson regretted that Virginia could not contribute a sufficient number of men to make active resistance possible. "I sincerely and anxiously wish you may be enabled to prevent Lord Cornwallis from engaging you till you shall be sufficiently reinforced and be able to engage him on your own terms," he told Lafayette. The foreigner who had fallen in love with America extemporized well, harassing the British and preventing them from penetrating deeper into Virginia and pushing north.

On May 28, 1781, a powerless Governor Jefferson appealed to Washington to lead the bulk of his army to Virginia. The reappearance of their long-absent native son would, he said, "restore full confidence of salvation." To this he added with extreme pathos: "A few days will bring to me that period of relief which the Constitution has prepared for those oppressed with the labours of my office." Two weeks later, when Jefferson was no longer governor, Richard Henry Lee would propose in no uncertain terms that Washington return to his state as a military dictator. Now a militia colonel who had seen some action himself, Lee appealed to Madison and the rest of the state's delegation to lean on Washington: "Let Congress send him immediately to Virginia, and as the head of the Foederal Union let them possess the General with Dictatorial power until the General Assembly can be convened." He expected Washington to retain this singular power for up to ten months and insisted that precedent for such action could be found in ancient as well as modern history. "There is no time to be lost," Lee urged, "for the enemy are pushing their present advantages with infinite diligence and art."[65]

Jefferson and the Virginia assemblymen with him in Charlottesville knew that the enemy was closing in. Pendleton had mistakenly conveyed intelligence to Madison that Tarleton had been killed in North Carolina, his legion "wholly cut to pieces." But on Sunday, June 3, 1781, one day after Jefferson's second term as governor came to an end without a successor having been chosen, an alarm was sounded. Captain Jack Jouett of the Virginia militia overheard the plans of several horsemen in Tarleton's regiment. Familiar with local roads, he raced to Monticello in the predawn to alert Jefferson, then rode on to warn the exposed legislators in Charlottesville. After sending his family to safety, Jefferson remained on his little mountain long enough to gather up papers he did not want the enemy to capture. He then made a dash to nearby Carter's Mountain, where he saw through his telescope that Charlottesville was crawling with British.

Tarleton's men took seven state legislators prisoner in town. Those British soldiers who reached Monticello threatened the lives of Jefferson's house servants as they stood guard over their master's valuables. Fortunately for the now ex-governor, Tarleton gave orders to leave the estate intact. Cornwallis, who occupied Jefferson's Goochland County property, Elk Hill, behaved less magnanimously, plundering at will. When he departed, nineteen of Jefferson's slaves went with him. Four Monticello slaves took advantage of the invasion and ran away as well. Upward of eighty thousand slaves left their owners during the war years.[66]

Jefferson recorded an innocuous entry for June 4 in his account book: "British horse came to Monticello." Rumors flew, and "intelligence" reached Philadelphia that exaggerated the impact of the assault on Charlottesville. Many read that Jefferson had been captured. We do not know whether or for how long Madison might have bought into this rumor, only that a month after the event he communicated with Philip Mazzei in Europe and noted that Jefferson had had a "very narrow escape." He would not escape his critics, however, as stories of his management of the crisis began circulating.

Jefferson's movements are actually easy to chart. After his brief reprieve on Carter's Mountain, he rode on and met up with Patty, their daughters, and twenty-two-year-old William Short. Short was one of Jefferson's select law students, a protégé like James Monroe. This handsome, honor-bound young man would be at Jefferson's side a great deal more than either Madison or Monroe during the 1780s, and at this fretful moment the family must have seen him as a godsend.

The Jefferson party traveled south together for two days, arriving at their Bedford County plantation, Poplar Forest, where the pursued politician cooled his heels. A fall from his horse kept Jefferson in Bedford longer than he might otherwise have planned to stay. The state legislature, which had assembled on the western side of the Blue Ridge, in Staunton, could not help but notice his absence.[67]

Jefferson felt he had performed his patriotic duty for two years as governor, and he wanted nothing more to do with management of the war. But before long he was compelled to answer for his conduct. On June 12 Thomas Nelson, Jr., an old friend of Jefferson's and a signer of the Declaration of Independence, took over as governor; Assemblyman George Nicholas, a young representative with interests in Patrick Henry's Hanover County as well as Jefferson's Albemarle, moved that an inquiry be made into Jefferson's actions. The clear imputation was that Jefferson had failed to do his duty in arranging for a proper defense of Richmond at the time of Arnold's invasion. Everything had gone downhill from there.

In July, once the damage was already done to Jefferson's reputation, Nicholas wrote to the accused that he had not intended personal insult. By autumn Nicholas would admit that he had overreacted. And at year's end both houses of the Assembly voted unanimously to commend Jefferson for his service as governor, wording the resolution so as to praise him for his "ability, rectitude, and integrity."[68] Nevertheless, people believed what they wanted, and over the years the story would enlarge: Was it ineptness that

Jefferson had displayed? Was it cowardice? Did he precipitously flee from Arnold, instead of remaining at his post and directing the militia? Did he do something weak in running from Tarleton's men as they approached Monticello? The rap on Jefferson was that he cared too much for his own safety and too little for that of others.[69]

In this time of panic, someone besides the enemy had to be blamed for what befell Virginia, thus Jefferson was made the scapegoat. But no one person was at fault for the thinning of the ranks. Over the course of the war, neither Jefferson nor any of Virginia's legislative leaders did anything to substantially change men's attitudes about military service. Washington had stated unabashedly that the "lower class of people" should serve as Continentals; he did not realize that these tended to be the men with the least resolve. Few cared to fight outside their state, and the Virginians who were drafted into the Continental Army became disaffected quickly. They demanded and received higher bounties than Virginia militiamen, but despite receiving incentives for their service, many still ended up deserting. Resistance to conscription exposed tensions between the ruling gentry and nonslaveholding whites who felt they bore the greater burden in keeping the Revolution on track. The fault lines grew wider as the war progressed. Not inconsequentially, and without the intention of vindicating Jefferson, Pendleton told Madison on the eve of Tarleton's entry into Charlottesville that the Pennsylvanians, instead of speeding their troops to Virginia, "were throwing out Insulting speeches that Virginia was too grand—let her be humbled by the Enemy, & such like."[70]

The fact remains that protesting the burdens of his office and lacking real military knowledge, Jefferson lost stature by acquiescing to a second term. If he had been more aggressive in raising and deploying militia the story of his wartime governorship might have been different. Nor can we say whether his predecessor would have done any better. Patrick Henry was back with the legislature in Staunton, known to have encouraged, if not goaded, Assemblyman George Nicholas to go after Jefferson.

No matter what grudging respect for the Revolutionary orator Jefferson might have retained up to this point, he unmistakably regarded Henry as his chief antagonist now. Writing to the sympathetic Isaac Zane, whose iron manufactory was much in demand during the war, he held Henry accountable for the investigation into his conduct. The "trifling," pitiable Nicholas, Jefferson said, was "below contempt," "the tool worked by another hand." Then, if the artisanal metaphor were not transparent enough, he left solid ground for his next, comparing the unnamed Henry to a whale, "discoverable enough by the turbulence of the water under which he moved."[71]

Finding "neither accuser nor accusation" when he arrived in Richmond to defend himself that fall, Jefferson stayed on for two weeks and turned his attention to science and study. He ran into the trailblazing Daniel Boone and gave him a letter for George Rogers Clark, then in Louisville, Kentucky. Jefferson requested of Clark "teeth of the great animal whose remains are found on the Ohio." He was in the process of writing *Notes on Virginia* and was eager to collect mammoth bones and other specimens from the West; his fellows in the American Philosophical Society awaited his findings.[72]

"The Hostile Machinations of Some of the States"

The future of the West was not merely a matter of science and exploration, of course. When the Assembly met in Staunton after Jefferson stepped down from the governorship, the state's attorney general, Edmund Randolph, was newly elected to Congress. He joined Madison in Philadelphia in July, and the two bonded quickly. They lived together at the House-Trist establishment and, by day, weighed the touchy matter of Virginia's western land cessions, a matter of unending concern to the planter class.

Poorly defined boundaries in vaguely worded royal charters had resulted in claims by Virginia, Massachusetts, Connecticut, and New York to some of the same territory. After more than a century and a half of jealously guarding its legal authority to land adjacent to the Mississippi River and the Great Lakes, Virginia now agreed in principle to give over to the United States the portion of its territory that encompasses modern Ohio, Indiana, and Illinois. Maryland, possessing no territory beyond its current borders, most resented neighboring Virginia's long reach. The Virginians had to satisfy Maryland if that state was to agree to the Articles of Confederation and define the wartime union as a constitutional authority and not merely a league of states.

Virginia's offer of a land cession was framed in terms of a common fund to be administered by Congress. It would not allow its western land to be divided among existing states, expecting instead that new states would be formed from it. This had been Virginia's position since 1780, when George Mason proposed using western land for the war effort—sales of public lands benefiting the national government.

From the perspective of Mason and others, the cession had to involve shared sacrifice. It had to void private land company acquisitions and questionable agreements with Indian tribes—all that continued to motivate the various non-Virginia claimants. Virginia would not permit private land companies to challenge its sovereignty in the West, nor should Congress even be able to consider these private claims. One such company, the Indiana, brought in a hired gun, the polemical Tom Paine, to argue against Virginia's interest. The author of *Common Sense* had spoken to common purposes in 1776, but in this instance Paine's prose served only to irritate the Virginians and increase their still-simmering suspicions about the motives of their sister states.

Virginia consented to an Ohio River boundary line, that is, to the westward extension of the Mason-Dixon Line, which officially divided Maryland and Pennsylvania. By this consent, Virginia gave away disputed portions of western Pennsylvania, at the same time stipulating that George Rogers Clark and his men receive from Congress the land bounties Virginia promised them. Crucially, Maryland dropped its objections to Virginia's expansionism; with their long coastline, Marylanders were spooked by British maneuvers offshore in 1781, and were suddenly eager for friends. That is how the last holdout among the so-called landless states agreed to sign the Articles of Confederation. America had its first national constitution.[73]

But that agreement did not end the contest over western lands. The congressional debates of 1781 marked but one phase in a protracted struggle by the small states to convince Virginia to adjust its sights in order to make for a less lopsided Union. As various members of Congress pressed Virginia to give up more of its rights to the "Western Country," Madison wrote to Jefferson that the proceedings "clearly speak the hostile machinations of some of the States against our territorial claims." George Mason warned Jefferson as well, using highly dramatic language when he portrayed the move in Congress as a conspiracy: "factious, illegal, & dangerous Schemes now in Contemplation in Congress, for dismembering the Commonwealth of Virginia."

At the time when Madison asked for guidance on land cessions, he and Jefferson had had no direct correspondence for several months. The congressman warned the ex-governor that the rise in discord threatened to bring an end to the Union just as soon as the war ended. While insisting that their state should reserve the right to withdraw its agreement to any cession at all, he asked Jefferson to convey to fellow Virginians "the necessity of great temper and moderation." Madison knew that any diplomacy he undertook would have to have full support in Richmond, and he still considered Jefferson's influence strong there.[74]

Despite Madison's historical reputation for reserve, he showed no reluctance to vocalize his strong pro-Virginia outlook in the face of skeptics. Along with his colleagues Edmund Randolph and Joseph Jones, the now thirty-year-old Madison had the presence of mind to strike a delicate balance between talking tough and urging patience. He saw a real possibility that the Confederation might dissolve right after it had begun, but he also thought it possible for Virginia to get what it wanted even as the central government gained new powers.[75]

The convergence of two fundamental ideas—negotiated boundaries and federal power—occurred to Madison before it did other Virginians. Did he envision, even remotely, where the road would lead in six years? As the historian Peter Onuf has put it quintessentially, "Jurisdictional confusion created a mandate for a stronger central government." And that is precisely where Madison stood. Once the Articles of Confederation were ratified, he immediately perceived the need for an amendment calculated to "cement & invigorate the federal Union" by asserting what he described to Jefferson as "the coercive power of Congress over the States." Jefferson did not respond to Madison's centralizing proposal for months, suggesting that in 1781 he may have been reluctant to engage fully with Madison's philosophy of government.[76]

The Revolution had profoundly affected the ways in which the former colonies related to one another. Independence required not just mutual military dependence but a moderation of the power differential among the states. The United States had only the shell of a government, because the collective states had not forged a sustainable political community. As Pendleton revealed when he gave credit to the rumor that Pennsylvania was withholding troops because it hoped to see Virginia weakened, trust was wanting.

"The Honorable Acquittal of Mr. Jefferson"

In October 1781 the Franco-American alliance culminated in a combined siege by land and sea, and the surrender of more than seven thousand of the enemy. With a feint toward the British position in Manhattan, Washington had marched south to Virginia, joining Lafayette, as the French navy sailed up the Chesapeake and put the squeeze on Lord Cornwallis at Yorktown. Though Washington would have preferred that Lafayette capture and execute the traitor Benedict Arnold, he was satisfied to get his hands on Cornwallis. After expressing confidence that the collapse of Virginia would effectively end the American rebellion, the British earl found his forces pinned down. On October 17 he capitulated so as to avoid unnecessary bloodshed. Virginia was saved, though not by Virginians. Out of a force of fifteen thousand that mustered to fight at Yorktown, only fifteen hundred or so were from the Old Dominion. As it was, the British would hold on to New York and Charleston for two more years, until a formal peace treaty was signed.

The defeat of Cornwallis changed the domestic conversation only to the extent that His Majesty's armed forces were no longer a threat to the sovereign states. Two issues, western land cessions and economic recovery, kept Congress hard at work. But persistent uneasiness in the political process does not take away from the meaning of Yorktown. As Dr. David Ramsay, the Revolution-era historian, wrote of this extraordinary moment: "The people throughout the United States displayed a social triumph and exultation, which no private prosperity is ever able to fully inspire." While Jefferson licked his political wounds at Monticello, Madison joined the Philadelphia celebrations.[77]

Shortly after Jefferson became governor in 1779, Edmund Randolph had visited Washington's headquarters as Virginia's attorney general. From there he reported back dutifully to Jefferson on the progress of the war. But now, laboring in Congress beside Madison in the fall of 1781, Randolph struck a very different tone. "I was much distressed," he wrote ex-Governor Jefferson, "to find your irrevocable purpose of sequestering yourself from public life." With a combination of flattery and frustration unlike anything Madison would have written, Randolph berated Jefferson: "If you can justify the resolution to yourself I am confident that you cannot to the world."

In his letters, Madison held back when it came to personal matters. In November 1781, before the Virginia Assembly dealt officially with the inquiry into Jefferson's conduct in office, he wrote to Jefferson on the western question as though nothing had changed since May. He signed off: "With great respect and sincere regard." The following month, after Pendleton relayed news that the embarrassed ex-governor had escaped censure in the Assembly, Madison was clearly delighted. "It gives me great pleasure to hear of the honorable acquittal of Mr. Jefferson," he told Pendleton. "I know his abilities, & think I know his fidelity & zeal for his

Country so well, that I am persuaded [the acquittal] was a just one." Madison's exoneration of Jefferson reads as heartfelt, yet we cannot overlook his choice of words: by his own testament, he had to be "persuaded" that Jefferson's actions were justifiable.[78]

During the first two years of the Madison-Jefferson correspondence, most letters concluded with some version of the conventional, "I am, dear sir, your obedient servant." That of May 5, 1781, was the first in which Madison placed "yr. sincere friend" above his signature. This was a few weeks before Jefferson's near-capture at the hands of Tarleton's dragoons. In the months following, an odd, indefinite silence disturbed the progress of the relationship. A half-year went by before all appeared well again. Whatever Madison was to Jefferson or Jefferson to him at the end of 1781, the next few years would see their collaborative purposes enlarge and their trust deepen.

CHAPTER THREE

Partners Apart
1782–1786

I thank you much for your attention to my literary wants.

—MADISON TO JEFFERSON, IN PARIS, APRIL 27, 1785

They yesterday finished printing my notes . . . I beg you to peruse it carefully
because I ask your advice on it and ask nobody else's.

—JEFFERSON TO MADISON, ON THE PENDING PUBLICATION OF
NOTES ON VIRGINIA, MAY 11, 1785

AS THE YEAR 1782 BEGAN, JEFFERSON HAD NO INTENTION OF RE-
entering politics. Madison, well adjusted to the legislative routine in
Philadelphia, did not know how hurt and angry Jefferson was upon his return to Monticello. On January 15 he wrote to Jefferson for the first time
since the Virginia Assembly proffered its outwardly conciliatory grant of
absolution to its former governor.

Madison had no illusions about the nature of politics. From this moment on he would never again confine himself to polite language in his
private correspondence with Jefferson. He called the Assembly's inquest
an "attack," without acknowledging that he had required "persuasion" to
re-embrace Jefferson. "The result of the attack on your administration was
so fully anticipated," wrote Madison, "that it made little impression on
me." These words would have been solace enough, but he wanted to say
more. Virginia had retracted the insult by electing Jefferson to Congress;
Jefferson had declined the honor. If Jefferson had agreed, Madison now
told him, "it would have afforded me both unexpected and singular satis-

faction." He needed a strong ally to bolster his efforts, and no one would have been a more resolute defender of greater Virginia than Jefferson.

His purpose in writing Jefferson at this time, however, was not to ruminate on the personal dimension of political life but to move ahead. Madison was uncertain that the delegation as constituted would be able to protect Virginia's distant territory from the "machinations" of "interested individuals." The other states were ganging up on Virginia. Even John Witherspoon, Princeton's president, whom Madison looked up to, was now his adversary in Congress, representing the small, landless state of New Jersey and supporting the claims of private land speculators against the arguments of Virginia. Madison charged that Virginia was being "persecuted" by its sister states, and he meant it literally.

If Jefferson refused to join Congress, then Madison at least wanted him to use his research skills to fortify the state's position on the land cession issue. Convinced that he had proof of a conspiracy against their state beyond what the Assembly in Richmond could help to offset, Madison explained why he needed Jefferson. Everyone else thought Virginia too big for its britches; they had no second thoughts about cutting Virginia down to size: "We have no hope at present of being enabled from any other sources than the voluntary aids of individuals to contradict even verbally the misrepresentations and calumnies which are daily leveled against the claims of Va." In the present environment, "calumnies" could stick.

As his trusted friend Edmund Randolph prepared to leave Congress after only eight months (Joseph Jones would be gone as well), Madison felt that the hopes of Virginia rested on his shoulders alone. He had in his possession a collection of papers and judgments from both George Mason and Edmund Pendleton, that he called "valuable"; but Jefferson was the one best equipped to assist him in winning back the respect for Virginia that he believed was practically depleted as the war neared its end. There is a tone of desperation in his January 15 letter, bidding Jefferson "spare as much time as would survey the whole subject, beginning with the original [1609] charter." He was asking for a lot: a multifaceted argument that drew on nearly two centuries of written history.[1]

Jefferson was an ardent collector not just of books—he possessed a trove of state historical manuscripts. Finally responding to Madison's January letter in late March, he acknowledged the importance of the issue Madison presented but explained that the materials he needed had been taken across the Blue Ridge Mountains to Augusta County for safekeeping when the British raided Charlottesville. He would be unable to begin addressing the legal aspects of the case until his papers were returned to him. This was not a rejection, as Madison well understood. In fact, James's brother William Madison was coming to Jefferson's neighborhood to study law; now that he was "retired from public business," Jefferson explained, he would have leisure to mentor William, as he had done with James Monroe and William Short.

Madison had no choice but to be patient. With guarded optimism he wrote to Edmund Randolph on May 1 that he expected Jefferson to "lend his succor in defending the title of Virginia . . . I have exhorted him not to drop his purpose." Randolph, considerably less patient with what he characterized as an "unpardonable rage for retirement," replied promptly: "Mr. Jefferson must undertake the guidance of the work; or, I fear, the deviation will be great from the path of argument, which ought to be trodden on this occasion." Randolph was clearly less sympathetic toward Jefferson, thinking him selfish for staying at home when Virginia needed him. But it was Madison who struggled most with the urgency of the situation. Despite his own good instincts and insights, he was unable to come up with another candidate—a distinguished enough mind and pen—for the job at hand. The combination of scholarship and persuasive power that Jefferson possessed was second to none in the state of Virginia.[2]

"Weaning Him from Those Attachments"

Two months after taking a lead part in the surrender ceremony at Yorktown, the Marquis de Lafayette, who would name his next daughter Virginie, returned home to France. He was not the only marquis with whom Jefferson had been communicating: there was the Marquis de Barbé-Marbois and the Marquis de Chastellux. The first, a chargé d'affaires in Philadelphia, had earlier passed to Monroe's uncle, Congressman Jones, a somewhat generic list of queries about Virginia, the answers to which were to be conveyed back to the French government. The queries ended up in Governor Jefferson's hands. While Marbois expected a dry, factual account, Jefferson's resulting product would be an encyclopedic work of natural history and politics titled *Notes on the State of Virginia*. The other marquis, Chastellux, like Lafayette, had had a role in the victory at Yorktown and was in the process of touring North America when he visited Jefferson at

Monticello on April 13, 1782, his host's thirty-ninth birthday. Thirty-three-year-old Patty Jefferson was expecting another child and was in the eighth month of her pregnancy.

In his *Travels in North America*, published in 1786, Chastellux described Jefferson as Madison was also often described on first encounter: "grave and even cold." But after two hours touring the house and property and conversing philosophically, the Frenchman felt "as if we had spent our whole lives together." He complimented Jefferson on his study of the fine arts in conceiving Monticello, and he wrote preciously that "no object has escaped Mr. Jefferson; and it seems indeed as though, ever since his youth, he had placed his mind, like his house, on a lofty height, whence he might contemplate the whole universe."[3]

That is, more or less, what Jefferson had in mind. Whereas Madison could easily don the armor he needed in the political trenches, Jefferson aimed for greater privacy, for a life spent reading, philosophizing, and improving the productivity of his farms, with perhaps occasional forays into the political field. The investigation into his conduct as governor had so shaken and so disturbed him that six months after his exoneration he rationalized his withdrawal from public life in an emotive letter to James Monroe that was clearly meant to be shared with political colleagues. "Before I ventured to declare to my countrymen my determination to retire," Jefferson said, "I examined well my heart to know whether it were thoroughly cured of every principle of political ambition, whether no lurking particle remained which might leave me uneasy when reduced within the limits of mere private life." In one of the most vibrant passages of any in his writings since the Declaration of Independence, he described his trauma: "I had been suspected and suspended in the eyes of the world...I stood arraigned for treasons of the heart and not mere weaknesses of the head. And I felt that these injuries, for such they have been since acknowledged, had inflicted a wound on my spirit which will only be cured by the all-healing grave."

Monroe knew that his mentor held on to his resentments, though he would have read "treasons" and the "wound" that only death could heal as examples of Jefferson's literary hyperbole. As a new member of the House of Delegates, Monroe was undoubtedly disappointed by Jefferson's retreat from the public; but Madison, still in Philadelphia, had not seen Jefferson in more than two years and had to have been perturbed when he heard that Jefferson had declined election not just to Congress but to the Virginia Assembly as well. He told Edmund Randolph bluntly: "Great as my partiality is to Mr. Jefferson, the mode in which he seems determined to revenge the wrong received from his Country, does not appear to me to be dictated either by philosophy or patriotism." He thought Jefferson should recognize that the Assembly had relented and stop fixating on the injustices some of its members had earlier committed.[4]

Lucy Elizabeth Jefferson was born on May 8, 1782, an hour after midnight. But after childbirth Patty, who had never been robust, failed to regain her strength. After languishing four months, she died in their bed on September 6, 1782. Her husband buried her in the shady grove down the sloping walk that led from the classically inspired house. After ten and a half years of marriage, she was "torn from him by death"—this is what Jefferson ordered carved on her tombstone. The epitaph, borrowed from the *Iliad,* was inscribed in Greek, a language Jefferson celebrated for its purity: "Nay if even in the house of Hades the dead forget their dead, yet will I even there be mindful of my dear comrade."

What is striking about this passage is that it does not place the survivor, Jefferson, among the living, but has him anticipating his own end and vowing that he will even then remember his Patty. The words of Achilles certainly suggest that the Jeffersons enjoyed an intense closeness. In the memoir of his active years written late in retirement, Jefferson referred to their years together as "unchequered happiness."

Reflecting on her mother's death in later years, Jefferson's eldest daughter, Patsy, recalled her father's depressed state. About to turn ten, she saw her father faint during her mother's last moments, then watched him walk about inconsolably for days thereafter. Witness to "the violence of his emotion," as she put it, Patsy could not bear to describe the scene beyond that—even after her father's death forty-odd years later.[5]

On the day Patty Jefferson died, Congress agreed to a conciliatory proposal made by John Witherspoon. In the case of state cessions of western lands, Congress would not reverse any state's decision on the legitimacy of private claims without that state's concurrence. While this was only a step in the right direction, it gave Virginia the flexibility its defenders wanted and removed most of Madison's fears of persecution. How the wary Virginia Assembly would act remained in doubt, but the lead Virginia congressman was relieved.[6]

A few days later Randolph heard of the tragedy at Monticello and wrote to Madison from Richmond: "Mrs. Jefferson has at last shaken off her tormenting pains by yielding to them, and has left our friend inconsolable." The phrasing indicates that Jefferson's associates all anticipated Patty's death but not her husband's reaction. "I ever thought him to rank domestic happiness in the first class of the chief good," Randolph adjudged. "But I scarcely supposed, that his grief would be so violent, as to justify the circulating report, of his swooning away, whenever he sees his children."[7] Madison's reply to Randolph shows how he gauged Jefferson's emotional constitution at this time: "I conceive very readily the affliction & anguish which our friend at Monticello must experience at his irreparable loss," he wrote. "But his philosophical temper renders the circulating rumor which you mention altogether incredible." Madison may have miscalibrated Jefferson's philosophical temper when it came to the manifestation of grief, but he was right in surmising that the loss of Mrs. Jefferson presented a silver lining. "Perhaps," he suggested somewhat indelicately to Randolph, "this domestic catastrophe may prove in its operation beneficial to his country by weaning him from those attachments which deprived it of his service."

While Madison lobbied Congress to send Jefferson, a southerner, to France, to augment the peace-negotiating team of northerners Benjamin Franklin and John Adams, he bade Randolph to make the overture to Jefferson "as soon as his sensibility will bear a subject of such a nature." The third negotiator in France, John Jay of New York, wished to be relieved of his duty, and so the timing seemed right. "Let me know," Madison pressed, "whether or not his aversion is still insuperable?" The question mark and the word *insuperable* tell us that despite his eagerness to employ Jefferson, Madison was well aware of the ultimate contradiction in his character: a desire to retreat from contentious society, an abiding preference for privacy and quiet, joined somehow to a strong political will.[8]

It took the death of his wife to convince Jefferson to leave Monticello, where so many bittersweet memories lingered. Madison, now an old hand in Congress, orchestrated the move and kept after Randolph for two months to persuade Jefferson to agree to a diplomatic posting. This was, in fact, the second attempt to lure Jefferson away. Shortly after the end of his governorship, he had been asked to go to France as a peace commissioner but refused the posting by stating ambiguously that a "temporary and indispensable obligation" would force him to remain in Virginia. This time, as there was no credible obligation, he consented and prepared to leave his native state for the first time in six and a half years. He would head first to Philadelphia to consult with Madison and others, before embarking on his European mission.[9]

"To Forget Their Local Prejudices"

On December 19, 1782, Jefferson jotted in his account book, "set out from Monticello for Philadelphia, France, &c." Accompanied by Patsy, the eldest of his three daughters, he ferried across the Potomac and traveled by way of Baltimore, arriving on the twenty-seventh in Philadelphia, where he visited a barber for a needed shave and took up lodgings with Madison at the House-Trist boardinghouse. On the thirtieth Madison informed Randolph that Jefferson had gotten down to work, "industriously arming himself for the field of negotiation."[10]

As the congressman and the would-be foreign negotiator shared confidences during their month together in Philadelphia, Madison renewed his interest in Catherine "Kitty" Floyd, the daughter of his fellow boarder, William Floyd of New York. Kitty may have been half his age, but at this time a sixteen-year-old girl was marriageable. Though Patsy Jefferson was but ten, she was much closer in age than Madison was to his intended, and she found friendship with Kitty and her older sister.[11]

On January 26, 1783, Jefferson left for the port of Baltimore, along with Major David Salisbury Franks, a Jewish, Montreal-born former aide-de-camp to Benedict Arnold, who was meant to serve as Jefferson's secretary in Paris. Franks and Jefferson were not well matched, in part because the major was suspected of being complicit in Arnold's treason (despite having been cleared by a military court). Franks was so eager to overcome the taint of his past association that he was driven to render services to American generals, diplomats, and financiers. From Baltimore, Jefferson confided to Madison, writing in a cipher they had devised, that he thought Franks competent but loose-lipped, a poor trait for one who was to be situated among foreign diplomats. "I have marked him particularly in the company of women," Jefferson related nervously, "where he loses all power over himself and becomes almost frenzied." They were testing not just a diplomatic code but a confidential vocabulary about the people who surrounded them. In public, the two Virginians came across as cordial and proper; in private, they could sound hypercritical and even cruel.

Madison chose figures of speech less colorful than Jefferson's, but he disparaged with the same degree of candor. He wrote to him: "Congress yesterday received from Adams several letters dated September not remarkable for any thing unless it be a display of his vanity, his prejudice against the French Court and his venom against Doctr. Franklin." Madison had not as yet met John Adams, but he felt free to conjecture. Replying in code, Jefferson took pleasure in Madison's tone of derision and answered in kind: "From what you mention in your letter I suppose the newspapers must be wrong when they say that Mr. Adams, had taken up his abode with Dr. Franklin . . . He hates Franklin, he hates Jay, he hates the French, he hates the English. To whom will he adhere? His vanity is a lineament in his character which had entirely escaped me. His want of taste I had observed. Notwithstanding all this he has a sound head on substantial points, and I think he has integrity." Jefferson's faint praise of Adams does not put much of a dent in the litany of hatreds that precedes it.

Had Jefferson left for Europe as planned, Madison and he would no doubt have continued to write candidly about issues and personalities. As things turned out, though, the vessel Jefferson and Franks intended to sail on was delayed because the predatory Royal Navy was in close proximity. Not long afterward, Jefferson received word that a peace treaty with Great Britain was soon to be finalized and America's independence recognized. As his mission now appeared unnecessary, he returned to Philadelphia and cemented the bond with Madison over the ensuing six weeks.[12]

The year 1783 marked a turning point in the political collaboration of Madison and Jefferson. Until now Madison had relied primarily on the two Edmunds, his dear friend Randolph and the veteran politician Pendleton, to communicate his views on the increasingly intense debates in Congress over the distribution of power in a disjointed republic struggling to make the transition from war to peace. With the widower Jefferson no longer distracted by home life and no longer reluctant to enter the fray, a warm and natural conversation developed between them.

Colonel Alexander Hamilton, Washington's wartime aide, joined the New York delegation in Congress in late November 1782, and immediately recognized James Madison as a colleague worth knowing. It seems likely that Jefferson's arrival on the scene a month later marks the moment when Hamilton and Jefferson met for the first time, quite possibly in the company of Madison. Though a new member of the national legislature, Hamilton was active and forceful in debate. His name appears frequently in Madison's notes on the deliberations of Congress; the two generally agreed on the issues, but Madison's commentary also hints that as the weeks passed, he saw Hamilton as deficient in tact and reluctant to compromise.

The questions of greatest interest to Madison and Hamilton at this moment were how to add revenue to the national government and how to strengthen Congress. They agreed on the desirability of an impost, or duty, on such imported commodities as coffee, wine, and spirits, to be collected from all the states. An impost would enable the United States to repay its war debts. But when Madison's plan came up for a vote, Hamilton would not go along—in Madison's words, because he had a plan "which he supposed more perfect," that is, which invited even greater encroachments on state sovereignty.

Hamilton wished centralization to exceed what Madison had worked out. He wanted federal revenue collection to be aggressive and far-reaching, with tax collectors appointed by Congress to ensure that their allegiance would be to it rather than to the individual states. All but New York and Rhode Island supported the impost; three years later, when Rhode Island finally came around, New York was still being criticized in the press for resisting "the united views and wishes of almost every other part of our foederal government." It was hard for those who agreed with Hamilton and Madison to understand how anyone could oppose such a "salutary expedient to retrieve the credit of America" and believe instead that an impost was the same as congressional despotism over the states.[13]

Madison followed up with an "Address to the States," a statement of principle, ostensibly drafted by a committee of three (with Hamilton of New York and Oliver Ellsworth of Connecticut) but in fact written by Madison alone. He wished that the states would be less self-interested and that Congress would lead in assuming and paying off the states' war debts—the national debt. Madison was cautious about giving Congress complete power over commercial treaties, cautious as well about sacrificing Virginia's planter economy to a northern commercial perspective. But in his mind, building up national revenues was a matter entirely separate from state posturing. And so he appealed to the states to commit to the larger cause of restoring the public credit. His choice of words was atypically emotional: "If justice, good faith, honor, gratitude & all the other Qualities which enoble the character of a nation, and fulfil the ends of Government, be the fruits of our establishments," he wrote, "the cause of liberty will acquire a dignity and lustre, which it has never yet enjoyed." But if the states refused to cooperate, he warned, "the great cause which we have engaged to vindicate, will be dishonored & betrayed."[14]

Madison's "Address to the States" was supplemented by Washington's "Circular to the States" six weeks later, in which the military commander insisted that America's well-being could not be sustained without an unbroken spirit of cooperation among the states, a move "to forget their local prejudices and policies, to make those mutual concessions which are requisite to the general prosperity, and in some instances, to sacrifice their individual advantages to the interest of the Community." Madison had stood up for Washington at times during the war when some of his congressional colleagues expressed doubts about the general's effectiveness. After Yorktown, when Washington came to Philadelphia and stayed for a few months, he and Madison interacted for the first time and occasionally saw each other socially. Around then, too, Madison recommended to the Virginia Assembly that something be done to honor Washington's favorite, the triumphant Lafayette. Madison had done everything he could to please Washington by cultivating the young French nobleman. Now, a year and a half after Yorktown, Washington wrote to Madison requesting that Congress consider Major James McHenry, his former aide (subsequently a Lafayette aide), for a ministerial position in London or Paris. Demonstrating Madison's fast-growing national importance, the illustrious Washington was seeking *his* favor.[15]

One other thing Madison did while Jefferson was on hand in Philadelphia was to propose a permanent resource for Congress: a depository of books on international law, history, world geography, and natural history, for use in politics and diplomacy. For this purpose he tapped a list of 2,640 books cataloged by Jefferson, which Madison amended and expanded to include numerous titles by radical religious skeptics. Unfortunately, the idea of a Library of Congress was ahead of its time; it would not be established until the last year of John Adams's presidency.[16]

Before Jefferson departed Philadelphia in April 1783, the month the "Address to the States" was issued, he observed a spark between the teenaged Kitty Floyd and Madison. In the letters he wrote to Madison while traveling, Jefferson did not fail to send his compliments to "Miss K." He had been privy to the teasing that went on inside the boardinghouse, which must have made Madison uncomfortable. Jefferson had apparently not pressed Madison about his feelings; but now, at a distance, he admitted that he had expressed to their other housemates his high regard for the match. "I know it will render you happier than you can possibly be in a singl[e] state," Jefferson assured.

The cat was out of the bag. Madison had made overtures to the Floyds in April and used their cipher to give Jefferson a blow-by-blow account: "Before you left us I had sufficiently ascertained her sentiments. Since your departure the affair has been pursued. Most preliminary arrangements although definitive will be postponed until the end of the year in congress."

He added a note of gratitude: "The interest which your friendship takes on this occasion in my happiness is a pleasing proof that the disposetions [*sic*] which I feel are reciprocal." In his reply, Jefferson "rejoiced" twice: "I rejoice at the information that Miss K. and yourself concur in sentiments. I rejoice as it will render you happier and will give me a neighbor on whom I shall set high value." Anticipating that the couple would settle in Virginia at the conclusion of Madison's time in Congress, Jefferson extolled the institution of marriage, though he himself, at this point seven months a widower, would ultimately choose not to remarry.[17]

Before returning to Monticello, Jefferson stopped at Edmundsbury, in Caroline County, and visited with Pendleton.[18] There was talk of a new Virginia convention. Madison would soon have to leave Congress, according to guidelines, when his third consecutive year there ended; Jefferson planned to go to Philadelphia in his stead. So in June 1783, thinking ahead, Jefferson presented Madison with an amended version of the state constitution, hoping for his friend's aid in selling it to their fellow Virginians. He wished for Madison to review and comment freely on it, and to discuss its features with capable men in Congress, but not to show it to any other Virginians. Jefferson felt certain he would meet resistance at home.

This episode reveals something else important. Already in Jefferson's mind, there was no one else of their generation at Madison's level of competence whom he could count on to design new policy. The plan was for each to continue the other's work. Madison had eclipsed Pendleton, Wythe, and even Mason as the pivot on which state-building was to occur.[19] Though for the moment the influential, if not always organized, Patrick Henry was relatively quiet, Madison and Jefferson still expected that he would have to be neutralized if their program was to obtain the support of a majority in Richmond.

One piece of correspondence reveals how Jefferson operated. Trying to stay one step ahead of Henry, he gave George Rogers Clark a guide to who Clark's friends were and who was secretly undermining him. To do this meant resorting to invective without sounding petulant, a delicate move for any political opportunist. Writing to one whose susceptible nature he had earlier flushed out, Jefferson stepped gingerly across the page. Clark would, of course, know that Henry was meant when Jefferson damned a certain someone as "all tongue without either head or heart," whose "schemes" were "crooked" (meaning wily and unpredictable). Exposing Henry's betrayal of Clark, Jefferson feigned surprise at Henry's hostile turn; he inserted the clause "as far as he has personal courage to shew hostility to

any man" to show the courageous soldier that he could write off his political rival with one deft twist of the knife. Jefferson divulged as much of
Henry's apparent duplicity as would serve to make the frontier fighter feel
the affront at a distance. The idea was to secure an ally.[20]

The Clark letter is meaningful as a template, because this was how
Jeffersonian-Madisonian politics would be constructed in coming years:
first identifying friends and enemies; then molding opinions, building alliances, and forging plans in coded letters or in small conclaves; and last,
presenting those well-formed plans to large deliberative bodies. In general,
it would be Jefferson who issued the controlling statements, goading their
allies, while the approving Madison maintained a temperate pose in all his
prose.

"His Judgment Is So Sound and His Heart So Good"

Like the federal constitution that Madison would support in 1787–88,
Jefferson's 1783 plan for the Commonwealth of Virginia endorsed three
distinct branches: legislative, executive, and judiciary. It differed from the
scheme then in force, because the governor would serve a single five-year
term, without any chance at reelection. The Executive Council would remain, and its advice to the governor would be, as Jefferson put it, "a sanction to him." The council's "sanction," or consent, was not meant as a stop
to executive authority, however. Jefferson wanted the governor to have
more, not less, power than he himself wielded when he was the state's executive. While opposing giving the governor a direct veto power, he did
recommend granting him more control over the militia, an area in which
he had felt his hands were tied.

A liberal feature in Jefferson's draft was the extension of voting privileges to "all free male citizens of full age and sane mind" after only one
year's residence in the state. But he did not believe the governor should be
popularly elected; rather, he should be chosen by the elected members of
the two houses. Jefferson did not want the legislature to have any opportunity to reverse his main agenda. It could not, for example, "abridge the civil
rights of any person on account of his religious belief" or compel anyone to
contribute to a church; it could not "ordain death for any crime but treason or murder"; it could not "prescribe torture." The slavery provision is
especially noteworthy: it made gradual emancipation a top priority. He
would constrain the General Assembly from introducing any more slaves

to Virginia; and he would not permit it to authorize "the continuance of slavery beyond the generation which shall be living on the 31st Day of December 1800." All persons born beginning January 1, 1801 would be, without exception, free. In this way the proposal marks Jefferson as an early abolitionist, though he did not elaborate on where freed slaves would be permitted to reside, and he certainly did not advocate a Virginia with self-sustaining black communities.

The proposed state constitution was a liberal document, concerned with fair and impartial government. Believing a better power-sharing arrangement could be achieved than that which the 1776 constitution provided for, Jefferson (even before Madison) put forward what amounts to a system of checks and balances. He was full of hope.[21]

Madison, still in Philadelphia, was greatly pleased that Jefferson had decided to reenlist in Congress. One way or another they would be crossing paths soon. In the interim, though, he suffered a personal setback when Kitty Floyd called off their engagement. At the behest of Kitty's father, the renowned portrait artist Charles Willson Peale had composed miniatures of Madison and his intended bride, which the couple ritually exchanged and now had to return to each other. Madison conveyed his disappointment to Jefferson by letter. He had not "calculated" on being jilted, he said—the word *calculated* itself a calculated means of avoiding emotional expression. It was, rather, "one of those incidents to which such affairs are liable." Any other description would have to await their next meeting. Madison expected he would visit Monticello in the coming weeks.[22]

Instead, Jefferson made his way to Philadelphia. He took a roundabout route of nearly two weeks through the Shenandoah Valley so that he could inspect caves and other natural formations that he would detail in *Notes on Virginia*. He was accompanied on his journey by his daughter Patsy and two servants, brothers Bob and James Hemings. Bob, now twenty-one, had been fourteen in 1776, when he traveled to Philadelphia as Jefferson's personal attendant; James, eighteen, served the master in that capacity now, while his older brother began his training as a barber. Both were the biological children of the late John Wayles, who was the late Patty Jefferson's father. These two slaves had come to Jefferson as part of an inheritance.[23]

It turned out that Jefferson did not stay long in Philadelphia, because Congress was on the move. The Revolution may have ended in triumph, but the unpaid soldiery had some sticky issues to resolve with their representatives. An irritated bunch of veterans had poured into Philadelphia in June 1783 to make their grievances known to the assembled Congress, causing the delegates to remove to the modest town of Princeton. There they reconvened temporarily.[24]

Though his seat in Congress would be fixed elsewhere, Jefferson settled his motherless, eleven-year-old daughter in the City of Brotherly Love. During her father's absence, Patsy would be exposed to the best of Philadelphia society, including the children of astronomer David Rittenhouse, a man whom Jefferson ranked among the world's geniuses. He gave his daughter money for music lessons and arranged for her to study drawing with Pierre du Simitière, the Swiss designer of the American and Virginian great seals, who proved impatient with children and would find her wanting in talent.

Having done what he could for Patsy, he rode on to Princeton. He learned there that Congress was doing little and would reconvene in Annapolis a bit later on. So he returned to Philadelphia, spending two weeks there with Madison, buying and discussing books, synthesizing Madison's experience over the past three years, and agreeing on an agenda so that Jefferson could further what Madison had begun. Then the two rode to Annapolis together, where Jefferson was finally able to join the roaming Congress.[25]

Ex-Congressman Madison had no reason to remain in Annapolis. He left Jefferson after a short stay and stopped briefly in northern Virginia to talk politics with George Mason at his estate, Gunston Hall. He informed Jefferson that Mason was amenable to a state convention to consider Jefferson's proposed constitution, though the touchy politician was perhaps less committed than either Madison or Jefferson to solidifying the national union. After he left Mason, Madison rode on to Montpelier. It was now December 1783 and the first time he had been at home with his family since departing for Philadelphia at the beginning of 1780. Easing Jefferson's loss of good company, James Monroe had moved from his position on the Governor's Council in Richmond to a seat in Congress at Annapolis, where they lodged together.

Not to be long diverted from his favorite subjects, Madison spent the snowy months studying constitutions and laws of nations. As things stood, no one was more familiar with the federal system under the Articles of Confederation, and Jefferson often sought his counsel by letter. Noting the absence of many of the states' delegates and expressing frustration over the slow pace of deliberations, he queried Madison about the extent of congressional influence: "Did not you once suppose in conversation with me that Congress had no authority to decide any cases between two differing states, except those of disputed territory? I think you did."

Madison responded with a dissertation upon government. He gave an interpretation of Benjamin Franklin's 1775 "Sketch of Articles of Confederation," looked closely at the role of Congress in treaty making, and weighed precedents in determining where a simple majority of states and where a two-thirds majority was required to enact law. He dwelled at length on the uncertain posture of Virginia, Maryland, and Pennsylvania when it came to any prospective cession of western territory to the federal government. "As all the *soil* of value has been granted out to individuals," he argued, "a cession of the *jurisdiction* to Congress can be proper only where the Country is vacant of settlers." He knew Jefferson would have to deal with this issue at length, and he harbored doubts as to Virginians' understanding of the true complexity of the matter of land cessions. Madison and Jefferson appreciated—but did their fellow Virginians?—the degree of compromise with neighboring states that was yet required to cement the Union.[26]

The Madison-Jefferson alliance was thriving. At the end of increasingly long letters, Jefferson expressed warmth and devotion directly. He invited Madison to ride over to Monticello in his absence and make use of its library, and at one point he ramped up his appeal for steadier companionship. While certainly appreciative of such sentiments, Madison remained tentative at best. In mid-March 1784, explaining that snowy conditions prevented him from accessing Monticello, he addressed Jefferson's larger object of bringing them permanently closer: "I know not my dear Sir what to reply to the affectionate invitation . . . I feel the attractions of the particular situation you point out to me; I can not altogether renounce the prospect; still less can I as yet embrace it."

The "particular situation" he projected was for Madison to move from the family plantation, where his still-healthy father managed everything well. "Monroe is buying land almost adjoining me," Jefferson taunted him. "Short will do the same. What would I not give [if] you could fall into the circle. With such a society I could once more venture home and lay myself up for the residue of life, quitting all it's contentions . . . Think of it. To render it practicable only requires you to think it so."

Madison was not always stirred by Jefferson's wistful themes, but on this occasion he was responsive. They were both without wives, Jefferson hinting that he could "once more venture home" only when Monticello no longer wore the pallor of irreparable loss. A Dutch observer at Congress who spent time with Jefferson in Annapolis presumably heard him refer to his bereavement and recorded these comments: "Retired from fashionable society, he concerned himself only with the affairs of public interest, his sole diversion being offered by belles lettres . . . His mind, accustomed to the unalloyed pleasure of a lovable wife, was impervious[,] since her loss[,] to the feeble attractions of common society, and that his soul, fed on noble thoughts, was revolted by idle chatter." Allowing for overstatement in the service of literature, G. K. van Hogendorp was apparently able to glimpse the intellectual passion Thomas Jefferson exuded as well as the tautness that brought on his fierce tension headaches and disrupted his famously unruffled bearing.

"To render it practicable only requires you to think it so": Jefferson's notion that Madison would be well served by erecting an estate independent of Montpelier obliged Madison to at least ponder the possibility. "Life is no value but as it brings us gratifications," Jefferson orchestrated. "Among the most valuable of these is rational society. It informs the mind, sweetens the temper, chears our spirits, and promotes health." He prodded with Epicurean accents—Epicurus was Jefferson's constant guide to the ideal life. And then he coaxed: "There is a little farm of 140 a[cre]s, and within two miles, all of good land . . . It is on the road to Orange." "Think of it," he pressed a second time, "and Adieu."[27]

In April 1784 Madison was elected to the Virginia House of Delegates. As his accomplishments in Congress were widely known, no one in Virginia doubted that his presence would make a great difference in all matters of state policy. He was a "general" in the eyes of Edmund Randolph, who wrote Jefferson with complete assurance that "our friend of Orange will step earlier into the heat of battle, than his modesty would otherwise permit." Jefferson, for his part, had written to his teenage nephew Peter Carr that he should look up Madison from time to time; while absent in Congress, he wanted a means to confirm that the lad's education was proceeding as it should. "His judgment is so sound and his heart so good," Jefferson urged Peter. "I wish you to respect every advice he would be so kind to give you, equally as if it came from me." For starters, Madison was conveying a copy of Homer for him to read. And though Madison had traded Philadelphia for Richmond, Jefferson, as his promoter, was making the case that he should be accorded membership in the American Philosophical Society.[28]

"Lopped Off from Other States"

As a member of the Confederation Congress from Virginia, Jefferson was front and center when George Washington came to Annapolis and on December 23, 1783, formally resigned his commission as commander in chief of the Continental Army. It was a more than symbolic rejection of military dictatorship before civilian authority; it was a pointed, if rhetorical, corrective to an incipient spirit of defiance that had sprung up among some of his officers. The Newburgh Conspiracy, so called, had been a drama staged for a slow-moving Congress during the spring of 1783, a devious ploy by some, including Alexander Hamilton, to fund the nation's debt and strengthen the federal structure. Its purpose was to change the direction of the country.[29]

Washington had acquitted himself well in the Newburgh episode, using the power of his personality to calm a discontented but ultimately loyal officer corps, and he continued to display dignity and self-possession. In November 1783 Jefferson met him for the first time in seven years and remarked to Virginia's present governor, Benjamin Harrison, that Washington looked healthier than before, despite the many trials he had endured. Jefferson was present at the spectacle in December, when the imposing, six-foot-three-inch Washington resigned his commission and brought his listeners, "especially the fair ones," to tears. Announcing his decision to "retire from the theatre of action" and return to a simpler private life, Washington spoke in a weak and wavering voice, his unexpected humanity electrifying those in attendance. Wise though intellectually unexceptional, eager for respect and admiration, and susceptible to sycophancy, George Washington had learned political savvy over the course of the war. Now fifty-one, he was secure as the preeminent symbol of the American Revolution.[30]

During his months in Congress, Jefferson was involved in the official approval of the Treaty of Paris, which affirmed American independence. That seemingly customary legislative function was complicated by the lack of signatures from some state delegations, prompting Jefferson to consult with Madison on the constitutional questions involved. It was a symptom of the country's lack of cohesion that nine states could not be corralled long enough to attain official recognition of the union of states that had been declared on July 4, 1776.

A certain amount of discussion in Congress dealt with housekeeping issues—anything could become political—so that Jefferson found himself taking part in conversations about where Congress should meet next. While every section of the Union had a favorite site convenient to its own delegation, the choice was narrowed down to an as-yet-unnamed town on the Delaware or one on the Potomac. Trenton, New Jersey, finally won out. Seeing how fractured Congress was, Jefferson could only think of America's domestic ills, its "politics and poverty," when he wrote to the America-loving Marquis de Chastellux, who had recently returned to France.[31]

The most significant matter Jefferson took up in Annapolis was the disposition of western land. This was the final stage in the debate over land cessions, and his communication with Madison was critical in giving Jefferson full confidence in the road that lay ahead. With the largest claimant, Virginia, ready to cede its rights to the Northwest, an efficient, government-controlled process of settlement could begin, moderating the lawless speculation that had muddied the waters for years. Imposing order on a certain hypothetical westerner, the unruly "adventurer," was now the consensus view. Federal land would be sold in stages, to avert a land rush and keep prices relatively high. All parties to the negotiation figured that by preventing the haphazard settlement of widely separated communities, the likelihood of armed conflict with Indians would also be reduced.

As Virginia's historic claim to the West, based on its seventeenth-century charter, dissolved as an issue, peace among the states appeared to be at hand. But below the surface, sectional problems remained, because New England expected Ohio to be settled by northerners, who would impart their values to the new West, while Virginia expected the majority of new states to be politically and commercially aligned with it, as its offspring Kentucky was. Not until the Constitutional Convention of 1787 would the large state–small state rivalry be conclusively dealt with; and by then there would be nothing left to mask the intense, competing visions of North and South.

Congress passed the interim Land Ordinance in April 1784. As chair of the committee that formulated the draft resolution, Jefferson was instrumental in drawing up a plan to divide the new western territories into distinct forms with known boundaries. After reaching an established level of population, each would then attain statehood on an equal basis with the original thirteen. Without detracting from Jefferson's efforts, it can be said that the 1784 ordinance was no less the culmination of Madison's previous work in Congress to federalize expansion without compromising Virginia. Congressman Monroe was on board too, taking the issue so seriously that, after the close of the congressional session, he traveled to westernmost New York State and as far north as Montreal. The next year he visited Pittsburgh and then floated down the Ohio to Kentucky, where he himself had land interests.

Madison regularly compared notes with Monroe on western affairs. He saw immediate prospects for adding new states to the republic, writing in May 1785 of the possibility that Kentucky might be the first, its delegates to the Virginia Assembly having already been instructed to propose "the separation of that Country from this, and its being handed over to Congress for admission into the Confederation." In Madison's estimation, as soon as the Kentuckians went through the process, others would see how smoothly it could be done: "They will not only accomplish it without difficulty but set a useful example to other Western Settlemts. which may chuse to be lopped off from other States."

This did not make Madison and Monroe clones of each other. Madison was, at this point, the more comfortable with prompt and decisive action. He considered the "lopping off" a natural act of evolutionary growth; and when a congressional committee proposed setting up an established church in each township of the newly created western territories—"smelling so strongly of an antiquated Bigotry"—he groaned audibly, finding Monroe ambivalent, if not sympathetic, to the friends of religious establishment. There was no other subject on which Madison took so unconditional a stand. When it came to the cause of religious liberty, Madison and Jefferson alike never relented. They were merely waiting for the moment to be right.

Madison and Monroe did see eye to eye on the enlargement and improved management of land. On his travels in 1784, Monroe had learned firsthand about Indian affairs and protested ongoing British interference along the ill-maintained frontier. When he observed land-redistribution methods under federal guidelines, he took heart. In 1785, then, Monroe followed in Jefferson's footsteps and chaired the committee assigned to reexamine the 1784 ordinance.

Fortune smiled on Jefferson, Madison, and Monroe. Though none of them was present when the Northwest Ordinance of 1787 passed and Congress finally and firmly established the means for new state formation, the document was to a significant degree the product of the three Virginians' collaborative efforts. Not only did the ordinance contain Jefferson's stricture against slavery's expansion; it also marked the first time that the third, fourth, and fifth presidents, whose terms would collectively comprise the "Virginia Dynasty," worked closely together.[32]

It was much more than the Virginians' land hunger that made the West central to political discourse. Americans' sense of their future greatness as a people had been tied to the land for some time. During the French and Indian War, in *The New American Magazine*, "Sylvanus Americanus" (literally, "American Woodsman") sang the praises of the happy, neighborly cultivator, "boast of our nation." The *Boston Gazette* told readers that agriculture was "the most solid Foundation on which to build Wealth," ensuring "the political Virtue of a Common Wealth." In 1775 Alexander Hamilton found a "dawning splendour" in the "boundless extent of territory we possess, the wholesome temperament of our climate, the luxuriance and fertility of our soil." And in 1784 the author John Filson made a national hero of the pioneering Daniel Boone, who spoke of Kentucky as "a second paradise." Western settlement was seen as regenerative.[33]

The new nationalism involved a certain amount of hypocritical thinking. The "virtuous" Washington had been, for years, among the hungriest of the speculators, a typical land-loving American ever on the make. He was now cautioning others to avoid rampant speculation, as if recognizing, belatedly, that the public's interest was always meant to supersede private gain. Jefferson, whose land was inherited, insisted that he did not profit from speculation. In a letter to Madison, he vehemently denied that he deserved to be classed with the speculators. He had withdrawn from a land company a few months after his wife's death, he said, thinking it a conflict of interest if he should go to Europe and be party to negotiations over the disposition of western lands. He had, he noted further, taken "a single step" toward speculating in the West, only to "retract" at the "threshold" of opportunity. Madison was in a less certain position, and he clearly did not share in Jefferson's moral outrage. His father was deep in speculation, and he himself wanted to cross that "threshold," in order to free himself from dependence upon his family. Yet being Madison, he would not enter into any venture unsystematically.[34]

"Civilian and Politician"

In the middle of 1784 an ocean came between Madison and Jefferson. From Annapolis that May, Jefferson notified his friend in Orange that Congress had authorized him to join Franklin and Adams in Paris as a commercial negotiator. Not knowing how long his mission would last, he set terms for Madison and himself: "I pray you to continue to favor me with your correspondence . . . On my part I shall certainly maintain the correspondence." He repeated his desire to operate as a purchasing agent for Madison, employing words that sound formal to us but were, in fact, entirely unceremonious: "If moreover you can at any time enable me to serve you by the execution of any particular commission I shall agree that my sincerity may be judged by the readiness with which I shall execute it. In the purchase of books, pamphlets, etc. old and curious, or new and useful I shall ever keep you in my eye."

Moreover, Jefferson wanted to make certain that the plan he had in mind for his closest political colleagues bore fruit. "I think Col. Monroe will be of the Committee of the states," he related to Madison, underscoring the line that came next: *"He wishes a correspondence with you."* Keeping secrets was one key to Jefferson's political style, which is what he was referring to as he recommended Monroe. "The scrupulousness of his honor will make you safe in the most confidential communications," he told Madison. "A better man cannot be."[35]

There was still time for several more exchanges, as Jefferson took to the road and headed north. From the General Assembly in Richmond, Madison related his intention to sound out his colleagues on the merits of Jefferson's revised state constitution. Whether the political climate in Virginia proved friendly or unfriendly, Madison wanted "license," he said, "to make use of the ideas you were so good as to confide in me." He would carry on, regardless of impediments. In the Madison-Jefferson political playbook, opposition was real but temporary.

The question at hand, Virginia's constitution, hinged on two men above all others: the generally positive Richard Henry Lee and the ever-wavering Patrick Henry. The eloquent Lee had yet to arrive in Richmond, so his mood could not be characterized. The influential Henry was another story. As Madison put it to Jefferson after a short conversation with Henry, "I find him strenuous for invigorating the federal Government though without any precise plan, but have got no explanation from him as to our internal Government. The general trend of his thoughts seemed to suggest favorable expectations." As things turned out, Madison was too optimistic. Just as Jefferson set sail for Europe, the matter of changing the constitution was brought before the legislature. On that day Lee unexpectedly took ill, and Madison, trying to read Henry, figured he had best remain silent. It was a wise move, for as he subsequently reported to Jefferson, "Mr. Henry shewed a more violent opposition than we expected."

Jefferson would not have been surprised. Taking the pulse of Virginia's leaders on another matter sometime earlier, he had complained to Madison: "Henry as usual is involved in mystery: should the popular tide run strongly in either direction, he will fall in with it." Henry had a knack for keeping people on edge, which Jefferson hated. He certainly refused to credit Henry's political abilities, distinguishing between principled secrecy in defense of just causes (his and Madison's way) and a barren lack of principles (Henry's demagoguery) that manifested itself through underhandedness.[36]

Jefferson would not have a chance to see Virginia respond to his ideas for an improved state constitution. No convention was ever called, which he naturally attributed to Henry's opposition. In fact, the constitution adopted in 1776 was to remain in force until after Jefferson's death. He did, however, take such pride in his 1783 plan that he decided to include it as an appendix in his *Notes on Virginia,* under the title "Draught of a Fundamental Constitution."

He picked up Patsy in Philadelphia. From there, waited on by the Hemings brothers, Bob and James, father and daughter traveled through New York to New Haven and from there to Rhode Island. The Providence newspaper reported the visit in the most complimentary terms: "Governor Jefferson, who has so eminently distinguished himself in the late glorious revolution, is a gentleman of a very amiable character...a mathematician and philosopher as well as a civilian and politician."

The word *civilian* retained a meaning we no longer recognize: a legal scholar, conversant in the laws of classical antiquity as well as those of the modern world. Jefferson's role as law tutor to James Monroe is one way of seeing his "civilian" rank. And the word *politician* referred not so much to one who campaigned for elective office as to a student of government who was potentially a statesman. In the early and mid-eighteenth century, *politician* denoted a refined breed of Roman, but it could also be used satirically in referring to ravenous colonial officials who were more ambitious than wise. By calling him a politician, the Providence notice clearly meant to honor Jefferson as a man of elegance and experience.[37]

Civilian and *politician,* seemingly generic terms, actually tell us a lot about Jefferson's reputation on the eve of his assignment abroad. For possibly the first time in a public paper, his name was directly linked to authorship of the Declaration of Independence. The statement was cast in the passive voice by an editor whose knowledge was secondhand: "the memorable Declaration of American independence is said to have been penned by him." The former Virginia governor was seldom in the news outside his native state, so when the Rhode Island newspaperman wanted to make him known to readers, he added the noteworthy line associating the new "minister plenipotentiary" with the famous Declaration. The Fourth of July was annually celebrated and the final text of the Declaration widely heralded, but few beyond the elite circle of Revolutionary leaders could have connected Jefferson to the document. His signature did not stand out as John Hancock's did, and the act of Congress overshadowed the contribution of any one individual, penman or not. Not until the 1800 campaign would Jefferson's supporters broadcast his authorship nationally. As late as the 1810s, his actual role would still come into question, one of the many annoyances he would have to contend with in a partisan environment.

In Boston, the vessel *Ceres* awaited. Bob Hemings was to return south, bearing a businesslike letter for Madison, while James Hemings accompanied the Jeffersons to Europe. He had no time to provide details, Jefferson explained to Madison, noting only that he had taken down his observations of the "commerce and other circumstances" of the northeastern states. Experiencing New England for so short a time was a kind of cultural limbo for him, a way station, as his first ocean crossing loomed.

As well read as Jefferson was, his spoken French was halting, and until he arrived in Paris, the only notable French contacts he had had were those titled gentlemen who had attached themselves to America's cause: Lafayette, Chastellux, and Marbois. He had left his most trusted allies, Madison and Monroe, with gentle directives. He also left behind in Philadelphia a surrogate family, including the upright Mary House and her amiable daughter, Eliza House Trist, proprietors of the boardinghouse to which Madison had introduced him. And he had deposited his two youngest daughters with his late wife's relatives in Virginia.

The Jefferson party left Boston on July 5, enjoying sunny skies and a smooth, brisk voyage to England, then crossing the channel to France. Other than the briefing he was to receive from Franklin and Adams in matters of public duty, one of Jefferson's top priorities after getting settled was to scope out scientific curiosities and acquire books for himself and his most favored friend in Virginia. And instead of bothering with exchange rates and payments, Jefferson told Madison that his expenditures in Europe on Madison's behalf would be offset by Madison's payments for the education and boarding costs incurred by Jefferson's fatherless nephews Peter and Samuel Carr. They would sit down and figure it all out after he returned home.[38]

"Devoutly to Pray"

Jefferson was delighted to have for his private secretary in Paris his protégé William Short. When his other "adoptive son," Short's friend (and now congressman) James Monroe, declined the offer to accompany him to Europe, Jefferson had turned to Short, whose career in Virginia politics was just getting under way. The companionable Short had taken the same road

Madison had at a similar age, serving as a member of the Governor's Council, and Jefferson fully expected him to go the distance, just as Madison had, by joining Congress.[39]

At the College of William and Mary, under the wartime leadership of Reverend Madison, Short had helped to found the Phi Beta Kappa Society that survives to this day. He also was a student of Jefferson's greatly admired law professor, George Wythe. Jefferson was his second examiner, alongside Wythe, when, in 1781, Short was granted his license to practice law. John Marshall, future chief justice of the Supreme Court and Jefferson-hater-in-chief, was another of the William and Mary band whom Jefferson and Wythe qualified for the law around this time.[40]

Short did not arrive in Europe until three months after Jefferson. When he did, he bore a letter from Madison. From the beginning, the young aide proved indispensable to the first-time diplomat. His conversational French was as proficient as Jefferson's was uncertain. In addition to his linguistic talent, he was a natural charmer, if unlucky in love. Short's modern biographer believes that the chief reason he agreed to give up on Virginia and seek a new life in France was the rejection he suffered in Richmond at the hands of a woman who was not his social equal. In France he would move to the other extreme and fall deeply in love with a married duchess.

The letter from Madison that Short carried was put in Jefferson's hand after three subsequent Madison letters had already come by public vessels. The combined product, nearly twenty pages, much of it encoded, made for essential reading that fall. For one, Madison reported on the effort of Virginia Episcopalians to refortify the religious establishment and Patrick Henry's exertions on their behalf. Well-publicized petitions complained about "the present state of neglect of religion and morality."

The fight that Madison and Jefferson had long anticipated was brewing. The church faction was so nervy, Madison reported, that it should have gone down to defeat without much work. It was "preserved from a dishonourable death," he said, "by the talents of Mr. Henry." This elicited what has to be considered Jefferson's most ill-tempered harangue of his competition: "While Mr. Henry lives"—the preceding three words were encoded—"another bad constitution would be formed, and saddled forever on us. What we have to do I think is devoutly to pray for his death." The last phrase was also in code.[41]

In the next paragraph of his letter to Madison, Jefferson moved from venomous talk to a reembrace of manly society. Without any idea of the length of his diplomatic tour, he updated his friendly proposal of ten months earlier: "I once hinted to you the project of seating yourself in the neighborhood of Monticello . . . Monroe is decided in settling there and is actually engaged in the endeavor to purchase. Short is the same. Would you but make it a 'partie quarree' I should believe that life still had some happiness in store for me." Jefferson was engaged in clever wordplay when he stretched the meaning of the French *partie carrée*, a four-way unit –which ordinarily referred to two male-female couples, as in a dance. The dance he had in mind was a power move, an appeal meant to build their collective political clout in Virginia over the long term.

Concerning bonds of love and friendship, with or without political overtones, Jefferson was emotionally demanding and a hard bargainer. Either Madison told him he felt isolated at Montpelier, or Jefferson had convinced himself that this was the case. He drew on their personal affinity and asked whether it did not mean more to Madison than financial gain through some distant land speculation: "Agreeable society is the first essential in constituting the happiness and of course the value of our existence," he wrote, extending his plea, "and it is a circumstance worthy great attention when we are making first our choice of a residence. Weigh well the value of this against the difference in pecuniary interest, and ask yourself which will add most to the sum of your felicity through life." And then the final push: "I think weighing them in this balance, your decision will be favourable to all our prayers." As a man who discounted the power of prayer, Jefferson did not rely on faith but instead on emotional persuasion. Sharpening his point, he urged Madison to spend five months in France: "You shall find with me a room, bed and plate, if you will do me the favor to become of the family."

Owing to the lag time in overseas mail, Madison's reply did not arrive for nearly six months. He reminded Jefferson that he was eager for treatises on "the antient or modern federal republics, on the law of Nations, and the history natural and political of the New World." To this he added a request for a "portable glass" (pocket telescope) to enliven his solitary walks in the neighborhood of Montpelier. Only at the end of the letter did he address the matter of travel, begging off the invitation to visit Paris: "It would break in upon a course of reading which if I neglect now I shall probably never resume." There was a second rationale: "I have some reason also to suspect that crossing the sea would be unfriendly to a singular disease of my constitution." Madison's postscript listed several notable deaths and ended with a question that might have been commonplace at the time and now seems precious: "What has become of the subterraneous City discovered in Siberia?"[42]

Jefferson's bed and plate proposal had been turned down, and his "partie quarree" was stalled. But he would have fresh ideas to report on as he became immersed in French culture and saw more of the country.

"As Sincere an American as Any Frenchman Can Be"

As Jefferson was crossing the ocean one way, the American Revolution's beloved benefactor, the Marquis de Lafayette, had arranged his own return to the United States. Without either of them knowing it, they were on the high seas together and reached land at nearly the same time.

Though he was just twenty-six, Lafayette was making his third crossing since the beginning of the Revolution. The immensely wealthy young aristocrat possessed a fund of honor and determination as well as land and connections. Supremely self-confident, he had sought a letter from Washington in 1783 that he expected would lead to his inclusion in ratification proceedings related to the Anglo-American peace treaty. Lafayette's ambition was of concern to diplomat John Adams, and even Washington was not entirely comfortable with the idea of a Frenchman representing the new nation. At the same time no one wished to dampen the spirit of the brave marquis, who continued to act as a useful liaison in political and commercial matters affecting France and America.[43]

Landing in New York in mid-1784, Lafayette headed south as quickly as he could to pay a visit to George Washington at Mount Vernon. Everywhere he went, he was banqueted. Returning north, he chanced to meet James Madison in Baltimore. The Virginian, who feared the perils of a voyage to France, responded nevertheless to an invitation from Lafayette to accompany him to Philadelphia and from there to central New York State, where the Frenchman was to help in negotiating an agreement with Indian tribes that had remained loyal to the British during the Revolution. The Iroquois retained warm recollections of the French from years of friendly intercourse, and they knew a great deal about Lafayette's exploits during the American Revolution. This is how Lafayette finally got his wish and a private citizen of a foreign nation came to represent the United States in an authoritative treaty.

The land-hugging Madison, who would never even see the burgeoning

West, experienced horrible seasickness as they sailed up the Hudson to Albany. Back on solid ground, the party was met by the Marquis de Barbé-Marbois of the French legation in Philadelphia, the instigator of Jefferson's soon-to-be-published *Notes on Virginia*. Arriving among the Indians, Madison heard several refer to young Lafayette improbably as "my father." The treaty was concluded. It secured long-term peace, while unevenly dividing lands between the tribes and the U.S. government.

Madison and Lafayette grew close as they were roughing it in the woodlands. Afterward Madison wrote to Jefferson about their time together and marveled at the Frenchman's ability to interact with Indians. The friendly Oneidas claimed that it was Lafayette's words to them during the war that had kept them from allying with the losing side. In Madison's view, Lafayette was "as sincere an American as any Frenchman can be; one… whose future friendship prudence requires us to cultivate." The Virginian was particularly struck by the strong stand Lafayette took against the institution of slavery. Said Madison charitably, "It is a proof of his humanity." Forty years later, after the two presidents had been long retired to their respective plantations, sustained by slave labor, Lafayette would still be pursuing an argument with them about America's greatest failing.

When he wrote of Lafayette to Jefferson, Madison was blunt about the Frenchman's less attractive but equally pronounced traits, especially his vanity. It was the same quality that had caused Madison to be repelled by John Adams. But it had to be said that Adams never curried favor from anyone, and Lafayette, Madison concluded, had "a strong thirst of praise and popularity." Reading Madison's letter, Jefferson agreed with his friend's assessment: "I take him to be of unmeasured ambition but that the means he uses are virtuous." To which Madison answered that he since had "further opportunities of penetrating [Lafayette's] character." His "foibles" had not disappeared, but his positive traits were that much more in evidence. He was power-hungry, but he wished to apply power to right ends. And crucially, "his disposition is naturally warm and affectionate and his attachment to the United States unquestionable." Madison was telling Jefferson that once Lafayette returned to France, the American minister should make good use of him. The two were clearly on the same page. "I am persuaded," Jefferson wrote next, "that a gift of lands by the state of Virginia to the Marquis de la fayette would give a good opinion here of our character." Without knowing the full extent of what was brewing in France, he added intriguingly that Lafayette might have a future need to find refuge in America.[44]

While keeping company with the marquis, a hardy traveler not easily deterred, Madison was obliged to endure chilly nights and high winds, as well as long hours sitting and observing ceremony. Though weather-beaten at the end of it all, he emerged from his northern trek attracted to land offerings in the Mohawk region of New York; he now saw investment opportunities there as the best means to secure his fortune. Though a national figure, he was still hopelessly dependent on his father, who had just given him 560 acres of Montpelier land. More to the point, he was a professional politician uninterested in establishing a private law practice.

At this point Madison invited fellow Virginians Monroe and Jefferson to invest in upstate New York along with him. To Monroe, he wrote: "My private opinion is that the vacant land in that part of America opens the surest field of speculation of any in the U.S." To the investment-shy Jefferson, he phrased his appeal a bit differently: "There can certainly be no impropriety in your taking just means of bettering your fortune." But Jefferson continued to find speculation in northern land unappetizing, and he refused to let go of his hope that Madison would buy property and settle near Monticello. No matter what he said, though, he could not convince Madison to do as Monroe was doing. Short, the other member of Jefferson's imagined "partie quarree," would end up investing elsewhere.

While away in France, Jefferson did not know that Madison was focusing his attention on land speculation nearly as much as he was reading up on the law. His father and two brothers, Ambrose and William, had purchased sixteen thousand acres in Kentucky while James, Jr., was serving in Congress; now the ex-congressman wanted to make up for lost time. It was risky business, he well knew, because in the midst of a fluctuating economy most people borrowed on credit in order to buy land.

His gaze was northward first, westward second. One reason the Mohawk Valley appealed to him was that onetime surveyor George Washington assured him it was a good investment. During 1784–85, in the wake of Lafayette's tour, Madison made repeated visits to the retired commander at his Mount Vernon estate, and the two graduated from a proper and respectful acquaintance to a warm and affectionate friendship. Accepting Washington's advice, Madison prepared to take the plunge with his cash-poor friend Monroe. They resolved to buy one thousand acres located between what would soon become the towns of Utica and Rome; but they could not settle their finances in a timely way and subsequently decided to wait until they could travel there together. In mid-1785 Madison let his friend Edmund Randolph in on the scheme, saying that he planned to take up Monroe on his invitation to join him for "a ramble of curiosity." One thing or another prevented them from carrying out their plan. Later, the two did invest on a very small scale. While Madison remained convinced that Mohawk lands would bring massive profit, in the end he was too cautious to risk any more of his small fortune.[45]

"Almighty God Hath Created the Mind Free"

In November 1784, after a five-year hiatus, Patrick Henry was once more elected governor, without opposition. In some ways it strengthened him. But given the executive's limited power under the state constitution, he was in a weakened position when issues he had previously championed were raised again in the House of Delegates. He had recently brought to the floor a bill to strengthen "Teachers of the Christian Religion" through a general tax, unleashing what historian Ralph Ketcham has termed "a torrent of eloquence" to make his case. But without his vocal attention to it, the same bill proved unsustainable in 1785, paving the way for Madison's reintroduction of its opposite: the bill for religious freedom that Jefferson had drawn up early in the war, nearly a decade past.

Firm in his belief, eager in his resolve, and nonconfrontational in his personal style, Madison authored one of the most vivid and striking position pieces of his long political career. His "Memorial and Remonstrance Against Religious Assessments" roused his colleagues to immediate action. It was so strongly worded, in fact, that he told his friends he wanted his name disassociated from it. Although many, as far away as New England, knew that Madison's hand had penned the "Memorial and Remonstrance," it was not until after Jefferson's death in 1826 that he unequivocally admitted his authorship to the grandson of its chief promoter, George Mason. The other prime mover in the effort to disallow state-subsidized religion was George Nicholas, the young legislator previously allied with Patrick Henry who, in 1781, had launched the investigation into Jefferson's conduct as governor but had since reconciled with both Madison and Jefferson.

The Anglican church in Virginia was weaker now than it had been before the Revolution, in spite of the honest determination of such advocates of establishment as Edmund Pendleton and John Page, the staunch friends of Madison and Jefferson. Richmond itself, the state capital, had only one church in 1784. Madison declared in his "Memorial and Remonstrance" that to make any civil magistrate a judge of religious life was not just "an arrogant pretension" and "an unhallowed perversion" but "a contradiction of the Christian Religion itself," which "disavows a dependence on the powers of this world." He argued that religious life had historically "flourished...without the support of human laws," while "rulers who wished to subvert the public liberty...found an established Clergy convenient auxiliaries" as they formed their ignoble plans. What had religious establishment brought to civilization in past centuries? Madison pressed. His unequivocal answer: "Superstition, bigotry, and persecution."

Ecclesiastical establishment not only destroyed the purity of religion, he insisted, it also contributed to "pride and indolence" in the favored clergy and stood to "erect a spiritual tyranny on the ruins of the Civil authority." Establishment lessened the chance that a lawful post-Revolutionary society could sustain "moderation and harmony," and it threatened America's image as a sanctuary for the victims of religious oppression abroad. This is vintage Madison. He argued principles and tried to hide his scorn.

Madison successfully contested Henry by showing that a bill in support of any one Christian sect was a violation of the 1776 Virginia Declaration of Rights, which he himself had helped to draft in his first season as a member of the Virginia Convention. He could now say, with much greater clout than before, what he could only mildly offer in 1776: that religion was not the business of political society, period. A religious establishment covets power. And that cannot be good.[46]

Madison's writings were of a piece with Jefferson's, who wrote incisively in his *Notes on Virginia:* "Was the government to prescribe to us our medicine and diet, our bodies would be in such keeping as our souls are now."[47] The Virginia Statute for Religious Freedom passed easily. It would stand as a model for the First Amendment to the United States Constitution and a primary accomplishment of the Madison-Jefferson partnership.

Its long preamble rolls flamboyantly: "Well aware that the opinions and belief of men depend not on their own will, but follow involuntarily the evidence proposed to their minds; that Almighty God hath created the mind free, and manifested his supreme will that free it shall remain by making it altogether insusceptible of restraint..." The statute goes on to assert that "civil rights have no dependence on our religious opinions any more than [on] our opinions in physics or geometry"; and it warns against "coercions" and the "impious presumptions" of "fallible and uninspired men." Its sharpest rebuke comes in the phrasing: "To compel a man to furnish contributions of money for the propagation of opinions which he disbelieves and abhors, is sinful and tyrannical." All citizens were free to profess their religious views without these having any effect on their rights or civil capacity. Elated, Madison told Jefferson that Virginia had "extinguished for ever the ambitious hope of making laws for the human mind." They were alike convinced that the "multiplicity" of religious sects would support the cause of religious liberty in America.[48]

With this important victory, a majority of the other, less contentious bills that Jefferson composed from 1776 to 1779 were destined to sail through the Virginia Assembly.

"Too Valuable Not to Be Made Known"

What Jefferson termed his "seasoning" in Paris took a good many months. When he was not too sick to go outdoors, he communed with fellow commissioners Franklin and Adams, still on hand, who hoped to conclude treaties of amity and commerce with friendly states in Europe. Franklin, troubled by gout and bladder problems, was always being sought out by his French admirers, which left the senior statesman a modest amount of time for his Virginia associate. In the spring of 1785, entering his eightieth year, Benjamin Franklin sailed home one last time. Jefferson succeeded him as the U.S. minister to France, while Adams accepted appointment as minister to England.

Jefferson had come to speak passable French. He placed Patsy in a well-regarded convent school, apprenticed James Hemings to a French chef, hired a valet, Adrien Petit, and eventually took out a lease on the two-story Hôtel Langeac, located at one corner of the Champs-Élysées. He tried to live well off his meager salary, doing what an eighteenth-century aesthete could scarcely avoid and what Jefferson did most of his life: overspend. His immediate family and the people he legally owned would pay the ultimate price after his death, but for now Jefferson was obliged to live like those in his social circle.

In France, as in America, he was an accomplished host. Living at the center of a great city, he became an incurable collector of paintings, wines, objects, and curiosities. He commissioned from the sculptor Jean-Antoine Houdon busts of Washington, Franklin, Lafayette, and himself, all for display at Monticello; plus a large statue of Washington for the statehouse in Richmond.[49]

Once Lafayette returned to France in 1785, he and Jefferson saw a good deal of each other. Upon his return, however, the marquis delivered a letter that imparted sad news from Virginia: the death of two-year-old Lucy Jefferson, the daughter of Thomas and Patty born a few short months before her mother's death. She and one of her Chesterfield County, Virginia, cousins had succumbed to the whooping cough. Jefferson would now insist on having his six-year-old daughter Maria join him in Paris, to be reunited with her sister Patsy, who was receiving a superior education at a convent school that catered to the French nobility.

Lafayette and Jefferson became regular companions. The marquis used his influence to help Jefferson advance America's commercial interests: duties placed on American whale oil were removed, as Jefferson sought to direct more of the trade in tobacco to France that was presently going through English intermediaries. Lafayette wrote glowingly of Jefferson to Marylander James McHenry, his wartime aide: "No better minister could be sent to France. He is every thing that is good, upright, enlightened and clever, and is respected and beloved by every one that knows him." Jefferson favored Lafayette with one of the first copies of his momentous book, which had been incubating for several years. He brought the manuscript with him to France, where he had put the finishing touches on what was now so much more than the gift ("a dozen or 20 copies to be given to my friends") that Jefferson first envisioned.[50]

As a composition modeled on Enlightenment philosophy, *Notes on the State of Virginia* is one thing on the surface—geography, products of nature, customs and manners of the inhabitants—and quite another as one reads into it: an inquiry into the human condition, an exploration of social policies, a work meant to illuminate. It captures Jefferson's obsession with detail and marks his desire to pronounce the merits of the part of America that he was proud to call home. His ambition was nothing less than to define the contours of Virginia in cultural and political as well as topographical terms.[51]

While an encyclopedic work, *Notes on Virginia* exhibits clear biases. As such, Jefferson first placed the revised and enlarged version in the hands of a small number of liberal European intellectuals whose opinions he wished to shape. It is significant that the only two copies that he sent to the United States went to Madison and Monroe. He asked Madison to judge whether any wider publication would give too much offense to certain Virginia politicians. In Jefferson's words, "There are sentiments on some subjects which I apprehend might be displeasing to the country perhaps to the assembly or to some who lead it. I do not wish to be exposed to their censure." This was more than idle concern, just as his request for Madison's editorial suggestions represented more than good manners. "Answer me soon and without reserve," Jefferson pleaded. "Do not view me as an author, and attached to what he has written. I am neither."

In their still-secure cipher, Madison replied that he, in consultation with "several judicious friends," recognized the risk of placing Jefferson once again in the center of controversy, but he and they considered *Notes on Virginia* "too valuable not to be made known." Reverend Madison was even more definitive than his cousin, goading Jefferson: "Such a work should not be kept in private. Let it have ye broad Light of the American Sun." After receiving his copy of the edition produced in London, Reverend Madison beamed: "Your Notes on Virginia I shall always highly esteem not only on Account of their intrinsic worth, but also, the Hand from which they came . . . I hope your Notes judiciously distributed among our young Men here, will tend to excite the spirit of philosophical observation amongst us.—Never was there a finer Range for the Exercise of such a Spirit, than this Country presents."[52]

Though Jefferson repeatedly called his book "imperfect," it is emphatically the product of a methodical mind that is equally concerned with natural (physical) phenomena and human agency. When Madison learned from Jefferson of its impending publication in French, he recommended that Jefferson authorize an English-language publication to prevent misinterpretation of its more delicate content. Late in life Jefferson recounted what happened next: a Frenchman to whom he had given an original copy died, and the book came into the hands of a Parisian bookseller, who took it upon himself to translate the *Notes* from English into French and print it himself. "I never had seen so wretched an attempt at translation," Jefferson would write in 1821. "Interverted, abridged, mutilated, and often reversing the sense of the original, I found it a blotch of errors from beginning to end." So he consented to publication in London, hub of the printing trade, accepting that he could not control its circulation.[53]

While the book is best known today for its unpalatable remarks about racial differences, it was regarded at the time as a celebration of America's attributes as much as Virginia's and as a defense of republicanism. Taking up the blessings of an agriculturally based economy, Jefferson offered a mild critique of Virginians' indolence and extravagance; yet the Virginia of his imagination was indisputably his idealized America, where westward settlement would add power as well as population amid the peaceful exploitation of a naturally rich and promising continent.[54]

The lists Jefferson compiled show his fascination with cataloging nature. Of rivers, between the Atlantic coast and the Mississippi, he indicates depths and breadth, navigability, rapidity of flow, frequency of floods, and varieties of fish; without apology for his hyperbole, he called the Ohio, which he had never seen, "the most beautiful river on earth." Of mountains, he was similarly thorough and similarly rapturous in description: "The passage of the Patowmac through the Blue ridge is perhaps one of the most stupendous scenes in nature." The Natural Bridge, which the young surveyor George Washington had seen at midcentury and Jefferson himself purchased from King George III in 1774, lay eighty miles southwest of Monticello, an impressive earth and limestone arch and "the most sublime of Nature's works," according to Jefferson in *Notes*. He rhapsodized: "It is impossible for the emotions, rising from the sublime, to be felt beyond what they are here."

As a scientific investigator, Jefferson doubled as a promoter. As part of his celebration of the land, he wanted his readers, men of broad interests, to register what it meant that the United States possessed buried treasure. Reserves of coal, iron, copper, limestone, and marble were abundant in Virginia and the western Alleghenies; there were precious stones to be found as well. Jefferson touted the climate of his own backyard: "I have known frosts so severe as to kill the hickory trees round about Monticello, and yet not injure the tender fruit blossoms then in bloom on the top and higher parts of the mountain." He had discerned which of Virginia's medicinal springs were "indubitably efficacious" and which owed their popularity to mere whimsy. Page after page, he named the plants native to Virginia's vast holdings (those territories that the state still claimed in the early 1780s). He gave both local and Linnaean designations for each, ranging from yellow pine to black birch and from wild cherries to whortleberries.

He applied the rigorous eighteenth-century perspective on the aesthetics of power, an understanding of which brings us a step closer to the psyches of eighteenth-century elite men and women. As the ornamental gardens of English manors showed (on an even larger scale than Jefferson's Monticello), social authority accrued from the collection of seeds and grafts, and from the cultivation of rare and beautiful plants. The Euro-American aesthete tamed nature by knowing what to expect of it. Nature, as spectacle, was convertible into personal, but also public, power. That was what Jefferson was reaching for in his *Notes*. He thought of himself as the assembler of a catalog of knowledge. He quietly boasted America's healthful surroundings and listed the relative sizes and weights of the animals of the Old and New worlds, in order to contest the assumption made by Europe's greatest authority, the Count de Buffon, that animals common to both continents were smaller in America.[55]

In this same vein, Jefferson defended the Native American against Buffon's claim that the Indian, though not shorter in stature, was "feeble," with "small organs of generation...and no ardor whatever for his female." Jefferson wrote at length of the affectionate character, admirable capacity for friendship, and healthy passions of the American Indian. And he famously retold the story of Chief Logan, who on the eve of the Revolution justified his act of vengeance against the whites for murdering his family. The speech of Logan, directed to Lord Dunmore, was, Jefferson asserted, an example of eloquence not excelled by the classical oratory of Demosthenes and Cicero.

History has not forgiven Thomas Jefferson for his comparative treatment of Indians and African Americans in the *Notes*. Indians, he stated, were ignorant because of their lack of exposure to the word of letters; the climate of America did not hold them back, as Buffon and others had insisted. On the other hand, Jefferson construed that blacks were of diminished capacity, a "blot" on America, whose numbers were growing only because they were well cared for: "Under the mild treatment our slaves experience, and their wholesome, though coarse, food, this blot on our country increases as fast, or faster, than the whites." While he acknowledged that slavery was a "great political and moral evil," he could not acknowledge blacks' potential in any meaningful way.

For Jefferson, white faces varied in appealing ways. Was their natural expressivenesss, he posed, not "preferable to that eternal monotony which reigns in the countenances, that immoveable veil of black which covers all the emotions of the other race?" The delicacy of description—this "immoveable veil" of the "other" race—made use of the vocabulary of sensibility through the imagery of light versus darkness, in order to suggest the alien character of the African without making Jefferson sound entirely devoid of compassion.

Claiming that the African was outwardly unappealing, he added "scientific" observations revealing of essential deficiencies. He felt that blacks' inelegance and lack of reasoning ability were natural traits rather than the result of their oppression; this made them incapable of genuine love, which Jefferson defined, in the spirit of his times, as "a tender delicate mixture of sentiment and sensation." Accepting that blacks equaled whites in memory, or "recollection," he still did not consider them to be as educable as Indians. "Their griefs are transient," he insisted; "in imagination they are dull, tasteless, and anomalous." In this way, he placed in opposition the African's depressing dreariness and the Indian's cleverness, artistry, and imaginative speechmaking.

For Jefferson, the African lacked a poetic consciousness. If his lovemaking was a matter of ardent impulse only, and enlightened emotions no part of his makeup, then banal communication was all the African could ever know. Wrote Jefferson, with an appalling provincialism: "Never yet could I find that a black had uttered a thought above the level of plain narration." He concluded that, when freed, all slaves must be returned to Africa or recolonized elsewhere, "beyond the reach of mixture," where, he assumed, they could be coaxed into remaining allies of the United States—albeit distant allies.

Jefferson's was a peculiar calculus of race, reflecting a unique combination of "enlightened" science and "enlightened" sensibility. How he constructed his argument was unusual—his racism was not. Even Madison did not think to rein in Jefferson when he floated preliminary ideas about racial difference that were bound to stir up political passions later. In fact, at this moment, Jefferson was more intent on speaking his mind about religion and power than about race and power. He expected to anger conservative forces by insisting on the rights of conscience in his merciless appraisal of state-sponsored religion. As for race, he did not fear northern mockery of his assumptions any more than he feared an angry African-American reaction to his language; but he anticipated that he would be alienating many in the South for bringing up emancipation at all. In the 1780s few northern whites would have taken offense at what Jefferson imagined as scientifically based conclusions. But he knew that his fellow southerners would react harshly to his recognition of the "ten thousand recollections, by the blacks, of the injuries they have sustained," unenumerated but undeniable wounds that Jefferson deemed likely to "produce convulsions which will probably never end but in the extermination of the one or the other race." In his later section on the manners of the American people, he returned to the issue and unabashedly stated that the institution of slavery had so poisoned America that it stood as "unremitting despotism" at odds with republicanism. White children, "nursed, educated, and daily exercised in tyranny," learned by "odious" example to ignore the humanity of the slave. Indeed, he pondered in this regard, "I tremble for my country when I reflect that God is just."[56]

John Adams notably called Jefferson's observations on slavery "gems," without discriminating between those that appealed for eventual emancipation and those that belittled the natural capacities of African Americans. Adams himself, in defending the British troops accused of murder in the 1770 Boston Massacre, had focused on the part-black, part-Indian provocateur Crispus Attucks, one of the dead, "whose very looks," Adams claimed, "was enough to terrify any person." To make his case, he said that the others who faced down the redcoats included "saucy boys, negroes and molottoes." New Englanders had little sympathy for the disadvantaged African American, felt science had yet to clarify the nature of racial difference, and exhibited no particular discomfort with most racial stereotypes.[57]

By modern standards, or even mid-nineteenth-century standards, Madison and Jefferson did not do nearly enough to relieve suffering and extend rights—certainly not if we compare their dynamic efforts as critics of organized religion, a cause they prioritized. Jefferson could easily have downplayed the problem of race in his native state, but instead he addressed it head-on. He ventured his opinions as one of a distinct community. It would be some time before a significant number of his fellow citizens found his opinions troubling.

In debating with himself and relying on Madison's counsel, Jefferson probably would have preferred to leave his name off the title page of his *Notes*. Even if he had, and removed first-person references in the text, certain passages would instantly have given away the book's authorship. Yet in his approach to the work, Jefferson was trying to signal that he was interested in promoting himself as a thinker only. Like any author, he wanted a certain amount of exposure, but he was not concerned with financial profit—only with reaffirming his status as a Virginia gentleman whose mind was comprehensive and whose purpose was to be useful to society.[58]

"The Present Paroxysm of Our Affairs"

At the end of the year 1785, Madison wondered whether significant agreement among the states was still possible. The wartime consensus had receded, and the voices of his strongest allies were hushed. George Mason wrote from Gunston Hall that he was suffering "Fits of the Convulsive Cholic." George Washington was supportive of Madison's efforts in the Virginia Assembly but impatient with the provincialism prevailing in that body: "We are either a United people or we are not," he fulminated. "If the former, let us, in all matters of general concern act as a nation . . . If we are not, let us no longer act a farce by pretending it." The subject at hand was commercial policy. Madison too feared for the health of the confederacy, given the "caprice, jealousy, and diversity of opinions" that abounded, plus Virginia's "illiberal animosities...towards the Northern States." He was uncertain what to expect from other states, but did not hesitate in condemning Virginia's immobility either.[59]

Also at the end of 1785, the District of Kentucky announced its aim to separate peacefully from its parent Virginia. It would become the first state west of the Appalachian Mountains. Its leaders determined to set up a number of constituent counties, including one called Fayette, after the marquis, where the town of Lexington lies; one called Madison, where Daniel Boone built his fort in 1775; and one called Jefferson, in which Louisville, the town founded in 1778 by George Rogers Clark, is situated. These names and associations, all precious to Virginia, were now to be associated with a new sovereign state. But much work remained to be done to advance the union of the states.[60]

"Everything is quiet in Europe," Jefferson wrote Madison early in 1786. It would be an entirely different picture three years later, of course, when he would be witness to the noisy beginnings of an increasingly bloody and turbulent revolution in France. He was becoming progressively more comfortable in Paris, though he was unimpressed with King Louis XVI and the ceremonies he attended at Versailles. Among the many social opportunities he enjoyed, none surpassed his visits to the Duc de La Rochefoucauld, the intellectually gifted humanitarian whose neighbors and tenants alike appreciated his reformist ways; nor did the duke seem to be concerned by the attentions that Jefferson's secretary, William Short, paid to his second wife, the blue-eyed Rosalie. The duke was fifty-four and she twenty-four, theirs an expedient, rather than romantic, *mariage de convenance*. Short, at twenty-seven, was beloved. Everyone seemed happy.[61]

As spring neared, Jefferson traveled to London, where he rejoined John and Abigail Adams. He was presented to, and disdainfully treated by, the same King George III whose tyrannical ways he had censured so unsparingly in the Declaration of Independence ten years earlier. If Adams-Jefferson diplomacy had no appreciable effect on the British, whose anti-Americanism flowed liberally from the royal court, Jefferson profited from his weeks in England in other ways. He became quite chummy with Mrs. Adams, visited exquisite gardens that he never forgot, and attended a series of plays and operas. His account books show that he did a fair amount of shopping.

Later, Jefferson gave Madison a blunt (encoded) reappraisal of the man he called "my friend Mr. Adams." For reasons that seem a bit disingenuous, he reminded Madison that he had been blind to Adams's shortcomings before Madison and Edmund Randolph jointly persuaded him of the New Englander's vanity. As a consequence, the self-appointed investigator Jefferson had felt it incumbent to look more closely at a man he continued to call "disinterested," "profound," and "amiable." Time, he now told Madison, had confirmed Adams to be "vain, irritable, and a bad calculator of the force and probable effect of the motives which govern men." He was a good judge of most things, reported Jefferson, but a bad judge "where knowledge of the world is necessary." This stinging evaluation suggests that he had sized up Adams as a man who sifted through learned treatises with deftness and decision but had no patience with, or was oblivious to, anything that required an understanding of personality or culture. In other words, he was likable but thick. In the same paragraph, Jefferson outlined the idiosyncrasies of other "public characters" Madison might want to know about, and he updated his opinion on the zealous and "efficacious" Marquis de Lafayette: "His foible is a canine appetite for popularity and fame. But he will get above this."[62]

While Jefferson was accepting the Adamses' hospitality, Madison and Monroe were growing closer too, though there was one piece of crucial intelligence Monroe chose to hide until the last minute: in February 1786 he married a New York merchant's daughter, Elizabeth Kortright, but he only intimated the event to Madison a few days before he tied the knot, saying nothing more than "I will present you to a young lady who will be adopted a citizen of Virga."

Henry "Light-Horse Harry" Lee, fellow Princetonian, Revolutionary general, and new member of Congress, reopened a correspondence with Madison by frivolously labeling Monroe a "Benedict," by which he meant the traitor Arnold. The quip from Lee was a reference to the newly wedded legislator's betrayal of the fraternity of single men. Monroe was six years Madison's and five years Lee's junior and was therefore, by his comic calculation, acting out of turn. Madison read of Monroe's nuptial in the newspaper and duly congratulated his friend on his "inauguration into the mysteries of Wedlock." William Grayson, another of Virginia's representatives in Congress and an old friend of Washington's, supplied Madison with a longer list of congressmen who had recently married, describing the trend coarsely as "a conjunction copulative." He prodded Madison: "I heartily wish you were here: as I have a great desire to see you figure in the character of a married man."[63]

As Jefferson roamed the streets of London, Madison wrote from Orange, telling his unofficial overseas agent how much he appreciated his many book purchases—"the literary cargo for which I am so much indebted to your friendship." In the same letter, he informed Jefferson about an upcoming convention of the states in Annapolis, designed as a "remedial experiment" to put the shaky national economy on surer footing. He anticipated that the addition of western states to the Confederation would make unanimity even less likely than it already was, reducing the amount of legislation that would pass Congress. Westerners, Madison said, possessed "sentiments and interests" that were not "congenial" with those of the Atlantic states. "I almost despair of success," he sighed. He conveyed the same apprehension to Lafayette, unsure whether the branches of the Mississippi would spawn "so many distinct Societies, or only an expansion of the same Society." So as Madison pondered the future in 1786, he imagined that state jealousies would only get worse as the West developed. Virginia's land cessions had eliminated one thorny problem and created another.[64]

Madison was just as explicit about the states and their disparate aims when he addressed Monroe on the subject of a hoped-for, but as yet amorphous, "Continental Convention." "I am far from entertaining sanguine expectations from it," he remarked doubtfully. "Yet on the whole I cannot disapprove of the experiment." A few days later he wrote again to Monroe: "I am not in general an advocate for temporizing or partial remedies. But a rigor in this respect, if pushed too far may hazard every thing."

He wondered whether the means existed to point the states toward consensus. What prudent strategy could Virginians pursue that would not be rejected by their distrustful sister states? The language he used at this moment was a type that Madison rarely resorted to, as nervous and angst-ridden as when he told Jefferson in 1782 that Virginia was being "persecuted" by the rest of the states on the land cession issue. "If the present paroxysm of our affairs be totally neglected," he warned Monroe, "our case may become desperate." Crucial change lay on the horizon: "If any thing comes of the Convention it will probably be of a permanent not a temporary nature, which I think will be a great point." A "great point" did not mean a positive outcome, but a major watershed that would either help or humble Virginia.

After the Civil War, scholars began to refer to the immediate post-Revolutionary years as "the critical period" in American history. One reason is that many of Madison's cohort shared his concerns about the destabilizing factors facing them: money matters within and among the states and their tenuous commitment to nationhood. Madison's general pessimism was offset only by his belief that "the trouble & uncertainty" of having to proceed in small steps would make the delegates of the various states psychologically disposed to negotiating a coherent, systematic treatment for the many palpable defects in the existing Confederation. This marks the first moment when we can identify Madison's dynamic commitment to what, in the end, became the Constitutional Convention.[65]

Finance was always at or near the head of the list of concerns. Some Americans owing British creditors rationalized that depredations during the war negated their prewar debts, but both Madison and Jefferson were among those who acknowledged the rights of the creditor and wanted Anglo-American commercial relations to get back on track. Interest that accrued on Americans' debt during the war was a hazier ethical question. The British expected the interest to be paid. All knew that America needed to trade.

Domestic debt was hardly a simple matter either. The states were ineffective in their attempts to pressure debtors or even to collect taxes. Part of the problem was the decline in output among small-scale farmers who had been away from home serving in the army. Another problem was the declining value of paper money. In Virginia, the gentry accepted the higher taxes the Assembly demanded of them, agreeing in principle that their relative power in state politics should be matched by a higher tax rate. This alleviated, to a certain degree, the burden on those with fewer advantages. But it did not end complaints or bring real stability.

"No supplies have gone to the federal treasury," Madison lamented. "Our internal embarrassments torment us exceedingly." He would feel this torment in spades as Patrick Henry tried to push through the Virginia Assembly a new issuance of paper money, which Madison was sure would "rather feed than cure the spirit of extravagance."[66] Experiments in paper money would fail everywhere: it was "morally certain," as he put it to Jefferson. And Virginia was only a small part of the problem. The sovereign states, taken together, were not contributing enough to the Union. The general government was fiscally unsound.

International repercussions were real and immediate. When Jefferson wrote to Madison from London that the British "sufficiently value our commerce; but they are quite persuaded that they shall enjoy it on their own terms," both understood that America's standing among the nations of Europe would be seriously hurt if discordant notes at home ruined the chance to build a sustainable union. Somewhat later, after negotiating alongside John Adams in Holland on behalf of the U.S. Treasury, Jefferson would remind George Washington of the danger of losing credit in Europe: "Were we without credit we might be crushed by a nation of much inferior resources but possessing higher credit . . . It remains that we cultivate our credit with the utmost attention."[67]

The foreign policy issues that preoccupied Madison were invariably ones with sectional ramifications. John Jay, in his role as secretary for foreign affairs of the Confederation Congress, was engaged in negotiations with Spain's envoy, Diego de Gardoqui, concerning the boundary between U.S. and Spanish possessions in the Southwest. The specific point of argument rested upon whether U.S. commercial traffic was to be permitted along the Mississippi River. On other commercial subjects, Gardoqui extended rights that the United States desired, but he held firm that the Confederation should agree to a twenty-five-year waiting period before navigation rights on the Mississippi were granted.

Jay and the New England interests were content with such an arrangement, believing the Southwest of little value in the short run—plenty of upstate New York land remained to be settled. Madison and the Virginians were outraged. To them, the Mississippi symbolized a future of agricultural wealth and a replication of the South's economy on contiguous lands. Madison had vehemently opposed Vermont's admission to the Union back in 1781, so as not to add another northern vote in Congress. Now, in the spring of 1786, Virginians could read the Jay-Gardoqui recommendation as proof that the Northeast wished to dominate the Union. Terming the negotiations "a ticklish situation," Madison proposed that Congress transfer responsibility from Jay to Jefferson, sending the Paris-based minister directly to Madrid. Meanwhile Monroe told Patrick Henry that men of Massachusetts were openly speaking of a separate northern confederacy if Virginia and the South continued to resist them.[68]

Madison gave Jefferson a lengthy report. As he digested the news, Jefferson painted an equally bleak scenario: the western settlers would recognize that they had been sold out by the United States. Prone to feelings of vengeance, they would then launch an attack on the militarily underprepared Spanish, to "rescue the navigation of the Missisipi River out of Spanish hands, and to add New Orleans to their own territory." In the process they would cease to identify with the eastern states and would move to establish a separate confederation. If the United States helped westerners in their war with Spain, they might rethink; but there would be no certainty of reunion once the ball started rolling.[69]

All this was happening as Madison readied himself for the special convention held in Annapolis in September 1786. Eight states sent delegates to consider the intertwined issues of commercial policy and regionalism. It was clear that without larger common purposes, without a sense of justice transcending sectional interests, the Union was doomed to fail. Unable to proceed very far in their deliberations, the delegates who met in Annapolis resolved that a more thoroughgoing convention would have to be organized. They announced that it would take place in Philadelphia in May 1787.

"In Imagination"

During the summer and autumn of 1786, five years after the death of his wife, Jefferson entered into an intense, if short-lived, relationship with the London-based Anglo-Italian artist Maria Hadfield Cosway. She was sixteen years younger than he, charming by all accounts, and in a loveless marriage with a successful painter, the miniaturist Richard Cosway, who is often depicted as sexually ambiguous and outlandish in his tastes.

The complete character of Jefferson's relationship with Mrs. Cosway cannot be known. But the tenor of the correspondence, and the fact that the more passionate of their letters were intentionally excluded from the posthumous multivolume collection of Jefferson's writings edited by his grandson, suggest a romantic relationship. They picnicked as a couple, attended museums and plays, and observed the city's architecture when Richard Cosway was elsewhere engaged.

Jefferson was acutely aware that in France the meaning of marriage was not quite the same as in America. Members of the nobility with whom he interacted married for social and economic reasons. Husbands and wives had sexual partners other than their spouses. The prim, more rigid Adamses flatly disapproved. In letters to fellow Virginians, Jefferson, at least rhetorically, also rejected this aspect of the French way of life and love. Marriage always had to have a moral component, he insisted.

How sincere was his protest against "a passion for whores" when he discussed the prospect of a young American seeing Europe and facing its temptations? Years later his correspondence shows him condoning French license—for the French, at least. It was fine for them to distort what nature intended, but Americans could not live that way. So it became something of a mantra for Jefferson to use the French example as a contrast when he wished to paint American manners as pure.

He complained reflexively of "female intrigue," because he subscribed to the medical Enlightenment no less than to the liberal political Enlightenment. The prevailing literature categorized the female constitution in sexual language, as prone to powerful urges and needing her natural curiosity gratified. Men, for their part, required an outlet; they could not abstain from sex without forfeiting their mental and physical health.

On this foundation, eighteenth-century philosophic medicine had fashioned an elite culture that did not view sex as sinful, in the way the later Victorians would. A man of breeding, especially a widower like Jefferson, could rationalize his engagement in discreet sexual activity with an available, attractive young woman of any social station. In the world he knew, the educated and privileged made their own rules; they escaped the kind of censure that the courts imposed on those, male and female, who were presumed vulgar and bad and whose individual efforts to resist laws concerning adultery or interracial sex received little sympathy.[70]

In one of his many letters to Maria Cosway, Jefferson complained about the prurient eyes that he feared would waylay any of their letters that were committed to the public post. A diplomat had to shield himself from possible blackmail. As the lover of a married duchess, William Short was no prude; constantly at Jefferson's beck and call, completely trusted by him, Short had to have been privy to whatever was happening in the relationship. Imploring Jefferson to visit her in London, Mrs. Cosway flirtatiously brought up Short's amorous tendencies, informing Jefferson that "the beauty he lost his heart by," the duchess Rosalie, "is here keeling [i.e., killing] every body with her beweching Eyes." Jefferson wrote to Maria that he wished he could fly to her side: "I am always thinking of you. If I cannot be with you in reality, I will in imagination." As the Jefferson-Cosway correspondence proceeded, there was usually a hint of romance, or else of disappointed yearnings.[71]

At no time did Jefferson commit to paper the name "Maria Cosway," even to note her existence, when he wrote to his intimates Madison and Monroe. Only the cautious couriers of their private letters knew anything.

CHAPTER FOUR

The Division of Power
1787

Nothing can exceed the universal anxiety for the event of the meeting here. Reports
and conjectures abound . . . The public, however, is certainly in the dark with
regard to it. The Convention is equally in the dark as to the reception
which may be given to it on its publication.

—MADISON TO JEFFERSON, FROM THE CONSTITUTIONAL
CONVENTION, SEPTEMBER 6, 1787

It is my principle that the will of the Majority should always prevail.
If they approve the proposed Convention in all it's parts, I shall
concur in it chearfully, in hopes that they will amend it
whenever they shall find it work wrong.

—JEFFERSON TO MADISON, FROM PARIS, DECEMBER 20, 1787

THE FEDERAL SYSTEM SET FORTH IN THE ARTICLES OF CONFED-
eration was unproductive. The United States of America was not being governed effectively. Frustration had been slowly building, and financial
hardship made it difficult to sustain either the confidence expressed in
print or the thanksgiving expressed in sermons of 1783, when the war
ended. Nor did the wanderings of Congress encourage great confidence.

As George Washington surveyed the postwar world, bidding farewell to
Lafayette at the end of 1784, he wrote to General Henry Knox, the Boston-
born artillery specialist who had spent much of the Revolution by Washington's side: "Would to God our own countrymen, who are entrusted with
the management of the political machine, could view things by that large

and extensive scale upon which it is measured by foreigners, and by the statesmen of Europe, who see what we might be, and predict what we will come to." It was not an optimistic appraisal of the American spirit.

Others expressed the same sentiment. Looking ahead to the Constitutional Convention, Madison wrote to Jefferson in March 1787: "What may be the result of this political experiment cannot be foreseen." Contrasting Washington and himself with those who feared a too-powerful federal system, Madison saw a certain inevitability facing the states: "The difficulties which present themselves are on one side almost sufficient to dismay the most sanguine, whilst on the other side the most timid are compelled to encounter them by the mortal diseases of the existing constitution."

Real change would have to come. Knox refused to hedge his bet when he told Washington that the Articles of Confederation would have to be altered "by wisdom and agreement, or by force." Here was one of General Washington's most trusted, noting the reluctance of some states to send delegates to a national convention of any kind; he found himself recommending that Washington assume the presidency of the convention, so as to lend it greater legitimacy.[1]

Richard Henry Lee, relieved to learn that George Mason had agreed to attend, vowed that he would be amenable to "alterations beneficial" in the Articles. He suspected, though, that the real problem government faced was in the hearts and minds of citizens. "I fear," he wrote, "it is more in vicious manners, than mistakes in form, that we must seek for the causes of the present discontent." Lee went on to voice the same complaint Madison had over the noncompliance of the independent states when it came to necessary federal expenditures, especially debt repayment and matters of trade. In Virginia and elsewhere, leading voices argued that the states were powerless as agents of moral correction.[2]

As for Madison, the busy constitutionalist continued to lay the groundwork for his performance at the upcoming convention. He had formulated two essentials: first, to attain national strength by creating a national legislature with sufficient weight to counteract "dangerous passions" at the state level; second, to empower the center to expand national power westward. In devising his strategy, Madison was thinking of protecting a national intellectual elite class of men. He was less concerned with the financial health of the common man, and still less with democratic principles.

Jefferson was too far from home to feel the pressure as Madison did. In fact, he was acquiring in France a strong sense of the damage done to society by ever-widening distinctions between those possessing land and those without land or opportunity. In 1786 Madison received a letter from Jefferson, written with extreme pathos, that recounted a solitary walk he had taken while aiming to discover something about the laboring poor. Encountering a "wretched" French peasant woman, he listened to her tale of woe and gave her a sum of cash; she burst into tears of gratitude. Why was her life this way? Because most of the French people had no choices. "The property of this country is absolutely concentrated in a very few hands," he explained. "These employ the flower of the country as servants." The poorest of the poor could not find work and lived close to starvation. He prescribed an axiom: "The earth is given as a common stock for man to labour and live on." Government had to provide opportunities for the poor to become industrious. Morality and the presumption of natural rights demanded it.

Responding eight months later to the story of his encounter with the peasant woman, Madison agreed with Jefferson that America had to avoid the trap France had fallen into. "I have no doubt," he wrote, "that the misery of the lower classes will be found to abate wherever the Government assumes a freer aspect, and the laws force a subdivision of property." But Madison also believed that the more consequential factor in explaining why the mass of Americans lived better than their European counterparts was their low population and not any political advantages they might claim. Feeling less than Jefferson did the struggle of the poor, Madison continued to concentrate his thinking on the imposition of a guiding structure that would condition citizens' behavior.

It was not simply that Madison had little desire to reduce inequality. He was fearful that a state legislature composed of less elite men would eventually result in a dangerous leveling of society, with the jealous poor demanding a redistribution of property. He did not agree with Jefferson that the poor represented the nation's potential, or that they were the glistening "flower of the country."

If Jefferson could derive a universal truth from a single encounter, Madison could not. Refusing to think in terms of human perfectibility, Madison spoke philosophically to principles of political economy. He surmised that no form of government could cope with a surplus population ("the redundant members of a populous society"), no matter what land distribution laws were in place. He concurred with Jefferson only to the extent that "a more equal partition of property must result in a greater simplicity of manners" and fewer idle poor. But the improvement must be partial, not general. There were no absolutes to be found in Madison's thinking, because there was no perfectibility to be had. He suggested to Jefferson that, before he jumped to conclusions, he should compare French conditions to those of other societies—"the indigent part of other communities in Europe where the like causes of wretchedness exist in a less degree." With sufficient data, they would then be able to direct American lawmakers toward practical policies.[3]

"A Negative in All Cases Whatsoever"

When James Madison left for Philadelphia to attend the Constitutional Convention in the spring of 1787, he was eager to debate the science of government. Four years earlier, after his retirement from Congress, he had committed himself to an intense course of legal study, spurred on by any new book Jefferson sent his way. Jefferson supplied him with the principal texts of the French Enlightenment, which supplemented works in classical political theory that he already owned. Madison then began to compile notes on the "defects" (the word he and Jefferson both used) of confederated governments throughout history. His collected papers show that he relied on extensive outlines whenever he was gathering his thoughts for a public presentation. In this instance he produced thirty-nine pages of notes, which he titled, "Of Ancient and Modern Confederacies." By exposing what had gone wrong in the past, he would make sense of the defects in America's imperfect union of states.[4]

Building a case against the Articles of Confederation, he needed to explain why the United States was so ill equipped to accomplish the basic tasks of raising money, making treaties, and regulating commerce. By April 1787 he had a diagnosis in hand. He called it "Vices of the Political System of the United States," and it became his working manifesto, a summary view at the end of his first decade as a state and national politician.

Chief among the vices Madison identified was the undue power lodged in the individual states. Having held a seat in Congress longer than anyone else (four years), he had come to feel that the Confederation was barely a government at all. Like most confederations, the U.S. system was a voluntary compact, a weak "league of friendship" among the states, and subject to internal dissensions. It lacked executive and judicial components; it rarely if ever represented the collective will of the people.

At best, Congress was an auxiliary arm of the thirteen states, a quasi-diplomatic body whose members were emissaries. The Articles of Confederation granted Congress certain prerogatives but no real authority. Madison had seen revenue legislation blocked at every turn, often because one or two states voted against tax bills endorsed by the majority. States routinely violated treaties, while imposing commercial restrictions on each other. Such "irregularities," Madison complained in "Vices," damaged the reputation of the United States in Europe. Beyond his extended term in Congress, his three years in the Virginia state legislature had exposed him to what he called the "imbecility" of government on the local level. Laws were "indigested," rather than carefully devised, and often rushed through the legislature at the last minute. He adjudged many of his fellow state representatives to be intellectually meek and unable to appreciate the elements of good government.[5]

Madison saw little to be gained in rescuing the Confederation. It was a dysfunctional system, its flaws too ingrained for it to be made energetic or even stable. Congress was a headless body, and the Confederation a government at war with itself. Moreover, the aggrandizing state legislatures of the 1780s resembled nothing so much as a group of rambunctious children refusing to play together fairly. They endangered property rights and by undoing one session's laws the next year failed to take their own legislation seriously. Damning the states unmercifully, Madison found his solution in a centralizing government.

Paternalism and moralism ran deep in his assessment. He found "want of wisdom," "vicious legislation," and "impetuosities" in the state legislatures. By this Madison meant rash, unthinking, and impulsive behavior. Virginia assemblymen struck him as uninformed and undisciplined, their actions dictated by selfish motives. He envisioned a strong central government with the authority to give guidance and even provide moral supervision.

Anger lurks below the surface of Madison's austere prose. It was not simply that the Confederation was inefficient: the childlike states wielded power unwisely, and they were too easily misled by self-serving demagogues. If the states could not be trusted to govern themselves, how could they unite a nation? Madison explained his thinking to George Washington shortly before the Constitutional Convention was set to open. There was only one way to save the nation, he said. The states had to be made "subordinately useful."[6]

Washington was instrumental. Any cause was helped by his participation. His national stature as the soldier-turned-statesman and his reputation for promoting national unity were invaluable assets. As a member of the Virginia Assembly in 1785, Madison had urged the state to dispatch commissioners to meet with representatives from Maryland at Washington's Mount Vernon home. The immediate agenda of the meeting was to convince the two states to agree on navigational rights along the Potomac. The meeting was, in fact, a preview of the Annapolis convention of 1786, where several more states came together to discuss commercial remedies for defects in the Confederation. Step by step, and with growing purpose, Madison rose to advocate decisive, large-scale government reform, with Washington on his side.[7]

A number of historians have dismissed the Annapolis meeting as a ruse, whose only purpose was to justify calling a second, more representative convention in Philadelphia. But for Madison, the value of Annapolis derived from his success in corralling members of the Virginia Assembly. Their unanimous recommendation to proceed made him more optimistic about the Philadelphia convention. As he put it to Jefferson, even the "most obstinate adversaries to reform" were now in agreement that the Confederation suffered from "dangerous defects."[8]

With Jefferson abroad, Madison turned to his friend Edmund Randolph, the former state attorney general who was Virginia's governor in 1787. Randolph had attended the Annapolis meeting, where he convinced Alexander Hamilton to revise his heavy-handed draft of the call for a Philadelphia convention. Convivial yet cautious, Randolph possessed other skills that appealed to Madison. In a world where eloquence mattered, he was a natural orator, more fluid and pleasing in his style than Madison, whose manner of speech was impressive and methodical but unexciting. As governor of their state, Randolph was able to shape the delegation that went to Philadelphia. He was Madison's point man as well as the head of Virginia's delegation. He would be the one to present Virginia's proposal to the convention.[9]

Washington had to be recruited. Both Madison and Randolph bombarded him with letters, urging him to attend. Eventually Madison persuaded Washington that his presence in Philadelphia was essential—not as a Virginian but as a unifier. He would reinforce the bond between the Virginia and Pennsylvania delegations. The Virginians could accomplish little unless another large state backed them, and their most likely ally was Pennsylvania. Madison would cozy up to Robert Morris, former superintendent of finance for the Confederation. Since 1782, as Morris called for the federal impost (tax on imports), a funding program, and a national bank,

Madison had consistently defended his agenda. This kept the flagging finances of Congress afloat in the crucial days before Yorktown. Both Robert Morris and Gouverneur Morris (no relation) would be delegates from Pennsylvania to the Constitutional Convention, two men who shared an economic outlook and were extremely close to Washington.[10]

George Mason was another major player. Mason, Madison, and Washington were all aggressive promoters of western expansion, envisioning commercial growth based on a direct water route from the Chesapeake Bay to the Ohio River. As a prominent speculator in western lands, Mason had had a material stake in securing an agreement with Maryland at the Mount Vernon meeting. Both inside and outside the state, he was respected for his draft of the Declaration of Rights and for his help in shaping the Virginia Constitution of 1776. But at sixty-two, Mason was the oldest member of the Virginia delegation. Madison knew he was unpredictable, "not fully cured of Antifederal prejudices" with respect to national control of international trade; but on the "great points," as he told Jefferson, Mason could be counted on.[11]

Virginia sent three other men, George Wythe, Judge John Blair, and James McClurg, to Philadelphia, for a total of seven. The final three, however, contributed little at the convention. Wythe was still a professor of law at the College of William and Mary. Blair was recognized for his superior legal training at Middle Temple in London; his uncle was a founder of the College of William and Mary. Madison had put McClurg's name forward after Patrick Henry, then former governor Thomas Nelson, and finally Richard Henry Lee all turned down the appointment. "He was on the spot," Madison confessed to Jefferson. McClurg had earned an M.D. at the prestigious University of Edinburgh and had no legal training at all.

When, in April 1787, the Virginia delegation was complete, Madison sent carefully crafted letters to Randolph and Washington, prodding them again to think about what the convention should accomplish. He told Washington forthrightly that he felt radical change was needed; but he took a slightly softer tone with Randolph, arguing that the most "valuable articles" of the Confederation should be preserved, but only as part of a new system that did more than simply "engraft" onto the old.[12]

The first change had to be in the principle of representation. The unicameral Confederation Congress, in which the vote of Delaware meant as much as the vote of Virginia or Massachusetts, was acceptable no longer. "No one," he told Washington, "will deny that Virginia and Massts. have more weight and influence." Proportional representation made the most sense: the number of legislative seats should be allocated according to a state's total population or its aggregate wealth.

This was not a new idea. It had been raised in 1774, at the First Continental Congress, but had been dismissed because of the pressing need for unanimity as war loomed. Rather than estrange delegates from smaller, less populated states, Congress had agreed to the practice of granting to each colony (later each state) one vote. Aware that a precedent had been set, Madison knew how persuasive he would have to be to end the practice of equal representation. At the same time he knew that delegates from the large states would not automatically be Virginia's allies. They had to be assuaged on other matters. If the new system granted the federal government the power to tax and to regulate commerce, as Madison proposed, then vital economic interests would be at stake. Some laws were bound to favor some states or regions, and discriminate against others.[13]

How could he make a majority of the delegates comfortable? And why would the large states agree to dramatic change? He observed that the northern states were the most populous, while the southern states were projecting faster growth in the future. Both would see their interests served, if he played his cards right.[14] There would be holdouts among the small states, but he dismissed them as irrelevant. The small states "must in every event yield to the predominant will," he pronounced coldly in a letter to Washington, assuring him that New Hampshire, Delaware, and the like could be pressed into agreement.[15]

Madison immediately saw the need for a federal judiciary, but he was noncommittal on the organization of the executive branch. He did see the value, at least, in a "council of revision," as he called it at the time, through which members of the judiciary and executive would come together, with the power to veto legislation. Congress would still be the main pillar of government, as it was under the Confederation. But to be a well-ordered government with extensive powers, Congress had to be composed of two branches. Increased powers required a smaller, more select body of men in the upper house, or Senate. They would watch over and curb the less steady, more impulsive lower house of Congress.[16]

The central government that Madison envisioned had a clear capacity for coercion. It would, without question, exercise authority over the states. He proposed to both Randolph and Washington that the federal government be granted "a negative *in all cases whatsoever*," that is, a U.S. Senate with the same power to override state legislation once reserved for the king of

England. Although having a check on the states would constitute a form of paternalism at odds with the democratic impulse, it would "controul the necessary vicissitudes" of the irresponsible states and overturn unjust law-making.[17]

Madison's sponsorship of the Senate's absolute negative rested on the theories of John Locke—not on the more often cited *Two Treatises on Government*, but on *Some Thoughts Concerning Education*. During his college years at Princeton, Madison had been attracted to enlightened pedagogy, and Locke's influence remained with him. Good government was meant to steer and to guide; the invisible hand of moral authority conditioned citizens, like children, to reach proper decisions; only tyrannical parents and despotic governments relied on brute force. Persuasion, or a well-defined guardianship, held out the likeliest chance of seeing good results. In defending the negative to Jefferson at the end of the Constitutional Convention, Madison adopted the Lockean vocabulary: "guardianship" produced good government by influencing the "disposition" of wayward states.[18]

Supervision was central to Madison's thinking about the U.S. Senate. A senatorial negative offered the "mildest expedient" to state "mischiefs," a deterrent to those who might otherwise be impelled to rash actions. Military force against the states was impractical and unwanted in a republican form of government; Madison knew Americans would never tolerate it. So like a good parent, the central government would use its negative to publicly chastise misbehavior. Bad laws would be vetoed, the states shamed into right action.[19]

The negative was a radical idea. Jefferson frowned on so sweeping an innovation, telling Madison unequivocally in June: "I do not like it." Employing the metaphor of an old outfit that was to be stitched back together, he wrote, "Instead of mending the hole, the proposed patch would cover the entire garment."[20] Randolph and Mason were less troubled by the proposition but not entirely on board. By the time of the convention, they supported a modified version of Madison's plan. Washington did not weigh in.

"Rambling Through the Fields and Farms"

Jefferson gave Madison his thoughts about the negative after returning from a four-month tour of the south of France and northern Italy. It may be pure coincidence, but just as he had escaped the memories of his deceased wife by leaving Monticello for an extended period after September

1782, he left Paris for the south as he was fighting off his feelings for the married artist Maria Cosway. He all but ceased writing to her.

William Short took charge of official business and was in constant communication with his boss. Meanwhile Jefferson the contemplative traveler recorded his days in great detail: vineyards, canals, castles, Roman ruins. To Short and others he was effusive, but his tone was subdued when he finally wrote again to the forsaken Maria Cosway. When she retorted with short, pouty letters, he assured her that he remained devoted, but it was not the passionate refrain it had been previously. As he distanced himself from her, his imagination found other channels of enjoyment and instruction.[21]

When he left on his tour, Jefferson also left his fifteen-year-old daughter Patsy behind at her convent school. Upon his return, he learned that his younger daughter Maria (at this age called Polly) had sailed from Virginia, according to his instruction, and was en route to England. There she was met and cared for by the maternal and always forthright Abigail Adams, who praised the child's good sense. Maria's inexperienced fifteen-year-old maid, Sally Hemings, who had shared the five-week ocean passage, came with her to Paris, where Patsy was reunited with her sister and Sally with her brother James.[22]

One month after this alteration in his domestic life, Jefferson wrote to an Albemarle neighbor: "All my wishes end, where I hope my days will end, at Monticello." It had been three years since he left America, and he was detached enough from past frustrations that he took pleasure in nostalgia. In part, this was made possible by his recent travels. He had ridden on mules and drifted on the water; he had stared at people and they had stared back. Something clicked, and he turned his mind to the creative opportunities ahead of him in exploiting the productive potential of his Albemarle and Bedford County lands. Seeing the output of the French and Italian countryside inspired him to perform a service for the economies of South Carolina and Georgia by supplying those states with olive plants and a particular strain of rice. Seeing the trouble their plows were causing farmers in the vicinity of Nancy, he drew a rough sketch of what would later become his award-winning design of a "mouldboard plough of least resistance." His excursions ("rambling through the fields and farms," as he put it in a letter to Lafayette during his road trip) taught Jefferson to appreciate the spirit of agricultural enterprise in a new way.

Always reaching out, he felt compelled to share what he had learned. He put up with filthy lodgings, one after the next, to gain a unique education. When, as a part of his study, he spied on simple farmers, he figured they saw him, too, as a curiosity. He cast himself almost as the hero of a first-person novel, a truth seeker wrapped up in nature, as Jean-Jacques Rousseau was in his late years. This was a uniquely meditative period of Jefferson's life, not to be so well exhibited in correspondence again until his postpresidential retirement. As one who frequently complained that political ambition was a disease that, once contracted, resisted treatment, he apparently thought he had found the cure through travel. His hatred of politics appeared less of a rhetorical ploy amid exposure to the byways of western Europe. Diversion always seemed to do him good.

Jefferson was now rich in information about the European landscape as well as the European mind. He was attuned to advances in science and economy, and he could characterize the poisoned political scene better than any other living American. In his well-appointed quarters at the hub of Paris, when not entertaining the local literati, he was receiving visitors from home—notably the sons of Philadelphians and the sons of southern gentlemen. In letters home, he touted America's superiority to Europe. Inviting James Monroe to visit him, he indulged in quintessentially Jeffersonian hyperbole, writing: "I will venture to say no man now living will ever see an instance of an American removing to settle in Europe and continuing there."[23]

It can be said that by the middle of 1787 the author of the encyclopedic *Notes on Virginia* was past the peak of his fascination with the Old World. When consulted by the compiler of the authoritative *Encyclopédie méthodique*, he made a concerted effort to correct what he regarded as inaccuracies about the United States. He was careful to absolve his Virginia colleagues and himself from foot-dragging on legislating an end to slavery. Meanwhile, impressed with South Carolinian David Ramsay's strategy of pairing an account of his home state during the Revolution with a thoroughgoing history of the American Revolution, Jefferson helped arrange a French translation. He was taking no chances as to how America's war for independence would be drawn for a scholarly European audience.[24]

For the determined diplomat, America's image abroad was no less consequential in 1787 than it had been when he composed the Declaration of Independence for a "candid world." Yet Jefferson had clearly come to view the Old World as America's inferior. He wrote to Monroe of the "utility" in seeing Europe, but the ultimate result of the experience was to remind him of what he had left behind. "My God!" he declared. "How little do my countrymen know what precious blessings they are in possession of, and which no other people on earth enjoy. I confess I had no idea of it myself."[25]

It is of interest that Jefferson did not write to Madison even once during his four-month excursion, though he continued to collect books for him. Back in Paris, Jefferson examined all that Madison had written that arrived in his absence, so that he was generally aware of preparations for the Constitutional Convention. With the average transatlantic voyage requiring five or six weeks, though, he would not see news from Philadelphia for some time to come.

"An Assembly of Demigods"

Madison came to town earlier than most, on May 3. He settled in, as before, with the House-Trist family. Intent on a strategy, he began consulting with members of the Pennsylvania delegation right away. He dined lavishly at Robert Morris's impressive three-story mansion. There he was introduced to the Scotsman James Wilson, another member of the so-called financiers' faction. Wilson was hard to miss, with a stocky build and a ruddy face like a workingman's. Thick glasses, however, marked him as a man of letters. He had studied at three different colleges in Scotland without ever earning a degree. Highly knowledgeable about world history, law, and government, he was an articulate advocate of national reform and one of the stars of the convention.[26]

Madison visited with Benjamin Franklin for the very first time. Entertaining the delegates at his home, Franklin had little trouble demonstrating that his mind was as sharp as ever. He told amusing stories and showed that he still relished a good glass of porter. But at eighty-one, he was physically frail. For most of the convention he remained seated, and often relied on others to read his prepared statements.[27]

Madison was especially pleased by the warm welcome accorded Washington on his arrival in Philadelphia. He was met with cannon fire, the ringing of bells, and huzzas from the crowd. Beyond the giddy "acclamations of the people," Madison informed Jefferson, the retired general was also shown "more sober marks of affection and veneration."

Sobriety, gravity, and steadiness were the qualities Madison had come to expect of the leadership corps in the new national system he visualized, and Washington embodied them all. Robert Morris conveyed the "First of Men" to his fine mansion, where the general would reside for the duration of the convention. Blair and Wythe landed in Philadelphia a week after Madison, establishing a quorum for the Virginia group. As a sign of things to come, the two most energetic delegations, Virginia and Pennsylvania, officially opened the convention on May 14. The next day Randolph and McClurg rode into town, and as Mason finally showed up, the Virginia contingent was complete.[28]

On May 20 all of the Virginia delegates, save Washington, attended a Catholic mass. They did so, as Mason reported, "more out of Compliment than Religion, & more out of Curiosity than compliment." The constant "Tinckling of a little Bell" reminded him of nothing so much as the curtain's rise at a puppet show. In his next letter home, Mason's tone was heavier. He felt a weight upon him, realizing that he was in the company of the "first Characters" of the country. "The Eyes of the United States are turn'd upon this Assembly, & their Expectations raised to a very anxious Degree," he surmised. "The Revolt against Great Britain, & the Formations of our new Governments at that time, were nothing compared with the great Business now before us." Though debate had just gotten under way, he already sensed that the convention's decisions would affect the lives of "millions yet unborn."[29]

On May 25, seven state delegations being present, the convention took up formal business. Its first task was to elect Washington as the presiding officer, which was done "una voca" (by unanimous voice vote), as Madison reported to Jefferson. Like Mason, Madison was impressed with the talent that surrounded him. Jefferson gushed in a letter across the Channel to John Adams: "It is really an assembly of demigods."[30]

The fifty-five men who sat in convention were, without exception, drawn from a ruling elite. None of them could be called representative of the common man. Most had received a superior education, having attended the finest colleges in Great Britain or the best schools in the colonies—Princeton, Harvard, Yale, and William and Mary. Hardly a disinterested lot, they were either wealthy merchants or large planters with experience in overseas trade. Many were large-scale speculators in land and government securities.[31]

Even the few delegates whose origins were humbler had married into families with large fortunes and imposing connections. Up-and-coming lawyers Alexander Hamilton and Rufus King wed the daughters of two of New York State's richest men. James Wilson had studied the law with Philadelphian John Dickinson, now a delegate from Delaware; Virginia-born John Francis Mercer, a member of the Maryland delegation, had Jefferson to thank for his legal apprenticeship. New Jersey sent its chief justice and its former attorney general. Maryland's attorney general, Luther Martin, was present. Connecticut dispatched Roger Sherman and Oliver Ellsworth, both of whom sat on the superior court. All were committed to the protection of property rights and class privilege. Madison had reason to expect that they and he were of one mind.[32]

A considerable number of delegates had been officers in the Continental Army, or had served in state militias. There were brigadier generals, majors, cavalry and garrison commanders, one military chaplain, and a quartermaster for the Continentals. John Langdon of New Hampshire combined his service as a regimental commander with blockade running and privateering, amassing great wealth during the war. For others, personal fortune and military service were foreordained. General Charles Cotesworth Pinckney, born to one of the first families of South Carolina, had commanded an elite regiment of grenadiers before joining Washington's staff.

As defenders of the law and as military men, the delegates came to the convention hoping to restore social order. Forty-one of the fifty-five had served in the Continental Congress and were well aware of the existing government's weaknesses. At sixty-six, Connecticut's Roger Sherman was the second-oldest member and had probably held more posts than anyone but the oldest member, Benjamin Franklin. He had been a county surveyor, justice of the peace, superior court judge, assemblyman, state senator, and delegate to the Continental Congress; he had joined Jefferson and Adams on the committee to draft the Declaration of Independence and subsequently helped to draft the Articles of Confederation. He and his colleagues were comfortable wielding power. They were prepared to take action. Like Madison, they were deeply disturbed by the social and economic turmoil brewing in the states.[33]

That turmoil was not imagined. Though pockets of unrest existed elsewhere, Shays's rebellion created havoc in Massachusetts in 1786–87 and formed the backdrop of the convention—the most immediate and compelling evidence that the Confederation was in trouble. The rebellion began when a group of armed men marched in military array to shut down several courts and stop foreclosures on debtors' property. Their protest was sparked by high taxes worse than any stamp requirement or duty on tea that the British had formerly imposed. At the first sign of trouble, the governor of the Bay State took punitive action and called out the militia to suppress the rebels. When the militia showed itself well disposed toward the insurgents and failed to make arrests, the governor hired a private army. A Revolutionary War veteran, Captain Daniel Shays, somehow came to be called "generalissimo" of the uprising and lent his name to it for the history books. Hearing that a large contingent of troops was headed their way, the rebels moved to seize the federal arsenal in Springfield.[34]

News spread quickly throughout the country. Washington was horrified by the men's blatant disregard for law and order. He told Henry Knox that he feared "combustibles in every state." His views were widely shared. More than any other factor, it was the actions of the Shaysites—Regulators, as they called themselves—that had convinced Washington to attend the convention in Philadelphia.[35]

The Regulators hit a nerve, raising the specter of class warfare. Even Madison believed early rumors that the revolt was connected to a secessionist plot to reunite with Great Britain by forming an alliance with British Canada. Shays's Rebellion earned a place on Madison's list of "political vices," when he ruefully observed that the Articles were silent on the point of mobilizing the government against "internal violence."[36]

For Madison, the Massachusetts uprising was a symptom, not a cause, of the Confederation's maladies. Although the Shaysites lost on the ground, they won at the ballot box: all the governor's men who bore responsibility for tax hikes, and who had backed the military response, were voted out of office. In March 1787 Madison informed Jefferson that many of Shays's men refused the offer of a conditional pardon, because in so doing they would have been disenfranchised. While that may sound noble to us, Madison was appalled that they appeared in public wearing their "insolence" as a badge of honor to win popular favor and got elected to "local offices of trust and authority." As new legislators, they granted debt relief and drastically cut direct taxes. Madison regarded this as a perfect example of the "perfidious" irresponsibility and instability exhibited in state legislatures. He feared democracy's power.[37]

While Madison regarded debtor-relief legislation and debtor-court closures as "vices" of the Confederation, it was not Massachusetts but little Rhode Island where he found the most glaring display of a state's weakness on this score. In 1781 Rhode Island had single-handedly derailed passage of the impost bill in Congress, though every other state had backed the funding measure. In 1786 its state legislature issued paper money, stipulating that such currency could be used to pay off debts. But paper currency suffered rapid depreciation, and as Madison told Jefferson, "shops were shut," "supplies were withheld from the Market," and the state was thrown into "a sort of convulsion." The same year that Rhode Island issued its paper money, New Jersey refused to make voluntary payments to Congress to settle the nation's war debt—it seceded (in fiscal terms, at least) from the Confederation.[38]

The allure of paper money reached into Virginia. In 1786 Madison defeated one effort in the legislature to issue paper money, only to see another campaign mounted in early 1787. As plans for the Constitutional Convention were being laid, Patrick Henry backed a new paper money scheme, leading Madison to update Jefferson on the activities of their chronic political adversary. Who would be able to stop the emission of paper money if Henry was pushing it? he posed. In June, as his anger rose, Madison wrote Jefferson that Henry could not be stopped unless the voters of his county "shall bind him hand and foot by instructions."

It turned out that paper money was the tip of the iceberg. Not only was Henry hostile to a bill introduced by Madison to reorganize the courts and ensure a more efficient system of debt collection; he was opposed to the stated goal of the Constitutional Convention. Madison was convinced that Henry was engaged in nothing short of fomenting a state rebellion (albeit one waged with words, not arms) and in promoting *"either a partition or total dissolution of the confederacy."* When the subject was Patrick Henry and the intended recipient of Madison's letter was Jefferson, an ordinarily calm pen could become quite agitated.[39]

It is not an exaggeration to say that Madison considered Patrick Henry's political style, in and of itself, to be one of the major vices of the Confederation. In his treatise on political vices, he spelled out why it was dangerous to trust in the state legislatures: "How frequently too will the honest but unenlightened representative be the dupe of a favorite leader, veiling his selfish views under the professions of public good, and varnishing his sophistical arguments with glowing colours of popular eloquence?"[40] Henry was the archetype for this scathing portrait. Genuine reform demanded a political mechanism that would check the seductive sway of the popular orator over his comparatively unenlightened colleagues. It also explains why Madison was so insistent that the federal government exercise an absolute negative over all state legislation.

Modern Americans would, of course, prefer to focus on the nobler motives of the framers, but money matters doubtless roused most of the delegates to come to Philadelphia. With only a few exceptions, they despised paper money and recognized debt as a combustible issue capable of fomenting class war. Most felt, as Madison did, that Congress needed additional power in order to raise revenue, protect property rights, and discipline rogue state legislatures. Rhode Island became the symbol of everything that was wrong with the Confederation—a small state with more power than it deserved, whose local representatives actually courted disaster by the degree to which they were responsive to their constituency. Rhode Island was the only one of the thirteen states that refused to send any delegates to Philadelphia.[41]

A minor diversion pertaining to the composition of Virginia's delegation rattled an already tense situation. James Monroe believed that Edmund Randolph, the governor, and Madison, his bosom friend, had turned on him. In the summer of 1787 he wrote to Jefferson of his dismay at being excluded from the Virginia delegation: "The Governor I have reason to believe is unfriendly to me and hath shewn (if I am well inform'd) a disposition to thwart me; and Madison, upon whose friendship I have calculated, whose views I have favored, and with whom I have held the most confidential correspondence since you left the continent, is in strict league with him and hath I have reason to believe concurr'd in arrangements unfavorable to me." Monroe often jumped to conclusions and was prone to feeling slighted. His relations with Madison would suffer, time and again, from these tendencies. In fact, many in Virginia believed that Monroe was unavailable for the convention. Neither Randolph nor Madison harbored any ill will toward him.[42]

"I Do Not, Gentlemen, Trust You"

As the convention opened for business, Madison took his seat front and center in the room. He wanted to be certain he could hear the speakers on his left and right and take down notes of the proceedings. He later explained that his notes were for "future curiosity," preserving for history an "authentic exhibition" of the road map that led to an improved republican government.

Scholars have long debated whether the account Madison kept was completely authentic. Some praise his meticulous and honest reporting, while others charge him with a deliberate manipulation of the record. He probably did edit portions of his notes later in life, but he certainly did not alter the evidence so flagrantly as to paint himself in the most favorable light. His notes from the convention belie the customary portrait of Madison as the "Father of the Constitution." The patriarchal metaphor is itself false, because even in *his own* telling Madison is clearly *not* the hero of the convention. He is shown to be less adept than Connecticut's Roger Sherman in getting his way. James Madison emerges not as the proud parent of a government made in his image but as a frustrated composer whose grand symphony has been left unfinished.

Nevertheless he tried aggressively to direct the course of the convention. Well before the other state delegations had assembled, he was already busy convincing his fellow Virginians to put together that agenda that came to be known as the Virginia Plan. And while Madison did the most to shape the proposal, the final draft shows the marked influence of Randolph and Mason. Deciding how to present their case to the convention was very much a collaborative effort.

Rules for the convention were largely the same as those used in previous congresses. The votes of all state delegations would be of equal weight, a concession the Virginians felt was necessary to avoid alienating the small states too soon. A simple majority would carry the day. Though the most visible of the Virginians, Washington, came with no intention of presenting to the convention, he was given the royal treatment—rules of adjournment dictated that "every member must stand in his place, until the President shall pass him." One can visualize the tall and sturdy general rising from his chair at the end of each day's discussion, marching from the room with all eyes upon him as delegates waited a decent interval before moving toward the door.

The most celebrated rule was seemingly the hardest to guarantee: preserving the secrecy of the proceedings. Nothing that emanated from the convention could be published, and delegates were constrained from discussing the debates in their confidential communications. As Madison explained to Jefferson, an "expedient" was needed "to secure unbiased discussion within doors, and prevent misconceptions and misconstructions without." Jefferson was dismayed and told John Adams that it was an "abominable" precedent, this "tying up the tongues" of the delegates. But he conveyed none of his displeasure to Madison.[43]

With rules in place, business began in earnest. On May 29 all eyes and ears were directed at Edmund Randolph, as he took the floor and gave an elaborate speech. He told his audience that he was opening the "great subject" of the convention as head of the Virginia delegation, in view of the fact that the very idea of the convention had originated in his state. To avoid launching into controversy on day one, he emphasized national security rather than economic measures as a means to strengthen the Union, wondering aloud what was to be done collectively in the event of a foreign in-

vasion. As things presently stood, Congress could not prevent a war if provoked by a state or states, and the Articles of Confederation conferred no
authority to fund any response to external threats. Additionally, the existing forms prevented government from checking quarrels between states or
intervening in the case of a domestic rebellion.

Madison's argument differed from Randolph's only in a tactical sense.
He would have begun by rejecting the "incroachments" of the states. Had
he done so, expressing opposition to the monetary policies of single states
that adversely affected other states—and a Congress unable to put a stop to
such disruptions—he would surely have had some delegates squirming in
their seats. Randolph's was a more diplomatically framed argument. Only
gradually did he move toward Madison's position, when he linked monetary issues to the larger cause of collective security.[44]

Having established a mild persona, Randolph presented the Virginia
Plan in full. Its fifteen resolutions showed that the "corrected & enlarged"
Articles of Confederation was in fact a radically new system of government.
Here Randolph incorporated Madison's key principles. He would establish
a bicameral national legislature and proportional representation in each
chamber, based on state population or wealth. Direct election by the people would be the rule for the House of Representatives, and the Senate
would be comprised of those elected *by the House* from a list of nominations
submitted by the state legislatures.

As to Madison's insertion of the absolute negative, or nullification of
state laws by the Senate (Resolution 6), Randolph and Mason established
boundaries that Madison would have done without. The negative, they
said, would apply only to those laws "contravening the articles of the
Union"—what we call "unconstitutionality." Madison's unyielding phrase
"in all cases whatsoever" was modified to read: The new national legislature
would interfere in "all cases to which the separate states are incompetent."
The absolute authority of Congress would apply *only* to matters deemed
outside the purview of the states. The central government would exercise
coercive force when a delinquent state "failed to fulfill its duty" to supply
funds as required. By minimizing the Senate's veto power, Madison's two
colleagues increased the possibility that Congress would resort to military
power against recalcitrant (presumably small) states.[45]

The Virginia Plan also called for officers of the national executive and
judicial branches to be chosen by Congress. A council of revision (composed of members of the executive and judiciary) would be given authority
to veto acts of Congress. The chief executive would serve a single term. As

for defining the states' eventual role in weighing what was agreed upon in Philadelphia, the Virginia Plan stipulated that as the convention completed its business, the new federal Constitution would have to go through an approval process in special ratifying conventions rather than in their existing state legislatures.

The guiding principle of the Virginia Plan was still Madison's: the desire to limit the influence of state legislatures on national policy. The new House of Representatives would be elected by the people, unlike the Confederation Congress, whose delegates were named in the state legislatures. The Senate would be elected *by the House,* and the president and judiciary voted into office by the Congress. The only influence the states could exert was to submit nominations to the House of potential U.S. senators.

Defending the Virginia Plan two days after Randolph announced it, Madison described the whole system as one that provided "successive filtrations." Once the sentiments of the people were expressed in the composition of the House, decisions and appointments would be filtered, or refined, through ascending branches of government. As the most powerful branch, the bicameral Congress would have broad authority in making national policy, vetoing state laws, and appointing the president and federal judges. If the Senate failed to check the House, and a bad law slipped through, then the joint executive/judicial council of revision would serve as a second filter in eliminating the unwise legislation.[46]

The Virginia Plan was bold and far-reaching. Madison counted on a coalition of southern states and large northern states to back it. He underestimated his opposition. The small states had no intention of bending to the will of the large states. Almost immediately a bloc formed to challenge the Virginia Plan. Delegates from Delaware, Connecticut, and New Jersey whittled away at the Virginians' design and eventually dismantled it. Madison was getting an education.

First the Delaware delegation threatened to leave the convention; only after some cajoling did its members change their minds. Picking up the pace, Roger Sherman of Connecticut fixed attention on the composition of the Senate: he proposed that the state legislatures—not the House—elect its members. The Senate was the body Madison was most intent on separating from state control, but Sherman had other plans.

The Connecticut delegate was gearing up to be his main rival at the convention. In appearance, they were an odd match-up. Sherman's manner of address was described as unschooled, "laughable & grotesque." But he was a very shrewd politician; no one understood the dynamics of the convention floor better. Over the course of the debates, he would speak, make motions, or add his second to motions 160 times, nearly as often as Madison himself.[47]

Chinks appeared in the armor of the Virginia Plan. Dickinson of Delaware proposed that the state legislatures be given the power to impeach the president. Madison quickly dismissed the idea as one that would grant small states excessive influence while corrupting a president who would be beholden to favorites in certain states. Not to be outdone, Dickinson and Sherman teamed up to press again for state legislatures to determine the composition of the Senate. Dickinson found Madison's successive filtration theory untenable. And he insisted that there was no logic in having proportional representation in both branches of the national legislature.[48]

Madison rushed to defend his plan. To eliminate proportional representation in the Senate was, he said, "inadmissible" and "unjust." He battled tooth and nail to realize his vision of a small body of senators able to govern "with more coolness, with more system, & with more wisdom, than the popular branch." Dickinson was unwilling to concede.[49]

With this heady debate, the tide began to turn against Madison. Things got worse on June 7 when one of his closest colleagues, George Mason, rose and acknowledged the merit of Dickinson's argument. Dickinson was the author of Revolutionary essays in opposition to British taxation. Mason was one to listen respectfully to a gentleman scholar, an elder statesman like himself. So after Dickinson had had his say, Mason conceded that the state legislatures needed the power to defend themselves against encroachments, just as much as the national government did. Madison's system was one-sided, because it recognized only the trespasses of the states against the national government. The Virginia Plan did not provide for "self-defense" all around, Mason reasoned. "Shall we leave the States alone unprovided with the means for this purpose?" he questioned. Clearly Mason's conversion tipped the scale in favor of Dickinson's motion, and the convention voted unanimously to permit state legislatures to appoint members of the U.S. Senate.[50]

Madison had lost ground, though one of his undeterred supporters, Charles Pinckney of South Carolina (cousin to General Charles Cotesworth Pinckney), stepped forward with a modified Virginia Plan, which endorsed Madison's expansive version of the absolute negative. At twenty-nine, Pinckney was one of the youngest members of the convention. He shared Madison's love of learning, would master five languages, and eventually acquired a two-thousand-volume library, nearly as diversi-fied as Jefferson's collection. (At the convention both he and Madison ad-vocated the establishment of a national university.) Building on Pinckney's motion, then, Madison returned to the theme of finding means to control the "centrifugal tendency" of the states, which were prone to spin away from their proper orbits. The choice of metaphor was deliberate: Dickin-son had just compared the states to planets as part of his defense of state influence.[51]

Elbridge Gerry of Massachusetts, a signer of the Declaration of Inde-pendence, was to be Madison's on-again, off-again, ally (and many years later his second-term vice president). At this moment he confessed to find-ing difficulty in imagining how the absolute negative would work, given that the states and their laws were so diverse. It would be onerous, if not impossible, for the national legislature to supervise them all. Gerry was re-vealing a glaring hole in Madison's theory.

The unapologetic nationalist James Wilson rose to Madison's defense. He reminded the delegates of the "impotent condition" of the Confedera-tion. State jealousies were responsible for frittering away national unity, each one cutting "a slice from the common loaf" to enrich itself. To correct vices was the business of the convention, Wilson reiterated, and one of the most prevalent vices was the absence of "effectual control in the whole over its parts."[52]

An unheralded delegate to the convention, Gunning Bedford, Jr., saw in this view a poorly concealed plan of attack on the small states. Under pro-portional representation, his state of Delaware would have no redress, a one-ninetieth share in the "General Councils" of government, while Vir-ginia and Pennsylvania would together possess one-third of the vote. In pursuing their ambitions, he said, the large states would "crush" the small ones. Where military action was taken against a defiant state, the Virgini-ans would have "an enormous and monstrous influence." Instead of calm-ing him, Madison chided the Delaware delegate with imagery no less extreme. Would the small states, he posed, be any safer from the "avarice & ambition" of the large states if the Union collapsed?[53]

As the debate wore on, Madison could see that his reasoning was failing to convince. It was entirely obvious that the large states benefited exclu-sively from having proportional representation in both houses of Con-gress, and that Virginia had the most to gain. Madison was juggling contradictory theories: it was impossible to keep the Senate small and ap-portioned by population, and at the same time grant the small states a real voice in government. Madison's basic problem was his lack of sympathy for the small states; it was to them that he had assigned the largest share of the Confederation's failures. The large states would continue to make the greatest contributions to the Union, and thus they deserved more of a say in policy. But who else could he convince?

Madison's plan continued to lose traction as the New Jersey delegation did the math. Under proportional representation, Virginia would have sixteen votes in the House, and Georgia only one. William Paterson, a Princeton graduate like Madison, bluntly charged that the Virginia Plan struck at the very existence of the small states. He deliberately provoked Madison by proposing, tongue in cheek, that the states should all be dissolved at once and reconstituted along new boundaries to create fair and proportional units. New Jersey refused to be "swallowed up," as Paterson put it, saying he would rather "submit to a monarch, to a despot," than consent to the Virginia Plan. He then presented what became known as the New Jersey Plan, drafted by a coalition of small-state delegates and rejecting virtually every major tenet of the Virginia Plan. Dickinson of Delaware pulled Madison aside and lectured him: "You see the consequence of pushing things too far."[54]

By this time the motion to expand the absolute negative (*"in all cases whatsoever"*) had failed by a vote of seven states to three. More disturbing to Madison was the fact that Randolph and Mason had deserted him, and Washington did not vote. Few of Madison's colleagues felt comfortable with the absolute negative once they considered its potential for abuse. Some saw his plan as a Virginia power grab, and others thought it a simply unreasonable answer to the weaknesses of the Confederation.[55]

On June 19, four days after Paterson introduced it, the New Jersey Plan was voted down. But it had achieved its purpose of dividing the ranks of delegates and weakening the resolve of the moderates in Madison's coalition.[56] The course of debate was not very productive at this point—one step forward, two steps back—principally because the issue of representation refused to die. On June 29, as the convention voted to grant the lower house proportional representation, Connecticut delegate Oliver Ellsworth took up the small-state cause: equality in the Senate. He called for a "middle ground," making the new government "partly national; partly federal." Some powers would be retained by those at the seat of government, while in other respects, built-in limits would guarantee that the states could never be consumed by an omnipotent power center. To deny the small states an equal vote in the Senate would be, Ellsworth claimed, just like "cutting the body of America in two"; three or four large states would end up governing the rest. At this point, the small-state advocates were sounding the most republican.[57]

Madison was not beaten, not yet. He refused to acknowledge that the small-states faction owned the moral high ground, and he accused the Connecticut delegates of inconsistency, if not rank hypocrisy. While they were claiming to have supported the Confederation government in principle, they refused to pay their tax requisitions. According to his logic, the New Jersey Plan would create a national government with no more teeth than what the Confederation had.

Rufus King of Massachusetts (who would be on the opposing ticket when Madison ran for president) was his staunch ally at the convention. He called the idea of an equal vote in the Senate a "vicious principle." But Delaware's Gunning Bedford, a rotund character who dwarfed Madison, stole the show by resorting to theatrics and threatening secession. "The large states dare not dissolve the Confederation," he bellowed, for if they do, "the small states will find some foreign ally of more honor and good faith." He was tired of talk and dubious assurances, stating unequivocally: "I do not, gentlemen, trust you." Paterson, too, complained of Madison's rudeness.[58]

The Virginian was abnormally contentious when he openly accused the small states of endangering the Union. Now in the minority, all he could do to turn the tide was to paint as bleak a picture as he could conjure and hope it reached the doubters. He made a dire prediction: republican liberty would yield to militarism. Left to their own devices, the disunited states would resort to standing armies and foreign alliances; they would form "partial confederacies," constantly at war with one another. All of this would occur, he claimed, unless the small states accepted their vulnerability and saw that they were in no position to make demands.[59]

As provocative as Madison's approach already was, he stirred up a hornets' nest when he shifted the terms of debate to the volatile subject of North-South differences. In one day's session at the end of June he declared that regionalism actually mattered more than the sizes of states. The three largest states were, he insisted, "as dissimilar as any three other states in the Union." They were more prone to "rivalships" than to "coalitions," because of slavery.

He had touched the third rail of American politics by conceding that the most fundamental socioeconomic distinctions in the country lay between North and South, "principally from the effects of their having or not having slaves." Upon acknowledging the central role of slavery, he was able to propose an unusual new configuration: apportionment in the lower house based on free inhabitants; apportionment in the upper house based on free inhabitants plus three-fifths of the slave population. If proportional representation in the Senate had passed on the strength of this reasoning, Virginia's control of the Senate would have been ensured. But once again Madison's argument fell on deaf ears.[60]

Out of the deadlock emerged the Connecticut compromise, granting proportional representation in the House. To appease the southern delegates, it counted three slaves to every five free inhabitants in constituting that body. It also established, once and for all, equal representation in the Senate. When a committee was formed to determine the number of seats in the House, the large-state advantage could not be missed: the three largest states held 43 percent of the seats. Sherman of Connecticut protested, and another committee was organized, which crunched the numbers again and donated a few more seats to the smaller states and New England.

Gouverneur Morris of Pennsylvania was horrified by what was happening. Trusting in a chosen few more than in an expanding union, he wanted to restrict the number of seats granted to new states. He saw danger in making population, instead of wealth, the standard for representation in the House, fearing this would allow the western states eventually to overpower the Atlantic states. Elbridge Gerry imagined that empowered western legislators would conspire to "drain our wealth into the Western country." He believed, as well, that the West would be flooded with foreigners.[61]

Gouverneur Morris was a famously captivating speaker. He would come up with the preamble of the Constitution, "We the People." As sardonic as he was charming, he exuded a robust self-confidence in spite of a crippling calamity: he had been one-legged since 1780, when in a freak accident his own horse-drawn chaise had run him over, and his doctor saw amputation as the only option. Though he could be reckless with language, irreverent, and often abrasive, Morris was an attention-grabber. As an unrepentant elitist, he contended that "remote wilderness" was not the "proper school of political talents," and that westerners were pretty much all backward. He was just as perturbed that the Constitution would protect slavery, and that slave-owning southerners were to be rewarded with added seats in Congress. He would abide by the compromise but continue to make himself heard.[62]

Madison, Mason, and Randolph all responded to Morris's geographical absolutism by defending the principle of treating all new states as equals. Madison, thoroughly exasperated by this time, scolded Morris for his tendency to measure the human character "by the points of the compass." Westward migration, he contended, could not be stopped, and it was only natural for people to move into less populous places where land was cheaper. True, the West was bound to grow at a rapid rate, as Spain yielded to America's demands and the Mississippi opened up. But the Atlantic states, north as well as south, Madison argued, would all reap tremendous economic benefits by supplying commercial goods to the western states. It was the same cause he had taken up in Congress in years past, and he kept on doing so for one simple reason: it was in the best interest of Virginia.[63]

North and South could not agree on the apportionment of representatives in Congress. Each section feared that the other was to gain the upper hand. It was Pennsylvania's James Wilson who finally provided the compromise solution in this instance, proposing that population-based representation also be tied to taxation and to a motion Congress had considered in 1783, which recognized the three-fifths principle. Northerners would be less offended if it appeared that counting southern slaves was a quid pro quo for taxing them. Wilson's maneuver was less a concession than a performance, though. No one expected to realize federal tax revenues from slaves after the new government was established.[64]

The rancor of some debates, especially over slavery and the West, demonstrated the instability of Madison's original coalition. Gouverneur Morris went so far as to accuse southerners of being unwilling to settle for anything less than a majority in Congress. He peered into the future and saw them conspiring with westerners to stage a war with Spain in order to secure the Mississippi. Northerners would be spilling blood in needless wars, just to satisfy the land-hungry South. He was not far off.[65]

Madison could not get his mind off proportional representation in the Senate and made one last attempt to salvage his plan. On July 14 he backed a motion presented by Charles Pinckney that would have recalibrated the system: no state, no matter how small, would be assigned any less than *one-fifth* the number of representatives of the most populous state. It was too little too late. On the sixteenth the convention voted to accept the Connecticut compromise—proportional representation in the House (counting slaves as three-fifths of a citizen for the purpose of apportioning seats), and equal representation in the Senate. Deeply troubled, Edmund Randolph asked for an immediate adjournment. Delegates from the large states met in private but failed to reach a consensus. Their coalition had dissolved. A modified version of the absolute negative contained in the Virginia Plan was decisively voted down the next day.[66]

After his study of constitutions, after all of his outlinings of a grand plan, and after a month and a half of debate, James Madison had witnessed the rejection of virtually every one of his ideas. The council of revision was the first to go. His absolute negative was quashed and its modified cousin faded away, as proportional representation in the Senate fell by the wayside. The Senate, his repository of "virtue & wisdom," was now his worst nightmare: a hapless pawn of the state legislatures.

"The Builders of Babel"

If Madison won over few of his peers, it was not because his arguments were all unappealing—he had prominent defenders. But fears among the states which he had not prepared for ultimately redirected the course of debate. In a private letter to a friend, Washington, who sat silently through most of the proceedings, expressed his despair over the sectional sparring. Benjamin Franklin, though hardly a man of faith, put it best on June 28, when he proposed that each subsequent day of the convention should begin with a prayer. If his colleagues paused for a moment to give over their thoughts to a higher power, they might then, he said, rise above their "little partial local interests" and avoid behaving like "the Builders of Babel." Regional bias had blinded delegates to the greater good.[67]

After his vision of a Senate comprised of an intellectual elite went down in flames, one might have expected Madison to pack his bags and leave the convention. Others did. But realizing that he would have to work with what he was given, he regrouped. For the remainder of the convention, he did everything possible to *reduce* the power of the Senate, looking to other branches to take on the responsibilities he had earlier assigned to the upper house.

He still faced an uphill battle. The tedium of the hot summer months brought a discernible impatience among the delegates. Speeches were shorter, and so were Madison's notes. An August 6 report of the Committee of Detail gave the Senate sole authority to select Supreme Court judges and U.S. ambassadors, to make treaties, and to resolve disputes between states. If the president died or had to be removed for some reason, the president of the Senate took his place. Meanwhile, in addition to the direct appointment of U.S. senators, state legislatures were to have new tools at their disposal: they could regulate the time and place of elections, determine districts, and set voter qualifications for House elections. Madison worried about abuses that were bound to occur if states had an uncontrolled right over election planning. They could corrupt the process by showing favor to one or another candidate. Equally galling to him, the Committee of Detail placed within the states' grasp one very tight purse string: control over congressmen's compensation.

Many besides Madison felt that after denying the Senate the power to police the states, the convention had gone too far in the other direction. So when the relentless Virginia delegate addressed these details, he obtained minor successes. He faced scant opposition when he motioned to reject the regulation of congressional elections by state legislatures. Even Roger Sherman, who agreed with Madison on little, concurred. And control over compensation of the officers of government was returned to Congress with virtually no protest.[68]

Madison's strongest statement in the midsummer debates came after Oliver Ellsworth motioned to empower the state legislatures to approve the federal Constitution, rather than submit it to special ratifying conventions. Here, dismissing the legislatures as "incompetent" to weigh the issues at hand, Madison developed his theory of constitution writing: *Only a ratifying convention gave legitimacy to any new government wherein new powers were to be based on the supremacy of the laws.* This point was crucial to him. He felt that "the people," not the states, must found the government. Popular ratifying conventions, like proportional representation, called forth the majority will. States, by definition, lacked a national focus. Their interests were naturally circumscribed, and they would only interfere with the duties, encroach on the powers, and clog the operations of the national government.[69]

After losing the Senate to the states, he argued that the office of the president was now the principal guardian of national interests. In appointing judges, for instance, "the Executive Magistrate would be considered a national officer, acting for and equally sympathizing with every part of the United States." Madison held that the president would transcend the "selfish motives" and partiality of the Senate, whose loyalties were divided between state and nation.[70]

To make things right, some kind of popular authority had to be employed in choosing the president. Early in the convention James Wilson had been the first to bring up the idea of electors, but his proposal was dismissed without much debate. It was revived in late July, when Madison recognized that temporarily chosen electors were less likely to corrupt the process than if the president were named by Congress directly. He would have preferred direct election of the president by the people at large—that is, all freemen in the United States without regard to state boundaries and without filtering their vote through any intermediate body. But he also knew that this method would favor the northern states, where the right of suffrage was, as he put it, "more diffusive." The South's three-fifths advantage would be eliminated in the direct election of the president, because the unfree cast no ballots.[71]

Little by little Madison and his allies chipped away at opposing arguments and made the idea of *some form* of popular election acceptable. Hugh Williamson of North Carolina and Gouverneur Morris of Pennsylvania came up with the solution whereby each elector would choose two candidates, one of whom could not be from his home state. This would oblige everyone to settle on a nationally respected figure. Madison endorsed this device, seeing its potential to defeat local prejudice. As he wryly (and somewhat cynically) put it, "The second best man in this case would probably be the first."[72]

The delegates also moved away from the proposal made by the Committee of Detail that would have had the president serve one seven-year term. Delegates had already toyed with the idea of extending that term to eleven, fifteen, or even twenty years. Gouverneur Morris warned that this was a recipe for creating a "despot of America," who would have the armed forces behind him if he should refuse to quit office. The delegates ultimately opted for a short presidential term and reelection.[73]

As delegates began arguing in favor of making the president eligible for reelection, Madison was even more convinced that Congress ought to be constrained from direct involvement in presidential politics. Every reelection contest would "agitate & divide" both houses, he said, and create a situation in which the candidate would be tempted to "intrigue" with the legislature. He would derive appointment not from the people but from the "predominant faction." Or as Gouverneur Morris concisely put it: "Make him too weak: The Legislature will usurp his powers. Make him too strong: He will usurp the Legislature."[74]

In September the delegates finally agreed to have the president serve a four-year term, with the possibility for continual reelection. He would be chosen by electors under rules decided by each of the state legislatures. This could include direct election by the people if the state so chose. The number of electors would be determined by the total number of representatives in Congress; each elector would vote for two candidates, one not from his state. If no candidate had a majority, the Senate would choose the president from the five top vote-getters.[75]

While this plan overcame the impasse over election of the president, it also left considerable power in the hands of the Senate. Madison spoke to the issue. So did James Wilson, who claimed that the president "will not be the man of the people as he ought to be, but a Minion of the Senate." Roger Sherman, the master of compromise, came up with the solution: If there was no clear winner, the House of Representatives would decide among the top five, voting as state delegations rather than as individuals. Each state delegation would have one vote, ensuring equality for the small states. Sherman's revision passed by a vote of 10 to 1.[76]

So now Madison would seek to vest in the presidency the powers he originally wanted to confer on the Senate. As a paternal guardian of the national interest, the chief executive would be wise enough to filter out bad laws and strong enough to control the propensity of the states to enact "pernicious measures." Madison would then strengthen the presidential veto, compensating for the loss of the absolute negative that he had originally intended for a Senate that no longer resembled his guardian ideal. Here, when all was said and done, he made out well.[77]

Madison could only feel pleased that the president was to have "more latitude and discretion" than Congress or the judiciary. The president would be able to make treaties and appoint ambassadors and judges. In insisting on the president's veto authority, Madison was willing to grant the Senate the right to override that veto on the strength of a two-thirds vote (though he preferred a three-quarters vote). The president could be impeached for "incapacity, negligence, or perfidy," Madison wrote—a more colorful rendering, perhaps, than the eventual phrase, "high crimes and misdemeanors."

In the short run, at least, he was not deeply concerned about presidential "perfidy" and was content to confer to the president power over the military. This was because George Washington was the model (and likeliest candidate) for the office. Since 1779, Americans had been celebrating his birthday and calling him "godlike" for the constancy of his devotion to the nation.[78]

In this and other ways Madison was sensitive to appearances. He opposed a prohibition against the foreign-born holding offices, suggesting (it sounds quaint today) that such a pose would "give a tincture of illiberality" to the Constitution and discourage the most desirable class of people from immigrating. Madison also supported an immediate prohibition on the importation of slaves, but he did not have an answer, or even the beginning of an answer, to the larger sectional issue of slavery.

It was not Madison, whose strongest feelings concerned the division of power in a federal system, but Rufus King of Massachusetts who ignited discussion of the slave trade. King was furious when the Committee of Detail refused to place any restrictions on the importation of slaves. George Mason voiced his own strong disapproval of this "infernal traffic," only to be mocked by Ellsworth of Connecticut, who reminded the Virginian that if slavery was truly to be regarded in a moral light, "we ought to go farther and free those already in the Country." South Carolina and Georgia refused to budge on the importation of slaves, and the dispute was handed over to the Committee of Eleven. Madison was a member of the committee, which voted to forbid Congress from interfering with the slave trade until 1800, though it did approve a duty on imported slaves. But even this was not enough for the Deep South. Charles Cotesworth Pinckney called for extending the deadline to 1808, at which point Madison took offense. He countered, without the least subtlety, that "twenty years will produce all the mischief that can be apprehended from the liberty to import slaves" and would seriously tarnish the national character. He reported to Jefferson: "S. Carolina and Georgia were inflexible on the point of slaves." The Deep South got its way.[79]

As of early September, Madison could not have been feeling triumphant. The coalition of Virginians he had worked to create no longer existed. He was unable to convince Mason and Randolph to embrace his way of thinking about the presidency—they instinctively distrusted the office. In Randolph's words, making one man the chief executive would constitute the "Foetus of Monarchy." To protect sectional interests, the pair preferred a three-person executive, with a representative from each of the coastal regions—New England, the Middle States, and the South.[80]

By midsummer Mason and Randolph were railing against the "aristocracy" of the Senate. They insisted that money bills and the taxing of exports be kept out of its "mischievous" (read: northern) hands. In the final days of the convention, trying to salvage some of his ideas for weakening power at the top, Mason called for a privy council, comprised of six regional advisers, to surround the president. This idea gained no ground either. When all was said and done, Randolph and Mason were left even more dispirited than Madison. The convention's refusal to make commercial treaties negotiated by the executive subject to a two-thirds approval in Congress was, for both men, the last straw.[81]

Thus Edmund Randolph, Virginia's current governor, and George Mason, Washington's longtime neighbor, both refused to sign the Constitution. Randolph demanded that participants in the upcoming ratifying conventions be authorized to add amendments. Mason made an even more improbable demand, calling for a second convention. Madison informed Jefferson, somewhat colloquially: "Col. Mason left Philadelphia in an exceeding ill humour indeed." Among the remaining delegates, Elbridge Gerry of Massachusetts was the only other one to refuse to sign the Constitution.[82]

Given the sour atmosphere and the almost constant wrangling, it is remarkable that only these three voiced their dissent at the end of the convention. To read the proceedings as "the miracle at Philadelphia," as tradition has dubbed it, is a willful oversimplification, if not a delusion. The participants in debate found it a byzantine experience, more wearisome than glorious. As for Madison, it was as a Virginia partisan that he attended the convention; given the utter failure of the Virginia Plan to take root, it was as a Virginian, once again, that he saw the presidency as the one office wherein his state might still retain preeminence.

On September 17, the last day of the convention, Benjamin Franklin offered up a conciliatory speech, admitting that the document to which those assembled had just agreed possessed flaws. But he was astonished, he said, that it approached "so near to perfection as it does." Looking around the room, the eighty-one-year-old Boston-born Philadelphian implored the delegates to join him in expressing their unanimity by putting their names to it.[83]

One can only assume that George Washington was inspired by Franklin's words when, as president of the convention, he rose for the first and only time to address the delegates. He said he hoped they would not be offended by his decision to break his silence, but he felt compelled to speak. A Massachusetts delegate had moved to change the ratio in the House from one representative for every forty thousand persons to one for every thirty thousand, and Washington wished for the delegates to back this proposal.

Why had he chosen this moment to say something? Washington had more than the one, relatively minor, alteration in mind when he spoke up. It was his subtle way of announcing to his colleagues that he endorsed the Constitution and that they should do so as well, before it went to the states for ratification. As the convention was adjourned, delegates dined together one last time before they parted company and returned home.[84]

On September 25–26, 1787, one week after the Constitutional Convention ended, Princeton College held its graduation, which was reported in newspapers as "a large and polite, and learned assembly." A series of orations were given, some of them delivered in Latin and Greek. One addressed "the Abuses of Independence"; another took as its subject religious liberty. Before the event concluded, a doctor of laws degree was conferred on a distinguished member of the class of 1771, "the Hon. James Madison, Esq."[85]

Just days before, Madison had stopped briefly in Princeton, as he hurried from Philadelphia to New York City to resume his duties in the old Congress—the Confederation Congress. There he had to protect the Constitution from any who would undermine it. Virginian Edward Carrington sent him an urgent letter warning that Richard Henry Lee was going to stir up trouble, offering amendments to the Constitution that would actually be used to oppose it.

A heated debate took place in Congress before it was agreed that no amendments would be added to the text of the Constitution. Congress would remain neutral, then, and send the Constitution on to the states without directly endorsing it. In Philadelphia, Madison had stood firmly behind the principle of ratifying conventions and now helped to word the congressional resolution so that it expressed unanimous agreement to the procedure. He confessed to Washington that a "more direct approbation" would have been better for their home state of Virginia, but he hoped that the indirect endorsement from Congress would be enough. Carrington wrote to Jefferson in the same vein: "The people do not scrutinize terms: the unanimity of Congress in recommending to their consideration, naturally implies approbation." Others disagreed. R. H. Lee wrote to George Mason that approval was of a limited character, applying only to "transmission" of the Constitution to the states. Battle lines were already being drawn between so-called federalists and antifederalists, proponents and skeptics of the new Constitution.[86]

Forbidden to divulge anything of substance during the debates, Madison finally wrote to Jefferson at length in October, elaborating on what he saw as imperfections in the final document. Madison's tone was one of anger and frustration. Unlike Randolph, Mason—or even Jefferson, as he would soon learn—Madison felt the new government was going to be too weak. He remained convinced that his fellow delegates had acted foolishly in rejecting the absolute negative, the only conceivable tool for subordinating the states and bringing selfish local interests under control.[87]

CHAPTER FIVE

The Addition of Rights
1788–1789

The founders of our republics have so much merit for the wisdom,
which they have displayed, that no task can be less pleasing than that of
pointing out the errors into which they have fallen.

—JAMES MADISON, IN *FEDERALIST* 48 (FEBRUARY 1, 1788)

Were I in America, I would advocate it warmly till nine should
have adopted & then as warmly take the other side to convince
the remaining four that they ought not to come into it
till the declaration of rights is annexed to it.

—THOMAS JEFFERSON TO WILLIAM S. SMITH,
FEBRUARY 2, 1788, CONVEYING HIS STRATEGY FOR
APPROACHING THE RATIFICATION OF THE CONSTITUTION

ON NEW YEAR'S DAY 1788 AN ODE APPEARED IN THE *VIRGINIA Journal,* celebrating the statesmen of the commonwealth and the glory and splendor of the Revolution. It recognized several members of the state's delegations to earlier congresses, but the choicest lines were reserved for the Virginian who had made his voice heard most often at the convention in Philadelphia. His physical meekness made his accomplishments all the more dramatic:

> *Maddison, above the rest*
> *Pouring from his narrow chest*
> *More than Greek or Roman sense*
> *Boundless tides of eloquence.*

Next in the poetic procession came the fatherly legal scholars: Wythe, who "drank the source of truth"; and Pendleton, who, "with locks of age," seemed so wise as to have been "lent from other worlds." The Lee family was "a glorious band," but only one of its sons was singled out, Richard Henry Lee, for he had "spoken an empire into birth." In case the reference was unclear to some, the anonymous versifier added a footnote: "R. H. Lee made the motion in Congress for the declaration of Independence, July 4, 1776."

But R. H. Lee was not a proponent of the Constitution. Given his illustrious role in the Revolution, "millions" (according to the poet) mourned his "loss," or defection, to antifederalism. He was, in fact, the only antifederalist who received mention in the poem: former governors Patrick Henry, who refused to attend the convention, and Edmund Randolph, who did but decided not to sign, were ignored.

The absent Thomas Jefferson was given his due some lines later: "Light and glory of the age / Jefferson the learned sage." His association with the Declaration went unmentioned, as it was not yet a part of the national lore. Washington, so revered that he need not even be mentioned by name, was symbolized by his capital achievement: "PRIDE of PEACE and STRENGTH of WAR!" The essence of the poem was its prediction that brighter days lay ahead on the western horizon, and that a golden age loomed for America.[1]

But the human character is mixed, and the conduct of politics is never as tidy as patriotic poetry teaches. From early 1787 to late 1788—pre-convention through ratification—Madison and Jefferson expressed significantly different views about republican government, the American character, and majority rule. As confidential correspondents, they could read each other's ciphers, but their master narratives for America had diverged.

"No Country Should Be So Long Without One"

Their lack of common ground was most striking in their dueling attitudes toward Shays's Rebellion. When he corresponded with Washington, Madison rebuked the Regulators as a band of traitors; to another ally, he identified the Shaysites as a "diseased part" of the body politic and contended that they were "secretly stimulated by British influence." But he must have known what to expect from the pen of the American minister to France, because he censored himself when writing to Jefferson.

Their disagreement was a fundamental one. Madison was guarded about the wisdom of the people. They could be duped and misled by colorful personalities or by foreign powers; they were vulnerable to bribes and alluring promises. Jefferson rejected this jaundiced view when he blithely wrote Madison in February 1787 that "a little rebellion now and then is a good thing, and as necessary in the political world as storms in the physical." He liked to infuse his metaphors of nature with therapeutic possibilities and saw the Shaysites as "a medicine necessary for the sound health of government," a natural elixir that kept the state honest. But Madison believed the Regulators' haughty defiance of established order threatened the very survival of government.[2]

Drawing from natural history, Jefferson reasoned like an anthropologist. People were conditioned by their surroundings, as he reminded Madison in the February letter, and societies arose in three ways: the Indian style of no government (a faulty assumption on Jefferson's part); monarchies, predicated on force; and republics, which allowed for greater liberty, promoted happiness, and occasionally endured disturbances from below. These disruptions were worth the price of freedom, Jefferson assured, quoting the Roman historian Sallust: *"Malo periculosam, libertatem quam quietam servitutem"* (I would rather have hazardous liberty than quiet slavery). The most dangerous encroachments, he said, were those made by the state against the rights of the people.[3]

No doubt reflecting his exposure to the courts of Europe, Jefferson was concerned about the new Society of the Cincinnati, a league of Revolutionary War veterans that was limited to officers. Its membership was hereditary, and Jefferson imagined it as a model for an American aristocracy. When queried, he warned George Washington to keep his distance from the society. Seeing little likelihood that Shays's rebellion was a herald of anarchy, Jefferson counseled that America should be more wary of a monarchical backlash. Or as he wrote to Edward Carrington: "The natural progress of things is for liberty to yield, and government to gain ground." Tyranny came from the top.

On this subject, he was rigid in his judgments. The difference between the American republic and the monarchies of Europe was the difference between heaven and hell, he told a fellow Virginian. Addressing Washington in late 1786, he had dismissed as "light" the "inconveniences" of the Articles of Confederation. Inconveniences? What could be a greater heresy to his friend Madison?[4]

Thus the erstwhile partners, still apart, routinely expressed their diametrically opposed philosophies regarding the dangers inherent in political society. Madison: Popular commotion weakened a republic. Jefferson: The people should stand guard against all encroachments on their liberties. Reflexive in their dissimilar outlooks, they agreed only that corruption was human.

Whereas Jefferson spoke out for majority rule, Madison understood how difficult it would be to restrain a majority from oppressing any minority. He told Jefferson that factional majorities were no different from the soulless mob, both of them unable to work for the good of the whole. In a similar sense, religion, which should have been a force for the cooling of passions, actually did the reverse, encouraging religious fervor (then called "enthusiasm"). Their philosophical conflict is again apparent in Madison's reference to the democratic-sounding "sympathy of the multitude"—he was warning Jefferson about sheeplike behavior: when a citizen became part of a crowd, he often went against his own conscience. In these several ways, then, Madison challenged Jefferson's defense of benign popular majorities, telling him pointedly that a "simple Democracy, or a pure republic, actuated by the sense of the majority," was unrealizable.

With his experience in Philadelphia weighing heavily, Madison also sketched out for Jefferson his theory of the extended republic, which he would soon publicize in *Federalist* 10. To forestall the formation of dangerous factions, he advised spreading the unruly classes across a "sphere of a mean extent." Scattered across physical space, "broken into so many interests and parties," they would resist the otherwise natural impulse to coalesce as a dangerously large faction. At the same time the people would not be spread so far apart as to lose a sense of unity if they should have to defend themselves against an oppressive administration. Madison's idea was to achieve a balance of political forces. As he explained to Jefferson after the close of the Constitutional Convention, a federal government functioned best as a neutral arbiter among contending interests.[5]

Here too we can isolate the influence on Madison of the skeptic David Hume. As scholars have long observed, the Scottish philosopher convinced him that in a large commonwealth factions were inevitable. But Madison was equally convinced that dangerous combinations were preventable. He had long admired Pennsylvania for its policy of religious toleration and could see how religious and religious pluralism might thrive side by side.[6]

In addition to Hume, when he wrote of factions occupying a spatial dimension, Madison reflected his engagement with Benjamin Franklin's 1751 *Observations Concerning the Increase of Mankind,* a study of population growth and American expansion, well known at this time. Franklin's focus was on productivity: as plants and animals flourished in a wide expanse, so would Americans prosper as they spread outward, married young, and farmed their land. In answer to a letter from Jefferson on poverty in Europe, Madison adopted Franklinian reasoning, arguing that America's limited population gave it political advantages over the Old World: "misery seems inseparable from a high degree of populousness." Indeed, in this case both Madison and Jefferson accepted the premise that concentrated urban populations were a key cause of human misery. Jefferson made a crude but effective analogy in *Notes on Virginia:* "mobs" in overcrowded cities did as much to advance good government across space as "sores" contributed to the health of the human body. Crowding and competition made for a delicate subsistence, slowed population growth, and impeded the pursuit of happiness.[7]

What Franklin saw in terms of "a general happy Mediocrity," Madison referred to as the "sphere of a mean extent." (The eighteenth-century words *mediocrity* and *mean* had the same connotation.) But Madison took Franklin's argument a step beyond. Territorial expansion not only reduced social conflict, he said; it also checked the growth of political discord. Not only was it the case that Old World cities, manufacturing economies, the consumption of luxury items, and the unequal distribution of resources all corrupted governments, it was also true that factious leaders acquired their greatest sway in small, homogeneous, densely crowded societies, using what Madison called "vicious arts" to kindle class hostilities. Expansion was a means of reducing "mutual animosities"—it provided an emotional safety valve.[8]

Franklin's theories may have repaired the perceptual gap in Madison's and Jefferson's thought. But when Madison told Jefferson he thought of the new federal system as a "feudal system of republics" with a weak central authority (hardly a ringing endorsement for the Constitutional Convention!), he reframed the argument once again. He predicted the emergence of collaborative groups within Congress that would eventually steamroll over unaligned states. It would begin with an amalgamation of the interests of the original southern states and their offspring (Virginia's hold on Kentucky, North Carolina's on Tennessee). Eventually, multiple-state alliances—shared identities—could develop and undermine the spirit of Union. It was not simply the North-South dichotomy that he saw threatening the longevity of the United States.

Madison granted that the Constitution was a "material" improvement over the "Confederacy of independent States" that had preceded it. But it had not corrected the problem that bothered him most: "sacrifices of national to local interests." Abuses would occur even as the republic grew to occupy an extensive sphere. Majority rule was not enough to correct it; it would never be a reliable source of political justice. But Jefferson was quite explicit: "The will of the Majority should always prevail."[9]

Trying to be both thoughtful and careful, Jefferson gave voice to his divergence of opinion with Madison. He was "captivated," he wrote, by the compromise between the large and small states (unaware, perhaps, of how painful a defeat this had been for Madison). He approved the overall balance among the three branches of government, the reduced dependence on state legislatures, and the popular election of members of the House of Representatives. This last, for Jefferson, preserved "the fundamental principle that the people are not taxed but by representatives chosen immediately by themselves."

As he noted what he disliked most about the Constitution, Jefferson sounded very much like George Mason and Edmund Randolph. "Omission of a bill of rights" worried him, and so did the absence of term limits for the chief executive: he predicted that the continual reelection of the president would result in his becoming "an officer for life." And for as long as America remained weak, a president might be persuaded to take money and arms from the European powers and become the pawn of one or another. For Jefferson, as for Mason and Randolph, the chief magistrate, as defined in the Constitution, resembled nothing so much as an elected monarch.

Jefferson repeated his argument as to Shays's rebellion, which could not but have disquieted Madison. The Shaysites had provoked more alarm than was warranted, he said, and he invoked France, where in the three years of his residency three violent insurrections had occurred. In Massachusetts little blood had been spilled, which prompted him to do a quick calculation: "One rebellion in 13 states in the course of 11 years, is but one for each state in a century and a half." To this he added, with an almost fanatical satisfaction: "No country should be so long without one." And if his rebellious streak was not bad enough, Jefferson allowed that he would be perfectly comfortable promoting the cause of a second constitutional convention, so as to amend the first.

To Madison, nothing could be more wrongheaded. If the country was unsatisfied with the first convention, a second would find the states even less willing to reach compromises. They would dismantle the federal system altogether. Of this he was utterly convinced.[10]

"Can This Possibly Be Jefferson?"

By the time Jefferson had answered Madison's post-convention letter, Madison had already written several of his *Federalist* essays, including the oft-quoted number 10. Hamilton had come up with the idea of the collaborative series, asking Madison, John Jay, and Gouverneur Morris to participate. Morris turned him down. Jay suffered a debilitating attack of rheumatism and could contribute only five pieces.

The eighty-five *Federalist* essays were printed in several New York City newspapers, then in two book-length volumes. Intended to be used in support of the Empire State's ratification alone, the essays were to be signed "A New Yorker." The addition of Madison required a different pseudonym, and thus was born (or reborn) "Publius," by which name was meant Publius Valerius Poplicola, an antimonarchical Roman official of the sixth century B.C. Hamilton penned the majority of the *Federalist* essays, fifty-one, and Madison wrote twenty-nine. They were done so quickly, Madison told Jefferson, that one author had almost no time to review another's work, or even to appraise his own, before the press demanded final drafts.[11]

Hamilton and Madison were an odd couple to combine on this project, given their common estrangement from the new constitution. Madison had watched as the delegates tore down his Virginia Plan; and Hamilton had considered that plan too accepting of the electoral process, blithely calling it "democracy checked by democracy, or pork with a little change of the sauce." His only significant proposal at the convention was a half-hearted effort to strengthen the chief executive by granting him veto power over state and federal laws. He was shot down. Consequently Hamilton retreated from the debates, floating a few minor resolutions before letting out his displeasure in a perplexing six-hour-long speech on June 18, in which he pronounced a plan of his own and praised the British government as "the best in the world." In Hamilton's plan, senators (necessarily men with extensive landed estates) were appointed for life; and the single executive was appointed for life too.

Hamilton was even more distrustful of the American people than Madison was. He wanted the central government to be the strongest possible. His June speech was met with indifference, causing Samuel Johnson of

Connecticut to quip: "The Gentleman from New York is praised by every gentleman, but supported by no gentleman." Unlike Madison, who stayed on despite setbacks, Hamilton left Philadelphia on June 29 and did not return until September 2.[12]

Hamilton's almost complete abandonment of the convention has never been adequately explained. He was hypersensitive by nature. Compromise did not come easily to him, and he was no doubt vexed when his biggest speech fell flat. He lacked the diplomatic skills needed to abide the constant give-and-take of the convention, and he informed Washington, under whom he had long served, that his continued attendance in Philadelphia would be a "waste of time." Washington chastised Hamilton for his desertion and urged him to return to Philadelphia. When he finally did, he lent his support to a federal constitution that he termed "better than nothing," later adding that "no man's ideas were more remote from the plan than [my] own." Nevertheless he soldiered up, called for unity, and gamely signed the Constitution.[13]

It was a short time later, in early October 1787, that Hamilton took the field with pen in hand. Writing as "Publius" was probably therapeutic for him, as it was for Madison, since neither wholeheartedly believed in the form the Constitution had taken. They found novel ways to justify the design of the new government, able to convince themselves that the "frail and worthless fabric" (to use Hamilton's words near the end of his life) was more robust than they had earlier imagined it.[14]

For his contributions, Madison tapped his extensive notes on ancient and modern confederacies. Public debate spurred him on, and one antifederalist essayist in particular got to him. "The Newspapers in the middle & Northern States begin to teem with controversial publications," he informed Edmund Randolph, "and one new combatant, with considerable address & plausibility, strikes at the foundation." That writer, who signed his essays "Brutus," made a strong case against any system of representation that encompassed an extended republic. It was after reading "Brutus" that Madison drafted *Federalist* 10, and he continued to debate this formidable adversary in subsequent essays.[15]

"Brutus" raised a concern that was common to the antifederalist critique: the Constitution created a government of "great and uncontrollable powers." Its powers to tax, to regulate the militia and raise armies, to overrule state laws through the federal judiciary, and to increase its authority at will through the "necessary and proper" clause posed a danger to individual liberty and to the very survival of the states. But his main concern was that in an extensive republic the people would lose touch with their rulers as their rulers lost touch with them.[16]

Madison defended the extended republic by arguing that the distance between rulers and ruled actually improved the quality of representation: the scattering effect would make it impossible for an "overbearing majority" to exploit passions and impose its will. The representatives in Congress would be "fit" characters, whose views were "consonant with the public good."

The notion of democracy has been made part of James Madison's reputation as the "Father of the Constitution," when democracy is, in fact, irrelevant to any understanding of his thinking in 1787–88. He disputed the idea advanced by "Brutus" (and maintained by Jefferson as well) that the only proper guardians of the public good were the people themselves—or representatives so sympathetic and beholden to the people that they mirrored their sentiments. Madison attributed little virtue to the force of popular opinion, as we understand it, instead embracing the social order that "Brutus" feared most: the creation of a separate, elite ruling class.[17]

Madison was not about to win over any antifederalists. Few of his contemporaries sufficiently understood the argument about diffusion, and fewer still bothered to repeat it in the debates over ratification. Even Jefferson did not seem to fully grasp its meaning at first. Not until the twentieth century did scholars, in rediscovering *Federalist* 10, transform Madison into a modern-day champion of pluralism. Downplaying his antiquated emphasis on virtue and elite rule, they presented the false idea that *Federalist* 10 was seen as something vital at the time it was written.[18]

The real impact of *The Federalist* is hard to measure. While many around the country claimed that the series, as a whole, was effective in demolishing the arguments of its enemies, all who made this claim were Madison and Hamilton partisans, writing to silence critics of the Constitution.[19] Only a small number of the essays were republished outside New York City; their turgid style limited *The Federalist*'s appeal to a narrow reading public. A Marylander remarked that it was not written "as a pamphlet ought to be" and failed to "force the attention, rouze the passions, or thrill the nerves."

Its main target was New York, but even there the series received mixed reviews. Melancton Smith, the leading antifederalist spokesman in that state's ratifying convention (who was possibly "Brutus" himself), dismissed "Publius" as irrelevant. Friends and foes alike found the work tiresome. A Philadelphian who signed his name "SQUIB" wished "Publius" would "rest his arm and let the people draw their breath for a little." Entirely unimpressed with the scholarly pretense of the windy essays, he let a bit of verse speak his mind: "His labour'd nothings, in so strange a stile, / Amaze th'un-learn'd, and make the learned smile." "SQUIB's" point was that the essays displayed empty erudition—the unlearned were bowled over, but the edu-cated were not fooled.[20]

Madison made a point of getting copies of his essays into the hands of prominent Virginians, notably George Washington and Edmund Ran-dolph. He was most eager to persuade Randolph to return to the federalist fold.[21] Madison had written for the New York newspapers with Virginia in mind, knowing he had one dragon to slay: the sixty-two-year-old George Mason, who had circulated "Objections to this Constitution" among a net-work of influential men inside and outside their state. After reading Mason's laundry list of complaints, Madison was hot under the collar, writing to Washington that Mason seemed obsessed with minutiae and unable to put a "proper gloss" on the text of the Constitution.[22]

There was nothing in Mason's written objections that Madison and his fellow delegates had not heard from him at the convention. Madison bris-tled in the letter to Washington, because he and Washington were kindred spirits, and Madison needed to vent. Washington himself would never quite reconcile with Mason, convinced that his neighbor's objections were aimed at alarming southerners about some imagined northern power play. No matter what the issue at hand was, fear of a predatory North was a con-venient refrain that worked effectively in Virginia. Mason's maneuver proved to be a major problem for Madison, who watched uncomfortably as his state divided into rival camps.

At the same time as he was doing battle with Mason, Madison received reports that Patrick Henry was taking jabs at the Constitution and stirring up the Assembly. Madison was certain that Mason was supplying the fod-der for Henry's attacks. This was precisely what Madison meant when he theorized that the people followed their favorite leaders unthinkingly and could not be trusted with power. As he put it to Edmund Randolph: "Had yourself, Col. Mason, R.H. L[ee]., Mr. Henry & a few others, seen the Con-stitution in the same light with those who subscribed to it, I have no doubt that Virginia would have been as zealous & unanimous as she is now di-vided on the subject."[23]

Madison took his first stab at Mason in *Federalist* 38. He submitted that the relationship between the executive and the Senate was harmless. He reasoned, too, that a bill of rights was unnecessary because issues of rights had not arisen under the Articles of Confederation—not one of Madison's most effective arguments. But Madison sidestepped Mason's loudest complaint: the notion that out-of-state tax collectors would invade Virginia and that in matters of commercial treaties the South was destined to become the pawn of the North. Mason imagined legislation being passed that would somehow undercut Virginia's tobacco trade with England. Oliver Ellsworth had ridiculed him on this very point in a widely (and anonymously) published essay that reached into Virginia.

So why did Madison fail to weigh in and take apart Mason's argument? Did he think that sectional rivalry was all right to introduce behind the closed doors of the convention, but was too combustible an issue to bring up in public afterward? Or was he embarrassed that Virginians should have to acknowledge their selfish provincialism in refusing to accommodate the interests of other states? Whatever the case, "Publius" refused to touch this question.[24]

But Madison did not dodge the highly controversial three-fifths clause. In *Federalist* 54 he defended the computation of slave numbers in the apportionment of House seats. The timing was curious. Only two days before, a New York critic had pointed out that "three-fifths" existed solely to equalize the "loaves and fishes," giving an artificial parity to North and South. It rewarded slave states for their "infecundity" and idleness. If southerners were given the privilege of counting each slave as three-fifths of a freeman, he reasoned, the northern states should be able to count "three-fifths of their live stock."[25]

Whether or not Madison had access to this piece, he dismissed the charge that slaves were solely property. Instead, through the use of a legal fiction, he explained that the slave was of a "mixed character," a person who was part property. He used the same expression in *Federalist* 39. Mixed character was, for Madison, the key to the whole federal system. The American Union was no longer "a *confederacy* of sovereign States" but a "*consolidation* of the States" predicated on the states' assent. The House of Representatives derived its powers from the people; the Senate derived its powers from the states; and the executive derived its powers from "a very compound source," reflecting "coequal bodies politic." The government, Madison wrote, "appears to be of a mixed character, presenting at least as many *federal* as *national* features." The Constitution had created a polity "neither wholly *national* nor wholly *federal*." He was drawing upon the distinction Oliver Ellsworth had made: in certain matters the states rule; in others, the national government decides for all. The government's "mixed character" was how it would preserve domestic peace. Madison had not embraced Ellsworth's argument in Philadelphia, but it resonated with him now.

As to the mixed character embodied in the slave, Madison applied a different logic, readily admitting that slavery was an arbitrary and unnatural condition. Laws had "transformed the negroes into subjects of property," he explained, before making the startling admission—startling for a Virginian—that their condition might be altered: "If the laws were to restore rights which have been taken away, the negroes could no longer be refused an equal share of representation with other inhabitants." If slaves were potentially free, legal inhabitants of the United States, then the Constitution had to recognize such an outcome: one cannot treat exclusively as property the person who might one day possess all the rights of citizenship.

The implications of Madison's legal thinking are substantial. Slaves could acquire legal identities similar to those of other inhabitants of the nation who were dependents: women, children, and aliens. (Not accidentally, it is called "emancipation" when a male child comes of age.) All of them lacked the full rights claimed by citizens. In Madison's construction, the peculiar legal nature of slaves had led to an "expedient" compromise— the three-fifths rule. The slave, then, was a strange hybrid, "debased by servitude below the equal level of free inhabitants, which regards the *slave* as divested of two fifth of man."

We should pause for a moment to consider how the logic worked, or didn't work. After just having, in effect, scheduled the end of the overseas slave trade for the year 1808, twenty years after adoption of the Constitution, politicians might have seized upon the calculations of "Publius" and pressed for a future date at which to convey "free inhabitant" status to the remainder of those born into slavery. Whether he realized it or not, Madison had devised a *constitutional* basis for the emancipation of slaves. The way he wrote about slavery, race almost appeared irrelevant: civil law had transformed African Americans into a species of property, and natural law had nothing to do with their status.[26]

His intellectual argument sidestepped the reality on the ground, of course. The indebted southern planter was anxious about the fluctuating value of his crop, and about preserving a certain quality of life; the human drama of slavery was tied to his fears. If Madison's "mixed character" thinking was a theoretical exercise, it was also divorced from the elaborate taxonomy of race that Jefferson had spelled out in *Notes on Virginia.*

For Jefferson, differences were dictated by nature. He never strayed from this judgment. But Jefferson's logic was also a series of psychological justifications. He regarded the original crime of capture, kidnapping, and enslavement as experiences indelibly imprinted on the African American and comparable, in this way, to skin pigmentation. The memory of abuse, he allowed himself to think, made it dangerous for manumission to occur without a complete separation of the races. Jefferson saw slavery as the suspension of a state of war—race war—that would break out at some point after mass emancipation.[27]

While both Virginians' formulations were fairly abstract, Jefferson's was framed by emotions he assumed were felt by both whites and blacks. Madison's dispassionate *Federalist* 54 saw slave status as something arbitrary and temporary. His "mixed character" designation for slaves could hardly have been comforting to southerners who read his essay, and were asked to accept the idea that only a legal fiction separated slaves from freemen. While Madison appears to have drawn up his argument for hypothetical purposes, we must recall that in the midst of the Revolution, he had been prepared to grant freedom to the slaves who served in the Virginia militia.

Madison read *Notes on Virginia* while engaged in writing his *Federalist* essays. Overlooking his friend's racial theories, he drew on Jefferson's words in an unrelated context to point to the danger of legislative tyranny. Naming the U.S. minister to France in the text of *Federalist* 48, Madison wrote: "The authority in support of [Virginia's state constitution] is Mr. Jefferson, who besides his other advantages for remarking the operation of the government, was himself the chief magistrate of it." Madison's point: The constitution-writing Governor Jefferson had understood—though Ambassador Jefferson apparently did not—that "173 despots would surely be as oppressive as one." Instead of criticizing Jefferson, Madison let Jefferson's language in *Notes* criticize Jefferson and the many other Virginians who, in 1787–88, reflexively warned about tyranny from the top down.

Madison opened *Federalist* 49 with a second reference to the author of "that valuable work," *Notes on Virginia.* This time it was to register disapproval of Jefferson's proposal for constitutional revision. Jefferson favored the calling of a popular convention at times when two of the three branches of Virginia's state government agreed that fundamental change was needed. Madison allowed that there was "great force in this reasoning," but he still had "insuperable objections" to it. If a constitution could be altered too easily, he said, it would become a mere tool of party politics. Regular conventions introduced "the danger of disturbing the public tranquility by interesting too strongly the public passions." Once again it was Madison's conviction that the people should be kept at bay.[28]

Madison was engaged in a virtual debate with his friend Jefferson, though not a virulent one. Curiously he did not reveal his authorship of *The Federalist* to Jefferson until the summer of 1788, a considerable time after he began writing the essays, and a month *after* Virginia's ratifying convention had ended. Edward Carrington, a Virginia delegate to Congress, had already let Jefferson in on the more or less open secret of "Publius's" identity, forwarding him copies of *The Federalist.* But Madison appeared in no hurry to acknowledge his views to Jefferson at this crucial moment.[29]

Since quitting Philadelphia, Madison had been living in New York. He finally headed back to Virginia in March 1788. He was not looking forward to his state's ratifying convention, telling Washington it would inevitably involve "very laborious and irksome discussions." In order to secure a seat at the Richmond gathering, he felt compelled for the first time in his life to give a lengthy political speech to the voters of Orange on Election Day. He spoke in the open air, on a windy day, aiming to dispel some of what he described to Jefferson as "absurd and groundless prejudices" circulating in central Virginia. He was elected as a delegate by a comfortable margin.

In Richmond Madison found himself battling more than antifederalists Patrick Henry and George Mason. Just as an intense debate opened, he became seriously ill and missed several days of the convention. While recovering, he had to listen in silence; each time he tried to raise his voice, he was barely audible.[30]

Aware that the vote on the Constitution would be close in his native state, he identified three factions right away: those, like himself, who unconditionally supported the new plan of government; those who would approve if it accepted amendments; and Henry's coalition, which sought to derail the proceedings. Madison placed Randolph and Mason in the middle group, unaware that the embittered Mason was moving closer to Henry's position.[31]

Jefferson told one of his correspondents in December 1787 that he expected Madison to be the "main pillar" of defense at the ratifying convention, but he also questioned whether Madison would be able to "bear the weight." He predicted that Virginia would reject the Constitution—and he would not be at all alarmed if that were the result. Madison would have been deeply troubled if he had known that Jefferson was devising a solution to the likely impasse that flew in the face of all that he hoped to accomplish.

Jefferson was not just expressing his disappointment with aspects of the Constitution; he was putting pressure on Madison directly. He submitted critical letters to a Maryland antifederalist and a Virginian, both of whom were then in London. These individuals were meant to take charge of circulating the letters, while keeping Jefferson's name out of the newspapers. To the Virginian, Alexander Donald, a tobacco broker whom Jefferson had known since youth, he was the more direct: "I wish with all my soul that the nine first [ratifying] Conventions may accept the new Constitution, because this will secure to us the good it contains, which I think great and important. But I equally wish that the four latest conventions, whichever they be, may refuse to accede to it till a declaration of rights be annexed." He knew that Maryland and Virginia both might reject the Constitution, and he deliberately targeted them because that was where his influence was greatest. He hoped to prompt a supplementary second convention. This strategy placed Jefferson closer to the middle group of Madison's three-way valuation: the group that sought amendments. But he was also unknowingly close to Henry in his comfort with a second convention.

Several months later, as Jefferson's disruptive letter was making the rounds, one flustered Marylander wrote to Madison and asked incredulously: "Can this possibly be Jefferson?" At the Virginia Ratifying Convention, Patrick Henry invoked Jefferson's name with perverse pleasure: "This illustrious citizen advised you to reject this government till it be amended." He was claiming that the two of them occupied common ground, and it certainly looked that way. Henry's words pained Madison, whose only recourse was to counter by saying that Jefferson's position was being misconstrued. But Madison did not delude himself: Jefferson was secretly working against him.[32]

"A Good Canvas"

The Virginia Ratifying Convention lasted from June 2 to June 25, 1788. Both sides already knew how most of the delegates would vote, and few changed their opinions even after three weeks of grueling debate. A handful of undecideds kept the others in suspense, knowing their votes could decide the fate of the Constitution. As a Madison supporter put it, all was "suspended upon a single hair." An increasingly skeptical Madison did not surrender his doubts until nearly the end of the convention.[33]

The gathering was a grand opera of strong personalities. By unanimous decision, Edmund Pendleton reprised his role of a dozen years earlier as convention president. His health was impaired and he stood on crutches, but he showed, in the words of moderate antifederalist James Monroe, "as much zeal to carry [the convention], as if he had been a young man." Henry, always entertaining, quickly grabbed the spotlight, sometimes speaking for hours at a time. But Pendleton's influence was equal to that of Henry, given the length to which the competing sides went to gain his support. As president of the Virginia Convention in 1776, he had led the state to declare its independence from Great Britain. Now the grand old man was to preside over the adoption of a brand-new form of government.

Ordinarily a harmonizer, Governor Edmund Randolph found himself a man misunderstood. Though he had turned down the Constitution in Philadelphia, he changed his mind over the intervening months and was calling for ratification, agreeing with Madison that amendments could wait. His turnabout meant he had to fend off brutal swipes from the voluble Henry. At one point Henry went so far that the convention demanded he apologize for his rudeness.[34]

Henry assumed the role of master of ceremonies at the convention, dictating the order of debate in spite of the will of the majority of delegates. They wanted to discuss the Constitution clause by clause, but he somehow outmaneuvered them all, identifying topics of interest as he saw fit and spelling out every possible danger he believed to be lurking in the language of the document. Mason and Henry proved a formidable tag team. Their themes were these: the federal government threatened Virginia's status as the most powerful state in the Union; the state's economic welfare would be seriously jeopardized as the North gained in population and secured control in Congress; and slavery, the source of Virginia's tremendous wealth, lay politically unprotected. Henry assured the delegates that Virginia could refuse to ratify and the other states would still welcome her back into the Union with open arms. But first she had to make her point and vote no. Monroe spoke relatively little, and any influence he had only underscored Henry's importance.

Of the subjects taken up, slavery proved the most contentious. Mason repeated what he had said during the Constitutional Convention: that the new government failed to provide for "domestic safety" if there was no explicit protection for Virginians' slave property. Henry called up the by-now-ingrained fear of slave insurrections—the direct result, he believed, of Virginia's loss of authority over its own militia (because the president, as commander in chief, could conscript all militias). Congress, if it wished, could draft every slave into the military and liberate them at the end of their service. If troop quotas were determined by population, and Virginia had over 200,000 slaves, Congress might say: "Every black man must fight."

For that matter, a northern-controlled Congress might tax slavery out of existence.[35]

Mason and Henry both ignored the fact that the Constitution protected slavery on the strength of the three-fifths clause, the fugitive slave clause, and the slave trade clause. Their rationale was that none of this mattered if the North should have its way. At length Madison rose to reject their conspiratorial view. He argued that the central government had no power to order emancipation, and that Congress would never "alienate the affections of five-thirteenths of the Union" by stripping southerners of their property. "Such an idea never entered into any American breast," he said indignantly, "nor do I believe it ever will." Madison was doing his best to make Henry and Mason sound like fear-mongers. Yet Mason struck a chord in his insistence that northerners could never understand slavery; and Henry roused the crowd with his refusal to trust "any man on earth" with his rights. Virginians were hearing that their sovereignty was in jeopardy.[36]

To Randolph and Madison, the antifederalists sounded arrogant, insular, and isolationist, their posturing unproductive, even foolish. Madison reminded the convention how "notoriously feeble" America was under the Articles of Confederation. Its deranged finances, its dubious reputation with foreign nations, and its troubled military defenses during the Revolution made a strong federal system absolutely essential. He reminded the delegates of General Washington's incontrovertible statement at the end of the Revolution, when he publicly voiced his disapproval of the Confederation as he lay down his arms. It was most probably Madison's tribute to Washington's resolute character that prompted Henry, the very next day, to embarrass Madison by bringing up Jefferson's criticism of the Constitution.[37]

Near the end of the convention, Henry launched into his longest discourse on slavery. The generally placid and greatly esteemed legal scholar George Wythe had had enough. Years before, Wythe had refused to certify Henry's admission to the bar, doubting the young man's academic credentials. Now, believing that Henry had nothing of relevance to add to the proceedings, he moved to cut off debate and vote for unconditional ratification.

Newspapers were reporting that the federalists would win by six or eight votes, and their prediction proved remarkably accurate. On June 25, after the convention rejected two lists of proposed amendments submitted by Henry, it voted and, by 89 to 79, Virginia became the tenth state to ratify. A special committee met to draft a list of constitutional amendments that it wished to have incorporated in the future, and on the twenty-seventh, the Virginia Ratifying Convention adjourned.[38]

The federal moment had arrived, and the press came alive. Though still in its infancy as a channel for shock and awe, the American newspaper effectively covered the clash of well-known personalities. Throughout Virginia's convention, readers followed the vigorous language of Patrick Henry and pored over the arguments of James Madison. One published letter explained that the Constitution had passed because of the latter's intellectual reach, "notwithstanding Mr. Henry's declamatory powers—they being vastly overpowered by the deep reasoning of our glorious little Madison." Reason had outlasted passion. David had slain Goliath.[39]

Antifederalists saw a different contest, to be sure, praising Henry's genius as well as his eloquence. To this loyal opposition, he was victorious even in defeat. When Henry railed against the "bloodsuckers" (tax collectors, excise men) trudging south to drag Virginians into federal court, he reached into the impressionable minds of debtors and small farmers. He showed large planters that they faced financial ruin if unsympathetic federal judges forced them to pay their British creditors. To Kentucky and frontier Virginia delegates, he sounded out a warning: when a northern-dominated Congress threw Virginia's "Western brethren" into the "arms of Spain" and surrendered all access to the commercial lifeline of the Mississippi River, they would be left high and dry. A French observer remarked of Henry: "He was always attacked, but never conquered." But he *was* conquered. He lost out to a Virginian who was not a delegate or even in Richmond at the time of the convention: George Washington, whose presence was felt, and whose support for the Constitution was well known. Monroe told Jefferson: "Be assured his influence carried this government."[40]

A month after Virginia ratified, when Madison got around to writing Jefferson, he was in a better mood than he had been up to that point. Yet he remained fatigued, if not alarmed, by all it had taken to turn back the antifederalist challenge. He expressed relief that Mason and Henry "will give no countenance to popular violences," but neither were they truly reconciled to the results. Informing Jefferson that Henry had brought up the contents of his letter to Alexander Donald as proof of Jefferson's antifederalism, Madison explained that he had attested to the falsity of those attributions that he knew misrepresented Jefferson's position. Beyond that, he said, he "took the liberty" to credit Jefferson for his opinions in support of the Constitution.

As their relationship allowed for candor, Madison criticized Jefferson for his recklessness—in language that was gentler than it might have been. He explained that Jefferson's antifederalist tone was not only recognized by Henry but had spread through Maryland even earlier, "with a like view of impeding the ratification" in that state. The minister's preference for amendments prior to ratification had revived the antifederalist cause in Maryland, but ratification did take place there, nonetheless, at the end of April. No harm done.[41]

Before he received Madison's reprimand, Jefferson had already responded warmly to news that ratification had succeeded in nine states (including Maryland, but prior to Virginia). "I sincerely rejoice at the acceptance of our new constitution," he wrote Madison. "It is a good canvas, on which some strokes only want retouching." In Jefferson's mind, some added strokes of the pen were needed both for Virginia's sake and also to sustain America's growing reputation for representative government among the liberal minds of Europe.

In fact, while Madison was dealing with Mason and Henry, Jefferson in Paris had been amicably debating the Constitution with Tom Paine and the Marquis de Lafayette. He had to deal with French displeasure at America's inability to pay the interest on its loans at a time when the French government itself struggled with an acute financial crisis. Ordinary French people were the ones who suffered the most. The French problem was, for Jefferson, another lesson in what can go wrong when government is deaf to the voice of justice and of consanguinity.[42]

He was witnessing up close how a government routinely violated individual rights. Naturally he expected America to do better, and for the U.S. Constitution to afford specific protections to individuals through a bill of rights. In writing to Madison, he outlined his reasons for favoring a precise delineation of basic individual rights, fixing on one that had been of deep concern to both of them, freedom of religion, and another that would be of mounting concern in the near future, freedom of the press. In both cases, he explained, government authority would not be compromised. For one, "The declaration that religious faith shall be unpunished, does not give impunity to criminal acts dictated by religious error." Second, "A declaration that the federal government will never restrain the presses from printing any thing they please, will not take away the liability of the printers for false facts printed." Jefferson's prescriptions were moderate ones: freedom of religion did not imply that one's faith protected him or her against prosecution for criminal behavior inspired by some imagined duty to God; freedom of the press did not imply that libel laws could be circumvented.

While forgiving of Jefferson's poor judgment in saying things that Henry could exploit in the two letters concerning ratification, Madison remained loose with his own language in those letters to Jefferson in which he passed judgment on political men. In the fall of 1788, as speculation about the new government began to spread, he named some of the likely officers to take their place in a government directed by George Washington. A southern president required a northern vice president, and Madison thought the leading contenders would be John Hancock and John Adams, both from Massachusetts. The two were equally objectionable to Madison, who reserved his choicest words for the latter: "J. Adams has made himself obnoxious to many, particularly in the Southern states." Besides, his "extravagant self importance" suggested that he had his eye on the presidency. "He would not be a very cordial second to the General," Madison predicted. "An impatient ambition might even intrigue for a premature advancement." It seems remarkable, in retrospect, that Madison should believe Adams capable of acting to push Washington out of the way; but his vast experience among delegates and congressmen had made Madison a harsh judge of human nature.[43]

Occupying different continents, Madison and Jefferson kept different company, so it is hardly surprising that they were not always on the same page. They had come to prioritize issues differently. Jefferson embraced his Americanness most when he found the political society of Europe wanting. To the Philadelphia satirist Francis Hopkinson, he compared the situations of France and the United States with mordant wit worthy of his correspondent: "The king and the parliament are quarrelling for the oyster. The shell will be left as heretofore to the people. This it is to have government which can be felt; a government of energy. God send that our country may never have a government, which it can feel. This is the perfection of human society." It was going to take time before Madison and he would be able to agree on the proper reach of government. They had been an ocean apart for four full years now.[44]

As Jefferson was collecting seeds and sampling wines and fixing his gaze on the bubbling political cauldron inside France, Madison faced an uncertain future. He was wondering whether, in the aftermath of two conventions, he was destined to sit in the Senate, as Washington wished and as Patrick Henry would do his best to subvert; or if he would stand for a

House seat by contesting his friend James Monroe. After all Madison had been through, this was hardly an enviable position to be in at the dawning of a new age in government. But Henry had seen to it that his and Monroe's home bases would be part of the same congressional district.

"Finesse"

George Washington possessed the confidence of the American people. Immediately after the ratification process was complete, he received letters urging him to accept the presidency that was to be offered him. It was not a question of running. Reading a copy of the Constitution "with An unspeakable Eagerness and Attention," Lafayette wrote to him that the executive seemed to be more powerful than it should be in a republic; thus, the country would be in good hands only if he should assume the office. "You Cannot Refuse Being Elected," the French-American general declared. For their part, Fourth of July celebrants in 1788 toasted "Farmer Washington," as they bade him return to the seat of government. The newspapers clamored for him.[45]

When the presidential electors cast their votes, Washington was unanimously chosen. He had expressed doubts about his age, and he was afraid of being thought of as lusting for power, but these concerns eventually dissipated. He prepared to leave Mount Vernon for the temporary national capital of New York, aware that he would have to endure celebratory cannon fire and widespread idolatry, as young girls scattered flowers along his route and amateur poets enlarged his victories into godlike triumphs. He was being widely referred to as a "saviour." Americans were an enthusiastic bunch.

Washington was cool to having John Adams as his vice president, but he appears to have preferred the testy New Englander to New York's longtime Governor George Clinton, an antifederalist whose friends were aggressively promoting him. Washington knew Clinton well from their wartime association, and together they had purchased some land in upstate New York. But Adams was smarter and more industrious. A student of government with solid experience abroad, he had proven his commitment to American independence many times over.

Destined, in his own mind, to be unpopular, Adams wrote and said what others may have thought but could not articulate with equal relish. This is how he became associated with the desire to foster aristocracy in

America when he believed he was merely acknowledging social inequality that already existed. Similarly, he wrote of his irritation with the ever-ballooning superlatives being given to both Franklin and Washington. As a result, he was thought peevish. Madison's and Jefferson's disparaging characterizations of Adams were echoed by others within Virginia and beyond its borders. Patrick Henry, as a Virginia elector, cast his second vote for Clinton.[46]

William Stephens Smith had been one of Washington's wartime aides-de-camp and was, since 1786, John Adams's son-in-law. He brought Jefferson up to speed in a letter of February 1789, reporting that Adams would be elected vice president, but that he might accidentally be made president in Washington's stead. The system of balloting gave the electors two votes but failed to discriminate between the votes for president and vice president—and so deftness was required. Connecticut's electors withheld two votes from Adams "from an apprehension that if the state of Virginia should not vote for General Washington that Mr. A. would be President, which would not be consistent with the wish of the country and could only arise from the finesse of antifoederal Electors with a View to produce confusion and embarrass the operations of the Constitution."[47]

There is irony here on three counts: first, that Adams, not a popular figure to begin with, stood a chance of leapfrogging over Washington; second, that Virginians might elect a New Englander over one of their own; and third, that the balloting system that the framers had failed to perfect would come back to haunt Jefferson a dozen years later during his own quest for the presidency, when, in opposing Adams, his party miscalculated and gave vice-president-designate Aaron Burr an equal number of votes. Their electoral tie in 1800–1801 did exactly what Smith had predicted in 1789, producing "confusion" and "embarrassing the operations of the constitution"; and it brought into play Jefferson's staunchest opponents, who used "finesse" to extract concessions from the incoming president. The problem of separating the votes for president and vice president would have to be resolved by constitutional amendment in 1804.[48]

"The Complexion of the New Congress"

Patrick Henry's animus toward Madison was entirely undisguised. He had promoted to the U.S. Senate two antifederalists with strong credentials, Richard Henry Lee and William Grayson. Not only had Henry threatened to move to North Carolina if Virginia ratified the Constitution, he also called candidate Madison "unworthy of the confidence of the people" and went so far as to charge that if Madison went to the Senate, it would "terminate in producing rivulets of blood throughout the land."[49]

Of the 324 votes cast in the Senate race, Lee received a plurality, though not a majority, and Grayson only nine votes more than Madison. One member of the Virginia Assembly was perturbed enough with Henry's actions that he wrote a letter, ostensibly to a friend, but meant for as many newspapers as would carry it. It bemoaned Henry's deviousness in attacking Madison. "I feel much for Mr. Maddison," the assemblyman cried, "but more for my country, for I considered this the trumpet of discord, a daemon which will destroy that domestic peace and happiness, which unanimity of sentiment has hitherto secured to us." Federalist or antifederalist was not supposed to matter, now that deliberations were past.[50]

Having succeeded in keeping Madison out of the Senate, Henry redoubled his efforts. Pitting Madison against Monroe, he quite nearly succeeded in barring Madison from the House of Representatives. Madison was forced to participate in staged debates in antifederalist strongholds. While the candidates maintained good relations, Monroe challenged Madison on the need for amendments, an argument that was easy to grasp. Madison understood that his countrymen would require explicit assurances that their liberties were not to be trampled on by a greedy government; he responded to political necessity by addressing concerns about a comprehensive bill of rights. Writing letters to influential friends, he overcame the fears of just enough voters to defeat his friend Monroe.[51]

The vote tally for Virginia's fifth congressional district was 1,308 for Madison and 972 for Monroe—Madison won 57 percent of the vote. In the process, he won 62 percent of Jefferson's Albemarle County, where Monroe was building a modest home for his family. Just a year earlier Jefferson had described his affection for Monroe in a letter to Madison: "Turn his soul wrong side outwards and there is not a speck on it." He was grave in appearance but amiable in company, ardent and somewhat restless compared to most of his political peers. Even friends saw that he was lacking in originality, and so to divert attention from his intellectual limitations, they stressed Monroe's sincerity—his speck-free soul. He was workmanlike as well as warm, a combination Jefferson liked when combined with trustworthiness.[52]

In addressing Jefferson on the national vote, it was unavoidable that Madison would bring up the delicate subject of his own campaign. "It was my misfortune to be thrown into a contest with our friend, Col. Monroe," he explained. "The occasion produced considerable efforts among our respective friends. Between ourselves I have no reason to doubt that the distinction was duly kept in mind between political and personal views, and that it has saved our friendship from the smallest diminution. On one side I am sure it is the case." On one side. He did not know for certain what Monroe was writing to Jefferson separately.[53]

In due course, Madison was able to rebuild his relationship with Monroe. And though Henry's means of seeking political advantage were fairly crude, he should not have to accept all of the blame for what happened. There was something already present, something in the stubborn egos of both Madison and Monroe, that would rise and challenge their bond more than once. Not insignificantly, each time the fourth and fifth presidents were placed in direct competition, the more sensitive Monroe would get the short end of the stick.

In 1789 George Washington was probably the only Virginian with a larger national reputation than James Madison, Jr. The inauguration of the first president took place in New York on April 30 of that year, at the remodeled City Hall on Wall Street. Based on a design by the Frenchman Pierre L'Enfant, the new building was renamed Federal Hall and completed in time for Washington to stand on the balcony and take the oath of office. Festivities concluded with a banquet thrown by George Clinton, whose antifederalism did not interfere with his admiration for Washington. Madison was present in New York from the beginning of the month, as Congress was already in session. He was Washington's most trusted adviser and, initially, the president's principal speechwriter.[54]

Madison had the odd task of preparing the official House response to the inaugural address that he had played a lead role in drafting. In the official rejoinder to his own handiwork, he ceremoniously flattered the chief executive with congressional attestations to the "pre-eminence" of his "merit" and "reverence" for his "wisdom," assuring Washington that the country regarded him as "the most beloved of her citizens." It is of no small moment that as the federal Constitution took effect, James Madison was dexterously orchestrating relations between the executive and legislative branches of government.[55]

He clearly enjoyed his privileged position, finally putting the menace of Patrick Henry behind him. In differentiating between federalist and antifederalist members of the Virginia delegation of the incoming First Congress, he was strikingly positive. He used the word *temperate* to describe one of those who had opposed the Constitution but was pleased to join the new government; and he described the least contented antifederalist as "not...inveterate." While he cautiously informed Jefferson, "It is not yet possible to ascertain precisely the complexion of the new Congress," he was confident that a few "conciliatory sacrifices" would "extinguish opposition to the system."[56] After debate in the House of Representatives began, Madison reported to Jefferson that any fears of congressional votes being split too neatly along sectional lines had been removed, and that so far "members from the same State, or the same part of the Union are as often separated on questions from each other, as they are united in opposition to other States or other quarters of the Continent. This is a favorable symptom." Those who have traditionally painted Madison as a hardheaded pragmatist tend to ignore these moments of enthusiasm.[57]

The congressman from Orange, Virginia, showed little restraint on the floor of the House. He was vigorously opposed to the use of illustrious titles for officers of the national government, and the vote on how to address the president and vice president pleased him. "I am not afraid of titles because I fear the danger of any power they could confer," he said with a grand gesture after the Senate's suggestions were sent to the House, "but I am against them because they are not very reconcilable with the nature of our Government or the genius of the people." With a clear majority in agreement, the First Congress rejected monarchical and aristocratic pretension.[58]

When he related the debate to Jefferson, Madison used the phrase "degrading appendages" for titles such as "Excellency." The top officers in government would be known with "republican simplicity" as "President" and "Vice President" and nothing more. Madison was not surprised by stuffy John Adams's preference for the cumbersome "His Highness the President of the U.S. and protector of their liberties"; but he had not expected Senator Richard Henry Lee of Virginia, an old enemy of aristocracy, to go along. For Jefferson, the episode corroborated his growing critique of Adams, whose scholarship stirred him, whose quirks did not sour him, and whose company he genuinely enjoyed. Still, the title proposed for the president—"superlatively ridiculous," Jefferson erupted—prompted him to repeat for Madison the words Benjamin Franklin had used to describe Adams: "Always an honest man, often a great one, but sometimes absolutely mad." Edmund Randolph subsequently reported to Madison that a greatly perturbed Washington was rumored to have written Adams that if titles were employed in the American republic, he would resign.[59]

Madison's influence over Washington was profound and would not be eclipsed by Hamilton's for some time yet. In the opening year of Washington's presidency, Madison was the president's closest confidant; and in the first two sessions of the First Congress of the United States, he was the dominant force. In the busy first month after Washington's inauguration, he virtually dictated the legislative agenda. He argued for the creation of the three cabinet departments—State, Treasury, and War—while reasoning in Congress that the president was vested with the authority to remove the appointed heads of executive departments whenever he chose. This would make the president responsible for the conduct of his top appointees. The president would subject himself to impeachment if he should countenance the commission of any high crime or misdemeanor by any of these individuals. In crucial ways, Madison was shaping the new government.[60]

Madison schooled himself, as he had throughout the 1780s, before taking his initiatives to the Congress. He never aimed to convince by harangue or bluster. He did not make loud, disapproving signs, and he rarely made exaggerated claims. Though his voice was naturally calm, there was no docility to him at all. He concentrated his thoughts and spoke to influence. His was the art of persuasion rather than the art of captivation. As the anti-Henry, he exhibited little of the nervous energy that wowed a crowd. Requiring few notes, Henry tended to listen to his opponent and then respond as if out of hunger. In contrast, Madison was all about note-taking, thinking through his points in advance. Since he had years in the state legislature and national congresses to his credit, and with a well-earned reputation for meticulousness and thoroughness, others allowed him to set the legislative agenda.

We have to read between the lines of the sober record-keeping that descends to us from that First Congress to recognize that Madison was not all business. Among his peers he was quite personable; he may have been warmer and more demonstrative, in this way, than his outwardly undisturbed friend Jefferson. He found the time to write to his longtime landlady, Eliza House Trist, of quirks and eccentricities he found among the congressmen, and at moments such as this his personality can be captured.

The blunt Virginian William Grayson was someone he and Eliza knew well. A former delegate to the Confederation Congress and now a U.S. senator, Grayson called attention to himself with his liberated language. Newly published proceedings of the Virginia Ratifying Convention of 1788 made this abundantly clear to Madison, who quoted back Grayson's remarks to his landlady: were Virginia to reject the Constitution, Grayson was to have said, "Penna. and Maryland are to fall upon us from the North like Goths & Vandals of old . . . And the Carolinians from the South, mounted on Alligators I presume, are to come & destroy our corn fields & eat up our little children." As a politician, Madison may not have been known for his use of hyperbole, but he clearly got a kick out of the tendency in others to get carried away.[61]

"Frenchified"

This is not to say impressions of Madison were unmixed. A new House colleague from Massachusetts, Fisher Ames, later a political foe of his and Jefferson's, sized him up to a friend after their first divergence of opinion. Describing him as "a man of sense, reading, address, and integrity" who spoke in soft tones and used language concisely, Ames was suspicious of Madison's "Frenchified," or liberal-activist, style of politics. "Pardon me if I add that I think him a little too much of a book politician," Ames confided. Madison's responsiveness to the needs and wants of his fellow Virginians troubled Ames as well: he "thinks that state the land of promise, but is afraid of their state politics and of his popularity there more than I think he should be."[62]

"A book politician" did not mean simply bookish. It meant that his range of social engagement was too circumscribed and his knowledge of human emotions weak. In truth, Madison was not as provincial or as awkward as Ames ungenerously implied. He socialized. While Congress was in New York, he became enamored with the widow Henrietta Colden, a Scottish émigrée attached to a prominent Loyalist family. Manhattan insider Samuel L. Mitchill, Columbia College professor of medicine and later a congressman, described her as "celebrated" for a "masculine understanding," which meant a rich intellect that combined nicely with the feminine graces.

Little is known of Henrietta Colden, and less is known of her relationship with Madison. She was friendly with Madison's Princeton classmate Henry "Light-Horse Harry" Lee and Lee's wife, Matilda. If it was not the Lees who introduced Madison to the widow, then he likely met her at one of the polite gatherings taking place in the city. As the first seat of the national government, New York had a vibrant salon culture. Martha Washington staged drawing-room receptions every Friday night, in which men and women drank tea and conversed. In May 1789 Madison asked Jefferson to provide introductions for one of Mrs. Colden's sons, who was traveling to France. As he neared forty, Madison was not about to give up on the idea of marriage or the pleasures of female company.[63]

He was receiving a steady stream of correspondence from Virginia. With his regular salutation to "My dear friend," Edmund Randolph opened a letter to Madison noting that Assembly elections had taken place in a "tolerably judicious" manner, though the hostile Henry (with whom he had traded personal barbs at the ratifying convention) would not back off. He was brief in characterizing their common foe: "Mr. H___y is said to have made a great parade in refusing to be reelected; but reelected he is, and will serve." For a while, anyway.

This was to be Henry's last hurrah as a Virginia legislator. He could no longer deny the dismal state of his personal finances. With a large family to support, he would have to return to his law practice full-time. For Randolph, the wait paid off. That summer he was able to gloat after a three-day trial, during which, as opposing counsel, he had tangled with the famed pleader over a land issue. Randolph won the case for his client. Henry, he told Madison, was "mortified" on being bested.

His home base still in Williamsburg, Randolph would shortly be asked by President Washington to come north and serve as the first attorney general of the United States. As he did on all pressing appointments at the start of his administration, Washington consulted with Madison before acting, though in this instance he hardly needed to. The president knew how close Randolph and Madison were and confessed to Madison at the close of one letter that he preferred Randolph to other prospective candidates for the job, "from habit of intimacy with him."[64]

There were other vacant posts in the executive branch. Madison had sent three letters to Jefferson during May. Using their cipher, the influential congressman passed on an inquiry from the president: "whether any appointment at home would be agreeable to you." He explained the need to fill "auxiliary offices to the President," as the cabinet was tentatively being described. "One for finance" would go either to John Jay or Alexander Hamilton. "The latter is perhaps best qualified for that species of business," Madison remarked fatefully.[65]

At this point Jefferson expected that he would return to America for a short sabbatical and then sail back to France. The pace of events required a diligent and perceptive diplomat on the scene, and he had come to understand well the social forces operating in Paris. He compressed his news of European affairs in the spring of 1789 by deriding the madness of King

George III, which had left the unlamented monarch "in a state of imbecility and melancholy." And he lauded the incipient revolution in France, proceeding as it was, he said, "with the most unexampled success hitherto." In June and the early days of July, Jefferson pinned his hopes on the Marquis de Lafayette, his frequent companion, as the two exchanged opinions on how best to present republican ideas to a nation caught up in "unexampled" unrest. Based on the conversations he had had already, Jefferson believed that cautious and gradual political change would take place. He did not see an armed insurrection coming.

One of Jefferson's warmest friends in France was an eyewitness to the attack on the Bastille. Ethis de Corny, an aide to Lafayette during the American Revolution, a state prosecutor in Paris in the mid-1780s, watched from close by as a small number of people took control of the seemingly impregnable fortress. Once Jefferson had learned, firsthand, of the dramatic events of July 14, 1789, he gave a blow-by-blow account to John Jay, secretary of foreign affairs under the old Confederation Congress, whom he would replace the following spring when he became secretary of state in the Washington administration. He explained to Jay that prisoners were freed, arms and ammunition taken, officials put to death—and that competing explanations made it hard to know for certain how it all had come about.

Writing Madison the following week, Jefferson declared that events already past would be "for ever memorable in history." Lafayette was in command of the militia, riding at the head of a train of joyous citizens. A number of the king's ministers had fled the country, but the uninspired Louis XVI, having submitted to the popular will, was safe for the moment. So were those members of the nobility and clergy who, as a measure of self-protection, voiced their support for the aims of the revolution.

When the Declaration of the Rights of Man and the Citizen was adopted in August, Jefferson had new reason to hope that law would triumph and that the republican transformation of France would proceed without any major disruptions. At Lafayette's beckoning, he hosted a secret dinner for a group of political leaders that lasted six hours. All matters of constitutional change, a favorite subject of Jefferson's, were on the table. In the summer of 1789, then, Jefferson was not just of value to France as one familiar with the character of America's republican revolution; he may be said to have symbolized the stature of an American in that country in that unforgettable year.[66]

In the second letter he wrote to Madison after the fall of the Bastille, Jefferson responded to Madison's report on John Adams's proposal of a lavish title for the U.S. president, bombastically telling Madison that he wished Adams had witnessed the events in Paris: "If he could then have had one fibre of *aristocracy* left in his frame he would have been a proper subject for *bedlam*." A month later, writing again to Madison, he was wildly optimistic that there would soon be a new system of justice in France, "a good deal like ours, with trial by jury in criminal cases certainly, perhaps also in civil. The provinces will have assemblies for their provincial government, and the cities a municipal body for municipal government, all founded on the basis of popular election." Concerning America's reputation among the French, he was no less ecstatic: "It is impossible to desire better dispositions towards us, than prevail in the [national] assembly. Our proceedings have been viewed as a model for them on every occasion."

Jefferson envisioned a new order of things and wished to project a U.S. foreign policy that gave preferential treatment to its proven friend over its proven adversary. Lafayette's countrymen had voluntarily exposed themselves to a "ruinous war" with Great Britain to save America. France had "opened her bosom to us in peace," while England "moved heaven, earth and hell to exterminate us in war...and libeled us in foreign nations." A new nation that behaved according to high principles showed itself to the world as "honest, masculine and dignified," he told Madison. Gratitude should occupy an important place in foreign affairs, and on this basis the Washington administration should back France and discriminate against England until England mended its ways.

Without as yet knowing of the fall of the Bastille, Monroe was telling Madison the same thing. He observed that "without restraints from us, we have nothing to expect from the liberality of G.B." Monroe's was a no-nonsense approach: giving advantages to the commerce of France "as well to compensate for those benefits she has already extended to us, as to induce her to grant others." If seen by his peers as unoriginal, Monroe certainly had an adept understanding of power.[67]

"I Like It As Far As It Goes"

One of Madison's first pieces of business in the House of Representatives was the Bill of Rights. As one might expect, he found himself in a difficult position. Between the convention and ratification, he had added up the reasons why constitutional amendments were unnecessary. He had dismissed the idea in *The Federalist*. Now, in a strange turn of events, it was

Madison who took charge of the issue in the First Congress, pushing and prodding the unenthusiastic national legislature to add amendments. Without his doggedness, in fact, the Bill of Rights that modern Americans venerate would never have become a part of the constitutional system.[68]

Madison had neatly summarized his objections in October 1788, after Jefferson directly told him that the omission of a bill of rights was unacceptable. At the time Madison felt that individual liberties were secure under the Constitution, because all rights not enumerated in the document were reserved to the states. He had calculated, too, that the New Englanders would oppose any guarantee of religious liberty. And he judged that the federal system, with its built-in tension between the states and national government, would be able to provide more protection than any of what he called "parchment barriers" might achieve. Finally, and more cynically, he explained that declarations of rights were routinely violated at the state level, and that the real danger came from a majority oppressing a minority—not the central government infringing on those below. For Madison, a bill of rights had no real power in a republic.

Despite this seemingly uncompromising outlook, he was willing to concede that some social benefits were to be had from such a charter. The most promising was that it could be used as a tool to educate the public and shape the opinion and manners of the American people generally. "Political truths declared in a solemn manner" could be woven into the "national sentiment," he told Jefferson. Although he believed it highly unlikely that the federal government would abuse individual liberties, he conceded that a bill of rights might prove useful in mobilizing the public to resist such encroachments. Otherwise, "parchment barriers" had limited force, and national emergencies might demand the temporary suspension of rights, such as habeas corpus (protection from unlawful detention), if another Shays's Rebellion were to occur.[69]

Months went by before Jefferson answered Madison. He did not, as some have suggested, convince Madison to support a bill of rights. But he did provide Madison with ammunition to use before the new Congress. A bill of rights in the hands of a judiciary composed of such independent men as "Wythe, [Williamsburg jurist John] Blair, and Pendleton" (Jefferson's examples) could be an effective check. Lacking Madison's automatic trust in the Constitution, Jefferson regarded a bill of rights as a "supplement" to contend with any unforeseen deficiencies in the text. "Half a loaf is better than no bread," he wrote, certain that a perfect bill of rights was not to be drafted all at once.

Jefferson believed that a bill of rights would reinforce the tension that naturally existed between the federal government and the states. Amendments would enable each to defend its guaranteed powers against incursions from the other. Although bills of rights were not "absolutely efficacious under all circumstances," he argued that they acted as a kind of architectural "brace" supporting the government. On the subject of rights, Jefferson was at his best, and Madison found his friend's line of reasoning astute. As a result of their correspondence, he inserted Jefferson's concern with judicial review into a speech before Congress.[70]

Though less theoretically committed to a bill of rights than Jefferson, Madison made a campaign pledge in January 1789 to support it, circulating letters to this effect. A man of conviction, he was also a determined politician. He knew that there were still those in Virginia pressing for a second convention. By supporting uncontroversial amendments aimed at protecting individual liberties, he was able to put a stop to the disruptive tactics of Henry's allies who preferred to see him retired from politics.[71]

Madison's maneuver went far beyond electioneering, though. He recognized that the legitimacy of the Constitution rested on the central government's responsiveness to the ratifying conventions. The Constitution was approved in Virginia because of the implicit quid pro quo that amendments would be introduced soon after. If he had tried to sidestep the issue, Madison would have alienated a large and influential contingent of principled moderates. To ignore their verbal contract would have made most antifederalists permanent enemies of the federal government.[72]

Madison saw to it that Washington's inaugural address included a statement sympathetic to amendments. Through the mouthpiece of the first president, he urged Congress to show "a reverence for the characteristic rights of freemen." Prudently, he announced his plan for amendments very early in the First Congress. Timing was critical, because on the very next day a fellow Virginian, Congressman Theodorick Bland, proposed calling a second constitutional convention.[73]

In composing his list of amendments, Madison carefully weighed more than two hundred amendments proposed at the various ratifying conventions. But he did more than synthesize when he presented eight amendments to Congress on June 8, 1789. Two were of his own invention: equal rights of conscience along with freedom of the press and trial by jury, and protection of property from state seizure. The rest of the amendments Madison proposed were drawn from the states' ratifying conventions. These included prohibitions against excessive bail, double jeopardy, and unreasonable searches and seizures; guarantees of due process of law, a speedy trial, right of assembly and petition, and the right to bear arms (a well-regulated militia). Finally, limits were placed on the size of congressional districts. Any powers not delegated by the Constitution were to be reserved to the states.[74]

Madison wanted these amendments woven into the body of the Constitution in the various places where each appeared to fit, rather than adding them as a codicil at the end of the document. The "most valuable amendment on the whole list," he contended, was one he drafted himself to protect *from state exploitation* the equal rights of conscience, freedom of press, and trial by jury. This was Madison's last attempt to safeguard the rights of the minority against a dangerous popular majority within individual states.[75]

As it turned out, there was little support in Congress for Madison's proposals. Federalists chastised him publicly as well as privately, claiming, as one Pennsylvanian wrote, that he was "so far frightened with the antifederalism of his own state" that he had thrown a "tub to the whale." More than one congressman approved this popular allusion to Jonathan Swift's satirical tale, in which sailors distracted a whale with a barrel, keeping the beast from destroying the ship. Madison, they said, had offered amendments in order to silence opposition, dispensing imaginary pills to cure antifederalists of their fear of the Constitution. Others dismissed his "water gruel" amendments as useless and unnecessary. Virginia antifederalists had little faith in Madison, believing he had turned a blind eye to other, more substantive amendments designed to curb federal power.[76]

It would be an uphill battle. His eight proposed amendments first went to a select committee of the House. During the second week of August, they were fiercely debated on the House floor, revised, and redrafted as seventeen amendments. Madison's old nemesis Roger Sherman, now a Connecticut congressman, insisted that the amendments, when passed, be added at the end of the Constitution. The majority agreed, and Madison deferred to his colleagues. The Senate made twenty-six changes to the House version and reduced the number of amendments from seventeen to twelve, ten of which were finally ratified by the states.[77]

The first ten amendments to the Constitution did not come about simply. Instead, they define the legislative process colloquially referred to in more recent times as "making sausage." Madison never looked kindly on butchering and was not at all pleased by the Senate's alterations. He winced at the loss of what he considered his "most salutary articles," in particular the one that dictated against state interference. But he was glad when the whole ordeal ended, writing to the two Edmunds, Randolph and Pendleton, that the work had been "exceedingly wearisome"; he had had to endure "dilatory artifices" and a "diversity of opinions & fancies."[78]

Madison backed the Bill of Rights to fulfill promises he had made—not only to his constituents but also to his closest friends and political allies. Like George Mason, Thomas Jefferson was a hard man to please. When he saw Madison's list of amendments, he gave it only a tepid endorsement. "I like it as far as it goes," he wrote, "but I should have been for going further."[79]

The U.S. minister to France was only one of many Virginians Madison had to consider. New Englander Fisher Ames only slightly overstated the situation when he wrote that Madison was afraid of losing his popularity among Virginia state politicians. Madison depended greatly on the Virginia circle. He listened to their complaints and remembered his promises to them. When he stood before Congress, he never forgot that he was a Virginian first.

"By Degrees"

As autumn arrived and the first session of the First Congress ended, Jefferson packed his trunks and prepared to sail for America, accompanied by his two daughters and the two Hemingses. Patsy and Polly had been taking regular guitar lessons; James had been trained in French cooking. Little is known about Sally's life in France other than the plausible assertion by one of her sons, eight decades hence, that she first became pregnant by Jefferson there. We do know that her master did a good bit of shopping before leaving Paris: books and political pamphlets, mathematical instruments, linen, a "macaroni machine" (courtesy of his secretary, William Short, who had recently traveled as far as Naples), and an assortment of clothing for Sally. We know nothing more about the pairing of a forty-six-year-old man and his sixteen-year-old servant.[80]

Madison remained in Philadelphia, thinking Jefferson would be sailing there and they would make the trip back to Virginia together. While waiting, he spent considerable time with Dr. William Thornton, a fellow boarder at the House-Trist residence. He had known Thornton for two years, and was impressed with his wide-ranging knowledge and intense passion for reform. The Edinburgh-trained physician was a man of many parts: a painter, a poet, a naturalist, and an early promoter of steamboat technology. He would author a treatise on language and design the U.S. Capitol.

Born in the British West Indies, Thornton came from a family that owned a large plantation. He arrived in America in 1786, with a grand scheme to liberate his slaves and lead an expedition of free blacks to Sierra Leone. Raised a Quaker and influenced by British abolitionists, he was not long in America before embarking on a tour of New York and New England, making speeches and looking for recruits and backers for his plan. The year he became acquainted with Madison, he was elected to the American Philosophical Society.

They may have conversed about slavery at the time of the Constitutional Convention, but it was in 1789 that Thornton persuaded Madison to write a memorandum on the viability of colonization. Thornton forwarded it to the president of the recently established French abolition society, Les Amis des Noirs, a group influenced by the Quakers and a group Jefferson had refused to join, despite an invitation from Lafayette.[81]

Madison wrote the unsigned and unpublished memorandum while Jefferson was at sea. In it he calculated that there were "not less than 600,000 unhappy negroes" in the South. But he was wary of any emancipation plan undertaken too soon or before appropriate measures were applied; he cited the "ill effects suffered from freedmen who retain the vices and habits of slaves." Neither the general happiness of society nor the happiness of individual slaves was served, Madison wrote, by "humane masters" who unconditionally freed their slaves. He held that differences caused by color were "permanent and insuperable" (just as Jefferson did) and that an integrated society would be virtually impossible in the South.

To the extent that free blacks found themselves trapped in the status of permanent aliens, Madison considered colonization along the west coast of Africa or "some other foreign situation" to be the only practical solution. He presumed that removal to America's "interior wilderness," the area beyond white settlement, would expose former slaves to Indian raids. He figured that Indians would resent the blacks' presence and develop their own "peculiar antipathy" toward them.[82]

Madison is rarely examined under the sharp lens that history has focused on Jefferson. In spite of his ruminations in *Federalist* 54, where the "mixed character" designation made enslavement appear to be a temporary condition, he held on to many of the prejudices that limited Jefferson's imagination and that persisted across the South. Whether he did so consciously or unconsciously, the pressure against real social change must have been powerful. All we have to do is to think of James Madison, Sr., the foremost planter in the county. James, Jr., grew up accepting his father's traditional role in county politics and his supervisory control over extensive lands. The eldest son knew what it would mean if he were to exercise his intellectual freedom in such a way that it threatened his own family, for the sake of bringing justice to African Americans. He had just been through the Virginia Ratifying Convention, listening to the likes of Henry and Mason raising fears of northerners taxing slavery out of existence. Bowing to prejudice afforded psychological protection.

That said, Madison's view diverged from Jefferson's in significant ways. Whereas Jefferson completely closed off the possibility of whites and blacks peacefully occupying the same continent, Madison gauged that it was unlikely at present but not impossible over the long run. A settlement of free blacks on the African coast could serve as a worthy "experiment" that would "induce" the master to see his human property in a new light.

In his 1789 memorandum, Madison allowed for the possibility that both masters and slaves were capable of achieving internal control over their less admirable passions. He thought of slaves more as wayward (but still educable) pupils, servants in need of regular guidance. In a rare Madison text from this period, handwritten instructions to the overseer at Montpelier in 1790, he delivers a message of gentle discipline, requesting that the man "treat the Negroes with all the humanity & kindness consistent with their necessary subordination and work." For "necessary subordination" to demand a reciprocal "humanity & kindness" neatly places Madison in his century.[83]

During their years living in Philadelphia, Madison and Jefferson routinely encountered free blacks as productive members of society. But Jefferson refused to abandon his theory that at some future point "convulsions" would end in the "extermination of one or the other race." Madison alone foresaw that "by degrees, both the humanity and policy of the Government" could "forward the abolition of slavery in America." Both were dealing in eventualities, not immediate prospects.[84]

Jefferson's republican political philosophy featured a union based on affectionate relations, one he saw in terms of an emotional inheritance. Madison's union occurred as a result of setting in motion safely counteracting, or neutralizing, forces—positive and negative energy. Consequently Jefferson identified history's beneficent tendencies as well as its destructive power, which influenced his views on race. Madison's view of history as a more fluid process (and a source of vitality) allowed him to anticipate the tempering effect of time and experience. In racial terms, Madison was less puzzled than Jefferson, or at least less troubled, by evidence of blacks' successful acculturation. The impact of historic memory was deeper for Jefferson than it was for Madison.

"Just Indeed in Their Intentions"

Before his departure from France, Jefferson tried to talk to William Short about the future. He liked writing the script of his friends' lives and wanted Short to think about returning to Virginia sooner rather than later. Jefferson had concluded that his bachelor secretary needed to run for political office back home or Virginia would forget that he was once a prodigy.

As proficient as Short was in his public duties, he was rebellious in other matters. He remained stuck on France and would not leave his duchess, though the likelihood of their ever marrying was slim. He imagined that Jefferson could put in a good word and see him elevated to the ministerial level. That was Short's counterproposal.

Without marriage thoughts of his own, Jefferson was still ruminating on the *partie carrée* proposal—the foursome of Jefferson, Madison, Monroe, and Short—living and thriving in the same neighborhood. That vision of the future still roused him in 1789, five full years after he had sailed to Europe. He figured that another of his intimates, the Harvard-educated painter John Trumbull, would perform Short's secretarial duties while Short forged an American career.

Aware that President Washington could not be pressed too hard, Jefferson did not insist that Short succeed him in Paris. Short (and some of the French too) actually assumed that Madison would be Washington's choice. But it was the experienced, one-legged Gouverneur Morris of New York, a standout at the Constitutional Convention, who was to perform in that role. Short was named minister to The Hague.

Gouverneur Morris was one of the republic's great characters, a man of culture possessing a keen sense of humor. He was also touchy, impatient, and unapologetic. Trained at King's College (Columbia) before the Revolution, he had, along with his friends Robert Livingston and John Jay, contributed significantly to New York's wartime constitution. Washington was impressed by Morris's eloquence and unfazed by his lack of delicacy as a diplomat. If the president's choice as minister to France was insensitive and in the main unfriendly to the aims of the French in the 1790s, it would do his career no harm.[85]

After a harrowing end to an otherwise smooth transatlantic crossing, in which strong headwinds nearly toppled his ship, Jefferson docked in Norfolk and returned home by way of Richmond. He had a great deal on his mind. Besides having to reacquaint himself with the productivity of his farms, his elder daughter, Patsy, seventeen, was to be married shortly to a Randolph she had known when young and who had visited Paris while they were there.[86]

Madison and Jefferson were reunited at Monticello just after Christmas 1789. After five years apart, Jefferson had to have noticed that Madison's hair was thinning. His own was still red and plentiful. What they dined on cannot be established, but we must assume it was capped off by French wine. Enjoying once more the splendid view from his mountaintop ("How sublime to look down into the workhouse of nature," he had written Maria Cosway), Jefferson mulled over President Washington's recent offer that he come to New York and take up the duties of secretary of state. In the days he spent with Madison at Monticello, comparing notes on politics at home and politics abroad, Jefferson must have absorbed a lot of information concerning the operations of Congress and the executive. Madison's chief concern at this time was to convince his friend, as Pendleton had once urged back in 1776, not to "retire so early in life from the memory of man."

Because of the obvious difficulty in getting mail to him while he traveled, it was not until Christmastime that Jefferson saw Madison's appeal that he enter the president's cabinet. The congressman had written at Washington's behest on October 8, 1789, the very day that Jefferson set sail from the French port of Le Havre: "It is of infinite importance that you should not disappoint the public wish on this subject," he said. By "public," Madison meant that he had sounded out those whose votes in the national legislature he most counted on. "The Southern and Western Country have it particularly at heart," he assured Jefferson, adding: "To every other part of the Union it will be sincerely acceptable." He had brought Jefferson out of retirement after his wife's death in 1782, and he was attempting to do so once again.

Shortly before he and Madison met up at Monticello, Jefferson had received word directly from the president that his services were desired. Replying in a tone of respect, he showed that he was of two minds. By accepting the position, Jefferson wrote Washington, "I should enter on it with gloomy forebodings from the criticisms and censures of a public just indeed in their intentions but sometimes misinformed and misled." His explanation revealed that he was still reflecting on his traumatic time as governor. In fact, in his first draft Jefferson left out the phrase "just indeed in their intentions"; only after rereading did he decide to retreat from his self-pitying language. His first thought, in any case, was to expose his fear of criticism and admit that he still felt a nagging hostility toward former critics.[87]

Jefferson would likely have acquiesced to the president's call even without Madison's argument. He appears to have resigned himself to his fate by New Year's Day 1790, just after Madison's visit was concluded. Jefferson could not have sounded very excited, because Madison wrote to Washington from Georgetown shortly thereafter, saying that he was "sorry to find him so little biased in favor of" the secretaryship. Apparently Jefferson took to heart the concept of "public servant" when he said he would allow the president to decide "what is to be done with me."

"In Usufruct"

Though Madison and Jefferson had drawn especially close in 1783–84 and shared confidences at length from 1785 to 1789, we know that their philosophical differences were not insignificant, but also not deep or disruptive. After meeting at Monticello in December 1789, they were still conversing about unfinished business two months later. As much as they might differ, they would not sacrifice their alliance for anything.

After the outbreak of the French Revolution in July 1789, Jefferson had written a letter to Madison that he did not send but eventually handed to him in Virginia. In it he hazarded a new and experimental view, rooted in the principle that "the earth belongs in usufruct to the living." He argued that contracted debts should be dissolved at the end of each generation, which he defined as nineteen years. According to Jefferson's logic, any public or private debt should be paid in full with moderate interest before nineteen years had expired. Contracts would then be renegotiated and laws and constitutions revised.

To think in terms of generations suited Jefferson's mind. Upon his return from Europe, he went back to the drawing board and scoped out a plan to tear up and rebuild Monticello, based on what he had seen in France. One might say that he was launching a generational restructuring of his home: architectural historians identify the pre-1790 house as the "first" Monticello, managed jointly by Patty and him, and the post-1790 house as the "second" Monticello, doubled in size and more dignified in appearance.

More to the point, when Jefferson thought of the structure of a generation, he was thinking legalistically. The theory he embraced was an extension of his earlier attempts to reform the laws of Virginia by ridding society of entail and primogeniture. Entail had allowed the dead to control the destiny of future generations by circumscribing how land could be distributed; primogeniture in effect disinherited younger offspring by automatically bequeathing the main estate to the eldest son.

When he imagined being able to reshape society, Jefferson was, on some level, thinking as a lawyer. The concept of "usufruct," originally part of Roman law, dictated that land, houses, slaves, and livestock (property not consumed by use) were to benefit the user only until his death. Each generation enjoyed the profits and advantages of a piece of property, but no person should be burdened by unfair debts or legal restrictions left over from the past. Jefferson believed that one generation could not be trusted to safeguard the interests of the next. As in 1776, when he undertook his revisal of the laws of Virginia, once again Jefferson was convinced of the need for moral constraints to be imposed by law—he continued to believe in social engineering.[88]

While he was largely thinking of usufruct metaphorically, Jefferson was making the case to Madison that the people deriving benefits from the federal Constitution had to be the *living* users of the text. The Constitution's meaning could not be stagnant; its understood benefits had to be progressively redefined. "No society can make a perpetual constitution, or even a perpetual law," wrote Jefferson unambiguously. He meant, too, that *there was no original intent:* the founding generation could not make the Constitution into a property monopolized by its authors, eternally empowering themselves to control its value and its application.

Jefferson's letter to Madison has been dissected by various historians for its intrinsic meaning and what it says about their opposing perspectives on the world. It is easy to jump to the conclusion that Jefferson was dreaming, or preparing to unleash social and political chaos, needing Madison to talk him out of it. But Jefferson was not prescribing policy so much as opening a conversation about an issue he and Madison both cared about: possible ways to fix limits on public debt so as to keep the people from having to face unending taxes. But he did, as well, consider his theory as a way to move in a new political direction—government flexibility on issues affecting the happiness of future generations. Even Dumas Malone, Jefferson's most prolific and adoring twentieth-century biographer, described his subject as a man who was married to his theories. "Few men in American public life," Malone wrote, "have taken general principles more seriously; more often than he should, perhaps, he regarded these as universal truths." Though he did not agree with his friend's prescription, Madison surely understood why Jefferson was thinking in the manner he was.[89]

In his measured reply to Jefferson's letter, Madison cautioned against too much mutability or volatility in government. Seeing monarchical Europe as moribund, Jefferson warmed to the notion that each generation had to shake things up, and that society would profit from the exercise. But Madison read past his curious proposition and saw what was dangerous and disruptive in it. As each generation prepared itself to redraft its constitutional charter, factions would inevitably form for the express purpose of manipulating the process. To undermine property law would destroy land values; to eliminate all debts would negate the social good that grew from the protection of contractual obligations.

As a realist, Madison disagreed strongly with the idea that the nation could, in effect, return to the state of nature every nineteen years, rebuilding governing institutions and sanctifying new laws with the active consent of the people. He thought Jefferson too enamored with the principle of majority rule, by which governments attained legitimacy only through the consent of their living subjects. Drawing on Locke and other social contract theorists, Madison defended the idea of civil society and the rule of law, whereby citizens voluntarily gave up some of their natural rights in exchange for civil protections.

As every constitution relied on, in Madison's words, "tacit and implied consent," he had to reject Jefferson's contention that majority will superseded all other law. There was only one conclusion to draw: if it were to be implemented, Jefferson's theory would require that every new member of society (every person who came of age) give his consent to every law. That was impractical, if not impossible.

Madison tried to mollify Jefferson, acknowledging that it was easier to criticize than to create a new theoretical framework. But he knew all too well that Congress had no taste for what he called "philosophical legislation"; Jefferson's unfiltered theory could never get off the ground. The prevailing wind in the First Congress was for curtailing the "licentiousness of the people," not for trying out an ideal notion of majority will, Madison explained. It would be a good long time before "the sublime truths which are seen thro' the medium of Philosophy, become visible to the naked eye of the ordinary Politician." He was letting Jefferson down easy.[90]

Madison was predisposed toward a structure that bent but did not break. No matter the issue, he always sought to uphold the usefulness of civil institutions. Jefferson, in contrast, celebrated the unfettered freedom of natural rights, the sovereignty of the individual, and his entitlement to protest whatever law curtailed personal liberty. Madison and Jefferson did not merely have different priorities; their manner of thinking was fundamentally different.

"Our Country Is Already Sufficiently Large"

Madison and Jefferson had shared purposes that transcended their differences. This was not at all the case with Hamilton, whose first inclination that Madison and he had a different agenda came five months into Washington's presidency, if not before. In October 1789 Hamilton had a long conversation with George Beckwith, the unofficial British minister to the new government. Fresh from London, Beckwith relayed his nation's displeasure with Congress's attitude toward commercial arrangements. In the course of their conversation, as Beckwith alluded nonspecifically to the hostility of some members of Congress to British interests, Hamilton reflexively answered him: "You mean Mr. Maddison from Virginia. I confess I was likewise rather surprized at it, as well as that the only opposition to General Washington was from thence." Madison's opposition to reasonable policy was, according to Hamilton, a manifestation of his provincialism: "He is very little Acquainted with the world."

The words sound flippant, so it must be allowed that some part of Hamilton's posturing may have been by design: to tell the Englishman what he wanted to hear. The treasury secretary was not above trying to soften up a British diplomat. If opposed on principle, he went on to say, Madison was "uncorrupted and incorruptible." It would appear that there was still a basis for mutual respect to develop, if Hamilton and Madison alike chose to move in that direction.[91]

Hamilton's ungenerous remark about Madison's experience was a close cousin to Jefferson's statement to Madison three years earlier about John Adams, whom he had called a poor judge "where knowledge of the world is necessary." The difference between Jefferson's and Hamilton's jibes lay in Jefferson's assumption that Adams was not naïve but misguided. Hamilton seemed to be claiming that Madison was ignorant of how the real world worked. Jefferson needed to get something off his chest when he wrote to Madison, while Hamilton's words show the condescension and self-importance that would soon come between the Virginians and him and influence national politics for an entire decade.

Hamilton told Beckwith of his own fondness for all things English. "I have always preferred a Connexion with you, to that of any other Country," he said, notably, changing back and forth from "I" to "We in America," as he gave encouragement to his visitor. "*We think in English,* and have a similarity of prejudices, and of predilections." Hamilton took liberties that President Washington would hardly have approved: "I am free to say, that Although France has been indulgent to us, in certain points, yet, what she can furnish, is by no means so Essential or so suited to us as Your productions, nor do our raw Materials suit her so well as they do you . . . We wish to form a Commercial treaty with you to Every Extent, to which you may think it for Your interest to go." As yet, the U.S. government had no commercial treaty with its late enemy.

Revolutionary France was still in its republican phase and largely in the hands of the liberal nobility. Lafayette, who was Hamilton's friend as well as Madison's and Jefferson's, represented the hope of a successful transformation. Yet Hamilton made his prejudices to Beckwith plain and would at no time give positive signals to the French. Moving to a discussion of Spain's control of the lower Mississippi, he assured Beckwith that the United States had no ambition to expand into the northern reaches of the magnificent river, where London maintained interests. But he was clear that western settlers would not accept Spain's refusal of navigation rights. At this point in the conversation, Hamilton made another obsequious remark, which Beckwith recorded alongside the others: "Our Country is already sufficiently large, more so perhaps than prudence might wish." Its extent *weakened* the federal government, Hamilton assured the Briton.[92]

At nearly the same time as Madison was reading Jefferson's letter recommending that the new administration show a clear preference to its wartime ally France, Hamilton was telling a high-level British representative the complete opposite. Battle lines were being drawn in this and other ways. While the secretary of the treasury aimed to concentrate investment in northeastern cities, Madison and Jefferson were intent on privileging southern interests and westward expansion. Simply put, as Jefferson prepared to enter the cabinet, the Washington administration was already speaking with more than one voice.

THE PATHOLOGICAL

DECADE AND

BEYOND

CHAPTER SIX

Attachments and Resentments
1790–1792

Every man seems to think himself born a Legislator, and is generally
so tenacious of his own darling sentiment, that unless it is adopted,
he is continually complaining.

—"POLITICIANS—A SCRAP,"
NEWPORT (PA.) HERALD, APRIL 8, 1790

Be ADAMS to your nation still endear'd!
And be the powers of JEFFERSON rever'd!
Be MADISON for eloquence renown'd!
Still various worth in HAMILTON be found!
Truth soon must flourish, enmity decrease—
They come, the patrons of true worth, and peace!

—STANZAS ON THE MOVEMENT OF THE FEDERAL GOVERNMENT
FROM NEW YORK TO PHILADELPHIA, AND THE ARRIVAL THERE
OF CONGRESS, *FEDERAL GAZETTE*, DECEMBER 6, 1790

JEFFERSON REMAINED AT MONTICELLO THROUGH FEBRUARY 1790, as his daughter Patsy married her second cousin, Thomas Mann Randolph. He then traveled to Richmond to arrange for payment of outstanding debts to British creditors (the interest now representing more than half of the principal). Afterward he rode north, stopping in Philadelphia to pay his respects to Benjamin Franklin, eighty-four and near death.[1]

The colorful, garrulous Senator William Grayson of Virginia, age fifty, predeceased Franklin by a few weeks. There was talk of a contest for his seat between Madison and Patrick Henry, but it was just talk. Madison wrote to

William Short, matter-of-factly, that Henry would be offered first, was likely to refuse, and that "Col. Monroe has been spoken of" also. For reasons not immediately apparent, Madison was at the same time querying Edmund Pendleton as to whether Henry's role in calling for resistance to the Stamp Act, a quarter-century before, had really been preeminent. The rationale he gave Pendleton for posing the question was that the American Revolution was such a consequential event for the world that "every circumstance connected with it...will be more and more a matter of investigation." As to the Senate seat, George Mason was offered it first and declined. John Walker, Jefferson's Albemarle neighbor, filled the vacancy. A year later James Monroe would inherit the office.[2]

On March 21, 1790, Jefferson reached New York City and joined the president's cabinet. Secretary of the Treasury Alexander Hamilton, his co-equal counterpart (it was too soon to describe him as Jefferson's opposite number), had had a number of months to adapt and to initiate. Hamilton was regarded as highly knowledgeable yet entirely tactless; the Madisonians in Congress were offended by him even before Jefferson arrived on the scene.

If the incoming secretary of state was exhibiting signs of strain, Hamilton had nothing to do with it. As Madison reported to Edmund Randolph, Jefferson's final push north had been slowed by the appearance of his "periodical head-Ach," devastating migraines that kept him out of the public eye for weeks. Madison himself was suffering from an attack of dysentery for the second time that year. The good-hearted Reverend Madison gave his cousin some encouragement: "The Disappointments of the best Politicians are not perhaps less frequent than those of other Men; but they must console themselves with having erected Lights, which tho' the unwary Mariner may not avail himself of at present, will, most probably be of future Utility." The question before James Madison the politician was whether his guarded approach to government would persuade in an age of heightened passion.[3]

Dissent and social conflict are as much a part of America's historical landscape as the hunger for land itself. Sectarians challenged the religious establishment; freethinkers scoffed at biblical revelation and church dogma; provincials decried English arrogance. The Revolution had had multiple purposes: it was fought to liberate colonial elites from constraints put upon them by officials in distant London. It was fought for the right to induce the Indians to part with more land. It was fought against whatever stood in the way of greater prosperity.

Among the middling sorts of people, hope of a new social order died hard. But as the average soldier found out, the ruling gentry had not gone to war to make liberty infectious or democracy possible. The egalitarian ideal proved useful in rallying support for independence among a wider public, but the simple fact was that colonial elites aimed principally to replace the British as America's lawgivers. They went to war for themselves.

The stakes had been high in 1775–76 and remained high in 1789–90, as power was being negotiated. We are often told that the debate over the Constitution divided the republic, momentarily, neatly, into two camps: federalists and antifederalists. But that way of seeing the founding generation misses what could not be intellectualized—it misses all that lay submerged.

Once George Washington became president, the Constitution of the United States was no longer a theory of government. The federal republic had to undergo field trials. And so the decade of the 1790s was reactive: it saw conflicts instigated by words as well as events. Even when it seemed to be otherwise, the most important catalyst behind the traumatic disturbances of the 1790s remained state jealousies and sectional identities, in no small measure due to the tenacity of Virginians. But even that did not explain the violence of mind and the nearly nonstop public bickering of a nation in flux, in what deserves to be dubbed the pathological decade of American history.

"A Public Evil"

When he assumed the presidency, Washington intended to preside, not to command or demand. The federal Constitution implied that Congress would be the most active of the three branches of government, and in 1789 Washington had no ambitious legislative program to push. It was, instead, Secretary of the Treasury Alexander Hamilton who promptly took up the nation's fiscal health and charted a dynamic course for the administration. That eager embrace of power during the first year of Washington's presidency set a tone for the fractious decade by creating a permanent distance between Madison, the leading voice in Congress, and Hamilton, the leading voice in the administration.

When Hamilton had his conversation with George Beckwith in October 1789, he was still getting a feel for Madison's position on the credit and debt issues. But by the time he introduced his *Report on Public Credit*, in January 1790, he must have known that Madison would lead the opposition in Congress. Hamilton wanted the federal government to assume not only its debts to European bankers (which all parties agreed was a matter of national honor) but also the states' remaining debts, which were considerable. The plan became more controversial when Hamilton announced how he intended to fund these debts: renegotiating interest rates and terms of repayment to the states' creditors. The government was to issue new securities to existing creditors, which could be easily sold and traded—an attractive opportunity for investors because the interest rates were generous and the government's backing was real.[4]

Madison took it hard. He immediately revolted against the injustice of rewarding the holders of the outstanding securities, who were wealthy speculators, predominantly northerners, some of them members of Congress. They had bought up the notes from the original holders: ordinary farmers, the financially strapped veterans of the Revolutionary War. These men had sold their government IOUs for ready cash, and many had received only ten cents on the dollar. Madison insisted that they receive fair compensation. When his motion on behalf of America's neglected citizens failed to impress a majority, the *Pennsylvania Gazette* printed a satirical poem that exposed a heartless Congress with this couplet: "In *war*, to heroes let's be just / In *peace*, we'll write their toils in dust."

Madison received acknowledgment from Philadelphia's noted professor of medicine Benjamin Rush, who reminded him that there were "More Widows—Orphans—& Soldiers among us who have parted with their Certificates than any city in the Union." Hamilton, he said, was influence-peddling on a scale "more dishonourable" than that used by any British minister. President Washington, rich in land bounties bestowed as compensation for his war service, sympathized with impoverished vets but sided with his treasury secretary for the sake of the national interest. As a Virginian, he was sensitive not to appear to be favoring a Virginia constituency.[5]

Even more controversial than the gift to wealthy speculators was Hamilton's plan to absorb all remaining public debts. While nationalizing debt strengthened the federal government, it favored northern speculators and hurt the interests of states such as Virginia that had already paid off what they owed. Debate on assumption of the state's debts began in March 1790 and went on for months, keeping Hamilton from realizing his objective of concentrating power in a tightly run central government while reducing the influence of the states. Hamilton's larger goal was to provide America with the power sought by modern nation-states: a managed public debt that would create capital for investment, spur commercial growth, and enable the United States to secure loans in times of war. It was, in short, a British model for raising revenues that he believed America would need to pursue imperial ambitions on the North American continent.[6]

Colonel Edward Carrington had taken part in the Battle of Yorktown and served in the Confederation Congress at the time of the Constitutional Convention. He wrote from Richmond in early April, informing Madison that assumption was a subject of widespread discontent in the Virginia capital and had already raised the old fear of "consolidation"—a national government that swallowed up the states' individual identities. Another worried Madison supporter reminded him that Virginians had worked hard to pay their debts: "Every creditor appears satisfied." So why should Virginia receive no dispensation for having paid up? And "Why in heaven then shou'd Congress interfere with us?"

The member of the Virginia House of Delegates most opposed to assumption was antifederalist Patrick Henry, who almost never saw eye to eye with Madison. Still furious over Congress's power to tax, he continued to hear the death knell of the Union. Secrecy and ambition were a volatile combination, and that is what many Virginians saw coming about in the U.S. Senate. The state's two antifederalist senators, along with skeptic William Maclay of Pennsylvania, were the only ones to vote in favor of opening the Senate's doors to the public. Sounding like George Mason, Henry Lee declared disunion preferable to life under "an insolent northern majority."[7]

Madison prepared to square off with Hamilton on assumption. His outline notes for the speech he gave on April 22, 1790, have survived and represent good evidence of the way in which he systematically built a case. Numerals 1 through 9 cover general principles as well as specific state experiences with specie and paper payments. This is followed by a comprehensive balance sheet, down to the dollar. Hamilton's plan was riddled with inconsistency and injustices, he scribbled; proposed excise taxes were "obnoxious," "arbitrary & vexatious." There were "frauds & perjuries" to account for, distinctions to be drawn between public and private debts, means of enforcement to be clarified. He planned to argue that Hamilton's plan was neither impartial nor enforceable.

But when he took the floor of the House, Madison played down his annoyance, trying to show instead that he felt no personal antagonism and was motivated solely (as he was with the war veterans and their government

IOUs) by practicality and propriety. "I am not insensible that an assumption of the state debts is under certain aspects, a measure not unworthy of a favorable attention," he said modestly. "If it had not at least plausible recommendations, I do not think it could have obtained so respectable a patronage here." But then he went on to present the flaw in the logic behind assumption: if the debts of the particular states, in the hands of its citizens, were nothing more than the debts of the United States "under another denomination," then should not any individual citizen's debt be defined as the debt of the United States? When the Constitution was adopted, no one understood the state debts as adhering to the Union. "Was it ever supposed that they were to be thrown into one common mass, and that the states should be called on collectively to provide for them?" He was hinting that he was not the centralizer Hamilton understood him to be, but a nationalist who was at once sensitive to the states' desire to retain their cultural identities and not surrender control over their destinies to an aggrandizing central power. In the relationship between money and power lay the fundamental difference between the federalist visions of Hamilton and Madison.

Addressing his colleagues in the House, Madison explained at length why he believed the inequity in Hamilton's program was deliberate. States that were greatly in arrears would do well with assumption, rewarded for having been irresponsible. Somehow Virginia, after demonstrating fiscal responsibility, would be bearing one-fifth of the national burden if assumption passed—rather than one-seventh, its just portion based on population and economy.

More and more Madison's argument became one of defending his home state by contrasting it with another. As Massachusetts was "getting rid of its embarrassments," he said, Virginia would be forced to relieve her. Madison offered a moral to this story: "If the public debt is a public evil, an assumption of state debts will enormously increase, and, perhaps, perpetuate it." The national and state governments could, independently of one another, discharge their debts "with greater ease and in less time" than the national government alone could do. Through this line of argument, he achieved one small but notable victory: Congress would conduct an accounting that showed what each state had paid during the war, to ensure that the contributions of states such as Virginia would be fairly displayed before assumption occurred. In all, Madison spoke for over an hour.[8]

It was on this date, too, that he rose to report the death of Benjamin Franklin. Madison proposed that members of Congress wear badges of mourning for one month, a practice that would continue in future years as the principal founders passed on. In Philadelphia, where Franklin had attained renown as a printer and a scientist, public ceremonies following the funeral attracted thousands of onlookers. The outpouring was perhaps even greater in France, where the good Dr. Franklin was especially revered. The National Assembly recalled his "sublime mission" during the American Revolution, praised "the charms of his mind," and declared a belief that "great men are fathers of universal humanity."

The National Assembly's message was formally addressed to the U.S. Congress. It went on to proclaim that as the world rejoiced in America's liberty, "the hour of the French has arrived:—we love to think, that the citizens of the United States have not regarded with indifference our first steps toward liberty." Jefferson was delighted at the French statement, writing: "It is, I believe, the first instance of that homage having been paid by a public body of one nation to a private citizen of another." As time would show, however, official mourning over Franklin served only to bring into sharper relief the increasingly mixed feelings in America toward the French, as their revolution departed from its earlier course.[9]

"A Lesser Evil"

Amid stalemate over Hamilton's proposals, an increasingly hostile climate developed in Congress. If something did not give, the machinery of government would become idle. New Englanders threatened to block any solution to the matter of public credit that did not include assumption of the states' debts. The situation could lead to a breakup of the Union, Madison told Monroe.

The migraine-prone Jefferson was still not well; nor was he fully acquainted with the details of debates in the House. But he obliged others by attending dinners, where President Washington was said to carry himself with all becoming dignity. Two months after his arrival in New York, Jefferson's head finally stopped throbbing. Madison reported to Eliza House Trist: "He is over the worst of his fit of the Head-Ach. He has had a severe time of it."[10]

At the beginning of June 1790, as Jefferson accompanied Washington on a three-day fishing trip on the Atlantic, Madison revealed to Monroe that he was planning to take action to get past the logjam in Congress over Hamilton's assumption proposal. He thought he would be able to get most of what he wanted, though Hamilton would not fold easily. Presumably, this was one of those field trials by which the practical operations of republican government were to be worked out.[11]

There remains an aura of some mystery surrounding accounts of the so-called dinner-table bargain. It occurred sometime after mid-June, on a day when Jefferson encountered an agitated Hamilton on the street outside the President's House and invited him to dine at his residence with only one other guest: Madison. The episode is related by Jefferson, based on a scrap of paper he took notes on in 1792. The agreement itself can be described simply: Hamilton was to convince a few holdouts to back a plan to situate the nation's capital on the Potomac. Meanwhile Madison, though he personally would not vote for assumption, would persuade two other Virginians in the House to change their votes.[12]

A bargain did take place as a result of the now-famous dinner, but we must question the simplicity of the interpretation. These three men, as highly placed as they were, lacked the influence to determine by themselves the vote on two such controversial pieces of legislation. Besides, well before the dinner, Pennsylvanians and Virginians in Congress had already reached agreement on a plan that would permanently situate the capital on the Potomac. Senator William Smith of South Carolina described that joint decision as the "offspring of a political cohabitation" between the two states. Philadelphia would have ten years as the national capital, while the federal city was being planned and built. The Pennsylvanians no doubt were hoping that once the capital was removed to their state, events would lead to its remaining there.

The monolithic model of the dinner-table bargain ignores the real fluidity of the situation. Madison and Jefferson probably did discuss with two Virginia congressmen, Alexander White (later to become a commissioner assigned to laying out the plan for Washington, D.C.) and Richard Bland Lee (brother of now-General Henry "Light-Horse Harry" Lee), a deal that aided passage of Hamilton's plan. But their two votes hardly decided the fate of the assumption bill. And there is no evidence whatsoever that Hamilton rounded up votes for the southern-based capital.

The "big names" did not call the shots in 1790. Compromise was the result of messy politics, then as now: unglamorous work that required time. It seems less likely that the compromise in question was reached at an exclusive dinner, or on the basis of a smooth formula obtained by three political geniuses one balmy evening. It should be underscored, too, that the crucial votes on both the assumption and the residence bills occurred in the Senate, which means that it took more than the assent of Virginia Representatives White and Lee for Hamilton to obtain the votes he needed to move forward with his fiscal plan. The neatly packaged story of the dinner-table pact glosses over the reality of how the First Congress operated.

Neither Hamilton nor Madison ever claimed there was a secret agreement between them. Madison's words to Edmund Pendleton, well before Congress took action on the residence bill, may best describe what actually took place: "a coincidence of causes as fortuitous as it will be propitious." He was not alluding to any backroom deal. Rather, he saw fate and fortune in operation, forces beyond his or Jefferson's ability to maneuver, which resulted in the Potomac site's being designated as the national capital.[13]

What we can also see in this process, if we look closely, is Madison's stubbornness. He refused to cast his vote for assumption. He never agreed to place the nation's capital in New York, Philadelphia, or any other city or town in the area of thickest settlement.

Madison had first sounded an alarm to Washington in the summer of 1788, before the ratification debates were even over. New York was an "extremely objectionable" choice for a capital, he had said then, and he wished to "shun Philada. at all events." He believed that representatives from the interior would become increasingly averse to repeated trips to and from the Northeast. So, he urged instead that the "convenience" of the "Western country" be taken into account, to prevent centrifugal tendencies and the inevitable breakup of the United States into separate countries. Why add new fuel to the West's jealousy, Madison reasoned, by summoning its congressmen to the "sea-shore" and at the same time give the southern states "decisive proof of the preponderance" of the Northeast within the Union? Despite its proximity to the Atlantic, and its convenience to Virginia politicians, he construed the Potomac as a gateway to the West.[14]

In September 1789, once debate over the Bill of Rights was behind him, Madison had again taken up the question of where the permanent national capital would be placed. Arguing before Congress, as he had in the letter to Washington, that the West needed easier access than New York or Philadelphia would afford, he pushed for the Potomac site. The Pennsylvanians in Congress countered that the Susquehanna was a more navigable waterway. Madison's position that the Potomac was probably "farther from tide-water" was not persuasive, and the House, at least at that point, looked more favorably on the Susquehanna.[15]

What, then, had changed? In July 1790, when the issue came up again, Madison toned down his Virginia partisanship and began to appear an honest broker. Forced to deflect the suggestion of another rival site, Baltimore, he touted the Potomac for its relative safety from invasion—which would prove ironic, of course, during the War of 1812. He rhapsodized the "great range of rich country that borders on it" and the "salubrity of air," politely assuring his colleagues that he was not "disparaging the pretensions of Baltimore." Since Jefferson's arrival in New York, Madison's desire for a healthful climate became more important to his calculus.[16]

Jefferson's contribution to Madisonian rhetoric was modest but meaningful. For Jefferson, no compromise was possible on the subject of concentrated cities: they spread diseases and reeked of death. He had seen the malignant effect of centralization in impoverished parts of Europe. He was sickened by the airless workhouses he visited, fearful of overpopulation, and repelled by filth. That is what urban life represented to him. The American way of life would be advanced amid rustic beauty, or else it would be lost.

Neoclassical Monticello was the definitive place of repose for him, of course, and pastoral agriculture the healthful alternative to urban-based production. Hamilton wanted government to actively stimulate the economy, especially in the manufacturing sector, and to promote internal improvements such as roads and canals. While a canal enthusiast himself, Jefferson wanted government to interfere as little as possible. There was a fundamental contradiction between Madison and Hamilton on matters of constitutionality and principles of economics. For Jefferson, more than constitutional principles, matters of social health dominated the real economy.

Washington signed the residence bill into law on July 16, 1790. It ensured that the federal city, as it was first known, would be built on the banks of the Potomac. The aging warhorse Edmund Pendleton chose the obvious metaphor when he wrote to Madison: "I am happy to find the Potowmac stands on so good grounds as the Permanent seat of Congress." Madison told Monroe that the assumption plan, as agreed to, "will very little affect the interest of Virginia," because, he rationalized, the numbers had been crunched in such a way as to reduce the state's responsibility from what had been previously calculated.

To his father, Madison wrote that acceptance of the adjusted assumption plan was "a lesser evil" than a deepening of state antagonisms. Patrick Henry disagreed with the "lesser evil" rationale and subsequently introduced a resolution in the Virginia House of Delegates calling assumption "repugnant to the Constitution." It would pass the Assembly in December 1790, by a vote of 75 to 52, representing the first step in a reassertion of state sovereignty.[17]

In mid-August 1790, as assumption became law, Madison and Jefferson packed their books for the move from Manhattan to the next temporary capital, Philadelphia. Then they rode south together, stopped at Mount Vernon to visit the president, saw George Mason at nearby Gunston Hall, and proceeded on to Orange, after which Jefferson continued on to Albemarle by himself. Also over that summer, taking no chances, Madison orchestrated his reelection to Congress, recruiting his younger brothers Ambrose and William as his campaign managers. Unlike the troubled campaign of 1788, when he had to face off against Monroe, this time he ran largely unopposed.[18]

"The Praetorian Band of the Government"

To solidify his plan for a vigorous economy, Hamilton had one more maneuver in mind: the establishment of a national bank, which he presumed Congress had the right to undertake. His notes to Washington in March 1791 spell out his reasons for recommending such an institution. It would circulate more money, given the limited amount of specie on hand; it would facilitate loans to emerging industries and to merchants who paid duties; it would make tax collection more routine and make funds available in case of national emergencies, by which he meant wars. "Lastly," Hamilton wrote somewhat heavy-handedly, "an attentive consideration of the tendency of an institution, immediately connected with the national Government which will interweave itself into the *monied* interest of every State, which will by its notes insinuate itself into every branch of industry . . . ought to produce strong prepossessions in its favor in all who consider the firm establishment of the National Government as necessary to the safety & happiness of the Country."

For Madison and Jefferson, "safety & happiness" could only mean a benign central government with well-defined powers and well-defined limits, resisting the tendency to favor the interests of factions. For Hamilton, "safety & happiness" directed government toward a comprehensive involvement in high finance, promoting industrial growth through central banking while attaching greater military control to the presidency and undermining all democratic inclinations. The word *democratic* had the connotation of a breakdown in government and a transfer of power to the ignorant masses.

Not surprisingly, Hamilton envisioned the bank as an instrument at the disposal of the treasury secretary. Only one-fifth of its money would be the government's, and most of the bank's directors would be private individuals empowered to make government loans. Hamilton figured these people would be so enmeshed in government policy that they would be agreeable to his goals, if not downright compliant. Madison rose in the House to assert that at the state ratifying conventions even the supporters of the Constitution did not think that Congress had any right to charter corporations. To establish a national bank would be to grant excessive power to the federal government. Madison was being less than fully honest at this moment, because it was he who had introduced the idea of giving government the power of incorporation at the Constitutional Convention.[19]

In a strictly sectional vote, the House rejected Madison's call to quash the bank bill. Now Washington sought the views of Jefferson and Randolph, both of whom opposed the measure, and promptly conveyed their opinions to Hamilton. It was Hamilton's custom to respond to challenges with overly long papers in his own defense; in this case, over the course of a week, he drafted a document that laboriously asserted the constitutionality of bank creation. Washington took it under advisement, asking Madison to draft a veto message, in case he should reject the bill on the basis of its questionable constitutionality.

The president waited until the last day possible under the Constitution before signing the bill into law. If, in this instance, he eventually gave Hamilton what he wanted, it was not necessarily because he was in agreement. With a relative detachment that Jefferson would not subsequently be known for, he had suggested to Washington that, unless he felt strongly that the bill was unconstitutional, the president should go along with Congress's decision. And since Congress had voted in favor, on February 8, 1791, Washington accommodated.[20]

Madison's concern with men of money, begun at the time of the debate over assumption, rose to a new level of outrage now. He was concerned that a group of merchants and speculators *beholden* to the government would in fact end up *controlling* the government. The national bank was the last straw in his conversion from trusting a strong central government to deeply fearing government corruption.

The focus of Madison's concern was the new environment Hamilton was creating, in which speculators in government paper—stockjobbers— were forming a class (or political faction) of their own. A significant number of these people were members of Congress. Madison believed that if

Hamilton had his way, as it appeared he would, Philip Schuyler, his father-in-law, would be at the head of the New York subscribers to bank stock.

In May 1791, Congress having adjourned, Madison was back in the soon-to-be banking mecca of New York, whence he sounded an alarm. He complained to Jefferson of the "licentiousness of the tongues of the speculators and Tories" who were bad-mouthing Washington for waiting so long to sign the bank bill. They had held over his head, Madison wrote, "the most insolent menaces." It suggested a threat to the president's legitimacy, while defining the emerging speculator class as a matured "party," at least in Madison's mind. He invoked the word *party* as it was generally understood in the years before the formal establishment of a two-party system: a self-interested group of men, inherently corrupt in their dealings. Hamilton was blatantly purchasing their support. In accepting the munificence of Hamilton, he and they became inseparable.

A few months later, again from New York, Madison warned Jefferson that "the stockjobbers will become the praetorian band of the Government, at once its tool and its tyrant." The Praetorian Guard, in its well-known classical sense, was a dictator's private army, and the current version of the guard was liable to plot a financial coup in America. "Bribed by [the Government's] largesses, and overawing it by its clamours and combinations," the corrupt class was proving to be the embodiment of those "factions" Madison had nervously written about in *The Federalist*.[21]

We need to understand what Madison was thinking. As he had explained to Jefferson in a long letter of 1787 and incorporated into *Federalist* 10, the central government was to play the role of impartial arbiter among competing interests: rich and poor, creditors and debtors, speculators, merchants, planters, and manufacturers. Government, he wrote Jefferson, was meant to be "sufficiently neutral between different parts of Society to control one part from invading the rights of another, and at the same time sufficiently controuled itself, from setting up an interest adverse to that of the entire Society." Nothing could have been clearer. Hamilton's policies upset that balance by favoring the growth of a "monied interest," or commercial class, over others in society. This was obnoxious for many reasons, not the least of which was that the chosen class of people was concentrated in northern cities. By compromising its integrity, the government endangered society. Madison had to stick to his principles, or Hamilton would ride roughshod.[22]

Pennsylvania senator William Maclay noted in his illuminating, if caustic, diary how the treasury secretary dominated in 1790–91. Protesting the way Hamilton manipulated members of Congress ("all the business is done in dark cabals, on the principle of interested management"), he expressed frustration with the results: "Mr. Hamilton is all-powerful and fails in nothing he attempts." Though the senator did not characterize Madison, he peppered his diary with references to the congressman's central role in all political activities. John Adams, with little disguise, wrote at about the same time that Madison's abilities were overrated—he was "a Creature of French Puffs"—and his proposals in Congress adequate proof of his "Infamy." An almost magnetic repulsion continued to operate between Madison and the nation's first vice president.[23]

Hamilton may have bullied as he sought to persuade, but he had his reasons. For him, moderation did not win wars on battlefields or wars over policy. While it may be true that he, Madison, and Jefferson all hoped to establish the character of the chief executive as an embodiment of the popular will—an accountable political actor who was also a moral protector—Hamilton was clearly attempting to deny the legislative branch preeminence and making as many of its members as possible personally beholden to him. Madison fought Hamilton tooth and nail. The illustrious face-off between Hamilton and Jefferson, a political battle that tore apart the executive, is better known, but for many months before Jefferson appeared on the scene, it was Madison who was Hamilton's adversary. It was he who witnessed Hamilton behaving as though he were a king's prime minister. It was he who led the counteroffensive. Madison gave Jefferson a vocabulary with which to scold Hamilton and those attracted to him.

Once Jefferson became part of the equation, Hamilton saw the obstructionist threat increasing and began more intently to count administration allies. Around the same time, in an institutional move, Washington shifted ghostwriting assignments—such as the president's annual message—from Madison to Hamilton and Jefferson. He did so not because of any falling out with Madison but because he recognized that such assistance should properly come from within the executive branch. This seemingly innocent move helped to change the dynamic.[24]

"The Indiscretion of a Printer"

As we have seen, Madison's and Jefferson's minds were on different trajectories as they embarked, with little certainty, on a major experiment in government—life under the Constitution. Philosophically, the Jefferson of 1790 was probably closer to the perspective of the Revolutionary gadfly Tom Paine than he was to the constitutional concerns of his friend Madison. But by the middle of 1791 both were finding Paine's sweeping arguments in favor of social equality crucial to their program. A new militancy in the political world served to deemphasize the remaining differences between Madison and Jefferson, as the methods of Alexander Hamilton rankled both of them equally.

After publication of the first volume of *The Rights of Man* in that year, Paine once again became a symbol of resistance to despotism. *Common Sense* had bolstered America's Revolutionaries in the months leading up to the Declaration of Independence. At the time John Adams had taken exception to the consensus view, calling Paine "a disastrous meteor," whose wildly successful pamphlet was hardly more than icing on the cake. It was only fitting that Vice President Adams's name should become enmeshed in the controversy over Paine's latest publication.[25]

The pamphleteer had left America in 1787, returning to his native England. Jefferson and he met up in Paris and remained in touch; when Adams departed London and sailed back to Boston the next year, Jefferson relied on Paine for information on British political developments. In 1790, with Jefferson in New York, Paine went to press with *The Rights of Man,* a defense of Revolutionary France; it would eventually result in his expulsion from England.[26]

The impetus for *The Rights of Man* was Edmund Burke's equally inflammatory *Reflections on the Revolution in France,* which demeaned even the auspicious energy of Lafayette and his allies of 1789. Writing with a heavy hand, Burke thought it prudent to "suspend" his congratulations to the French until they had proven that their movement was "something deeper than the agitation of a troubled and frothy surface." For Burke, the anti-Christian agitation associated with the French Revolution exposed hypocrisy. "These Atheistical fathers have a bigotry of their own," he railed, doubting the collective vision of popular politicians and their intellectual backers. "With them it is a sufficient motive to destroy an old scheme of things, because it is an old one . . . They think that government may vary like modes of dress, and with as little ill effect." Dismissive and tart in his repudiation of what he viewed as democratic tyranny, Burke celebrated the balance and resilience of the British model.[27]

Paine rejected his adversary's association of the French Revolution with fanatics bent on tearing society apart. Burke was ignorant of what was truly happening in France: cleansing a nation of autocratic government. Even if Louis XVI, whose reign seemed mild, was not an evil man, he symbolized "hereditary despotism"—nothing prevented worse rulers from arising in the future. Echoing Jefferson's thinking about generational tyranny, Paine wrote: "Every age and generation must be free to act for itself *in all cases*... The vanity and presumption of governing beyond the grave, is the most ridiculous and insolent of all tyrannies."[28]

He pitied the British subjects of the "feeble and crazy" George III for their learned passivity. And echoing Madison's criticism of Hamilton's strategic plan, he attacked the funding system in Britain for accruing a large debt in order to pay for wars, increase taxes, and cultivate "a monied interest of the Nation" in support of state-sponsored aggression. It was almost word for word the danger to the republic that Madison (and, in due course, Jefferson) saw in Hamilton's assumption plan. "It is power, and not principles, that Mr. Burke venerates," taunted Paine, as he questioned his opponent's moral sensibility.

The suspicions of Burke and Paine would be reproduced in the United States. In both the Old and New worlds, the politics of the 1790s were beset by premonitions of civilization's collapse. According to Paine's diagnosis, those who could still feel had no problem perceiving the justice of popular resentment. The Revolution in France, like the Revolution in America, was a "renovation of the natural order of things..., combining moral with political happiness." He dedicated the first volume of *The Rights of Man* to George Washington and shipped him fifty copies. Washington may not have extolled the British political model as Burke did, but he certainly shared neither the radical intellectualism nor the moral imagination of the campaigning Tom Paine.[29]

The life of Paine's friend Jefferson was about to change. Giving little thought to a brief cover letter that he wrote to a man he had never met, he passed on an early copy of the first (British) edition of *The Rights of Man*, which Madison had loaned to him. Jefferson had merely followed Madison's instructions. Or so he thought. Unbeknownst to him, the recipient of the book was the brother of the man who intended to publish it in America, a man who clearly saw publicity value in using Jefferson's words as a prefatory recommendation for the book. "I am extremely pleased," Jefferson had casually penned, "that something is at length to be publickly said against the political heresies which have sprung up among us." He was disturbed by the rise of pro-British feelings among those in government whom he would soon be referring to as "Anglomen."

When the American edition came out, Jefferson acknowledged, to Washington as well as to Madison, the accuracy of the quote. It was, he explained, a dissent from the unrepublican notions of John Adams, who appeared to have renounced his Revolutionary principles in favor of a government steeped in privilege. The vice president had just published *Discourses on Davila,* a labored work on appetites and ambition in which he expressed his reservations about popular government. His ultimate reasoning may have elicited questions, but it was hard for an honest politician to object to his realism. "National passions and habits are unwieldy, unmanageable, and formidable things," Adams wrote. No other member of the Washington administration was as yet prepared to acknowledge, as Adams was, that where competition among political parties existed, "the nation becomes divided into two nations, each of which is, in fact, a moral person, as much as any community can be so, and are soon bitterly enraged against each other."

Jefferson regarded as political heresy Adams's solution to the foibles of human nature. In any society, Adams wrote, famous figures attracted a following, such that it was irresistible for people to want to emulate them. Conferring rank and distinction restricted an otherwise out-of-control ambition among men, just as democratic impulses produced a "sordid scramble for money." Rank and distinction preserved stability so that good things got done. By seeking to abolish social distinctions, the Revolution in France was attempting the impossible, because wealth, honor, and beauty never went out of fashion. Without some kind of paternalistic intervention, new rivalries always formed. For Adams, inequality was natural and should be preserved. The U.S. government should bestow titles upon the "natural aristocracy" of America. He wanted state conventions called for the purpose of appointing hereditary U.S. senators.

Adams did not consider himself unrepublican, but his definition of a republic was rather unusual: "a government whose sovereignty is vested in more than one person." On this basis, Britain's government was a "monarchical republic," and as he phrased it in a letter to Roger Sherman, the United States would remain a republic whether power was invested "in two persons, or in three millions." Republics, according to Adams, were no less productive of inequality than despotisms, only less cruel. The policies and institutions he favored would defeat socially disruptive impulses but also retain a class hierarchy.[30]

John Adams, then, was the individual Jefferson was thinking of when he wrote of "political heresies"—and he meant nothing more than that. To Madison: "I tell [Adams] freely that he is a heretic, but certainly never meant to step into a public newspaper with that in my mouth." Addressing President Washington, the secretary of state was less piquant and more circumspect. It was, he said, "the indiscretion of a printer" that had unfortunately resulted in his sentiments spilling out onto the page. Adams and he differed "as friends should do." He hoped it would end there.

Something like this did not disappear overnight, however, and a flurry of newspaper commentary ensued. One series of articles, signed "Publicola," took Jefferson to task for sponsoring Paine's obnoxious ideas and labeled Jefferson the real political heretic. The aggressive style of "Publicola" resembled that of John Adams. Jefferson did not weigh in; nor did he immediately contact Adams. Writing supportively to Paine after the initial storm over *Rights of Man* had subsided, he reported optimistically that the author's friends were winning the battle for public opinion over the friends of "Publicola." He did not identify by name those who constituted the opposing side, referring instead to a "sect..., high in names but small in number."

Madison's response to the incident showed that he and Jefferson were on the same wavelength. Seeing the preface to the American edition of Paine's work and the quote from Jefferson, he correctly put together all the circumstances that had produced an unsolicited controversy. Writing Jefferson, he could not resist adding his own strong critique of the "anti-republican discourses" that he regarded as an endorsement of the royal court. Madison viewed Adams's ideas as irrelevant, if not ridiculous, and was confident that the vice president was incapable of convincing public men of anything at this point. It was Hamilton's pro-British attitude that struck Madison as most unsound and no less ridiculous. Yet Hamilton was succeeding in convincing public men of the justness of his policies. And Madison had run out of patience.

Two more months passed before Jefferson sought to clear the air with Adams, dexterously explaining the motive behind his letter: "to write from a conviction that truth, between candid minds, can never do harm." His notorious quote to the printer had been a throwaway line, he reiterated, never meant to see the light of day. Adams, as ingenious as he was spontaneous, replied to Jefferson with an affectation of surprise, claiming that they had never really discussed their respective views on government. He was telling Jefferson that it was dangerous to assume too much about another person's beliefs. And indeed, Jefferson may not have known that the vice president, for all intents and purposes excluded from major policy discussions, cared little for Hamilton's economic proposals, which he saw as a "swindle" of ordinary Americans that only gave license to a "mercenary spirit of commerce." Nor did Adams approve in the least the closer ties Hamilton wanted with England.

No doubt Jefferson made it a point to show Madison this letter, in which Adams denied that he was "Publicola." It was, in fact, his twenty-five-year-old son John Quincy, as yet unnamed, who had embarked on his column without his father's immediate knowledge. Jefferson, more ready than Madison to maintain a courteous conversation with the vice president, reaped what he had sown, as Adams, after lecturing, gave him warm assurances: "The friendship which has Subsisted for fifteen years between Us, without the Smallest Interruption, and untill this occasion without the Slightest Suspicion, ever has been and Still is, very dear to my heart."[31]

"A Very Respectable Mathematician"

Much of the *Rights of Man* controversy had taken place while Madison and Jefferson were traveling. In 1784 Madison had visited upstate New York with Lafayette, but Jefferson was as yet unfamiliar with the region. In May 1791, after conversations in lower Manhattan with Madison's college friend and roommate Philip Freneau, a poet, and U.S. senator Aaron Burr, who had recently bested Hamilton's father-in-law, Philip Schuyler, in a tense election, the two Virginians sailed up the Hudson. In the state capital of Albany, on a day when the temperature reached ninety-four, one of the city's newspapers announced that it was "honored with the presence of Mr. Jefferson, Secretary of State, accompanied by the *Charles Fox* of America, the celebrated Madison." Fox was a Whig leader in the British Parliament who had vocally supported the American Revolution and who now, no less controversially, welcomed the French Revolution.[32]

Their trip was billed as a nature expedition, and the travelers' journals suggest that it truly was, though it would be absurd to think that political strategizing had not occurred to them as they took in their surroundings and met with prominent citizens. Beyond rumors that flowed through the pen of a Hamilton intimate, there is no evidence of machinations, no meeting to establish an alliance with Governor George Clinton of New York, who eventually would serve as vice president under both Virginians. But there is, ironically, a record of a cordial get-together with the defeated Senator Schuyler.[33]

Madison and Jefferson traveled as far north as Lake Champlain, visiting

Fort Ticonderoga and the Revolutionary battlefield of Saratoga. They paddled a canoe and went fishing on Lake George. They took in Bennington, Vermont, site of another battle of the Revolution, and traversed western Massachusetts and the Connecticut Valley. They then sailed forty miles across Long Island Sound to pay a visit to William Floyd, the former New York congressman whose daughter Madison had unsuccessfully courted. Madison biographer Ralph Ketcham has sardonically, yet aptly, described this crossing as "probably the longest sea voyage of his life." Altogether Madison and Jefferson traveled nearly one thousand miles before they ferried from bucolic Brooklyn and ended up again in busy Manhattan.[34]

At every stage of their journey, the two paid close attention to the regional economy. Madison's notes make reference to a thriving free black farmer who employed white laborers, "and by his industry and good management" operated an efficient farm. The congressman was impressed by the man's native intelligence as well as his accounting skills. Jefferson's notes were dominated by scientific measurements and rigorous observations on trees and fruits, so we have no way to know whether the farmer made an impression on him.

But there are other indications of Jefferson's fairly static thinking about race. Shortly after he and Madison returned to Philadelphia, he had an exchange of letters with the Baltimore-area mathematician Benjamin Banneker, a sixty-nine-year-old free black. Jefferson's one-page reply to Banneker stands alongside *Notes on Virginia* as our best evidence of his perplexity with regard to African Americans' intellectual attainments.

The mathematician's prose is wrapped in the gallantry that eighteenth-century epistolary culture favored. His uninvited communication implored Jefferson to recognize an essential equality among all peoples: "I suppose it is a truth too well attested to you, to need a proof here, that we are a race of beings, who have long labored under the abuse and censure of the world; that we have long been looked upon with an eye of contempt; and that we have long been considered rather as brutish than human, and scarcely capable of mental endowments." He presumed that Jefferson was better than most whites, "a man far less inflexible in sentiments of this nature, than many others; that you are measurably friendly, and well disposed towards us; and that you are willing and ready to lend your aid and assistance to our relief, from those many distresses, and numerous calamities, to which we are reduced." Quoting back the self-evident truths contained in the text of the Declaration of Independence, Banneker counted on Jefferson to call publicly for an end to the "inhuman captivity, to which too many of my brethren are doomed."

The largely self-taught Marylander, having illustrated his literacy and refinement, enclosed a copy of the almanac he had published. It revealed complex mathematical calculations and indicated his skill in the science of astronomy, a favorite pastime of Jefferson's since his days as a student. In his reply, the secretary of state appears magnanimous, commending Banneker on the quality of his work: "No body wishes more than I do, to see such proofs as you exhibit, that nature has given to our black brethren talents equal to those of the other colors of men; and that the appearance of the want of them, is owing merely to the degraded condition of their existence, both in Africa and America."

On the same day that he sent his compliments to Banneker, Jefferson wrote to the fervently pro-American French philosopher Condorcet, his good friend and one of the great optimists about human nature. The statement was framed as if it were announcing a scientific discovery: "I am happy to be able to inform you that we have now in the United States a negro, the son of a black man born in Africa, and a black woman born in the United States, who is a very respectable Mathematician." Repeating the language he had used in his *Notes on Virginia*, he expressed hope that science would eventually reveal that "the want of talents observed in [blacks] is merely the effect of their degraded condition, and not proceeding from any difference in the structure of the parts on which intellect depends." This may have qualified as liberal sentiment in the eighteenth century, but it showed too that Jefferson was separating science (or philosophy of the mind) from the politics of emancipation.

In fact, Jefferson thought that one almanac and one well-written letter constituted but little proof of the qualities of mind attaching to a whole race of men. His reservations became clearer in his comments to others, wherein his first line of defense was to rationalize that Banneker's ancestry contained European blood. Or perhaps a white associate had helped him. Or perhaps the taste of trigonometry he offered was the extent of his natural gift. Justifying his doubts in later years, after Banneker was dead, Jefferson recalled that his impression of the mathematician was "a mind of very common stature," and he went so far as to claim that there was a "childish and trivial" quality to Banneker's writing.[35]

In that Jefferson's history shows a constant suspicion about the African's mental powers and a fixed disregard for any evidence offered to him, the letter to Condorcet appears to have been a momentary detour. Madison's greater curiosity and openness with regard to the black farmer in upstate New York attests to the suppleness of his thought; yet it would be wrong to see him as an integrationist either. He might have been entirely comfortable living in the North, but he never strayed far from Jefferson's call for the recolonization of blacks beyond America's borders.

"Public Opinion"

In early 1791, as the contradiction between the Madison-Jefferson and Hamiltonian visions for America became impossible to resolve through cordial means, Madison encouraged his college roommate Philip Freneau to open a newspaper that would talk back to the administration. John Fenno's *Gazette of the United States* was staunchly defending whatever Hamilton proposed. Fenno was of modest means, an entrepreneur who identified with the interests of the ruling circle and saw profits flowing from being its mouthpiece. He had, as yet, no competitor in the marketplace of ideas.

Freneau was just scraping by when Madison and Jefferson agreed to assist him in signing up subscribers. They also guaranteed that any losses would be covered. Though a Princetonian with literary gifts, Freneau did not come from wealth. The son of a New York merchant, he had been the captain of a privateer during the Revolution and was captured by the British. Confined to a noxious prison ship in the Hudson River, he made a daring escape. Even more important to his patrons than his Revolutionary heroism, Freneau was a time-tested republican, an intellectual who despised banks and speculators and had published articles on the subject. Madison fully trusted him, which was why Jefferson did as well. Another of the Princeton legion, General Henry "Light-Horse Harry" Lee, eagerly signed on to the project.[36]

Financing problems delayed publication for some months. Naysayers, Madison wrote, "practiced some artifice" in their attempt to scare off the would-be editor. But in the end Freneau, like Jefferson before him, found Madison's call to service overpowering. Freneau accepted a low-paying position in the State Department as a translator—incontrovertible proof of how closely Madison and Jefferson were cooperating at this moment. The noncoincidence would be exploited by an outraged Hamilton, who naturally read intrigue into the Freneau appointment. Jefferson maintained just enough distance that he could deny any unseemly involvement, while

Madison agreed to stay abreast of all financial details of the prospective opinion journal. He even enlisted his father to round up subscribers in central Virginia.[37]

The *National Gazette* published its first issue in Philadelphia on October 31, 1791. Three weeks later Madison anonymously authored the first of eighteen essays for his friend's paper. It was titled "Population and Emigration." Essentially nonpartisan, it revisited Benjamin Franklin's observations on the safety-valve effect of westward expansion. Madison described migration from the Old World to the New as a natural process that stood to benefit both the United States and Europe. Creating a healthier, happier Euro-American population would add eager new consumers of European goods while ridding Europe of its laboring poor. According to Madison's theory, immigrants would continue to desire what Europe produced, even as they became American in their pursuit of economic uplift. While it appeared politically innocuous, the essay established a template, a guide for further argument.[38]

As a political journalist, Madison was to offer step-by-step instruction in republicanism—how to talk back, how to push back against Hamilton's British-style plan of government. Given Hamilton's consolidation of power in the executive branch, normal checks and balances embodied in the federal system were no longer adequate, and quiet tactics were outmoded. Madison's unceasing work in Congress had failed to stop an agenda overtly aimed at Anglicizing the new republic; so he would now tap the best minds in the country to help him salvage the constitutional framework. His answer to Hamilton was simple and straightforward: "public opinion."

Madison did not employ the term in the way we understand it today, as raw poll data. By public opinion, he meant *educated* opinion, the output of influential critics. His earlier conception of the federal republic, the carefully drawn, thoroughly unpopular Virginia Plan, had hoped to empower an educated class of people's representatives to filter and refine the collective opinion of "the people." Now, disappointed in the overall output of the people's elected representatives, he turned to what he called "the class of literati," enlightened opinion makers, cultivators of ideas and manners, who he hoped would use the press to educate.[39]

There were few self-imposed limitations in what he wrote. In the notes he took as he conceived the *National Gazette* essays—ideas that he thought twice about and abandoned—Madison showed that he wanted to blast slavery for perpetuating aristocracy in the state governments of the South. He could not have done this in Congress without losing his southern allies, but in the "public opinion" format he thought, for a moment at least, that he would speak truth to power. In the end, he realized he could not risk what would happen if his anonymity were compromised—alienating the southerners whose opinions he and Jefferson wished to mobilize against Hamilton's policies.[40]

On December 5, 1791, two weeks after "Population and Emigration," Madison contributed his second essay, "Consolidation." It extended his theory of public opinion by focusing on the role it played in securing the republic. "Consolidation" regarded Hamilton's capture of executive energy as an incipient move in the direction of monarchy, which stood to dissolve the states and consolidate (or concentrate) wealth and power at the center. Congress would lose its effectiveness; the people's voice would go silent. Citing values of "reason, benevolence, and brotherly affection," Madison drew upon the vocabulary of political sympathy (ordinarily Jefferson's specialty), calling on the "great body of the people" to transcend their state identities, sympathize, and act in concert. When the federal government overstepped its authority, the collective people had to become a truer union than the established structure and "*consolidate* their defense of the public liberty." Madison's sense of collectivity described a people enlightened by public opinion; Jefferson's described a people actuated by their native intelligence. Rethinking his definition of "the people," Madison found himself philosophically closer to Jefferson and increasingly remote from Hamilton.[41]

He enlarged on the same question two weeks later as he opened a new *National Gazette* editorial with an axiom: "Public opinion sets bounds to every government, and is the real sovereign in every free one." There were instances, he explained, when government must obey public opinion and instances when public opinion would be influenced by government. In the coming years, his and Jefferson's detractors would obsess on the first instance and challenge their belief in the second.

This essay is significant, because it was a departure from Madison's argument in *Federalist* 10, wherein he had relied on the widening contours of the republic to prevent the abuses caused by factional majorities. In 1787 he had thought that geography held the key to preventing demagogic appeals from spreading. Now he believed something different: that circulation of public opinion over that broad expanse—the addition of critical voices—was the essential balancing element in political society. He endorsed "a general intercourse of sentiments, as good roads, domestic commerce, a free press, and particularly a *circulation of newspapers through the entire body of the people.*" In Congress, he argued for lowering the postage on newspapers.[42]

After justifying the power of public opinion, Madison gave his attention to all things British in Hamilton's policies. In the essay "Universal Peace," he contested the practice of perpetual debt to facilitate wars. "Each generation should be made to bear the burdens of its own wars, instead of leaving the expense for other generations," he wrote. He thought there was something sinister about Hamilton's ploy to keep taxes low and indirect while allowing the government to mobilize large sums for war or other empire-building activities. It was not the prize—western land—that Madison objected to, of course, but the necessary by-product of funding a great military machine: the all-powerful central government, mirror image of Great Britain.[43]

On December 5, 1791, the day Madison published "Consolidation," Hamilton gave him further cause for grievance with the release of his long-researched *Report on Manufactures.* Confirming Madison's worst suspicions, the treasury secretary laid out a complex plan to enlist the federal government in promoting new industries. Madison's objection was to financial inducements from the government. The practice, as he understood it, would create an entrenched cadre of moneyed patrons or, in modern parlance, lobbyists. Earlier in the year, as an experiment, Hamilton had backed a state-chartered cotton textile firm in Paterson, New Jersey, which was capitalized at $1 million and incorporated shortly before the *Report on Manufactures* was announced. So the report was more than theoretical.[44]

For Madison, the evidence was clear. Each of Hamilton's programs sucked the United States deeper into the British orbit of foreign investment and capital. The republic would soon become a miniature version of its once and future enemy. Hamilton was extending the government's powers beyond what the Constitution allowed, interpreting the preamble's call to "promote the general Welfare, and secure the Blessings of Liberty" as a blank check. Madison wrote Henry Lee, who was about to become Virginia's governor, that any executive seizure of power could be justified based on Hamilton's unrestrained reading of the republic's charter. He concluded ruefully: "The parchment had better be thrown into the fire at once." Lee's response was even more cynical. He charged that Hamilton was trying to create a new species of American, a more docile race. Instead of the "stout muscular ploughman full of health...with eight or ten blooming children," the secretary seemed to prefer "squat bloated fellows all belly & no legs who...manufacture a little."[45]

As a member of the president's cabinet, Jefferson was in a difficult position. He could not oppose Hamilton's report directly. Washington had made it clear that the development of a manufacturing economy was a high priority of his presidency; he asked the secretary of state to cooperate with particular inventors and artisans who were bringing British technology to America.

The most aggressive promoter of manufactures in the government was Tench Coxe, Hamilton's associate at Treasury, with whom Jefferson was friendly. This made the process bearable. So while Jefferson carried out the president's orders, Coxe ran interference between Jefferson and Hamilton, taking the lead in organizing the Paterson corporation (called the Society for Establishing Useful Manufactures). Jefferson, who exhibited an intellectual interest in all technological innovation, accompanied President Washington, the first lady, and Secretary Hamilton and his wife to visit the "cotton manufactory," or machine shop, in Philadelphia, where the new and improved double looms for Paterson were being constructed. He did not do so as a concession to Hamilton—it was a command performance at the behest of the president of the United States.[46]

Jefferson knew full well that Washington was the force behind manufactures, which meant that Madison knew it too. Yet Madison had no qualms about attacking the *Report on Manufactures* in several of his later *Gazette* essays. In one notable instance, he returned to the cause of agrarianism, a subject generally associated with Jefferson. Praising the health, virtue, intelligence, and competence of the husbandman, Madison drew a contrast between the contentment of the self-employed and the pitiful condition of the exploited sailor—his symbol of the pervasive inequality within Britain's maritime economy. "His mind, like his body, is imprisoned in the bark that transports him," Madison wrote of the sailor, echoing Jefferson's theory as he equated social well-being with freedom of movement and the creative exercise of human faculties.

More hard-hitting essays followed. In "Fashion," Madison described the capricious character of manufacturing in merry old England. He recounted the plight of twenty thousand buckle factory workers who suddenly found themselves on the streets in 1786, owing to the fickleness of fashion. This highly specialized kind of production was exactly what Hamilton wished to encourage, but for Madison it represented the "lowest point of servility." In his avid embrace of the rurally based economy and the healthy physical environment that promoted contentment among the masses, Madison continued speaking in Jefferson's voice. Jefferson, meanwhile, was either under an official charge to remain silent on this issue or was uncharacteristically detached from it.[47]

"Its Real Friends"

Madison and Hamilton had diametrically opposed views of economic expansion, but both men wore ideological blinders. Madison saw what was wrong: government should benefit a majority of the people and not artificially stimulate the economy in ways that favored one class over another. But in his calculation, he missed the real losers in a Hamiltonian universe: women, children, and the poor who were to be exploited as factory laborers as America developed its industrial economy. Hamilton relegated these elements of the white population to the status of surplus labor—virtual slaves. For his part, Madison invoked the independent yeoman as a hero without seeing how small farmers were turning increasingly to slave owning.

The point is simple. All American economic theory at this time was mechanistic; none of it was humanistic. The independent yeoman had to produce—to use Henry Lee's words—"eight or ten blooming children." In the yeoman's paradise to which Madison and Jefferson subscribed, women were breeders; they were reproducers more than producers (though wives were, in fact, the chief producers of homespun clothing). This was not independence. It is curious that in post-Revolutionary America, enlightened men failed to think more creatively with respect to the physical costs of childbirth in a medically dangerous environment. Jefferson had lost his wife Patty in 1782, after a series of difficult pregnancies. In 1790 Henry Lee mourned his "Divine Matilda," when she succumbed after the birth of her fourth child. Postpartum death was a common occurrence. Yet somehow the fantasy of the happy and fecund farmer's wife persisted, as attention was redirected to Hamilton's ostensibly unhealthy plan of federally supported industries.[48]

In another *National Gazette* piece, with the unambiguous title of "The Union: Who Are Its Real Friends," Madison sketched out a partisan creed, rendering his argument in the negative. The Union's real friends were "not those who charge others with not being its friends, whilst their own conduct is wantonly multiplying its enemies"; "not those who favor measures, which by pampering the spirit of speculation within and without the government, disgust the best friends of the Union"; "not those who promote unnecessary accumulations of the debt of the Union, instead of the best means of discharging it as fast as possible"; "not those who ... pervert the limited government of the Union, into a government of unlimited discretion, contrary to the will and subversive of the authority of the people." So, finally, who were the real friends of the Union? Madison's positive answer: "friends to the authority of the people," "friends to liberty," "friends to the limited and republican system of government," and "enemies to every public measure that might smooth the way to hereditary government."[49]

Jefferson would soon coin the term *monocrat* to describe the proponents of Hamiltonianism. But it was Madison who, at this juncture, publicly associated himself with a philosophy of republicanism and denounced those who would sabotage it. President Washington could not have been pleased by what was happening. He supported Hamilton's general plan to strengthen the national economy, though he continued to hear the opinions of both Madison and Jefferson. For as long as Jefferson and Attorney General Edmund Randolph remained in the cabinet, Washington would try not to take sides.

Shortly after Madison's combustible "The Union: Who Are Its Real Friends" appeared, the president met with the congressman and brought him into a conversation he had hitherto carried on only with individual cabinet members. He was collecting opinions: Should he resign the presidency at the conclusion of his term? According to Madison's notes of their meeting, Washington said he was "disinclined" to continue in office another four years. He saw Adams, Jefferson, and John Jay as potential successors. He noted Jefferson's vaunted "repugnance to public life & anxiety to exchange it for his farm & his philosophy." He also alluded to the "obnoxious" views of Adams and Jay: the former's positions were generally repellent because of unconcealed "monarchical principles"; the latter disqualified himself because of his unpopular diplomatic activity in selling out western interests by supporting Spanish rights to navigation of the Mississippi. The president did not mention Hamilton as a potential successor. And if he was upset about Madison's intimacy with Freneau, he did not show it.

As each member of the president's cabinet had done, Madison too pressed Washington to remain in office and try to conciliate the competing interests in the federal government. The president, in turn, asked Madison to help him draft a message to Congress, one that sidestepped the issue of his desire to leave office. In delaying his decision on a second term, Washington appears to have felt he could do little to avert the ripening disagreement he saw coming, and he was not eager to preside over it.

Jefferson was beginning to express his vexation, at least in private correspondence, by identifying Hamiltonian politicians as "tories" and "monarchists." Meanwhile the "tories" and "monarchists" belittled the critics of Hamilton's centralizing program as an illegitimate "faction" of antifederalists. The name-calling had begun.[50]

In 1792 the volume of party strife grew louder. Using a variety of pseudonyms, Hamilton took up his pen in July and August, targeting Madison and Jefferson in the *Gazette of the United States*. He went easier on Madison, mentioning only Jefferson by name. Perhaps Hamilton recognized that Madison had a well-defined legislative role to play, whereas the secretary of state, as a member of the executive cabinet, competed directly with him for the president's ear. But that is a rational explanation, and politics is an irrational business driven by strong personalities and skewed perceptions. Hamilton may also have thought Madison's ambitions stopped at the national legislature, and that Jefferson more directly threatened him because of his "worldly" experience.

Hamilton understood perfectly well that Madison posed at least as great a threat to him as Jefferson. Privately he said so. It was only in the public press that he placed Jefferson ahead of Madison in the symbolic hierarchy of the anti-administration bloc. Madison and Jefferson had not established a chain of command, and their circle was at this point comprised of select Virginians only; it did not even include a majority of their state's assemblymen, whose focus, with the exception of the assumption issue, remained local. The so-called republican interest had yet to develop a national character.[51]

But Hamilton made it apparent in his newspaper offensive that he thought of Jefferson as a man whose pretension to literary and scientific erudition covered up what were really "weak judgments." He was ready to go toe-to-toe with Jefferson on intellectual matters, but he reserved his sternest criticism for Jefferson's political performance, enlarging the Freneau appointment into a symbol of sleaze and the *National Gazette* as a "pernicious" instrument, "eminently calculated to disturb the public peace, and corrupt the morals of the people." The essay was meant to expose Jefferson as a backhanded operator, a flat-out deceiver, who did what he did out of personal animus toward Hamilton. Freneau had been Madison's friend, a fellow Princetonian. Hamilton could just as easily have pointed to Madison, but he chose Jefferson instead.[52]

In the piece he signed "An American," Hamilton accused Jefferson of being a weak patriot, objecting to the Constitution in the main and having recommended it only "on the ground of expediency, in certain contingencies." This was an obvious exaggeration, but an effective slur. At the end of the long essay, Hamilton went the distance: "Mr. Jefferson is emulous of being the head of a party, whose politics have constantly aimed at elevating State-power, upon the ruins of National Authority."

Again in the fall of 1792, Hamilton wrote contemptuously of Jefferson as a selfish and covetous plotter, "the ambitious and intriguing head of a party," a demagogue. The contempt compounded: "Plain Thomas J—; wonderful humility on all occasions—the flimsy veil of inordinate ambition." One can only imagine the level of Hamilton's exasperation, as well as scorn, when he wrote: "Mr. Jefferson fears in Mr. Hamilton a formidable rival in the competition for the presidential chair."[53]

This was the quintessential Hamilton, a warrior. "Plain Thomas J" did not answer in kind, but Madison did. Two more contributions to the *National Gazette* guaranteed the dynamic congressman his central position in the war of words. "A Candid State of Parties" declared that there was a "Republican" party comprised of those who wished well to republican government; and an "antirepublican" party (no one yet mentioned the word *federalist* as a party designation) that accepted the "active and insinuating influence" of the moneyed men to whom they were beholden.

Madison's next essay, "Who Are the Best Keepers of the People's Liberties?" was an inelegant debate between a generic republican and antirepublican, in which one embraced the "sacred trust" of a liberty-loving people and the other attacked the masses as a "stupid, suspicious, licentious" group that needed to be taught submission and obedience. Madison saw the emergence not so much of a two-party *system* as of two party *personalities*—one patriotic and republican, the other "debauched" and weak, having turned traitor to the ideals of the republic. Madison's moralism had reached what was, for him, an extreme.[54]

A political war was now unavoidable. The colicky George Mason, whose unending opposition to the Constitution had soured him on the new establishment, must have been pleased by the fight he saw in Madison. On most occasions when he traveled south, Madison dutifully stopped at Gunston Hall to consult and would likely have done so again. But in October 1792 Mason died at home, age sixty-seven. Jefferson had seen him just a week before, finding Mason "perfectly communicative" though weak.

Jefferson knew he needed to enlist influential allies if he was to counteract Hamilton's defamatory labors effectively. Yet he remained intent never to write for the partisan press. Aiming to set the record straight, he went from

Gunston Hall to Mount Vernon to see Hamilton's boss. As usual, Washington was cooperative, and Jefferson thought he had gotten through. He told Madison he had enjoyed a "full, free, and confidential conversation with the President" and would fill him in on the details when next they met.[55]

"A Plot Thickens"

A lot was happening beyond the power struggle between Hamilton and the two Virginians. As the election of 1792 approached, the lines of division began to play out on the state level in the large states of New York, Pennsylvania, and Virginia. Those who did not care for John Adams's so-called heresies hoped to replace him as vice president with a different northerner.

New characters were emerging. Jamaica-born Philadelphian Alexander James Dallas, who had edited the successful antifederalist *Columbian Magazine,* traveled to a gathering in New York in 1792, where he and like-minded men launched a concerted effort to unseat Vice President Adams. Dallas was confident that Senator Aaron Burr possessed the credentials that Pennsylvania republicans were looking for. The Philadelphia physician and educator Benjamin Rush, who over the course of a lifetime maintained friendships with Adams, Jefferson, and Madison, urged Burr: "Your friends everywhere look to you to take an active part in removing the monarchical rubbish of our government."

New York was another battleground, where antifederalist George Clinton, the incumbent governor, faced an intense reelection bid in 1792. His two likeliest competitors were the unaligned moderate with antifederalist leanings, Senator Burr, and the prominent federalist, Supreme Court chief justice John Jay. At that point, none of the three was identified with a national party: in the press, there were only "Jay-ites," "Clintonians," "anti-Clintonians," and in time "Burrites" as well. Before the contest heated up, Burr withdrew; he felt he could not get enough backing. But he refused to transfer his support to either of the other two.

The New York gubernatorial election was dogged by charges of corruption. Clinton won, but only after the votes of three upstate counties were thrown out because of a technicality. Burr was asked to take part in its adjudication. While there appears to have been no impropriety, the tenor of state politics was affected. Even Jefferson thought that Clinton should yield to Jay to avoid any unseemliness.

Practiced at pulling strings, Hamilton paid close attention to what was taking place in his home state. Though he held a national appointment, he resolved to blunt the electoral careers of the New Yorkers he opposed. With so many hostile forces present, suspicions stretched up and down the state. Postelection Clintonians saw the federal government ever more as a corporation that would attack liberty and plunder the states. Jay was compared to a crocodile lying in wait. And Hamilton did not quite know what to expect of Burr, who had ties to Madison and Jefferson and could not be forgiven for ending Philip Schuyler's political career. Everything Burr did seemed to produce some misgiving in Hamilton's mind.

A few months after Clinton's reelection, Madison and Jefferson began to seek opinions on whether to run Clinton or Burr against Adams. There was a vice-presidential contest only in 1792, as no elector would think of withholding his vote from the incumbent president. Monroe entered the conversation with Madison and Jefferson, and the three Virginians ultimately opted to support Clinton. While Clinton's questionable reelection had left a bad taste, Burr was only thirty-six, seventeen years Clinton's junior, and considered too green for the vice presidency. The youngest in the triumvirate, Monroe, was relatively comfortable with Burr as a national candidate, aware that in the key state of Pennsylvania Burr had support and Clinton did not. But Madison and Jefferson were the heavyweights; they overruled the Pennsylvanians and insisted on Clinton, proving that long before there was a "Virginia Dynasty" of presidents, and even before there was a Democratic-Republican Party, there was a "Virginia interest" managing politics at the national level.[56]

Hamilton suddenly warmed up to the man who appeared the least objectionable at the moment. He wrote to Adams to commiserate on the Clinton challenge. Cultivating an us-against-them mind-set, Hamilton made reference to the nastiness in the newspapers, Freneau's in particular, as he egged on the irritable Adams with a panicky view of the situation: "You will have perceived that a plot thickens & that something very like a serious design to subvert the Government discloses itself." Though the plot was, indeed, thickening, Adams received a good many more votes than Clinton and retained his second position in the federal system.[57]

"I Like His Manners Better"

During Jefferson's nearly four years as secretary of state, one of his critical duties was to receive French and British envoys and to discuss political and commercial topics with them before reporting to the president. Where matters of trade intervened, Hamilton met with the same envoys. The first official French minister to the United States was Jean-Baptiste Ternant. He was fiftyish and had taken part in the American Revolution. Lafayette thought highly of him. The first British minister was the under-thirty George Hammond. Neither was on the scene during the inaugural year of Washington's administration.

Jefferson and Hamilton saw foreign representatives separately and sometimes spoke at cross-purposes. Hamilton suspended payment of outstanding U.S. debts to Revolutionary France until a government deemed legitimate was installed. Not surprisingly, he and Jefferson disagreed on what defined political legitimacy.

While the United States was struggling to speak with a single voice at home and abroad, relations among the nations of Europe remained in flux. Distances made the dissemination of essential information slow and uncertain, and diplomacy took place in multiple stages with changing personnel. In 1791 the unofficial British envoy George Beckwith, closely connected to the governor-general of Canada, remained a fixture on the American scene. He took up lodgings in Philadelphia at, of all places, the House-Trist establishment. Jefferson thought this might make Madison uneasy and, with his usual aplomb, suggested that they move in together. He had refrained from making the proposition while Madison was daily enjoying "agreeable Congressional society"; but now that the complexion of things had changed, he urged: "Come and take a bed and plate with me." Jefferson was living a few short blocks away and had four spare rooms in his rented house, any of which Madison could have moved into at a moment's notice. "Let me intreat you, my dear Sir, to do it," he repeated. "To me it will be a relief from a solitude of which I have too much." He bribed Madison with the convenience of an exceptional private library.

But Madison did not take the bait. He was content to take bed and plate under the same roof as the British envoy. Aware that he was sacrificing many "hourly enjoyments" in Jefferson's company by remaining where he was, he explained that he did not wish to upset his routine: "My papers and books are all assorted around me." Nor did he wish to give Beckwith the impression that he was moving out so he would not have to board with an enemy.

It made sense. Any apparent incivility would spoil the chance to make diplomatic inroads. As long as Madison was staying put, Jefferson prevailed on him to informally discuss with his English housemate the

British-Indian arms trade that was threatening America's position along the northwestern frontier in the area of British-occupied Detroit. Britain still maintained eight of the fortifications it had agreed to give up when it acknowledged American independence in 1783.[58]

It is unclear the extent to which Congressman Madison and Secretary of State Jefferson were aware of Hamilton's communications with Beckwith. The latter two held private meetings over the eighteen months since Hamilton first suggested Madison's limitations by pointing to his lack of worldliness. Some of the issues Hamilton took up with Beckwith belonged within the proper scope of the State Department, although it must be said that the duties of the two department heads overlapped more than they would in future presidencies.

George Hammond arrived in Philadelphia as the first *official* minister from Great Britain in November 1791, and the treasury secretary cozied up to him. Hammond confirmed Beckwith's impression of Hamilton, writing home that the New Yorker had a "liberal" attitude and shared England's larger interests, whereas Jefferson was an obstructionist. Hammond admitted his bias to a U.S. senator from New Jersey in March 1792, in a statement sounding like that of Hamilton's comment to Beckwith about Madison. "The Secretary of the Treasury is more a man of the world than Jefferson," Hammond said, "and I like his manners better, and can speak more freely to him." To which he added, significantly: "Jefferson is in the Virginia interest and that of the French." It would appear that *worldliness* was a code word for accommodating England's geopolitical strategy.

Following up on Madison's unprofitable discussions with Beckwith, Jefferson sounded out Hammond on what mattered most to America's government over the long term: the fulfillment of treaty obligations and the removal of British posts and troops from U.S. territory in the West. He also pressed for direct U.S. access to the British West Indies trade, which had been long denied. London's position was that it would not abandon the western posts until southern planters had paid their prewar debts, with interest, to British merchants; but southerners would not go ahead on debt payments until they received compensation for their loss of slave property during the war. Anglo-American talks did not progress far.[59]

Jefferson heard bad news from overseas. In the late summer of 1792 his successor as U.S. minister to France, Gouverneur Morris, notified him that Lafayette had fallen into enemy hands. Earlier that year France had declared war on Austria and Prussia, partially out of a fear that émigré armies would crush the Revolution. Partisans of Lafayette were among the pro-war coalition. The marquis would spend the next five years in a series of prisons, under the control of both the Austrians and the Prussians. "He has spent his Fortune on a Revolution," the unsympathetic Morris wrote to Jefferson, "and is now crush'd by the wheel which he put in motion."[60]

Not long after Jefferson received this intelligence, he got word from the new U.S. minister to the Netherlands, his former secretary, William Short, that the king of France and his family faced execution—or as Short put it, "assassination." Distrusting Morris, Lafayette had written to Short just before being jailed, asking to be "reclaimed" by the U.S. government. In identifying himself as "an American Citizen, an American officer," he expected Short to find some way to pursue his release through diplomatic channels. Short did the only thing he could under present circumstances, which was to appeal to Gouverneur Morris, aware that Lafayette detested Morris. This whole string of events placed America's Francophiles, such as Madison and Jefferson, on the defensive.[61]

As he brought Hamilton up to date on all that he was witnessing, Morris queried his correspondent on partisan developments back in the United States. "What will be the republican Sense as to the new Republic?" he posed sarcastically. "Will it be taken for granted that Louis the sixteenth was guilty of all possible Crimes and particularly of the enormous one of not suffering [i.e., allowing] his throat to be cut which was certainly a nefarious Plot against the People and a manifest Violation of the Bill of Rights." Later in life, thinking about the French patriots' unreal expectations from their Revolution, John Adams would enjoy a chuckle when he wickedly pressed Jefferson to acknowledge the truth about the self-destructiveness of the French at this time in their history.[62]

"Womanish"

Hamilton feared outbursts of passion among the common people of America and advocated strong measures to keep the masses quiet. Madison was similarly attuned to the need for lawful control, but he no longer feared to the same degree as Hamilton what popular resistance might entail. The danger of an executive bent on domination was now his primary concern.

Ten years after the end of the Revolution, Jefferson still espoused a soaring rhetoric of equality and natural rights, continuing to embrace a comprehensive theory of moral equality, educability, and humane interaction, at least among free whites. This subjected him to the charge of being an airy philosopher, too carefree for the tastes of many northern men of business. For the likes of Hamilton, Jefferson was something else entirely: a panderer, a demagogue, routinely engaged in behind-the-scenes arm-twisting and playing politics with craft and cunning. Once his pretty language was stripped away, he was like everyone else.

The most telling of nationally significant communications in this transformative year of 1792 may be the letter that Hamilton, prickly and proud and never reluctant to acknowledge his drive, wrote to Edward Carrington on May 26. It was one of the longest and most illuminating letters of his career. He was hoping to make inroads with Carrington, then supervisor of revenue for the Commonwealth of Virginia, whom he had met during the Revolution when together they carried out a prisoner exchange. Hamilton knew that he could not "turn" Madison or wean him away from Jefferson; but he thought a reasoned appeal to Carrington might at least succeed in gaining support in a state he had not visited since the Battle of Yorktown: the home state of the president, the secretary of state, and the single most prominent congressman.

He began his letter by extending the wish that good feelings still subsisted between Carrington and himself, "persuaded also that our political creed is the same on *two essential points,* 1st the necessity of *Union* to the respectability and happiness of this Country and 2 the necessity of an efficient general government to maintain that Union." Hamilton got right to the crux of his complaint: Aware, early on, of Madison's power of argument, he would not have accepted his position in the executive branch had he not believed firmly in their political compatibility. Funding the national debt by co-opting the speculating note holders, along with the assumption of state debts, were two vital areas in which Hamilton believed he and Madison shared a vision dating back to 1783. They had had a long conversation about state debts in Philadelphia during the Constitutional Convention and were, he said, "perfectly agreed." Something had happened, and Hamilton wished to understand it. Of course, he had his own theories, which was where his letter was heading.

With a habit of claiming victimhood, Hamilton warranted that it made perfect sense for him to have lost respect for "the force of Mr. Madison's mind" after Madison's unexpected about-face on the assumption issue. Yet he had not doubted Madison's "good will" at the time this occurred. After a while, he explained, he finally recognized that "Mr. Madison, from a spirit of rivalship or some other cause had become personally unfriendly to me." Rivalship? According to Hamilton, Madison had admitted to an unnamed individual his fear of being supplanted. It was through this conduit that Madison's improper and vilifying words had reached Hamilton.

Pursuing his narrative of honorability, wounded innocence, and sudden surprise, it had dawned on Hamilton that *"Mr. Madison cooperating with Mr. Jefferson is at the head of a faction decidedly hostile to me and my administration, and actuated by views in my judgment subversive of the principles of good government and dangerous to the union, peace and happiness of the Country."* As if his underlining pen were shaking from having to revisit the moment of a painful realization, Hamilton rhetorically stepped back, offering Carrington a line that reeks of eighteenth-century literary pathos: "These are strong expressions; they may pain your friendship for one or both of the Gentlemen whom I have named. I have not lightly resolved to hazard them. They are the result of a *Serious alarm* in my mind for the public welfare."

It is hard to say who in the early American republic privileged the public welfare over more parochial, or even egoistic, concerns. In his newspaper attacks, Hamilton had already shown how much personal investment he had in the outcome of his battle with "Plain Thomas J." He saw theirs as a true test of wills, possessing the character not of a sibling rivalry but of a landmark crusade; or a race to determine, right from the starting line, the direction government would take. With Madison, Hamilton thought the problem was one of an intellectual competition, at least until Jefferson intervened. He believed that Madison and he could at least tolerate each other. With Jefferson it was more elemental, something deep-seated, a never-ending duel.

"Mr. Jefferson," Hamilton prodded Carrington, "with very little reserve[,] manifests his dislike of the funding system generally; calling in question the expediency of funding a debt at all ... In various conversations with *foreigners* as well as citizens, he has thrown censure on my *principles* of government. He has predicted that the people would not long tolerate my proceedings & that I should not long maintain my ground."

He held Jefferson solely responsible for Freneau's "malignant and unfriendly" newspaper. In accepting that Madison had made vicious remarks about him in rumored conversations, Hamilton wanted Carrington to know, should Carrington be able to intercede, that "I cannot persuade myself that Mr. Madison and I, whose politics had formerly so much the *same point of departure*, should now diverge so widely." If he really did believe that their political rupture might be healed, Hamilton undercut his purpose by once again personalizing the problem: "The opinion I once entertained of the *candour* and simplicity and fairness of Mr. Madison's character has, I acknowledge, given way to a decided opinion that *it is one of a peculiarly artificial and complicated kind.*" By "artificial and complicated," Hamilton meant "tactical," in a Machiavellian sense—this is the nearest modern equivalent to his words.

What would these tactics have been aimed at? Having thought things through, Hamilton concluded that James Madison was involved in nothing less than a conspiracy to force the treasury secretary's resignation from the president's cabinet, perhaps to clear the way for Jefferson. Warning Carrington of "unfriendly intrigues," Hamilton noted Madison's "abuse of the Presidents confidence in him." Presumably Washington was coming to see things as Hamilton did, forbearing as long as possible until no other inference was possible. Madison's pose, like Jefferson's, was duplicitous: his "true character is the reverse of that *simple, fair, candid one,* which he has assumed."

While Hamilton incorrectly assigned to Jefferson primary responsibility for the establishment of Freneau's anti-administration newspaper, he did include Madison in "the consequences imputable to it." Moving on to foreign policy, Hamilton predicted that, left to their own devices, Madison and Jefferson would, within six months, resort to an "open war" with England. *"They have a womanish attachment to France,"* he declaimed, *"and a womanish resentment against Great Britain."* This insult to their collective manhood was the ultimate dishonor.

In Paris, according to Hamilton, Jefferson "drank deeply of the French Philosophy, in Religion, in Science, in politics," and returned to America "with a too partial idea of his own powers, and with the expectation of a greater share in the direction of our councils than he has in reality enjoyed." In fact, Hamilton surmised, Jefferson may actually have "marked out for himself" Hamilton's job. This was a first thought, before Hamilton arrived at the grander suspicion that Jefferson actually wanted to contest him for *Washington's* job.

Hamilton characterized the bond between his two Virginia adversaries: "Mr. Madison had always entertained an exalted opinion of the talents, knowledge and virtues of Mr. Jefferson. The sentiment was probably reciprocal." Aware of their warm correspondence while Jefferson was abroad, he offered a pair of explanations for what happened after Jefferson's return: either Jefferson had redirected Madison's political sentiments (Jefferson being "more radically wrong" in politics than Madison); or else "Mr. Madison was seduced by the expectation of popularity" into changing his opinions. Whatever the case, Hamilton judged: "The course of this business & a variety of circumstances which took place left Mr. Madison a very discontented & chagrined man and begot some degree of ill humor in Mr. Jefferson." It is curious that Hamilton saw Madison, and not Jefferson, as the generator of ill humor.

Yet he perceived in Jefferson a worse trait than any of Madison's: the lust for power. As he flailed away, Hamilton went from suspecting to proclaiming that Jefferson owned an "ardent desire" to occupy the "Presidential Chair." This was, for him, the ultimate proof that Madison and Jefferson were engaged in "party-politics"—meaning political dissension. Hamilton had pieced it all together, he explained, after hearing that some in Virginia were anxious lest the state governments were to be subsumed into a behemoth of a national government.

The foregoing was a roundabout way for Hamilton to tell Carrington that Virginians needed to be reassured by someone they trusted—Carrington—that their fears of consolidation were entirely off base. "As to my own political Creed, I give it to you with the utmost sincerity," pronounced Hamilton. "I am *affectionately* attached to the Republican theory." It was, he pledged, "the real language of my heart." He knew there were men "acting with Jefferson & Madison" who saw him differently. "I could lay my finger on them," he said boldly and, perhaps, a little roguishly.

Feeling entirely justified in his disappointment with Madison, and no less confident in his reconstruction of events to which he had no proximity, Hamilton thus made his case before those in Virginia who were still willing to listen. Wrapping up the long letter, he indulged in a momentary reconsideration of the two Virginians who, motivated by irrational fear, had dangerously determined to "narrow the Federal authority." If, in fact, Madison and Jefferson had not meant to go so far as to accuse him of promoting monarchy, Hamilton would admit that he had treated them in print "with too much severity." He did not wish to do them any injustice, he professed to Carrington, but he would retreat from his argument no more than that. "From the bottom of my soul," he swore, "I have drawn them truly." And so he brought to a close more than twenty pages of exceedingly strong invective.[63]

Hamilton was convinced that the antifederalist Jefferson had had it in mind to "turn" Madison even before he left Paris. He was reaching too far here, wrong about the course of events: Madison had become suspicious of Hamilton's motives entirely on his own. He had not needed Jefferson to instruct him. Indeed, by the end of 1792 Madison was convinced that Congress needed to look into Hamilton's secret expenditures and possible misuse of Treasury Department funds. The prime mover was Madison, not Jefferson.

Adding to existing suspicions, allies of Madison and Jefferson had learned that Hamilton was paying blackmail to a man who had attempted to defraud the U.S. government. That man, James Reynolds, was the husband of a woman with whom Hamilton had engaged in a protracted sexual affair. Senator James Monroe was among a small delegation from Congress to meet with Hamilton in December 1792. They accepted Hamilton's explanation that no federal funds were involved in the payments. For the moment Hamilton's critics resolved that, as gentlemen, they would keep quiet about his private problem. And they decided that there was no cause to notify the president.[64]

Apparently Hamilton felt safe, or at least unconcerned that his risky actions would come back to haunt him, because he did not let up in his efforts to discredit Jefferson. The secretaries of state and treasury may have held a grudging respect for each other's intellectual range. But if they did, it did nothing to slow down the ever-growing conflict in the cabinet. As much as Jefferson despised Hamilton for his transparent bid to shape the federal government in his own image, Hamilton suspected Jefferson of plotting to do the same. Where policy differences fail to expose the whole truth, personal foibles may complete the picture, at least in explaining how Hamilton could have been led to overstate Jefferson's role in Madison's rejection of his basic programs. It could always be said of Madison that he was direct; but he was also subtle enough in his nonverbal communication that Hamilton did not follow the trajectory of his thinking (since publication of *The Federalist*) until they were past being able to communicate.

Hamilton had a need for vindication and found it as he wrote Jefferson into the history of Madison's drift. He would not, by any means, be the last to paint the history of the 1790s with this broad brush. Eventually the perception of Jefferson's consummate role in the development of a partisan mind-set would be chiseled in stone.

"A Tissue of Machinations"

Second in its revelatory content only to Hamilton's letter to Carrington was Jefferson's to George Washington of September 9, 1792, in which he defended himself against Hamilton's newspaper attacks. In a memo not long before, the president had asked for "liberal forbearances" from his feuding secretaries. There were matters of national urgency that required cooperation, not the least of which was Spanish, French, and British collusion with hostile Indians. Washington appealed unequivocally: "How unfortunate...whilst we are encompassed on all sides with avowed enemies and insidious friends, that internal dissentions should be harrowing and tearing our vitals."

Writing from the quiet of Monticello, Jefferson spelled out just how offensive he felt Hamilton's efforts to intrude upon State Department matters were and how inflammatory the newspaper attacks had been. "I am so desirous ever that you should know the whole truth," he petitioned the president. He started with the state of affairs in Congress and, denying any attempt of his own to influence votes, cast suspicion on Hamilton's motives and actions.

The flaw in Hamilton's system was painfully simple, Jefferson said. It was rooted in "principles adverse to liberty, and was calculated to undermine and demolish the republic, by creating an influence of his department over the members of the legislature." Calculated to undermine and demolish the republic? Under such terrifying circumstances, there could be no compromise between them. Hamilton's unethical relations with members of Congress, his "dealing out of Treasury-secrets among his friends," his destabilizing discussions with the ministers from England and France—there was no better term than *cabals* to describe such underhanded pacts.

In spite of the clear and present danger, Jefferson hinted at a final retirement from all public business. "When I came into this office," he wrote, "it was with a resolution to retire from it as soon as I could with decency . . . I look to that period with the longing of a wave-worn mariner, who has at length the land in view, and shall count the days and hours which still lie between me and it." If he was ready to call it quits, he could not sign off before he had thoroughly discredited his rival: "I will not suffer my retirement to be clouded by the slanders of a man whose history, from the moment when history can stoop to notice him, is a tissue of machinations against the liberty of the country which has not only received and given him bread, but heaped it's honors on his head." With a grand gesture drawn from classical oratory, alluding at once to Hamilton's common and foreign origins (born on the island of Nevis, in the Caribbean, and abandoned by his father), Jefferson penned a most memorable slur of the man who had repeatedly attacked his political dignity and moral worth.[65]

As it happens, Hamilton addressed Washington on the same delicate subject on the very same day. "I *know* that I have been an object of uniform opposition from Mr. Jefferson, from the first moment of his coming to the City of New York," he wrote. "I *know,* from the most authentic sources, that I have been the frequent subject of the most unkind whispers and insinuating from the same quarter." He claimed that while Jefferson was plotting against him, he "never directly or indirectly retaliated," remaining for too long a "silent sufferer" of calculated injuries. Most important, Washington needed to know that as a veiled conspirator, Jefferson was behind "a formed party" bent on dismantling the government.[66]

Jefferson thought himself a guardian of liberty. Hamilton thought himself a model of patience. Washington did not wish to investigate the claims of either of his headstrong advisers. He was interested not in assessing motives but in governing.

CHAPTER SEVEN

Party Spirit

1793

Every consideration private as well as public require a further
sacrifice of your longings for the repose of Monticello. You must
not make your final exit from public life till it will be marked
with justifying circumstances.

—MADISON TO JEFFERSON, MAY 27, 1793

To my fellow-citizens the debt of service has been fully and
faithfully paid. I acknoledge that such a debt exists: that a tour
of duty, in whatever line he can be most useful to his country,
is due from every individual. It is not easy to say perhaps of what
length exactly this tour should be. But we may safely say of
what length it should not be. Not of our whole life,
for instance, for that would be to be born a slave.

—JEFFERSON TO MADISON, JUNE 9, 1793

IN JANUARY 1793 LOUIS XVI WAS GUILLOTINED, AS THE VOLATILE
Jacobins took control of government and buried the liberal ideals of 1789.
When the news reached Philadelphia in March, Jefferson told Madison
that he felt a sense of relief because America's "monocrats" were not deeply
troubled by this latest report of Revolutionary violence. He had just dined
with a large and diverse group of politicos whose casual colloquy ran the
gamut of opinion, from "the warmest jacobinism" to "the most heartfelt
aristocracy"; but not a one was roused to anger, or the kind of condemnation he expected. It appeared to him that it was only the town's squeamish

society women who were shocked by the manner in which the French king had been dispatched. At home in Orange between legislative sessions, Madison took the pulse of "the mass of our Citizens" and discovered that Virginians had bought into "spurious" accounts of the king's innocence that were printed in some newspapers. They felt for Louis the man but not for Louis the monarch.[1]

Even after the execution, many Americans had hopes for the Revolution. General Henry "Light-Horse Harry" Lee, a recent widower and the present governor of Virginia, made plans to sail to France and offer his services on the battlefield. Not until March did he begin having second thoughts about the idea, and only at the end of April did he inform his old comrades Washington and Hamilton of his preparations. Washington replied, with some understatement, that the French faced more significant domestic threats than foreign ones at that moment. There would be "much speculation" if a U.S. governor were to enlist in the armed services of a foreign power. Lee got the message. Instead of sailing, he stayed home and remarried. In the decade that followed, Ann Carter Lee bore Light-Horse Harry a son, Robert Edward, whom he scarcely knew but who was destined to outdo his father on the battlefields of America.[2]

In February 1793 England was officially added to the French Revolutionaries' list of belligerents. Americans learned of the new Anglo-French war in April. Inside France, defense of the state became the justification for revenge against supposed enemies. Aristocracy became, literally, a crime. Civil rights were ignored. This was the age of the Terror, and it would reach high tide in mid-1794. After trials at which defendants were denied counsel, upward of fifteen thousand of the politically suspect met their deaths in a widespread purge.

These events would transform American politics. No power in the United States was capable of calling in a favor with the government during this phase of the Revolution. Based on his intimate knowledge of French politics, William Short saw the Jacobins as demagogues. From his perch in The Hague, he predicted correctly that their reign would be brief: they knew how to inflame the mob but not how to cool it down.

He learned this firsthand. As his beloved Rosalie watched helplessly, her charitable husband, the Duc de La Rochefoucauld, was dragged from their carriage, stoned, and slashed to death. Obtaining passports that permitted him to cross French and Austrian lines, Short left the Netherlands, where he continued to serve as U.S. minister, and sped to Rosalie's side. He proposed marriage to the now-widowed duchess; she refused him but signed over a large portion of the estate to her American lover, who successfully protected the majority of it from confiscation.[3]

The Marquise de Lafayette pleaded with President Washington to send an envoy to arrange her husband's release from prison. Lafayette was under close guard, deprived of many necessities, and for the most part unaware of what was going on in the wider world. She was frustrated because, at this dire moment, the American president seemed inattentive. The marquis had been, as she wrote, "in the chains of the enemy" for six months and the marquise herself under virtual house arrest. She had been able to smuggle out of the country only the one letter to Washington, with the help of an English farmer. At once haunted and disbelieving, the marquise wondered where Washington was when Lafayette needed him: "I confess to you, Sir, that your silence … is perhaps of all our evils the most inexplicable to me."

The president did the only thing he thought possible: he sent her money, in case it was needed. But he did not see that he had any other options. Upon receiving her first letter, he had asked Jefferson to draft a reply, offering "all the consolation I can … consistent with my public character and the National policy." In its final form, it read: "Be assured that I am not inattentive to his condition, nor contenting my self with inactive wishes for his liberation. My affection to his nation & to himself are unabated, & notwithstanding the line of separation which has unfortunately been drawn between them, I am confident that both have been led on by a pure love of liberty & a desire to secure public happiness." Jefferson enclosed a copy to Gouverneur Morris, reminding him to undertake "all prudent efforts" to aid Lafayette.[4]

"Half the Earth Desolated"

War between England and France placed Americans in one of two camps— and for the next several years made political life especially challenging for the Madison-Jefferson coalition. The "rights of man" remained an attractive-sounding slogan, but those who had predicted a smooth course for the progress of liberty struggled now to find in the French experiment the obvious appeal it once had had. When Jefferson learned from William Short of the inhumanity displayed toward their celebrated friends, his instinct was to shame Short into recanting. "You have been … hurried into a temper of mind which would be extremely disrelished if known to your countrymen," he lectured.

Jefferson counseled patience with the Jacobins, convinced that the French nation stood behind them. But his thinking was flawed insofar as he was unable to separate the fate of the French Revolution from the fate of republican principles in America. For Short he defined his domestic opponents: "characters of opposite principles; some of them are high in office, others possessing great wealth, and all of them hostile to France and fondly looking to England as the staff of their hope." He claimed that these usurpers of the American republic were a "little party" but a dangerous one.

In the same letter, composed just after New Year's Day 1793, Jefferson contributed to America's political vocabulary his most unfortunately phrased maxim with respect to the cause of republicanism. Rather than watch the French Revolution fail, he said, "I would have seen half the earth desolated; were there but an Adam & an Eve left in every country, & left free, it would be better than as it now is." Gore Vidal has called this wording "raging melodrama." In defense of the Jacobins, Jefferson was willing to accept the loss of the liberal aristocrats as martyrs in the struggle for a better world.

Conventional hyperbole aside, Jefferson could be mistaken about major matters, as he was here. His habitual hatred of monarchy combined with his compulsive fear that the Hamiltonians espoused republican government "only as a stepping stone to monarchy." As Short remarked at the time of Jefferson's death: "It was most difficult to make him change an opinion." Madison knew this too: both he and Short found ways to accommodate Jefferson's foible. But as a subordinate, Short could say only so much.[5]

Jefferson's cavalier allusion to mass extermination can be explained, but it remains disturbing. He conceived of republican revolution as a global battle against the corrupting power of monarchy. Its success in France would ensure the survival of republicanism in America. Writing to Lafayette a short time before the marquis became a prisoner, he resorted to hyperbolic language when he praised the Frenchman for undertaking heroic efforts toward "exterminating the monster of aristocracy, and pulling out the teeth and fangs of it's [sic] associated monarchy." Jefferson compared the French beast to the "sect" of aristocrats and monocrats he faced in the United States. Not shying from the word *extermination*, though, Jefferson came dangerously close to condoning the actual murder of flesh-and-blood royalists.[6]

His point was that death was part of the price of freedom. It had always been so. Revolution required purification, and sometimes innocent blood was sacrificed in the process. Because he had not yet discovered effective medicine to combat the political contamination introduced by Hamilton, he could envision only a macabre end to the American experiment.

His Adam and Eve allusion, at once a dystopian and a utopian nightmare, was not meant to sound quite as fatalistic as it does today. He summoned up the promise of republicanism, and not just the threat to it, when he called forth the Garden of Eden, a golden age of innocence, a return to first principles and first parents, a perfect, natural relationship untainted by the sins of the flesh. Republicanism required naked simplicity, a state of being in which time-honored virtue was transparent, artifice was stripped away, and even the proverbial lust for power could be overcome. The Enlightenment that Jefferson breathed sometimes took for natural science, or political science, what was in fact a romance of the mind. That deficiency— moralism masquerading as science—was what spawned his eccentricities, sanctioned his rationalizations, hardened his prejudices, and encouraged extravagant language.

Recall that in 1787 Jefferson had justified to Madison "a little rebellion now and then" in defense of Shays's Rebellion, comparing it to the occasional disturbance caused by an ordinary storm. In six years that small storm had magnified into a natural disaster of cataclysmic proportions when he suggested to Short that he was willing to tolerate "half the earth desolated" rather than the failure of the French Revolution. In fact, though, in pursuit of a romantic truth, Jefferson was mixing his biblical allusions, because the image of God decontaminating the earth has more in common with the story of Noah than the Garden of Eden. The metaphorical ark of Jefferson's imagination contained, instead of animals, male and female representatives of every nation.

It is always hard to voice opinions in politics and achieve consistency. It was especially hard in an age of revolutions.

"With a Bleeding Heart"

Toppling monarchy and aristocracy in faraway France was one thing. Responding to an incipient revolution in St. Domingue (now Haiti) was quite another. St. Domingue was the most valuable French outpost in the West Indies. Taking up approximately one-third of the island of Hispaniola, just slightly larger than the state of Vermont, it produced most of the sugar and coffee that European and U.S. markets required, reducing Americans' need to trade with the British and Spanish Caribbean colonies. This made it an important partner to the United States in the post-Revolutionary decades.

The alliance with France at the time of the American Revolution had opened up a thriving trade, which also made it possible for slavery to expand rapidly on the island. Power was concentrated in the hands of a ruthless planter elite, creating a stark demographic imbalance: 35,000 white residents, 30,000 *gens de couleur* (those of mixed-race ancestry), and nearly half a million black slaves.[7]

This oppressive slave system was responsible for the rebellion that swept through the island colony in 1791, but events in France had a decisive impact too. After the French Assembly proclaimed the Declaration of the Rights of Man and the Citizen in 1790, the abolition society Amis des noirs organized a campaign, with the help of *gens de couleur* on both sides of the Atlantic, to grant political rights to free blacks on the island. When this effort failed, a mixed-race militant named Vincent Ogé, fresh from France and in possession of American arms, mounted an insurrection, which was crushed. But then a much larger slave revolt broke out, and hundreds of plantations were destroyed; blacks and whites alike were slaughtered.[8]

Secretary of State Jefferson kept a cautious eye on these events. He sensed that unilateral American action would be seen as interference, and he did not wish to offend the Revolutionary French government. But as news of the rebellion spread, and as whites' accounts of death and destruction (many of them exaggerated to win outside support) reached both France and the United States, Jefferson changed his mind. He felt that the white planters of St. Domingue might turn to London for backing if their appeals were ignored. And if the British were to gain a foothold on the island, U.S. commercial interests would be seriously threatened.[9]

That change of mind is of consequence to the course of American history. "A man attacked by assassins will call for help to those nearest him," Jefferson wrote to William Short, as grim reports came to his desk.[10] Viewing this as the moment to extend meaningful assistance to the colonial government on St. Domingue, he argued that the law of self-defense applied to colonies as well as nations and that in an emergency the nearest ally should come to the aid of the endangered population. It was the early 1790s, and Jefferson was already laying the foundation for what would become known three decades later as the Monroe Doctrine. By identifying a sphere of influence in the Caribbean, he drew a line: America's national interest was at stake wherever instability and violence appeared in its hemisphere.[11]

In a rare moment of agreement in the executive branch, Jefferson, Hamilton, and Washington all concurred that the United States should aid the island's white colonists by selling arms and making money available to the colonial government. The amount expended would be deducted from Revolutionary War loans that the United States still owed France. It was a risky proposition. The French Assembly might reject America's terms, and no one wished to become embroiled in an unpleasant diplomatic dispute with France over money. But Jefferson felt something had to be done. The white islanders were vulnerable and growing increasingly desperate. If they became "disgusted with either France or us," he told Short, Great Britain waited in the wings and would take advantage.[12]

To prevent worse violence, Jefferson wished for the French Revolutionary government to negotiate a compromise with the St. Domingue rebels.[13] Instead, Paris acted aggressively, sending fresh troops to the Caribbean while establishing a commission to oversee the colonial government. The head of that commission, Léger-Félicité Sonthonax, was both a Jacobin and an antislavery advocate. His priority was to destroy royalism and defend French rule at all costs.

A majority of the white planters on St. Domingue were strongly opposed to French Revolutionary policies. Jefferson was correct in his assumption that as early as 1791, some of these planters viewed secession and an alliance with Great Britain as their only hope of retaining power. Sonthonax put down the first planter coup, deporting hundreds of whites in the process. Then after France declared war against England, and British forces made plans for an invasion, Sonthonax called on black insurgents to rally to his side and defend the French Republic. In the summer of 1793 he decreed that all slaves in the colony were free.[14]

Many white planters abandoned the island. Their refuge lay in the United States. Congressman Madison did not appear especially alarmed, but as he corresponded with Edmund Pendleton about the "gloomy" conditions on St. Domingue, the Virginia Assembly passed legislation prohibiting free blacks from entering the state. They feared, of course, that the contagion of rebellion might reach their shores.

Jefferson's reaction to the white immigrants was mixed. He wrote to Monroe that the "fugitives (aristocrats as they are) call aloud for pity and charity." But he preferred that the state governments, not the federal government, provide assistance to them. He claimed that as secretary of state, it was "with a bleeding heart" that he had resolved to deny the refugees any assistance. When a bill came before Congress to support them, Madison took a different position. He did not believe that the Constitution sanctioned congressional funds for acts of charity, but he conceded that the government could draw on the existing U.S. debt to France to provide assistance to the royalist refugees. The bill passed, and money was charged against the debt.[15]

Jefferson was crying crocodile tears for the refugees when he called them "fugitives" (which, to him, connoted criminals of the state) and "aristocrats" (a term obviously indicating that he did not regard their arrival on American shores as a hopeful addition to the young republic). To his daughter Patsy, he was rather more blunt. Informing her that four hundred "aristocrats and monocrats" were to be sent to the United States, he snapped: "I wish we could distribute our 400 among the Indians, who would teach them the lessons of liberty and equality." It is hard to resist smiling at Jefferson's tongue-in-cheek suggestion that the royalist planters be humbled through an internment process and treated as political criminals to be reconditioned in camps run by Native Americans, whose equality was unsupported and whose liberty was routinely threatened.[16]

Even as he mourned slavery's long-term effect on morals, Jefferson condoned the sense of superiority bred among slave owners. Caught between his devotion to the French Revolution and his wariness of slave rebellions, he felt something between contempt and dismay toward the white refugees. He admitted to Monroe that, down deep, he feared "all the West Indies islands will remain in the hands of people of colour, and a total expulsion of whites sooner or later will take place." Seeing St. Domingue in grander terms than others did, Jefferson recalled the dark vision he had put forth in *Notes on Virginia*, in which an eventual race war on the North American continent would lead to the extermination of one or the other race. If St. Domingue was an omen, growing the slave population in the South was a risky prospect. To Monroe again: "It is high time we should foresee the bloody scenes which our children, and possibly ourselves (South of Patowmac) have to wade through, and try to avert them."

Jefferson could not accept that the revolutionary ideology he had for so long embraced—the overthrow of an aristocracy by those who felt oppressed—lay behind the eradication of slavery on St. Domingue. Blaming royalists came naturally to him, but he could not make a real adjustment in his thinking as to the destructive force of racial antagonism. Drawing on his earlier imagery, could he have said that there would be no one left in the Caribbean but a black Adam and Eve? He was unable to reconcile the two global forces of republicanism and racial justice. Jefferson's blind spot caused him to perceive racial conflict as a force beyond human agency, when in fact free blacks and slaves exercised agency as positive revolutionary actors in St. Domingue.[17]

"Hotheaded, All Imagination, No Judgment"

The Western world was trembling. As the Revolution in France grew bloodier and more muddled, Madison and Jefferson needed each other's support more than ever. In April 1793 the political balance in America entirely shifted, as President Washington declared a neutral position with respect to the belligerents. To Madison and Jefferson, it meant that the president had effectively rescinded the 1778 treaty of alliance with France, a diplomatic retreat orchestrated, no doubt, by Hamilton. The larger problem, for Jefferson especially, was less that the Neutrality Proclamation directly harmed France than that it signified Hamilton's full-scale entry into foreign policy making.[18]

The Virginians were backed further into a corner when the new French minister arrived in America and took matters into his own hands. Charles-Edmond Genet landed in South Carolina in April and swept north, addressing crowds in a most undiplomatic voice. Actively encouraging U.S. citizens to pressure their government into abandoning neutrality, Genet transgressed. He annoyed Thomas Jefferson, the best friend Revolutionary France had, by proposing to use U.S. ports to outfit French warships or otherwise prosecute the war against England. Already French privateers were showing off captured British vessels to American crowds.

Jefferson, restless in Philadelphia, wrote to Madison, at Montpelier, about Genet's activities: "Never, in my opinion, was so calamitous an appointment made . . . Hotheaded, all imagination, no judgment, passionate, disrespectful and even indecent to the P[resident] . . . , urging the most unreasonable and groundless propositions, and in the most dictatorial style etc. etc. etc." In early American politics, the terms *all imagination* and *passionate* meant essentially the same thing: lacking the emotional balance required for rational (republican) policy choices. Jefferson was sure that the fanatical French emissary would only play into the hands of the "Anglomen" in America.

Urgent communications moved north and south. Each was a week in transit and confided to trusted servants and reliable Virginia gentlemen who happened to be on the road. Taking no chances, Madison and Jefferson wrote in code where prominent names were mentioned. They knew a crisis was at hand and that they had to do something. At the same time, both understood that any problems caused by Genet would land in the lap of the secretary of state, and Madison could only advise from a distance. After one maddening encounter with the Frenchman, Jefferson admitted to his foremost ally: "He renders my position immensely difficult." Madison, predictably, encouraged Jefferson to talk Genet out of his "folly" before he did any more mischief. Jefferson tried, but the quarrelsome envoy would not listen. He remained a loose cannon.

Washington would not stand for Genet's insulting behavior. Hamilton and Secretary of War Henry Knox took advantage of the situation and went public. Jefferson reported that the two "pressed an appeal to the people with an eagerness I never before saw in them." He had to endure it silently, because public criticism of Genet came with the president's seal of approval.

Madison consulted with Monroe at the Highlands, the latter's place near Monticello, and came up with the only possible solution: an active defense. Genet was, in this calculation, irrelevant. A "republican interest" was under siege in Philadelphia; a gang of pro-English Virginians (the term Madison used for them was "Anglicans") were working up strategies to embarrass any Virginian still attached to the French cause. "The only antidote for their poison," Madison resolved, "is to distinguish between the nation and its Agent"—to insist that Genet did not represent a France that American republicans recognized. Faced with no good choices, Jefferson joined his cabinet colleagues in criticizing Genet, urging his recall, and predicting in a confidential letter to Madison that if Genet were allowed to continue as France's voice in the United States, "he will sink the republican interest."[19]

Neither Madison nor Jefferson was surprised by what happened next: Hamilton set out to destroy what remained of pro-French sentiment in America by writing once again for the newspapers. Waiting until the president had left town to prosecute his case, he used the pseudonym "Pacificus" to inflame opinion. Interpreting the Neutrality Proclamation his own way, he wrote that it was expressly designed to renounce the Franco-American alliance. For those who retained fond memories of French aid in the American Revolution, Hamilton corrected the record by illustrating French compulsions: vengeance and a need to "repair the breach" in "the National glory" brought about by an ignominious defeat at British hands in the colonial war that ended in 1763. America's revolution happened to come along at a time that suited French "calculations" of self-interest. Reminding his readers that King Louis XVI was a "humane kind-hearted man," Hamilton asked rhetorically how Louis could be a "Tyrant," and Lafayette a "Traitor." Genet had opened the door, and Hamilton was the first to walk through.[20]

Jefferson fought back by giving his political allies a rhetorical weapon, premised on his conflation of pro-British policies with corruption. In the first of his several bold outlines characterizing the duality of American politics, he explained: "The line is now drawing so clearly as to shew, on one side, 1. the fashionable circles of Phila., N York, Boston, and Charleston (natural aristocrats), 2. merchants trading on British capitals. 3. paper men, (all the old tories are found in some one of these descriptions). On the other side are 1. merchants trading on their own capitals. 2. Irish merchants. 3. tradesmen, mechanics, farmers and every other possible description of our citizens."

Drawing a line in the sand, Jefferson claimed for his side the small, provincial, modest, and hard-working of the nation. (Of course, when he used the innocuous word *farmers*, he concealed the truth about his prime constituency: wealthy, slave-owning, aristocratic Virginians.) As he promoted the average freeholder's values, he identified his enemy as two essential types: the armchair speculator, a pompous, ineffective, and parasitic species that produced nothing of value; and the men of commerce who thrived on their association with the British juggernaut and had transferred loyalty to London.

Jefferson was uncompromising when he relied on classification systems, a tendency explained by his comfort with the order and methods of eighteenth-century science. He took his formulation to a private meeting with Washington and complained about "the wealthy Aristocrats, the Merchants connected closely with England, the new created paper fortunes." At a time when France was mired in confusion, would the president see through the smoke screen, as he did, and understand who actually posed the greatest threat to the young republic? All Jefferson could reasonably hope was that Washington kept an open mind.[21]

The spring and summer of 1793 were long months of nervous anticipation for Madison and Jefferson. For as long as possible, Washington had resisted taking sides in the conflict between France and England. But as Hamilton amassed influence, the two realized that they would be unable to stem the tide. The 1792 elections had not appreciably changed the composition of the national government, which, to Jefferson especially, meant that popular opinion was excluded from the halls of power. From this perspective, it seemed no exaggeration to suggest that monarchy might result if Congress did not reconstitute itself as a popular body, as the Constitution intended. Outsiders needed an uncorrupted friend among the insiders. That was who Jefferson had convinced himself he was.

Madison also adopted the term *monocrats* to describe a party so enamored with combinations of power that it would at some point find a comfortable consensus in monarchy. To Monroe, he was perhaps even more unreserved than he was in writing to Jefferson: Genet was "a madman," he charged; and "Anglicans and Monocrats from Boston to Philada" were running off at the mouth. Madison's vocabulary most often expressed the philosophical script of the thinking man's founder, the Madison whom history remembers; but at times such as these the largely unrecorded vernacular of the political activist surfaced. This was the Madison known only to his immediate political circle.[22]

At Jefferson's request—"For god's sake, take up your pen," he cried out—Madison rose to the occasion as "Helvidius," rebutting Hamilton's "Pacificus" in August and September 1793. He questioned the extent of the president's authority, arguing the law of nations in five prominently featured newspaper articles. He charged that the arguments of "Pacificus" represented nothing less than a reiteration of British modes of conduct. What Madison wrote as "Helvidius" was good political science, highly legalistic and, as such scholarship often is, outstandingly uninspiring.

Still, these essays matter. The two who had collaborated as "Publius" were meeting again in print, this time as dire opponents. Madison's main objection was Hamilton's twisting of the Constitution's language. In reassigning to the executive primary power in all foreign policy matters, he was relegating Congress to a subordinate (and ineffectual) role. In making his case, Madison used Hamilton's own words from *The Federalist* against him, because "Publius" had clearly stated that the power to make treaties was "to partake more of a legislative than of the executive character."

Washington's Neutrality Proclamation made the president the "organ of disposition" with regard to war and peace and in so doing seriously undermined the ability of Congress to act independently. This, Madison insisted, was wrong. Now Congress faced the unpleasant prospect of offending the president by opposing him; or it could avoid conflict and passively acquiesce to the executive's announced policy. The republic was untested, and the first president had not been criticized in this way before.

Congress had been granted the power to declare war—a logic repeatedly defended during the Constitutional Convention—in order to prevent the executive from using wars to augment its power. Foreseeing potential danger if Congress should sacrifice its duty to stop the executive from making unilateral decisions regarding war, Madison was cautioning against what critics since the Vietnam War era have come to regard as the modern imperial presidency.[23]

The Latin pseudonym "Helvidius" was not capriciously chosen. Madison's alter ego, in this instance, was a Roman official of the first century A.D. who promoted *demokratia,* was exiled for his opinions, and eventually executed by order of the emperor. Identifying with the honorable Helvidius, Madison was saying that "Pacificus" was something other than a peacemaker: he was a monarchist threatening republican ruin.[24]

"Inveloped in the Rags of Royalty"

Madison was Jefferson's pillar of support during these tense times. But how long could Jefferson withstand the infighting? He was getting nowhere in cabinet debates and was sick of the increasingly hostile environment. During the summer of 1793 he told the president that he wished to resign his office effective September 30. He had let Madison know of his resolve back in May; and Madison, predictably, refused to let him off easily. "Every consideration private as well as public require a further sacrifice of your longings for the repose of Monticello," he maintained. It was not the first time he had met Jefferson's protest.

Jefferson came back with a literary defense of his right to the "tranquility" of home. He argued, in an affecting if weepy style, that his debt of public service had been paid in full. "The motion of my blood no longer keeps time with the tumult of the world," he said. This letter, with its poetic effusions, was something different from what Jefferson typically wrote to Madison, presumably because he expected it to find its way into the public press.

The motion of his blood? The tumult of the world? Where did this gut-wrenching language lead? "It leads me to seek for happiness in the lap and love of my family," he wrote, "in the society of my neighbors and my books, in the wholesome occupations of my farm and my affairs, in an interest or affection for every bud that opens, in every breath that blows around me, in an entire freedom of rest or motion, of thought or incogitancy, owing account to myself alone of my hours and actions." Contrasting his domestic ideal with the political scene, he built up to a mighty expression of regret: "Worn down with labours from morning till night, and day to day...committed singly in desperate and eternal context against a host who are systematically undermining the public liberty and prosperity..., cut off from my family and friends, my affairs [i.e., his plantation economy] abandoned to chaos and derangement, in short giving every thing I love, in exchange for every thing I hate." For Jefferson, a son of the Virginia gentry, national politics had become a barren profession as well as an unbearable personal sacrifice.

He moved from self-pitying speech to a nearly analogous worry for the health of George Washington—and by its language, this part of the letter was not intended for public eyes. The office of president had become onerous: "Little lingering fevers have been hanging about him for a week or ten days, and have affected his looks most remarkably. He is also extremely affected by the attacks made and kept up on him in the public papers. I think he feels those things more than any person I ever yet met with."

If one accepts Jefferson's view, the president's so-called supporters were hampering him by elevating him. Jefferson recalled Madison saying to him sometime before that "satellites and sycophants" pushing the ceremonial trappings of the presidency could not but have ill effect. Jefferson was now suggesting to Madison that Washington might be trapped in those trappings: "Naked he would have been sanctimoniously reverenced. But inveloped in the rags of royalty, they can hardly be torn off without laceration."

The rags of royalty. It was a perfect paradox for the republican thinker to bring into play. In his tacit acceptance of a quasi-royal court, Washington could no longer be seen as an innocent. In 1793 the executive branch was bound to those whom Hamilton had openly and wantonly embraced two years earlier as "the *monied* interest of every state." America was heading in the wrong direction, and as president, Washington was doing nothing to resist.[25]

Madison and Jefferson saw the world around them as one where power corrupted. They seemed not to grasp that Washington was a serious-minded man of business who hated inefficiency. What made him a mature military commander had also made him amenable to a central government with a dynamic executive. The raw material he had at his disposal—the citizenry—was a hodgepodge he could not count on to mobilize effectively. People needed direction, and government required good organization. Madison had believed this too, not long ago. But as Madison rejected the Hamiltonian vision in favor of the Republican theory of checks on the concentration of power, Washington did not veer from the Federalist assignment of power. Madison and Jefferson prized efficiency, just as Washington did. The difference arose over the emphasis they placed on the principle of constitutional balance—Madison and Jefferson felt they were engaged in preserving it while Hamilton was shamelessly defying it.

One sign of the uphill struggle that Virginia Republicans faced was the failure of the Giles resolutions to result in Hamilton's censure. Like Madison, William Branch Giles was a graduate of Princeton; like Jefferson, he had studied the law under George Wythe. The Virginia native had recently arrived in the House of Representatives, full of boisterous energy and unafraid of tangling with Hamilton. Early in 1793, whether or not he was aware of the treasury secretary's adulterous liaison and resulting payments to the offended husband, which the Republicans had decided to bury, Giles proposed a detailed investigation into Hamilton's conduct while in office. Could the secretary submit evidence to verify that he was not misusing public funds?

Congressman Giles was speaking for the silent Madison and Jefferson—quite literally. Notes in Jefferson's hand have survived. He appears to have penned many of the resolutions Giles read in the House, which were filtered through Madison before being finished by Giles. Madison believed that Hamilton had taken funds borrowed in Europe to discharge America's foreign debt and placed that money in the national bank "for the benefit of speculators." In his dramatic letter to Washington of September 1792, in which he complained of Hamilton's "tissue of machinations" against his country, Jefferson had also accused his high-and-mighty colleague of "shuffling" millions between U.S. and European accounts without reporting on what he was doing. Giles served as messenger to make this suspicion public.

Early in 1793 Jefferson had asked Washington to open a separate executive branch inquiry into Hamilton's financial dealings, and Washington refused him. Was Jefferson being paranoid? In this case, the answer is no. He had every reason to suspect Hamilton's motives. The treasury secretary unapologetically meddled in the business of every department within the executive branch. Some people are happy to be team players; Alexander Hamilton was not. He did not understand boundaries. He assumed he knew best, and he did what he wanted.

Passion-driven, hard-nosed, and perhaps less brilliant than his academic pedigree implied, William Branch Giles introduced a cluster of resolutions at different times during the early months of 1793. When all was said and done, though, the Virginians came up empty. They were outdone by the inspired and imperious treasury secretary. With great dispatch, Hamilton provided facts and figures that made the allegations appear weak, or at least unproven. The Giles resolutions made Hamilton pause, but they did not stop him for very long.[26]

Still, the ranks of activist Virginians swelled. Edmund Pendleton's nephew and protégé, redheaded, thirty-nine-year-old John Taylor of Caroline, was a U.S. senator and an increasingly important Madison-Jefferson ally. In May 1793 he began work on what would be, when complete, a stinging pamphlet condemning Hamilton's vision of the banking system. Monroe immediately saw its promise, alerting Madison to Taylor's talent and praising the "many useful & judicious observations addressed in his humorous style concluding in the sentimt. that the bank shod. be demolished." After Monroe had weighed in, Taylor asked Madison to review his work and help to improve it; he asked the same of his venerable uncle. He initially hesitated to present it to Jefferson, but only because he did not wish to add to the secretary of state's burdens. Eventually he asked Madison to forward it. A preview of Taylor's pamphlet appeared in Freneau's *National Gazette* under the unassuming heading "Reflections on Several Subjects." It was an anonymous column, printed without Taylor's permission. Madison rejoiced to Monroe: "Mr. J. is in raptures with the performance of our friend."

Freneau introduced the unnamed author to his readers, saying there was a certain party in America whose "persecuting spirit" was more akin to the Vatican than to any more modern political body. It was a mere "party" though it styled itself a "government"; it was a religion established by law, demanding faith ("blind idolatry") while refusing to confront truth. In taking on the national bank, Taylor explained that instead of acting in the public's interest, it was deviously contrived by the party in power "to accelerate . . . a political moneyed engine." The previously unheralded polemicist loaded his pamphlet with ready axioms: "If a bank will stick by a minister, a minister will stick by a bank." In short, the institution was a "blot" on America's republican character.[27]

Around the same time Taylor's uncle wrote a warm but testy letter to his old acquaintance George Washington. In the space of a page or two, the veteran Revolutionary concisely outlined what he saw as Hamilton's power-amassing moves, asking Washington, in effect, whether he could see what was happening around him. Referring to the treasury secretary not by name but only as "the Gentleman at the head of that Department," Pendleton urged a thorough probe. Then, to soften his message, he concluded by telling the president that he would not feel hurt if all his suggestions were ignored, provided they were accepted as "the well meant reveries of a Fireside Politician, who never had much Pretentions to the Character of a Statesman, but cordially hates all Intrigues, Finesse and Strategems in Government." Edmund Pendleton had lost neither his commitment to principle nor his ready wit.[28]

"Fermentation"

Before his friend from Orange would allow him to retire, Jefferson was obliged to sit through a good many more cabinet meetings, all of them unpleasant for him. The meetings of August 1793 pivoted on what he described to Madison as "three speeches of ¾ of an hour each" by Hamilton, outlining possible ways to respond to the dangers posed by French ideas. Each argument was aimed at convincing Washington to "dismount" as "head of the nation" and take up as "the head of a party"—in effect declaring war against "the Republican party." As he committed these words on the page, Jefferson made it clear to Madison that he was not just airing private grievances to a friend—no, these were the very words he had uttered to the president *in Hamilton's presence*. For once, he had not held back. There was no point in maintaining false courtesies anymore.[29]

Washington and Jefferson met prior to one of those August cabinet meetings in which Jefferson was monitoring his timepiece to chronicle Hamilton's long-windedness. The president confessed to him that he did not know what to make of the "fermentation" taking place in political society. Jefferson tells us—we have no evidence other than his private notes—that he tried to assure Washington that the emerging Republicans continued to esteem their president and trusted fully in his republican sympathies. Responding to Washington's unhidden concern that what he saw printed in the newspapers could easily spin out of control, Jefferson reminded him how his own words, ever since the *Rights of Man* blowup, had been "caught, multiplied, misconstrued, and even fabricated and spread" to do him injury. Though Jefferson continued to go through the motions of trying to persuade Washington that he should see Hamilton's crowd as "the monarchical party," nothing in Jefferson's notes suggests that he believed their meeting convinced the president of anything. Washington did, however, convince the secretary of state to stay on through the end of 1793.[30]

Jefferson had previously given Washington his reasons for resigning. Hamilton too expressed his intent to leave within a year. The two senior cabinet officers possessed superior managerial expertise, and yet the executive was in shambles. Washington would not have agreed to a second term if he had known in advance that Jefferson and Hamilton would depart early. Now he had three more years in office and, under these inflamed circumstances, did not know who had the right skills and the right temperament to take over at State and Treasury. He told Jefferson that his first choice for State was Madison but held out little hope that Madison would oblige him.

Jefferson was not angered just by Hamilton, who could not be reasoned with in the least. He was also greatly disappointed in Madison's old friend Edmund Randolph, the first attorney general of the United States, and roundly criticized him for his wishy-washy whiggism. In the cabinet, after Jefferson made his final stand against Hamilton and Knox, who always voted as a bloc, Randolph, instead of helping him, hedged.

For Jefferson, the most exasperating thing Randolph did was to suggest that Washington delay (not dismiss) carrying out Hamilton's proposition that the president issue a public message, instructing the American people to guard against French principles. Jefferson interpreted the move as rank hypocrisy: Randolph was saying, in effect, that it was all right to alienate the French in stages. "He is the poorest Cameleon I ever saw," Jefferson fumed in a letter to Madison. The sticky-tongued attorney general had no color of his own but reflected his environment: "When he is with me he is a whig, when with H[amilton] he is a tory, when with the P[resident] he is what he thinks will please him." This was an insurmountable problem for Jefferson. Randolph's inconsistency gave Hamilton a clear edge. Randolph was the swing vote in the cabinet, and the president, Jefferson stressed, "acquiesces *always* in the majority."[31]

But nothing really suggests that Randolph was indecisive, or chameleonlike, as Jefferson was charging. He was his own man, apt to follow Jefferson in many, but by no means all, policy disputes in the cabinet. Jefferson was being a bit cranky in expecting Randolph to agree all the time. Anyway, it is perfectly clear that Hamilton never mistook Randolph for an ally.[32] Nor did Madison automatically endorse Jefferson's view. When the president sent his attorney general to Virginia to get a sense of popular opinion on the neutrality issue, Jefferson urgently appealed to Madison to contact Randolph's brother-in-law, Wilson Cary Nicholas, and to make sure that Nicholas persuaded Randolph that Virginians were unified in their support of France. Madison did not see the same urgency Jefferson did and reassured him that Nicholas would "fairly state the truth & that alone is wanted." But even after hearing from Madison, Jefferson left nothing to chance. He considered compromise under present circumstances a sign of weakness and vacillation. In simple terms, Jefferson was reproaching Randolph for getting in the way of his war on Hamilton.[33]

Adding to Jefferson's woes, Citizen Genet still refused to calm down. The notorious French minister came before the public again and again, financing the defense of an American who stood trial for enlisting on a French privateer. With Attorney General Randolph arguing the government's case, and Hamilton aiding him, Genet's side still won. Being linked to Genet was a "cruel dilemma" for him, Jefferson told Madison. Emboldened after the trial, the Frenchman placed ads in American newspapers soliciting new recruits and comparing them to those French who had served in the American Revolution.

Genet repeatedly circumvented Jefferson, as he set out to humiliate Washington. During that already wearisome month of August, he insisted that the president publish in the papers an unambiguous statement in defense of the envoy's right to continue on the same course. "My conduct," Genet informed the president, "has accordingly been marked with all the energy and frankness which ever characterize a true republican." It fell to Jefferson to admonish Genet that it was "not the established course" for any diplomat to correspond directly with the president.[34]

As if this were not enough, Genet offered French government backing to military expeditions designed to capture the Spanish territories of Louisiana and East Florida. He contacted George Rogers Clark in Louisville, who was ready to lead the assault on New Orleans. This was not a new idea. There is circumstantial evidence that before Genet arrived on the scene, Jefferson was consulted on Clark's suitability for such a mission. Jefferson, like Madison, was concerned about the fading attachment of America's western settlers to a federal government unresponsive to their quest for land and need for protection against Indians. The French government had no qualms about providing such support.

The Virginians were as keen as ever to secure the rights of Americans to ply the Mississippi. What may have happened is that the secretary of state, initially open to westerners' claims, changed his mind after Genet embarrassed him, then forbade American citizens from joining any Louisiana filibuster in violation of neutrality laws. Under the circumstances, he had little choice but to make it clear that the United States was not at war with Spain.

The ironies compounded. As the Jacobin leader Robespierre took over in Paris, France exited the filibuster game. Calling off the Louisiana and Florida projects, the Jacobins demanded Genet's return in shackles. The move came in large measure as a result of a letter Jefferson wrote at the behest of the president and a united cabinet, recommending the minister's recall. Genet's failure to respect American neutrality had led him to poor judgments. He had not alienated all parts of the country, but he had embarrassed Jefferson. Genet had no choice now but to act to save his own skin; and so the obnoxious emissary of republican brotherhood fled to New York State. Next, the French demanded the recall of the unrepublican Gouverneur Morris. Tit for tat.

All ended well for Genet. President Washington magnanimously granted him political asylum, and in 1794 he married a daughter of Governor George Clinton, earning American citizenship ten years later. Once a provocateur, Genet spent the remainder of his life farming in well-deserved obscurity except for occasional labor as the publisher of others' pamphlets. His replacement, Jean-Antoine-Joseph Fauchet, though more prudent than his predecessor, would prove equally controversial and equally enfeebled by the Hamiltonians.[35]

"A Man As Timid As He Is"

In mid-1793 Madison's longtime Philadelphia landlady, Mary House, died. "She extinguished almost like a candle," Jefferson apprized him in June. Her daughter Eliza House Trist would sell the boardinghouse where, since he first joined Congress, Madison had resided for a greater amount of time than he lived with his family at Montpelier.

The sale of the House-Trist establishment redirected the life of Madison's former slave Billey Gardner. Brought north by his master in 1780, Billey had run away three years later, only to be recaptured and sold, without acrimony, but sold nonetheless, into a servitude in Pennsylvania of seven years' duration. After 1790 he found jobs in Philadelphia. Mrs. House employed him for a period of time, and Madison occasionally paid him to carry goods to Virginia. Jefferson interacted with Billey as well, utilizing the services of his wife, Henrietta, a washerwoman. Finally Billey found work as a merchant seaman, while his parents remained as slaves at Montpelier. Tragically, he would perish off the coast of Louisiana not long after.[36]

Billey Gardner's conditional existence—his curious passage from slavery to freedom—was acted out on a larger scale in Congress, but with far less humanity than Madison had shown. A court case in Pennsylvania involving the rendition of a fugitive slave from Virginia resulted in the passage of the Fugitive Slave Act of 1793, fortifying the constitutional understanding that slaves were property and not afforded the rights of U.S. citizens to a fair trial. The *Annals of Congress* denoted it "an Act respecting fugitives from justice, and persons escaping from the service of their masters." Anyone who tried to rescue or in any way interfered in the return of a "fugitive from labor" was to be fined $500. Without any protest over its constitutionality, and few votes in opposition, President Washington signed the bill, and it became law.[37]

In August and September 1793 death descended on Philadelphia. While Jefferson was still dealing with repercussions of the Genet fiasco, an epidemic of unprecedented proportions struck the city of thirty thousand. Though fairly common in the tropics, yellow fever had not been visited upon Philadelphia for some thirty years. Nearly half the city fled to the uninfected countryside, among them the president of the United States. Government was at a standstill. By the time the contagion passed, several thousand were dead, including the attorney John Todd, who left behind a wife, Dolley (the future Mrs. Madison), and their one-year-old son. What made the fever "yellow" was the discoloration of the skin of its victims; in the final phase of the disease, nausea and internal bleeding led to delirium and coma.

Death on so large a scale produced scenes of daily horror, with many more rotting corpses in sight than there were brave nurses. Approximately half of those who exhibited symptoms eventually died from the yellow fever. While it raged, Jefferson refused to flee the stricken city and in the midst of the horror found a new way to unload on his chief adversary. Writing to Madison in early September, he announced, almost giddily, that Hamilton was ill. From sources close to the patient, Jefferson had learned that Hamilton's life was in danger. But Jefferson had his doubts. He knew Hamilton's tendencies as well as anyone and figured he could read meaning into his ailing enemy's behavior: Supposedly, an overwrought Hamilton had been pacing back and forth in recent days, certain that he was going to catch yellow fever and die. Friends of Hamilton's presumed that he was in fact suffering from nothing more than the common, nonlethal "autumnal fever."

All this gave Jefferson license to slur Hamilton. In a letter to Madison, he wrote offhandedly: "A man as timid as he is on the water, as timid on horseback, as timid in sickness, would be a phænomenon if the courage of which he has the reputation on military occasions were genuine." This was a rejoinder to a little newspaper nastiness Hamilton was responsible for under the pseudonym of "SCOURGE," which sarcastically celebrated Jefferson for his exemplary bravery as governor.

It had not been that long since Hamilton had mocked Madison's and Jefferson's "womanish" resentment toward England. All who knew the slightly built Madison would have been aware of his exaggerated health fears—*he* could legitimately be called timid according to that definition. But Jefferson, aside from his migraines, was a healthy specimen. Of the two Virginians whom Hamilton had termed "womanish," Jefferson took insults less well. His definition of manliness did not require participation in warfare or private duels, which he regarded as barbaric rather than brave. And despite his bookishness, Jefferson did not lead a sedentary life by any means; he was a man who knew lust. If he had been cowardly in the way that "SCOURGE" implied, he would not have been able to devise the icy tactics he did to combat Hamilton, well knowing that Hamilton would take extreme measures in return. Jefferson was not one to panic.

He was clearly glad for the opportunity to refute the headstrong Hamilton's wide reputation for machismo, and it is hard to imagine anyone other than Madison with whom he could so easily share such a cruel joke. Four days after his "timidity" letter he was obliged to amend his diagnosis in a quick update on the situation in Philadelphia. "The fever spreads faster," he jotted to Madison. "Deaths are now about 30. a day. It is in every square of the city. All flying [i.e., leaving] who can." And as to Hamilton: "H had truly the [yellow] fever, and is on the recovery, and pronounced out of danger." So it was more than "autumnal fever." Hamilton had contracted the deadly virus and survived it.

Nevertheless Jefferson had proved his own resolve, and courage, by standing his ground. As Washington and Secretary Knox left town, and as Hamilton lay ill, he remained behind so as to avoid, he said, an even greater panic. He told Madison that "serious ills" would have ensued if the entire executive were absent from Philadelphia. And yet this political soldier wanted nothing more than to finish his tour of duty and to retire, once and for all, to Monticello.[38]

Having made his point, Jefferson left Philadelphia mid-September and visited with Madison at Montpelier. Not long afterward, Madison followed up with a visit to Monticello, where Monroe joined them to strategize. Before they returned north in November for another session of Congress, a dramatic change occurred that would profoundly affect Madison's future. His younger brother Ambrose, age thirty-eight, died at the family estate. Ambrose had run the Montpelier plantation; now that duty passed to James, Jr., who soon learned of a small reversal of fortune: most of his Kentucky land was improperly surveyed and the purchase thereby voided. He proceeded to sell his land in the Mohawk region of New York in order to put up a gristmill at Montpelier, passing up the chance for substantial profit if he had only held on to it for a few more years. Responsibilities and misgivings multiplied.[39]

"What Caused the Fall of Athens?"

Philadelphia's self-anointed "republican interest" was the first to establish a "democratic society," and the Hamiltonians promptly claimed that Genet had started it. It was just too easy to bestow the label "Jacobin" on them, and soon "American Jacobin" became a common slur applied to the Madison-Jefferson axis. In 1793 democratic societies spread across the country, a network of popular political assemblies akin to the committees of correspondence that had flourished on the eve of the American Revolution. While not directly the arm of a named party, the members of these societies were all critics of Hamiltonian policies. Madison would report to Jefferson that in the case of the New York Democratic Society, Edward Livingston, a prominent member, could not have been elected to Congress in 1794 without its exertions. Livingston's older brother Robert was a signatory of the Declaration of Independence, and Edward, a Princetonian, had the talent and enthusiasm to jump right into the fracas as a key Madison ally.[40]

With 33,000 inhabitants, New York had recently surpassed Philadelphia as the most populous U.S. city and was beginning to rival it in political speech as well. A characteristic example of what was happening is contained in the published address of William Wyche, a liberal-minded

British-born attorney who immigrated to America, attained citizenship, and now resided in Manhattan. At Tammany Hall (as yet more a social than a political gathering place), he made an appeal for calm and cautioned against "the influence of interested faction on the mind of man." With strength of mind, he declared in favor of a new brand of independence: "The idle distinctions of aristocrat and democrat I would bury in oblivion, and treat no one as enemies but those who would deprive me of my liberty." In a time of intense competition, the attorney's message—"Liberty ought to have no enemies"—was modest and conciliatory. The distinctions drawn between Whig and Tory, Clintonian and Jay-ite, and, most recently, aristocrat and democrat, served only to destroy the general good, he said.

His oration was titled "Party Spirit," a phrase with a long history, and for the next several years it was used steadily as an admonition to both sides on the American political scene. The original was penned by Joseph Addison in London in 1711, as part of the *Spectator* series of essays, which were still widely read and greatly admired in America in the mid-1790s. As relations within Congress and the executive, and between those two bodies, deteriorated, U.S. pamphleteers and newspapermen cribbed this passage most often:

> There cannot a greater judgment befall a country than such a dreadful spirit of division as rends a government into two distinct people, and makes them greater strangers and more averse to one another, than if they were actually two different nations. The effects of such a division are pernicious to the last degree..., fatal both to men's morals and their understandings; it sinks the virtue of a nation, and not only so, but destroys even common sense.
>
> A furious party-spirit, when it rages in its full violence, exerts itself in civil war and bloodshed; and when it is under its greatest restraints, naturally breaks out in falsehood, detraction, calumny, and a partial administration of justice. In a word, it fills a nation with spleen and rancour, and extinguishes all the seeds of good-nature, compassion and humanity.[41]

In an "unseasonable" state assembly contest that heated up in 1747, the *New-York Gazette* had editorialized against "violent party spirit." The *Boston Evening-Post* had seen the writing on the wall in 1772, when a devotee of the penetrating style of *Spectator* appealed to enlightened morals: "A FURIOUS party spirit, when it rages in its full violence, exerts itself in civil war and bloodshed." In July 1776, while contemplating the shaky partnership among leading gentlemen in Virginia, Edmund Pendleton was reminded of "the Spirit of Party, that bane of all public Councils," in a letter he wrote to Jefferson. The concept lived on as a reminder, an oracle. Its resurfacing in the mid-1790s, though, was different, because the Addisonian admonition suddenly became pervasive.

Left unchecked, the spirit of party had always brought chaos to a liberty-loving republic. "What caused the fall of Athens?" the lawyer Wyche posed: "Faction: the spirit of discord prevailed, and liberty was destroyed." Party spirit had a "pernicious" tendency to "make honest men hate one another," another wrote, reiterating the message of *Spectator*. "A man should not allow himself to hate even his enemies." *Spectator* provided the code words meant to prompt a softening of the accusatory script, but it was all to no avail.

By the end of 1793 it had become axiomatic that partisan "zeal" led to "calumny"—defamation and misrepresentation. But that is all that the two sides in political debate agreed on. Each denied that it was doing anything to contribute to the problem. As a species of invective belonging to their mutual blame game, the acrimonious "party-spirit" may have been used equally by those supportive of the Washington administration and those critical of it, but the term was used more excitedly in pro-administration publications. For instance, the *Mirrour,* a conservative newspaper published in Concord, New Hampshire, would open the year 1794 with a warning about democratic societies, "detached clubs…constantly involved in contradictions" (which meant hypocrisy). The "boisterous republicans," "mighty liberty folks," merely pretended to support a generous "rotation in office," when what they really aimed for was the opposite: "They exert every nerve to keep their own party in office for life." For papers like the *Mirrour,* the Republicans alone were spreading hate: "This party spirit is blind and headstrong; it never seeks truth; but with a mind made upon every subject it seeks for facts and opinions that favour his premature judgment." The piece concluded with *Spectator*'s warning that party spirit "extinguishes all the seeds of good nature, compassion, and humanity."

Shouts in earnest, appeals to common sense, came at a time of increasing alienation. Each side claimed legitimacy when it branded the other a "faction." Words carried weight. John Adams adopted the prevailing vocabulary in a perplexed letter to his wife, Abigail, in late 1792: "I am really astonished at the blind Spirit of Party which has Lived on the whole soul of

this Jefferson. There is not a Jacobin in France more devoted to Faction."
The New Yorker Washington Irving, who came of age in the 1790s and first
came to prominence as a political satirist, fed the following line to the pro-
tagonist of one of his later, lesser-known tales: "The republic of letters is
the most factious and discordant of all republics, ancient or modern." The
bookish men whom history chooses to remember as political geniuses were
really gladiators, as frantic and fearful as they were inspired.[42]

Public discord was of more than rhetorical concern: it went against
everything the leadership group had been taught growing up. Rational discourse was at the heart of the eighteenth century's ideal of civil society. Enlightenment thinkers had imagined that the free exchange of ideas in
public forums, whether set in type or voiced in small gatherings of educated citizens, created an environment conducive to intellectual and moral
progress. Those who joined the democratic clubs drew upon this ideal.
They defended themselves with appeals to open and transparent debate
and freedom of speech—only to be labeled destructive to civil society. Who
was right and who was wrong? Both sides could not be right.

This conundrum explains why Madison and Jefferson were so invested
in public opinion. In their world, productive conversation took place on
neutral terrain (beyond the control of government) where government
abuses could be safely exposed. Faction, on the other hand, poisoned the
body politic. It blinded and it inflamed the worst passions of the people.
The American republic shook when vehicles of public opinion such as Freneau's *National Gazette,* designed to advance debate, became virulent organs
of factional rage. The dissemination of knowledge quickly turned into
something else, as a new breed of journalist, influenced by the London tradition of slander and satire, took center stage. Refusing to adhere to the
conventions of civil discourse, the partisan editor served up scandal to
readers whose appetite for salacious news appeared insatiable. Faction,
once ignited, stayed lit.

This was how the two political parties known as Federalist and Republican came to be. "In every political society, parties are unavoidable," Madison had stated in January 1792. But when his statement proved true over
the ensuing year, most did not like what they saw; the organized party was
not greeted as a healthy means of managing political competition.

As two national tickets slowly but inexorably took form, a quiet war
arose over whose definition would ultimately apply to quintessential political labels. Freneau's *National Gazette* used the term *federalist* inclusively, tak-

ing in every devotee of republican government; but John Fenno, editor of the pro-administration *Gazette of the United States,* would not cede the term to Freneau's readers: "The federalists, as they call themselves, speak of the constitution as a thing full of dangerous principles." Fenno then identified the opposition's stand as "pretend federalism."

Thomas Greenleaf's *New-York Journal,* friendly to Madison and Jefferson, took the next step in party definition in the summer of 1793, by explaining the absorption of former antifederalists into the Madisonian position: "In the year 1788 every one knew how to define an antifederalist . . . The constitution once adopted, the appellation should have ceased . . . A modern anti-federalist, then, is one who is sincerely attached to the constitution of his country, which proceeded from the people." In contrast were former federalists who had made government the "servant" of "a host of speculators." They were not to be called federalists, because Madison's supporters had never abandoned the name. The *New-York Journal* offered an easy definition: *federal* was "an English word, strictly meaning a leagued confederacy, a compact."[43]

But as the months went by, the word *republican* became the first choice of the widening anti-administration alliance, while those who supported the administration identified themselves with the "benign influences of the federal government" that extended to all states of the Union. They referred to themselves as "true friends of the constitution" and "friends to peace freedom and government" but saw no need to contrive any fancier name for their creed than *federal* or *federalist.* Initially some experimented with the more comprehensive *federal republican,* which did not stick at the time but would revive on conservative newspaper banners during Jefferson's and Madison's presidencies.

The banner of a newly established newspaper in Baltimore read *Federal Intelligencer.* Its editorial policy was to reveal the hypocrisy in its opponents' naming practices and to expose the crankiness of those out of power: "It might seem, from the outs, or Antifederalists, as they were called, that they are the only friends of liberty and the constitution, while the federalists are become enemies to liberty and the government . . . Instead of Antifederalist you are to use the word republican, and in place of federalist you are to use the word aristocrat." Lumping together all self-styled republicans as disorderly "democrats," many of whom were recent arrivals to America (which, to most minds, meant quarrelsome Scots and Irishmen), the *Federal Intelligencer* insisted that no "democrat" had ever taken part in "one single act to advance the independence of America"; yet these same troublemakers were trying to convince native-born citizens that "the old federalist cares nothing about the people, and wishes to destroy the government."[44]

American newspapers were not great profit centers, but hard-working and increasingly contentious printer-editors believed that their aggressive efforts to earn the public's trust were paying off for them in other ways. People paid attention. Politicians could not ignore them. During the next two years the editors' role in electoral politics enlarged as they set the country's Republicans and Federalists against one another. Accusing and satirizing at will, the partisan press moved from population centers into smaller and smaller communities.[45]

Party spirit had transformed the landscape. Fearless and full of life, the American newspaper of the 1790s merrily rejected long-established modes of public decorum and took a sledgehammer to the character and dignity of *homo politicus*.

CHAPTER EIGHT

The Effects of Whiskey on Reputation
1794–1795

*On the subject of the Debt, the Treasury faction is spouting on the
policy of paying it off as a great evil . . . Hamilton has made a long
Valedictory Rept. on the subject. It is not yet printed, and I have not
read it. It is said to contain a number of improper things.*

—MADISON TO JEFFERSON, JANUARY 26, 1795

*Hamilton is really a colossus to the antirepublican party.
Without numbers, he is an host within himself.*

—JEFFERSON TO MADISON, SEPTEMBER 21, 1795

ON JANUARY 3, 1794, MADISON OPENED A NEW SESSION OF CON-
gress by introducing a bill that discriminated against nations with which
the United States had no commercial treaty. Without naming Britain, the
proposed legislation was meant to serve as a bargaining chip in ongoing
negotiations. Madison reasoned that trade policy should be based on reciprocity, not fear.

New England merchants carried on a thriving business with Great
Britain, which they did not want to see disturbed. Ninety percent of American imports of manufactured goods were British. Twice as much was imported than sold to Britain. In contrast, France purchased from the United
States seven times what she sold to it. Even as he brought these statistics to
the attention of Congress, Madison felt he was making little headway. He
wrote to Jefferson of "vast exertions by the British party to mislead the people of the eastern states." By "British party," he meant, of course, the pro-
British element in Congress.

No longer in the cabinet since the first of January, Jefferson had removed himself from active politics. He was a full-time planter again, secure in the separate world he had fashioned for himself at Monticello. Though he and Madison had formulated the commerce bill in tandem, he fully expected Madison to bear the brunt of their opponents' criticisms—"the most artful and wicked calumnies," as Madison was soon telling him. It was Madison's name that was associated with the universally discredited Genet mission now. Farmer Jefferson was happy to be out of contention; a few white hairs had begun to appear on his head, and his married daughter Patsy had given him a granddaughter, Anne, and a grandson, Thomas Jefferson Randolph.[1]

As Madison pursued his agenda, a New York newspaper commented on his oratory. He spoke in Congress on trade matters for two and a half hours during which, it was said, "one might hear a pin fall."[2] Yet for all the encomiums heaped upon him as a force in the legislature, he did not universally impress. A new representative from Connecticut wrote to a friend: "A hollow, feeble voice—an awkward, uninteresting manner—a correct style without energy or copiousness—are his distinguishing traits." While crediting him for precision and judgment that were "solid," the critic could not understand why Madison had received so much acclaim for his forensic abilities: "He is wholly destitute of vigour or genius, ardour of mind, and brilliancy of imagination. He has no fire, no enthusiasm, no animation." The new legislator did not deny, however, that the Virginian retained "the most personal influence of any man in the House of Representatives."[3]

Madison's experience in Congress would not be enough to give his party the edge. The various characters we identify as the leaders of the Revolutionary generation understood their peers to be men driven by complex motives. They recognized the growth of partisanship as more than a momentary phenomenon. No one could predict at this point how long the United States would hold together. Allegiances were shifting; schooldays and wartime friendships cooled.

With Jefferson's departure from Philadelphia and the sinking of Madison's proposal to impose discriminatory duties on British merchant ships, a distinct change took place in the executive. As the generally moderate Edmund Randolph tried to fill Jefferson's shoes at the State Department, and the increasingly persuasive Hamilton continued to advise the president, the power dynamic should have been instantly obvious. It was obvious, at least, to George Nicholas, the attorney general of the newly admitted state of Kentucky, whose brother Wilson Cary Nicholas was a standout in the

Virginia House of Delegates. Writing to his old acquaintance Madison, he likened Randolph's new situation to a "bed of thorns," convinced that the exchange of cabinet positions would make him "the mark at which all who are dissatisfied with public measures, will aim their shafts." Nicholas was right on target. What awaited Randolph was sheer misery.[4]

Another change in the executive was the addition of William Bradford. Madison's best friend from Princeton days moved into the attorney generalship. These days, Bradford's politics were much closer to Hamilton's than to Madison's, and the old friends appear not to have had any meaningful contact. From Jefferson's perspective, Washington was being inundated with advice from one side only. Many years later, in his desire to shape historical memory, Jefferson would look back on this time and decide that the president had sunk into senility—for how else could a true republican have bowed to Tory principles?

The senility rationale is not convincing. Washington was not browbeaten into submission: he had expressed plenty of anti-English views over the years. More important, though, the politician-general was greatly sensitive to reputation and wished to be known for wise decisions. Neither Madison, nor Jefferson, nor anyone else could have convinced him that Revolutionary France was moving in the direction of greater stability. As a surrogate father to the inspired Marquis de Lafayette, he appreciated that the wide-eyed French teenager had first sailed to America because he believed in the words of the Declaration of Independence and in national self-determination. But something else prevailed in Washington's mind now: the unruliness of Lafayette's people. This judgment, combined with his recognition of the value of commerce to America's fiscal health, amended his earlier conviction that the United States should not yield to pressure from Britain. In spite of London's refusal to allow American vessels to trade directly with the British West Indies, and in spite of its refusal to abandon the western forts, Washington lent a willing ear to Hamilton, digested his appeals, and decided to risk a less-than-ideal agreement with the late enemy.

It was a foregone conclusion that the president was willing to distance himself from Madison, whose supple mind he had counted on most in 1789–90, while laboring over how to erect a practical, functioning executive. The two would never reconstitute the relationship they had earlier enjoyed, or anything close to it. Their diametrically opposed outlook on democratic speech and democratic societies was leading the president to doubt the congressman's personal loyalty. By 1794 Washington and Madison no longer interacted outside of public functions. Otherwise secure in his judgments, Washington had one weakness that he readily acknowledged: an insufficient knowledge of matters legal and constitutional. Without Madison, he turned almost exclusively to Hamilton for guidance.[5]

At Monticello, Jefferson was making up for the time he had spent away. He paid his back taxes to the county, hired a Scottish gardener, experimented with seeds, set up a nail manufactory manned by teenage slaves, and produced his "mouldboard plough of least resistance," for which the French bestowed a prize. He was also remodeling the house to include its signature dome, based on a design he had seen in Paris. A month into his retirement, he wrote to Edmund Randolph and reiterated how happy he was to be divorced from political squabbles: "I think it is Montaigne who has said that ignorance is the softest pillow on which a man can rest his head. I am sure it is true as to every thing political, and shall endeavor to estrange myself to every thing of that character." Being Jefferson, he could not stop there and ended up confessing to the man who had inherited his position that he still had leftover concerns: "I indulge myself on one political topic only, that is, in [dis]closing to my countrymen the shameless corruption of a [por]tion of the representatives in the 1st. and 2nd. Congresses and their implicit devotion to the treasury." He would not lay his head on that pillow of ignorance.[6]

Madison kept in constant touch. In March alone he wrote to Jefferson seven times, largely to report on the mood in Philadelphia. To undermine Madison's agenda, Hamilton was feeding speeches to William Loughton Smith, a congressman from South Carolina. "Every tittle of it is Hamilton's except the introduction," Jefferson assured Madison after reading one of these. "The sophistry is too fine, too ingenious even to have been comprehended by Smith, much less devised by him." Jefferson also told Madison: "I have never seen a Philadelphia paper since I left it, till those you inclosed me . . . and believe I never shall take another newspaper of any sort. I find my mind totally absorbed in my rural occupations."[7]

Whether or not Jefferson was inviting news briefs, the reports from Philadelphia were not all bad. Madison told him that the new French minister, Jean-Antoine-Joseph Fauchet, was reversing the errors of Genet: "He has the aspect of moderation. His account of things in France is very favorable on the whole. He takes particular pains to assure all who talk with him of the perseverance of France in her attachment to us." However, Madison had also heard that arms for the British were being purchased in New York and elsewhere in the Northeast and shipped on American vessels to the

British West Indies. "This is really horrible," he wrote. "Whilst we allow the British to stop our supplies to the French Dominions, we allow our citizens to carry supplies to hers."

Jefferson proposed taking a hard line and challenging Britain militarily if it decided to go after French possessions in the Caribbean. "Not that the Monocrats and Papermen in Congress want war," he said snidely, with Hamilton's Anglophilia in mind. "But they want armies and debts." It was hard to say what bothered him more: maintaining a national debt that could be used to build a menacing national military, or repressing the military option by making allowances for British power.

To understand why Jefferson felt this way is to grasp a key feature of American politics in the 1790s. If Hamilton were to control America's destiny, the new nation would emulate the British model of courtly power and courtly corruption. To a republican, a powerful central government built up the public debt and funded aggressive standing armies—this was how Tom Paine had explained the workings of the British government in *The Rights of Man*.

From a purely financial standpoint, Hamilton's system threatened to keep the debt growing. Jefferson's deepest fear was that the engine of debt was being passed on to the next generation, making citizens the pawns of a Hamiltonian quasi-king bent on pursuing power-engrossing wars. The secretary of state had clamored for retirement and finally had his wish, but his irritation was not checked by an altered schedule and rural circumstances. Eager to convince himself that he was done with politics, he was doing his best to keep Madison fired up.[8]

He did not have to. Even Federalists in Congress were ready to take action when the British stepped up their belligerent activities in the Caribbean. In April 1794 a thirty-day embargo was passed. "French arms continue to prosper," Madison wrote tentatively, apprising Jefferson that the prospect of another American war against England so alarmed Washington that a special diplomatic mission to London was in the works. The president's choice to head the mission would be John Jay of New York.[9]

"Bad Precedent"

In this season of debate, Madison still had the presence of mind to devote himself to personal considerations. How long his attraction to a certain young lady had been building one can only guess. Dolley Payne Todd had been living in Philadelphia since the age of fifteen, after a childhood in Hanover County, Virginia. Her Quaker father opposed slavery and had emancipated the slaves he owned before moving north. In this way, the twenty-six-year-old widow already had a firsthand acquaintance with America's homegrown tyranny when, in May 1794, she met "the great little Madison"—this was how she reportedly spoke of her forty-three-year-old suitor. Madison had earlier approached a mutual friend of theirs, the recent widower Aaron Burr, and requested a formal introduction.

It had been a decade since Madison's abortive courtship of Kitty Floyd. Aside from his undefined friendship with the widow Henrietta Colden in Manhattan, no evidence exists to suggest romantic (or sexual) activity of any kind prior to the congressman's courtship of Dolley, which did not drag out very long. "He thinks so much of you in the day that he has Lost his Tongue," the wife of a Virginia congressman wrote to Dolley. "At night he Dreames of you and Starts in his Sleep a Calling on you to relieve his Flame." While this tender account is entirely undependable, the embattled legislator married the young mother at the home of Dolley's brother-in-law, a nephew of George Washington's, who was living in what is today West Virginia.

That was not the only curious element in Dolley's genealogy. Her great-grandfather, a Virginia Quaker, was also the grandfather of Patrick Henry. Among the Virginians, such ties were to be expected. Recall that a similar connection existed between the Madison and Pendleton clans, and between the Jeffersons and the Randolphs. Jefferson had knowledge of the Madisons' courtship in advance, though any written mention of it has been lost. Two weeks after the ceremony, when Madison next wrote to Jefferson, he denoted September 15, 1794, his wedding date, as "the epoch at which I had the happiness to accomplish the alliance which I intimated to you I had been some time soliciting." Dolley was less circuitous. Without waiting, she wrote to a close friend on the fifteenth: "In the course of this day I give my hand to the man of all others I most admire." Before sealing the letter that evening, having taken his name, she added an emphatic postscript: "Dolley Madison! Alass! Alass!"[10]

Politics did not take a honeymoon, because America's relationships with the warring European powers remained unresolved. The two main branches of government were still trying to establish credit abroad and grow maritime commerce. President Washington counted on his London-bound envoy to make things right. He had been personally comfortable with John Jay ever since the late 1770s, when the Revolution was in trouble and Jay, then president of Congress, staunchly supported the commanding general against those who wanted him replaced. To some, Jay was vain, condescending, and aristocratic in manner, but Washington had known him only as a well-trained, right-thinking public servant. During the Confederation period, Jay served as U.S. secretary of foreign affairs and, since 1789, as chief justice of the Supreme Court. The Court was not nearly as active as it would later be, and Washington thought that Jay could be spared from judicial duties long enough to travel to London to negotiate a commercial treaty and avert war.

The appointment would prove to be a bad choice for a president who was pushing against the increasing pressure of faction. But this did not matter to Washington. A letter he wrote to Hamilton toward the end of his presidency, marked "Private," summed up his turn of mind: "I have a very high opinion of Mr. Jay's judgment, candour, honor and discretion (tho' I am not in the habit of writing so freely to him as to you)." In or out of office, Hamilton was the president's chief aide. It was Hamilton, in fact, who first proposed Jay's name to Washington when his own selection became unlikely. The consequence of the Virginian Washington having thrown in with New Yorkers Hamilton and Jay would prove far-reaching.[11]

James Monroe, soon to be dispatched to Paris to placate the French, stood in opposition to Jay's confirmation. As a U.S. senator, he had also voted against Morris's appointment as minister to France. His reasons for opposing Jay now were no different from Madison's and Jefferson's: Jay's weakness in dealing with the Spanish in the past made it doubtful that he could be a tough negotiator with the British. If less obnoxious than Hamilton, Jay was nonetheless one of those "Anglomen" whom Jefferson, Madison, and Monroe all distrusted. The ostensibly objective Edmund Randolph advised Washington not to send Jay because it would be a "bad precedent that a chief justice should be taught to look for *executive* honors . . . while he retained his judicial seat." Good reasoning, perhaps, but it went unheeded. Republicans in the Senate would make sure this violation of the separation of powers remained an issue.

Aware that the United States was divided into two rival camps, the British were in no hurry to allay its concerns. Washington hoped that Jay, accommodating by nature, would convince the British to abandon the western forts, as they had consented to do a decade before. He hoped too that both sides would reach an agreement to grant American vessels easier access to the British West Indies. He could not ignore the growing number of incidents in which British warships had captured American merchant ships.

The chief justice sailed to London in mid-May 1794 and followed his instructions closely. But as the British would not bend much, Jay fell short of everyone's expectations. Rather than express outrage over British depredations, as Madison would have preferred, he remained circumspect, attuned to British sensibilities and driven by a concern that a commercially isolated United States would be at a disadvantage.[12]

Meanwhile, Monroe left for Paris, accompanied by his wife and young daughter. He knew why he had been chosen for the assignment. The president, he told Jefferson, wanted "a republican character" to serve as his special envoy in order to repress whispers about his own political drift. Not surprisingly, Hamilton proposed Edmund Randolph for the assignment. Randolph, in turn, proposed Monroe. Monroe had offered Burr's name, which would have made Madison perfectly happy. But Burr was a New Yorker, as Jay was, and Robert Livingston, another New Yorker, had already refused the assignment. So after consultation with Madison and others, Monroe had accepted the appointment "upon the necessity of cultivating France," as he put it, "and the incertainty of the person upon whom it might otherwise fall."[13]

Benjamin Franklin Bache, grandson of the late Dr. Franklin, was the editor of the pro-French Philadelphia *General Advertiser*. On learning of Monroe's mission, he gloated in his paper that a "DEMOCRAT" was going to France who would "supersede" the authority of Gouverneur Morris, Federalist. This was a rare, early evocation of the word *democrat* in a prideful light. The Federalists were using it as a defamatory term, equating the mobs of Revolutionary France with the "mad democrats" in America. It was the beginning of Bache's short but colorful reign as the one editor who could intimidate the president of the United States.[14]

At the end of 1794 Bache's *General Advertiser* became known as the *Aurora*, projecting the dawn of a new age as its anti-administration bent became more purposeful. The editor proved so infatuated with the Revolution in France that he became a complete apologist. He failed even to pick up on Jefferson's abandonment of Genet. Imbued with an excess of optimism, Bache fed the once popular sentiment that time was accelerating and world historical events multiplying because of the French Revolution. Politicized readers nervously awaited each new piece of intelligence—

rumors first, and then corroborations from abroad—which Bache added to an already impassioned American stew.

In 1795, as he began personalizing his attacks, Bache went right after the greatly admired president. Stoking the fires of partisanship, he pronounced that "a good joiner may be a clumsy watch-maker; that an able carpenter may be a blundering taylor; and that a good General may be a most miserable politician." In time, when he ran out of coy metaphors, Bache would directly assail Washington's generalship.[15]

"God Save King George!"

In September 1794 President Washington became General Washington again, and rode at the head of an army. Hamilton rode with him. Another of his generals, Virginia governor Henry Lee, who just a year before had fantasized joining the French Revolutionaries, went along—all of them in pursuit of a domestic enemy. The improbable "enemy" was a nearly invisible corps of western Pennsylvania whiskey distillers who were refusing to pay taxes on their product—taxes established by Hamilton in 1791. At some point between 1791, when he attacked Hamilton in the strongest terms, and 1794, when he decided that the threat of the mob was the greatest threat America faced, "Light-Horse Harry" Lee had turned away from Madison and Jefferson to become an ardent Federalist.[16]

In the whiskey rebels' corner were two prominent Republicans from western Pennsylvania: Hugh Henry Brackenridge (another of Madison's Princeton classmates) and the Swiss-born Albert Gallatin, who was just beginning an illustrious career in politics and finance. As the tax resisters made theirs an issue of freedom from oppressive government, they found solidarity all across the backcountry of western Pennsylvania, Maryland, Virginia, and Kentucky.

Washington called up nearly thirteen thousand militiamen, larger than the size of his entire force during the Revolution. With Hamilton at his side, he led a large contingent of them toward Carlisle, Pennsylvania, and Hagerstown, Maryland. These were sites of resistance, to be sure, but only two of many locations in the trans-Appalachian counties of states where the federal government was too weak to make a real show of force. Rural populations communicated easily across state lines, facilitating the movement of arms while giving the backcountry a sense of the government's weakness. Washington faced the logistical nightmare of feeding and marching an undisciplined army during a change of seasons in the mountains. As they moved about, government troops encountered sporadic protests from plain people in Philadelphia, Norfolk, Baltimore, and other places. In Baltimore a dissenter cried out "God save King George!" and was tarred and feathered by his social betters, who evidently did not appreciate political satire when the butt of the joke was George Washington.

In this phase of the conflict, shots were fired but few casualties resulted. The whiskey men, who had resorted to strongly worded petitions in the early days of the protest, saw themselves as reborn Sons of Liberty, those roguish heroes of the American Revolution whose legend loomed large. But Washington and Hamilton were not in a conciliatory mood, though they might have been: the army they raised was comprised of the kinds of people they were opposing, not those whose interests they were defending. Brackenridge and Gallatin, seeing the hopelessness of outright rebellion, delivered a message of moderation to the disaffected, pleading with them to reject radical methods and exhibit loyalty to the government.

In fact, no rebel army ever took the field against federal conscripts. Madison wrote to Monroe that the whole episode was a ploy by Hamilton to add military despotism to the catalog of powers he wanted the executive to engross. It was clear that aside from a handful of identifiable mischief-makers, there were no rebel leaders. That did not stop Hamilton from ordering the arrest of 150 men, all of whom Washington eventually pardoned. Under these circumstances, the administration's response to the rebels was an obvious case of overkill.

The president had had to report to Philadelphia, because Congress was back in session. He left the army in Hamilton's hands. After a month the troops returned east, having accomplished nothing that could reflect well on the administration. Some two thousand of the tax resisters had by this time moved into deeper frontier, where the army of the federal government could not reach them. Once the threat of force ended, the distillers resumed their normal operations, and no one came back to enforce the excise laws.[17]

The war on the whiskey rebels served the purposes of Madison and Jefferson, who saw value in exploiting social division in the North. The president laid blame on the democratic societies for having fomented the rebellion, a position from which he could not turn away. The only member of his cabinet to oppose a military response was Edmund Randolph, who advocated the use of commissioners to negotiate a peaceful solution—he listed eleven solid reasons in support of his opinion. Randolph, the former attorney general and now secretary of state, argued that the rebellion did not meet the constitutional standard of treason. Washington had not wanted to act precipitously, so he gave Randolph's plan a chance to work.

Randolph never looked so good as he did at this moment of decision. He had told the president the unvarnished, embarrassing truth—that there was no crisis. But then Hamilton stepped in front of him, outmaneuvering Randolph by refusing to give the commissioners time to do their job. Pretending that negotiations had failed, Hamilton brought the president on board with his plan and called up the militia. Randolph had no traction left after this.

The problem was compounded by the president's poor judgment. Indeed, the sequence of events revealed Washington's tragic flaw: he was not one to admit defeat. Randolph was not merely sidelined; he was forced to submit, to demonstrate his loyalty to Washington by retreating from his principled stand. He went on the record agreeing with his president that the democratic societies had stirred up all the trouble. Randolph went so far as to say that the "late insurrection" had "threatened the authority of the government" and "degraded the American character."[18]

If ever there was a moment when Jefferson could have been justified in suspecting Randolph of "Cameleon" tendencies or a lack of backbone, this was it. In November 1794 Randolph served as ghostwriter of the president's attack on what were now being called "self created" societies. Congressman Madison did not at all like the implication of the phrase and led an effort in Congress to remove "self created" as a designation for what were, in fact, civil gatherings of republicans. Politically charged words continued to drive debate.

With Randolph neutralized, Madison refused to let the matter go. This generally unheralded moment actually serves to define Madison's centrality in national politics over the first five years of rule by the Constitution. For when Washington came into office in 1789, it was Madison on whom the first president relied most; and in 1794 the same man was defining Washington's failure as a leader. The fact that Greenville, South Carolina, called its democratic society the "Madisonian," and Fenno's *Gazette of the United States* identified the political clubs en masse as "Madisonian," probably contributed to the president's apprehension that his agreement to serve a second term could ruin him. Neither said so, but Madison and the president were now pitted against each other directly. And in 1794, as in 1789, Jefferson was absent from the government and Madison most formidable as a one-man political force.[19]

As soon as he heard of Washington's assault on the "self created" societies, Jefferson related to Madison his astonishment that the president would allow himself "to be the organ of such an attack on the freedom of discussion, the freedom of writing, printing and publishing." If the "democratical societies" plotted anything, he wrote, it was "nourishment of the republican principles of our constitution." Never one to lose hope, Jefferson took solace in reports from militiamen just back from service who said that the frontier resisters were at no point cowed by the overwhelming show of federal force. *They* had let the army escape harm, not the other way around. But he also took the reports to mean that a more coordinated western separatist movement was in the offing—a possible dismemberment of the Union. "The excise-law is an infernal one," Jefferson growled, perversely encouraged that further frontier disturbances would be blamed on the administration.[20]

At this moment especially, Madison and Jefferson recognized the value of a critical public to their cause. Two of the leading Republicans in Pennsylvania, Alexander James Dallas and Albert Gallatin (both born outside the United States), were active members of democratic societies. Gallatin spoke with a noticeable French accent and had already made himself a symbol of the French menace among Federalists in Congress. In 1793, thirteen years after emigrating from Switzerland, he found his election to the U.S. Senate overturned on the basis of his qualifications for citizenship.

In many ways, Gallatin was more American than the provincials who went after him. He had spent his first years in Revolutionary America tutoring French at Harvard. He knew from firsthand experience how western land was a magnet for Virginians, having traveled to the Ohio River in the mid-1780s and having speculated, without much success, in the vicinity of some of Washington's properties. Before permanently settling in Pennsylvania, he thought for a time that he would acculturate among Virginians who had migrated west. When the Federalists rewrote the law concerning citizenship, they were unequivocally conniving to exclude the Gallic Republican.

Elected to the House in 1794, Gallatin began his long political career by speaking out against Jay's mission and writing against Hamilton's economic system. Like Madison and Jefferson, he was leery of the long-term national debt that Hamilton so enthusiastically embraced. Federalists could tout their magical-sounding "sinking fund" all they wanted, just as William Pitt had done in England, but there was, Gallatin said with wry insistence, only one way for a nation to pay its debts and that was to "spend less than you receive." Reporting to Jefferson on Congressman Gallatin's specialized skills, Madison credited him for being a "real Treasure" as a colleague, "sound in his principles, accurate in his calculations and indefatigable in his researches." They had found someone they could rely on to undo the Hamiltonian system.[21]

"An Impenetrable Secret"

In London, John Jay was well treated. The British considered him second only to Hamilton among England's American friends. Lord Grenville, their chief negotiator, had been a member of Parliament since the age of twenty-three and was a self-possessed political operative. Concerned with U.S.-Canadian issues for a decade already, he was well enough aware of America's exploitable weaknesses to have thought it possible to wean Kentucky away from the eastern states. Grenville gave Jay few nonnegotiable demands, which made the American's acquiescence to British power seem less dramatic than it would appear to his many critics back home.[22]

In Paris the Terror was finally past, but anxiety was still rampant. As Washington's envoy, James Monroe faced a skeptical leadership set, men who wondered whether he represented the administration or just imagined he did. Monroe sought to allay these fears by assuring his hosts that the United States would always support its sister republic. "Their governments are similar," he volunteered. "They both cherish the same principles and rest on the same basis: the equal and unalienable rights of man."

His passionate address was immediately reprinted. Monroe's diplomatic counterpart in London was irritated, and when a transcript arrived stateside, Madison felt obliged to inform Monroe that the Federalists had found his tone "grating." Secretary of State Randolph reprimanded him for going too far: his instructions had been to assure the French of America's attachment without suggesting any abandonment of U.S. neutrality at a time of Anglo-French hostilities. Whereas Jay was expected to negotiate a treaty, Monroe was expected to give the false impression that the administration was guileless in conveying its respect for France.[23]

While the Monroes were in Paris, the newly wedded Madisons occupied their Philadelphia home during the congressional session. Madison asked Elizabeth Monroe to make purchases for him in Paris: curtains, carpets, and furniture "in a stile suitable to my stile and fashion." In the months since the "self created" societies reanimated him, Jefferson returned to commenting on his farming activities. Now, when Madison heard from him, the lead subject was usually a mix of weather reports and corn or wheat prices. Lest Madison allow himself to think that his friend was ready to return to the fracas, Jefferson would request a pamphlet on crop rotation. It was Madison who saw to it that the conversation never strayed from national affairs for long. He kept Jefferson current on the "Treasury faction," as he called the Hamiltonians; he wrote of state elections and the changing shape of parties. While he had not heard privately from Monroe, Madison seemed to think that France was strong and the rest of Europe resentful of the fact.[24]

Shortly after New Year's 1795, without specifying his sources, Madison told Jefferson that he believed the Jay mission to London would bear fruit. "It is expected," he wrote, "that he will accomplish much if not all he aims at. It will be scandalous, if we do not under present circumstances, get all that we have a right to demand." He was setting them both up for disappointment.

In early spring Jay returned with treaty in hand. Its terms were not immediately made public, forcing Madison to change his tune. "It is kept an impenetrable secret by the Executive," he noted scornfully in a letter to Jefferson.[25] For more than two months, the country waited to learn what Jay had negotiated, because President Washington was reluctant to endorse what he knew was a less-than-perfect treaty; he finally came to the decision that if the Federalist-led Senate approved it, he would go along. And that is precisely what occurred. By the terms of the treaty, the British agreed to evacuate the same Northwest frontier posts they had already agreed to abandon in 1783, something Lord Grenville had been prepared to do even before Jay arrived. But England made no new commercial concessions. It did not agree to stop taking American merchant vessels and confiscating their cargo. It did not even begin to recognize the rights of neutrals during wartime. The treaty did reduce the chance of Anglo-American war, which was Washington's first priority. And Jay did not suffer much for his weakness as a negotiator: he was elected governor of New York while abroad. It pleased him to step down from the bench in order to assume the office he had wanted three years before, when he narrowly lost it to George Clinton.[26]

Despite Monroe's efforts in Paris, an undesired consequence of the Jay Treaty was that it intensified resentment toward the United States on the part of the French. The treaty was not neutrality to them; it was subservience to England, a resumption of the colonial relationship. American professions of friendship would no longer be deemed credible. No one could have expected the French to take a nuanced view at this time, with Hamilton, who wished to model America's economy on Britain's, steering U.S. foreign policy. His pending retirement from the cabinet would not put an end to his influence.[27]

"A Real Farmer"

The time had come for Madison and Jefferson to discuss the future of the presidency after Washington. At the end of 1794, precisely one year after he resigned from the cabinet, Jefferson pleaded that the nation could not afford for both of them to retire. If Madison ever left the House, he said, it should be to accept "a more splendid and a more efficacious post." He meant, of course, the presidency. Madison took several months to answer, and when he did, he said only that his reasons for shrinking from higher ambition were "insuperable" and "obvious" and would be spelled out when they had the "latitude of a free conversation." Jefferson should prepare himself "to hear truths, which no inflexibility will be able to withstand."[28]

Madison would win the argument, as he had in the past when he brought Jefferson out of retirement. In an awkward reprise of his emotional letter to Madison of June 1793, when he had maintained that the motion of his blood no longer kept time with the tumult of the world, Jefferson acknowledged on April 27, 1795, that while he was still in the cabinet, he had been approached (by whom he did not say) to run for president. To do so, then or now, would be to give his enemies the satisfaction of being able to say that they were right about his presidential ambitions. That was not the full explanation, however. At fifty-two, he claimed he was beginning to feel the effects of growing old: "My health is entirely broken down within the last eight months; my age requires that I should place my affairs in a clear state." He protested to Madison that "the little spice of ambition, which I had in my younger days, has long since evaporated." Knowing how adept his associate was in putting pressure on him, Jefferson punctuated his statement with the most definitive line he could summon: "I do not mean an opening for future discussion, or that I may be reasoned out of it. The question is forever closed with me." Somehow Madison still talked him into challenging John Adams for the presidency.[29]

Jefferson and Adams had continued to maintain cordial relations through the mails. Late in 1794, fresh from a long vacation back home in

Massachusetts, the vice president wrote the former secretary of state from Philadelphia: "I have Spent my Summer So deliciously in farming that I return to the Old Story of Politicks with great Reluctance. The Earth is grateful. You find it so, I dare say. I wish We could both say the Same of its Inhabitants." Agriculture was a convenient subject for two who might otherwise step on each other's principles. Jefferson gamely replied to Adams: "I have found so much tranquility of mind in a total abstraction from every thing political . . . Tranquility becomes daily more and more the object of my life." If he really wished it so, he wished in vain. To a fellow Virginia planter, he feigned: "I am encouraging myself to grow lazy." Insisting that he was no longer attempting to steer the ship of state in any particular direction, he sang his own dirge: "I consider myself now but as a passenger, leaving the world and it's [sic] government to those who are likely to live longer in it."[30]

In a letter to the apolitical Maria Cosway, who knew him much better as a man of the arts than as a politician, Jefferson could not resist making reference to the "great buz about Mr. Jay and his treaty." But then he recovered his familiar pose, resolutely describing the transition from a "public life which I always hated" to "the full enjoiment [sic] of my farm, my family, and my books." He was, he said, eating the peaches, grapes, and figs of his own garden: "I am become, for instance, a real farmer, measuring fields, following my ploughs, helping the haymakers, and never knowing a day which has not done something for futurity. How much better this than to be shut up in the four walls of an office, the sun of heaven excluded, the balmy breeze never felt." Before he was finished, he reclaimed the nostalgic feeling that had been a part of his romantic letters to Mrs. Cosway when he was in Paris and she in London: "In truth whenever I think of you, I am hurried off on the wings of imagination into regions where fancy submits all things to our will."[31]

Jefferson may have had a carefree side, but his carefully cataloged correspondence suggests that he rarely showed it in this most demanding decade. Much as he tried, he could not remain aloof from politics.

"Intestine Convulsion"

Hamilton's men were concerned that the unpopularity of Jay's treaty might swing opinion back to France, in which case Monroe's representations to that country's new leaders would become a self-fulfilling prophecy. And that could not be allowed to occur.

Secretary of State Edmund Randolph was the only Virginian in national office who might still have imagined there could be a middle ground. But his drumming out of office in 1795 ended Randolph's career in politics and instructed Madison and Jefferson that it was time to acknowledge that they were building a distinctive party and not simply putting forward an opinion.

Randolph's downfall was set in motion in August when a letter written by the French minister, Baron Fauchet, to his government, was intercepted at sea by a British warship. The letter was then translated and presented to President Washington. It showed Randolph in a questionable light. He appeared to have revealed sensitive information to the French minister. At best, Fauchet was overstating what Randolph had said to him in order to impress his superiors in Paris. But there could be no gray area in these black-and-white times.

Washington did not understand French, and the translation he read was defective. Hamilton's handpicked successor, Oliver Wolcott of Connecticut, and the man who replaced Henry Knox in the War Department, Timothy Pickering of Massachusetts, deliberately made it appear that Randolph had committed treason. Wolcott and Pickering confronted the unsuspecting cabinet officer, in a scene they staged for the president's benefit. Blindsided, the unoffending Randolph had no time to react. He could see that Washington, whom he had known since his Williamsburg boyhood, was already convinced of his guilt. The nation's second secretary of state promptly resigned his office. He drew up papers freeing the slaves he had brought with him to Philadelphia and rushed to New England to track down Fauchet. There he found the French minister and obtained from him an affidavit to prove his innocence of any charge of collusion with the French.

That December the disgraced cabinet officer released a statement in his own defense. *A Vindication of Mr. Randolph's Resignation* was a nearly hundred-page pamphlet, giving a blow-by-blow account of his untarnished patriotism, his relations with Fauchet, and the unraveling of his career within the executive. Son of a noted Tory, Randolph had been a Washington aide early in the war, a governor of Virginia, and the first public servant to hold two different cabinet-level appointments. Over the course of his career, he had always sought to steer a middle course. He believed in facts. He aimed to be fair.

The *Vindication* is more than a denial of wrongdoing; it is a testament to unselfish public service. Highlighting his long and honorable devotion to one man, Randolph addressed that man directly, insisting that the two cabinet posts he held were positions "which I did not covet, and which I would not have accepted, had I not been governed by my affection for you, my trust in your republicanism, and your apparent superiority to the artifices of my enemies." Sensitive to the need to keep Washington from political harm, Randolph had acted as a best friend did, persuading the president "to abhor party" and forestall "intestine convulsion." He had done all he could to see that Washington went down in history as "a bulwark against party-rage." Despite such carefully wrought well-wishes, readers were meant to conclude that the president had submitted to a party, to the detriment of the country.[32]

With a single swipe, ignoring facts and fairness, the Hamiltonians had undone the many years of trust between Washington and Randolph. In simple terms, they wanted the last Virginian out of the cabinet. Wolcott had been, until lately, comptroller of the treasury, in charge of putting Hamilton's national bank into operation. It is no exaggeration to say that he was completely indebted to Hamilton and completely responsive to him. Pickering, once adjutant general of the Continental Army, had a strong mind and blustery personality and would be an outspoken and unforgiving critic of the Republicans for years to come. These two combined to put the squeeze on Randolph when they introduced the poisonous Fauchet letter to a gullible president.[33]

So although Randolph was innocent of all charges, his pamphlet contained enough venom to ensure his political exile. Jefferson dissected the work and sent a critique of it to the restless Virginia Republican William Branch Giles. The gist of Jefferson's argument was that political neutrality was useless and that Randolph's failure showed why the establishment of a party was sometimes necessary. He wrote: "Were parties here divided merely by a greediness for office, as in England, to take a part in either would be unworthy of a reasonable or moral man. But where the principle of difference is as substantial and as strongly pronounced as between the republicans and the Monocrats of our country I hold it as honorable to take a firm and decided part, and as immoral to pursue a middle line." This one statement captures Thomas Jefferson's political creed more succinctly than any of his better-known or more eloquent texts.[34]

Another who took an interest in Randolph's pamphlet was Federalist-friendly "Peter Porcupine." This barbed quill of a pen name belonged to a newcomer to Philadelphia, William Cobbett, a thirty-year-old British Army veteran who had been stationed in Canada for several years before deciding to try his luck in the United States. A robust critic of the emerging Democratic-Republican Party, he hit the ground running, disputing Randolph point by point. Writing to Jefferson, Madison acknowledged the impact of "Porcupine's" treatment of the *Vindication:* "It is handled with much satirical scurrility . . . , ingenuity and plausibility." To Monroe, he was rather more severe, calling Cobbett's piece a "malignant attack."[35]

Meanwhile, the bruised author of the *Vindication* wrote his old and trusted friend Madison and confessed to how deeply he had experienced Washington's betrayal. "I feel happy," he said, "at my emancipation from an attachment to a man, who practiced upon me the profound hypocrisy of Tiberius, and the injustice of an assassin." It was Randolph's way of telling Madison that he knew he had just written his own political obituary.[36]

Given the rich educations that the gentry received, their classical allusions tend to be illuminating, and Randolph's invocation of the Emperor Tiberius is no exception. For what turned out to be his last hurrah as a member of the administration, he had taken the pseudonym "Germanicus," virtuous nephew and adopted son of the Roman emperor, in a series of letters he published in defense of Washington's "firmness" during the Whiskey Rebellion. It was in the "Germanicus" letters that Randolph had yielded to the term "self created societies," accusing the democratic societies of planting the seeds of America's destruction. Such societies were fit for Revolutionary times, he wrote, but "ought to be avoided in seasons of tranquillity because they may be easily abused." He was wrong about the tranquillity and wrong about who was committing abuses.

But that is not why Randolph's pseudonym of 1794 revealed so much in 1795. "Germanicus" symbolized competence and loyalty—especially loyalty. As he prepared his *Vindication,* Randolph could only have been shocked by the supreme irony in his choice of pen name. Or perhaps he had forgotten how the story ended: the emperor repaid Germanicus for his honorable service by attaching him to an officer who despised him and had him poisoned. Tiberius was thought to have been behind the conspiracy, though it was never proven.[37]

In unsubtle ways, Randolph had paternal expectations from Washington. Their break—his shaming—was catastrophic for him; but in politics, suspicion could kill a friendship or an alliance in an instant. So Randolph consciously wrote his *Vindication* as a life-affirming experience—an "emancipation," as he told Madison. Washington's decision to abandon Randolph is harder to explain. He had never had occasion to question the younger man's integrity. And yet he convicted Randolph on the flimsiest of evidence: a report he never verified, a report that had passed through British hands. Why did he suddenly accept this dark portrait of his long-trusted subordinate? The answer may lie in the Revolutionary past, in an incident known as the Conway Cabal. In 1777–78, at a low point in the war, a number of prominent civilians and military men were writing openly of Washington's incompetence. The Continental Congress was all abuzz with news of infighting. It came to Washington's attention that one general in particular, Thomas Conway, had circulated sharp criticisms of his military prowess. So the commander in chief dismissed him with contempt, rallied support, and ruined Conway's career. In both that instance and this one Washington acted impulsively, apt to believe he was being betrayed.[38]

Madison was kind to Randolph, agreeing that Washington's overreaction was inexcusable. He wrote Monroe that the *Vindication* redeemed Randolph's honor, proving his innocence, so that even "his greatest enemies will not persuade themselves that he was under the corrupt influence of France." But at the same time Madison read the pamphlet as the confession of a failed politician, saying that not even Randolph's "best friend" could "save him from the self condemnation of his political career as explained by himself." Madison used the third person singular: *his* best friend. It is an oddly detached construction, because Madison was really talking about himself; he had long been Randolph's best friend in the carnivorous land of politics.[39]

Edmund Randolph's star had finally faded. Born to privilege and known to the movers and shakers in Virginia from the time he learned to write, he would never be asked to hold high office again—not under Jefferson, not under Madison. Burdened by personal financial concerns, he returned to the practice of law. He amused himself by writing a history of Virginia, though it would not be published until after his death. Adding insult to injury, when Washington considered a replacement for Randolph as secretary of state, he thought first of Patrick Henry—a peculiar choice at this or any moment—before settling on the redoubtable Timothy Pickering.[40]

"Red-Hot Democratic Fools"

Washington had made his choice. Hamilton had rendered it impossible for Jefferson to remain in the cabinet once Washington had chosen Hamilton over him; Hamiltonians had made it impossible for Randolph, whose one ally in the inner circle was the president himself. It was a purge of Virginia Republicans.

No Republican anywhere had influence with Washington anymore. The president got his European news from the brilliant, idiosyncratic, ungovernable Gouverneur Morris, a Federalist who predicted that France was tired of experiment and would restore the monarchy before long. Morris acknowledged (and he said the same to Hamilton) that England was not the perfect ally; but, he added, any injuries America suffered from that quarter could be endured.[41]

Out of government, Hamilton made sure that he was still heard from. He kept in close touch with the president and the new cabinet. "When shall we cease to consider ourselves as a colony to France?" he posed in a letter to Attorney General Bradford, when Randolph's purported treason came to light. Hamilton's unambiguous goal was the total eradication of pro-French feeling in America.[42]

In July 1795 Hamilton challenged James Nicholson to a duel. A naval officer during the Revolution, Nicholson was active in the Democratic Society of New York. He was also Albert Gallatin's father-in-law. Nicholson had annoyed Hamilton with the tenor of his arguments against the Jay Treaty, which somehow proved hurtful enough for Hamilton that he resorted to a deadly challenge. "The unprovoked rudeness and insult which I experienced from you," wrote Hamilton, "leaves me no option."

Hamilton proceeded to make out his will. This time, at least, his impulsiveness ended without bloodshed. On the day following the above exchange, without knowing how the challenge would play out, Hamilton (as "Camillus") began what would turn into a long series of newspaper pieces in defense of Jay's treaty. "No one can be blind to the finger of party spirit," he wrote in the first of the series, accusing the "leaders of clubs" of criticizing Jay in order to elevate Thomas Jefferson and George Clinton.[43]

Moved by Hamilton's enthusiasm, and having taken a liking to Jay, President Washington came to view the imperfect treaty as a lesser evil. Debate would drag on during the second half of 1795 and into the early months of 1796; and though confidence in Washington diminished in some quarters, conservative voices stayed on the attack. This was perhaps best expressed in Noah Webster's *American Minerva,* where it was written that opposition to the treaty was "begotten in cabal—supported by knavery" and sustained by a minority.[44]

The newspaper was a partisan feast, dripping with political bloodlust.

Federalists found satirical poems to be a particular delight. They contained every slur and every slight of the times, mocking the "servile" American Jacobins and the foreign origins and foreign principles of every so-called Antifederal dissenter. The foreign-born ("A medley mixed from every land") were dangerous because they produced unrest.

> *Scotch, Irish, renegadoes rude,*
> *From Faction's dregs fermenting brewed;*
> *Misguided tools of antifeds*
> *With clubs anarchial for your heads . . .*

And whenever "self created societies" were mentioned, James Madison was found making excuses for them. The misdirected rabble were

> *Well pleas'd as* Madisonian *tools*
> *Or red-hot democratic fools.*

This devastating satire distinguished the Madisonian trash from America's better prospects under a President John Adams, who was by now regarded as Washington's presumptive successor. A New England paper, meanwhile, came up with a devious abbreviation of "Madisonian" when it denominated the "Jaco-Demo Crats" as "Mads." Other critics would pick up on the useful nickname.[45]

Aurora editor Benjamin Franklin Bache was not the only "Franklin" in Philadelphia to take on John Jay and George Washington in 1795. In the spring of that year Pennsylvania Republican Alexander James Dallas adopted the name of the late Dr. Franklin, whom he had met years before at the University of Edinburgh. The *Letters of Franklin, Or, the Conduct of the Executive, and the Treaty Negotiated by the Chief Justice of the United States,* did not deny the constitutional powers of the executive and the U.S. Senate in treaty making but emphasized the unresponsiveness of both to the will of the American people. "This Treaty is of a piece with the other perfidies of Great Britain," Dallas criticized, while praising Madison for seeking a way to regulate America's commerce with Britain that would control the "hostile spirit of that nation." Dallas posed the question of the decade: "How comes it that every man who prefers France to Great Britain—republicanism to monarchy—is denominated *Antifederalist, Jacobin, Disorganizer, Miscreant,* &c., while men of another humour arrogantly and exclusively assume the titles of *Federalist, Friends to order,* &c. &c.?"[46]

Terms of abuse were tossed around with irreligious fervor. Though most of the "self created" democratic societies would disappear by the end of 1796, Cobbett's "Peter Porcupine" identified a conspiracy against the government when he repeated the toasts delivered by southern Republicans at a Franco-American function. The first glass was lifted to "Democratic Societies throughout the world—may they be the watchful guardians of Liberty"; the second to "Citizen *Maddison* and the *Republican party* in Congress." In a long, discursive pamphlet titled *A Little Plain English,* "Porcupine" mocked the all-too-clever names Republicans had come up with for their domestic enemy: "Aristocrat, King's man, Loyalist, Royalist, Clergyman, Englishman." Cobbett happily embraced the last of these, as he wrote in support of social distinctions: "As an Englishman, I shall be excused for not thinking myself upon a level with every *patriot,* every *negro,* and every *democrat,* that pleases to call me his *fellow citizen.*" Democracy meant erasing all social distinctions.

According to Cobbett, the "French faction" in America was "perverse" in its thinking; the treaty's opponents thrived on "frothy declamation and vaunting bombast...ambiguity and confusion...every passion that can disgrace the heart of man." Directly disparaging the author of *Letters of Franklin* as "this fawning mob orator," Cobbett insisted that President Washington had done the right thing by resisting the mob's demand for a pro-French policy. To condemn Washington was to imitate the ungrateful pirate crew "who, having safely arrived in port, cut the throat of their pilot."[47]

"To Generalise a Whole Nation"

As the parties were forming and newspapers waged partisan warfare, American slavery received relatively scant attention. In July 1795, however, once Washington had submitted Jay's treaty to the Senate and recommended its passage, Hamilton, as an informal legal adviser to the president, responded to the president's solicitation of advice on how to treat southerners' claims against the British for "seducing away our negroes during the War." It was one of the issues Jay was meant to have addressed during negotiations.

Hamilton called the wartime seduction of slaves "infamous" behavior, "an indelible stain" in the annals of the British Empire. But it would have been "still more infamous" if, after defeat, the British had returned the runaways to their masters. Within the law of nations, he wrote, restoration of property was one thing, and "the surrender of persons *to slavery*" quite another. Citing Emerich de Vattel, the eighteenth century's foremost expert in international law, Hamilton maintained that to keep slaves was to maintain a state of war with them—this interpretation more or less coincided with Jefferson's theory of African Americans as a captive nation. Hamilton raised but did not resolve the question, "Is there any thing which exempts negroes more than other articles of personal property from capture & confiscation as booty?" In the end, he gave Washington some law to chew on, without recommending a clear course of action.[48]

In December 1794 Jefferson freed Robert Hemings, age thirty-two, who as a teenager had accompanied him to the Continental Congress in Philadelphia. Bob was the first slave Jefferson formally, if reluctantly, emancipated. Just over nine months after Bob's emancipation, in October 1795, his younger sister Sally delivered a daughter at Monticello. It was the first of her children whose birth Jefferson recorded in one of his domestic account books. Sally and her infant, despite their slave status, were tended to full-time by a nine-year-old slave girl, possible evidence of special treatment ordered by Jefferson. Over the next thirteen years the biracial Sally Hemings, described by one who knew her as "mighty near white," would bear five more Jefferson children. And all who survived to adulthood would be freed.[49]

Though he did not have the responsibilities placed upon him that Jefferson did when he came into his patrimony, James Madison, Jr., was now a husband with concerns beyond public service. He contemplated farming experiments to be tried at Montpelier when he left Congress for good, and his wife Dolley, despite her antislavery Quaker education, recognized that she was in no position to question the labor arrangements in Orange, Virginia. There she made a home for herself and her fatherless son and accepted the reality of slavery.

If anyone could have made inroads at this time, it was Dolley's husband. Back in 1785, at the height of his interest in acquiring land in New York's Mohawk region, he said he wished "to depend as little as possible on the labor of slaves." Although Madison did not often discuss his private misgivings about slavery, he set down in a private journal a year or so before he and Dolley met: "In proportion as slavery prevails in a State, the Government, however democratic in name, must be Aristocratic in fact." Refusing to shrink from the implications of his words, he acknowledged directly that the northern states were more democratic than the southern. While many of the thoughts in this particular notebook found their way into his newspaper pieces, the slavery passages did not. Madison obviously felt it would have been imprudent for him to introduce a subject on which Virginians were so vulnerable. Political society was already in great flux. He would not consciously spark new unrest.[50]

Madison was thinking of the word *democratic* in its classical sense and not as a partisan slur used by northern Federalists in the mid-1790s. As election year 1796 approached, the "democratic" North of his theorizing had its share of democracy-hating, Republican-baiting men. Made defensive by those who tarred them as aristocrats, the Federalists conventionally declared themselves to be people of good sense; they assumed the collective mantle of a deserving leadership corps, a steadying influence in government. Anxious about the visibility and rising popularity of men of "indecent" ambition, the Federalists tried to shout them down; they claimed that the "Mads" did not even care if their actions served to break down the structure of government. A representative newspaper stated that protest over the Jay Treaty proved that "Jefferson, Madison, and Burr, itching for high offices in our government, will leave untried no probable means of accomplishing their views." In linking the cagey Virginians with one cagey New Yorker, Federalists assumed that the Democratic-Republican Party had devised a North-South plot.

This was much overstated; it was a tentative alliance. Just a half year earlier Jefferson had identified the "Southern interest" as the segment of the political population that he was principally concerned about. If the "Southern interest," he told Madison, had "any chance of prevailing," the executive could not be allowed to fall into northern Federalist hands. The Federalists saw a marriage in the works that Jefferson, at least, was shying away from.[51]

It would be wrong to read too much into Jefferson's choice of words, but it would be just as unwise to ignore it. His supposedly undeviating plan of retirement contained many holes and detours. As he contemplated how to respond to a German historian and geographer who was undertaking a multivolume work on the North American continent, Jefferson rejoined the conflict. Christoph Daniel Ebeling had written to the author of *Notes on Virginia* asking for information. Made aware that two northern Federalists who had toured the South were supplying the German professor with material from their travels, Jefferson instinctively disputed their findings by declaring that one cannot know a region just by staying at inns along the road and communing with "idle, drunken individuals who pass their time lounging in taverns." Without even knowing whether the professor's correspondents had characterized the southern political economy in critical terms, Jefferson warned against what it would mean "to generalise a whole nation from these specimens." But then he did some general cataloging of his own, presenting a conspiratorial picture of the essential division between republican and antirepublican in the United States. As before, he identified the misdirected people ("old tories," "timid whigs," and "American merchants trading on British capital") who worshipped the British model; he claimed they were "hoping monarchy might be the remedy if a state of complete anarchy could be brought on." In contrast, true republicans could be defined as "the entire body of landholders" and "the body of labourers, not being landholders, whether in husbandry or the arts." This would seem to exclude only Americans of an urban and speculating character. Jefferson was designating the Federalist as substantially a northern creature, who up to this point had monopolized the power in government and who would ultimately be upended by a republican electorate.

Taken together, Jefferson's confidential evocation of the "Southern interest" in the letter to Madison, and his notes for the German historian, suggest that he envisioned a solid South that would combine in the political furnace with landed yeomen of the North, South, and West to forge an electable consensus. From their no-less-heated perspective, the Federalists saw a Frenchified America waiting in the wings. Having witnessed the birth and expansion of democratic societies, a rebellion among taxpayers in the backcountry, and agitation against a commercial treaty with England, they were now concerned with the prospect of the Republicans gaining adherents in Pennsylvania, New York, and interior parts of New England. They saw their opposition as moblike.[52]

Angry as he was over Hamilton's orchestrated takeover, Jefferson was genuinely repelled by politics and reluctant to reenter the lists. Madison was able to wear down his resistance only because he knew that his semi-retired friend saw the situation as desperate. We are left with the question of why Madison did not pick up on Jefferson's suggestion that *he* seek the presidency. Given Madison's personality, it is possible that he regarded himself not as a singular administrator but as a floor manager. He would not envision otherwise until he had labored by a president's side for eight years.

CHAPTER NINE

Danger, Real or Pretended
1796–1799

*[I] begin to entertain serious doubts whether this is the country we inhabited
12. or 15. years ago: whether we have not by some accident been thrown to
another region of the globe, or even some other planet.*

—JAMES MONROE TO JAMES MADISON, DECEMBER 10, 1797

*There never was perhaps a greater contrast between two characters than
between those of the present President [Adams] and of his predecessor,
although it is the boast and prop of the present that he treads in the steps of his
predecessor. The one cold considerate and cautious, the other headlong and
kindled into flame by every spark that lights on his passions.*

—JAMES MADISON TO THOMAS JEFFERSON, FEBRUARY 18, 1798

IN THE SPRING OF 1796 JAMES MADISON LED THE FINAL FIGHT IN
the House of Representatives to stop the Jay Treaty. He argued that while
the Senate alone ratified treaties, the House, due to its role in appropriat-
ing public funds, had a right to review this or any treaty before its implementation. It was a novel approach, and although a majority in Congress
sided with him, some Republicans, even at this late date, chose not to humiliate Washington, who claimed executive privilege and contested their
right to inspect his instructions to Jay or any notes or correspondence relating to treaty negotiations.[1]

Madison sent Jefferson a copy of Washington's challenge to Congress.
The president's "absolute refusal" to show his hand was, he charged, "as
unexpected as the tone and tenor of the message [was] improper and in-

delicate." Madison felt cheated. He saw the hand of Hamilton in the president's gambit, but he believed Republicans in Congress would muster "sufficient firmness" to face down the threat, without having to stage a direct confrontation with Washington. But whatever subtlety Madison might choose to employ, Benjamin Franklin Bache had his own strategy: to inflame the public further, he decided to publish the debates over the treaty.[2]

Washington's challenge should not have surprised Madison, who was, after all, stretching the meaning of the Constitution. Hamilton had assured the president that the House was to be excluded from the treaty process on the basis of the one precedent Madison ought to have understood and yielded to: the original meaning of the Constitution as established by the debates at the Constitutional Convention. While Madison's allies begged him to draw on his detailed notes from the convention, he had to realize that it would have been a lost cause to do so. Instead, he invoked the ratifying conventions, and especially Virginia's. These conventions, he now held, were responsible for breathing life into the Constitution. They had called forth the "voice of the people" and had transformed a "dead letter" into a living document. Therefore one could obtain a properly nuanced interpretation of the Constitution only by reckoning how the states understood it. Refusing, in his words, to treat the Constitutional Convention as an "oracular guide," Madison creatively countered the Washington-Hamilton line by insisting that the Constitution had acquired "validity" only through its reception in the popularly elected ratifying conventions. He was improvising, of course, because at this moment his political agenda took precedence over constitutional correctness.[3]

Madison was wrong to substitute the ratifying conventions for the authority of the federal Constitution, and he was wrong as well about the firmness of the Republicans in the House. He pressed his colleagues to refuse appropriations and force renegotiation of the treaty, just as he told Jefferson he would do; but two unexpected absences and "a few wrongheads," as he put it, finally sank his hopes. He gave Jefferson news of "defections among our friends," which he said was owing to an unfounded fear of war with England.[4]

After a close vote, resistance to the Jay Treaty died. And once again it was Hamilton who worked hardest to keep the Federalist position in public view. Writing as "New Yorker," he prepared a broadside that raised the fear of what would happen if the treaty were not implemented: "The CONSTITUTION and PEACE are in one scale—the overthrow of the CONSTITUTION and

WAR in the other. Which do you prefer?" Lest there be any doubt who represented the domestic problem, he ended his piece with an unabashed attack on the Madisonians: "Do not second the ambition of a VIRGINIAN FACTION, constantly endeavoring to govern the United States."[5]

In the early months of 1796, Madison thought he had rallied his forces effectively but found that he could not arrest their inclination to accommodate Washington. As a result, he grew deeply disillusioned. "Alas! Poor Madison!" one Federalist proclaimed. "He seems to have dwindled into nothing." The Federalists had won the battle, without a very sophisticated argument. The Republicans looked weak.[6]

"How Political Plants Grow in the Shade"

Madison led the Republicans in Congress, but he did not control them. Sometimes they reacted too impulsively for his taste, as Edward Livingston of New York and William Branch Giles of Virginia had recently. But Madison adapted, as he always did, and resumed an active role in debate. These days, Albert Gallatin was his most trusted ally. Jefferson was not there, but he reinforced Madison's instincts by telling him that if Gallatin would only look into the chaotic state of the nation's finances and make better sense of them, "he will merit immortal honor." Quick to launch into a republican refrain, Jefferson reduced his thought to a straightforward maxim: "The accounts of the U.S. ought to be, and may be, made, as simple as those of a common farmer." When it came to fiscal health, he demanded transparency, literally wanting the government's records so basic that the average cultivator understood them. This, he believed, would weaken the grip of the commercial class on the national government.

Jefferson's hostility toward the central government had had time to incubate over the past two years of a midcareer retirement to Monticello. Hoping to see the national budget shrink—to see less government—he chided Madison for supporting a post road bill. "Boundless patronage" would result, he feared, in "jobbing to members of Congress." No good could emerge from a "bottomless abyss of public money." It pleased him that Virginia's roads were administered by each county. "The roads of America are the best in the world," he cooed, "except for those of France and England." It was an admission that America had far to go, but the devotee of yeoman decency saw no reason to hurry things along.

Here Madison thought Jefferson all wrong. The good roads were in the northeastern states. Those south of Richmond were vastly inferior, and the roads west were the worst. Massachusetts Federalist Chauncey Goodrich described southern roadways as "little better than in a state of nature." Madison would put the government in charge so that, in carrying newspapers far and wide, post offices could keep postage low. As impossible as unity was for the time being, his priority remained to bring Americans closer. An efficient system of communication would ensure the vigorous dissemination of news and public opinion.

But what if someone from New Hampshire were to "mark out a road" for Georgia? Jefferson fretted. In much the same way Patrick Henry, at the Virginia Ratifying Convention, had imagined swarms of northern tax collectors imposing themselves on the hospitality of the South. Restless about others' meddling intentions, Jefferson aimed to convince Madison that the states should be self-sufficient in all their domestic matters. He had been away from Philadelphia long enough to see through southern eyes exclusively.[7]

With passage of the Jay Treaty, Madison began to count the days to Washington's retirement. All he could look forward to now, as he confirmed to Monroe, was the hope of a Jefferson presidency. But this seemed doubtful, as Federalists controlled the New York legislature, which would determine presidential electors. The use of a general ticket in Pennsylvania—giving all of its electoral votes to the person receiving a plurality—also seemed to favor the Federalists. Jefferson could not win without some northern support.[8]

Madison was convinced, even as John Jay's name was being floated as a possible Federalist presidential candidate, that John Adams would run. It is not clear whether Adams knew the extent to which Madison disliked him. He had dined with James and Dolley at the end of February 1796, writing to his wife that "Mrs. Madison is a fine Woman." Insofar as he and Jefferson were still corresponding cordially, he may have assumed that the straight-shooting Madison shared some of Jefferson's forbearance. But as the treaty vote loomed, he classed Madison among his hardened, habitual foes. "The Anarchical Warriours are beat out of all their Entrenchments by the Arguments of the Friends of Peace and order," he told Abigail colorfully. "But Party Spirit is blind and deaf, totally destitute of Candour, unfeeling to every candid sentiment." He observed the toll it was taking on his recent dinner companion: "Mr. Madison looks worried to death. Pale, withered, haggard." And of Madison's vocal associates, new congressmen

Edward Livingston and Albert Gallatin: "They have brought themselves into great Embarrassment."[9]

It was the "great little Madison" who put the Republican engine in motion, who argued, strategized, and paved the way for Jefferson in 1796. Although Aaron Burr made a pilgrimage to Monticello at the end of 1795, hoping to win Virginia's support in his vice-presidential bid, Jefferson's correspondence reveals that he did precious little to shape the Republican organization or to promote himself personally. While he acquiesced to Madison's management of his candidacy for high office, he certainly did nothing to encourage it—even in the middle months of election year 1796. There was only one party leader now: Madison.[10]

Within the Commonwealth of Virginia, Jefferson was largely inactive, while Madison kept an eye on the county-level political organizations. But whereas Madison and Jefferson were focused on national issues that they saw as potentially ruinous for the country, Virginia voters of 1796 were largely apathetic. Elite men were elected and reelected to the state assembly based on their social stature rather than their political viewpoints. County-level Federalists, whose Federalism consisted of little more than opposing anyone who criticized Washington, were content to tread water.[11]

Once the campaign season began, coordinating Virginia Republicans across twenty-one far-flung electoral districts was no simple matter for the Madison-Jefferson interest. Knowing that Adams's candidacy excited almost no one in the Old Dominion, Federalists turned their eyes toward Patrick Henry, whose statewide popularity, even now, probably exceeded Jefferson's. Before he finally, grudgingly, offered his support to Adams, Hamilton covertly sought a southern Federalist to run for president. He asked Virginians John Marshall and Henry Lee whether Patrick Henry might be drafted. The game was to divert just enough votes to Henry to deny Jefferson the presidency. But Henry was unresponsive.[12]

A handful of political operatives knew quite well that Jefferson was *in* the running, even if he was not running. Most notable was London-born John Beckley, a former indentured servant, now clerk of the House of Representatives. Though of humble stock, Beckley had climbed the political ladder through access to the Virginia gentry. His first patron, Edmund Randolph, brought him to the attention of Richmond politicos, and he was named clerk of the Virginia House of Delegates. It was Madison who spoke for him in 1789 and helped to facilitate his clerkship in the national legislature. Despite his visibility, Beckley never escaped his lowly origins; he occasionally performed errands for the powerful, for example, racing about Philadelphia trying to track down a suitable house for the Madisons to rent. He communed easily with the tavern-going crowd, warming up to radical émigrés in the Tom Paine mold. He was the bridge between the Baches of the political world and the Madisons and Jeffersons, making sure that gentlemen who had political axes to grind, but did not wish to get their hands dirty, had someone to run interference for them.[13]

So Jefferson stood for high office as "the man of the people" without having to run with a plebeian crowd. A letter to Monroe in September 1796, if it is to be taken literally, suggests that even at this late date Madison was conspiring to keep Jefferson from resisting his own election. "I have not seen Jefferson," Madison wrote—Dolley helping him to encode the letter—"and have thought it best to present him no opportunity of protesting to his friends against being embarked in the contest." As the times seemed to demand, Madison added with a groan: "His enemies are as indefatigable as they are malignant."[14]

Slow to accept Adams, Hamilton urged his Federalist friends to favor Thomas Pinckney of South Carolina, who he hoped might yet attract more electoral votes than either Adams or Jefferson. For the moment, Pinckney was a hero to many across America for his having negotiated a favorable treaty with Spain that opened the Mississippi River to commerce. It had occurred just as John Jay was being accused of folding his cards in London.

Inflexible in his beliefs, but prescient about many things, Adams reckoned he knew what James Madison's future held. He told his wife that Madison would soon leave Congress, return to his Virginia plantation, and eventually reenter national politics and run for president. "It seems the Mode of becoming great is to retire," he noted on the eve of his own inauguration. "Madison I suppose, after a Retirement of a few years, is to become President or V.P. It is marvellous how political Plants grow in the shade." Of course, that last line may have been penned with Jefferson in mind.[15]

"This Disgusting Dish of Old Fragments"

Jefferson's last interaction with George Washington occurred in June 1796. Until then, they had been safely exchanging intelligence on farming methods, and Jefferson scrupulously avoided any allusion to unpleasant political matters. But in the letter of June he opened with a resolute denial of having leaked a paper to Benjamin Franklin Bache, which was published in the *Aurora* and showed the president to have been contemplating an anti-French policy in 1793: "I can say with truth that not a line for the press was ever communicated by me." The only person with whom he might have shared the leaked text, Jefferson said, was the "one person who possesses all my confidence as he has possessed yours." Washington, of course, knew that he meant Madison. "I was in the habit of unlimited trust and counsel with him." Note that Jefferson said Madison "has possessed" rather than "possesses" Washington's confidence. Why should he pretend otherwise? The relationship between Washington and Madison, once reckoned as indissoluble, no longer rose to the present tense.

Delicacy was Jefferson's epistolary bottom line. The recipients of his letters, he believed, understood that sincerity declared above his signature was the same as a sworn affidavit. On that basis, he could not resist taking a last stab at convincing Washington of the purity of his motives and the integrity of his principles. Someone, he said (without naming), "has thought it worth his while to try to sow tares between you and me, by representing me as still engaged in the bustle of politics, and in turbulence and intrigue against the government ... Political conversation I really dislike ... But when urged by others, I have never conceived that having been in public life requires me not to bely [*sic*] my sentiments, nor even to conceal them." Jefferson was often in the habit of explaining himself, something that Madison almost never felt the urgency to do. Leaping to a new paragraph, Jefferson breathed a figurative sigh as he took an easier tack: "I put away this disgusting dish of old fragments, and talk to you of my peas and clover."[16]

Washington replied generously and with apparent candor. He had been told of Jefferson's remarks, he acknowledged, the gist of which was that as a lame duck president, he was "a person under a dangerous influence; and that, if I would listen *more* to some *other* opinions all would be well." This certainly appears to be an accurate representation of what Jefferson had been saying. But, Washington went on, shifting his emphasis, "My answer invariably has been, that I had never discovered any thing in the conduct of Mr. Jefferson to raise suspicions, in my mind, of his insincerity."

What came next is no less interesting. Denying that he was in such isolation that any person or faction could capture his political mind, Washington contended he was "no party man myself," and "if parties did exist" he wished only "to reconcile them." He expressed amazement at what had taken place: "I had no conception that Parties Would, or even could go, the length I have been Witness to," or that he would ever be accused of favoring Britain over France, or doing anything other than "steering a steady course, to preserve this Country from the horrors of a devastating war." And then, like Jefferson, he launched into a discussion of peas and clover.[17]

Madison, for his part, offered Washington one final supportive gesture. He endorsed the plan for a national university that the president had put forward in his last annual address to the Congress. Washington wished it built in the federal city, on land he himself would donate. While many Republicans were wary of the plan, Madison made two speeches in its favor—not surprising, since it was Madison who had first made such a proposal during the Constitutional Convention. (Washington had to have remembered this.) Symbolically, at least, the two were able to put aside "party spirit" to speak briefly to their common agenda. Neither was able to rally his followers behind the initiative, however, and the national university idea died.[18]

In 1792, before he reluctantly consented to a second term in office, Washington had relied on Madison to draft a valedictory that the president intended to deliver to the nation as he went into retirement. He retained Madison's draft over the next four years and then turned it over to Hamilton. For the greater national interest, Washington hoped that Hamilton would acknowledge Madison's contributions to the Farewell Address.

Some historians have concluded that President Washington sought to reverse the trend toward a cynical politics and permanent party alignments by inviting Madison to see him in mid-May 1796. Doubt remains, however, as to whether the two former intimates met at this time or whether Washington was even predisposed to try. It is recorded that he wanted Hamilton to insert Madison's name into the text of the updated address—which, more likely than not, was a tactic to neutralize Madison rather than credit him justly. In any case, Hamilton would not comply. The untidy dispute over Jay's treaty had made even the smallest accommodation objectionable. In the end, Washington accepted Hamilton's revisions to the text, leaving only faint traces of Madison's original language.[19]

The president's Farewell Address, completed in the fall of 1796, said nothing of the emotional bond with France dating to the Revolutionary War. Rather, it set America on a middle course, avoiding "entangling alliances" with any foreign power. The U.S. ought to have healthy commercial ties and "as little political connection as possible" with Europe. It was his desire, he said, to see a moderation in "the fury of party spirit" in American life. Not only were the president's words disingenuous; they were, in fact, the obvious contrivances of Hamilton, who gave Washington the means to renounce the Republicans. They were, allegedly, the ones solely responsible for domestic discord, "designing men," organizers of "faction," "cunning, ambitious, and unprincipled." He did not have to say "Republican"; he did not have to name Jefferson. But that was what was meant by his warning: "sooner or later the chief of some prevailing faction" would fulfill his private ambition "on the ruins of public liberty."[20]

Virginia Republicans were decidedly unimpressed with Washington's insincere appeal to harmony. Others were disturbed by the president's call for "religion and morality as indispensable supports" of the national government, which sounded too much like a plea for a national religion. Washington had lost his ability to rise above party squabbles, and the Farewell Address did little if anything to heal wounds. George Washington was a Federalist first and a Virginian second.[21]

"The Sublime Delights of Riding in the Storm"

The 1796 presidential campaign featured newspaper attack ads that modern Americans would recognize. "Will you," a Philadelphia handbill asked rhetorically, "make the avowed friend of monarchy, President?" John Adams had sons who might succeed him, the paper reminded voters, while Jefferson had only daughters. One candidate was the "fond admirer" of the British system; the other "likes better our Federal Constitution, and thinks the British full of deformity, corruption, and wickedness."[22]

Both sides applied scare tactics. Jefferson came under fire for views critical of organized religion, as gleaned from *Notes on Virginia*—views fortified during his five years in France. The *Gazette of the United States* noted with disdain Jefferson's witticism, "It does me no injury for my neighbour to say there are twenty gods or no god. It neither picks my pocket nor breaks my leg." "What?" the shocked editor exclaimed. "Do I receive no injury as a member of society if I am surrounded with atheists?"

According to the *Gazette,* Jefferson had been heard to say that his philosophical Parisian friends were atheists. Both he and his protégé, fellow Francophile "Citizen Monroe," were intimates of Tom Paine, who in 1793–94 had followed up his *Rights of Man* with *The Age of Reason*. The latter work was regarded as a frontal assault on Christianity. Were Jefferson returned to the executive and promoted to the first rank, the "impious and blasphemous" Paine would take a seat at the president's dinner table. As kindred

philosophers and tools of French Revolutionary atheism, they would unleash chaos in America. There was a real difference between freedom *of* religion and freedom *from* religion. Was Jefferson the fit successor to the
"virtuous" Washington? And what "good effects" were ever produced by
his Virginia Statute for Religious Freedom?[23]

If atheism were not enough of a disqualification, Jefferson could be
charged with "timidity" and "cowardice" for having abandoned the governor's chair in the midst of the British invasion of Virginia. He had resigned
his position as secretary of state at a critical moment as well. To such
charges, his defenders reflexively answered that a lack of ambition to govern men was a mark of trustworthiness, not timidity. And when Jefferson's
deviation from Washington's line of thinking was used as a rationale for
denying him the presidency, an incredulous columnist quickly countered:
Who differs from Washington more than John Adams?[24]

Republican newspapers were beginning to make casual references to Jefferson's role in the Second Continental Congress. In Savannah, Georgia, he
was toasted on July 4, 1793, as "chairman of the committee that reported
the declaration of independence"; in Bache's *Aurora*, and in neighboring
New Jersey, in 1795, he was "the illustrious framer of the declaration of
independence"; and again, a few months later, "he who penned the declaration of independence."[25]

As the French Revolution cast a shadow over political discourse in
America, the durability of the two young republics remained a central question. Newspapermen intent on making their mark reckoned with extremes
only, which they could do because it was impossible for anyone to predict
what a post-Washington government would look like. In a sense, the public's anxiety boiled down to the question of who was able to distinguish between what was real and what was illusory. Those with their heads in the
wrong books became "crazy projectors."

Abstract ideas feed speculation in any age, but they were never so vio-
lently imagined as they were in the period that is imperfectly remembered
as the Age of Reason. In Boston, New York, Philadelphia, Richmond,
Charleston, and other places, the talk of the town consisted of a vocabulary
that is in less frequent use today: "innovation" courted "instability," "imagination" clouded "judgment," and "effete" or "decadent" tendencies (or in
individual cases, "relaxed nerves") led to unproductive behavior or the
blind acceptance of unrepublican rule. All recognized that change was
coming, but what kind of change? Good order devolving into chaos? Freedom dissolving before monarchical tyranny? There was no in between. One

was either attached to the old order or willing to bear a dangerous political experiment. Partisan oversimplification had become a contagion.[26]

Sectionalism shaped the election season as much as personalities or foreign alliances. "Pelham," a writer for the *Connecticut Courant,* saw the contest on a grand scale: northerners would have to decide whether they wanted to stay in the Union and remain accomplices of the institution of slavery. "Pelham" was offended by the unwieldy clause in the Constitution by which House seats were apportioned and electoral votes assigned preferentially to the South—each slave state inflating its population by adding three-fifths of a person for every noncitizen kept as property. Years before arch-Federalist Timothy Pickering tarred Jefferson as the "negro president," elected only because of the three-fifths advantage, a host of New Englanders were already expressing ample resentment over the inequity.

As the "Pelham" essays made the rounds in Virginia, Joseph Jones wrote to Madison about them. The sarcastic Connecticut columnist had charged that slaves were "the CATTLE of citizens of the Southern states"—and if their self-indulgent masters had found them "good for food," they would surely have eaten them already. Jones's reaction was tongue-in-cheek: "He does not degrade us to the servile office of toad eaters [i.e., toadies], but exalts us to the honourable Station of Can[n]ibals." Not in the least uncomfortable, Jones presumed that the writer's feeling was dictated by partisan, not ethical, considerations. Whether or not spoken of directly, North versus South was clearly the subtext when the presidential choice was between Adams and Jefferson.[27]

Though he was the ostensible leader of the Republicans, Madison had to admit to one Virginia ally that he was "little informed on the present state of electioneering politics, either in or out of Virginia." Having been unable to do very much to coordinate a Republican ticket in his home state, he could not prevent many Virginia electors from throwing away their second votes. Consequently, they wrote in Samuel Adams, George Clinton, or George Washington and gave only a single vote to Aaron Burr.

Electoral votes divided, for the most part, along sectional lines. Pennsylvania went Republican; New York, New Jersey, and New England went Federalist; and Maryland was split. Adams received 71 electoral votes to Jefferson's 68. The South Carolina Federalist Thomas Pinckney came in third, Burr a distant fourth. Because the framers had not anticipated strict party competition, the Constitution did not as yet provide for tickets and running mates. As the second highest vote-getter, Jefferson was awarded the vice presidency.

"The event [i.e., result] of the election has never been a matter of doubt in my mind," Jefferson wrote to Madison on New Year's Day 1797. "Indeed the vote comes much nearer an equality than I had expected." Though he said he could not decide whether the vice presidency, a largely powerless office, was in the least attractive to him, he accepted his role: "The General of to-day should be a soldier tomorrow if necessary." Acknowledging that he was Adams's "junior" in age and experience, Jefferson submitted to fate. He was hopeful, he said, that the incoming president would relinquish his pro-England bias and govern as a republican.

In accounting for his willingness to serve with Adams, Jefferson added something else: "He is perhaps the only barrier against Hamilton's getting in." Jefferson was apparently thinking ahead to 1800, suggesting to Madison that if the relatively moderate Adams failed, Hamilton would be pulling the strings of a Pinckney; or perhaps he meant that Hamilton himself stood a chance of being elected president, because, after Adams and Hamilton, the Federalists' choices were all lesser men.

Jefferson enclosed the draft of a congratulatory letter to President-elect Adams so that Madison could comment before it was sent. Its tone was genteel, its conventional rejection of political ambition a rhetorical but still meaningful peace offering. "In the retired canton where I am," wrote Jefferson, "I learn little of what is passing: pamphlets I see never; papers but a few; and the fewer the happier." With an ironic metaphor suited to an age of risky travel, he continued: "I leave to others the sublime delights of riding in the storm." Rationalizing his preference for the less taxing second position, he wanted Adams to know that he would rather have as his neighbors "fellow laborers of the earth" than the "spies and sycophants" who surrounded whichever man possessed real power. He did not envy Adams his job, and while he expected no one would believe him, he said he had no wish to be president.[28]

Madison, in Philadelphia, read the letter and without hesitation instructed Jefferson not to send it. As Jefferson had entrusted the draft to his most dependable friend, Madison in turn did what he thought a friend should do. "In exercising this trust," he said, "I have felt no small anxiety." He told Jefferson that it was unnecessary to express conciliatory views directly to Adams—others could be relied on to let Adams know that, as runner-up, he harbored no jealous feelings. Eventually, Madison himself took on this duty, making a point of leaking the letter by way of the harmony-seeking Benjamin Rush of Philadelphia, an intimate of both

Adams and Jefferson. Rush did as Madison expected he would, transmitting to Adams a detailed summary of the contents of the unsent letter.

Madison's second critique of Jefferson's offering to Adams was its "general air," which sounded labored to him. He believed that Jefferson was protesting too much his dislike of politics and lack of ambition. Given Adams's "ticklish" temper, one could not at all predict how the new president would read Jefferson's intent. Madison put forward, all together, six arguments against sending the letter. The last and most direct of his arguments was the "probability that Mr. A's course of administration may force an opposition to it from the Republican quarter." Though he said he appreciated the desire to give the president-elect "a fair start to his Executive career," Madison returned Jefferson's draft knowing full well that Jefferson would follow his recommendation. Their relationship was entering a new phase. To use modern parlance, Madison had become Jefferson's "handler," sensitive to the missteps his enthusiastic friend was prone to and eager to help him avoid embarrassment. As such, Congressman Madison may be described as the first presidential campaign consultant.[29]

Even without the written note of congratulation that Jefferson had wanted to send, the new president and vice president started out the year at ease with each other. On March 4, 1797, in an otherwise-opaque inaugural address, Adams pledged his devotion to republican government. He castigated all the evils known to political man: "the spirit of party, the spirit of intrigue, the profligacy of corruption, and the pestilence of foreign influence, which is the angel of destruction to elective governments." It was an effort to appease.

Adams wanted to include Jefferson in his administration in a visible way, but Jefferson backed off. He was candid with Madison as to why: he refused to "descend daily into the arena like a gladiator to suffer martyrdom," as he had been obliged to do in Washington's cabinet. As far as Vice President Jefferson was concerned, his sole duty would be the constitutional one of presiding over the Senate.[30]

"This Lying Wretch of a Bache"

The spirit of party was not to recede. Broadly considered, neither side wished that any level of comfort should exist between the two leading members of the executive branch, whose principles were so incompatible.

In fact, what the president and vice president had most in common at this juncture was their aversion to one man, Alexander Hamilton. In the letter he composed but never sent, Jefferson assumed that Adams would appreciate his characterization of Hamilton as "your arch-friend from New York."

Philadelphia was a pressure cooker. On the same day that he took the oath of office as vice president, Jefferson paid Benjamin Franklin Bache for a year's subscription to his ultra-Republican newspaper. He stayed in the city only nine days, returning to Monticello for nearly two months. On arriving back in Philadelphia in May, ever righteous in denying his own contribution to conflict, Jefferson wrote to Elbridge Gerry of Massachusetts, a signer of the Declaration of Independence and a friend to both Adams and himself: "I consider as a certainty that nothing will be left untried to alienate him from me. These machinations will proceed from the Hamiltonians by whom he is surrounded, and who are only a little less hostile to him than to me."[31]

President Adams did not need to confer with his vice president to come to the same conclusion. Early on he was certain that Hamilton would stop at nothing to sink his chances for a second term. As his term proceeded, his cabinet repeatedly heard him blast Hamilton for his treachery; the cabinet, which Adams had inherited from Washington, kept no secrets from Hamilton. It took far too long for Adams to realize that cabinet selection was his prerogative and not his esteemed predecessor's.

Years later, after Hamilton's death, the battered New England patriot would pour out his heart in an autobiography that one historian has aptly called less a literary text than "an open wound." Hamilton was "infamous," Adams railed, a being caught up "in a delirium of Ambition," who yet "hated every man young or old who Stood in his Way." Hamilton, Adams insisted, was far less courageous than he was given credit for—the very same critique Jefferson had leveled when he wrote Madison that Hamilton was "timid on horseback" and easily taken sick.[32]

Combustible elements combined to defeat the hope of a presidential honeymoon. As Adams was trying to constitute an embassy to France to include at least one moderate who was not an extension of Hamilton (it would turn out to be Elbridge Gerry), he was being told that Jefferson did not want him to succeed in his efforts toward peace. Adding fuel to the fire was the *Aurora*, Bache's newspaper, which gave the new president almost no time at all before printing inflammatory stories. William Cobbett, in his rival Federalist paper, *Porcupine's Gazette*, fought fire with fire: "The most infamous of the Jacobins is BACHE," he pronounced, "Distributor General of the principles of Insurrection, Anarchy and Confusion." Franklin's grandson was cartooned as a "haggard-looking hireling of France."

At the center of the firestorm, Abigail Adams was taking the insults to her husband worse than the president himself did. She saw the Republicans collectively as agents of the French and believed that "this lying wretch of a Bache," as she called the editor, was only the most easily detectable member of a devious band trying to force the president's resignation. "And then they will Reign triumphant," she railed, *"headed by the Man of the People."* She meant, of course, Thomas Jefferson, whom she had once adored. The confidences they had shared as Americans abroad in the 1780s were memories of a bygone era. Madison's prediction had come true. Both Adamses assumed that Jefferson burned with the same ambition that his Republican minions harbored for him. Mrs. Adams saw Bache's work not simply as libelous and the atmosphere as lawless; she predicted that if his newspaper was not suppressed, the United States would succumb to civil war.

Cobbett's newspaper was widely read. The first lady remarked with pleasure that "his shafts are always tipt with wit." But Cobbett, clever as he was, had no substantive connection to Hamilton or any other leading Federalist. He was unable to coordinate his writing with those in Congress who might otherwise have helped to offset the shock value of Bache's fear-inspiring pronouncements.[33]

The Fifth Congress of the United States convened in the spring of 1797, the first, since government under the Constitution began in 1789, to open without James Madison as a member. Home at Montpelier with Dolley, Madison had ended his long congressional career feeling that the Hamiltonians had succeeded in compromising republican principles. The struggle would have to continue without him. Federalists, glad to see Madison replaced by others, quickly began referring to the opposition as "Gallatin & Co."

Madison and Jefferson would remain Republican lightning rods. This time, though, Madison was out of government, and Jefferson back in. Like Jefferson in 1794, Madison wanted so badly to stay out that he wrote to his father urging him not to listen to any entreaties from Jefferson. The courier for Madison's letter was none other than Jefferson, who was heading south a few weeks sooner. Although they dined together at House clerk John Beckley's home the day it was penned, we can safely assume that Madison did not allow Jefferson to peek at the letter. Madison had wanted his father to know that he had decided not to stand for election to the Virginia House of Delegates. "If Mr. Jefferson should call & say any thing to counteract my determination," he averred, "I hope it will be regarded as merely expressive of his own wishes on the subject, & that it will not be allowed to have the least effect."[34]

After they visited some of Dolley's Virginia relatives, the Madisons came to live with his parents, who had arrived at their fiftieth year of marriage. James, Jr., in his mid-forties, would father no children, though he and Dolley had been trying; but he remained surrounded by family and helped to raise Dolley's son Payne. There was his thirty-five-year-old brother William; his two sisters and their children; and his late brother Ambrose's daughter Nelly, named for her paternal grandmother (reputedly Madison's favorite among his younger kin). All lived in the vicinity of Orange. As he established a new domestic routine, Madison implemented a system of crop rotation—wheat, corn, peas, and clover—recommended by Jefferson. He solicited architectural designs from his accomplished friend, bought nails from the Monticello manufactory, and scheduled work on an addition to the Montpelier mansion.[35]

Meanwhile, as president of the Senate, fifty-four-year-old Vice President Jefferson swore in eight new members of that body and delivered a formal address in which he apologized in advance for any procedural error he might commit. He had been so long away from legislative functions that he was rusty. Adams, of course, had lately served in the position he now took up, and Jefferson seized this formal opportunity to praise his old friend the president as "the eminent character...whose talents and integrity have been known and revered by me thro' a long course of years."[36]

Their shared sense of honor stood no chance of auguring a time of reconciliation. Not just the partisan press at home but also liberals abroad demeaned Adams. From France, Tom Paine wrote to advise Jefferson that America's reputation was deflated, and there was little hope of improvement under an Adams regime. "You can have but little conception," Paine testified, "how low the character of the American Government is sunk in Europe." Where it was not despised for its impotence, he said, it was being written off for its ignorance of how to conduct meaningful diplomacy: "England laughs at her imbecility, and France is enraged by her ingratitude, and Sly treachery."[37]

Politics inside the United States was still conditioned by manifestations of unfriendliness emanating from the Old World. There were clear signs of troubles yet to come in U.S. relations with an exasperated French government, which had begun to threaten American shipping. There was some talk of war. Britain remained surly and unbending, which hardly bothered the ruling Federalists but made Republican heads spin. As the Federalists stepped up their philippics against "foreign influences," Jefferson, Madison, and Monroe were to gather on a number of occasions between 1797 and 1799, meeting at one or another's home in Albemarle or Orange to assess developments. With impending crises at home and abroad, they tried to figure out what the Republicans could do as a minority party.

"La catin Angleterre"

One hazard of possessing a gift for powerful figures of speech is the tendency to go too far and later feel regret. Jefferson had that tendency and on occasion felt that regret. It is what tempts historians to probe his mind and uncover his prejudices. In March 1796, for example, in a letter to political ally William Branch Giles on a subject of no particular consequence to his reputation, Jefferson speculated on the difficulties associated with the protection of American sailors against impressment by the Royal Navy. One would not expect a champion of tradesmen to express open disdain for the merchant seaman, but here is Jefferson objecting to a plan under review to issue them certificates of citizenship: "But these certificates will be lost in a thousand ways. A sailor will neglect to take his certificate. He is wet twenty times in a voyage. If he goes ashore without it, he is impressed, if with it, he gets drunk, it is lost, stolen from him, taken from him, and then the want of it gives an authority to impress which does not exist now." Rather than entrust American sailors with paper, the cynical Jefferson would have the men "parade" on deck, while three foreign officers boarded the U.S. vessel to hunt for any non-Americans who might be concealed below.[38]

As patronizing and demeaning as this sort of statement may appear now, it would never come back to haunt him. On the other hand, one portion of a single paragraph in a letter he wrote a few weeks later to Philip Mazzei would carry tremendous weight from the moment of its inconvenient publication until the end of his days. Mazzei was the chatty Italian who had resided near Monticello before the Revolution and who, though long since back in Tuscany, still had unfinished business in Virginia. Together Madison and Jefferson were handling Mazzei's finances, which explains why Jefferson was writing. He was retired from politics in April 1796, when he wrote the letter; but when Mazzei allowed its publication in a Paris newspaper in January 1797, Jefferson was about to reenter the executive.

His letter was translated from French back into English, imperfectly but not inaccurately, and published in early May in Noah Webster's *American Minerva,* a successful New York newspaper. Webster was a confirmed Federalist.

It was nothing Jefferson had not said before: "In place of that noble love of liberty and republican government which carried us triumphantly thro' the war, an Anglican, monarchical and aristocratical party has sprung up . . . , all timid men who prefer the calm of despotism to the boisterous sea of liberty." But this time, in suggesting that some who had fought for a republic had now conceded to a corrupt British-style regime, he drew inferences. Readers of the *Minerva* took Jefferson's plural to be singular, when he said: "It would give you a fever were I to name to you the apostates who have gone over to these heresies, men who were Samsons in the field and Solomons in the council, but who have had their heads shorn by the harlot England." The French had printed "la chevelure a été coupée par la catin Angleterre"; retranslated, it read, less beautifully: "whose hair had been cut off by the whore England."[39] There could be only one man Jefferson was referring to: George Washington. As Samson, he had wrestled the British lion and crushed enemy armies; as wise Solomon, he built a temple to republican values. Jefferson might protest the translation, but the ex-president certainly thought Jefferson's reference was to him; the benefit of the doubt he had granted Jefferson after their most recent exchange quickly dissolved into anger. He never said anything publicly, but others intervened to make certain that Washington stayed irate.[40]

Jefferson was torn. He wanted to own up to his authorship of the letter and control its meaning so as to minimize damage. As he put it to Madison, "The general substance" was his, but in one place or another "very materially falsified." He was splitting (Samson's) hairs, of course, and realized that "nine tenths of the people of the U.S." would recoil at anything he might publish in an attempt to rationalize his stated opinion of the retired president. "Think for me," he implored Madison, "and advise me what to do, and confer with Colo[nel] Monroe on the subject."

Madison responded promptly. Eager to manage his friend's career before the Federalists had their chance to end it, he undertook damage control. He confirmed what Jefferson knew, that any hint of a confession would be exploited, and advised silence. In that Monroe had already suggested to Jefferson that he go public, Jefferson was less likely to follow Monroe's advice unless Madison independently concurred.

While this was going on, Gallatin of Pennsylvania, the most prominent

Republican in Congress, rose to defend what he interpreted as Jefferson's spirited opposition to an ill-conceived foreign policy. He protested the stigmatization of being labeled "Jacobin" simply for perceiving the world differently than the party in power. His Federalist colleagues did not allow Gallatin's remarks to stand unanswered, broadly hinting that Jefferson's language was at least indecent and maybe conspiratorial. In the political climate of Washington's retirement years, one did not overcome an insult to the supreme founding father. As for President Adams, the Mazzei letter confirmed his larger feeling that the Republicans had lost all sense of national fidelity in their blind devotion to France.[41]

Shortly after the Mazzei letter's publication, Alexander Hamilton returned to the public eye, this time without having solicited the attention. The Reynolds affair, as it became known, was a tale of adultery and blackmail that scandalized the ultimate symbol of Federalism. But Hamilton seemed incapable of experiencing embarrassment, and the whole sordid mess ultimately had little impact on party politics. Madison and Jefferson were only peripherally involved, but as interested onlookers they captured the moment in their correspondence.

Angelica Schuyler Church was Hamilton's sister-in-law—they quite adored each other—and also a close friend of Maria Cosway's in London. After one of the newspapers he subscribed to reported that Angelica and her English husband had docked in New York, Jefferson took the time to write to her. Separating friendship from politics, he wrote delicately: "Your affections, I am persuaded, will spread themselves over the whole family of the good, without enquiring by what hard names they are politically called. You will preserve, from temper and inclination, the happy privilege of the ladies, to leave to the rougher sex, and to the newspapers, their party squabbles and reproaches." It was Jefferson at his peace-making best.[42]

When he resumed his correspondence with Mrs. Church, Jefferson could not have known that the five-year-old story of Hamilton's adulterous romp was about to make the rounds again. In the summer of 1797 the dangerous liaison he had embarked on with Maria Reynolds in the summer of 1792 found a wider audience at the apparent prompting of a Virginian or two. Angelica's husband, John Barker Church, conveyed a piece of gossip to Hamilton that raised his hackles. According to Church, Virginians Madison and Giles, along with Pennsylvania Republican William Findlay, had "used a variety of Perswasions [sic]" to pressure a former Treasury Department clerk into accusing Hamilton of financial misconduct while in office.

It was not in James Madison's direction, or even Giles's, that Hamilton looked to blow off steam. Instead, he goaded James Monroe, accusing him of having leaked the story to James Thomson Callender, a scandal-seeking writer who had arrived from Scotland in 1793 and who lacked all capacity for restraint. Monroe was the most suitable target, because only he, in this group, was a Revolutionary War veteran—and, like all veterans, familiar with dueling culture. Madison was notably unmartial, and it was absurd to think of anyone enticing him into an "affair of honor" that might lead to the dueling ground.

Hamilton called for an urgent "interview" with Monroe. When these two equally stubborn men met, both grew enraged. In the next phase of negotiation Aaron Burr took on the role of intermediary. The accusatory game ended in stalemate, but at least a duel was averted. A caucus of Republicans, including Jefferson, Madison, Burr, and others, assembled in Philadelphia and devised a strategy to quietly end the Hamilton-Monroe affair. In its wake, Hamilton published an exculpatory pamphlet (at least that is what he thought it was) copping to a lesser charge. He declared to the world that he had not committed "improper pecuniary speculation," as alleged; he had merely committed adultery, with the "privity and connivance" of the blackmailing husband.

Hamilton's self-assessment reads preciously today. "I can never cease to condemn myself," he explained unconvincingly, protesting his love for the wife he had hurt and previewing all such apologies in the history of American political scandal. But the gist of his published appeal was not a plea for forgiveness; it was a quest to put to rest all rumors that he had done the public any wrong. The opening words of the pamphlet pointed to the real culprit: "the sprit of jacobinism," which posed a larger threat to the world than "WAR, PESTILENCE and FAMINE." Jacobinism's weapon of choice was "calumny." It was the "jacobin news-papers" and their "odious insinuations and charges against many of our most virtuous citizens" that had cornered him.

Writing to Jefferson in October 1797, Madison mocked Hamilton's effort to turn the tables on the Republicans as a poorly managed rhetorical ploy designed "to excite the spirit of party to prop up his sinking reputation." Madison found it incredible that the Washington administration's persecutor-in-chief was complaining of persecution and milked it for all it was worth. How perfect that the constant supplier of pseudonymously authored newspaper columns attacking Jefferson by name, and the Republicans at large, now disapproved the "system of defamation" that made him "so peculiarly an object of persecution." Here he was, charging that "no character, however upright," was to be spared the imputation of guilt under that "dark" system. What gall!

To Jefferson, Madison gloated in describing Hamilton's pathetic overreaction. The adulterer's long pamphlet, with its long appendix, proved that he did not know when to shut up. "Next to the error of publishing it at all," Madison observed, "is that of forgetting that simplicity and candour are the only dress which prudence would put on innocence." Hamilton went so far as to print a third-party letter reputing to show that Jefferson was somehow involved in the conspiracy against him. "Its *impotence* is in exact proportion to its venom," charged Madison, doubting Hamilton's vaunted masculinity as he and Jefferson both liked to do in such instances (italics supplied).[43]

Callender's exposé of Hamilton came in the form of his grandiosely titled *History of the United States for 1796*. In June 1797 Vice President Jefferson purchased it, paying the author directly—and paying an amount much larger than the cost of a pamphlet, suggesting that he bought multiple copies or, more likely, made a charitable donation to a politically useful writer. As one who sought to stir the pot of political passions indiscriminately, Callender would prove one of Jefferson's worst investments.

In the midst of the Reynolds affair fallout, a wedding took place at Monticello. Maria Jefferson, nineteen and by all accounts pretty, married her cousin John Wayles (Jack) Eppes, of whom Jefferson was already quite fond. When she was much younger, before being sent to France to join her father and older sister, Maria had lived under the same roof with her Eppes relatives—her mother's side of the family. Now, ten years after being separated from the estate of Eppington, below Richmond, she returned there as the wife of her childhood playmate. Jack Eppes, twenty-five, had a good mind, and later, as a member of Congress, would be an effective Virginia Republican.[44]

"Disgusting Proceedings"

On February 15, 1798, President Adams and Vice President Jefferson dined together. At one point in their conversation, Adams quoted a writer whose name Jefferson could no longer recall when he got home and jotted down what he could piece back together of the vignette. The quote was: "Anarchy did more mischief in one night than tyranny in an age." To which Adams had added: "In Modern times we might say with truth that in France anarchy had done more harm in one night than all the despotism of their kings had ever done in 20. or 30. years." The words certainly sound like they could have come from the fabulously blunt Adams. If we accept Jefferson's transcription, this fragment well sums up their difference in outlook on the world. Of course, we don't know whether Jefferson smiled, frowned, or concealed his emotions; whether he expressed a contrary opinion, or opted for silence.[45]

Writing from central Virginia, ex-Congressman Madison believed to a greater degree than did Jefferson, situated in the national capital, that war with France was likely. He even thought it possible that the Adams administration would enter into war with Spain at the same time. Long suspicious of Adams, Madison denounced him now as a "perfect Quixotte" whose brinksmanship could not be predicted.[46]

Then came more bad news. In March President Adams revealed that the mission to France had failed. The three envoys, Charles Cotesworth Pinckney of South Carolina, Elbridge Gerry of Massachusetts, and John Marshall of Virginia, were Federalists of various stripes—Gerry the most moderate. Three officials, referred to only as "X, Y, and Z," had prevented them from meeting with Talleyrand, the foreign minister. X, Y, and Z were demanding a bribe, which the insulted U.S. team refused to give over. Pinckney and Marshall were sailing home, and only Gerry remained to see whether war could be averted.

As the partisan free-for-all continued, a wild sideshow took place in the House when Vermont Republican Matthew Lyon responded to an insult he had received from Connecticut Federalist Roger Griswold by spitting in his face. A few days later Griswold clobbered Lyon with a cane. While under attack, Lyon squirmed free and fought back. A former paper mill owner and printer, Lyon was over fifty; Griswold, a classical scholar at Yale, was thirty-five. It could only have looked ridiculous as Lyon eyed his surroundings and found a makeshift weapon. A satirist of the day, alluding to the Vermonter's Irish origins, put the event into verse: "The knight of *Hibernia,* to avenge all his wrongs / In passing the fire, had snatch'd up the tongs." Griswold's hard wooden cane came in contact with Lyon's metal fireplace tongs, as the two continued to tangle. Onlookers stood "quivering and quaking," and unless the poet was exercising too much license, the eminent Dr. Rush was sought, to bandage the warring pair.

By the time of the inconclusive brawl, the Federalist majority had already voted to expel Lyon from Congress but did not obtain the necessary two-thirds. Jefferson fretted over the "disgusting proceedings" in a gossipy letter to Madison, privately hoping that the violence in Congress would "degrade the General government, and lead the people to lean more on their state governments." Madison was no less dismayed by the lack of decorum, preferring that nasty business be removed from the public forum, the way honor-bound gentlemen ordinarily disposed of such matters. "No man ought to reproach another with cowardice, who is not ready to give proof of his own courage," he submitted.[47]

Thus did the even-tempered Madison, presumed the least sadistic man in an age of revolutions, occasionally show the limits of his patience as well as a readiness to countenance dueling as the proper recourse for a certain breed of men. Sometimes the leadership corps of the early American republic—even the skilled constitutionalist Madison—faced unheroic choices. When he was talking to an intimate such as James Monroe, his words could have an acerbic edge indistinguishable from Jefferson's. "If events should not be unpropitious to the Monarchical party," he wrote after Monroe's recall from France, "you may prepare yourself for still more wonderful indications of its spirit & views . . . Let us hope however that the tide of evil is nearly at its flood." Monroe, as easily, approached Madison for advice when Adams publicly branded him "a disgraced minister." He knew he could not address the perceived damage to his reputation by engaging in an affair of honor with Adams, as he might have done with Hamilton. "He is an old man & the Presidt," Monroe explained, unnecessarily, to Madison.

Monroe allowed both Madison and Jefferson to see how impulsive he could be. What should he do? Ignore Adams's insult? Or assume an accusatory attitude in a public venue, "ridicule his political career, shew it to be the consummation of folly & wickedness? Is the present a suitable time for this?" Jefferson counseled him to get back at the president by entering Congress and going on the public record—not the most noble reason to run for national office. Monroe concluded that such a course would only expose him to the "lesser knaves" who were stand-ins for Adams, and that would not deliver satisfaction.[48]

The politics of the 1790s must be viewed through the prism of "manly" pride. Refined comportment or reserve was, more than ever, a shell. Of those who would eventually constitute the Virginia Dynasty of presidents, Madison seems to have been the least prone to mood swings, though he was far less dispassionate than history records. Jefferson, who suffered migraines, was always prepared to enlist surrogates to publish attacks on his behalf. Monroe, at least prior to his presidency, was the most easily upset and the quickest to lock horns with a perceived enemy. A modern historian has described the political elite of this tortured decade almost as passengers on a runaway train: "They were constructing a machine already in motion, with few instructions and no precise model. The result was a politics of anxious extremes."[49] The psychodrama enlarged as the vulgarity of attacks in print produced one-on-one violence.

"An American in Heart"

The Federalists deftly employed the XYZ Affair to expand their power at the national level. Jefferson predicted that if war with France came, the "Tory" point of view would sweep the nation. On March 22, 1798, he indicated to Madison that he thought Congress should expose the reckless approach of the executive to foreign policy. He proposed two ways to subvert the warmongers: prohibit the executive from arming for war, and have Congress adjourn so that its members could solicit the views of their constituents. This was another illustration of Jefferson's belief that state governments should curb the excesses of the federal government. Madison fully concurred with his anxious friend in this instance, both as to the prohibition and as to the delaying tactic. But even before Jefferson heard back from his chief counselor, he dashed off a letter to another old friend who, he knew, recalled vividly what it was like to stand on the precipice of war. The next few weeks would be "the most eventful ever known since that of 1775," he told a still-energetic seventy-six-year-old Edmund Pendleton.

We know that Jefferson was prone to hyperbole, but this was no sudden emotional flare. The danger of war over XYZ appeared great because the French government, buttressed by Napoleon's recent victories, may actually have seen a benefit in taking on the United States, believing what the Federalists claimed with respect to the Republicans—that "an attachment to France and hatred to the Federal party, and not the love of their country [was] their first passion." As on past occasions, Jefferson declined to write for public consumption, and as it was not Pendleton's habit either, he urged Madison to do so.[50]

Though Madison did not comply in the near term, he could not rest either. He doubted that the Adams administration was being truthful in its dealings with Congress. The focus of his irritation was the presumption that Foreign Minister Talleyrand had been complicit in the insulting treatment America's envoys received, especially the demand of a kickback. Talleyrand had recently spent two years in the United States. "Is it possible," Madison posed to Jefferson, "that a man of sagacity as he is admitted to be, who has lived long eno. in this Country to understand the nature of our Govt...could have committed both his character and safety by such a proposition?"

Madison was prepared to listen to "evidence," he said, but he was not to be moved by "infatuation"—which is what he deduced as he read the newspapers. Though ordinarily slow to embrace conspiracy theories, he went so far as to speculate that the Jay-ites in New York saw that their governor, seeking reelection, was in trouble because of the unpopularity of the treaty that bore his name; it was the eve of the election, and they had ample motive to exaggerate facts so as to influence a suggestible population. Monroe spent a night at Montpelier later that month and agreed with his host that the XYZ charges were greatly exaggerated. They were satisfied that envoys Pinckney and Marshall would meet "derision" when the full truth was known.[51]

In fact, though, the forty-two-year-old John Marshall sailed from Bordeaux aboard the *Alexander Hamilton* and received a tumultuous welcome when he returned home. While sharing a carriage from New York to Philadelphia with ardent Republican Edward Livingston, he admitted that the French people had no thought that war with America was brewing. The Marquis de Lafayette, recently released from prison, wrote to George Washington and appealed for calm. Nevertheless, the High Federalists continued to spread the word that the United States was under a very real threat of invasion.

Jefferson had not completely given up on Marshall, at least not yet. He hoped to have direct contact with him to see whether, like Elbridge Gerry, this envoy could keep an open mind about France. He assumed that Hamilton would coach Marshall on the tone to adopt to advance the party line, but he still had doubts that Marshall would follow Hamilton's script to the letter. Although Jefferson was on hand to observe Marshall's reception, the two Virginians were unable to meet in Philadelphia. Jefferson reported uneasily to Madison that a concourse of cavalry had formed, a large crowd had turned out, and bells rang through the night.[52]

Marshall aimed to capitalize on this career-making moment, believing he could transcend party. Seeking a seat in Congress some months later, he advertised his qualities in the Virginia newspapers. "In heart and sentiment ...I am an American," he wrote proudly, steering a middle course. For his principled resistance to French intimidation, Marshall had become a national hero.

A young lawyer named John Thomson was deeply angered by what seemed to him a mania over Marshall. As "Curtius," he published a series of letters in the *Virginia Argus,* demanding that the rising star of Virginia Federalism answer the charge that the ruling party had hijacked the term *federalism* while engaging in "a rancorous persecution of every enlightened republican." How can you be "an American in heart," he wrote, denouncing the candidate, when you possess principles "most warmly admired by persons who are Englishmen in heart and sentiment?" Marshall was on the fast track to high office, and "Curtius" felt it was incumbent upon him to explain himself first. In successive letters to the *Argus,* he mocked the "abject and oriental adulation which you have lately received," and would not let it rest. "Vanity can be forgiven," he posed, "but malignity cannot be excused."

Either Marshall was liberal-minded or he was a Federalist tool—he could not have it both ways. To show the contrast between the parties, "Curtius" took as his model of republican decency the constant object of the Federalists' anti-Gallicism, Albert Gallatin. After demanding an explanation of what it was that made Marshall a hero, he reversed his argument: Why was Gallatin *not* a hero? Why was he, instead, the convenient target of mean-spirited Federalists? "Mr. Gallatin has been persecuted with all the detestable rancour of envy and malice," observed "Curtius"; and yet this brilliant man remained "serene in the midst of clamours," "attached to the constitution because it is free, [attached] to the people because they are generous and amiable, and to the country because he has found in it, an asylum from oppression and misery." For the opinion writer, a beautiful irony lay in his magnificent truth: "The conduct of Mr. Gallatin is his best vindication," "Curtius" concluded. "The foreigner has defended the constitution against the attacks of native [born] Americans." Perhaps the Federalists were "formidable in their numbers," but they were iniquitous in their rule.[53]

Now, and for some years to come, Republicans would have to remind their enemies that Hamilton, reared in the West Indies, had come to America at the age of eighteen; Gallatin, educated in freedom in Switzerland, arrived at the age of nineteen. Who, then, was more American?

"Who Can Object to a Sedition Bill?"

The issue was far from simple. Jefferson had recently revealed the nativist strain in his thinking when he drafted a petition in opposition to the action of a federal grand jury in Virginia. He objected to the grand jury's presentment against a Republican congressman who used anti-administration language in a circular to his constituents. When judges or grand jurors were made "inquisitors," violations of free speech would receive sanction. Jefferson diagnosed the problem correctly but went too far in the cure he recommended. He wanted the grand jurors impeached by the Virginia House of Delegates. And he further argued that the jury pool should be restricted to "native citizens of the United States." He must have been told that one or more members of this particular grand jury were not U.S.-born.

Madison gently urged Jefferson to reconsider. The state assembly was not the proper venue for his complaint—and Monroe agreed. The operation of a federal grand jury was a federal, not a state, matter. Madison worried about the precedent Jefferson would be setting if his plan were enacted: it could only result in the "partial disenfranchisement" of naturalized citizens. Would this not apply to a Gallatin? Jefferson had not thought everything through. In any case, even with changes, his radical remedy was rejected by the Virginia House of Delegates.[54]

In May 1798 the Federalist-led Congress moved in a darker direction when it settled on a plan that would give Federalists the power to rid the country of the pesky Gallatin and others they perceived to be dangerous foreigners. A Francophobic impulse (or conspiracy, as Madison would have it) put the country on a war footing, at the same time as it made into suspects foreign-born persons whose political views threatened the administration. After the Alien Acts were adopted, the Federalists in Congress capitalized on their momentum and passed a Sedition Act, legitimizing the harassment and curtailing the liberties of native-born citizens.[55]

The Alien Acts represented the first act in the unrepublican episode that Jefferson famously dubbed "the reign of witches."[56] It would now take fourteen years to attain citizenship, he reported to Madison, owing to the fear that "a deluge of democrats" would reach America's shores as a result of continued political conflict and confusion across the Atlantic. The Alien Enemies Act would give the president, during wartime, the power to identify, arrest, and deport any alien whom he considered a threat. For Madison, the new legislation was "a monster that must forever disgrace its parents," and he believed (wrongly) that Washington would disapprove of the "hot-headed proceedings" of John Adams in taking the country in the direction of war. A number of Republicans in Congress, outnumbered by the Federalists and afraid of being associated with the French enemy, kept quiet. President Adams learned from his son John Quincy, then in Berlin, that the French had designs on American territories. Acting on this intelligence, and responding to the patriotic professions of various local militias, he authored a series of presidential statements, which were disseminated through the nation's newspapers.[57]

The Sedition Act was the most extreme manifestation of panic politics. Its unusual provision was to declare that publishing, or even verbalizing, "scandalous and malicious" statements about the president or Congress would result in a stiff fine and imprisonment. The carefully worded statute did not, however, protect the *vice* president from libelous insults, which was presumably intentional. By June 1798 a good number of congressional Republicans were running scared, afraid of appearing unpatriotic. William Branch Giles went back to Virginia. Edward Livingston returned to New York. Only Gallatin remained in town to monitor the Federalists in their moment of uncontested power.[58]

Newspapers took up the slack. *Carey's United States' Recorder,* published in Philadelphia, right away understood the sedition legislation as a "nefarious" instrument meant to establish "presidential infallibility" while rendering the federal Constitution "a dead letter, or a piece of musty parchment." It vowed: "The people may be gagged by alien and sedition bills, but at elections they will make their voice heard." On the other side of the lopsided equation, the *Columbian Centinel* of Boston asked rhetorically: "Who can object to a Sedition Bill," when American newspapermen were calling for subservience to France, and when such "wretches in this country... openly profess to wish the United States *may be punished,* and that all may terminate to the *glory of France.*"[59]

To combat the threat to national security, President Adams established a provisional army, for which he planned to enlist tens of thousands of men. He dutifully named George Washington as commander. To Adams's dismay, Washington said he would come out of retirement only if Hamilton were his second in command, at the rank of major general. Adams despised Hamilton for what he described as "debauched Morals" as well as a limitless ambition, but he swallowed his pride. It could not have been easy. He now had a Hamiltonian cabinet and a Hamiltonian army, while attempting to exercise executive authority over events that were spiraling out of control. Adams wanted his old friend Henry Knox, the former secretary of war, to be Hamilton's superior, and Knox himself expressed disgust with Hamilton's grand maneuver. But neither Hamilton nor Washington would accept an arrangement whereby Hamilton would have to answer to anyone—for it was unlikely that Washington would ever take the field.

Demonstrating just how solitary Adams's voice was, he had intended to appoint battle-hardened Aaron Burr a brigadier general, but Hamilton's men squelched the appointment. Before long Federalist mainstays began to ask what Hamilton's real motives were. Jefferson wryly called him "our Buonaparte," and Adams, in private, likened him to Julius Caesar. Yet as much as he longed to ride at the head of an expanded army, Hamilton did not instigate, or even advocate, the Alien and Sedition Acts. He worried about a political backlash, and he felt that the common law would be plenty effective in putting anti-administration newspapers out of business.[60]

Able to resist expressing sympathy for John Adams under any circumstances, Madison scoffed at the notion, then in vogue, that the president deserved credit for keeping the problem from getting worse. When the "infatuation of the moment" was past, Madison told Jefferson, it would be clear that the executive had deviously manipulated the public into doing what the government wanted. "Perhaps it is a universal truth," he argued most forcefully, "that the loss of liberty at home is to be charged to provisions against danger, real or pretended, from abroad." Keeping America safe was a sham justification for measures denying free speech, consolidating power, and impeding open debate in Congress.[61]

The undeclared war that followed became known to history as the Quasi-War. A few naval engagements between U.S. and French warships occurred, but casualties were light. The provisional army never fought. The most important result of the Quasi-War was the executive's consolidation of power in the conduct of foreign policy. Congress could request documents relating to diplomatic instructions, but it could do little to prevent any administration from charting a belligerent course. As things turned out, though, after the president returned to Massachusetts in July and was removed from the pressure put on him by his Hamiltonian cabinet, he determined that France had no intention of invading America and that it would be wise to restart diplomacy.

For Republicans, however, the summer did not pass quietly. In late June anticipation was already high as to the Federalists' plans to shut down dissent. Senator Henry Tazewell of Virginia had a dark sense of humor, which he expressed when he sent Madison a copy of the just-published Sedition Bill. He presumed that once Jefferson left Philadelphia and returned to Virginia, Madison would need a reliable source of news. Tazewell volunteered to be that source: "I will send you an account of whatever may occur that can be interesting," he said, "if I am not guillotined."[62]

Madison indulged his taste for humor. In advance of the Fourth of July 1798, he drafted a long list of mock toasts. It was a tradition in every town in America to lift glasses to the president, the Union, the Constitution, and other national symbols. Lists of toasts were published in the newspapers. Madison had his fun with the standard format: "The P. & V.P. may the [latter] never feel the passion of J.A. nor the [former] forsaken by the philosophy of T.J." Next, the ironist lifted his metaphorical glass to the Sedition Law: "The freedom of speech; May it strike its enemies dumb." And fixing on solid ground the loftiest of Americans: "G.W. the hero of liberty. May his enemies have the justice to applaud his virtues, and his friends the candor to acknowledge his error." This was as close as one could come before crossing the line with respect to the esteemed Washington.[63]

Madison's toasts never made it into print. While Jefferson was on a visit to Montpelier during that first week of July, a paper in Boston, the heart of Adams country, celebrated "that deathless instrument, the Declaration of American independence" by affirming that its inspired author, "the immortal Jefferson," deserved praise for the inspiration he brought to its composition.[64] Bache's paper added an impressive two hundred new subscribers in response to the enactment of the Sedition Law. "Thus," the editor wrote of those who sought to enfeeble him, "the daring hand of persecution already counteracts its own designs." Bache's exuberance did not last. After years of polemical writing, Benjamin Franklin's undiplomatic grandson was finally indicted for seditious libel. But in September 1798, a month before he was scheduled for trial, the defendant contracted yellow fever and died. By coincidence, one week later John Fenno, the Federalists' favorite editor, died too.[65]

It was not President Adams so much as his abrasive secretary of state, Timothy Pickering, who spearheaded the prosecutions for seditious libel. Pickering lumped together all Irish as dangerous elements and recommended drastic restrictions on immigration. Among those put on trial during the second half of the Adams administration were the Scottish pamphleteer James T. Callender, the Irish newspaperman John Daly Burk, and the fireplace-tong-wielding Matthew Lyon of Vermont. For libeling the president, Callender was fined $200 and sentenced to nine months in prison. Burk was bullied into shutting down his presses, as Aaron Burr sent him to the friendlier clime of Virginia to avoid deportation. Lyon, who bore a noticeable Irish accent, was fined $1,000 and jailed for four months after writing that the executive had "an unbounded thirst for ridiculous pomp, foolish adulation, and selfish avarice." He was reelected to Congress from his cell, and Jefferson was among those in Philadelphia who made contributions to the fund that paid Lyon's fine. Lyon had become a symbol in America of the price one paid for being outrageous in the act of seizing one's liberty.[66]

"The Residuary Mass of Right"

Edmund Pendleton's nephew John Taylor had left the U.S. Senate and was now a Virginia assemblyman. When he assured Taylor in June 1798 that "the reign of witches" would not last, Jefferson knew that he and Madison would be brainstorming shortly. After their days together at Montpelier on Jefferson's way home from Philadelphia, they determined to spend the Virginia summer drafting countermeasures to the clearly unconstitutional Alien and Sedition Acts.

Their answer became known as the Kentucky and Virginia Resolutions. Jefferson had originally intended to send his draft to the North Carolina legislature. But the fortuitous appearance in central Virginia of Kentucky's John Breckinridge led Wilson Cary Nicholas, to whom Jefferson had confided the work, to change the plan. As Kentucky was already actively protesting the Alien and Sedition laws, Breckinridge assured Nicholas that his state would be a more receptive forum in which to pass judgment on the administration's excesses. Jefferson agreed to the Kentucky strategy.

Breckinridge's credentials were strong. Jefferson's neighbors could attest to his character. He was born in Augusta County, Virginia, west of Albemarle (as the Reverend James Madison was), and had attended the College of William and Mary. In 1785, when Jefferson was in Paris, Breckinridge opened a law practice in Charlottesville, relocating to Kentucky in 1793, where he served as the state's attorney general for two years before entering the state House of Representatives. He had already drafted resolutions and public protests against the Alien and Sedition Acts before he made his trip to Virginia. His major ally in this effort was the brother of Wilson Cary Nicholas.[67]

By late October, after reviewing Jefferson's resolutions, Madison had prepared a separate text for Virginia. The resolutions were presented to the two state legislatures by Breckinridge and Taylor, respectively, so as to shield the actual authors. Secrecy was maintained; it would be a good many years before Madison and Jefferson were publicly identified with the texts.[68] Despite their well-laid plans, rumors circulated almost immediately that

Jefferson was behind both the Kentucky and Virginia Resolutions. Boston's *Columbian Centinel* reported: "The disorganizing Resolutions introduced into the Legislature of *Virginia*, have passed.—And—Mr. Jefferson has arrived in *Philadelphia*."[69]

Jefferson's underlying principle was laid out in the opening sentence of the Kentucky Resolutions: the United States was "not united on the principle of unlimited submission to the general government." As equal parties to the federal compact, the individual states had delegated certain enumerated powers to the federal government, while reserving to themselves "the residuary mass of right to their own self-government." If the federal government tried to exercise "undelegated powers," its actions were immediately to be considered "unauthoritative, void, and of no force." Therefore, the power to decide what those delegated powers were could not reside in the federal government; each state had "an equal right to judge for itself."[70]

The theory had much in common with the Declaration of Independence. Recall that Jefferson conceived of the Declaration as a kind of divorce petition, in which the natural rights of one of the parties within the British-American union (the colonies) had been violated repeatedly. The condition of the states in the federal Union was similar to that of the colonies in that they were united by compact with a central authority. In ratifying the Constitution, each state had given its consent, but as with any compact or contract, it could be annulled or amended. A breach of contract, a violation of its specific terms—in this case the federal government's use of an unauthorized power—meant the state could refuse to abide by that part of the contract which the other party had twisted and corrupted. *Nullification* was a form of veto power, normally reserved for the executive. But as Jefferson saw it, that power now belonged to each of the individual states and was to be exercised solely within its jurisdiction.[71]

Jefferson had retreated to his earlier thinking on the division between federal and state functions, which he had sketched out to Madison in 1786. At that time he had said: "To make us one nation as to foreign concerns, and keep us distinct in domestic ones, gives the outline of the proper division of power between the general and particular governments."[72] Now he was insisting that each state warranted a powerful form of redress: to declare any law null and void that compromised its ability to protect the rights of its citizens. Because the states had a natural right to nullify on their own authority, any state that lost its autonomy sacrificed itself to the dominion of another. Like an individual, a state was either free and independent or in a state of submission. There could be no middle ground.[73]

For Jefferson, a strict division between federal and state authority had to be preserved. Any trespass of this rigid boundary was a slippery slope. The Alien and Sedition laws were the beginning of a long train of abuses that would lead from deportation of the "friendless alien" to persecution of the average citizen. The central government could do anything it wanted if the states did not have some check on its authority. It appeared to him that if Congress could claim any power, or transfer its authority to the president or any other person, then that person, as "the accuser, counsel, judge and jury," could turn "suspicion" into "evidence," reduce anyone to an "Outlaw," and place anyone under the "absolute dominion of one man." In short, without a check, the United States could become a dictatorship.

Part of this thinking was personal. Certain Federalists were looking for any excuse to turn Jefferson into an "Outlaw." He hoped to make Virginia his sanctuary, a legal fortress, his protection from their predatory grasp. He wanted the Constitution to be a straightjacket, capable of undermining any attempt at a power grab by government officials. Constitutional checks had no appreciable force in the current political environment, or as Jefferson put it: "The barrier of the constitution thus swept away from us, no rampart remains against the passions and the power of a majority in Congress." The states' last defense was to nullify illegitimate laws.

Madison began the Virginia Resolutions by repeating some of Jefferson's ideas. He agreed that the federal government was based on a compact "to which the states are parties." As the Constitution was limited by "enumerated powers," if the government engaged in a "deliberate, palpable and dangerous exercise of other powers not granted by the said compact, the states who are parties thereto have the right, and are duty bound, to interpose for arresting the progress of the evil." After three opening paragraphs, all nodding in Jefferson's direction, Madison diverged somewhat. His constitutional argument focused on "forced constructions" of the charter—Hamilton's misreading of the "necessary and proper" clause that pointed toward a consolidation of the states into "one sovereignty."

He framed his opposition to the Alien and Sedition Acts differently than Jefferson did. The Alien Act violated the separation of powers, he said, by transferring both judicial and legislative powers to the executive. This gave the president the judicial power to set up hearings to judge whether a person could be deported; the president alone determined proof of guilt without having to follow any congressional guidelines on what constituted a danger to the public safety.[74]

While the Sedition Act relied on an undelegated power, Madison considered its more egregious transgression to be that of violating what was "expressly and positively forbidden" in the First Amendment to the Constitution. Quoting from the Virginia Ratifying Convention, he reiterated that freedom of conscience was the "guardian of every other right." By showing an "indifference" to this guaranteed freedom, the Sedition Act was a "mark of reproachful inconsistency and criminal degeneracy." But he stopped short of calling for nullification. He wished instead for other states to join with Virginia in declaring the acts unconstitutional; they would offer a united front and publicly espouse a common interpretation of the "rights reserved to the States, respectively, or to the people."[75]

The point is that Madison's text was a limited, not a total, endorsement of Jefferson's principles. He intentionally avoided use of the words *null, nullify,* or *nullification*. He substituted the word *interpose,* which, according to Dr. Johnson's *Dictionary,* meant "to mediate, to act between two parties; to put in by way of interruption." These are gentler terms than what Jefferson opted for, and they opened the door to negotiation. To nullify was to annul—to declare that the government never had this power in the first place.

Madison's solution was intentionally more ambiguous. He proposed no coherent legal strategy; he did not explain precisely what the states must do to arrest the "evil" before them. He refused to weigh in on the power of an individual state to curb the excesses of federal power, which was so central to Jefferson's strategy. For Madison, the states—the collective body of the states—would take the appropriate (but unspecified) action.[76]

Although Madison and Jefferson diverged, several state legislatures failed to draw a distinction between the two sets of resolutions. These states criticized both for advocating "the *dangerous doctrine,* that the State Governments are the constitutional judges of the Acts or Laws of the Federal Government." Madison's subtle word choices did little to quell the larger fear of disunion that was seen in the call to grant states "unwarrantable power" to interpret federal laws.[77]

After just a few days of debate, both houses in Kentucky passed the resolutions in November 1798. Breckinridge made changes to Jefferson's draft, dropping the language of nullification. Then the resolutions were forwarded to Kentucky's two U.S. senators and its two congressmen, who were instructed to work for the repeal of the Alien and Sedition Acts in Congress. Jefferson's staunchest allies in Kentucky understood that the protest should be aimed at Congress, even if Jefferson intended for Congress to be bypassed and for the state to take matters into its own hands.

The Virginia Assembly passed its version of the resolutions on December 21, 1798.[78]

After all was said and done, not a single state rallied to Virginia's side. Nine northern states renounced the resolutions, and only one southern state, North Carolina, bothered to respond at all (and still its Senate would not approve the resolutions).[79] Changing the debate, "Peter Porcupine" lashed out at the Virginians for their hypocrisy in claiming to be "actuated by a *love of liberty*" when they "live on the sweat of *slaves*." A Connecticut critic brought up Jefferson's history of slinking away from manly engagement by calling the resolutions "cowards huffs," empty threats spun by the "insidious sophistry of the *Mazzei* tribe of philosophers." Since the Virginia Resolutions were followed by a bill for arming the state's militia, some accused Richmond of preparing to use the threat of military force to intimidate other states. Madison's and Jefferson's enemies flatly declared the "Ancient Dominion" to be in opposition to the Union.[80]

"A Foreign Poison Vitiating the American Sentiment"

Rather than help the Republicans' cause, the Kentucky and Virginia Resolutions served only to stiffen the Federalists' resolve. Fisher Ames of Massachusetts assailed Madison's surrogate for the Virginia Resolutions, John Taylor of Caroline: "Virginia, excited by crazy Taylor, is fulminating its manifesto against the federal government." Former president Washington was so disturbed that he appealed to Patrick Henry to reenter politics in order to turn back the tide. In a letter marked "confidential," he bemoaned "the endeavors of a certain party among us, to disquiet the Public mind with unfounded alarms." No longer even mentioning the names of former intimates Madison and Jefferson, he expressed regret that Virginia had "taken the lead" in protesting "every act of the Administration."

Like the most inveterate of Federalist propagandists, Washington accused those whom he would not name but called generically "this Party" of preferring "the interest of France to the Welfare of their own Country." Pages into his anguished letter to Henry, the "First of Men" brought his list of charges to an end and opened a new paragraph: "I come now, my good Sir, to the object of my letter—which is—to express a hope, and an earnest wish, that you wd come forward at the ensuing Elections (if not for Congress, which you may think would take you too long from home) as a candidate for representation, in the General Assembly of this Commonwealth." He flattered Henry: "Your weight of character and influence... would be a bulwark against... dangerous Sentiments."[81]

Henry, so long out of government, could not say no to George Washington. He refused to stand for Congress, given his declining—what he called "very indifferent"—health, but he did agree to serve in the Virginia Assembly. He despised the Republicans as much as Washington did for the disrespect they had shown to the government, but as a devout Christian, he cast his fears in religious language. "The Foundations of our Morality and Government" had been sacrificed to "French principles," Henry said, because "those who nickname themselves 'Democrats'" were turning their backs on "Truths which concern our Happiness in the World to come, alike with our Happiness in this."[82]

Many others would launch public attacks on Jefferson and the Republicans for their dangerous critique of religion, but the well-developed network of Republican papers fought back. "The spirit of party has converted the elegant reasoning of Mr. Jefferson against *religious establishments* into a blasphemous argument against *religion* itself," wrote one supporter in the *Baltimore Telegraph,* an opinion picked up by newspapers in other parts of the country. And the *Bee,* of New London, Connecticut, proclaimed: "How ridiculous and contemptible do our newspaper scribblers of the present day appear in their endeavours to detract from the literary and moral character of Mr. Jefferson!"[83]

The Alien and Sedition Acts complicated life for Federalists much as the Terror had complicated life for Republicans a few years before. John Marshall, a favorite of Washington's, claimed that he would have voted against the Alien and Sedition Acts though they were constitutionally sound; he authored a pamphlet on the subject. Washington had urged Marshall (in addition to Henry) to run for Congress and now had to be disabused of his belief that Marshall had adopted, undiluted, the High Federalist creed. Like President Adams, John Marshall did his own thinking.

Writing from Philadelphia, Adams explained to his predecessor why he had decided on a new approach to the French. Talleyrand himself had assured him that a decent reception awaited his next envoy. This did not prevent Adams from launching into a rant about the Republicans for having urged good Franco-American relations all along: "I wish the babyish and womanly blubbering for Peace may not necessitate the Conclusion of a Treaty that shall not be just nor very honourable." Also from Philadelphia, two days later, Secretary of State Pickering wrote Washington of the Hamiltonians' annoyance with Adams for agreeing to take up diplomacy with the despicable French. "The Jacobins alone are pleased," Pickering alleged. "The *honor* of the country is prostrated in the dust."[84]

Wading into the brawl in which his political offspring were engaged, an honored elder urged reason and forbearance. In his *Address of the Honorable Edmund Pendleton of Virginia to the American Citizens, on the State of Our Country*, published in Federalist Boston, the old Revolutionary pointed out how futile it was for the United States to engage in provocation with France when France was sending signals that its demand was for nothing more than "placing our commerce with Britain and France on the same footing." He dismissed the notion that there was somehow a "French party" in America, and he explained that no Republican wanted any connection with France more "intimate" than the quality of the relationship America enjoyed under the 1778 treaty through which the French proved themselves willing to fight for American independence. Pendleton defended Jefferson, not by name but as "the gentleman who is honoured by being placed at the head of this supposed party," and pleaded with a divided people to take a breath and look for peaceful, constitutional remedies for the nation's domestic ailments. As he had been in 1775, Pendleton attempted to be in 1799: the cooler head that he hoped would prevail. What he did not say in his address was that Jefferson had explicitly asked him to write something that would have the effect of "exposing the dupery being practised" on the American people by a cynical government. "Nobody in America can do it so well as yourself," Jefferson had coaxed.[85]

The year 1799 saw a continuation of confrontational politics. In January and February Madison decided to go after the malefactors. Twice he wrote surreptitiously for the *Aurora,* using the signatures "Enemy to Foreign Influence" and "A Citizen of the United States." In the first, he used an uninhibited metaphor—"the most jealous lover never guarded an inconstant mistress with a more watchful eye"—to complain about Britain's "rigid and compulsive monopoly" over transatlantic trade, dating to the colonial period. "But the most powerful, perhaps, of all her motives," Madison charged, "is her *hatred and fear* of the *republican example* of our governments." He updated the old imagery of Tory perversion, warning that trade and profit had been concentrated in the hands of merchants who were bound to British capital and credit: "Thus it is," he wrote spectacularly, "that our country is penetrated to its remotest corners with a foreign poison vitiating the American sentiment, recolonizing the American character." This piece of polemic may be the most eloquent single line Madison ever wrote. He did not take, and has never received, credit for it.

In the second of his *Aurora* essays, Madison tried to reason his way through the generally distasteful course of the French Revolution. Demonstrating his caustic wit, he explained that it was not unusual for governments in the process of consolidating power to cultivate fear among the populace, mixing real threats with "jealousies, discontents, and murmurs." Subversion of public opinion was, he wrote sharply, a tactic to which the United States was no more immune than the French Republic.[86]

Jefferson saw and approved the essays before they were printed, and he visited Madison in early March as he traveled south from Philadelphia. In the early years of the republic, Congress might be out of session for entire seasons, and in 1799 Vice President Jefferson remained at home from March until mid-December.[87] After his late-winter stopover in Orange, there is a mystifying six-month gap in the Madison-Jefferson correspondence, due perhaps to both men's apprehensions about the security of their communications. It is likely that messages were conveyed through private messengers and not retained.

In April 1799, a month into this epistolary drought, John Taylor and others expressed to Madison their concern about Patrick Henry's return to politics. They convinced Madison to serve once again in the House of Delegates as a foil to the seductive orator, who rarely did as expected and who now supported the repressive Alien and Sedition Acts. But the drama never played out. On June 6, before the state legislature had even met, Henry died.[88]

In August, from Monticello, Jefferson reopened his correspondence with Madison. Dolley was in Jefferson's neighborhood at the time and could, without harassment, carry home a letter containing dangerous sentiments. The letter of August 23 was arguably the most radical that Jefferson ever wrote to Madison or to anyone else. It envisioned conditions under which he would be willing to sanction the dissolution of the Union. In Jefferson's estimation, the resolutions he and Madison had authored for the states to consider were good, but not good enough. Kentucky and Virginia had not sparked the kind of outcry he had hoped for; he wanted now to reexamine what might be done in a worse instance, if the states too easily acquiesced after the federal government clamped down on them, "disregarding the limitations of the federal compact."

His prescription was dire. He seemed to strain to get the words out, and when he did, he could not find an effortless way to finish the opinion. Express in "affectionate and conciliatory language," he proposed, "our warm attachment to union with our sister-states..., that we are willing to sacrifice to this every thing except those rights of self government the securing of which was the object of that compact: that not at all disposed to make every measure of error or wrong a cause of scission, we are willing to view with indulgence and [to] wait with patience till those passions and delusions shall have passed over which the federal government have artfully and successfully excited to cover it's own abuses and to conceal it's designs." Jefferson was writing a new, less beautiful declaration of independence—or declaration of divorce. "But determined," he plodded on, "were we to be disappointed in this, to sever ourselves from that union we so much value, rather than give up the rights of self government which we have reserved, and in which alone we see liberty, safety and happiness." And then he added bizarrely: "These things I sketch hastily."[89]

Madison did not go to his desk and compose a systematic reply. He rode to Monticello instead, where they conferred face-to-face. Jefferson rethought what he had written and agreed with Madison that disuniting was a faulty prescription for present—or future—political ills. It was a rare instance of Jefferson's reversing himself. But as he explained to Wilson Cary Nicholas of Albemarle County, his close ally in the state legislature, Madison had not needed to argue to convince him. He realized on his own that he had momentarily gone astray.

As the year wore on, Madison and Jefferson did not even have the luxury of paying visits to each other at will. The reason was not just the insecurity of the postal service, where seals and handwriting were recognized, and letters were purloined and their contents fed to unprincipled newspaper editors. This time Monroe took the initiative, cautioning Jefferson and Madison to avoid being seen together. In a place with few country roads and little anonymity, it was hard to hide comings and goings. It would not take much for them to stand accused of brewing conspiracies. Jefferson agreed with Monroe's logic.[90]

Madison, Jefferson, and Monroe were more a triumvirate now than they had been at any time past. The Monroes were spending more and more time on the Albemarle property.[91] In a heavily Republican House of Delegates, late in 1799, Madison proposed Monroe for the governorship of Virginia. His activities in France earlier in the decade had annoyed Washington while greatly pleasing most of the rest of Virginia. As a result, Monroe won the governor's job by a significant margin over the Federalist candidate. The Virginians were on the move again. Stymied by Federalist gains in the last few years, they were buoyed now by confusion in the Federalist ranks, after President Adams rebelled against his cabinet and restored balance in foreign affairs. Virginia was eager to reclaim its accustomed rank among the states.

"Death Has Robbed Our Country"

The new century drew near. And as it did, the Revolutionary generation bade farewell to two senior Virginians. Six months after the loss of the daring, erratic Patrick Henry, George Washington died at Mount Vernon on December 14, 1799, at the age of sixty-seven. Had he lived a few more months, he would have had his immediate successor as a neighbor, when the Adamses moved from Philadelphia to the new Federal City on the Potomac.

Before he died, Washington was able to resume a correspondence with the youngest general in his Continental Army. Despite his long confinement, Lafayette had emerged from prison with as dynamic a commitment to American-style liberty as he possessed before his ordeal began. He loved the Americans and vowed to return to the United States for a long visit. Washington discouraged him from coming, citing the "present political agitation," but Lafayette, as stubborn as he was affectionate, still planned to sail, saying that he wished to enjoy moments of seclusion at Mount Vernon with his treasured friend. In truth, Washington feared that Lafayette was too close in sentiments to the Republicans, or could be manipulated by them. Lafayette did not accept "no" easily. "I long to be in America," he cooed.

No one else addressed Washington with the fervor of Lafayette. "I know you long to fold me to your paternal heart," he pressed. In the last letter of his that Washington would ever read, Lafayette acknowledged his ambition to play a role in negotiating an improvement in Franco-American relations. To an American diplomat at The Hague, he suggested that the unique understanding he shared with lead participants in the American Revolution might be enough to bring peace to the warring factions, Federalist and Republican.[92]

It was the height of nerve and perhaps the best example of Lafayette's "canine" appetite for fame that Jefferson had long before described in a letter to Madison. Still, the Frenchman had a sincere and irreducible commitment to the United States. Only the death of George Washington could stop him from sailing. As a result, he would not cross the ocean again for another quarter-century, at which time he who was once the youngest

American general would be within a year of the age Washington was when laid to rest.

Lafayette's only open criticism of America concerned the sin of slavery. In the mid-1780s he had urged the land-rich Washington to resettle slaves as tenants on his property in the West—an experiment other planters could imitate. But the suggestion fell on deaf ears. At the time Washington claimed that his financial future remained in some doubt, and he saw slave ownership as an "imperious necessity" for him.

Washington, credited in history for having resolved to free his slaves after his death, could do so because he had no sons or daughters of his own and had earned an income from lands he leased out over the years, lands he had surveyed or received as bounties for his military service. The ambivalent emancipator made it clear that Mount Vernon would retain its slaves while his widow Martha lived. He claimed to have done all he could to provide an "easy and comfortable" way of life to those whose "ignorance" prohibited the adoption of any more liberal policy. He did nothing as president to draw the public's attention to the politics or morals of race enslavement.[93]

Other matters took precedence. It is tempting in the twenty-first century to collapse time, reduce the distant past to an easy logic, and assign the greatest share of blame for slavery to certain well-known names or to censure the entire Revolutionary generation for failing to live up to its grand ideals. But doing so risks imputing to them a sense of priority and a vision of collective action that matches our own cherished cultural views. While it is true that Quakers and Methodists agitated for an end to slavery, widespread prejudices such as those George Washington unhesitatingly voiced always stood in the way. We may never really know what conscience dictated to historical actors, but a wise beginning for the modern questioner would be to assess everyday fears and political pressures and to analyze, in this context, how they rationalized their behavior.

Nor was Washington's passing an occasion on which to reexamine the slavery issue. It was, however, a time when many chose to recall the Revolution appreciatively. As one would expect, the second half of December 1799 and the first part of the year 1800 produced an outpouring of ceremony and tribute, the most memorable of which was the succinct phrasing of Henry Lee: "First in war, first in peace, and first in the hearts of his countrymen." Less well known is the more hyperbolic language contained in General Lee's address: "When our monuments shall be done away; when nations now existing shall be no more; when even our young and far-spreading empire shall have perished, still will our Washington's glory un-faded shine, and die not." Other eulogists went even further to paint the first president as an instrument of God's providence. As hard as it is to imagine in light of Washington's posthumous reputation, there was back-lash in select places too. At the College of William and Mary, Bishop James Madison—the reverend had been named bishop in 1790—authorized black armbands to be worn, but a number of students refused.[94]

In the Virginia House of Delegates, Madison rose to report the tragic news: "Death has robbed our country of its most distinguished ornament, and the world one of its greatest benefactors." As he had done in Congress on the death of Benjamin Franklin in 1790, in Richmond now he intro-duced a motion calling on the members of the legislature to wear badges of mourning for the length of the current session.

On the day before Washington's death, in curious contrast, a similar res-olution honoring the "eloquence and superior talents" of Patrick Henry was put forward. It was rejected. Fifteen years earlier, when Henry was frus-trating reform in the Assembly, Jefferson had said in a letter to Madison: "What we have to do I think is devoutly to pray for his death." Perhaps Henry's *political* death was all he meant. Now Henry was in all ways dead, and a new era had arrived in Virginia politics in which the party of George Washington was a dwindling minority.[95]

Though their politics had diverged sharply, Madison could not dislike Washington the man. He convinced himself that Washington's opinions were similar to his own, and that the older man had little patience for John Adams's argumentative manner and less adept management of the presi-dency. Madison surely believed that Washington had been misled by the High Federalists, and while he did not describe the phenomenon as a func-tion of senility, as Jefferson later did, he preferred not to think that Wash-ington was lumping Madison together with all those who had made his second term unpleasant. But the truth is, he was. He did not, however, con-sider Madison sneaky or dishonest.

Jefferson was a different story. At the end of his life, Washington refused to forgive Jefferson for the betrayal that the Mazzei letter represented, thinking little more of him than he did the newspaper editor Benjamin Franklin Bache, whose fulminations in print soured his moods and caused him to question the longevity of the Union. Madison, it appears, was caught keeping company with those who most infuriated Washington, and it served to end too soon what had been a good and vigorous collaboration.

CHAPTER TEN

Inhaling Republicanism
1800–1802

*The late brilliant triumph of republicanism appears to have
given to the public mind an animation only equalled by that
which attended our revolutionary struggle.*

—*NATIONAL INTELLIGENCER* (WASHINGTON, D.C.),
MARCH 13, 1801, ONE WEEK AFTER JEFFERSON
TOOK THE OATH OF OFFICE

*Our republic is undoubtedly "the world's best hope"; the elysium
of earthly residence. If it perish, twenty centuries more may
elapse before another arise.*

—*AMERICAN CITIZEN* (NEW YORK), FEBRUARY 8, 1802

A NEW, MORE FORWARD STYLE OF POLITICAL ACTION HAD COME
into vogue that centered on the understood power of print in the enterprise of party building. By this measure, Republicans were gaining. They
communicated. They knew how to organize.

The discourse of election year 1800 retained a vocabulary of extremes.
To the Federalists, if Jefferson defeated Adams, upending a government of
"order," he would introduce in its place a government of dangerous "experiment," with the country devolving into atheism and anarchy. To Republicans, of course, "order" had slaughtered liberty. Madison, Jefferson,
and their allies felt temperatures rising.

Republicans never doubted that Thomas Jefferson was to be their national candidate in 1800. No one within the party preferred another or be-

lieved anyone else could defeat Adams. During the months when government business kept him in Philadelphia, Vice President Jefferson began to take an unusually direct role in raising funds for a new Republican newspaper. The paper never got off the ground, but he was not deterred. In the coming year, both he and Madison would contribute to emerging newspapers in the federal city of Washington, where the next president would be taking the oath of office. And they would pay close attention to the activities of Republican organizers.[1]

While he sat in the Virginia House of Delegates, Madison continued to function as Jefferson's campaign manager. He felt he had to clear up any remaining confusion about the Kentucky and Virginia Resolutions, the true authorship of which remained a closely guarded secret. His *Report of 1800,* passed by the state legislature on January 7, essentially disavowed the nullification principle; at the same time, it went to great lengths to show how the Sedition Act threatened a fair presidential election. There had to be open discussion about the candidates—he meant, of course, an open discussion of Adams's record—without critics having to fear prosecution for "freely examining" the president's public character and decisions.

Madison put forward an unambiguous definition of free speech, more far-reaching than he had ever done before. Freedom of speech was the foundation of republicanism, a principle "*equally* and *completely* exempted from all authority whatever of the United States." Neither federal nor state law could restrict it. Subversive ideas had fueled the American Revolution and circulated again during the ratification period. Had a sedition act been enforced against the press at such times, he asked, "might not the United States have been languishing to this day, under the infirmities of a sickly confederation? Might they not possibly be miserable colonies, groaning under a foreign yoke?"

He was not forgetting the Kentucky and Virginia Resolutions. Rather, he was softening those elements contained in them that might otherwise be found dangerous to the health and well-being of the Union. By the end of the report, Madison reduced the Virginia Resolutions to mere "expressions of opinion," with no presumed effect greater than "exciting reflection." States could and should communicate freely with other states; their legislatures could "originate amendments to the constitution," without being deemed radical or destructive. Jefferson read Madison's report with satisfaction and had high hopes for it, but it sparked little reaction outside of Richmond. The Kentucky and Virginia Resolutions were already old news.[2]

With that matter taken off the table, attention turned to Europe. Once again domestic politics must be understood in the light of developments abroad. Foreign intelligence ordinarily reached Philadelphia first, yet it was Madison, in Orange, who approached Vice President Jefferson in February 1800 with the observation: "We see by the late papers that a new scene is presented on the French Theatre, which leaves the denôuement more a problem than ever." He hesitated to say that absolutism would be the result of the ten-year-old French Revolution, but "melancholy evidence appears that the destiny of the Revolution is transferred from the Civil to the military authority." The facts did not suggest to Madison that Republicans in the United States would have more to explain on the subject of their identification with the French. Rather, the lesson to be drawn from Napoleon's rise to the rank of first consul (after a coup that overthrew the constitutional government) was that the American public needed to be more wary of military usurpation coming from within its own government.[3]

Jefferson was counting heads, examining the balance of power in Congress. To an even greater degree, perhaps, he was assessing the balance of power in key state legislatures, particularly New York, where presidential electors were about to be chosen. "All depends on the success of the city election," he told Madison encouragingly, noting that Aaron Burr and Edward Livingston, the primary and secondary strategists there, "entertain no doubt on the event of that election." They had assured him that Republicans were in a position to reverse the 1796 result, when Adams and Pinckney had won all of the state's electoral votes.

Victory in New York was critical, because Pennsylvania, the one northern state Jefferson had carried in 1796, remained in jeopardy. Its state legislature was engaged in a sharp debate over the method by which presidential electors would be chosen. New Jersey, where Philadelphians exerted influence, was leaning Republican, if not yet in the composition of the state legislature, then certainly in congressional contests. Clerk of the House of Representatives John Beckley, a key Jefferson ally, coordinated with the Garden State's leading voice, thirty-year-old Princeton graduate Mahlon Dickerson, who practiced law in Philadelphia and wrote for the *Aurora*.

Chastened, no doubt, by the sectional results of the election that relegated Jefferson to the vice presidency, the southern-dominated party was embracing new elements and rallying support beyond its home base. "Peter Porcupine" saw the trend. The Philadelphia Republicans were making his blood boil, and he vented to a friend in England: "If I could exterminate the whole race, I know not how I should set bounds to my vengeance . . . Damnation seize them, body and soul! If I can give them a foretaste of the torments of hell, I will do it." After doing the math, Jefferson reconfirmed that New York City held the key to the election of 1800.[4]

There Burr was outmaneuvering Hamilton. He had built a party organization in Manhattan and selected an unbeatable slate of candidates. Energetically addressing citizens on the importance of the upcoming election, he got the results he wanted: the Republicans carried all thirteen assembly seats in the city, which assured that they would get to name the state's presidential electors. Caught off guard, Hamilton rushed off a letter to Governor John Jay, requesting a lame duck session of the legislature. He wanted Jay to change the rules so that the Federalists would not be deprived of seats—Hamilton was trying to overturn a fair election. Jay recognized the ploy as a mere "party measure" and refused to go along. His sense of ethics salvaged Burr's victory and seems to have convinced Virginians that Burr deserved to be Jefferson's running mate.[5]

In April 1800, Jefferson reported on a stimulating visit he had had from the French political economist Pierre Samuel Du Pont de Nemours, a near victim of the guillotine who became his lifelong friend—"one of the very great men of the age," he told Madison. Nonetheless, Jefferson refrained from expressing sentiments about the larger picture in France. It was Madison who reopened the subject. Without crediting Adams (who had already dispatched a pair of unprejudiced envoys), he expressed comfort with the new approach to Old World diplomacy. "The posture of Europe," wrote Madison, "tho' dreadful to humanity in general, will I trust enforce the disposition of France to come to a proper adjustment with us."[6]

This did not mean that the Republicans, as the antiwar element in the country, should or would let their guard down. The first year of a new century was, after all, an election year, or as it was also called, an "Electoral epoch," and in times such as these nothing could be taken for granted. Madison was candid about his concern. The Federalists might provoke a war hotter than "quasi-war" in order to create an atmosphere that would dictate against changing administrations. "The situation of the party bent on war is such," he said, "that every stratagem ought to be suspected that may afford a chance of prolonging their ascendancy. The horrors which they evidently feel at the approach of the Electoral epoch are sufficient warning of the desperate game by which they will be apt to characterize the interval." He promised to enlighten Jefferson on the appointment of presidential electors by the Virginia Assembly. Both men were equally focused on the electoral count.

In a close campaign, every vote counted. Because they had control of the legislature, Virginia's Republicans opted to amend the system that had been in place in 1796. At that time, the vote of each electoral district was separately tallied, making it possible for the state's electoral votes to be divided among the candidates. In 1800 all of Virginia's electoral votes, undivided, would be awarded to the candidate who won a majority. (This is the general ticket system, comparable to the system under which electoral votes are counted in modern U.S. presidential elections.) Predictably, Jefferson was strongest in heavily agricultural districts: Albemarle (563 votes to 33), Orange (337 to 7), and Pendleton's and Taylor's Caroline County (370 to 5). Richmond was almost evenly divided, owing to the strength of pro-Federalist commercial interests there; and the busy port of Norfolk went for Adams. The electors, chosen by the voters of each district, included the names of men long associated with Jefferson: Edmund Pendleton, George Wythe, John Page, Joseph Jones, William Branch Giles, and James Madison. All of Virginia's twenty-one electoral votes were going to the native son, and none to Adams.[7]

Virginia was not representative. Jefferson knew that as the campaign proceeded, he would have to withstand another wave of newspaper assaults. Every aspect of his past that was contained in the public record would be exploited for partisan purposes. And so Jefferson's supporters turned to 1776 as a protective device, and the Declaration of Independence as a sacred symbol. Nearly a quarter-century had passed without his being known widely as the author of the Declaration. By July 4, 1800, this fact had become an integral part of his reputation; it also generated significant blowback from the other side. As Rhode Island's *Providence Journal* indifferently reported, "From the frequent mention that Jefferson was the author of the Declaration of Independence, ignorant people might be led to doubt whether others, who were esteemed patriots, approved the measure. If Jefferson penned the declaration, it probably was an accidental honour in the arrangement of committees." The distinction drawn between authorship and penmanship was a meaningful one.[8]

Demonstrating just how much tabloid fascination drove the press in 1800, a rumor begun in Virginia reached Philadelphia, New York, and outlying areas by midyear, claiming that candidate Jefferson had died. Eventually the story unraveled: "A negro man who formerly belonged to the family of Mr. Jefferson, and had taken the family name, died very suddenly near Winchester, where a young lad thought it a good Virginia Joke to spread a report of the death of Citizen Tom Jefferson, without comment;—the report spread like wildfire." The article went on to accuse Madison of having callously fancied himself in the "great chair" before ultimately discovering the inaccuracy of the report.[9]

The Hamiltonian explanation of Madison's desertion of his *Federalist Papers* coauthor—his supposed seduction by Jefferson—had by now become central to the Federalist critique. "No sooner did Mr. Jefferson return from Europe," reported both the *New-York Spectator* and *Courier of New-Hampshire*, "than Mr. Madison commenced an opposition to the measures of government." The conspiratorial tone of the article intensified as it took on the delicate subject of sectional prejudice and the common assumption that Virginia planters possessed a proud air of inherited superiority, which they had transferred to their state: Virginia had developed such "pride in her greatness" that "she cannot brook the idea of losing…her supposed right to command."

A presidential election is a zero-sum game. For someone to win, someone else must lose. To this terrified writer, Madison and Jefferson both appeared amenable to social revolution; and so an adverse outcome could only mean national catastrophe. "Mr. Jefferson's men declare there is no conciliation," he interpolated from rumors and questionable news sources. Unless the Federalists held on to power, the best America could expect was an uneasy peace between North and South and a return to state sovereignty as it existed under the Articles of Confederation. Then a series of popular disturbances would result either in a military takeover or in a brutal civil war.[10]

The incumbent president was forced to endure a comparable amount of vindictive press. From the Richmond jail where he had been confined after calling Adams a "hoary-headed incendiary," James T. Callender published a further harangue, maintaining a sarcastic tone over 152 pages. He mocked Adams's professions of Christianity—the same grounds on which Jefferson was so often attacked—by asking: "What is the religion of that man, who swears to support a constitution, and then breaks it?" Adams had "prattled so loudly of his reverence for the Christian religion" upon entering office; but his legislative initiatives since then belied the claim.

Callender defended Virginia republicanism, and Jefferson, in turn, defended Callender though he knew the man was vulgar. He might have listened to John Taylor of Caroline, who cautioned against involvement with one so unscrupulous and so dominated by self-interest that he was likely to turn on his benefactor at the first sign of neglect.[11]

"Forever and Inseparable, the Names of Independence and Jefferson"

In the fall of 1800, Madison and Jefferson shared news of the ever-tightening race. Burr's soon-to-be son-in-law, a South Carolina planter heading home from a tour of the northern states, carried a letter from Montpelier to Monticello, relating Burr's optimism about the votes of Rhode Island. Yet some of the strongest repudiations of Jefferson were just then appearing in the Federalist press in that tiny state: He was the "patron of disorganization," the "American philosopher...convicted of cowardice," the hypocritical slave owner who degraded the capacity of blacks while pretending to favor manumission, "a man who has, in his writings, proclaimed himself to the world a *Deist,* if not an *Atheist*...and ridicules the Bible with wanton malignity." In contrast, it reported, "Who ever heard it said of Mr. Adams that he was an infidel in principle, a coward in the hour of dangers, or a dupe to the wild anti-christian, and demoralizing theories of the age, which have corrupted mankind?" The article, dateline Newport, was signed, "INVESTIGATOR."[12]

Reports from Burr on Republican inroads in New England were hard for Jefferson to accept as certain indicators. Meanwhile Madison conveyed to Jefferson the concerns of Burr's allies that after having been abandoned by Virginia Republicans in 1796, when he was Jefferson's putative running mate, the New Yorker might not be able to count on the "*integrity* of the Southern States" in 1800 either. To Monroe, Madison wrote asking that "all proper measures" be taken to ensure that Burr did not lose the vice presidency because of some mix-up in Virginia. Indeed, one of the stipulations that Burr himself made on accepting his role as running mate was that the traditionally ungenerous Virginians hold up their end of the bargain and this time back him without reservation.[13]

As election time approached, Jefferson's later biographer George Tucker found James Madison at the home of Governor Monroe, and penned a description of him: he was "nearly fifty years of age, dressed in silk stockings and black breeches, and wore powder according to the practice that still prevailed in full dress. The first [impression] he made on me was that of sternness rather than of the mildness and suavity which I found afterwards." A few months later Margaret Bayard Smith, the energetic wife of newspaper editor Samuel H. Smith, gave a singular account of her first encounter with Vice President Jefferson. Congress had only then completed its inaugural meeting in the "infant city" of Washington, when a stranger presented himself in her parlor. After the initial chill of his exceedingly dignified bearing, she found that "he turned towards me a countenance beaming with an expression of benevolence and with a manner and voice almost femininely soft and gentle." They began to converse more affably, as he drew her into a discussion of substance. "I know not how it was, but there was something in his manner, his countenance and voice that at once unlocked my heart." Some time later her husband appeared and told her, to her great surprise, who the captivating conversationalist was.[14]

Clerk of the House John Beckley was the Republicans' most ardent campaigner. In this age when candidates "stood" rather than "ran" for election, and remained at home, Beckley pseudonymously composed a thirty-eight-page pamphlet that we would call a campaign biography. "The probationary period of ten years, since the institution of the federal government, affords much ground to hope and fear," it began. During those ten years, the experiment in liberty was being slowly subverted by "the painful spectacle of political apostacy, amidst the wreck of principle." And where should America look for relief? he asked. To Jefferson, "mild, amiable, and philanthropic, refined in manners as enlightened in mind, the philosopher of the world, whose name adds lustre to our national character." To which he added breathlessly: *"Jefferson, yet lives."*[15]

In September 1800, utterly surrounded in ultra-Federalist Connecticut, Republican Abraham Bishop spoke out against the social class that was doing all it could to prevent the popular voice from receiving a fair hearing: "The agents of delusion are the great, the wise, rich and mighty of the world," he censured. History showed that men with "charming outsides, engaging manners...fought like blood hounds, in defense of despotism and tyranny." Federalists, in this case, promised citizens that they would establish good social order, but they were creating instead a culture of slavish ignorance. Bishop predicted a worse future if the Federalists continued to get their way: "What infant in his nurse's arms is to be the progenitor of an illustrious race of AMERICAN MONARCHS is yet unknown." If the origins of political division were social, the distance between the people and their present rulers was a function of psychological manipulation. This was all that the election of Jefferson was meant to nullify.[16]

In October 1800, less powerful than he had been at any time since Washington's presidency began, "Boss" Hamilton aimed to recover his influence by publishing a fifty-four-page attack pamphlet against John Adams. He focused on "the defects in his character" and his unsuitability for a second term, finding, with little introspection of his own, that Adams's "extreme egotism" and "gusts of passion" made him an alienating character. The reconstituted *Aurora* publicized Hamilton's damaging text, as the New Yorker revealed his preference for Charles Cotesworth Pinckney of South Carolina, whose brother, Adams's 1796 running mate Thomas Pinckney, had declined to run again. Madison, in a sense, had predicted Hamilton's move four years earlier, when he told Jefferson that Adams was "too headstrong to be a fit puppet for the intriguers behind the skreen." Did Madison appreciate the irony that the qualities he most disliked in Adams were those that inoculated him against the political malignancy that was Hamilton?

By the time of Hamilton's pamphlet, it had been five months since Adams unceremoniously fired Secretary of State Timothy Pickering, who was all too obviously undermining him. He replaced that brash cabinet officer with Virginian John Marshall. In spite of Hamilton's power play, Adams did what was possible to keep his temper in check, rebuild his command within the executive branch, and combat division within the party. He retained support among a great majority of southern Federalists. But Pinckney, his ostensible running mate, did not care much for him, and as a result, the New Englanders thought their southern allies might withhold votes from Adams; so they, in turn, began discussing the possibility of doing the same.[17]

On November 24, 1800, Jefferson packed up and left Monticello. On his way to Washington to preside over the Senate as vice president for a final, three-and-a-half-month session, he had one more opportunity to confer with Madison. His arrival in Washington was reported by the newly established Republican organ, Samuel H. Smith's *National Intelligencer*. Otherwise he tried to stay out of trouble. Living temporarily at Conrad's boardinghouse, one of several atop Jenkins—renamed Capitol—Hill, he appears not to have paid a visit to President Adams. He also appears to have done everything possible to avoid giving his fellow politicians, in their rural, rudimentary federal city, the impression that he had immediate expectations. His housemates must have formed a protective circle around him, for they included Gallatin of Pennsylvania and several southern Republicans.[18]

Residents of the federal city would have to wait. On the third day of

December, the electors of the states gathered around the country to cast their votes for president and vice president. After much back-and-forth among Jefferson, Madison, Monroe, and their political allies regarding the convolutions of the several states with their differing means of granting votes to their electors, it became clear that those states voting exclusively for the Republican ticket had voted for both Jefferson and Burr; those that split their votes between the Federalist and Republican candidates— Pennsylvania, Maryland, and North Carolina—also voted in like numbers for Jefferson and Burr. A sitting president had lost reelection. But it would take weeks more before Jefferson could affirm his own election.

One of the most dramatic elements in the overall contest took place in South Carolina. There Republican Charles Pinckney, an old friend of Monroe's from their days in the Confederation Congress, was instrumental in delivering the toss-up state to Jefferson and Burr, sinking the chances of his Federalist second cousin; he was to South Carolina what John Beckley was to Philadelphia or Aaron Burr to New York. From the vibrant port city of Charleston to the interior capital of Columbia, Federalists and Republicans alike were making promises of patronage, and both Pinckneys were on hand to manage their party's respective efforts. During the last three months of the year, Pinckney the Republican wrote to Jefferson repeatedly, the anxiety in his tone increasing in each letter. Madison, who knew Pinckney from the Constitutional Convention, saw him as hotheaded and entirely untrustworthy. Like Burr, he could possibly be a future Republican rival for the Virginia-controlled presidency. Yet at this moment Madison must have been counting on Pinckney's impassioned campaigning as much as Jefferson was.[19]

Because the Virginians were under strict instructions not to withhold any votes from Burr, the contrivance of giving Jefferson the slight edge over his vice president was meant to have been taken care of in one of the other southern states. This was not done, however, and so there was neither a president-elect nor a vice president–elect. On December 26, 1800, after final results had come to Washington from all parts of the Union, Jefferson wrote to Madison, with apparent lack of concern, from his lodgings near the half-finished Capitol: "There is no doubt that the result is a perfect parity between the two republican characters."[20]

Bishop James Madison of the College of William and Mary penned a letter to his cousin two days later, punctuating it with an insouciance Jefferson could in no way have mustered: "Will it not be a strange Vagary in Fortune to place Burr in the presidential Chair?" he posed. "I can hardly suppose such an Event possible, & yet so various are Reports, that I fear, our Friend Jefferson is not so sure of it, as America." In South Carolina, under the direction of the restless Republican Pinckney, one vote was meant to have been withheld from Burr, to avoid a tie. Instead, Republican unity took precedence over calculation, resulting in the embarrassing tie.[21]

"Speculative Theorists and Absolute Terrorists"

For six years the Congress of the United States had been solidly Federalist. The election of 1800 reversed that. For the first time the U.S. Senate would contain a majority of Republicans; the House of Representatives would be composed of a nearly two-thirds Republican majority. But that Congress—the Seventh Congress—would not convene until December 7, 1801, nine months after Jefferson took the oath of office. Until then, for its last hurrah, the Federalist-led House primed its members to exploit the Republicans' discomfiture in having failed to withhold one vote from Vice President–designate Burr.

Madison termed the Federalists "the adverse party," as it worked to draw out the process of resolving the tie. Certain Federalists were so embittered that they were receptive to absolutely any idea that would confound their opposition. If it would undermine the Republican triumph and sow dissension, they would willingly reverse the order intended by the Republicans, making Burr president. They entertained, as well, the prospect of a delay past inauguration day that would place either the lame-duck Adams, Chief Justice John Marshall (whom Adams had just moved from the Department of State to the Supreme Court), or some other Federalist in the presidential chair for an indeterminate period. Jefferson thought that a candid conversation with Adams might lead to some cooperation, and Madison, as he had done four years before, rejected any overture to Adams. After Jefferson's election was finally secured, Madison reflected on the outgoing president's lame-duck appointments and general disregard for the Constitution: "The conduct of Mr. A. is not such as was to have been wished or perhaps expected," he wrote to Jefferson. "Instead of smoothing the path for his successor, he plays into the hands of those who are endeavoring to strew it with as many difficulties as possible."[22]

Contrary to subsequent histories, which were too accepting of secondhand gossip, neither Madison nor Jefferson suspected Vice President–designate Aaron Burr of bad behavior. The Federalist press in Washington urged congressmen, in rather stark terms, to choose Burr over Jefferson: "Col. Burr is not a Virginian. This is a reason of primary importance." Besides, the article read, he was "a person of a cool, clear head," not a "professed deist; nor a scoffer at religion." To this, a hopeful scenario was added: "Col. Burr has been abused by no party, and stands committed to no party." Committed to no party? Though entirely unsubstantiated, many a desperate Federalist bought into this notion, and many subsequent historians have deemed it credible too.[23]

Burr stayed away from Washington, where he might have embroiled himself in the election controversy and subverted the intended order, had he chosen to do so. He remained in close touch with Jefferson and Gallatin, resenting the impertinence of the more distrustful Republicans whose fears of a Federalist "usurpation" led them to suspect the worst of him. No firm evidence exists to prove that either Burr or Jefferson made any meaningful promises to any Federalist electors. As a result, the House Federalists ultimately surrendered the presidency to Jefferson on the thirty-sixth ballot.[24]

John Page, a congressman from Tidewater Virginia through most of the turbulence of the 1790s, had been Jefferson's close friend since their late teens. He identified the offenders in the House of Representatives as "the insolent faction" and recited a long train of abuses of power by Federalists in Congress. He included in the list "their utter Contempt of the Opinions & Wishes of the People," which was causing even "their best Friends" to "give them up to the Censure they deserve." Convinced that the "Friends of Man throughout the World will hate them," Page projected his wish that "in their eagerness to grasp at the Shadow [they] have lost the Substance. Their Power & Influence is gone forever." Honoring "the Commencement of a new Aera," as many other Republican enthusiasts would, he signed off the letter to his old college chum with a fanciful gesture, if not a Frenchified wish: "Health & Fraternity."[25]

An English visitor to the new national capital as it existed in Jefferson's first term described its "dreary" atmosphere: "There were no objects to catch the eye, but a forlorn pilgrim forcing his way through the grass that overruns the streets." He was not the only one to write of the rudeness of Washington, D.C., but if we accept that a certain amount of literary license is taken with these words, we should read the same into his fascination with the U.S. Capitol, "rising with sacred majesty above the woods," which he viewed from a sailing vessel on the Potomac.[26]

Madison was unable to come to Washington for Jefferson's March 4 inauguration. His father died in late February, at the age of seventy-seven, and he was executor of the estate. Though he had to tend to his sixty-eight-year-old mother, Madison himself was in ill health, referring nonspecifically to "several complaints" when he wrote to Jefferson. Burr arrived in the national capital on March 1, and in thanking the citizens who gathered to welcome him, he affirmed: "No person could have supposed that I would have stepped in between the wishes of the people and the man whom they have looked up to."

The new order was slow in getting under way. Albert Gallatin, whose mere presence on the scene had irked Federalists for the better part of a decade, was within reach. He was to hold only an interim appointment as secretary of the treasury until the Republican-led Congress finally met and approved him. Personally incorruptible and opposed to the culture of public debt and speculative risk, Gallatin would go on to serve with distinction in the cabinets of both Jefferson and Madison, reducing government expenditures and improving efficiency. This would be done to the detriment of the War and Navy departments, where the most obvious cuts were to be made. Gallatin was, after Madison, Jefferson's most influential adviser in Washington.[27]

With little fanfare, Madison's name was safely given to Congress the day after the inauguration. Despite the fact that Madison had never left American shores, the president could not conceive that anyone would question his choice for secretary of state, and indeed, unanimous approval was given. The same was true with his nominations for secretary of war and attorney general. The first of these was Henry Dearborn of Maine, a farmer by birth, physician by training, and a Revolutionary officer who had taken part in key battles from Bunker Hill to Yorktown; the second, Levi Lincoln of Massachusetts, was a Harvard graduate and an early convert to the political perspective of Madison and Jefferson. Until Madison took up his post, Lincoln served as acting secretary of state as well as attorney general.[28]

Jefferson did not move from the boardinghouse on Capitol Hill into the large, but largely vacant, President's House on Pennsylvania Avenue until he had been in office two weeks. He engaged Captain Meriwether Lewis, a twenty-seven-year-old from Albemarle, as his private secretary. The president's salary of $25,000 was quite ample, but Jefferson applied a good portion of it to the support of his French steward, French chef, and other staff. Jefferson's noted love of good wines extended his financial outlay, while providing guests with stories of his epicurean table. The inauguration itself was a more modest affair than the first two presidents' had been. This was a symbol of change in keeping with Jefferson's anti-aristocratic principles. John Adams did not stay in town for the ceremony. He and his wife left before dawn, riding north into a less-than-ideal retirement.[29]

The third president was sworn in by Chief Justice Marshall, who that very day paid Jefferson a backhanded compliment in a letter to the disappointed candidate Charles Cotesworth Pinckney: "The democrats are divided into speculative theorists and absolute terrorists," he wrote. "With the latter I am *not* disposed to class Mr. Jefferson."[30] Marshall had honed his political skills before his appointment to the High Court, and Jefferson did not know how to neutralize him. As a result, Marshall would occupy the spot on Jefferson's enemies list that Patrick Henry and Alexander Hamilton had held before. With Henry entombed and Hamilton ineffectual, Marshall had taken their place. He was a Virginian who possessed the kind of popularity that could threaten the Republican mission, and he had no second thoughts about flexing his legal muscle.

President Jefferson would have to contest men younger than himself who did not subscribe to older models of deference. Yet whatever bitterness he felt concerning his predecessor's appointments, he did not show it in (to draw on Marshall's phrasing) the theoretical speculation contained in his cheerful, stirring, almost sermonic inaugural address.

"Harmony and Affection"

On March 4, 1801, the incoming president carried on his person an address that had gone through several drafts. The House chamber was still unfinished, though the Capitol's physical incompleteness did not detract from the dignity of the occasion. With gravity, and in a small voice, Jefferson read to a full Senate chamber that contained members of both sexes.

"Friends and Fellow Citizens," he saluted, exalting his country as a "rising nation, spread over a wide and fruitful land... advancing rapidly to destinies beyond the reach of mortal eye." As many before have argued, the first inaugural was Jefferson's most eloquent public address. With hope and the promise of forgiveness, he proposed to his countrymen: "Let us restore to social intercourse that harmony and affection without which liberty and even life itself are but dreary things." Alluding to both the Virginia Statute for Religious Freedom and the Alien and Sedition Acts, he continued: "And let us reflect that having banished from our land that religious intolerance under which mankind so long bled and suffered, we have yet gained little if we countenance a political intolerance as despotic, as wicked, and capable of as bitter and bloody persecutions." But then he softened his language again: "Every difference of opinion is not a difference of principle. We have called by different names brethren of the same principle. We are all republicans: we are all federalists."[31]

The message of political toleration and social harmony was a hypnotic suggestion meant to bring about Jefferson's therapeutic solution to the diseased imagination of the pathological decade. It recalled the imagery of 1776, when the union of the states was depicted as thirteen clocks that chimed together and thirteen hearts that beat as one.[32] Much in the way that his 1786 "Head and Heart" letter to Maria Cosway made friendship and commitment a visceral matter by invoking "generous spasms of the heart," his inaugural sentiments bespoke a kind of manic compassion, an inventive altruism, by ignoring the fact that the emerging two-party system had up to that point made political cooperation impossible.

This was Jefferson at his best. With a lyrical energy that none of his contemporaries could even try to imitate, he relegated the "agonizing spasms of infuriated man" to the "throes and convulsions of the ancient world." In saying this, he gave a kind of presidential blessing over a hopeful new world poised for change, for humane progress.

If we are to believe that Jefferson's offer was legitimate, "We are all republicans: we are all federalists" was the high point of his optimism and his fondest vision for a democratic republic. These were not words that Madison would have uttered, because Madison did not recur to the kinds of rhetorical constructions Jefferson found irresistible; nor did he believe that such a healing could take place. Madison's influence is absent from this production; he was, it appears, too preoccupied with family matters at the time to restrain the prose of the incoming president. Madison did not dream as Jefferson did, and Madison would not have declared, as Jefferson did in a letter of 1819, that his election symbolized a revolution—"the Revolution of 1800"—as real as that of 1776 had been.

As the inaugural address returned to like themes, the third president enlarged on his America, "the world's best hope . . . , the strongest government on earth," "a chosen country, with room enough for our descendants to the thousandth and thousandth generation." For the sake of promoting harmony, uplifting images eclipsed any and all suggestions of a specific policy direction. Still, it was the effusive appeal of "We are all republicans . . ." that readers of his speech focused on most intently, then as now. It was an offering, an olive branch after nearly ten years of an interparty communication breakdown—a decade of "agonizing spasms," crowned with spite and satire.

These outpourings do not quite reveal what was in the politician's head. Jefferson was anticipating improved conditions that would take place over a number of years, once the bitterest Federalists, an illegitimate, unrepresentative ruling group, were dethroned, and moderate Federalists, as a political minority, accepted a kinder and gentler oppositional arrangement until they ultimately merged with the Republicans. His unrelenting, long-term political strategy of eliminating all vestiges of monocracy and toryism—the extreme, minority element among those who identified themselves as Federalists—was disguised in his inaugural address as a mellow retreat from politics as usual. When the new order he envisioned came to be, the election of 1800 would stand as a testament to national redemption after a time of national delusion. The Republicans' triumph meant that America was being restored to its first principles.[33]

But none of this was apparent as citizens found themselves focusing on the attention-getting phrase "We are all republicans: we are all federalists." Jefferson's clever composition worked not because it was original or visionary but because it was an easy concept for people to relate to who had been weaned on models of enlightened humanity in a colonial setting. Precisely one century earlier, in 1701, William Penn concluded a momentous agreement with the Conestoga tribe and declared that relations between his people and theirs would henceforth be governed by something even greater than filial affection. As the following generation of Indians remembered it, Governor Penn said that he would reckon whites and Indians as "one Body, one Blood, one Heart, and one Head." At a council in Philadelphia, another Indian speaker qualified shortly thereafter, "William Penn said, We must all be one half Indian & the other half English, being as one Flesh & one Blood under one Head." Peace between the cultures lasted for six decades, until white Pennsylvanians massacred the head-and-heart metaphor when they dispatched the Conestoga tribe. But for the white Pennsylvanians of 1801, the lesson drawn from history was that harmony was worth striving for.[34]

Additionally, both Penn and Jefferson were using the "one flesh" metaphor, a biblical allusion to marital accord and productivity. As he had done in the Declaration of Independence and in his original version of the Kentucky Resolutions, Jefferson again found a matrimonial parallel to help him redefine the body politic. The Federalists could join under the Republican banner, strengthening the country by bringing harmony. Doing so would produce "descendants to the thousandth and thousandth generation." This theme of fertility corresponded easily with Jefferson's bucolic vision of a future America, expansive and fruitful, no longer held back by partisan divisions, a nation in which kinship gradually supplanted the artificial boundaries that faction sustained.

A week after the inauguration, his old friend Dr. Benjamin Rush of Philadelphia excitedly praised the new president: "It would require a page to contain the names of all the citizens (formerly called Federalists) who have spoken in the highest terms of your speech." Another who appreciated the gesture was Henry Knox, secretary of war when Jefferson was secretary of state, who wrote graciously from Boston: "I cannot refrain from expressing to you, the heart felt satisfaction I have experienced in perusing your address . . . The just manner in which you appreciate the motives of the two parties, which have divided the opinions, and which sometimes have seemed to threaten to divide the territory and government of the Country . . . evince conspicuously, at one view, your intelligence patriotism and magnanimity." He made a point of telling Jefferson that he had preferred Adams for a second term; but he accepted Jefferson's words as literal and wished him "a richly merited reward, similar to that bestowed by a grateful people on the much loved Washington."[35]

Just three days after his inaugural address, Jefferson gave Virginia governor James Monroe his recapitulation of the months of turmoil preceding it. He thought he understood the psychology of the average Federalist: weak-minded, easily led, and (most important) so afraid of social anarchy that he was capable of being manipulated by whomever was in power. After months of calling Jefferson an anarchist, these people, "from timidity of [physical] constitution," had come to fear "anarchy" and now "only wanted a decent excuse" to reembrace government; they had laid down their arms, as it were, because they "wished for a strong executive," one way or the other. "Timidity" needed to believe in a leader.

This was hardly the way to establish a hybrid Republican-Federalist regime. To longtime confidant John Page, Jefferson significantly toned down his language, which he certainly did not have to do in light of Page's recent harangue against the Federalists in the House. "My dear friend," he wrote with generous intent, "I am very much in hopes we shall be able to restore union & harmony to our country." Unlike the "desperado" leaders—the "incurables" among the High Federalists—middle-of-the-road Federalism consisted of many "real republicans" who had merely been "carried over from us by French excesses" and might now, without too much struggle, be won back.[36]

That bastion of Federalist journalism, Philadelphia's *Gazette of the United States,* decided to give Jefferson a chance to make good on his promise. His accession to the presidency gave the party of "good order" a chance to demonstrate its devotion to the high principles of "religion, morality, and laws" rather than any "blind attachment to particular men." Federalists were not Jacobins, the paper insisted, and would therefore honor the constitutionally elected chief executive as long as he proved himself worthy of the public's trust. It was up to Jefferson to hold in check "the factious, the impious, the rapacious, the clamorous, the ambitious, and the turbulent"— those Republicans whom Chief Justice Marshall had termed "terrorists." It was up to Jefferson to imitate George Washington.[37]

On the other hand, many prominent Federalists were unconvinced from the outset of the new president's sincerity. They suspected that Jefferson was thinking deviously, if not thinking of outright revenge. They understood power, and Jefferson understood power. The real test would come when Federalist officeholders were either retained or dismissed by Jefferson's administration.[38]

"We are all republicans..." was a form of idealism foreign to most Federalists' way of thinking. If Jefferson embraced that hybrid political entity he seemed to be calling for, it would be as an opiate to ease the pain of a nervous transition. How long would Jefferson be patient with the Federalists, if he was really thinking, deep down, that their party would have to fade away for his vision to be realized? Even the most charitable interpretation of the "one flesh" metaphor as a model for Jeffersonian bipartisanship assumed a natural subordination amid unity. As partisan feuds gave way to marital felicity and public tranquillity, the reins of power would remain in the firm but gentle hands of the Republican head of family. In their prospective marriage, the dominant, or male, persona was to be the Republican; the subordinate, or female, the Federalist. Why should Federalists not be skeptical of a promise of equality that was not really equality?

What, then, to do about Federalist officeholders? Albert Gallatin, despite having been tossed from Congress by illiberal Federalists who regarded him as an untrustworthy foreigner, took a moderate position and for years to come would privilege competence over ideology in appointments.[39] Governor Monroe was less magnanimous and proposed that a slow testing-of-the-waters approach made the most sense. Laying out his thoughts in a stream of consciousness, he reminded his friend the president (unnecessarily) that "the royalist party has committed infinite crimes and enormities." But he reckoned that if Republicans maintained their cohesion, Federalism would never rise to challenge again.

For Monroe, the administration's first responsibility was to leave no cause for discontent among Republicans by extending the olive branch too far. But he also believed, as Gallatin did, that Federalists who had performed their offices competently and without political prejudice should be retained; and he predicted that most victory-savoring Republicans would not object to this middle way. But there were also Republicans who would not appreciate *any* concession to *any* Federalist, he said, and it was with these people that Monroe was most concerned. He concluded the letter with an assessment of Madison's Department of State, where he was sure a complete overhaul would be needed. Owing to the intensity of anti-French feeling, which had long festered, Monroe presumed that the incoming administration would uncover "the most gross and depraved kind" of abuse in State Department files.[40]

"Prejudice and Passion, Which Never Can Be Friendly to Truth"

Letters poured in from around the country recommending candidates for federal appointment. Some used colorful language in making their partisan points; men with Republican credentials blatantly asked for appointments to bail them out of the financial straits in which they were caught. A Philadelphian who had served as a commercial agent for Virginia during the Revolution said he was compelled by his "present unfortunate situation" to "throw" himself upon the president's "indulgence" after his estate had been seized.

Another correspondent wanted nothing for himself but had plenty to say. He described himself as a man "who inhaled with his first breath the genuine spirit of republicanism" and thought he should write to warn Jefferson about the dangers of continuing Federalists in office. He was a Vermonter and a "warm friend" of the recently liberated Matthew Lyon, the Irish pugilist representing that state who had wielded fireplace tongs against an upraised cane on the floor of the House. He wanted the president to know that there were still those in office who had labeled Jefferson "an anarchist and an atheist." Whether by chance or by design, the never-boring Lyon wrote to Jefferson with encouraging reports at just about the same time. While on the road in Pennsylvania, he had heard a confirmed Federalist decrying all those who had spoken ill of Albert Gallatin. Everyone had an opinion.[41]

For several months Jefferson's correspondence with political allies was filled with such discussion. To Gallatin, the president reasserted his basic principle for staffing federal positions: "We must be inflexible against appointing federalists till there be a due portion of republicans introduced into office." He divided the various interests into categories of "Monarchical federalists," the salvageable "Republican federalists," the uncompromising "*Sweeping* republicans," and the deserving "moderate & general republicans," who invariably saw things his way.

Certain executive acts of an overtly partisan nature would not wait. Even before Madison arrived in Washington, Jefferson rewarded the electioneering energies of South Carolina's Charles Pinckney by appointing him U.S. minister to Spain. He also pardoned several who had been convicted under the Sedition Act, including the notorious James T. Callender. Somehow, though, Callender concluded that Jefferson was standing in his way and delaying his release from prison.[42]

Reestablishing former connections, the president wrote to friends abroad. He humbly announced his change in status and conveyed his "constant & sincere affection" to William Short, Thomas Paine, and the Marquis de Lafayette. He promised fair decisions and "sentiments worthy of former times." As he weighed fairness against sentiments, he continued to collect letters of recommendation and compiled careful lists of candidates for office. Who was to be hired, who was to be fired? The page was divided into columns, marking each individual's residence, the position requested, the recommender's name, and the date of the recommendation letter. Elaborating on his comment to Secretary Gallatin, the president explained to any who inquired what his guiding principle would be. Appointments made by John Adams after his electoral defeat in December were deemed unacceptable; and partisan imbalances within the federal judiciary were to be corrected through appointment of Republicans as state attorneys where the courts were presently dominated by Federalists.

Nevertheless Jefferson retained a majority of the justices of the peace for the District of Columbia whom the Senate had confirmed only days before he took office. One of those to whom he denied office, William Marbury, would shortly become a sizable footnote in history. Adams himself appeared not to have anticipated the hubbub surrounding his "midnight" appointments, having written to his successor, with considerable grace, on his arrival back in Massachusetts: "I See nothing to obscure your prospect of a quiet and prosperous Administration, which I heartily wish you."

Another Adams, the ex-president's cousin, was decidedly Jeffersonian in his political spirit and plainly philosophical in the last years of his life. Samuel Adams had entertained the Virginian at his home in Boston on the eve of Jefferson's departure for France in 1784. He addressed him now as "my very dear friend" and presented a maritime interpretation of the challenges before the country: "With you, I hope we shall once more see harmony restored; but after so severe and long a storm, it will take a proportionate time to still the raging of the waves." He recognized in the nature of conflict the power of self-deception: "The World has been governed by prejudice and passion, which never can be friendly to truth." And he closed his letter tenderly: "You have devoutly my Blessing and my Prayers."[43]

Jefferson saw Madison at Montpelier one month after the inauguration, as he rode back to Albemarle for a two-week working vacation. He spent the night at the Madisons' again when he returned north—the new Congress was still months from its first meeting. When Madison joined the administration on May 1, the oath of office was administered to him by Abigail Adams's nephew, Judge William Cranch, whom Jefferson would later name chief justice of the Federal District Court.

Initially, James and Dolley lodged at the President's House, moving several blocks uptown as Madison's physical condition improved. For now, the State and War departments were housed together. Between there and Capitol Hill lay rough country, as Pierre L'Enfant's radiating street design had not yet been carved out. Indeed, the formless look and feel of low-lying Washington obliged Madison and Jefferson to leave town for the healthier air of central Virginia during the "bilious" summer months.[44]

The new secretary of state was intricately involved in all appointments and dismissals, especially the choice of some fifty U.S. consuls stationed abroad. Notwithstanding Monroe's warning about the number of State Department employees whose loyalty was to the other side, Madison by and large retained the staff. One clerk, Daniel Brent, proved such an efficient manager of communications that he would still be at State during the administration of Martin Van Buren. Another, Jacob Wagner, was an out-and-out Federalist, but Madison perceived in him a rare combination of integrity and administrative ability.

Madison was easy to work for, his manner so accommodating, in fact, that the caustic pamphleteer Callender proclaimed that the secretary of state was the only cabinet officer he felt he could trust, the only man "whom I could without hypocrisy profess to feel an attachment for." When Jefferson sent Meriwether Lewis to the agitated Callender, bearing fifty dollars and an explanation for the delay in relieving his pecuniary concerns, Lewis returned to the president with Callender's demand for—as Jefferson repeated to Monroe—"hushmoney." He could not imagine what intelligence Callender possessed that could do him damage and wrote fatefully: "He knows nothing of me which I am not willing to declare to the world." It is curious that the pamphleteer, who was not beyond threatening the president directly, fully expected Madison to see to it that Jefferson named him postmaster of Richmond, which was at that time a quite lucrative position.[45]

In spite of the abuse he had earlier suffered at the hands of Federalists in Congress, the fair-minded Gallatin took Jefferson's inaugural optimism to heart. He prepared a circular announcing that his door was open to all political opinions, and he would staff the Treasury Department with men of talent, regardless of previous partisan attachment. Madison and Jefferson were together when Gallatin sent his circular to the president for approval. Madison was probably the more reticent about releasing the document to federal employees, but it was the president who instructed Gallatin to withhold it until it was deemed safe to proceed with a truly nonpartisan policy.

The Federalist press did not take long before announcing that it had sniffed out dissension among the chief players in the administration. As early as mid-1801 the *Philadelphia Gazette* raised the specter of a dissolution of the Virginia–New York axis: "It is whispered among MR. JEFFERSON's friends, that he will not be nominated four years hence for re-election . . . Those who say this also say that MR. MADISON will be his successor.—The friends of Col. BURR are not pleased with this arrangement, and think he ought to succeed to the Presidency . . . but Virginia never will support for the Presidency any man who is not a Virginian." In New England, similar reports circulated.[46]

If the story seems entirely made up, and it may be, this Federalist wish-fulfillment contained elements of truth. Madison and Jefferson were in agreement that they should not shore up Vice President Burr's patronage power in his home state of New York. Of the other men of influence there, Robert Livingston was in France and his brother Edward was soon to come under a cloud as mayor of New York City. George Clinton had been returned to the governorship. His publicity-seeking nephew DeWitt Clinton waited in the wings, no less desirous of being a political "boss" than Hamilton ever was.

Even before any overtures were made to the Clinton family (the Burrites' strongest rivals), Jefferson acted to derail the political advancement of Matthew Livingston Davis, Burr's closest associate. Davis went so far as to pay Jefferson a visit at Monticello, where he stated the case for his appointment as second in command to the collector of customs. Within the administration it appears that only Gallatin protested the snubbing of Davis, unabashedly asking Jefferson whether denying him office was tantamount to announcing that Burr would not be on the Republican ticket in 1804.

The Virginia interest prevailed over the unifying interest—at least, that was how things must have appeared to Gallatin. As time went on, Jefferson's agenda got people wondering. The administration-friendly *Aurora* persisted in linking Burr with the Federalists, questioning whether the Burrites had "negociated" with the opposition. The powerful newspaper claimed that the vice president's refusal to respond to any and all rumors was a black mark against him.[47]

It did not take Jefferson long to realize that New York's Republicans could be kept at bay if they remained disunited. The three Republican factions that vied for power during the election of 1800—Clintonians, Livingstons, and Burrites—were held together by a tenuous alliance. By refusing to help Matthew Davis, Jefferson was sending a strong message: Burr's group no longer had the favor of the administration. He and they were fair game. Stealthily, the president decided he would back the Clintons, while giving a few patronage positions to the Livingstons to keep them happy. The Clintons hired English émigré James Cheetham, editor of the *American Citizen,* to wage an unrelenting campaign against Burr, at which point Jefferson became a new subscriber and welcomed Cheetham to the President's House.

Neither Madison nor Jefferson could convincingly claim that he was being evenhanded when it came to Republican interests in New York. Jefferson did not intend to permit any northern Republican to gain control of the party or the presidency, and Madison seemed not to object. While it is true that the administration showed restraint by minimizing the number of Federalists it dismissed from federal offices, the president was too much a Virginian to de-sectionalize his republican theory. Federalism was effete and nonthreatening in his calculations; he saw a greater future threat from the prospect of former Federalists and disgruntled northern Republicans teaming up against Virginia. Keeping the New Yorkers divided was thus a necessary move to prevent the formation of a cross-bred party.[48]

Of course, the Federalist Party had no plans to dissolve. Its members did

not respond to Jefferson's effort to limit dismissals from office by shower-
ing the Republican president with expressions of their appreciation. Taking up where "Peter Porcupine" left off, "Oliver Oldschool" began in 1801
to satirize the Republicans, and Jefferson in particular, in the pages of the
Port Folio. "Oldschool" was Boston-bred Joseph Dennie, Harvard class of
1790, whose disenchantment with democratization was equaled only by
his compulsion to illustrate a counternarrative to the American Revolution. While publishing a newspaper in Walpole, New Hampshire, in 1797,
he had written to his mother castigating the "hoary traitor" Samuel Adams
and the Tea Party militants, without whom, he said, he might have been "in
the service of my rightful King and instead of shivering in the bleakness of
the United States, felt the genial sunshine of a Court." These were strong
words and gave credence to Jefferson's characterization of some incorrigible Federalists as "Tories."

In 1799 Dennie found a sponsor when the snobbish secretary of state
Timothy Pickering, a New Englander, brought him to Philadelphia and
made him his private secretary. It was Dennie's moment to shine, or so he
thought. Once President Adams "shamefully and fatally banished" Pickering (as Dennie described the firing), his patron left him high and dry in
Philadelphia. Dennie rebounded by finding his voice as the opinionated
"Oliver Oldschool."

The writer was already priming for political battle with Jefferson in February 1800, when he gave his impressions of the then–vice president:
"From his sullen & retired habits, few know more than myself. I have frequently listened to his sophistry." Before the election Dennie authored a
pamphlet in which he predicted that the "infidel" Jefferson would rule as "a
Chinese or Russian despot." A few months later, when he began the *Port
Folio*—he termed it "not quite a *Gazette* nor wholly a *Magazine*"—Dennie
asked his self-selected readership to submit "*political* observations, from
sober, reflecting men of *old fashioned* principles." He was confident that a
"formidable" minority might yet prove more powerful than the "jacobin interest" that was poised to take over the government.[49]

Dennie's unexpurgated manner of speech appealed to an angry readership. "There is a spirit of domination engrafted on the character of the
southern people," he impressed upon them, insisting that relocation of the
nation's capital to an "obscure village" on the Potomac was Virginia's
means of drawing power and population away from the North. He may
have been right. On the other hand, he showed little restraint on any topic.
He questioned the propriety of hallowing the Fourth of July, because it poi-

soned the minds of "the ignorant and brutal mob" against the British nation, which had never "manifested a wish unfriendly to our independence." This was a rarely heard sentiment, even in Federalist circles.

But Dennie was just warming up. He made a mockery of Jefferson's language in the Declaration of Independence, pointing out that "some hundreds of negroes are constantly at work, making nails, or wading through rice-swamps, at Monticello, the favourite haunt of philosophy, liberty, and other French fairies." The same week that Madison left Orange and went to work in Washington, Dennie deconstructed Jefferson's first inaugural address from a rhetorician's perspective, remarking on improper syntax and figures of speech that gave the oration "an air of juvenility." Jefferson's "throes and convulsions of the ancient world," for example, led the audacious editor to observe that the only "throes" he knew in English concerned "the image of a woman in child-birth." President Jefferson might still have hoped for civility. With the likes of Dennie stirring the pot, that hope would fade fast.[50]

"A Large Detachment of Republican Blacks"

The State Department was in charge of a variety of domestic matters in addition to administering the foreign policy of the United States. Madison and his staff were responsible for coordinating the U.S. Census, assigning lucrative publication projects to private printers (what the Government Printing Office does in-house today), and operating the Patent Office. This last function was placed under the care of William Thornton, Madison's housemate of 1789, a Quaker who had urged a humanitarian policy of emancipation and colonization of enslaved blacks.

Thornton charmed George Washington with his design for the Capitol in the early 1790s. The idea to erect a rotunda was his. After Madison and Jefferson brought him into the administration, he proved so tireless that he helped in the redesign of Montpelier, and in later years Jefferson would consult with him on a layout for the University of Virginia. The choice of the polymath Thornton for a supervisory role in the State Department (a position he held throughout the Virginia Dynasty of presidents) reminds us how mutable and experimental this moment really was.[51]

As secretary of state, Madison felt free to adopt a neutral position with respect to the European powers. Napoleon's military ambitions had effectively ended the Republicans' tortured defense of France; for the better part

of Jefferson's first term, this relegated England to merely secondary concern in the shaping of U.S. foreign policy. The Anglo-French war that had
begun eight years before, when Jefferson held Madison's post, came to an
end during Madison's first year at the State Department. In a very real
sense, Madison and Jefferson felt they faced a new world order.

The challenge that arose, then, was an unexpected one. Spain was handing over to Napoleon the strategic territory of Louisiana. It was a "retrocession," insofar as France had ceded Louisiana to Spain four decades earlier,
after its disastrous defeat in the French and Indian War. A mingling of
races—French, Spanish, Indians, Anglo-Americans, free and enslaved
blacks—made for a polyglot population in Louisiana and seemed to increase the potential for conflict. Even so, Spain was not maintaining a large
force there when a revitalized France under Napoleon eyed the western
hemisphere with renewed interest.

If, because of Madrid's desire for New Orleans, the United States had an
uncomfortable relationship with the Spanish in the 1790s, the French now
looked as if they would be a far more formidable threat to American political and commercial development along the southern Mississippi than
Spain ever was. Were French armies to encroach on land that the United
States coveted, the Republicans would find themselves hard-pressed not to
warm up to Great Britain. It would be a marriage of convenience, to be
sure, but a "marriage"—to echo Jefferson's phraseology—nonetheless.

In a closely related theater, Napoleon had set his sights on St.
Domingue (the future Haiti) where a successful slave revolt in 1797 had
placed a former slave, Toussaint Louverture, in power. The question at
hand was a delicate one: would the Jefferson administration continue to
recognize the black republic? The Adams administration had opened
diplomatic and trade relations with St. Domingue, a policy Jefferson felt
was dangerous to southern interests. Commerce flourished during the Federalist period, and the U.S. Navy even backed Toussaint against a rival
leader.

For a brief period, the British attempted to occupy the nominally
French island. They were forced out by the islanders themselves. Toussaint,
the same age as Jefferson, kept all options open; Jefferson tried to do the
same. Not surprisingly, to the minds of most Virginians, close, respectful
ties with a former slave boded ill. The prospect of black crews carrying seditious ideas—abolitionist ideas—to southern ports was menacing.[52]

Although he shared those exaggerated fears, Jefferson proceeded slowly,
combining prudence on economic matters with aggressive diplomacy. He

could read a balance sheet and had no desire at this point to alienate American merchants by shutting down the profitable Caribbean trade. In July 1801, meeting with Edward Thornton, the British chargé d'affaires (no relation to William Thornton), Jefferson made clear that he supported the Adams policy of "free and open trade" with the island, but he also said that he wished to prevent "all maritime exertion on the part of the Negroes."

Striking a delicate balance, the administration hoped for improved relations with France too, declaring a policy of neutrality toward all powers on the island and all powers interested in its future. As secretary of state, Madison gave detailed instructions to Tobias Lear, formerly George Washington's private secretary, who had replaced the Federalist consul on St. Domingue in mid-1801. Taking care not to offend the French, Lear was given the title of commercial agent (instead of a diplomatic title) and was, at least on the surface, to have no formal connection to Toussaint.[53]

By the time Madison and Jefferson met with Louis Pichon, the French chargé d'affaires in Washington, their position was less clear. Pichon first called on Madison and left the meeting feeling troubled by the secretary of state's "equivocal and reserved language," as he later informed Jefferson, and Madison's willingness to leave things in St. Domingue as they were, "without pretending to judge." Madison had told Pichon that, for commercial reasons, the administration would not cut off Toussaint, because northern Federalists would turn an anticommercial policy into an inflammatory sectional issue. But the most jarring exchange between Madison and Pichon occurred when Madison pressed him on French designs in Louisiana. He claimed that serious "collisions" between the two countries would be inevitable if France were to become too near a neighbor of the United States.

Pichon received a different message, at least on the status of St. Domingue, from President Jefferson. Commercial ties with the island were indeed important, he asserted, confirming what Madison had said. But when queried about the U.S. response to a French military expedition to the island, Jefferson gave the impression that he would support an occupation and that he wished to see an unofficial alliance involving France, England, and the United States. All three would come together to crush the island republic, and as Pichon reported home, Jefferson agreed that they would "reduce Toussaint to starvation."[54]

By the end of 1801 Jefferson once again changed his tune, complaining to Pichon about the size of the French expeditionary force en route to St. Domingue. Reports had circulated that Napoleon would send as many as

twenty thousand troops, far more than was required to subdue a single island. So the president brought forth a new proposal: St. Domingue should
declare formal independence and be placed under the combined protection
of France, England, and the United States.

It must have appeared to Pichon that Jefferson was taunting him at this
point, because the American president would have known that Napoleon
would never agree to such an arrangement. Fresh, seemingly reliable rumors were circulating, to the effect that French forces would topple Toussaint and proceed on to Louisiana. So Jefferson warned Pichon that France
would remain in formerly Spanish Louisiana only as long as it pleased the
United States. He then threatened to align with Great Britain if Napoleon
refused to back down.[55]

This progression makes sense given that news of the peace treaty between France and England arrived at a crucial moment in the fall of 1801.
It forced Madison and Jefferson to reconsider their view of the extent of
Bonaparte's ambition. Prior to this, Madison had believed that France's
motivation for reclaiming Louisiana was simply to make sure Great Britain
would never control it. The theory no longer made sense with Britain out
of the picture.[56]

The U.S. minister in London, Federalist holdover Rufus King, wrote
Madison in early October that with peace, St. Domingue and other
Caribbean islands would engage Napoleon's attention and result in
Louisiana becoming even more a place of exiles. To make matters worse,
Madison was deeply troubled by the French government's behavior in refusing to confirm the retrocession of Louisiana from Spain to France. King
called it "extraordinary" that London had remained silent on Louisiana
during peace negotiations with its old and inveterate enemy. Rumors held
that Britain was supplying ships for the French campaign against Toussaint. This was too much to take. The administration did not want to
adopt a passive, wait-and-see posture. Jefferson tried saber rattling, but his
threat to ally with England could not have given Napoleon any pause, since
England and France could no longer be played off against each other. The
administration needed a new approach to disturbances in its southern
neighborhood.[57]

If French occupation of Louisiana was inevitable, as Madison felt it was,
then the United States might buy western Florida from France, in order to
preserve at least one avenue for getting agricultural produce down the Mississippi and out to sea. Jefferson slowly became convinced that the situation in St. Domingue might actually help America's cause. Napoleon

announced that a force was being assembled, led by his brother-in-law, General Charles Leclerc. Hearing this, Jefferson told Pichon that French forces would fail miserably if they tried to reinstitute slavery on the island. In the early months of 1802 they did, in fact, become bogged down, at which point the administration saw its opportunity to put pressure on.[58]

The policy that emerged had teeth: it declared neutrality while defiantly refusing to restrict American shippers from freely trading with the island. The French government demanded an end to this trade, and the administration refused to comply. At the same time, when Pichon begged for loans from the United States to assist the French forces, Madison coolly rejected his proposal.

Though General Leclerc was promised American food and supplies, he soon found himself in an impossible situation on St. Domingue. Without U.S. assistance, he could neither feed his own massive army nor curtail the flow of U.S. contraband to Toussaint's army. By May 1802, Leclerc had confiscated American cargo, thrown two captains in the brig, ejected Tobias Lear from the island, and lodged complaints against the United States for intentionally assisting the rebels. American public opinion quickly turned against the high-handed French commander. Madison and Jefferson kept their passive-aggressive trade warfare going. Their silence encouraged more U.S. trade. In fact, rather than starve Toussaint, as Jefferson had originally pledged, U.S. obstruction of Leclerc reduced the French forces to near starvation.[59]

The administration's failure to maintain a consistent, coherent policy suggests either that Jefferson and Madison did not precisely mirror each other's understanding or else they had devised a very shrewd diplomatic strategy. Jefferson confronted Napoleon, while protesting (for effect) that any break with France would pain him. Such were his words to Robert Livingston, his minister to France, in a long letter of April 1802. Anticipating the end of Franco-American amity, the president adopted a plaintive tone: "It compleatly reverses all the political relations of the U.S. and will form a new epoch in our political course. Of all nations of any consideration France is the one which hitherto has offered the fewest points on which we could have any conflict of right, and the most points of a communion of interests."

As we have seen many times already, Jefferson used letter writing as a means to convey sentimental attachments or, as in this instance, his professed shock in having to face up to a major disappointment. Perhaps it is going too far to say that he enjoyed the semantics of bold reprisals; but at virtually no time were the theatrics of his shifting moods meant to lead to the use of military force. Madison preferred a subtler approach to foreign policy making, finding ways to manipulate neutrality—here it was to undermine General Leclerc. To a greater extent than Jefferson, he believed in economic retaliation as America's only good weapon against hostile imperial powers.[60]

Jefferson and Madison were equally worried about the appearance of a large French army in their neighborhood. It fell to Rufus King to encapsulate brilliantly the predicament of their lifetime, when he quoted for Madison the Enlightenment-era political philosopher Baron de Montesquieu: "It is happy for trading Powers, that God has permitted Turks and Spaniards to be in the world since of all nations they are most proper to possess a great Empire with insignificance." Replacing the weak Spanish presence with the French was a dangerous prospect. From Tobias Lear, Madison learned that the French army in St. Domingue was filled with "anti-republican venom" and was committed to forcing monarchy on those whom it conquered. This was what Louisiana appeared to be facing as well. Madison avowed to Robert Livingston that a contingent threat existed to America's security: any French colony in Louisiana would become a haven for runaway slaves, who had already been taught "to regard the French as the patrons of their cause."[61]

Race-baiting messages from national political figures of all stripes streamed in. Philadelphian Tench Coxe, a former Hamilton associate now in the Republican camp, laid out the worst-case scenario for Madison when he predicted that Bonaparte would send "a large detachment of republican blacks" from St. Domingue to Louisiana. This, he said, would lead to the "sudden emancipation" of the blacks there, and Madison could count on their becoming "warlike." To Coxe, St. Domingue could no longer be considered an isolated island, safely removed from American shores. As ideas of emancipation and racial equality were carried to New Orleans, the vibrant, growing port would keep up its "extensive constant intimate connexion with the great Negro state," to the detriment of the entire U.S. South.[62]

The situation in St. Domingue also pained the humanitarian Benjamin Rush, who wrote to his friend Jefferson: "Does our globe, like a diseased body, stand in need of a perpetual issue of blood? I tremble for the consequences everywhere and particularly in our own country. Can nothing be done by concession and partial emancipation to avert the storm from the southern states?" It is hard to overstate the apprehension Jefferson, Madison, and their political friends all seemed to share.[63]

At least rhetorically, the idea of emancipation was hard for liberal Republicans to declaim against. As long as it did not produce violence inside the United States, the anticolonial objective of the blacks on St. Domingue was easy to appreciate. But as more reports circulated, rumors spread far and wide. In 1800 the Richmond-based conspiracy known as Gabriel's Rebellion, though stopped in its tracks, shook Virginia to its core. Gabriel was well built, literate, and a skilled blacksmith who, like many slaves, was able to move freely about the state. His men had contemplated taking Governor Monroe hostage as a means of securing their freedom and advancing the cause of emancipation more generally. To make matters worse, some white Frenchmen were thought to be associated with Gabriel. After the conspirators were hanged, new legislation required every manumitted slave to leave the state within one year.[64]

Dr. Rush was known for his warm attachments. He knew firsthand that churchgoing free black families were at least as stable as working-class white families. But whites' fears of their black neighbors were rising even in Philadelphia, where abolition had a consistent following. After years of mutual accommodation, the combination of events on St. Domingue and the influx of less-skilled, southern-born ex-slaves had produced a tense environment in the city. It would find expression in militant demonstrations and counterdemonstrations in the streets, warnings about sex across the color line, and an increase of forthright sermons in black churches on captivity in Egypt and the eventual deliverance of the people of Israel.[65]

Proslavery arguments took root in Virginia as never before, assisted by such campaigning writers as Edmund Pendleton's nephew John Taylor of Caroline. Mainstay Republicans such as Taylor mingled racial fears with economic logic, and Madison and Jefferson were not the sort to risk alienating the majority in the South—even though other Virginians believed gradual emancipation would be a prudent policy and would have responded positively to encouragement from the president and secretary of state.

No matter what his thoughts were on black republics, Jefferson never seriously entertained emancipation as a policy option. He took comfort in his prediction that Bonaparte's plan to reestablish slavery in St. Domingue would lead to his army's ultimate demise. In this, he was at least partially correct. Violent resistance to reenslavement mired French forces in a prolonged and very bloody conflict. Not even the capture of Toussaint in May 1802, and his removal to France, slowed the resistance. Only when tropical disease thoroughly decimated his troops did Napoleon realize the island campaign was headed for defeat. Among the dead was General Leclerc.[66]

Jefferson's growing complacency in the period after Leclerc's death is captured in the observations of an Englishman. John Davis, who spent the years 1798 to 1802 touring the United States, north and south, relished his time in Virginia and heralded its culture of hospitality. "I never saw slavery wear so contented an aspect," he observed after visiting a plantation. "The work of the slaves was light, and punishment never inflicted." With Jefferson's concurrence, the author dedicated his book to him.[67]

"Conciliatory Manners, Examplary Morals"

Virginia was at the helm—that much was clear. During Jefferson's first term, northern Federalists kept up a steady stream of criticism. They reflected uneasily upon the surrender to southern sensibilities that took place at the Constitutional Convention. Their acceptance of the three-fifths compromise had tilted the scales in favor of southern interests, and it was not clear that political balance would ever be restored.

Prejudices hardened, and not merely because of the impact of flame-throwers such as Joseph Dennie. "In the conception of a Virginian it is merely the object of *Liberty* to secure independence to Planters," wrote Connecticut's Oliver Wolcott, Jr., Hamilton's successor as treasury secretary, now out of a job. The old refrain was repeated in more than one anti-administration newspaper: if human property counted toward representation, then why shouldn't New England horses, hogs, and oxen? Jefferson was the most obvious beneficiary and most visible practitioner of a grotesque and hypocritical system.[68]

In the war of words, the president was ably defended by the administration's main organ, the *National Intelligencer*. But Madison fared better in the press, in general. The otherwise unfriendly *Connecticut Courant* and *Massachusetts Spy* noted at the end of Jefferson's first year in office that "the conduct of Mr. Madison and Mr. Gallatin towards the clerks in their departments, is admitted to have been fair and impartial." But they were as sure to append that the Republicans never acknowledged the same about former secretary of state Timothy Pickering, who retained clerks that had worked under his predecessors, Jefferson and Edmund Randolph. If his two top advisers were comparatively fair-minded, reported the newspapers, Jefferson himself was intolerant and mean-spirited, as his affronts toward Washington and Adams proved.[69]

After a visit to the President's House in 1802, a southern traveler published his observations on the chief officers of the government, stressing Jefferson's artificiality and Madison's relative openness, Gallatin's compulsive work habits and Dearborn's nepotistic hiring practices. Starting with Jefferson, he followed every detail: "Mr. Jefferson is most affectedly plain in his dress; the morning I waited on him, he wore cut shoes as slippers, and very coarse brown stockings." According to the traveler, Meriwether Lewis, Jefferson's "awkward and stiff" secretary, was on hand to interpret the president's outfit, stating that the stockings were not imported fineries, but the product of a Germantown, Pennsylvania, factory.

Jefferson's commitment to democratic self-deprivation was undeniable: "The president rides out every day, unattended by any servant . . . I saw him at the Capitol . . . He hitched his horse amongst twenty others, at the row of pegs which are placed before the Capitol door in the manner you have seen at country taverns." His right and left hands were a study in contrast:

> Mr. Gallatin is a little man with a monstrous nose and large black piercing eyes, has long hair, which he wears in a queue of great length; he is as brown as a man of colour, and has lost most of his teeth. [He] sees no company and is said to be constantly in his office smoking and writing.
>
> Mr. Madison is the only one of the ministers who sees company; he gives a dinner once a week, in a very plain and frugal manner; but his lady and himself both do the honours of his house handsomely, and his parties are said to be pleasant. Mr. Madison has not turned one of the clerks in his department out of office, and I am told was opposed decidedly, and actively to the dismissals which have been made.[70]

These descriptions may not be the real Madison and Jefferson, but they reveal a general impression of Madison's independence from Jefferson, as the idea lodged in the minds of those who encountered them briefly or imagined their perspectives and governing styles from a distance. Madison was not necessarily seen as complicit in the actions Jefferson took that annoyed the opposition.

A friendly northerner's portrait was printed in newspapers of western

Massachusetts and Vermont around the same time, under the heading "Biography of Mr. Madison." It plainly shows that, at least in some places, the secretary of state was not regarded as subordinate to Jefferson—in fact, he was just as instrumental in the triumph of republicanism as Jefferson. Because of Madison's leadership on contentious issues, the short biography states, this "bosom friend" of the president was subject to "federal abuse," all of it undeserved. He gave evidence of "conciliatory manners, examplary [sic] morals, unimpeachable integrity, a luminous understanding, indefatigable industry, and long experience." There was nothing artificial and everything honorable about him. One could not hope for better press.

The same writer gave Madison credit for every important advance in the cause of union. In the "Old Congress," he had moved for a general convention to amend the Articles of Confederation. He had gone on to help draft the Constitution, the greater part of which was in his own words. "The Constitution owes more to Mr. Madison than to any other man," the author declared. Though Madison was not yet being hailed as the "Father of the Constitution," this was as close as he had yet been to having his paternity established.

In this published portrait, Madison comes across as something of a prophet. On Hamilton's economic plan, it read, Madison "early perceived the *anti-republican* tendencies of that *deep laid* system. He considered it a deviation from the spirit of the Constitution." During the battles over funding and assumption, it was not Jefferson but Madison who discerned the problems, and Madison again whose oppositional politics was "artfully ascribed to a spirit of rivalship with Mr. Hamilton." The mini-biography converted Jefferson into a figurehead, with Madison as the prime mover behind the current administration's policies and the man whom Hamilton was right to think of as his main rival: "Long may our country be benefitted by his patriotic services."[71]

The Louisiana Purchase was a collaboration involving Madison, Jefferson, Robert Livingston, and James Monroe; no one man deserves preponderant credit for the literal doubling of America's territory. It was Madison who, in the spring of 1802, started the ball in motion by asking Livingston, America's minister in Paris, to ascertain what Napoleon's price would be for the city of New Orleans. Madison assigned relative values to the real estate he most desired: East Florida was worth half as much as West Florida (the latter consisting, more or less, of the land between Pensacola and Baton Rouge); and the Floridas combined were one-fourth as valuable as New Orleans. With his own penchant for calculation, Jefferson expressed

to Livingston his firm belief that the Crescent City was of supreme commercial importance, because "the produce of three-eighths of our territory
must pass to market" through it.

Jefferson's words to Livingston summed it up. "Spain might have re-
tained [New Orleans] quietly for years," he wrote. But not the "new" France.
"The impetuosity of her temper, the energy and restlessness of her character," had made it imperative that the United States redirect the course of
Franco-American relations. "We must be very improvident," cautioned Jefferson, "if we do not begin to make arrangements on that hypothesis."
Without warning, in November 1802 the Spanish authority closed New
Orleans to American vessels—a purely local decision, as things turned out,
and not an idea emanating from Madrid.

Since Thomas Pinckney's Treaty of 1795, Spain had granted Americans
unrestricted navigation of the Mississippi and a duty-free right of deposit
at New Orleans. Madison wrote urgently to Charles Pinckney, cousin of the
earlier negotiator and present U.S. minister in Madrid, that he was deeply
concerned about what France and Spain were cooking up. He had already
alerted Pinckney that the administration was committed to acquiring all of
the land from East Florida to the Mississippi, and that no nation with
claims in North America should consider denying the United States access
to any navigable river. With some subtlety (though he meant something far
more aggressive), he said that the administration desired "a natural and
quiet boundary with Spain."

Having reached this point, Madison and Jefferson resolved to send their
trusted friend Monroe to France to augment Livingston's efforts to purchase New Orleans. Coordination between Washington and European capitals was difficult. Given the length of time required for transatlantic
communication, the president and his secretary of state could not be certain that some intelligence might not arrive in the meantime that would
end up redirecting their efforts. They had no greater priority and every reason to worry.[72]

Soon, however, they would find out that Napoleon had resolved to
forgo further efforts to resecure St. Domingue. Another pending conflict
with Great Britain made whatever vision he had of a North American empire appear impractical. Talleyrand, once (at the time of XYZ) and yet again
the French foreign minister, approached Livingston with a proposition:
selling not simply New Orleans but the entire Territory of Louisiana. Livingston and the newly arrived Monroe circumspectly regarded this unexpected opportunity. Unnecessarily, though understandably, the process

was complicated by the New Yorker's resentment that the Virginian, a far younger man, had arrived on the scene, at this pregnant moment, with diplomatic seniority over him.

The cast of characters in the Louisiana drama included the Marquis de Barbé-Marbois, at whose behest Jefferson had written *Notes on the State of Virginia* and with whom Madison and Lafayette had once traveled at length through New York's Indian country. Having since that time held a key post in St. Domingue, and having opposed the abolition of slavery there, Marbois had a unique perspective on current events. It was as a top aide to Napoleon that he visited with Livingston and Monroe and reconfirmed the offer, leaving the impression that Napoleon might change his mind if the United States delayed its decision. Despite their strained personal relations, which lasted for as long as both remained in Europe, Livingston and Monroe combined to complete the historic transaction.[73]

SIGNS OF A
RESTLESS FUTURE

CHAPTER ELEVEN

The Embryo of a Great Empire
1803–1804

In the bickerings of party animosity Americans do not
sufficiently value the unrivalled happiness they enjoy . . .
Taxes are lighter than in any nation on earth,
while labor is more productive.

—PRO-ADMINISTRATION *NATIONAL*
INTELLIGENCER, MAY 30, 1803

The present government has long ago discarded the
slavish principle of letting the people participate in
a knowledge of our foreign relations.

—SARCASTIC COMMENT FROM THE FEDERALIST
NEW-YORK EVENING POST, AFTER THE LOUISIANA
PURCHASE, NOVEMBER 9, 1803

AT SOME POINT DURING 1802 AND CULMINATING AT THE START
of 1803, President Jefferson resolved in his own mind to accelerate the policy of securing U.S. control over western territory. But he would have to be
quite clever if he was to move in this direction without Federalist interference and without alerting European governments to his actual motives. He
could not just outwait the British, French, and Spanish; he had to outwit
them.

Even before the Louisiana Purchase was finalized, while French and
British territorial claims still overlapped a good portion of the presumed
route, Jefferson devised what became the Lewis and Clark Expedition. The

young army captain from Albemarle, Meriwether Lewis, had been the president's trustworthy private secretary; William Clark, Lewis's old army buddy, was the younger brother of George Rogers Clark, the Revolutionary War hero whose ambitions Jefferson had warmly supported.

The president had recently read Alexander Mackenzie's *Voyages from Montreal,* in which the author-explorer openly appealed to Great Britain to invest more in strengthening its position in western North America. This could only have exacerbated Jefferson's existing fears. So when he approached the British representative in America, Edward Thornton, and his French counterpart, Louis Pichon, he secured passports for his explorers by camouflaging his intentions and convincing both that the mission was scientific. It made perfect sense that the naturalist who had authored *Notes on Virginia* would want to mark his presidency by acquiring a better understanding of the continent's plant and animal life.

In approaching Congress to fund a federal mission of discovery, Jefferson was more practical and honest. He confided that the explorers were principally meant to map a river route to the Pacific for the expansion of commerce and U.S. settlement. He slyly told Thornton and Pichon that he would have to emphasize commerce when he went to Congress or else face strong public opposition to so whimsical an expenditure as the one he had planned.[1]

At this time only Kentucky and Tennessee were considered western states and their populations were growing fast. Ohio attained statehood in 1803, its state seal featuring a rising sun, a sheaf of wheat, and a bundle of arrows. Within two decades the river city of Cincinnati would have a greater population than Washington, D.C. Jefferson, the son of a mapmaker, had grown up around the organizers of the Loyal Land Company in Virginia, which was small in scale next to what he now envisioned: the beginnings of a broad agricultural empire.

In April 1803 the quite sizable price tag of $15 million was agreed upon for Louisiana, encompassing the land between the Mississippi River and the Rocky Mountains. Because the trans-Mississippi West was largely unmapped, Jefferson and most others imagined that the Rockies were far less formidable than they are, and that the Missouri and Columbia rivers joined in some way. The president was convinced that his explorers would find familiar settings matching the geography of western Virginia as well as pliant Indian tribes, curious new species of crops, and navigable waterways.[2]

If $15 million for an unknown land was a gamble, it was an irresistible one for Jefferson. Issuing instructions to Meriwether Lewis, he was not just fantasizing what the expedition would bring back; he was also thinking of domestic politics. "The acquisition of the country through which you are to pass," he wrote the captain, "has inspired the public generally with a great deal of interest in your enterprize . . . The Feds. alone still treat it as philosophism, and would rejoice in it's failure." That "philosophism" was Jefferson's acknowledgment that his enemies liked to portray him as a hopeless dreamer, and westward movement as a distraction from eastern commerce, the real lifeblood of the nation's economy. Curiously, while Secretary Gallatin shared the president's excitement over plans for the Lewis and Clark expedition, Secretary Madison added little to the president's instructions to the two captains and remained largely uninvolved until the successful completion of their journey. But the trio was in the explorers' minds when they named three rivers they discovered that branched off the Missouri: the Jefferson, the Madison, and the Gallatin.[3]

"The Rule of Nature"

Here is where theory informed practice. The acquisition of Louisiana accorded with the theory Jefferson had advanced in his *Notes,* that an agrarian empire supported a republican political economy better than the urban-dominated manufacturing alternative.

For as long as he owned land, Jefferson could not divorce himself from the culture of the earth. In Washington, D.C., as at Monticello, the president charted growing seasons and changes in the weather, literally tracking when various vegetables were picked and came to market. He luxuriated in this kind of thinking and planning, as though keeping tabs on the predictable and unpredictable would lead to a more appreciable control over the course of life.

That same mind-set magnified when he conceived the mission to settle the West. The creative possibilities in land organization and land cultivation stood in marked contrast to the sterile progress he associated with a manufacturing economy. His "Revolution of 1800" was meant to redirect the people's energies and to make positive use of America's most tangible asset—land. For someone who had earlier denied to Madison having any interest in land speculation, Jefferson was presiding over the greatest land speculation in American history.

Outside the context of America's competition with European colonizers, westward expansion served other, equally critical purposes. Jefferson, who had fought to abolish entail and primogeniture, had never given up thinking about the tyranny of inheritance. A dozen years before, Madison had forced him to confront practical problems associated with his theory that "the earth belongs in usufruct to the living"—his ideal for canceling out debts to the past. But Jefferson continued to insist on the uniqueness of generational identity; he was persuaded that each generation needed a fresh start if it were to avoid being unjustly held back. He was not sure precisely what the West would look like in one or two or five generations, but he was convinced that it would be clay in America's hands. He believed, as Benjamin Franklin had, that the strength of the continental nation could be measured by its fertility rate—presupposing, of course, that this growth took place in a healthy environment. The right thing to do was to grow the republic.

Attachment to a fertile, fruitful land was perhaps Jefferson's strongest faith. America would be most peaceful and resilient as a breeder nation. The president's political vocabulary was rich in allusions to affection, attachment, health, good air, natural abundance, and the almost hysterical rejection of bad blood. It all added up to propagation of a certain (white republican) species and the dissemination of those ideas that bred a healthy spirit of personal independence.

When the Louisiana Purchase became fact, the president decided that Indians would best breed west of the Mississippi. Here, he rationalized, they would find "asylum" from conflict with whites. Here, over time, they would develop "useful arts" and "civilized" habits. This convenient formula for producing assimilable "yeoman" Indians ignored what he already knew: that tribes south of the Ohio River were confirmed agriculturalists. From 1803 Jefferson's salutations in letters addressed to tribal leaders changed from "Friends and Brethren" to "My children," symbolizing a paternalistic turn. Indians could wait. White landed interests came first.

Cold and calculating as his policy was, he remained as convinced as he had been when writing *Notes on Virginia* that Indians were willing to accept instruction. They were prone to violence but easily weaned from it; they demonstrated a "natural" kindness toward strangers and a strong commitment to friendship. It was for those Indians who still needed time in the endless hunting lands of the trans-Mississippi frontier (for the "manly amusement" of the chase) that eastern Indians were to sacrifice their property that abutted white towns.

Only the timeline had changed. No one said it outright, but that was the effect of the Louisiana Purchase. Jefferson's earlier intellectualization of the Indian's humanity in the tribute he paid to Indian eloquence yielded easily to practical concerns of land use and political reorganization. Indians might be physically and sexually suited to an amalgamation with the white race, but as an unlettered race they still lacked cultural complexity. The collection of Indian artifacts on the wall of the entry hall at Monticello represented objects of curiosity, not evidence of refinement. Indians lagged. They were now the virtual counterpoint to prevailing notions of social progress. It was a conclusion more easily arrived at because Federalists and Republicans alike believed it.[4]

Jefferson's faith in republican empire did not reveal itself to him overnight. Persons and books not generally accounted for in modern histories influenced him. While he was living abroad, Jefferson had befriended Pierre Samuel Du Pont de Nemours, a French official who subsequently emigrated to America in 1799. He and Jefferson remained regular correspondents for years. Du Pont was so trusted, in fact, that on a return visit to his homeland in 1802, he was the courier for private letters to America's chief diplomats.

Du Pont was of the physiocratic school, which had flourished for a time in France and which had great appeal to Jefferson. The word itself meant "the rule of nature," and the physiocrats considered theirs the science of nature. They extolled the productive class, the active agriculturalists, whom they ranked above the physically inactive (those whose "product" had no tangible value). They believed that farming's contribution to society was far greater than that of the money-oriented occupations. In the larger cause of social justice, they approved of free trade and opposed taxes and monopolies. Jefferson's vision of republican empire was an adaptation of physiocratic thought: an empire without a metropolis. In the city, disease festered, and the air became noxious. Expansion was healthy, compression unhealthy.[5]

William Coleman, editor of the *New-York Evening Post*, the long-running newspaper founded by Alexander Hamilton, expressed full support for the Louisiana Purchase. "In future the navigation of the Mississippi will be ours unmolested," he wrote with relief. But for the next year or more, he repeatedly mocked Jefferson's fanciful assumptions about the region's abundance. For instance, when the president informed Congress that the trans-Mississippi would yield *"all the necessities of life and almost spontaneously,"* Coleman jumped on the overconfident prose and took even greater literary license when he suggested that Jefferson meant to say that "not only *salt,* but bread and meat, and some other necessaries grow 'of their own accord,' in this vast garden of Eden ... Methinks such a great, huge mountain of solid, shining salt, must make a dreadful glare in a clear sun-shiny day." Add to this "an immense lake of molasses" and "an extensive vale of hasty pudding, stretching as far as the eye could reach," and one sees how physiocratic thinking would automatically strike busy Federalists as glowing fiction. They would never let Jefferson live down his reputation for dreaming on about the West's breadth and beauty and productive potential.[6]

Despite its basis in pragmatism, Madison was less attached to Jefferson's adaptation of physiocratic thinking and the sanitation-based moral calculus that Jefferson attached to it. Both men endorsed territorial expansion, a reliance on agricultural production, and freedom from British trade monopolies, but Madison was more comfortable with Newtonian physics for his model of westward expansion. Seeing the larger forces of attraction and repulsion in play, he felt that government should act to avert "collisions" along national borders (as he had warned the French when they considered occupying Louisiana); it should preempt the kinds of disruptions that were induced by population density and that gave rise to competing political factions. In Newtonian terms, he was monitoring gravitational pull, making certain that the planets remained in their proper orbits. In other words, his emphasis was on avoidance of conflict.[7]

"Probationary Slavery"

The Louisiana Purchase challenged the philosophies of both men. Jefferson was preoccupied with its constitutionality; after learning that the treaty had been signed, he convened his cabinet to discuss the legal ramifications and quickly drafted a detailed constitutional amendment, which he thought could and should be passed *ex post facto* (after the fact of the purchase). He defended his actions on the basis of national urgency, as he voiced his concern over how to rectify the unusual but necessary move.

His letter of August 1803 to Senator John Breckinridge on this subject was meant as both clarification and self-justification. Once again, Jefferson's surrogate in promoting the Kentucky Resolutions would prove himself a trustworthy ally. In 1799, as a leading state legislator, Breckinridge had worked to limit federal authority. Now as a U.S. senator, he would be doing the opposite: aggrandizing the power of the executive.

Jefferson felt the need to document his apprehension. The treaty would have to be ratified by the Senate and the purchase funded by the House. Nonetheless he thought he should entertain one additional step. "I suppose," he wrote Breckinridge, with reference to the members of Congress, "they must then appeal to *the nation* for an additional article to the Constitution, approving and confirming an act which the nation had not previously authorized." His tentative "I suppose" was followed by a clear recognition that "the Constitution has made no provision for our holding foreign territory, still less for incorporating foreign nations into our Union."

Jefferson's underlying premise in the letter was that the West was inseparable from the nation's destiny, whether new territories entered the Union or established themselves as independent republics allied with it. Fate and foresight gave him the right to seize this "fugitive occurrence"—a fleeting opportunity—to advance the good of the country: "It is the case of the guardian, investing money of his ward in purchasing an important adjacent territory; & saying to him, when of age, I did this for your good." Adopting this paternal tone, he insisted that Congress must now do "what we know they would have done for themselves had they been in a situation to do it."[8]

Before even a week went by, though, the president was forced to adjust his thinking. A nervous letter from Robert Livingston led him to confer with Madison, then to issue a reclarification to Breckinridge: he should put off any discussion in Congress of the "constitutional difficulty" he had raised just days earlier. The administration's position was that any delay could prove costly, and the treaty might be lost. An ominous-sounding letter to Madison from French foreign minister Talleyrand removed all remaining doubt: the administration had no time to consider a "safe & precise" construction of the Constitution.[9]

Treasury secretary Gallatin also played a role in the president's decision not to seek authorization by means of a constitutional amendment. Gallatin felt there was no legal necessity to pursue such a course, and he told Jefferson so. He succeeded in leaning on Jefferson to borrow a portion of the funds that enabled the $15 million purchase; then he prevailed upon him to expand federal powers by establishing a branch of the National Bank in New Orleans—mainly as a way to secure more firm connections with the new, culturally diverse, and politically uncertain possession.[10]

Jefferson called for a special session of Congress to convene on October 17, 1803. The Senate ratified the treaty in three days, and both houses

swiftly passed the Enabling Act that allowed the president to take possession of the territory. The speed with which Congress acted demonstrated
just how tightly Jefferson held the reins over the Republican Party at that
moment. Nothing was left to chance. His draft of the bill was forwarded to
Breckinridge, leaving the Federalist minority to grumble from the sidelines. There was no real deliberation on the treaty's provisions.[11]

As Congress weighed the acquisition of Louisiana that month, the
country learned of two deaths of national significance. On October 3 the
eighty-one-year-old Revolutionary patriot Samuel Adams "paid the last
tribute to nature," as the newspapers were wont to phrase it; and on the
twenty-third, when eighty-two-year-old Edmund Pendleton followed him,
it was broadcast that "another star has fallen from the splendid constella-
tion of virtue and talents which guided the people of the United States in
their struggle for independence." The House of Representatives instructed
each of its members to wear a "badge of mourning" for thirty days, to show
their veneration for both men. Some in the U.S. Senate balked at the suggestion, leading the *Aurora* to shudder that such an abhorrent act was "almost too malignant even for federalists." As the nation's boundaries
expanded, the battle over the Revolution's meaning went on.[12]

The bill Jefferson signed on October 31 was a temporary measure. It allowed Madison to notify William C. C. Claiborne that he had been appointed the territorial governor of Louisiana; but the government itself
was without form or substance. Claiborne, a less-than-poised twenty-eight-
year-old former congressman from Tennessee, had been serving as governor of Mississippi Territory since 1801. Moving over to New Orleans, he
was accompanied by five hundred troops, in case the Spanish attempted to
resist the transfer of power. The show of force was meant as well to awe Indians of the region and curb potentially rebellious slaves.

Claiborne found the Crescent City prosperous and bent on improvement, its buildings "elegant." But he also found the displaced French to be
of a "disorderly disposition"; those among them whom he called "warm
imprudent young men" seemed spiteful toward Americans. If the French
had to be watched, so did "adventurers...from several different nations—
of various characters, and among them many vagabonds." The young
governor-in-waiting was unsure how far he should go to demonstrate his
authority. Illustrative of the problems he had to confront, Claiborne did
not speak French.

In early December 1803, at long last, the Spanish in New Orleans staged
an official retrocession to France, though at that time no French mili-

tary presence was in the area. Cannon fire sparked the event, and the celebrants toasted both Bonaparte and Jefferson. Then, on December 20, the Louisiana Territory was formally conveyed from France to the United States, and its Virginia-born, Tennessee-bred governor addressed the people of New Orleans: "The American people receive you as brothers; and will hasten to extend to you a participation in those inestimable rights which have formed the basis of their own unexampled prosperity." In the middle of January, when word of the peaceful transfer finally reached Washington, members of Congress hosted a festive dinner for the president and his cabinet; a ball in Georgetown brought out close to five hundred gentlemen and ladies.[13]

In framing a government, Jefferson turned yet again to Senator Breckinridge, insisting this time that anything he told him was to be kept in the strictest confidence. "Never let any person know that I have put pen to paper on this subject," he wrote, and enclosed his draft of the bill he wanted. Breckinridge, who conveniently chaired the committee on Louisiana, followed instructions, returned the original letter to the wary chief executive, and made few changes in the blueprint for a new political order in this most extensive territory.

It was a good thing for Jefferson that he concealed his authorship. Debate on the Louisiana Ordinance of 1804 began in the Senate in early January and was immediately controversial. It pleased few members of Congress from either party. It was, in fact, a rather "unJeffersonian" creation: autocratic and oligarchic. The governor was appointed, not elected, and the thirteen councilors whom Jefferson designated were drawn from the ranks of "notables." In effect, President Jefferson was reinventing the British colonial model.

In keeping with that model, ordinary citizens had no voice in government. The outspoken Matthew Lyon, formerly of Vermont, sat in Congress these days as a Republican representative from Kentucky. He could not restrain himself from griping that the Louisianans were being reduced to "probationary slavery." For all intents and purposes, in crafting America's first colony, Jefferson was giving its residents fewer rights than the rebellious patriots of 1776 owned.[14]

Those in Congress who defended the undemocratic ordinance rationalized that the people were not ready for self-government. In a display of nativism, men in Washington pronounced that New Orleanians were different from citizens of the United States, their character marred by too much exposure to colonial Spanish (and before that French) rulers. They were prone to unrest; they had to be weaned off bad habits. Native Louisianans sought audiences with President Jefferson in order to convince the administration that their cultural forms were consistent with the American understanding of free republican government. He politely heard their pleas but was unmoved.[15]

Jefferson continued to be guided by the metaphor of the guardian and his ward. He told DeWitt Clinton of New York of his reluctance to experiment with democracy in Louisiana. "Our new fellow citizens as of yet are incapable of self government as children," he stated, disagreeing with those in Congress who refused to "suspend its principles for a single moment." Jefferson was saying that as children, or wards of the government, these dependents were to be regarded as aliens to republican values, who therefore could not act in their own best interest. This logic was oddly reminiscent of the hated Alien Acts of 1798, which had extended the naturalization period for aliens.[16]

"Another St. Domingo"

The political taint would wear off once Virginians, and others like them, migrated into the Louisiana Territory and replicated "American" forms. In the "empire for liberty" that Jefferson envisioned, vast open spaces invited new opportunity for a decent and deserving people who were meant to spread west and republicanize. Cultural dominance was built into that grand vision. It was impossible not to look to the future, as Jefferson mused to James Monroe in 1801, "when our rapid multiplication will expand itself beyond our limits, and over the whole northern, if not southern continent, with a people speaking the same language, governed in similar forms by similar laws." They would, of necessity, comprise a homogeneous population.[17]

The only thing that threatened demographic conquest was, said Jefferson, racial "mixture"—which could only "blot" the pristine "surface" of his hoped-for American sphere of influence. And so he rejected the notion, held by some would-be emancipators, that parts of the trans-Mississippi West could be colonized by free blacks. He was thinking of the interests of a growing planter class poised to spread across newly acquired territories, and of the white yeomanry who aspired to slave ownership.

But the theory of the yeoman republic of the West had a basic flaw. It would never be racially pure, due to the white landowner's ambitions.

Booming fields of cotton and sugarcane had already made the slave system nonnegotiable in the Southwest. In Claiborne's relatively brief time as governor of Mississippi Territory, he had learned how profitable it was to own and sell slaves, reporting to Madison in early 1802 that the "culture of cotton is so lucrative, and personal labor so valuable, that common Negro Fellows will generally command five hundred dollars a head." Arriving in New Orleans, he discovered that similar sentiments existed among the planters of Louisiana. The domestic slave trade would have to be protected.[18]

In his confidential letter to Breckinridge, Jefferson made clear that he thought domestic slaves would satisfy the demand created when the supply of slaves from overseas dried up. White Virginians would reap the greatest benefits from this approach, because at least 45 percent of all slaves lived in the Old Dominion, where domestic slave traders carried on a brisk business. Virginians had long opposed the foreign slave trade, which kept the price of slaves from rising, and Madison had pushed hard at the Constitutional Convention to curtail imports of Africans. As early as 1784, he anticipated that westward movement would change the demographics of slavery. Tobacco cultivation, so destructive to the soil of Virginia, would find a more receptive environment to the west, as Virginia, in Madison's words, was "disburdened of the slaves who will follow the culture of that plant." As slaves were moved to new tobacco fields, many more would go where cotton and sugar grew.

Virginians struggled with their mounting debts, increasingly selling off their "surplus" slaves. The buyers believed domestic slaves to be safer—that is, less likely to rebel—than slaves brought from the West Indies. As the mayor of New Orleans concluded in early 1804, "domesticated" slaves drawn off the eastern states would ensure his city's security; he was prepared to welcome "a race of servants already acquainted with our habits and attached to our country."[19]

The Louisiana Ordinance triggered a fractious debate on slavery in the U.S. Senate. Few were fooled by the suggestion that shutting down the foreign slave trade would benefit the nation. William Plumer got straight to the point: "It is obvious that the zeal displayed by the Senate from the Slave States, to prohibit the foreign importation of Slaves into Louisiana, proceeds from the motive to raise the price of their own slaves in the market— & to encrease the means of disposing of those who are most turbulent & dangerous to them." James Jackson of Georgia summarized the national dilemma: "You cannot prevent slavery—neither laws moral or human can do it. Men will be governed by their interest, not the law." Regardless of what laws Congress passed, unless the government enforced them with overwhelming military force, Louisianans would buy as many slaves as they wanted, from Virginia or from abroad.

Defending Jefferson's position, Breckinridge raised the specter of slaves in the South producing "another St. Domingo," and Republican John Smith of Ohio backed him up, imagining what would happen if foreign slaves overran Louisiana. If the "negroes were scattered more equally" throughout the states and territories, he said, everyone would feel better. Samuel White of Delaware chimed in, reminding his colleagues of Gabriel's Rebellion in Virginia. Breckinridge had no problem supplying the real rationale for the proposed redistribution of slaves: it was to "disperse and weaken the race—and free the southern states from a part of its black population, and of its danger." Anything less and Congress would be prohibiting "men of wealth from the southern states" from settling in the territories. This was the idea of "diffusion," lessening the evil of slavery by siphoning off the increasing population of slaves from the Atlantic states. As the Upper South became whiter, the pressure of simmering racial hatreds that Jefferson had referred to in *Notes on Virginia* would find a release. Simply put, the West was to serve as a safety valve for the South. Given this understanding, the impulse to "disperse and weaken the race," as obnoxious as it is to us, could be spoken of openly. At the start of the nineteenth century, the "dispersal" or "diffusion" of blacks framed a convincing logic for many white Americans who considered themselves enlightened.[20]

Defending the manner in which the president had acquired Louisiana, Breckinridge relied on the line of reasoning presented by Madison in *Federalist* 10. The senator dismissed the "old and hackneyed doctrine" that "a Republic ought not to be too extensive." Madison's premise was that factions ought to be diffused across space to make it more difficult for demagogic leaders to manipulate the passions of the people; small, crowded republics were more vulnerable to disruptive factions. Owing in large part to events in St. Domingue, Madison's theory had become racialized. On a small, crowded island, violent passions had been unleashed.

As top national executives, Madison and Jefferson were in positions of power and might have looked for an innovative approach to the moral menace of slavery. But in complicated times, politicians do not typically reach for the hardest, longest-insoluble problem to confront. Instead, they act in their own best interest—their immediate interest—and serve their closest constituency. They rationalize doing little by acknowledging the uncertainties that remain. To Monroe, in 1801, Jefferson could write that the West Indies were provided by nature as a "probable & practical retreat" for America's free blacks, offering "climates congenial with their natural constitution." The sea was a better racial barrier, a better means of quarantine, than the trans-Mississippi West. In the 1810s Jefferson would react to the problem of slavery in familiar language when he remarked to another Virginian: "Where the disease is most deeply seated, there it will be slowest in eradication." The "curative process" required, he said, "time, patience, and perseverance." This was how he rationalized. Neither he nor Madison nor their peers, meditating often on what loomed, persevered to posterity's satisfaction.[21]

In acquiring Louisiana, the United States did not fully understand the uniqueness of the place it had sought for years and finally won through diplomacy. Louisianans would be hard-pressed to convince the federal government that free men of color, who had previously served in the local militia, should continue in that function. Congress promptly barred free blacks from serving on juries. "With respect to the importation of Slaves from Africa," Claiborne informed Madison in March 1804, "the people generally appear to feel a lively interest, and the prevailing opinion expressed here is, that a prohibition would tend greatly to the injury of the Province." The governor was following his southern instincts in keeping the peace by interfering little. Some months passed before he was able to assure Madison that "calm" prevailed in the region: "I do believe," he wrote, "if the natives of the United States should not excite discontents, the Louisianans will become well pleased with the temporary Government which Congress has prescribed." And that is where things stood, for a while anyway.[22]

"The Etiquette Story"

One need only peruse the published letters of Madison and Jefferson at any point in the first decade of the nineteenth century to see that foreign diplomacy never ceased to be of great concern to them. Amid the extraordinary transition from a Federalist to a Republican order, the new style of governance in Washington produced all kinds of problems. Small gestures could be interpreted as major slights. The offended parties were the usual contending parties, the envoys from England, France, and Spain.

As Anglo-French war renewed in mid-1803, the rights of neutral shipping came to the fore, as did the British practice of impressment. Neither Madison nor Jefferson was inclined to do the Royal Navy any favor by handing over deserters. Resentment built as the British defended their right to board American ships virtually anywhere in search of British subjects, who could then be hauled away and impressed into service. Americans naturalized as citizens after 1783, when the War for Independence ended, were deemed fair game.

Madison was stubborn in his view on neutrality, but he was disinclined to respond at length to the first rumblings of impressment. Perhaps he did not want to get into a shouting match, but even so, his initial note to the British chargé d'affaires Edward Thornton proved fiery enough to anger Thornton, who had previously informed London that he considered Gallatin, not Madison, the heavyweight in the cabinet. Now he scoffed at what he described as Madison's "bitterness of tone and of insinuation."

The Briton was aware that Madison had taken it upon himself to address the diplomatic note without conferring with the president, and he convinced himself that Jefferson would not have approved such language. But Thornton did not perceive the nature of Madison's and Jefferson's relationship. If forced to take charge, Jefferson would have stated U.S. opposition to British policy in complete detail and with no more reticence than Madison, feeling it was necessary to do so before anything took place on the high seas that threatened to spiral out of control.

At times the president preferred to guard his opinions. In this case, Madison was present to commit them to paper at his behest and run interference with a foreign representative. Jefferson rarely made a policy decision without soliciting Madison's counsel, and Madison would not pledge the United States to a position that he did not already know Jefferson approved. As a result of misperception, Thornton was made decidedly uncomfortable by Madison, while remaining remarkably unperturbed by Jefferson's policies. Thornton felt the same way about the president's unpretentious dress and bearing. He and his wife had visited Monticello, and if its unfinished condition (which Jefferson seemed perfectly at ease in) made their stay imperfect, they had grown to understand that whether at home or inside the President's House, their host did not entertain in the ostentatious manner to which most European diplomats were accustomed, and to which George Washington had adhered.[23]

Edward Thornton did not have a full opportunity to judge President

Jefferson's policy toward neutrality and impressment, because his successor arrived in early 1804. Although envoy extraordinary and minister plenipotentiary Anthony Merry was not of especially high rank, he had previously been in the diplomatic service in Spain. He came with expectations of grand treatment, as did his wife, Elizabeth, who reportedly sailed to America with servants and baggage overflowing.

Jefferson detested high court culture and felt no need for ceremony. The Merrys were taken aback by the lack of formality at the President's House, as when Jefferson greeted them in bedroom slippers. Learning that this was not an insult but the way he had appeared before a Danish minister as well, the Merrys still found ways to complain in letters home. It irked them (as it had the Spanish minister) that President Jefferson paid no mind to seating arrangements at his dinner table. Merry had assumed he was the guest of honor, only to find that the French minister had been invited to the same gathering, in spite of the fact that their two nations were at war. Hannah Gallatin had to give up her place at the table to Mrs. Merry, to help the Englishwoman overcome her discomfort.

Madison was present on these occasions, as was Dolley. The secretary of state was not concerned enough to contradict the president's routine, and he may not have detected the problem right away either. For her part, Mrs. Madison was not squeamish in the least, nor reared among the highborn. "She is still pretty," Aaron Burr wrote to his daughter, "but oh, that unfortunate propensity to snuff-taking." Jefferson, not one to police his letters to trusted friends, was reacting to Elizabeth Merry's diamond-studded attire and overstated requirements from etiquette when he told Monroe, who remained abroad, that she was an alienating force in Washington. Burr, curiously, had an impression of Elizabeth Merry very different from Jefferson's: "Much of grace and dignity, ease and sprightliness; full of intelligence . . . an amiable and interesting companion."

To call this a crisis over etiquette misses Jefferson's state of mind. He did not care to be subtle in demonstrating his contempt for a female who insisted on speaking her mind, calling Elizabeth Merry a "virago"—a shrewish woman. Though accustomed to female-orchestrated salons in Paris, Jefferson as president had little patience with a diplomat's forceful wife attempting to insinuate herself into what he regarded as a strictly masculine political setting. Madison reported to Monroe, with similar dismissiveness, that the Merrys' expectations amounted to a "display of diplomatic superstition, truly extraordinary in this age and country." In his official role, taking no chances, he bade Monroe to assure the British government that there was no reason for the Merrys' eccentricity to lead to any worsening of Anglo-American relations.[24]

Though Madison and Jefferson were in general agreement, the incident with the Merrys again suggests differences in the two Virginians' personalities. Jefferson had the habit of looking to define people on the basis of preconceived categories; he dismissed those who annoyed him and denied his own agency in the process. Madison was less of an essentialist, with a less deterministic way of mulling over human foibles—or at least, less of a tendency to vent. As importantly, he appears to have had less of a need to have the last word.

The so-called Merry Affair echoed all the way to London, though fortunately its effect did not linger long. Monroe reported to Madison from the British capital after meeting with one of the Lords: "He knew nothing of the Etiquette story tho' he is in the diplomacy of the country . . . I inferred from that circumstance that the government gave no eclat to the incident." This was one Anglo-American diplomatic squabble that could be put to rest easily.[25]

The administration continued to cope with foreign policy standoffs, all of which landed on Madison's desk. U.S. merchant ships were harassed by the British whenever they dared to conduct business with the French. New Yorkers became especially irate when British warships hovered not far off Manhattan Island, spying on a French frigate that was in port to take Jerome Bonaparte back to France. The French, for their part, took offense at America's posture in the Caribbean, where armed merchant ships continued to convey supplies to the black forces in Haiti. Madison worked out an elaborate argument, trying to convince the French that by forbidding Haitians to trade freely with the United States, they would only be "embittering the minds of the inhabitants against France." His logic had no immediate effect. And despite the Louisiana exchange, Spain and the United States remained at odds over the Florida boundary.[26]

Neutrality was a lot easier to proclaim than to maintain. Madison tried to preserve balance: keeping the peace and avoiding looking weak. He and Jefferson read each other's mail when one was at Washington and the other at home, or one at Montpelier and the other at Monticello; and we can assume that they did so when they were laboring near at hand in Washington. But exertions toward making America's positions matter in a Eurocentric world were onerous when the nature of diplomacy was slow and deliberate and every word took a month or more to cross the Atlantic.[27]

"River of Thieves"

Jefferson's handling of the Tripolitan War has to be one of the most instructive episodes in early U.S. foreign policy. Often seen as a diversion, the administration's conflict with the Barbary powers was actually central to Jefferson's and Madison's philosophy of statecraft. For both of them, the principle of neutrality was automatically coupled with an implied threat of commercial retaliation. But economic pressure could work only on nations such as France and England, where there was a considerable volume of trade; the same strategy was useless in dealing with smaller states that disrupted American commerce. Jefferson had concluded as early as the 1780s that in such situations brute force was the only option.[28]

The Barbary States of North Africa, which included Algiers, Tunis, Tripoli, and Morocco, had a long-established practice of attacking American ships in the Mediterranean. They demanded tribute—bribes to ward off assaults on American merchantmen—and when it seemed expedient, they took American sailors captive. Forced to do backbreaking slave labor, the prisoners were punished with the infamous *bastinado,* one hundred blows to the feet for even minor offenses. Angered when President Adams failed to pay tribute as expected, the *bashaw* of Tripoli (the word for "high official" comes from either Persian or Turkish) impulsively declared war on the United States just as Jefferson assumed office. Unwilling to continue the past policy of "tributes and humiliations," Jefferson told Madison that only military force would stop "the eternal increase of demand from these pirates."

After consulting with his cabinet, Jefferson decided to send a squadron to the Mediterranean. This initiated the Tripolitan War (1801–05), best described as a naval war of intimidation and harassment. The captain of the American squadron carried clear instructions: to fight any or all of the Barbary States if they should declare war; and to safeguard commerce and "chastise their insolence—by sinking, burning or destroying their ships" wherever they might be found. The navy's goal was to establish a blockade of Tripoli and protect American vessels at the lowest possible cost.[29]

Jefferson may have had qualms over the constitutionality of the Louisiana Purchase, but he was little troubled by his unsanctioned use of military force in this instance. Did he possess the authority to go to war without first consulting Congress? Attorney General Levi Lincoln was the only member of his cabinet to urge caution. Both Gallatin and Madison eagerly endorsed an unmitigated show of force. Surprisingly, Congress put up little resistance to Jefferson's naval war, granting him complete control over the Mediterranean operation in 1802. The following year Gallatin set up a special fund that the president could use at his discretion and without further congressional oversight. Jefferson never made a formal declaration of war and kept a tight rein over relations with the Barbary States until the day he left office.[30]

The war with Tripoli was not just about protecting American commerce; it was a statement to the world about American fortitude. In a letter to Secretary Madison, David Humphreys, U.S. consul in Spain, expressed his concurrence with a policy designed to "chastise that haughty but contemptible Power." The military response would, he said, serve "not only as salutary example to the other piratical States, but it would produce an almost incalculable effect in elevating our national character in the estimation of all Europe." He echoed what poets and political figures had been saying for two decades already: that "National Character and public opinion are far from being unimportant objects, and more particularly as they respect a rising People." The "rising" United States still had a great deal to prove in Europe.

Madison shared these sentiments, advising Jefferson to display the flag and use force strategically, to help improve relations with England and France. He insisted that the administration broadcast the deployment of its navy so as to let every nation understand its purpose. Gallatin may have said it best when he claimed that the decisive use of force proved that the United States was "prepared, like the Great Powers, to repel every injury by the sword." Madison, Jefferson, and Gallatin all wished to prove America's virility.[31]

Between 1801 and 1804 the American squadron in the Mediterranean showed off its nautical skill and military muscle. In its first engagement, the schooner *Enterprise* won a quick and decisive victory over a Tripolitan cruiser. Jefferson heralded the bravery of the crew. The enemy suffered heavy casualties without the loss of a single American life. This victory helped the president convince Congress to pass the 1802 authorization bill that gave him unrestricted control over Barbary policy.

American exploits continued to receive favorable press at home and abroad. When the American frigate *Philadelphia* ran aground near Tripoli in October 1803, defeat was turned into a spectacular success. The captain and crew had become captives, their ship taken over and used against other U.S. vessels. In February 1804 Captain Stephen Decatur of the *Intrepid* earned his nation's gratitude by overtaking the Tripolitans, who held the *Philadelphia,* and then setting the ship ablaze. This even earned him accolades from the acclaimed English admiral Lord Nelson, who termed Decatur's feat "the most bold and daring act of the age." In case doubts remained as to America's long-term resolve, Decatur's commander, Edward Preble, launched a large-scale assault on Tripoli. The war officially ended in 1805, when a combined sea and land offensive brought the prostrate ruler to terms.[32]

The administration's understanding of its distant enemy was filtered through predictable stereotypes about Arabs and Muslims. U.S. diplomats contemptuously dismissed the Barbary powers as a thuggish "handful of banditti" and their area of operations as a "river of thieves." In Anglo-American lore, inhabitants of the Barbary States were rude barbarians and superstitious heathens who reversed history by enslaving Christians. But some observers used images of Islamic slavery to highlight the gap between American rhetoric and reality. In his last publication before death, Benjamin Franklin produced a scathing satire on this very subject, in which a fictitious North African Muslim defended slavery. Though his tale was set in 1687, Franklin was actually mocking the speech of a southern congressman.

Jefferson and Madison refused to comment on the moral implications of the enslavement of white Americans. They may even have understood that Muslim slavery was a more limited and, in some respects, less repressive regime from what was practiced in parts of the U.S. South. Those doing forced labor in the Barbary States were not of a particular race or religion; and manumission was not just possible but quite common. There were nearly three-quarters of a million slaves of African descent in the United States in 1803, and only a few hundred Americans held in bondage in North Africa.

The administration was equally careful not to turn the war into a holy crusade. Despite the fact that Pope Pius VI, learning of Tripoli's surrender, had praised the Americans for doing more than any other nation to protect Christianity, neither Madison nor Jefferson saw any advantage in furthering religious prejudice. In appointing Tobias Lear (formerly assigned to St. Domingue) as the consul general in Algiers, Madison reminded him that "universal toleration in matters of religion" was official policy. That said, the secretary of state's decision had less to do with a high-minded view of religion than with the practical benefit America gained over other Christian nations when it dealt in simple terms of power and interest with Islamic cultures.[33]

Confident that he was pursuing an able and intelligent policy, Jefferson was convinced that rogue states should be chastised like unruly children. He generalized about weak polities as illegitimate territories that could be manipulated. He called Haiti the "American Algiers" and wrote off Spain's provincial governments in North America with similar contempt. For President Jefferson, though he probably would not have said so, a distinctive hierarchy of nations existed. At the top were the "Great Powers," England and France, which extended their rule through war and conquest. Next he ranked the United States, a nation morally superior to the imperial powers and commercially strong but unwilling (as long as it adhered to its republican form) to become a full-fledged, tax-and-borrow, military behemoth. At the bottom of Jefferson's hierarchy of states were the small and insignificant. For them, independence had minimal bearing on their historical destiny. Offering little to the world, these states remained potentially destabilizing and were to be ignored, subjected to persuasion, and when required dealt with by force. Jefferson's system of nations fell neatly into a classic republican division of social classes: the corrupt, bloated, but still dangerous elite; the honest and morally upright middle ranks; and the primitive, if not hopeless and contemptible, lower class.[34]

In his thinking, the adoption of a more forward international posture would reinforce American liberty. By showing it had no reluctance to use military force where it saw advantages in doing so, the United States stood to free itself from subservience to British maritime policy. The British still ruled the high seas, but the United States had begun its climb toward greater respectability by controlling its destiny in one corner of the Mediterranean. For his part, Madison was convinced that America's show of strength would help its relations with London and silence those Federalist critics who liked to paint Jefferson as a feeble president.

Refusing to go along with the status quo and pay tribute to the Barbary States, the administration had begun to reverse a trend. Jefferson had earlier considered the possibility that an informal league with Russia and Sweden could help curb the excesses of the Barbary States and shift the maritime balance of power in America's favor. Consul David Humphreys voiced this very opinion when he told Madison that the United States could start a "new aera in the naval history of mankind."

After signing a treaty with Tripoli in 1805, President Jefferson defended his actions to the English émigré Thomas Cooper, concluding that the nations of Europe needed to take a fresh look at the United States. They had mistakenly believed that America was "entirely Quaker in principles & will turn the left cheek when the right has been smitten." This opinion, according to Jefferson, "must be corrected"; the Tripolitan War had provided a "just occasion" to undo the error in perception. Putting Tripoli in its place gave America an upper hand in diplomacy, not just in the Mediterranean but also on the Continent, where it counted most.[35]

"Repugnant to the Constitution"

A few other events that stigmatized the years of Jefferson's presidency warrant consideration because they affected Jefferson's and Madison's respective—and joint—legacies. The Marbury court case, which came to a head in 1803, pitted the administration against the Federalist-dominated Supreme Court. James T. Callender's newspaper columns prying into the president's personal behavior unleashed a scandal that continues to resonate into the twenty-first century. And the Yazoo corruption controversy forced the administration to confront the American passion for speculation in frontier land. It also brought to the fore John Randolph of Roanoke, exemplar of Old South political eloquence, who went overnight from Republican stalwart to administration critic.

William Marbury is known to history not for a distinguished career but for a career interrupted. Named by John Adams as a justice of the peace for the District of Columbia on the eve of Jefferson's inauguration, he never received his commission. He sought redress from the Supreme Court, hoping the justices would hear his case and force Secretary of State Madison to hand over his commission.

The question seems almost trifling: Was Marbury entitled to his job as promised? Was the lack of delivery of his commission a meaningful omission or a meaningless detail? Chief Justice John Marshall, who ruled on the case, was at the time of Marbury's appointment President Adams's secretary of state—it was *he* who had not completed the arrangement. Yet his successor in that office, Madison, was being held accountable for failing to follow up.[36]

It was Jefferson, and Jefferson alone, who had decided to withhold Marbury's commission. Madison had still been in Virginia at the time and had not yet taken up the duties of his new office. The third president considered the second's last-minute appointments "nullities" and felt no qualms, as he told Madison, in dismissing those persons "indecently appointed and not yet warm in their seat of office." "Indecency" made an impression on Jefferson.

Though duly summoned in December 1801, Madison never appeared in court; Attorney General Levi Lincoln made his excuses. One must wonder whether, in urging his secretary of state to boycott the proceedings, Jefferson was afraid that Madison might take a moderate line and find some common constitutional ground with Marshall. Or perhaps he was simply so outraged by Marshall's forward and presumptuous action in summoning Madison that he wanted to snub the Court. Either way, in this case Madison allowed himself to be muzzled by Jefferson.[37]

Soon enough the Republican press went on the attack, haranguing Marshall for his "ludicrous" attempt to "stigmatize" the executive. With two of three branches of government in Republican hands, Jefferson complained that the Federalists had "retired to the Judiciary as a strong hold," from which "battery" the good works of a Republican administration were to be "beaten down & erased." The president's recurrence to a metaphor of warfare was no accident; he planned to subject the High Court to a long siege. It seemed Americans were not "all Republicans, all Federalists" after all.[38]

Jefferson's initial gambit was the repeal of the Judiciary Act of 1801, for which he relied on his allies in Congress. The Judiciary Act, passed during the lame duck session at the end of the Adams administration, increased the number of federal district court judges. At the same time the District of Columbia was formed, creating forty-two new judgeships, among which was the position that went to William Marbury. In Jefferson's mind, these so-called midnight appointments constituted a flagrant form of court packing. It placed a "phalanx" of disruptive Federalists—again, his sense of political warfare—at the hub of his administration. In early 1802 Breckinridge of Kentucky took the lead in dismantling the bloated judiciary. Federalists became defensive. Accusations flew that Jefferson was threatening the independence of the courts.[39]

When the repeal bill moved to the House, James Bayard of Delaware (one of the Federalists who had tried to put Burr in the presidential chair) accused Jefferson of demagoguery. Bayard called his Republican colleagues puppets of the president, presuming them subject to the same vindictive spirit. In time, he predicted, as the executive succeeded in stripping the courts of competent judges, the real power would be lodged in "one man." Only the judicial branch was capable of "rising above the storm" of partisanship, he said; only the judiciary could keep the "fierce passions of a victorious faction" at bay.

Republicans shot back. Could anyone forget the sordid legacy of the Alien and Sedition Acts? John Randolph of Roanoke bitingly remarked that the judiciary did nothing when the people's liberties were at stake. And now, touch but "one cent of their salaries, abolish one sinecure," and they suddenly become great champions of the Constitution. Surely Madison's summons to appear in the Marbury case was in Randolph's mind when he accused the Federalists of trying to establish an "inquisitorial authority over the Cabinet of the Executive."[40]

The Republicans overturned the Judiciary Act by the slimmest of margins, 16 to 15, in the Senate; but they had a healthy margin of 59 to 32 when the House voted. After Jefferson signed the bill, sixteen district court judges (fifteen of them Federalists) were shorn of their lifetime appointments. Republicans then passed their own Judiciary Act, reestablishing the circuit court design that existed prior to 1801. Supreme Court justices, not only district judges, would suffer the indignity of having to ride the circuit, which meant traveling on horseback long distances to preside over district court sessions. On the Senate floor, sharp-witted Gouverneur Morris of New York derided the change, noting that judges required "less the learning of judge than the ability of the post-boy"—the youths who delivered their newspapers. Meanwhile, in eliminating the June 1802 session of the Supreme Court, Republicans in Congress found a way to postpone the Marbury hearing. On February 10, 1803, when the Court finally met, it was clear that long delays had done nothing to cool partisan animosity. Two weeks later, Marshall issued his decision.[41]

Madison and Jefferson must have expected Marshall to rule in favor of Marbury, in order to dictate the limits of executive authority. Instead, the chief justice ruled in favor of Madison. But there was a twist—or perhaps more than one. Asserting that the judicial branch of government was entrusted to explain the meaning of the law, Marshall overturned a portion of one section of the 1789 Judiciary Act, a piece of legislation that had authorized the Supreme Court to deliver a writ of mandamus (an order to hand over a document) to a federal officeholder. According to Marshall, the Supreme Court lacked authority to issue the writ; Congress had assigned jurisdiction to the Supreme Court when the federal Constitution stipulated otherwise. Marbury would have to seek redress from a court other than the Supreme Court.

Marshall could have limited himself to this ruling. But his real intent, as both a politician and a jurist, evidently was to lecture the current president and secretary of state. And so he elaborated. They were wrong to maintain that an appointment was not official until delivery of the commission, he said. The appointment could not be annulled. It was official, because it had

President Adams's signature on it and the seal of the government, which Marshall himself had affixed as secretary of state, in early 1801. The next president had no right to "sport away the vested rights of another." So as he chided Jefferson, he also took Madison to task for his passivity in confusing his political obligation to the president with the performance of the separate and distinct legal duties of his office. Twenty of the twenty-seven pages of Marshall's opinion were devoted to showing how Jefferson had violated the law. Madison, in this construction, was a mere pawn.

In response to Jefferson's offensive against the Federalist-controlled judiciary, Marshall had turned the bench into his bully pulpit. Unafraid of his Republican critics in Congress, he passionately defended judicial scrutiny of the executive. In his ruling, though he wrote on behalf of the entire Court, Marshall gave conspicuous evidence of his personal sense of outrage. He called Republicans' accusations of partisanship "absurd and excessive"—allegations that the Court refused to entertain, even for a moment. But of course, that was precisely what Marshall was doing when he decided to introduce the subject into his official opinion.

He was not quite finished with Congress either. The Court had every right to reject laws "repugnant to the Constitution," he explained, saying that to ignore his responsibility would be to subject the government to "legislative omnipotence." He took particular umbrage at the remarks of John Randolph, saying that by weakening the courts the Republicans were no less responsible for curtailing the rights of others than those who enacted the Sedition Acts were.[42]

What Marshall did not say in *Marbury v. Madison,* though modern interpreters have claimed he did, was that the Court's decisions were binding on the two other branches of government. He was far more concerned with protecting the boundaries of the judiciary from legislative and executive encroachments than he was in elevating the Supreme Court above the other federal departments. Marshall even conceded important ground to the Republicans: Supreme Court justices agreed to ride the circuit without complaint. And in another decision, *Stuart v. Laird,* the Court agreed that the legislative branch, in certain instances, could restructure the judiciary. As the legal historian Kent Newmeyer has concluded, "Survival was the order of the day . . . not supremacy."[43]

The case of *Marbury v. Madison* was decided in the administration's favor, but the lecture Chief Justice Marshall gave was more than a contingency. It symbolized his wish to shed a critical light on the Jefferson administration and intimate that it needed to remain under close scrutiny.

The Republican press saw the decision as an example of judicial overreach. Jefferson saw it as an affront, and it stuck in his craw until the end of his days.

Jefferson might well have preferred for Chief Justice Marshall to have compelled Madison to hand over the commission. As president, he would then have persisted in withholding it, rejecting the court's authority to question his discretion. Or perhaps, he would have agreed to hand over the commission but issued a statement of his own against judicial interference, using his own lawyerly erudition to pick apart the logic Marshall applied in his ruling.[44] In any event, the official whose name was associated with the Marbury case, James Madison, was barely harmed by it. And even the snappish Joseph Dennie, who was not beyond diagnosing hard-working diplomat James Monroe's "mental imbecility," noted in his *Port Folio:* "It is a justice due to the present secretary of state, Mr. Madison, to observe that the disgrace [of *Marbury v. Madison*] is not entirely imputable to him."[45]

"Surely a Philosopher May Kiss His Wench"

James T. Callender presented a much different problem. Back in May 1801, Jefferson had shrugged off Callender's crass assertion that he could embarrass the president if his demands for office were not met. "He knows nothing of me which I am not willing to declare to the world," Jefferson confidently told Monroe. Callender made good on his threat in September and October 1802, when he published a series of articles in the Federalist *Richmond Recorder,* ridiculing Jefferson for keeping an "African Venus" as his concubine at Monticello.

Even the friendly travel author John Davis, in the book he dedicated to Jefferson, sexualized female slaves. He described the "liberty" they enjoyed on the Sabbath, and how they dressed up in "garments of gladness, their bracelets, and chains and ear-rings, and deck[ed] themselves bravely to allure the eyes of the white men." Nor, he went on, did they fail to please, "for as the arrow of a strong archer cannot be turned aside, so the glance of a lively negro girl cannot be resisted."[46]

Callender had never seen Sally Hemings; he identified her based on the accounts of unidentified citizens of Albemarle County. As Federalist newspapers lapped up each report, the Republican press reacted: "From four to eight columns of newspaper which ought to be devoted to useful information are filled with low and venomous slander against *Mr. Jefferson.*" As to the "abandoned libelers," the *Republican Star* vented: "False, base, wicked, and malicious, indeed they are." Republicans claimed that they scarcely took the time to think about invented stories aimed at the president's "private feelings" because they were undoubtedly designed for a gullible Federalist press by the crass Callender, "whose infamy is proverbial." That did not stop the Federalists from having their fun. One paper went so far as to record the president's purported monologue on learning what Callender had done: "He broke into a violent passion, and so far forgot the dignity of office as to call him a damn'd rascal, a damn'd eternal miscreant, and other such polite christian phrases."[47]

Joseph Dennie printed "original poetry" on the subject, all of it laden with an undisguised repugnance toward dark skin. Even before the scandal broke, he told sexually charged anecdotes. One concerned a "celebrated surgeon" whose apprentice had run off with his wife: "The lady complained that her husband's *practice* was on the *decline.*" In one of his many efforts to satirize Jefferson, Dennie mocked the Jeffersonian truth that all were created equal—in black-speak. One stanza credited the generic slave "Quashee" with the logic that his natural equality should permit him to cross the color line in choosing a mate:

> *And why should one hab de white wife,*
> *And me hab only Quangeroo?*
> *Me no see reason for me life!*
> *No! Quashee hab de white wife too.*

Once Callender's reports began circulating, Dennie was amused that the president would lie with a slave after having written in *Notes on Virginia* that blacks emitted "a *strong and disagreeable odor*" (the italics are Dennie's). Prefacing verse imported from the *Boston Gazette*, he remarked: "If, according to the elegant proverbs of Dr. Franklin, 'a man may *kiss his cow*,' surely a *Philosopher* may *kiss his wench.*"

> *Dear Thomas, deem it no disgrace*
> *With slaves to mend thy breed,*
> *Nor let the wench's smutty face*
> *Deter thee from the deed.*

Showing the famously philosophical Jefferson stepping out of character gave the defeated party means of gratification.[48]

As the much-publicized scandal relates to the partnership of Madison and Jefferson, we have no evidence of how the two treated the matter in their private moments; but it seems unlikely that they would have been uncomfortable discussing it. As a man habituated to the ways of Virginia plantation life who did not marry until he was in his forties; and as one who was on familiar terms with the house servants at Monticello, James Madison obviously knew Sally Hemings and knew the truth. Having been just as deeply involved with Callender as Jefferson, Madison would have confirmed for Jefferson that the best way to deal with the writer was to publicly ignore the charges.

Callender's intelligence coup went beyond what took place on Jefferson's property. As good as the tale of "copper colored Sally" was, moralizing editors found in Jefferson's "more criminal and flagitious" behavior—the attempted seduction of his neighbor John Walker's wife Betsy, in 1769—even better fodder. The picture of "a certain moral man being forced out of a gentleman's house with an insulted husband's foot at his crupper" (a horseman's slang for rump) was irresistible.[49]

Dennie continued to needle the president into 1803, compiling a host of barbs he had used over the years, in another, intentionally mediocre, ode:

> *Of wit and folly, genius void of sense,*
> *Malicious deeds, and mildness in pretense,*
> *And* pious *Atheism, profligate and grave,*
> *Serenely pure, and wenching with a slave.*[50]

As the months passed, Republican newspapers were still smarting from Callender's handiwork. One of these was New York's *American Citizen,* which indulged in sexual smears itself, shamelessly calling Aaron Burr debauched—even homosexual. In July 1803 its aggressive editor, James Cheetham, saw fit to remind readers of the "foul slander about Sally," as he compared Callender to one Richard Croucher, a convicted rapist and murderer whose name was known to all Manhattanites. "The whole federal party have looked up to Callender as the wretch deputed by Hell to overturn the present administration," Cheetham wrote scornfully.[51]

On July 17, 1803, Callender drowned in the James River. According to the *Virginia Gazette,* "The water being shallow where it happened, 'tis supposed he was affected either by the cramp or a fit. He went into the water for the purpose of bathing, which was his regular practice." The sensation-driven writer was, the paper assured, "decently interred" on the day that he died. A letter from Richmond, published in New England, had something else to add to initial reports: Callender was seen on the morning of his death "much intoxicated." While the coroner's report declared the death "accidental," the deceased had been embroiled in a very public argument over money at the time of his demise. This was all anyone knew. Apparently, whether or not his drowning was an accident, there were people other than supporters of the president who wished to see harm come to James Callender.[52]

Even afterward Jefferson haters posted occasional reminders of Callender's work. The *Trenton Federalist* argued, in a religious tone, that what those who lived near Monticello said about Jefferson carried the weight of truth: "In the immediate neighborhood of the President, the same allegations against him, which are impudently contradicted at a distance, are still recapitulated in the most circumstantial manner. Does not this manifest the warmest confidence in their truth?" The New Jersey editor compared Jefferson's neighbors to the apostles: they were as incapable of misrepresenting "Lord Jefferson" as the latter were of misrepresenting the character of Jesus.[53]

New England Federalists savored the poetic justice. Jefferson had previously attempted to deny or downplay his prior connection to Callender, when Callender was conveniently targeting President Adams. Jefferson the "virtuous philanthropist" had posed for citizens as something he was not—detached and disinterested. That is how the most eager of the Federalist editors viewed him. So from the pen of the once-trusted Callender, the two-faced politician had gotten his comeuppance.

People believed what they wanted. Many years later, when Jefferson was past eighty, an apologetic colleague of Callender's bemoaned the "paroxysms of inebriety" that had elicited the mercenary writer's most noxious stories. By then Jefferson undoubtedly believed that his private life would never again be the subject of lurid speculation. We, of course, know otherwise. Callender's columns outlived not just their author but everyone else who was alive at the time of their publication, remaining so much a part of the nation's tortured conversation about race relations that science finally turned to DNA to establish the paternity of Sally Hemings's children.[54]

"Yazoo Man"

In 1789, the year George Washington became president, the Yazoo Company of Virginia, led by Patrick Henry, petitioned Georgia for land grants to settle its western parts. Similar companies formed in South Carolina and Tennessee. Ignoring Washington's displeasure with the plan, Georgia consented in 1794 to put millions of acres in private hands.

Three years later Congress reversed the sale and redefined the Mississippi Territory to encompass a considerable chunk of the Yazoo lands. By this time many would-be settlers had already paid the original speculators for their land, and no one could say who held valid title. The worst part of the business was what had happened in Georgia's state legislature in 1794: the Yazoo land syndicate bought the votes of most of the representatives, so that investors could obtain land grants at an exceedingly low price. Georgians smelled a rat right away.

The Jefferson administration inherited this knotty problem. A fraud had taken place; no one was trying to deny it. When national attention turned to the Louisiana Purchase, relations with Spanish-held lands, and the future of the Deep South and Southwest, the cabinet took up the Yazoo matter. Madison, Gallatin, and Attorney General Levi Lincoln put their heads together and worked toward a resolution. In 1802 Georgia was compensated for its cession to the federal government of the millions of acres in question, in what is now Alabama and Mississippi. The three cabinet officers revisited the claims of private individuals and came up with a compromise that apportioned land and money, though no party was entirely happy with the result.

At this moment John Randolph of Roanoke, a Virginia planter with a rich genealogy, made himself heard. Tall, awkwardly formed, and boyish in appearance owing to a genetic condition, he was noticed even before he opened his mouth—which he did often and for hours at a stretch. He happened to be in Georgia at the time the scandal broke, and the display of corruption forever marked him. Randolph's standard of republican purity was impossibly high; he could not consent to any administration that compromised on such an issue. For some years friendly toward Gallatin, and as yet unready to see Jefferson as a betrayer, the theatrical young congressman with the high-pitched voice directed his criticism toward the generally unassailable Madison, whom he knew less well.

Randolph was one of the most temperamental persons ever to serve in Congress. He was trained for Virginia politics from early on, because the field was open to any Randolph, certainly one of such ambition. In 1790 he studied law with then–Attorney General Edmund Randolph in Philadelphia. His forensic talent was legend: he knew instinctively how to apply his splendid memory when he felt inspired to cite classical verse or unleash spontaneous invective. He treated hyperbole as an obligatory first step in any argument. Randolph also had the tendency, once he formed an objection to someone, to allow the feeling to fester and grow; there was no turning back for him. In identifying Secretary of State Madison as a "Yazoo man," Randolph refused to let go of the image in his mind. It would color his actions for years to come, as his power as a provocateur increased and placed him front and center in the sensationalizing columns of the American press. In Randolph's lexicon, once you were a "Yazoo man," you could not be a real republican anymore.[55]

It hardly matters why he identified Madison as corrupt or at least complicit in a fraud. In an age of malcontents, Randolph was arguably the most malcontented; in a time of Republican ascendancy, he held out impossible expectations of political purity, which ultimately served to marginalize him. The movement he started took Virginia provincialism to unprecedented lengths and complicated the lives of Madison and Jefferson— precisely what the pesky congressman intended.

"I Feel Relief from Being Unbosomed"

The year 1804 was one of mixed emotions for President Jefferson. In April his younger daughter was in failing health. "Our spring is remarkably uncheary," Jefferson wrote to Madison from Monticello on the day he turned sixty-one. "A North West wind has been blowing for three days. Our peach trees blossomed on the 1st. day of this month, the poplar began to leaf . . . But my [flower] beds are in a state of total neglect."

He was watching Maria, at twenty-five, succumb to the effects of a difficult childbirth, as her mother had done when she was a toddler. She had been a charming and delicate child and, over the years, the recipient of her father's most indulgent letters. Now she was the wife of her cousin, the thirty-one-year-old first-term Virginia congressman John Wayles Eppes. Maria's death on April 17 left Jefferson bereft. It meant that the only surviving child of his ten-year marriage was Patsy, also thirty-one, and the mother of six living children. His old friend John Page wrote a letter of condolence, and in his response Jefferson lamented their having outlived so many beloved friends and family: "When you and I look out on the country over which we have passed, what a field of slaughter does it exhibit." Thinking toward final retirement, the president acknowledged that Patsy was "the slender thread" on which his "evening prospects" now hung, and he tempted fate by questioning whether she would outlive him.[56]

Maria's death led to one of the most moving of epistolary exchanges in the literal republic of letters. On reading of Jefferson's personal loss in a newspaper, Abigail Adams opened a straightforward dialogue with the man who had ousted her husband from office. She had adored nine-year-old Maria in 1787, caring for the child in London while she and her husband were residing there and Maria was en route from Virginia to Paris to rejoin the father she had not seen in three years. Maria had clutched her when it was time to leave, crying out: "O! now that I have learnt to Love you, why will they tear me from you?" That memory was why the former first lady put pen to paper now, in spite of the ill will she harbored toward Jefferson the president.

"Reasons of various kinds withheld my pen," she admitted, until "the powerfull feelings of my heart, have burst through the restraint." Jefferson responded feelingly, and with the assurance that "the friendship with which you honoured me has ever been valued." He assigned responsibility for the ugliness of politics to unnamed others and expected her to appreciate his version of his history with her husband when he said, "We never stood in each other's way." Jefferson's letter was twice the length of hers and professed near the end: "I feel relief from being unbosomed." Then he asked her forgiveness for turning from subjects of grief and loss to the unkind nature of politics.[57]

Mrs. Adams answered promptly, in a letter nearly twice the length of his, which picked apart much of what Jefferson had said. She introduced matters he had failed to bring up that continued to gnaw at her, and told him exactly how she felt as the election of 1800 unfolded. Her phrases contained no softness and nothing of Jefferson's apologetic tone. "I have never felt any enmity towards you Sir for being elected president," she affirmed. "But the instruments made use of, and the means which were practised to effect a change, have my utter abhorrence and detestation." And then she announced: "I will freely disclose to you what has severed the bonds of former Friendship."

Dropping all affectation of politeness, she confronted Jefferson directly. The subject was Callender. "One of the first acts of your administration," she charged, "was to liberate a wretch who was suffering the just punishment of the Law due to his crimes for writing and publishing the basest libel, the lowest and vilest Slander, which malice could invent, or calumny exhibit against the Character and reputation of your predecessor, of him for whom you profess the highest esteem and Friendship." She devoted three paragraphs to the man she termed "the serpent you cherished and warmed," finding ways to vary her epithets and reminding Jefferson that the spiteful snake had "bit the hand that nourished him." Having scolded him enough, she concluded her letter with charitable lines—"I bear no malice I cherish no enmity"—leaving Jefferson seriously wounded, as she put down her pen.

His reply on the Callender matter was weak. He claimed to have cared no more for the adjudication of Callender's case than for that of anyone else who had been imprisoned under the Sedition Law. "I knew nothing of his private character," he wrote, clearly hoping that she would see his relationship to Callender's attacks on her husband as no different from John Adams's relationship to the poisoned arrows aimed at Jefferson by Federalist newspaper editors "Peter Porcupine" or John Fenno.

The exchange continued. Her next letter addressed the state of parties concretely and contained some harsh words that Jefferson could not but have agreed with: "Party spirit is blind malevolent uncandid, ungenerous, unjust and unforgiving." It was no more welcome for her in Federalist papers than in Republican papers. "Party hatred by its deadly poison blinds the Eyes and envenoms the heart . . . It sees not that wisdom dwells with moderation."

Jefferson ended his part in this flurry of letters with one political and one personal sentiment. The political sentiment was his decided belief that both parties pursued the public good, differing because the Federalists feared the ignorance of the people at large, whereas the Republicans feared the selfishness of rulers not accountable to them. The personal sentiment was his appreciation for her "candour" and "sincere prayers for your health and happiness that yourself and Mr. Adams may long enjoy the tranquility you desire and merit."

Abigail Adams had opened their correspondence, and she would bring it to a close. It was six months now since Maria's death. "Affection still lingers in the Bosom, even after Esteem has taken flight," she wrote, disliking Jefferson less yet standing at a distance from any more yielding embrace. As to the distinction he drew between the two political parties, she had an effective rejoinder: "Time Sir must determine, and posterity will judge with more candour, and impartiality I hope than the conflicting parties of our day, what measures have best promoted the happiness of the people." To show Jefferson—who must have been wondering—that the second president had had no hand in any of the preceding compositions, John Adams scrawled at the bottom of the final letter: "The whole of this Correspondence was begun and conducted without my Knowledge or Suspicion. Last Evening and this Morning at the desire of Mrs. Adams I read the whole. I have no remarks to make upon it at this time and in this place." And so things would stand for another seven and a half years.[58]

Overall, Jefferson appeared the more accommodating. But the authenticity of some parts of his self-vindication (and not just as to Callender) remain open to question. Was he really as prompt to forgive lame duck John Adams for his "midnight" appointments in 1801 as he maintained? He was dexterous, but how genuine? Was he trying, and failing, to match Abigail Adams in emotional genuineness? In the words of historian Edith Gelles: "She measured justice by its impact on people, not by abstract principle." Jefferson argued from principles while he worked to gain the political upper hand, whereas Mrs. Adams, in this case, framed her argument on the basis of a belief that personal relationships were meant to be defended and friendship preserved at all costs.[59]

"The Sun of Federalism Is Indeed Set"

Senator William Plumer of New Hampshire provides us with an apt generalization of where partisan politics stood as the election of 1804 approached. A Federalist who socialized with the political opposition, he confided to a friend: "The southern Democrats fear New England Federalists. Though our numbers are small, we are both feared and respected. We can seldom carry any measure; but we prevent the ruling party from doing much mischief." Plumer, relatively new on the national political stage, was still optimistic.[60]

Joseph Dennie was another story. The *Port Folio* had been hammering away at southern democrats week by week. "In Virginia, where churches are out of fashion," he wrote in July 1804, "democracy is most in fashion. In Connecticut, where they have yet more room for their Meeting Houses and Schools and less for whiskey shops and brothels, there is less of democracy and more of federalism." Right when the Republicans were beginning to take pride in the unpopular word *democrat*, Dennie grabbed onto it and tried to pull it backward so that it could only connote chaos.

In the following issue, he called up some of the shibboleths of election year 1800, hoping to get new traction by renewing his critique of *Notes on Virginia*—especially its "tendency to Subvert Religion." Jefferson's "tendency" could be traced back to another whom the cranky critic deemed morally suspect. "Whereas Franklin has made one man frugal," Dennie wrote aphoristically, "he has converted a hundred to Deism." But what Dennie appeared to despise most about Thomas Jefferson was his stealthy and manipulative vocabulary, and here the *Port Folio* went on a tear: "With respect to Mr. Jefferson's style, I cannot better express my opinion than by saying, that it is just such a style as Betty, my cookmaid, uses, in writing to her lovers . . . Betty is a long-sided, red-haired slut, and, like Mr. Jefferson always hankering to have a mob of dirty fellows about her." New England Federalism of the Dennie sort found most appalling what it saw as the vulgarity of popular appeal.[61]

Alexander Hamilton was yet another story. Despite regular opinion pieces in the newspaper he had founded in Manhattan, Hamilton was long out of office and had less influence than ever. His correspondence suggests he was feeling sorry for himself. He continued to distinguish between the "cool and discerning Men," whom he called "real friends to the national government," and those who had been "successful in perverting public opinion, and in cheating the people out of their confidence." These "mad Democrats" were now "advancing with rapid strides in the work of disorganization—the sure fore-runner of tyranny," which for Hamilton meant "the horrors of anarchy."

Hamilton's fear-mongering language was the equal of Jefferson's. The difference was that when Jefferson invoked his "reign of witches" imagery to symbolize High Federalist rule, he immediately predicted that the reign would soon end, and the republic would be saved. Hamilton had no such vision. But he did have salient points to make, because he still hoped to quiet the pro-administration press before it could completely rewrite the founding and make the Hamilton of 1788 into a moribund monarchist. The problem, he wrote in one sharp editorial, lay with the arbitrariness of terminology: *monarchy* did not necessarily connote *despotism*. It could as easily mean any government in which the executive was a single individual, even an elected one. Great Britain, with its hereditary king, was easily spoken of as a commonwealth and as a republic. And so to try to distance the Hamilton of 1788 from the Madison of 1788 by describing the former as an exponent of monarchical government was fatuous.

Hamilton knew the Republicans in power were trying to discredit his political theory as something morally inferior to their supposedly genuine republicanism. This, he charged, was "worse than arrogance." The Virginia delegation at the Constitutional Convention, Madison prominent among them, had voted for "the most energetic form of government"—for a strong national authority. Showing that old disputes persisted, some months after Hamilton wrote these words, the *National Intelligencer* explained that when Federalists used the term *energetic government,* "they mean that government which shall introduce privileged orders, and the oppression of the poor and industrious." It was a good comeback, but by then Hamilton was already dead.

All this swatting around of political language eventually led the Jefferson administration to become proactive. A paragraph of Dennie's printed in April 1803, and largely ignored by Republican newspapers at the time, would later become evidence in the editor's trial for seditious libel. "A democracy is scarcely tolerable at any period of national history," wrote Dennie. "Its omens are always sinister, and its powers are unpropitious . . . It has been tried in France, and has terminated in despotism. It is on trial here, and the issue will be civil war, desolation, and anarchy."

While Dennie raged, Hamilton was too realistic to calculate on an end to Democratic-Republican rule. Insisting "mine is an odd destiny," he wept for his own fallen star in a pair of letters to Gouverneur Morris, now U.S. senator from New York: "What can I do better than withdraw from the Scene? Every day proves to me more and more that this American world was not made for me."[62]

Of course, he was right about that, but not as he intended. In the spring of 1804 the doomed partisan turned his attention to Aaron Burr's campaign for the governorship of New York. Jefferson's vice president had long since been shown the door, as it were, given clear signals that Madison and Jefferson did not want to cede the national stage to any but a trusted Virginian. Looking to reestablish himself in his home state, Burr was drawn into an affair of honor with his old colleague and occasional cocounsel. It was not the first time that Hamilton had sought to deny Burr elected office by resorting to character assassination—their political competition went back a full decade. In the past Hamilton had apologized. But not this time. The result of his stubbornness in the affair with Burr was an avoidable duel and Hamilton's untimely death at the approximate age of forty-nine.[63]

Neither Madison nor Jefferson left their true feelings about the death of

Hamilton to the historical record, just as they were careful not to publicly comment on Callender's drowning. Senator Plumer, however, noted with disquiet when members of the administration who had formerly distanced themselves from Burr began to embrace him. "I never had any doubts of their joy for the death of Hamilton," he wrote of congressional Republicans; "my only doubts were whether they would manifest that joy, by carressing [sic] his murderer. Those doubts are now dispelled." Gallatin, who had long looked favorably on Burr's republicanism, was known to have spent two hours meeting privately with the vice president. William Branch Giles, the impulsive Virginia congressman, now U.S. senator, was urging the governor of New Jersey—in whose state the duelists met for their "interview"—to void the pending indictment of Burr and declare the duel fair. But Madison had "taken his murderer into his carriage," on a ride that mystified Plumer, because it brought them to the home of the French minister. And Jefferson had "shewn more attention" to Burr than was becoming, inviting him into the President's House. It amazed Plumer what had happened to the U.S. government: "The high office of the President is filled by an infidel, and that of Vice President by a murderer." Yet the day after he penned this last sentiment, he dined with the infidel and found him "dressed better than I ever saw him"; his scarlet vest new, his hair powdered, and his stockings clean. Not to disappoint the Federalist fashion police, Jefferson's slippers were old, the senator reported, and his coat "thread bare." No secrets fell from the president's lips.[64]

Though Dennie had long kept alive his hopes for a Federalist revival, he was forced to admit in September 1804, on lamenting the death of Hamilton: "The sun of federalism is indeed set, and unless it rise again, nothing remains for us but to be subjected to the dominion of Virginia." The Federalists remained active with their pens but were unable to stir the electorate. Jefferson, renominated by his party in February 1804, awaited a reelection that was all but inevitable, and the Washington newspaper that routinely defended him, the National Intelligencer, celebrated the prospect of a second term: "While the world around him has been in a state of mutation, it is his distinction to have remained the same. Who more fit to preside over the destinies of a republic than such a man?"[65]

Republicans were a bit complacent. That fall the newspaper Republican Farmer, in Federalist Connecticut, challenged the neighborhood gossip concerning Jefferson's alleged failure to appoint northerners to key posts by pointing to his cabinet. "His magnanimity and impartiality are conspicuous," the editor proclaimed.[66]

"Fields of Futurity"

The president issued his fourth annual message on November 8, 1804, presenting the executive's outlook on the still-simmering issues of France and Haiti, Spain and Florida. Senator Plumer expressed frustration at the lack of substance in the address. Bringing up the U.S. boundary with Spanish Florida, Jefferson stated that America's object had been "misunderstood on the part of Spain"; on the related matter of Madrid's discomfort with America's title to the larger Louisiana Territory, he expressed equal confidence that the issue would be easily resolved. But to Plumer, this was all wishful thinking. Only the "irresistible arm" of France had convinced Spain to accede, he wrote, and only for the moment.

Jefferson was feeding Congress mere crumbs of information. Probably his secretary of state was the one who made sure that nothing more specific was being conveyed. Madison had been unyielding in his posture toward France, but especially toward Spain. He preferred to negotiate with Madrid to buy the arc of land abutting the Gulf of Mexico; but in letters to diplomats Monroe and Pinckney, his language suggested that, with or without an agreement, and lest it fall into British hands, he would have the United States move into the disputed borderland that was known as West Florida—east of New Orleans, past Mobile and Pensacola, and nearly to Tallahassee. His claim to this land was certainly debatable; but just as he had few qualms about proceeding with the Louisiana Purchase without consulting Congress, he put the law second after what he regarded as national security.

Senator Plumer was not fully aware of Madison's role when he took out his pique on Jefferson alone. He jotted in his private journal that the president's message contained such outright ambiguity that his words could be interpreted however one chose. The annual address that marked the end of his first term was, the senator said, "more empty & vapid, & wrapt in greater obscurity than any of his preceding messages." So much for the positive gloss Federalists were meant to place on the emblematic first inaugural.[67]

Though it could not completely drown out the opposition, the administration's voice carried the farthest. In his 1804 *Defence of the Measures of the Administration of Thomas Jefferson,* Virginia's John Taylor enumerated the successes of Jefferson's first term. The man the Federalists painted as a dangerous radical was in fact, he wrote, a prudent administrator of the general government, paying down the interest on the federal debt ("retrenchment of unnecessary expence") while seeking to preserve peace with the European powers and pointing the executive branch away from any tendency toward "criminal excess of power" at home. Similarly, Secretary of State Madison had done nothing to undo his own long-held reputation for mildness. He operated "by the force of argument and truth," said Taylor, who went on to contradict the Federalists' appraisal of the foreigner Gallatin. Differentiating between France, which provided a language, and the canton in Switzerland where Secretary Gallatin was born, Taylor reflected: "the air he there inhaled was that of liberty."

In the sentimentally assertive rhetoric of republican empire, Americans found a way to minimize their protectiveness of region and declare their superiority as a nation. They were accustomed to hearing patriotic oratory and reading patriotic pamphlets protesting their fervent desire for peaceful expansion for the good of all. Since the middle of the prior century, sylvan America had been known as an "asylum" for those oppressed elsewhere in the world. A cheerful folk, full of energy and enterprise, they had learned not to crave the "gaudy superfluities" of foreign manufacturers, but to reap satisfaction in their plain possessions. Jefferson himself had early on hailed the "elegant simplicity" of his countrymen. This was the America a young Vermont lawyer named Orsamus C. Merrill evoked in his Fourth of July oration in 1804, when he alluded to "fields of futurity" and extolled his nation's mission to diffuse knowledge and virtue "through mankind generally." That same America was the one John Taylor of Caroline County, Virginia, was proud to associate with the first Republican-led administration.[68]

Emphasizing the calm acquisition of Louisiana as a triumph of peace through manly diplomacy, Taylor invoked Alexander Hamilton as a highly useful, if supremely ironic, example in support of his position. Quoting at length from Hamilton's defense of the Jay Treaty negotiations, he demonstrated the reasonableness of Republican methods. "A very powerful state may frequently hazard a high and haughty tone with good policy," Hamilton had stated in 1795. "But a weak state can scarcely ever do it without imprudence. The last is yet our character, though we are the embryo of a great empire."

Hamilton had recognized how the United States was to walk a fine line in diplomacy: "If there be a foreign power which sees with envy or ill will our growing prosperity, that power must discern that our infancy is the time for clipping our wings." Navigating well what was—and not even

Hamilton could have denied it—a dangerous situation, the Jefferson administration had adhered to the tried-and-true foreign policy of George Washington and kept America at peace. Yet the domestic opposition was brazenly, jealously contending that the president and his secretary of state deserved no credit for what had occurred through pure happenstance.

According to Taylor, the Jefferson administration had taken treaty-making authority out of the hands of a single executive and made it republican through the combined efforts of a trusted group of diplomatic strategists. It was, he wrote, "a new political era" in America. Grumbling Federalists exhibited, he said, "a temerity unprecedented" in their knee-jerk criticism of the improvements made since 1800. They could not acknowledge the truth about Republican rule: it was not imperious but collaborative. This was, at any rate, the shiny surface John Taylor held up to his readers' view.[69]

In the election of 1804 Jefferson and his running mate, George Clinton, won handily, defeating the ticket of Charles Cotesworth Pinckney of South Carolina and Rufus King of New York. Even New England went Republican, save for the dissenting state of Connecticut. The electoral vote (162 to 14) showed just how low Federalist fortunes had sunk. The party's leaders had predicted four years earlier that a President Thomas Jefferson, hopeless visionary that he was, would tear apart the religious fabric of the country and Frenchify American political culture. He had turned out to be far more down-to-earth than his enemies billed him. In response, the most embittered of the Federalists, at a loss to do anything productive, entered into conversation about a New England secession movement.

John Taylor's pamphlet was a first-rate defense of political doctrine. Unfortunately for Madison and Jefferson, it did not anticipate where things were already heading.

CHAPTER TWELVE

Years of Schism, Days of Dread

1805–1808

> *Mr. Madison's election is . . . recommended because it*
> *will be the best fitted to the destruction of schism*
> *among the republicans.*
>
> —*NATIONAL INTELLIGENCER, JULY 8, 1808*

> *Virginia . . . saw with indignation, the rising greatness and the pre-eminent*
> *rank New-York would assume among the individual states; and in all the*
> *blackness of malevolence and envy, immediately plotted her dismemberment,*
> *and the establishment of two distinct states in her stead. This plan now in*
> *possession of James Madison, Secretary of State, was submitted by him to the*
> *inspection of several members of congress, a scheme as diabolical in practice as*
> *the heart of man could conceive.*
>
> —*GEORGE CLINTON NEXT PRESIDENT . . . OR, JAMES*
> *MADISON UNMASKED, A PAMPHLET PUBLISHED*
> *IN NEW YORK, 1808*

AS THE YEAR 1805 BEGAN, A POLITICAL POET DELIVERED THE doggerel to which newspaper readers had grown accustomed at New Year's time. On a fairly regular basis, cartoonish verse made hay with men and events. None of it was any good. Heady rhymes unevenly philosophized the nature of man and led inexorably to grandiose statements about the American republic.

This one, penned by an avowed Republican, bemoaned the failure of France to live up to expectations after "bright freedom's early dawn" in

1789. The unnamed poet laughed off the revolution in St. Domingue as a pitiful attempt of unlettered blacks to imitate a mature government. Proceeding from the insensitive to the bombastic, he asserted America's virtues by contrasting rustic pleasure with effete arrogance:

> *Thy hardy children here deride*
> *Old Europe's folly, and her pride.*

And how had America already come to supplant Europe? Why, owing to the talent at the top of the Republican Party. In a quick cadence, the poet went down the list:

> *Lo, Gallatin sublimely stands,*
> *While* finance *brightens in his hands.*
> *His grateful country proud to own*
> *And smile on her adopted son.*
> *No less great Madison shall claim*
> *Of public gratitude and fame.*
> *But more the MAN whose lofty soul*
> *O'erlooks, combines, directs the whole!*
> *Yes, Jefferson . . .*

There was no complexity to the effort. The long poem recounted the ways in which impertinent Federalists regularly berated the Republican president for his unpretentious manner, his unpowdered hair, and his simple corduroy pantaloons. They had "stamp[ed] him Infidel," and persisted in disseminating "old threadbare tales" of his sexual past, without offering proof. They had gone so far as to issue the absurd claim that he "fell in love, too, with a negro!"

Federalists had resorted to these blundering attacks on the president only because Jefferson had turned his back on the "courtly pomp" that noble, dignified Federalism sorely missed. For the ousted party, according to the Republican playbook, Jefferson's biggest crime was his naturalness—his reputed comfort with commonness, his mass appeal.[1]

It is hard to perceive either Jefferson or Madison as men with a common touch. Their social identities as members of a cognitive elite made them no closer to common farmers than a neighborly, condescending smile demanded of them. Yet as often happens in politics at moments of change, style can trump every other consideration. The truth is that although they were power brokers, the Virginia Dynasty of presidents—Jefferson, Madison, and Monroe—had no impact on the composition of the Virginia delegation in Congress. Fully 60 percent of the state's congressmen during their three successive presidencies were men whose close relatives had previously served in the House or Senate. But that did not stop the discredited party from making Jefferson out as a man who pandered to the democracy.[2]

Madison did not arouse the same degree of resentment. And it was not only because Jefferson held the chief executive position. Madison was just not scandal-prone; nor did he reveal in his correspondence a sentiment that could be turned against him. Jefferson's gestures got him into trouble. His humane vocabulary struck some as less than sincere. Whether or not he intentionally did so, he appeared to court popularity, an indicator of cunning of which Madison could not be accused.

Of course, the Republican takeover of the executive linked the names of Madison and Jefferson in the partisan press as never before. As friends, their interdependence was fortified by regular social contact, and given Jefferson's widower status, the convivial Dolley Madison occasionally took up duties as hostess at official gatherings in the President's House. Jefferson's surviving daughter Patsy spent the majority of her time in central Virginia.

Jefferson almost never missed a stopover at Montpelier when he rode to and from Washington City, and the Madisons typically visited Monticello every summer. In September 1804, a slow time in national politics with Jefferson's reelection widely assumed, the Madisons came to stay with him. House servant Sally Hemings was pregnant. The following January she gave birth to a son, who was given the name James Madison Hemings. Though he bore his mother's surname, he was, almost unquestionably, the master's son, and it seems inconceivable that by this time the Madisons did not know. It was Mrs. Madison who suggested the name, as Madison Hemings informed a reporter late in life.

Precisely one year later, in January 1806, Patsy gave birth to a son at the President's House, Jefferson's eighth grandchild and second grandson (the first since 1792). That child too was named after James Madison. His father, Thomas Mann Randolph, was a high-strung congressman and future Virginia governor, far less talented than the man under whose roof he was sleeping or the man whose name his son had borrowed. Randolph's temperament often gave his father-in-law cause for concern, and during this otherwise tranquil interlude he came close to fighting a duel with another whose name he shared, the routinely abusive Congressman John Randolph. Complex circumstances, personal as well as political, must have given President Jefferson fresh reasons to appreciate the steadfastness and trustworthiness of James Madison.[3]

"The Artillery of the Press"

Jefferson's second inaugural address appears on the surface as workman-like as the first was vivid and dramatic. He showed his draft to Madison, who suggested alterations to two sections: the free exercise of religion and Indian policy. This time the rich Jeffersonian phrasings most likely to invite satirical responses were removed, quite likely by Jefferson himself.

If there was a single boast in the message, it was the rhetorical claim: "What farmer, what mechanic, what laborer, ever sees a tax-gatherer of the United States?" Translation: The Jefferson-Madison-Gallatin partnership was a hands-off central government, which suited a quiet, industrious people. State and national governments could coexist peacefully. This was what it meant to live as a republican.

Jefferson wrote out several drafts of the second inaugural, just as he had done with the first inaugural, and with the Declaration of Independence before that. Because he retained these pages, it is possible to probe his thinking—which is especially useful in identifying his initial tendency to emotional expression, which he then repressed, or at least compressed, in the final (published) text.

His "Notes on a Draught for a second inaugural Address" appears to be the earliest outline. It clarifies Jefferson's assumption that the first inaugural address was "an exposition of the principles on which I thought it my duty to administer the government." The second, he noted, should "naturally" be a rectification of accounts, "a statement of facts, showing that I have conformed to those principles. The former was *promise:* this is *performance.*" Here was Jefferson recurring to his experience as a lawyer, seeing his first inaugural in terms of a contract or a formal vow—an oral promise made in public and fulfilled.

Jefferson conceived of inaugural addresses as a ritual practice. They were different from his policy messages to Congress. He reminded himself (or Madison and other cabinet members, if he intended them to see the "Notes on a Draught") that details were not called for. In listing the chief subjects he would be addressing, he privileged foreign affairs, followed by domestic affairs, taxes, national debt reduction, Louisiana, religious freedom, Indians, and the press. For the section on Indians, he called on citizens to show the tribes humanity, so as to ensure their continued "good opinion" of white America. This is a hard pill for the modern reader to swallow, though it once reflected a standard of "philanthropy" toward Indians.

Jefferson saved the best for last: the press. The subject of newspaper opinion was absent from his first outline, but he devoted a good bit of time to crafting this section in a subsequent draft that contains the most cross-outs and insertions. "During this course of administration," he began the fitful paragraph, "the artillery of the press has been levelled agt [against] myself personally agt my executive associates, & the members of the legislature." Then, upon rereading, he eliminated the "myself personally" while still underscoring the nefarious character of the Federalist press.

The uncensored "Draught" read:

> During the course of this administration and in order to disturb it the artillery of the press has been levelled agt myself personally agt my executive associates, & the members of the legislature charged with every thing which malice could inspire, fancy invent, falsehood advance, & ridicule & insolence dare. treason itself...

After thoughtful editing, it became:

> During this course of administration, and in order to disturb it, the artillery of the press has been levelled against us, charged with whatsoever its licentiousness could devise or dare. These abuses of an institution so important to freedom and science are deeply to be regretted, inasmuch as they tend to lessen its usefulness and to sap its safety.

It was a larger "us" who were being mistreated, and free institutions suffered for it. Luckily, he wrote, "wholesome punishments" were available to the state governments for prosecuting those guilty of "falsehood and defamation." But (and here he tried to sound magnanimous as he issued a veiled threat) "public duties more urgent press on the time of public servants, and the offenders have therefore been left to find their punishment in the public indignation." It was his way of saying that he was attentive to published slurs.

His larger message to the nation was really self-congratulatory, because it claimed that his political opposition was ever-diminishing. As a republican, it was mandatory that he should congratulate the citizenry at large instead: "Contemplating the union of sentiment now manifested so generally as auguring harmony and happiness to our future course, I offer to our country sincere congratulations." The "harmony and affection" of his first inaugural had become "harmony and happiness" here, as he celebrated a return to the course set forth in 1776, when the states had been genuinely, and not just rhetorically, united.

The text that the president actually read from on March 4, 1805, was, for convenience, a single long page, written in a shorthand that Jefferson had developed. There were indicators of where to pause—the word closest to the right margin was the final word in the sentence, with two slash marks placed after the period. In this, his speaking copy, Jefferson drew subject headings such as "Press" in clear boldface characters. Although he is universally depicted as a soft-spoken individual whose public addresses were difficult to hear, Jefferson's intense, controlling method of preparing the speaking text shows that he cared enough about its reception to see that those in earshot were not disappointed.

As he delivered his inaugural message, he took a bow in the direction of Madison's initially ignored and now much-heralded *Federalist* 10. (Jefferson did not explicitly acknowledge the source.) Given the enormity of the Louisiana Purchase, it seemed to him useful to assure the public that expansion west was in the interest of all Americans. "Who can limit the extent to which the federative principle may operate effectively?" he posed. "The larger our association, the less it will be shaken by local passions; and in any view, is it not better that the opposite bank of the Mississippi should be settled by our own brethren and children, than by strangers of another family?" But of course, Jefferson did not mention the slaves being sold west, as he did not consider them part of the national family. His words highlight the tone of a young government still very anxious about European designs on portions of the continent.[4]

Former vice president Aaron Burr, despite having been rejected by Jefferson, was in attendance at the inauguration and paid the president a visit afterward to offer his congratulations.[5] On the surface at least, Burr was ready to demonstrate his acceptance of the reality that a different New Yorker, older and less threatening to the Virginia presidency, was his heir to the job. Like Madison and Jefferson, Burr had a sense of the potential of so vast a territory as Louisiana and would be making his way down the Mississippi shortly. Less than two years later, at Jefferson's instigation, he would be awaiting trial for treason. The "happiness and harmony" that the president preached and, in his own secular way, prayed for, was not to be seen in his second term.

"The Thousand Insulting Insinuations"

The trans-Mississippi West was not the only source of anxiety within the administration. As Chief Justice Marshall swore in Jefferson for a second time, sectional tension existed not only between northern Federalists and southern Republicans but also between northern and southern Republicans. The Republican editor of the *Vermont Journal* responded to the stirrings of Virginians who had openly conveyed their eagerness to alter the federal Constitution by pushing through amendments after Jefferson's re-election. The plan was supposed to make the republic more democratic, but its covert design was perceived as undoing the careful balance among large and small states, giving Virginia even more weight than it presently carried. Reducing U.S. senators' terms from six to two years would go far toward eliminating aristocratic pretense in that body. Direct election of the president would be an obvious improvement on the Electoral College. No longer giving judges lifetime appointments seemed a sensible move. But in all of these instances the small states would lose. "May the Constitution and the Union be perpetual!" cried the fearful Vermont editor. As to the kinds of people who made up the best republic, he concluded his piece with a personal statement: he owned a mere fourteen acres, which he farmed with his own hands—and what could be more republican than that? What claims to the republican spirit did his "brother of the south" have who possessed fourteen thousand acres, which his slaves worked for him?[6]

One of the most privileged of slave owners, the gangly, garrulous John Randolph of Roanoke, cared little how many northern Republicans he upset. On the heels of the Yazoo compromise that so offended him, he went on the warpath again in the cause of justice. As House manager of the impeachment of Associate Justice Samuel Chase of the U.S. Supreme Court, he drew up a list of offenses meant to show that the public good was at peril because Chase held obnoxious opinions. Impeachment was a new instrument, and the standard of "high crimes and misdemeanors" was barely tested. The offenses inventoried by Randolph included the judge's behavior when he presided at the trial of James Callender in 1800 for seditious libel—and so the martyred Callender was resurrected and dissected yet again.

The Republicans in Congress had been encouraged to go after Chase by none other than President Jefferson. After a mentally unstable judge, an easy target, was removed in New Hampshire, the president eagerly took aim at more valuable prey. If the Chase trial had gone his way, he might well have urged proceedings against Chief Justice Marshall himself. He desperately sought means to purge incorrigible Federalists who enjoyed lifetime appointments to the bench.

What angered the president most was Chase's 1803 instruction to a Baltimore jury that struck him as seditious speech. The justice had warned of "mobocracy," while directly condemning the administration's approach to judicial appointments and removals as "mighty mischief." Chase was indeed guilty of having a big mouth, but was that enough to remove him from the bench?

Jefferson had to be careful not to have his imprint on the investigation into the judge's conduct appear obvious. Hinting strongly to a friendly congressman that he wanted Chase gone, he made it clear that, as president, he had to maintain a polite distance from the prosecution. The irony was rich but was lost on Jefferson: he who had done so much, upon entering office in 1801, to see that the Sedition Act was struck down now wanted, in effect, to revive the same charge in individual cases, as a tool for getting rid of political enemies.

Samuel Chase of Maryland was something of a political prodigy. He had been admitted to the bar the year Jefferson matriculated at the College of William and Mary. The republic's self-anointed guardian against "mobocracy" in 1804 had been a firebrand during the Stamp Act protests in 1765, accused at that time of being a "ringleader of mobs." He went on to serve in the Continental Congress, signed the Declaration of Independence, and in 1788 became, of all things, an outspoken antifederalist. Nevertheless he was a staunch supporter of the first president, and Washington trusted Chase's judgment well enough to appoint him to the Supreme Court in 1796. Justice Chase appears not to have made any intemperate remarks on the High Court itself; but on the circuit he proved himself as contentious a speaker as John Randolph was in Congress. That was what got to Jefferson.

The Chase Senate trial unfolded during the interval between the election of 1804 and the second inaugural. Presiding over the impeachment was Vice President Burr's last duty before stepping down. His fair-minded treatment of the parties impressed those otherwise predisposed to demean his character. In the late nineteenth century the discerning historian Henry Adams, descendant of two presidents, described Chase's defense team as "a body-guard of the ablest lawyers in America." Prominent among them was Luther Martin, the attorney general of Maryland, a critic of Madison's at the Constitutional Convention, and a hard-drinking man whom Adams called a "reprobate genius," "rollicking, witty, audacious . . . , shouting with a schoolboy's fun at the idea of tearing Randolph's indictment to pieces."

Eccentric John Randolph was a colorful but rambling speaker and no match for the defense. He conferred at length with his counterpart in the Senate, fellow Virginian William Branch Giles, whose emotional makeup as well as political positions seemed to match Randolph's. But neither man could construct a linear argument, and even before the issue came to a vote, Madison confided to the historian's grandfather, John Quincy Adams, then a member of the Senate, that he was unhappy with the "petulance" of the Virginians who were managing the impeachment.[7]

When the Senate put partisan preferences aside and voted for acquittal based on a strict adherence to the law, the Republican press gloried in its elected representatives' decency. "Republican Senators," one Maryland column ran, "notwithstanding the thousand insulting insinuations leveled at them by Mr. Chase, have magnanimously discarded the angry passions of human nature, and strictly (perhaps too strictly) confined themselves to the law."[8]

Jefferson hid his disappointment in the outcome. Randolph of Roanoke sulked for a while before returning to Washington with renewed purpose. He was already anticipating a Madisonian presidential succession, and it stuck in his craw. He started referring to those who would join his resistance to the established order as "the old Republicans," alternatively as the "Tertium Quids" ("third something"), a third political party. Randolph had James Monroe in mind as a proper successor to Jefferson and stepped up his flattering correspondence with this other Virginian, who remained abroad, dutifully carrying out the will of Madison and Jefferson.

Randolph was seeding the ground for a competition that Monroe almost certainly had not considered. The envoy was, at the time, writing frequent long letters to his boss—the secretary of state—on affairs in Europe. It is hard to say precisely why Randolph was convinced that Monroe represented his views better than Madison did. Monroe and Randolph did not know each other well; but Randolph's prejudices tended to have quirky origins. In this case, there are a handful of clues to his thinking: the natural affinity of the South and the emerging West was of principal concern to him, and in 1803 he quoted at length from a Monroe speech to support his position on this subject. More recently, he was touched by the generous attention Monroe had shown toward a relative of his in England who was deaf and mute. Additionally, Randolph would not have easily forgotten the ostracism that the moody Monroe suffered after imperfectly representing President Washington in Revolutionary France. Sympathy had a reciprocal quality for the Byronic Virginian.

The political game was getting more unpredictable and no easier. When Randolph became irritated, he became irritating—especially so at this time, as he fixed his attention on foreign policy issues. Provoked by Madison, he read secrecy and dishonesty into behind-the-scenes efforts to convince France to advise Spain to sell West Florida to the United States. Undisclosed approaches to foreign governments issued, he said, from the "weak, feeble, and pusillanimous spirit of the keeper of the Cabinet"; he upbraided Madison for carrying out a "base prostration of the national character, to excite one nation by money [France] to bully another nation [Spain] out of its property." Randolph had made up his mind that Madison was not only untrustworthy but unrepentant.[9]

He expressed his isolationist viewpoint on the floor of the Congress in early March 1806, when he officially broke with the administration. "What!" Randolph exclaimed. "Shall this great mammoth of the American forest leave his native element and plunge into the water in a mad contest with the shark?" Fixing the republican moment as the year 1798, he vowed he would resist any alteration from the Madison-Jefferson pose in that year; he had stood with them then against the witches of the Adams administration, and he would hold their feet to the fire now.

Randolph had come to see the partnership of the president and his secretary of state as phony republicanism. He could have been talking about either of them when he warned his colleagues: "You give him money to buy Florida, and he purchases Louisiana." Sensitive to any perceived abuse of power, this man of strange sympathies but deep nostalgia vowed to reawaken "the spirit of inquiry" on behalf of an honest people, "now at home at their ploughs." Randolph spoke, he insisted, in defense of the South. More agrarian than even Jefferson, he abhorred what anyone else would have seen as progress.[10]

Louisiana was easy pickings for Randolph because of its remoteness from the nation's capital and its admittedly confused politics. Territorial Governor William C. C. Claiborne, Jefferson's appointee, was under fire from some highly placed enemies. Claiborne had served in the belligerent U.S. Congress of 1798 and had tried to break up the fight when Congressmen Lyon and Griswold scuffled on the House floor (literally, on the floor). His mediating skills had been insufficient then and were insufficient now in the existing power vacuum of territorial New Orleans. Local newspapers berated him as unsuited to the town's cultural scene; he divulged to Madison that the combination of "newspaper scribbling" and "licentiousness" offended him deeply. The criticism became even more personal when he was rumored to be shopping for a rich wife, dissatisfied with his attractive $5,000 annual salary.

Unconcerned who it was that he offended, John Randolph actively cultivated Claiborne's detractors. He listened to the territory's representative in Congress, Irish-born Daniel Clark, who, like Lyon and Randolph, had a reputation for an unregulated mouth. At the same time as he turned on the president and secretary of state, Randolph attacked their instrument Claiborne, calling him a "miserable" administrator, entirely ineffective against the Spanish. He acknowledged Daniel Clark as his source, referring to him as "an enlightened member of that odious and imbecile Government." Clark had organized a volunteer militia in 1803 and was taking credit for the peaceful transfer of Louisiana from France to the United States while disparaging a governor who, he felt, had come late to the scene, reaping an undeserved reward.

Reinforced by Randolph's performance in Congress, Clark returned south. Over the next several months he continued to taunt Claiborne, alleging in the newspaper that the Orleans militia was in disorder. Tapping into obvious prejudices, he insisted that Claiborne favored a Negro militia unit. The affronted governor challenged Clark to a duel; they fought, and Claiborne received a serious wound to the thigh. Jefferson was relieved when he finally learned that Claiborne, in whom he continued to lodge his trust, was able to resume his duties.[11]

This was just one of the ways in which Randolph's prominent and repeated ridicule of fellow Republicans had a ripple effect. After his first momentous speech in March 1806, newspapers in various areas of the country reported that in breaking from the administration Randolph had used language "unequalled by the most virulent federalist writers." It was enough evidence to convince many that "a complete schism in the party has taken place." Just across the Potomac, the *Alexandria Gazette* observed that Jefferson's conduct and character were "most severely handled" by Randolph, while Madison was "treated with sovereign contempt."[12]

As yet, however, Randolph's amorphous faction had few adherents. One of those inclining in his direction, however, was John Taylor of Caroline, so recently the author of a tough-talking pamphlet defending the policies of the first Jefferson administration. Here was a classic case of strange bedfellows: the late Edmund Pendleton's nephew Taylor had come to believe that Treasury Secretary Gallatin was refusing to undo Hamilton's economic policies. Meanwhile Randolph was still communicating his opinions to Madison's warm ally Gallatin.

Taylor, no hothead, clearly had misgivings about Randolph's lack of subtlety and restraint, but he tried to put ideas ahead of style. And Randolph somehow avoided alienating Taylor, who in 1808 would still be on Randolph's rickety Quid bandwagon, criticizing Madison for adhering to the big-government thinking contained in *The Federalist*. Ironically, they were suspicious of Madison's Hamiltonian tendencies.

Republican defections began to add up. In the troubled years preceding the election of 1800, no one had been more loyal to Madison and Jefferson than the clerk of the House of Representatives, John Beckley; he did not oppose the administration as Randolph did but nonetheless wrote to James Monroe in July 1806: "Madison, is deemed by many, too timid and indecisive a statesman, and too liable to a conduct of forbearance to the Federal party, which may endanger our harmony and political safety." At the other end of the political spectrum, Federalists seemed to enjoy speculating on rumors that Jefferson's putative successor was dismayed and overwhelmed by internal Republican politics and ready to bow out.[13]

"Fools, Geese, and Clodhoppers"

The Franco-American relationship may have soured considerably with the rise of Bonaparte, but a sense of debt to the Marquis de Lafayette remained constant. In fact, Jefferson was reported to have had Lafayette in mind as his foremost choice to serve as the first U.S. governor of the Louisiana Territory. Lafayette maintained a fairly regular correspondence with both Madison and Jefferson; they learned from him that while he held on to the family's magnificent estate, La Grange, he had otherwise been broken by the destructive force of the French Revolution. During the years of imprisonment, his considerable fortune had vanished. In 1803, as a bounty for having served as a U.S. major general, Congress voted to award him a tract of land (without stipulating where) that was approximately equal to all that Jefferson—and more than Madison—possessed. Such a quantity of land was available only north of the Ohio River or in Louisiana. In 1805 the matter was resolved when Madison and Jefferson, acting as Lafayette's agents, arranged a purchase close to the city of New Orleans. A few years later these lands were valued at $200,000, the very sum Lafayette had taken from his once-limitless store of capital to fund the American Revolution.[14]

The unprecedented addition of territory may have encouraged disputation within Congress, but it made little impression abroad. With the spectacular victory of Admiral Lord Nelson over a combined French and Spanish force off the coast of Spain, England was able to restore its dominance on the high seas. And in December Napoleon's success at Austerlitz gave France control of the European continent. As these two military giants continued to fight for global hegemony, foreign policy again took center stage in Washington. Though the administration wished otherwise, the inclinations of neutral nations mattered little to England and France. Jefferson's theory that a muscular Barbary policy would counteract the denigration of America's capacity was yet to be proven.

Madison responded to the changing scene by retreating to his library, where he prepared a 204-page pamphlet protesting the British disregard for neutral nations. Attacking London's justifications for the capture of neutral vessels in times of war, he asserted that the policy had no basis in international law but was *"a mere superiority of force."* Several members of Congress waded through the overwritten treatise, few of whom found anything quotable or politically useful in it. John Randolph resorted to his usual antics, throwing the document on the floor as he scoffed at "a shilling pamphlet hurled against eight hundred ships."

In his annual message that December, Jefferson called for a better organized militia, ready for any "sudden emergency." He asked Congress for gunboats to meet the dangers posed by the European belligerents. "We should have a competent number of gunboats," he said, "and the number, to be competent, must be considerable." As a purely defensive measure, the small, maneuverable boats were meant to patrol the nation's coastline and northern border lakes.

To suit his vision of a volunteer republican army, Jefferson hoped that the naval militia would be manned by local militia regulars. He knew that the gunboats were inadequate by themselves, so he asked Congress to fund the construction of more substantial warships, a policy backed by his usually tightfisted treasury secretary. Republican legislators flatly rejected the idea. The president and his secretary of state were ready to expand the peacetime navy, but their southern allies were refusing to follow their lead. This refusal would have dire consequences.[15]

The party of Madison and Jefferson was so strong in the South that by the congressional campaign season of 1806, there was only one incumbent Federalist below the Potomac. In all but four of the South's forty-six congressional districts, no Federalist even made the effort to run for a seat.[16] In Massachusetts, Senator John Quincy Adams found himself agreeing with the administration's foreign policy. But rather than herald an era of muted partisanship, the younger Adams's turnabout served only to isolate him.

No sooner had the Republicans proven that they could best the Federalists nearly everywhere than they began battling among themselves. It went beyond John Randolph. The word *schism* appeared more frequently in the nation's newspapers. The *Republican Spy,* in Northampton, Massachusetts, tried to deny the trend, complaining in September 1805 that the Federalists were the real troublemakers, their papers "full of hopes and wishes about 'the third party' in New York and Pennsylvania . . . They hope that Col. Burr will create a schism in Louisiana and the western states." Anything that might "perplex the administration" would suit the unseated party just fine, warned the *Spy.* The Burrite newspaper in Manhattan hoped to deflate at least some of the rumors about their champion, assuring New Yorkers the following spring that the dismissed vice president was back in the Republican fold. "The friends of freedom who lamented a schism . . . will rejoice," reported the *Morning Chronicle.*[17]

The "schism" turned out to be more real than the optimists thought. As the party in power, the Republicans could no longer define themselves as outsiders. With their archenemy Hamilton gone, they took chances, exercising free speech in rowdy ways while showing less of an inclination to maintain party solidarity. The *Republican Watch-Tower,* a New York newspaper, urged that "passion should yield to justice and calm reflection" if society was to uphold "the cause of *civil liberty,* of *social happiness,* of our *country,* and of *man.*" Casting the issue in these cosmic terms, the paper admitted that "an extensive schism has long existed among us," while agreeing with the *Republican Spy* that it had been "artfully fomented by our antagonists." Regardless of its cause, the *Watch-Tower* warned, the internecine feud was being conducted "with too much heat and animosity."

The spirit of party had turned in on itself. Republicans were called upon to "sacrifice resentments upon the altar of your country's welfare." But the resentments were too real for noble appeals to reverse what was happening. A year after Randolph's break with the administration, the language of schism persisted. The *Tickler*, in Philadelphia, printed a column titled "The New Split," noting that "much interest has been excited by a new schism among the democratic republican party." No one was tickled.[18]

We must recognize where this was coming from. An intensification of state politics not only reflected but also in some ways preceded activity at the national level. In the case of Pennsylvania, Jefferson had told Gallatin as early as March 1803 that "a schism was taking place...between moderates and high flyers." Clearly, there was more than one understanding of how the Democratic-Republican vision was to be realized in practice. Pennsylvania had a "Chase trial" all its own in the impeachment of Judge Alexander Addison, who had been overzealous in his enforcement of the Alien and Sedition Acts. In the Keystone State, the name *Quid* was assigned to those who sought to restrain radical democrats from undermining a structure that already supported prosperity for the many. As respectable merchants and manufacturers, political liberals who extolled "the blessings of republican government," the Quids feared turbulence coming from public figures who were pushing for too much too fast. For their part, the radicals complained that political offices were still occupied by an exclusive corps of elite names and should be opened up to more ordinary citizens. In 1805 the radical Society of the Friends of the People claimed it represented the undervalued majority against aristocratic tendencies. Although the pro-administration governor Thomas McKean defeated the radicals' candidate and was reelected, the vote was extremely close.

Ironically, McKean could not have won without the votes of Federalists. He was an old warhorse, a signer of the Declaration of Independence well known to Madison and Jefferson and respected by them. Both had served with him in Congress—in fact, in 1781 McKean was president of Congress. In the 1790s he reigned as chief justice of the Pennsylvania Supreme Court, and in 1801 he was as eager as any to remove Federalists from office. But as soon as William Duane, editor of the newspaper *Aurora* since 1798, turned against McKean for being too moderate, he was pursued relentlessly. After his reelection as governor in 1805, the defeated radicals, bolstered by Duane, went about examining the grounds on which they could possibly impeach the now seventy-year-old executive. Duane would keep the movement alive through 1807.[19]

Benjamin Rush put it tartly in a letter to John Adams during the acrimonious gubernatorial campaign of 1805: "We have four distinct parties in Pennsylvania: 1. old tories, 2. honest Federalists, 3. violent Democrats, 4. moderate Republicans." Later, as McKean's three-year term wound down,

Rush agreed with the governor's classification of the diverse population of their state (now divided merely in two): "one part of them 'Traitors, tories, apostate whigs, and British agents,' and the other 'Fools, Geese, and Clodhoppers.' " Stripped of its hopeful-sounding vocabulary, this was the naked state of politics in what has been designated Jeffersonian America.

For the Madisonian perspective in the midst of schism, we turn again to Dr. Rush, who informed Adams that the secretary of state was in a generous frame of mind. When James and Dolley visited Philadelphia in August 1805, the former spoke of the second president in unusually sympathetic terms. "He dwelt largely upon"—and here Rush quoted word for word—"your 'genius and integrity,' and acquitted you of ever having had the least unfriendly designs in your administration upon the present forms of our American governments." Apparently, ex-President Adams, now that he was removed from the political game, could be seen as something less monstrous than a monarchist.[20]

"The Transactions of Colonel Burr and Others"

The Federalists who were still actively engaged in battling the administration had long considered those they dismissively called "democrats" as a species prone to emotionalism. They had been anticipating "schism" since the Jefferson-Burr electoral tie and followed the competition between Burrites and Clintonians in New York with great glee. It was not just the case in the North, where anti-Virginia sentiment ran strong. South Carolina Federalists noted the quarrels between Burrites and Clintonians as they were developing, and they interpolated from this intelligence that there were quarrels among "partizans of the Cabinet." More than one paper deduced "a schism in the party at large and division has got among them."

This "storm of democratic madness... often predicted" was now widely recognized. As John Randolph's attacks on the administration added to intraparty feuds in Pennsylvania and New York, the Federalists' anxious prophecy had come true. In March 1806 the *Aurora*'s editor Duane wrote Jefferson that rumors were circulating to the effect that the president had gone soft, and that among the members of the cabinet only Madison still had any confidence as to the direction in which the administration was heading. But in reading the letters that Madison and Jefferson were writing on political subjects during this period, one cannot find even a glimmer of concern beyond the ordinary.[21]

The administration was hopeful that Monroe's diplomatic efforts in London would bear fruit. And in Louisiana, General James Wilkinson was being instructed to take care to avoid hostilities with neighboring Spanish forces. The president officially informed Madison that there was a "great probability of an amicable and early settlement of our differences with Spain," and that the boundary between U.S. and Spanish spheres of influence in the Southwest was to be negotiated. Jefferson was cautiously optimistic, and Madison guarded, writing to one general that it was "premature to draw any positive conclusions."[22]

Hopes vanished in the waning weeks of 1806, when the best-laid plans for peace and growth dissolved, and Jefferson's second term set a course for catastrophe. Madison and Jefferson found their lives increasingly complicated, once former Vice President Burr and the powerful General Wilkinson presented the administration with two possible scenarios, both drastic. One or the other was lying about a plan to circumvent federal policy and use military means to acquire land across the Spanish frontier. The scandal that ensued preoccupied Jefferson for many months, at a time when the secretary of state could not be sure of the trajectory of ongoing U.S. talks in London and Madrid.

But before the so-called Burr Conspiracy could be resolved, an incident of British impressment off the coast of Virginia resulted in three deaths and sparked a contest of national honor that tied up the administration for the balance of Jefferson's presidency. London's unsatisfactory response would raise the specter of a second Anglo-American war and prompt Jefferson to step up his plan to act out a continental vision. During the summer of 1807 he confided in Madison the following thought:

> I had rather have war against Spain than not, if we go to war against England. Our southern defensive force can take the Floridas, volunteers for a Mexican army will flock to our standard, and rich pabulum will be offered to our privateers in the plunder of their commerce and coasts. Probably Cuba would add itself to our confederation.

This noteworthy statement signals the president's comfort with a southern-directed lust for land. It exposes, as well, his readiness to employ U.S. power to take advantage of a fluid situation. Uniquely capturing Jefferson's zealotry, these few sentences occupy the foreground as we unravel the events of 1807.[23]

There can be no mistake about it: Thomas Jefferson entertained grand expansionist plans, and James Madison was in favor of them all.[24] Neither Jefferson nor Madison was opposed to what Burr was preparing for south of the border. What bothered them, and the president especially, was that Burr, only recently out of government, was already a step ahead. Jefferson, who never doubted Burr's capabilities, feared that his rejected running mate was in a strong position to reap political gain from his independent efforts.

Recent history offered solid examples of filibusters waiting to happen, proving that Burr's idea was not original. Other influential men had crossed the line from ordinary land speculation to assemble private armies and conduct foreign policy on their own. Virginia's George Rogers Clark, the frontier fighter whom Jefferson had consistently supported, once sought French aid to oust the Spanish from Louisiana. During the Adams presidency Tennessee Republican William Blount, Andrew Jackson's patron, approached the British in a bid to obtain the same result; he was removed from the U.S. Senate when word got out. Even Alexander Hamilton thought of leading troops into Mexico.

War would present opportunities to enlarge America's borders. And filibustering was not illegal in a time of war. As long as Burr was in a wait-and-see mode, he was not guilty of treason or anything else. And no one really doubted that America would eventually, one way or another, oust the Spanish from the continent. From the perspective of Madison and Jefferson, the only question was the role of diplomacy in setting up the operation.[25]

Early in 1805 Burr met with General Wilkinson in Washington. Together they discussed the prospects for expansion. When Burr traveled to New Orleans not long afterward, he seeded the ground. He saw opportunities every step of the way and gained support from western politicians. In Nashville he met with a former congressional colleague, Andrew Jackson, a rough-hewn man of definite likes and dislikes who detested the pretentious, overfed Wilkinson but was drawn to Burr. Poised for action as major general of a division of militia, Jackson hoped for assurances that the administration would welcome a force of Tennesseans in the larger effort to oust the Spanish.

On Burr's second trip west in the autumn of 1806, things suddenly changed. He began to raise eyebrows; rumors were fed to one newspaper after the next. Suggestions that he was forging a third party of disgruntled Federalists and Republicans blossomed into the new charge that he was plotting treason. Suspicion led from there to exaggerated claims of a massive recruitment effort and an even larger army, whose object—Burr's object—was nothing less than an empire to rule over. Wilkinson recognized that it was time to disassociate himself from Burr, to save his own skin.[26]

Jefferson decided to accept whatever General Wilkinson had to say about Burr. He needed Wilkinson to maintain a professional fighting force in the strategic Southwest, and to coordinate, if necessary, a larger campaign to seize all of Florida; he also needed Wilkinson to keep Burr at bay.

In the final two months of 1806 Washington's *National Intelligencer* reprinted rumors of a "western" conspiracy. Its headline: "AARON BURR." "Two distinguished federalists," the paper reported, "are parties to the contract for furnishing provisions on the waters of the Ohio." The tension built: "Rumors have reached us from so many parts of the continent, respecting the transactions of Colonel Burr and others ... calculated to excite much curiosity and interest." Said the *Scioto Gazette*, in Ohio: Burr has "formed an Association for the purpose of making war against Spain." And finally came a headline in a Massachusetts paper that committed a host of other newspapers to an unretractable position: "BURR'S CONSPIRACY." The story below began: "We have hesitated to believe; because we thought that no man, possessing the cunning and intrigue of Burr, could be so far infatuated by a mad ambition, as to enterprize the seduction of a people from the rational government of their choice." This remark was followed by a passage in Latin, taken from the *Aeneid,* that was meant to underscore Burr's infatuation with personal gain: *"Quid non mortalia pectoral cogis! Auri sacra fumes!"* (To what lengths will man's passion for gold not lead him?) "It is true!" the widely reprinted article asserted. "Burr has conspired to sever the western states from the Union, and join them with Louisiana; and by the conquest of Mexico, to establish a great Western Empire." Words, in this case, meant more than actions; the absence of hard evidence almost did not matter.[27]

General Wilkinson did not like being identified as Burr's main partner in a greedy filibuster. To save himself, he wrote directly to President Jefferson, swearing loyalty as he conveyed knowledge of Burr's bold intentions. He went so far as to declare that the "arch-conspirator" threatened the security of New Orleans. Trusting in Wilkinson completely, Jefferson announced to the nation in January 1807 that the disreputable Burr was guilty of treason. All that remained was to capture him and put him on trial.[28]

Whether Burr's design was in fact a quest to develop and populate western land, a staging action in case the opportunity arose to seize undergoverned Spanish territory, or a conspiracy to foment a war with Spain, it was an outright conspiracy in the mind of the president. Madison appears to have fundamentally agreed with Jefferson's assessment of the situation; he gave no one any contrary indication, though the written record is otherwise silent.

Captured in Mississippi Territory and brought east, Burr stood accused. He gathered a stellar defense team that included Luther Martin, who had been a thorn in Jefferson's side as Justice Samuel Chase's defense attorney. To make matters worse for the administration, the presiding judge at Burr's Richmond trial was none other than the circuit-riding chief justice of the United States, John Marshall.

In charge from start to finish, Marshall defined treason as an overt act of military aggression, which would be difficult to prove in this case. Nonetheless the trial dragged on through the spring and summer months of 1807. No one the prosecution brought in to testify could do better than level accusations. Wilkinson was forced to admit that he had tampered with the encoded letter Burr had sent him, altering what it said to make Burr look guilty. General William Eaton, another man of inflated self-importance in whom Burr was alleged to have confided, claimed that Burr was not content to stop with a western empire—he aimed to lead his forces to Washington and overthrow the government! Eaton's credibility was properly doubted, even by administration partisans.[29]

Then there was Andrew Jackson, who was subpoenaed from Nashville to testify. Jackson could see that Jefferson had been tainted by his connection to Wilkinson, and that Burr was being unfairly portrayed. The frontier general took to the courthouse steps to broadcast his disgust with the administration. It did his career no harm. At his trial, Burr spoke in his own defense, asking where the war was that he was supposed to have manufactured. As far as he could tell, it existed only in newsprint.

In the end Burr went free, though his public career was finished. The grand jury foreman, none other than Congressman John Randolph, called Wilkinson "the only man I ever saw who was from the bark to the very core a villain." Luther Martin concluded the case for the defense with a fourteen-hour summation. William Wirt, a Maryland-born Virginia lawyer just beginning work on his Patrick Henry biography, was one of the lead attorneys for the prosecution; while eloquent, he did not present nearly so compelling a case as Martin. From Wirt's perspective, the "not guilty" verdict was attributable to the chief justice and his narrow definition of treason. "Marshall has stepped between Burr and death," he wrote to his friend (and Jefferson's nephew) Dabney Carr, himself a future judge.[30]

The president played an active role in the trial as it unfolded. He sent suggestions to lead prosecutor George Hay on how to secure a conviction. He authorized nearly $100,000 in federal funds to bring one hundred or more witnesses to Richmond. Jefferson even had hopes of prosecuting Luther Martin, whom he called a "federal [i.e., Federalist] bulldog." When a rumor that Martin was aiding and abetting Burr came to Jefferson's desk, he promptly bought into it.

As the case against his former vice president crumbled, Jefferson gave thought to whether Congress might take action to remove Chief Justice Marshall for twisting the law. His hatred for Marshall was intense—it might be said that Jefferson feared him. Whereas John Jay had considered the position of chief justice inert, Marshall was inclined to challenge executive authority. Allowing his pique to dictate his actions, Jefferson repeated the error of President Washington in the bullying of Edmund Randolph. Seeing political vulnerability through the lens of personal disloyalty caused both to overreact.

The seditious libel trial of Joseph Dennie took place around the same time, though it was a minor sideshow compared to Burr's trial. Jefferson's second inaugural, a speech that deliberately lacked specificity, had contained an implied threat: that the executive would go after those in the press who crossed the line from reasonable disagreement into depraved and harmful activity. The cause for the Dennie indictment was a single paragraph in an 1803 issue of the *Port Folio,* but it could have been any one of Dennie's loose terms of abuse. "A democracy is scarcely tolerable," he had written, predicting (though no one could possibly construe that he was fomenting) "civil war, desolation, and anarchy."

The editor, like the vice president, was found not guilty. His prosecution came late anyway, as Dennie's invective had mostly dried up by 1805. When he died in 1812, his monument would read, in part: "A wit sportive, not wanton."[31]

"Bring the Mad King to His Senses"

One month into the Burr treason trial, even worse news arrived at the President's House. The *Chesapeake,* a forty-gun American frigate bound for the Mediterranean, had come under fire a few hours after it sailed from the port of Norfolk. The captain of a British vessel, the fifty-gun *Leopard,* was under orders to search the *Chesapeake* for deserters, and he blew holes in the American ship when it resisted. The British boarded, and a single deserter was taken off the ship, along with three American sailors who had been impressed into the Royal Navy—improperly taken off another U.S. vessel—some months earlier.

This outrage was as severe an insult to U.S. sovereignty as an American president could imagine. The American flag was meant to be insurance against impressment, both for U.S. citizens and for foreigners aboard an American ship. No international law stipulated otherwise. The *Carolina Gazette* hit the nail on the head when it described the "dogma of Britain" as a mockery of civilized life: "Once a subject always a subject" was ludicrous. How could a nation that called itself free say, in essence, that no man is free to emigrate?[32]

Jefferson's reaction to the *Chesapeake* incident was immediate. As the boarding occurred off the Virginia shore, he urged the governor of his home state, William Cabell, to "prevent future insults." Then on July 2, 1807, he and his cabinet issued a public proclamation ordering all armed British ships from American harbors. The statement reminded the world that ports within the United States had maintained, in times of Anglo-French war, a just neutrality, carrying on "with all the belligerents, their accustomed relations of friendship, hospitality & commercial intercourse." This being the case, the *Leopard* had acted "without provocation" at Norfolk, hovering about with predatory purpose, scoffing at America's generosity.

Newspapers exploded with calls for war to avenge the dishonor. The *National Intelligencer* likened the crisis to the immediate causes of the Revolution: "What we did in the weakness of infancy, it will be strange if we cannot repeat in the vigor of manhood." Rumors circulated that Britain had declared war on America. Many residents of Virginia believed that the British had already invaded.

As unrelenting as Jefferson was in his mistrust of the British, the strongest lines in his July 2 proclamation belonged to Madison, who seems to have wished that the wording could have been made even stronger. His proposed draft contained the accusatory "Jeffersonian" phrase "lawless & bloody purpose" in characterizing the "uncontrouled abuses" and "injuries & irritations" perpetrated by the British. Madison and Jefferson recognized this as a moment when heightened security and bold diplomacy would be equally critical.[33]

Others sent supportive letters to the secretary of state, urging him to stand up to any and all insults. From Boston, Elbridge Gerry wrote: "The public indignation is universally excited." It was Gerry whose presence in France during the XYZ Affair had helped to prevent a worse result than "quasi" war. "If redress... cannot be obtained," he said now, "will not a state of warfare be preferable to such a state of national insult & degradation?" John G. Jackson, a western Virginia congressman who was married to Dolley Madison's younger sister, brought unrelated imagery of military adventuring into his wide-ranging anti-British comments: "A tame submission to such outrages will be the signal for every species of insult until the national spirit, broken, sunk & degraded, will return with loathing & abhorrence from the Republican system we now so fondly cherish, & take refuge against such wrongs in a military despotism, where another Buonaparte or a Burr will give Law to the Republic." The congressman was unremitting: "At no period has the Eyes of the Nation—of the World—been more anxiously looking for your decision."[34]

On July 11 President Jefferson addressed his thoughts to Barnabas Bidwell, a Stockbridge, Massachusetts, Republican who was leaving Congress to become attorney general of his state. Referring to "the atrocious acts committed by the British," he stated his principles: first, to give London an opportunity to "disavow & make reparation"; second, to take as much time as it took for America's seaborne vessels to return home, before any hostile act was even considered; and third, to commit to no course of action before Congress could choose "between war, non-intercourse, or any other measure." He had decided to wait until October to call Congress into session, because he did not expect to have a clear response from London until then.

A few days passed, and the president received a letter from Richmond in a recognizable handwriting. His boyhood friend John Page, who had succeeded Monroe as governor in 1802, now held a lucrative federal appointment, courtesy of the president, as commissioner of loans. It was not the first time that Page had exhorted Jefferson to take decisive action. In April 1776 he had written to him in the Continental Congress: "For God's sake declare the Colonies independent at once, and save us from ruin." Now it was: "I have heard it repeatedly said that 'an immediate Embargo is necessary'... to retrieve our lost honor & to bring the mad king to his senses." Page reminded Jefferson that George III still harbored personal animus toward him, and he underscored the fear "that you will lose by delay, & it is evidently certain that *he* is bent on a war with the U.S., relying on the support of federal partizans... *Burr's Choice Spirits,* & I suppose Insurrections of

Slaves in the Southern States." It is curious that Virginians John G. Jackson and John Page could not but see the British threat in conjunction with domestic instability.

Madison would not have trusted such wayward thoughts to the mails. But Jefferson and Page had shared confidences since their days at William and Mary, and Page's fond and faithful letters over the years contained undisguised emotion. Madison issued instructions to the U.S. minister in Madrid to suspend his efforts to purchase the Floridas, East and West. His thinking was twofold: war with England, if it came, would require massive expenditures; and with war, the Floridas would be had for a lower price, because the United States would be doing Spain and France a favor by keeping it out of British hands.[35]

Back in Virginia for August and September, Madison and Jefferson paused to consider a strategy. During these two months they wrote constantly, weighing information received from Secretary of War Henry Dearborn concerning the number of troops that could be raised if war took place. It was at this time, too, that Jefferson explored with Madison the prospect of simply taking the Floridas from Spain, confiding that he had "rather have war against Spain than not." On October 1 Jefferson stopped at Montpelier to pick up Madison, and they returned to Washington for the first session of the Tenth Congress.[36]

The British proved that they were not in a conciliatory mood. The men taken from the *Chesapeake* were brought north to Canada and subjected to what Madison termed "an insulting trial." The British subject among them was executed. Word soon reached him that London was equivocating in its renunciation of the "pretension" that it could search ships of war for deserters. Madison wanted demonstrable "atonement," he said to Jefferson. It was not forthcoming.[37]

Treasury Secretary Gallatin was especially concerned about the nation's readiness for war, having warned in 1805 that a strong navy was required if U.S. foreign policy was to have real teeth. Otherwise, he wrote the president, "we must be perpetually liable to injuries and insults, particularly from the belligerent powers, when there is a war in Europe." The United States had an impressive merchant presence on the high seas but a very modest navy. During his first term Jefferson had deliberately reduced naval expenditures, considering defense of the home shores a much higher priority than an offensive fleet. When, at the end of 1805, he called for both gunboats and larger warships, and the Republican Congress balked at the latter, Jefferson vigorously pressed the case for more gunboats. After the attack on the *Chesapeake,* his Federalist critics mocked him with an insincere toast: "The President of the United States—First Admiral of American Gun-Boats!"

It was clear in the fall of 1807, as the dust began to settle, that in spite of the tough talk, neither the Congress nor the executive branch really wished to go to war. The Republican governor of Massachusetts, James Sullivan, wrote to Jefferson in a state of panic, warning that many in the eastern part of his state would likely act to undermine U.S. interests: "To send our sons into the field against an invading enemy, & to leave a great number of the enemies friends in the rear, as orators, scriblers, & printers, would never do." He asked the president to consider carefully.[38]

Madison and Jefferson agreed that a meaningful form of commercial retaliation was called for. The United States would stop trading with the world—shock tactics—in a unilateral attempt to obtain what ordinary diplomacy could not. Madison drafted an Embargo Message for the president, and on December 22, 1807, it passed Congress easily, despite outcries from entrenched Federalist Timothy Pickering and the Republicans' expert in harassment, John Randolph. Within days Gallatin, who was an early critic of the embargo, notified Jefferson that he had information about the tricks being employed to evade the law: laden vessels were registering their destinations as domestic ports and then actually heading out to foreign destinations.[39]

Just after New Year's Day 1808 Morgan Lewis addressed his concerns to Madison. The New Yorker who defeated Aaron Burr in the gubernatorial contest of 1804, though known for his political independence, had been, by process of elimination, the Clintonian candidate that year. He was now a bitter critic of George Clinton, the sixty-eight-year-old vice president, and felt the need to apprise Madison of his strong feelings.

Lewis's immediate alarm was tied to the embargo. It was throwing out of work a lot of good family men who labored at New York's harbor, "dependent on the wages of the day for subsistence." Seamen, shipwrights, rope-makers and sail-makers, riggers, caulkers, and draymen were being lost to the economy—150 such men had just sailed to Canada, where their labors were much needed. Lewis saw huge implications as the new coercive policy went forward: Republicans should not be alienating their natural constituency. Lewis had good Republican credentials; he was also the husband of Robert and Edward Livingston's sister. Would Madison listen?

Lewis wished for Madison to succeed Jefferson. He saw that Clinton would profit from the embargo's unpopularity. So he made his remarks blunt: discouraging working-class citizens aided not only the Federalist cause but also Clinton's presidential hopes and would work to Madison's detriment. This was when Lewis's repugnance for the vice president came out. "Is it possible," he posed nervously, "that a Man of such feeble Intellect, of so few Acquirements, can be thought of" as presidential timber in a time of national crisis?

Lewis had known Clinton for a good many years and recognized that the "encomiums" lavished on him as a soldier and statesman were pure embellishment. The man's "unfitness" for the presidency was unquestionable; he was a military "blunderer," unable to serve as an effective battalion commander, let alone as commander in chief. Never mind that Madison had never been anywhere near combat. As a Revolutionary colonel, and before that a Princetonian like Madison, Lewis asked the man-who-would-be-the-next-president to keep his reproachful letter in the strictest confidence. He assured Madison that he would repair to Washington immediately if his personal attendance at the seat of power would be of use.[40]

It seemed to this New Yorker, and to many others less friendly, that the embargo was ill conceived in every respect. Morgan Lewis's counsel notwithstanding, Madison remained convinced that a full-scale embargo was the best approach to the present predicament. Since the 1790s, he had advocated commercial discrimination (higher tariff duties) as a means of sending a signal to nations refusing to sign reciprocal trade agreements with the United States. Time would prove, he was certain, that America, north, south, and west, would not have to rely upon foreign manufacturing, and he calculated that commercial coercion would gradually become less unpopular. Once England and France saw that the states stood united, they would wake up to the rights of neutrals and play by Washington's rules.[41]

The embargo program was a bad miscalculation on Madison's part; Jefferson was equally committed to it. Britain could have been seriously hurt only if its exports were prevented from reaching America—something that never really happened. Backed into a corner, Jefferson and Madison's presidencies, from this point forward, would be defined by what they did not accomplish and by how they alienated segments of the population.

Proactive yet nonviolent, the embargo appeared viable to Madison and Jefferson for another reason. In their minds, Monroe's efforts in London had come up empty. At a hopeful moment in the spring of 1806, when Madison thought that the issues of impressment and neutral rights would be discussed seriously, Baltimore attorney William Pinkney was dispatched to assist Monroe.[42] But the treaty that the two American envoys sent by special messenger early in 1807 proved, under Madison and Jefferson's inspection, to be little better than the hated Jay Treaty. It did not address impressment. The president did not even bother to show it to the Senate.

Monroe and Pinkney, unaware how disappointed Madison and Jefferson were, thought that their treaty was a step forward in trying times. Britain was blockading ports that had no evident stake in the Anglo-French conflict; Napoleon's Berlin Decree barred allies of France from conducting trade with England. British naval chauvinism was resurgent, and America's self-respect was of secondary concern at best to those who needed every advantage in a brutal struggle with the raging French emperor. London's ministers were already predisposed against Jefferson in view of his previous pro-French bias, and they were most certainly aware of "schisms" within the Republican Party. The administration's negotiating position was never as strong as Madison and Jefferson imagined.

Monroe was treated warmly by his English counterparts. From where he sat, it was necessary to compromise. He continued for some time to believe the Monroe-Pinkney Treaty "an honorable and advantageous adjustment with England." It would have provided the nation's maritime commerce with "ample protection" from harassment, and it would have convinced France that she should tread lightly with the United States. In his own words, Monroe felt that he had been "put into a state of duress" by Madison, who "criticized the treaty with Great Britain in terms which I thought it did not deserve." He regarded Jefferson as the less forward critic.[43]

While unable to shield Monroe from embarrassment, Madison managed a few conciliatory sentences for his old friend when he wrote of the administration's decision: "The President & all of us are fully impressed with the difficulties which your negociations had to contend with, as well as with the faithfulness & ability with which it was supported, and are ready to suppose, in as far as there may be variance in our respective views of things, that in your position we should have had yours, as that in our position, you would have ours." Madison assumed agency for the president: "If he has been silent it is because he assures himself, that his sentiments cannot be misconceived by you." If this was true, it was not apparent in Jefferson's remarks to a congressional committee on March 3, 1807, when he showed little sympathy for the situation Monroe and Pinkney were in and laid considerable responsibility on them for the failure to secure better terms.

When he finally arrived back in the United States in December 1807, Monroe hurried to Washington, only to realize that the two he counted on most were treating him differently. In his presence, the president and secretary of state seemed to direct conversation away from delicate political matters. At first Monroe tried to convince himself that their concern with dissension in the party and Madison's uncertain prospects in the election of 1808 were making them nervous. Likely Monroe also recalled Jefferson's offer (in a letter he received in London) to serve as governor of Louisiana, an offer that, if accepted, would have placed him at great distance from the presidential campaign.

Monroe's doubt and confusion are understandable. He was unaccustomed to being placed at arm's length from his closest political allies. Rather than confront them, though, he waited three months, until they were both in Albemarle, before baring his feelings to his neighbor the president. Monroe let Jefferson know, first of all, that he had interpreted Pinkney's arrival in London as a strong hint that his services abroad were no longer required. He was, he said, "struck with astonishment and deeply affected" at the time. And he was persuaded upon arrival home that "your friendship had been withdrawn from me." Jefferson's famously placid countenance hid whatever disturbance he felt; as he heard Monroe out, he nimbly repaired the breach between them in no time at all.[44]

Monroe's adherence to the culture of honor and reputation was strong and his sensitivity to criticism severe, but he may not have been inventing the tension he perceived. His proneness to injury must have been of enough concern to Madison and Jefferson that as they awaited his appearance, after so long abroad, they cooked up a conciliatory strategy that they carried off poorly. Beyond that, Madison was capable of exhibiting a blend of hard-headedness and resentment, which Monroe would have easily detected. Monroe's position was that Madison should have communicated the administration's requirements more clearly over the course of negotiations. So for now Jefferson was off the hook, and Madison and Monroe remained at an impasse.[45]

"Our Weapon Recoils"

In March 1808, in advance of scheduled communications with U.S. ministers in London and Paris, Jefferson issued formal instructions to his secretary of state. On the subject of neutral rights, England and France were showing no signs of bending to U.S. demands, and the president wanted the two belligerent nations to understand his resolve. "Without assuming the air of menace," he told Madison, "let them both percieve [sic] that if they do not withdraw their orders and decrees, there will arrive a time when our interests will render war preferable to a continuance of the embargo." The language was meant to be absolute. "When that time arrives," added Jefferson ominously, "if one has withdrawn and the other not, we must declare war against that other; if neither shall have withdrawn, we must take our choice of enemies between them." If this pronouncement was Jefferson's, and not jointly conceived, it effectively painted his successor into a corner. Jefferson had previewed this mind-set two months earlier, when he wrote on the embargo to John Taylor of Caroline: "Keeping at home our vessels, cargoes & seamen saves us the necessity of making their capture the cause of immediate war." It was a puzzling, even perverse, way of looking at his options.[46]

Certainly the embargo was accomplishing less than the Jefferson administration imagined. The *National Intelligencer* insisted defensively that Virginia would experience the most "inconvenience" from the measure, but even this, the administration's paper, went from consoling itself that "the temper of the nation remains unruffled" to acknowledging that news of the embargo "made no impression on the political circles in London." The question was simple and fairly obvious: How long would Americans, no matter how incensed they were with Europeans' might-makes-right posture on the high seas, remain willing to endure privations?[47]

Newspapers to the north, particularly those of the port cities, regularly expressed their concern that the embargo would be never-ending. The *North American and Mercantile Daily Advertiser,* a Baltimore paper, was one of these, reporting that the administration ignored sincere communications of friendship from London while permitting "breaches of the embargo law" by French privateers. British policy, it sought to explain, was "not meant as an injury or insult to America, but as a measure of self-defense for Great Britain." The enemy to fear was Napoleon Bonaparte, who had overrun Spain and might well have designs on the United States.

How could the Republicans continue to overplay the threat of one power and underplay the threat of the other? A letter to the *Salem* (Massachusetts) *Gazette* from a presumably reliable source in Washington assured readers: "We shall have peace with Britain. War with France will follow . . . It is confidently said that Mr. Jefferson has declared his dread of the enormous and preponderating power of France!" Others accused the administration of deliberately playing into Napoleon's hands, which led a New York paper sympathetic to Madison and Jefferson to grouse: "The old story of French influence is again resuscitated, in the vain hope of enlisting odium against the embargo and the administration." The *New-York Evening Post* offered a pithy prediction from its Connecticut correspondent: "Jefferson's Embargo is an excellent mother, for she brings forth federal children in abundance."[48]

Boston's *Columbian Centinel* insisted that embargoes solved nothing and only destabilized. "How are the Poor to be fed?" it asked, with Virginia in its sights and satire on the tongue: the North's poor, after all, were not as lucky as southern slaves, whose masters would always make sure they had their hominy grits to eat. For the equally unforgiving *Albany Gazette,* the embargo was an intentional ploy meant to maintain Virginia dominance. "Where are our defences?" it asked nervously, as it described the vulnerability of Manhattan and interior portions of the state. "Behold the effects of an *anticommercial* spirit—behold the effects of a deadly and unnatural hostility to the *State of New York.*" An interstate rivalry came into sharper focus: "Yes yes, the growing wealth and strength of New York must be checked! The omnipotence of Virginia must be maintained." In this instance, Jefferson escaped mention, but the presumptive fourth president, coarchitect of the embargo, did not: "Let Mr. Madison look to it; let his supporters pause—for his French predilections may lead to the ruin of our Independence." Madison and Jefferson did little to disabuse northerners of their apprehensions, convinced as they were that all sections of the country were in fact making equal sacrifices.[49]

On the Fourth of July, in the last year of his presidency, Thomas Jefferson opened the doors of the President's House to citizens of the young national capital. He was dressed in "a neat suit of homespun," the *National Intelligencer* reported, "in conformity to the spirit of the times." A cavalry paraded before the Madisons' home, and Dolley emerged to give a patriotic address to those assembled. In Charleston and Columbia, South Carolina's two largest towns, celebrants selflessly toasted the embargo. "Its injurious effects will be borne with patience by every real friend of his country," ran the one. "Better it is to bear all its attendant evils than to lay prostrate our dear bought independence," proclaimed the other.[50]

Despite such gestures as these, the spirit of the times was not at all what Madison and Jefferson had prepared for. Their misplaced confidence in commercial restrictions soon led them to turn to more draconian enforcement measures along the coasts and on the Canadian border. In August

1808, while at Montpelier, Madison urged that Jefferson waste no time in deploying every available gunboat to attend to "the suspicions situations along the New England Coast." That section's much-valued lumber and flour were being smuggled into Canada and from there to the West Indies. Madison wanted a show of force to suppress all who were, as he stressed, "in collusion with British smugglers." It took a Newark, New Jersey, newspaper to direct attention to an increasingly conspicuous problem of perception: "In order to render our embargo an effectual instrument against Great Britain, it ought obviously to operate more strongly upon her than on ourselves." The Newarker restated his point neatly: "Our weapon recoils."[51]

There were small signs of hope. Senator John Quincy Adams went against the New England grain and would eventually be rewarded for his courage in a Madison administration. This new, unexpected ally was toasted in the unlikeliest of places, such as Charleston, South Carolina, for his refusal to conform to "the dictates of party spirit." But as the sole Federalist to vote in favor of the embargo, he succeeded only in guaranteeing the loss of his Senate seat.

The other Massachusetts senator, former secretary of state Timothy Pickering, had been fired by Adams's father. Pickering could plainly see that his party would not regain the presidency, and he hoped in vain that Monroe (now presumed cured of his partiality toward France) might stand a chance against Madison. Just as Federalists once thought they could influence Aaron Burr if they should connive to sneak him into the presidency past Jefferson, there was thought that Monroe could be shaken loose from his Republican connections.

One of Pickering's steady correspondents was Chief Justice John Marshall, who presumably was not wearing his judicial robe when he predicted where things were heading. The embargo, he wrote Pickering, "will impel us to a war with the only power which protects any part of the civilized world from the despotism of that tyrant [Napoleon] with whom we shall then be arranged." Pickering had made noises about disunion in 1804, and now, four years later, his compatriot Harrison Gray Otis, ex-congressman and current state legislator, wrote suggesting a convention of New Englanders—inviting select New Yorkers too—to find ways of fighting the embargo. Others may have had secession in mind, but that was not Otis's purpose. He simply wanted northern Federalists to show nerve. Some in the Northeast were threatening to nullify the embargo law, using Jefferson's theory of states' rights against him.[52]

Cotton producers of the Carolinas and Georgia, stuck with an unsold crop and unpaid debts, saw their circumstances uniquely. Their trade was exclusively with England, while New England had access to a number of markets. They also believed that a restoration of normal trade would benefit northern consumers more than it would southern producers. Placed in what they saw as the most unenviable position, cotton producers boasted their greater patriotism in putting up with trade restrictions. The Charleston papers in 1808 vowed that the Carolinians would hold on longer if the administration demanded.[53]

Resistance was not confined to the North, however. When the administration-friendly *Richmond Enquirer* finally admitted that "the inhabitants of the United States appear to differ from the government, with respect to the efficacy of the embargo," it was all right to acknowledge publicly that it harmed neither Britain nor France. Softening the blow, the *Enquirer* reported at the same time that the Virginia House of Delegates had voted its "approbation" of President Jefferson's policy, reminding citizens of their duty to rally round the measures of the government when the flag was insulted and commerce menaced by the "iniquitous edicts" of the European powers.[54]

"I See with Infinite Grief a Contest Arising"

Madison's role in the embargo earned him a good many enemies, and not only in New England Federalist circles. As Morgan Lewis rightly construed, Republicans from Manhattan to Albany and beyond were cool to the plan of succession. The port of New York had eclipsed Philadelphia as a center of population, commerce, and finance. Its entrepreneurs were being held back, the city's growth impeded. New Yorkers naturally resented the impotence of Vice President Clinton inside the Jefferson administration. Refusing to solicit Clinton's advice as it plunged ahead with a destructive policy, the Virginia faction was showing that it did not care about anyone but themselves.

Activists who wished to end the stranglehold Virginia had on the rest of the country reminded voters that George Clinton had been a "friend and companion" to George Washington. By some unexplained logic, they maintained that this made him Washingtonian in his leadership skills, "as wise and discerning a statesman as he had been an expert and courageous soldier." For a time even some Virginia Republicans recognized the legiti-macy of New York's grievance: U.S. senator William Branch Giles and Rich-mond newspaper editor Thomas Ritchie, both deeply respectful toward President Jefferson, at least entertained the idea that it was New York's turn to supply a Republican president.

But then the Clintonians got nastier, portraying the secretary of state as a shady character. The worst of these stated: "No man ever injured the United States in an equal degree with James Madison . . . The awful crisis in our public affairs: impending war, internal broils, the defenceless state of our country, are all the dreadful consequences of a system organized by this man." That dread had grown from unmet expectations. Clinton sup-porters had hoped, if they did not assume, that their champion's elevation to the vice presidency in 1805 was meant to groom him for the presidency when Jefferson retired. For those who distrusted the Virginians, and for the Madisonians who distrusted the Clintonians, the Republican Party did not appear to be national in character.[55]

The Republican nominating caucus was held in Washington on January 23, 1808, two days after the Virginia Assembly nominated Madison for the presidency. The *Virginia Argus* defined *caucus* as a "voluntary association of individuals agreeing to abide by the will of the majority" and (a bit too con-fidently) "the only proper way" of uniting Republicans. Knowing the fore-ordained outcome of the caucus, supporters of Clinton in New York and John Randolph's pro-Monroe crowd in Virginia both registered their ob-jections to the staged event and refused to attend. By now Senator Giles and editor Ritchie were staunch Madisonians, no longer flirting with the idea of being fair to New York. The new Madisonian John Quincy Adams took part in the caucus as well, and while his mother looked askance, his father warmly approved his son's independent streak and declared that he himself had "renounced" those who went, these days, by the name of Fed-eralist.

Candidate Madison won 83 of 89 votes cast at the Republican caucus. George Clinton and James Monroe received 3 each. On the ballot for vice president, Clinton was awarded 79 of 88 votes. The administration wing of the party had spoken.

Rather than agree to run for four more years of subordination, Clinton expressed personal dissatisfaction with the process in a letter to the *Ameri-can Citizen*, the New York City newspaper edited by James Cheetham. The paper had vocally supported the Jefferson administration in the past, but it decided to withdraw support from Jefferson's handpicked successor. If

Madison was elected, Cheetham said, "nothing short of a miracle can save the republican party from destruction." And so he came out for a Clinton-Monroe ticket.

Not all New Yorkers took up Clinton's cause—a sizable number stood behind Madison. By July these people were declaring that the two newspapers edited by Cheetham were "no longer to be considered by us as republican papers, and that they ought not to be any longer esteemed as organs of republican opinions." Cheetham, undeterred, promulgated his reasoning as to why a vote for Madison, twelve years Clinton's junior, was unsafe: "He is sickly, valetudinarian [obsessed with health issues], and subject to spasmodic affections [convulsive disturbances], considered by philosophers as one of the most powerful agents of our intellectual faculties." Madison did, indeed, have a reputation for a weak physical constitution, but suggesting that his past medical history pointed to a deterioration of mental acuity was a stretch.[56]

The reality was that the aging George Clinton was a stand-in for his thirty-nine-year-old nephew DeWitt Clinton, mayor of New York for the past four years. It was he who pulled the strings. Four years later, in fact, DeWitt Clinton would nearly succeed in unseating President Madison. But at this moment, if he lacked national stature, the younger Clinton did not lack guile. Morgan Lewis thought he saw credible evidence of this when New York State's presidential electors were about to be chosen. He warned Madison that DeWitt was changing the "game" so that Republicans—all of whom wanted a New Yorker on the ticket—could have their choice between his uncle George for president or, if a Virginian was at the top of the ticket, DeWitt himself as vice president.

Convinced that once he was elected, Madison would know how to handle "the federalists and British apologists" who gnawed at him, Lewis issued a warning of Shakespearean dimensions in case Madison still thought it possible to make an arrangement with DeWitt Clinton: "Those who approach and assail you under the disguise of friendship will be most to be dreaded. A vice president certainly has great opportunities for intrigue . . . Be assured I know his Character well. He is mischievous, intrigueing, impatient of a Superior, and attached to nothing in this world but himself." Morgan Lewis was obsessed with the Clintons. But he would prove prescient.[57]

After the Republican caucus, John Randolph's men circulated a carefully worded dissent: "We . . . protest against the nomination of James Madison, as we believe him to be unfit to fill the office of President in the present juncture of our affairs." A number of Clintonians added their signatures to the document. William Duane, editor of the nationally influential Philadelphia paper *Aurora*, initially supported George Clinton; he now switched over to Madison's side.[58]

The administration paper, the *National Intelligencer*, maintained a steady stream of articles lavishly praising Madison. "The page of history glows with the achievements of the hero who has fought," it pronounced, "but its brightest effulgence beams around the individual who ranks as the founder of a fundamental system, which adjusts for ages the limits of power and its application to the varied and complicated wants of man." According to the *Intelligencer*, Madison's consistent performance guaranteed that he would "pursue the straight line of honest policy, without being led astray by the false lights of sinister ambition."

The easiest way to promote Madison's candidacy was to enlarge upon his painstaking work at the Constitutional Convention, which the *Intelligencer* did with its accustomed flamboyance: "Every eye was fixed on Madison . . . The task was Herculean; but it was performed with zeal and dignity." In this rendering, his energetic mind was supported by "candor and moderation"; and in subduing passions, he symbolized the "calmness and sobriety" that the emerging nation needed in 1787. The editor of the *Intelligencer* did not want to hear of Madison's defeats in Philadelphia—all that mattered was the legend.[59]

Not since Monroe lost to Madison in the election for a House seat in 1789 had the two been so visibly pitted against each other. This time, of course, the presidency was at stake. Madison and Monroe were careful not to say anything publicly, and none of the newspapers promoting Madison criticized Monroe at any time. The *Argus* clarified: "Being sincerely convinced (as we have always been) of the exalted merit of Col. *Monroe*, we shall not attempt to detract from it in the least; but we wish to know in what respects he excels Mr. *Madison*? Does he possess greater natural talents? More learning?" This was a direct response to the friends of Monroe who were, according to the *Argus*, parsing words in their effort to find "an essential and radical distinction" between the two by elevating Monroe above Madison in terms of his "purity of principles" and "patriotism." One who signed his contribution "An American of '76" wrote that it was not Monroe but Monroe's supporters who were inventing the division between them by accusing Madison of having subverted Monroe's diplomatic mission, setting Monroe up for failure. Monroe, the writer assured, could not possibly have been complicit in any underhanded attack on Madison.[60]

There was a real possibility of confusion at the polls. The adoption of the Twelfth Amendment in 1804 now provided separate slates for president and vice president. Clintonians could vote for Clinton on the presidential slate and choose someone else for vice president, while the Madisonians were expected to vote for Clinton as their vice-presidential choice. Morgan Lewis's dreaded scenario could arise if the Republicans were not careful.

Monroe himself remained torn. He wanted to be president, but he did not wish to create bad blood that might permanently deny him the office he aspired to. In a piece designed for the newspapers that he penned but ultimately did not send, he said he did not think of himself as a candidate for president but would serve if his fellow citizens went so far as to elect him. President Jefferson, with evident discomfort, wrote to him: "I see with infinite grief a contest arising between yourself and another, who have been very dear to each other, and equally so to me." Insisting that he was maintaining perfect neutrality—it was to be a "sacred observance" for him, owing to their long association—Jefferson was nonetheless disturbed that "painful impressions" remained on Monroe's mind that could tear apart critical friendships. He urged him not to believe the malicious messages that he knew Monroe was receiving from third parties, which did more than hint at the lame duck president's partiality toward Madison. "I feel no passion, I take no part, I express no sentiment," Jefferson wrote. He was being truthful only insofar as party regulars had already acted to secure the succession in the manner Jefferson preferred. His will was being enacted without his having to say or do more.

Jefferson and Monroe were kindred spirits. Both had lost a father at an early age, had raised daughters but no sons, and nurtured a healthy appetite for political revenge. Both had been tapped by President Washington to serve the nation (Jefferson in the cabinet and Monroe as an envoy); and both had lost Washington's confidence owing, they believed, to the machinations of Hamilton. Monroe was, without exaggeration, Jefferson's protégé, his career overseen by his mentor ever since 1780, when he read the law under then-Governor Jefferson's watchful eye.

Jefferson used delicacy whenever he wrote to Monroe, a pose he rarely found necessary when he wrote to Madison. In the early months of 1808, Jefferson assured Monroe that Madison and he were equal in his esteem, "two principal pillars of my happiness." But even with the exiting president's effort to reunite them, Madison and Monroe refrained from interacting. When Madison visited Monticello that summer, he did not go the extra mile, literally, to see Monroe at home; nor did Jefferson extend Monroe an invitation to join them on the mountaintop. Bad feelings lingered.[61]

As the election neared, the language used by interested friends of the Republican competitors remained sharp. Some Federalists sought the role of spoiler by suggesting that Jefferson's partiality for his secretary of state was a form of tampering with the election process. When Federalists in Richmond met to endorse Monroe, they took extreme positions, claiming that Madison was under French influence and Monroe under British. According to their extended logic, Madison had abandoned the principles of George Washington, whereas Monroe, conciliatory toward Federalists during his governorship (1799–1802), was long known for his honesty and could be counted on to act with restraint. As the *Virginia Gazette* reported: "We have no fears of his marking out the federalists as a political sect *upon whom he shall have vengeance!!*" In joining a brand of Federalist to a brand of Republican, the Monroe phenomenon constituted a fairly unique event in American history, a function of minority fears and prejudices on opposite sides of the political spectrum.[62]

With all parties acknowledging the near certainty of Republican victory at the polls, one Federalist adopted as his nom de plume "Richard Saunders," the folksy alter ego of Benjamin Franklin in his long-running annual (1732–57), *Poor Richard's Almanack*. Weighing in on Jefferson's presidency, "Saunders" opened with feigned praise for the first inaugural and its call for unity: "I declare I would have given Thomas Jefferson the best calf on my farm for speaking such good words, had he come and asked for it. But talking is one thing, and acting another."

For "Saunders," James Monroe's unappreciated exertions abroad constituted the only harmony seeking in Jefferson's eight years. For all his sincerity and hard work, Monroe had been "blackguarded" by his supposed friends. At this point, "Saunders" surmised, the Jay Treaty had to look good, even to Republicans. As to the ill-conceived embargo, he pretended to be confused, mock-innocently addressing the Republicans: "The French want money, said Madison, and they must have it; John Randolph heard him say these very words . . . And now Bonaparte says we must go to war with England; and if Madison or Clinton or any of your leaders get to be president, to war we shall go."[63]

As the year of embargo progressed, even Dr. Benjamin Rush of Philadelphia, a moderate Republican who had initially favored the measure, was ready to throw up his hands. He wrote to a favorite correspondent, ex-president John Adams: "Could the absurdities in principle and conduct of our two great parties for the last 12 years be laid before the world in a candid and dispassionate manner, we should be ashamed to call ourselves MEN. The disputes of children about their nuts and gingerbread have less folly and wickedness in them."[64]

Dr. Rush could only offer a diagnosis; he knew of no cure for America's political ills, beyond suturing the rupture between two old Revolutionaries who were his friends. It was his desire to restore the friendship of Adams and Jefferson, an historic mission he would embark on once Jefferson left office and Madison inherited the problems of the presidency.

"What I Had Foreseen Has Taken Place"

The coolness that subsisted between Madison and Monroe cast a pall over the presidential transition. Though the Jefferson administration ended poorly, as a whole it did not resemble the picture of anarchy and atheism painted by the advocates of order and firmness eight years earlier. Until the embargo was instituted, opposition congressmen recognized the methodical and responsible approaches that the president and his cabinet took to issues of administration and economy. Though Federalists were removed from office for political reasons, no members of the despised "mobocracy" were elevated to federal office. Hot issues such as the Samuel Chase trial reminded Federalists that Jefferson had an obnoxious agenda and they needed to be wary of him. But in spite of core disagreements, Jefferson and Madison and Gallatin ultimately did little to upset the structure the Federalists had put in place.[65]

At a later period Madison was fond of telling one particular joke to demonstrate Jefferson's disarming manner as president. A new congressman who had been led to expect a man of rigid opinions walked away from a meeting with him saying, "He is the most pliable *great* man I ever met with." Owning that Jefferson was persuaded by his argument on a political subject, he boasted to his friends: "I verily believe I could change his mind on almost any point." The joke, as Madison related it, was that the new congressman had in fact been converted to Jefferson's side of the issue without even knowing it.[66]

Until the embargo went into effect, all sections of the Union had thriving economies. By the end of Jefferson's two terms, weakened northern

Federalists were left with much to protest. Southern Federalists were equally nervous and even less visible. The number of their party's newspapers in the South had declined from sixteen in 1800 to twelve in 1808. In the same region during the same period, Republican papers grew in number from thirteen to twenty-three. Perhaps owing to the disastrous embargo policy, four new southern Federalist papers raised enough funds to go into business between January 1808 and January 1809. Still, the Republican Party was in the ascendant. Every southern state legislature remained in Republican hands. As the historian James Broussard sees it, "It would not be an exaggeration to say that without its vigorous partisan editors, the southern Federalist Party would scarcely have existed at all."[67]

Once Monroe enthusiasts saw their chances shrink, the election of 1808 became anticlimactic. The character of Virginia's congressional delegation remained Republican, of course, yet pockets of resistance remained. Both northern and southern districts of Virginia voted in Federalists in 1808, among them one Daniel Sheffey of Wytheville, in the southwest portion of the state. Sheffey began his career as a shoemaker's apprentice (an atypical Federalist profile); he worked his way up by studying the classics and the law and entered Congress at age thirty-nine, in 1809. The invective-hurling John Randolph was known to refer to Sheffey as "the shoemaker" when they disagreed on the floor of the House.[68]

Randolph of Roanoke was not about to scale back on the fury of his speeches or the provocations in his letters; he would remain newsworthy for another quarter century. But the time of his being considered a leader, or even a legitimate critic in national affairs, was past, save for his usefulness to Federalists, who could count on his vote in opposition to war measures. Henceforth the defective philosopher would be portrayed in caricature: the obstructionist as entertainer.

Nationally, the Federalists ran Charles Cotesworth Pinckney again. He did little better against Madison than he had done four years before against the incumbent Jefferson. The South Carolinian was not even able to win his home state, and though George Clinton siphoned off 6 of New York's 19 electoral votes, Madison still received 122 of the 169 electoral votes cast.

But how strong a president would he be? During the last week of December 1808, Albert Gallatin sized him up. "Mr. Madison is, as I always knew him, slow in taking his ground, but firm when the storm arises. What I had foreseen has taken place. A majority will not adhere to the embargo much longer, and if war be not speedily determined on, submission will soon ensue." It was not a sanguine picture.[69]

Madison and Jefferson had persisted with the embargo to the detriment of their political reputations. That measure was to be repealed by Congress, and there was little they could do about it. Jefferson had come into office a hero to his party, and he left it wounded but with honor intact; even "schism" had not reduced him. In Madison's case, a paradox presented itself: rejection accompanied by electoral victory. He had much to prove.

CHAPTER THIRTEEN

Road to War
1809–1812

The pillars of Democracy begin to fall away;
But you're no novice in the art of bolst'ring the decay;
Grease well their palms, *you little rogue, as I have had to do;*
They follow only for the loaves, James Madison, my Joe.

—AN "INTERCEPTED LETTER FROM TALL TOMMY TO
LITTLE JEMMY," FEDERALIST SATIRE IN THE
ALEXANDRIA (VA.) *GAZETTE*, 1810

God bless you and send you a prosperous course through your difficulties.

—JEFFERSON TO MADISON, MARCH 26, 1812

THE MARCH 3, 1809, ISSUE OF THE *NATIONAL INTELLIGENCER*
marked the transition in Republican administrations. "This day will form
a bright aera on the page of history. Never will it be forgotten as long as liberty is dear to man, that it was on this day that THOMAS JEFFERSON retired
from the supreme magistracy amidst the blessings and regrets of millions."
He had strengthened liberty, while creating an environment in which
wealth had "outrun every calculation." Had he chosen to serve a third term,
the editor volunteered, Jefferson would have had no competition.

The following issue of the same paper came out on the sixth, two days
after Madison became president. It related the events of inauguration day,
from the "federal salutes" of navy guns to the cavalry troops that escorted
the modest man's carriage to Capitol Hill. The streets of Washington had
been filled with inquisitive citizens. Some ten thousand people crowded

around the Capitol, most of them unsuccessful in obtaining access to the ceremony. Jefferson made his entrance as inconspicuous as possible, opting to ride his own horse to the event. He hitched it to a post and moved inside, so that he was already at the front of the House chamber when Madison entered and approached.

The incoming president took his seat beside the outgoing one. Chief Justice John Marshall rose to perform the swearing in. Marshall had recently completed the fifth and final volume of his widely read biography of George Washington, in which he painted Thomas Jefferson as a man of ambition who had tried to erase his countrymen's love of the national father. Madison's name was scarcely mentioned in Marshall's work.

After the chief justice administered the oath of office, "two rounds of minute guns were fired." Thomas Ritchie, whose Richmond newspaper, the *Enquirer*, was the only paper Jefferson would admit to reading in his retirement years, sat beside a thirty-one-year-old Virginia-born Kentuckian, already a U.S. senator and soon to be Speaker of the House. America would hear often from Henry Clay during the ensuing four years. Some argue that he influenced the nation's political direction in ways Madison could not.[1]

The time arrived for Madison to deliver his inaugural address. It was a colorless speech, in which he soberly recognized his inheritance: "The present situation of the world is indeed without a parallel, and that of our own country full of difficulties." The first, more substantive section of his address dealt with world affairs. He wanted nothing to do with Europe's "bloody and wasteful wars," he said, and he would seek "peace and friendly intercourse with all nations." He claimed that his nation was righteous in its demand for neutral rights: "It has been the true glory of the United States to cultivate peace by observing justice, and to entitle themselves to the respect of the nations at war by fulfilling their neutral obligations with the most scrupulous impartiality." To which he appended the morally assertive line: "If there be candor in the world, the truth of these assertions will not be questioned."[2]

He dwelled on this subject long enough to provide evidence of America's continuing concern with the two belligerent powers. Turning to domestic affairs, he had only platitudes to utter, evocations of the small-government, liberty-loving philosophy associated with republicanism: seeing the Constitution as "the cement of the Union, as well in its limitations as in its authorities"; deferring to the states instead of lording over them; avoiding "the slightest interference with the right of conscience or the functions of religion, so wisely exempted from civil jurisdiction"; observing

"economy in public expenditures"; and keeping "within the requisite limits" a standing army, that is, recognizing state militias as "the firmest bulwark of republics," instrumental in the preservation of liberty. There was
no indication of any alteration in the thinking that had governed the moderate Republicans before this.

As to the Indians of North America, Jefferson had left a memo regarding
unresolved intrusions by whites on Cherokee and Chickasaw lands in
Georgia. The third president's thinking was that Indians should choose
either incorporation into white society as individual farmers, or eventual
banishment across the Mississippi, where a mobile, hunting society could
be sustained for a period of time. The new chief executive, lacking, as the
vast majority of his generation did, the impulse to accommodate alternative cultures on terms of political equality, vowed in his inaugural message
to "carry on the benevolent plans which have been so meritoriously applied
to the conversion of our aboriginal neighbors from the degradation and
wretchedness of savage life to a participation of the improvements of
which the human mind and manners are susceptible in a civilized state."[3]

America's priorities lay with Europe. The nation's immediate future was
thought to be most closely linked, economically and militarily, to Old
World power relations. In such a political climate, dutiful attention was to
be given, but little real sensitivity shown, to the needs of Indians and those
with detectable African origins still in bondage in the South. An indulgent
vocabulary of Christian charity coexisted with, but did little to counteract,
common depictions of Indians and African Americans. This reading of race
was manifest in visual, spoken, and written stereotypes destined to thrive
in both North and South for many decades. In the minds of those who
directed U.S. policy in Washington, Indian traditionalists were buried by
material progress; blacks were adjudged by nature less attractive than
whites and were assumed biologically distant as well. With such stereotypes ingrained, government policy in years to come was to center on Indian removal and black recolonization, accompanied by an upsurge in
miscegenation fears. Laws that rendered mixed-race offspring as bastards,
deprived of any inheritance, would outlast slavery itself. When freedom
was defined exclusively as a white inheritance (though no one said so explicitly), Indians and blacks were seen not just as inferiors but also as social
deviants who posed a credible danger to the wholesome vigor as well as necessary security of American expansionism.[4]

Congress had recently terminated the overseas slave trade in accordance
with the twenty-year postponement written into the Constitution. But this

did not do much to stimulate thinking that a political solution might be found over the short term. To the extent that the politics of race was on the minds of Virginians and others in 1809, it was the frightening example of the black republic in Haiti. With attention focused on the future of Spanish Florida and the unsettled Louisiana Purchase lands, some began asking whether the black population might be relocated from the Atlantic states onto lands still populated by Indians.

New territory meant more opportunities for speculating slave owners, but it also meant new problems. In the commercially attractive, soon-to-be state of Louisiana, for instance, sugar plantation owners anxiously viewed the end of slave imports from abroad. When the embargo was declared, officials were forewarned that Louisiana could become another Haiti, and so they attempted to cut off smuggling. Slaves were arriving in New Orleans in substantial numbers from Africa, the Caribbean, and South Carolina. What would be considered the right balance between public safety and private profit? Edward Livingston, the prominent Republican congressman (and DeWitt Clinton's predecessor as New York City mayor), had removed to New Orleans in the wake of a financial scandal, where he married an attractive young French widow, a refugee from Haiti, whose father had owned a sugar plantation there. A constitutional scholar as well as land developer, Livingston, as an adoptive southerner, challenged the prohibition on importation of slaves from Africa.[5]

Since Gabriel's Rebellion in Virginia and the bloody course of events in Haiti, the possible growth and expansion of slavery appeared more unsettling than the possible relocation of Indians. That was why Madison found it easier, in the text of his inaugural address, to direct his attention to the relatively benign project of making Indians "white." Indians were a mobile race, whereas slaves were bound to the land because their owners needed them to render it fruitful. Slavery remained a blight on the cultural landscape and an issue that was too huge to tackle head-on in the lead-up to the War of 1812.

As he approached the end of his address, the new president added a personal sentiment. He praised his immediate predecessor, asking to be "pardoned for not suppressing the sympathy with which my heart is full, in the rich reward he enjoys in the benediction of a beloved country." Margaret Bayard Smith, wife of the editor of the *National Intelligencer,* described with pathos the affectionate respect Jefferson received from the ladies who visited the President's House expressly to see him one last time. At the evening's inaugural ball, Jefferson, who was among the first to arrive, seemed uncomfortable and was heard to inquire: "You must tell me how to behave for it is more than forty years since I have been to a ball."[6]

A month from his sixty-sixth birthday, Thomas Jefferson had been writing home frequently in eager anticipation of his return. "My heart beats with inexpressible anxiety and impatience," his daughter appealed in mid-February, hopeful that his retirement might be passed "in serene and unclouded tranquility." The mayor of Washington City presented a letter of farewell on behalf of the local citizenry, all of them members of a "great and flourishing nation," the "solitary republic of the world." They would "pray" for his "felicity," and his release from the world of contention: "Happy, thrice happy retreat! where patriotism and philosophy, friendship and affection will animate, direct and soften the purest feelings of the heart!" Jefferson responded the same day with only slightly less florid language.[7]

"Father Never Loved Son More Than He Loves Mr. Madison"

A number of vignettes descend to us in which Jefferson's quiet dignity yields to tenderness in conversation, and strangers (men and women alike) find an immediate attraction to his passion for knowledge. No one ever described a personal encounter with James Madison as an inspirational moment. He seemed too small to fill Jefferson's shoes. At a glance, the Adamses, John and John Quincy, hardly seemed built of presidential materials, but the latter's wife, Louisa Catherine, regarded Madison's physique as almost cartoonish. He was, she wrote, "a *very* small man in *person*, with a *very* large *head*." The agreeable Dolley Madison, "tall, large and rather masculine in personal dimensions" made her husband look that much odder. To Mrs. Adams, James was "her little man"; but she acknowledged too that once one got over his appearance, he could be a "lively" and "playful" conversationalist.[8]

The closest to a portrait of warmth comes from Albert Gallatin's sister-in-law Frances Few, whose commentary differs somewhat from Mrs. Adams's. The day before the inauguration, Few noted in her diary that Madison, up close, looked like "parchment," his face so weather-beaten that he first appeared to have had smallpox. But after observing him a short while, she looked past his wasted appearance and discovered eyes that were "penetrating and expressive," a smile that was "charming"—and once again, "his conversation lively and interesting." Though Dolley's complexion was "brilliant" and stood in stark contrast to that of her husband, the first lady struck Mrs. Few as tasteless in her choice of wardrobe and opaque as a human being. "She is all things to all men," the diarist recorded.[9]

President Madison did not wish to be all things to all men, certainly not in the sense that Jefferson had tried, when in his first inaugural address he reached out to the Federalists who distrusted him. Madison was rather less interested in force of personality and more interested in carrying out his duties. As he was eight years younger than Jefferson, he was the same age now as his predecessor had been when he first took the oath of office. He dressed routinely in dreary-looking outfits but was capable of flashing a warm and welcoming smile. At Montpelier he was known not only to tell good stories to his guests but also to send them into fits of laughter in the telling. With a less-than-formidable presence, he was nonetheless comfortable as a host and had a taste for fine foods and Madeira wine.[10]

The Madisons did not move into the President's House until the outgoing president had vacated. After the inauguration, Jefferson needed time to gather up his belongings and take care of essential correspondence. Before leaving town a week later, he brought his account with Joseph Milligan, his preferred Washington bookseller and leather binder, up to date. Accompanied by two slaves, the now ex-president paid the toll at the Georgetown ferry and headed out in snowy conditions. Owing to the weather, it took a good bit longer than usual to reach Monticello.[11]

He would never return to the nation's capital; he was finished with Washington. Yet his closeness to his successor prevented him from turning a deaf ear to political news. He intended to find more innocent diversions and told Madison that he was "reading the newspapers but little and that little but as the romance of the day." But given the state of the nation, this inattention could not last.[12]

Dolley Madison was forty when she became the first lady. She took great pains to make the President's House a place for socializing. Whereas Jefferson had laid out gardens, she redesigned the interior. In a few short months the state dining room, accented with portraits of the first three presidents, and Mrs. Madison's sunflower-yellow parlor were readied for company. Fireplaces in the halls were supplemented by sunken stoves, keeping the downstairs warm. At regular Wednesday drawing-room gatherings, guests sported their best clothes and helped themselves to whiskey punch. For domestic help, the Madisons called upon the Montpelier house servants. Outside, a packed gravel driveway led to the main (north) entrance, over which a pair of stone eagles stood watch.[13]

In his first letter to Madison after turning over the keys to the President's House, Jefferson reported on how bad the roads had been as he trudged south on his "very fatiguing journey" back to Albemarle. Once home he regained his strength, though his return to the life of a farmer was anything but smooth. "The spring is remarkably backward," he testified. "No oats sown, not much tobacco seed, and little done in the gardens. Wheat has suffered considerably."

Despite his wish to leave all political matters to Madison, Jefferson divulged his concerns for the near future, fearing the country's unpreparedness for a major foreign conflict. He was quick to blame both the newspapers and credulous congressmen for the state of things: "I feel great anxiety for the occurrences of the ensuing 4. or 5. months. If peace can be preserved, I hope and trust you will have a smooth administration." But nearly everything he wrote to his successor dictated against that hope and trust. Thinking of how the nation had divided over the embargo, he growled: "I know no government which would be so embarrassing in war as ours. This would proceed very much from the lying and licentious character of our papers; but much also from the wonderful credulity of the members of Congress in the floating lies of the day. And in this no experience seems to correct them." Unsparing in his censure, Jefferson identified "the present Maniac state of Europe" as another unknown variable. Madison absorbed these anxious comments but replied to Jefferson's letter without addressing any particular concern. Other than the cumbersome "I wish your exemption from ill effects from the snow storm may be permanent," he limited himself to matters of an almost clerical nature.

Jefferson could not rest. To a Philadelphia physician with similar political leanings, he wrote as of old, warning that the "monarchists of our country" still had to be watched. But he said he had no fears that Madison would cave in to pressure from them: "Our enemies may try their cajoleries with my successor. They will find him as immoveable in his republican principles as him whom they have honored with their peculiar enmity."[14]

There must have been days when Jefferson did succeed in forgetting the larger world. Turning his attention to matters of the field, the kitchen, and other domestic concerns, he bought a new plow, ordered cotton seed, and hired a man to dig brick cisterns to store fresh water. He bought considerable quantities of beef and fish and brought in his chef from the President's House to complete the training of two of his accomplished female servants in the art of French cooking. Then he gave his thoughts over to his Poplar Forest retreat, an octagonal house on his productive farms in Bedford County, ninety-odd miles southwest of Monticello, where he was to spend months at a time throughout his retirement. It was an even quieter place than his much-venerated mountaintop estate, which was ever under construction. As the years passed, legions of curious citizens would arrive at Monticello unannounced, disturbing the family's privacy. When he wished for an even more remote existence—though even there he could not remain anonymous—Jefferson would escape to Poplar Forest. There, granddaughters and books would be his chief amusement.[15]

But Jefferson would not be Jefferson if he could resist having a hand in solidifying political friendships. It was a talent Madison did not possess, or at least not in the same degree. On March 30, 1809, Jefferson wrote to his successor with hopeful signs for the reanimation of the Madison-Monroe alliance, the fount from which Republican power had to flow: "Colo. Monroe dined & passed an evening with me since I came home. He is sincerely cordial: and I learn from several that he has quite separated himself from the junto which had gotten possession of him."

"Sincerely cordial" was one thing; a willingness to reconcile with Madison was quite another. Monroe and the prickly John Randolph had parted ways. That was what Jefferson meant when he said "the junto." But he also had to acknowledge that Monroe was not his source. "I did not enter into any material political conversation with him," he explained, while eagerly predicting: "I have no doubt that his strong & candid mind will bring him to a cordial return to his old friends." Monroe was returning to Highland, his home down the road from Monticello, and Jefferson, with paternal care, had resolved to lean on him gently and orchestrate a Madison-Monroe rapprochement.[16]

Before long Jefferson weighed in on foreign developments. He envisioned opportunities to absorb the rest of the North American continent, incorporating all reachable territory that did not require a large, expensive navy to stand guard against European schemes. Conquest of the underpopulated expanse would perfect the American republic, he said epigrammatically, yielding "such an empire of liberty" that the founders' dream would be fulfilled and their posterity forever rescued from the European extremes of luxury and squalor: "I am persuaded no constitution was ever before so well calculated as ours for extensive empire and self government." He believed deeply in the inevitability of American empire.

Napoleon's recent conquest of Spain made Jefferson think that the

French emperor would be willing to accept America's "moral right" to Florida, East and West, as well as Cuba. "Napoleon will certainly give his consent without difficulty to our recieving [sic] the Floridas," he wrote confidently. Cuba, he said, might take a little more work. To this, Madison replied that he expected Napoleon to dangle the Floridas before him in order to extract concessions on America's right to trade with Haiti, which the French emperor still aimed to reconquer.

Feeling he understood the nature of Napoleon's ambition, Jefferson anticipated a French takeover of Spain's colonies in South America. He considered it in America's best interest to position itself so that Napoleon would have to curry favor as his armies established a presence in the southern hemisphere. The ex-president envisioned a scenario in which the French would turn over the Floridas and Cuba to the United States, and the Madison administration, prudent and practical, would take Canada, finally eliminating all colonial threats in the vicinity of the United States.

Jefferson came close to meddling in his successor's foreign policy. He had an unguarded conversation with the French ambassador, Louis-Marie Turreau, affirming American designs on Cuba. When Turreau, posted to Washington since 1803, evinced concern, Secretary Gallatin was obliged to disavow his former boss and to state that President Jefferson no longer spoke for the government. To calm Turreau, Gallatin said that even if Cuba were offered to the United States, the administration would refuse it.[17]

The Virginia presidents were hesitant, lest they upset the French. They were far less concerned about antagonizing the notoriously weak Spanish. Yet policy with respect to the future of the western hemisphere was dictated by more than the comparative strength of colonial regimes. Madison and Jefferson alike differentiated between two kinds of republican revolutions in America's neighborhood: white and black. The United States would maintain outward neutrality, with Monroe at the helm, when the colonies of Latin America rose up against Spanish rule, beginning in 1818. It would embrace the new governments that formed, whose leaders bore European features. All the while, under Presidents Jefferson, Madison, and Monroe, the United States consistently withheld recognition of Haiti. It had nothing to do with Napoleon and the French. A nearby black republic was simply too disturbing.[18]

Though dreams of empire were never far from the minds of Madison and Jefferson, they required a greater military than the two presidents had provided for, a sense of national unity that did not exist, and a spirit of concession that the European powers would not exhibit. Although England was prepared for some accommodation with the United States amid the shock of Spain's capitulation to France, Madison's administration was off to a rocky start in all other respects. In congressional elections that took place in April 1809, the Federalists picked up twenty-four House seats, three in Virginia alone.[19]

These factors were on Jefferson's mind when it appeared that London was encouraging its U.S. minister, David Erskine, to find a broad-based solution to Anglo-American maritime problems. The Washington-based diplomat had worked out an agreement by which his government's 1807 Orders in Council (the edict that threatened all neutral shipping) would be lifted. Even so, a cynical Jefferson doubted this would happen and showed his annoyance to Madison. The British "never made an equal commercial treaty with any nation," he contended, "& we have no right to expect to be the first." Convinced that he had seen through yet another British ploy, Jefferson hazarded a prediction: "It will place you between the injunctions of true patriotism & the clamors of a faction devoted to a foreign interest." In other words, he figured that London and the Federalists were in cahoots, and that those at home who wished to wreck Madison's administration would rebuff any tough talk directed at the British.

Madison announced the imminent restoration of trade with Great Britain, and Jefferson was aggrieved. To his mind, America had no leverage anymore. He went so far as to compare the maritime policies of the British ministry to an "Algerine system"—its methods as unprincipled as those of the Barbary pirates. Jefferson believed the embargo had worked, though it had needed two years to succeed. Now, with the renewal of commerce, he sighed, "we never can have them [any] more in our power."

If Jefferson was correct, Madison was in a bind. With Anglo-American relations in limbo, Napoleon would choose to toy with America. Madison agreed with at least one of Jefferson's assessments: as France displayed the arrogance the United States generally expected of Britain, it would now hold hostage Americans' desire for Florida until the administration agreed to an unequal commercial relationship. The young United States was still not considered a significant enough threat that the European powers gave a second thought to Madison's proclamations.

As to London's diplomatic initiative, Madison felt none of Jefferson's concern—at least for the moment. The new president was certain he could be neither manipulated nor bullied. He reassured Jefferson that no matter what the British proposed, the United States would prepare itself with "a prudent adherence to our essential interests." His optimism was atypical

when he insisted: "The case of impressments, hitherto the greatest obsta-
cle, seems to admit most easily of adjustment." On the same day that he
wrote the above to Jefferson, Madison penned a letter to Lafayette expressing his hope that the French emperor would change course and recognize
neutral rights. "It will be a source of deep regret," he said, if Napoleon did
nothing to alleviate the "very obvious and painful dilemma" that the administration faced in navigating (on the high seas, as well as diplomatically) between the European belligerents.[20]

There were other demands on the president's time, not all of which
commanded a response. Within days of his taking office, Madison received
a letter from Rebecca Blodgett, daughter of the Reverend William Smith,
late provost of the University of Pennsylvania. A noted wit and beauty,
Blodgett was not on intimate terms with Madison, though she had been,
by her own account, acquainted with Dolley Madison, who had always
greeted her on the streets of Philadelphia with affectionate smiles. With
unapologetic bluntness, Blodgett called on the president to show compassion for the "lovely drooping" Theodosia Alston and end the persecution
of Theodosia's father, the exiled Aaron Burr. Blodgett termed the former
vice president a faithful friend of many years, to whom she owed, she said,
"whatever is valuable in myself." In crediting Burr (a champion of gender
equality) for enlightening her mind, she petitioned Madison to "begin your
Administration with an act of generosity & Magnanimity." But she did her
cause no great service by explaining why she had waited until this moment
to plead on Burr's behalf: "I despised your predecessor too much to conde-
scend to become his petitioner—to beg a favour infers an inferiority on the
part of the petitioner—& Heaven forbid that I shou'd ever place myself in
the light of an inferior to Thomas Jefferson, a *thing* whose principles religious, moral & political, are alike weak & wicked. A shifting, shuffling Visionary. An old woman in her dotage! A wretch without nerve!" This was
not tact. "Pardon me Sir," she affixed to her mockery. "My pen has a strange
trick—& 'tho I often caution it, it will tell all the secrets of my heart." She
hoped that it was not the president of the United States so much as an old
and forgiving friend of Aaron Burr's, who was to attend to her heated letter. Burr would eventually return from Europe and take up residence in
New York during Madison's presidency, but without any assistance or assurances from him or from his administration.[21]

As spring proceeded, Madison was still assembling his cabinet. He did
not have the luxury Jefferson previously had in selecting men he trusted.
First and foremost he wanted to make his closest adviser, Treasury Secre-

tary Albert Gallatin, his secretary of state. A small but influential faction led by Maryland senator Samuel Smith and Virginia's William Branch Giles—both experienced wheeler-dealers—would not hear of it. They had previously defended Gallatin against Federalist slurs regarding his un-American character, but things were different now. According to a nineteenth-century Smith descendant, the objection to Gallatin's assumption of the secretaryship of state was once again his foreign birth—which, for some unexplained reason, seemed less of an issue if he were to remain in charge of America's financial well-being.

It was probably not that simple and more about political jockeying. For his part, Giles wanted the appointment for himself. He had been a useful auxiliary in Congress for several years and tried to take credit for smoothing Madison's way to the presidency. But if John Randolph can ever be regarded as a reliable source of information, it may have been that Giles was not quite as competent as he thought he was. At least Smith "can spell," wrote Randolph, and thus "he ought to be preferred to Giles." (Giles had earlier flirted with Randolph's Quiddism, distancing himself when it came time to throw his support to Madison over Monroe.)

Madison did not wish to provoke Senator Smith or to alienate Giles. Smith's brother was Jefferson's secretary of the navy, Robert Smith, yet another Princeton graduate. He definitely lacked the will to perform administrative duties with Gallatinian energy. Jefferson had found his secretary of the navy to be a pleasant but not particularly dynamic cabinet officer, and Madison probably shared his opinion. As early as inauguration day former senator Wilson Cary Nicholas, now a congressman and one of Madison's and Jefferson's most trusted Virginia colleagues, had alerted Madison to the existence of an anti-Gallatin wing in the Republican Party; yet it was Gallatin himself who forced Madison's hand and sanctioned the appointment of Robert Smith to State. The loyal Gallatin opted to remain at Treasury rather than stir up more dissension in the Republican ranks.

It was left up to Jefferson to make nice with the Smiths. He wrote to Robert after his appointment, saying that he was able to "look back with peculiar satisfaction on the harmony & cordial good will which, to ourselves & our brethren of the Cabinet so much sweetened our toils." The irony of this sentiment would become evident in little more than a year, as conflict between Smith and Gallatin escalated. Hoping to avoid problems, Madison had opted to placate; he had already seen too much of confrontation, schism, and faction.

It bought him time, but not much. His politically drawn cabinet choices, beginning with Robert Smith, were to prove ruinous to the president in his first term. And it made Madison's life no easier when it became apparent that nothing he did allowed him to escape Jefferson's shadow—many, even his political admirers, assumed that the retired president was still calling the shots.

Madison was, to many, the sickly heir apparent, a pale copy of the controversial but inspirational former president. Margaret Bayard Smith even suggested that the new president was more like a child than an equal of Jefferson's. "Father never loved son more than he loves Mr. Madison," she recorded, imagining paternal pride on Jefferson's face. Lacking the party-building skills of Jefferson, Madison would find it difficult to claim the initiative.[22]

The most decisive difference between the two presidents lay in their approaches to party leadership. Jefferson cajoled his Republican allies into doing what he wanted, sharing secrets and demanding loyalty. Madison did not have this ability. To put it indelicately, only Jefferson knew how to seduce. He courted the faithful and sought out the young, the suggestible. His skill as a letter writer enabled him to convince his associates that their ideas and services were important. He knew how to soothe wounded egos—a political skill not sufficiently appreciated.

Madison had been successful in drawing close to elder statesmen such as Edmund Pendleton and George Washington because he could get things done for them. He held others to the same standard. Jefferson had the personal touch, Madison much less so. While Madison scripted Jefferson's political ascendancy in the 1780s and 1790s, it was Jefferson, not Madison, who conceived and built the Virginia Dynasty of presidents. Another way to interpret Margaret Bayard Smith's bubbly comment—"Father never loved son more"—is to imagine Madison inheriting his office in the sense that a prince succeeds the king. As all familiar with that story know, the younger man never quite measures up to the patriarch.

Coming into office, Madison was not the head of the party in the same way he had been in Congress in the 1790s. Deferring to others when he did not appoint Gallatin to the State Department, he did little to incline the members of Congress to do his bidding. It was a fainthearted approach and tactically unwise. Nor did he reach out to the compromise candidate, Robert Smith, as Jefferson did. It is hard to imagine Jefferson allowing Congress to derail him; it is harder still to imagine Jefferson failing to welcome a new cabinet member and soliciting his loyalty, which Madison evidently did not adequately do. When it fell to Jefferson to write to Smith, he attempted to conciliate, to reach out to him on an emotional level.

We know that Jefferson was often irked by the hostile attacks—"the floating lies"—that drew near him, just as we know that Madison was largely able to shun all of that species of torment. But Jefferson conveyed affectionate thoughts to the members of his party; in so doing, he succeeded in convincing them that he should be looked up to as the party's leader. Ironically, Madison was closer to the Adams model, a president who was most popular when America was on the verge of an international crisis but who, in the normal course of administration, was less intimate with his fellow politicians.

"I Consider War with England Inevitable"

On the Fourth of July 1809 President Madison and his cabinet attended church on F Street in Washington, where the ardent Republican poet Joel Barlow gave a patriotic oration. A band played, and as was customary, the Declaration of Independence was read. Toasts were presented, and enumerated in order of importance, to "the cardinal principles of democracy"; the office of the presidency; the memory of George Washington; "our beloved fellow citizen Thomas Jefferson"; and with an apparent flourish, while still identifying the new president as the untried heir, "James Madison, the Friend of Jefferson—That he may equal the virtues of his predecessor, is our sincere hope; that he will emulate them is our firm belief; may his life be happy and his memory revered!" At an Ohio gathering of Federalists, the message was somewhat different: the toast went out to "Thomas Jefferson—may his shin bones be converted into drumsticks, to beat the triumph of federalism in the U. States!"[23]

In August, approaching six months on the job, President Madison paid a visit to Monticello in the company of Albert and Hannah Gallatin. There is no record of what transpired, but the familiar threesome no doubt covered a wide range of policy issues, foreign and domestic, giving considerable attention to the warring Europeans and only somewhat less attention to unresolved bad feelings within the Republican Party. In all, it was a busy month. Margaret Bayard Smith and her husband, editor Samuel Harrison Smith, stayed several days at Monticello—welcomed, she wrote, by her host's "benignant smiles & cordial tones." And as the Madison-Gallatin party rode off, Jefferson welcomed another fond visitor, the widowed Eliza House Trist, his and Madison's Philadelphia landlady of years past. Three weeks later, not quite the detached farmer he claimed to be, Jefferson rode the twenty-five miles to Montpelier for one last visit before Madison had to return to Washington to take up troubling new developments relating to Anglo-American affairs.[24]

In his letters to Madison, and no doubt in private conversation as well, the scenarios Jefferson spun all pointed to war with England. He called British foreign secretary George Canning (whose very name seemed a blend of "canny" and "cunning") a man of "unprincipled rascality." Canning's "equivocations" degraded an already "shameless" government, Jefferson prodded Madison, adding without hesitation: "I despair of accommodation with them, because I believe they are weak enough to intend seriously to claim the ocean as their conquest, and think to amuse us with embassies and negociations until the claim shall have been strengthened by time and exercise, and the moment arrive when they may boldly avow what hitherto they have only squinted at." By "weak," Jefferson meant morally weak and brutally simple. He was most incensed by Britain's denunciation of all sense of honor in its dealings with Washington.[25]

Canning had told U.S. envoy William Pinkney the previous autumn that Jefferson's embargo meant nothing to him; it was "only to be considered as an innocent municipal Regulation, which affects none but the United States themselves." Canning's may have been the most incendiary public voice emanating from London, but the fact was that England had no fear of America. If the leadership, concentrating on Napoleon, saw the United States as too insignificant a power for London to have to attend its demands, then we should not be surprised that Jefferson continued to see a British regime bound to its hostile foreign secretary as irredeemable.

Madison was wrong to believe that the all-important impressment issue would be solved during the first year of his presidency. Congress had put an end to the unpopular embargo in the finals days of Jefferson's second term, and Madison entered office wanting to show no signs of weakness. He believed he had done just that over the course of his first months on the job. The British, however, did not see things the same way. Madison stood behind the Non-Intercourse Act of March 1809, which replaced the embargo but was still meant to close to U.S. commerce those ports that remained under British or French control. In fact, though, the Non-Intercourse Act contained enough loopholes that U.S. vessels were able to trade with the

British in neutral ports. In London, it appeared that the Madison administration had blinked.

Until July, Madison could not have known that his reliance on David Erskine, the British minister in Washington, was ill considered. When it became clear that Erskine had gone beyond what his superiors intended, and that Canning saw no reason to bend, the menacing Orders in Council remained in place and Erskine was recalled to London. Jefferson first learned of this and wrote Madison with an I-told-you-so self-satisfaction: "I never doubted the chicanery of the Anglomen."[26]

With firm resolve, Madison communicated to Secretary of State Robert Smith the proper posture he should take toward Erskine's replacement, Francis James Jackson, whose reputation for stuffiness and callousness Gallatin had earlier related. "From the character of the man, and the temper of his superiors," wrote Madison, "any thing beyond that politeness which explains itself, and is due to ourselves, is more likely to foster insolence than to excite liberality or good will." Whereas Jefferson never expected anything like a peaceful overture from London, Madison was aggravated because he had been deceived. Henceforth there would be no compromise. As long as Madison, like Jefferson, aimed to enlarge the borders of the United States, the British would remain the principal enemy, and Napoleon would be treated as the lesser of two evils. Not only were the British in Canada and in league with western Indian tribes; they appeared, at this point, more likely than Napoleon to advance into Spanish-held territories on America's frontier.[27]

Jefferson was extremely forceful. "Should Bonaparte have the wisdom to correct his injustice towards us, I consider war with England inevitable," he goaded Madison, expecting that the president would wait for the inevitable seizure of a France-bound American vessel to claim a pretext for war. "I have no doubt you will think it safe to act on this hypothesis, and with energy." He did not expect that Madison would shy from confrontation, but he wanted to be sure.

If A, then B. As much for his own clarification as for Madison's, Jefferson tried to foretell the course of events: "The moment that open war shall be apprehended from them, we should take possession of Baton rouge. If we do not, they will, and New Orleans becomes irrecoverable and the Western country blockaded during the war." Baton Rouge was the westernmost point of Spanish West Florida, perched on the commercially and militarily vital Mississippi and, despite its proximity to New Orleans, not in Ameri-

can hands. Jefferson wanted Madison to take advantage of the first opportunity to occupy and annex all of Florida and fulfill America's destiny.[28]

In early November 1809 Madison vowed to Jefferson that he would
"proceed with a circumspect attention" and "a just sensibility" that America's interest should not be sacrificed to either England or France. We
should not misread these words. For if Jefferson expressed his resentment
in unmistakable terms and Madison sounded "circumspect," Madison was
just as deeply concerned about national humiliation and felt no pressure
to reconcile with England.[29]

"But Madison Must Also Die"

With Madison's administration showing early signs of vulnerability, Federalists looked for new ways to strike at the Republican core. Well into Madison's second year in office, they continued to assume that Jefferson was
pulling the strings.[30] With perverse pleasure, they asserted that what the two
administrations had in common was the habitual waste of public funds.
Not only were dishonest appointees deliberately pilfering, they claimed, but
the Republicans were blatantly incompetent in managing money. The most
flagrant examples lay in the realm of military expenditures, where waste was
apparent in the procurement of supplies—inexplicably, the quartermaster's
office had been eliminated. The notorious reliance on the expensive, lightly
armed gunboats, meant to defend American harbors against larger, deadlier
European war vessels, made no sense at all.

Madison was less committed to the fifty-foot gunboats than Jefferson
had been, but neither, as president, made a concerted study of what should
be done to ensure an economically sound, militarily effective naval strategy
in the period after the *Chesapeake* incident. In 1807 then-Secretary of the
Navy (now Secretary of State) Robert Smith appears simply to have ratified
what the president and secretary of state desired. Jefferson clearly did not
wish at any time to participate in an "arms race" with Great Britain. Madison also appears to have believed that eventual U.S. expansion into Spanish
Florida and western destinations required vessels equipped for service
along the shallow rivers of the continent. Beyond that, privateering seemed
a cost-effective solution. In sum, a British-style naval force was more than a
pay-as-you-go government was willing to bear.[31]

The Federalists' hectoring satires did not let up either. The later months of 1809 saw the publication of *Memoirs of the Hon. Thomas Jefferson,* a two-volume send-up of the retired president meant to reflect equally on his hapless successor. The name of the anonymous author was exposed by the *Carolina Gazette* as one Stephen Cullen, alternately described as a "renegade Englishman," "a foreign hireling," and the "secret emissary" of Great Britain, who had lived in Charleston before removing to New York. "O my country!" the Republican newspaper claimed, "how art thou debased when such wretches find countenance and support from men who disgrace the name of AMERICANS by assuming it." Amid the crisis of impressment, Cullen's ability to pass for American reinforced the ambiguity of citizenship at this time of heightened Anglo-American antagonism.[32]

The two volumes purport to be Jefferson's actual memoir, though it is highly unlikely that anyone read ten pages into it without getting the joke. Jefferson's achievements were noted, and then immediately discounted. The magnificent first inaugural address was "hypocrisy," coming from a man who stood at the head of a political sect. Jefferson then "fell upon" the Federalists and "laid aside all decency, all shame" in persecuting them. Protesting that the third president misread British policy, Cullen made the actions of the *Leopard* in firing on the *Chesapeake* appear a reasonable action. Perhaps the most lurid characterization in the mock-memoir, though, was that of the proto-Jacobins who purportedly "joined in the diabolical orgies held at the house of Jefferson."

Moving on to Madison, Cullen found a "versatile president," by which he meant wavering and lacking in the masculine qualities of firmness and resolve. "General Hamilton," Cullen reminded, "declared that Mr. Madison was, during the agitation of the important question of a Constitution, far more zealous for monarchy than any other active public character in America." It was Hamilton, not Madison, who had been so inclined in 1787; but by 1809 the Federalist narrative incorporated many such spurious charges.[33]

Around the same time a long poem, printed as a broadside, lamented the death of Washington and the Republican era that opened in its wake. Like Cullen's nasty memoir, it brought up every old charge against Jefferson before turning to the new Republican president:

> *The* Sage *of Monticello's run*
> *And left the throne to* Madison
> *His talents small, his courage less*
> *Has brought us all into distress.*

The partisan poet concluded that liberty was fading and would expire in Madison's arms. How could America have gone from the sturdy Washington to the scrawny Madison in so short a time?

> *Great Washington, our friend, is dead,*
> *And Madison reigns in his stead;*
> *Much reason then to mourn and sigh;*
> *But Madison must also die.*[34]

Of course, no Republican could ever be a Washington. Some Federalists, in the Joseph Dennie mold, had by now devised a kind of political eugenics. For them, the weak-kneed Madison was a worse incarnation—a lesser Jefferson. Politically powerless themselves, mock-poetry and song served as a kind of voodoo chant: it was meant to put a curse on Madison, the heir who lacked any part of the vitality of the foremost Federalist.

"The Militia of Georgia Will Do It in a Fortnight"

The executive branch closely monitored news out of Europe, but it was in Congress that headlines were made. The 1809–10 winter session witnessed vigorous debate in both houses over England and France, America's commercial life, and national honor. What he read irritated Madison, who wrote at the end of January to a group of Maryland Republicans that national unity was the only means of securing respect for "our National character & rights." If foreigners were encouraged by "internal discords & distrusts," then safety, honor, and the national interest would all be endangered. To William Pinkney, still trying to negotiate with the British, Madison blamed Congress for its "passive spirit" and predicted a pendulum shift in the next session when it became clear that Britain would respond only to measures that had bite: "Every new occasion seems to countenance the belief, that there lurks in the British Cabinet, a hostile feeling towards this Country, which will never be eradicated . . . but by some dreadful pressure from external or internal causes."[35]

Madison wrote to Pinkney just as Congress repealed the Non-Intercourse Act and replaced it with Macon's Bill no. 2, named after North Carolina Republican Nathaniel Macon. This clever but ultimately inconclusive piece of legislation was designed to exert psychological pressure on England and France by restarting formal trade between the United States

and the two belligerents in anticipation of the Europeans' removal of restrictions against the United States. It did so while stipulating that Washington was prepared to reimpose sanctions on whichever of the two would
not comply or attacked neutral commerce. The French responded with
what turned out to be a hollow gesture: announcing an intention to abide
by Macon no. 2 and requesting that the Madison administration do its part
by reinvoking nonintercourse with Britain. Madison, who did not expect
London to rescind the Orders in Council to begin with, and who had written Pinkney that he was "equally distrustful" of France, fell for Napoleon's
gambit nonetheless and played into French hands.[36]

If there was one piece of communication that mirrored the state of
Madison's mind during these months, it was that which he received from
his attorney general, Caesar A. Rodney of Delaware. The son of a signer of
the Declaration of Independence, Rodney had come to Jefferson's attention in 1802, after winning a seat in the House. He actively supported Jefferson's effort to impeach Justice Samuel Chase. Upon Rodney's defeat at
the polls, Jefferson appointed him attorney general, and he retained that
position when Madison became president.

Rodney's supportive letter was more the work of a stirring essayist than
that of a legal adviser. "We live in an age without precedent in history," he
wrote, "a solitary neutral, amid a warring world." International law had
come to be irrelevant in the face of "arbitrary orders & decrees of the belligerents." He condemned a world that would force America to stand alone
on principle: "It is in this unexampled state of things, that we are struggling to preserve the moral rule of action." For Rodney, the choice was clear
and there was no turning back: "If we unsheathe our sword, I am most decidedly for selecting our foe . . . England is our old & inveterate enemy. She
has done us more injury. The impressment of our seamen alone is worse
than all we have sustained from France." For this attorney general, it was
worth plunging the nation into war just to protect the doctrine of neutral
rights. He too believed strongly in the efficacy of privateers as a counter-
force to the all-powerful Royal Navy.[37]

At this point President Madison finally proved himself an unabashed
expansionist. To demonstrate, we must begin by asking a seemingly obfus-
cating question: Who was the Virginian Fulwar Skipwith, and how did he
become, ever so briefly, the head of government of an independent republic in North America? In 1810 Skipwith had lived in the neighborhood of
Baton Rouge, then a part of West Florida, for only one year when he
emerged as the beneficiary of a rebellion against Spanish rule

In more ways than one, the West Florida Republic foreshadowed that of the Republic of Texas a quarter-century later—including the symbol on its flag, a lone star. The difference between the two minirepublics was Mexican independence from Spain, which occurred well after the West Florida events and long before Texas separated itself. Also of historical note, the ordinarily aggressive president Andrew Jackson proved reluctant, in 1836, to trigger war with Mexico by annexing Texas (annexation did not occur until 1845); and the ordinarily law-abiding James Madison, the president of the United States in 1810, did not wish to wait nine years to annex Spanish territory.

Fulwar Skipwith was well known within the Madison-Jefferson circle. As a young attorney, courting his future wife, Jefferson had been friendly with the Skipwith clan. Patty Jefferson's half sister married Henry Skipwith, and when Jefferson became an executor of the estate of Patty's father, he carried on an extensive correspondence with Henry over their common problems as inheritors of John Wayles's debt. Jefferson most likely came to know his legal protégé and secretary in Paris, William Short, through the Skipwiths: Fulwar was William's cousin and confidant, Henry his uncle, and they all had financial dealings.

In the mid-1780s, when Jefferson and Short went to Paris, Fulwar Skipwith went to London as a representative of Virginia tobacco merchants, placing clients' tobacco on the market and overseeing shipments. Jefferson relied on him for occasional favors. More important, when James Monroe sailed to Paris in 1794, at the behest of President Washington, Skipwith accompanied him as secretary of the legation. He remained in Paris for several years after Monroe returned home, rising to U.S. consul general. When Monroe sailed again to France to assist Robert Livingston in managing the Louisiana Purchase, Skipwith was his main contact. An insider to the negotiations, Skipwith was clear when it came to U.S. designs on the Floridas. He understood that no precise delimitation of West Florida's boundary was ever made, though Monroe had requested it of the French.

Skipwith had a temper. He tangled with Robert Livingston, whose personal honor was wounded as a result of Skipwith's actions—the consul general, technically Livingston's subordinate, engaged in discussions with the French to which Livingston was not immediately privy, and wrote to then–Secretary of State Madison on his own. Livingston responded by reducing Skipwith's salary. Madison was concerned enough about the incident to raise it with President Jefferson.

In 1806 a new round of discussions over the future of West Florida took place in Paris between U.S. representatives and Napoleon. Skipwith was front and center. So was special envoy James Monroe, with whom he again cooperated closely. The pair found themselves equally at odds with Robert Livingston and John Armstrong, who were not only New Yorkers but also brothers-in-law. In succeeding Livingston as U.S. minister, the notoriously prickly Armstrong questioned Skipwith's financial ethics. This occasioned Monroe, at the start of 1809, to attest to Skipwith's "perfect integrity and patriotism." The Virginians were sticking together.[38]

With his knack for irritating important people, Fulwar Skipwith relocated to West Florida later that year. But before his removal to Baton Rouge, he paid a visit to the State Department in Washington, and we must presume he called on the president. As he was establishing himself as a Louisiana cotton planter and making himself known to his neighbors, it is unclear whether he was in communication with Madison or Monroe. Were they at all surprised, in November 1810, when Skipwith was named governor of the newly self-proclaimed West Florida Republic? It appears not. But if no paper trail exists to suggest that Madison directed Skipwith to do anything, the events that occurred did eventually play into the president's hands.

In the months leading up to the West Florida takeover, Madison and Jefferson were both giving considerable attention to the politically stressed, militarily vital region where Skipwith had gone. West Florida was a prize oft-mentioned, a prize yet to be won; and New Orleans was an obvious target for an invader, if war were to occur. At the same time Jefferson necessarily brought President Madison in on his nasty little legal battle with Edward Livingston over ownership of the batture, disputed land on the fringes of the Crescent City. Back in 1803, when he was mayor of New York and his brother was in Paris, one of Livingston's clerks had misused government funds and left a shortfall in the tens of thousands of dollars. Additionally, Edward Livingston was one of five legal scholars to offer advice to the Spanish minister, a business that placed him at odds with the Jefferson administration. At the time Madison and Gallatin urged Jefferson to hold Livingston accountable, and to prosecute him, if feasible, under a law barring ordinary citizens from entering into diplomacy.

The disgraced mayor arrived in Louisiana not long afterward (allegedly with only $100 in cash) and rebuilt his career and reputation in no time flat. Flash-forward to 1810, when he interrupted the third president's retirement by bringing suit against him, because, as president, Jefferson had contended that some valuable batture land Livingston had purchased for himself was public and not private property. The politics of land was, as always in early America, a tangled web.

The situation gets even more complicated. As a longtime supporter of fellow New Yorker Aaron Burr, Edward Livingston bore little sympathy toward Governor Claiborne of the Territory of Orleans, the native Virginian whom Jefferson had appointed and whom Madison left in charge of territorial politics. In May 1810 Claiborne made the long trip to Washington in order to meet with Madison. Not surprisingly, then, Madison reflected the southern governor's perspective when referring to the anti-Claiborne faction as a "combination" whose aims were not entirely clear. New Yorkers versus Virginians.

That summer the battles involving personalities and politics enlarged. Madison was in regular touch with the Department of State over fallout from the bitter dispute that had earlier occurred between Skipwith and Armstrong in Paris. In mid-August Jefferson was at Montpelier, and just after he departed, the *National Intelligencer* reprinted a proposed constitution for West Florida, put together by area settlers. (Skipwith may or may not have been directly associated with this document.) Reading intelligence communicated to him by Harry Toulmin, a superior court judge in the Mississippi Territory, Madison expressed concern about the region's volatility and sent Toulmin's letter to the State Department, saying it was of pressing interest. This prompted further discussion about the means to suppress filibustering enterprises against the Spanish.

By mid-September ideas gave way to what is today referred to as actionable intelligence. Madison learned of the burning hunger for revolution among Americans in West Florida. He knew (or assumed) that something was to be staged in the hope that the United States would respond with military aid. But the anxious West Florida plotters also acknowledged that significant numbers in the region leaned toward Great Britain, and still others were not prepared to forswear allegiance to the Spanish Crown. In mid-September, before returning to Washington, Madison visited Monticello. Claiborne had not yet left the East Coast. Madison sent word to the acting governor of the territory to keep a "wakeful eye" on Baton Rouge, but nothing more.[39]

To bring down Spanish colonial rule, a band of American rebels attacked the garrison at Baton Rouge, on the banks of the Mississippi, and forced the Spanish out. Militia loyal to the Spanish were stripped of their weapons and placed under house arrest. On October 27, in convention, the rebels approved a constitution. Three weeks later Fulwar Skipwith was

elected governor. His talents were well enough known even before the rebellion that he had been put forward for a judgeship on the highest court
of the territory. At that time the Spanish governor rejected his nomination
on the grounds that he had been a resident for too short a time and, no less
meaningfully, that Skipwith had never declared his loyalty to Spain. Soon
afterward the former U.S. consul in Paris was helping to declare West
Florida independent.

The declaration he issued was based on natural rights doctrine, stating
that because Spain was in political turmoil, responsibility for West
Florida's protection was returned to its people. It was not quite as convincing as Jefferson's grand appeal to the "candid world" in 1776, but Skipwith
knew how to dress a text in colorful garb: "Having been abandoned by a
sovereign, whose system and principles of colonization grew up in the past
ages of bigotry and persecution; our rights of self-government will not be
contested." So he told the assembled legislators of the new republic in his
inaugural address.[40]

Madison had to appear to honor America's proclaimed neutrality. He
pretended to distance himself from what was happening in Baton Rouge,
until the smoke had cleared. As soon as he could, though, he issued a presidential proclamation asserting that the United States already had title to
this territory on the strength of the Louisiana Purchase. He made this announcement on October 27, by coincidence the same day that a convention
in West Florida adopted a constitution. In his decree, Madison stated that
the land from the River Perdido (situated between Pensacola and Mobile)
to the Mississippi was a part of the purchase. The United States had not
taken possession of it before but would now. It was, he said, "a satisfactory
adjustment, too long delayed" and "suspended by events."

Madison's claim was debatable. In fact Spain did not agree, and would
not agree, to America's interpretation of the Louisiana Purchase until
James Monroe was president. Annexation took place because England and
France were otherwise engaged—in 1810 West Florida was a meaningless
distraction from the war in Europe. Still, in the mind of Madison no less
than Jefferson, the entire Gulf Coast remained potentially an operational
base for hostile Europeans. He had acted accordingly.[41]

The West Florida Republic elected its governor and legislature in late
November. The next month, back in the region, Governor Claiborne presented Madison's proclamation to Fulwar Skipwith. At first Skipwith
balked. But Claiborne talked sense into his fellow Virginian, and the West
Florida Republic breathed its last. In later years Skipwith told the story dif-

ferently, asserting that he had always looked favorably upon the president's policy of immediate annexation of the territory. The precise truth—what went on behind the scenes—cannot be known.

Madison floated the idea that East Florida might also be wrested from Spain during his presidency, though preferably through negotiation. Just after West Florida's annexation, he gave Georgia's seventy-one-year-old former governor, George Mathews, the leeway to negotiate with the Spanish for East Florida. In the spirit of the times, Mathews, in spite of his advanced age, interpreted his instructions as permission to lead an army south and to take the land by force if necessary.

Of Irish extraction, Virginia born and Georgia bred, General George Mathews was thoroughly familiar with the Georgia-Florida border, East and West Florida. He had fought the Shawnees in 1774, was wounded on a Revolutionary battlefield, and languished on a British prison ship for two years before witnessing the Yorktown surrender ceremony. Though tarred by his association with the Yazoo fraud, he continued to have friends in high places. Madison had served with Mathews in the First Congress. At a meeting in the President's House in early 1811, Mathews outlined the dangers emanating from a pro-British faction in East Florida, and Madison listened.

From that point on, as Madison kept his ear to the ground, Mathews remained ready and eager. At the first opportunity he tried to engineer a rebellion in St. Augustine and install a friendly government. But the candidates Mathews had in mind were wary of him and revealed his plot to Spanish authorities. Whether the plot was officially sanctioned or a self-supporting filibuster did not matter to old George Mathews. He wanted to move in and to turn over East Florida to the United States. The Spanish consul, Juan de Onís, caught wind of what was happening and strongly protested. He wanted to know whether Mathews represented the Madison administration.[42]

"I go to St. Augustine," Mathews declared, just as the administration realized it had to disavow his activities. "From there our victorious men move on Mobile and Pensacola. But we will not stop. On to Venezuela, to rout the autocratic Spaniards and plant the flag of freedom over all of South America." It was the wrong time to rely on intimidation as a regular form of policy, and Madison knew it.[43]

In the case of the West Florida Republic, Madison had felt less encumbered. Baton Rouge was only nominally Spanish. In that sense, he had a good understanding of what Burr's alleged conspiracy had really been about—like Skipwith's ploy, it was concerned with growth opportunities in southeastern Louisiana and the volatility of Spanish lands generally. In authorizing Governor Claiborne to intercede in Baton Rouge, Madison was generally wary of what could happen when land-hungry frontier types joined their fortunes to a fearless expansionist. He wanted to take no chances that what Burr was *thought* to have been plotting might occur again under Skipwith's auspices and spin out of control. In truth, then, Madison was doing in West Florida just what Burr had wanted: permitting a filibuster to open the door to territorial annexation.

Madison committed the United States to the filibuster and gave Skipwith an honorable way out. He could do this because both Claiborne and Skipwith were Virginians—politically nonthreatening ones, at that. Burr, of course, was a New Yorker and a latent threat to Jefferson's vision of a Virginia Dynasty. Had the battle-hardened Colonel Burr, a company commander during the Revolution, taken Mexico, his political fortunes in the United States might well have revived. Jefferson, as president, had acted out of fear and distrust, doing all he could to scare off any who might otherwise have glorified Burr. Charging Burr with treason and putting him on trial—a political show trial—backfired on him; Marshall had seen to that. In 1810 Madison was at the helm, less impulsive than his predecessor had been three years before. The result was the disempowerment of Fulwar Skipwith and his fellows and the successful incorporation of a piece of Spanish territory.

As for Jefferson, whose retirement was meant to take him out of politics, Baton Rouge appeared to be a clear harbinger of things to come. He advocated a forward policy when he wrote to his former son-in-law John Wayles Eppes, the cousin and husband of his late daughter Maria, and a member of Congress since 1803. Just as Mathews was meeting with Madison in Washington, and aware that Eppes was to be in charge of the House Foreign Affairs Committee, Jefferson urged action: "I wish you would authorise the President to take possession of East Florida immediately." He was convinced that as soon as England learned that Baton Rouge was taken, it would move on Florida—from St. Augustine on the Atlantic west to Pensacola—and do it "pretendedly for Spain."

If Madison questioned the timing of so forward a move in East Florida and thus proceeded with caution, Jefferson weighed the situation differently. Based on his long-cultivated suspicion of British intentions—always good grounds for a land grab—he thought any Florida gamble worthwhile. Reading in stark terms the mind of the enemy, he wanted the government to provide for the security of its territory. "The militia of Georgia will do it in a fortnight," Jefferson assured Eppes. We do not know for certain whether Madison's initial appeal to George Mathews involved Jefferson's input, but it is reasonable to conclude that Madison knew precisely where Jefferson stood when he stopped short of giving Mathews the green light. It was too soon for East Florida.[44]

Once again it is the southern mind, its long-prevailing sense of opportunity, competition, and risk, that explains all governing motives in the Gulf area drama of 1810–11. Madison understood and supported the impulse to acquire new land and banish foreign influence; but he seems to have been sensitive to appearances and unwilling to rile Britain, France, or Spain without sufficient cause. Jefferson's motives typically involved fears of encroachment, which in this case was the fear that his nation's freedom of movement was to be somehow restricted by Great Britain. Madison did not see quite the same threat. Yet in the end he came away with West Florida, using a convenient *legal* interpretation of the Louisiana Purchase to justify an *extralegal* filibuster. This was political canniness, if not political genius.[45]

Militancy made sense to a certain breed of American—generally, though not exclusively, southern Republicans. They were motivated by the desire for land on which to cultivate cotton and other cash crops; they were motivated by the desire to sell surplus slaves in the West. In 1802, while trying to squeeze Napoleon to give up New Orleans, then–Secretary of State Madison had capitalized on the same phenomenon when he advised U.S. minister to France Robert Livingston to drop hints that disgruntled Americans might provoke incursions of their own into Louisiana. James Monroe was another who long favored strong action with respect to Spain. They all had a convenient rationale: men like George Mathews were everywhere. Government officials wanted it understood that forces operating in and around the Gulf were too large and too random for them to control. General Andrew Jackson would be next, and the most successful of all, finally securing East Florida and becoming its first territorial governor in the years immediately after Madison left the presidency to Monroe.

"Silence the Growlings"

Among the younger generation of Virginians who were increasingly involved in Madisonian-Jeffersonian politics, Congressman John Wayles

Eppes is one of the least remembered. In the lead-up to the War of 1812, however, he was a valuable liaison between the executive and legislative branches of government, no mere mouthpiece of the administration.

From the moment of Madison's accession to the presidency, Eppes took an interest in both military and civilian appointments as they related to Louisiana and U.S. relations with Spain. Early in 1810 he alerted Madison to information reaching him from army circles that rates of desertion were high among U.S. troops in New Orleans, and that General Wilkinson was responsible for the deaths of many of those in his command by exposing them to unsanitary conditions and stationing troops in swampy areas. Eppes advised Madison that the shady general, an alleged pensioner of Spain, had by this time "lost completely the confidence of nine tenths of all persons with whom I am acquainted." Wilkinson would be brought up on charges and, in spite of the efforts of those like Eppes, somehow survive long enough to embarrass himself anew as a wartime commander.

Eppes was one of the Jefferson intimates invited to comment on the batture case. In addition, he kept his former father-in-law up to date on partisan debates in Congress over West Florida annexation. Expressing himself with no less reserve when he spoke to the sitting president, Eppes urged Madison in early 1811 to wait for evidence of French cooperation before strengthening the terms of nonintercourse with England. His established position in Congress underscored the slow but steady shift in policy formulation from the Revolutionary generation to its successor: men born in the early 1770s, bearing no memory of life as colonial subjects, were grabbing national headlines.[46]

With Jefferson in retirement, Madison in Washington, and the Federalists diminished in number but not in noise-making, the third and fourth presidents knew that history was chronicling their career achievements and shortcomings and would continue to do so whether or not they weighed in. As a compiler of notes and an inveterate record-keeper, Jefferson is known for his many vocations: He accumulated thousands of books in several languages; he studied and savored wines; he carefully annotated his correspondence, made architectural drawings, undertook encyclopedic studies of flora and fauna, and pursued Indian vocabularies. He recorded all expenditures made for his farms when he stayed at home, and he kept track of expenses large and small on the road, when he traveled near and far, down to the cost of a shave and the tips he gave to Madison's servants when he visited Montpelier. But he also, and with extreme care, put his political house in order between 1809 and his death seventeen years later. His purpose in the reorganization and recalibration of the past was collective as much as it was personal: he wished to ensure that America's founding era was painted with a Republican rather than a Federalist brush.

For years already Jefferson had been appealing to the poet Joel Barlow to write an authoritative political history. Though Connecticut-born and Yale-educated, Barlow was of a modest genealogy and a Republican in temperament. He had lived long in France before returning to the United States in 1802. "Mr. Madison and myself have cut out a piece of work for you," then-President Jefferson had appealed. "We are rich ourselves in materials, and can open all the public archives to you." He insisted that Barlow move to Washington, "because a great deal of knoledge of things is not on paper, but only within ourselves for verbal communication." It is hard to know for sure whether the sly and seductive tone we automatically read into Jefferson's language bore an equally conspiratorial flavor for Barlow as he read the letter. The poet kept Jefferson on hold, and when he was about to embark on a diplomatic mission for Madison in 1811, Jefferson appealed to him one last time: "What is to become of our Post-revolutionary history?" Joel Barlow died in 1812, while on that mission. And the history Jefferson wanted written would not appear in his lifetime.[47]

Because of Madison's more guarded manner, far less is known of his predilections in this regard, though we have Jefferson's testimony that the two of them were equally involved in the solicitation of Barlow. For some reason President Madison was poring through his papers at Montpelier during the summer of 1810 and was upset not to find among them "a delineation of Hamilton's plan of a Constitution," in Hamilton's own hand, dating to the time of the Constitutional Convention. In 1791 he had asked Jefferson to make copies of his notes from the convention, for safekeeping, and in 1810 bade Jefferson to help him look for the missing Hamilton document. Jefferson in turn asked his son-in-law Eppes, who as an eighteen-year-old had written out the copies; he amazingly recalled the pin that fastened these particular pages. Writing Madison directly, the now-thirty-seven-year-old congressman Eppes detailed the procedure by which he undertook the "entirely confidential" trust of making the copies. All these years later he was able to assure Madison that he had returned the Hamilton piece with the rest of the papers, and indeed Madison took another look and found what he sought.[48]

Whatever it was in the historical record that concerned Madison at that moment, his history could not be completely written before relations with England and France were resolved. And for now he was strapped to a secretary of state who was sapping the strength of the executive. Robert Smith demonstrated loyalty only to his senator-brother, Samuel, who had grown increasingly resentful toward Gallatin, the only cabinet member to whom Madison accorded real power. Gallatin knew infinitely more about international affairs than his rival Smith did, but he was convinced that the Smiths were conspiring to make Robert president in 1812. Jealousy was clearly a factor in the Smith-Gallatin rift. Even their wives quarreled. After one extremely bitter social encounter, Smith said he would have shot Gallatin if given the chance. Dolley Madison sought to calm matters between the Smiths and Gallatins, but to no avail.[49]

During the spring of 1811, when the administration could little afford it, its family squabble reached the breaking point. Smith revealed information about U.S. distrust of the French to a British representative, implying that the British had cause to question the president's candor. Madison confronted Smith, denouncing him both for undermining Gallatin and for making the president's job difficult by operating behind his back. Smith denied that he had any bad intent.

Technically, it was Gallatin who offered his resignation. But he may have done it as a ruse, in consultation with the president, to bring matters to a head and yield the result Madison wanted. Gallatin could not be spared, of course, and Smith was dismissed. Madison offered him, as a consolation prize, the St. Petersburg ministry, currently occupied by John Quincy Adams, who disliked Russia intensely. After initially expressing interest, Smith thought twice before rejecting what he termed an "insidious" offer. Next, he set out to repudiate Madison before the public, vowing to his brother that he would "overthrow" the president. The forty-page pamphlet he published in July 1811 was aimed at personal vindication, but it went so far as to label the president "unmanly" for conducting a weak foreign policy. Madison prepared to defend himself, drafting a memorandum on Smith's activities in case public opinion turned against him or he was forced to answer charges before Congress. He told Jefferson that much of what Smith wrote could be answered only by "disclosures" from himself, which the duties and decorum of his office precluded. He could only hope, he said, that others would see to it that the "whole turpitude" of Smith's conduct was exposed.[50]

How unmanly Madison was by the standard of the day is best measured in political terms, because that was what his opponents really meant by their insults. Madison was slender and never hearty, of course. The prolific Washington Irving, not yet thirty when he met the president, was already a popular satirist, but his world-famous short stories were yet to be conceived. Introduced around Dolley's drawing room, "hand in glove with half the people in the assemblage,"* he pronounced upon the president: "Poor Jemmy! he is but a withered little apple-John." Shriveled up perhaps, but Madison was a fan of Irving's and approved his spicy attitude. Literature, he knew, could not exist without quirks and humorous distortions.[51]

Political emasculation was another matter entirely. Madison's critics took aim at those they referred to as "submission men," whose cowardly subservience left the country without a manly defense or its national honor. The so-called invisibles or malcontents who rallied round the Smiths demanded some form of military retaliation against Great Britain in place of passive economic coercion. Surprisingly, Madison's old Virginia friend Wilson Cary Nicholas abandoned him in protest against the administration's relatively modest commercial warfare policies. As Nicholas put it, "Every expedient short of war was submission."[52]

To Madison's dismay, Philadelphia *Aurora* editor William Duane, a longtime ally, became an angry opponent after 1809. Taking the side of the Smiths against Gallatin, he roundly criticized Madison. So despite a tormented history with printers and editors, Jefferson decided that this was one time when it made sense for him to get directly involved. He enjoyed a good rapport with Duane and felt he might persuade the editor to return to the fold.

In March 1811, only days before his first appeal to Duane, Jefferson received a letter from Jack Eppes that may have convinced him to pursue the course he ultimately took with Duane. "The rancor of party was revived with all its bitterness during the last Session of Congress," Eppes wrote. "I consider the scenes of 1798 & 1799 again approaching." No one else had presented such imagery to Jefferson—summoning back the "reign of witches"—and it had to have affected him in some way. Concerned about the election of 1812, Eppes laid out the risks and the possibilities: "Our principles are staked on the support of Mr. Madison—A change in our foreign relations would enable him to ride triumphant, put down his opponents in Congress & silence the growlings of those who ought to possess his entire confidence."[53]

Jefferson knew that Madison could not afford to lose the state of Pennsylvania, where "growlings" were coming from the presses of the *Aurora*. Writing on March 28, he asked Duane to reconsider, and to indulge differences in political outlook that Jefferson considered relatively minor. "I believe Mr. Gallatin to be of as pure integrity...as [the] most affectionate native citizen," he testified. During his eight years as president he had come to know the character of his treasury secretary "more thoroughly perhaps than any other man living"; and, he amplified, "I have ascribed the erroneous estimate you have formed of it, to the want of that intimate knoledge [*sic*] of him which I possessed."

Jefferson's exhortation to Duane continued for pages, emphasizing the need for Republicans to recover their common purpose. "If we do not act in phalanx," he wrote, "I will not say our *party*, the term is false and degrading, but our *nation* will be undone." Alluding to the ambiguities that had resulted in schism, he added with conviction, if with a less than fully honest recollection: "I have ever refused to know any subdivisions among [the Republicans]."[54]

Jefferson sent Madison a copy of his letter. "I shall make one effort more to reclaim him from the dominion of his passions," he said of Duane after several weeks had gone by. And when he did, he tried both stick and carrot, informing the editor that Virginians had lost both sympathy and respect for the *Aurora*. Jefferson appealed first to conscience, and then to a sense of honor, before suggesting to Duane that the mind can be led, "step by step, unintended & unpercieved by itself," to self-destructive acts. "The example of John Randolph, now the outcast of the world, is a caution to all honest & prudent men," he pressured, adding a personal touch before he closed: "It would afflict me sincerely to see you ... become auxiliary to the enemies of our government." This was a letter written with extreme care, but not without a tone of finality. Duane would recognize it as an ultimatum. After waiting another month for the answer that never came, Jefferson told Madison: "It probably closes our correspondence as I have not heard a word from him on the subject." In the interim Jefferson redoubled his effort to see that Thomas Ritchie of the *Richmond Enquirer* was "correct as to the administration generally." It was essential to shore up Virginia Republicanism before any other advantage could be sought.[55]

Madison had been far less sanguine all along. While he credited Duane as "a sincere friend of liberty," he did not regard him as "rational or friendly" when it came to the team of Madison and Gallatin. Nor did Madison expect the editor ever to be anything but a slave to his passions. "He gives proofs of a want of candor, as well as of temperance," the fourth president unloaded to the third. In the end Jefferson had to agree. When May rolled around, he told an ally, attorney (and future attorney general) William Wirt: "It is possible Duane may be reclaimed as to Mr. Madison, but as to Gallatin I despair of it." In the same letter he echoed Madison's belief as to Duane: "His passions are stronger than his prudence, and his personal as well as general antipathies, render him very intolerant." The Smiths and William Duane had succeeded in producing a schism in Madison's first term to equal that which Jefferson had endured in his second. And the partisan newspaper, an American institution that Madison and Jefferson could not say they were entirely innocent of promoting, had become the channel through which President Madison—whose circle of friends was now much constricted—had to fight for his political life.[56]

Robert Smith's long-overdue departure from State made it possible for Madison to redefine administration foreign policy. He did so by repairing, once and for all, the personal breach his predecessor had cared about most. Madison wrote Jefferson laconically: "You will have inferred the change which is taking place in the Department of State. Col. Monroe agrees to succeed Mr. Smith." Jefferson was able to read into those two sentences everything Madison intended him to know. His reply was elaborate: "I do sincerely rejoice that Monroe is added to your councils. He will need only to perceive that you are without reserve towards him, to meet it with the cordiality of earlier times. He will feel himself to be again at home in our bosoms, and happy in a separation from those who led him astray." There is an indication that before Madison made this appointment, he had asked Jefferson whether *he* would like to serve as secretary of state, in which case Monroe would have been placed at the head of the War Department.

Why would Madison have wanted Jefferson back at the State Department? Was it not obvious to him that if Jefferson rejoined the government, "Little Jemmy Madison's" image problem would only have deepened? Or perhaps Madison's ego was not so sensitive that he would be concerned about that. Surely his enemies would have termed the appointment an admission by Madison of his own incompetence. On the other hand, Madison's motivation is fairly obvious: after all the problems caused by the Smiths, he wanted a reliable Virginian, someone he completely trusted, in key posts. Jefferson had to have thought Monroe the perfect candidate and was not being merely rhetorical when he said he was tired of the daily routine of government and unwilling to subject himself to further mutilation in the press. Refusing to reenter the maelstrom, Jefferson noted of Monroe's new situation: "I learn that John Randolph is now open-mouthed against him."[57]

The oft-dismissed Monroe had eased his way back into government. For nearly five years, from the time he had toiled in London, struggling to achieve better Anglo-American relations, through his lukewarm welcome home and his acquiescence to the Old Republicans in the 1808 presidential campaign, he had wallowed in disappointment. His bruised feelings started to heal in 1810, when he campaigned successfully for a seat in the Virginia House of Delegates and announced: "Mr. Madison is a Republican and so am I." He had smoothed his way back into the good graces of regular Republicans, without alienating his 1808 supporters, by taking advantage of the peace-making skill of his and Madison's old friend—turned Old Republican critic—John Taylor of Caroline. Taylor had been wary of Madison's ascendancy in 1806, when he urged Jefferson to run for a third term. In the 1808 election, though closer in thinking to Monroe, he had chosen party unity over ideological purity. Endorsing the addition of Monroe to the cabinet, Taylor anticipated that the new secretary of state would keep the nation out of war, while dissuading Madison from consolidating the powers of the federal government. He guessed wrong.

Monroe had accepted election as governor of Virginia in January 1811. It was a job he had performed a decade before, at the time of Jefferson's election; but he would have little time for it as the Smith catastrophe played out and Madison sought a ready replacement at State. Given Robert Smith's insult to Madison, it is altogether fitting that Monroe, as the incoming secretary of state, wrote to Jefferson of the president's offer: "The manner in which the proposition was made to me, was liberal and manly." This "manly" meant respectful, fair-minded, and morally self-assured. As he entered Madison's fractured cabinet in April, Monroe hoped he could fulfill the president's wish to see a more conciliatory spirit emanate from London.[58]

"Whiffling Jemmy"

It would not be easy. In November 1811 a new Congress convened. Eppes had lost his seat, and there was no Virginian in the House with whom Madison could as comfortably sit down and chat. John G. Jackson, Dolley Madison's brother-in-law, was defeated by a Federalist. Indeed, the Virginia delegation in Congress was, as a whole, a less impressive bunch than Madison had known at any previous time. Only a little more than half of the Eleventh Congress was returned in the Twelfth.

The most outspoken member of either branch of the national legislature in 1811–12 was Henry Clay. His mostly southern Republican cohort was soon to be known collectively as the War Hawks. Until recently a member of the Senate from Kentucky, the Virginia-born Clay had moved over to the House and was promptly elected Speaker. Despite prior national service and training in the law from George Wythe (who had trained Thomas Jefferson a generation earlier), Clay was not especially well known until this moment. But from 1811 until his death four decades later, he would remain at the very center of national life.[59]

This son of a Baptist preacher had "a genius for self-dramatization," as the historian Merrill D. Peterson has written of him. After leaving Virginia and settling in Lexington, Kentucky, Clay had distinguished himself as a criminal lawyer. There, in 1806, he successfully defended Aaron Burr against the U.S. attorney, a Federalist, who was hoping to prove that Burr aimed to sever the West from the Union. Arriving in Washington, Clay quickly acquired a reputation for dueling, cavorting, and gambling at cards—and predicting that America would have an easy time taking on the British military. He did not possess a military mindset, any more than Madison could be called a military adventurer; but both were not-so-secretly desirous of acquiring territory for the United States. While in the Senate, Clay had pushed for defiance of the Spanish and annexation of West Florida. He said he believed Madison was giving "proper energy" to the prospective acquisition of East Florida and would take a more aggressive stance with respect to Great Britain. Among his Federalist colleagues—though, of course, they opposed his policies—many called Clay well informed, allowing that he had assumed the Speaker's role with customary dignity. He was the man to lead the War Congress.[60]

And Madison? In midsummer, looking ahead a year, the anti-administration *Alexandria Gazette* resorted to doggerel verse:

> *Who will be the next President causes great doubt,*
> *As all parties agree whiffling Jemmy goes out.*

To whiffle was to waver. The *Gazette* proposed no Federalist names, nor likely Republican alternatives, for the first position. Its only requirement was that the next president not be "led by the nose" (whether, one presumes, by congressional War Hawks or by ex-President Jefferson), as Madison allegedly was.[61]

How much more forbearance would the United States have to exhibit, while England laughed at its feebleness? That question, in one form or another, made the rounds as Congress and the executive readied the populace for a war that was now more widely believed to be unavoidable. Though military preparations were all too few, the president was willing to force the issue if the Orders in Council were not rescinded by spring and neutral commerce given proper protection.

Madison had returned to Washington from Montpelier in October 1811, in order to present his third annual message to Congress. He called for a buildup of regular troops in anticipation of war. Despite U.S. efforts to achieve "all the mutual advantages of reestablished friendship and confidence," he said, the British had consistently upheld measures that bore "the character as well as the effect of war on lawful commerce." He appealed to the legislative branch to heed the facts and authorize war preparations: "With this evidence of hostile inflexibility in trampling on rights which no Independent Nation can relinquish, Congress will feel the duty of putting the United States into an armour, and an attitude demanded by the crisis, and corresponding with the national spirit and expectations."[62]

Madison's message of firmness belied the "unmanly" smear that had long followed and besmirched him. One who offered praise was Constitutional Convention colleague Elbridge Gerry of Cambridge, Massachusetts. Gerry was an Adams Federalist in the 1790s who became a Republican on the eve of the 1800 election. "I have read your message, with great attention & pleasure," he wrote now. "It is clear, candid, firm & dignified." Gerry told Madison not to worry too much about the "british subjects, traders & partizans" of Boston. They would make themselves scarce if war erupted.[63]

The current British minister in Washington, Sir Augustus John Foster, gave an inch when he came through with an agreement to make reparations for the *Chesapeake* incident of 1807. But for Madison it was too little too late. It took "one splinter out of our wounds," he wrote to John Quincy Adams. France had done precious little to satisfy U.S. requirements either, but there seemed to be a moral difference between the two situations—or perhaps, better put, a less unpleasant history.[64]

Canada again loomed large. In Indiana Territory, America's northwestern frontier, fighting broke out at the end of 1811. While the Shawnee leader Tecumseh was attempting to build a tribal confederation for defensive political purposes, his more bellicose brother Tenskwatawa believed it was possible to turn back the onslaught of white settlers. Tenskwatawa ran into the crusading William Henry Harrison, who achieved a resounding victory at the Battle of Tippecanoe. Word reached Washington that the British to the north were supplying the Indians and stopping at nothing— which ballooned into emotional cries comparable to the extreme symbolism of impressment.

President Madison was even more cautious in his approach to the Northwest than he was with respect to the Gulf Coast. But he was hopeful that war with England would cause Canada to fall into U.S. hands. Andrew Jackson, at this time still an untested Tennessee militia general, commanded an army of volunteers who were ready and willing to march north. He wrote to General Harrison, asking whether he needed a resupply of forces. As the year 1812 began, boundary matters were again on the table.[65]

Louisiana was shortly to become a state. Territorial governor Claiborne reported a month before Tippecanoe that the newspapers reaching him all said war was likely. "The pulse of the English Government seems high for War," he advanced in a letter to the president, "and instead of receiving reparations for the Many Wrongs offered our Country, we hear daily of further Aggressions." Nothing of a deadly nature was happening in Louisiana other than "that dreadful Scourge, the Yellow Fever," he said. But war fever was as prevalent, and building.[66]

Secretary of State Monroe was taking charge of negotiations with the British minister, fruitless though they appeared to be. And no American counterpart was left in London, once William Pinkney had returned home. Madison used Monroe as a liaison with Congress, improving relations with the House Foreign Affairs Committee, which allowed Madison to shape war measures that had a better chance of gaining majority approval. It did not take long before John Randolph began complaining about Monroe's war politicking in the House.[67]

Madison's annual message helped salvage his reputation. His bold language began the process of convincing reluctant Republicans that war was necessary, while solidifying his image as a man who was prepared to face military challenges. John Randolph still did what he could to derail war preparations, calling the Canadian invasion a "war of conquest" and declaring unequivocally: "Our people will not submit to being taxed for this war." Combining race-baiting rhetoric with his penchant for the colorful and the absurd, he raised the specter of slave rebellions if the southern states were left unprotected after their militias were dragged to the "deserts of Labrador." He ruminated aloud on what would happen if Frenchified Canadians, attracted to the same dangerous doctrines that had inspired the Haitian Revolution, should be incorporated into the "Anglo-Saxon" United States.

Randolph's scare tactics did not work. His oratorical skills could not drown out the chorus that now backed the president. British aggression had pushed the country to the "brink of a second revolution, as important as the first," said Congressman Richard Mentor Johnson of Kentucky, praising Madison's message for its "manly and bold attitude of war." If Congress failed to follow through, he went on, it might as well "annul the Declaration of Independence" and acknowledge the states, "devoted colonies."[68]

The War Hawks used Madison's tough talk to good advantage. Madison's enemies could no longer mock him as a "submission" man. This enabled his congressional supporters to shift the conversation away from ridicule of Madison's weakness and toward the more positive metaphor of the president as "oracle" of a second War for Independence. In mid-December 1811, by overwhelming majorities, the House passed resolutions fashioned by its Foreign Affairs Committee that increased the regular army, called out fifty thousand volunteers, outfitted the navy, notified the militia, and armed merchant ships.

Henry Clay was so pleased with the message that he sent Madison a bottle of Maderia the next day. Outside Washington the message was as warmly received. A regiment of the Virginia militia in Lexington prepared its own address to the president, which praised him for his "laudable zeal & devotion" and then launched into militaristic flights of fancy: "Our swords leap flaming from their scabbards and cannot be returned appeased." Repeating Madison's phrase, "We have 'put on the armour,' " they promised to fight "on the shores of the Atlantic or in the wilderness of Canada," determined, they said, to relive the glory of Bunker Hill and Saratoga.[69]

While President Madison generally receives little credit either for his thinking or for his conduct in this time of high tension, his private secretary's 1856 retrospective presents evidence of a different side of the war president. According to Edward Coles, Madison was "less rampant" than the "noisy politicians" in advance of the war; and later, in the midst of hostilities, he was "less crouching under difficulties" than these same individuals. As we have seen in other contexts, Madison was dogged and relentless but never hasty. He used war fever to political advantage.[70]

"Take DeWitt Clinton"

As Madison and Monroe were repairing their relationship, Jefferson and John Adams succeeded in repairing theirs as well. The same Edward Coles was on a tour of New England when he paid a visit to the Adams household in Braintree, Massachusetts. The subject of politics came up, as it naturally would, and Coles heard Adams remark on the uncomfortable transition of power in 1801. As their conversation proceeded, Coles made it clear that Jefferson (who was also his Albemarle neighbor) had only kind things to say about Adams. As Coles subsequently explained, Adams became effusive: "I always loved Jefferson, and still love him."

Benjamin Rush, the good friend and regular correspondent of both ex-presidents, had been trying to bring the two aging Revolutionaries back together for some time—at least through the mails, since travel was impossible for both. Rush had seen the abortive exchange of letters of 1804, between Jefferson and Abigail Adams, that were triggered by the death of Maria Jefferson Eppes: if Coles had gotten the ball rolling, Rush refused to drop the ball and persisted in coaxing the principals. On December 5, 1811, after Coles had spoken with him, Jefferson wrote to Rush, confirming the conversation as Coles had repeated it to him. Without waiting, Rush wrote to Adams, quoting back Coles's recording of Adams's "I always loved Jefferson" just as Jefferson had given it to him. Nothing, it seems, was left to chance.[71]

On January 1, 1812, Adams made the next move, writing to Jefferson directly: "I wish you Sir many happy New Years"; and Jefferson answered him by retrieving memories of 1776, "recollections very dear to my mind." Momentous events had brought them to Philadelphia at the same time, all of which constituted a bond that ought not to be broken. By anchoring their destinies to the same cause, Jefferson fashioned Adams and himself as metaphorical mariners on the ocean of life: "We rode through the storm with heart and hand, and made a happy port." Still cautious about reopening political wounds as he brought history forward, the Virginian pretended to be more remote from issues of national power than he actually was, claiming: "I have given up newspapers in exchange for Tacitus and Thucydides." At least the second part was true.[72]

Jefferson's home life was never as relaxing as he wished, or claimed. Suffering from rheumatic joints, his hip ached terribly when he walked. His indebtedness continued, though he claimed he was on the path to extinguishing all financial obligations. In 1812 he was convinced that his annual income from tobacco and wheat production in Bedford County was considerable enough to get him out from under. He was wrong. Adding to the imperfection of daily life, Jefferson's slave Jame Hubbard, a habitual runaway, fled Monticello, and when he was found and returned, Jefferson ordered him flogged and jailed. Not always a pretty picture, the Virginia idyll.

More was happening to divert Jefferson from his Tacitus and Thucydides. After he learned that Edward Livingston's case against him over disposition of the batture had been dismissed, he prepared a lawyerly pamphlet on the subject, constituting his defense. When it went to the printer, he made a list of seventy-seven names, in addition to the members of Congress, to whom it was sent. The list took in the obvious, such as the president and his cabinet, Governor Claiborne, and other governors, judges, and national figures; it included some who might have been on the other side: Edward's brother Robert Livingston, the critical William Duane, and John Wickham, one of Burr's prominent defense attorneys. The pamphlet went out as well to one present and one former son-in-law, several nephews, and other family members. The one female on the list was Madison's and Jefferson's Philadelphia landlady, Eliza House Trist, so often in the midst of political talk, but whose use of the turgid treatise on property law is harder to gauge.[73]

One (unstated) reason for Jefferson to have committed himself to the batture pamphlet is that he wished to place his legal erudition before Chief Justice John Marshall. He believed that Livingston had taken up his suit in the hope that Marshall would preside in the case and intercede on his behalf. So often goaded by thoughts of his enemies' maneuverings, Jefferson griped to Madison that the chief justice was prone to "reconcile law to his personal biases." He was no doubt thinking of both *Marbury v. Madison* and the Burr trial.

As the batture matter simmered, Jefferson found cause to rebuke Marshall for his "twistifications" of the law. He badly wanted Madison to give Marshall competition by appointing a strong Republican to the Court. Jefferson's attorney general, Levi Lincoln, turned down the offer, and so did another New Englander, John Quincy Adams—the appeal to whom showed President Madison's predisposition to go outside Jefferson's narrowly conceived list of acceptable justices. In the end Madison chose Joseph Story, who was possibly the last person Jefferson wanted to see on the High Court. He had specifically warned Madison about Story, calling him an outright "Tory" and no friend to the embargo. While the latter was true, Story, a Harvard graduate, had defended Jefferson in 1801 from the most hostile corner of New England.[74]

The war on John Marshall was not going Jefferson's way. Nor was the war-in-waiting. In his correspondence of 1812, he stepped up his harangues about English arrogance, surmising that problems in Congress were preventing an early declaration of war: "That a body containing 100.

lawyers in it, should direct the measures of war, is, I fear, impossible," he told Madison in February. A month later, he related the anxious sentiment that permeated central Virginia: "Every body in this quarter expects a declarance of war as soon as the season will permit the entrance of militia into Canada." Madison replied to him that the decision for war or peace was in the hands of the British, who, he thought, "prefer war with us, to a repeal of their Orders in Council. We have nothing left therefore but to make ready for it." In the final analysis, Madison judged that in ignoring the rights of neutrals Britain stood ready to "recolonize" America's commerce and probably stood in the way of America's continental ambitions as well. Westerners, meanwhile, wanted Indians cleared out, and they figured an invasion of Canada would achieve that object. To war-bent Americans, liberty, at this moment, meant the ability to spread in all directions without having to face domestic resistance or foreign pressure. Madison was with the hawks.[75]

Not content to wait for events to take their course, he upped the ante in March when he made a Jefferson-like move, declaring the existence of a disunionist plot, hatched by New England Federalists with British connivance. An Irishman named John Henry, who had lived in America for some years before migrating to Montreal, had been hired in 1808 by the governor of Lower Canada to discover whether disgruntled Yankees, angered by the embargo, might be interested in secession. When he could not get the kind of money he felt he deserved for his services, Henry decided to sell his correspondence to the United States. Somehow he convinced the Madison administration to pay him the incredible sum of $50,000, which reportedly drained the entire fund set aside for secret services.

Madison wrote to Jefferson that the documents obtained gave "formal proof, of the cooperation between the Eastern Junto [of Federalists] and the British Cabinet." He sent the packet of materials to Congress, but John Henry's papers turned out to contain no smoking gun, no names of Federalists willing to betray the Union. Madison turned next to New Jersey Federalist Jonathan Dayton, an old friend of Aaron Burr's, convinced that Dayton was just disaffected enough from his party to reveal the names of secessionists. But Dayton had nothing to say, and Madison lost ground. The Federalists accused the administration of using the Henry incident as an "electioneering trick" to drum up Republican support in New England.

And perhaps it was. Monroe described these events to the French minister as "a last means of exciting the nation and Congress" to get on with the inevitable. The president hoped that by hinting at treason he would silence

New England; and he probably expected, too, that news of the intrigue with Henry would force London's ministers to act with dispatch in resolving its dispute with the Madison administration. But once Henry broadcast how much he was paid, Madison suddenly looked foolish, if not crooked. Combined with the abortive attempt of George Mathews to wrest East Florida from the British-allied Spanish (called off by Madison), the president's position was suddenly dubious, even in the South.[76]

Then again, Madison may have thought he had a very good reason to play up the Henry affair. A threat of disunion—an espionage caper originating in Canada, where many Loyalists had lived since the Revolution— would be quite enough to justify a northern invasion. This, plus British-inspired Indian attacks in the West, and Canada would no longer be a passive country. With a firm push north, the border would dissolve.

On June 1, 1812, Madison came forward with a definitive list of unredressed grievances against Great Britain. These included impressment, the Orders in Council, and incitement of Indians in the Northwest. The House Foreign Affairs Committee met and agreed that London's hypocrisies could no longer be tolerated. The long period of anxious anticipation ended, as both houses of Congress voted for war. The tally was 79 to 49 in the House, 19 to 13 in the Senate (coming on June 17, and only after extended debate).

Madison sent Jefferson a copy of the war declaration. Without hesitation, Jefferson conveyed his overall strategy for success. "To continue the war popular two things are necessary mainly: 1. to stop Indian barbarities. The conquest of Canada will do this. 2. to furnish markets for our produce." As to the first, he did not have to elaborate, because Madison and he were equally eager to see if, in fact, the Canadians could be prodded to rise up against the empire. But on the matter of maintaining markets for U.S. production, Jefferson went into greater detail. It did not concern him whether U.S. carriers, neutral vessels, or even enemy ships under neutral flags were under sail, just so long as America's commerce remained healthy. The one "mortifying" possibility, which he knew would cause farmers to turn against the war, was for their surplus wheat, meant for export, to rot in their barns.[77]

It was hard to fight a war when the excitement was short-lived. Few Americans were willing to make significant sacrifices over maritime rights alone. Embargo had made that clear. And if one region of the country suffered a disproportionate burden, the war effort would certainly suffer. Madison and Jefferson both knew this. John Marshall exposed underlying tensions when he wrote in early 1812: "There would be a great majority for war if it could certainly be carried on without money." Bellicose words cost Virginians nothing, a Norfolk newspaper observed, but many cared more for their pocketbooks than for "the liberty of which they so much boast."

Jefferson's strategy was to keep the South and West happy. He was willing to concede that the Northeast was a lost cause. Madison saw things differently, by necessity. Regulars and volunteers from New England would be needed for the Canadian invasion, and he prayed that "the zeal of the S. & W. could be imparted to that region." He assessed the situation in a letter to a friend in Massachusetts: the war would be "short and successful," he said guardedly, if the enemy could be convinced that it was fighting "the whole and not a part of the nation."[78]

The underlying theme in Madison's war message to Congress was that England's refusal to treat the United States as an independent nation challenged the nation to demonstrate its honor and self-worth. Seeing America as a rival, kidnapping its sailor-citizens, inciting "Savages" to attack women and children, stealing "the products of our soil and industry," Great Britain would bully and intimidate for as long as the United States allowed the "spectacle of insults and indignities" to continue. As an individual, Madison, of course, had never even come close to engaging in a duel. But he understood the emotive force of this language. War Hawks in Congress had beaten their drums with such overwrought phrases as "the honor of a nation is its life" and to "abandon it is to commit political suicide." They had compared America to a young man, kicked and cuffed, or robbed and stabbed, whose one recourse was to respond with force. Americans as a group had endured "mental debasement," a prolonged state of humiliation. "To step one step further without showing that spirit of resentment becoming freemen," as one congressman contended, "would but acknowledge ourselves unworthy of self-government." The president and Congress had transformed the war into a coming-of-age story, a metaphorical battle for manly vindication.[79]

Reading much about neutral rights, Federalists had no idea that Jefferson was writing to Madison about improvements to the farm-based economy if the war should go as well as he expected. The voice of antiwar New England put forward a different logic: Madison was using "dark, ambiguous, and unintelligible" language to fabricate a threat of invasion where there was none. How could a "Quixotic expedition" into Canada, a foreign country, by American fighters, be called self-defense, or "proof that America was in danger"? Madison was susceptible to the same charge he had leveled at John Adams in 1798, when criticizing "hot-headed proceedings" in advance of the Quasi-War with France.

The Federalists experienced a different reality. In 1812 they believed that Britain was willing to modify its stand on impressment. The great stumbling block, the Orders in Council, was finally being repealed. This being the case, the "rights" the president was poised to go to war over were "barren and useless" rationalizations, not real rights. The rejected Monroe-Pinkney Treaty could have achieved a reasonable settlement of Anglo-American conflict in 1807—Monroe had certainly thought so. He was cognizant of the unpreparedness of the U.S. military and sensitive to the vulnerability of U.S. coastal cities. Monroe, now a key member of Madison's cabinet, had to know that the War of 1812 was pure folly.

But the problem went deeper. Madison was calling state militias into service, a move the Federalists judged to be unconstitutional under existing circumstances. They urged the states to resist the president's instructions. Several New England governors did just that, refusing to hand over their militia to federal control—especially for a far-flung campaign into Canada. State sovereignty, the old Republican calling card, was now the Federalist mantra. As unlikely as it seemed, given his past behavior, Madison was, to his northern opponents, the architect of a "consolidation" of the military power of the country.[80]

Southern Federalists saw the irrationality of the president's course with the same clarity. Waging war meant increasing the national debt that Gallatin was working so hard to retire. It also meant raising taxes on commerce, and Republicans were supposed to be staunchly opposed to taxes. The War Hawks seemed oddly unconcerned about these things. From Virginia to Georgia, Federalist newspapers pointed out that the president's policy was upside down: Anglo-American trade was nearly ten times the volume of Franco-American trade, and worth protecting. U.S. interests would be served in allowing England to concentrate fully on defeating Napoleon, the real tyrant and only real threat in the long run.

For Federalists, north and south, then, the Republican majority was temporarily out of its senses and trapped in an uncompromising position. Former North Carolina governor William Richardson Davie, a Revolutionary War hero, saw an opportunity in the midst of upheaval. "We must touch an extreme point of public wretchedness," he wrote, "before the people could be set right." If enough Americans were killed in the war, the Federalists would be voted back into power. This is where politics stood.[81]

From the start, Vice President George Clinton had played no role whatsoever in the Madison administration. When Jefferson wrote of his own impairments to Benjamin Rush, he ventured into the subject of human nature and the aging mind, and while on the subject he offered a medical opinion of Clinton, his own former vice president: "Our old revolutionary friend, Clinton, for example, who was a hero, but never a man of mind... tells eternally the stories of his younger days, to prove his memory. As if memory and reason were the same faculty, nothing betrays imbecility so much as the being insensible of it." George Clinton's value to Madison, as to Jefferson, was his "imbecility."[82]

His nephew, New York mayor DeWitt Clinton, was quite a different story. A patron of the arts, surly, boastful, yet widely respected for his intellect, this Clinton was a crafty politician. In 1812, at the age of forty-three, he believed his time had come. Though a Republican, he thought he could defeat Madison by forging a coalition with New England Federalism and launched his campaign when Madison opted for war.

It did not take long for word to spread. New Englander Henry Dearborn, who had been Jefferson's secretary of war, informed the ex-president in March that the "Clinton party" was stopping at nothing to defeat Madison. Then in April 1812 George Clinton died, still holding office, and more than symbolically passed the torch to the next generation. In what might be considered bad taste, the Madisons hosted a party at the President's House just two days after the vice president's funeral.

DeWitt Clinton's core constituency was the Republicans (and not only New Yorkers) in Congress who opposed going to war with England. They would orchestrate his candidacy just as they had tried four years earlier to substitute his uncle for Madison at the top of the Republican ticket. "If a man of the Washington school cannot be brought forward with any success, take DeWitt Clinton," the *Trenton Federalist* urged in August. "Take any sensible and honest American, not a Virginian of the present ruling party, and we shall do better."

Federalists had tried a similar kind of rationalization in backing "honest" Monroe over the supposedly less reasonable Madison in 1808. It had not worked. But this time New Jersey Federalists succeeded in the same way that Aaron Burr had in 1800, taking their activism to the elections for seats in the state legislature, where presidential electors were chosen. Clinton forces not only positioned themselves to deliver the state to their candidate; they also gerrymandered New Jersey so as to deprive the state of a Republican majority in the House of Representatives. Madison acknowledged to Jefferson that he understood the contest with DeWitt Clinton as a referendum on the war. He called this "the Experimentum crusis," or critical experiment, upon which the fate of his administration would hinge. Clinton proved a formidable opponent. Although in the general election he did not pick up any states south of New Jersey, he did win in seven.[83]

The gerrymandering phenomenon may not have been the invention of Elbridge Gerry, precisely, but it was he whose name became most closely associated with the maneuver. The same Elbridge Gerry was now to provide the North-South balance traditionally sought in the executive, when he agreed to serve as Madison's second-term vice president. As old John Adams wrote to Madison in May 1812, Gerry remained "one of the firmest pillars of that system which alone can save this Country from disgrace and ruin." Recently defeated as he sought reelection as his state's governor, Gerry was sixty-eight years old and unmistakably meant to serve as an unambitious caretaker vice president under an embattled president who wished to be on hand to see the war through.[84]

"This Most Disgraceful Event May Produce Good"

The lack of self-censorship in the Madison-Jefferson correspondence is more apparent at this juncture than at almost any other time. Jefferson repeatedly and optimistically urged war. Madison was less cheerful about the subject but was unrestrained in expressing anxiety about all he had unleashed.

Among his uppermost concerns was New England's all-too-obvious resistance, which led Madison to fear that not many men would volunteer for the military. Before there were even battles to report on, he wrote Jefferson that "seditious opposition" in Massachusetts and Connecticut, with "intrigues elsewhere insidiously cooperating with it," had "so clogged the wheels of the war that I fear the campaign will not accomplish the object of it." With loose language, Jefferson called for different measures in different parts of the country: "A barrel of tar to each state South of the Potomac will keep all in order," he ventured in August. "To the North they will give you more trouble. You may have to apply the rougher drastics of . . . hemp and confiscation"—by which he meant the hangman's noose and the confiscation of property. This marvelous example of Jefferson's gallows humor is a clear sign of the unguarded style he brought to his communications with Madison. His untied tongue was meant to encourage firmness, rather than literally to prescribe retaliation. He knew he could speak maliciously because he knew that Madison, and not he, was now in charge of strategy. Meanwhile the antiwar activist John Randolph found himself the target of physical threats; one of Madison's Virginia correspondents wrote unsympathetically that Randolph should be struck down, if not by "the vengeance of heaven" then by the "the hand of his country."[85]

A series of riots broke out in Baltimore between June and August after a pro-war mob destroyed the print shop of a Federalist newspaper, the *Federal Republican*. The Virginian Henry ("Light-Horse Harry") Lee was the editor's friend and happened to be at the scene. The noted general and memorable eulogist of George Washington had recently emerged from prison, where he had been incarcerated for debt after poorly juggling his land investments. As his world was crumbling, Lee had asked his old friend Madison to assign him to a consular post in the Caribbean, so that he could keep the law from his door. Madison did nothing. While the used-up general sat in prison and paid off his debt to society, his hatred for Jefferson and the embargo caused him to seethe. It was Jefferson's fate to be the focus of prying eyes and negative attention, and Madison's better fortune to escape the harshest criticism.

Henry Lee appeared in bellicose Baltimore in the summer of 1812, for the ostensible purpose of selling his memoir of the Revolution, which he had written in prison and which revisited the charge that Governor Jefferson had failed Virginia. As a guest in the house of Alexander Contee Hanson, the *Federal Republican*'s editor, Lee sought to restrain those present from provoking the rock-throwing miscreants who clamored outside. But as the mix of boys, middle-class men, immigrant laborers, and others invaded the house, Lee defied them and was badly beaten on the head and face as a result of his courageous stand. When the militia was called out, its members decided they would not risk themselves to protect Federalists; so they stood by the pro-war mob and evinced little sympathy for the victims—or the free press. With such activity occurring, Secretary of State Monroe warned Madison that a sedition law of some kind might be needed to avert an escalation of violence. Madison was unmoved. He would not repeat the missteps of President John Adams by sacrificing civil liberties, even in a time of war.[86]

Two months after Congress had declared that war, the president still had no inkling of the enemy's reaction. "We have had no information from England since the war was known there, or even, seriously suspected, by the public," he wrote. As a result, he was having a hard time justifying any offensive. In fact, Lieutenant General Sir George Prevost, the man in charge of Canada's defense, learned in May that no troops would be sent from England for the foreseeable future. Henry Dearborn, who had developed the basic three-prong strategy—committing forces to the theaters of Detroit, Niagara, and Montreal—was put in charge of the planned assault on Montreal from northern New York State. He received and accepted a proposal from Prevost to cease hostilities. Madison rejected it and ordered Dearborn to prepare a northern invasion as soon as possible. He wanted Canada.[87]

Committed to the cause, former president Jefferson had no choice but to sit on the sidelines. He read, more than he wrote, on the subject. Enlistee Isaac Coles updated him from Buffalo, complaining that he and his fellow soldiers were getting mixed messages: either they were to hunker down in the woods without adequate supplies or launch an invasion of Canada. Coles was less than sanguine. "In truth," he wrote, "the regulars here ... are without discipline & could by no means meet an equal number of British troops—You can form no conception of the irregularity and disorder that exist in every branch of the service—every one prates & no one acts."

Initial news from the Detroit frontier was disappointing. Michigan territorial governor William Hull, a Jefferson appointee and a colonel in the American Revolution, was given responsibility for the Northwest campaign. At the first sign of trouble, he froze, exposing his men to British-led Indian attacks. Monroe reported to Jefferson that he regarded Hull as "weak, indecisive, and pusilanimous," but concluded: "This most disgraceful event may produce good. It will rouse the nation. We must efface the stain before we make peace, & that may give us Canada."

Jefferson, so long mocked by the Federalists for his alleged cowardice as a Revolutionary War governor, saw events much as Monroe did. In the case of Hull, Jefferson displayed a cruel streak. "The seeing whether our untried Generals will stand proof is a very dear operation," he observed to Madison in November. "We can tell by his plumage whether a cock is dunghill or game. But with us cowardice and courage wear the same plume." Though he looked the part, Hull had proved to be "dunghill." He would subsequently be tried and convicted, and his life spared only after his service in the Revolution was recalled. Whereas Jefferson preferred to have him shot "for cowardice and treachery," Madison was willing to pardon him.[88]

The fiasco in the Northwest sent Madison's administration into a tailspin. Monroe insisted that the government should not accept blame for what had happened, and he presented Madison with a better solution: send him out west. Seeing an opportunity to shine, Monroe proposed to leave

Washington, take charge of the army Hull had mismanaged, and undertake decisive action to, in Monroe's words, "support the cause of free government." Monroe was worried that his own reputation would suffer if the war did not go well. In his mind, military heroics would win him the presidency.

Richard Rush, son of Dr. Benjamin Rush of Philadelphia, was another of Madison's confidants at this time, and his future attorney general. He endorsed Monroe's plan and proposed bringing Jefferson out of retirement to fill the empty slot in the cabinet if Monroe were to go west. Extolling the "illustrious" and "venerable" Jefferson, Rush assured Madison that if he were to fill the position of secretary of state, "millions" would rejoice, and the administration would regain the confidence of the country. Rush informed Madison that the prominent Pennsylvania Republican Alexander James Dallas agreed with him that "the return of Mr. Jefferson to the Cabinet" was a perfect answer to the current malaise; while reluctant to see Monroe leave the president's immediate circle, Dallas was confident that everything would work out. To Madison's chief supporters, once Jefferson's celebrity power was added to the administration, the public relations nightmare of Hull's defeat would be erased from the national memory.

At first Madison backed the Monroe-Rush-Dallas plan, but then he had second thoughts: recalling Jefferson could easily be seen as a sign of desperation and weakness. At this crucial juncture in his presidency, he was unwilling to hand over the spotlight to either Monroe or Jefferson. He would press on for as long as possible without making any major personnel changes.[89]

Bad news continued to roll in. Hull's defeat was followed by two more failed campaigns into Canada. The first was a crossing of troops from New York, over the Niagara River. The commander in this instance was Major General Stephen Rensselaer, a prominent Federalist with no prior military experience. Nearly 950 Americans were captured. Then Henry Dearborn, Jefferson's secretary of war over his two terms, led a feeble attempt to take Montreal. Over sixty and rather portly, the lackluster general did not inspire confidence.

Many Americans had come to believe that simply by marching across the border, Canada would be won. These early defeats proved otherwise. The War Hawks, it had turned out, were all talk. U.S. forces had poor leadership at every level. Dearborn's successor as secretary of war, William Eustis of Massachusetts, had witnessed battle up close; he was on the scene at the dramatic and bloody Battle of Bunker Hill in 1775. But he was a marked man now, soon to become the sacrificial lamb for the botched invasion of Canada. Rumors circulated that either James Monroe or John Armstrong should replace him.

The administration's only reprieve came from the navy. Impressive victories at sea breathed life back into the deflated American public. The USS *Constitution,* under the command of Isaac Hull, nephew of the man who had disgraced his country in Michigan, defeated a British warship at close range 750 miles east of Boston. President Madison was rowed out to a ship anchored on the Potomac, where a celebration of the event was held before a merry crowd. Dolley Madison did her part during a second Washington gala that fall, commemorating Stephen Decatur's victory over a British frigate east of the Canary Islands. He brought the enemy vessel home as a prize, and a navy lieutenant laid its flag at the feet of the first lady.[90]

Amid his heavy concerns, the president found time to read and enjoy a farce on the coming of the war, which he recommended to Jefferson. Though Madison mistook *The Diverting History of John Bull and Brother Jonathan* as the work of Washington Irving, its actual author, James Kirke Paulding, was Irving's lifelong friend, a fellow New Yorker, and himself a man of many talents. In time Paulding would come to work for President Madison, be charmed by him, visit Montpelier, and contemplate writing his biography.

The *Diverting History* was aptly titled. It found its mark by reducing global rivalry to family bickering. John Bull was the personification of England, and Brother Jonathan the predecessor of Uncle Sam. Paulding's parable converted the Atlantic Ocean into a millpond and explained the American Revolution in comic miniature: "Squire Bull sent Jonathan to settle new lands," only to be "handsomely rib-roasted [while] attempting to pick Jonathan's pocket." France was transcribed as "Frogmore," and when John Bull tried to pick Jonathan's pocket again, Jonathan penned him a professedly "respectful" letter: "Honoured Father, 'Sblood, wha d'ye mean, you bacon faced son of a horned cow, by telling me I shant visit Beau Napperty [Napoleon] when I please!"

As Madison gave Jefferson his copy of Paulding's satire, he told him what to expect. "It sinks occasionally into low and local phrases, and some time forgets Allegorical character; But is in general good painting on substantial canvas." While Madison critiqued Paulding's "low and local" provincialism, we need to underscore that firsthand reports also attribute a taste for low humor and ribaldry to the fourth president—a style not associated with the third at any time.[91]

Having defended Jefferson's political reputation on the floor of the House, Speaker Henry Clay now gave his full support to the Madison administration. Over the months leading up to the declaration of war, and in the months after, Clay and Madison became comfortable in each other's company. Madison opened his mouth more after he had wine at dinner, which may also have helped to bring the two closer. Privately, Clay expressed admiration for Madison's mind; but in December 1812 he confided to Caesar Rodney, who had resigned as attorney general a year before: "Mr. Madison is wholly unfit for the storms of war." Others had the same impression of him, no matter how aggressive a posture he took toward Great Britain.[92]

The president had not been blamed for Hull's failure in the Northwest. But unless he could find able generals, James Madison would be unable to escape condemnation as new charges of incompetence surfaced.

CHAPTER FOURTEEN

Road Out of War
1813–1816

We have hardly enough money to last till the end of the month.

—ALBERT GALLATIN TO MADISON, MARCH 5, 1813

*I sincerely congratulate you on the peace, and more especially on
the éclat with which the war was closed.*

—JEFFERSON TO MADISON, MARCH 23, 1815

THE FEDERALISTS HUNKERED DOWN AND PREPARED THEMSELVES for a second term. Playing off the royal Stuarts of seventeenth-century England, they found a way to make a mockery out of America's "King James," the democratic monarch. A Hartford, Connecticut, paper provided the verse, which was reprinted across two columns of the *Federal Republican*—published, ever since its editor was run out of Baltimore, just down the road from the President's House, in Georgetown.

The *Federal Republican* was the opposition's answer to the fawning paper of the Madison court, the *National Intelligencer*. With the president's reelection, its Federalist poet noted that Madison's natural constituency was thriving:

> *Ye vagabonds of every land,*
> *Cut-throats and knaves—a patriot band—*
> *Ye demagogues lift up your voice—*
> *Mobs and banditti—all rejoice!*

Associated with the riff-raff of society, Madison was now being subjected to the same treatment as his predecessor had been, the difference
being that Madison was seen not as the originator of bad policy so much as
a stand-in for others. Forced into an unenviable position by events, he was
a willing dupe of the ambitious and the unrestrained. As the Federalists
saw things, the war was not going as planned, and the president could not
figure out what to do next:

> *Now deep despair, and dire disgrace,*
> *Commingle in King James's face.*
> *The war was solely undertaken,*
> *In hopes to save his royal bacon.*[1]

The Madison administration needed a more forward posture. One of
the central players in national politics at this time was the Pennsylvania-
born New Yorker John Armstrong. A Princetonian before the Revolution
and a staff officer to General Horatio Gates at the Battle of Saratoga, he became connected to one of the most powerful families of New York State
when he married the sister of Edward and Robert Livingston. He succeeded
the latter of his brothers-in-law as U.S. minister to France, serving from
1804 to 1810.

Historians have called Armstrong moody, self-protective, and ambitious—adjectives that probably describe most of the political characters of
the Revolutionary generation. His letters to Madison, and especially to Jefferson, are finely crafted and more than just courteous. He could use
strong words at times and had a habit of fault-finding, which eventually
caught up with him. The Virginians would never quite trust his motives.

Like Speaker of the House Henry Clay, Armstrong seems to have had
doubts about Madison's fitness as a wartime president. One of his more
caustic comments, though it was not aimed at Madison directly, came in a
private letter of 1811. "We are a nation of quakers," he noted, "without either their morals or their motives." Friendly with the Smith brothers of
Maryland, Armstrong was thought a potential troublemaker during the
lead-up to war, opposing, as he did, a continuation of the Virginia Dynasty.
For this reason, Madison's choice of Monroe as secretary of state did not
please him. Yet in a meaningful turnabout, Armstrong pointedly criticized
the divisive strategy of DeWitt Clinton in 1812, seeing the importance of a
unity government in time of war. His reward was an appointment as
brigadier general and commander of forces in New York City.

As 1813 began, practical solutions took precedence over partisan plans. Although Treasury Secretary Gallatin had nothing close to a warm relationship with Armstrong, his strong recommendation helped convince the president that the high-handed general could help the war effort. The administration's strategy involved taking the war to Montreal through New York State. This required a secretary of war with a strong political base there—at the moment there were only 20,000 men in the entire American army, a mere 2,400 of whom were stationed in this theater. So in January 1813, and despite the fact that he was reckoned a likely presidential contender in 1816, General John Armstrong was named secretary of war.[2]

Secretary Eustis had resigned without complaint several weeks earlier. Even so, the transition was not smooth. At Madison's request, Monroe had stepped in to fill the vacuum; but Monroe, too, presented problems because he had been giving Madison conflicting signals as to his own path to the presidency. Did he want the War Department? A battlefield appointment? Or to remain at State? So the choice of Armstrong may have reflected Madison's annoyance with Monroe. For in spite of Armstrong's flaws, Madison convinced himself that he could regulate the man's "objectionable peculiarities," as he later put it, with a deft combination of conciliation and control. He was conscious that Armstrong was capable of reining in Monroe and unlikely to tolerate his interference. And that is precisely what happened.

In February 1813, when Armstrong took up his post, he quashed Monroe's plan to head the army in the Northwest by persuading the president that in making Monroe a lieutenant general and outranking all others, he would stir resentment in the officer corps. To keep the peace, Armstrong recommended that Monroe settle for the rank of brigadier general. Had he agreed, he would have been subordinate to the less-than-competent Dearborn.

Predictably, Monroe was outraged. To add insult to insult, he next discovered that Armstrong intended to head the new Canada campaign himself, prompting an emotion-charged letter to Madison in which Monroe accused Armstrong of fusing the roles of commander of the army and secretary of war and usurping the duties of the commander in chief. Madison was unmoved; he would uphold the principle of checks and balances within his cabinet, much as George Washington had done when the Hamilton-Jefferson feud first reached his desk.[3]

Accusations against Monroe came from several places. Federalist congressman Josiah Quincy of Massachusetts alleged that Monroe was at the center of the cabinet's machinations to prolong the war. Seeking popularity as a war leader, he claimed, the secretary of state was laying the groundwork for something potentially more dangerous than a Monroe presidency—a military dictatorship. Quincy was right about one thing: Monroe had put forward an audacious proposal to Congress, to raise an army of an unheard-of size, 55,000 troops, which he apparently expected to command. Gallatin and Congress trimmed down the proposal, and Monroe reluctantly went along. Ridiculed by Quincy as "James the Second" and chastised for his vanity, Monroe retreated from the spotlight, at least momentarily. Still, the "deadly feud," as John Randolph described the Armstrong-Monroe competition, came to consume both men. Overlapping ambitions bred contempt, as both thought they could step over the unmartial Madison on the way to the presidency.[4]

Quincy's scornful speech in Congress ignited a second scandal. Calling those New Englanders who sought patronage from the president "reptiles," he suggested that they had left "slime" in the drawing room of the executive mansion. Several congressmen were appalled by the remark; one of these exploded, calling Quincy "filthy." It was obvious to them (though not to a modern audience) that their colleague's insinuation was aimed at Dolley Madison. At her weekly Wednesday drawing room gathering, young and old alike attended, all looking for favors as well as a good time. What Quincy was doing was joining a biblical metaphor to libertine fiction. Snakes oozing slime called up the history of European palace intrigues, where sexual liaisons were common. "Queen" Dolley was the Eve-like seductress, turning the President's House into a harem.[5]

Such innuendo did not stop there. Alexander Contee Hanson, the Federalist editor whose establishment had come under attack in the Baltimore riots, was now a member of Congress. He showed little fear and no shame as he took up Quincy's outrageous theme in his Georgetown-based newspaper. Hanson ran what purported to be an advertisement for a forthcoming book written by Madison's new attorney general (and Monroe's former diplomatic partner) William Pinkney. It was a work said to have been funded by his "illustrious patroness," the first lady. One of the imaginary chapters publicized the concept, *"L'Amour et la fume ne peuvent se cacher"* (Love and smoke cannot be concealed), constituting a defense of polygamy and infidelity.

Was Hanson's *Federal Republican* accusing Mrs. Madison of having an affair with Pinkney? It seems quite likely. The elegant Marylander was a favorite among the ladies, who filled the courtroom to hear his colorful orations. Dolley was one of his admirers and attended court sessions with her retinue of family and friends. Hanson dropped a strong hint in his column, one that his classically trained readers would have easily recognized: he identified Dolley as "Corinna," the Roman poet Ovid's famous married mistress.[6]

Pinkney lasted only one more year in Madison's cabinet. He was forced to resign after the House passed a law requiring cabinet members to live in Washington. It was a law written for him. With a flourishing law practice in Baltimore and Annapolis, he had no desire to move. Though considered one of the most talented lawyers in the nation, the House had little trouble passing this dubious piece of legislation, suggesting that Pinkney's scandalous reputation—Hanson charged him with introducing the ways of "Modern Sodom" into a "chaste republic"—may have caught up with him. Pinkney would be succeeded, in 1814, by the reliable Richard Rush.[7]

Madison made one more change in his cabinet. Secretary of the Navy Paul Hamilton, like Pinkney, had become the focus of damning rumors. Washington was as yet a small town with few secrets, and all could see that Hamilton was an alcoholic who fell asleep at his desk and made a spectacle of himself at social events. The navy had been the only branch of the U.S. armed forces to perform admirably, but Hamilton had little to do with it. He begged Madison to keep him, desperately needing the income; but Madison forced him out, assuming that Congress would withhold funds to a department headed by an embarrassing drunk.

Madison offered the Navy Department to William Jones, whom Jefferson, in 1801, had tried unsuccessfully to recruit for the same office. A Pennsylvania merchant and former sea captain, Jones had been involved in the opium trade in southern China as recently as 1805. A man of pronounced wit and strong connections to the Pennsylvania Republicans, he promised to end the chaos in his department. Jones understood that the navy had to play a bigger role in the war, and he resolved to enlarge it by encouraging more privateers to harass British ships. After Hull's devastating defeat, Madison had concluded that "ascendancy over those waters" was essential to any future Canadian campaign. Under Jones's watch, a major program got under way to build warships on both Lake Ontario and Lake Erie.[8]

Madison was growing more daring. When he called for an enlarged navy and praised the crews of the victorious American ships for their gallant reprisals, he defended the war as one of "manly resistance" to British tyranny. The United States would remain "colonists and vassals," he said, as long as the nation submitted to British domination of the high seas—"that element which covers three-fourths of the globe." He had begun to confront one of the unsound premises of Jefferson's administration: that the United States did not need a navy of significance. The Royal Navy, with some thousand warships, completely outclassed the U.S. fleet, with barely five seaworthy frigates. A naval presence large enough to stand up to an aggressor had to become part of the American arsenal, not merely to carry on war but to prevent it. As Gallatin admitted to his brother-in-law at this time, the growth of the navy would be an essential ingredient in America's autonomy after the war. "Taught by experience," he wrote, the government would be channeling public resources into the navy so that "within five years" it would be in a "commanding position" in its Atlantic neighborhood.[9]

During the American Revolution, Madison had recognized the need for a strong navy. His assessment of the conditions the nation faced in 1813 marked a revival of that earlier commitment. In fact, war caused Madison to change his opinion about several articles of the Jeffersonian faith: no direct taxes, no national bank, and a reliance on gunboats. When he appointed Jones secretary, Madison selected a man who despised gunboats. Of the one hundred coast-hugging gunboats on the water in 1813, Jones took more than half out of commission, asking Congress to grant the president permission to sell boats not in use. They were "sluggish in their movements," he said, and were no match for warships. Scattered about the country, the gunboats were mere "receptacles of idleness and objects of waste and extravagance without utility." Jones did not mince words.

Madison backed him fully. When Jefferson wrote in May, pleading for "the humble, the ridiculed, but the formidable gunboat" to defend the Chesapeake, going so far as to send Madison a detailed map of how they might be positioned, he did not receive the reply he expected. Softening the blow, Madison told him a little white lie, that "the present Secretary of the Navy is not unfriendly to gunboats." He then repeated Jones's critique almost verbatim: gunboats were "too slow in sailing, and too heavy for rowing, they are limited in their use to particular situations, and rarely for other than defensive co-operations." While Federalists mocked the country's "formidable armada of gunboats," Madison decided to quietly phase them out of existence. In 1815 he secured congressional approval to sell all that remained.[10]

"Repent Even at the Eleventh Hour"

By the early spring of 1813, Madison's two newest cabinet members had brought energy and order to their troubled departments. Jones took the first step in constituting a naval bureaucracy by overseeing shipbuilding at the Washington Navy Yard and acting to eliminate sources of friction over rank—navy captains had hitherto been subordinate to army commanders. Armstrong was just as busy reorganizing the War Department. Less than half of the regular forces were under arms at the time he took over. An army needed a supply system to operate effectively as it advanced, and so he named quartermasters for each military district to arrange for the purchase of food, clothing, arms, and ammunition.

But Madison's cabinet was no more united than it had been. Just as Monroe exhibited jealousy and suspicion of Armstrong, Gallatin watched nervously as Armstrong used the power of appointment to build up a personal base, giving important posts to Gallatin's foes in Pennsylvania. This included editor William Duane of the *Aurora*. And as his personal secretary, Armstrong named Robert Smith's nephew. Gallatin was regretting his earlier endorsement of the wily New Yorker.[11]

But a more serious crisis confronted Gallatin. Five days into March he informed the president: "We have hardly enough money to last till the end of the month." Any future military operations would be threatened, he warned, if the government could not find funds soon. Republicans in Congress had made the problem worse by mulishly rejecting, in their last session, his proposal for direct taxes. This left Gallatin with little choice but to cultivate private investors. His main prospects were the German-born New York merchant John Jacob Astor and the Philadelphia banker Stephen Girard—ironically, the kind of speculators Madison had dismissed in the 1790s as depraved "gamblers" and Hamiltonian tools. Astor offered little encouragement. He explained that most financiers were skeptical of the way the administration was handling the war and proposed a radical, entirely unrepublican solution: the administration should charter another bank of the United States, and borrow from the bank to finance the war.[12]

The bank would have to wait, as the nation learned of Napoleon's crushing defeat in Russia. Republican newspapers assessed the implications of the shocking news. Some claimed that the reports had been exaggerated in the British press; others anticipated a likely increase in British operations against the United States, as military operations against France were scaled back. As one New York editor concluded: "Every defeat sustained by Bonaparte in Europe is a victory gained not by Russia, by Spain, but by our *own* enemy England."

An unusual proposal came from Alexander I of Russia. The tsar offered to mediate the conflict between Great Britain and the United States. Madison wasted little time before accepting the offer and appointed his ever-controversial, French-speaking right-hand man to the diplomatic mission. Albert Gallatin would join John Quincy Adams, already in Europe, and they would end impressment and bring the war to an honorable end. At least that was the plan.

Madison's choice made strategic sense. Gallatin was more than a diplomat—he was the president's most trusted adviser. Astor and his friends would take heart. Having Treasury Secretary Gallatin on the commission said to these tightfisted financiers that the government was serious about the mission. Indeed, the sudden prospect of peace convinced the wary investors to agree to $10.5 million in urgently needed loans, most of which was promptly allocated to the War Department.[13]

Old resentments toward Gallatin quickly resurfaced. This time a group of malcontents headed by Virginia Republican William Branch Giles, taking their cue from New York Federalist Rufus King, questioned whether the president had the authority to appoint one man to two such important positions. Madison assumed he did, and on June 3, 1813, one month after Gallatin and fellow negotiator Federalist James Bayard of Delaware set sail for St. Petersburg, the president notified Congress that Secretary of the Navy Jones would serve as acting treasury secretary during Gallatin's absence.

Madison, overworked, took ill at this time. Rumors that he was dying spread across Washington. At the end of June, on the fifteenth consecutive day of a "remittent" bilious fever, Madison remained under the simultaneous care of three physicians. Dolley was constantly by her husband's bedside. Monroe gave Jefferson a blow-by-blow account of the president's condition; the *National Intelligencer* issued daily bulletins. One cold-blooded critic, who signed his name "Virginius," diagnosed Madison's disease as one caused by a mass of "parasites, sycophants, and flatterers"; he hoped that as Madison faced his maker he would see the error of his ways and "repent even at the eleventh hour." If he should escape death, the president would then return to the world of the living ready to end the war.

Next, Vice President Elbridge Gerry fell ill, and Monroe conjured a darker plot. He believed that the Senate wished to elevate the unfulfilled Giles first to president pro tem of the Senate and then to the presidency, along the line of succession established in the Constitution. Monroe pictured Giles, Madison's most virulent enemy at this moment, maneuvering to sink his own chances of winning the presidency in 1816. It was an extreme scenario, but Monroe's lurid imagination was engaged, as rancor coming from the Senate remained intense.

Even as he fully recovered in July, Madison did little to alleviate the schismatic situation. He agreed to informally discuss the Gallatin appointment with members of the Senate committee who were then considering how to respond to it. But in explaining his position to them in writing in advance of the meeting, Madison ultimately left no room for argument. He insisted that the Senate might advise, but could not dictate, to the president. The committee, as a body, marched over to the executive mansion prepared for a showdown. They presented their resolutions, and Madison rejected them. A prolonged silence ensued. The president's stubbornness fed their anger, and enemies old and new, offended by his brusque treatment, mustered enough support to defeat Gallatin's diplomatic appointment by one vote.[14]

The spring and summer of 1813 were precarious months in the war effort. While Armstrong attempted to bring order and system to land-based forces, Britain stepped up efforts to blockade U.S. ports, from New York to the Chesapeake, Charleston, Savannah, the Mississippi, and anywhere American privateers set sail. By late spring, British raids along the Maryland and Virginia shores were being met with little opposition.[15]

Whether or not owing to Napoleon's setbacks, the British had become more aggressive. Former British foreign secretary Lord Wellesley provoked members of Parliament by asking: "What have we done? Nothing—nothing to intimidate—nothing to punish." Americans had to suffer, or the war would drag on. Jefferson recognized that Virginia and Maryland would become prime targets for the enemy. Random raids of towns along the Chesapeake would have their desired effect on the middle states—"the most zealous supporters of the war," as he reminded Madison. The Virginia militia ably defended Norfolk, but Hampton was not so lucky. Reports of British outrages circulated: rape and murder as well as plunder.

Men of Virginia were called to arms to rise in defense of American womanhood. The House of Representatives issued a report on "British Barbarities," highlighting the "shrieks of innocent victims of infernal lust at Hampton." Some six hundred Virginia slaves fled to the British, reawakening Virginians' fears from the days of Lord Dunmore. As British ships appeared at the mouth of the Potomac in July 1813, clashing cabinet members Monroe and Armstrong rushed out to meet the danger, with their companies of volunteers and regulars respectively. Hearing this, Secretary of the Navy Jones observed with more than a hint of sarcasm that the two were really "running for the Presidential purse."[16]

Although Republicans were opposed, on principle, to raising taxes, British raids so close to Washington may have prompted Congress to accept what Gallatin had earlier called "necessary evils." Congressman Charles Jared Ingersoll disputed his fellow Pennsylvanian's choice of words but not his policy. There was nothing evil about taxes, even direct taxes, he argued before the House: "War cannot be waged without finances." He saw a silver lining in the cloud of battle, if the United States emerged from the fight with "a good system of permanent internal revenue."

Few would agree openly with Ingersoll. The Republicans seemed hopelessly divided. So when they rallied to pass revenue bills, they caught the Federalists off guard. With lobbying help from Acting Treasury Secretary Jones, the Pennsylvanians were able to nudge the legislation through, though the taxes imposed would not go into effect until 1814. Madison strongly endorsed the tax increase, taking a decisive step away from Jefferson's minimalist approach to federal government.[17]

One bright spot for Madison and Jefferson was the victory of Jefferson's son-in-law, the since-remarried John Wayles Eppes, who bested John Randolph of Roanoke in a House contest that bore symbolic weight for the administration. The isolationist Randolph had campaigned vigorously. In spite of his soaring rhetoric and captivating storytelling, the establishment triumphed over the carnival act. Congressman Eppes served as chair of the powerful Ways and Means Committee.

Eppes had his doubts about the Gallatin-Jones tax package. He felt that the constitutional rule of using population to apportion direct taxes (from which the insidious three-fifths clause was derived) was flawed. His Virginia instincts kicked in, as he alluded to disparities between old and new, and agricultural and commercial, states. He wrote to Jefferson that he saw no just reason why "a given population in an uncultivated Forrest" should pay the same tax on personal property as an advanced manufacturing and commercial center, or a more productive agricultural community. Why, he posed, should the state of Ohio, "just arriving into political existence," pay the same tax as the state of New Jersey? Only indirect taxation (customs fees, for example) ensured that the system of taxation would not oppress the people. But even with his strong reservations, Eppes had to acknowledge that direct taxation was "unquestionably the best" means to balance the budget. So he decided to remain silent during the House debate and to vote for most of the revenue bills. It was by no means easy to navigate between the old Jeffersonian philosophy of limited taxes and Madison's pragmatic new approach to prosecution of the war.[18]

Eppes was torn, but his father-in-law was plainly disgusted. In a long letter of June 1813, Jefferson gave vent to his mounting concerns about government finances. He feared, he wrote frantically to Eppes, "debt, bankruptcy—and Revolution." To explain the problem, he repeated his 1789 theory that "the earth belongs to the living," restating that the debts of one generation must never burden the next. Funding war through debt, like a dependency on paper money, was, he insisted, a discredited way of thinking, in "slavish imitation" of Great Britain. He believed that the United States had already grown too fond of banks—state banks were generating an uncontrollable inflation. The charter of the first national bank had expired in 1811, and Jefferson did not think that chartering another national bank was the solution to anything.

He proposed alternatives, willing to do virtually anything at this point to minimize the power of banks and bankers. First, the government had to stop borrowing money from "self-created money lenders," and here he had the likes of John Astor and Stephen Girard in mind. With any loan, he said, Congress should pass an accompanying tax (he did not specify what kind), guaranteeing that the loan was redeemed within a reasonable amount of time. Then instead of piling up debts, the government would issue short-term Treasury notes to further help cover the expenses of war. He believed that such a program would obviate the need for banks and keep the federal budget balanced.

Jefferson did not seem at all alarmed that he would be granting Congress the power to control the circulation of money—at least during times of war. He imagined that the states south and west of New England would all be willing to rescind state bank charters and redirect their hard coin, or specie, to the coffers of the federal government. When Washington controlled most of the specie, it could offer Treasury notes at good rates, eventually forcing even the holdout states to join in, putting many state banks out of business. Every generation had a natural right to be free from its parents' debts, Jefferson reasoned, but "no one had a natural right to the trade of the money lender." Increasing the power of the federal government by giving it complete control over the money supply, he was willing to adopt an essentially Hamiltonian structure, solely in order to rid the nation of avaricious bankers and their unhealthy profits. As he envisioned it, his plan would provide a healthy cleansing of the economy, while preserving the United States as a more moral, and essentially agricultural, nation.

As before, Jefferson was preoccupied with patrolling boundaries. In *A Summary View* in 1774 he had defined America's distinct corporeal identity: a country created on its people's own blood-drenched soil, a country enriched by the sacrifices of generations past. It was what endowed this people with inalienable rights. Then in contemplating the federal Constitution in 1789, he had sought to "guard the people against the federal government" by supplying a "parchment barrier" in the form of a bill of rights. Turning his attention to the states in 1798, he had claimed in the Kentucky Resolutions that each state's corporate identity was unassailable and that, in the name of self-defense, any state could reject invasive federal laws.

Now in 1813, as he worried about the federal debt, he set out to protect future generations, each of which, in his words, constituted "a distinct nation." One generation could no more bind its successor than it could pass laws for the inhabitants of a foreign country. When a generation ended, so did its sovereign debts. In Jefferson's thinking, the boundary between generations was a natural chasm; it could not be crossed any more than the dead could return to the living over the river Styx.

As much as it made him secure in purging an evil, Jefferson's plan was not at all democratic and stood in marked contrast to the democratic theory he was and is widely known for. In his own state of Virginia, many of the existing state banks were established to extend credit to those beyond the governing class. Jefferson's view of lending perversely assumed that only individuals with money should be able to borrow. By this logic, he would restrict yeomen farmers from the purchase of land and equipment, or any sort of self-betterment; or, crucially, from picking up stakes and relocating west. Extending the privilege of borrowing money only encourages social mobility.

Jefferson had taken the time to write a long and polished disquisition, which he expected Jack Eppes to circulate among Republicans in Congress. "Use them or not as they appear to merit," he said, a standard way of telling someone to spread the word. Jefferson needed congressmen in his corner before he would broach the subject with Madison. He would be sadly disappointed. Though Eppes did push the Treasury notes strategy and did oppose the charter of a new national bank, he gained few converts in Congress. Of the prominent Virginians in Washington, only Monroe seriously considered the ex-president's approach. It would be another year before Jefferson decided to write to Madison on these subjects, when he knew that the administration had every intention of backing a new national bank.[19]

"Such Gossiping Trash"

Madison did a most un-Republican thing when he raised taxes in order to conduct an aggressive war. Banking on an invasion of Canada to improve U.S. prospects, he simultaneously hoped that diplomacy, assisted by Tsar Alexander, would bring an end to impressment and obtain peace with honor. During the first half of 1813, the British buildup on the northeastern shore of Lake Ontario and along the St. Lawrence River was matched by an American buildup at Sackets Harbor, in New York State, on the eastern shore of the lake, some forty miles south of the St. Lawrence.

In the West the Shawnee leader Tecumseh proved as courageous as he was impatient with the tentative British commander with whom he was meant to coordinate operations. On the American side, William Henry Harrison seemed to be wasting money as he wasted time; the *Virginia Argus* thought of this native son as an inept watchmaker, "always winding up, but...never striking." East and west, British and American forces alike exhibited their share of disorderly conduct, on and off the battlefield. In July 1813 Secretary of War Armstrong removed an increasingly despondent General Henry Dearborn ("Granny Dearborn," to the Federalists) from his command.[20]

During the second half of the year, the United States gradually achieved naval supremacy on Lake Ontario, though the balance of power there kept shifting. On Lake Erie America's newest naval hero, Oliver Hazard Perry, redefined coolness under fire as he braved some of the heaviest fire of the war and destroyed the best of the British fleet. As he reduced their profile, the British thought it prudent to abandon Detroit. This opened the door for William Henry Harrison. Boosted by Kentucky riflemen, he crossed into Canada in pursuit of the enemy; and at the Battle of the Thames in October, Tecumseh, the eloquent spokesman for pan-Indian alliance and most formidable of warriors, was killed. Montreal and Quebec remained too heavily defended to pose a real opportunity, even for a resilient American force.

General James Wilkinson, who tainted everything he touched, replaced

Dearborn. In the spring of 1813 he was called from New Orleans to New York State and took charge at Sackets Harbor. The army assembled there was weakened by a health crisis caused by the consumption of food polluted by water that flowed through the soldiers' latrines. But it was not long before Wilkinson was claiming that he was primed to take the war to the enemy.

His survival as an active general, despite years of harassing civilian leaders and tormenting troops, is a remarkable story. Useful to Jefferson when he gave dubious substance to the rumors of Aaron Burr's treasonous intent, Wilkinson found himself the subject of serious inquiry, and then a court-martial, in 1811. An investigation launched by President Madison himself found irregularities in the general's behavior with respect to Burr and, ultimately of greater importance, in playing both sides in his dealings with Spanish authorities. But the evidence fell short of what was required to convict, and he retained his position in Louisiana, where he was universally despised. Armstrong's decision to reassign Wilkinson to the Canadian front was done to take him out of harm's way, politically speaking.

From Sackets Harbor, then, Wilkinson menacingly moved his force of seven thousand up the St. Lawrence in October and early November 1813, aiming for Montreal. Taking ill, the portly general self-medicated with the opiate laudanum, which slowed his thinking and slowed the advance. His senior officers favored continuing engagements along the river, but Wilkinson proved less bold than his rhetoric and returned to winter quarters. With all his ribbons, he revealed himself a rather indecisive soldier. Like Secretary of War Armstrong, he had never commanded an army in battle and left it up to a heartier breed to engage directly.[21]

These were the kinds of men who directed Mr. Madison's ground war. Slowly, as significantly higher bounties led more and more men to enlist, better soldiers rose in the ranks and replaced Wilkinson, Dearborn, and their like. In the West, the British-Indian alliance had weakened. Any northern push would now have to come from that direction.

Meanwhile, as he surveyed the failed Canadian campaigns, Armstrong became convinced that conscription was needed to produce a superior force. He published an editorial in a New York newspaper, calling for a regular army of 55,000 men, because the voluntary regular army and state militias had proven unreliable. Monroe, now sensitive to the political cost of such a move, persistently warned Madison against listening to his secretary of war—Monroe was convinced that militia units would fight as well as regular army. Madison ignored these warnings and allowed Armstrong to

James Madison (1751–1836),
as a member of the House of
Representatives. Painted by
Charles Willson Peale, 1792.
Courtesy Gilcrease Museum

Thomas Jefferson (1743–1826),
as secretary of state under
George Washington. Painted by
Charles Willson Peale, 1791.
Courtesy Independence National Historical Park

Edmund Pendleton (1721–1803),
Virginia's foremost politician at the time of
the Revolution, was a crucial resource
for both Madison and Jefferson.
William Mercer miniature, ca. 1790.
Courtesy Virginia Historical Society

Edmund Randolph (1753–1813),
a friend and ally to both Madison and
Jefferson, held such positions as governor of
Virginia and attorney general of the
United States before succumbing to
political assassination at the hands of
highly placed Hamiltonians.

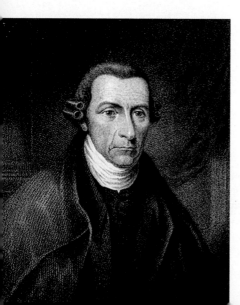

Patrick Henry (1736–1799),
the most popular man in Virginia,
was for many years the formidable
opponent of Madison and Jefferson.

Marquis de Lafayette (1758–1834), French aristocrat whose ties to Madison and Jefferson, as to the American Revolution itself, were lifelong. Engraving from an 1857 text, based on a portrait of 1790.

William Short (1759–1848), Virginia-born diplomat who studied the law under Jefferson, became his secretary in Paris, and transcended Virginia parochialism. Painted by Rembrandt Peale.

Courtesy Muscarelle Museum of Art at the College of William and Mary; gift of Mary Churchill Short, Fanny Short Butler, and William Short

James Monroe (1757–1831), Jefferson's protégé, Madison's friend and sometime rival, who succeeded Madison as president.

National Portrait Gallery, Washington, D.C.

John Taylor of Caroline (1753–1824),
the nephew of Edmund Pendleton, was a
nationally known promoter of agrarianism
and an apologist for the institution of slavery.

William Jones (1760–1831),
a proactive secretary of the navy
during the War of 1812, was one of
the few cabinet members Madison
came to trust as president.
Courtesy Historical Society of Pennsylvania

Albert Gallatin (1761–1849),
born in Geneva, Switzerland, was a
western Pennsylvania politician despised by
the Federalists. He served as treasury secretary
in the Jefferson and Madison administrations
and was an irreplaceable policy advisor
to both presidents.

A newspaper welcomes Madison, Jefferson, Adams, and Hamilton to Philadelphia in an entirely too optimistic poem, as the federal government sets up its temporary capital in the City of Brotherly Love at the end of 1790. This is the start of what grew to be the most emotionally exhausting decade in American political history prior to the Civil War.

FOR THE FEDERAL GAZETTE.

Stanzas on the arrival of Congress in Philadelphia, December 1790.

WELCOME, ye former *warriors!—statesmen* too!
  Superior objects ye have now in view.
Ye come our former triumphs to complete,
And prove our city FREEDOM's fav'rite feat.
Ye come to bid all doubt, all clamour cease;
Ye come, securing LIBERTY and PEACE.
  Ye legislators!—warriors now no more;
Till foreign rage shall bid your cannon roar,
Henceforth be discord to those realms confin'd,
Where haughty despots rule the human mind—
Welcome! may ev'ry earthly bliss encrease!
Ye come to strengthen COMMERCE, VIRTUE, PEACE.
  Ye patriots! who defi'd external powers,
And nobly struggled for your rights, and ours;
Who in the scenes of battle or debate,
Guided true Freedom, and preserv'd each state;
Freedom ye love; a suffering world release, *
Till all shall boast tranquility and peace.
  Be ADAMS to your nation still endear'd!
And be the powers of JEFFERSON rever'd!
Be MADISON for eloquence renown'd!
Still various worth in HAMILTON be found!
Truth soon must flourish; enmity decrease—
They come, the patrons of true worth, and peace!
  GERRY! thy talents knowledge has refin'd——
How many statesmen rush upon my mind!
Our southern brethren ev'ry praise demand,
In council wise, they dar'd each hostile band.
With WASHINGTON's lov'd name my verse shall cease;
IN WAR OUR CHIEF; OUR PRESIDENT IN PEACE!

* *By examples of heroism, virtue, and wisdom.*

PROVIDENCE, June 19.
Wednesday last the Hon. Thomas Jefferson, Esq; late Governor of Virginia, arrived here by land from that State, on his way to Boston. He is shortly to embark for Europe, as a Minister Plenipotentiary from the United States, in the room of the Hon. John Jay, Esq; who is to return to America. Governor Jefferson, who has so eminently distinguished himself in the late glorious revolution, is a gentleman of very amiable character, to which he has joined the most extensive knowledge. He is a Mathematician and Philosopher, as well as a Civilian and Politician, and the memorable Declaration of American Independence is said to have been penned by him.

"The memorable Declaration of American Independence is said to have been penned by him." In June 1784, a Providence, Rhode Island, newspaper takes note of Jefferson's arrival in town en route to Boston and his first transatlantic voyage.

"Intercepted Letter from Tall Tommy to Little Jemmy." Federalist contempt for the diminutive President Madison is unmistakable in the opening lines of a satirical poem published in the *Alexandria Gazette* in 1810.

Poetry.

FROM THE ALEXANDRIA GAZETTE.

INTERCEPTED LETTER

FROM TALL TOMMY TO LITTLE JEMMY.

(*It goes in a fine old Tune.*)

JAMES MADISON my Joe, Jim, when I gave up the chair,
Thee I bequeath'd my old blue cloak, a mantle for thy wear;
And thank *the gods*, thou didst possess a double portion too,
Of my good spirit in thy bones, James Madison my Joe.

From Monticello's Octagons, th' abode of peace and me,
This pledge of ancient friendship then comes *hopping* straight to thee;
So store its beauties in thy heart, and never let them go;

"I met the P[resident] on the road. . . . Always & affect[ionate]ly yours." The congress-man shares news with his chief political ally. Madison to Jefferson, June 12, 1792. *Library of Congress*

"The motion of my blood no longer keeps time with the tumult of the world." The secretary of state explains why he is leaving government. Jefferson to Madison, June 9, 1793. *Library of Congress*

"The conduct of Mr. A. is not such as was to have been wished or perhaps expected. Instead of smoothing the path for his successor, he plays into the hands of those who are endeavoring to strew it with as many difficulties as possible." Madison complains about John Adams's behavior in the days before Jefferson's inauguration as president. Madison to Jefferson, February 28, 1801. *Library of Congress*

"Take care of me when dead." Sensing that he will not survive much longer, Jefferson asks his trusted friend of fifty years to defend his historical reputation. Jefferson to Madison, February 17, 1826. *Library of Congress*

Montpelier, Madison's home. Photograph taken prior to 1884.

Monticello, Jefferson's home. From an engraving in *Gleason's Pictorial* (Boston), 1854.

make his case to Congress. On December 7, 1813, Madison gave an address to the national legislature, in which he endorsed conscription. He was ready for drastic measures, even if it meant raising the specter of a standing army, so long anathema to republicanism.

The collapse of the northern campaign made Monroe angry again. He demanded Armstrong's removal. In fact, during Armstrong's absence at the front, Monroe ordered all correspondence dealing with the 1813 campaign transferred to the State Department. His method for collecting evidence against Armstrong struck Madison as unsavory—in fact, the chief clerk at the War Department later recalled that he had never seen Madison "more in a passion." The president was not likely to listen to a new round of Monroe's complaints. Though wary of Armstrong, he was willing to give him another chance, believing that every move in the direction of Canada strengthened America's hand in negotiations with England.

With Armstrong and Monroe jockeying for power and Gallatin overseas, Madison put greater trust in the loyal, enterprising, but less personally ambitious William Jones. When Gallatin's appointment as a peace negotiator was officially approved in Congress, Jones finally stepped down as treasury secretary, leaving that key administration position open. Madison tried to enlist the Pennsylvanian Alexander James Dallas, an outspoken Republican since the mid-1790s, who was a close friend of Jones's. But Dallas despised Armstrong and refused to serve in the cabinet with him. The president then settled on Senator George Washington Campbell of Tennessee, a man with little skill in the area of finance. His appointment was largely cosmetic, as it relieved Jones of the bureaucratic burdens of running two departments, though the president still came to him for economic advice.[22]

In the latest round of cabinet shuffling, Madison got rid of Postmaster General Gideon Granger, a DeWitt Clinton ally, after Granger attempted to use his patronage power to humiliate his boss. Instead of ratifying Madison's choice for postmaster of Philadelphia, he had named one of Gallatin's archenemies. Granger's petty maneuver was, in Dolley Madison's words, an "insult to *us* all." Seeing what might occur next, Madison warned Jefferson to be wary of any "artful" letter he might receive from the outgoing official. Incredibly, Granger thought he could blackmail Jefferson into defending him. He directly threatened to publicize allegations about the sexual diversions of both the first lady and her sister. And he even insinuated that he might have to remind the public of Jefferson's attempted seduction of his neighbor's wife, a charge dating to the late 1760s, first leveled by James Callender, which Jefferson had owned up to.

Jefferson did not take Granger's threats lightly. He replied to the unwelcome letter with a stern warning: If he dared to circulate "such gossiping trash," Granger would quickly find himself ostracized by the Republican Party. With Granger out of the way, Madison appointed Ohio governor Return J. Meigs as postmaster general. It did not go unnoticed that after the death of Dolley Madison's sister, the husband she left behind, John G. Jackson, congressman from Virginia, had recently married Meigs's daughter.[23]

"Inertia"

As president, Madison was not pressed by his fellow Virginians, or even by prominent northerners, to devise a remedy for slavery—except in private by his personal secretary Edward Coles. Madison did, however, witness during his second term the beginnings of what would become the South's antebellum defense of slavery as a creditable institution. The man responsible was the quintessential Old Republican, Edmund Pendleton's nephew and Madison's longtime acquaintance, former U.S. senator John Taylor of Caroline.

In 1813 Taylor published the influential *Arator* (Latin for "cultivator"), a guide to healthy agricultural practices that was equally a defense of Virginia tradition. In the essays, Taylor showed no sympathy for African Americans. Claiming a realist perspective, he dismissed the arguments of humanitarians and insisted that slavery was an evil that could never be "wholly cured"; "to whine over it is cowardly," he insisted, "to aggravate it, criminal." The realist's solution was to perfect slave owning and contain its violent potential. For this, Taylor drew a transparent analogy: "The history of parties in its utmost malignity is but a feint [*sic*] mirror for reflecting the consequences of a white and black party." He played upon memories of the worst of the French Revolution, referencing the poorest and most shabbily dressed of the Jacobins: "For where will the rights of black sansculottes stop?" It was critical that slaves remained docile and disciplined, because slavery remained the only means to wealth in the South, and Taylor could see no better option than to maximize the efficiency of farms.[24]

Taylor was convinced that free blacks were "an unproductive class" and, lacking full political rights, turned easily to vice. Their "mingling" with enslaved brethren "mutually excit[ed] each other to rebellion." The visibility of free blacks damaged the planter's efforts to keep his slaves happy and productive. The national government, he said, as a composite of North and

South, was collectively ignorant of agricultural science and incapable of acting in the interest of the cultivator.

Taylor joined two themes: exhaustion of the soil of Virginia and big government's taking the side of the moneyed interest over that of the endangered cultivator. Entranced with the banking community, government only added to the southern farmer's woes by victimizing him for owning slaves, while at the same time consigning his agriculture to "contempt and misery." Outside the United States, according to Taylor, the agricultural interest was "a slave"; "here she is only a dupe..., deluded by flattery and craft." If nothing were done to reverse the trend, in the end the South's entire wealth would be squandered.[25]

He had thrown down the gauntlet. Either Washington must protect the true, tangible wealth of the nation, or it would wreak economic havoc and increase the potential for widespread racial violence. Taylor insisted that the republican form of government was entirely compatible with the institution of slavery. "Slavery was carried farther among the Greeks and Romans than among ourselves," he argued, "and yet these two nations produced more great and good citizens, than, probably, all the rest of the world." Accordingly, Taylor rejected Jefferson's warning in Notes on Virginia that slavery corrupted the manners of whites. Even Madison, despite an inclination to find comfort in the demonstrated abilities of free blacks in the North, would return before long to the familiar stereotype, praising the benevolent Virginia master and saying that emancipation was not likely to remedy the slave's "natural and habitual repugnance to labour."

President Madison did not entirely escape condemnation for his support of slavery. His papers reveal that at least one representative abolitionist was irate enough to write to him directly and expose the hypocrisy in his complaining about Britain's "pressing and enslaving a few thousand of your seamen," while "you southern Nabobs, to glut your avrise [sic] for sorded [sic] gain, make no scruple of enslaving millions of the sons and daughters of Africa, & their descendants."[26]

While demeaning descriptions of the character of a slave fed the many rationalizations for the institution's persistence, most everyone in the South agreed that a concentration of slaves in any one place increased the possibility of social unrest. The colonization/removal option, whether arising out of ostensibly humane concern for the enslaved or selfish motives on the part of whites, remained alive from the Revolution through the deaths of Jefferson and Madison.

Jefferson's clearest reflection during these years on the problems associated with slavery and emancipation appears in two exchanges: one with the businessman John Lynch, founder of Lynchburg, in 1811; and another, the more famous, with Edward Coles, in 1814.

Late in 1810, a Philadelphia Quaker had been in the area of Jefferson's Poplar Forest retreat and had hoped to find Jefferson on his property. Failing this, she conveyed her ideas to Lynch, "with a request that I would Lay the matter before thee." Anne Mifflin, like Lynch, wished that Virginians would coordinate with existing British efforts to colonize African Americans on the West Coast of Africa. During Jefferson's presidency, she had written to a member of Congress, asking that the plan be presented to Jefferson and had heard nothing since.

Replying to Lynch, Jefferson explained what he had sought to do as president. His views concerning "the people of color of these states" had never really changed, he said. He had long favored "gradually drawing off this part of our population" and "transplanting them among the inhabitants of Africa." In 1801 Virginia's legislature, through the office of then-Governor Monroe, had requested presidential action, and Jefferson in turn recommended following the plan of the private English company that was colonizing former American slaves in Sierra Leone; or if that was logistically infeasible, to look to "some of the Portuguese possessions in South America." Monroe raised the possibility of colonization closer to home—west of the Mississippi—which Jefferson rejected outright. He wrote to the U.S. minister in London, who informed him that the Sierra Leone enterprise was opposed to including any more African Americans in their colony, owing to their reputation for disruptiveness. The colony was by then in financial straits, what Jefferson called "a languishing condition." His effort, as president, to interest the Portuguese "proved also abortive." He was now a private individual, unable to perform officially, though he believed that the commercial prospects were equal to the humanitarian value in setting up an African colony. "But for this the national mind is not yet prepared," he concluded. He spoke in favor of "the experiment," but urged prudence and caution.[27]

The more famous exchange of this period was Jefferson's with his wealthy young neighbor Edward Coles. Born in Albemarle when Jefferson was serving as the U.S. minister to France, Coles grew up identifying with the first families of Virginia and, like Jefferson, attended the College of William and Mary. This privileged young Virginian, as secretary to President Madison, felt comfortable sending Jefferson a pressing appeal to help him bring an end to slavery in their home state. Coles planned to emancipate his slaves, bring them to Illinois, and give them land—it would be 160 acres each when he succeeded in realizing his plan a decade later.

Telling Jefferson in his letter of July 31, 1814, that he had had such an enterprise in mind ever since he was old enough to grasp the meaning of the "rights of man," Coles admitted he was uncertain as to the reception of his ideas. But he could not contain himself in seeking aid from his famous neighbor. "The fear of appearing presumptuous" would have deterred him, he wrote, "had I not the highest opinion of your goodness & liberality . . . My object is to entreat & beseech you to exert your knowledge & influence." Do not refuse out of a fear of failure, he ventured.[28]

Jefferson understood the passion that went into Coles's composition and wrote feelingly in reply three weeks later: "The love of justice & the love of country plead equally the cause of these people, and it is a moral reproach to us that they should have pleaded it so long in vain." He owned that his passages on slavery in *Notes on Virginia* remained the best synthesis of his beliefs, as he recounted for Coles his own early activism: as a colonial legislator he had appealed to a senior statesman, Colonel Richard Bland, to seek "certain moderate extensions of the protection of the laws to these people." Bland followed through, embracing Jefferson's idea in a public forum, only to be "denounced as an enemy of his country, & treated with the grossest indecorum." Whether or not Jefferson was suggesting a direct parallel, he was insisting that his time to make waves was past. His preferred analogy was to Virgil, the epic poet of Rome, whose *Aeneid* related the fall of Troy. Were he to enter the lists with Coles, Jefferson would be King Priam, long past his fighting days when he ridiculously strapped on a set of useless armor and attempted to save the city. The ex-president claimed he was too old to accomplish anything significant. "This enterprise is for the young," he told Coles, adding: "It shall have all my prayers."

Coles allowed three weeks to pass before he addressed Jefferson once again. He refused to let him off the hook. "Your prayers I trust will not only be heard with indulgences in Heaven," he said, "but with influence on earth. But I cannot agree with you that they are the only weapons of one of your age, nor that the difficult work of cleansing the escutchion [*sic*] of Virginia of the foul stain of slavery can be best done by the young." The old must combine with the young, he coached, because the old had achieved a high social station and still held the power to change course—providing that the will remained healthy. Joining together, old and young could combat the unfortunate human tendencies of "apathy," "habit," and "inertia."

Coles explained again his reasons for turning to Jefferson, whom he termed "the first of our aged worthies." He did not invoke Madison in these letters, but Coles must have presumed—or been told directly—that the war president was in no position to tackle so contentious an issue at this moment. He seemed undeterred, though, by Jefferson's alert rationalizations, and with an utter lack of inhibition, he reminded the ex-president that Benjamin Franklin, at a greatly advanced age, had spoken out against slavery and had the degree of influence over Pennsylvanians that Coles hoped Jefferson might have over their fellow Virginians.[29]

Jefferson was not inclined in the least to accommodate Coles. In the letters of his retirement years, he wrote so often of his "love of tranquility" that the phrase became automatic. During the presidencies of Madison and Monroe, he commented at will on national and international affairs, expecting his successors as president to treat all such letters as confidential. To others, he routinely protested his desire to spend his final years away from the public eye, as a farmer, a gardener, and a family man. When the subject was slavery and race, he would listen to those whose fertile thoughts of dramatic possibilities would one day improve America. It was an extension of his theory of generational distinctiveness: the successors would shape a different destiny for themselves, based on the will of a new majority unencumbered by the yoke of the past.

"The President—Lost!"

As 1814 opened, news arrived that Napoleon had suffered more serious reverses and was retreating into France. His abdication in early April improved British military prospects in America. Men and ships previously committed to Europe would now be able to come to the aid of Canada. Russian mediation had collapsed late in December, but the British still expressed a readiness to restart negotiations in Sweden. That was where the American negotiating team went—a group that had grown to include J. Q. Adams, Albert Gallatin, and James Bayard, with the new addition (so as not to appear too conciliatory) of Speaker of the House Henry Clay.

Federalists assumed that the recent course of events would prompt Madison to press for peace on just about any terms. But that was wishful thinking on their part. For one, American sailors, as a rule, were happy with their commanders and nationalistic in spirit. Privateers were having a tremendous impact on the war: the more than five hundred authorized privateering vessels had captured more than thirteen hundred British prizes and earned considerable financial rewards in so doing. In the view of the enemy, these motley crews did greater damage than the U.S. Navy.[30]

The United States was now fielding disciplined forces. They were led by men in their twenties and thirties: Winfield Scott, Jacob Brown, and Edmund Pendleton Gaines (named after, but not directly related to, the Revolutionary), all of whom came under heavy onslaughts from the north but whose decisions and determination had secured the strategic Niagara region. The British had some success as they pressed south from Montreal, until routed at the Battle of Plattsburgh at the end of summer. This was more than tit for tat, as the casualty rate along the Canadian frontier was severe on both sides.[31]

The state of affairs to the north was eclipsed in August 1814 by the more than symbolic British assault on the Chesapeake and the wanton destruction of Washington, D.C. The man at the helm for the British was forty-two-year-old Rear Admiral George Cockburn, who had seen considerable action against Napoleon before coming to America. Though some under his command felt a kinship with their American cousins, Cockburn was well known for his near-obsessive need to punish the upstarts for their challenge to British preeminence. Secretary Armstrong, to his discredit, believed the federal city safe and focused on the defense of Baltimore. Madison himself appears to have been watching and waiting more than he might have. From Montpelier in May, he apologized to Jefferson that he would be unable to visit Monticello anytime soon. "I am obliged," he wrote, "to hold myself in readiness," in the event that he was called to Washington on short notice. Absent from their correspondence was any concern with brutality or loss of life on the battlefield. In their letters, war had become not an abstraction, but a predominantly political issue. Madison relished relating the defeat of antiwar Federalists at the polls in New York. He did not feel hamstrung by factions in Congress and the states, believing more than ever that he could direct the course of political measures and make political appointments.[32]

He took his life in his hands simply by returning to Washington as the hot, sticky, "bilious" months began, when acute gastrointestinal ailments ravaged the area. The president was sixty-three, far from robust, and accustomed to spending his summers, as Jefferson had, in the healthier setting of Piedmont Virginia. But having returned at this unseasonable time, Madison got straight to business. He called together the members of his cabinet, who were still focused on prosecuting the war for Canada.

Over the course of June and July, Armstrong continued to plod along, while Madison and Monroe, wary of that gentleman's motives, increasingly feared that Washington itself was the prize Cockburn sought. Madison began to inspect War Department records more closely, trying to read into the secretary's routine, and realized that Armstrong had communicated with his generals on subjects of critical importance without showing that correspondence to the president.

All intelligence suggested that the enemy was strengthening. The capital was "in a state of perturbation," Dolley Madison wrote to Hannah Gallatin in late July, openly wishing she were back in Philadelphia. As Cockburn's warships hovered nearby, the first lady stated that her husband had resolved to stay at his post in the event of an invasion and go down with the ship of state. From Boston, Vice President Gerry wrote the president that he approved strong war measures to match "mad" Britain's "vindictive feelings..., pride & vain glory." Meanwhile, news arrived that fifteen thousand more British troops had landed in Montreal.[33]

A test was coming. The British invasion force landed on August 17, southeast of Washington along the Maryland shore. Armstrong was uncertain whether Baltimore or Washington was the immediate target. Secretary of State Monroe, a Revolutionary cavalry colonel, mounted his horse and reconnoitered personally. On the twenty-fourth the British broke camp and descended on Bladensburg, Maryland, just above the state's border with the District of Columbia. Monroe joined the commander of the Baltimore militia and tried to direct the defense. But there was no time to rally the troops or even maintain order, as the British launched rockets and the American militia took to their heels. Cockburn himself rode a white steed and took charge of artillery at considerable personal peril. One bullet just missed him; another killed a marine standing beside him. While they lost more men than the Americans, who held the high position, the British routed the inexperienced militiamen. The road to the President's House lay open to them.[34]

Incredibly, there was no one left to defend Washington. When he returned to the executive mansion late that afternoon, the president learned that Dolley had fled with the army. She and their servant Paul Jennings had saved one canvas from the expected onslaught, refusing to leave George Washington's portrait for the invaders. A week earlier a State Department clerk had taken care to remove the original of the federal Constitution for safekeeping. The president had nothing to gain by waiting around.

It was not yet dark when Royal Marines reached the Capitol. A pyrotechnics expert was on hand to oversee its destruction. The Library of

Congress, housed in the Capitol, went up in flames, and the whole could be seen for many miles into the night. According to Major General Robert Ross, who accompanied Cockburn up Pennsylvania Avenue, Madison was expecting a fine dinner and plenty of friendly company. Instead, the president's table, laid out for forty, was the scene of a rollicking celebration by British raiders, who enjoyed Madison's wine almost as much as they enjoyed the irony of it all. While Washington's citizens were physically unharmed, the president's domicile was consumed by flames, along with the other public buildings.[35]

The *Baltimore Patriot* had its story ready the very next day but could only speculate as to the full damage. "The Navy Yard, report says, is burnt," it read. "Whether the Capitol is destroyed is not known, though it is believed to be." When the smoke cleared and the whole series of events became known, a militiaman's letter expressed a loss of composure as yet unrecovered: "I do not pretend to censure any one in particular; but a dread responsibility rests somewhere. I almost blush to put on the American uniform." As was customary in times of war, the fate of women and children framed the emotion of the memoirist: "I cannot describe the distress of the female part of our inhabitants, many of whom flew into the country without a hiding place or a protector."

A few days later, in receipt of the *Boston Centinel* issue covering the rout at Bladensburg, the *Patriot* editor lashed out at his New England Federalist counterpart, whom he called a "veteran news-perverter," for striving "to gull his willing dupes" with assertions that those who led and fought bravely were Federalists, and Federalists alone. To set the record straight, the *Patriot* editor expressed pride that Republicans and Federalists were fighting side by side; it hardly mattered to them who officered a company, so long as it acquitted itself well in battle. This was no time, he charged, for any to promote "distrust and dissention, when all should unite for the public safety"; and it was no time for Americans anywhere to have to suffer a "bloated ignoramus" of an editor who would act to undo the growing fellowship claimed by citizens of different regions of the country.[36]

That newspapermen could be cruel no one doubted. A Federalist paper in Delaware printed a couplet to memorialize Bladensburg: "Fly Monroe, fly! run Armstrong, run! / Were the last words of Madison." On first reports, the *Salem Gazette*, in Massachusetts, ran the headline, "THE PRESIDENT—LOST!" It went on to elaborate: "Ever since the Battle of Bladensburg, MADISON has been missing—he does not even know where he is himself—entirely lost and bewildered!" Cowardice had always been a favorite charge of Federalists, and now Madison had become as susceptible to the charge as Jefferson. The unoriginal Delaware paper was quick to assign blame to "the idolators of Jefferson and Madison" for the military catastrophe: the "jacobin administration," "feeble, improvident, disgraced," had reduced the nation to a shadow of its former self, "by driving from our councils the pupils of Washington!"[37]

The psychological power of the press can be acute in a time of war. Preliminary intelligence reaching Keene, New Hampshire, a full week after the burning of Washington, reported with horror what its distant citizens could only imagine happening at the seat of power:

> The British commander was issuing his Proclamations and orders from the President's House! Public credit must receive a shock. A crisis is at hand. Let James Madison and Elbridge Gerry either resign (if they wish to save their country from further disgrace) and let Congress elect from the Senate better men—or let Mr. Madison, if he wont resign, dismiss his present weak and inefficient ministers, and appoint such as all parties must have confidence in.[38]

Madison was not concerned at this point with the battles being waged between rival editors. He had to reassemble his government. Though he and Dolley had made prior arrangements to meet in the event that they were separated, it took a full day before they found each other at a tavern on the Virginia side of the Potomac. The British, having accomplished what they came for, pulled out. Now Madison could inspect the damage and begin to deal with the conditions Washingtonians faced. He would send for Dolley when convinced that the way was clear for her return.

On August 28, after going their separate ways for a time, Madison and Monroe returned together to the charred city. Added to the intimate circle was Richard Rush, the president's third in a line of attorneys general. He stayed close as the short and scrawny commander in chief rode from place to place seeking information. Ferried across the Potomac, Madison was deeply angered to view the destruction all around him. He was irritated, too, by reports that came to him from residents of the District who expressed disgust with the government for its failure to stage any meaningful defense.

The *National Intelligencer*, its office ravaged during the invasion, reopened with a vengeance a few days later, and reported that the British commander had confronted its editor with the "peculiar slang of the Common Sewer." Countering the expected condemnation of Madison, the first postinvasion issue assured: "The President of the United States was not only active during the engagement but...has been personally active ever since. Everyone joins in attributing to him the greatest merit."[39]

Armstrong came under heavy fire from residents of Washington and from Congress. His effigy was etched in the walls of the burnt Capitol building, where he was shown hanging from a gallows. At this low moment, the president recommended to Armstrong that he take temporary retirement. Madison then made Monroe acting secretary of war, so that his fellow Virginian held two cabinet positions simultaneously.

Before John Armstrong exits the narrative too abruptly, there is reason to believe that his firing may not have been quite as simple as a pro-Madison position would describe it. In June, when the D.C. militia mustered, Armstrong expressed disapproval of Madison's choice to lead that body—indeed, it was by all accounts a poor choice. Discomfort grew. Two months later, when the nation's capital proved indefensible, Madison and Monroe must already have been calculating that Armstrong could be made into an easy scapegoat. Better this than to leave an impression that the presidential hopeful from New York was ousted for strictly political reasons. In this alternative narrative, Armstrong was really no less competent than Madison or Monroe. It can be argued that he was simply not given enough of a chance to prove himself in the months leading up to Cockburn's landing.[40]

On the other hand, if Madison wanted to be rid of his disagreeable secretary of war, why would he have suggested only a *temporary* retirement from the office? Was Madison letting him down in stages, or biding his time and leaving his options open? The president's own memorandum of their last meeting states that they parted on friendly terms. Navy Secretary William Jones, who was close by, thought differently, recapping events in great detail to Alexander Dallas in Pennsylvania. He bemoaned the lack of a response to the British landing and wrote that Armstrong's impulse was to "divest himself of all responsibility" for the failure to protect Washington. To Jones, the story Armstrong told was built on a combination of "cunning" and "insufferable...vanity," anything but "candour." Armstrong's only qualification for high office, according to Jones, was his bluster. "This man imposed himself on society without one useful, valuable quality, either social, civil or military," he upbraided, explaining what really happened: "The President stated facts to Armstrong" and referred to a

widening prejudice against him, shared "to a certain and considerable degree" by the president himself; then on grounds of "expediency," Madison
asked Armstrong to retire from his duties "until those passions had subsided."

This would seem to have been the gist of Madison's temporary, or not so
temporary, dismissal of Armstrong—a few words that could be interpreted
in more than one way. Jones, as one of those highly prejudiced against
Armstrong, concluded his statement to Dallas with the simple and dismissive "I am glad we are clear of him." His remarks about Monroe, in the same
letter, were hardly more complimentary: "He has a strong military passion
but without the requisite qualifications." If Monroe moved back to the War
Department, Jones ventured, "I predict his fall . . . His judgement I think in
most things extremely feeble." It did not stop there. Overall, Madison's secretary of the navy had little confidence in the cabinet. "With due humility I
feel my own nakedness," he wrote, "and perceive that the costume of my
colleagues is not of the firmest texture." At this low moment in the war, he
itched to return to private life, but rather than abandon Madison, he
agreed to wait until December to end his public service.[41]

Whatever the ultimate truth may be, Armstrong headed for Baltimore,
no longer a factor in the war. The Madisons, meanwhile, had no home and
moved in with Dolley's sister and her husband. Though James Madison
had never given an indication that he possessed a military mind, he understood the necessity at this moment to show that he was in command.
Aided by the pen of Attorney General Rush, he issued a presidential proclamation on September 1, in which he accused the British of a "deliberate
disregard of the principles of humanity and the rules of civilized warfare"
and appealed to citizens to "unite their hearts and hands" and come to the
defense of "exposed and threatened places." As they dutifully published the
proclamation, Federalist newspapers took pains to agree with Admiral
Cockburn that the burning of Washington was done for a particular reason and strictly in retaliation for the U.S. "conflagration and destruction of
property" inside Canada; on that basis, Madison had shown "audacity" in
claiming that the fault lay on one side only.

It took all capital letters to describe Madison's contemptible crusade: it
was "A WICKED, CAUSELESS WAR," designed only to help one political party.
"Not a finger will be raised in support of Mr. Madison's grounds of war, nor
his honour," declared the editors of the *Boston Spectator*. As the president
ranged about the scorched city, they would hold his feet to the fire, as it
were.[42]

Opposition newspapers suddenly had a warehouseful of material to use against Madison and his top appointees. They would see to it that the sack of Washington defined his presidency. Hanson's *Federal Republican* giddily interpreted the president's mind in the wake of the British invasion. In "Little Jemmy, or Poor Madison," the Georgetown editor assumed that the president was "terrified" lest the people realize that he and the unworthy Armstrong had "consorted together in the ruin and betrayal of the capital"; for how could such self-immolation have taken place, if not on purpose? As absurd as that sounded, the same newspaper looked for new ways to mock and found solace in song as the increasingly unpopular war continued. One particular satire, with its added allusion to Jefferson, was meant to be sung to the tune of "Yankee Doodle":

> *Since* Madison *has held the helm*
> *And steer'd by Jeff's old notions,*
> *Afflictions dire have spread the realm,*
> *Now goading to commotions.*

Without money enough to wage war, it went, "Jemmy's plans are all blank."[43]

Under the pressure he now faced, and amid the devastation, Madison, by all accounts, retained his full presence of mind. Though he did not entirely trust Monroe, under these circumstances he had to rely on him more; and Monroe's confidence in his own abilities as a war chief filled whatever gap existed in Madison's battle plan. One can only surmise how Madison greeted news of the successful defense of Baltimore's Fort McHenry in September, a defense led by none other than the now sixty-two-year-old Maryland militia general (concurrently U.S. senator) Samuel Smith. In spite of past differences over Robert Smith's performance at State and the brothers' constant sniping at Gallatin, Smith struck Monroe as able, and the president was now letting Monroe make more war-related decisions.[44]

Madison and Jefferson had been out of contact during the months when Chesapeake communities were feeling the might of the British forces. On September 24 Jefferson reopened communications. "It is very long since I troubled you with a letter," he noted. The decision not to write had been based on "discretion, and not want of inclination." He knew that Madison had more than enough concerns, but he was too moved to let any more time pass: "In the late events at Washington I have felt so much for you that I cannot withhold the expression of my sympathies." He absolved

Madison of responsibility for the burning of the federal city, assuming he had done all he could and relied on others to execute his orders.

Jefferson understood that words would be little solace. "I know," he said, "that when such failures happen they afflict even those who have done everything they could to prevent them." As a proud man who, as governor, fled to the hinterlands when Benedict Arnold ravaged Virginia, he added meaningfully: "Had General Washington himself been now at the head of our affairs, the same event would probably have happened." It seems unlikely that Madison would have thought to compare his predicament to anything Washington had faced in the Revolution; but he must have been comforted, at least a little, by Jefferson's proposition that some military setbacks were unavoidable. Never one to admit defeat easily, Jefferson predicted that the naval war on the Canadian frontier would continue to give the British pause. "While our enemies cannot but feel shame for their barbarous atchievements at Washington," he assured, "they will be stung to the soul by these repeated victories over them on that element on which they wish the world to think them invincible . . . We can beat them gun to gun, ship to ship, and fleet to fleet."

Time had come for Madison and Jefferson to address their differences on wartime finance, which Jefferson had remarked upon without detailing. The National Bank begun by Hamilton had not had its twenty-year charter renewed. Jefferson had opposed it in 1791, and nothing for him had changed. He wished to find a means of paying for the war other than the issuance of state bank notes (in the absence of a national bank). Paper money always made him uneasy, and state banks had recently stopped specie payments. But for Madison, times had changed, and he was no longer opposed to the bank, as he had been in 1791. For the United States to conduct its war, it would have to borrow. Rather than write bluntly to Jefferson, he communicated only in general terms: "To a certain extent, paper, in some form or another, will, as a circulating medium, answer the purpose your plan contemplates."

When financing of the war was debated in Congress in 1814, Dolley's former brother-in-law James G. Jackson proposed a new national bank, and Jefferson's son-in-law Eppes opposed it. Through their proxies, then, the bank was a point of contention for the third and fourth presidents. When Madison dismissed his plan to privilege Treasury notes over all other sources of funding for the war, Jefferson was stunned. But Madison explained that relying on Treasury notes would only replicate the unhappy situation during the Revolution, when currency issued by the Continental

Congress rapidly depreciated in value. He even told Jefferson that he felt the national bank of Great Britain was the best model to follow! Perhaps there was no time when Madison and Jefferson's economic thinking was farther apart than this.[45]

Meanwhile, in the latter months of 1814, Monroe was far more interested in being secretary of war than secretary of state. If he had his druthers, he would ride at the head of the nation's ground forces. He preferred this role to the presidency itself and had decided to disavow any interest in 1816 if he could just take over the army. But Madison had other ideas. He believed that under present circumstances, northerners would react with unprecedented hostility to a Virginian as secretary of war. Monroe had to work hard to convince Madison otherwise; he succeeded, and the Senate promptly confirmed Monroe as secretary of war, without his having to disqualify himself from the presidential race.

Looking for a successor to Monroe at the State Department, Madison considered the diplomatic choice of Rufus King, the Federalist U.S. senator from New York. But then he approached another New Yorker, Governor Daniel Tompkins, who had taken on the Clinton coalition in 1812 and 1813, and had retained office in spite of his association with Mr. Madison's unpopular war. But Tompkins did not feel like picking up and moving his family to the burned-out national capital. When he rejected the president's offer, Monroe again took to wearing two hats: secretary of war and acting secretary of state.[46]

"That Little Man in the Palace"

The autumn of 1814 was stressful. Madison hoped for a negotiated peace, but the reports from Gallatin in Europe, even before the burning of Washington, were decidedly pessimistic: "Great Britain wants war in order to cripple us: she wants aggrandizement at our expense."[47]

The president found a new secretary of the navy in Benjamin Crowninshield, a native of Salem, Massachusetts, the very nucleus of New England Federalism, and this took a bit of the heat off the power-wielding Virginians. But the British spirit had risen since Napoleon's defeat, and it seemed that nothing less than America's submission would satisfy the government in London. Adding to the president's burdens, Elbridge Gerry died in late November while on his way to Capitol Hill. Edward Coles informed Madison that death came quickly, "after a few moments illness, with a kind of paralytic fit." With Gerry's passing, the vice presidency would remain vacant for the remainder of Madison's second term.[48]

The party out of power had its own ideas at this mouthwatering moment. With the destruction of Washington and the loss of Gerry, some Federalist senators tried a coup of sorts, pressuring for Rufus King to be made president pro tem and for Madison to resign the presidency. Their power grab was transparent and led nowhere fast. It revealed only that the party of Washington and Hamilton was clinging to life.[49]

There were no moderate Federalists anymore and had not been for some time. Those such as Dr. Benjamin Waterhouse of Harvard, who refused to toe the party line, were ostracized. "Until the memorable affair of the *Chesapeake*," Waterhouse wrote to Jefferson, "I was considered as a moderate federalist"; but since defecting to the Republicans, "a secret and not an open persecution has followed me." His medical research came under attack, and he soon realized that New England's Federalists would stop at nothing: "When I expressed my disgust at the attempt to prostitute truth & science to the purposes of party, they discovered I was not a fit instrument for their purposes, & a species of warfare ensued." After giving details of the whisper campaign against him, Waterhouse apprised Jefferson that the youth of the region were being militarized, but not to fight the British. He thought arch-Federalist Timothy Pickering was behind it, and that Pickering was in league with the Clintonians. He urged Jefferson to give President Madison a true account of these occurrences.[50]

Wilson Cary Nicholas had been critical of Madison's deliberative foreign policy at the outset of his presidency but returned to the fold once the war was launched. In 1809 he was a "malcontent," like the Smith brothers, to whose sister Nicholas was married; in 1814, however, their daughter was being courted by Jefferson's eldest grandson, as Nicholas was elected governor of Virginia. The new state executive wrote fearfully to Madison that the "discontented and factious of the eastern States" concerned him as much as the British military did. While he had no concrete information from New England beyond the public papers, he had read enough to raise suspicions, and like Dr. Waterhouse, he assumed clandestine goings on. "It is the characteristic of treason to be secret," Nicholas forewarned: "I love the union and have a strong attachment to the eastern people. It was not until very recently that I could be brought to distrust them to the extent I now do . . . I do not believe national antipathy was ever stronger in an Englishman towards a Frenchman than which is felt by them towards us." It was probably true that the Federalist leaders' feelings of resentment toward Virginia had never been greater.

Nicholas, a staunch Madison-Jefferson ally in the decade 1798–1808, could not have found a more receptive audience than the man who was president in 1814. As Gerry was laid to rest in the Congressional Cemetery, Madison vented: "You are not mistaken in viewing the conduct of the Eastern States as the source of our great difficulties in carrying on the war." Just as Federalists had, until lately, accused him of playing into the hands of Napoleon, he saw a coalition of High Federalists and their anti-Republican "priests," as he still called the New England clergy, looking for a British victory to enable a complete separation from Virginian rule. Their delusion, Madison told Nicholas, was "scarcely exceeded by that recorded in the period of witchcraft." He depended, he said, on the "vigorous support of the well-disposed States," more now than ever before, and he pleaded for "zealous exertions" from Virginia.[51]

The bitterest Federalists referred disparagingly to the president as "that little man in the Palace" and felt an obligation to make his life a living hell as the war trudged wearily on. They believed it an act of virtue to trade with the enemy. Upon the downfall of Bonaparte, Boston threw a massive public celebration.

The war forged a strange alliance and fruitful correspondence between the opinionated John Randolph and former Massachusetts congressman Josiah Quincy, who bore the distinction of having proposed Jefferson's impeachment during the third president's final months in office. When Massachusetts state senator and future U.S. senator Harrison Gray Otis, a prime mover in the DeWitt Clinton coalition of 1812, voiced a states' rights argument in 1813, Randolph laughed his way through a letter to Quincy. Resisting "Federal usurpation" in 1798–99, Randolph had been with the Virginians in supporting the same concept these New Englanders now embraced. "I rejoice," he told Quincy. "Pray give me some light on the subject of your proceedings. It was always my opinion that Union was the *means* of securing the safety, liberty, and welfare of the confederacy, and not in itself an *end* to which these should be sacrificed."[52]

The proceedings to which Randolph alluded were Otis's call to organize a convention, which opened in Hartford on December 15, 1814. The Hartford Convention is infamous in American history for the loud whispers of secession that emanated from it. It was conceived as a meeting in which the northern Federalist minority could air its collective grievances and consider options in dealing with what was, for them, an unresponsive central government. It did not advocate outright violence, though one delegate recklessly recommended a return to the original thirteen states, leaving the West (and the territories formed out of the Louisiana Purchase) to their own devices. The Federalist press was responsible for airing the most extremist ideas that attached to the Hartford Convention.

What the meeting did do, significantly, was to propose a new constitutional convention to reconsider the justice of that representation arrangement that gave the slaveholding South a distinct advantage in the House of Representatives. Another agenda item certain to harden Madison's resolution to silence New England's bold resisters was the convention's call to limit the chief executive to a single term and to deny any state the right to provide two presidents in direct succession—in other words, no Virginia Dynasty. Monroe was concerned enough that he began to prepare a military response in the event that a secession plan actually went into effect.[53]

If slightly less incendiary than history imagines, the Hartford Convention gave substance to the fears expressed by Governor Nicholas, President Madison, and many other Republicans. In the end, though, its timing could not have been worse for the Federalists, given the news that started to circulate across the United States shortly after the final gavel fell. Peace was at hand, and Federalism would be unable to survive it.

"The Republic Is Safe"

Along the southern frontier, a showdown was about to occur. Major General Andrew Jackson had removed the British from Pensacola in November 1814, where they had been guests of the ruling Spanish government. He had not waited for orders from Washington. (Indeed, Secretary of War Monroe had cautioned against irritating Madrid, fearing it might more overtly join in the war.) But historians generally agree that Monroe anticipated Jackson's actions and saw no real urgency to interfere. Any letter of caution to him was merely pro forma.

As the tall, gaunt Tennessean headed for the ethnically mixed, incompetently policed city of New Orleans, he well knew its history of petty crime and the potential for violence. But he was prepared to use anyone he could find who was willing to fight the British. Worn down by dysentery, Jackson arrived there on December 1. Despite unpropitious circumstances, he rallied his forces and two weeks later declared martial law. While on the lookout for spies and traitors, he sought advice from an old ally, Edward Livingston, the adoptive Louisianan who had been Jackson's New York Republican colleague in the House of Representatives seventeen years earlier. He made Livingston his speechwriter and a colonel.

A man for desperate times, Jackson went so far as to release prisoners from jail if they agreed to join the militia. He enlisted friendly Indians and African Americans in his army. Slaves did the hardest work, digging trenches and raising fortifications. With Livingston's negotiating assistance, he bargained with the pirate Jean Lafitte, who had fought Governor Claiborne of late, but whose artillery would prove instrumental against the British invaders. When he took charge, Jackson sidelined Claiborne, adding to the list of public officials whose resentment he earned through his impetuousness. All that Jackson was concerned with at this moment was giving America's overconfident enemy a rude welcome to the Crescent City. His lines extended a mile and a half, from forest to swamp, and five miles southeast. Because of the many approaches, and the rivers, creeks, and bayous, it was hard to know precisely where the British would attack. In Washington, Madison waited nervously for updates.[54]

Britain's invasion force was composed of veterans of the Chesapeake offensive, veterans of the war with Napoleon, and African-born soldiers belonging to two West Indies regiments. London was so sure of victory that it sent along civilian officials meant to make the arrangements for a new colonial government. Here Jefferson's admonitions as to the true extent of British ambitions proved justified. Since the defeat of Napoleon, the War of 1812 had become, for London's ministers, a war of territorial capture and subjugation. Andrew Jackson put a stop to that, though the result would have been the same if he had not, as the peace treaty signed at Ghent, in Belgium, on Christmas Eve denied the British the city of New Orleans.

The Battle of New Orleans, the stuff of legend, is a rare historic event so spectacular that it could not be ruined even by generations of overeager storytellers. Disciplined British columns advanced through a dense early morning fog in the direction of the American lines, as artillery exploded in several directions. From their defensive positions, Jackson's motley frontiersmen, inadequately trained, mowed down the brave British. The commanding general, Sir Edward Pakenham, was among the dead, and along with him a number of colonels, majors, and captains. American losses were in the tens, whereas British losses stood in the hundreds.

The entire battle lasted under two hours. As a result of what appeared to most a providential victory, Andrew Jackson earned a lifetime of celebrity and political capital that his future enemies could not discount. Caught up in the moment, even the anti-administration *New-York Evening Post* saw fit to praise his "unstudied simplicity and modesty." Former *National Gazette* editor and now aging national poet Philip Freneau wrote to tell his friend the president that he was applying all his "poetical energy" to the production of epic verse on "the grand subject of the Repulse of the British army at New Orleans."[55]

General Jackson complicated things, however, by refusing to lift martial law after news reached him that the war was over. Assuming dictatorial power, he imagined mutinies brewing around him and justified himself to Governor Claiborne: "This Sir is not a time for Complaint, or equivocation." Jackson and Claiborne were both Tennesseans and veterans of affairs of honor, but Claiborne saw no excuse for the general's pugnacity. Jackson clamped down on militiamen for neglect of their duties and desertion. He jailed resident aliens based on only weak suspicions and ordered the arrest of a prominent state legislator who had openly criticized his repressive methods. Then he arrested the federal judge who challenged that action, banishing him for "exciting mutiny." The judge in question turned the tables on Jackson, citing him for contempt, and Jackson was eventually obliged to pay a substantial fine. A letter from Claiborne reached President Madison, characterizing Jackson's imperious manner; and while sympathetic to the general's apprehensions, Madison could not understand the lengths to which he went. Through the War Department, he expressed his disquiet and requested of Jackson that he show more discretion in his treatment of the people of Louisiana. Fortunately for all concerned, the glory of victory drowned out these untoward memories; they only resurfaced years later when Jackson pursued the presidency.[56]

After the dust had settled, Jefferson wrote Madison a letter of congratulation. The glorious end of the war reaffirmed, in his mind, the country's ability to take up arms against a perceived threat to its continental destiny. "The affair of New Orleans was fraught with useful lessons to ourselves, our enemies, and our friends," he said. "It will show [Europe] that we mean to take no part in their wars, and count no odds when engaged in our own." Years before, in Paris, he had rhapsodized to Maria Cosway that America took on the world's fiercest army in its Revolution because of heart, not logic. Whether or not this second war for national independence was prudently undertaken, Jefferson rightly concluded that it fed an ever-widening sense of popular entitlement to still uncharted land and winding riverways. And the high seas would be safer too. Though the matter of impressment was unresolved, the Royal Navy no longer needed to impress American sailors into service, because Britain was at peace for the first time in more than twenty years.[57]

Jefferson's letter the same week to "Granny" Dearborn emphasized other lessons of the Battle of New Orleans—"truths," he pronounced, "too important not to be valued." He felt, for one, that his trust in the patriotism of the people of Louisiana was not misplaced. The city had defended itself, the militia had proven resolute, and the British were revealed to be beatable without outside assistance, something that could not have been said in 1783, after the French had come to America's rescue in the Revolution. Moreover, Jefferson reveled, "we have officers of natural genius now starting forward from the mass." He regarded New Orleans as a triumph of Republican politics.

Dearborn had told Jefferson that his native state of Massachusetts was now "humbled & degraded," an acknowledgment that presented an opening for Jefferson to speak of sectional politics. "Should the state once more buckle on her republican harness," he assured, "we shall recieve [sic] her again as a sister." In his assessment, it was only a wayward wing of the New England tribe, which he labeled "the parricide party," who qualified as "venal traitors"—those who would have "basely sold what their fathers had so bravely won from the same enemy." The moralistic ex-president expected "repentance" from them as a recognition that the clearer-headed politicians who opted for embargo and took the nation to war had been correct all along.[58]

The peace treaty was received in Washington in the second week of February, about a week after the magnificent news from New Orleans had arrived. According to the terms of the Treaty of Ghent, no exchange of territory took place. The treaty was acceptable to nearly all, yet no one was particularly pleased with it. Henry Clay was the American peace negotiator who should have been the most disappointed in the indefinite outcome of the conflict; after all, from 1811 forward, he had forcefully called for a war of conquest. But even Clay was buoyed by the thought that the British upper crust regarded the treaty as a loss. Recent defeats were left unavenged. And the Americans had had the last word. President Madison sent the treaty to the Senate on February 15, 1815, where it was immediately ratified. Two days later he announced to the country that the war was over.[59]

Patriots came out of the woodwork. Recall that the contrarian *Virginia Patriot* had mocked Madison and Jefferson as "false prophets" in 1814. Now, from Rhode Island, the *Providence Patriot* put the exclamation point on Mr. Madison's War. "The tools of royalty have never ceased prating against the imbecility and weakness of republics," it taunted. "Where are these false prophets now? The republic is safe. Surrounded by internal traitors—a whole section of the country basely devoted to the cause of the enemy—we have entered into a conflict with one of the most powerful nations on earth; destitute of men, of money, of the munitions of war, & of military science, and yet before three years have rolled away, we have beaten and discomfited that enemy by sea and by land." It was a hyperbolic defense of a war that should not have been waged. But that did not mute the satisfaction many Americans were feeling. The year 1815 saw a boost in morale, which did much to salvage Madison's reputation.[60]

His legacy meant a great deal to Madison. Before the war had come to an end, he coordinated the production of a white paper, an official justification—"a correct and full view of the war," as he put it to Jefferson in March 1815. Though it was for all intents and purposes Madison's work, the ostensible author was the Pennsylvanian Alexander James Dallas, his new secretary of the treasury, known for his close ties to Gallatin. The president stopped publication once the Senate ratified the Treaty of Ghent, figuring it would be counterproductive to issue an aggressive pamphlet just when peace had been restored. He needed time to think about what to do with the several hundred copies he was sitting on.

For the much-harried war president, this was no ordinary writing. A little more than a year away from the next presidential election, he had said little publicly in his own defense. How many times he went through and evaluated the argument Dallas and he had constructed we cannot know; but the 1815 text makes plain that Madison meant to emphasize the moral component of the War of 1812 as indistinguishable from that of the American Revolution—a war that no one in America, save the late Joseph Dennie, would have seen as anything but honorable.

This was how the Madison-Dallas text read: "Great Britain has violated the laws of civilized warfare by plundering private property, by outraging female honour; by burning unprotected cities, towns, and villages, and houses; and by laying waste whole districts of an unresisting country." Compare that to the damning language, directed at the king of England, which was contained in the Declaration of Independence: "He has plundered our seas, ravaged our coasts, burnt our towns, ... circumstances of cruelty & perfidy scarcely paralleled in the most barbarous ages ... We have petitioned for redress in the most humble terms." In both cases, as the innocent victim of crimes against humanity, America had had little recourse but to fight back.[61]

Madison was naturally incensed by the destruction of the capital, especially his own abode. More from the same text: "They set fire to the edifice, which the United States had erected for the residence of the chief magistrate." This and the other public buildings that were lost represented "progress of the arts, which America had borrowed from her parent Europe." All had been "consigned to the flames, while British officers of high rank and command, united with their troops in riotous carousal, by the light of the burning pile." Hurt and indignation undercut any defense of its conduct that London could dream up.

Once again targeting the South with special vengeance, the invaders of 1814 had incited the slaves to revolt. As the pamphlet tells it: "In a formal proclamation issued by the commander in chief of his Britannic majesty's squadrons ..., the slaves of the American planters were invited to join the British standard, in a covert phraseology, that afforded but a slight veil for the real design ... But even the negroes seem, in contempt, or disgust, to have resisted the solicitation; no rebellion or massacre ensued." In other words, the British professed to care about the lives of America's slaves, when all they really wanted was to provoke violence and allow the chips to fall where they may. To achieve the same effect, the analogous section of the Declaration of Independence had cited "domestic insurrections" and "merciless Indian savages." But whereas the frontier of 1776 described an ever-present danger, in the Madison-Dallas narrative's far-fetched defense of the southern way of life, the slaves were able to see through the British ruse and remain at peace with their masters.[62]

There was evidently something very personal and cathartic for Madison in seeing this pamphlet through production. By invoking "a decent respect to the opinions of mankind," the Declaration of Independence had been directed to a "candid world." Similarly, in writing Jefferson about the unpublished paper, Madison labeled it an "Exposé" meant as an antidote to "misstatements which had poisoned the opinion of the world." As he originally conceived it, the pamphlet was to have been released in "the usual demiofficial form"; he explained that he had since given much thought to its reception in a postwar environment. He had toyed with the idea of issuing it with a prefatory explanation that it had been written prior to receipt of the peace treaty.

Madison must have had an inkling of how Jefferson would respond, when he wrote coyly: "I have thought a perusal of it might amuse an hour of your leisure." He asked that the enclosed sample be returned to him (in Washington) or put in safekeeping, where it would be "in no danger of escaping." He was explicit in saying that he wished the abortive pamphlet retained for its value to future historians; but he felt it was no longer prudent to issue it: "You will observe, from the plan and cast of the work, that it was meant for the eye of the British people, and of our own, as well as for that of the Neutral world." In other words, for every imaginable audience: present opinion makers and posterity alike. Yet he had withheld it.[63]

Within days Jefferson wrote back. He fully appreciated Madison's need to have history told "right," for that was his fear every bit as it was Madison's. He worried—and would long continue to worry—that the history of the 1790s, and of his own administration, would be told to his detriment. He wanted the world to see Madison's pamphlet sooner rather than later: "I have read it with great pleasure, but with irresistible desire that it should be published. The reasons in favor of this are so strong, and those against it so easily gotten over . . . 1. We need it in Europe. They have totally mistaken our character . . . 2. It is necessary for the people of England, who have been deceived as to the causes and conduct of the war . . . 3. It is necessary for our own people, who . . . have been so plied with false facts and false views by the federalists." If some of the "roughnesses" in the text were "rubbed down" to give the appearance of moderation, and a "soothing" postscript added to mollify the British people, who were no longer America's enemy, then he believed the whole should be printed and liberally distributed. In fact, he urged, "Mr. Gallatin could have it translated into French." Publication went forward the following month.[64]

The Federalist *Alexandria Gazette* could not accept that the United States was any better off for having gone through the war. In a squib titled "Impromptu," a mock-conversation between Madison and Monroe was recorded:

> *Says Jemmy Madison to James Monroe,*
> *I've flogged the British rascals Jim, by Jo,*
> *Have you so, says he? And after all what's gain'd?*
> *What by your war, good sir, have you obtain'd?*[65]

For a moment, when reports arrived of Napoleon's escape from exile and return to France, Madison and Jefferson fretted that the United States would have to face a new wave of uncertainty in balancing its policies toward England and France. Monroe expressed doubts that America's maritime shipping would be respected in any new Anglo-French conflict, and as the president wrapped up a visit to Monticello in late April, Monroe warned him that England would be tempted to restart impressment and blockade. To Jefferson, Monroe wrote similarly: "We have treaties with none, and not much kindness to be expected from any." But Napoleon's defeat at the Battle of Waterloo in June 1815 brought finality to the question, allowing the Madison-Jefferson exchange to focus again on less troubling matters.[66]

"As Ever Became a Great Man"

Was the war a failure? Coming into office, Madison had been forced to confront the fact that the United States was unprepared to engage in war. He had had to make adjustments, and he privately recognized how much he had to learn. Few were willing to rise or fall along with a president's decisions. The proverb is apropos: it was lonely at the top.

One who knew this firsthand would have seemed a most unlikely supporter of the war president. In January 1814, rather than write directly to Madison, John Adams sent a letter to Richard Rush with the understanding that its contents would be shared. The second president encouraged the fourth with reminders of how the Revolution had been won despite the immensity of debts outstanding, a Congress chased out of Philadelphia by British troops, and a commanding general who was on the run—not to mention a long list of incompetent generals who had to be eased out of their commands.

Madison may have hoped, in 1812, that a declaration of war would force the British into making diplomatic concessions. In this case, the president's strategy would have amounted to a masterful bluff. It is more likely, though, that Madison wanted to fulfill a long-held desire to secure national economic sovereignty. For him, a "common sovereignty on the high seas" was as essential as territorial sovereignty. The embargo having failed, war remained the only way to obtain any leverage. Otherwise, the United States was destined to become the permanent pawn of England's empire.[67]

Although Jefferson's fiscal conservatism kept voters happy and suited a young republic, it led to miserable shortages in funding and bureaucratic inefficiency in wartime. Along with a strong navy, the United States required an overhaul of its financial system. The answer was direct taxes and a British-style national bank. Madison understood these things and turned his back on the Republican ideology of the 1790s. But it took him time to get there.

From the beginning, America's offensive war was flawed. It was, in effect, a filibuster disguised as a defensive war, justified on the faulty premise that the British would hand over Canada much as Napoleon had relinquished the Louisiana Territory. But the British were not the French. They resented American politicians' braggadocio and were prepared to give the British public what it wanted—that is, to give the United States a good drubbing.

The War Hawks may have plotted their crusade as yet another land grab, justifying military aggression in the name of national honor. But the war quickly devolved into a family soap opera, in which the estranged parent and bratty child lost the ability to negotiate peaceably. They issued warnings. They pressured. They crowed. Theirs was a war that revisited family secrets and opened up old family wounds. The English torched the nation's capital mainly to humiliate the president—and perhaps more than one president. For in reducing Washington the city, they were symbolically reducing Washington the general who had reduced Lord Cornwallis at Yorktown. Madison was made to appear a befuddled executive, unable to defend his hearth and home. In a fitting way, his escape from Rear Admiral Cockburn was a rerun of Jefferson's flight from Monticello, as the cowardly governor of Virginia.

Madison lacked swagger, let alone a military reputation. He did not know how to rally the public or mobilize enough regulars. That is why he needed so badly to win over New England. Though he never took a hard line against governors who refused to send their militias to the front, neither did he give them any leeway to work out an honorable compromise with the government. New Englanders backed the U.S. Navy, but that was as far as they went. With his mishandling of the so-called John Henry plot, Madison alienated many New Englanders before the war had even begun, trying to make them appear as traitors. Playing the "sectional card" backfired.[68]

For the war to have succeeded, Madison needed more than propaganda. He needed a just cause, such as an attack on the United States. The impressment issue lacked the symbolic resonance to rally support for a prolonged war. Secretary of the Navy William Jones seems to have come up with a more likely scenario: if U.S. ships had refused to allow the British to search their crews and impress their sailors, forcing both sides to resort to arms, then the war might have risen to a higher moral station in the public's imagination. A series of "*Chesapeake* Affairs" might have made the conflict more of a national crisis.[69]

Another problem was that the United States was fighting two wars. One was initiated by westerners in a scheme to subdue the Indians. It was a frontier war, really nothing more than a filibuster to obtain desired land still lodged in hostile hands. The western theater had little to do with actual grievances against the British. The British were blamed for encouraging Indian atrocities during the war, but that did not move many residents along the East Coast. The other war, the one Madison cared about most deeply, stemmed from a diplomatic conflict with Great Britain over control of the high seas, which mattered more in the older, more politically savvy parts of the republic. Attempting to forge two different national threats into one grand narrative, the Madison administration convinced too few that there was a coherent logic behind the War of 1812.[70]

Another problem for Madison was that he was no Jefferson when it came to writing emotional texts. As a *litterateur,* he had no finesse. The War Hawks, with their overblown rhetoric, had greater influence over the narrative of war, but their rhetoric was out of touch with the actual military or fiscal strength of the government. The proud declaration of war may have secured Madison's reelection, but a meaningful victory remained beyond his grasp. In the end, he failed to secure free trade or the acknowledgment of sovereignty on the high seas. Impressment ended when England and France stopped going to war, not because of anything Madison did.

Did he oversee a losing war? It is closer to the truth to say that Madison shook off a near defeat and ultimately survived the war. He disciplined his unruly cabinet. He gradually dislodged the congressional malcontents. He moved the federal government toward fiscal stability by turning away from the Virginia model and being more receptive to his Pennsylvanian advisers. Forced to learn lessons the hard way, he emerged intact. One thing can be said about James Madison: He was a political survivor.

Pennsylvania senator Jonathan Roberts may have captured Madison's survival instincts best when he described a series of 1814 visits. Though they met two or three times a week that year, and Roberts typically brought "gloomy forebodings" to the president's desk, he observed nonetheless: "I found him cheerful, he look'd through the pass'd [*sic* for past], and passing events; as ever became a great man." Was greatness simply a refusal to cave in to pressure in the midst of war? Or was it something more: an ability to see the bigger picture? The pettiness of personal rivalries that plagued his administration would have overwhelmed a less supple mind. Suffice it to say that if the war failed in its projected goals, that failure did not completely tarnish Madison's reputation.[71]

"The Sun Itself Is Not Without Spots"

It was a time to rebuild. Jefferson had volunteered to replenish all that was lost when the Library of Congress burned, by selling his Monticello library if the members of Congress were so inclined. For decades he had scoured Europe and America for titles and collections on subjects ranging from architecture to zoology. Some dated back to the seventeenth century. He possessed accounts of voyages encompassing every corner of the globe; atlases and travelogues in English, French, Spanish, and Italian; an array of dictionaries and encyclopedias; ecclesiastical histories in Latin; dozens of volumes on British history and an equal number on classical antiquity; and studies of jurisprudence, moral philosophy, gardening, mathematics, surgical manuals, literary criticism, and epic poetry.

He proceeded to catalog it all—6,487 volumes. The Federalists in Congress, to a man, voted vindictively to reject Jefferson's library. One even called the books "infidel" in nature. By a partisan vote, then, the measure passed, and Thomas Jefferson allowed his books to be packed and shipped to Washington in the nine-foot-high pine cases in which they had been displayed in his private study. The new Library of Congress now contained twice as many books as it did before the war.[72]

Jefferson had badly needed the funds from the sale of his library in order to pay back outstanding loans. At the same time he continued to oppose rechartering of the national bank. He was wary of the wild issuance of credit and unreliable circulating paper. Monroe was a cautious ally, but both Madison and Treasury Secretary Dallas had come around to the idea of a second national bank as a check on inflation—the direct opposite interpretation to Jefferson's.

Madison vetoed the bank recharter bill in its first incarnation in 1814, not on constitutional grounds, but because he felt it did not adequately invest the bank with the power to preserve a uniform (national) currency. Ten months later, in his annual message, he urged Congress to draft a new bill in which he ignored the rationale that the bank was primarily needed to borrow money (the argument in 1791) or collect taxes (the argument in 1814). And he gave a slight nod in Jefferson's direction by claiming that whether the means was through Treasury notes or a national bank, the goal in either case was to establish a uniform currency. Madison would recharter the bank, but not on Hamiltonian terms.

Congress voted in favor of recharter in April 1816, but the Bank of the United States proved to be a mixed blessing. At first a great boon to the postwar economy, rapid expansion would prove catastrophic by 1819, when prices fell, credit tightened, and the bank called in its loans. Overborrowed Americans, north, south, and west, were ruined. Smarter banking practices were then put in place, and the 1820s saw healthier growth and expansion.

But for the moment President Madison was convinced that the bank he had once thought unconstitutional was constitutional after all—and a good way for the United States to restore pubic credit abroad in peacetime. The president was at Montpelier, during what had become the government's traditional summer/early autumn recess, when Monroe informed Jefferson that little could be done to change minds about the bank. Any subsequent discussion the third and fourth presidents had on the bank question was verbal and remains lost to history. It was a unique state of affairs when Jefferson's position on the bank was adopted by southern Federalists, who voted against recharter in 1816 and made noises about limiting its powers in the months preceding the Panic of 1819.[73]

In 1815–16, for the first time in his long-embattled presidency, James Madison had a cabinet with which he felt comfortable. Madison and Monroe forgot the past disturbances in their relationship. Alexander Dallas was the new Gallatin, reliably reporting from Washington in the months when the president relaxed on his plantation. Senator William Harris Crawford of Georgia, a rising star, filled the opening at War, as Monroe reembraced the State Department. John Quincy Adams was the new minister to Great Britain, and Gallatin minister to France.

An interesting transition was under way. Federalists were muting their Federalism and recommending party "amalgamation," under the banner of nationalism, as the way forward. The more vigorous government symbolized by Madison's acceptance of the bank led many to perceive a mitigation of the Republican ideology. New Hampshire governor William Plumer, a Monroe supporter, had been a Federalist senator during Jefferson's presidency. He now believed that both the Federalist and Republican parties had "expired" with the end of the war, each having "absorbed into itself much of what was best in the policy of its opponents."[74]

In spite of the remaining fire-eaters on both sides of the political divide, a consensus appeared to be slowly forming. It delivered no appreciable power to a Federalist, however, unless he explicitly abandoned his original creed first. And while that consensus began to take shape in Madison's shadow, it would emerge as a Monrovian, not Madisonian, persuasion. Still, Henry Adams recognized what happened when he later wrote of Madison's good fortune: "Few Presidents ever quitted office under circumstances so agreeable." The restoration of the financial system was, to this Adams, the most noteworthy element in a new calculus. "In a single day, almost a single instant," he declared, "the public turned from interests and passions that had supplied its thought for a generation." As the war's outcome provided the catharsis citizens needed, Madison's sense of urgency vanished, allowing him to reason through the science of constitutional government and preview his future "job" as elder statesman.[75]

The decline of Federalism allowed for a brief respite from the politics of "faction." As he neared his sixty-fifth birthday, Madison presided over a slowly strengthening nation. Public servants became professionals, and Congress, for the first time, voted its members a regular salary, replacing the negligible per diem meant to offset expenses. This had the added bonus of enabling more members of Congress to bring their wives and children to Washington, D.C., helping to make it more livable.[76]

Although James Monroe was destined to be the last U.S. president to have participated directly in the American Revolution, the inclusiveness newly possible in political life gave indications that a generation less encumbered by Republican-Federalist wrangling was coming into its own. In that sense, Virginia-born William Crawford might have been a more representative choice to succeed Madison. He had worked his way up in the ranks from farmer to schoolteacher to lawyer, then from Georgia state legislator to U.S. senator during the middle years of Jefferson's presidency. Madison respected his talents enough to send him to France as U.S. minister during the trying years of the War of 1812, before naming him to the cabinet.

But there were other considerations. Those who wielded power in the federal government were leaving little to chance. The wheels had been set in motion some time back, and Madison clearly wanted Monroe's ambition to be fulfilled. Thus, in early April 1816, the Republican caucus nominated James Monroe for president. "The service of his country has taken up a large share of Mr. Monroe's active and well spent life," the *National Intelligencer* recorded, as it showed Crawford of Georgia surprisingly close behind in votes.[77]

Lest one believe that all political wrangling was past, the *Virginia Argus* found it necessary to rebuke as "false and malevolent calumny" a story in the *Boston Gazette* claiming that Crawford's supporters in Congress had resolved to cast their lot with the Federalists. Governor Daniel D. Tompkins of New York, meanwhile, agreed to be Monroe's vice-presidential running mate, reaffirming the Virginia–New York chain of command. And Crawford settled in as secretary of the treasury, always a prominent post in the early republic. He would hold on to it for the duration of Monroe's two-term administration.[78]

As James Madison planned a peaceful final year in office and a smooth transition, he continued to come under attack from certain enclaves in New England where the past hung on. If Jefferson could boast a cabinet with little turmoil and little turnover for eight years, Madison had seen a long succession of short-lived cabinet officers and unsuitable field generals. The *Massachusetts Spy* took joy in trying to list them all—dredging up the Robert Smith imbroglio and the names of military mediocrities such as Dearborn, Hull, and Wilkinson. It was all meant to show that Madison was a poor judge of character.

Unanimity was not then, or ever, an American trait. Even among Monroe's supporters, there were those who estimated him according to his less commendable traits: hypersensitivity, hastiness, a lackluster intellect. Typical of the shrill voices that continued to personalize politics, the *Alexandria Gazette* maintained a constant drone from the south side of the Potomac. "As to Mr. Monroe, there is little we know that should entitle him to the high distinction he covets," read a representative article, "unless it is playing the fawning parasite." In 1808, the *Gazette* reminded readers, the parasitic Monroe was "in disgrace with the old man of the mountain"—Jefferson the puppeteer. Making fun of politicians still sold papers.[79]

According to the anti-administration *Nantucket Gazette*, while the *National Intelligencer* "prattled about the purity of election," pressure had been applied to the electors of at least two states in order to push Monroe past Crawford. Under the Republicans, the Constitution was ignored, and free suffrage was a myth: "These men carry all their elections by corruption." Federalist holdouts took the position that there was hypocrisy galore among the Republicans, whether pro-Madison in 1808 or pro-Monroe in 1816. But that was all the discredited party could do now; its editorializers shook their heads at unmannerly democrats and charged that "Peter Porcupine" and Joseph Dennie had been right all along: the party of Jefferson, Madison, and Monroe encouraged profligacy in America.[80]

The prevailing spirit among Republicans comes alive in the Fourth of July 1816 oration given in Windsor, Vermont, by a War of 1812 army officer named Selleck Osborn. As a Jeffersonian newspaper editor in Federalist Connecticut, Osborn had spent much of the year 1806 in jail for his supposedly libelous writings. He was a marvelous satirist who poked fun at the disgruntled Federalists who mechanically labeled Republicans as infidels and libertines. Osborn described his home state as "a country conquered by lawyers" and did not shy from exposing a justice of the peace who dispensed injustice. For speaking the truth he had to be punished most cruelly. It was not enough to lock him up—Osborn was given a mentally disturbed cellmate who had raped and murdered.[81]

The Republican editor was much restored by 1816 and living in the free state of Vermont. That year he delivered a Fourth of July oration lacking none of the pizzazz that had earlier gotten him into trouble. Painting the Federalist residue as men of gloom and doom, he berated their "idle talk" about the taxes of 1816 by asking them to remember the taxes of 1799, when their party had been in charge. They could speak at length about the faults of democracy but made no acknowledgment of democracy's merits. "We shall hear many dismal prophecies," he said pertly, "but nothing about the falsehood of all their preceding ones." The one line summed up his critique of an effete ideology.

He did not profess that the Republicans were perfect. "The sun itself is not without spots," he assured. But in praising the Virginia presidents for their efforts to see that independence stood "deeply rooted where it was planted forty years ago," Osborn drew an unusual comparison between the wars waged by two chief executives: "In a second struggle for independence, we have, some of us, been prone to lay our misfortunes at the door of our best and ablest friends—The same spirit that would have consigned a Washington to oblivion and disgrace . . . , would have deposed and sent a Madison to Elba [Napoleon's place of exile], and placed in his station, it is difficult to say whom, but certainly not a better man." The comparison was meant to level the playing field of history: Madison had his detractors, and so did Washington.[82]

On that same Fourth of July, the Madisons threw what Dolley described as a "profuse and handsome" picnic dinner on the shady lawn of Montpelier. Ninety of their country neighbors attended. Jefferson was not present, being then at his Poplar Forest retreat, more than one hundred miles away. Returning to Albemarle, he paid the Madisons a visit at Montpelier in mid-August.[83]

Little could be done to stop one more Virginia Republican triumph. In the last year of his presidency, Madison spent June through early October in Virginia, his longest absence from the capital since 1800. It was a sign of his impending retirement and also a recognition that he was likely to spend the rest of his term without having to face any sudden crises. Entering the presidency at a time of acute anxiety, he exited it amid a growing sense of possibility. Meanwhile, to no one's surprise, Monroe soundly defeated his Federalist rival, New York senator Rufus King, failing to win only the states of Massachusetts, Connecticut, and Delaware. Perhaps the oddly indifferent Federalist nominee said it best, as he explained why his loss was foreordained. Monroe, King observed, "had the zealous support of nobody, and he was exempt from the hostility of Everybody."[84]

"Internal Improvements"

Before Madison took his leave, the overall atmosphere of experiment and renewal brought the constitutional issue of "internal improvements" (highway and canal building) front and center for the first time since 1808. Back then, with Jefferson's blessing, and in a desire to secure the Union, Treasury Secretary Gallatin had prepared an elaborate report for Congress with a series of recommendations detailing the practical means and probable expense involved in linking North, South, and West. With the retirement of the national debt there would be fewer barriers to public works projects; and with its responsibility for appropriations, Congress could enact legislation without stepping on the rights of the states whose land and navigable waterways were involved in the prospective projects.

Like Jefferson, Madison favored internal improvements in principle. All understood that good roads contributed to an increase in land values. Local authorities had traditionally built and maintained roads through taxes, but work usually stopped at the county line. Internal improvement, as a unifying national program, was something different, and the problem that concerned both the third and fourth presidents was whether a constitutional amendment was necessary to enable the federal government to undertake large projects. But whereas Madison embraced a federal responsibility for road building in service to national security and mail delivery, Jefferson was less committed to the principle; both were skeptical about internal improvements for strictly commercial ends.

As Madison completed his second term, the age of the canal and steamboat was getting under way. The expansive energy that these innovations were to provide to a generation of settlers, and to towns all along the Ohio and Mississippi rivers, was entirely unprecedented. DeWitt Clinton, Madison's opponent in the last presidential election, was, after many years of brash maneuvering, finally to achieve greatness as the lead proponent of the Erie Canal. When the federal government refused to offer support, he established a canal commission composed equally of Federalists and Clintonians. At the end of 1815 he began appealing for funds from within the Empire State.

Monroe's running mate from New York, Governor Tompkins, was less than wholly enthusiastic about the project. Jefferson, on the other hand, looked over the plans Clinton had sent him and replied with zest: "The conception is bold and great, and the accomplishment will be equally useful." Always eager for proofs of America's superiority to the Old World, he added: "The works of Europe in that line shrink into insignificance in comparison." For Jefferson, in so many ways a Virginia apologist, progress was, on certain occasions, a matter of national pride.

The New York canal commissioners went ahead with a memorial to Congress in December 1816, offering an attractive cost-benefit analysis. But their final gambit yielded nothing, because the outgoing president made the matter moot. Just one day before Monroe's inauguration, Madison vetoed the Bonus Bill championed by Henry Clay and John C. Calhoun, which would have taken the first steps toward defining a permanent federal role in this crucial arena of national development and national prosperity. Meanwhile the Erie Canal, as an entirely state-sponsored enterprise, went on to make a profit even before completion, spurring Ohio and other states to imitate it, while making the federal government appear inept in the realm of internal improvements.

Madison shocked his allies in Congress when he issued the veto.[85] It was he, after all, who had urged Congress to take up the issue in his final annual message on December 3, 1816. And it was only after considerable wrangling that the House and Senate were able to come up with an agreement on the internal improvements dilemma. During those weeks of debate, the president reached the conclusion that the Bonus Bill was unconstitutional, that it undercut, in his words, the "definite partition" between the "General and State Governments." It appeared to him too incoherent, too nonspecific, to accomplish its noble goal. It might feed dishonest dealings between national legislators and interested state officials looking for advantages.

Jefferson, and later Gallatin, agreed with Madison's second reading of the Bonus Bill. The most respected analyst of the subject, historian John L. Larson, offers a somewhat cynical interpretation of what went on in President Madison's mind: he had come to distrust the founders' successors. Writes Larson, "Madison watched young men with no roots in the founding take up the game of constitutional construction . . . Madison hoped to bind the rising generation with the authority of the Union's creators." If true, it might have reflected his fear of the future, but it also shows a lack of introspection on Madison's part—for he had broken with his own past views more than once.[86]

Another executive decision that Madison reached at the end of his tenure in office spoke to his interest in the authority of the Union's creators, this one far less complicated. He directed the patriotic John Trumbull to paint four large murals for the Rotunda of the rebuilt Capitol building, taking as their subject what Madison viewed as the most memorable events of the Revolution: the signing of the Declaration of Independence, the resignation of George Washington from the Continental Army, the surrender of General John Burgoyne after the Battle of Saratoga, and the surrender of General Charles Cornwallis at Yorktown. They would be life-size representations of dynamic proceedings, each one twelve by eighteen feet.

Jefferson had played an unconscious role in Madison's executive decision. Trumbull had conceived his iconic *Declaration of Independence* and *Surrender at Yorktown* in 1786–87, while a guest at Jefferson's home in Paris. *The Resignation of General Washington* was of particular significance to Jefferson: as a member of the Confederation Congress, he had been present at the ceremony in Annapolis, in December 1783, bearing witness as the victorious general, speaking in slow, hushed tones, resigned his military commission and acknowledged civilian authority over the United States. "Having now finished the work assigned to me, I retire from the great theatre of action," Washington had recited at that time. And now Madison was to do the same.[87]

CHAPTER FIFTEEN

Madison Lives to Tell the Tale
1817–1836

To myself you have been a pillar of support thro' life. Take care of me
when dead, and be assured that I shall leave with you my last affections.

—JEFFERSON TO MADISON, FEBRUARY 17, 1826

You cannot look back to the long period of our private friendship and
political harmony, with more affecting recollections than I do.

—MADISON TO JEFFERSON, FEBRUARY 24, 1826

MADISON AND JEFFERSON EACH KEPT UP A SPIRITED CORRESPON-
dence with state and national figures. But as their friend and neighbor
Monroe assumed the presidency, their impact on current political debates
was less direct and, to a certain degree, self-limited. When asked by the
younger generation to clarify some past action or intent, they would do
what they could to give a durable answer. As gentlemen, it mattered to
them how they were received; as Revolutionaries who had lived through a
highly partisan age, they cared how they would be thought of by posterity.

The political environment in which they had come of age was fast re-
ceding. Men born in the 1770s, and even the 1780s, were now the dominant
voices in statehouses and the U.S. Congress. In 1813, when Benjamin Rush
passed away, Jefferson and John Adams were already tallying the names of
those signers of the Declaration of Independence whose obituaries had yet
to be published. "I am the only one South of the Patomac," Jefferson reported.[1]

As, one by one, the Revolutionary generation began to die off, Madison and Jefferson both took more of an interest in replenishing the earth—that is, in scientific farming. Some of their most involved correspondence addressed matters of agriculture, and Madison became president of the agricultural society of Jefferson's Albemarle County. The pair were as concerned now with the exhaustion of Virginia's soil as they had been with Virginia's stake in the American Union.

On March 4, 1817, outgoing President Madison was on hand for his successor's inaugural address. It was delivered outdoors because the rebuilt Capitol would not be reoccupied until 1819. "National honor is national property of the highest value," Monroe pronounced. "The sentiment in the mind of every citizen is national strength." The style of address was not Madisonian, but it expressed a continuation of policy. At the end of Monroe's oration, just as Madison had used the same occasion eight years earlier to ask to be "pardoned for not suppressing" his heartfelt sympathy with the retiring President Jefferson, Monroe said: "Of my immediate predecessor..., I shall be pardoned for expressing my earnest wishes that he may long enjoy in his retirement the affections of a grateful country, the best reward of exalted talents and the most faithful and meritorious service."

Like Jefferson in 1809, Madison in 1817 remained in Washington to participate in celebrations in honor of the new president. And like Jefferson, he would never return to Washington after his retirement to central Virginia. "I shall hasten my departure from this place as much as possible," he told Jefferson in mid-February, "but I fear I shall be detained longer after the 4th of March than I wish." In fact it was a whole month into the Monroe administration before Madison rode home.[2]

The New Yorker James Kirke Paulding accompanied him by steamboat along the Potomac on the first leg of the journey. Nationally known for both political satire and romantic fiction, Paulding had pseudonymously authored a lovely farce, *The Diverting History of John Bull and Brother Jonathan*, as the War of 1812 began. Madison enjoyed it immensely, complimenting it before knowing its author and calling it to Jefferson's attention. In 1815 he gave Paulding his first Washington job, an appointment to the Board of Navy Commissioners. In the waning months of the Madison presidency, they relaxed on a good many evenings, after the day's business was behind. "I have several times made the President laugh in a way altogether unbecoming a great man," Paulding wrote then. "He enjoys a joke hugely." Aboard the steamboat on his way to retirement, Madison was, Paulding reported, "as playful as a child." He "talked and jested with every body on board, & reminded me of a school Boy on a long vacation." Later in 1817 the author of *The Diverting History* found that he could be easily diverted himself. Jim Paulding spent several leisurely weeks in Madison's company at Montpelier, as much taken by Madison's wit as by his stock of old anecdotes—"for he was a capital story teller." Others said the same thing about this man whom history has painted too soberly.

The ex-president's mother, Nelly Conway Madison, was then in her mid-eighties and would thrive for another dozen years. James and Dolley called on her each day in the wing of the mansion where she sequestered herself. Mornings, as Madison and the affectionate Paulding rode out the front gate of the estate for a tour of farming operations, the younger man was enthralled by his host's dexterous use of a crooked stick to pry open the gate from atop his horse. As they discussed the past, Paulding was particularly struck by the ex-president's insistence that accounts of historic events written by political men tended to be unreliable. It was difficult, Madison said, even for one at the center of unfolding events to remember how a course was chosen—how, "from a multiplicity of motives," one thing led to another.[3]

"Heretofore Ascribed to Mr. Hamilton"

Jefferson the inveterate letter writer and seasoned communicator never denied that he wished to have an impact on the future. It was in the very fabric of his being. By 1817, when he was seventy-four, the executive experimenter had turned executive educator. What he had early conceived and fancifully termed "an Academical Village" became precisely that and more. Mr. Jefferson's university, as it would be familiarly known, used space in new ways. A combination of classical architecture and creative design, it began as a horizontal society, splendid pavilions spread across a lawn, rather than a conventional college revolving around an administrative core. Its villagelike setting encouraged it to function as a diverse community. Beyond the lecture halls, library, and student and faculty residences, a proctor, serving as a kind of permanent contractor, kept the "village" in shape. Vegetable gardens, farm animals, storage structures, washhouses, and other outbuildings were to support a growing student and faculty population and a paid and unpaid workforce. Some of the self-sufficiency Jefferson had developed on his mountaintop he sought to build into his university plan.[4]

From the purchase of acreage to its opening not long before Jefferson's death, the University of Virginia took eight years to build. In the spring of Monroe's first year as president and Madison's first year of retirement, Jefferson staged a meeting in Charlottesville, making sure to involve both men as members of the governing Board of Visitors of what was at that time still known as Central College. On the very day of their meeting, Jefferson wrote of Madison's retirement prospects to John Adams: "Such a mind as his, fraught with information, and with matter for reflection, can never know ennui. Besides, there will always be work enough cut out for him to continue his active usefulness to his country." And then, with wonderful understatement, he gave Adams a suitable example of their collaborative "usefulness": "a collegiate institution to be established in our neighborhood."

After prevailing on his fellow presidents to attend the foundational gathering in person, Jefferson gradually came to demand less of their time and attention as he saw the necessity that he make the day-to-day decisions himself. Jefferson wrote of his university-in-embryo with a gardener's loving concern: "I look to it as a germ from which a great tree may spread itself."

Jefferson's pet project did more than take up his time—it enthralled him. He designed the curriculum, cast a wide net in search of worthy professors, and monitored all expenditures. He would not resist having "Father of the University of Virginia" (though not "President of the United States") carved into his tombstone. Jefferson had been contemplating the establishment of a university since his unhappy term as vice president. He had cultivated a young state senator, Joseph Carrington Cabell, during the years of Madison's presidency. Cabell obligingly served as Jefferson's surrogate in Richmond, stepping forward and squeezing essential funds out of the parsimonious Virginia Assembly. Many years later, Cabell would preside over Mr. Jefferson's university as rector. The land itself, once but no longer owned by Monroe, was close enough that Jefferson could peer through his telescope from the lawn of Monticello and watch construction as it unfolded.[5]

While engaged in building his university, Jefferson made a concerted effort to forget all political contention. The one and only newspaper he read in the years after the War of 1812 ended was Thomas Ritchie's *Richmond Enquirer*. When Ritchie began sending him a new offshoot of that paper, the *Richmond Compiler*, which focused attention not on national news but the Virginia economy, Jefferson politely declined it. He discontinued his subscription to William Duane's Philadelphia *Aurora*. To the always-friendly publisher of Washington's *National Intelligencer,* he was unequivocal when he rejected that paper too, saying, "It is useless to be recieving newspapers which I never open." He explained that he read Ritchie's *Enquirer* "chiefly for the advertisements"; of outside events in general, he insisted, "I scarcely enquire or wish to know what is passing." He did not allude to the nine essays published in the *Enquirer* that were authored by William Branch Giles, a longtime ally, who had now turned to mocking Jefferson as the "prince of philosophers" and an eccentric. Giles strongly opposed the ex-president's activism when it came to overhauling Virginia's system of education. But this was one field in which Jefferson's passion to chart a course and build a legacy was unstoppable, as Giles would learn.[6]

At the time he was swearing off newspapers, Jefferson was compiling his *Anas,* piecing back together the fragmentary notes of conversations and meetings that had taken place while he was secretary of state. He believed that this record was superior to anyone's memory, and that it could and should be used by historians to recount Alexander Hamilton's power-hungry designs and Jefferson's purposeful embrace of real republicanism. Not long afterward, in 1819, at the age of seventy-six, he described his accession to the presidency as the "Revolution of 1800," a transformational moment. History was meant to record the change in the principles and functions of government that took place then. In Jefferson's reconstruction of events, from 1801 forward, the federal government began to favor the interests of ordinary citizens rather than accord artificial advantages to a moneyed elite.

It is in his final years' correspondence that we see Jefferson's most concerted effort to enlist others in drawing on original documents, stored at Monticello, to contest Federalist historiography. Madison is harder to assess, because as usual the records he left are more subtle. He clearly evidenced pride in the outcome of the War of 1812, though without directly claiming that success had been a function of his stewardship. In a retrospective glance at the two wars he had lived through, written less than a year after his presidency came to an end, he unostentatiously donned the laurels of the victorious commander in chief and gave what amounted to a benediction. "If our first struggle was a war of our infancy," he said of the Revolution, "this last was that of our youth; and the issue of both, wisely improved, may long postpone, if not forever prevent a necessity for exerting the strength of our Manhood."[7]

We do know that getting history "right" had long mattered to Jefferson.

Recall that as president, in 1802, he tried to induce the poet Joel Barlow to compose the counternarrative to Chief Justice John Marshall's biased *Life of George Washington,* the last (and most offending) volume of which was not published until 1807. Jefferson was still seeking vindication nineteen years later, in the weeks before he died, when he pressed the volatile son and namesake of the volatile General Henry Lee to inspect his papers at Monticello. In between, he leaned on several others, including an associate justice of the Supreme Court, to draw on his handwritten records and prepare a history akin to what he had expected of Barlow. Marshall, who would still be on the bench several years after Jefferson's death, tormented him. Jefferson wanted a Republicanized "History of Parties," as he termed it, to serve as the antidote to the "five volumed libel" of the long-active chief justice.

Henry Lee IV pursued both Jefferson and Madison. The former may have been desperate enough to count on the first-time biographer's objectivity, but the latter was a good deal less encouraging. This gifted but unpredictable scion of an old and distinguished Virginia family appealed to Madison in altogether flattering terms, saying that if he were allowed to write the president's biography, he would "make your memory as illustrious as your life has been distinguished and useful." He was ambitious enough to say that he planned to write the biographies of the greatest living Virginians: Jefferson, Madison, Monroe, and Marshall.

Madison's rejoinder to Lee was to say that he did not want his life examined except posthumously. He explained that the best material was already in the public record and would constitute an intellectual history at some later date. That was far from the whole story. Madison was not about to reveal to Lee what he really felt.[8]

In 1818 William Plumer of New Hampshire, contemplating an end to public life, wrote Madison familiarly: "Like you I hope to devote the remainder of my days to agricultural & historical pursuits." He was probably referring to the reading of historical works, a sentiment Madison had shared with him. But Madison was not merely a passive reader of history in his early retirement years. Unlike Jefferson, he never explicitly forswore newspapers, and he carried on avid conversations concerning matters of constitutional law and policy. He remained issue-oriented.[9]

At nearly the same time as Plumer's letter came to him, Madison received a "handsome copy" of a brand-new edition of *The Federalist,* published in Washington by Jacob Gideon. It was the third edition and, surprisingly, the first that Madison had had a hand in. That is why it matters. He had been in transit when Alexander Hamilton made arrangements for the 1788 printing and, for partisan reasons, was not consulted at the time Hamilton authorized the 1802 revised edition. So when Gideon had approached him and asked for the loan of a first edition, Madison had happily obliged, supplying an annotated copy, corrected to show who had actually authored each of the numbers. This time Hamilton was not around to oversee the process. Had Hamilton intentionally, or the initial publisher inadvertently, assigned authorship of some Madison numbers to Hamilton? Or was Madison's memory imperfect? The most accomplished modern editor of *The Federalist* sides with Madison in most cases.

Gideon responded favorably to Madison's recommendation that he include for added interest and clarification the Articles of Confederation that the Constitution was designed to replace. He also took it upon himself to include the "Pacificus" and "Helvidius" letters of 1793, in which Hamilton and Madison had argued key constitutional issues. At that time Hamilton, striking first, had asserted that the executive's role in the making of foreign policy was paramount; Madison gave as good as he got, as certain that the executive's aggrandizement of powers reserved for Congress threatened to ruin the constitutional balance the framers wished to preserve. The substance of their debate, as things turn out, remains current in the twenty-first century.

Madison was initially opposed to the insertion of the point-counterpoint of "Helvidius" versus "Pacificus" and told the publisher so. In Madison's mind, *The Federalist* showcased a collaboration; the 1793 essays, though constitutionally relevant, pitted the same pair in opposition—to add them, he said, would be a "double incongruity," serving to confuse the reading public. But Gideon had gotten his idea from the last edition (1802), inspired by Hamilton, which highlighted "Pacificus" by itself, without Madison's counterargument. Gideon wanted to give Madison equal time. Madison dropped his protest; he ended up correcting errors from a previous publication of "Helvidius" and submitted an authorized version. The 1818 edition of *The Federalist*, with its additions and alterations, advertised Madison's involvement on its title page.

The exchange of letters between Madison and Gideon confirms Madison's interest in seizing every opportunity to set the record straight. In the end, the publisher flattered both himself and the ex-president when he assured Madison that the public welcomed the new edition as "the first work of merit published within the district of Columbia." Its historical value was already being felt, he added, in that the new edition would "tend much to stop the many misrepresentations" by which several numbers "heretofore ascribed to Mr. Hamilton" would now be known to have been written by Madison.[10]

"Interference & Excitement"

After perusing Gideon's edition of *The Federalist,* Madison rode to Monticello and accompanied Jefferson west to the Blue Ridge Mountains. There, at Rockfish Gap, Jefferson made a personal appeal to a special state commission on education and secured for Charlottesville the permanent location of the state's university, which until that moment had yet to be formalized. The towns of Staunton and Lexington presented themselves as alternative sites, but the mere presence of the two former presidents seemed to be enough for the commission to grant them their wish. Unfortunately for Jefferson, rather than ride home with Madison, he opted to travel north to Virginia's Warm Springs, to treat his rheumatism. And instead of getting better, he contracted a fever along with a painful skin infection. Boils broke out across his backside—"a large swelling on my seat," he informed his daughter. He required months to recuperate.[11]

Meanwhile President Monroe earned short-lived credit for ushering in the "Era of Good Feelings," after his postinaugural tour of Federalist New England restored faith that the business of America lay in creating new opportunities for growth. The president's tour included dinner with John Adams and other former adversaries. Amid the healing that took place, the President's House received a postwar makeover and was painted a vivid white, making it possible for citizens to begin to call it the White House. Social events there in the Monroe years lacked the warmth and amusement that the bubbly Dolley Madison had famously provided; the current president and first lady were both widely regarded as colorless and preferred to keep to themselves. It was Monroe's dynamic cabinet members who maintained ties with congressional allies, allowing the president his executive privacy, when he wanted it, without alienating lawmakers.[12]

During Monroe's two terms in office, it became increasingly apparent that the immediate future of the republic lay in the hands of those who had not been schooled in the Virginia way. It was the beginning of a long slide for the Old Dominion. Its planter gentry was treading water as the North developed vibrant new industries and the West took on a life of its own—

America's fastest-growing city at this time was Cincinnati, Ohio. Canals and railroads were bound to connect the diversifying West to the Northeast, leaving the once-mighty South behind. Dependence on slavery intensified, old fears and jealousies refused to die, and the members of one section called into question the character and intentions of the other.

Though a southerner himself, a slave owner, and an ardent expansionist, Andrew Jackson made Thomas Jefferson politically uncomfortable. Nor did he relate easily to the mind of James Madison. The one occasion, in late 1815, when Jackson sat with the fourth president, their conversation was less than lively, and the frontier fighter's eyes wandered to the ruins of public buildings. This brief vignette, recorded by a Jackson aide, does not say a lot, though perhaps it symbolizes the lack of connection between two who did not quite see eye to eye.

On the other hand, General Jackson believed that he had, in President Monroe, a man he could work with and, hopefully, influence. On the fifth president's inauguration day, before launching into a long, advice-filled letter on everything from enforcing loyalty to directing policy, Jackson noted, with what sounds like mere formality: "Your Predecessor accomplished much for his country. None could have served with more virtuous zeal—yet there still remains undone, much for you to perform." What he expected of Monroe was the cultivation of peace and safety on Jackson's terms, which meant allowing his major general to push for wider national boundaries.[13]

Before he became president himself, the irrepressible Jackson had a way of courting sitting presidents and their secretaries of war until all disappointed him. At the time of his first militia command, he had made hopeful appeals to Jefferson, only to be disgusted by the president's embrace of the dishonest General Wilkinson. He found little to criticize as long as Madison condoned an aggressive Indian policy; but he never believed Madison at all skilled in war management. Monroe was different because he was the only member of the Virginia Dynasty who had been a soldier and had seen action on a Revolutionary battlefield. "I have waited with anxious solicitude," he flattered Monroe, "for the period to arrive, when I could congratulate my Country and myself on your being placed in the Presidential Chair of this rising republic." He despised Monroe's secretary of the treasury (Madison's last secretary of war) William H. Crawford of Georgia, and he did not know enough to distrust Monroe's secretary of war, John C. Calhoun, who successfully hid his condemnation of the general.

Jackson sometimes misjudged men. Authorized by Calhoun, in 1818, to cross into Spanish East Florida for the sole purpose of pacifying the Seminole Indians, he interpreted his orders loosely and launched a complete invasion, refusing to stop until he had embarrassed the administration. Monroe's instinct was to accept his explanation that Indian aggressiveness was the result of "interference & excitement" by the Spanish authorities. But after word arrived that the Tennessean had reduced the Spanish forts, Monroe wrote to Madison: "The fact is, that genl Jackson was not authorised to take them, & did it on his own responsibility." When Jackson hanged two British subjects for their collaboration with the Seminoles and caused an international uproar, Madison and Jefferson both rationalized that they were not close enough to the action to determine whether Jackson had overstepped his authority; they gave the general some leeway. A British political cartoonist labeled Jackson a "butcher," while depicting President Monroe as manic, wild-eyed, and eternally grateful to the pitiless soldier.

To all appearances, President Monroe, like President Madison during the West Florida Republic interlude, was uninvolved in the action—reluctant to disturb relations with the Spanish and British. Most likely aggressive actions were condoned in both incidents because communications were slow and insufficiently specific: Madison, in 1810, and Monroe, in 1818, both enjoyed what is today called plausible deniability.

At the time of Fulwar Skipwith's brief tenure as chief executive of the West Florida Republic, the Spanish military presence had been negligible, requiring nothing more than a token U.S. force to bring the disturbance to a resolution. In the case of Jackson's bloodier invasion of East Florida, when the cabinet weighed in privately on the general's behavior, Secretary of State John Quincy Adams, whose background and personality was the least Jacksonian, proved to be the one voice, and yet an overpowering one, in favor of his precipitous move. It was in the nature of frontier warfare, he said, for "retributive justice" to be applied. Monroe adopted a neutral pose until Adams made his case. But Jackson allowed himself to believe that Monroe had been in his column all along.

Congress investigated, and Jackson, facing censure, was obliged to come to Washington to explain himself. Monroe told Jefferson that if Jackson had been brought to trial for exceeding his orders, "the interior of the country would have been much agitated, if not convulsed by appeals to sectional interests." Most everyone believed it was high time that Madrid was pushed to negotiate a firm boundary between U.S. and Spanish possessions. Madison and Jefferson were on board with this policy, adding their tacit approval to an illegal invasion that ended with the long-sought acquisition of the whole of Florida, in the Adams-Onís Treaty of 1819.[14]

Events had played into Monroe's hands. In the next phase of declaring American muscle, Monroe's name would be affixed to a doctrine that rightly should have been named after his Federalist-born-and-bred secretary of state.

"The Blot on Your Person"

If any "good feelings" remained from Monroe's Northeast tour, they were greatly shaken in 1819. A financial panic that year disrupted the nation's sense of its unbounded economic promise. Credit suddenly tightened, banks called in loans made to farmers and land speculators, and western land values plummeted. Expansionists blamed the Bank of the United States and eastern money men rather than their own greed. On the heels of the panic, the Territory of Missouri applied for statehood. Congressional debate centered on whether, or how long, slavery would be permitted to exist in the new state. A New York member of the House, James Tallmadge, urged his colleagues to vote to prohibit the further importation of slaves into Missouri and to arrange for the gradual emancipation of those already present. At this time, according to the national census, there were 1.5 million slaves in the United States, more than double the number there had been in 1790, and southern representatives argued that Congress lacked the authority to impose conditions on the admission of new states. In point of fact, the South was afraid of losing ground, as well as population, which would be reflected in future censuses and thus in the future composition of the House of Representatives.

As it was, northerners had every right to grumble about the three-fifths clause in the Constitution. In 1820 the slave population accounted for nearly half of South Carolina's electoral votes. When Senator Rufus King of New York declared that slavery was "contrary to the law of nature, which is the law of God," southerners feared for their safety; the Speaker of the Virginia House of Delegates responded that King would bring on "the tragical events of St. Domingo" in America. Virginia's reliance on tobacco production was lessening as the number of slaves in the state increased through normal procreation. Thus slave owners in need of capital insisted on retaining the right to sell slaves to new western settlers. Eventually a compromise was reached that allowed Missouri to come into the Union as a slave state, while Maine (until this time part of Massachusetts) entered as a free state. The balance between slave and free remained unchanged for the time being. A line was drawn west from Missouri's southern border, defining where, if not precisely how, future slave and free states would be carved out.[15]

At this point Jefferson decided to weigh in on the Missouri question, writing a much-quoted letter to John Holmes of Massachusetts/Maine. When Jefferson was president, Holmes had been a Federalist member of the Massachusetts state legislature; since 1817, however, he had been serving as a Republican member of the House of Representatives, resigning in 1820 in order to participate in Maine's state constitutional convention. To advance statehood, he pragmatically adopted the compromise position on Missouri, though the citizens of Maine opposed slavery. With Maine's admission to the Union, Holmes was elected as one of its first two U.S. senators. He took up his new duties just as Jefferson's letter arrived in the mail.[16]

Holmes had sent Jefferson a copy of his address to his constituents on the vexing problem of Missouri, in which he argued that the question was more complex than many of his neighbors realized. "The Constitution of the United States was a compromise of conflicting rights and interests," he reminded them. No one wanted slavery to become intractable, he assured; allowing slaves to be "carried" west was a means "to disperse but not to increase" their number.[17]

Jefferson answered Holmes's welcome essay by expressing his fears for the future of the nation. The heated debate over Missouri was "a fire bell in the night," he wrote, which "awakened and filled me with terror." Unfortunately, he went on, its resolution was a temporary solution, a "reprieve" only: "As it is, we have the wolf by the ear and we can neither hold him, nor safely let him go." True to the spirit of his worried prognostication in *Notes on Virginia* so many years before, Jefferson underscored two, and only two, words in the letter to Holmes: *practicable* and *expatriation*. The only feasible long-term solution was the removal of black Americans—the same belief, subscribed to by a majority of whites, that had brought the purportedly philanthropic American Colonization Society into being three and a half years earlier. As the historian Francis Cogliano recently observed of the "wolf by the ear" metaphor: "It invites sympathy for the man holding the wolf and understanding of his unwillingness to let it go."[18]

Holmes was entranced by Jefferson's reasoned reply, which emphasized the moral necessity to end slavery and deemphasized the comments on black inferiority in *Notes on Virginia* that are so repellent to the modern reader. The letter was vintage Jefferson, cleverly constructed to communicate broad-mindedness and an essential humanity. He called the "cession" of his slaves—their complete emancipation—a "bagatelle," a matter so simple to conceive and carry out that it was scarcely worth the thought. He was saying, of course, that emancipation would be simple *if* the ex-slaves' removal from white society was accomplished at the same time. And that was all he was really saying.

While he and Holmes were exchanging letters, Jefferson wrote offhandedly to Jack Eppes: "I consider a woman who brings a child every two years more profitable than the best man on the farm." Whether or not Jefferson did anything to encourage their fertility, it has been shown that slave women on his plantations began bearing children at a younger age than slaves on most other southern farms, and three years earlier than the average northern woman. But it was Jefferson's literary hyperbole that Senator Holmes found especially appealing. He had captured Jefferson saying that he would be delighted—it would not "cost" him "a second thought"—if all the slaves of the South were freed. The Missouri Compromise could be twisted to mean that its supporters did not in all ways sanction slavery.[19]

After he had pored over the "wolf by the ear" letter, the Maine senator wrote back enthusiastically, telling Jefferson, as was customary in the republic of letters, that he had shared their correspondence with "a few select friends" who could be relied on to be discreet. Jefferson's was too good a letter to be filed away. It deserved to be widely publicized, and Holmes wanted his permission to release it to the press. But having endured much abuse as a result of the publication of his indelicate, undiplomatic, or thoughtless speech, Jefferson was loath to give his consent. He had memories of the controversial preface to Paine's *Rights of Man;* and the notorious Mazzei letter, with its implied insult to George Washington. So when the former president addressed Holmes again, he begged to be allowed to enjoy some tranquillity in his old age. "Some, I know, have forgiven, some have forgotten me," he wrote preciously, "but many still brood in silence over their angry recollections. And why should I rekindle these smoking embers?"[20]

There is a Madisonian parallel to Jefferson's Holmes letter. Indeed, nothing demonstrates the unseen side of James Madison quite so well as a literary exercise he engaged in as the Missouri crisis was concluding. Without intending it for any eyes but those he most trusted, he composed "Jonathan Bull and Mary Bull," a kind of soap opera inspired by Paulding's War of 1812 parable, *The Diverting History of John Bull and Brother Jonathan.* Both were absurd perspectives on old rivalries—except instead of England and America, this time it was North versus South.[21]

In Madison's version, more legalistic and less droll than Paulding's, Jonathan and Mary were "distant relations of" (which he crossed out in favor of "dependants of") "old Mr. Bull." They had inherited "contiguous estates" and moved naturally toward matrimony despite the meddling of Old Bull, who used his ample purse and his knowledge of the "subtleties of the law" to come between them. Seeing rationally, the couple devised a plan, and "an intermarriage was determined on & solemnized with a deed of settlement as usual in such opulent matches." In Madison's rendering, the marriage is decidedly not based on affectionate ties, though it does seem to make sense.

"The marriage of J. & M. was not a barren one," he continues puckishly. "Every year or two added a new member to the family," each of whom received "a good farm, to be put under the authority of the child on its attaining the age of manhood." As the "estates" were separately controlled by Jonathan and Mary, "tenants" issued forth from one or the other's original terrain. Competition ensued.

Clumsily, Madison assigned an unfortunate trait to Mary, a "stain" from "a certain African dye" that had disfigured her left arm in childhood. The arm was "perfectly black" and consequently weaker than the other arm. Jonathan had been well aware at the time when the dye, this "noxious cargo," had entered the river running through Mary's estate; but she possessed a "comely form" otherwise, and so he had not allowed the one imperfection to dissuade him from marrying her.

There came a time, however, when all he could think about was the "black arm" of his bride. He taunted her unmercifully, reminding her of his "long forbearance," and demanded that she "tear off the skin from the flesh or cut off the limb." In Madison's blunt reconstruction of the debate among the members of Congress, he insisted that the North's sense of moral superiority was as arrogant as it was unjust. "White as I am all over," Jonathan declares, "I can no longer consort with one marked with such a deformity as the blot on your person." He is the aggressor, of course: "Mary was so stunned by the language she heard that it was some time before she could speak at all."

Madison's refusal to acknowledge the North's right to speak out against southern slavery is matched by his feminization of the South, vulnerable if not wholly innocent and routinely subjected to unwarranted pressure. In his awkward script, it is the North that is unfeeling (as "our British brethren" were in the Declaration of Independence); it is the North that contemplates divorce; and the North that demands of its erstwhile partner nothing short of a voluntary dismemberment—sectional suicide—if the marriage is to be saved.

Mary alone appreciates the "good feelings" that are meant to characterize relations between husband and wife. Her "generous & placable" temper was being tested, her "proud sensibility" to "unjust & degrading treatment" an utterly reasonable response. She is calm as she tries to talk sense to Jonathan, whom she continues to refer to respectfully as "my worthy partner." Don't forget our original "deed of settlement," she reminds him, that which constituted "our Union." She bade him remember that at the time of their joining together, "you yourself was not entirely free of a like stain on your own"—and here Madison could not decide whether to use the word "person" or "color." On their wedding day, Jonathan had had "spots & specks" as black as Mary's.

The next of Madison's transparent metaphors drew upon the still highly uncertain practice of medicine. "If so cruel an operation were to be tried," as attempting all at once to remove the black from Mary's arm, no one could say what might happen. Jonathan was asked to reflect on what "the most skilled surgeons" were predicting: that the result would probably be fatal—"a mortification or bleeding to death." And if the experts were wrong and surgery did not in fact result in death, Mary would still be left "mangled or mutilated." Would you like me better in such a condition? she asks her husband.

Next, she asks him a rhetorical question: Would divorce make your estates stronger than they are as one half of our union? She did not deny that his protective arm made her stronger; she readily admitted that his "aid & counsel" made her a better household manager. Jonathan should, for his part, admit that her "purse" was valuable to him in the event of future "litigious" actions by "Old Bull" or anyone else.

Madison's parable lacked a rousing conclusion, and the compromise worked out over Missouri statehood proved to be nothing more than a holding action. As every student of history knows, the estrangement of North and South resulted four decades later in the unimaginably bloody Civil War. Not until 1835, the year before he died, did Madison finally permit the *Southern Literary Messenger* to publish "Jonathan and Mary Bull."[22]

The reactions of Madison and Jefferson to the crisis of union were dissimilar. The two shared a "foreboding" about the future, as the historian Peter Onuf has written, but whereas Madison remained privately cynical, Jefferson was jumpy. He had slipped into the radical Old Republican camp of John Taylor of Caroline and Virginia Appeals Court judge Spencer

Roane. At the height of the Missouri debate, the latter cautioned President Monroe that Virginians were already surrounded by blacks and refused to be "dammed up in a land of slaves." Jefferson was, in Onuf's words, "self-dramatizing" and "dangerously doctrinaire," as he pursued a "solipsistic fantasy of death and destruction." He supposed that the republic founded on common consent and common lineage was now held together by mere threads. Acknowledging that the Missouri question had aroused him from political slumber, he wrote nervously to his onetime protégé William Short, who now lived in Philadelphia: "The old schism of federal & republican, threatened nothing because it existed in every state." Partisanship along sectional lines spelled a far greater danger, and Jefferson knew it.[23]

After 1821 the sound of the "fire bell" was more muffled, and while Jefferson's alarmed sense of an overreaching federal power did not quiet much, he was able to reinvest his heart in the university and in watching his grandchildren (and even great-grandchildren) grow. He turned his financial affairs over to his eldest grandson, Thomas Jefferson Randolph. Though in earlier years "Jeff" had proved less studious than his grandfather had hoped, he resourcefully negotiated with bankers and worked tirelessly to manage the former president's mounting debts.

The slave economy did not offer Jefferson any comfort in his retirement. Madison too encountered significant problems of economy as he aged. Whereas Jefferson had his large family to think about, Madison, like Washington before him, had no children to whom he would will his land. Just as Washington had freed his slaves, effective upon the death of his widow, Madison anticipated that he would be able to do the same. But even he would find such a plan impossible to carry out, as the Virginia economy continued to experience decline.[24]

"Civilities and Softness of Expression"

During the Monroe years, politicized Virginians could not help but notice Judge Spencer Roane. Residing in John Marshall's hometown of Richmond, he had become the southern states' rights answer to the chief justice. It was Roane who had the loudest voice among the alliance known as the Richmond Junto, speaking through Thomas Ritchie's *Enquirer.* Even the *National Intelligencer* had come to support Marshall's rulings, causing Roane to perceive the nationalizing trend in dire terms. His opinion pieces grew more and more acerbic; his appeals always sounded ominous.[25]

During the middle months of 1821, at his wit's end, Judge Roane tried to convince Madison to take a public position against the Marshall Court. Two Marshall decisions in particular alarmed him so much that he solicited the man whom, he said, Virginians regarded as the greatest living constitutional thinker, to come out of retirement. "They see in your pen," he coaxed, "the only certain antidote" to Marshall. The case of *McCulloch v. Maryland* (1819) privileged the national bank by refusing to allow the states to tax any of its branches that operated within their borders. The case of *Cohens v. Virginia* (1821) asserted the right of a lottery firm set up by Congress to practice in contravention of Virginia law, thus thoroughly demeaning states' rights theory. Both decisions expanded federal power and undermined the strict construction of the Constitution that Madison and Jefferson had favored.[26]

Before he decided to address Madison, Roane had published several newspaper essays under the pseudonym of "Algernon Sydney," in which he called *Cohens v. Virginia* a "most monstrous" decision. He hearkened back to what he termed "the glorious revolution of 1799," the Kentucky and Virginia Resolutions, which had affirmed the state legislatures' right to overturn unpalatable acts of Congress. The judge was hoping that Madison might reenlist in the same cause now. But it had been twenty years, and Madison now considered the situation of the states far from dismal. Writing out of respect to Roane, he agreed that "the Gordian Knot of the Constitution seems to lie in the collision between the federal and State powers." But going into great detail to explain his current perspective, he seemed entirely comfortable with a nationalist agenda: Marshall's lack of tact was unfortunate but not unconstitutional. "It is to be regretted," he said, "that the Court is so much in the practice of mingling with their judgments pronounced comments and reasonings of a scope beyond them; and that there is often apparent disposition to amplify the authorities of the Union at the expense of the States . . . The constitutional boundary between them should be impartially maintained." He did not give Roane any further support.[27]

It is ironic that at this moment Jefferson was closer to Judge Roane in his thinking than to Madison, given how quickly Roane came to the defense of the memory of his late father-in-law, Patrick Henry. But Roane and Jefferson shared a strong personal antipathy toward Chief Justice Marshall. And they were deeply concerned that strengthening the federal government through judicial decisions made more intrusive constitutional revision in the future—such as the abolition of slavery—likely. "The great object of my fear," Jefferson wrote Roane in March 1821, "is the federal judiciary. That body, like Gravity, ever acting with noiseless foot, & unalarming advance, gaining ground step by step, and holding what it gains, is ingulphing [*sic*] insidiously the special governments [i.e., the states] into the jaws of that which feeds them." Like Henry's son-in-law Roane, and like Pendleton's nephew John Taylor, Jefferson took sustenance in the "recall to first principles" and hoped their combined call would be "heard & obeyed" by Virginia. "Let the eye of vigilance never be closed," he intoned.

From this impassioned charge, Jefferson went on to divulge to Roane what he could not block out of his mind. "Last and most portentous of all is the Missouri question. It is smeared over for the present: but it's geographical demarcation is indelible. What is to become I see not; and leave to those who will live to see it." Having emptied his gut of its fears, he had finally landed in a sentimental place. "The University will give employment to my remaining years," he breathed, "and quite enough for my senile faculties. It is the last act of usefulness I can render, and could I see it open I would not ask an hour more of life. To you I hope many will still be given." But Roane, nineteen years Jefferson's junior, died in 1822.[28]

Curiously, as all of this was occurring, Jefferson was moved to undertake what is now referred to as his autobiography. He did not mean to advertise it either as a concrete whole or as a self-exposition, as modern memoirists do. De-emphasizing its public value, he opened with a disclaimer: "At the age of 77. I begin to make some memoranda and state some dates & facts concerning myself for my own more ready reference & for the inform[atio]n of my family." Doubtless, his extended "memoranda" were meant to be available to friendly historians, as an authoritative record to form a part of a larger work on founding-era politics.[29]

After the disclaimer, he detailed the Jefferson family's Welsh ancestry and his mother's Randolph lineage to England and Scotland. He outlined his father's role in Virginia settlement and his own formal education; his awareness, as a young attorney, of the issues that led to the Revolution; and his interactions with the key figures, older than himself. Jefferson's anatomical dissection of his time in the Continental Congress is perhaps the most self-indulgent portion of the "memoranda," though his assignment and writing of the Declaration of Independence is cast in the humblest of language: "The committee for drawing the declaration of Independence desired me to do it. It was accordingly done." The superlatives employed in Jefferson's ostensible autobiography are reserved for his introduction of James Madison into the narrative:

Mr. Madison came into the House in 1776. a new member and young; which circumstances, concurring with his extreme modesty, prevented his venturing himself in debate before his removal to the Council of State in Nov. 77. From thence he went to Congress, then consisting of few members. Trained in these successive schools, he acquired a habit of self-possession which placed at ready command the rich resources of his luminous and discriminating mind, & of his extensive information, and rendered him the first of every assembly afterwards of which he became a member. Never wandering from his subject into vain declamation, but pursuing it closely in language pure, classical, and copious, soothing always the feelings of his adversaries by civilities and softness of expression, he rose to the eminent station which he held in the great National convention of 1787, and in that of Virginia which followed, he sustained the new constitution in all its parts, bearing off the palm against the logic of George Mason, and the fervid declamation of Mr. Henry. With these consummate powers were united a pure and spotless virtue which no calumny has ever attempted to sully. Of the powers and polish of his pen, and of the wisdom of his administration in the highest office of the nation, I need say nothing. They have spoken, and will forever speak for themselves.[30]

This is the tenderest tribute Jefferson ever wrote about anyone.

After six months on the project, Jefferson gave up—or felt he had done enough to advance his perspective on the history of the Revolution. He completed the work with an extensive accounting of his five years in Europe, finally putting down his pen after noting his arrival in New York in the spring of 1790. Presumably he meant for the already collated *Anas* to serve as a companion to the memoranda, a primary source of importance in exposing the delicate history of his conflict with Hamilton in Washington's cabinet. As to his two terms as chief executive, Jefferson must have expected his biographer to find materials in the vast correspondence that his grandson would eventually publish, beyond what lay in public archives.[31]

Benjamin Franklin's famed autobiography was also left incomplete, though probably not by its author's design. So did Jefferson and Madison discuss what each was doing independently to speak to future generations? There must have been moments when they did, though we have no clear record.

"A Subject Which Ruffles the Surface of Public Affairs"

Madison and Jefferson actively reviewed the names of prospective faculty for the university. Both men considered it essential that the professors should be amenable to their political as well as pedagogical perspectives. This was especially true in the case of the law faculty. "The most effectual safeguard against heretical intrusions into the School of Politics," wrote Madison, "will be an Able and Orthodox Professor, whose course of instruction will be an example to his successors."

The ex-presidents took special interest in the law and government texts they would assign to the first crop of students. In conceiving a curriculum, Madison displayed his fear of declension from republican traditions. He wrote that John Locke and Algernon Sydney, a seventeenth-century critic of the British monarchy (whose name Spencer Roane had adopted in his newspaper essays), were "admirably calculated to impress on young minds the rights of Nations to establish their Governments, and to inspire a love of free ones." But he also noted that these same thinkers "afford no aid in guarding our Republican charters against constructive violations." And "tho' rich in fundamental principles," the Declaration of Independence, he said, "falls nearly under like observation." Thinking of Jacob Gideon's recent republication of *The Federalist,* he commented that as a text for law students, it "may fairly enough be regarded as the most authentic exposition of the text of the federal Constitution...Yet it did not foresee all the misconstructions which have occurred; nor prevent some that it did foresee." It seems Madison was still wishing to refine, as well as redefine, the work.[32]

As Madison contemplated the meaning of *The Federalist* for a new generation, Jefferson had to fight revisionism in order to reclaim the Declaration of Independence. In 1823 the hostile and unrepentant Timothy Pickering delivered a provocative Fourth of July address, announcing that the Declaration was as much Adams's as Jefferson's and a rather undistinguished piece of work besides. Jefferson, despite his declared ignorance of what was in the newspapers, assured Madison that he retained his original drafts—self-evident historical truth—and "written notes, taken by myself at the moment and on the spot." He dredged up every past criticism that came to mind, not just Pickering's. "Richard Henry Lee charged it as copied from Locke's treatise on government," he recalled. "Whether I gathered my ideas from reading or reflection I do not know. I know only that I turned to neither book or pamphlet while writing it." Madison, obligingly, replied:

"Nothing can be more absurd than the cavil that the Declaration contains known and not new truths. The object was to assert not to discover truths, and to make them the basis of the Revolutionary Act. The merit of the Draught could consist only in a lucid communication of human rights... in a style and tone appropriate to the great occasion." Jefferson could not have said it better.[33]

Although Madison held firm in the conviction that his notes from the Constitutional Convention should remain unpublished until after his death, both he and Jefferson retained personal measures of political orthodoxy. Jefferson's was to ensure that his story of the Declaration remained the standard; and Madison's was to privilege *The Federalist* in sanctifying his plan of government. The primary texts at the University of Virginia were to be, then: "1. The Declaration of Independence, as the fundamental act of Union of these States." "2. the book known by the title of the 'Federalist,' being an authority to which appeal is habitually made by all... as evidence of the general opinion of those who framed and those who accepted the Constitution of the U. States on questions as to its genuine meaning." "3. the Resolutions of the General Assembly of Virg^a in 1799, on the subject of the Alien and Sedition laws . . ." "4. The Inaugural Speech and Farewell Address of President Washington, as conveying political lessons of peculiar value." These texts would enshrine the spirit of 1776, Madison's moment as a nation builder, and Jefferson's self-proclaimed Revolution of 1800, all the while reclaiming the republican heart and mind of George Washington, a man whose farewell address actually reflected Hamilton's critique and who died rejecting the common vision of Madison and Jefferson.[34]

While Jefferson concurred with Madison's selections, this did not mean that their perspectives on a party-free, or post-party, America were identical. In an 1822 letter to Gallatin that was more panic-stricken than politically perceptive, Jefferson saw a clandestine resurgence of the Federalist threat, which had been thought defunct: "You are told indeed that there are no longer parties among us..., [that] the lion and the lamb lie down together in peace. Do not believe a word of it. The same parties exist now as ever did." No one would get a single vote running as a Federalist after 1820; but Jefferson still insisted that those who had once been avowed monarchists were settling now for "consolidated government"—an overbearing federal presence, undermining states' rights. In Congress, he asserted, "you see many, calling themselves Republicans, and preaching the rankest doctrines of the old Federalists." It was more than the punishing presence of the Marshall Court that he feared. For Jefferson, the battle was far from over.[35]

In the autumn of 1823 Jefferson saluted a foreign friend. "We have gone through too many trying scenes together, to forget the sympathies and affections they nourished," he addressed the Marquis de Lafayette, before going on to describe the latter-day "agitation" in American political life. "The Hartford Convention, the victory of [New] Orleans, the peace of Ghent, prostrated the name of federalism," he declared. "Its votaries abandoned it through shame and mortification; and now call themselves republicans. But the name alone is changed, the principles are the same." The morbid tone resembled that of his warning to Gallatin, but this time Jefferson found a universal truth: "The parties of Whig and Tory, are those of nature. They exist in all countries, whether called by these names or by those of Aristocrats and Democrats, Coté Droite et Coté Gauche, Ultras and Radicals, Servile and Liberals. The sickly, weakly, timid man, fears the people, and is a Tory by nature. The healthy, strong and bold, cherishes them, and is formed a Whig by nature."

Back to the particulars of American politics, he called up the Missouri question yet again, insisting that it had been raised as a "false front" by those who pretended to care about ending slavery but who actually intended to produce "a geographical division of parties, which might insure them the next President." Predisposed, as he had been in the 1790s, to mourn the opposition's ability to dupe a part of the public, he charged: "The people of the North went blindfold into the snare." At the end of the 1790s, in Jefferson's political lexicon, the people had "recovered their sight"; after Missouri they gradually saw through "the trick of hypocrisy." He was apparently accepting that his correspondent Senator John Holmes of Maine represented a broader awakening. "The line of division now is the preservation of the State rights, as reserved in the Constitution, or by strained constructions of that instrument, to merge all into a consolidated government. The Tories are for strengthening the Executive and General Government." With consolidation in place, Jefferson warned, there was only one direction the United States could head in: it "must immediately generate monarchy."[36]

At the end of the 1790s Madison might have regarded monarchy as a distant possibility for Federalist America, if trends were not reversed; he might have thought *Tories* a still-relevant term. But in the 1820s such thoughts were extreme, and Jefferson's imagery unconvincing. Their divergence as retired presidents is evident in the letter Madison wrote to Lafayette as the Missouri debate was still simmering late in 1820. Allowing that he was keenly aware of Lafayette's strong abolitionist sentiments, we can see, even so, Madison's acceptance that the issue was neither simple nor stark. Missouri was, he wrote, "a subject which ruffles the surface of public affairs"—not a subject tearing apart the nation's viscera. "A Govt like ours has so many safety valves giving vent to overheated passions that it carries within itself a relief ag[ain]st the infirmities from which the best of human Institutions can not be exempt." The republic in the 1820s was, for Madison, a system prone to internal convulsion, but a self-healing system nonetheless.

He coolly reported to Lafayette that the question of Missouri centered upon "whether a toleration or prohibition of slavery Westward of the Mississippi would extend its evils." He had no easy answer: "The humane part of the argument against the prohibition turns on the position that...a diffusion of those in the Country tends at once to meliorate their actual condition, and to facilitate their eventual emancipation." That was Madison's conviction as well. Like Jefferson, he did not want to see the black population grow for any reason. He figured that national debate would continue until the fate of free blacks was resolved. Missouri's constitution excluded free blacks from the state, which was not unusual. Surveying the Union, Madison told Lafayette: "The Constitutions & laws of the different States are much at variance in the civic character given to free people of colour; those of most of the States, not excepting such as have abolished slavery, imposing various disqualifications which degrade them from the rank & rights of white persons. All these perplexities develope more & more the dreadful fruitfulness of the original sin of the African trade." He was saying that ambiguities in the laws made America's race problem more complex than a good-hearted republican would prefer to imagine. He may have come down on Jefferson's side of the argument, but it was not a "fire bell in the night" to him. The Missouri question did not destroy Madison's calm. To judge by his epistolary persona, he remained solemn, unexcitable, and unafraid.[37]

"All Power in Human Hands Is Liable to Be Abused"

The election of 1824 was one of the most thrilling and contentious in the annals of U.S. history. Campaigning began even before Monroe embarked on a second term, when newspapers decided to speculate on the future prospects of a new breed of politician. Change was eagerly anticipated.

For one of the few times in the quadrennial election cycle, party identities were indistinct and there were more than two viable candidates in the running. John Quincy Adams had New England locked up, but not much else; Henry Clay of Kentucky, Andrew Jackson of Tennessee, and William Crawford of Georgia vied for the South and West. Three of the four had been overseas envoys during the Madison administration; the fourth was the most conspicuous military hero since George Washington and had recently entered the U.S. Senate for the purpose of announcing his availability.

Jefferson hoped for Crawford, who seemed most likely to protect Virginia's interests—and in fact, the Georgian would go on to win Virginia's electoral votes. And while he said nothing for public consumption, Jefferson's feelings about Andrew Jackson were shaped by his knowledge of the general's ungovernable temper and lack of intellectual curiosity. The rough and ready Tennessean was an admirer of Napoleon and known in some circles as *"Napoleon des bois,"* or "Napoleon of the woods." Jefferson despised the French emperor and held nothing back when he labeled the Corsican a "scoundrel." Daniel Webster of Massachusetts, who visited Monticello prior to the election of 1824, heard Jefferson express his distaste for Jackson. Webster quoted him as having called the general a "dangerous" man.

Jefferson did not live long enough to see Jackson inaugurated, so it is difficult to say whether he would have been more gracious in evaluating the energetic and imposing seventh president. Jefferson's unofficial private secretary, Nicholas Trist, who married one of Jefferson's granddaughters, served as a State Department clerk in the John Quincy Adams administration before becoming a trusted Jackson aide. Madison, who lived until the end of the Tennessean's second term, did nothing to steal his thunder and earned the respect of the hard-edged old general as the years went by. It was indeed a time of flux in American politics.[38]

Madison and Crawford got on well, and in April 1824, when the candidate asked the ex-president to help him refute charges of improper ambition—solicitation of office—dating to Madison's second term, Madison responded promptly and positively. Madison was not as close to Clay, but they communicated unceremoniously. When in the midst of the 1824 campaign, Clay shared with Madison his argument in favor of a protective tariff, Madison explained collegially, candidly, and at length why he could not support the plan. Though Jefferson had always been more at ease with the elder Adams than Madison had been, Madison was decidedly more comfortable with John Quincy than Jefferson was. Monroe was not only pleased with the performance of the younger Adams, his secretary of state, but was personally fond of him too; and he had rather mixed feelings about Crawford, his secretary of the treasury, whom he came close to firing. Monroe strained to do all he could not to play favorites in his second term.[39]

Jefferson thought he was sorting out a mess when, in advance of the election, he viewed the competition to succeed Monroe and predicted that it would come down to two candidates: "a Northern & Southern one, as usual."[40] No one at the time could have predicted the course of this extraordinary political contest—whose result was as unplanned as the awkward tie between Jefferson and Burr in 1800.

Variables were present that Republicans in the past had not encountered. The nominating caucus no longer meant what it had. Ohio had more electoral votes than any southern state except Virginia. Crawford, the Virginians' favorite, suffered a stroke in 1823 yet remained on the ballot. And in eighteen of twenty-four states, popular votes were translated into electoral votes for the first time. But when all ballots were cast, none of the four leading candidates had received enough to win the presidency outright, though Jackson led all competitors by a clear margin in both popular and electoral votes. According to the Constitution, the House of Representatives would have to determine Monroe's successor.

Newspapers around the country indulged in speculation but with less acrimony than in past elections. Far from the action, in Maine, editors collected their thoughts as they collected the newspapers of Boston, New York, and points south. The *Portland Advertiser,* while lauding Jackson as "the candidate of the people," noticed "the superior popularity of Mr. Adams, above that of General Jackson, with the members of the House of Representatives." The *Advertiser*'s editor absorbed reports in Thomas Ritchie's *Richmond Enquirer.* Reading what he called the "Oracle of the Ancient dominion," the New Englander sensed correctly that Virginia's House delegation would deny Jackson.[41]

When the election was thrown into the House of Representatives, the fourth-place finisher, Henry Clay, was excluded from the three-person runoff, according to the rules laid down in the Constitution. Clay used his influence as longtime Speaker of the House to deliver key state delegations to Adams. And Adams, never afraid to act in accordance with the dictates of his conscience, committed a massive political error. By making the capable but controversial Clay his secretary of state, cries of a "corrupt bargain" rang out, which pretty much assured that the stubborn sixth president would be a one-term president, as his father was before him.[42]

Though Madison and Jefferson were largely spectators to the 1824 election, they shared a certain defensiveness on behalf of their native state. In February 1825, as Adams's controversial victory was broadcast through the national press, Madison wrote to Jefferson about the viability of one particular candidate for the professorship in moral philosophy at the university. The choice had to be made carefully, he said, because responsibilities included the teaching of finance; and the gentleman in question exhibited a doubtful adherence to the "Virginia Creed," after having become "a convert to the constitutionality of canals." It was quite unusual for Madison, not just in his retirement years but at any time, to state directly that he looked for evidence of the "Virginia Creed" when assessing a person's political character.

The professor he was writing about was George Tucker, a three-term Virginia congressman. Whether the "Virginia Creed" had any relationship to one's view of slavery is unclear. But Tucker had just published a novel, *The Valley of the Shenandoah,* that told of the deterioration of a Virginia plantation family and illustrated the wretchedness of slavery. When all was said and done, Madison and Jefferson agreed that it was worth taking a chance on Professor Tucker, despite the one "flaw," as Madison referred to his position on internal improvements. His educational "fitness," combined with a "great amiableness of temper," helped them overcome their suspicions. From the Virginia perspective, their trust was rewarded: in 1837, Tucker published a friendly biography of Jefferson. And he remained on the university faculty until 1845.[43]

In 1825 the constitutional question of funding improvements to the growing nation's transportation networks dominated Madison's thoughts. "It seems strange," he wrote to Jefferson, "but it is a certain fact, that there are several instances of distinguished politicians who reject the general heresies of federalism, most decidedly the amalgamating magic of the terms 'General Welfare,' who yet admit the authority of Congress as to roads and canals, which they squeeze out of the enumerated articles." He was wary of *utility,* a seductive word that could be used to rationalize any departure from constitutional correctness—what he now called "Constitutional orthodoxy." Both Madison and Jefferson felt that the current craze of canal building was a state and not a national responsibility. Using the same argument they did in opposition to federal interference with slavery in the territories, Madison feared that the popularity of a measure would overcome any constitutional objection, even when the Constitution was impossible to misconstrue. This was why his last act as president had been to veto the popular but, to him, unconstitutional Bonus Bill. Eight years later he was hopeful that the Supreme Court would steer clear of this issue. "The will of the nation being omnipotent for right, is so for wrong also," he opined for Jefferson.[44]

At the end of 1825 Madison was still on the case. Jefferson considered the matter as desperate. On Christmas Eve he wrote to Madison, enclosing a paper he had been asked to write by a neighbor who sat in the House of Delegates. It disavowed the notion that Congress had authority under the "General Welfare" clause to fund canals, and it assured skeptics at the same time of Virginians' continuing commitment to the Union. Written, Jefferson said, as "an example of a temperate mode of opposition," he thought it might at best "intimidate the wavering," and at worst "delay the measure a year at least." He wanted Madison to look it over. If Madison approved it, Jefferson would pass it on; if he frowned on it, "it shall be suppressed"; if it had merit but needed work, "make what alterations you please." Their collaborative engine was still in operation.[45]

Madison thought that Jefferson's paper, titled a "Solemn Declaration and Protest," was too strongly worded. He was worried that Jefferson would only be adding to the animosity many northerners felt toward Virginia. But he could hardly have disapproved of Jefferson's conclusion that a constitutional amendment was required to extend the canal-building power to the federal government. Madison himself had proposed at the Constitutional Convention a clause that would have empowered Congress to build canals.

What concerned him was Jefferson's reference to the "sister states" as "co-parties" to the constitutional compact. These terms were dangerously close to the extreme states' rights language that supported a state's right to nullify acts of Congress. Jefferson also used the inflammatory words *usurpation* and *degeneracy* when he referred to the increased use of federal power—language that Madison, the more cautious constitutionalist, would never have approved. Language one might expect to find in a Jefferson production was missing here: he did not mention "majority will," presumably because the majority will was now united against him. As Madison picked apart the proposed document, he showed Jefferson how it could do more harm than good.

Unbeknownst to Jefferson, Madison had already been asked by Ritchie, of the *Richmond Enquirer,* to prepare a like paper. The state legislature was in session, and as much as Jefferson's local delegate was feeling anxious, the politically savvy editor wanted to reach as many decision makers as he could. Madison sent Jefferson what he had sent Ritchie, a carefully outlined brief designed to aid the legislature in deciding what to do (and what not to do) to express Virginia's opposition to federally funded roads and canals. "All power in human hands is liable to be abused," he wrote epigrammatically. But if Virginia was free to exercise its right to call attention to a constitutional violation, that was all it could do.

For supporters of internal improvements, the federal government had every right to appropriate funds, just as, in regulating foreign commerce, Congress was authorized to deepen harbors and establish roads to assist in developing trade with Indians. Madison was not prepared to go back to the Virginia Resolutions, where the threat posed by the Alien and Sedition Acts struck him as a "deliberate, palpable, and dangerous" extension of federal power. The present issue did not rise to that level of danger; nor could it be described in dire terms.

His opposition was intellectually rooted, though of more than intellectual interest. But if he saw eye to eye with Jefferson on internal improvements, he still recognized that his state was on the losing side of this particular battle and should acquiesce. One thing had not changed: Virginians were still trapped in their inherited sense of bigness, as much as they were in 1776 and 1787; they were poised to defend against a tyranny that was unlikely ever to present itself.

Madison concluded his letter to Thomas Ritchie with a humble admission: "I find myself every day more indisposed, and, as may be presumed, less fit, for reappearance on the political Arena." He was accepting of the shift that was under way.[46]

"Mr. M. Feels His Departure Dearly"

In his letter to Lafayette on the Missouri question in 1820, Madison had written that if the Frenchman ever paid a visit to Montpelier, he would find "as zealous a farmer, tho not so well cultivated a farm as [Lafayette's estate] Lagrange presents." Madison, who had never made an ocean voyage, knew he was too old to give it a whirl. Nor did he expect the marquis, now in his sixties, to find his way back to Virginia. He wrote, without expectation: "I may infer from a comparison of our ages a better chance of your crossing the Atlantic than of mine." Lafayette had not set foot in America since 1784.[47]

As it happened, Madison and Jefferson would twice more be able to cast their eyes on their old friend. In advance of the fiftieth anniversary of the American Revolution, Congress and President Monroe had invited Lafayette to return to the United States to see how it had grown, and how beloved he still was. It was no exaggeration. During his thirteen-month tour, from August 1824 to September 1825, the last surviving commander of Continental Army troops grabbed headlines week after week. Accompanied by his son, George Washington Lafayette, he was heralded everywhere as "the nation's guest." In spite of the wear and tear on his aging frame, he obligingly visited every one of the twenty-four states.

Plainly dressed, with ample belly and undistinguished features, Gilbert du Motier de La Fayette was, all the same, an icon. Mothers presented their children to him, that he might confer his blessing; adulatory crowds spontaneously formed wherever he was spotted. Young ladies competed to set flower wreaths upon his head; balls were held and toasts drunk. In Newburgh, New York, citizens impulsively took to the streets in protest when it was learned that Lafayette was to shorten his stay and depart at night, before they could glimpse him.[48]

In mid-October 1824 the marquis was joined by Chief Justice Marshall and other notables at the Yorktown battlefield. From there he traveled west to Richmond, where he was again feted and where, in his aide's words, he witnessed "those bursts of frank and hearty merriment so distinctive of the inhabitants of Virginia." Finally the general was able to satisfy his desire to see Monticello, riding up the mountain in early November and embracing his host outside the columned home. Eyewitnesses were moved to tears. Jefferson took "the nation's guest" to the university, largely completed but for some of the brickwork and plastering of interior rooms. At the banquet staged at the unfinished Rotunda, Lafayette sat between Jefferson and Madison, the latter of whom toasted the Frenchman with memorable words: "To liberty, with virtue for her guest, and gratitude for the feast." Jefferson, protesting that his voice was too weak to be heard, had his prepared remarks read aloud by someone else.

Departing Monticello, Lafayette rode on to Montpelier, where the Madisons proved themselves ideal hosts. "Mr. Madison at the time of our visit was seventy-four years of age," recorded Lafayette's aide, Auguste Levasseur, "but his well preserved frame contained a youthful soul full of sensibility." Despite the "severity" of his outward appearance, "all the impressions of his heart are rapidly depicted in his features, and his conversation is usually animated with a gentle gaiety." At both Monticello and Montpelier—Lafayette stayed for several days at each—the subject of slavery came up more than once in conversation. Lafayette did not hold Madison and Jefferson personally responsible for the persistence of slavery; but he did not disguise his discomfort and, in his evening conversations with Madison's planter neighbors, voiced disgust that such a class of men could so easily condemn their fellow human beings to lives unfree and degraded.[49]

Once he had finished touring the interior states, Lafayette returned to Virginia in the late summer of 1825, before sailing back to France. Madison accompanied him through the Virginia countryside to Monticello, and Monroe, still in office when Lafayette first landed and now an ex-president, joined them there. Over the intervening months Jefferson had become quite frail and was confined to the house. Their visit took on a woefully expectant air. "I shall not attempt to depict the sadness which prevailed at this cruel separation," wrote Levasseur.[50]

The University of Virginia opened in May 1825. The curriculum of Jefferson and Madison was broader than that offered by older American colleges. For several years now the pair had scoured the national book market for seed texts to fill the shelves of the university's library. The faculty, largely imported from Great Britain, was meant to train a native corps of professors who would eventually succeed them. Among these men was a young professor of medicine, Robley Dunglison, who became Jefferson's personal physician as he went into decline.

In September 1825, shortly after Lafayette's departure, Jefferson informed Madison: "The state of my health renders it perfectly certain that I shall not be able to attend the next meeting of the [Board of] Visitors *at the University*." And so he called for the meeting to take place at Monticello. Madison was his designated successor as rector of the university, just as he had been preselected to succeed Jefferson in the presidency.[51]

Even in the first year of the school's operation, the students who came together in Charlottesville had more on their minds than an education. The ailing Jefferson had worries beyond those of finance and general administration. He may have delighted in having the faculty wives join their husbands for dinner at Monticello, but if he allowed himself to think his job of extending enlightened society was finished, events soon proved otherwise. Liquor, gambling, tobacco, and weapons were all prohibited on the grounds; but the students were not well behaved, and Jefferson himself reckoned that one-third could be best described as "idle ramblers." At length it became clear that alcohol had been smuggled into students' rooms, when someone launched a bottle through a window. Two professors were physically harassed, one of them hit by a rock. It was night when this occurred; the offenders stole away, and no student could be found to betray his classmates. A few days later the students were assembled, and with the eminent founders Madison and Jefferson both present, the culprits came clean.

According to one who was there, Jefferson attempted to address the students, but because of his deep and wounded feelings, he said little before he felt impelled to turn over control of the meeting to another of the Visitors. In pain when he walked and taking regular doses of the opiate laudanum, he was forced to confront anarchy in his own backyard during the last autumn he was to see. It could not have been easy.

Looking over a lifetime of his correspondence, one cannot but conclude that Jefferson's pen was most animated when he was able to express optimism. Once faculty authority was reasserted a short time later, his mood improved. "Every thing is going smoothly at the University," he told Madison. But then he added ominously: "My rides to the University have brought on me great sufferings, reducing my intervals of ease from 45. to 20. minutes. This is a good index of the changes occurring."[52]

On February 17, 1826, Jefferson wrote Madison a letter that began, as much of their correspondence had of late, with remarks about hiring faculty and constructing more classrooms. As the second year of instruction was to begin, the number of students continued to grow, and the dormitories would be filled. At this point, though, Jefferson broke into a long explanation of his personal finances, at the end of which he said: "But why afflict you with these details? I cannot tell, indeed, unless pains are lessened by communication with a friend." There was a tone of anticipation, if not finality, in his words: "The friendship which has subsisted between us, now half a century, and the harmony of our political principles and pursuits, have been sources of constant happiness to me through that long period. And if I remove beyond the reach of attentions to the University, or beyond the bourne of life itself, as I soon must, it is a comfort to leave that institution under your care."

Jefferson did not stop there; he wanted to record some testament to their larger purposes as public men. "It has also been a great solace to me," he said earnestly, "to believe you are engaged in vindicating to posterity the course we have pursued for preserving to them, *in all their purity*, the blessings of self-government." Though, in his mind, no satisfactory history of their collective labor had yet been published, he knew he could count on Madison to interpose, should his character again come under attack. "To myself you have been a pillar of support through life," he said as he concluded the richly appreciative letter. "Take care of me when dead, and be assured that I shall leave you with my last affections." A short time after this, Thomas Jefferson sketched his own tombstone, a small, crudely formed obelisk.[53]

Madison's reply echoed the sentiment. Assuring Jefferson of his commitment to the university, he compared himself unfavorably to his friend—"the Tutelary Genius of the Sanctuary"—and bade Jefferson hang on until the institution was strong enough that it did not need either of them. His own health was flagging, Madison said, empathizing: "The past year has given me sufficient intimation of the infirmities in wait for me." Turning, as Jefferson did, to their common political legacy, he added warmly: "You cannot look back to the long period of our private friendship and political harmony, with more affecting recollections than I do . . . And I indulge a confidence that sufficient evidence will find its way to another generation, to ensure, after we are gone, whatever justice may be withheld whilst we are here." It is hard to imagine a better testament of mutual devotion.[54]

At the end of his days Jefferson stood straight and continued to read eagerly. His mind was vigorous, his memory good, and his eyesight remarkable for a man of eighty-three. As the month of May 1826 began, he was able to report to Madison that "in comparison with my sufferings of the last year, my health, although not restored, is greatly better." He wished he could be spending more time reading and less answering letters, as civility demanded. Madison suggested that he should deal with his "epistolary taxation" by relying on a young family member to acknowledge his correspondence and to limit each reply to an expression of thanks. This was their last exchange of letters before Jefferson took a turn for the worse.[55]

The octogenarian moved slowly, while facing prostate problems and episodes of gastrointestinal distress. He was fortunate to have a physician on call. Robley Dunglison, born in Cumberland County, England, was just twenty-seven when he became the first professor of anatomy and surgery at the University of Virginia. Though they had known each other for only one year, he and the man who was both his employer and his patient built a close relationship. They talked textbooks and pharmacology.[56]

If only that had been all. Before he sank into his grave, Jefferson was forced to confront the result of a lifetime of indebtedness. Since at least the early 1790s, when he argued against Hamilton's view of the utility of a public debt as a key to long-term prosperity, he remained troubled by thoughts of the republic losing its way. He was, even then, sinking under his own interest-payment obligations. In 1809, at the end of his presidency, he was completely conscious of the distance he had to go before his debts were retired, and he vowed to his daughter that he would alter his spending habits. It was easier said than done. In 1818 he added to the nightmare by imprudently cosigning a sizable loan at the behest of his old friend Wilson Cary Nicholas, whose daughter had recently married his grandson. Nicholas defaulted and soon after died.

Retired from public life, Jefferson had held on to his hopes as long as he could, continuing to operate the Monticello nailery and to lease out his nearby mill. Year by year he waited to see greater profitability on his farms. Gradually he disposed of thousands of acres; but even this could not rescue the future. A state-sponsored lottery was launched in the early months of 1826, aimed at saving Monticello for his surviving family. One who contributed to the rescue effort was the wealthy William Short. He and Jefferson had remained warm friends and regular correspondents over the years, but Short had soured on the slave economy and saw states' rights thinking as stingy and backward. He was a staunch advocate of federally funded internal improvements and had made a fortune in New York land, Mississippi River steamboats, and other investments in the North. Not so Jefferson, who had first introduced Short to the engineering marvel of canals in France but who, with respect to personal investments, preferred to think small.[57]

The insolvent patriarch was spared the knowledge that the lottery effort had failed in its purpose. Monticello was lost, his daughter left with little. The slaves of Monticello faced the auction block, and families were split up. It was a most unbecoming conclusion to a life devoted to the promotion of fiscal discipline, modest government, and a serene vision of contentment in the bosom of a prosperous and productive nature. Jefferson's example proved that Virginia's economy would be in trouble for as long as slaves represented a commodity of comparable value to the planter as his actual crops.[58]

In a flight of fancy back in 1771, Jefferson had recorded a romantic idea in his account book: "Chuse out for a Burying place some unfrequented vale in the park where 'No sound to break the silence but a brook.' " Here among "antient and venerable oaks" and "gloomy evergreens," he would lay his family to rest and apportion half the area to "strangers" and "servants." The grave of his favorite slave would support a pyramid of "rough rock stone." But as things turned out, only immediate family were interred in that cemetery, and only Jefferson's plot featured that "rough rock stone" capped by a small pyramid. No servants were ever interred in the family plot.[59]

Dr. Dunglison recorded that Jefferson "spoke freely of his approaching death" and that his mind remained clear at all times. On his last night the dying man slept fitfully, even after the doctor had administered laudanum. He imagined himself back in the Revolution and thrashed with his hand, half-consciously calling for the Committee of Safety to prepare for attack. At around four A.M. on July 4, 1826, he called to his servants "in a strong and clear voice," though none of his words were recorded. He was conscious enough at ten A.M. to signal that he wanted his pillow adjusted. Then his breathing slowed, and he finally gave in at fifty minutes past noon. It was the day on which patriotic citizens across the country were gathering to celebrate the fiftieth anniversary of American independence; and the day on which ninety-year-old John Adams died as well.[60]

Madison had been prepared for Jefferson's death by the detailed prognosis he received from Dr. Dunglison on July 2. A note from grandson-in-law Nicholas Trist confirmed that Jefferson had died on the fourth—no comment was needed as to the significance of the date. Madison was unable to attend the July 5 funeral, but he commiserated with Trist in a letter of July 6: "We are more than consoled for the loss ... by the assurance that he lives & will live in the memory and gratitude of the wise & good as a luminary of Science, as a votary of liberty, as a model of patriotism, as a benefactor of human kind."[61]

In the will Jefferson had composed three months before, he left to Madison a "gold-mounted walking staff of animal horn, as a token of the cordial and affectionate friendship which for nearly now an half century, has united us in the same principles and pursuits of what we have deemed for the greatest good of our country." It was delivered by Dr. Dunglison, on instructions from Thomas Jefferson Randolph, who requested of Madison that he continue to make Monticello his "head quarters" whenever he visited the university. "The article bequeathed to me by your grandfather," Madison wrote in reply, "was received with all the feelings due to such a token of the place I held in the friendship of one whom I so much revered & loved when living, and whose memory can never cease to be dear to me." Dolley Madison confirmed the sentiment in a letter to her son, then in New York: "Mr. M. feels his departure dearly."[62]

"That Peculiar Feature in Our Community"

As he promised he would, Madison took over Jefferson's responsibilities as rector of the University of Virginia, holding that position for eight years—until he was the age Jefferson was when he died. In an extended visit to Charlottesville at the end of 1826, he endured winter storms and presided over students' examinations. He was constantly in communication with the other, younger members of the Board of Advisors, seeing to it that they did not convert a secular institution into one with a religious affiliation. He watched the library expand to ten thousand volumes. During difficult times Madison remained a resource for his late friend's family; but there was only so much he could do, writing to Lafayette of the "pinching poverty" that the white family of Monticello faced, as Jefferson's creditors descended upon them.[63]

He helped to oversee the preparation and publication of Thomas Jefferson Randolph's *Memoir, Correspondence, and Miscellanies, from the Papers of Thomas Jefferson,* which was printed and bound in Charlottesville in 1829; in Boston shortly after; and subsequently in Paris. At first Randolph planned just to publish Jefferson's partial autobiography (the *Memoir* that appears in his eventual title). Asked to pen a preface to it, Madison did so punctually. But then Jeff Randolph was persuaded that the autobiography was too little for a hungry public; and for a good many months he took pains to pore over his grandfather's lifetime of stored correspondence, selecting the letters and official addresses that ultimately came to comprise four volumes. He chose to include the lengthy dialogue between "My Head and My Heart," a letter of longing that Jefferson wrote to Maria Cosway in 1786, because it would be read as a proper treatise on friendship; but he appended none of the widower's more suggestive notes to the unhappily married Anglo-Italian artist. Also, Randolph failed to include the long, accusatory letter of September 1792 to George Washington, in which Jefferson referred to the foreign-born Hamilton as "a tissue of machinations" against the country that had "heaped" honors on his head. In an effort to avoid controversy, Randolph also removed any evidence of Jefferson's support for James T. Callender, the stubborn journalist who had first exposed Hamilton's extramarital affair, then called John Adams, when he was president, a "hoary-headed incendiary," and went on to publicize President Jefferson's long-standing relationship with Sally Hemings. Any criticism of the still-living Chief Justice John Marshall, whom Jefferson had regularly and roundly criticized in highly partisan literary rants, was excluded too.

Despite these editorial decisions, Randolph was less careful in his selections than Madison would have preferred. Prompted by Nicholas Trist to examine some passages, the former president called Randolph's attention to questionable remarks about John Adams that reflected poorly on both Jefferson and himself. Madison also worried about reaction from Hamilton's defenders, of whom there were yet many. In Hamilton's handling of the 1794 Whiskey Rebellion and his "dishonorable agency" in the election of 1800, Madison felt that "the implied charge of corruption" could "hardly fail to produce calls for proofs by those sympathizing most with the fame of the accused." He did not wish to open up his own cache of letters to refight old battles.

Although the *Memoir, Correspondence, and Miscellanies* brought remuneration to the Randolphs, the four volumes breathed new life into old debates over Jefferson's politics and personality. The collection contained the highly politicized *Anas,* "scraps" of unedited notes in "three volumes bound in marbled paper," detailing Jefferson's early suspicions about Hamilton's policies. As an editor, Randolph dropped sentences in the middle where they alluded to nasty business. And it was impossible not to notice that despite the insertion of sixty-nine letters from Jefferson to Madison, years go by in the chronology without the inclusion of any letters crucial to an understanding of the development of the Democratic-Republican Party or intra-party politics. There are none from September 1789 to April 1794, or from August 1804 to March 1809.[64]

In retirement, Jefferson had articulated his concerns rather differently from Madison. Most notable was his extraordinary fear of consolidated government. One of the last letters in Jefferson Randolph's collection, dated December 26, 1825, is addressed to William Branch Giles. Here, Jefferson expresses his fear for the "plundered ploughman and beggared yeomanry" subject to the rule of a monied aristocracy; he wants the federal "usurpation" of states' rights to be denounced "in the most peremptory terms."

Madison, of course, refrained from such language. He clarified the difference in their styles most instructively in a letter of 1832 to Nicholas Trist. One had to be careful, he said, not to read too much into Jeffersonian hyperbole, especially when it came to his fearful prognoses of sectional discord. "As in others of great genius," he explained, Jefferson had the habit "of expressing in strong and round terms, impressions of the moment."[65]

Probably the most crucial rescuing of Jefferson's reputation that Madison undertook during Andrew Jackson's two terms as president was his insistence in 1831 that Jefferson would have had nothing to do with South Carolina's nullifiers. The issue that grew into the nullification crisis had materialized three years before, when William Branch Giles and Thomas Ritchie combined in an effort to divide the third and fourth presidents. These staunch defenders of what Madison not too many years before had praised as the "Virginia Creed" now claimed Jefferson for themselves and hoped to wrest his legacy from Madison, if Madison should refuse to side with them in a highly explosive debate on tariffs.

Giles was Virginia's governor from 1827 to 1830, while Ritchie remained at the helm of the *Richmond Enquirer*. Congress had passed a protective tariff, a patchwork of high and low duties on a range of goods and manufactures—wool, woolens, iron, hemp, and molasses—which no one entirely understood and many in the South feared would impoverish their section and enrich New England, the Middle States, and the West. Earlier in the decade Madison had politely but firmly disagreed with Henry Clay's aggressive approach to tariff policy, but Clay was not involved in the present mess. Weighing in on the constitutional principle, Madison felt strongly that there was already ample precedent in favor of congressional justification in using tariffs to regulate commerce when these were shown to be in the *national* interest.

The problem for Madison arose only because Giles was armed with a letter Jefferson had written to him that construed tariffs as unconstitutional. Madison agreed (privately) that Jefferson had used "unguarded" language in a "hasty" letter, but he refused to give Jefferson over to the Richmond Junto. He felt it was incumbent on the political world to appreciate Jefferson's ideas in toto and not to dwell on one ill-formed, overinterpreted statement made in 1825. Jefferson's view on the tariff, Madison assured, was framed in terms of his warnings against abuses of power more generally. And so just as Jefferson had enlisted his protégé Joseph Cabell to sell the University of Virginia to the state legislature, Madison now turned to the same gentleman to publicize his thoughts and counter the voice of Governor Giles, who was by now imagining, without the slightest dread, the eventual breakup of the Union into regional confederacies.[66]

The matter of the tariff lingered, indeed festered. Flags on ships in Charleston harbor were lowered to half-mast to protest this "Tariff of Abominations." Looking to the past for sustenance, and reading the Madison of 1798 creatively, a prominent faction in South Carolina proceeded to relate the Kentucky and Virginia Resolutions to their larger complaint against the federal government. With Jackson's South Carolinian vice president, John C. Calhoun, fast losing influence to Secretary of State Van Buren, the movement gathered steam. But as Madison would insist, there was a marked difference between the philosophies of 1798 and 1831. The first theorized that a majority of state legislatures might nullify a generally despised act of Congress; the second supposed that the principle of state sovereignty allowed a single state to withdraw from the Union if it could not find a majority of states to agree with its rejection of an act of Congress. He called the South Carolinian construction "preposterous" and a misreading of Jefferson's thinking.

The nullifiers mined the *Memoir, Correspondence, and Miscellanies* for added support from Jefferson. Some of their faith turned him into a prophet, designating him as the "high priest" of the South Carolina doctrine. It was at a Jefferson's birthday celebration in Washington that President Jackson famously toasted "Our Union: It must be preserved," and Vice President Calhoun, recently reborn as a nullifier, came back with "The Union: Next to our liberties the most dear." Nothing so plainly symbolized the fissure. As the nationalist Jackson confronted the hardened resisters from his native state, Madison—and Ritchie—became aware that Jefferson's long-unattended-to, unpublished draft of the Kentucky Resolutions in fact contained the word *nullification*.

Madison's job now became to broadcast his intimate knowledge of Jefferson's true intentions in 1798, when he committed to paper the language the nullifiers were now seizing upon. Nothing could be further from the truth, Madison cried out, than a Jefferson embracing the notion that nullification extended to the right to secede from the Union: "No man's creed was more opposed to such an inversion of the Repub[lican] order of things." But when South Carolina resorted to nullification of the tariff in 1832, a nullification proponent contrived a whimsical dialogue between Jefferson and Jackson, in which the former rejects the latter's principle of majority rule: "Why the Federalists, with Tim Pickering at their head, never published a more offensive libel against me and my principles."

Congress passed a compromise tariff in 1833, mollifying South Carolina enough that the legislature agreed to withdraw its nullification ordinance. But the bad taste did not disappear. Madison's outspokenness enabled the likes of U.S. senator John Tyler—the next president to hail from Virginia—to condemn the last of the founders as a consolidationist. Tyler said that Madison had forsaken Virginia and that his authority could no longer be relied upon. It seems that he had created more problems for himself by "Madisonizing" Jefferson, who at the time of the Kentucky and Virginia Resolutions had thought more about the right of a state to secede from the Union than Madison was willing to admit. He hated the nullifiers and wanted Jefferson to hate them too.[67]

In the midst of this sectional impasse, Virginia revisited its state constitution, and Madison willingly served as the delegate from Orange. Chief Justice John Marshall, Senator John Tyler, Congressman John Randolph, and Governor Giles were also delegates. Oddly enough, among these names, it was Marshall the Federalist whose constitutional views Madison felt closest to. Even before this time Madison had told a northern visitor to Montpelier that the chief justice no longer reflected those heavily partisan impressions he had recorded in the fifth volume of his *Life of Washington*, which had driven Jefferson to actively solicit a Republican counterhistory.[68]

Although his health was beginning to deteriorate, former president Monroe was in attendance at the state convention. Serving on the Board of Visitors for the university since his retirement in 1825, Monroe was accustomed to seeing Madison at their periodic meetings. Madison was, not surprisingly, the only one of the ninety-six members of the 1829 convention to have taken part in the Virginia Convention of 1776, which had adopted the current state constitution.

Ongoing tension between eastern and western Virginia interests had triggered the new convention. Representation in the state legislature was unequal, and the westerners had become increasingly agitated. The decisive factor in their understanding of power was the counting of slaves in determining the composition of the state legislature. There were nine times as many slaves east of the Blue Ridge as west. Thus, the western Virginians reprised, on the state level, the role of the northern states as to representation in the national legislature.

Madison called the convention to order on October 5, 1829, promptly nominating Monroe as presiding officer, a largely ceremonial job. The motion was agreed to, and Madison and Marshall conducted Monroe to the chair. A lively debate got under way, which grew more heated as the weeks passed. Despite his advanced age, Madison took part in every meeting. On the key issue he favored compromise, modestly reducing the eastern majority in the House of Delegates, while retaining the existing measure of representation in the Senate. He spoke at length only once, on December 2. As he rose, the convention recorder noted, "the [other] members rushed

from their seats and crowded around him." He appears to have been neither surprised nor even bothered by John Randolph's rambling of that day,
in which the obstructionist congressman took direct aim at the ideas of
Thomas Jefferson, mocking his populist language in *Notes on Virginia*. "We
all know he was confident in his theories," Randolph said of Jefferson, "but
I am a practical man and have no confidence *a priori* in the theories of Mr.
Jefferson, or of any other man under the sun."

Madison ignored the inconsequential and chose to focus instead on
slavery, "that peculiar feature in our community, which calls for a peculiar
division in the basis of our Government." It was crucial to their character
that Virginians, he said, in apportioning power in the legislature by assigning a value to slaves for the purpose of representation, should not ignore
the slaves themselves. They should be seen in the light of their humanity,
he commanded, and not simply as property, so that whatever determination was made as to representation, the quality of life for African Americans would be improved. "The mere circumstance of complexion cannot
deprive them of the character of men," he said meaningfully. In 1801, at the
time of the death of Madison's father and nearly at the height of his slave
owning, Montpelier's unfree taxable population stood at 108; at the time
of the 1829 convention it was 61—a result of financial setbacks and not
manumissions. "We must agree on some common ground, all sides relaxing in their opinions," he urged.

Madison's refrain made sense. Compromise had brought about the federal Union; compromise should prevail in Richmond as well. He concluded
his address to the delegates with a bid for calm: "I have now more than a
hope—a consoling confidence, that we shall at last find, that our labors
have not been in vain." His voice was low, and many of his hearers could
not make it out; still, none could have been confused by his message. Virginians needed to overcome their passion and provincialism. This was the
sentiment on which he chose to end his career as a statesman.[69]

"Pandora with Her Box Opened"

Monroe's health had been steadily deteriorating since Richmond—he had
had to step down from the chair before the close of the convention. In September 1830 he lost his wife of forty-four years and subsequently moved in
with their daughter and son-in-law in New York. In April 1831 he wrote to
Madison, stating that he would be unable to attend any more meetings of

the Board of Visitors, and tendering his resignation. In reply, Madison told him: "The effect of this, in closing the prospect of our ever meeting again afflicts me deeply, certainly not less so than it can you." Of his own condition, Madison claimed "comfortable health" for the moment, but he reminded his old friend that he had already lived "a decad beyond the canonical three score & ten, an Epoch which you have but just passed." Despite the inauspicious tone of Monroe's letter, Madison held out a hope that the commencement of spring would restore his strength and he might yet undertake a journey south. His own "stiffening fingers" were making for a smaller handwriting, and he noted that "my feet take shorter steps." But he seemed reluctant to accept that Monroe, seven years his junior, was dying. On July 4, 1831, five years to the day after Jefferson and Adams died, James Monroe's life ended in New York.[70]

Even as Madison was reading Monroe's last letter, James K. Paulding, archetype of the Knickerbocker school of writers and once Madison's close companion, was feeling him out on the subject of a "life and letters" biography. Born during the Revolution, Paulding appears never to have seen Jefferson in the flesh. He wrote Madison now, asking for unique anecdotal materials on the primary founders and especially himself.

He received a surprisingly tepid reply, similar to what Madison had earlier written to Henry Lee IV. He was not interested in conveying his life according to the self-revelatory model of Benjamin Franklin. He admitted to "awkwardness" about the prospect of preparing a personal sketch, even for his friend Paulding: "My life has been so much of a public one that any review of it must mainly consist of the agency which was my lot in public transactions . . . Any publicity of which selections from this miscellany may be thought worthy, should await a posthumous date." Asked about Franklin, Madison said he had nothing to add to what was already known. Regarding John Adams, he said simply that they did not meet until 1789, adding, with intentional vagueness, that he knew nothing of his private character, "which was not visible to all." "Of Mr. Hamilton," Madison wrote with greater honesty, "I ought perhaps to speak with some restraint though my feelings assure me that no recollections of political collisions could controul the justice due to his memory."

Most surprising, though, were his remarks about Jefferson, which were not just undramatic but entirely commonplace. He directed Paulding to "the obituary Eulogiums" that "multiplied" the meaning of his life after the epochal coincidence of his and Adams's deaths on the fiftieth Fourth of July. Wrote Madison:

It may on the whole be truly said of him, that he was greatly eminent for the comprehensiveness & fertility of his genius for the vast extent & rich variety of his acquirements, and particularly distinguished for the impress left on every subject which he touched. Nor was he less distinguished for an early & uniform devotion to the cause of liberty . . . In the social & domestic spheres he was a model of all the virtues & manners which most adorn them.

At the end of his deficient statement, he wrote: "I am sorry Sir that I could not make a better contribution to your fund of biographical matter."[71]

It surely would have pleased those living if Madison had had something more precious to convey about his and Jefferson's long partnership. Though uninhibited and at times ribald among friends, his reserve when it came to publication marked him as a cautious actor. When Paulding read too much into his letter, believing there was more to come and that it would be a substantive history of the Revolution and the constitutional era, Madison wrote back: "I did not mean I had in view a *History* of any sort, public or personal, but only a preservation of materials of which I happened to be a Recorder, or to be found in my voluminous correspondence."[72]

In 1832 and 1833 Madison was called upon to offer judgments on nullification, slavery, and other weighty matters. Along with John Marshall, who was concurrently chief justice and president of the American Colonization Society, Madison defended the society's project of relocating American blacks to West Africa. He saw this imperfect option as the best alternative to the "convulsions" that he believed inevitable if simple, across-the-board emancipation were to take place. He recognized as a central problem "the consent of the individuals to be removed," for which he could offer no possible resolution; but he held out hopes of seeing "gifts & legacies from the opulent, the philanthropic, and the conscientious." He counted on the state legislatures to provide funds, and he saw that, even with such funding, West Africa was too distant a destination for easy coordination to be undertaken in the United States. Madison's "auxiliary" plan would involve colonization on those Caribbean islands "where the colored population is already dominant." When Marshall stepped down in 1833, Madison accepted his turn as president of the American Colonization Society. And in October 1834, to balance his accounts, Madison *sold* sixteen of his slaves to a relative.[73]

When the English writer and abolitionist Harriet Martineau visited Montpelier in February 1835, she found the last of the Revolutionary patriarchs amiable and attentive, though he complained of deafness in one ear. "He talked more on the subject of slavery than any other," Martineau noted. But Madison did not retreat from colonization. He pointed out "how the free states discourage the settlement of blacks; how Canada disagrees with them; how Hayti shuts them out; so that Africa is their only refuge." To Madison's remarks, Martineau added her own commentary: "He did not assign any reason why they should not remain where they are when freed." He also confessed to her that his own slaves were relieved to learn that they were not to be colonized in West Africa, which they much feared.

These contradictions bothered Martineau. Madison might rationalize that conditions had improved for the slaves of Virginia, but such wishful thinking did nothing to comfort the abolitionist, and she ultimately found a tragic depth to his feelings about slavery. She added pathos to the scene she witnessed at Montpelier by describing how "his little person [was] wrapped in a black silk gown," propped up by a pillow, as his wife read to him.[74]

That summer Madison described his mixed feelings about the state of the nation to another elderly Virginian. He foresaw disunion as a real possibility, but at the same time he refused to surrender his hope for "a more tranquil and harmonious course of our public affairs." He evidently had his own infirmities on his mind as he theorized about sectional politics: "A sickly countenance is not inconsistent with a self-healing capacity of a Constitution such as I hope ours is; and still less with medical resources in the hands of a people such as I hope ours will prove to be." To those who inquired after his well-being in the summer and fall of 1835—President Jackson, John Quincy Adams's son Charles Francis, and others—Madison offered the same refrain: his health was "broken by chronic complaints," mainly rheumatic joints. Warm weather offered some reprieve, but by November 1835 he was unable even to walk across his bedroom.[75]

In July 1835 Chief Justice Marshall died. Lafayette had passed away the year before. Randolph of Roanoke had met his fate in 1833, telling his doctor at the end: "I have been an idiosyncrasy all my life."[76] There was really no one of the Revolutionary generation left, save for Madison and Aaron Burr, who was in New York and destined to outlive the Virginian by only two and a half months. Like Madison, the political exile, once prosecuted for treason, and who for two decades had maintained a steady, if understated, law practice, accepted the energetic, if intellectually deficient, Andrew Jackson as president. But unlike Madison, Burr was not called upon for his expert opinion anymore. History had cast its vote against him.

At Christmastime 1835 Madison was still answering his correspondence. He responded to a report from Secretary of the Treasury Levi Woodbury: "The exuberant prosperity of our Country is a happy illustration of the beneficent operation of its political Institutions." After New Year's he received a policy update from Vice President Van Buren, and information on the planning of the Washington Monument from William Cranch, a longtime federal district judge related to Abigail Adams. A professor sent him his "Geological Reconnaissance of the State of Virginia," and many others wrote for his views on constitutional matters. Madison's eyes had weakened, and it became difficult for him to read for any length of time. At eighty-five, he had been worn down by successive winters of rheumatic pain. Yet he faithfully answered his mail, sometimes through dictation, other times in his own hand.[77]

In the years since Jefferson's death, Madison had given regular attention to their combined legacy as well as their individual legacies. Like Jefferson, he made certain to prepare his papers for posterity. Conscious of a duty to history, he had shared letters from the era of the founding with Jared Sparks, a Harvard graduate born in the year George Washington became president, who in the 1830s reigned as the most prolific chronicler of the founders. He welcomed to Montpelier the historian George Bancroft, who would go on to produce a massive history of the United States.

He was doing all he could to stay involved. Dolley kept watch and doted. In his last will, prepared in April 1835—expecting that his collected papers would fetch a good price for his widow—Madison felt secure in bequeathing substantial sums to the American Colonization Society, the University of Virginia, and his alma mater, Princeton.

He received a visit in May 1836 from Charles Jared Ingersoll of Philadelphia, a War of 1812–era congressman whose father had served alongside Madison in the Continental Congress during the Revolutionary War. After a bumpy ride from the Orange Court House, Ingersoll described the surrounding countryside: "The woods were in foliage, the white-thorn and red-bud trees in greater number than I had ever seen them, giving a pleasant coloring to what was otherwise a wild, poor, and uninteresting region. Nearer Mr. Madison's, the country is more improved, and the mountain scenery is very agreeable." On the property itself, Ingersoll found "signs of ornamental agriculture," but the brick mansion was "decayed and in need of considerable repairs." Inside were French carpets and tall mirrors, and a table "handsomely provided" with an impressive array of foods and wines.

As the two men spoke of current affairs, Madison made it a point to bemoan the fate of the slave economy. He was somewhat less sanguine than he had been when the Englishwoman Harriet Martineau recently visited. To Ingersoll, he predicted "troubles and explosions," and while willing to discourse on any and all political subjects, Madison left his guest feeling that the nullification controversy had sent a shock through his system. But there was one subject about which he felt no indecision. "You perceive directly that Mr. Jefferson is the god of his idolatry," Ingersoll wrote. Madison kept several Jefferson portraits on the wall, and while he referred to his friend the fifth president simply as "Monroe," he never mentioned his predecessor except as "*Mr.* Jefferson." When pressed on past actors, Madison refused to speak ill even of Hamilton. In a tribute subsequently published in a Washington, D.C., newspaper, the Philadelphian concluded of Madison: "A purer, brighter, juster spirit never existed."[78]

During Ingersoll's visit, Madison's rapidly deteriorating health concerned Dolley. He was unable, she wrote, "even to exert his thoughts without oppressive fatigue." Breathing was becoming more difficult. By the time Jefferson's physician, Dr. Dunglison, was called to Montpelier, there was nothing to be done.

The last obligation Madison accepted was to review the biography of Jefferson by Professor George Tucker, while in manuscript. Learning that it was being dedicated to him, he penned a note of gratitude to the author on June 27, 1836. "Apart from the value put on such a mark of respect from you in a dedication of your Life of Mr. Jefferson to me, I could only be governed in accepting it by my confidence in your capacity to do justice to a character so interesting to his country and to the world; and I may be permitted to add with whose principles of liberty and political career mine have been so extensively congenial." Tucker advised him that the proof sheets were with the printer in Philadelphia, and Madison could expect to receive his copy "as soon as it can be bound."[79]

It may have been Madison's wish to expire on Independence Day, as the second, third, and fifth presidents had all done, ten and five years earlier. But that did not occur. On Tuesday, June 28, at breakfast, and attended by a niece, the fourth president spoke a few words to reassure her that he was feeling fine, then slumped over and quietly left the world. It was, officially, the end of the Virginia Dynasty of presidents.

In the U.S. Senate, on the thirtieth, Virginian William Cabell Rives, a protégé of Madison's and Jefferson's alike, could not resist invoking the providential deaths of Adams, Jefferson, and Monroe. Referring to Madison's "trembling and unsteady signature" at the end of the letter he held in his hand, dated just the week before, Rives expressed his personal sorrow, adding: "Still I trusted that his light might hold out to the 4th of July, that he might be restored on that glorious anniversary to an immortal companionship with those great men and patriots. But it has been ordered otherwise."[80]

The *National Intelligencer* declared: "JAMES MADISON is no more!" It celebrated Madison's genius, as "the last of the great lights of the Revolution, the brightest of those great minds," and gave him the serene end he deserved: "He expired without a struggle, free from pain, free from regret, and from cause of reproach." The same newspaper had proclaimed ten years before: "THOMAS JEFFERSON is no more!" The metaphors of light were equally resplendent then: "His weary sun hath made a golden set, leaving a bright tract of undying fame to mark his path to a glorious immortality." At moments such as these, the press routinely called upon all Americans to count themselves as constituents of a sentimentally united nation.[81]

Dolley Madison received only $30,000 rather than the $100,000 her husband had calculated on for his papers—which included the much-awaited notes that Madison took at the Constitutional Convention in 1787. Though she was not saddled with the degree of debt and hardship that Jefferson's family immediately faced upon his death, she did struggle considerably. After enjoying forty-two years of marriage, and left with a compulsive spender for a son, the sixty-eight-year-old Mrs. Madison kept her Washington connections alive and bore up under the strain.

She honored her husband's wish not to break up slave families when potential buyers approached with offers to relieve her of her financial burden. Jefferson's heirs had been obliged to sell their nearly two hundred slaves in 1827; the families of all concerned suffered deep heartache at the inhumanity of the spectacle. Mrs. Madison, despite mortgage assistance from the New York millionaire John Jacob Astor, lost Montpelier in 1844. When she died at eighty-one, in 1849, she was returned there and buried beside her husband and his parents in the small cemetery on the property.[82]

At midcentury, as the crisis of the Union worsened, Madison's second-term attorney general, Richard Rush, publicly revealed a previously unknown text, a single page, that Madison had composed a year or so before his death. Dolley had sent it to Edward Coles, who in turn had passed it on to Rush. It bore the title "Advice to My Country," and it contained a poignant personal message:

As this advice, if it ever see the light will not do it till I am no more it may be considered as issuing from the tomb, where truth alone can be respected, and the happiness of man alone consulted.

The advice nearest to my heart and deepest in my convictions is that the Union of the States be cherished and perpetuated. Let the open enemy to it be regarded as a Pandora with her box opened; and the disguised one, as the Serpent creeping with his deadly wiles into Paradise.[83]

This was a very different parable from "Jonathan Bull and Mary Bull," the bizarre tale of North versus South (and the nasty black stain) that he had earlier written. This was no allegory with a happy ending; it was, rather, a sharp admonition from a guarded man, sober and fearful, who had seen too much to be resting easy as he read the newspapers. The aged Madison invoked Pandora's box to warn that talk of disunion, taken one short step further, would bring on an unstoppable train of events. The Serpent in Paradise was a stern reminder that those who severed the Union would be subject to everlasting shame and scorn.

He had finished fighting battles. He could do no more than to wish his nation the self-possession and self-control it needed to recalibrate political and constitutional balance as it moved ahead.

LEGACY

CHAPTER SIXTEEN

Thawing Out the Historical Imagination

*Jefferson and Madison . . . recognized and adhered to the political party
that elected them; and they left it united and powerful when, at the close of
public life, they carried into their retirement, and always enjoyed,
the respect, esteem, and confidence of all their countrymen.*

—MARTIN VAN BUREN,
INQUIRY INTO THE ORIGIN AND COURSE OF POLITICAL PARTIES

*Calm authority sat in Jefferson's eye, and lurked in the firm intonations
of his voice . . . Madison, in public, appeared to a stranger like a
polished and contemplative professional man or student,
who was taking a look out on the busy world.*

—HENRY S. RANDALL, JEFFERSON BIOGRAPHER, 1858,
REPEATING THE OBSERVATIONS OF THOSE STILL LIVING
WHO WERE THE PRESIDENTS' INTIMATES

IN THE NINETEENTH CENTURY MADISON AND JEFFERSON WERE
often spoken of in a single breath. Most regarded their administrations—
wrongly—as an unbroken chain. Their penchants and policies while in
office were lumped together, but their personalities were as readily differentiated: Madison was said to be naturally noble, Jefferson classically creative; Madison cool, Jefferson cordial. But none of the many descriptions of
Madison and Jefferson by their contemporaries would strike the modern
reader as detailed and unbiased. Indeed, despite all that has been written
over the past two hundred years, the two Virginians descend to us as men
with secrets, contradictory attitudes, and unknowable thoughts.

It is that conclusion which we have been strenuously writing against in these pages. Our twofold object has been to get inside the all-important political culture of the Revolutionary generation and to resist, as much as possible, favoring one actor over another. If Americans' historical understanding is to benefit, we must find a way to engage in a legitimate amount of speculation while stopping short of making the glib assertions and assumptions that always seem to attach to the founders.

"Moved As They Were by a Common Impulse"

Martin Van Buren was a U.S. senator from New York when he visited Virginia and conferred with Jefferson at Monticello. Though he had supported DeWitt Clinton over Madison in the election of 1812 and felt lukewarm toward President Monroe, he had, by 1820, perceived Virginia as the linchpin of his own national political ambition. In 1824 Van Buren invited Jefferson to refute charges recently made by the still vocal, still tactless New England Federalist Timothy Pickering, to the effect that Jefferson was covetous of power and a deliberate seducer of the unwitting public.

Pickering and Jefferson were civil with each other in person, though two more bitterly opposed in political sentiments could hardly be found. "He arraigns me on two grounds: my actions and my motives," Jefferson wrote back to Van Buren. "The very actions, however, which he arraigns, have been such as the great majority of citizens have approved." All together Jefferson's letter ran eleven pages, typical of the lengths to which he went when it was a matter of defending his historical reputation. Once he had cited page numbers and passages he objected to, and systematically tore apart Pickering's "diatribe," he left Van Buren the quintessential Jeffersonian statement as to his regard for historical vindication and his means of attaining it:

> Altho' I decline all newspaper controversy, yet, when falsehoods have been advanced, within the knoledge of no one so much as myself, I have sometimes deposited a contradiction in the hands of a friend, which if worth preservation, may, when I am no more, nor [are] those whom it might offend, throw light on history, and recall that into the path of truth, and, if of no other value, the present communication may amuse you with anecdotes not known to every one.

This broad hint-prescription-decree comprises a single tortuous sentence. Jefferson might have restrained himself here, and he might have compressed the eleven pages into three or four, had not his purpose been so far-reaching. His "contradiction" of Pickering's testimony was thus left to Van Buren to release at the moment when it could have the greatest effect on posterity.[1]

Although not a Virginian, Van Buren was, as it turned out, the right man for the job. After Jefferson's death, the New York Democrat and future president increasingly looked up to Madison as a constitutional authority, whether on matters of federal support of roads and canals or on federal-state relations generally. As Jackson's first-term secretary of state, he volunteered himself as a forwarder of Madison's letters to Europe; and as vice president during Jackson's second term, he sent Madison presidential messages in published form as well as political pamphlets of various kinds, inviting the founder to comment.[2]

It was toward the end of his own life, as the Civil War approached, that Van Buren composed the texts that became his own historical search for vindication. His *Inquiry into the Origin and Course of Political Parties* traced his political lineage to the third and fourth presidents. Its first chapter opens with the lines: "There has been no period in our history, since the establishment of our Independence, to which the sincere friend of free institutions can turn with more unalloyed satisfaction, than to that embraced by the administrations of Jefferson and Madison, moved as they were by a common impulse." Van Buren was unsparing in his characterization of Alexander Hamilton's disgust for democracy. He pointed, as Jefferson would have him do, to Patrick Henry's foolish (or greedy) attraction to Hamilton's system. And he deployed Jefferson's response to Pickering in the most persuasive way he knew how.

In his narrative of the rise of the Republican Party in the 1790s, Van Buren chose to depict Jefferson as the "head" and Madison as the "laboring oar." The party, he wrote, was "warmed into action by Jefferson's more fervent though not more deeply seated patriotism." Madison was "simple, practical, and direct," and his report on the Alien and Sedition Acts "the flag under which the Republicans conquered." The eighth president thus made the pair into righteous pugilists, delivering a one-two punch to the political sect that stood in the way of progress.[3]

Henry S. Randall was too young to have met either Madison or Jefferson. Raised in a Hamilton-worshipping community in New York, he grew into a Van Buren Democrat, but one who resisted the antislavery turn Van

Buren took in 1848. Regarding northerners' distaste for southern culture as a "disease," he was the first in a series of sympathizing biographers who told the story of the early republic as Madison and Jefferson preferred it to be understood—if, that is, Madison did not mind his friend receiving the lion's share of attention. As he researched his three-volume history, Randall remained in close touch with Jefferson's grandchildren, and as his epigraph to this chapter suggests, he sculpted the third and fourth presidents as though they were posing for national monuments.[4]

No Madison study ever really caught on during the formative period of patriotic biography. Madison had no children with Dolley who might have functioned as Jefferson's daughter, grandson, and granddaughters did. John Payne Todd, Dolley's son from her first marriage, turned out to be a great disappointment in all respects. A tag-along member of the diplomatic staff that sailed to Europe to negotiate the Treaty of Ghent that ended the War of 1812, he often disappeared from the entourage and over the years became increasingly self-destructive. Madison himself spent thousands of dollars paying off his stepson's gambling debts. After Madison's death, Todd auctioned off thousands of his stepfather's letters to cash in.[5]

While Jefferson may have ultimately triumphed among biographers, Madison was the clear favorite of James Kirke Paulding. Writing in the 1840s, he acknowledged Jefferson's primacy as "the Great Apostle of Democracy" but at the same time expressed his reservations about the third president's occasionally immoderate prescriptions. He saw no genius in Jefferson's management of policy in the lead-up to the War of 1812, and he did not acknowledge Madison's share in responsibility for it. Writing of the "twinkle" in Madison's "small bright blue eyes," he made it abundantly clear how much he preferred the fourth president's well-composed views of democracy. "His mind was more consummate and his faculties more nicely balanced than those of his predecessor," Paulding wrote.[6]

Recall the bookseller quoted in the preface to this book, who observed in 1824 that Jefferson possessed "more imagination and passion," while Madison was the "more natural, candid and profound." To these remarks, Samuel Whitcomb appended one other: that Madison, in spite of his "excellences," had "a quizzical, careless, almost waggish bluntness of looks and expression."

We have, then, the perspectives of the writer Paulding and the bookseller Whitcomb to describe the artificial competition between Madison and Jefferson. Paulding added his observation of the "twinkle," the spark, to the "waggish" or mischievous quality that Whitcomb saw in Madison. Perhaps it only grew on Madison in later years, but there was definitely a flash, a flicker, an irreverence that radiated from him, which history ignores. For whatever reason, modern scholars have made Madison not only full of thought, which he was, but a stone-faced politician, which he was not; and they have, with comparable ease, rendered Jefferson as the Federalists so often branded him, a confused idealist.

These are one-dimensional judgments. Before he was an idealist, Jefferson was a student of the physical world. He was always picking up his pen to record a thought, a design, an expenditure; he was always buying guides, collecting seeds, and describing nature. Whether the subject was farming or politics, he conducted experiments to satisfy his curiosity, always hoping to discover principles or verify hypotheses. And though his theories might at times have been flawed, he was critical of unscientific approaches to knowledge—views that were, as he saw it, counter to nature. Madison understood this about his friend, though his own inclinations were somewhat different. Madison was wary of excesses in experimentation and was more willing to compromise. He disliked inefficiency in any system. And he was intolerant of those in the political world whom he saw as uninspired or driven by narrow interests.

With impressive variety in his routine, Jefferson yearned to extend knowledge. However, his need for rules and method also led him to impose an often arbitrary order on the world, inadvertently setting limits to knowledge. He chased consonance and fled dissonance. Though the language of harmony and affection supported his ambitious lifetime project, he was neither the anarchist that the angriest Federalists imagined him to be nor the bright-eyed New Deal liberal that the generation that consecrated his Tidal Basin memorial in Washington, D.C., proclaimed him. He was an introvert with a stubborn streak and a clear compulsion to have himself proven correct in the unfolding story of American politics. He had Madison, Van Buren, and grandson Jefferson Randolph, among others, to help him do the job. But the deterioration of historical memory deprives us of detail and context and makes a truthful translation from one generation to the next unlikely. When historians take shortcuts, they de-emphasize one trait by emphasizing another. Much interpretive power is forfeited as time presses on.

Biography is a tricky thing. Privileging one source over another inevitably alters conclusions. The particular problems among biographers of Madison and Jefferson are those caused by too much license being taken with too little information. As Benjamin Rush said so incisively in 1808, believing in the "great man" theory of history makes as much sense as believing in "witches and conjurors." The celebratory biographer exists because nostalgia adheres to every generation.

"L'Amour Propre Blessé"

There is rarely a single moment in historical research, a smoking gun, that immediately and irreparably changes our knowledge of the past. The Madison-Jefferson relationship is too complex to be understood in that way. No one vignette encapsulates all the political twists and turns as two Virginians—two from the rural central counties of Virginia—sought to influence the domestic balance of power. For most of their careers, Madison and Jefferson were intent on rescuing the people of the United States of America from oppressive government. But they were not heroic. In the prime of their lives they acted out of an attachment to Virginia as much as a desire to defend the Union.

It was Jefferson's particular habit to personify his political enemies, to give them a physical form through corporeal metaphors. For him, the "monocrat" Federalist's ailment had its own unique pathology: it was a feminine disorder, embodied in a "timid" nervous constitution and a parasitic desire to worship the strong. These pseudo-aristocrats were backward in their thinking and out of step with the times, both dysfunctional and doomed. Like the dinosaurs of Jurassic Park, Jefferson's effete monocrat was a monstrous re-creation, at once a poison introduced into a natural environment and an unnatural entity unable to progress, unable to adapt. "Doctor" Jefferson aimed to create new, healthy cells so that the body would heal completely once the diseased and anachronistic minority died off naturally. Or in the case of African Americans, unloved offspring of the institution of slavery, he preferred to purge the body of them, to expel them altogether, and to replace them by transfusion—new blood in the form of white European peasants or laborers.

Madison did not ignore personal flaws, such as Patrick Henry's demagoguery and John Adams's vanity. But he was less likely to blame policies on inherent defects or psychological failings. He focused instead on social forces, errors in reason, and balances of power that demanded structural solutions. He would reorganize the political dynamics of the national environment through reeducation. This was how, early in his congressional career, he could envision a homeland for former slaves in Sierra Leone or Liberia; for him, a concerted experiment in recolonization and economic uplift stood a better chance of changing white racist attitudes than any other solution he could imagine. Later, growing from his conviction during the Constitutional Convention that the absolute negative made the most sense for an immature political society, he embraced a paternalistic model for the American republic: the invisible hand of educated public opinion. He was perfectly willing to confront enemies who violated the law of nations or constitutional principles—these were Madison's sacred rules--but he lacked Jefferson's need for visceral release in the process.

So Jefferson saw politics as an experimental physician recommending a healthy lifestyle, and Madison saw politics as an accomplished chess master with his steady eye on the moves of the most valued pieces and with the people as so many pawns. Regardless of the metaphor we select, though, theirs was a cutthroat business. Consequently, their often devious political strategizing does not have to diminish the achievements of either Madison or Jefferson. In writing the story of their rise to power, we have tried to shift emphasis from the less tangible (judgments of their private character) to the culture of competition amid a nationwide struggle to define how a republic should constitute itself.

The most extraordinary misjudgment in the historical record is, of course, the portrayal of the cerebral Madison as the perennial dullard among the founders. While it is true that he was opaque to many observers, he was not unemotional by any stretch of the imagination. Those who saw him up close over time, particularly in the context of political performance, knew that he could become flustered, frazzled, and, every so often, quarrelsome.

Like his friend from Albemarle, he did not admit wrong easily, and he held grudges. His misgivings toward John Adams and his instinctive mistrust of others serve as only the most obvious examples. In 1802, on returning from his eighteen years in France and the Netherlands, William Short was at Monticello enjoying a reunion with his patron Jefferson in the company of then Secretary of State Madison. They fell into a discussion about French Revolutionary politics. Short straightened Madison out on a matter concerning the personalities in charge at the time of the XYZ Affair and Quasi-War. Madison, who never saw Europe, still believed the French leaders of that time to have been "a quintette of good honest souls"—or so

Short reminded Jefferson a decade and a half after the 1802 incident. "I discounted the vision and assured him they were really and bona fide most consummate villains," the former diplomat said. As Short saw it, "Mad's idea was to me...so absurd and fell on me so abruptly that I probably betrayed some kind of ridiculing sneer, without intending one. But *l'amour propre blessé* [wounded self-esteem] seldom forgets and never forgives." Since then, Madison had never again exhibited any warmth toward Short.[7]

Thin skin attaches to portraits of Jefferson in some historical accounts, but never before to Madison. In this context, the Madison-Monroe relationship is a highly interesting one. Beyond their occasionally clashing ambitions, and unprovoked hurt feelings generated by Monroe, Madison may have breathed an air of entitlement in advance of the 1808 election. Madison's greater intellectual reach did not have to diminish Monroe's political prospects, but there was clearly a Republican hierarchy as well as an inherited Virginia notion of deference.

Jefferson felt that Madison should be next in line to succeed. In all likelihood, it was not just Monroe who felt himself subject to a hierarchical classification of political talent that Linnaeus might have understood. Jefferson never considered Monroe ill suited for the office. But while his ambitious protégé must have thought himself ready, Jefferson may simply have considered Monroe not quite ripe—still in training—for the Virginia-bred presidency. This makes sense if we consider that Jefferson described himself as John Adams's "junior" in rationalizing the denial of the presidency to him in 1796; and it seems probable that Madison stepped aside that year for the same reason, when Jefferson suggested that his younger friend accept a draft and run against Adams. It may not be entirely by coincidence that none of the first five presidents was younger than fifty-seven when he assumed office; and all retired from public life when they were either sixty-five or sixty-six.

It was not just wounded self-esteem that these political actors were occasionally subject to. Both Madison and Jefferson were men of intensity. They were inner-directed, exacting, and self-demanding. Madison's early "epileptoid hysteria" (convulsive fits) and frequent "bilious complaints," and Jefferson's "periodical headaches" (which ended when his presidency ended) and abdominal upset that worsened with age, all suggest that public life exposed both to such stress as put pressure on the body. When we think of Madison's humanity or Jefferson's psychology, such factors as these do matter, though they are less obvious in the historic record.[8]

"The Impulse to Unmask"

As communicators, Madison and Jefferson were both highly effective, despite the obvious difference in their styles. They circulated their ideas eagerly—this was what made them national figures in the first place—and they took care to adhere to principles of rhetoric in order to achieve elegance of thought and presentation. From the time they were children, they were steeped in the spectacle of classical oratory and taught to be clever by reading the *Spectator* essays of Oxford-educated Joseph Addison and Richard Steele. Written in the 1710s and still read with zeal a century later when Madison heartily recommended them to his young nephew, *Spectator* observed and critiqued the practices of daily life, at once symbolizing refined taste, good humor, and public commitment. *Spectator* taught young men how to live in society, how to describe pleasure, and how to befriend. We have seen how one *Spectator* essay on "party-spirit" became the preoccupation of political writers in the 1790s.

Beyond the power of the partisan press, a variety of texts shaped formal argumentation in the world Madison and Jefferson inhabited: the republic of letters. Madison, though less known for his literary skill, relished the study of eloquence and persuasion. While Jefferson's pathos was finely balanced, and his rhythmic arrangement of words and phrases was a gift no other political writer of his day could equal, Madison's *control* of language was exemplary, which was one of the reasons Jefferson turned over so much of the responsibility for newspaper essay writing to him.

Jefferson reached for beauty as he expressed his ideals. He enriched his prose with metaphor and hyperbole, none of which really interested his partner. Jefferson's use of hyperbole both intrigued and annoyed his contemporaries; it makes him endlessly fascinating for us moderns as well. Madison has always been harder to read, and harder to love or hate, because he shunned all extravagance. His blend of eloquence and wisdom was quieter. He had had to compete against the unparalleled eloquence, absent of wisdom, that attached to Patrick Henry. If not eloquent, James Madison became competitive through long deliberation, precision, and application.[9]

Jefferson has been so painstakingly analyzed by serious researchers and polemicists alike that it is nearly impossible to address the multiple personalities attributed to him across the generations. Henry Randall set the tone for all Jefferson hagiography in his portrait of the people's hero, proclaiming: "There was a sympathy between his heart and the great popular heart, which nothing ever did, ever can, shake." In the early twentieth century Charles Beard associated Jefferson's political thinking with economic naïveté, an unreasonable fear of banking and government involvement in capitalist development. His Jefferson lacked the prescience to lay the groundwork for modern capitalism, just as today's Jefferson fails to adopt enlightened ideas about social equality for African Americans, Native Americans, and women. While these criticisms are valid, we must acknowledge that it is easier in hindsight to identify shortcomings in historical figures. What we need to do is to question what caused their blind spots and narrowed their thinking.[10]

The Jefferson image remains a contested site for sensitive cultural issues. Each time America reawakens to issues of social justice, more people ask how Jefferson is to be evaluated. As University of Virginia historian Peter Onuf has noted of the most recent generation of scholars and pundits: "Jefferson's fitness as a national icon has been cast as a question of character . . . The impulse to unmask Jefferson, to make sense out of his complex career, is a mark of his continuing significance in our public culture." It seems Jefferson is always on trial.[11]

Those who prefer the headstrong John Adams or the unrelenting Alexander Hamilton as solid, no-nonsense characters principally see Thomas Jefferson as an extravagant, unmanly, secretive, insincere being. Other students of the Revolutionary generation see Aaron Burr as a "rogue founder": a lovable scoundrel or a cold-blooded murderer. And nearly all who have formed any opinion about James Madison have chosen to accept him as a Jeffersonian cipher, all brain, no emotion. We can no longer accept these time-saving devices as legitimate determinations.[12]

Generations have combined to make the American founding appear timeless. In this nebulous chronicle, Madison's personality is frozen at the time of the Constitutional Convention. Since constitution writing is seen as his greatest contribution, everything afterward becomes irrelevant. His growth as a politician is stunted, just as his physical size seems to suggest of him. The shriveled-up figure, Washington Irving's "Poor Jemmy . . . a withered little apple-John," becomes the standard pose for Madison. In metaphysical terms, he is Jefferson's pale shadow. The dynamic force of Jefferson is the shining sun, while Madison appears cold and desolate, a lonely minor planet. He is frozen in the historical imagination in 1790, at the moment Jefferson reheats.

A related problem is the historian's need to label. Must we choose between "Jeffersonian democracy" and "Madisonian democracy"? Must we have one brilliant, commanding mind at the center, one master architect of what was, in fact, a complex political movement?

In writing a book about a partnership, we have discovered that Madison's and Jefferson's contributions to history have an essential equality. We have also weighed their differences and come across significant disagreements. More purposefully, perhaps, we have encompassed the larger cast of characters who mattered to the course of human events. When Americans look for their favorite founders and judge them based on personality, they lose sight of the real dynamic of history: relationships of power.

In these pages, Madison and Jefferson exist as political thinkers and tacticians rather than as symbols. Jefferson strikes us as an exacting natural philosopher who, though he dreamed incessantly, simultaneously cultivated a stern moralism that yielded a binary outlook on many subjects. Yet he was not a purist. Purists reject history. Jefferson's celebrated appeal to "harmony and affection" in his first inaugural address reflected his desire to forge a history in common. Similarly, his desire to reform Virginia's laws shows that he believed it was possible to engineer change over time.

He was invested in the cause of education, and in encouraging freedom of conscience. But what makes the freethinking "Father of the University of Virginia" less admirable is his capacity for loathing. Jefferson's primal fear of regal government conditioned much of his partisanship. He was afraid, perhaps rightly so, of the marriage of money power and the secret management of government. But the lengths to which he took his fears resulted in his applying a political litmus test of a most rigid kind. Purging the Supreme Court of Federalists is extreme (and unrepublican) behavior.

On the other hand, at the most charged moment of partisan contention in mid-1798, he told arch-Republican John Taylor of Caroline that New England Federalism actually kept the southern states from fighting among themselves. In Jefferson's view, political society naturally led to passionate bickering: "Seeing that we must have somebody to quarrel with, I had rather keep our New-England associates for that purpose." Later in the same paragraph, he adopted an aphoristic tone: "If the game runs sometimes against us at home, we must have patience, till luck turns." This statement suggests that while he was preoccupied with the need to defang and declaw the enemy, he also gave ample evidence of a philosophical fortitude. It is a curious combination: Jefferson understood the psychology of needing an enemy and he was able to rhetorically heighten or de-emphasize the threat almost at will.[13]

Thomas Jefferson's master plan thought small and remained provincial: every man the master of his own domain, every understood right protected. He visualized an American future that acknowledged regional differences and did not threaten his Virginia pastorale. As long as the federal government was relatively weak, his people could expand west without restrictions, and Virginia would remain strong. Madison was different. He never tried to create an ideal environment. Though he supported Virginia's political interests every step of the way during his long career, he felt less impelled to protect Virginia as a "culture" distinct from others. He came to believe that national unity relied on circulating information, and he wanted to develop an infrastructure that allowed for more exchange of news and culture. Whereas Jefferson wanted to establish boundaries, fearing contamination, Madison resisted isolationist tendencies. In several different instances, he spoke in favor of establishing a national university, hoping for opportunities to create and sustain public opinion nationwide.

"Which Do You Prefer?"

In 1789–90, when Jefferson was first back from France, Hamilton still felt that Madison and he envisioned a similar role for the federal government. Could Madison and Jefferson have made a more concerted effort to work with Hamilton? Probably they could have, though only in a limited way.

The "Hamilton problem" remains fascinating. Jefferson's strong antipathy to him is understandable. Hamilton had a lifelong habit of spreading vicious gossip (something Jefferson did too, though less uncontrollably). It was Jefferson's opinion that Hamilton sucked all the air out of the room when the Washington cabinet met; he had a pile of ideas and plans ready for implementation that undercut everything Jefferson believed in.

But what does it tell us about George Washington that, as president, he allowed his senior minister to feed his fear of declining popularity? The historian of the Revolution John Ferling points to Hamilton's deviousness from as early as the Newburgh Conspiracy episode in 1783, when the young officer helped promote a protest among the officer corps only to control its outcome. Hamilton essentially played Iago to General Horatio Gates's Othello, prompting Gates to place himself on the wrong side of history when the ostensible threat to civilian authority was removed. Ferling concludes that Washington, no innocent himself, was aware of Hamilton's handiwork and overlooked his aide's willingness to sacrifice the army's interest to serve personal ends.

Washington was a clever politician; as such, he probably caught on to Hamilton's repressed dislike of him. The "First of Men" may not have minded Hamilton's envy of the general's (later, president's) power, just as he did not mind Hamilton's arrogance. So long as the aide did his work effectively and shielded his hypersensitive commander by bottling up all potential political competition among the general officers, Washington was happy. Theirs was a relationship built on expedience. They used each other equally.[14]

Later, in the Whiskey Rebellion of 1794, Hamilton once again roped Washington into confronting a minor protest that was built up to appear a major threat to civil order. Hamilton's magic, for as long as it lasted, was the ability to make himself appear essential to the Federalist cause, or to a forceful government run by the "right" men. He exploited the Washington image as no one else could. By the mid-1790s neither Madison nor Jefferson, old and trusted associates of Washington's, could reverse what was happening; but they clung to their former view that Washington, deep down, was still one of them, still a Virginia republican.

Had Madison been in Jefferson's place in the cabinet, perhaps the dynamic would have been slightly altered. Madison maintained what Jefferson described in his autobiography as "a habit of self-possession"; and so while he would have argued at least as forcefully against Hamilton's ideas, he might not have reacted with the level of outrage Jefferson exuded. But as public outcry over the Jay Treaty reached its zenith in 1796, Hamilton had Madison in mind no less than Jefferson when he laid down the gauntlet in a major broadside: "The CONSTITUTION and PEACE are in one scale," he charged, "the overthrow of the CONSTITUTION and WAR in the other. Which do you prefer?" It was, he insisted, "the ambition of a VIRGINIAN FACTION" that threatened the Constitution.[15]

For a time, Hamilton maintained the erroneous belief that Madison concurred in his desire for "energetic" government. In fact, though, Hamilton looked to the creative possibilities in constructing a powerful machine, whereas Madison saw government's role as that of moral disciplinarian, acting to trim excesses and check the impulse to magnify power. For Hamilton, when government ran into a problem the answer was always to enhance its authority; for Madison, the threats to government came from different places, which made government most effective when it mediated, when it adapted. In that Madison allowed for fluidity, he was able to come to terms with Jefferson's instinctive fear of monocrats and embrace of an educable citizenry.

History has imagined that Madison looked up to Jefferson, read his mind, and found ways to pursue policies in partnership without any concern that he was subordinating himself. Reading backward, students of history want to see Jefferson as the executive, the primary instigator, because he was in Washington's cabinet and he was president for eight years before it was Madison's turn. Madison, with the less pronounced ego, did not serve as an executive until a decade after Jefferson, when Jefferson appointed him secretary of state, a position Jefferson had occupied and therefore knew how to instruct his friend in.

As the reader now knows, nothing in the historical record supports the convenient narrative in which Madison yields to Jefferson's stronger position or stronger views. Indeed, from 1793, when Jefferson lost his influence with Washington and the executive branch lost Jefferson as a counterweight to Hamilton's aggrandizing interpretation of governmental authority, Madison became the clearest voice of a spirited resistance. Unquestionably, Jefferson remained instrumental behind the scenes, but Madison led.

There were qualitative differences—meaningful differences—in these two friends' approaches to friendship. Jefferson was drawn to men whose intellectual curiosity matched his, but also to those whom he could mentor or make into useful political allies. The special friendship he developed with Madison was probably more important to him than it was to Madison, if only because Madison more typically centered his friendships upon commitment to an agenda: *he liked people because they could get things done.*

In such matters, the record is always incomplete, but as it stands, Madison exhibited less of a need for emotional reinforcement than Jefferson (again, his "habit of self-possession" that Jefferson remarked upon). In advance of the Constitutional Convention, Madison was close to elder statesman George Mason, knowing Mason's unpredictability but still expecting that they would be able to collaborate. He was closest to George Washington in the period 1787–90, when they saw eye to eye on the need for a take-charge government. No doubt Madison could express personal warmth—that is not at issue. But he seems to have preferred a business model to other approaches. That is, personal warmth grew over the course of business. And when business was finished, as in the case of Washington's complete surrender to the Hamiltonian system, the warmth receded. Yet

Madisonian relationships did not turn acrimonious. Here is another instructive example: When Jefferson blamed Edmund Randolph for failing to uniformly echo his vote in cabinet meetings, he abandoned Randolph completely; it was highly personal. Madison did not turn against Randolph. He did not feel the same degree of animus, not nearly.

As an adviser to Jefferson during wartime, Madison initially looked for common ground so that they could coordinate policy together. There does not appear to have been an emotional connection until sometime later, and it no doubt arose at Jefferson's bidding. It was Jefferson who repeatedly advanced the idea of a "partie quarree," permanently bringing Madison, Monroe, and Short to Albemarle to form his ideal neighborhood. Madison resisted, or at least was not inspired to change his circumstances in order to fulfill Jefferson's dream.

The story of the long friendship of Madison and Jefferson was embellished as the years went by in order to suit the Republican narrative—and, eventually, to give historians what they craved. As we have shown, however, the relationship, as close as it was, was not the symbiosis imagined. Jefferson was more dependent on Madison than Madison was on Jefferson. In a sense, Madison was Jefferson's political crutch. He would put himself in Madison's hands, let Madison decide the tenor of debate. A prime example is Jefferson's willingness to give Madison the last word when it came to the conciliatory letter Jefferson wanted to present to John Adams just after the election of 1796. Jefferson wrote with emotion; Madison censored Jefferson's emotion. This was how they worked best, and it was what Jefferson agreed to. To the extent that Jefferson found he was unable to contain himself when he took pen in hand, Madison stopped him before he made his next mistake. Jefferson miscalculated, or fell into error, because he wished to trust others. Madison had fewer illusions. For this reason, he did not need Jefferson in the same way—as insurance against overcommitment and disappointment.

"Different,—Yet Equal"

Beyond the famous twosome were many others, more than minor characters in our narrative of the "Age of Madison and Jefferson." After the Virginians and their presidential dynasty, the most critically important of the politicos was the Swiss-born Pennsylvanian Albert Gallatin, who had a lasting influence on Madison and Jefferson and on the politics and economy of the early republic. His voice was routinely heard, his ideas seriously weighed; he cannot be called an adjunct or mere subordinate any more than Madison deserves to be reduced in stature by being called Jefferson's lieutenant. The Lee dynasty of Virginia and the Livingston dynasty of New York were dynasties of a different sort, but they and others like them mattered on both the state and national scene. As Clintonians and Burrites crossed swords with the Livingstons, they fell in and out of line with the Virginia Republicans.

Madison and Jefferson did not exist in a bubble. They might have expected that anything they did would be opposed by a Patrick Henry or mocked by a Timothy Pickering, but they could never afford to operate as though larger family- or issue-based groups—entities that cannot be strictly defined as political parties—did not exist. Add to these elite groupings the Shaysites and Whiskey rebels and others like them, and the picture only sharpens. An unvarnished portrait of politics shows us how incomplete the singular political biography can be.

Benjamin Franklin's grandson, Benjamin Bache, traded on his family name, as did the Lees and Livingstons, and established the fact that historic "great men" did not act alone. Newspaper editors and pamphleteers, though attached to parties, were far from pawns. Some were ambassadors to the expanding electorate, others independent critics, still others irrepressible troublemakers who took American politics to new levels of partisanship from the 1790s on. The nation would have been a much different place without the less-than-deferential Bache or the Jefferson-baiters William Cobbett, Joseph Dennie, and James T. Callender.

What do we mean? Simply that Madison, Jefferson, and the founding generation represented not a school of philosophy, as *The Federalist Papers* would have us believe, but a school for politics. Though the third and fourth presidents did not always agree, they developed a unique and powerful trust. They took up their pens or came together to confer every time an issue arose or one or the other saw a trend that he disliked. They shared observations. They tested theories. They reinforced each other.

Henry Clay of Kentucky was as well known for his personal warmth and sociability as he was for his deeply affecting oratory and political acumen. In 1829, at an informal gathering in Washington just days after his nemesis Andrew Jackson was inaugurated as president, he entertained company with his personal reflections, repeating the almost clichéd distinction we have heard others relate: that Jefferson possessed "genius" and Madison "judgment and common sense." When Clay elaborated, saying that Jefferson was "a visionary and theorist, often betrayed by his enthusiasm into rash and imprudent and impractical measures," the man sitting beside him, Samuel Harrison Smith, founding editor of the *National Intelligencer,* vigorously defended Jefferson. According to Smith, Jefferson's remarkable "power and energy" enabled him to steer his country through crises that Madison was less well equipped to handle. Clay disputed him, saying: "Prudence and caution would have produced the same results." At the end of their protracted dinner debate, Clay and Smith agreed on the essentials: Madison and Jefferson were *"different,—yet equal."*[16]

How much do we actually learn from this argument? In terms of detail, quite little. As meaningful as the access to Madison and Jefferson was that each enjoyed, Clay and Smith appear not to acknowledge that the "power and energy" of Jefferson's presidency was no less Madison's than Jefferson's. Jefferson would not have undertaken any of the measures he did if Madison had strongly opposed him.

What Jeffersonian act could be considered "rash" that Madison did not have a hand in? There are perhaps two, and two only, of enduring significance: the prosecution of Justice Samuel Chase in 1805 and the prosecution of Aaron Burr in 1807, which Madison would not have embarked on but evidently did not contest. During Jefferson's two terms as president, the historic record shows no "daylight" between their perspectives. The differences to which Clay and Smith were alluding appear to be matters of style more than substance.

"The Negro Is an Accident"

Thirty-five years ago the historian David Brion Davis noted that in the Age of Revolution, antislavery was merely "one of the many harmless philanthropic fashions of the late Enlightenment," until the issue was addressed head on at the Constitutional Convention and in deliberative bodies in France and England. We would shift the date from 1787 to the start of the Revolution, when slavery became politicized in the patriots' rhetoric; but it is true that humanitarian concern stood little chance of being translated into concerted action in Congress at any time prior. A poignantly worded 1786 petition to the Virginia Assembly cast the matter in terms of the political values of the Revolution: "What doth plead with greater Force for the emancipation of our Slaves in proportion as the oppression exercised over them exceeds the oppression formerly exercised by Great Britain over these

States." Davis spoke to the "perishability of Revolutionary time," in identifying a disturbing phenomenon: as memory of the Revolution receded, a creed extolling liberty and an economy based on slavery coexisted without embarrassing its practitioners.[17]

Virginians were not blind to the problem. Half of America's blacks lived in the Chesapeake in 1776, and the free black population of Virginia grew nearly tenfold from the end of the Revolution to the end of Jefferson's presidency. This was in large measure due to individual manumissions and the commitment of slaves, once freed, to work and save in order to free their loved ones. But the issue of race and citizenship was never taken up. Free blacks and biracial Americans were understood, in civic terms, to be of a "degraded" character—mere "denizens" of America, unequal before the law and perennially lacking the rights of citizens. And it was never suggested in Congress that the federal government could interfere with any slave owner's personal property.[18]

Madison and Jefferson were party to a general failure to combat slavery. If we remove moral considerations from the calculus, their participation can be boiled down to a problem of logic. They believed the southern agrarian economy, with its dependence on slave labor, was viable; if so, why were they not troubled enough by their own unmet financial obligations and the debts accrued by their fellow planters to question the system on grounds of its practicality? There had always been fluctuations in market prices, so principles of credit and borrowing alone could hardly explain Virginia's economic decline as the North prospered.

In 1808 slave imports from abroad ended because of a provision in the federal Constitution. Afterward, as a matter of planters' short-term economic self-interest, Virginia became a site for slave breeding and increased sales to other, newer states. In conjunction, whites' rhetorical abhorrence for race mixing intensified. Expulsion (colonization abroad) became a fantasy solution, because all southerners understood that white-black unions—sex across the color line—was otherwise unstoppable.

The end of 1791 was the last time either Madison or Jefferson thought of criticizing slavery publicly. That was when Madison prepared notes for a *National Gazette* essay, never published, in which he asserted that slavery and republicanism were incompatible. It was not until after 1820 that Lafayette, an advocate of emancipation since at least the 1788 founding of the group Amis des noirs, demanded of the pair some justification for their inaction. As post-Napoleonic France enjoyed a new dawn, and the Virginia Dynasty of presidents neared its end, he pressed Jefferson to become again the activist he had been when they first met. Recalling conversations they had had in Richmond in 1781 and outside Paris in 1789, Lafayette gloried that their world was a safer place now, and in his opinion "The Great Work of General Enfranchisement" could start over.

The French patriot said he was uncharacteristically tongue-tied on the subject of American slavery. "While I feel an inexpressible delight in the progress of every thing that is Noble minded, Honourable, and Useful throughout the United States," he wrote, "I find, in the Negro Slavery, a Great draw Back Upon My Enjoyments." Friends who knew of his affection for the United States frequently asked him to account for the persistence of slavery, and he had to admit that he had no defense. "Let me Confess, My dear friend," he addressed Jefferson, "I Have Not Been Convinced, and the less as I think More of it, By Your Argument in favor of dissemination." Understanding that it was easier to criticize from abroad, he gently but firmly protested that "this wide Blot of American Philanthropy is ever thrown in My face."[19]

Today the problematic character of "American philanthropy" is often thrown in *Jefferson's* face. He has been the target of intense criticism because of both his candor and his confusion. He never reconsidered the repugnant view he espoused regarding the presumed intellectual inferiority of Africa-descended Americans. He was not above suggesting that the free black mathematician Benjamin Banneker was an anomaly, or even a fraud. When his mentor George Wythe was murdered in 1806, a new Wythe protégé, the biracial Michael Brown, was killed along with him. Wythe's will provided for Jefferson to oversee Brown's further education, and Jefferson wrote that he would gladly have taken on the responsibility. The irony, of course, is that Wythe undertook Brown's education to disprove the general assumption of black intellectual inferiority endorsed by Jefferson. Jefferson's motivation in stating that he would have honored Wythe's will speaks not to his concurrence with Wythe's hypothesis about racial equality but only to his sympathy and devotion to Wythe himself.[20]

On the solution Jefferson promoted from the 1780s until his retirement years, the gradual but certain expulsion of blacks through colonization abroad, he did not stop to consider the needs and wants of free Negroes. Too few white Americans did. Jokes based on stereotypes mocking black pretensions to gentility were common across the North—not just the South—from the Revolution to the Civil War. Not even the European critics who left Lafayette speechless exhibited the nuanced perspective of the modern scholar who, in tracing the rise of abolitionist sentiment, is able to show that in New England the end of slavery was not simply a function of popular belief in the natural rights of all people. Historian John Wood Sweet describes the reality of it: "As the value of slaves in the northern states fell, incentives for selling them southward rose."

North of the Mason-Dixon Line, it is not clear that a majority reflected the culture of sensibility (cultivated sympathy) or even the slightly less noble emotion of pity. Nor was it just men of business who refused to feel for African Americans. In 1795 John Adams wrote of the situation in Massachusetts, where he adjudged slaves to have grown "lazy, idle, proud, vicious, and at length wholly useless to their masters, to such a degree that the abolition of slavery became a measure of œconony." So much for pure motives, at least in the first half-century of Madison's and Jefferson's lives.[21]

Pennsylvania was the first state to rule in its courts that free blacks were not citizens and were ineligible to vote. Massachusetts, in 1786, passed the Solemnization of Marriage Act, forbidding interracial unions. Rhode Island's state assembly, in 1800, constrained black women from suing white men for child support. In 1821, just after the Missouri Compromise was hammered out, a good many delegates to New York's constitutional convention agitated for the disenfranchisement of free blacks—one contended that they were "a peculiar people" lacking "discretion, prudence, or independence" of thought. In sum, the legal degradation of African Americans was not simply a function of the institution of slavery.[22]

Jefferson never doubted that the descendants of those who had been kidnapped from West Africa deserved better. On his own lands, he mixed patience and a system of rewards with expectations of industry and devotion. He regarded himself as a kind patriarch and his biracial slaves as subordinate family members. He, and Madison too, reckoned there were many in Virginia who acted in this way. But when thinking generically of the dark skinned in their midst, they were unsentimental and legalistic.

Jefferson saw nationhood in racially untainted hues. He feebly addressed outsiders' concerns, offering bland wishes. Madison did not do much better. Returning blacks to West Africa was costly and unrealistic, even as the American Colonization Society was thriving during Monroe's two terms as president. That society, founded in 1816 and heavily invested with Virginia slave owners, proposed to organize regular, voluntary removals of African Americans to Liberia. Madison lent his name to the organization and never abandoned it, while Jefferson steered clear of commitment. To offer the reader a longer view, it bears saying that for most of his career in politics, the "Great Emancipator," Abraham Lincoln, saw the merits of a voluntary removal plan.

Colonization as envisioned by white reformers encroached on free blacks more than it consulted their interest. Between 1782 and 1802 private manumissions occurred with regularity, but after 1802 state law required that emancipated slaves leave Virginia within one year. From this moment on, it became increasingly difficult for Virginians to conceive of a way to phase out slavery. Their uncertainty as to a proper course of action made room for a new southern literature. That literature described an illusion: contented slaves and a sinless, or at least humane, white planter class.

The slow pace of sailings under the auspices of the American Colonization Society, relative to the growth of the African-American population, made it perfectly plain that the society had limited hopes of succeeding. Like most of their cohort, Madison and Jefferson were ready to put off doing anything of substance. The covertly hostile program of colonization relied on the regular publication of poems and essays glorifying the prospective return of a long-lost people to their roots: "Oh, unhappy Africa," one representative writer lamented in 1825. "How long must thy soil be washed with the tears of those who weep for their nearest and dearest relatives, who have been torn away from them, and dragged into bondage."[23]

In 1829, three years after Jefferson's death, Virginian John Hartwell Cocke sat on the Board of Visitors of Jefferson's university. A devout Presbyterian, he wished to couple emancipation with colonization and in later years was to bemoan the example set by Jefferson in having had a slave concubine. William Short, seventy years old in 1829 and living in Philadelphia, wrote to Cocke and expressed puzzlement over Jefferson's original formulation in *Notes on Virginia*. As Jefferson's personal secretary when *Notes* was first printed, he revealed his dismay in unambiguous language. "Sending vessels charged with a number of one color & bringing back the same number of another [i.e., European peasants] always appeared to me to be among the wildest & most impracticable that could be imagined," he wrote, with respect to Jefferson's scheme. Short believed that "the best remedy" for the evil of slavery was for Virginia's state legislature to convert slaves into "serfs" in the manner that they existed in northern Europe. This, he said, would constitute "the gentlest alleviation" of slaves' current status as property, while saving their masters from having to acknowledge moral accountability in being born to slave ownership. He doubted that the Virginia Assembly would countenance even this small alteration in the status of Virginia's enslaved population. Nor would a redefinition of this sort whiten Virginia, which the planter elite wished to accomplish. So if his notion was no more practical than Jefferson's was in the 1780s, William Short's thinking does serve as a guide to the limits of imagination prior to the explosion of abolitionist sentiment in the North.[24]

Shortly after the Missouri crisis, Jefferson's favorite granddaughter, the most intellectually resilient of the family, married and became a Bostonian. Seeing a society without slaves, she expressed disgust with the perpetuation of slavery in the South. The females in her family at Monticello felt similarly. The patriarch of that family, who had found a way to validate the violence that attended the French Revolution, and who believed that rebellion against tyranny was justified, did nothing to address how future catastrophe might be averted or how Virginians could avoid being classed with the world's tyrants. The "mildness" of the slavery that Virginia planters practiced was one of several convenient rationales for continued delay.

Madison appears not to have internalized Jefferson's assumptions about black inferiority. He did not fixate on racial "amalgamation" or "blood admixture" as his friend did. Madison's personal behavior is demonstrably less troublesome than Jefferson's: he behaved more than courteously to freed Virginia slave Christopher McPherson, who became a clerk in the Virginia High Court of the Chancery in 1800. When McPherson delivered a packet of books and a letter sent by Jefferson, the Madisons invited him to stay for dinner, and they treated him as an equal at their table. The ex-slave described the encounter: "I sat at Table Even[in]g & morn[in]g with Mr. M and his Lady & Company & enjoyed a full share of the Convers[ation]." Jefferson apparently felt less comfortable with McPherson as a free man. Writing Madison that same year, he used McPherson's slave name, identifying him as "Mr Ross's man Kitt," thus reaffirming his status as an inferior.[25]

Madison looked past color and saw intelligence and ability, but he did not think that the vast majority of white Americans ever could. Like Jefferson, he was quick to defend his fellow Virginia slaveholders for consistently acting to improve the lives of those they owned. Since the Revolution, he wrote in 1819, slaves were "better fed, better clad, better lodged, and better treated in every respect." Gradual improvement was good enough for him. His compromise solution to slavery was similar to that of slave-owning Colonization Society supporters Henry Clay and John Randolph: colonization would improve the ratio of whites to blacks. These national politicians had convinced themselves that *some* blacks would be grateful after receiving a new lease on life on the coast of West Africa.[26]

Madison and Jefferson attended to the needs of those of their color and class. They could not betray their own kind, those agreeable white landowners with whom they had interacted closely since youth, who wanted the good life to continue. Nor could they ignore the aspirations of their neighbors' land-hungry offspring who would be taking their slaves west. This dual biography, after all, is as much a collective biography of the Virginians whose weight and whose prejudices were brought to bear on their state and nation: Edmund Pendleton and Edmund Randolph, John Randolph of Roanoke and John Taylor of Caroline, Patrick Henry and his son-in-law Judge Spencer Roane, George Mason and George Washington. Friendly congressmen and loyal state legislators who regularly corresponded with Madison and Jefferson influenced their thoughts and conditioned their actions. Add to the list John Page and Wilson Cary Nicholas, John Wayles Eppes and William Branch Giles, and append to them the unnamed subscribers to Thomas Ritchie's Richmond newspaper.

These men's common conviction was that every free American's birthright was an opportunity for advancement and renewal through land ownership. Property conferred honor. If they had a choice between freeing their slaves and sustaining their fathers' vision of the good life, they, like Madison and Jefferson, chose the latter. It was a rare individual, such as Edward Coles, who made common cause with the men and women he had inherited as property.

Looking back to the first chapter of this book, we can ask: Would the common desire to uphold white power in Virginia have been so entrenched if the British had not fomented slave defections in 1775–76; and if, as General Washington reluctantly acknowledged, southerners had grown comfortable with blacks fighting for their freedom as patriot soldiers? It is impossible to answer with certainty, though at the time of the Revolution, Jefferson was more open to extending legal protections to African Americans than he subsequently became. After America's independence was recognized, southern discomfort grew by the decade. In 1792, at a time when Madison was in Congress and Jefferson in the executive, the state assembly in Virginia defined, for legal purposes, what "white" meant. In 1805 the same assembly updated a colonial injunction against teaching slaves to read by extending the ban to free black children. This was the spirit of the times.[27]

Does the evasiveness, the ambivalence, of a Jefferson or a Madison make them loathsome? Or simply weak? Their political generation, like every generation, worked around ethical issues when clarity was not immediately forthcoming. Slavery may be the most striking example, but it is only one of many examples of Madison's and Jefferson's indecision—because theirs, as ours, was a wait-and-see, reactive political world. Public men did not necessarily take collective public action at the first sign of trouble or the first recognition that a moral dilemma existed. That is not an explanation for the persistence of slavery, but it is the way of American politics. Our expectations from past historical actors are ultimately irrelevant, and our final judgment on them brings us satisfaction only insofar as it reflects on how we wish to change the world *we* inhabit for the better.

No one denies that white Americans have been responsible for the telling of U.S. history for most of the past 250 years, and they have shaped the story of national origins in ways that protected (when they did not justify outright) white jurisdiction over that past. In a recent investigation of what he refers to as "the absence of black people in the master narrative," the historian Clarence Walker neatly synthesizes the problem of ownership when he cites the words of a white southern editor in 1902, in disavowing African Americans: "The Negro is an accident—an unwilling, a blameless, but an unwholesome, unwelcome, helpless, unassimilable element in our civilization." These words are emblematic of an anxious, needy strain prevalent among racists and nativists of the twentieth century, and one that echoes as well the attitude Jefferson came to symbolize. When his former presidential secretary freed his slaves and moved with them from Virginia to Illinois in 1819, Madison was up front about the long-term implications of white prejudice. "I wish your philanthropy could compleat its object," he told Edward Coles, "by changing their colour as well as their legal condition."[28]

Despite their common inability to address issues of race in a truly enlightened way, Madison and Jefferson subscribed to the Enlightenment in ethereal form: its adoration of science and philosophy and its treatment of religious dogma as hopeless fallacy; its focus on grand nature and human nature; its teaching that we should privilege rational understanding over passionate conviction.

The Paris Jefferson inhabited in the 1780s was a congenial city, the modern Athens, a place of soaring aesthetics and cultivation of the broadest kind. He brought it home to Madison through the books he sent, which Madison hungrily consumed. *Belles lettres* and scholarly treatises were equally the ornaments of their private libraries. Books inspired the two Virginians to do practical things as well as to philosophize: aside from constitutional considerations, for instance, making scientific farming an essential course of study helped them draw up economic plans and regard the prospects of rural America. As collectors of the latest research, they maintained a constant correspondence with other readers and thinkers, bringing the wider republic of letters closer while saving them from boredom.

At its root the Enlightenment ideal was just that: an intellectual's ideal, a visionary program combining individual awareness with the impulse to engineer social improvement. Politics, on the other hand, was a cumbersome process involving methods of organization that philosophy did not easily address. As they sought to implement a better system of governance than what they had inherited, Madison and Jefferson understood that man's failings lay in his ignorance—and ignorance, they knew, was no less a function of democracy than it was of monarchy. That is why their cause began with an appeal to those whose educational opportunities resembled their own, whose experience within book culture made them receptive to new ways of thinking.

Their affinity for books also fed a strong sense of justice and injustice. Madison and Jefferson adopted an enlightened approach to freedom of conscience, as they spoke out against religious bigotry. This was how their relationship began. They rejected the notion that anyone knew the right way to be a Christian. As an ex-president, Madison was prouder of his forward role in support of freedom of religion, which ended the colonial-era persecution of religious dissenters, than he was of any other accomplishment. Jefferson's self-composed epitaph pronounced him "Author of the Virginia Statute of Religious Freedom." His words of 1800 to Benjamin Rush wrap around the interior of his domed monument in Washington, D.C.: "I have sworn upon the altar of god eternal hostility against every form of tyranny over the mind of man."[29]

What held true for clerical imitators and imposters held true for kingly inheritance too. No English monarch or aristocratic body had ever welcomed progress. On the strength of this simple formulation, Madison and Jefferson advocated a republican government that kept power out of the hands of the undeserving and transferred it to new guardians of the public trust. Republican government extended happiness by minimizing taxes and maximizing individual freedom. This is their legacy. But in doing almost nothing to advance the cause of liberty for those enslaved, Madison and Jefferson also knowingly acquiesced to an American tyranny.

It is hard for most to think of Madison and Jefferson and admit that they were Virginians first, Americans second. But this fact seems beyond dispute. Virginians felt they had to act to protect the interests of the Old Dominion, or else, before long, they would become marginalized by a northern-dominated economy. Virginians who thought in terms of the profit to be reaped in land were often reluctant to invest in manufacturing enterprises. The real tragedy is that they chose to speculate in slaves rather than in textile factories and iron works. They convinced themselves (with help from some sympathetic northerners) that the moral foundation of their economy lay in the fact that their slaves were well provided for in youth and old age. The white laboring poor in the North had no such provision. And so as Virginians tied their fortunes to the land, they failed to extricate themselves from a way of life that was limited in outlook and produced only resistance to economic development. Even Madison condoned this activity. Even Madison evidenced no entrepreneurship.[30]

Madison lodged trust in the political vision of many northerners; Jefferson never really trusted the northern states. When he spoke abstractly of the "people," Jefferson thought of Virginians first, though he was always prepared to include those northerners who agreed with him in the means of constructing his imagined community that left the southern states to their own devices. For Jefferson, right thinking on the part of the people could be lost and then regained; the election of 1800 marked the people's conscious desire to return to an earlier republican vision after letting their guard down and letting the monocrats hoodwink them.

Jefferson thought of politics as an ongoing cyclical process of revolutions and resistance to encroachments. As organic creatures, bodies politic were capable of self-destruction if destabilized by unnatural mixtures and nervous imbalance. In contrast, Madison talked about the "mixed character" of the federal government as "co-equal bodies politic," a stabilizing element representative of a healthy interaction of forces. Madison emphasized good chemistry, and Jefferson emphasized the need to patrol social boundaries, keeping alien and combustible elements apart.

"A Coup de Grace"

In history there is enough dark emotion to cause us to question the moral makeup of our species. While the founders are still a pantheon of heroes for many Americans, today's scholars increasingly disparage them for a *lack* of foresight and humanity. This degradation in the historical imagination is largely a result of their compromise position on slavery, a subject to which we have given a good many pages, with the idea that our treatment of slavery should be thorough and systematic, but not exceed the amount of attention Madison and Jefferson gave to it relative to their other priorities as public men.

While they sought to remake their world, and make it freer, Madison and Jefferson grew up believing that authentic Americans were white men, most of them thrifty farmers. Even the white yeoman's wife was reduced to a breeder, which reflected Madison's and Jefferson's common obsession with demography—they believed that the strength of the nation was tied to its ability to reproduce and expand westward.

Madison and Jefferson had a constituency that is not ours. They do not know us, and we know them only slightly. It goes without saying that they remained oblivious to the shape of the world to come. We admire them for focusing attention on the rights of conscience; but we would be wrong to associate them with today's progressive agenda, just as Hamilton is wrongly credited for pointing the United States in the direction of the modern economy. Their psychic distance from us cannot be ignored.

The whole concept of original intent, therefore, makes no sense. It is a legal fiction that grossly oversimplifies Madison's thinking. The truth is, his interpretation of the Constitution changed over the course of his lifetime, and original intent assumes that Madison's views were permanently fixed in time. His earliest sense of what the Constitution should mean was expressed in his support for the Virginia Plan and the absolute negative, both of which were rejected. So which Madison do we claim was right? Madison at the beginning of the convention? Or Madison at the end? Or when he was writing his *Federalist* essays? In 1793, when Hamilton and he were engaged in combat in the newspapers as "Pacificus" and "Helvidius," Madison deployed one of Hamilton's *Federalist* essays against him. In the last stages of the Jay Treaty debate, Madison tried to say that original intent began with the ratifying conventions, and that meaning was not inherent in the Constitution itself but came instead through the exegesis of the states, beyond Philadelphia. Madison resorted to this tactic only because the so-called original meaning contained in the Constitution that he had signed did not support his position on the Jay Treaty eight years later. Thus, the only way to appreciate Madison's constitutional thinking is to measure comprehensible changes in his views in response to specific political problems.

Madison's and Jefferson's concerns had an immediacy that was far more central to the contests of their lives than to any thoughts of legacy. The demons they faced were the forces they considered hostile to republicanism or that threatened to compromise American independence as they conceived it. This begins to explain their do-or-die contest with the High Federalists and the hysterical labeling that accompanied it. It also explains their eagerness to bulldoze over traditional Indian lands and lawfully Spanish lands, which they did to prevent the mere possibility of future British or French expansionism.

England's bullying on the high seas challenged a sense of national honor. Fear of perpetual vassalage was a humiliating thought as well as an effective legal limitation on national sovereignty. It led Jefferson to embark on the Tripolitan War, and it led Madison to envision the conquest of Canada. They and their associates adopted an inflated rhetoric meant to overcome concerns about the vulnerability of the Union; and they justified acts of aggression in order to prove their manhood on an international stage. In their retirement years, Madison and Jefferson were able to witness the fundamental collapse of the world system they abhorred. The iniquitous routine of impressment eventually ended; and the prejudicial navigation laws that had for decades caused Anglo-American relations to alternate between wary and unfriendly finally moderated.

Despite Virginia's monopolization of the executive branch of government from 1801 to 1825, southerners remained transfixed on the economic engine of the North. They saw themselves losing ground. In this environment, with all their nationalistic pronouncements, Madison and Jefferson did not simply transfer allegiance to the nation on the basis of abstract republican theory. Jefferson's retreat to the theory of nullification in 1798 is only the most obvious example, showing the extent of his preoccupation with protecting Virginia rather than protecting his earlier vision of union. Virginia was on Madison's mind when he battled to situate the national capital on the Potomac—he wanted Virginia's river to be America's Amazon, its primary economic artery.

Politics always trumped abstract ideas for Madison. *The Federalist Papers* belonged to a very small fraction of his career, and yet they constitute at least 50 percent of modern scholars' efforts to describe his mind. What he wrote as "Publius" was simply meant as propaganda for passage of the new Constitution and certainly did not represent the pure distillation of his thought—there was nothing timeless about it. The political wisdom he demonstrated as a partisan writer after 1790 was far greater, and should be more valuable to us today, than his studies of government in 1787–88. If the writings of those few years made him a better politician, it was because he discovered which of his ideas worked and which did not. And just as important, he discovered which of Jefferson's most cherished ideas had to be countered. He was a problem solver.

Jefferson took more chances. He often believed he could actualize what he read in books. At times he was impulse-driven and highly inventive; in other ways he refused to unglue himself from outmoded thinking. He was hardheaded, and Madison was one of a very few who could move him to question basic assumptions. Yet he was also a superb manager of personnel; he was a doer, not just a thinker.

Jefferson's words have malleable meaning. They have provided much fodder for students in disciplines such as botany and architecture, in addition to history and politics. As an indebted slave owner recording his day-to-day accounts in portable notebooks, he was weighed down by an anxious regard for the meaning of human happiness that was anything but abstract. At times he got lost rhapsodizing the healthful life amid the gently sloping landscape and red clay soil of Virginia's Piedmont. And then there was his final experiment—a university.

That does not mean that the legacy Madison and Jefferson left behind is a cloudy one. In a multitude of ways, they confronted old ideas with sobriety and commanding commitment. They did what the celebrated in all historical eras do: they fought passivity. They did not claim to have performed miracles; but they did claim to have fought superstition, ignorance, and corruption—all servile forces besetting the world into which they were born. For better or worse, they gave the United States its profoundly paradoxical character, enabling the nation to claim itself a generator of positive change in the world, at the same time rendering it a world unto itself.

As serious as they were in their mission, we should not forget the other, less well known side of their collaboration—the spirited. In 1830 Madison wrote to the Washington grande dame Margaret Bayard Smith with reference to the journey he and Jefferson took to upstate New York back in 1791. At a dinner party in an unspecified town, they were engaged in polite conversation with one who assured them that the new nation would be best served by having a hereditary chief executive. As Madison tells it, "At the close of an eloquent effusion against the agitations and animosities of a popular choice, and on behalf of birth as, on the whole, affording even a better chance for a suitable head of the Gov't, Mr. Jefferson, with a smile remarked that he had heard of a University somewhere in which the professorship of Mathematics was hereditary. The reply, rec'd with acclamation, was a coup de grace to the anti-republican Heretic." Now that reveals more of the real personality of two who are ordinarily depicted in stern, classical poses—it speaks both to the narrator's sublime memory and to his friend's sublime wit.[31]

James Madison and Thomas Jefferson were durable, purposeful men and politicians to the core. Their handling of the historical record helped guarantee that posterity would remember the Revolution and what followed as a triumph of enlightened idealism. They wished for us to become their disciples, and whether or not they intended it directly, they ensured that the history of the United States would be told in nostalgic strains. But they were not prophets, nor high-flown storytellers. Once again, they were politicians, who knew enough about the nature of tyranny to renounce complacency when it hindered the honest pursuit of truth.

Acknowledgments

One positive aspect of a collaborative study—drawing our analogy from the U.S. Constitution—is that the process involves a balance of power. Like those who met in Philadelphia in 1787, we have sparred constructively, paragraph by paragraph, over the narrative. We dare not say that the exercise has produced a "more perfect union," but we trust it has resulted in less arbitrary and better reasoned conclusions. And we hope, of course, that it has provided a meaningful and provocative engagement for the reader.

Over the years, we have profited greatly from spirited conversations with other specialists in the field of early American politics. We open our acknowledgments with names associated with the history of the ambitious and irreplaceable documentary editions of the James Madison and Thomas Jefferson Papers. Of the generation of scholars who preceded us, we were fortunate to have had Robert A. Rutland as a friend and colleague in the last year of his life. Bob was a pioneer at both the Madison and George Mason Papers projects in the 1960s. Another editor-turned-biographer, Ralph Ketcham, knows the mind of Madison as few others do, and it was good to have him just an email away. The late Merrill Peterson also offered considerable encouragement.

Taking care not to conflate scholarly generations and prematurely age our colleagues, we insert this paragraph break before expressing gratitude to the current editors of the Madison, Jefferson, and Washington Papers projects, especially to David Mattern, Mary Hackett, Barbara Oberg, James McClure, Elaine Pascu, J. Jefferson Looney, and Ted Crackel, with whom we consulted at different stages of our own project. Because of their meticulousness, historians are able to research and write with greater confidence.

Of course, twenty-first-century methods are not without meaning to lovers of paper and ink. The wide availability of digitized early American newspapers, pamphlets, and broadsides makes it simpler than ever before to comb these critical sources. Mixing media at institutions that have adapted to the new conditions, we were able to move ahead with greater ease and energy. We owe much to the highly professional and knowledgeable staffs at the American Antiquarian Society, Worcester, Massachusetts; Alderman Library and Special Collections at the University of Virginia; the Jefferson Library at Monticello; the Huntington Library in San Marino, California; the Historical Society of Pennsylvania; and Hill Memorial Library at Louisiana State University.

Our colleagues at LSU have all helped us improve our focus. Special thanks go to Gaines Foster, Bill Cooper, Paul Hoffman, Charles Royster, Alecia Long, and Gibril Cole. We are grateful as well to Daniel K. Richter for including us in the McNeil Center seminar in Philadelphia, corralling an audience of scholars who read a compressed version of the manuscript in the autumn of 2009 and gave us much to think about.

In the wider community of early American scholars, we have significantly profited from the work of Peter Onuf, John Stagg, Drew McCoy, Jeffrey Pasley, Saul Cornell, David Waldstreicher, Eva Sheppard Wolf, Douglas Egerton, Woody Holton, Jack Rakove, Jim Broussard, William Howard Adams, and Charles Hobson. We were able to bounce ideas off a number of those immersed in the ever-vital field of Jefferson studies, most notably Daniel P. Jordan, Susan Stein, Jack Robertson, Mary Scott-Fleming, and Frank Cogliano. We owe a particular debt to the Anglo-Virginian Andrew O'Shaughnessy, director of the International Center for Jefferson Studies, for his critical reading of a portion of the manuscript; and to Beth Taylor at Montpelier, for her insights on Madison and slavery.

Our literary agent, Geri Thoma, has a strong sense of what makes a good book, and she has done much to lift our spirits through this and earlier book projects. Old friend and accomplished graphic designer Mark Nedostup tidied up the illustrations without compromising their historical character. Newer friend Jennifer Blakebrough-Raeburn has served as a guiding spirit in the writing process. Our editor at Random House, Jonathan Jao, is as astute as he is enthusiastic, having helped immensely to improve the book's readability. He envisioned a bold and comprehensive history of America's national beginnings, and we have done our best to deliver it.

Notes

Abbreviations

Brant   Brant, Irving. *James Madison.* 6 vols. Indianapolis: Bobbs-Merrill, 1941–61.

JMB   *Jefferson's Memorandum Books.* Edited by James A. Bear, Jr., and Lucia C. Stanton. 2 vols. Princeton, N.J.: Princeton University Press, 1997.

JMP-LC   James Madison Papers, Library of Congress. Digitized. Online at http://memory.loc.gov/ammem/collections/madison_papers.

Ketcham   Ketcham, Ralph. *James Madison: A Biography.* New York: Macmillan, 1971.

Malone   Malone, Dumas. *Jefferson and His Time.* 6 vols. Boston: Little, Brown, 1948–81.

PAH   *The Papers of Alexander Hamilton.* Edited by Harold Syrett. 27 vols. New York: Columbia University Press, 1962–87.

PGW-CS   *The Papers of George Washington, Confederation Series.* Edited by W. W. Abbot et al. 6 vols. Charlottesville: University Press of Virginia, 1992–97.

PGW-PS   *The Papers of George Washington, Presidential Series.* Edited by W. W. Abbot et al. 13 vols. to date. Charlottesville: University Press of Virginia, 1987–.

PGW-RS   *The Papers of George Washington, Retirement Series.* Edited by W. W. Abbot et al. 4 vols. Charlottesville: University Press of Virginia, 1998–99.

PGW-RW   *The Papers of George Washington, Revolutionary War Series.* Edited by W. W. Abbot et al. 16 vols. to date. Charlottesville: University Press of Virginia, 1987–.

PJM   *The Papers of James Madison.* Edited by William T. Hutchinson et al. 17 vols. Chicago and Charlottesville: University of Chicago Press (1961–77) and University Press of Virginia (1977–91).

PJM-PS   *The Papers of James Madison, Presidential Series.* Edited by Robert A. Rutland et al. 6 vols. to date. Charlottesville: University Press of Virginia, 1984–.

PJM-RS   *The Papers of James Madison, Retirement Series.* Edited by David B. Mattern et al. 1 vol. to date. Charlottesville: University of Virginia Press, 2009.

PJM-SS   *The Papers of James Madison, Secretary of State Series.* Edited by Robert J. Brugger et al. 8 vols. to date. Charlottesville: University Press of Virginia, 1986–.

PTJ   *The Papers of Thomas Jefferson.* Edited by Julian P. Boyd et al. 36 vols. to date. Princeton, N.J.: Princeton University Press, 1950–.

PTJ-RS   *The Papers of Thomas Jefferson, Retirement Series.* Edited by J. Jefferson Looney. 6 vols. to date. Charlottesville: University Press of Virginia, 2004–.

RL   *The Republic of Letters: The Correspondence between Thomas Jefferson and James Madison, 1776–1826.* Edited by James Morton Smith. 3 vols. New York: W. W. Norton, 1994.

TJP-LC   Thomas Jefferson Papers, Library of Congress. Microfilm and digitized. Online at http://memory.loc.gov/ammem/mtjquery.html.

Preface

1. William Peden, "A Book Peddler Invades Monticello," *William and Mary Quarterly* 6 (October 1949): 635. The bookseller, Samuel Whitcomb, was from Massachusetts.

CHAPTER ONE
The Virginians, 1774–1776

1. Jack P. Greene, "The Intellectual Reconstruction of Virginia in the Age of Jefferson," in Peter. S. Onuf, ed., *Jeffersonian Legacies* (Charlottesville, Va., 1993), 225–53. A Scottish physician who immigrated to Maryland and toured the colonies in the 1740s described ordinary people in Rhode Island as "rude" and the "middling sort of people" in Massachusetts as generally untrustworthy and suspicious of strangers; Pennsylvania merchants "will tell a lye with a sanctified, solemn face." See Elaine G. Breslaw, *Dr. Alexander Hamilton and Provincial America* (Baton Rouge, La., 2008), chaps. 9 and 10, quote at 132. In 1785 Jefferson wrote to a French aristocrat that northerners were "cool, sober, laborious" (the last of which meant "industrious") but also "chicaning," or tricky; southerners, he said, were "fiery, Voluptuary" (pleasure seeking), and "indolent" but also "candid." To Jefferson, these traits permeated the societies of the respective sections. See TJ to the Marquis de Chastellux, September 2, 1785, *PTJ,* 8:468.

2. Fred Anderson, *Crucible of War: The Seven Years' War and the Fate of Empire in British North America* (New York, 2000), chaps. 3–5; Kenneth P. Bailey, *Christopher Gist: Colonial Frontiersman, Explorer, and Indian Agent* (Hamden, Conn., 1976), 75–88; Louis Knott Koontz, *Robert Dinwiddie: His Career in American Colonial Government and Westward Expansion* (Glendale, Calif., 1941), 279–305.

3. John Richardson, "Atrocity in Mid Eighteenth-Century War Literature," *Eighteenth-Century Life* 33 (Spring 2009): 92–114; Peter Silver, *Our Savage Neighbors: How Indian War Transformed Early America* (New York, 2008).

4. John Ferling, *Setting the World Ablaze: Washington, Adams, Jefferson, and the American Revolution* (New York, 2000), 45.

5. James Parton, "Thomas Jefferson a Virginia Lawyer," *Atlantic Monthly* 29 (March 1872): 320. According to Parton's source, Madison was heard to speak of having observed Jefferson in court; this would have been sometime after 1767, when Jefferson began to practice law in Virginia.

6. David John Mays, *Edmund Pendleton, 1721–1803: A Biography* (Richmond, Va., 1952), 1:11–12, 238–39; 2:126–30; Robert Leroy Hilldrup, *The Life and Times of Edmund Pendleton* (Chapel Hill, N.C., 1939), passim; Jack P. Greene, "Society, Ideology, and Politics: An Analysis of the Political Culture of Mid-Eighteenth-Century Virginia," in Richard M. Jellison, ed., *Society, Freedom, and Conscience: The American Revolution in Virginia, Massachusetts, and New York* (New York, 1976), 14–76; Jefferson's Autobiography, Library of Congress.

7. The Boston Port bill used the British military to stop all trade and commerce in the harbor, thus crippling the entire Massachusetts economy; the Massachusetts Government Act annulled the colonial charter and vested the governor and council with virtually absolute political authority; the Justice Act, known as the "murdering bill," protected Crown officials from facing trial in the colony. See Alison Gilbert Olson, *Making the Empire Work: London and American Interest Groups, 1690–1790* (Cambridge, Mass., 1992), 167; *Massachusetts Gazette and Boston Weekly*, December 23, 1773, and *Boston Gazette*, December 20, 1773; *Virginia Gazette*, September 1, 1774; Jerrilyn Greene Marston, *King and Congress: The Transfer of Political Legitimacy, 1774–1776* (Princeton, N.J., 1987), 40–45; John E. Selby, *The Revolution in Virginia, 1775–1783* (Williamsburg, Va., 1988), 7–8.

8. Seven of the eleven members of the Committee of Correspondence were sent as delegates to the First and Second Continental Congresses (to the first: Peyton Randolph, Richard Bland, Richard Henry Lee, Benjamin Harrison, Edmund Pendleton, Patrick Henry; to the second: Thomas Jefferson). See "Resolutions of the House of Burgesses Establishing a Committee of Intercolonial Correspondence, 12 March 1773," "Resolution of the House of Burgesses Designating a Day of Fasting and Prayer, 24 May 1774," "Association of Former Burgesses...27 May 1774," and "Convention of 1774," in Robert L. Scribner et al., eds., *Revolutionary Virginia: The Road to Independence* (Charlottesville, Va., 1973–81), 1:90–102; "Resolution of the House of Burgesses Designating a Day of Fast and Prayer, May 24, 1774," in *PTJ*, 1:105–7; Andrew Burstein, *Sentimental Democracy: The Evolution of America's Romantic Self-Image* (New York, 1999), chap. 3; John E. Ferling, *A Leap in the Dark: The Struggle to Create the American Republic* (New York, 2003); Jack Rakove, *The Beginnings of National Politics: An Interpretative History of the Continental Congress* (New York, 1979), 21–25.

9. See "Extract of a Letter from Boston," in *Virginia Gazette*, October 27, 1774; *A Letter from a Virginian, to the Members of the Congress* (New York, 1774), cited in Rakove, *Beginnings of National Politics*, 38; "Extract of a Letter from Maryland, Sept. 28," in *Pennsylvania Ledger*, February 2, 1775; JM to William Bradford, November 26, 1774, *PJM*, 1:129; "The Convention of 1774: Instructions to the Deputies Elected to Attend the General Congress, 6 August," in Scribner et al., eds., *Revolutionary Virginia*, 1:237.

10. William Wirt, *The Life of Patrick Henry* (Hartford, Conn., 1832 [1817]), sec. 4.

11. "A Summary View," in *PTJ*, 1:121–35.

12. See especially Lynn Hunt, *Inventing Human Rights: A History* (New York, 2007),

116ff.; Jay Fliegelman, *Prodigals and Pilgrims: The American Revolution Against Patriarchal Authority, 1750–1800* (New York, 1982), chap. 5.

13. JM to Bradford, April 1, July 1, and August 23, 1774; Bradford to JM, August 1, 1774, *PJM,* 1:112, 115, 118, 121.

14. Jeffrey H. Morrison, *John Witherspoon and the Founding of the American Republic* (Notre Dame, Ind., 2005); John Witherspoon, "The Charge of Sedition and Faction against Good Men . . ." (1758); sermon dedicated to Hancock, *The Dominion of Providence over the Passions of Men* (1776), both in *The Works of the Rev. John Witherspoon,* 3 vols. (Philadelphia, 1800), 1:319–44, 2:407–36, quotes at 332–33, 427–28; David W. Robson, *Educating Republicans: The College in the Era of the American Revolution, 1750–1800* (Westport, Conn., 1985), 69–70; Ashbel Green, *The Life of the Revd. John Witherspoon,* ed. Henry Littleton Savage (Princeton, N.J., 1973), 146–47, 258; Ketcham, 41–44; Mary-Elaine Swanson, "James Madison and the Presbyterian Idea of Man and Government," in Garrett Ward Sheldon and Daniel L. Dreisbach, eds., *Religion and Political Culture in Jefferson's Virginia* (Lanham, Md., 2000), 119–31; Nancy Isenberg, *Fallen Founder: The Life of Aaron Burr* (New York, 2007), 10–11.

15. JM to Bradford, January 24 and April 1, 1774, *PJM,* 1:106, 112–13; Rhys Isaac, *The Transformation of Virginia, 1740–1790* (Chapel Hill, N.C., 1982), 278–82.

16. JM to Bradford, January 20 and July 28, 1775, *PJM,* 1:135, 161–62; Ketcham, 64–67; Brant, 1:106–11, 116–17; "Orange County Committee," from *Virginia Gazette,* April 15, 1775, in Scribner et al., eds., *Revolutionary Virginia,* 2:377–78, 386, 389.

17. JM to Bradford, November 9, 1772, *PJM,* 1:75; Anne C. Vila, *Enlightenment and Pathology: Sensibility in the Literature and Medicine of Eighteenth-Century France* (Baltimore, 1998), 104; G. J. Barker-Benfield, *The Culture of Sensibility: Sex and Society in Eighteenth-Century Britain* (Chicago, 1992), 24–27.

18. *PTJ,* 1:246; *PJM,* 1:163.

19. TJ to Wirt, August 4, 1805, and April 12, 1812; Wirt to TJ, September 16, 1805, *TJP-LC;* Frank L. Dewey, "Thomas Jefferson and a Williamsburg Scandal: The Case of Blair v. Blair," *Virginia Magazine of History and Biography* 89 (1981): 44–63, quote at 57. Jefferson (who was not in Philadelphia when Henry was) nevertheless informed Wirt that as a member of the First Continental Congress, Henry made a good first impression: "While general grievances were the topics, he was in his element & captivated all by his bold & splendid eloquence. But as soon as they came to specific matters, to sober reasoning and solid argumentation he had the good sense to perceive that his declamation however excellent in it's proper place, had no weight at all in such an assembly as that, of cool-headed, reflecting, judicious men." It was essential to Jefferson that the world know what Henry was *not.* "He squeezed exorbitant fees," Jefferson persisted, claiming that Henry shamelessly sought personal fame and giant wealth: "Mr. Henry's ravenous avarice, the only passion paramount." Wirt admitted his dilemma, Jefferson's disparagement having apparently been confirmed by some others—though only Jefferson, it appears, was fixated on Henry's supposedly indecent love of money. "Conflicting narratives are so equal in number and character," Wirt told Jefferson, "that I find it impossible to say directly where the truth lies."

Though he ended up writing a biography that Henry's descendants adored, Wirt confirmed Jefferson's assessment of Henry's lack of diligence. Unbiased former colleagues attested to Henry's own admission, in later years, of an "early neglect of literature" and the "indolence of his character." Attempting to rescue his subject, Wirt rationalized: "The people seemed to have admired him the more for his want of discipline." This was how early American biography was slanted. Oratorical genius was meant to range, not to be confined to paper; or as Wirt put it, to "revel in all the wildness and boldness of nature." Wirt, *Life of Patrick Henry*, esp. 25–26, 125–33.

20. Scribner et al., eds., *Revolutionary Virginia*, 1:227–28. Each of the more than one hundred members of the convention voted for seven individuals; because a nominee had to receive two-thirds of the convention's votes to be selected for Philadelphia, two ballots had to be taken before seven names were found. In the two ballots, Peyton Randolph received 104 and 107 votes, respectively (virtually everyone included him in the top seven); Lee received 100 and 102; Washington 98 and 104; Henry 89 and 104; Richard Bland 79 and 90; Benjamin Harrison 66 and 94; and Pendleton 62 and 100. Jefferson received 51 on the first ballot and merely 18 on the second.

21. JM to Bradford, August 23, 1774, *PJM*, 1:121; Diary of Silas Deane, September 10–19, 1774, in *Letters of Delegates to Congress, 1774–1789*, ed. Paul L. Smith (Washington, D.C., 1976–2000), 1:61; Elma Josephine Hege, "Benjamin Harrison and the American Revolution," master's thesis, University of Virginia, August 1939; Henry S. Randall, *Life of Thomas Jefferson* (New York, 1858), 1:155. Jefferson was impressed with Richard Bland as a source of knowledge on constitutions, "a great antiquarian, and possessed of many valuable public papers." TJ to Ebenezer Hazard, April 30, 1775, *PTJ*, 1:164. However, Ralph Ketcham speculates that the two men Madison wished replaced were Bland and Randolph, for being "timid," or insufficiently aggressive. Ketcham, 61. On Washington, see John Ferling, *The Ascent of George Washington: The Hidden Political Genius of an American Icon* (New York, 2009), 75–79.

22. *Pinkney's Virginia Gazette*, June 1, 1775, cited in Woody Holton, *Forced Founders: Indians, Debtors, Slaves, and the Making of the American Revolution in Virginia* (Chapel Hill, N.C., 1999), 152; *Providence Journal*, December 23, 1775; JM to Bradford, June 19, 1775, *PJM*, 1:153. The phrase a "devil more damned in evil," from *Macbeth*, is attributed to John Page; see Scribner et al., eds., *Revolutionary Virginia*, 4:21; *Virginia Gazette* (Purdie), May 31, 1776.

23. "Report of the Causes of the Late Disturbances," in *Journals of the House of Burgesses of Virginia, 1773–1776*, ed. John Pendleton Kennedy (Richmond, 1905), 237; Selby, *Revolution in Virginia*, 3.

24. JM to William Bradford, May 9, 1775; "Address to Captain Patrick Henry and the Gentlemen Independents of Hanover," *Virginia Gazette*, May 19, 1775, *PJM*, 1:144–47.

25. Pendleton to Joseph Chew, June 15, 1775, in *Letters of Delegates to Congress*, 1:486; TJ to Small, May 7, 1775, in *PTJ*, 1:166–67.

26. JM to Bradford, May 9 and June 19, 1775, *PJM*, 1:145, 151–52; Selby, *Revolution in Virginia*, 50. The charges against Bland were found to be baseless.

27. JM to Bradford, November 26, 1774; Bradford to JM, January 4, 1775, *PJM*, 1:129–32; Douglas R. Egerton, *Death or Liberty: African Americans and Revolutionary America* (New York, 2009), 60–61. Egerton also notes that in South Carolina in 1775, a slave was executed for preaching that King George III had "set the Negroes Free," while their white masters were ignoring the decree.

28. JM to Bradford, June 19, 1775, *PJM*, 1:153; Douglas B. Chambers, *Murder at Montpelier: Igbo Africans in Virginia* (Jackson, Miss., 2005), 5–7. Ambrose Madison may in fact have died of natural causes—the point is that his slaves were blamed, and the sinister art of poisoning (brought to Virginia from West Africa) immediately suspected.

29. Donald J. Gara, "Loyal Subjects of the Crown: The Queen's Own Loyal Virginia Regiment and Dunmore's Ethiopian Regiment, 1775–76," *Journal of the Society for Army Historical Research* 83 (2005): 30–42; John Wood Sweet, *Bodies Politic: Negotiating Race in the American North, 1730–1830* (Baltimore, 2003), 194–97; Selby, *Revolution in Virginia*, 50, 67; Washington to Joseph Reed, February 26–March 9, 1776, *PGW-RW*, 3:374. In his 1789 account South Carolina patriot David Ramsay wrote of the "headstrong passions" of Lord Dunmore during this period, and the general British view that an "easy conquest" of the American rebels would come as a result of the massive numbers of slaves and servants who seemed likely to join with His Majesty's forces. See Ramsay, *The History of the American Revolution*, ed. Lester H. Cohen (Indianapolis, 1990), 1:232–33. On the badge "Liberty to Slaves," see *New-York Gazette*, December 18, 1775.

30. TJ to Page, October 31, 1775; Robert Carter Nicholas to TJ and the Virginia Delegates, November 25, 1775; Pendleton to TJ, November 16, 1775, *PTJ*, 1:251, 260–61, 266–67. The falsity of Pendleton's claim as to Dunmore's intent to sell the escaped slaves is borne out in Cassandra Pybus, *Epic Journeys of Freedom: Runaway Slaves of the American Revolution and Their Global Quest for Liberty* (Boston, 2006).

31. In 1778 General Washington instructed his kinsman Lund Washington, who oversaw production at Mount Vernon, to "Barter for other Land" in Virginia by selling slaves. The only property he would not have Lund sell were "Breeding Mares and Stock of other Kinds." Read unsympathetically, it appears that Washington's human breeders were expendable to him, but his livestock was not. By war's end, there would be some five thousand African-American Continentals under his command. It was all done quietly and gradually. GW to Joseph Reed, December 15, 1775; to Lund Washington, August 15, 1778, *PGW-RW*, 2:553, 16:315; Egerton, *Death or Liberty*, 74–75. The most compelling recent analysis of Virginians of all ranks amid the crisis fomented by Dunmore's decisions is Michael A. McDonnell, *The Politics of War: Race, Class, and Conflict in Revolutionary Virginia* (Chapel Hill, N.C., 2007), chaps. 1–4.

32. Selby, *Revolution in Virginia*, 26–32; Holton, *Forced Founders*, 92–96; "Indenture," September 1774, in *PJM*, 1:123–24; Susan Dunn, *Dominion of Memories: Jefferson, Madison, and the Decline of Virginia* (New York, 2007), chaps. 1 and 2; Brant, 1:49.

33. Henry to Robert Pleasants, January 18, 1773, in James M. Elson, comp., *Patrick Henry in His Speeches and Writings and in the Words of His Contemporaries* (Lynchburg, Va., 2007), 66–68.

34. George Van Cleve, "Somerset's Case and Its Antecedents in Imperial Perspective," *Law and History Review* 24 (Fall 2006): 601–46; Jerome Nadelhaft, "The Somerset Case and Slavery: Myth, Reality, and Repercussions," *Journal of Negro History* 51 (July 1966): 196–97; *New-York Journal*, August 27, 1772.

35. Benjamin Franklin to Anthony Benezet, August 22, 1772, *Papers of Benjamin Franklin*, 19:269; "Extract of a Letter from Phillis, a Negro girl of Mr. Wheatley's of this Town, to the Rev. Samson Occom," *Boston Evening-Post*, March 21, 1774; Peter Dorsey, "To 'Corroborate Our Own Claims': Public Positioning and the Slavery Metaphor in

Revolutionary America," *American Quarterly* 55 (September 2003): 354, 366. The author of another article, signed "A Son of Africa," echoed the *Somerset* ruling, claiming that Americans could not enslave Africans without contradicting the British constitution, the laws of Great Britain and God. Only custom supported slavery, as there was no positive law in the Kingdom of Great Britain or the province of Massachusetts that upheld slavery. *Massachusetts Spy*, February 10, 1774.

36. "Number VI: A Few Political Reflections," *Pennsylvania Packet*, August 8, 1774; Dorsey, "To 'Corroborate Our Own Claims,' " 369; Eva Sheppard Wolf, *Race and Liberty in the New Nation: Emancipation in Virginia from the Revolution to Nat Turner's Rebellion* (Baton Rouge, La., 2006), 23–24.

37. *Virginia Gazette*, November 25, 1775, March 22, 1776, July 20, 1776, and October 4, 1776; *New-York Gazette*, December 4, 1775; see also issue of December 8 for a satirical poem, "A Proclamation Declaration," mockingly attributed to Dunmore. It reads in part: "Ye *convicts, servants and* ye *debtors,* / Ye sentenc'd *felons,* break your fetters, / And *slaves* of *rebels* hither come / And march with me at beat of drum." These caricatures tell only half the story. Dunmore was confident that colonial resistance would fail, because the Virginia planter elite had so little concern for both white and black underclass. "Slaves and the lower class of people," he wrote to the Earl of Dartmouth, would discover before long that they had been "duped by the richer sort" into doing their bidding. His letter found its way back to the *Virginia Gazette* and fed Virginians' fearful expectations. Dunmore was not merely inciting rebellion, they now heard, but planned to grant free blacks and white servants the much-coveted rights of Britons if they turned on the patriot crowd. See "Extract of a letter from the Earl of Dunmore to the Earl of Dartmouth, dated Williamsburg, December 24, 1774; laid before the House of Commons, February 15, by Lord North," *Virginia Gazette*, April 29, 1775.

38. *Virginia Gazette*, November 22, 1775, and April 13, 1776; Christopher Brown, "Empire Without Slaves: British Concepts of Emancipation in the Age of Revolution," *William and Mary Quarterly* 56 (April 1999): 285–86.

39. Journal entry of July 13, 1776, Robert Carter Papers, 1772–1793, Box 1, Folder 2, American Antiquarian Society, Worcester, Mass.; Andrew Levy, *The First Emancipator: The Forgotten Story of Robert Carter, The Founder Who Freed His Slaves* (New York, 2006). Yet when a British privateer landed a short distance from his plantation, thirty-two blacks were there to commit themselves to the British—much to Carter's surprise. See Egerton, *Death or Liberty*, 71.

40. See esp. Winthrop D. Jordan, *White Over Black: American Attitudes toward the Negro, 1550–1812* (Chapel Hill, N.C., 1968), 276ff., quote at 279.

41. Jack McLaughlin, *Jefferson and Monticello: The Biography of a Builder* (New York, 1988), chaps. 1–3; Lucia Stanton, *Free Some Day: The African-American Families of Monticello* (Charlottesville, Va., 2000), 17–18; Andrew Burstein, *The Inner Jefferson: Portrait of a Grieving Optimist* (Charlottesville, Va., 1995), 12–23; John Wayles to TJ, October 20, 1772, *PTJ*, 1:95–96; "Deed from Jane Randolph Jefferson for the Conveyance of Slaves," undated, *PTJ*, 27:675–76; Herbert E. Sloan, *Principle and Interest: Thomas Jefferson and the Problem of Debt* (New York, 1995), 14–18. Sloan shows that had Wayles's heirs kept his lands intact, their exposure to Wayles's British creditors would have been minimal; in receiving his portion of the Wayles property, Jefferson attached his own lands to the liability he bore in meeting his late father-in-law's debts. The Revolution did not change

this, and Jefferson spent the remainder of his life trying unsuccessfully to meet his obligations.

42. Malone, 1:30–32; Brant, 1:66, 407; Kenneth Bailey, "George Mason, Westerner," *William and Mary Quarterly* 23 (October 1943): 409–17; Shaw Livermore, *Early American Land Companies: Their Influence on Corporate Development* (New York, 1939); Kenneth P. Bailey, *The Ohio Company of Virginia and the Westward Movement, 1748–1792* (Glendale, Calif., 1939); Thomas Perkins Abernethy, *Western Lands and the American Revolution* (New York, 1959); Harriette Simpson Arnow, *Seedtime on the Cumberland* (New York, 1960), 183, 228; Peter S. Onuf, *The Origins of the Federal Republic: Jurisdictional Controversies in the United States, 1775–1787* (Philadelphia, 1983), 75–82; Anthony F. C. Wallace, *Jefferson and the Indians: The Tragic Fate of the First Americans* (Cambridge, Mass., 1999), 28–37; Holton, *Forced Founders*, 9–12, 32–33; TJ to JM, November 11, 1784, *RL*, 2:350.

James Madison, Sr., had extensive dealings with land investors. One of his closest friends was Joseph Chew (ca. 1725–98), who moved out of Orange County and engaged in commercial dealings in various colonial cities. In 1750 Chew revealed to him that he wished to become a manager of the Ohio Company, the land venture begun in 1749 and backed by George Washington. The elder Madison also had dealings with William Lee, younger brother of Richard Henry Lee, who acted as one of the principal agents of the Mississippi Company; see JM to James Madison, Sr., October 9, 1771, and January 23, 1778, in *PJM*, 1:68–69, 222–23; and Joseph Chew to James Madison, Sr., September 6, 1749, and May 21, 1750, in Madison Family Papers, Library of Congress; Washington to Joseph Chew, September 25, 1774, in *Letters of Delegates to Congress*, 1:102. The Virginia gentry had to effect a balance between their own financial interests and the financial and the social aspirations of increasingly disgruntled tenant farmers. See Thomas J. Humphrey, "Conflicting Independence: Tenant Farmers and the American Revolution," *Journal of the Early Republic* 28 (Summer 2008): 159–82.

43. Randolph C. Downes, "Dunmore's War: An Interpretation," *Mississippi Valley Historical Review* 21 (December 1934): 311–12, 321–23, 326–27; Holton, *Forced Founders*, 33–34; Richard White, *The Middle Ground: Indians, Empires, and Republics in the Great Lake Region, 1650–1815* (Cambridge, U.K., 1991); and Michael N. McConnell, *A Country Between: The Upper Ohio Valley and Its Peoples, 1724–1774* (Lincoln, Neb., 1992), 269–81.

44. Wallace, *Jefferson and the Indians*, 1–5; John Bakeless, *Background to Glory: The Life of George Rogers Clark* (Lincoln, Neb., 1957), 25–28; *JMB*, 1:385–86.

45. TJ to Frances Eppes, June 26, 1775; "Declaration of the Causes and Necessity of Taking Up Arms," June 26–July 6, 1775; TJ to John Page, August 5 and August 20, 1776, all in *PTJ*, 1:175, 217, 317, 485–86, 500.

46. *PTJ*, 1:123. Aptly, Jefferson's notion followed the logic of the embattled Shawnees of 1770, who justified their retention of the land according to the "Antient Right of Conquest." See Downes, "Dunmore's War," 316. To be clear, Jefferson's "adventurers" were direct ancestors of the landed elite of his own time. He was not celebrating the yeomanry of Virginia so much as he was defending the rights of the Madisons, Pendletons, and like-minded others.

47. *A Summary View of the Rights of British America*, in *PTJ*, 1:121–23, 133; Peter S. Onuf, *Jefferson's Empire: The Language of American Nationhood* (Charlottesville, Va., 2000), 21–23.

48. JM to Bradford, June 19, 1775, *PJM*, 1:153; also see Rhys Isaac, "Dramatizing the Ideology of the Revolution: Popular Mobilization in Virginia, 1774 to 1776," *William and Mary Quarterly* 33 (July 1976): 380-82.

49. Robert G. Parkinson, "From Indian Killer to Worthy Citizen: The Revolutionary Transformation of Michael Cresap," *William and Mary Quarterly* 63 (January 2006): 97-122; Robert McGinn and Larry Vaden, "Michael Cresap and the Cresap Rifles," *West Virginia History* 39 (1978): 341-47; also "Virginia Marksmanship: From Purdie's *Virginia Gazette*, November 17, 1775," in *William and Mary College Quarterly Historical Magazine* 20 (October 1911): 144-45.

50. Jefferson's published resolution on Lord North's proposal, July 25, 1775, is in *PTJ*, 1:233; TJ to Gilmer, July 5, 1775; and see a similar repudiation of Americans' alleged cowardice in TJ to John Randolph, August 25, 1775, ibid., 186, 241; for British statements, see "From London Evening Post. On Civil War in America," *Pennsylvania Ledger*, November 18, 1775.

51. Burstein, *Inner Jefferson*, 186; Burstein, *Sentimental Democracy*, 132-34; *PTJ*, 1:495-97, 510-11.

52. Selby, *Revolution in Virginia*, 88-89; Mays, *Edmund Pendleton*, 1:241-42, 2:5-7; McDonnell, *Politics of War*, 181-83.

53. Selby, *Revolution in Virginia*, 95-97; *Virginia Gazette*, May 17, 1776.

54. Robert A. Rutland, *George Mason: Reluctant Statesman* (Baton Rouge, La., 1961), 23, 26-27, 38-40; Moncure Daniel Conway, *Omitted Chapters of History Disclosed in the Life and Papers of Edmund Randolph* (New York, 1888), 20-26; Pendleton to TJ, May 24, 1776, *PTJ*, 1:296.

55. *The Papers of George Mason*, ed. Robert A. Rutland (Chapel Hill, N.C., 1970), 1:276-77; Brant, 1:238-41; Pauline Maier, *American Scripture: Making the Declaration of Independence* (New York, 1997), 126-27.

56. *Virginia Gazette*, June 1 and June 12, 1776; Selby, *Revolution in Virginia*, 106-8. The same argument would be made in the historic *Dred Scott* decision of 1857.

57. Brant, 1:241-48; Ketcham, 72-73; Richard R. Beeman, *Patrick Henry: A Biography* (New York, 1974), 103; Daniel L. Dreisbach, "Church-State Debate in Virginia: From the Declaration of Rights to the Statute for Establishing Religious Freedom," in Sheldon and Dreisbach, eds., *Religion and Political Culture in Jefferson's Virginia*, 135-41. Edmund Randolph in later years remembered Henry as the committee member who introduced the language on toleration; most scholars, however, believe Randolph's memory flawed in this regard.

58. TJ to Fleming, July 1, 1776, *PTJ*, 1:412-13.

59. J. Kent McGaughy, *Richard Henry Lee of Virginia: A Portrait of an American Revolutionary* (Lanham, Md., 2004), chap. 5; for hints of Lee's contentiousness, or divisiveness, which may or may not be exaggerated, see Randall, *Life of Thomas Jefferson*, 1:148-56.

60. Fleming to TJ, June 22, 1776; TJ to Fleming, July 1, 1776; to Lee, July 23, 1776; to Page, July 30, 1776, *PTJ*, 1:406, 412-13, 477, 482-83; Malone, 1:240-41.

61. On the larger similarities between Jefferson's and Mason's work, and their common sources, see Ronald Hatzenbuehler, *"I Tremble for My Country": Thomas Jefferson and the Virginia Gentry* (Gainesville, Fla., 2006), 39-43, 54-57.

62. The several versions of the Declaration of Independence, notably Jefferson's original draft and that adopted by Congress, are in *PTJ*, 1:315-19, 413-33.

63. Quote from Katherine Sobba Green, *The Courtship Novel, 1740–1820: A Feminized Genre* (Lexington, Ky., 1991), 66.

64. Sharon Block, *Rape and Sexual Power in Early America* (Chapel Hill, N.C., 2006), 230-31; Quentin Outram, "The Demographic Impact of Early Modern Warfare," *Social Science History* 26 (Summer 2002): 245-72, indicating that the English fear of mercenaries can be traced back to the Thirty Years War in Germany, 1618-48; Frank Whitson Fetter, "Who Were the Foreign Mercenaries of the Declaration of Independence?" *Pennsylvania Magazine of History and Biography* 104 (1980): 508-13; on the connection between rape and war, see also Nancy Isenberg, "Death and Satire: Dismembering the Body Politic," in Isenberg and Burstein, eds., *Mortal Remains: Death in Early America* (Philadelphia, 2003), 77-78. Joseph Warren's momentous oration on the occasion of the second anniversary of the Boston Massacre, in 1772, evoked the same imagery, justifying "alarmed imaginations" over the prospect of "our children subject to the barbarous caprice of the raging soldiery,—our beauteous virgins exposed to all the insolence of unbridled passion,—our virtuous wives, endeared to us by every tender tie, falling a sacrifice to worse than brutal violence." See Burstein, *Sentimental Democracy*, 68-69.

65. John Dunn, *The Political Thought of John Locke: An Historical Account of the Argument of "The Two Treatises of Government"* (Cambridge, U.K., 1969); Carole Pateman, *The Sexual Contract* (Stanford, Calif., 1988), 93; on Jewish divorce law, see Matthew Biberman, "Milton, Marriage, and a Woman's Right to Divorce," *Studies in English Literature, 1500–1900* 39 (Winter 1999): 131-53. Carl L. Becker has written of America's relationship to the king as a "thin gold thread of voluntary allegiance to a personal sovereign." See Becker, *The Declaration of Independence: A Study in the History of Political Ideas* (New York, 1922), 130-34.

66. Frank L. Dewey, "Thomas Jefferson's Notes on Divorce," *William and Mary Quarterly* 39 (January 1982): 216-17. Jefferson also recognized the voluntary nature of marriage when he wrote: "where both parties consent," the covenant "must be dissoluble from the nature of things. On the primacy of Jefferson's "tranquil permanent felicity," see Andrew Burstein, *Jefferson's Secrets: Death and Desire at Monticello* (New York, 2005).

67. Dewey, "Thomas Jefferson's Notes on Divorce," 218-19.

68. For an account of the king's speech, given in Parliament on October 28, 1775, but not reprinted in American newspapers until several months later, see the *Pennsylvania Packet*, January 13, 1776. The speech continued to be debated in the newspapers; see "Letter to Mr. Purdie," *Virginia Gazette*, March 8, 1776. See also Rakove, *Beginnings of National Politics*, 80-81, 92, 95.

69. *Virginia Gazette*, February 23 and March 8, 1776; "Some QUERIES offered to the FREEHOLDERS and PEOPLE of VIRGINIA at large," *Virginia Gazette*, April 19, 1776; Thomas Paine, *Common Sense* (Garden City, N.Y., 1973), 33. It is striking, too, that in one of Virginia's petitions, the king was accused of assigning the colonies the woman's role by "restraining her trade within the most narrow bounds," draining her, through internal taxes, "of the little circulating cash she had," all so that she would be bound "within her

little sphere..., contented with homespun." Reconciliation might preserve an unequal union, but it would also make the colonists cowardly and effeminate dependents.

70. On masculine English traits and manly public spirit, see Paul Langford, *Englishness Identified: Manners and Character, 1650–1850* (Oxford, U.K., 2000), 69, 96; and Lawrence E. Klein, *Shaftesbury and the Culture of Politeness: Moral Discourse and Cultural Politics in Early Eighteenth-Century England* (Cambridge, U.K., 1994), 184–85; also "An American," *Virginia Gazette,* January 1, 1776.

71. "Some QUERIES offered to the FREEHOLDERS...," *Virginia Gazette,* April 19, 1776; "Reasons for a Declaration of Independence of the *American* Colonies," *Pennsylvania Packet,* as reprinted in *Virginia Gazette,* March 25, 1776; on Jefferson's strategies in the Declaration for granting Congress its legitimacy as the king's replacement, see Peter S. Onuf, "Thomas Jefferson, Federalist," in *The Mind of Thomas Jefferson* (Charlottesville, Va., 2007), 89–90.

72. Note that in lowercasing "united," the parchment copy signed by the members of Congress denoted the primacy of the states over the nation at their moment of joining together. *PTJ,* 1:432. Compare Jefferson's "Original Rough Draft," which capitalizes "United," ibid., 1:427.

73. Pendleton to TJ, November 16, 1775, *PTJ,* 1:261. For an incisive discussion, see Sidney Kaplan, "The 'Domestic Insurrections' of the Declaration of Independence," *Journal of Negro History* 61 (July 1976): 243–55. Charles A. Miller shows that Jefferson fell short of calling chattel slavery a violation of natural law, in *Jefferson and Nature: An Interpretation* (Baltimore, 1988), chap. 3. Carl Becker diminishes the power of Jefferson's so-called philippic against slavery in the Declaration, writing: "It is indeed vehement; but it is not moving." Becker, *Declaration of Independence,* 220.

We should be careful not to generalize too much on this subject. For instance, some northern figures associated with an antislavery mentality were in fact much slower to become active critics than history imagines. Benjamin Franklin assumed black inferiority and is shown by the historian David Waldstreicher to have been extremely cautious, even ambivalent, in addressing the slavery issue. Franklin did not register disagreement with the slavery passage in Jefferson's draft of the Declaration of Independence that overdramatized both London's complicity in the colonial slave trade and Americans' desire to put an end to it. He had made the same argument himself four years earlier, in response to the *Somerset* case. "To free slaves," as Waldstreicher reminds us, "would infringe on the property rights of Britons—and thus effectively enslave the slaveholders." See Waldstreicher, *Runaway America: Benjamin Franklin, Slavery, and the American Revolution* (New York, 2004), quote at 180.

74. *PTJ,* 1:426–27.

75. See, for instance, the *Newport* [R.I.] *Mercury,* July 22, 1776.

76. *Pennsylvania Packet,* June 24, 1776, reprinted in the *New-York Journal,* July 4, 1776.

77. *New-York Journal,* July 11, 1776; *Virginia Gazette,* July 27 and August 10, 1776.

78. *Freeman's Journal,* July 6, 1776.

79. Michal J. Rozbicki, *The Complete Colonial Gentleman: Cultural Legitimacy in Plantation America* (Charlottesville, Va., 1998); Dunn, *Dominion of Memories;* Haztenbuehler, *"I Tremble for My Country."*

80. Pauline Maier contends that Congress's editing distinctly improved Jefferson's text. See Maier, *American Scripture*, chap. 3.

81. Pendleton to TJ, August 10, 1776, *PTJ*, 1:488–89.

82. David A. McCants, *Patrick Henry, Orator* (New York, 1990), chap. 1; Becker, *Declaration of Independence*, 218.

CHAPTER TWO
On the Defensive, 1776–1781

1. Charles Crowe, "The Reverend James Madison in Williamsburg and London, 1768–1771," *West Virginia History* 25 (1964): 270–78; Rhys Isaac, *The Transformation of Virginia, 1740–1790* (Chapel Hill, N.C., 1982), 203–5; Malone, 1:42. As a young lawyer, Jefferson traveled to Augusta County and had extensive dealings with Reverend Madison's father and brother (both named John). See numerous entries in *JMB* for the years 1767–69.

2. Brant, 1:251–71; Pendleton to TJ, August 10, 1776, *PTJ*, 1:489.

3. Henry S. Randall, *Life of Thomas Jefferson* (New York, 1858), 1:62–63; *JMB*, 1:424–26; Malone, 1:245–46.

4. Pendleton to TJ, August 10, 1776, *PTJ*, 1:489.

5. In this context, Peter Gay has written that Hume's view of politics was "realistic in its awareness of conflict, hard-headed in its call for order, but at the same time, liberal in its insistence on a domain of freedom, and above all, flexible in its very generality." He effectively sums up Madisonian political theory with these words. See Gay, *The Enlightenment: The Science of Freedom* (New York, 1969), 460–61.

6. Jefferson's "Autobiography," *TJP-LC*.

7. Holly Brewer, "Entailing Aristocracy in Colonial Virginia: 'Ancient Feudal Restraints' and Revolutionary Reform," *William and Mary Quarterly* 54 (April 1997): 313.

8. Ibid., 311, 315–18, 338.

9. On Jefferson's failed attempt to circumvent entail, see ibid., 327–28; Carter Braxton to Landon Carter, December 19, 1776, cited in John E. Selby, *The Revolution in Virginia, 1775–1783* (Williamsburg, Va., 1988), 140; Malone, 1:252ff.

10. On this subject, see esp. Eva Sheppard Wolf, *Race and Liberty in the New Nation: Emancipation in Virginia from the Revolution to Nat Turner's Rebellion* (Baton Rouge, La., 2006). In 1782 Madison willingly became involved in helping Pendleton's nephew recover an escaped slave and appears not to have been averse to promoting a fugitive slave law. Pendleton to JM, September 9, 1782; JM to Pendleton, September 24, 1782, *PJM*, 5:109–10, 157–58.

11. It is uncertain precisely how much original thought belongs to Jefferson in Bill no. 51, "A Bill concerning Slaves," prepared (but not introduced into the Assembly) prior to June 1779. See *PTJ*, 2:470–73. Virginia's General Assembly may have voted to end the state's participation in the international slave trade in 1778, but it continued to permit slave owners from outside the state to settle there without having to free their slaves. The Continental Congress had voted to stop the slave trade in 1774 (mainly to harm British merchants), but it may be that the states did not consider this vote as

binding after 1776, and several, individually, passed more decisive legislation to this effect. Virginia was the first to do so.

Jefferson's role in the process is not entirely clear. In June 1777 a bill was prepared in the Assembly for the purpose of ending the importation of slaves into Virginia. "Hereafter," it read, all persons "imported into this Commonwealth" would be "absolutely exempted" from bondage. Jefferson may or may not have been involved in its drafting—documentation is lacking—though he believed, when he was in his seventies, that he had been a principal in this legislation. The important points to make are, first, that he was associated with a push to curtail the slave trade from at least the time of his draft of the Declaration of Independence; and second, that his colleagues were well aware of his discomfort with slave trafficking. He took pride in his opposition, whether or not he misremembered his authorship of this particular bill. *PTJ*, 2:22–24; Selby, *Revolution in Virginia*, 158–61; John Chester Miller, *The Wolf by the Ears: Thomas Jefferson and Slavery* (New York, 1977), 20–21.

12. On the neurophysiological attributes inherent in Jefferson's political medicine, and its particular vocabulary, see Andrew Burstein, *Jefferson's Secrets: Death and Desire at Monticello* (New York, 2005); and for further contextualization, see Sarah Knott, *Sensibility and the American Revolution* (Chapel Hill, N.C., 2009).

13. Jefferson was not alone in his thoughts on education. At the very time the new state constitution was being drafted, one interested citizen sent an urgent appeal to the Virginia Assembly. "Academicus" wrote for the *Virginia Gazette* that "learning alone" stood to ensure the stability of the new state government. Relying on England for education was no longer possible and would perhaps even be detrimental—the writer expressed suspicion of those who "drank deep of the fountain of corruption." See "To the Honorable Convention of Virginia," *Virginia Gazette*, May 31, 1776.

14. Brant, 1:296–300; Malone, 1:274–77; Randall, *Life of Thomas Jefferson*, 1:203–5.

15. *JMB*, 1:70, 428–29. That same month Jefferson was repaid by Reverend Madison for a sum of cash he had loaned. The notation Jefferson made with respect to the purchase of books reads "Recd. of James Madison"; for the return of cash lent, "Recd. of Rev. Madison." The notations were made only days apart. The distinction suggests that the first transaction was indeed made with James Madison, Jr.

16. James M. Elson, comp., *Patrick Henry in His Speeches and Writings and in the Words of His Contemporaries* (Lynchburg, Va., 2007), 91.

17. John J. Reardon, *Edmund Randolph: A Biography* (New York, 1974), 35–37.

18. Selby, *Revolution in Virginia*, 124–27; John E. Ferling, *The First of Men: A Life of George Washington* (Knoxville, Tenn., 1988), chap. 7 and 199–200; *Patrick Henry in His Speeches and Writings*, comp. Elson, 92; Stephen to TJ, [ca. 20] December 1776, *PTJ*, 1:659; Paul K. Longmore, *The Invention of George Washington* (Berkeley, Calif., 1988), 64, 250n30. General Stephen was drummed out of the service a year later, and blamed for the American defeat at Germantown; Washington was glad to be rid of him. See John Ferling, *The Ascent of George Washington: The Hidden Political Genius of an American Icon* (New York, 2009), 136–37.

19. Selby, *Revolution in Virginia*, 131; Brant, 1:211, 323–26; Michael A. McDonnell, *The Politics of War: Race, Class, and Conflict in Revolutionary Virginia* (Chapel Hill, N.C., 2008), 247, 257, 265–76. Aware of the difficulty in recruitment, meaningful numbers of

slaves expressed a willingness to join the army, which legislators refused to allow; however, free blacks were enlisted, a practice sanctioned in Virginia but in no other southern state and many slaves pretended to be free and were aided by recruiters, who received ten dollars for each "free" person they brought into service. As of mid-1777, white indentured servants and apprentices could legally leave their masters without consent in order to serve in the military. Ibid., 261, 337–38.

20. David C. Hendrickson, "The First Union: Nationalism versus Internationalism in the American Revolution," in Eliga H. Gould and Peter S. Onuf, eds., *Empire and Nation: The Revolution in the Atlantic World* (Baltimore, 2005), 48–50; John Adams to Henry Knox, September 29, 1776, in *Letters of Delegates to Congress, 1774–1789*, ed. Paul L. Smith (Washington, D.C., 1976–2000), 5:260.

21. "Resolutions Urging Recruitment and Conferring Emergency Powers on the Governor and Council," December 21, 1776, *Papers of George Mason*, ed. Robert A. Rutland (Chapel Hill, N.C., 1970), 1:325–27; TJ to Adams, May 16, 1777, *PTJ*, 2:19.

22. *PJM*, 1:192–93; Mark W. Brewin, *Celebrating Democracy: The Mass-Mediated Ritual of Election Day* (New York, 2008), chap. 2.

23. *PJM*, 1:214–15; Brant, 1:316.

24. *PTJ*, 2:119, 122–24, 139–47. Characterization of Wythe is from TJ to Ralph Izard, July 17, 1788, *PTJ*, 13:372.

25. On the debates, see esp. Merrill Jensen, *The Articles of Confederation: An Interpretation of the Social-Constitutional History of the American Revolution, 1774–1781* (Madison, Wisc., 1940).

26. JM to JM, Sr., January 23, 1778, *PJM*, 1:222–23; Malone, 1:284–85; Brant, 1:292–93.

27. "Session of Virginia Council of State, April 7, 1778," *PJM*, 1:236–37. Henry was forced to admit his personal ineffectiveness in a letter to Congress: "no Efforts of the Executive have been sufficient," he wrote.

28. JM to Bradford, March 23, 1778; "Election to Virginia House of Delegates Voided," May 27, 1778, *PJM*, 1:235, 242–43; Brant, 1:337–38.

29. *JMB*, 1:468–69; Andrew Burstein, *The Inner Jefferson: Portrait of a Grieving Optimist* (Charlottesville, Va., 1995), chap 1; Malone, 1:287, 435–46; Jack McLaughlin, *Jefferson and Monticello: The Biography of a Builder* (New York, 1988), 143–45. The additional acreage was spread about Amherst, Cumberland, Goochland, Rockbridge, and Henrico counties, plus a small lot in Richmond.

30. Lee to TJ, May 2, 1778; "Bill for Raising a Battalion for Garrison Duty," May 16, 1778; TJ to Lee, June 5, 1778; to Fabbroni, June 8, 1778, *PTJ*, 2:174, 179–80, 194–96.

31. Frederick Doveton Nichols and Ralph E. Griswold, *Thomas Jefferson: Landscape Architect* (Charlottesville, Va., 1978), 139–42; Malone, 1:164–65.

32. TJ to Hancock, October 19, 1778, *PTJ*, 2:225. It is curious that Pendleton, these days Virginia's chief advocate for the established church, detested Philip Mazzei and suspected him of being an agent of the pope. It is interesting, too, that Richard Henry Lee proposed that Madison go with Mazzei on the mission to Italy. Madison, who in consideration of his inferior physical stamina would at no time agree to leave America's

shores, expressed confidence in Mazzei but refused to accompany him. See David John Mays, *Edmund Pendleton, 1721–1803: A Biography* (Richmond, 1984), 2:136–37; Ketcham, 85.

33. Richard R. Beeman, *Patrick Henry: A Biography* (New York, 1974), 109–10.

34. Lee to TJ, March 15 and May 3, 1779; Fleming to TJ, May 22, 1779, *PTJ*, 2:236, 262, 267.

35. Fleming to TJ, May 22, 1779, *PTJ*, 2:269.

36. JM to Samuel Harrison Smith, November 4, 1826, *JMP-LC*; Mason to Lee, June 4, 1779, *Papers of George Mason*, ed. Rutland, 2:506–7.

37. Rutledge to TJ, February 12, 1779, *PTJ*, 2:234.

38. Pendleton to TJ, May 11, 1779, *PTJ*, 2:266–67; Mays, *Edmund Pendleton*, 2:144–45.

39. Page to TJ, June 2, 1779; TJ to Page, June 3, 1779; "Message Accepting Election as Governor," June 2, 1779, *PTJ*, 2:277–79.

40. JM to Margaret Bayard Smith, September 21, 1830, *JMP-LC*.

41. Pendleton to TJ, May 11, 1779, *PTJ*, 2:266; "A Bill for the More General Diffusion of Knowledge" and "A Bill for Amending the Constitution of the College of William and Mary," ibid., 526–43; Harold Hellenbrand, *The Unfinished Revolution: Education and Politics in the Thought of Thomas Jefferson* (Newark, Del., 1990), 76–94; Ralph Lerner, *The Thinking Revolutionary: Principle and Practice in the New Republic* (Ithaca, N.Y., 1979), 75–87.

42. Pendleton to TJ, August 3, 1776; TJ to Pendleton, August 13, 1776, *PTJ*, 1:484–85, 491–93.

43. John Bakeless, *Background to Glory: The Life of George Rogers Clark* (Philadelphia, 1957), 15–17; Ketcham, 19–20.

44. Anthony Marc Lewis, "Jefferson and Virginia's Pioneers, 1774–1781," *Mississippi Valley Historical Review* 34 (March 1948): 551–88; Letter to Clark (in Mason's handwriting), January 3, 1778, *PTJ*, 2:132–33; TJ to Pendleton, August 13, 1776, *PTJ*, 1:494; Bakeless, *Background to Glory*, 33–39, 55–56. According to Lewis, Clark also knew Mason from the time of his youth. On the relationship between Virginians' land hunger and the politically complex, utterly brutal career of the Revolutionary Indian fighter Clark, see esp. Barbara Alice Mann, *George Washington's War on Native America* (Lincoln, Neb., 2008), 114ff.

45. Malone, 1:257–59; Lewis, "Jefferson and Virginia's Pioneers"; Peter S. Onuf, *Origins of the Federal Republic* (Philadelphia, 1983), 79–89.

46. Clark to George Mason, November 19, 1779, *Papers of George Mason*, ed. Rutland, 2:555–88; Selby, *Revolution in Virginia*, 192–203; Malone, 1:294–95, 308–13; Mann, *George Washington's War on Native America*, chap. 5; Bakeless, *Background to Glory*, passim; "Order of Virginia Council Placing Henry Hamilton and Others in Irons," June 16, 1779; and TJ to the Continental Board of War, June 18, 1779, *PTJ*, 2:292–95, 300–301; "Jefferson, Madison, and the Executive Council to General William Phillips," July 22, 1779, *RL*, 1:91–93.

47. James M. Gabler, *Passions: The Wines and Travels of Thomas Jefferson* (Baltimore,

1995), 3–8; Mazzei to TJ, March 4, April 21, and May 3, 1780, *PTJ,* 3:310–12, 360–61, 366–68; Mazzei to JM, November 30, 1780, *PJM,* 2:214–16; Brant, 1:340–52. Mazzei sailed through the Chesapeake, knowing that he might fall into British hands. So he concealed his commission and instructions in a sack containing a four-pound ball of lead. When the vessel was not long out of port, and the British boarded, Mazzei tossed the sack with his instructions overboard and had to go on to Europe without documentation. Once there, he learned Virginia had no credit to speak of among her presumed supporters.

48. TJ to Gálvez, November 8, 1779, *PTJ,* 3:167–69; Brant, 2:70.

49. Brant, 2:11.

50. JM to JM, Sr., March 20, 1780, *PJM,* 2:3; Brant, 1:365–67; *A Dictionary of the English Language* (Philadelphia, 1813); on Jones, see *Biographical Dictionary of the American Congress, 1774–1949* (Washington, D.C., 1950), 1388.

51. JM to TJ, March 27–28, May 6, and June 2, 1780, *RL,* 1:135–40.

52. TJ to JM, July 26, 1780, *RL,* 1:142–43.

53. Rev. JM to JM, August 3, 1780, *PJM,* 2:54–55.

54. *Pennsylvania Packet,* January 27, 1780.

55. Pendleton to JM, August 27, 1780, *PJM,* 2:66–67.

56. John Buchanan, *The Road to Guilford Courthouse: The American Revolution in the Carolinas* (New York, 1997); JM and Virginia Delegation to TJ, ca. October 5, 1780, *RL,* 1:146–47; TJ to Horatio Gates, September 3, 1780; to Lee, September 13, 1780, *PTJ,* 3:588, 642–43.

57. Harry Ammon, *James Monroe: The Quest for National Identity* (New York, 1971), chap. 2; Malone, 1:324–25.

58. Ammon, *James Monroe,* 32–33; Monroe to TJ, September 9, 1780, *PTJ,* 3:622.

59. Attending an official ball at the French legation, Madison struck Martha Bland as "stiff" and "unsociable" and appears to have been slow to warm up to strangers. But one should be careful not to overgeneralize, as there are earlier and later examples of his warmth around both men and women. Brant, 2:13, 16–17, 33; Jack Rakove, *James Madison and the Creation of the American Republic* (New York, 1990), 22.

60. JM to Pendleton, October 31 and November 7, 1780; Jones to JM, November 5 and November 10, 1780; Pendleton to JM, November 6 and November 13, 1780, *PJM,* 2:157, 161–71.

61. Jones to JM, November 18 and December 8, 1780; JM to Jones, November 28, 1780, *PJM,* 2:182–83, 209, 232–33. Madison may have borrowed the idea of freeing slaves who fought from a 1722 Virginia law upholding emancipation for "meritorious" service.

62. Selby, *Revolution in Virginia,* 216–26; Buchanan, *Road to Guilford Courthouse,* chap. 21, quote at 327; Bakeless, *Background to Glory,* 271–73; Malone, 1:338–43. In his conceit, Tarleton blamed his troops' "total misbehaviour" rather than credit Morgan for outthinking him.

63. Buchanan, *Road to Guilford Courthouse,* 383; TJ to Lafayette, March 12, 1781, *PTJ,* 5:130; JM to TJ, April 3, 1781, *PJM,* 3:45–46 (Jefferson's letter to Madison was not pre-

served); McDonnell, *Politics of War,* 410, terming Jefferson's remarks to Lafayette "somewhat disingenuous."

64. TJ to Virginia Delegates, April 6, 1781, *PJM,* 3:58–59.

65. Pendleton to JM, May 28, 1781; Lee to Virginia Delegates, June 12, 1781, *PJM,* 3:136–37, 156–58; TJ to Washington, May 28, 1781; to Lafayette, May 29, 1781, *PTJ,* 6:32–33, 35–36.

66. Pendleton to JM, April 7, 1781, *PJM,* 3:63; "Jefferson's Statement of Losses to the British," January 27, 1783, *PTJ,* 6:224–25; Malone, 1:352–69; Lucia Stanton, *Free Some Day: The African-American Families of Monticello* (Charlottesville, Va., 2000), 52–57; Sylvia R. Frey, *Water from the Rock: Black Resistance in a Revolutionary Age* (Princeton, N.J., 1991), 211. Despite the slave exodus, the black population of Virginia grew by 100,000 from 1776 to 1782. See ibid., 218.

67. *JMB,* 1:510–11.

68. "Resolution to Inquire into the Conduct of the Executive," and "Resolution of Thanks to Jefferson by the Virginia General Assembly," November 27, 1781, and December 12, 1781, *PTJ,* 6:133–36; Malone, 1:366.

69. In addition to his contemporaries, most historians have criticized Jefferson for reacting too slowly to the invasion that occurred under his watch. His protective nineteenth-century biographer Henry S. Randall reviewed the situation differently: "Virginia continued to pour every enlisted soldier she could raise into the Northern and Southern armies, leaving her own bosom naked." Randall likened Jefferson to Washington, who placed the national welfare over that of his home state, and there is a certain logic to the statement. Randall, *Life of Thomas Jefferson,* 1:291–92. A less charitable interpretation of Jefferson's performance is in John Ferling, *Setting the World Ablaze: Washington, Adams, Jefferson, and the American Revolution* (New York, 2000), chap. 8.

70. Pendleton to JM, May 28, 1781, *PJM,* 3:136.

71. TJ to Zane, December 4, 1781, *PTJ,* 6:143; Elson, comp., *Patrick Henry in His Speeches and Writings,* 100–103; Robert Douthat Meade, *Patrick Henry, Practical Revolutionary* (Philadelphia, 1969), chap. 17. A few months before the end of Jefferson's governorship, believing that ill health could well bring an abrupt end to his political career, Henry had warmly addressed his successor, writing of "virtue and public spirit" and signing off as "your affectionate friend."

72. TJ to Clark, December 19, 1781; to Charles Thomson, December 20, 1781, *PTJ,* 6:139, 142.

73. "Motion regarding Western Lands," *PJM,* 2:72–77; Jensen, *Articles of Confederation,* chaps. 11 and 12; on Virginia-Pennsylvania relations and the Mason-Dixon Line (the "Mason" in which bears no relation to George Mason), see Mason to Joseph Jones, July 27, 1780, *Papers of George Mason,* ed. Rutland, 2:655–59. Mason believed that Pennsylvania's commissioners for settling the disputed territory had "overmatched" Virginia's, but that to "remove any cause of ill will or disagreement with a sister state," Virginia should settle the matter as quickly as possible.

74. JM to TJ, November 18, 1781, and January 15, 1782, *RL,* 1:202–3, 211; Mason to TJ, September 27, 1781, *Papers of George Mason,* ed. Rutland, 2:679.

75. Reardon, *Edmund Randolph,* 41–43; Selby, *Revolution in Virginia,* 256–58.

76. Onuf, *Origins of the Federal Republic,* 8–17, 96–99, quote at 3; "Proposed Amendment of Articles of Confederation," March 12, 1781; and "Protest of Virginia Delegates," October 10, 1781, *PJM,* 3:17–19, 284–86. Madison's amendment would have authorized the central government to use force to "compel" the states "to fulfill their federal engagements." George Mason was less amenable to federal compulsion; in 1787, when the Constitution was adopted, he would become an antifederalist.

77. David Ramsay, *The History of the American Revolution,* ed. Lester H. Cohen (Indianapolis, 1990 [1789]), chap. 24, quote at 2:590.

78. Randolph to TJ, October 9, 1781, *PTJ,* 6:128; JM to Pendleton, December 25, 1781, *PJM,* 3:337.

CHAPTER THREE
Partners Apart, 1782–1786

1. JM to TJ, January 15, 1782, *RL,* 1:209–11; John J. Reardon, *Edmund Randolph: A Biography* (New York, 1974), 47–56.

2. TJ to JM, March 24, 1782, *RL,* 1:213; JM to Randolph, May 1, 1782; Randolph to JM, May 10, 1782; JM to JM, Sr., May 20, 1782, *PJM,* 4:195–96, 225–26, 256.

3. Marquis de Chastellux, *Travels in North America in the Years 1780, 1781, and 1782,* trans. and ed. Howard C. Rice, Jr. (Chapel Hill, N.C., 1963), 2:389–95.

4. TJ to Monroe, May 20, 1782, *PTJ,* 6:184–86; Andrew Burstein, *The Inner Jefferson: Portrait of a Grieving Optimist* (Charlottesville, Va., 1995), 118–19; Randolph to JM, May 5 and May 16, 1782, *PJM,* 4:208, 246. Monroe showed Jefferson's letter to Edmund Randolph, who quoted parts of it back to Madison. Randolph believed that Jefferson could help himself most by returning to Richmond and taking on his former enemies. Randolph to JM, June 1, 1782, *PJM,* 4:305–6; JM to Randolph, June 11, 1782, *PJM,* 4:333.

5. *JMB,* 1:508, 519; Karl Lehmann, *Thomas Jefferson, American Humanist* (Charlottesville, Va., 1985 [1947]), 54; Sarah N. Randolph, *The Domestic Life of Thomas Jefferson* (Charlottesville, Va., 1978 [1871]), 62–63; Burstein, *Inner Jefferson,* 60–63.

6. Peter S. Onuf, *Origins of the Federal Republic* (Philadelphia, 1983), 94–97, 240n98; JM to Randolph, September 10, 1782, *PJM,* 5:115–16.

7. As only immediate family and slaves were present at Jefferson's "swooning away," we must assume that either the house servants or the doctor was responsible for word reaching Richmond. It is interesting that this portion of Jefferson's private history, reconfirmed in later years by his eldest daughter, made the rounds so quickly.

8. Randolph to JM, September 20, 1782; JM to Randolph, September 30, 1782, *PJM,* 5:150–51, 170; Burstein, *Inner Jefferson,* 60–62.

9. "Resolution of Congress Appointing Peace Commissioners"; TJ to Thomas McKean (president of Congress), June 15 and August 4, 1781, *PTJ,* 6:94, 113; Malone, 1:398; Randolph to JM, November 8 and November 22, 1782; "Motion to Renew Thomas Jefferson's Appointment as Peace Commissioner"; JM to Randolph, November 12 and November 19, 1782, *PJM,* 5:262, 268, 272, 288–89, 307. As they were wearing Jefferson down, Madison proudly informed Randolph that not a single voice in Congress questioned the choice of Jefferson, while Randolph testified that "Monticello, which formerly was the great magnet, has lost its power."

10. JM to Randolph, December 30, 1782, *PJM,* 5:473; *JMB,* 1:524-25.

11. *JMB,* 1:527n.

12. JM to TJ, February 11, 1783; TJ to JM, February 14, 1783, *RL,* 1:221, 223; William Pencak, *Jews and Gentiles in Early America, 1654–1800* (Ann Arbor, Mich., 2005), 209-10.

13. Madison's Notes on Debates for April 18, 1783, *PJM,* 6:471; *Freeman's Journal* (Philadelphia), January 1, 1783; *Massachusetts Centinel,* March 1, 1786; *New-York Journal,* March 2, 1786; Brant, 2:209-36; Ketcham, 117-19.

14. "Address to the States," April 26, 1783, *PJM,* 6:494; Hamilton was already resorting to the authorship of anonymous newspaper essays to advance his aims. Our interpretation of Madison's differences with Hamilton at this early moment in their relationship draws significantly on Lance Banning, "James Madison and the Nationalists, 1780-1783," *William and Mary Quarterly* 40 (April 1983): 227-55.

15. Stuart Leibiger, *Founding Friendship: George Washington, James Madison, and the Creation of the American Republic* (Charlottesville, Va., 1999), 20-25; Washington to JM, April 22, 1783; JM to Washington, April 29, 1783, *PJM,* 6:484-85, 505. McHenry of Maryland would eventually serve as U.S. secretary of war.

16. Madison's Notes on Debates for January 23, 1783, *PJM,* 6:62ff.; Brant, 2:242-46, 288-90. The editors of *PJM* suggest that Madison considered the titles owned by Reverend Madison, John Witherspoon, and Theodorick Bland, in addition to those of Jefferson.

17. JM to TJ, April 22, 1783; TJ to JM, April 14 and May 7, 1783, *RL,* 1:242, 244-45; Brant, 2:283-87.

18. *JMB,* 1:531.

19. The tone of one letter should suffice to give evidence of Mason's attitude. When recruited for state office, he delivered his firm refusal on grounds of "don't call me, I'll call you," regarding the attempt as "an oppressive & unjust Invasion of my personal Liberty." Mason to Martin Cockburn, April 18, 1784, *The Papers of George Mason,* ed. Robert A. Rutland (Chapel Hill, N.C., 1970), 2:799.

20. TJ to Clark, November 26, 1782, *PTJ,* 6:204-5.

21. TJ to JM, June 17, 1783, *RL,* 1:252-60; Adrienne Koch, *Jefferson and Madison: The Great Collaboration* (New York, 1950), 11-13; David N. Mayer, *The Constitutional Thought of Thomas Jefferson* (Charlottesville, Va., 1994), 60-65; *PTJ,* 6:283, 308-16; "Resolutions on Private Debts Owed to British Merchants," and R. H. Lee to JM, November 20, 1784, *PJM,* 8:58-63, 144-45; Sylvia R. Frey, *Water from the Rock: Black Resistance in a Revolutionary Age* (Princeton, N.J., 1991), 211-12.

22. Theodore Bolton, "The Life Portraits of James Madison," *William and Mary Quarterly* 8 (January 1951): 25-27; JM to TJ, August 11, 1783, *RL,* 1:262.

23. *JMB,* 1:536-42; Lucia Stanton, *Free Some Day: The African-American Families of Monticello* (Charlottesville, Va., 2000), 104.

24. Madison's notes indicate that he felt little concern for his own safety in Philadelphia. The troops at large did not seem prone to violence, he wrote, "individuals only occasionally uttering offensive words and wantonly pointed their Muskets to the Windows of the Hall of Congress." But the wide availability of "spirituous drink from

the tippling houses" made him worry that the combustible combination of muskets and alcohol might lead to what he termed "hasty excesses." For his part, Jefferson considered the event "a very trifling mutiny of 200 souldiers." Why he believed that two hundred armed men did not constitute a threat is not entirely clear.

25. Madison's Notes on Debates for June 21, 1783; Brant, 2:294–95; TJ to Martha (Patsy) Jefferson, November 28, 1783, *The Family Letters of Thomas Jefferson*, ed. Edwin Morris Betts and James Adam Bear, Jr. (Charlottesville, Va., 1966), 19–20; Francis Hopkinson to TJ, January 4, 1784; TJ to Chastellux, January 16, 1784, *PTJ*, 6:444–45, 466; Malone, 1:404–5.

26. TJ to JM, February 20, 1784; JM to TJ, March 16, 1784, *RL*, 1:297–303.

27. Jefferson's appeals on paper were always crafted with sensitivity to the temperament of the other party. Just as he knew how to tap into George Rogers Clark's insecurity about his reputation back in Virginia by feeding antagonism toward Patrick Henry and promising to protect the frontiersman's interest, he knew Madison well enough to engineer an approach based on his friend's cautiousness—thus the allusion to "rational society." The only chance he had was to convince Madison that he would be looking after his own best interest when he established himself in Albemarle. JM to TJ, March 16, 1784, *RL*, 1:305; *PTJ*, 7:82. On Jefferson's epicurean side, see Andrew Burstein, *Jefferson's Secrets: Death and Desire at Monticello* (New York, 2005).

28. JM to TJ, December 10, 1783, *RL*, 1:286; TJ to Carr, December 11, 1783; Francis Hopkinson to TJ, February 23, 1784; Randolph to TJ, May 15, 1784, *PTJ*, 6:379–80, 556, 7:260.

29. Richard H. Kohn, "The Inside History of the Newburgh Conspiracy: America and the Coup d'Etat," *William and Mary Quarterly* 27 (April 1970): 187–220; Kohn, *The Eagle and the Sword: The Federalists and the Creation of the Military Establishment in America, 1783–1802* (New York, 1975), chap. 2; C. Edward Skeen, *John Armstrong, Jr., 1758–1843: A Biography* (Syracuse, N.Y., 1981), 8–17; Leibiger, *Founding Friendship*, 25–28.

30. TJ to Harrison, November 11, 1783; and "George Washington's Resignation as Commander-in-Chief," *PTJ*, 6:351–53, 402–7; Ronald Byrd, "George Washington and Wellness," in Kevin L. Cope, ed., *George Washington in and as Culture* (New York, 2001), 249–67; Joseph J. Ellis, *His Excellency: George Washington* (New York, 2004), 144–46; John E. Ferling, *The First of Men: A Life of George Washington* (Knoxville, Tenn., 1988), 263–65. For a nuanced reading of Washington's symbolic value during his lifetime, as well as insights into his intellectual life, see Paul K. Longmore, *The Invention of George Washington* (Berkeley, Calif., 1988), 213–26 and passim.

31. TJ to Chastellux, January 16, 1784, *PTJ*, 6:467.

32. "The Virginia Cession of Territory North of the Ohio," *PTJ*, 6:571–617; Onuf, *Origins of the Federal Republic*, chap. 7; Richard P. McCormick, "The 'Ordinance' of 1784?" *William and Mary Quarterly* 50 (January 1993): 112–22; JM to Monroe, May 29, 1785, *PJM*, 8:285–86; Harry Ammon, *James Monroe: The Quest for National Identity* (Charlottesville, Va., 1971), 41–45, 51–54.

33. Another promoter of the new America was Ezra Stiles, president of Yale College and a Congregationalist minister, who published a popular sermon just months before passage of the 1784 Land Ordinance, in which he proclaimed: "The whole continent is activity, and in the lively vigorous exertion of industry." Owing to the "enterprising

spirit of Americans for colonization and removing out into the wilderness," an invigo-rated population would "soon overspread the vast territory from the *Atlantic* to the *Mississippi.*" See Andrew Burstein, *Sentimental Democracy* (New York, 1999), 38–39, 88, 162–64; Stiles, *The UNITED STATES Elevated to GLORY and HONOUR* (Worcester, Mass., 1785), 12–13.

34. Peter S. Onuf, *Statehood and Union: A History of the Northwest Ordinance* (Bloom-ington, Ind., 1987), chap. 1; Onuf, *Origins of the Federal Republic,* 17, 99–102; TJ to JM, No-vember 11, 1784, *RL,* 1:350.

35. TJ to JM, May 8 and May 11, 1784, *RL,* 1:315–16.

36. TJ to JM, May 7, 1783; JM to TJ, May 15 and July 3, 1784, *RL,* 1:245, 318, 322. Underscoring Henry's dangerousness as an opponent, David A. McCants has written of how Virginia's model orator succeeded: "Henry pleaded causes, not cases; he presented dramas, not arguments." See McCants, *Patrick Henry, the Orator* (New York, 1990), 103.

37. Printers in Boston and Virginia picked up the story and reprinted it verbatim, which is what newspapers of this era typically did. The original dateline is Providence, June 19, 1784, but available copies are in Boston's *American Herald,* June 28, 1784; *Salem Gazette,* June 29, 1784; and *Virginia Journal,* July 15, 1784. On the definition of *civilian,* see Johnson's *Dictionary* (Philadelphia, 1813); on uses of *politician,* see the progression in various American newspapers between 1706 and 1786, including *Boston News-Letter,* September 9–16, 1706, *American Weekly Mercury* [Philadelphia], February 13–20, 19–26, 1722, *New-England Courant,* July 2–9, 1722, *Boston Evening-Post,* December 26, 1743, *Boston Gazette* and *New-York Mercury* for 1756, *Political Intelligencer* [New Brunswick, N.J.], May 11, 1784, *Independent Journal* [New York] issues of 1785, *Charleston Evening Gazette,* June 9, 1786. The *New-Hampshire Gazette* [Portsmouth], February 18, 1786, reprints an address by Benedict Arnold, from London, using the word dismissively to belittle the re-publican pretensions of Congress and the states: "The Americans are certainly the most extraordinary politicians in the world."

38. TJ to JM, November 11, 1784, *RL,* 1:350–51.

39. As early as May 1783, Jefferson had let Madison know that he considered Short an ideal person for him to work with in Paris: "You may know my high opinion of his abilities and merits," he said. "I will therefore only add that a peculiar talent for prying into facts seems to mark his character as proper for such a business." TJ to JM, May 7, 1783, *RL,* 1:245. Short took quite a chance, sailing to France before he had any assur-ance that he would be officially compensated by the U.S. government.

40. George Green Shackelford, *Jefferson's Adoptive Son: The Life of William Short, 1759–1848* (Lexington, Ky., 1993), 5–16.

41. JM to TJ, July 3, 1784; TJ to JM, December 8, 1784, *RL,* 1:322–23, 353–54; Brant, 2:322–23.

42. JM to TJ, April 27, 1785, *RL,* 1:367–71.

43. Louis Gottschalk, *Lafayette between the American and the French Revolution, 1783–1789* (Chicago, 1950), 23–25, 38–39, 63, 69, 73, 83–84.

44. JM to JM, Sr., September 6, 1784, *PJM,* 8:112; JM to TJ, October 17, 1784, *RL,* 1:347–49; TJ to JM, March 18, 1785, and February 8, 1786, *RL,* 1:365, 411; Gottschalk, *Lafayette between the American and the French Revolution,* chap. 8; Ketcham, 155–57.

45. Leibiger, *Founding Friendship*, 53–56; "Deed of Gift of Orange County Lands," August 19, 1784; JM to Randolph, July 26, 1785; to Monroe, March 14, 1786, *PJM*, 8:99, 328, 497; JM to TJ, August 12, 1786, *RL*, 1:432–33; Brant, 2:328–35, 340–41; Ketcham, 145–47. The Madison-Monroe purchase of nine hundred acres was not concluded until 1790, when they made their final payment—having only been able to raise $675 in 1786. See Monroe to JM, July 19, 1789, *PJM*, 12:297.

46. "Memorial and Remonstrance against Religious Assessments," ca. June 20, 1785, *PJM*, 8:295–304; Ketcham, 162; Koch, *Jefferson and Madison*, 27–30.

47. William Peden, ed., *Notes on the State of Virginia* (Chapel Hill, N.C., 1954), Query XVII, 159.

48. *Virginia Journal* [Alexandria], April 14, 1785; JM to TJ, January 22, 1786, *RL*, 1:402–3; Ketcham, 163–68. The Virginia Statute for Religious Freedom became law in January 1786.

49. George Green Shackelford, *Thomas Jefferson's Travels in Europe, 1784–1789* (Baltimore, 1995), chap. 1; William Howard Adams, *The Paris Years of Thomas Jefferson* (New Haven, Conn., 1997); Malone, 2:3–20, 44, 213.

50. Lafayette to McHenry, December 3, 1785, in Gottschalk, *Lafayette between the American and the French Revolution*, 208; TJ to Chastellux, January 16, 1784, *PTJ*, 6:467.

51. For modern commentary on the *Notes*, see Douglas L. Wilson, "Jefferson and the Republic of Letters," in Peter S. Onuf, ed., *Jeffersonian Legacies* (Charlottesville, Va., 1993), 53–57, 63–64; Charles A. Miller, *Jefferson and Nature: An Interpretation* (Baltimore, 1988), 15–19; Henry Steele Commager, *Jefferson, Nationalism, and the Enlightenment* (New York, 1975), 36–39; and Kevin J. Hayes, *The Road to Monticello: The Life and Mind of Thomas Jefferson* (New York, 2008), chap. 17.

52. TJ to JM, May 11, 1785; JM to TJ, November 15, 1785, *RL*, 1:372, 392; Rev. JM to TJ, March 27, 1786, and February 10, 1789, *PTJ*, 9:357, 14:534. In 1786 Reverend Madison was first shown a copy of the *Notes* by James Madison, Sr., and was not given time to read in depth. For a good analysis of Jefferson's self-conscious concern about the personal and political dimensions of publishing *Notes* on a large scale, see Douglas L. Wilson, "The Evolution of Jefferson's 'Notes on the State of Virginia,' " *Virginia Magazine of History and Biography* 112 (2004): 98–133.

53. TJ to JM, February 8, 1786; JM to TJ, May 12, 1786, *RL*, 1:410, 419; "Autobiography," *TJP-LC*.

54. See Introduction to Peden, ed., *Notes on Virginia*. For an examination of Jefferson's take on Virginia in the context of various published perspectives, see Jack P. Greene, "The Intellectual Reconstruction of Virginia," in Onuf, ed., *Jeffersonian Legacies*, 225–53.

55. Peden, ed., *Notes on Virginia*, Queries II, IV, VI, VII; on plants and power, see Richard Drayton, *Nature's Government: Science, Imperial Britain, and the "Improvement" of the World* (New Haven, Conn., 2000), esp. 44–49.

56. Peden, ed., *Notes on Virginia*, Queries VIII and XIV.

57. John Wood Sweet, *Bodies Politic: Negotiating Race in the American North, 1730–1830* (Baltimore, 2003), chap. 4, "Strange Flesh," and chap. 7, "Conceiving Race," quote at 189.

58. On this tradition, and the culture of patronage and publishing, see esp. Richard B. Sher, *The Enlightenment and the Book* (Chicago, 2006), chap. 3.

59. Washington to JM, November 30, 1785; Mason to JM, December 7, 1785; JM to Washington, December 9, 1785, *PJM,* 8:429, 433, 438–39.

60. "Act Concerning Statehood for the Kentucky District," December 22, 1785, *PJM,* 8:450–53. Kentucky statehood was delayed until 1792. Madison had long seen Kentucky as a virtual colony of Virginia and continued to assume that Virginians would sell goods to the settlers in the West, replicating the British model of center and periphery. Madison backed George Washington's idea of a Potomac canal for the same reason.

61. Shackelford, *Jefferson's Adoptive Son,* 111–13; William Howard Adams, *The Paris Years of Thomas Jefferson* (New Haven, Conn., 1997), 10.

62. TJ to JM, February 8, 1786, and January 30, 1787, *RL,* 1:412, 462–63; Shackelford, *Thomas Jefferson's Travels in Europe,* 37–39. The attitude of the English toward the United States persisted, as Britain-based American John Brown Cutting demonstrated in a subsequent letter to Jefferson on Americans' degradation in the press and government alike: "Why every species of contumely and abuse against the citizens of [A]merica is so much relished here it is obvious to discern." The king and his ministers had created a "political fashion": America-bashing. "To gratify the irascible feelings of the monarch," Britons would recommence hostilities, if they could be assured of only a minor derangement in their internal affairs. "I own in the present moment of [B]ritish insolence and royal hatred, a fresh conflict with us may not be very distant." Cutting to TJ, August 3, 1788, *PTJ,* 13:461–62.

63. Monroe to JM, February 11 and February 16, 1786; Lee to JM, February 16, 1786; JM to Monroe, March 19, 1786; Grayson to JM, March 22, 1786, *PJM,* 8:492–93, 504–5, 510. Lee, like Madison, would finally marry in his forties.

64. JM to TJ, March 18, 1786, *RL,* 1:413–16; JM to Lafayette, March 20, 1785, *PJM,* 8:250–55; Onuf, *Statehood and Union,* 54–58.

65. John Fiske, *The Critical Period in American History, 1783–1789* (Boston, 1888), Preface. Fiske found his title after considering Thomas Paine's comment when his wartime series, "The Crisis," ended, in 1783, and Paine asserted: "The times that tried men's souls are over." The historian differed, thinking the next five years were even more critical. JM to Monroe, March 14 and March 19, 1786, *PJM,* 8:497–98, 505–6; Ketcham, 175–76. Madison had referred to "the present paroxysm of jealousy" among the states as early as 1783.

66. JM to TJ, August 12, 1786 *RL,* 1:429–30.

67. TJ to JM, April 25, 1786, *RL,* 1:417; TJ to Washington, May 2, 1788, *PTJ,* 13:127–28.

68. Lance Banning, *The Sacred Fire of Liberty: James Madison and the Founding of the Federal Republic* (Ithaca, N.Y., 1995), 66–69; JM to TJ, April 23, 1787, *RL,* 1:475–76.

69. JM to TJ August 12, 1786; TJ to JM, January 30–February 5, 1787, *RL,* 1:431, 461–62.

70. TJ to John Banister, Jr., October 15, 1785, *PTJ,* 8:636–37; Burstein, *Jefferson's Secrets,* chap. 6.

71. Maria Cosway to TJ, April 29, 1788, *PTJ,* 13:116; Burstein, *Inner Jefferson,* 98–99.

CHAPTER FOUR

The Division of Power, 1787

1. Washington to Knox, December 5, 1784; Knox to Washington, April 9, 1787, *PGW-CS,* 2:170–72, 5:134; JM to TJ, March 19, 1787, *RL,* 1:470.

2. Madison called paper money "fictitious money," and Lee considered the fluctuation in currencies enough of a cause for alarm that he wrote: "Knaves assure, and fools believe, that calling paper money, and making it tender, is the way to be rich and happy; thus the national mind is kept in constant ferment." Congress, he warned, had to put its foot down so that the "continual disturbance by the intrigues of wicked men" would be stopped. Lee to Mason, May 15, 1787, *Papers of George Mason,* 3:876–79.

3. TJ to JM, October 28, 1785; JM to TJ, June 19, 1786, *RL,* 1:390, 423–24.

4. See "Notes on Ancient and Modern Confederacies," *PJM,* 9:3–24.

5. "Vices of the Political System of the United States," *PJM,* 9:348–50. For the importance of Madison's experience in the Virginia Assembly in convincing him of the need for a new federal system of government, see Charles F. Hobson, "The Negative on State Laws: James Madison, the Constitution, and the Crisis of Republican Government," *William and Mary Quarterly* 36 (April 1979): 223–24.

6. "Vices of the Political System," *PJM,* 9:353–54; JM to TJ, October 15, 1788 (containing Madison's observations on Jefferson's draft of a constitution for Virginia), *RL,* 1:555; JM to Washington, April 16, 1787, *PJM,* 9:383.

7. Ketcham, 169–70, 185.

8. JM to TJ, December 4, 1786, *RL,* 1:454.

9. It was Randolph's idea that the general propositions of reform should be "prepared for feeling the pulse of the convention," and that an "address" should accompany the Virginia plan. See Randolph to JM, March 27, 1787, *PJM,* 9:335.

10. Madison let Washington know that his name was needed to convince the Virginia legislature of the "magnitude of the occasion." See JM to Washington, November 8, 1786; also JM to Washington, December 7 and December 24, 1786, *PJM,* 9:166, 199, 224–26. Madison was concerned about the best way to capitalize on Washington's stature. In April he wrote to Randolph that it might be wise for the general to postpone his arrival, as it would be disastrous if he should be attached to "any abortive undertaking." Yet Madison also considered that his late arrival might keep him from presiding over the convention and subject him to a "less conspicuous" role. He thought Washington's delay might enable Pennsylvania to nominate Benjamin Franklin as chair. Madison was willing to sacrifice Washington's role, if it would reinforce the alliance with Pennsylvania. See JM to Edmund Randolph, April 15, 1787, *PJM,* 9:378. On Madison's relationship with Robert Morris, see Ketcham, 117, 130–35; David Brian Robertson, *The Constitution and America's Destiny* (New York, 2005), 78–79.

11. JM to TJ, May 12, 1786; JM to James Monroe, May 13, 1786, *PJM,* 9:50, 55.

12. Clinton Rossiter, *1787: The Grand Convention* (New York, 1966; revised ed., 1987), 121–23; JM to TJ, April 23, 1787, *RL,* 1:476; JM to Edmund Randolph, April 8, 1787, JM to Washington, April 16, 1787, *PJM,* 9:369, 382–83.

13. JM to Randolph, April 8, 1787, JM to Washington, April 16, 1787, *PJM,* 9:369–

70, 383; Jack N. Rakove, "The Great Compromise: Ideas, Interests, and the Politics of Constitution Making," *William and Mary Quarterly* 44 (July 1987): 427-28.

14. It was an accepted theory at the time that migration patterns overwhelmingly favored the Southwest, as available land there would lure Americans away from the northern states and toward the Gulf of Mexico.

15. JM to Washington, April 16, 1787, *PJM,* 9:383.

16. JM to Randolph, April 8, 1787; to Washington, April 16, 1787, *PJM,* 9:370, 384-85.

17. JM to Randolph, April 8, 1787; to Washington, April 16, 1787, *PJM,* 9:369-70, 383-84. Also see the discussion in Gordon S. Wood, *The Creation of the American Republic, 1776-1787* (Chapel Hill, N.C., 1969), chap. 12.

18. JM to TJ, October 24 and November 1, 1787, *RL,* 1:500; on the pervasive influence of Locke's educational theory, see Jay Fliegelman, *Prodigals and Pilgrims: The American Revolution Against Patriarchal Authority, 1750-1800* (New York, 1984), 13-15, 30-31; and on the importance of pedagogical discipline under Witherspoon at Princeton, see Christopher Castiglia, "Pedagogical Discipline and the Creation of White Citizenship: John Witherspoon, Robert Finley, and the Colonization Society," *Early American Literature* 33 (1998): 192-214.

19. Comments by JM, June 8, in *Notes of the Debates in the Federal Convention of 1787* (Athens, Ohio, 1966), 88-89.

20. TJ to JM, June 20, 1787, *RL,* 1:480.

21. Examples of the correspondence: Cosway to Jefferson, "I will write two words, to show you I can write *if I please* but as I dont please I shall say no More, as I wait to hear from you . . . tho' you neglect me, I force myself to your recolection." To which Jefferson replied, only half-convincingly, that she should cross the Channel again to see how well her paintings were being admired, whence he would "take refuge every day in your coterie." Of course, a coterie was a flock, and as such would prevent the two of them from sneaking off alone. He had moved from poetic longing to prosaic flattery. TJ to Cosway, April 24 and July 27, 1788; Cosway to TJ, June 23, 1788; Angelica Schuyler Church to TJ, July 21, 1788, *PTJ,* 13:103-4, 287-88, 391, 424.

22. Abigail Adams to TJ, September 10, 1787, *PTJ,* 12:112; Malone, 2:133-38.

23. TJ to Monroe, June 17, 1785; to Lafayette, April 11, 1787; to George Gilmer, August 12, 1787, *PTJ,* 8:233, 11:283-85, 12:26.

24. *Catalogue of the Library of Thomas Jefferson,* comp. E. Millicent Sowerby (Washington, D.C., 1952-59), 5:143-45; Francis D. Cogliano, *Thomas Jefferson: Reputation and Legacy* (Charlottesville, Va., 2006), 44-48.

25. TJ to Monroe, June 17, 1785, *PTJ,* 8:233.

26. Rossiter, *1787: Grand Convention,* 104-6; Ketcham, 191.

27. Carl Van Doren, *Benjamin Franklin* (New York, 1938), 744-45.

28. JM to TJ, May 15, 1787, *RL,* 1:477; Ketcham, 192-93.

29. George Mason to George Mason, Jr., May 20 and June 1, 1787, *Papers of George Mason,* ed. Robert A. Rutland (Chapel Hill, N.C., 1970), 3:881, 892-93.

30. JM to TJ, May 15, 1787, *RL,* 1:477; TJ to John Adams, August 30, 1787, *PTJ,*

12:69. On May 25 the southern states were present in force, whereas New England had not as yet assembled complete delegations. The most recent scholar to write on the convention sees this, in part, as a function of some New Englanders' "apathy" toward the proceedings. See Richard Beeman, *Plain, Honest Men: The Making of the American Constitution* (New York, 2009), 58–60.

31. After Elbridge Gerry of Massachusetts, Dr. McClurg of Virginia was the most conspicuous holder of state and continental securities at the convention. See Rossiter, *1787: The Grand Convention,* 124.

32. Nathan Schachner, *Alexander Hamilton* (New York, 1949), 102–3, 124–25; Robert Ernst, *Rufus King: American Federalist* (Chapel Hill, N.C., 1968), 66–68; Malone, 1:409; John E. O'Connor, *William Paterson: Lawyer and Statesman, 1745–1806* (New Brunswick, N.J., 1979), 88, 111, 130, 133–34; Christopher Collier, *Roger Sherman's Connecticut: Yankee Politics and the American Revolution* (Middletown, Conn., 1971), 102, 194, 234–35; Paul S. Clarkson and R. Samuel Jett, *Luther Martin of Maryland* (Baltimore, 1970), 41.

33. Collier, *Roger Sherman's Connecticut,* 7–15, 20, 26, 58, 90, 102, 110–11, 138, 189, 194, 230, 235.

34. Leonard L. Richards, *Shays's Rebellion: The American Revolution's Final Battle* (Philadelphia, 2002), 23, 26–27, 63, 83–88; Richard Buel, Jr., "The Public Creditor Interest in Massachusetts Politics, 1780–1786," in Robert A. Gross, ed., *In Debt to Shays: The Bicentennial of an Agrarian Rebellion* (Charlottesville, Va., 1993), 51, 55.

35. Washington to Knox, December 26, 1786; Randolph to Washington, January 4, 1787; Washington to Randolph, March 28, 1787, *PGW-CS,* 4:482, 501, 5:113; also Woody Holton, *Unruly Americans and the Origins of the American Constitution* (New York, 2007), 220; Richards, *Shays's Rebellion,* 131–32. Washington had initially told Governor Edmund Randolph that he wished to decline appointment to Virginia's delegation. Randolph waited three months, as the details of Shays's Rebellion had time to disseminate. Then Washington had his change of heart.

36. "Vices of the Political System," *PJM,* 9:350; JM to Edmund Pendleton, January 9, 1787, *PJM,* 9:245. Madison heard the rumors of British influence in Shays's Rebellion from William Grayson, who was serving in Congress. See Grayson to JM, November 22, 1786, *PJM,* 9:174–75; Richards, *Shays's Rebellion,* 127–32; Stephen E. Patterson, "The Federalist Reaction to Shays's Rebellion," in Gross, ed., *In Debt to Shays,* 105.

37. JM to TJ, March 19, 1787, *RL,* 1:473; Holton, *Unruly Americans,* 77, 155–56; Richards, *Shays's Rebellion,* 16–17, 118–19.

38. "Vices of the Political System," *PJM,* 9:349–51; JM to TJ, August 12, 1786, *RL,* 1:430; Holton, *Unruly Americans,* 158; Robertson, *The Constitution and America's Destiny,* 57. For Madison, New Jersey was another "salutary lesson" of the "impotency of the federal system," demonstrating how roles were reversed between Congress and the states. As he wrote to James Monroe, Congress was forced to "court a compliance with its *constitutional* acts," and what was more humiliating, it had to beg obedience from a state "not of the most powerful order." See JM to Monroe, April 9, 1786, *PJM,* 9:25.

39. JM to TJ, March 19 and June 6, 1787, *RL,* 1:473, 479; Ketcham, 172–73.

40. "Vices of the Political System," *PJM,* 9:354.

41. "Madness," "wickedness," and "folly" were the words Madison used to describe the tiny state, where, he said, "all sense of character as well as right is obliterated." He meant that the democratic impulse was strong and unhealthy—a matter of whim instead of reason. JM to Edmund Randolph, April 2, 1787; and "Virginia Delegates to Edmund Randolph," April 2, 1787, *PJM*, 9:362-63.

42. Monroe to TJ, July 27, 1787, *PTJ*, 11:631; Harry Ammon, *James Monroe: The Quest for National Identity* (New York, 1971), 66–67.

43. JM to TJ, June 6, 1787, *RL*, 1:478; TJ to Adams, August 30, 1787, *PTJ*, 12:69.

44. Speech by Randolph, May 29, *Notes of the Debates in the Federal Convention*, 28–30.

45. Virginia Plan, May 29, ibid., 30–31. We accept Charles F. Hobson's argument that Randolph and Mason were "probably responsible for the milder version of the negative" in the Virginia Plan. See Hobson, "The Negative on State Laws: James Madison, the Constitution, and the Crisis of Republican Government," *William and Mary Quarterly* 36 (April 1979): 215–35, quote at 226.

46. JM, May 31, *Notes of the Debates*, 40–41.

47. Reed and Sherman, May 31, ibid., 37, 39, 43; "Notes of Major William Pierce on the Federal Convention of 1787," *American Historical Review* 3 (January 1898): 326; Robertson, *Constitution and American Destiny*, 124–25; Beeman, *Plain, Honest, Men*, 114–18; Collier, *Roger Sherman's Connecticut*, 26, 194, 230.

48. Dickinson, June 2; Dickinson and Sherman, June 7, *Notes of the Debates*, 55–57, 82, 84.

49. Madison and Dickinson, June 7, ibid., 83–84.

50. Mason, June 7, ibid., 87; James H. Hutson, "John Dickinson at the Federal Constitutional Convention," *William and Mary Quarterly* 40 (April 1983): 257; Rossiter, *1787: Grand Convention*, 110–11.

51. Charles Pinckney, June 8; Madison and Pinckney, August 18, *Notes of the Debates*, 88, 477–78; Marty D. Matthews, *Forgotten Founder: The Life and Times of Charles Pinckney* (Columbia, S.C., 2004), 6, 11–12, 45; Mark A. Noll, *Princeton and the Republic, 1768–1822: The Search for the Christian Republic in the Era of Samuel Stanhope Smith* (Princeton, N.J., 1990), 92; JM, June 8, *Notes of the Debates*, 89. Richard Beeman discusses Pinckney's later claim that he had more to do with the convention—and more original ideas—than Madison gave him credit for. See *Plain, Honest Men*, 93–98.

52. Gerry and Wilson, June 8, *Notes of the Debates*, 89–91.

53. Bedford and JM, June 8, ibid., 91–92.

54. Bearly and Paterson, June 9, ibid., 94–97, 118–21, 127; Rosemarie Zagarri, *The Politics of Size: Representation in the United States, 1776–1850* (Ithaca, N.Y., 1987).

55. Bearly and Paterson, June 9, *Notes of the Debates*, 92. New Hampshire's delegation was late in arriving and did not vote; Delaware's vote was canceled because its delegates were evenly split.

56. The New Jersey Plan was so out of sync with Madison's viewpoint that it even rejected the idea of a bicameral Congress, which the astute Sherman found he could use as a wedge issue. By suggesting that he might be willing to consider a compromise on bicameralism, he was able to stick to his guns on more important concerns. In the days

that followed, the other two Connecticut delegates, Oliver Ellsworth and Samuel Johnson, stayed on message, repeating George Mason's words that small states deserved the
right to self-defense. Sherman, June 20; Johnson, June 21 and June 29; Ellsworth, June
29, ibid., 148, 161, 211, 218.

57. Ellsworth, June 29, ibid., 217–18.

58. JM, King, and Bedford, June 30, ibid., 224, 228, 229–30; for Paterson's complaint about the rudeness of Madison, see Paterson, July 5, ibid., 243; also see Robert
Yates's notes on the convention in Max Farrand, ed., *The Records of the Federal Constitution
of 1787* (New Haven, Conn., 1911), 1:500; for Madison's comment on Connecticut's refusal to pay its requisitions, see JM to James Madison, Sr., February 25, 1787, *PJM*,
9:297.

59. JM, June 29 and July 14, *Notes of the Debates*, 214–15, 293–95. Even before the
convention, he had raised the specter of the Union dividing into three sectional governments but at the time did not identify the small states as responsible. Rather, the
subject was sparked by the controversy over control of the Mississippi. See JM to Edmund Pendleton, February 24, 1787, *PJM*, 9:259, 264.

60. JM, June 28, June 30, and July 9, *Notes of the Debates*, 206, 224–25, 259; David
Waldstreicher, *Slavery's Constitution: From Revolution to Ratification* (New York, 2009), 82.

61. Morris, July 10; King, July 6; John Rutledge, July 5; Pierce Butler, July 6; Gerry,
July 14, ibid., 245–47, 265, 288–89.

62. A Georgian at the convention termed Morris "conspicuous and flourishing in
public debate." See "Notes of Major William Pierce on the Federal Constitution of
1787," 329; and William Howard Adams, *Gouverneur Morris: An Independent Life* (New
Haven, Conn., 2003), 96, 126, 159.

63. JM and Mason, July 11, *Notes of the Debates*, 266–67, 272–73.

64. Wilson, July 12, ibid., 279–280; also see Howard A. Ohline, "Republicanism and
Slavery: Origins of the Three-Fifths Clause in the United States Constitution," *William
and Mary Quarterly* 28 (October 1971): 580–81. Taxing slaves would realize revenues for
the states, not the central government.

65. Morris, July 10 and July 13, *Notes of the Debates*, 262, 285–86.

66. July 14, ibid., 290–91, 297.

67. Gerry, June 29; Morris, July 5; JM, July 11; Franklin, June 28, ibid., 209–10, 217,
240, 272; Beeman, *Plain, Honest Men*, 177–81.

68. At this point in the deliberations, Congress had the power to appoint the president, and if each house voted separately, the Senate could override the choice of the
House. JM, July 17, July 19, July 21, August 6, August 9, August 14, and August 23; JM
and Daniel Carroll, August 14; Report of the Committee of Detail, August 6, all in *Notes
of the Debates*, 311, 326–27, 344, 386–93, 423–25, 457–59, 520; Robertson, *Constitution
and America's Destiny*, 148.

69. Madison, July 23, *Notes of the Debates*, 352–53.

70. The Senate, by this reading, failed to embody the popular will. When Madison
used the term "popular will," he really meant southern approval, because northern
states made up the majority in the Senate in the current configuration. The Senate's

actions were not truly national in character because they were taken "by a minority of the people, though by a majority of the States." JM, July 21 and August 23, ibid., 344, 520.

71. It was hard to know precisely where prejudices lay on this issue. Gerry called popular election "radically vicious," pointing to the "ignorance of the people" who would be duped by some powerful group of men to vote for its handpicked candidate. Small state defenders were also skeptical of Madison's approach to national election. Ellsworth concluded that direct election would give the largest states the advantage in crowning a favorite son. JM, July 19 and July 25; Gerry, July 19; Gerry and Ellsworth, July 25, ibid., 327–29, 363–66, 368.

72. Williamson, Morris, and JM, July 25, ibid., 368.

73. King and Morris, July 24, ibid., 358, 361.

74. JM, July 21 and July 25; Morris, July 24, ibid., 338, 361–65.

75. August 31 and September 4, ibid., 569, 574.

76. Only Delaware voted against Sherman's motion. JM, September 5; Wilson and Sherman, September 6, ibid., 584, 587–88, 592.

77. JM, July 21 and July 25, ibid., 337–43, 364–65.

78. JM, July 17, July 20, August 15, August 17, September 7, and September 12, ibid., 311, 332, 465, 476, 599, 629; John Ferling, *The First of Men: A Life of George Washington* (Knoxville, Tenn., 1988), 319–20. Pierce Butler of South Carolina wrote in 1788 that the reason the delegates were willing to extend such power to the president was because they "cast their eyes towards General Washington as President." See Rossiter, *1787: Grand Convention,* 222.

79. JM, August 13, August 16, August 24, August 25, and August 29; King, August 8 and August 22, *Notes of the Debates,* 409–10, 445–47, 467–68, 503–9, 530, 532, 550; Robertson, *Constitution and America's Destiny,* 179–80; Beeman, *Plain, Honest Men,* chap. 17; JM to TJ, October 24–November 1, 1787, *RL,* 1:503.

80. Randolph, June 1; Mason, June 4, *Notes of the Debates,* 46, 64.

81. Mason wanted commercial treaties (or navigation acts that placed restrictions on foreign vessels carrying American exports) to require supermajorities, or two-thirds of each house, for passage. It was this issue that arguably resulted in his decision to oppose the adoption of the Constitution. It was not the absence of a bill of rights. See Peter Wallenstein, "Flawed Keepers of the Flame: The Interpreters of George Mason," *Virginia Magazine of History and Biography* 102 (April 1994): 241–42.

82. There were others, such as Luther Martin and John Francis Mercer of Maryland, who did not sign, having left Philadelphia before the end of the convention. Several delegates had already left for personal and political reasons. Thirty-eight of the original fifty-five delegates signed the constitution. Randolph, September 10; Randolph, Mason, and Gerry, September 15, *Notes of the Debates,* 612, 615, 651–52. JM to TJ, October 24–November 1, 1787, *RL,* 1:503.

83. Franklin, September 17, *Notes of the Debates,* 652–54.

84. Washington, September 17, ibid., 655, 659; Rossiter, *1787: Grand Convention,* 237–38.

85. Princeton dateline, as reprinted in the *Columbian Herald* [Charleston, S.C.], October 18, 1787.

86. Carrington to JM, September 23, 1787; JM to Washington, September 30, 1787, *PJM,* 10:172, 180–81; Carrington to TJ, October 23, 1787, *PTJ;* Richard Henry Lee to Mason, October 1, 1787; Paul H. Smith et al., eds., *Letters of Delegates to Congress, 1774–1789* (Washington, D.C., 1976–2000), 24:459.

87. JM to TJ, September 6, 1787, October 24 and November 1, 1787, *RL,* 1:491, 495–507.

CHAPTER FIVE

The Addition of Rights, 1788–1789

1. *Virginia Journal,* January 1, 1788.

2. JM to Edmund Pendleton, January 9, 1787; to Washington, March 18, 1787; and esp. to George Muter, January 7, 1787, *PJM,* 9:231, 245, 315; TJ to JM, January 30 and February 5, 1787, *RL,* 1:461.

3. TJ to JM, January 30–February 5, 1787, *RL,* 1:461.

4. TJ to George Wythe, August 13, 1786; to Washington, November 14, 1786, and August 14, 1787; to Joseph Jones, August 14, 1787, in *PTJ,* 10:532–33, 12:34, 36–38; JM to TJ, October 24 and November 1, 1787, *RL,* 1:496; for an interesting discussion of how European opinion colored Jefferson's views, see Lawrence S. Kaplan, "Jefferson and the Constitution: The View from Paris, 1786–89," *Diplomatic History* 11 (1987): 321–35.

5. JM to TJ, October 24–November 1, 1787, *RL,* 1:498, 500–502.

6. Douglass Adair was the first to stress the significance of Hume to Madison's *Federalist* 10. His interpretation was challenged by Edmund Morgan, who saw how Madison built upon Hume's view of factions but concluded that Madison had rejected Hume's solution. See Adair, " 'That Politics May be Reduced to a Science': David Hume, James Madison, and the Tenth *Federalist,*" *Huntington Library Quarterly* 20 (1957): 343–60; and Morgan, "Safety in Numbers: Madison, Hume, and the Tenth *Federalist,*" *Huntington Library Quarterly* 49 (1986): 95–112. For a thorough review of this debate, and his own emphasis on religion, see Marc M. Arkin, " 'The Intractable Principle': David Hume, James Madison, Religion, and the Tenth *Federalist,*" *American Journal of Legal History* 39 (April 1995): 148–76.

7. Benjamin Franklin, "Observations Concerning the Increase of Mankind" (1751) and "Information to those who would remove to America" (1782), in *The Papers of Benjamin Franklin,* ed. Leonard W. Labaree et al. (New Haven, Conn., 1959–), 4:225–34, 8:604; JM to TJ, August 20, 1784, June 19, 1786, October 24–November 1, 1787; TJ to JM, December 20, 1787, *RL,* 1:340–41, 423–24, 502, 514. Even before this, when he wrote to Jefferson about access to the Mississippi (just after Jefferson had sailed to France), Madison echoed Franklin, who had reasoned that any development of a manufacturing economy would be postponed naturally as a growing population along the eastern seaboard was kept under control by healthy numbers of westward-bound emigrants. For his part, Jefferson argued in *Notes on Virginia* that manufacturing in Europe was not a choice but a necessity, owing to surplus population.

Madison maintained a continuing interest in Franklin's and later the British writer

Thomas Malthus's argument on population growth. In 1791 he wrote an essay in the *National Gazette,* entitled "Population and Emigration," drawing on Franklin's thinking. See *PJM,* 14:117–22; for other scholars who recognized Madison's debt to Franklin, see Dennis Hodgson, "Benjamin Franklin on Population: From Policy to Theory," *Population and Development Review* 17 (December 1991): 639–61; also I. Bernard Cohen, *Science and the Founding Fathers: Science in the Political Thought of Thomas Jefferson, Benjamin Franklin, John Adams, and James Madison* (New York, 1995), 156–64; Drew R. McCoy, "Jefferson and Madison on Malthus: Population Growth in Jeffersonian Political Economy," *Virginia Magazine of History and Biography* 88 (July 1980): 259–76; *Notes on Virginia,* Query XIX.

8. For use of the terms "vicious arts" and "mutual animosities," and a more developed statement on "factional leaders," see "*The Federalist* No. 10," in Jacob E. Cooke, ed., *The Federalist* (Middletown, Conn., 1961), 64.

9. JM to TJ, October 24–November 1; TJ to JM, December 20, 1787, *RL,* 1:499–500, 514.

10. TJ to JM, December 20, 1787, *RL,* 1:512–14.

11. There is disagreement over the authorship of some of the essays, but the evidence favors Madison's claim to have written the disputed numbers (50–52, 54–58, 62–63). See Cooke, *Federalist,* xi–xv, xxvii; JM to TJ, August 10, 1788, and "Madison's Authorship of *The Federalist:* Editorial Note," *PJM,* 10:259–63, 11:226–27; on the pseudonym "Publius," see JM to James K. Paulding, July 24, 1818, *PJM-RS,* 1:310.

12. Hamilton, June 4, 18–19, *Notes of the Debates in the Federal Convention of 1787* (Athens, Ohio, 1966), 61–62, 66, 134–39, 152; Nathan Schachner, *Alexander Hamilton* (New York, 1946), 197–206.

13. Hamilton, September 17, *Notes of the Debates,* 656; Hamilton to Washington, July 3, 1787; Washington to Hamilton, July 10, 1787, *PGW-CS,* 5:245, 250.

14. Hamilton to Gouverneur Morris, February 29, 1802, in *PAH,* 25:544.

15. JM to Randolph, October 21, 1787, *PJM,* 10:199–200.

16. "The people in Georgia and New-Hampshire would not know one another's mind," "Brutus" reasoned, "and therefore could not act in concert to enable them to effect a general change of representatives." He felt that federal officials, no less flawed in character than those they governed, would be unable to resist personalizing power, and the people would be left out of public deliberations. See "Brutus I," *New-York Journal,* October 18, 1787, in John Kaminski and Richard Leffler, eds., *Federalists and Antifederalists* (Madison, Wisc., 1987), 6–13; Saul Cornell, *The Other Founders: Anti-Federalism and the Dissenting Tradition in America, 1788–1828* (Chapel Hill, N.C., 1999), 28–31, 95.

17. "*The Federalist* No. 10"; "*The Federalist* No. 57," in Cooke, ed., *Federalist,* 62–63, 384–85; also see "*The Federalist* No. 46," in which Madison stresses the need for more "impartial guardians of the public interest," ibid., 318; and "*The Federalist* No. 56," in which Madison argues that representatives will possess sufficient knowledge of state laws and local concerns to legislate for the nation; ibid., 378–86; for an excellent discussion of Madison's debate with "Brutus," see Emery G. Lee III, "Representation, Virtue, and Political Jealousy in the Brutus-Publius Dialogue," *Journal of Politics* 59 (November 1997): 1078–83.

18. For the most complete discussion of why *Federalist* 10 was not an influential piece of political theory during the Constitutional Convention or the debates over rati-

fication, but was elevated to its status as the "ur-text" only in the twentieth century, see Larry D. Kramer, "Madison's Audience," *Harvard Law Review* 112 (January 1999): 645–46, 657–58, 665–67, 670–71, 679.

19. One Boston paper claimed that "the arguments which have been adduced in support of [the Constitution] are conclusive and unanswerable; while *every objection* . . . has been fully and entirely answered, by that incomparable writer, PUBLIUS, the author of the FEDERALIST." Such blanket praise was purely partisan. A Philadelphia newspaper named "Publius," among other defenders of the Constitution, as "full of profound political wisdom," then dismissed the antifederalists for offering only "impudent assertions," "scurrility," and "seditious falsehood." In response, an antifederalist used the same wording but reversed the praise, highlighting "Brutus" and other critics as "full of profound political wisdom"; it dismissed the "dry trash of Publius in 150 numbers." See *Massachusetts Centinel,* May 7, 1788; *Pennsylvania Mercury and Universal Advertiser,* May 3, 1788; and *Independent Gazetteer,* May 9, 1788.

20. See "Aristides, Remarks on the Proposed Plan of the Federal Government," in John Kaminski and Gaspare J. Saladino, eds., *The Documentary History of the Ratification of the Constitution* (Madison, Wisc., 1984), 15:517; Kramer, "Madison's Audience," 665; Robin Brooks, "Alexander Hamilton, Melancton Smith, and the Ratification of the Constitution in New York," *William and Mary Quarterly* 24 (July 1967): 349; *Freeman's Journal; or the North-American Intelligencer,* December 12, 1787 (signed "SQUIB"); other essayists attacked "Publius" by assigning his "long winded publications" to paid "hirelings" and verbose lawyers hiding a weak case behind a smoke screen of words. See *New-York Journal,* February 4, 1788; and "Letter from a Gentleman in Dutchess County," *New-York Journal,* February 14, 1788.

21. See JM to Washington, November 18 and November 30, 1787; and JM to Randolph, December 2, 1787, *PJM,* 10:254, 283–84, 290.

22. Washington sent Madison a copy of Mason's "Objections." See Washington to JM, October 10, 1787; JM to Washington, October 18, 1787, *PJM,* 10:189–91, 196–98; Cornell, *Other Founders,* 74–75.

23. Washington to JM, October 10, 1787; Archibald Stuart to JM, October 21, 1787; JM to Randolph, January 10, 1788, *PJM,* 10:189–90, 202, 355. Stuart told Madison: "Mr. Henry has upon all Occasions however foreign to his subject attempted to give the Constitution a side blow." Charles Tillinghast reported that Mason "means to sound the alarm through the southern states." Madison received a letter from George Lee Turberville, a member of the Virginia House of Delegates, who echoed most of Mason's objections, demonstrating their influence among elite Virginians. See Charles Tillinghast to Hugh Hughes, October 12, 1787; Washington to Henry Knox, October 15, 1787, in Kaminski and Saladino, eds., *Documentary History of Ratification of Constitution,* 8:54, 57; and Turberville to JM, December 11, 1787, *PJM,* 10:315–24. For a revealing analysis of the elements leading to the eventual falling-out of Mason and Washington, see Peter R. Henriques, "An Uneven Friendship: The Relationship between George Washington and George Mason," *Virginia Magazine of History and Biography* 97 (April 1989): 185–204.

24. In *Federalist* no. 38 Madison made mention of many of Mason's objections, using some of the same language of his rival. He listed the "want of the bill of rights, the tendency toward monarchy or aristocracy, the Senate's dangerous power of trying im-

peachments, and the lack of a council of state." He also argued that another major complaint of Mason's, a restriction on the importation of slaves, was an improvement over the Articles of Confederation, which had no such limitation. In no. 44 Madison dismissed Mason's concern over the restriction placed on states in the collection of export duties; in no. 45 he refuted Mason's charge that out-of-state tax collectors would oppress the people; in no. 46 he refuted Mason's charge that the states would "dwindle into insignificance"; in no. 47 he rejected Mason's fear that the government would produce an aristocracy; and in nos. 53, 55, 56, and 57 he argued against the notion that the House would have only, in Mason's words, "a shadow of representation" and would lack the proper information to govern or to inspire confidence in the people; in his last essay, no. 63, Madison defended the Senate against the charge that it would possibly become a "tyrannical aristocracy." Out of Mason's twelve objections, Madison directly responded to eight. In addition to circulating his objections, Mason also wrote an anonymous newspaper essay in which he focused on the fear of New England revenue officers entering the homes of Virginians and dragging them off to court in another state. A friend sent Madison a copy of this essay. See Cooke, ed., *Federalist,* 244–47, 302, 312–31, 362–63, 372–83, 384–90; Mason's "Objections to the Constitution of the Government" and his anonymous essay, "Cato Uticensis," *Virginia Independent Chronicle,* October 17, 1787; and "Landholder IV," written by Oliver Ellsworth, in *Connecticut Courant,* December 10, 1787, all in Kaminski and Saladino, eds., *Documentary History of Ratification of Constitution,* 8:41–45, 73–75; John Dawson to JM, October 19, 1787, *PJM,* 10:198–99, 230–31.

25. "The Expositor, No. 1," *New-York Journal,* February 7, 1788. *Federalist* no. 54 was published on February 9, 1788; see Cooke, ed., *Federalist,* 359.

26. In these years, manumitters of slaves in Virginia rarely used the Enlightenment's secular precepts of sympathy and justice to overturn the accepted notion that their slaves were born *un*free. They tended instead to rely on their religious values to justify the humane action of releasing human property into the world and "recommending" them "to the publick" as people who could be counted on to contribute to society and not to cause trouble. It seems obvious that at this pregnant moment in history, the conversation was limited—too equivocal for the laws to advance far at all. "*The Federalist* No. 39"; "*The Federalist* No. 54," in Cooke, ed., *Federalist,* 253–57, 367–69; Malick W. Ghachem, "The Slave's Two Bodies: The Life of an American Legal Fiction," *William and Mary Quarterly* 60 (October 2003): 811–15; Eva Sheppard Wolf, *Race and Liberty in the New Nation: Emancipation in Virginia from the Revolution to Nat Turner's Rebellion* (Baton Rouge, La., 2006), 49–52.

27. Peter S. Onuf, *Jefferson's Empire: The Language of American Nationhood* (Charlottesville, Va., 2000), 147–51.

28. Nos. 48 and 49, in Cooke, ed., *Federalist,* 333–35, 338–43. In *Federalist* no. 63, Madison offered his strongest statement on the subject of limiting the people's capacity to restructure their government. He favored the "*total exclusion of the people in their collective capacity* from any share in" administration. See ibid., 428.

29. Carrington to TJ, May 14, 1788, *PTJ,* 13:156–57; JM to TJ, August 10, 1788, *RL,* 1:548.

30. JM to George Washington, February 20, 1788, JM to Eliza House Trist, March 25, 1788, *PJM,* 10:526, 11:5; on his attack of bilious fever, see JM to Alexander Hamilton,

June 9, 1788; to Rufus King, June 9, 1788; to Tench Coxe, June 11, 1788, *PJM,* 11:101–2; Ketcham, 258.

31. JM to TJ, December 9, 1787, and April 22, 1788, *RL,* 1:507–11, 534–35.

32. TJ to William Carmichael, December 15, 1787; to Uriah Forrest, December 31, 1787; to Alexander Donald, February 7, 1788, *PTJ,* 12:475–79, 570–72; Daniel Carroll to JM, May 28, 1788, *PJM,* 11:64–66; Eric Robert Papenfuse, "Unleashing the 'Wildness': The Mobilization of Grassroots Antifederalism in Maryland," *Journal of the Early Republic* 16 (Spring 1986): 92–95; "The Virginia State Ratifying Convention," in Kaminski and Saladino, eds., *Documentary History of Ratification of Constitution,* 9:1088, 10:1223.

33. To understand how the votes of the delegates could be accurately forecast a month before the convention, see the letter from David Henley to Samuel Henley, April 28, 1788, in which Henley compiled a record of 151 of 168 delegates, showing that 82 of 85 of the federalists voted as predicted. F. Claiborne Johnson, Jr., "Federalists, Doubtful, and Antifederalist: A Note on the Virginia Convention of 1788," *Virginia Magazine of History and Biography* 96 (July 1988): 333–44; Archibald Stuart to John Breckinridge, June 19, 1788, in Kaminski and Saladino, eds., *Documentary History of Ratification of Constitution,* 10:1651 (Stuart wrote "suspended on a single hare," but meant "hair"); JM to Ambrose Madison, June 24, 1788, *PJM,* 11:170–71.

34. Monroe to TJ, July 12, 1788, *PTJ,* 13:351. Richard Henry Lee urged George Mason to try to win over Pendleton; see Lee to Mason, October 1, 1787; and Pendleton's unanimous election as president, in Kaminski and Saladino, eds., *Documentary History of Ratification of Constitution,* 8:29, 9:897. Madison wrote Washington confidently that Pendleton viewed the Constitution "in its true light," and that "his support will have great effect." JM to Washington, October 18, 1787, *PJM,* 10:197. For praise of Henry's eloquence, see Spencer Roane to Philip Aylett, June 26, 1788; on Henry's harangues against Randolph and forced apology, see John Brown Cutting to TJ, July 24, 1788, in Kaminski and Saladino, eds., *Documentary History of Ratification of Constitution,* 10:1707, 1713.

35. Mason, June 11, June 17; Henry, June 16, June 17, June 24, Virginia State Ratifying Convention, in Kaminski and Saladino, eds., *Documentary History of Ratification of Constitution,* 9:905, 1159, 1161, 10:1338, 1341, 1476–77, 1688–90; see also Robin L. Einhorn, "Patrick Henry's Case against the Constitution: The Structural Problem with Slavery," *Journal of the Early Republic* 22 (Winter 2002): 556–59, 563.

36. Madison, June 20, June 24; Henry, June 20, Virginia State Ratifying Convention, in Kaminski and Saladino, eds., *Documentary History of Ratification of Constitution,* 10:1417, 1424, 1503; Einhorn, "Patrick Henry and Slavery," 555–56.

37. Randolph raised a pertinent national security question: Would not Virginia need the Union in order to survive? Seven years before, it was shown to be susceptible to military attack, and all the more vulnerable because of its huge slave population. Its white population was scattered. In this way, as they spoke to the convention, Randolph and Madison portrayed themselves as the realists. Randolph, June 6, June 7, June 9; Madison, June 7, Virginia State Ratifying Convention, in Kaminski and Saladino, eds., *Documentary History of Ratification of Constitution,* 9:973, 977–78, 983, 1016, 1028, 1086; 9:1033–34.

38. Alan V. Briceland, "Virginia: The Cement of the Union," in Patrick T. Conley

and John P. Kaminski, eds., *The Constitution and the States: The Role of the Original Thirteen in the Framing and Adoption of the Federal Constitution* (Madison, Wisc., 1988), 218–21. Another month would pass before New York ratified.

39. "Extract of a Letter from Richmond, June 18," *Pennsylvania Mercury,* June 26, 1788.

40. Henry, June 5, June 7, June 9, June 13, June 24; Mason, June 14, Mason and Henry, June 17, Virginia State Ratifying Convention, in Kaminski and Saladino, eds., *Documentary History of Ratification of Constitution,* 9:963, 1039, 1051, 10:1245, 1260–70, 1355, 1356–57, 1361, 1476–77; Monroe to TJ, July 12, 1788, *PTJ,* 13:352.

41. JM to TJ, July 24–26, 1788, *RL,* 1:541–42.

42. TJ to JM, July 31, 1788, *RL,* 1:543; William Howard Adams, *The Paris Years of Thomas Jefferson* (New Haven, Conn., 1997), 264–67.

43. JM to TJ, October 17, 1788, *RL,* 1:563.

44. TJ to Hopkinson, May 8, 1788, *PTJ,* 13:145.

45. Lafayette to Washington, January 1, 1788, *PGW-CS,* 6:5–6; Douglas Southall Freeman, *George Washington: A Biography* (New York, 1948–57), vol. 6, chap. 6. Lafayette's critique of the Constitution was, almost verbatim, the same as Jefferson's.

46. John E. Ferling, *The First of Men: A Life of George Washington* (Knoxville, Tenn., 1988), 314–15; Peter Shaw, *The Character of John Adams* (Chapel Hill, N.C., 1976); Joseph J. Ellis, *Passionate Sage: The Character and Legacy of John Adams* (New York, 1993); Stanley Elkins and Eric McKitrick, *The Age of Federalism* (New York, 1993), 532–37.

47. Smith to TJ, February 15, 1789, *PTJ,* 14:559–60.

48. History has made it appear that the election of the first president and First Congress was trouble-free. Like Smith, Madison was aware of the constitutional intricacy though he explained the problem to Jefferson in simpler terms: "The votes were unanimous with respect to General Washington ... in each of the States. The secondary votes were given, among the federal members chiefly to Mr. J. Adams, one or two being thrown away in order to prevent a possible competition for the Presidency." To "throw away" votes could not have sounded ideal to Jefferson, who had not wanted an open-ended presidency without term limits. JM to TJ, March 29, 1789, *RL,* 1:606.

49. Richard R. Beeman, *The Old Dominion and the New Nation, 1788–1801* (Lexington, Ky., 1972), 22–24.

50. *Herald of Freedom* [Boston], December 22, 1788, published in New York and elsewhere. The letter itself was dated November 8.

51. Beeman, *The Old Dominion and the New Nation,* 24–27; Roger H. Brown, *Redeeming the Republic: Federalists, Taxation, and the Origins of the Constitution* (Baltimore, 1993), 208–10; Robert A. Rutland, *The Presidency of James Madison* (Lawrence, Kan., 1990), 71.

52. *Virginia Gazette* [Winchester], April 2, 1789, in Lampi Collection of American Electoral Returns, 1788-25, American Antiquarian Society, Worcester, Mass.; TJ to JM, February 5, 1787, *RL,* 1:465.

53. JM to TJ, March 29, 1789, *RL,* 1:606–7.

54. On the renovation of City Hall/Federal Hall, see Agnes Addison Gilchrist, "John McComb, Sr. and Jr., in New York, 1784–1799," *Journal of the Society of Architectural Histo-*

rians 31 (March 1972): 14; John P. Kaminski, *George Clinton: Yeoman Politician of the New Republic* (Madison, Wisc., 1993).

55. "Address of the President to Congress," April 30, 1789; "Address of the House of Representatives to the President," May 5, 1789, *PJM*, 12:120–24, 132–33; on historiographical issues and attribution of the first inaugural address, see also *PGW-PS*, 2:152ff.

56. JM to TJ, March 29, 1789 *RL*, 1:606–7; Andrew Burstein, "Jefferson's Madison versus Jefferson's Monroe," *Presidential Studies Quarterly* 28 (Spring 1998): 394–408.

57. JM to TJ, May 9, 1789, *RL*, 1:608–9.

58. Madison cleverly illustrated the absurdity of titles: "One of the most impotent sovereigns in Europe has a title as high as human invention can devise … 'High Mightiness.' " To carry on this way seemed to him "to border on impiety." May 13, 1789, 1st Cong, 1st sess., *Annals of Congress* (New York, 1857), 1:67.

59. JM to TJ, May 23, 1789; TJ to JM, July 29, 1789, *RL*, 1:613, 627; Randolph to JM, September 26, 1789, *PJM*, 12:421.

60. "Removal Power of the President," May 19, 1789, *PJM*, 12:170–71.

61. JM to Trist, May 21, 1789, *PJM*, 12:175–76.

62. Ames to G. R. Minot, May 3, 1789, cited in Brant, 3:249.

63. Henrietta had married Richard Nicholls Colden, whom she met when he was stationed in the Isle of Man as an officer in the Royal Highlanders. Two of Richard's uncles, Cadwallader and David, were prominent New York Loyalists, whose land was confiscated during the Revolution. Both of Henrietta's sons, Alexander and Cadwallader, were born in New York early in the war. Her husband died in 1777, after which she returned to England. There she petitioned the government for a stipend, compensation for losses as the wife of a Loyalist. She was well versed in her family's finances and kept in touch with her husband's family in America. Returning in 1785, she was listed as head of household in the south ward of New York City in the first U.S. census in 1790. She was also one of the few women to purchase stock in the Ohio Land Company. See JM to TJ, May 23, 1789, *RL*, 1:612–13; JM to Henry Lee, June 21, 1789, *PJM*, 12:251; Henrietta Maria Colden to TJ, November 25, 1790, TJ to Henrietta Maria Colden, January 20, 1790, *TJP*, 18:70–71, 578; on Madison's fascination with Henrietta Colden, see Samuel Mitchill to his wife, January 3, 1802, in "Dr. Mitchill's Letters from Washington: 1801–1813," *Harper's New Monthly Magazine* 58 (1879): 743; Edward Purple, *Genealogical Notes of the Colden Family in America* (New York, 1873), 13; "Letter of David Colden, Loyalist, 1873," *American Historical Review* 25 (October 1919): 76–86; Mary Beth Norton, "Eighteenth-Century American Women in Peace and War: The Case of Loyalists," *William and Mary Quarterly* 33 (July 1976): 390–91; for notice of her arrival in New York City, see *Independent Journal*, July 23, 1785; *Heads of Families at the First Census of the United States Taken in the Year 1790* (Washington, D.C., 1908), 132; Anne Hollingsworth Wharton, *Salons Colonial and Republican* (Philadelphia, 1900), 40, 63–64; Edwin G. Burrows and Mike Wallace, *Gotham: A History of New York City to 1898* (New York, 1999), 301.

64. Randolph to JM, May 19 and August 18, 1789; Washington to JM, ca. September 23, 1789, *PJM*, 12:168, 345, 420.

65. JM to TJ, May 27, 1789, 1:614.

66. TJ to JM, July 22–23, 1789, *RL,* 1:625–27; Adams, *Paris Years of Thomas Jefferson,* 288–93; Malone, 2:222–28.

67. TJ to JM, May 11, July 22–23, July 29, and August 28, 1789, *RL,* 1:610, 625–32; Monroe to JM, July 19, 1789, *PJM,* 12:296–97.

68. On Madison's reservations, see Paul Finkelman, "James Madison and the Bill of Rights: A Reluctant Paternity," *Supreme Court Review* (1990): 302, 307–8, 318–19, 326–27.

69. TJ to JM, December 20, 1787, and July 31, 1788; JM to TJ, October 17, 1788, *RL,* 1:512–13, 545–46, 564–66.

70. TJ to JM, March 15, 1789, *RL,* 1:587–88; and see Madison's speech on June 8, when he introduced his proposed amendments. He argued: "If they are incorporated into the constitution, independent tribunals of justice will consider themselves in a peculiar manner the guardians of those rights . . . Beside this security, there is a great probability that such a declaration in the federal system will be inforced; because the state legislatures will jealously and closely watch the operations of this government, and be able to resist with more effect every assumption of power than any other power can do." See "Amendments to the Constitution," June 1789, *PJM,* 12:206–7.

71. For Madison's campaign pledges, see JM to George Eve, January 2, 1789, JM to Thomas Mann Randolph, January 13, 1789, and "To the Residents of Spotsylvania County," January 27, 1789, *PJM,* 11:404–5, 416–17, 428–29; 12:57. Joseph Jones wrote to Madison after seeing his proposed amendments: "They are calculated to secure the personal rights of the people so far as declarations on paper can effect the purpose, leaving unimpaired the great Power of the government—they are of such a nature as to be generally acceptable and of course more likely to obtain the assent of Congress." See Jones to JM, June 24, 1789, *PJM,* 12:258–59; also JM to Edmund Randolph, June 15, 1789, ibid., 219; on the proposed second convention, see Richard Labunski, *James Madison and the Struggle for a Bill of Rights* (New York, 2006), 129–32.

72. Madison made this point clear in remarks in Congress on August 15 in defense of the Bill of Rights: "It was wished that some security should be given for those great and essential rights which they had been taught to believe were in danger. I concurred, in the convention of Virginia, with those gentlemen, so far as to agree to a declaration of rights which corresponded with my own judgment, and of the other alterations which I had the honor to bring forward before the present congress." Madison also noted to Richard Peters, Speaker of the Pennsylvania House: "In many States Constn. was adopted under a tacit compact in favr . . . In Virga. It would have been *certainly* rejected, had no assurances been given by its advocates that such provisions would be pursued." See "Amendments to the Constitution," August 15, 1789; JM to Peters, August 19, 1789, *PJM,* 12:341–42, 347.

73. "Address of the President to Congress," June 8, 1789, *PJM,* 12:59, 123; Stuart Leibiger, "James Madison and the Amendments to the Constitution, 1787–1789: 'Parchment Barriers,' " *Journal of Southern History* 59 (August 1993): 460.

74. "Amendments to Constitution," June 8, 1789, *PJM,* 12:58, 200–203; Kenneth R. Bowling, " 'A Tub to the Whale': The Founding Fathers and the Adoption of the Federal Bill of Rights," *Journal of the Early Republic* 8 (Fall 1988): 235–36; Leibiger, "Parchment Barriers," 460–61.

75. "Amendments to the Constitution," August 17, 1789, *PJM,* 12:58–59, 344.

76. Bowling, " 'Tub to the Whale,' " 223, 233, 236–37.

77. Ibid., 236, 239, 241–42, 244–45, 247; also see Scott D. Gerber, "Roger Sherman and the Bill of Rights," *Polity* 28 (Summer 1996): 526.

78. JM to Pendleton, August 21 and September 14, 1789; to Randolph, August 21, 1789, *PJM,* 12:348, 402.

79. TJ to JM, August 28, 1789, *RL,* 1:630–31; Mason to TJ, January 10, 1791, *PTJ,* 18:484–85; Mason to Samuel Griffin, September 8, 1789, *The Papers of George Mason,* ed. Robert Allen Rutland (Chapel Hill, N.C., 1970), 3:1172. Edmund Randolph encouraged Madison to propose amendments, drawing a distinction between those "opposed on principle" and those driven by "virulence." See Randolph to JM, March 27, 1789, *PJM,* 12:31. Pendleton, too, supported amendments at the ratifying convention, writing Madison that they would have "a good effect in quieting the minds of many well meaning Citizens." As Madison explained to Richard Peters, he felt vindicated "as an honest man," having lived up to "assurances" given to delegates at the ratifying convention—not any pledge to his constituents. See George Nicholas to JM, April 5, 1788; JM to Nicholas, April 8, 1788; JM to Edmund Randolph, April 10, 1788; JM to Peters, August 19, 1789; Pendleton to JM, September 2, 1789, *PJM,* 11:9, 12, 19, 347, 368; also see Leibiger, "Parchment Barriers," 451, 467; Labunski, *James Madison and Struggle for Bill of Rights,* 114–15.

80. *JMB,* 1:732–43. Annette Gordon-Reed develops the argument for how Jefferson might have become intimate with a teenaged Sally Hemings in Paris. See Gordon-Reed, *The Hemingses of Monticello* (New York, 2008), 264–89.

81. For Madison's memorandum, see "Memorandum on an African Colony for Freed Slaves," ca. October 20, 1789, in *PJM,* 12:437–38; William Thornton to Etienne Clavière, November 7, 1789, in C. M. Harris, ed., *Papers of William Thornton* (Charlottesville, Va., 1995), 1:xxxi–liii, 105–6; H. N. Sherwood, "Early Negro Deportation Projects," *Mississippi Valley Historical Review* 2 (March 1916): 502–3. Thornton's proposal was more progressive than Jefferson's resettlement plan. He imagined a thriving free black republic—he would not call it a colony—that boasted an advanced system of education and a sound commercial economy. He predicted that Americans, "who had so strenuously contended for LIBERTY, and who have declared it to be the natural right of MAN," would be receptive to his ideals. See "Address to the Heart, on the Subject of Slavery," published in the *Herald* [Newport, R.I.], March 1, 1787; and Thornton to John Coakley Lettsom, July 26, 1778, and June 15, 1790, in Harris, ed., *Papers of William Thornton,* 1:49–53, 77–79, 113–14; Sherwood, "Early Negro Deportation Projects," 490–93; Wolf, *Race and Slavery in the New Nation,* 14, 102–3, 107.

82. "Memorandum on an African Colony," *PJM,* 12:437–38. Both Jefferson and Madison, schooled in Scottish moral philosophy, assumed that all human beings had an innate desire for sociability. Consistent with this principle, if whites refused to socialize with blacks, emancipating southern slaves threatened social cohesion. Humane treatment did not alter hierarchy. See Joyce Chaplin, "Slavery and the Principle of Humanity: A Modern Idea in the Early Lower South," *Journal of Social History* 24 (Winter 1990): 299–302.

83. "Memorandum on an African Colony"; "Instructions for the Montpelier Overseer," ca. November 1790, *PJM,* 12:438, 13:303; Christopher Castiglia, "Pedagogical Dis-

cipline and the Creation of White Citizenship," *Early American Literature* 33 (1998): 195, 197, 207. In 1773, two years after Madison left Princeton, two "Fanti-speaking" students (John Quamine and Bristol Yamma) were enrolled to study with John Witherspoon to prepare for being sent as missionaries to Africa. These young men were free blacks, sponsored by Reverend Samuel Hopkins, another early promoter of colonization. It is likely that Madison was aware of this bold experiment. See George E. Brooks, Jr., "The Providence African Society's Sierra Leone Emigration Scheme, 1794–1795: Prologue to the African Colonization Movement," *International Journal of African Studies* 7 (1974): 185–86; Sherwood, "Early Negro Deportation Projects," 497–500.

84. "Memorandum on an African Colony," *PJM,* 12:438; *Notes on Virginia,* Query XIV; Onuf, *Jefferson's Empire,* chap. 5. Madison meant that southern whites might eventually accept freed slaves as citizens. This desirable end would be achieved after news traveled across the ocean with proof that colonization worked and that blacks could lift themselves from a degraded state, adopting a republican character—slaves would not be remade in the eyes of slave owners until it was done first at a safe distance. In 1783, when Jefferson arranged his private library, he adapted the categories first used by Francis Bacon: memory, reason, and imagination. Of these faculties of the mind, he grouped memory with works of human and natural history (including medicine); philosophy with moral and mathematical concerns (including law); and imagination with literature and the arts. By placing memory and the human organism in the same category, he symbolically kept slavery apart from ethics and jurisprudence while associating blacks' physical constitution—those attributes that commanded them to return to their original continent—with the politics of memory. The analogy to Jefferson's library is not meant to be regarded as evidence of his racial science, so much as a curiosity in the context of his intellectual habits. See Charles A. Miller, *Jefferson and Nature: An Interpretation* (Baltimore, 1988), 35–37, 73; James Gilreath and Douglas Wilson, eds., *Thomas Jefferson's Library* (Washington, 1989).

85. William Howard Adams, *Gouverneur Morris: An Independent Life* (New Haven, Conn., 2003); Malone, 2:209–11, 400–401.

86. Henry S. Randall, *Life of Thomas Jefferson* (New York, 1858), 1:551, 558.

87. JM to TJ, October 8, 1789; *RL,* 1:638; TJ to Washington, December 15, 1789, *TJP-LC.* In Jefferson's reconstruction of the one sentence, certain unnamed people became a public "just indeed in their intentions," and his grievance against those who had once called for an investigation into his conduct suddenly weighed less. His rhetorical pose now said that he was capable of perceiving those who censured him as individuals lacking in objective information rather than impelled by malevolence. But the thought of further criticism, regardless of underlying motive, made him nervous and reluctant to assume so visible an executive role.

88. TJ to JM, September 6, 1789, *RL,* 1:632–37. In usufruct land ownership, whoever had a claim to a property was able to reap the benefits of it—a modified form of possession. If the land was not used regularly, one could lose the usufruct. Herbert E. Sloan has come up with a cultural explanation for Jefferson's nineteen-year cutoff for the span of one generation, seeing it in the context of a lifetime of number-crunching: Jefferson "hoarded numbers with unusual intensity," Sloan writes, so as "to control the world around him." Sloan, *Principle and Interest: Thomas Jefferson and the Problem of Debt* (New York, 1995), chap. 2, quote at 58.

89. Adrienne Koch, *Jefferson and Madison: The Great Collaboration* (New York, 1950), chap. 4; Dumas Malone, *Thomas Jefferson as Political Leader* (Berkeley, Calif., 1963), 6.

90. JM to TJ, February 4, 1790, *RL,* 1:652–55.

91. "Conversation with George Beckwith," *PAH,* 5:485.

92. Ibid., 483–85; Ketcham, 305.

CHAPTER SIX
Attachments and Resentments, 1790–1792

1. JM to TJ, October 8, 1789; TJ to JM, January 9, 1790, *RL,* 1:638, 650; TJ to Washington, December 15, 1789, *TJP-LC;* JM to Washington, January 4, 1790, *PJM,* 12:467; Malone, 2:249–55.

2. JM to Pendleton, April 4, 1790; to Short, April 6, 1790; Henry Lee to JM, March 13, 1790, *PJM,* 13:102–3, 138–41.

3. JM to Randolph, May 6, 1790; Rev. JM to JM, May 12, 1790, *PJM,* 13:189, 196.

4. *PAH,* 6:51ff.; Max M. Edling, " 'So Immense a Power in the Affairs of War': Alexander Hamilton and the Restoration of Public Credit," *William and Mary Quarterly* 64 (April 2007): 309–11.

5. Madison's proposal would give current note holders the highest market value and reserve the difference between the market price and par value for the original holders. See Edling, " 'So Immense a Power,' " 289–90; *Pennsylvania Gazette,* March 24, 1790, reprinted in the *New-Hampshire Spy* [Portsmouth], April 10, 1790; Rush to JM, April 10, 1790, *PJM,* 13:146; Jacob E. Cooke, *Tench Coxe and the Early Republic* (Chapel Hill, N.C., 1978), 145–48; Stuart Leibiger, *Founding Friendship: George Washington, James Madison, and the Creation of the American Republic* (Charlottesville, Va., 1999), 128–29; Ketcham, 314.

6. Edling, " 'So Immense a Power,' " 287, 292–96.

7. Carrington to JM, April 7, 1790; George Lee Turberville to JM, April 10, 1790, *PJM,* 13:142–45; Richard R. Beeman, *The Old Dominion and the New Nation, 1788–1801* (Lexington, Ky., 1972), 74–77; Ketcham, 311–12. Henry was predicting the "prostration of agriculture at the feet of commerce," along with the creation of a "large monied interest."

8. "Notes for Speech in Congress" and "Assumption of State Debts," *PJM,* 13:159–74.

9. Letter from the National Assembly of France, and TJ to Rev. William Smith, February 19, 1791, *PTJ,* 19:109, 112–13. For the complicated diplomatic dance over the mourning of Franklin, see "Death of Franklin," *PTJ,* 19:78ff.

10. JM to Trist, May 27, 1790, *PJM,* 13:231; Henry S. Randall, *Life of Thomas Jefferson* (New York, 1858), 1:612; Malone, 2:258–62, 267.

11. JM to Monroe, April 17 and June 1, 1790, *PJM,* 13:151, 233–34; John W. Kuehl, "Justice, Republican Energy, and the Search for the Middle Ground: James Madison and the Assumption of State Debts," *Virginia Magazine of History and Biography* 103 (July 1995): 327.

12. "Jefferson's Account of the Bargain on Assumption and Residence Bills" (1792?), *PTJ,* 17:204–8; Noble E. Cunningham, Jr., *The Jeffersonian Republicans: The Formation of Party Organization, 1789–1801* (Chapel Hill, N.C., 1957), 5–7; Adrienne Koch, *Jefferson*

and Madison (New York, 1950), 103–8. Jefferson's letters to the likes of George Mason and James Monroe from mid- to late June convey optimism and a conciliatory spirit. This makes it highly probable that Madison, without prodding from Jefferson, had been doing the most to stall the program Hamilton wished to push through Congress.

13. We consider the best explanation to be that offered by Jacob E. Cooke, "The Compromise of 1790," *William and Mary Quarterly* 27 (October 1970): 524 -45; the scholarly debate was extended in Kenneth R. Bowling, "Dinner at Jefferson's: A Note on Jacob E. Cooke's 'The Compromise of 1790,' " *William and Mary Quarterly* 28 (October 1971): 629–48. Stanley Elkins and Eric McKitrick wrote: "Jefferson, Madison, and Hamilton could not themselves impose a final resolution. But a fair guess, considering the circumstances, is that no settlement *not* acquiesced in by them was likely to occur." Elkins and McKitrick, *Age of Federalism* (New York, 1993), 156.

14. JM to Washington, August 24, 1788, *PGW-C,* 6:469–70. In July 1789, as Jefferson was watching the French Revolution unfold, Madison remained anxious about his northern colleagues' ignorance of westerners' sentiments. He wrote to Virginia ally George Nicholas of the many mistaken perceptions that "still lurk in the minds of those who view [the western country] at so great a distance and through the medium perhaps of local prejudices." Madison was eager for Kentucky to be granted statehood, believing it would focus renewed attention on augmenting American power up and down the Mississippi. When remarking on the interests of the West, his real meaning seems to have been the interests of Virginia and the South. See JM to Nicholas, July 5, 1789, *PJM,* 12:279–81.

15. *PJM,* 12:369–82.

16. "Location of the Capital," July 16, 1790, *PJM,* 13:264.

17. Pendleton to JM, July 21, 1790; JM to Monroe, July 26, 1790; to JM Sr., *PJM,* 13:282–85; Beeman, *Old Dominion and New Nation,* 78–81.

18. Ketcham, 316.

19. Hamilton to Washington, March 27, 1791, *PAH,* 8:218–23; Ketcham, 319–22.

20. On Madison's appeal to the Constitutional Convention, see Benjamin B. Klubes, "The First Federal Congress and the First National Bank: A Case Study in Constitutional Interpretation," *Journal of the Early Republic* 10 (Spring 1990): 28–31, 40–41; *RL,* 2:668. To Jefferson, the bank was a "convenient" instrument but not a "necessary" one. On Washington's political purpose in asking for his cabinet members' opinions, see Kenneth R. Bowling, "The Bank Bill, the Capital City, and President Washington," *Capitol Studies* 1 (Spring 1972): 66–68.

21. JM to TJ, May 1, July 10, and August 8, 1791, *RL,* 2:687, 697–98, 708.

22. JM to TJ, October 24 and November 1, 1787, *RL,* 1:501–2. Madison's famous definition of faction in *Federalist* 10 is: "a number of citizens, whether amounting to a majority or minority of the whole, who are united and actuated by some common impulse or passion, or of interest, adverse to the rights of other citizens, or to the permanent and aggregate interests of the community."

23. *Journal of William Maclay, United States Senator from Pennsylvania, 1789–1791,* ed. Edgar S. Maclay (New York, 1890), entry of February 9, 1791, 387; Adams to Trumbull, April 1790, cited in Ketcham, 311.

24. Karl-Friedrich Walling, *Republican Empire: Alexander Hamilton on War and Free Government* (Lawrence, Kan., 1999), 134–37, 141–42; Leibiger, *Founding Friendship,* 124–25; Joanne B. Freeman, "The Art and Address of Ministerial Management: Secretary of the Treasury Alexander Hamilton," in Kenneth R. Bowling and Donald R. Kennon, eds., *Neither Separate Nor Equal: Congress in the 1790s* (Athens, Ohio, 2000), 269–93.

25. Adams's Autobiography, in *The Works of John Adams,* ed. Charles Francis Adams (Boston, 1865), 2:507–9.

26. As the historian Eric Foner has put it: "The early 1790s saw Paine at his best—bringing radical ideas to a new audience, submitting contemporary institutions to a withering critique, raising the demand for far-reaching change." See Foner, *Tom Paine and Revolutionary America* (New York, 1976), 233.

27. Edmund Burke, *Reflections on the Revolution in France* and Thomas Paine, *The Rights of Man* (Garden City, N.Y., 1973), 19–20, 101, 124–26, 139–40, 315, 370, 380, 384–85.

28. Adrienne Koch noted the similarity in Paine's and Jefferson's language, in *Jefferson and Madison,* 82–85.

29. Burke, *Reflections on the Revolution,* and Paine, *Rights of Man,* 272–74, 277–78, 283–86, 294–96, 364, 383–84. The second volume of Paine's work, published early in the following year, would be dedicated to the Marquis de Lafayette. Paine would send twelve copies of part 2 of *The Rights of Man* to Washington when it was published. See Washington to Paine, May 6, 1792, *PGW-PS,* 10:357-358n.

30. *Discourses on Davila,* in *The Works of John Adams,* ed. Charles Francis Adams (Boston, 1851), 6:254–62, 270–75, 284; letter to Sherman, 428; Peter Shaw, *The Character of John Adams* (Chapel Hill, N.C., 1976), 230–36.

31. TJ to Washington, May 8, 1791; to Adams, July 17, 1791; to Paine, July 29, 1791; *PTJ,* 20:291–92, 302, 308; Adams to TJ, July 29, 1791, *PTJ,* 20:305–7; TJ to JM, May 9, 1791; JM to TJ, May 12, 1791, *RL,* 2:689–91; Malone, 2:355–59; John Ferling, *John Adams: A Life* (Knoxville, Tenn., 1992), 311–12, 316. See also the extended Editorial Note, "*Rights of Man:* 'The Contest of Burke and Paine…in America,' " in *PTJ,* 20:268ff.

32. "The Northern Journey of Jefferson and Madison," *PTJ,* 20:436. The other Albany paper had nothing to say about the Madison-Jefferson visit, while unfriendly newspapers that picked up the story reprinted it with a different purpose: to make the point that Charles Fox symbolized opposition to the established government.

33. "The Northern Journey of Jefferson and Madison," *PTJ,* 20:437–42; *JMB,* 2:819–25.

34. Ketcham, 323–26, quote at 325; Malone, 2:359–61.

35. This last remark is outright racism, not even credible as eighteenth-century logic. Banneker's astronomical calculations were corroborated and his intellectuality verified by none other than David Rittenhouse of Philadelphia, a scientist whom Jefferson quite literally worshipped, and whom he advertised in *Notes of Virginia* as "second to no astronomer living." See Banneker to TJ, August 19, 1791; TJ to Banneker, August 30, 1791; TJ to Condorcet, August 30, 1791, *PTJ,* 22:49–54, 97–99; Andrew Burstein, *The Inner Jefferson: Portrait of a Grieving Optimist* (Charlottesville, Va., 1995), 180–81; John Chester Miller, *The Wolf by the Ears: Thomas Jefferson and Slavery* (New York, 1977), 76–77.

36. Jeffrey L. Pasley, *"The Tyranny of Printers": Newspaper Politics in the Early Republic* (Charlottesville, Va., 2001), 51–66; Pasley, "The Two National Gazettes: Newspapers and the Embodiment of American Political Parties," *Early American Literature* 35 (2000): 66; Richard A. Harrison, *Princetonians, 1769–1775: A Biographical Dictionary* (Princeton, N.J., 1980), 149–53.

37. "Jefferson, Freneau, and the Founding of the *National Gazette*," *PTJ*, 20:718–56; Ketcham, 326–27; Pasley, *"Tyranny of Printers,"* 74–76. While Madison took the lead in recruiting Freneau, Jefferson did all he could to smooth the way. As parties became better defined in 1792, both Virginians insisted that they did not have in mind an anti-administration paper, only one that would criticize the political theory they saw as monarchism in Adams's writings. For an early elaboration, see Cunningham, *Jeffersonian Republicans*, 13–19.

38. "Population and Emigration," *National Gazette*, November 21, 1791, *PJM*, 14:117–22.

39. For more on "the class of literati" as "cultivators of the human mind—the manufacturers of useful knowledge," see Madison's "Notes for the *National Gazette* Essays," December 19, 1791–March 3, 1792, *PJM*, 14:168. The relevant books that Madison read were those sent by Jefferson from France. French thinkers associated public opinion with the growth of print media and the free exchange of ideas among enlightened men. They drew a sharp distinction between this and the other definition of popular opinion—the unsophisticated views of the masses. See Colleen A. Sheehan, "Madison and the French Enlightenment: The Authority of Public Opinion," *William and Mary Quarterly* 59 (October 2002): 925–56.

40. "Notes for the *National Gazette* Essays," *PJM*, 14:163–64.

41. "Consolidation," *National Gazette*, December 5, 1791, *PJM*, 14:137–39.

42. "Public Opinion," *National Gazette*, December 19, 1791, *PJM*, 14:170; on Madison's support for lowering the postage for newspapers, which failed to gain approval, see ibid., 186. He continued to denigrate orators, who he felt were the bane of society. He imagined that public opinion expressed in print was less likely to excite the passions and more reasonable than the inflamed rhetoric of public speakers such as Patrick Henry. The acerbic, highly emotionalized partisan direction of newspapers would soon show that Madison was wrong. For his continuing distrust of orators, see "Notes for *National Gazette* Essays," *PJM*, 14:165.

43. Madison sharpened his criticism in the essay "Spirit of Governments," leaving the impression that Hamilton was distributing "bounties" to "favorites" and converting republican government into the "real domination of the few." Here Madison took a swipe at Adams as well, warning that Americans would only remain "happy and honorable" if they "never descend to mimic the costly pageantry" of Old World forms. See "Universal Peace," "Spirit of Governments," *National Gazette*, January 31, February 18, 1792, in *PJM*, 14:207–8, 233–34.

44. Drew R. McCoy, *The Elusive Republic: Political Economy in Jeffersonian America* (New York, 1980), 148, 151, 159; Elkins and McKitrick, *Age of Federalism*, 258–63. Proponents of the Paterson experiment, including Hamilton, would be deeply troubled when they learned that some of the chief private investors—presumed friends of the federal

government—promptly sold off their subscriptions to others, before operations were even under way, so as to make a quick profit.

45. JM to Lee, January 1, 1792; Lee to JM, January 8, 1792, *PJM*, 14:180, 184. Madison told Edmund Pendleton that Hamilton's *Report on Manufactures* defied "the sense in which the Constitution is known to have been proposed, advocated and adopted. If Congress can do whatever in their *discretion* can be *done by money*, and will promote the *general welfare*, the Government is no longer a limited one possessing enumerated powers, but an indefinite one subject to particular exceptions." See JM to Pendleton, January 21, 1792, ibid., 195.

46. *PTJ*, 20:315–22; Jacob E. Cooke, *Tench Coxe and the Early Republic* (Chapel Hill, N.C., 1978), esp. chap. 9. Coxe had given his preliminary "Plan for a Manufacturing Society" to both Hamilton and Jefferson in April 1791. See ibid., 191.

47. "Republican Distribution of Citizens" and "Fashion," *National Gazette*, March 5 and March 20, 1792, *PJM*, 14:245–46, 257–59. The historian Drew R. McCoy has concluded that Hamilton was unconcerned about the dehumanization that attended progress. See McCoy, *Elusive Republic*, 149.

48. On the death of Lee's wife, see Paul C. Nagel, *The Lees of Virginia: Seven Generations of an American Family* (New York, 1992), 165.

49. *National Gazette*, December 5 and December 19, 1791, January 23 and April 2, 1792. See in this context Jack Rakove's appraisal of Madison's "calculated" but not "cynical" reassessment of the proper balance between national and state authority, in Rakove, *James Madison and the Creation of the American Republic* (New York, 1990), 99–102.

50. Madison's memorandum, dated May 5, 1792; Brant, 3:355–56; Malone, 2:420–21. When Washington some months later confided in a female friend, the wife of a Pennsylvania official, that he wished to resign, she wrote to him: "Your Resignation wou'd elate the Enemies of good Government and cause lasting regret to the friends of humanity . . . The Anti-federalist would use it as an Argument for dissolving the Union, and would urge that you, from Experience, had found the present System a bad one, and had, artfully, withdrawn from it that you might not be crushed under its Ruins." Elizabeth Willing Powel to Washington, November 17, 1792, *PGW-PS*, 11:395–96.

51. Beeman, *Old Dominion and New Nation*, 114–18.

52. "T.L. No. III," August 11, 1792, *PAH*, 12:193–94.

53. "An American, No. I," August 4, 1792; "Metellus," October 24, 1792, *PAH*, 12:157–64, 617; *Gazette of the United States*, September 22 and November 24, 1792.

54. *National Gazette*, September 26 and December 22, 1792.

55. TJ to JM, October 1, 1792, *RL*, 2:742.

56. Cunningham, *Jeffersonian Republicans*, 33–49; Raymond Walters, Jr., *Alexander James Dallas* (Philadelphia, 1943), chap. 4; *Albany Gazette*, June 28, 1792; JM to Edmund Pendleton, December 6, 1792, *PJM*, 14:421; Nancy Isenberg, *Fallen Founder: The Life of Aaron Burr* (New York, 2007), 108–19; Brant, 3:359.

57. Hamilton to Adams, June 25, 1792, *PAH*, 11:559.

58. TJ to JM, March 13, 1791; JM to TJ, March 13 and ca. April 18, 1791, *RL*, 2:682–85.

59. Brant, 3:337, 358–59; Malone, 2:393–99, 413.

60. Morris to TJ, August 22, 1792, *PTJ,* 24:313.

61. Tom Paine was as vocal as Lafayette in his opposition to the politically conservative Morris, appealing to Jefferson to reverse what he saw happening in U.S. foreign policy. See Paine to TJ, February 13, 1792; Short to TJ, July 26, September 18, and September 28, 1792, *PTJ,* 23:115; 24:252, 402, 425–26.

62. Morris to Hamilton, October 24, 1792, *PAH,* 12:618. On Adams's symbolic victory over Jefferson, see Ellis, *Passionate Sage,* 92–93.

63. Hamilton to Carrington, May 26, 1792, *PAH,* 11:426–44.

64. JM to Pendleton, November 16, 1792, *PJM,* 14:408–9; Maria Reynolds to Hamilton, June 2, 1792; Hamilton to James Reynolds, June 3–22, and June 24, 1792; *PAH,* 11:481–82, 558; Jacob Karz Cogan, "The Reynolds Affair and the Politics of Character," *Journal of the Early Republic* 16 (Autumn 1996): 398–417; Brant, 3:365–69.

65. Washington to TJ, August 23, 1792; TJ to Washington, September 9, 1792, *PTJ,* 24:317, 351–59. Jefferson was more cautious when he wrote to Edmund Randolph the following week. The latest in Hamilton's unsigned attack essays could easily be proven false, he said, but he had resolved to keep his anger in check. "For the present," Jefferson qualified, "lying and scribbling must be free to those mean enough to deal in them, and in the dark." He wished to give Randolph the impression that he could exercise control, whereas Hamilton could not. TJ to Randolph, September 17, 1792, *PTJ,* 24:387.

66. Hamilton to Washington, September 9, 1792, *PAH,* 12:347–49.

CHAPTER SEVEN

Party Spirit, 1793

1. TJ to JM, March 25, 1793; JM to TJ, April 12, 1793, *RL,* 2:765, 768.

2. Lee to Washington, April 29, 1793; Washington to Lee, May 6, 1793, *PGW-P,* 12:493–94, 533; Lee to Hamilton, May 6, 1793, *PAH,* 14:416–17. Lee was originally inspired by the prospect of serving with Lafayette and had asked the marquis for a commission.

3. George Green Shackelford, *Jefferson's Adoptive Son: The Life of William Short, 1759–1848* (Lexington, Ky., 1993), 64–67, 115.

4. Noailles Lafayette to Washington, March 12, 1793; TJ to Washington, March 15, 1793; Washington to Noailles Lafayette, March 16, 1793, *PGW-PS,* 12:307–9, 321, 331–32; TJ to Washington, March 13 and March 15, 1793; to Gouverneur Morris and Thomas Pinckney, March 15, 1793, *PTJ,* 25:382, 387–88, 390–92.

5. TJ to Short, January 3, 1793, *PTJ,* 25:14–16; Shackelford, *Jefferson's Adoptive Son,* 68–69; Gore Vidal, *Inventing a Nation: Washington, Adams, Jefferson* (New Haven, Conn., 2003), 57.

6. TJ to Lafayette, June 16, 1792, *PTJ,* 24:85.

7. Thomas O. Ott, *The Haitian Revolution, 1789–1804* (Knoxville, Tenn., 1973), 6–17; Laurent DuBois, *Avengers of the New World: The Story of the Haitian Revolution* (Cambridge, Mass., 2004), 29–33, 40, 45, 56; Donald R. Hickey, "America's Response to the Slave Revolt in Haiti, 1791–1806," *Journal of the Early Republic* 2 (Winter 1982): 362–63; John H. Coatsworth, "American Trade with European Colonies in the Caribbean and South

America, 1790–1812," *William and Mary Quarterly* 24 (April 1967): 245–47. For the most accurate account of the population of St. Domingue in 1789, see David P. Geggus, *Slavery, War, and Revolution: The British Occupation of Saint Domingue, 1793–1798* (Oxford, U.K., 1982), 405; for the repressive nature of the planter elite, see ibid., 6, 25.

8. Nathaniel Cutting to TJ, August 4, 1790, *PTJ,* 17:301; David P. Geggus, "Racial Equality, Slavery, and Colonial Secession during the Constituent Assembly," *American Historical Review* 94 (December 1989): 1297–98, 1300–1303; Ott, *Haitian Revolution,* 36–38. David Geggus observed that the insurrection "produced acts of great savagery from the slaves, as from whites and coloured." Geggus, *Slavery, War and Revolution,* 41. John D. Garrigus argues that racial reforms for free blacks were crucial in undermining the slave regime. Garrigus, *Before Haiti: Race and Citizenship in French Saint-Domingue* (New York, 2006), 227–63.

9. TJ to Short, November 24, 1791, *PTJ,* 22:330–31. Rumors of British intervention circulated in England's newspapers as early as October 1791, but Britain did not get involved until after France had declared war against it. See David P. Geggus, "The British Government and the Saint Domingue Slave Revolt, 1791–1793," *English Historical Review* 96 (April 1981): 289; Tim Matthewson, *A Proslavery Foreign Policy: Haitian-American Relations during the Early Republic* (Westport, Conn., 2003), 12, 20, 28–29.

10. Jefferson's use of the word *assassins* was not accidental but echoed what he was hearing. Jeremy Popkin argues that descriptions of the insurrection followed a rigid formula, focusing on the carnage, including the murders of women and children; blacks were denoted "assassins." The word *assassins* appeared in the first appeal for aid from the colonial assembly on August 24, 1791, and American newspapers carried similarly graphic accounts. Just days before Jefferson wrote to Short, the *National Gazette* reprinted a letter stating: "St. Domingo continues to bleed by the hands of the infatuated Africans, who have doubtless been led on by emissaries, to act this scene of murder and desolation." See *National Gazette,* November 17, 1791; and Jeremy D. Popkin, *Facing Racial Revolution: Eyewitness Accounts of Haitian Insurrection* (Chicago, 2007), 6–9; also Matthewson, *Proslavery Foreign Policy,* 12, 29.

11. Some reckoned that the United States might someday annex St. Domingue. That was certainly the conviction of Jefferson's principal informant on the island, Nathaniel Cutting, an American businessman who had done small favors for Jefferson in Europe. In 1790 he had sailed to Africa from Le Havre and was still actively engaged in the slave trade at the time he wrote Jefferson from St. Domingue that "every Free American who indulges Political Reflections must feel himself peculiarly interested in the Fate of this valuable and flourishing Colony of Saint Domingue, which at some future point may possibly fall within the Jurisdiction of the Thirteen United States!" While Jefferson would not speak of independence for the whites of the troubled colony, he did want to use leverage to pressure France into removing trade restrictions to benefit the United States. See Cutting to TJ, April 19, 1791, *PTJ,* 17:240; Simon Newman, "American Political Culture and the French and Haitian Revolutions: Nathaniel Cutting and the Jeffersonian Republicans," in David P. Geggus, ed., *The Impact of the Haitian Revolution in the Atlantic World* (Columbia, S.C., 2001), 73–74, 78.

12. TJ to William Short, November 24, 1791, *PTJ,* 22:331; Matthewson, *Proslavery Foreign Policy,* 25–26, 29, 38.

13. There was precedent for this. In Jamaica in 1739 the British resolved a rebellion

diplomatically by recognizing a completely separate maroon colony of free blacks in the mountains of the interior. Doing so, they secured the plantation economy, preserved the institution of slavery, and satisfied a defiant free black population all at once. The British strategy in Jamaica was consistent with Jefferson's thinking in *Notes on Virginia*: segregation, removal, and rejection of a biracial political unit ensured social stability. See TJ to Lafayette, June 16, 1792, *PTJ*, 24:85; Matthewson, *Proslavery Foreign Policy*, 39. Laurent DuBois has argued the importance of maroon communities, in DuBois, *Avengers of the New World*, 52–57.

14. Geggus, *Slavery, War and Revolution*, 42–45, 64, 78.

15. JM to Pendleton, March 25, 1792, and "Santo Domingan Refugees," January 10, 1794, in *PJM*, 14:263, 15:177–79; Eva Sheppard Wolf, *Race and Liberty in the New World: Emancipation in Virginia from the Revolution to Nat Turner's Rebellion* (Baton Rouge, La., 2006), 26–27, 115; TJ to James Monroe, July 14, 1793, *PTJ*, 26:503.

16. TJ to Martha Jefferson Randolph, May 26, 1793, in *The Family Letters of Thomas Jefferson*, ed. Edwin Morris Betts and James Adam Bear, Jr. (Charlottesville, Va., 1986), 119–20.

17. TJ to James Monroe, July 14, 1793, *PTJ*, 26:503. Jefferson did not consider that the principles which set in motion the American and French revolutions had meaning in St. Domingue; but Nathaniel Cutting did, blaming the French Revolution and its "leveling principles" for destroying St. Domingue. See Newman, "American Political Culture and French and Haitian Revolutions," 79.

18. See the extended discussion of the wrangling that took place over the neutrality proclamation in John Lamberton Harper, *American Machiavelli: Alexander Hamilton and the Origins of American Foreign Policy* (Cambridge, 2004), 104, 108–14.

19. TJ to JM, July 11 and August 3, 1793; JM to TJ, July 18 and September 2, 1793, *RL*, 2:792–93, 797, 814–15; Alexander DeConde, *Entangling Alliance: Politics and Diplomacy Under George Washington* (Durham, N.C., 1958), 206–13. Adding to the confusion, Genet's predecessor, Ternant, did not know which way to turn when the Jacobins refused to credit him for his work in America. Having sentiments for Louis XVI, Ternant turned for comfort to Hamilton, "put on mourning for the king, and became a perfect Counter-revolutioner." Then he received word from Genet that he might be given an army appointment under the Jacobins and did another turnabout. TJ to JM and Monroe, May 5, 1793, *RL*, 2:770–71.

20. The seven "Pacificus" essays were published between June 29 and July 27, 1793; quotes are from "Pacificus No. V," July 13–17, 1793, *PAH*, 15:90–91, 95.

21. TJ to JM, May 13, 1793, *RL*, 2:773; "Notes of a Conversation with George Washington," August 6, 1793, *PTJ*, 26:628; Brant, 3:377–79.

22. JM to Monroe, September 15, 1793, *PJM*, 15:110–11.

23. Madison wrote the "Helvidius" essays from August 24 to September 18, 1793. He published them in Fenno's *United States Gazette*, wishing for the essays to appear in the same publication as Hamilton's "Pacificus." See "Helvidius No. 1," August 24, 1793, "Helvidius No. 5," September 18, 1793, *PJM*, 15:67–68, 71, 73, 115–16; JM to TJ, June 19, 1793, *RL*, 1:786.

24. Madison's knowledge of Helvidius Priscus most likely comes from Book 4 of Tacitus.

25. JM to TJ, May 27, 1793; TJ to JM, June 9, 1793, *RL,* 2:776, 779–81.

26. Eugene R. Sheridan, "Thomas Jefferson and the Giles Resolutions," *William and Mary Quarterly* 49 (October 1992): 589–608; Malone, 3:14–33; Stanley Elkins and Eric McKitrick, *The Age of Federalism: The Early American Republic, 1788–1800* (New York, 1993), 295–301.

27. Taylor to JM, May 11, June 20, and September 25, 1793; Monroe to JM, May 18, 1793; JM to Monroe, September 15, 1793, *PJM,* 15:13–14, 17, 34–35, 110–11, 123; *National Gazette,* September 11, 1793. The pamphlet would be published as *An Enquiry into the Principles and Tendency of Certain Public Measures.*

28. Pendleton to Washington, September 11, 1793, *The Letters and Papers of Edmund Pendleton,* ed. David John Mays (Charlottesville, Va., 1967), 2:613–15.

29. TJ to JM, August 11, 1793, *RL,* 2:802–3.

30. "Notes of a Conversation with George Washington," August 6, 1793, *PTJ,* 26:627–30; *PGW-PS,* 13:312n.

31. TJ to JM, August 11, 1793, *RL,* 2:803–4. Jefferson first expressed frustration with Randolph a few months earlier, when Randolph came up with a compromise position for enforcement of neutrality laws in U.S. ports. Hamilton wanted the responsibility conferred upon customs officials, which meant shifting more power to the Treasury Department. To mollify Jefferson, Randolph proposed that all customs officials report instead to federal attorneys. Rather than see this as a workable solution, Jefferson came to resent Randolph's mediation. It appeared to him that Randolph was subtly outmaneuvering both Hamilton and him and puffing himself up.

32. TJ to JM, May 13, 1793, *RL,* 1:772–73. Randolph agreed with Jefferson on sixteen out of nineteen issues raised in cabinet meetings. When Hamilton attacked Jefferson for supporting Freneau's newspaper, Randolph was the first to defend him in print, calling his "calumniator" a "cowardly assassin." But Randolph refused to be bullied by Jefferson. In most of his disagreements with Jefferson, he had valid reasons. When Jefferson suggested sending the controversial Gouverneur Morris, currently the minister to France, to England, Randolph warned that such a move would insult France since that country might soon be at war with Great Britain. In 1793 Jefferson suggested a special Board of Advice to decide on constitutional questions, which would have usurped the duties of the attorney general. Randolph refused to allow this to happen. For a balanced view of Randolph's actions, see John Garry Clifford, "A Muddy Middle of the Road: The Politics of Edmund Randolph, 1790–1795," *Virginia Magazine of History and Biography* 80 (July 1972): 288–94.

33. TJ to JM, June 2, 1793; JM to TJ, June 13 and July 22, 1793, *RL,* 1:778, 783, 794–95; TJ to Monroe, May 5, 1793, *PTJ,* 25:661–62. Nicholas confirmed for Madison that Randolph's views on France were not different from theirs, and Madison continued to defend Randolph and Nicholas by blaming "tainted sources" for any errors in Randolph's report on the sentiments of Virginians. In September, though, he straddled the issue, defending Nicholas as a sound Republican while listing possible reasons that might "derogate from a full confidence in" Nicholas. See JM to TJ, July 30 and September 2, 1793, *RL,* 1:796–97, 816.

34. Genet to Washington, August 13, 1793, *PGW-P,* 13:436–37; TJ to Genet, August 16, 1793, *PTJ,* 26:684.

35. DeConde, *Entangling Alliance*, 214–16, 224–26, 235–39, 248–50; "The Recall of Edmond Charles Genet," and supporting documentation, *PTJ*, 26:685ff.; TJ to Isaac Shelby (first governor of Kentucky), November 6, 1793, *PTJ*, 27:312. Cynical in their assessment of the Republicans and too quick to credit or condone Hamilton, Elkins and McKitrick nevertheless present a thoroughgoing account of the politics surrounding the neutrality proclamation and the furor over Genet. See *Age of Federalism*, chap. 8. Contemptuous of Hamilton's motives, Malone predictably praises Jefferson as fair and realistic, "wise and patriotic," throughout this trying period. See Malone, 3:90–131.

36. Douglas B. Chambers, *Murder at Montpelier: Igbo Africans in Virginia* (Jackson, Miss., 2005), 131–32; Brant, 3:380; TJ to JM, June 2, 1793, *RL*, 2:779, and several references to Billey in the Madison-Jefferson correspondence of 1793. Douglas R. Egerton says of the decision to leave Billey in Philadelphia, "Madison was able to flatter himself a humanitarian even while turning a small profit." Egerton, *Death or Liberty: African Americans and Revolutionary America* (New York, 2009), 131.

37. *Annals of Congress*, 2nd Cong., 2nd sess., 1414–15; Paul Finkelman, *Slavery and the Founders: Race and Liberty in the Age of Jefferson* (Armonk, N.Y., 2001), chap. 4. Pennsylvania had had a Gradual Emancipation Act in force since 1780, after which time children born of slaves were free at birth.

38. TJ to JM, September 8 and September 12, 1793, *RL*, 2:818–19; Malone, 3:472–73. The classic treatment on the epidemic is J. H. Powell, *Bring Out Your Dead: The Great Plague of Yellow Fever in Philadelphia in 1793* (Philadelphia, 1993).

39. JM to James Madison, Sr., May 4, 1794, *PJM*, 15:322–33; Brant, 3:385; Ketcham, 375–76.

40. Noble E. Cunningham, Jr., *The Jeffersonian Republicans: The Formation of Party Organization, 1789–1801* (Chapel Hill, N.C., 1959), 63–66; Andrew Burstein, *Sentimental Democracy: The Evolution of America's Romantic Self-Image* (New York, 1999), 176–80.

41. *Spectator* no. 125, July 24, 1711, in Crissy and Markley edition (Philadelphia, 1851), 3:90–94.

42. William Wyche, *Party Spirit: An Oration* (New York, 1794), 8–15, 19; though Wyche's address was given in the spring of 1794, it reflected a state of affairs amply evidenced in public statements of 1793 as well; advertisement for its publication in *American Minerva* (New York), June 30, 1794; *New-York Gazette*, December 21, 1747; *Boston Evening-Post*, March 23, 1772; [Donald Fraser], *Party Spirit Exposed, or Remarks on the Times* (New York, 1799), 5–6; Pendleton to TJ, July 22, 1776, *PTJ*, 1:472; "Impartiality, No. 2, To the Mechanics of New-York," *Loudon's Register*, January 18, 1793; "Principles of the Democratic Society of Pennsylvania," in *Middlesex Gazette* [Middletown, Conn.], July 27, 1793; *Mirrour* [Concord, N.H.], January 6, 1794; *American Apollo* [Boston], January 9, 1794; *Philadelphia Gazette*, April 19, 1794; *Medley* [New Bedford, Mass.], October 31, 1794; John Adams to Abigail Adams, December 28, 1792, *Adams Family Papers: An Electronic Archive*, Massachusetts Historical Society (http://www.masshist.org/digital-adams); Franklyn George Bonn, Jr., "The Idea of Political Party in the Thought of Thomas Jefferson and James Madison," Ph. D. diss., University of Minnesota, 1964, chap. 2, showing the strict political usage of *faction* and the occasional nonpolitical usage of *party*; Washington Irving, "The Poor Devil Author," in *Tales of a Traveller*, ed. Judith Giblin Haig (Boston, 1987), 92.

43. *National Gazette*, January 12, 1793; *Gazette of the United States*, March 16, 1793; *New-York Journal* article first cited, as reprinted in the *National Gazette*, September 4, 1793; *New-York Journal*, August 13, 1794.

44. *Gazette of the United States*, June 19, 1793; *Federal Intelligencer*, January 10 and January 12, 1795. An early example of the use of *Federalist* in its eventual party context is a short piece placed in the *Federal Orrery*, published in Boston on October 20, 1794, which promoted the reelection of the Hamiltonian Fisher Ames; it was signed by "A True Fed-eralist." In this vein, see Gordon S. Wood's assessment of Ames as one who had lost confidence in the people, but not in the Revolution. Wood, *The Radicalism of the American Revolution* (New York, 1992), 230–31.

45. Jeffrey L. Pasley, *"The Tyranny of Printers": Newspaper Politics in the Early Republic* (Charlottesville, Va., 2001), esp. 62–78.

CHAPTER EIGHT

The Effects of Whiskey on Reputation, 1794–1795

1. Brant, 3:389–95; Henry S. Randall, *Life of Thomas Jefferson* (New York, 1858), 2:223–27; JM to TJ, March 2, 1794, *RL,* 2:832.

2. *Loudon's Register,* January 20, 1794.

3. Ketcham, 360.

4. George Nicholas to JM, February 9, 1794, *PJM,* 15:256.

5. Stuart Leibiger, *Founding Friendship: George Washington, James Madison, and the Creation of the American Republic* (Charlottesville, Va., 1999), 182–96.

6. *JMB,* 2:913, 918; TJ to Randolph, February 3, 1794; to John Adams, May 27, 1795, *PTJ,* 28:15, 363.

7. There is nice irony not only in Jefferson's professions of apathy toward politics but also in Congressman Smith's performance and Jefferson's reaction to it. Just prior to the start of Jefferson's conflict with Hamilton, the question had arisen in Congress as to who should perform as chief executive if both president and vice president died or were incapacitated. At that time Smith suggested that the secretary of state should step in and fill the position.

8. JM to TJ, March 2 and March 9, 1794; TJ to JM, April 3, 1794, *RL,* 2:832–35, 839; "Vacancy in the Presidency," *Annals of Congress,* January 10, 1791.

9. JM to TJ, April 28, 1794, *RL,* 2:841–42.

10. JM to TJ, October 5, 1794, *RL,* 2:847, 857; Brant, 3:404–12; Ketcham, 376–83; Catherine Allgor, *A Perfect Union: Dolley Madison and the Creation of the American Nation* (New York, 2006), 30–33. Despite her husband's prominence, Dolley was "read out" of Meeting and no longer considered a Quaker after her marriage to the non-Quaker Madison.

11. Washington to Hamilton, November 2, 1796, *PAH,* 20:365. The increasingly callous Madison needed to satisfy his and Jefferson's bloodlust in imagining their enemy squirming. And so, without knowing precisely what had transpired and unable to be objective, Madison wrote Jefferson that Hamilton had suffered "great mortification" when Jay was selected.

12. JM to TJ, April 14, April 28, and May 11, 1794, *RL*, 2:840–43; Harper, *American Machiavelli*, 130–42; Sandra Frances VanBurkleo, " 'Honour, Justice, and Interest': John Jay's Republican Politics and Statesmanship on the Federal Bench," *Journal of the Early Republic* 4 (Autumn 1984): 239–74; Francis X. J. Coleman, "John Jay on War," *Journal of the History of Ideas* 43 (January–March 1982): 145–51; Samuel Flagg Bemis, *Jay's Treaty: A Study in Commerce and Diplomacy* (New Haven, Conn., 1962), 253ff.; Moncure Daniel Conway, *Omitted Chapters of History Disclosed in the Life and Papers of Edmund Randolph* (New York, 1888), 220ff.

13. Monroe to TJ, May 27, 1794, *PTJ*, 28:86–87; Brant, 3:400.

14. *General Advertiser*, June 17, 1794. Bache's sense of enterprise may have been inherited from his grandfather, colonial America's most successful printer, but his patriotic optimism was a blend of Jefferson and Paine. As secretary of state, Jefferson had had doubts about Bache. He did not consider Bache's newspaper as accomplished as Freneau's *National Gazette;* but he came to feel for the contentious editor, fated to acquire more enemies than his famous grandfather and yet enjoy little of his financial success.

15. Jeffrey L. Pasley, *"The Tyranny of Printers": Newspaper Politics in the Early Republic* (Charlottesville, Va., 2001), 86–96; James Tagg, *Benjamin Franklin Bache and the Philadelphia Aurora* (Philadelphia, 1991), 101–2, 135–36 and passim. On the French Revolution and accelerated time, see Matthew Rainbow Hale, "On Their Tiptoes: Political Time and Newspapers during the Advent of the Radicalized French Revolution, circa 1792–1793," *Journal of the Early Republic* 29 (Summer 2009): 191–218.

16. Charles Royster, *Light-Horse Harry Lee and the Legacy of the American Revolution* (New York, 1981), chap. 4.

17. Thomas P. Slaughter, *The Whiskey Rebellion: Frontier Epilogue to the American Revolution* (New York, 1986), chap. 13 and passim; Ketcham, 354.

18. Mary K. Bonsteel Tachau, "George Washington and the Reputation of Edmund Randolph," *Journal of American History* 73 (June 1986): 21–23; [Edmund Randolph], *Germanicus* (1794), in Early American Imprints (Evans), no. 27597, quote at 4.

19. JM to TJ, February 15, 1795, *RL*, 2:852, 867, 873; Leibiger, *Founding Friendship*, 191–92; Brant, 3:415–22. Having been through a political conversion, and having overplayed his hand in facing down the whiskey rebels, Henry Lee took personal offense at Madison's public argument about the use of "self created" as a derogatory term. Lee believed that Madison had been making "frequent remarks" to his detriment, and he could not be convinced otherwise. When he composed his memoirs, the Virginia general would have his revenge only indirectly—striking at Jefferson and ignoring Madison.

20. TJ to JM, December 28, 1794, *RL*, 2:867. His ominous words on a possible dismemberment began: "That separation which was perhaps a very distant and problematical event, is now near."

21. Henry Adams, *The Life of Albert Gallatin* (Philadelphia, 1879); Raymond Walters, Jr., *Albert Gallatin: Jeffersonian Financier and Diplomat* (New York, 1957), 121–22; JM to TJ, January 31, 1796, *RL*, 2:917; Henry M. Dater, "Albert Gallatin, Land Speculator," *Mississippi Valley Historical Review* 26 (June 1939): 21–38. Gallatin's *A Sketch of the Finances of the United States* was published in New York in 1796.

22. Bemis, *Jay's Treaty*, 41–43, 206–13.

23. Harry Ammon, *James Monroe: The Quest for National Identity* (New York, 1971), 117–22.

24. March 26, 1795, *PJM,* 15:497–98; TJ to JM, December 28, 1794, and February 5, 1795, *RL,* 2:849, 866, 871. A suddenly needy-sounding Jefferson ("I have past [*sic*] my winter almost alone") invited James and Dolley, the latter of whom had yet to see Montpelier, to visit him at Monticello.

25. JM to TJ, January 11 and March 23, 1795, *RL,* 2:869, 876.

26. Bemis, *Jay's Treaty,* 232–51.

27. On Hamilton's goal to emulate England but also to exceed it in economic muscle, see Doron Ben-Atar, "Alexander Hamilton's Alternative: Technology Piracy and the Report on Manufactures," in Ben-Atar and Barbara B. Oberg, eds., *Federalists Reconsidered* (Charlottesville, Va., 1998), 41–60.

28. TJ to JM, December 28, 1794; JM to TJ, March 23, 1795, *RL,* 2:868; 875–76.

29. TJ to JM, April 27, 1795, *RL,* 2:877.

30. Adams to TJ, November 21, 1794; TJ to Adams, February 6, 1795; to Mann Page, August 30, 1795, *PTJ,* 28:207–8, 261, 440–41. Shortly after his midcareer retirement began, Jefferson had devised a standard for venturing political opinion and then promptly denying any interest in continuing to have an impact on public matters. To the president: "My opinion of the British government is, that nothing will force them to do justice but the loud voice of their people, & that this can never be excited but by distressing their commerce. But I cherish tranquillity too much, to suffer political things to enter my mind at all." TJ to Washington, May 14, 1794, *PTJ,* 28:75. Like Adams, Jefferson and Washington talked in detail about plants and seeds and soil and dung.

31. TJ to Cosway, September 8, 1795, *PTJ,* 28:455–56.

32. [Edmund Randolph], *A Vindication of Mr. Randolph's Resignation* (Philadelphia, 1795), quotes at 6–7, 78. He said he wished, even now, for the name of Washington to remain "untainted by the suspicion of being a favourer of party"; but of course, if Randolph still hoped to have his reputation restored, he would not have vilified the only person who had the power to do that.

33. The authoritative biography of Pickering is Gerald H. Clarfield, *Timothy Pickering and the American Republic* (Pittsburgh, 1980).

34. Giles to TJ, December 20, 1795; "Notes on Edmund Randolph's *Vindication,*" and TJ to Giles, December 31, 1795, *PTJ,* 28:558–59, 563–67. Giles provoked Jefferson with these words: "The Alarmists have commenced a most violent and unmerciful attack upon Mr. Randolph's vindication, and no doubt will keep it up, but no estimate can yet be formed of its effect upon the public mind."

35. JM to TJ, January 10, 1796, *RL,* 2:907; JM to Monroe, January 26, 1796, *PJM,* 16:204.

36. A number of Virginians weighed in, buoyed by so powerful a critique of the administration. Jefferson needed, on some level, to both gloat and moralize, having referred to Randolph's efforts to pursue a "middle line" as "immoral," when Randolph left him to battle Hamilton alone in cabinet meetings. Madison kept a close watch on the impact of the pamphlet. Joseph Jones wrote him that the *Vindication* was bound to make an "impression." See TJ to JM, November 26, 1795; JM to TJ, December 27, 1795,

RL, 2:901, 904; Randolph to JM, November 1, 1795; Joseph Jones to JM, February 4, 1796, *PJM,* 16:117, 211.

37. [Edmund Randolph], *Germanicus* (1794), in Early American Imprints (Evans), no. 27597, quotes at 8, 67, 72; Conway, *Omitted Chapters of History Disclosed in the Life and Papers of Edmund Randolph,* 359–61. For an excellent treatment of the value of classical antecedents on American political life, see Eran Shalev, *Rome Reborn on Western Shores: Historical Imagination and the Creation of the American Republic* (Charlottesville, Va., 2009).

38. Charles Royster, *A Revolutionary People at War: The Continental Army and American Character, 1775–1783* (Chapel Hill, N.C., 1979); John F. Ferling, *The First of Men: A Life of George Washington* (Knoxville, Tenn., 1988), 228–30, 459, 462. In the case of Randolph and the Fauchet letter, Washington was told that one of the intercepted dispatches rebuked him for his handling of the Whiskey Rebellion. Confronted with the challenge to his reputation, Washington took the bait, as he had when Hamilton exaggerated the rebels' threat. He imagined a conspiracy against him. Mary K. Bonsteel Tachau has pointed out that Washington underlined those portions of the questionable dispatches from Fauchet that painted him in a negative light. Fauchet had cast the president as Hamilton's dupe, leading a grand army against poor farmers simply to augment his administration's power. The Conway comparison is credible, because in both instances the attacks involved Washington's performance as a military commander. The suggestion that Randolph might have spread this information to Fauchet was thoroughly humiliating to the president and revived all of his earlier resentments about "secret enemies" under his command. Tachau, "George Washington and the Reputation of Edmund Randolph," 23, 26.

39. JM to Monroe, January 26, 1796, *PJM,* 16:204.

40. Henry's stated rationale for declining was fatherhood: "My domestic situation pleads strongly against a removal to Philadelphia, having no less than eight children by my present wife." See James M. Elson, comp., *Patrick Henry in His Speeches and Writings and in the Words of His Contemporaries* (Lynchburg, Va., 2007), 167.

41. William Howard Adams, *Gouverneur Morris: An Independent Life* (New Haven, Conn., 2003), 257–59.

42. Hamilton to Bradford, June 13, 1795, *PAH,* 18:374. The assertive, combative Hamilton was not loved by all Federalists. Take Secretary of War Henry Knox, probably the general officer most trusted by Washington during the Revolution. Just as he had earlier angered Jefferson by his intrusions into State Department matters, Hamilton alienated the accommodating Knox when he supplanted the War Department in the government's response to the Whiskey Rebellion by having the procurement of military supplies transferred to Treasury. It was the reason Knox left the cabinet and returned to Maine—to a home coincidentally named "Montpelier." See Knox entry in online edition of *American National Biography* (Oxford University Press, 1999).

43. Hamilton to Nicholson, July 20, 1795; "The Defence No. 1," July 22, 1795, *PAH,* 18:471–74, 479–83.

44. Todd Estes, *The Jay Treaty Debate, Public Opinion, and the Evolution of Early American Political Culture* (Amherst, Mass., 2006), 94–103.

45. *Columbian Centinel* [Boston], January 17, 1795, apparently originating in Hartford, Conn.; *Weekly Register* [Norwich, Conn.], February 17, 1795.

46. [Alexander James Dallas], *Letters of Franklin* (Philadelphia, 1795), esp. 7, 20, 27–29; [Dallas], *Features of Mr. Jay's Treaty* (Philadelphia, 1795), 12, 25. The letters were serially published in the newspapers first. Advertisement in the *Aurora* announcing publication of the collected *Letters of Franklin* in pamphlet form, July 30, 1795.

47. "Peter Porcupine," *A Little Plain English, Addressed to the People of the United States, on the Treaty Negotiated with His Britannic Majesty* (Philadelphia, 1795), Preface, 6–9, 89, 101–2; Brant, 3:417. *A Little Plain English* was published one month after *Letters of Franklin* appeared as a pamphlet.

48. *PAH,* 18:415–18.

49. *JMB,* 2:923; Lucia Stanton, *Free Some Day: The African-American Families of Monticello* (Charlottesville, Va., 2000), 102–7, 118–19; Jack McLaughlin, *Jefferson and Monticello: The Biography of a Builder* (New York, 1988), 114, 406–7; Annette Gordon-Reed, *Thomas Jefferson and Sally Hemings: An American Controversy* (Charlottesville, Va., 1997), 195; Gordon-Reed, *The Hemingses of Monticello* (New York, 2008), 497–501. Jefferson freed Robert Hemings after Bob made arrangements to remove to Richmond. In 1784, after seeing Jefferson off to Europe, he had been allowed to hire himself out. In this way he found a wife, Dolly, and during Jefferson's years abroad they had a child. Dolly was owned by a physician, who agreed to advance Bob the sum he needed to purchase his freedom, in order that the family could live together. Jefferson complained that Bob had been "debauched" from him—a remark that seems utterly cruel and selfish. Bob explained to Patsy that he did not wish to cause his master unhappiness, but he could not help choosing his immediate family over the one he had come into deprived of choice.

50. Drew R. McCoy, *The Last of the Fathers: James Madison and the Republican Legacy* (Cambridge, 1989), 233–36; Susan Dunn, *Dominion of Memories: Jefferson, Madison, and the Decline of Virginia* (New York, 2007), 40–41.

51. *Western Star* [Stockbridge, Mass.], December 15, 1795; James Roger Sharp, "Unraveling the Mystery of Jefferson's Letter of April 27, 1795," *Journal of the Early Republic* 6 (Winter 1986): 411–18.

52. Ebeling to TJ, July 30, 1795; "Notes on the Letter of Christoph Daniel Ebeling," [after October 30, 1795], *PTJ,* 28:423–27, 506–10; Andrew Burstein, *Jefferson's Secrets: Death and Desire at Monticello* (New York, 2005), 199–203.

CHAPTER NINE

Danger, Real or Pretended, 1796–1799

1. Todd Estes, "Shaping the Politics of Public Opinion: Federalists and the Jay Treaty Debate," *Journal of the Early Republic* 20 (Autumn 2000): 393–422; Estes, *The Jay Treaty Debate, Public Opinion, and the Evolution of Early American Political Culture* (Amherst, Mass., 2006); Jack N. Rakove, *James Madison and the Creation of the American Republic* (New York, 1990), 117–120; "Notes for Speech, Jay's Treaty, 1796," *JMP-LC.*

2. JM to TJ, April 4 and April 11, 1796, *RL,* 2:929, 931.

3. Jefferson egged Madison on, writing with grand gestures and extreme language. He would preserve the power of treaty making as a method of securing peace only, he said, seeing "no harm" in "annihilating" it if it was nothing more than a means to forge

permanent links between England and the Anglomen in Congress. This language of noncompliance was a clear preview of an even more radical position: the language of nullification which would dramatically challenge the sanctity of the Union. By his use of the word *annihilating* Jefferson was declaring that one party might reject a federal treaty or federal law, bypassing constitutional guidelines altogether. He regarded such a maneuver as the only way to stop Hamilton. See TJ to JM, March 27, 1796; JM to TJ, April 4 and April 11, 1796, *RL,* 2:928–29, 931. Washington cited the journals of the Constitutional Convention, as Hamilton did in his "Camillus" essays, written in an effort to defeat Madison's bill. For Madison's reliance on the state constitutional conventions (Virginia, North Carolina, and Pennsylvania), see "Note for Speech in Congress, March 23–April 2," and "Jay's Treaty," April 6, 1796, *JMP,* 16:274, 276, 296; Ketcham, 361–62.

4. JM to TJ, May 1, 1796, *RL,* 2:936.

5. Writing under a pseudonym, Robert Livingston observed the previous September, in a widely circulated opinion, that all Americans with unbiased judgment disapproved of what they saw happening. Of the deepening divisions around the country over the Jay Treaty, he wrote: "The states in which there is *least* of party spirit, manifest *most* warmth and most unanimity in their opposition." See Cato no. 8, *Philadelphia Gazette,* September 12, 1795. But this did not seem to matter in the end, as Hamilton's perspective won the day. "To the Citizens Who Shall Be Convened This Day in the Fields in the City of New York," April 22, 1796, *PAH,* 20:131–34.

6. JM to TJ, May 9, 1796, *RL,* 2:937, 940. Historian Todd Estes explains that Washington had an "extraordinary sense of timing and use of delay." He waited until anger had abated before publicly embracing the less than ideal treaty. Estes also believes that Madison recognized the uncertainty of his constitutional argument that the House, because of its role in appropriations, rightly deserved to be involved in monitoring the treaty. See Estes, *Jay Treaty Debate,* 154, 160–61.

7. TJ to JM, March 6, 1796; JM to TJ, April 4, 1796, *RL,* 2:923–24, 929. The post road bill was defeated because some New England Federalists saw it as a ploy for using northern tax dollars to pay for improving southern roads. See "Post Road Survey," February 5 and 11, and May 19, 1796, *PJM,* 16:213, 221–22, 363; Joseph H. Harrison, Jr., "*Sic Et Non:* Thomas Jefferson and Internal Improvement," *Journal of the Early Republic* 7 (Winter 1987): 340; on the poor state of southern roads, see Richard B. Kielbowicz, "The Press, Post Office, and the Flow of News in the Early Republic," *Journal of the Early Republic* 3 (Autumn 1983): 277.

8. JM to Monroe, May 14, 1796, *PJM,* 16:358; Noble E. Cunningham, Jr., *The Jeffersonian Republicans: The Formation of Party Organization, 1789–1801* (Chapel Hill, N.C., 1959), 80–85.

9. As Madison had taken an instant dislike to Adams years earlier, Adams had a particular aversion to Gallatin, Madison's chief lieutenant in Congress. He proclaimed that the congressman's "Ignorance" had been exposed in a speech—the same speech that so enchanted Thomas Jefferson when he read it in Bache's paper that he pronounced it worthy of being added to the *Federalist Papers*! Previewing a prejudice Adams would carry into his presidency, he added of Gallatin: "It is intolerable that a Forreigner, should act such a Part as he has done and yet go on." John Adams to Abigail Adams, February 27 and April 28, 1796, *Adams Family Papers: An Electronic Archive,* Massachu-

setts Historical Society (http://www.masshist.org/digitaladams); TJ to JM, March 27, 1796, *RL*, 2:927–28.

10. TJ to Monroe, June 12, 1796, *PTJ*, 29:124; Nancy Isenberg, *Fallen Founder: The Life of Aaron Burr* (New York, 2007), 145–46. Already among Burr's powerful friends in the state of Virginia were Governor Robert Brooke, Henry Tazewell, and John Taylor of Caroline—the latter two had served with him in the U.S. Senate.

11. Madison exercised a commanding influence in Jefferson's Albemarle, where admiring friends took charge of rallying freeholders; farther west the population was thin, and he had little influence. In other places where the Republicans held sway, he lacked personal connections and was unable to identify who the moderates were; as a result, some diehards took center stage and made the Republican cause vulnerable to charges of "jacobinical" radicalism. See Richard R. Beeman, *The Old Dominion and the New Nation, 1788–1801* (Lexington, Ky., 1972), 132–35, 143–66.

12. Ibid., 161; Brant, 3:440.

13. Jeffrey L. Pasley, " 'A Journeyman, Either in Law or Politics': John Beckley and the Social Origins of Political Campaigning," *Journal of the Early Republic* 16 (Winter 1996): 531–69; Brant, 3:445.

14. JM to Monroe, September 29, 1796, *PJM*, 16:404, and *JMP-LC*. The numerical code used breaks up certain words into syllables or even individual letters; "Jefferson," for instance, which is designated 581 798 604 146, translates into "Je" "f" "fer" "son."

15. Adams to Abigail Adams, as quoted in *PJM*, 17:xix, and *RL*, 2:895.

16. TJ to Washington, June 19, 1796, *PTJ*, 29:127–28.

17. Washington to TJ, July 6, 1796, *PTJ*, 29:141–43.

18. Madison consulted with District of Columbia Commissioner and Virginian Alexander White, in discussing possible strategies for gaining support in Congress. See Alexander White to JM, September 26 and December 2, 1796, and Madison's two speeches on the National University, December 12 and December 26, 1796, *PJM*, 16:401–3, 421–22, 425–26, 436–38.

19. Felix Gilbert, *To the Farewell Address: Ideas of Early American Foreign Policy* (Princeton, N.J., 1961), 123–26. Gilbert's treatment is sound, but Stuart Leibiger's analysis of Washington's attitude toward Madison is a good deal more persuasive. See Leibiger, *Founding Friendship: George Washington, James Madison, and the Creation of the American Republic* (Charlottesville, Va., 1999), 209–14.

20. Gilbert, *To the Farewell Address,* 137–47.

21. See esp. U.S. senator Henry Tazewell to JM, October 3, 1796, *PJM*, 16:406–7.

22. Cunningham, *Jeffersonian Republicans,* 97–99.

23. *Gazette of the United States,* October 27, 1796.

24. "Cassius, No. II," *New Jersey Journal* [Elizabethtown], November 16, 1796. This particular piece went on to assert: "Men of narrow minds are delighted with the exercise of power . . . But great men accept offices as painful duties." Crediting Jefferson with the courage of his convictions was a subtle means of counteracting the Hamiltonian definition of masculine authority. The writer praised Jefferson's resistance to the "detestable influence" of a certain "insidious foreigner," exaggerating the foreignness of the

Caribbean-born Hamilton, at the same time insisting that Jefferson's deviation from Washington's political line was not a disqualifier, because Washington was not the arbiter of the "eternal nature" of truth.

25. *Columbian Herald* [Charleston, S.C.], July 23, 1793; *Aurora General Advertiser,* July 7, 1795; *Jersey Chronicle* [Mt. Pleasant], July 18 and November 28, 1795, originating with the *Aurora.*

26. For a compelling discussion in this regard, see Susan Dunn, "Revolutionary Men of Letters and the Pursuit of Radical Change: The Views of Burke, Tocqueville, Adams, Madison, and Jefferson," *William and Mary Quarterly* 53 (October 1996): 729–54.

27. Jones saw "Pelham's" impulse as an urge to instigate "a separation from the Southern people." Recall that Jefferson had only recently (to Madison) identified the Republicans as the party of the "Southern interest." See *Connecticut Courant,* November 21 and December 12, 1796; James C. Welling, *Connecticut Federalism, or Aristocratic Politics in a Social Democracy* (New York, 1890), 10–16; James Roger Sharp, *American Politics in the Early Republic: The New Nation in Crisis* (New Haven, Conn., 1995), 158–59; TJ to JM, April 27, 1795, *RL,* 2:877–78; Sharp, "Unveiling the Mystery of Jefferson's Letter of April 27, 1795," *Journal of the Early Republic* 6 (1986): 411–18; Joseph Jones to JM, December 1796 or January 1797, *PJM,* 16:448–49.

28. TJ to JM, January 1, 1797, with enclosure, *RL,* 2:952–55.

29. JM to TJ, January 15, 1797, *RL,* 2:956–58.

30. John Adams Inaugural Address, March 4, 1797, in James D. Richardson, comp., *A Compilation of the Messages and Papers of Presidents of the United States,* 20 vols. (New York, 1897–1917), 1:218–22; TJ to JM, January 22, 1797, *RL,* 2:960.

31. *JMB,* 2:954–60; TJ to Gerry, May 13, 1797, *PTJ,* 29:361–64.

32. Joseph J. Ellis, *Passionate Sage: The Character and Legacy of John Adams* (New York, 1993), 61–62.

33. James Morton Smith, *Freedom's Fetters: The Alien and Sedition Acts and American Civil Liberties* (Ithaca, N.Y., 1956), 189–91; Kurtz, *Presidency of John Adams,* 141; Abigail Adams to Mary Cranch, May 7, 1798, in Stewart Mitchell, ed., "New Letters of Abigail Adams," *Proceedings of the American Antiquarian Society* 55 (April–October, 1945), 347; Karen List, "The Role of William Cobbett in Philadelphia Party Press, 1794–1799," *Journalism Monographs* 82 (1993): 1–23. James Roger Sharp also provides a good brief assessment of the Adams-Jefferson dynamic and the slow disintegration of the relationship as the embassy to France was being considered; see Sharp, *American Politics in Early Republic* (New Haven, Conn., 1995), 160–67.

34. JM to James Madison, Sr., March 12, 1797, *PJM,* 16:500; *JMB,* 2:956.

35. Ketcham, 365, 370–72, 386–87; TJ to JM, January 3, 1798, *RL,* 2:1012.

36. "Address to the Senate," March 4, 1797, *PTJ,* 29:310–11.

37. By Paine's accounting, Washington had failed as president. "How America will scuffle through I know not," he opined, persuaded that "John Adams has not Character to do any good." He repeated himself later in the same letter: "Your Executive, John Adams, can do nothing but harm." Even if the much-admired Madison were dispatched to Paris, as was still being rumored, he could expect to accomplish nothing of sub-

stance, just because Adams had sent him. Paine to TJ, April 1 and May 14, 1797, *PTJ,* 29:340–44, 366–67.

38. TJ to Giles, March 19, 1796, *PTJ,* 29:35.

39. "Jefferson's Letter to Mazzei," April 24, 1796; "A Native American" to TJ, May 19, 1797, *PTJ,* 29:73–87, 382–84.

40. To take the allegory further, Samson was blinded by the Philistines as a result of having his head shaved while he slept; Solomon, idolatrous and undependable, had his kingdom divided after he turned against the God of Israel. Regarding Jefferson's explanation of the Mazzei letter to Martin Van Buren many years later, see Andrew Burstein, *The Inner Jefferson: Portrait of a Grieving Optimist* (Charlottesville, Va., 1995), 222–23; also Henry S. Randall, *The Life of Thomas Jefferson* (New York, 1858), 2:371–73; Malone, 3:308–11.

41. TJ to JM, August 3, 1797; JM to TJ, August 5, 1797, *RL,* 2:985–86, 990–91, 996–97; Monroe to TJ, July 12, 1797, *PTJ,* 29:478. It is meaningful that as part of his effort to convince Jefferson to stay out of the papers, Madison invoked the example of Washington, who (from Madison's direct knowledge) had not responded to the publication of forged Revolution-era letters attributed to him.

42. TJ to Mrs. Church, May 24, 1797, *PTJ,* 29:396–97.

43. "David Gelston's Account of an Interview between Alexander Hamilton and James Monroe," July 11, 1797; John Barker Church to Hamilton, July 13, 1797; "Printed Version of the 'Reynolds Pamphlet,' " *PAH,* 21:159–63, 238ff, quotes at 238, 239, 243; JM to TJ, October 29, 1797, *RL,* 2:993; Malone, 3:327–31. Months after their shouting match, Monroe was still inquiring of his friend Madison: "You will be so good as to tell me frankly yr. opinion of the footing upon wh. my correspondence with that Scondrel stands, and whether it becomes me to pursue him further." Monroe to JM, October 15, 1797, *PJM,* 17:50.

44. *JMB,* 2:963, 972; Malone, 3:239–40. Jefferson gave the couple the estate of Pantops, in Albemarle, and thirty-one slaves, but Maria and Jack chose to spend most of their time at the Eppeses' ancestral home.

45. "Notes on a Conversation with John Adams," *PTJ,* 30:113.

46. JM to TJ, February 12 and February 18, 1798; TJ to JM, February 15 and March 2, 1798, *RL,* 2:1018–21, 1024.

47. "Geoffrey Touchstone," *The House of Wisdom in a Bustle* (Philadelphia, 1798), quote at 21; see also *The Spunkiad, or Heroism Improved. A Congressional Display of Spirit and Cudgel* (Newburgh, N.Y., 1798); TJ to JM, February 15, 1798; JM to TJ, February 18, 1798, *RL,* 2:1019–22.

48. JM to Monroe, December 17, 1797; Monroe to JM, June 8, 1798, *PJM,* 17:61–62, 145–46.

49. Joanne B. Freeman, *Affairs of Honor: National Politics in the New Republic* (New Haven, Conn., 2001), 10.

50. TJ to JM, March 21–22, April 6, and April 12, 1798; JM to TJ, April 2, 1798, *RL,* 2:1028–36; TJ to Pendleton, April 2, 1798, *PTJ,* 30:242; Alexander DeConde, *The Quasi-War: The Politics and Diplomacy of the Undeclared War with France, 1797–1801* (New York,

1966); Sharp, *American Politics in Early Republic,* 171–73. Curiously, Jefferson's most adoring modern biographer considered Jefferson's position on the XYZ Affair to be "labored and injudicious" and his expectations from the Adams administration unrealistic. See Malone, 3:374.

51. JM to TJ, April 15, 22, and 29, 1798, *RL,* 2:1037, 1041, 1043.

52. TJ to JM, June 21, 1798, *RL,* 2:1008–10, 1060–61; Jean Edward Smith, *John Marshall: Definer of a Nation* (New York, 1996), 234–36. Marshall may have refused to pay the French agents X, Y, and Z; but he himself was paid handsomely by the Adams administration for his time abroad, netting $18,000 after expenses. He owed interest on his Virginia estate at this time, so it is no wonder that he should have been in good spirits and eager to perform more public service. Jefferson's annual income as vice president was only $5,000. Ibid., 238.

On the very same weekend as Marshall docked, Jefferson's Philadelphia Quaker friend George Logan left for Paris on an ostensibly selfless personal mission to make peace with France; the *Aurora* published a secret letter from Talleyrand, and Secretary of the Treasury Alexander Wolcott, a Hamilton ally, rushed to New York to interview an American returning from France, in the hope of uncovering a damning letter showing Jefferson's connection to a French plot. He, of course, failed to find anything. See Malone, 4:377–78.

53. Leonard Baker, *John Marshall: A Life in Law* (New York, 1974), 303–4; [John Thomson], *The Letters of Curtius* (Richmond, 1798), 3–7, 26–27, 32–35. Addressing the Adams administration's aggressiveness, Thomson sharply challenged the abuse of language that went along with a perverse policy. The word *France,* he charged, was "the *cabalistic* word" by which the Federalists had "silenced all opposition." Rancor was extreme, moderation mocked. "This delusion cannot last," he vowed. On Thomson's brief career, see Edward A. Wyatt IV, "John Thomson, Author of the 'Letters of Curtius,' and a Petersburg Contemporary of George Keith Taylor," *William and Mary Quarterly Historical Magazine* 16 (January 1936): 19–25. Thomson died in 1799, but he was memorialized by his admirer John Randolph of Roanoke in the next decade.

54. TJ to JM, August 3, 1797; JM to TJ, August 5, 1797, *RL,* 2:973–75, 985–91. Jefferson's contention was that the federal grand jury had no "sanctuary," no separate standing in the state, and was under the jurisdiction of the Virginia Assembly.

55. For the logic regarding Hamilton and Gallatin, see for example the *Republican Star* (Easton, Md.), October 19, 1802.

56. TJ to John Taylor of Caroline, June 4, 1798, *PTJ,* 30:389.

57. JM to TJ, May 20 and June 3, 1798, *RL,* 2:1051, 1056; John Ferling, *A Leap in the Dark: The Struggle to Create the American Republic* (New York, 2003), 424–25.

58. Cunningham, *Jeffersonian Republicans,* 125. A New Jersey Republican versified his resentment in the face of Federalists' accusations that the party's political opposition was unpatriotic because of its reluctance to challenge France:

> *The* Federalists *call us a cowardly band;*
> *But we will be foremost when danger's at hand;*
> *And we'll never be partial to gain the feign'd smile*
> *Of ship-wrecked Britain, who would us beguile.*

Embracing the Union, the poet mentioned Jefferson, Madison, Livingston, and Burr by name, wishing success to their efforts on behalf of liberty. See *Centinel of Freedom* (Newark, N.J.), September 25, 1798.

59. *Carey's United States' Recorder,* June 7 and June 28, 1798; *Columbian Centinel,* June 20, 1798.

60. Sharp, *American Politics in the Early Republic,* 181–82; John E. Ferling, *The First of Men: A Life of George Washington* (Knoxville, Tenn., 1988), 497–99; Ferling, *Leap in the Dark,* 436–41. The widow of publisher Thomas Greenleaf was indicted under the federal Sedition Law, after which Hamilton initiated a state libel prosecution so as to put her paper out of business. See Smith, *Freedom's Fetters,* 400; Isenberg, *Fallen Founder,* 172. For a somewhat sympathetic look at Hamilton's behavior relative to Adams's diplomatic posture and arguments suggesting a moderating desire on Hamilton's part, see Aaron N. Coleman, " 'A Second Bounaparty?': A Reexamination of Alexander Hamilton during the Franco-American Crisis, 1796–1801," *Journal of the Early Republic* 28 (Summer 2008): 183–214.

61. DeConde, *Quasi-War,* 90–95; JM to TJ, May 13, 1798, *RL,* 2:1048.

62. Tazewell to JM, June 28, 1798, *PJM,* 17:159.

63. "Notes on an American Dinner," "Toasts for an American Dinner," ca. July 4, 1798, *PJM,* 17:160–61. Madison inadvertently reversed the order of "former" and "latter." Part of the list was copied at an unknown time in Dolley Madison's handwriting.

64. The Boston story was reprinted in the Salem, N.Y., *Northern Centinel,* July 23, 1798. A bit earlier, Benjamin Franklin Bache made the same observation in the context of berating the Federalist press for its "party fanaticism" (*Aurora,* May 30, 1798).

65. Some months before, rival editor William Cobbett ("Peter Porcupine") had crudely urged that Bache be dealt with as "a TURK, A JEW, A JACOBIN, OR A DOG." At any rate, Bache's death did not immediately kill the *Aurora.* His handpicked successor married his widow, adding another layer of scandal to an already scandalous paper. See Jeffrey L. Pasley, *"The Tyranny of Printers": Newspaper Politics in the Early Republic* (Charlottesville, Va., 2001), 100–103; Malone, 3:384, 387, 390–92.

66. Randall, *Life of Thomas Jefferson,* 2:417–19; Malone, 3:431; for sources on Callender's Richmond trial, see *RL,* 2:1137–38; Pasley, *"Tyranny of Printers,"* 125. John Daly Burk was editor of the *Time-Piece,* which he had taken over from Madison's Princeton friend Philip Freneau; *JMB,* 2:997; on the history and tone of the *Time-Piece,* see Frank Smith, "Philip Freneau and the *Time-Piece and Literary Companion,*" *American Literature* 4 (November 1932): 270–87. The British had their counterpart in the cross-eyed outlaw John Wilkes, supporter of universal male suffrage, defender of the American Revolution, hero of the working class, and noted libertine and duelist, whose writings were suppressed and who was reelected to the House of Commons from prison. See Arthur H. Cash, *John Wilkes: The Scandalous Father of Civil Liberty* (New Haven, Conn., 2006).

The absurdity of some of the prosecutions under the Sedition Law of 1798 makes it hard to believe that they actually went forward. A New London, Connecticut, newspaper publisher was incarcerated for agitating against enlistment in the army. An inveterate drinker in Newark, New Jersey, was fined and jailed for suggesting as a target John Adams's posterior, when the president passed by in his stately carriage to the accompaniment of ceremonial cannon fire. Edward Livingston wrote trenchantly: "We have . . .

nothing to do but to make the law precise, and then we may forbid a newspaper to be printed, and make it death for any man to attempt it!" From his perch at the front of the Senate chamber, Vice President Jefferson had seen the onslaught coming in April, when he prophesied all of this in a letter to Madison. As he made out the rumblings of a newspaper suppression campaign, he had learned that Bache's paper would be the first condemned. See Smith, *Freedom's Fetters*, 116–30, 180–81, 270–73; TJ to JM, April 26, 1798, *RL*, 2:1042. James Roger Sharp notes Jefferson's return to use of the term *whig* in 1798, symbolizing the ever-increasing division between the parties and akin to the desperate situation of 1776. See Sharp, *American Politics in Early Republic*, 174.

67. James Morton Smith, "The Grass Roots Origins of the Kentucky Resolutions," *William and Mary Quarterly* 27 (April 1970): 221–45; Adrienne Koch and Harry Ammon, "The Virginia and Kentucky Resolutions: An Episode in Jefferson's and Madison's Defense of Civil Liberties," *William and Mary Quarterly* 5 (April 1948): 155–56; Breckinridge entry in *Biographical Directory of the American Congress* (Washington, D.C., 1950), 884.

68. It is not far-fetched to suggest, as Dumas Malone did in 1962, that in the frenzied political climate of 1798–99, the vice president himself could have been brought up on sedition charges and impeached for authoring the Kentucky Resolutions; Malone, 3:400. Madison's authorship of the Virginia Resolutions became known in 1809; Jefferson finally acknowledged his authorship of the Kentucky Resolutions in 1821.

69. *Columbia Centinel*, January 5, 1799. Another Boston paper reported that Breckinridge had made a journey to Virginia, and brought back with him the nine resolutions; it identified Jefferson as the individual behind them. See *Russell's Gazette*, December 24, 1798.

70. "Jefferson Draft of the Kentucky Resolutions of 1798," *RL*, 2:1080–81; for the three different versions of the Kentucky Resolutions, see "The Kentucky Resolutions 1798," *PTJ*, 30:529–56.

71. What made Jefferson's premise radical was his claim that each state had an "equal right" to nullify a law, and that state law had created a distinct boundary around Virginia that superseded the authority of the federal government. Freedom of speech, freedom of the press, and laws pertaining to aliens belonged under the state's purview. Jefferson was thus creating two spheres of law with severely proscribed boundaries: the states claimed responsibility for most domestic regulations, leaving the national government with a limited range of powers.

72. TJ to JM, December 16, 1786, *RL*, 1:458.

73. "Jefferson Draft of the Kentucky Resolutions of 1798," *RL*, 2:1082–84. More specifically, Jefferson laid out his theory in these critical terms: "In the case of an abuse of delegated powers, the members of the general government being chosen by the people, a change by the people would be the constitutional remedy; but, where powers are assumed which have not been delegated, a nullification of the act is the rightful remedy."

74. Madison spelled this out in greater detail in his *Report of 1800*, drafted to defend the Virginia Resolutions. He explained that the failure of the Alien Act to offer detailed instructions gave the president too much latitude and transferred the legislative power to him: "His will is the law." He contended as well that the president was "to stand in the place of the Judiciary also . . . , his order the only judgment which is to be executed." See *Report of 1800*, and "Virginia Resolutions," December 21, 1798, *PJM*, 17:188–89, 324–25.

75. "Virginia Resolutions," December 21, 1798, *PJM,* 17:189–90. Though Jefferson and Madison both relied on the Bill of Rights, Jefferson based his argument primarily on the Tenth Amendment, that "the powers not delegated to the U.S. by the constitution, nor prohibited to the states, are reserved to the states respectively, or to the people." He did mention the First Amendment but mainly as a corollary to his ruling principle that the freedom of speech was reserved to the states. Madison never mentioned the Tenth Amendment. His main contention was that the First Amendment proved that the Sedition Act was unconstitutional. On Madison's deliberations during the period during which the Resolutions were drafted and considered, see also Lance Banning, *The Sacred Fire of Liberty: James Madison and the Founding of the Federal Republic* (Ithaca, N.Y., 1995), 388–93.

76. Directly disagreeing with the implications of Jefferson's message to the Kentucky legislature, Madison posed to him: "Have you ever considered thoroughly the distinction between the power of the *State* and that of the *Legislature,* on questions relating to the federal pact." He was arguing that the state ratifying conventions (not the state legislatures) had forged the Union; an individual state legislature was not the legitimate organ for declaring federal laws null and void. In asserting each state's right to nullify an act of Congress that it deemed injurious, Jefferson was very close to the perspective South Carolina was to take, more ominously, in 1831. JM to TJ, December 29, 1798, *RL,* 2:1085; Ketcham, 395–97, 400; Brant, 3:462. Adrienne Koch provided the earliest analysis of the Jefferson-Madison exchange over the resolutions; see Koch, *Jefferson and Madison: The Great Collaboration* (New York, 1950), chap. 7.

77. The Connecticut legislature claimed that "controlling the measures of the general government," as expressed in the Kentucky and Virginia Resolutions, was "foreign to the duties of the State Legislatures." The Maryland legislature resolved that the Virginia Resolutions "contain the unwarrantable doctrine, of the competency of the State Government, by a legislative act, to declare an act of the Federal Government unconstitutional and void." Massachusetts denied that its state legislature had the power to decide the constitutionality of the acts of the federal government. The Delaware and New York legislatures treated the two sets of resolutions as the same. See "Connecticut, versus Virginia and Kentucky," *Columbian Centinel,* June 6, 1799; "Virginia and Kentucky Resolutions," signed "Civis," ibid., February 2, 1799; *Vergennes Gazette* [Vergennes, Vt.], March 7, 1799; "Maryland Legislature," *Philadelphia Gazette,* January 1, 1799; *Gazette of the United States,* February 7, 1799; on New York, see *Providence Gazette,* March 2, 1799, and *Philadelphia Gazette,* March 3, 1799.

78. Smith, "Grass Roots Origins of Kentucky Resolutions," 238–40. There was a strange twist when it came to the Virginia Resolutions: two versions existed. Without consulting Madison, Jefferson had contributed a subtle alteration to his friend's draft, convincing Wilson Cary Nicholas and John Taylor to add the phrase "that the [Alien and Sedition Acts] are, and were ab initio null, void and of no force, or effect." This was what first appeared in the national newspapers. But it was not the official version. Whether he was influenced by Madison or reached the decision on his own, Taylor changed the draft back to its original form just before it passed the Assembly.

Annulment meant that the marriage never existed; to be void *ab initio* was to be automatically considered null and void. Jefferson seemed to be saying that, in effect, the Alien and Sedition Acts never existed, because they relied on unconstitutional powers.

His language was declarative—there was no room for debate: the acts were illegitimate, invalid, without legal standing. He was probably drawn to the concept of annulment because it was based on the idea of higher law. An annulled marriage was not recognized in the eyes of God, and thus distinct from the rule of human or civil law. "Virginia Resolutions: Editorial Note," *PJM*, 17:187–88; Koch and Ammon, "Virginia and Kentucky Resolutions," 159–60.

79. Kevin Gutzman, "A Troublesome Legacy: James Madison and 'the Principles of 98,'" *Journal of the Early Republic* 15 (Winter 1995): 581.

80. *Oracle of Dauphin* [Harrisburg, Pa.], February 2, 1799; "Virginia Resolutions," *Columbian Centinel*, February 2, 1799; *Albany Centinel*, January 1, 1799; reprint of Cobbett's essay in "Virginia Folly and Impudence," *Albany Centinel*, January 1, 1799; "Truth and Patriotism," *Weekly Oracle* [New London, Conn.], March 11, 1799.

81. Washington to Henry, January 15, 1799, *PGW-RS*, 3:317–20; Ames to Wolcott, January 12, 1800, *Works of Fisher Ames*, ed. Seth Ames (Indianapolis, 1983), 2:1347; Ketcham, 397.

82. Henry to Washington, February 12, 1799, *PGW-RS*, 3:370–72.

83. *Baltimore Telegraph*, as reprinted in the New York paper *American Citizen*, July 31, 1800; *Bee*, September 24, 1800; similarly, the *Carlisle* [Pa.] *Gazette*, July 30, 1800, denoted Jefferson an "inestimable patriot" and stated, "We are not afraid of the effect of false, scandalous and malicious writings."

84. Washington to Marshall, December 30, 1798; Marshall to Washington, January 8, 1799; Adams to Washington, February 19, 1799, *PGW-RS*, 3:297, 309–10, 387–88.

85. Edmund Pendleton, *An Address of the Honorable Edmund Pendleton of Virginia to the American Citizens, on the State of Our Country* (Boston, 1799); TJ to Pendleton, January 29, 1799, *PTJ*, 30:661–62. Jefferson took an active interest in the circulation of pamphlets that he approved of, not just Pendleton's; see Dumas Malone, *Thomas Jefferson as a Political Leader* (Berkeley, Calif., 1963), 41–42.

86. "Madison's *Aurora General Advertiser* Essays," *PJM*, 17:211–20, 237–43. The plural use of *governments*, in the first essay, represents the common device of referring to the now-fifteen states of the federal Union; similarly, the common syntactical expression of this period: "The United States are . . ."

87. *JMB*, 2:998–1013.

88. Brant, 3:465.

89. TJ to JM, August 23, 1799, *RL*, 2:1118–19.

90. Monroe to JM, November 22, 1799, *PJM*, 17:278–79; Freeman, *Affairs of Honor*, 68.

91. In the summer of 1798 the widowed Eliza House Trist and her grown son were also added to the neighborhood. For many years she had been like family to the Virginia delegation who lodged at her popular Philadelphia boardinghouse. In the spring of 1799 Dr. William Bache, another Franklin grandson, was lured to Albemarle by Jefferson, acquiring six hundred acres a few miles north of Monticello, which he unimaginatively named "Franklin." See JM to Monroe, January 30, 1799, *PJM*, 17:222; Ammon, *James Monroe*, 170–73; *JMB*, 2:1037n; *PTJ*, 33:241n.

92. Lafayette to Washington, May 9, 1799; Washington to Timothy Pickering, July

14, 1799; William Vans Murray to Washington, August 17, 1799, *PGW-RS*, 4:54–59, 187, 261–62; William Howard Adams, *Gouverneur Morris: An Independent Life* (New Haven, Conn., 2003), 261–62. Lafayette also received a letter from Hamilton beseeching him not to come to America.

93. Patrick Henry, despite his own earlier denunciations of slavery, conveyed his human property to his wife and children in his will, allowing only in a codicil that his widow might wish to "set free one or two of my slaves." That still left dozens in bondage. His words of 1773 to a Quaker, commending that sect for the "moral and political good" of practicing abolition and urging all Americans to do the same, ring hollow. But Henry's hypocrisy was typical. Like most Virginia planters, on acquiring new property in 1797, he wrote to the seller: "I will also hire the Negroes as they are desirous to stay together & be not parted, & I will use them well." He accepted slavery as a responsibility, that is, owning slaves was morally supportable if they were "used well." See James M. Elson, ed., *Patrick Henry in His Speeches and Writings* (Lynchburg, Va., 2007), 66–68 and Appendix D; Henry to William M. Booker, October 31, 1797, Patrick Henry Papers, Library of Virginia, Richmond, Va.; Matthew Mason, *Slavery and Politics in the Early American Republic* (Chapel Hill, N.C., 2006), 19–21; Ferling, *First of Men*, 474–76.

94. Andrew Burstein, "Immortalizing the Founding Fathers: The Excesses of Public Eulogy," in Nancy Isenberg and Andrew Burstein, eds., *Mortal Remains: Death in Early America* (Philadelphia, 2003), 97–98.

95. "Death of George Washington," *PJM*, 17:295; Beeman, *Old Dominion and New Nation*, 216–17.

CHAPTER TEN

Inhaling Republicanism, 1800–1802

1. Noble E. Cunningham, Jr., *The Jeffersonian Republicans: The Formation of Party Organization, 1789–1801* (Chapel Hill, N.C., 1959), 131–33. Jefferson would continue into the next year encouraging the likes of Irishmen Matthew Lyon and John Daly Burk to publish. See *JMB*, 2:1014n. He and Madison also supported Lyon's son's *Friend of the People* and Samuel Harrison Smith's *National Intelligencer*. See JM to TJ, December 20, 1800, *RL*, 2:1155.

2. Madison's report was long and detailed and focused heavily on the law, incorporating the arguments of Virginia jurist St. George Tucker, who had authored a *Letter to a Member of Congress; Respecting the Alien and Sedition Laws*. See "The Report of 1800," *PJM*, 17:303–51, esp. 338, 344–48. The *Columbian Centinel* may have been correct when it recorded a year earlier that the Virginia and Kentucky Resolutions "have had a rapid passage from *Contempt* to *Oblivion*." See *Columbian Centinel*, January 1, 1799.

3. JM to TJ, February 14, 1800, *RL*, 2:1126. Jack N. Rakove writes that the centrality of foreign policy disputes in shaping Americans politics for two full decades after 1793 was unexpected and made "control of the presidency the decisive fact of American politics and governance." See Rakove, "The Political Presidency: Discovery and Invention," in James Horn, Jan Ellen Lewis, and Peter S. Onuf, eds., *The Revolution of 1800: Democracy, Race, and the New Republic* (Charlottesville, Va., 2002), quote at 46.

4. TJ to JM, March 4 and March 8, 1800, *RL*, 2:1127–29; Carl E. Prince, *New Jersey's Jeffersonian Republicans: The Genesis of an Early Party Machine, 1789–1817* (Chapel Hill,

N.C., 1967), 54–68; Cobbett letter of March 6, 1800, in *Letters from William Cobbett to Edward Thornton, Written in the Years 1797 to 1800*, ed. G.D.H. Cole (London, 1937), 67–68. Jefferson won 14 of 15 electoral votes in Pennsylvania in 1796.

5. Nancy Isenberg, *Fallen Founder: The Life of Aaron Burr* (New York, 2007), 197–202.

6. TJ to JM, April 4, 1800; JM to TJ, April 20, 1800, *RL*, 2:1132–34.

7. Votes published in *Herald of Virginia* [Fincastle], December 5, 1800; Daniel P. Jordan, *Political Leadership in Jefferson's Virginia* (Charlottesville, Va., 1983), 17–18; Cunningham, *Jeffersonian Republicans*, 196.

8. *Providence Journal*, July 9, 1800. Suggesting how spotty knowledge of Jefferson's association with the Declaration was, a seemingly illogical sentence appeared obscurely in the middle of an unrelated story in the Federalist *Alexandria Advertiser* on December 18, 1798: "The violent antipathy of some men to *Thomas Jefferson* is accounted for by his having framed the Declaration of American Independence." The verb *framed* had not been used previously to describe Jefferson's role. The Philadelphia *Aurora* and smaller Republican presses around the country had more regularly, and always approvingly, credited "the immortal" Jefferson for writing the Declaration and his "co-patriots" for playing their part in the "deathless instrument" of national birth. See, for example, *Aurora*, May 30, 1798; and the Salem, N.Y., *Northern Centinel*, July 23, 1798, reprinting from a Boston paper. See also Robert M. S. McDonald, "Thomas Jefferson's Changing Reputation as Author of the Declaration of Independence," *Journal of the Early Republic* 19 (Summer 1999): 169–95; Simon P. Newman, *Parades and the Politics of the Streets* (Philadelphia, 1997), chap. 3.

9. *Oracle of Dauphin and Harrisburgh Advertiser* [Harrisburg, Pa.], July 21, 1800, attributed to an unnamed New York paper.

10. *Courier of New-Hampshire*, May 15, 1800, from the *New-York Spectator*.

11. [James Thomson Callender], *The Prospect Before Us*, vol. 2 (Richmond, 1800), quotes at 74, 111. On Virginia, Callender chortled: "It would almost be worth while to collect into one body the sum total of scurrilous appellations which the stock-jobbing faction has bestowed on this state." The phrase "hoary headed incendiary" appears on p. 143 of volume 1 of the same work. In October–November 1800, when volume 2 was published, Jefferson paid for fifty copies and forwarded nine to Madison that Madison had requested. See TJ to JM, November 9, 1800, *RL*, 2:1152; *JMB*, 2:1028; Cunningham, *Jeffersonian Republicans*, 170–72.

12. *Newport Mercury*, September 30, 1800. A series of articles under the headline "The Jeffersoniad" had appeared over the summer in Boston's *Columbian Centinel* and such Federalist newspapers as the *Gazette of the United States*. "The Jeffersoniad No. V," for example, appearing on August 1 in the *Gazette*, dissected *Notes on Virginia* in such a way as to show Jefferson to be a hater of American commercial enterprise, a dangerous deist, and a selfish "southern philosopher, who secure in his cool grotto at Monticello, and sunned by his slaves, who are the cultivators of HIS EARTH, looks down with tranquil indifference" on the industrious merchants he would suppress as president.

13. JM to TJ, October 21, 1800, *RL*, 2:1151; JM to Monroe, ca. October 21, 1800, *PJM*, 17:426.

14. Brant, 4:13; Margaret Bayard Smith, *The First Forty Years of Washington Society*, ed. Gaillard Hunt (New York, 1906), 6–8. Popular democracy seemed to demand that fa-

vored statesmen be given traits of sociability, which was generally accomplished through descriptions of their refined and charming conversation. Federalists, opposing popular democracy, preferred to tar Republicans as crazed, lawless ideologues and cold, calculating atheists—the reverse image.

15. Beckley also took on the "fanatics, bigots, and religious hypocrites" who seized upon Jefferson's efforts to secure religious freedom and exaggerated his words in order to raise the specter of enforced atheism. "Our civil rights have no dependence on our religious opinions," he explained, citing the Virginia Statute for Religious Freedom, the entire text of which he included in his pamphlet. He then reminded readers of the enduring meaning of 1776 and the Declaration of that year, which must "preserve in the American mind, *forever* and *inseparable,* the names of Independence and Jefferson." [John Beckley], *Address to the People of the United States with an Epitome and Vindication of the Public Life and Character of Thomas Jefferson* (Richmond, 1800), 3–7, 22.

16. Abraham Bishop, *Connecticut Republicanism. An Oration on the Extent and Power of Political Delusion* (Albany, N.Y., 1801), Preface, 8, 41, 46, 60.

17. JM to TJ, December 5, 1796, *RL,* 2:948; Cunningham, *Jeffersonian Republicans,* 186; John Ferling, *Adams vs. Jefferson: The Tumultuous Election of 1800* (New York, 2004), 140–44; James H. Broussard, *The Southern Federalists, 1800–1816* (Baton Rouge, La., 1978), 17–19. It was Adrienne Koch who referred to Hamilton as a "boss" (according to its later meaning) when he went after Adams. See her *Jefferson and Madison: Great Collaboration,* 217.

18. Malone, 3:491–92.

19. Marty D. Matthews, *Forgotten Founder: The Life and Times of Charles Pinckney* (Columbia, S.C., 2004), 36–37, 140.

20. Ferling, *Adams vs. Jefferson,* 162–66.

21. TJ to JM, December 26, 1800, *RL,* 2:1156; Rev. James Madison to JM, December 28, 1800, *PJM,* 17:450–51; Cunningham, *Jeffersonian Republicans,* 188–89, 231–40; Matthews, *Forgotten Founder,* 96–105.

22. Bruce Ackerman, *The Failure of the Founding Fathers: Jefferson, Marshall, and the Rise of Presidential Democracy* (Cambridge, Mass., 2005); JM to TJ, January 10 and February 28, 1801, *RL,* 2:1156–57, 1162. Exhibiting personal animus in his political analysis, Madison considered Adams by this time to have "sunk in the estimation of all parties."

23. *Washington Federalist,* February 2, 1801.

24. Isenberg, *Fallen Founder,* 202–20.

25. Page to TJ, March 5, 1801, *PTJ,* 33:185–86.

26. John Davis, *Travels of Four Years and a Half in the United States of America; during 1798, 1799, 1800, 1801, and 1802* (London, 1803), 208, 222.

27. Leonard D. White, *The Jeffersonians: A Study in Administrative History, 1801–1829* (New York, 1961), 140–47.

28. *National Intelligencer,* March 6, 1801.

29. Malone, 4:37–49; "Wine provided at Washington," *JMB,* 2:1115–17.

30. Marshall to Pinckney, March 4, 1801, *The Papers of John Marshall,* ed. Charles F. Hobson (Chapel Hill, N.C., 1990), 6:89.

31. The first draft and final text are reprinted in *PTJ*, 33:134–52.

32. See Andrew Burstein, *Sentimental Democracy: The Evolution of America's Romantic Self-Image* (New York, 1999), 112.

33. For a complete analysis of how Madison, Jefferson, and their fellow Republicans had come to this formulation, in which popular sovereignty would prevent a nonrepresentative political party from holding on to power, see Peter S. Onuf, *Jefferson's Empire: The Language of American Nationhood* (Charlottesville, Va., 2000), chap. 3.

34. Nancy Shoemaker, *A Strange Likeness: Becoming Red and White in Eighteenth-Century North America* (New York, 2004), 125–26.

35. Rush to TJ, March 12, 1801; Knox to TJ, March 16, 1801, *PTJ*, 33:260–62, 313.

36. TJ to Monroe, March 7, 1801; to Page, March 23, 1801, *PTJ*, 33:208, 422–23.

37. *Gazette of the United States*, March 11, 1801, reprinted in *Spectator* [New York].

38. When Marshall wrote to Charles Cotesworth Pinckney on March 4, he was thinking in these terms; so was the quintessential Boston Federalist Harrison Gray Otis when he wrote, resignedly, in anticipation of Jefferson's election, that "the love of change...is stronger and more natural than the love of system." Robert Goodloe Harper, a South Carolina Federalist, qualified: "Names may change; the denominations of parties may be altered or forgotten; but the principles on which the federalists have acted must be adopted, their plans must be substantially pursued, or the government must fall to pieces." (In 1800, Harper moved from South Carolina to Baltimore, where he became a successful attorney.) As he watched the new president's dismissals of Federalist officeholders, another South Carolina Federalist, John Rutledge, assumed that popular reaction would be felt at the polls, and Federalists returned to power. See Samuel Eliot Morison, *Harrison Gray Otis, 1765–1828: The Urbane Federalist* (Boston, 1969), 173, 185; Broussard, *Southern Federalists, 1800–1816*, 44.

39. Jay C. Heinlein, "Albert Gallatin: A Pioneer in Public Administration," *William and Mary Quarterly* 7 (January 1950): 64–94.

40. Monroe to TJ, March 12, 1801, *PTJ*, 33:257–59. William Branch Giles expressed sentiments akin to those of Monroe but with even less nuance. He told Jefferson outright that the "principle of moderation" should not be taken very far, and that if he were to show "too much indulgence" to the Federalists, his best political friends would be deeply resentful. "It can never be unpopular," Giles coached, "to turn out a vicious man & put a virtuous one in his room." It was one thing to allow the minority to retain its voice, and quite another to deny justice to those who had been waiting in agony for change to come. Whereas Monroe saw particular problems with State Department appointments, Giles urged a clean sweep; the president should use all means at his disposal to rid the judiciary of its Federalists and punish the late administration for its many outstanding abuses. The enemy faction was not dead, Giles declared. "They only sleep." Giles to TJ, March 16, 1801, *PTJ*, 33:310–11.

41. "Vermont Republican" to TJ, April 3, 1801; Oliver Pollock to TJ, April 4, 1801; Lyon to TJ, April 4, 1801, *PTJ*, 33:532–38.

42. TJ to Gallatin, August 14, 1801, *PTJ*, 35:85; Pinckney to TJ, March 12, 1801; "Pardon for James Thomson Callender" (signed by TJ and Acting Secretary of State Levi Lincoln); Callender to TJ, April 12, 1801, *PTJ*, 33:259, 309–10, 573–74.

43. TJ to Lafayette, March 13, 1801; to Short, March 17, 1801; to Paine, March 18, 1801; J. Adams to TJ, March 24, 1801; S. Adams to TJ, April 24, 1801; "List of Candidates," "Lists of Appointments and Removals," *PTJ*, 33:270, 337–38, 358–59, 426, 638–39, 665–67, 674–75. In letters to Short, Jefferson was the least self-censoring, glibly alluding to the Federalists' slow self-destruction in having abandoned themselves to "a perfect frenzy," a loss of caution, "madness," and "paroxysm."

44. *JMB*, 2:1036–41; Brant, 4:41–43; Malone, 4:64.

45. Robert Allen Rutland, *James Madison: The Founding Father* (New York, 1987), 176–77; Brant, 4:48–51; TJ to Monroe, May 26 and May 29, 1801, *PTJ*, 34:185–86, 205.

46. *Philadelphia Gazette,* June 29, 1801; *Salem Gazette,* June 26, 1801, printed in other New England newspapers as well. These reports expressed a concern not part of the Philadelphia piece: that the relative equality of the states under the federal Constitution was all that restrained Virginia from pressing its ambition to govern the country south of New England.

47. Isenberg, *Fallen Founder,* 227–31; Ketcham, 413–14; TJ to Burr, September 4, 1801, *PTJ*, 35:204; *Aurora General Advertiser,* February 3, 1804.

48. Isenberg, *Fallen Founder,* 227, 231, 243–45, 255–56, 299.

49. William W. Clapp, *Joseph Dennie* (Cambridge, 1880); "A Layman" [Dennie], *The Claims of Thomas Jefferson to the Presidency, Examined at the Bar of Christianity* (Philadelphia, 1800), 10, 17–18, 27, 44–45; letters from Dennie to his mother, April 26, 1797, and May 20, 1800; and to Roger Vose, February 7, 1800, *The Letters of Joseph Dennie,* ed. Laura Green Pedder (Orono, Me., 1936), 159, 179–81.

50. *Port Folio,* January 3, January 31, April 11, May 2, May 9, and May 16, 1801.

51. White, *Jeffersonians: Study in Administrative History,* chap. 14; Daniel Preston on Thornton, in American National Biography Online.

52. See TJ to JM, February 12, 1799, *RL,* 2:1095; and TJ to Burr, February 11, 1799, *PTJ*, 31:22. Northern Republicans opposed establishing close ties to Louverture's government. Even Gallatin claimed that to recognize the black republic would "excite dangerous insurrections" in the southern states. New York mayor Edward Livingston also demanded guards to prevent French sailors from escaping into the country. Philippe Girard has argued that the open-door policy of the Adams administration worked because of Louverture's diplomatic balancing act. He secured aid from Britain and the United States in anticipation of the island's declaring independence; but he never broke from France. Philippe Girard claims that the U.S. Navy's support of Louverture "must rank as the first U.S. intervention in a foreign conflict." See Girard, "Black Talleyrand: Toussaint Louverture's Diplomacy, 1798–1802," *William and Mary Quarterly* 66 (January 2009): 93–94, 99, 109–10, 115–16; Douglas R. Egerton, "The Empire of Liberty Reconsidered," in Horn, Lewis, and Onuf, eds., *The Revolution of 1800,* 314–15; and TJ to JM, September 13, 1802, *RL,* 2:1248.

53. Jefferson's remarks were reported by Edward Thornton to Lord Grenville, March 28, 1801. See Editorial Note: "Avoiding the Maelstrom of Saint-Domingue 1 May–1 June 1801," and JM to Tobias Lear, June 1, 1801, in *PJM-SS,* 1:128–29, 243–44.

54. For a partial account of Pichon's report of his conversation with Madison, see *PJM-SS,* 1:403–4n1; for accounts of his conversations with Madison and Jefferson, see Carl Ludwig Lokke, "Jefferson and the Leclerc Expedition," *American Historical Review* 33

(January 1928): 323–24; and Tim Matthewson, *A Proslavery Foreign Policy: Haitian-American Relations during the Early Republic* (Westport, Conn., 2003): 99–100.

55. Rumors concerning the size of the army were circulated in London newspapers as early as October 7, 1801. General Leclerc was appointed only a week after the peace treaty was concluded between France and England on October 1. Rufus King sent Madison a private letter, informing him that a "considerable expedition of land and Sea forces will proceed to St. Domingo, and perhaps to Mississippi." When Robert Livingston confirmed the reports of the size of the expedition on November 22, he claimed that the "armament... will consist of 40,000 men." Philippe Girard calculates the initial force at around 19,500 men. See Matthewson, *Proslavery Foreign Policy*, 107; Lokke, "Jefferson and the Leclerc Expedition," 326; Philippe R. Girard, "The Ugly Ducking: The French Navy and the Saint-Domingue Expedition, 1801–1803," *International Journal of Navy History* 7 (December 2008): 1–25; Rufus King to JM, October 31, 1801; Robert Livingston to JM, November 22, 1801, *PJM-SS*, 2:214, 265–66; for newspaper reports on the French expedition, taken from London newspapers of October 7, see *Philadelphia Gazette*, November 27, 1801, and *Gazette of the United States*, November 27, 1801; for the report that the expedition will go from St. Domingue to Louisiana, see *Newburyport Herald*, December 29, 1801.

56. Madison laid out his theory in detailed letters to Charles Pinckney, minister to Spain, and to his fellow Virginian Wilson Cary Nicholas. Madison's view was shaped by James Monroe's intelligence when he was minister to France under Washington. Madison also sent a strongly worded letter regarding Louisiana to Rufus King, warning off Britain. See JM to Pinckney, June 9, 1801; to Nicholas, July 10, 1801; to King, July 24, 1801; Monroe to JM, June 1, 1801, in *PJM-SS*, 1:315, 275–76, 394, 407; 2:309.

57. Rufus King to JM, October 9, 1801, November 20, 1801, in *PJM-SS*, 2:167, 254–55; Robert W. Tucker and David C. Hendrickson, *Empire of Liberty: The Statecraft of Thomas Jefferson* (New York, 1990), 112, 114, 127, 129. Tucker and Hendrickson state that Jefferson's threats of an alliance with Great Britain were a diplomatic "feint" because London had no intention of disrupting the peace agreement with France over Louisiana. Jefferson's threats did not stop the French—only weather and a renewed British blockade stopped Napoleon's army from heading to Louisiana. In his correspondence with Tobias Lear, Madison confirmed that England was not opposed to the French expedition, and he expected a part of that force to head to Louisiana. See JM to Tobias Lear, January 8, 1802, February 26, 1802, *PJM-SS*, 2:373, 490.

58. JM to Robert Livingston, September 28, 1801, *PJM-SS*, 2:145; Tucker and Hendrickson, *Empire of Liberty*, 208–9. Jefferson told Pichon on December 3, 1801, that the French would fail if they tried to reinstitute slavery; see Matthewson, *Proslavery Foreign Policy*, 107. Lear agreed with Jefferson that blacks would never submit to the yoke of slavery. See Lear to JM, January 17, 1802, *PJM-SS*, 2:404–5.

59. On the demand for an end to the trade, or embargo, see Robert Livingston to JM, March 27, 1802, and Louis André Pichon to JM, March 17, 1802; Pichon hoped the U.S. Treasury would buy French government bills for $400,000 to be used for purchasing supplies for the Leclerc expedition; for Madison's rejection of this request, see Louis André Pichon to JM, March 22, 1802, and April 4, 1802; for Madison's protests against the unjust treatment of the two captains, see JM to Livingston, May 7, 1802; for his condemnation of the French policy and his subtle rebuke of Leclerc's high-handed mea-

sures, see JM to Livingston, July 6, 1802; for Leclerc's public accusation that the United States was in the service of Toussaint, see Livingston to JM, July 3 and July 30, 1802, all in *PJM-SS*, 3:42–43, 62–63, 78, 98, 196–97, 365–68, 373–74, 443–45; Matthewson, *Proslavery Foreign Policy*, 109–10; Hendrickson and Tucker, *Empire of Liberty*, 127–28; Lokke notes that Napoleon in his secret instructions told Leclerc to expect supplies from American merchants—a conclusion based on Jefferson's earlier statement to Pichon. See Lokke, "Jefferson and Leclerc Expedition," 328.

60. See TJ to Livingston, April 18, 1802, *TJP-LC*. Madison did not discount the utility of threats, but he urged that they be used with "delicacy," as he told Livingston in his official instructions before the start of the diplomatic mission. See JM to Livingston, September 28, 1801, *PJM-SS*, 2:144–45. For a compelling discussion of this moment in diplomacy, see James E. Lewis, Jr., "A Tornado on the Horizon: The Jefferson Administration, the Retrocession Crisis, and the Louisiana Purchase," in Peter J. Kastor and François Weil, eds., *Empires of the Imagination: Transatlantic Histories of the Louisiana Purchase* (Charlottesville, Va., 2009), 117–40.

61. King to JM, June 1, 1801; JM to Livingston, September 28, 1801; JM to TJ, May 7, 1802, *PJM-SS*, 1:251; 2:144–45; 3:195.

62. Tench Coxe to JM, November 28, 1801, *PJM-SS*, 2:181–83; TJ to James Monroe, June 1, 1802, *TJP-LC*. Talleyrand had used the threat of recognizing Toussaint and the new "black Frenchman" in his effort to convince Great Britain to sanction the French expedition to St. Domingue. See Robin Blackburn, "Haiti, Slavery, and the Age of Democratic Revolutions," *William and Mary Quarterly* 63 (October 2006): 659–60. When he appealed to Madison to impose an embargo on American merchants, Pichon used racial unity as a point of argument. See Louis André Pichon to JM, March 17, 1802, in *PJM-SS*, 3:41–43.

63. Rush to TJ, May 12, 1802, *Letters of Benjamin Rush*, ed. L. H. Butterfield (Princeton, N.J., 1951), 2:847–48.

64. Douglas R. Egerton, *Gabriel's Rebellion: The Virginia Slave Conspiracies of 1800 and 1802* (Chapel Hill, N.C., 1993).

65. Gary B. Nash, *Forging Freedom: The Formation of Philadelphia's Black Community, 1720–1840* (Cambridge, Mass., 1988), esp. chap. 6.

66. Jefferson did not believe that the capture of Toussaint would end the conflict. "Some other black leader will arise, and a war of extermination ensue," he wrote, "for no second capitulation will be trusted by the blacks." John Chester Miller, *The Wolf by the Ears: Thomas Jefferson and Slavery* (Charlottesville, Va., 1991), 138–39; TJ to Robert Livingston, April 18, 1802, *PTJ-LC*.

67. Davis, *Travels of Four Years and a Half in the United States of America*, 366–67.

68. Linda K. Kerber, *Federalists in Dissent: Imagery and Ideology in Jeffersonian America* (Ithaca, N.Y., 1970), chap. 2, quote at 324; Garry Wills, *"Negro President": Jefferson and the Slave Power* (Boston, 2003).

69. *Massachusetts Spy*, April 28, 1802, originating in the *Courant*.

70. *Charleston Daily Advertiser*, April 14, 1802; also, *The Republican or, Anti-Democrat*, May 10, 1802.

71. *Weekly Wanderer* (Randolph, Vt.), April 17, 1802; also *Pittsfield Sun*.

72. TJ to Livingston, April 18, 1802, *TJP-LC;* JM to Livingston, May 1, 1802; to Pinckney, May 11, 1802, *PJM-SS,* 3:174–78, 215–16; Malone, 4:286–91.

73. Laurent DuBois, "The Haitian Revolution and the Sale of Louisiana," in Kastor and Weil, eds., *Empires of the Imagination,* 93–116.

CHAPTER ELEVEN

The Embryo of a Great Empire, 1803–1804

1. Donald Jackson, *Thomas Jefferson and the Stony Mountains: Exploring the West from Monticello* (Urbana, Ill., 1981), esp. chap. 7; James P. Ronda, " 'A Knowledge of Different Parts': The Shaping of the Lewis and Clark Expedition," *Montana: The Magazine of Western History* 41 (Autumn 1991): 4–19; Ronda, "Dreams and Discoveries: Exploring the American West, 1760–1815," *William and Mary Quarterly* 46 (January 1989): 145–62; William E. Foley, "Lewis and Clark's American Travels: The View from Britain," *Western Historical Quarterly* 34 (Autumn 2003): 301–24.

2. Charles A. Miller, *Jefferson and Nature: An Interpretation* (Baltimore, 1988), 238–43.

3. TJ to Lewis, January 13, 1804, *TJP-LC;* Jackson, *Thomas Jefferson and Stony Mountains,* 128–29. Jefferson was interested not only in the Northwest but in the Southwest too. That expedition, tackling the Red River and testing Spanish power, did not fare as well. See Dan Flores, "Jefferson's Grand Expedition and the Mystery of the Red River," in Patrick G. Williams, S. Charles Bolton, and Jeannie M. Whayne, *A Whole Country in Commotion: The Louisiana Purchase and the American Southwest* (Fayetteville, Ark., 2005), 21–39.

4. Harold Hellenbrand, "Not 'To Destroy But to Fulfil': Jefferson, Indians, and Republican Dispensation," *Eighteenth-Century Studies* 18 (Autumn 1985): 539, 542; Bernard W. Sheehan, *Seeds of Extinction: Jeffersonian Philanthropy and the American Indian* (Chapel Hill, N.C., 1973), esp. 89–91, 245–48; Eve Kornfeld, "Encountering the Other: American Intellectuals and Indians in the 1790s," *William and Mary Quarterly* 52 (April 1995): 287–314; Francis Paul Prucha, *American Indian Policy in the Formative Years* (Cambridge, Mass., 1962), 215–17, 225–27; Anthony F. C. Wallace, *Jefferson and the Indians: The Tragic Fate of the First Americans* (Cambridge, Mass., 1999), 276–80. Brian Steele has recently addressed Jefferson's sense that Indian culture remained inferior if it "forced" women to labor in the fields; once Indian women were removed from hard labor, they could "literally reproduce the nation," by equaling the fertility rates of white women. See Steele, "Thomas Jefferson's Gender Frontier," *Journal of American History* 95 (June 2008): 19–24. On Jefferson's ease in sacrificing Indian lands and cultures to whites' manifest destiny, see Robert J. Miller, *Native America, Discovered and Conquered: Thomas Jefferson, Lewis & Clark, and Manifest Destiny* (Westport, Conn., 2006), chap. 4. On the banishment of Indians from the narrative of American character, see Steven Conn, *History's Shadow: Native Americans and Historical Consciousness in the Nineteenth Century* (Chicago, 2004).

5. Peter Gay, *The Enlightenment: The Science of Freedom* (New York, 1969), 348–53; Miller, *Jefferson and Nature,* 205–6; Ketcham, 417–20. The observation that Jefferson conceived of an empire without a metropolis comes from Peter S. Onuf, *Jefferson's Empire: The Language of American Nationhood* (Charlottesville, Va., 2000), 45. Jefferson's physiocratic thinking was consistent with his neurologically based theory of partisan differences. It was axiomatic for him that Republicans were *naturally* of "sound minds

and bodies." In 1802 he classified those he identified with as "the healthy, firm and virtuous feeling confidence in their physical and moral resources." Federalists, by contrast, were "timid," constitutionally predisposed to yield to strong, subversive leaders or welcome a return to monarchy. It could well be that in Jefferson's mind, Federalists' lesser identification with agricultural enterprise related to how their neurological health suffered due to their contentment with the status quo. Though a tireless, wide-ranging reader, Jefferson needed fixed models to back up what he might have put more simply, in purely political terms: Federalists resisted mass movement west because they feared a loss of control, the breakdown of class barriers, and the imagined results of democratic uplift. See Andrew Burstein, *Jefferson's Secrets: Death and Desire at Monticello* (New York, 2005), esp. 201–2; TJ to William Branch Giles, undated, but sometime after October 15, 1795, *PTJ*, 28:423–27; TJ to Joel Barlow, May 3, 1802, *TJP-LC*.

6. Jerry W. Knudson, *Jefferson and the Press: Crucible of Liberty* (Columbia, S.C., 2006), 102–4.

7. Madison's thinking here relates, as well, to checks and balances in the federal system put in place in order to diffuse destabilizing concentrations of power.

8. TJ to Breckinridge, August 12, 1803, *TJP-LC*.

9. TJ to Breckinridge, August 18, 1803; TJ to Wilson Cary Nicholas, September 7, 1803, *TJP-LC*. In his letter to Nicholas, Jefferson referred to an "unusual kind of letter" from the French minister to Madison, admitting that he would "acquiesce with satisfaction" if Congress ignored the need for an amendment. The phrase "safe & precise" also comes from the letter to Nicholas. Also see Ketcham, 421.

10. Henry Adams, *Life of Albert Gallatin* (Philadelphia, 1879), 320–22.

11. William Plumer of New Hampshire pointedly observed that only the Senate rules requiring a treaty to be read three times, and once a day, had prevented the treaty's passage on the first day. According to Plumer, the president was handed his "vast wilderness world" without having to face any opposition. See *William Plumer's Memorandum of Proceedings in the United States Senate, 1803–1807,* ed. Everett Somerville Brown (New York, 1923), 13–14; also *RL,* 2:1290–91; James E. Scanlon, "A Sudden Conceit: Jefferson and the Louisiana Government Bill of 1804," *Louisiana History* 9 (Spring 1968): 141.

12. *Aurora General Advertiser,* November 7, 1803; *American Citizen,* November 7, 1803; *Republican Star* [Easton, Md.], November 8 and November 15, 1803; *Alexandria Daily Advertiser,* January 9, 1804.

13. *Aurora General Advertiser,* January 6, 9, and 19, 1804; *Republican Advocate* [Fredericktown, Md.], February 10, 1804; "The Governor's Address to the Citizens of Louisiana," (New Orleans, December 1803); Brant, 4:159.

14. TJ to Breckinridge, November 12, 1803. Congressman George Washington Campbell of Tennessee also claimed that the new government would put residents "under the lash of despotism," reduced to "chattel." See *Annals of Congress,* 8th Cong., 1st sess., 1060, 1064–65; and Scanlon, "Sudden Conceit," 142, 144, 149.

15. Peter J. Kastor, *The Nation's Crucible: The Louisiana Purchase and the Creation of America* (New Haven, Conn., 2004), 36–41, 55–66.

16. TJ to Clinton, December 2, 1803, *TJP-LC*.

17. TJ to Monroe, November 24, 1801, *TJP-LC.*

18. Claiborne to JM, January 23, 1802, *JMP-SS,* 2:416; Adam Rothman, *Slave Country: American Expansion and the Origins of the Deep South* (Cambridge, Mass., 2005), 45–51; Lacy Ford, "Reconfiguring the Old South: 'Solving' the Problem of Slavery, 1787–1838," *Journal of American History* 95 (June 2008): 103–4.

19. TJ to Breckinridge, November 12, 1803; JM to TJ, August 20, 1784, [draft portion of letter,] *PJM,* 8:108; Steven Deyle, "'The Irony of Liberty: Origins of the Domestic Slave Trade," *Journal of the Early Republic* 12 (Spring 1982): 43–44, 60–61; Lewis Kerr to Isaac Briggs, March 24, 1804, cited in Ford, "Reconfiguring the Old South," 105–6.

20. Everett S. Brown, "The Senate Debate on the Breckenridge Bill for the Government of Louisiana, 1804," *American Historical Review* 22 (January 1917): 345–47, 350, 353–54. In 1798 John Nicholas and William B. Giles, both Virginians, had appealed similarly when the subject was allowing slavery in Mississippi Territory. At the time Congressman George Thatcher of Massachusetts, who had proposed keeping the restriction on slavery from the Northwest Ordinance in the Mississippi Territory bill, reacted to the diffusion argument: "The gentleman from Virginia...contended that certain States were overflowing with slaves, and if not colonized by opening this wide tract of country to them, they would not be able to keep or manage them... The gentleman wished to take the blacks away from places where they are huddle up together, and spread them over this territory; they wished to get rid of them, and to plague others with them." *Annals of Congress,* 5th Cong., 2nd sess., 1308–11; Rothman, *Slave Country,* 24–26.

21. *Annals of Congress,* 8th Cong., 1st sess., 60. Tench Coxe had advocated diffusion to Madison in 1801, calling for tight restrictions on the foreign slave trade and a stronger militia to avoid the dangers previewed in the Caribbean; see Coxe to JM, December 12, 1801, *PJM-SS,* 2:307–8; TJ to Monroe, November 24, 1801, *PTJ,* 35:718–21; TJ to David Barrow, May 1, 1815, *TJP-LC.*

22. Joseph T. Hatfield, *William Claiborne: Jeffersonian Centurion in the American Southwest* (Lafayette, La., 1976); Kastor, *Nation's Crucible,* 36–41, 55–66; Claiborne to JM, December 27, 1803, January 31, February 4, March 1, and May 12, 1804, *PJM-SS,* 6:231, 416, 428–29, 525; 7:210.

23. Brant, 4:56–57, 160–70; Malone, 4:93–94, 376–77. As to Madison's reluctance to commit an opinion without first knowing Jefferson approved, see JM to TJ, April 24, 1804, *RL,* 2:1323, in an instance involving Governor Claiborne of Louisiana and Secretary Gallatin and the establishment of a state bank. Madison distinguished between private letters expressing "sentiments" and official letters expressing the government's position. It is also an example of the seamless communication of Madison, Gallatin, and the president.

24. Catherine Allgor, *Parlor Politics* (Charlottesville, Va., 2000), 34–47; Malone, 4:377–83; JM to Monroe, February 16, 1804, *PJM-SS,* 6:484–86. The French minister separately confirmed Madison's and Jefferson's assessment of the negative impact Mrs. Merry's resentments had on other Washington diplomat families.

25. Burr to Theodosia Burr, October 16, 1803, and January 17, 1804, in *Correspondence of Aaron Burr and His Daughter Theodosia,* ed. Mark Van Doren (New York, 1929), 129, 147–48; Catherine Allgor, *A Perfect Union: Dolley Madison and the Creation of the Amer-*

ican Nation (New York, 2006). Allgor's portrait of Dolley Madison is very insightful, though her penchant to diminish James in order to lift Dolley to preeminence amounts to caricature; Monroe to JM, July 1, 1804, *PJM-SS*, 7:404.

26. JM to Robert Livingston, January 31, 1804, *PJM-SS*, 6:411–12; *Albany Gazette*, December 19, 1805, reporting a decree from the French general governing Haiti, which stated that all American vessels bringing supplies to the "revolted Negroes" would face "seizure and condemnation."

27. Robert A. Rutland, who calls Secretary of State Madison Jefferson's "assistant chief executive," has pointed out the difficulty of knowing precisely what Madison and Jefferson discussed in private from 1801 to 1809; he cites Jefferson's letter at the end of his presidency, in which he reminded Madison: "A short conference saves a long letter." See Rutland, *James Madison: The Founding Father* (New York, 1987), 169–70. See TJ to JM, August 7 and August 18, 1804, *RL*, 2:1332–33, 1337–38, for pertinent examples (among many) of the transatlantic correspondence they shared and the opinions they hazarded to each other. They were open about their complaints against Livingston, whose letters to the State Department were deficient, in Madison's judgment, and whose "quarrelsome disposition" irritated Jefferson. See also JM to TJ, August 4 and August 18, 1804, and TJ to JM, August 18, 1804, ibid., 1331, 1338.

28. James R. Sofka, "The Jeffersonian Idea of National Security: Commerce, the Atlantic Balance of Power, and the Barbary War, 1786–1805," *Diplomatic History* 21 (Fall 1997): 519, 526.

29. TJ to JM, August 28, 1801, *RL*, 2:1193–94; Samuel Smith to Captain Richard Dale, May 20, 1801, in *Naval Documents Relating to the United States Wars with the Barbary Powers* (Washington, D.C., 1939), 1:467; Frank Lambert, *The Barbary Wars: American Independence in the Atlantic World* (New York, 2005), 124–25, 133; "Editorial Note: Dispatching a Naval Squadron to the Mediterranean 20–21 May 1801," *JMP-SS*, 1:198–99.

30. David A. Carson, "Jefferson, Congress, and the Question of Leadership in the Tripolitan War," *Virginia Magazine of History and Biography* 94 (October 1986): 410, 412, 415, 417–18; "Jefferson's Cabinet Notes, May 15, 1801," *TJP-LC*; Lambert, *Barbary Wars*, 126; Sofka, "Jeffersonian Idea of National Security," 538.

31. Humphreys to JM, April 24, 1801, *JMP-SS*, 1:92; "Jefferson's Cabinet Notes, May 15, 1801"; Gallatin to TJ, September 12, 1805, *TJP-LC*.

32. Decatur received a promotion and was commended by the secretary of the navy for his "gallant conduct" in a "brilliant enterprise." The president ceremonially awarded him a sword. See Michael Kitzen, "Money Bags or Cannon Balls: The Origins of the Tripolitan War," *Journal of the Early Republic* 16 (Winter 1996): 601–24; Robert J. Allison, *The Crescent Obscured: The United States in the Muslim World, 1776–1815* (New York, 1995); Gardner W. Allen, *Our Navy and the Barbary Corsairs* (Boston, 1905), 173–77; Lambert, *Barbary Wars*, 128–30, 142–44.

33. Humphreys to JM, April 24, 1801, James Leander Cathcart to JM, July 2, 1801, JM to Lear, July 14, 1803, *JMP-SS*, 1:92, 370–71; 5:178; G. A. Starr, "Escape from Barbary: A Seventeenth-Century Genre," *Huntington Library Quarterly* 21 (November 1965): 35–52. Franklin was not alone in criticizing southern slavery with his comparison to the Islamic practice. Royall Tyler's *The Algerine Captive* (1797) was the most popular American work on the Barbary captives, and he too emphasized that American slavery was no bet-

ter, and perhaps worse, than the Algerine practice. See Thomas S. Kidd, " 'Is It Worse to Follow Mahomet than the Devil?' Early American Uses of Islam," *Church History* 72 (December 2003): 766, 788. A former U.S. captive, William Ray, also published a memoir in 1808, in which he ridiculed the abuse of American sailors by their officers and compared them to African-American slaves; see William Ray, *Horrors of Slavery; or, the American Tars in Tripoli*, ed. Hester Blum (Troy, N.Y., 1808; rpt., New Brunswick, N.J., 2008), xix–xx; Lambert, *Barbary Wars*, 40, 110, 118, 120, 161; Sofka, "Jeffersonian Idea of National Security," 542. This was not the only kind of representation Americans had access to; a 144-page history of Barbary described a "tawny"-colored people both "superstitious and cruel." Its author led up to his explanation of current events with an account of the prophet Muhammad who, according to the Koran, urged his followers to fight to the death and fear nothing in so doing. The people of North Africa still, it was said, believed in evil spirits and in a destiny ordained by God; they acknowledged no law but "force and convenience." See Stephen Cleveland Blyth, *History of the War between the United States and Tripoli and Other Barbary Powers* (Salem, Mass., 1806), quotes at 4, 40, 127–28.

34. Jefferson's reference to St. Domingue as the "American Algiers" is in TJ to JM, February 5, 1799; his reference to the Spanish provincial governors as "pigmy kings" in TJ to JM, August 30, 1802, *RL*, 2:1093, 1242. He used similar language some years earlier in a letter to James Monroe, in complaining that the federal government was making an unlawful attempt to transfer power from the House of Representatives to the president, the Senate, or "any other Indian, Algerine or other chief." TJ to Monroe, March 21, 1796, *PTJ*, 29:41–42. Jefferson also expressed his willingness to use force against Spain, suggesting an attack on a Spanish garrison in 1792, and again while he was president. See Sofka, "Jeffersonian Idea of National Security," 528; and TJ to JM, October 23, 1805, wherein he claimed that if Spain interfered with the status quo, "we shall repel force by force." *RL*, 3:1395. Also see TJ to JM, September 14, 1803, *RL*, 2:1285–86.

35. JM to Levi Lincoln, July 25, 1801, Humphreys to JM, April 24, 1801, *PJM-SS*, 1:92, 476; TJ to Cooper, February 18, 1806, *TJP-LC*; Cooper was a staunch Jeffersonian found guilty of libeling President Adams in 1800 and was briefly imprisoned under the Sedition Act. On Jefferson's idea of informal leagues of nations, see Sofka, "Jeffersonian Idea of National Security," 534, 539.

36. William van Alstyne and John Marshall, "A Critical Guide to Marbury v. Madison," *Duke Law Journal* (February 1969): 3–8.

37. TJ to William B. Giles, March 23, 1801, *PTJ*, 33:413–14; TJ to JM, August 13, 1801, *RL*, 3:1186; William Marbury to JM, December 16, 1801, *PJM-SS*, 2:319–20. If Madison disagreed with the posture Jefferson took, there is no evidence of it. It is Bruce Ackerman who has suggested that Jefferson "muzzled" Madison; see Ackerman, *The Failure of the Founding Fathers: Jefferson, Marshall, and the Rise of Presidency Democracy* (New York, 2005), 191.

38. TJ to John Dickinson, December 19, 1801, *PTJ*, 36:165–66. Newspapers friendly to the administration saw Marshall's determination as a pathetic ploy to irritate the executive: "The Tories talk of dragging the President before the court, and impeaching him, and a wonderful deal of similar nothingness. But it is easy to see this is all *fume*, which can excite no more than a ludicrous irritation." See reprint from the *Aurora*, De-

cember 22, 1801, in *Centinel of Freedom* [Newark, N.J.], December 29, 1801. Other Republican papers reported "dark and mysterious appointments" as a desperate act by President Adams. See *American Citizen,* January 4, 1802; and *Aurora,* December 30, 1801.

39. Van Alstyne and Marshall, "Critical Guide to Marbury v. Madison," 4–5. According to Carl Prince, Jefferson was able to remove 18 of 30 Federalist judges, out of a total of 32 individuals appointed. He also replaced 13 of 21 district attorneys (11 of them Federalists) and 18 of 29 U.S. marshals. Of 316 offices, he forced out at least 146 incumbents (46 percent), at least 118 (37 percent) of whom were Federalists. Carl Prince, "The Passing of the Aristocracy: Jefferson's Removals of the Federalists, 1801–1805," *Journal of American History* 57 (1970): 565–68.

40. *Annals of Congress,* 7th Cong., 1st sess., 628, 662; also see Ackerman, *Failure of Founding Fathers,* 152, 154; and James M. O'Fallon, "Marbury," *Stanford Law Review* 44 (January 1992): 238.

41. Ackerman, *Failure of Founding Fathers,* 156; Charles Hobson, "John Marshall, the Mandamus Case, and the Judiciary System, 1801–1803," *George Washington Law Review* 72 (December 2003): 295; *Annals of Congress,* 7th Cong., 1st sess., 38, 82.

42. *Marbury v. Madison,* 5 (1 Cranch) (1803); also see Hobson, "John Marshall," 299.

43. Marshall personally felt that forcing Supreme Court judges to share the duties of district judges (which would eliminate the need for more district court judges) was unconstitutional, and he had discussed the possibility of a boycott with his colleagues on the bench. But the justices decided not to make it a political issue and resumed the duties of riding the circuit. See R. Kent Newmeyer, "Symposium: Marbury v. Madison and the Revolution of 1800," *George Washington University Law Review* 72 (2003): 312; Van Alstyne and Marshall, "Critical Guide to Marbury v. Madison," 35–37; Larry Kramer, "Understanding *Marbury v. Madison,*" *Proceedings of the American Philosophical Society* 148 (March 2004): 25–26; and for the importance of *Stuart v. Laird,* whose opinion was written by Justice William Paterson and not Marshall, see Ackerman, *Failure of Founding Fathers,* 185–89, 193–94.

44. While entirely speculative, this explanation is meant to provide additional insight into Jefferson's mind. That he might have handed over the commission with a statement designed to limit judicial interference with executive authority is inferred from Jefferson's action in 1807, when Marshall issued a subpoena *duces tecum* ordering him to hand over documents during Aaron Burr's treason trial. At that time the president gave the court the required documents, while reserving the right to withhold any document containing confidential information. See Nancy Isenberg, *Fallen Founder: The Life of Aaron Burr* (New York, 2007), 345.

45. *Port Folio,* January 22, 1803 (on Monroe), and December 8, 1804 (on Madison).

46. Davis, *Travels of Four Years and a Half,* 366.

47. *Republican Star,* September 21, 1802; *Trenton Federalist,* October 4, 1804. One of the "abandoned libelers" named was William Coleman, who had been set up in 1800 as editor of the *New-York Evening Post* by Alexander Hamilton.

48. *Port Folio,* July 10, July 17, October 2, and October 30, 1802. On the use of slave speech in satire during this period, see Robert Secor, "Ethnic Humor in Early American Jest Books," in *A Mixed Race: Ethnicity in Early America,* ed. Frank Shuffelton (New York, 1993), 172–76. For more on Dennie's mockery of Jefferson and Hemings, and a larger

discussion of Dennie's treatment of race and gender, see Catherine O'Donnell Kaplan, *Men of Letters in the Early Republic: Cultivating Forums of Citizenship* (Chapel Hill, N.C., 2008).

49. *United States Chronicle*, September 16, 1802.

50. *Port Folio*, February 19, 1803.

51. *American Citizen*, June 29 and July 5, 1803. Manhattanites knew Richard Croucher from a lurid trial of 1800, when Burr and Hamilton served as cocounsel for an accused young man who very likely killed his fiancée; in that instance one of the defense attorneys interrogated Croucher, a prosecution witness, and suggested that he was likelier than their well-groomed client to have done the deed. Croucher was subsequently convicted in the murder of a different woman.

52. *Hornet* [Fredericktown, Md.], August 2, 1803, taken directly from the *Virginia Gazette; National Aegis* [Worcester, Mass.], August 3, 1803; *Newburyport Herald,* July 29, 1803. The *Rhode Island Republican* had referred to Callender as a "notorious drunkard" in its July 16 issue, prior to Callender's drowning.

53. *Trenton Federalist,* January 2, 1804.

54. *Republican Star,* September 7, 1804; Robert Richardson to TJ, March 31, 1824, in Thomas Jefferson Papers, Tucker-Coleman Collection, College of William and Mary.

55. C. Peter Magrath, *Yazoo: Law and Politics in the New Republic* (New York, 1966); Daniel P. Jordan, *Political Leadership in Jefferson's Virginia* (Charlottesville, Va., 1983), 158–65; Robert Dawidoff, *The Education of John Randolph* (New York, 1979), 173–82 ; *Moultrie v. Georgia,* in *The Documentary History of the Supreme Court of the United States, 1789–1800,* ed. Maeva Marcus and James R. Perry (New York, 1985), 5:496–511; Malone, 4:448–57; Brant, 3:230–40.

56. TJ to JM, April 13, 1803, *RL,* 2:1307; Andrew Burstein, *The Inner Jefferson: Portrait of a Grieving Optimist* (Charlottesville, Va., 1995), 141–43, 191–92.

57. Abigail Adams to TJ, May 20, 1804; TJ to Abigail Adams, June 13, 1804, *The Adams-Jefferson Letters: The Complete Correspondence between Thomas Jefferson and Abigail and John Adams,* ed. Lester J. Cappon (Chapel Hill, N.C., 1959), 268–71.

58. A. Adams to TJ, July 1, August 16, and October 25, 1804; TJ to A. Adams, July 22 and September 11, 1804, ibid., 271–82.

59. Edith B. Gelles, *Portia: The World of Abigail Adams* (Bloomington, Ind., 1992), 103.

60. Plumer to D. Lawrence, December 27, 1802, in William Plumer, Jr., *Life of William Plumer* (Boston, 1857), 247.

61. *Port Folio,* October 29, 1803, July 28, August 4, and October 13, 1804. The sexual satire was written by Josiah Quincy, as "Climenole." A Connecticut Republican earlier explained the proper understanding of the word *democrat:* "The terms *republican* and *democrat,* are used synonimously [sic] thro'out, because the men who maintain the principles of 1776, are characterized by one or the other of these names, in different parts of the country." See Abraham Bishop, *Connecticut Republicanism* (Albany, N.Y., 1801), 9.

62. Hamilton to Morris, February 22 and February 29, 1802, "The Examination, Nos. XII & XIII," and "To the *New-York Evening Post,*" in the *New-York Evening Post,* February 23, 24, and 27, 1802, *PAH,* 25:527–45. A year and a half later Hamilton was still trying to prove that Madison had had strong monarchical tendencies in 1787–88. See

exchanges with Timothy Pickering, in which Hamilton concluded, "if I sinned against Republicanism, Mr. Madison was not less guilty." Hamilton to Pickering, September 16, 1803; Pickering to Hamilton, October 18, 1803, *PAH*, 26:147–49, 160–61; *National Intelligencer*, October 22, 1804; *Port Folio*, April 23, 1803.

63. Isenberg, *Fallen Founder*, 256–69 and passim. Hamilton's actual date of birth is uncertain. Many historians have accepted it as 1755; some take it as 1757.

64. *William Plumer's Memorandum of Proceedings in the United States Senate, 1803–1807*, ed. Everett Somerville Brown (New York, 1923), 193, 203–4; Brant, 4:246–47.

65. *Port Folio*, August 18 and September 1, 1804; *National Intelligencer*, March 2, 1804.

66. *Republican Farmer* [Bridgeport, Conn.], October 24, 1804.

67. *William Plumer's Memorandum of Proceedings*, 186–93. On the subject of Madison's aggressive foreign policy in 1803–04, see Ketcham, 421–25; also JM to Monroe, December 26, 1803, *PJM-SS*, 6:213. Envoys Monroe and Livingston also believed that West Florida was included in the Louisiana Purchase; see Charles Pinckney to JM, January 24, 1804, *PJM-SS*, 6:384; Tucker and Hendrickson, *Empire of Liberty*, 137–56.

68. Burstein, *Sentimental Democracy*, 224–25.

69. "Curtius" [John Taylor of Caroline], *A Defence of the Measures of the Administration of Thomas Jefferson* (Washington, 1804), 10–11, 16–17, 123–36. In arguing that the Jefferson administration had consistently acted in the national and not a partisan interest, Taylor reasoned that the emergent West would be the South's competitor and the North's partner in commerce.

CHAPTER TWELVE

Years of Schism, Days of Dread, 1805–1808

1. *Republican Farmer*, January 2, 1805.

2. Daniel P. Jordan, *Political Leadership in Jefferson's Virginia* (Charlottesville, Va., 1983), 99.

3. Annette Gordon-Reed, *The Hemingses of Monticello* (New York, 2008), 589–90; Malone, 5:65, 127–32.

4. "Notes on a Draught for a second inaugural Address" and extant drafts of the second inaugural address, March 4, 1805, *TJP-LC*.

5. *Morning Chronicle* (New York), March 12, 1805.

6. "Mr. Elliot to His Constituents," in *Vermont Journal*, as reprinted in *Albany Gazette*, June 6, 1805.

7. Henry Adams, *John Randolph* (1882; rpt. Armonk, N.Y., 1996), 94–106, quotes at 95, 99; Lynn Hudson Parsons, *John Quincy Adams* (Madison, Wisc., 1998), 77; Nancy Isenberg, *Fallen Founder: The Life of Aaron Burr* (New York, 2007), 273–79.

8. *Republican Advocate* [Fredericktown, Md.], March 5, 1805. The case against Justice Chase had been spelled out in the newspaper over the preceding weeks, in a series titled "Truth Stark Naked."

9. Ketcham, 436–38; Adams, *John Randolph*, 111–13, 123; Randolph speech citing Monroe commented on in *Charleston Courier*, February 9, 1803; Harry Ammon, *James*

Monroe: The Quest for National Identity (New York, 1971), 244–45. Federalists, too, were highly skeptical about the funds being used to bribe France to convince Spain to sell Florida. See James H. Broussard, *The Southern Federalists, 1800–1816* (Baton Rouge, La., 1978), 116; David A. Carson, "That Ground Called Quiddism: John Randolph's War with the Jefferson Administration," *American Studies* 20 (April 1986): 75, 84.

10. *Annals of Congress*, vol. 3, March 5, 1806, 424–33. In his nostalgia for 1798, Randolph invoked the name of the ill-fated young Petersburg lawyer John Thomson, author that year of the "Letters of Curtius," who had promoted Virginia republicanism while criticizing John Marshall upon his tumultuous welcome home as the hero of the XYZ Affair. Thomson was "the greatest man whom I ever knew," Randolph declared to his congressional colleagues. He now used Thomson's example to lambaste Madison and Jefferson for going behind the people's backs, which he characterized as "the proneness of cunning people to wrap up and disguise in well-selected phrases, doctrines too deformed and detestable to bear exposure in naked words."

11. Joseph T. Hatfield, *William Claiborne: Jeffersonian Centurion in the American Southwest* (Lafayette, La., 1976), 154–62.

12. *New-York Spectator*, March 12, 1806; *United States Gazette*, March 12, 1806; *Alexandria Gazette*, reprinted ibid.; similarly, see *Newport Mercury*, March 22, 1806, reporting that Randolph treated Madison with "the greatest contempt." The Federalist paper argued: "His whole speech was in total opposition to everything democratical."

13. Adam L. Tate, *Conservatism and Southern Intellectuals, 1789–1861* (Columbia, Mo., 2005), 15–16; Norman K. Risjord, *The Old Republicans: Southern Conservatism in the Age of Jefferson* (New York, 1965), 24–31; Ketcham, 436; Robert Allen Rutland, *James Madison: The Founding Father* (New York, 1987), 178; Ammon, *James Monroe*, 255.

14. *William Plumer's Memorandum of Proceedings in the United States Senate, 1803–1807*, ed. Everett Somerville Brown (New York, 1923), 219; Brant, 4:244–46.

15. Ketcham, 442–44; Jefferson's Fifth Annual Message, December 3, 1805, *TJP-LC*; Julia H. Macleod, "Jefferson and the Navy: A Defense," *Huntington Library Quarterly* 8 (February 1945): 173–77.

16. Broussard, *Southern Federalists*, 86.

17. *Republican Spy*, September 3, 1805; *Morning Chronicle*, March 10, 1806.

18. *Republican Watch-Tower*, January 6, 1806; *Tickler*, September 16, 1806.

19. Andrew Shankman, *Crucible of American Democracy: The Struggle to Fuse Egalitarianism and Capitalism in Jeffersonian Pennsylvania* (Lawrence, Kan., 2004), 1–2, 84–85, 96–102, 141–43, 154–60, 174.

20. Rush to Adams, August 14, 1805, April 22, 1807, and January 13, 1809, in *Letters of Benjamin Rush*, ed. L. H. Butterfield (Princeton, N.J., 1951), 2:900–901, 941, 993. Note that the plural form of *government* referenced the united *states* while expressing the meaning of federal union. The reason for the trip to Philadelphia was Mrs. Madison's health. The renowned Dr. Philip Syngh Physick was consulted to evaluate whether she would need surgery for a growth on her leg.

21. *South Carolina State Gazette*, May 20, 1802; *New-York Spectator*, March 14, 1804, announcing: "*Democrat* against *Democrat*—'a consummation devoutly to be wished.' "

Referring to the Burr-Clinton rivalry, the *Newburyport* [Mass.] *Herald*, on July 26, 1803, stated that "the schism is great, and the dissention sharp and severe." According to the *Connecticut Centinel* of June 22, 1802, that "schism in the democratic party has been maturing ever since the Presidential election." On Duane's impressions, see Noble E. Cunningham, Jr., *The Jeffersonian Republicans in Power: Party Operations, 1801–1809* (Chapel Hill, N.C., 1963), 224.

22. TJ to JM, November 8, 1806, *RL,* 3:1455–56; JM to General Williams, November 9, 1806, *JMP-LC.*

23. TJ to JM, August 16, 1807, *RL,* 3:1485–86.

24. Madison's bold actions in 1810, as president, in the seizure of West Florida, provide ample proof of this. See Chapter 13.

25. Isenberg, *Fallen Founder,* chap. 8, esp. 283–85.

26. Ibid., 286–311; Andrew Burstein, *The Passions of Andrew Jackson* (New York, 2003), chap. 3.

27. *National Intelligencer,* November 9, 17, 19, and 24 and December 5, 1806. The *Scioto Gazette* story is in the November 24 issue; the piece under the headline "BURR'S CONSPIRACY" was originally printed in *National Aegis* [Worcester, Mass.].

28. Isenberg, *Fallen Founder,* 312–15; Charles Henry Ambler, *Thomas Ritchie: A Study in Virginia Politics* (Richmond, 1913), 38–39.

29. In Eaton's case, the title of "General" was an honorary one, a testimonial to his ambitious march through the Libyan desert during the Barbary campaign, when he recruited a motley group of Europeans in an action best defined as a filibuster.

30. Isenberg, *Fallen Founder,* 307, 323–65, Randolph quote at 349, Wirt quote at 362.

31. Jefferson probably did not know that, at the time he wrote the offending comments on democracy, Dennie was living with Thomas Boyleston Adams, son of John and Abigail, brother of Senator John Quincy Adams, and in Dennie's words, "my constant friend." The pair, Harvard classmates some years past, were sharing their home with a family of Philadelphia Quakers—pacifists in a den of politics. William W. Clapp, *Joseph Dennie* (Cambridge, Mass., 1880), 36–37; letter of June 15, 1803, from Dennie to his mother, in *The Letters of Joseph Dennie,* ed. Laura Green Pedder (Orono, Me., 1936), 191.

32. *Carolina Gazette* [Charleston], March 4, 1808.

33. Proclamation in Jefferson's hand, July 2, 1807, and transcription of Madison's draft, in *TJP-LC; National Intelligencer,* July, 1, 1807; Ketcham, 452–53; Malone, 5:415–35; Edwin M. Gaines, "The Chesapeake Affair: Virginians Mobilize to Defend National Honor," *Virginia Magazine of History and Biography* 64 (April 1956): 134, 137.

34. Gerry to JM, July 5, 1807; J. G. Jackson to JM, July 5, 1807, in *JMP-LC.*

35. Bidwell to TJ, June 27, 1807; TJ to Bidwell, July 11, 1807; Page to TJ, July 12, 1807, *TJP-LC;* Andrew Burstein, *The Inner Jefferson: Portrait of a Grieving Optimist* (Charlottesville, Va., 1995), 137–43; Ketcham, 453.

36. See esp. TJ to JM, August 9, 11, and 16, 1807, *RL,* 3:1483, 1486; *JMB,* 2:1212; Isenberg, *Fallen Founder,* 284–85, 296. Jefferson had briefly considered a filibuster in Florida two years before.

37. JM to TJ, September 20, 1807, *RL,* 3:1499.

38. Sullivan to TJ, December 7, 1807, *TJP-LC;* Ketcham, 455–56; for the toast mocking Jefferson, see *Independent Chronicle,* July 27, 1807, cited in Thorp Lanier Wolford, "Democratic-Republican Reaction in Massachusetts to the Embargo of 1807," *New England Quarterly* 15 (March 1942): 42; Robert W. Tucker and David C. Hendrickson, *Empire of Liberty: The Statecraft of Thomas Jefferson* (New York, 1990), 208–10.

39. Bradford Perkins, *Prologue to War: England and the United States, 1805–1812* (Berkeley, Calif., 1961), 152–56; Gallatin to TJ, December 31, 1807, *TJP-LC.*

40. Lewis to JM, January 9, 1808, *JMP-LC.*

41. Perkins, *Prologue to War,* 168; Drew R. McCoy, *The Elusive Republic: Political Economy in Jeffersonian America* (New York, 1980), 138, 216–17.

42. No relation to the Pinckneys of South Carolina.

43. Monroe to John Taylor, September 10, 1810, in *Writings of James Monroe,* ed. Stanislaus M. Hamilton (New York, 1898–1903), 5:131–33.

44. Monroe to TJ, March 22, 1808, ibid., 5:27–35.

45. JM to Monroe, March 20, 1807, *JMP-LC;* Ammon, *James Monroe,* 254–70; Ammon, "James Monroe and the Election of 1808 in Virginia," *William and Mary Quarterly* 20 (January 1963): 40–42; Jack N. Rakove, *James Madison and the Creation of the American Republic* (New York, 1990), 142–44; Malone, 5:414.

46. TJ to JM, March 11, 1808, *RL,* 3:1514; TJ to Taylor, January 6, 1808, cited in Malone, 5:483.

47. *National Intelligencer,* January 18 and March 23, 1808.

48. Elsewhere, the opposition asked leading or rhetorical questions, or focused on the good and decent people who were being hurt. The merchant "sounds idle," the *Connecticut Courant* mourned. The mechanic was "obliged to dismiss his journeymen—his customers desert him"; the farmer "finds no market for his produce." Saddest yet was the "Poor Sailor, generous, honest, and unsuspecting." Into what "dreadful abyss" were "our democratic rulers" about to "plunge the American people?" See *North American and Mercantile Daily Advertiser,* March 19, March 23, and July 29, 1808, including articles reprinted from the *Courant* and *Evening Post; Public Advertiser* [New York], January 7, 1808; *Salem Gazette,* February 16, 1808; Jerry W. Knudson, *Jefferson and the Press: Crucible of Liberty* (Columbia, S.C., 2006), 156.

49. *Columbian Centinel,* January 2, 1808; *Albany Gazette,* August 1 and October 3, 1808.

50. *National Intelligencer,* July 6, 1808; *City Gazette* [Charleston, S.C.], July 6, 1808.

51. JM to TJ, August 10, 1808, *RL,* 3:1532; *New-Jersey Telescope,* November 8, 1808.

52. Parsons, *John Quincy Adams,* 91–95; *City Gazette* [Charleston, S.C.], July 6, 1808; Leonard Baker, *John Marshall: A Life in Law* (New York, 1974), 525–26; Samuel Eliot Morison, *Harrison Gray Otis* (Boston, 1969), 300–308; Donald R. Hickey, *The War of 1812: A Forgotten Conflict* (Urbana, Ill., 1989), 21.

53. Brian Schoen, "Calculating the Price of Union: Republican Economic Nationalism and the Origins of Southern Sectionalism, 1790–1828," *Journal of the Early Republic* 23 (Summer 2003): 173–206; Charleston's *City Gazette* editorialized: "If we have not

virtue to withstand a temporary embargo, how can we expect to support a war, which when once declared no person can say when and where it will end" (as republished in the *Republican Star* of Easton, Maryland, November 8, 1808). In its inaugural issue, the *Anti-Monarchist* of Edgefield, South Carolina, adhered to the administration line, while acknowledging Britain's preponderant power: "We are reduced to this situation," the editor explained: "submit to pay TRIBUTE to England, and be plundered by France, to go to WAR, or hold to the Embargo . . . France we cannot touch; and England, by her powerful navy, could soon sweep us from the ocean." *Anti-Monarchist, and Republican Watchman,* December 14, 1808.

54. *Enquirer,* December 10 and December 20, 1808.

55. Saunders Cragg, *George Clinton Next President, and Our Republican Institutions Rescued from Destruction* (New York, 1808), 4, 11–16; Ambler, *Thomas Ritchie: A Study in Virginia Politics,* 46–47.

56. *Virginia Argus,* January 1 and February 2, 1808; Cunningham, *Jeffersonian Republicans in Power,* 112–21; Parsons, *John Quincy Adams,* 92–93; Cheetham, reprinting a piece from the Troy, N.Y., *Farmer's Digest,* cited in Brant, 4:439–40.

57. Lewis to JM, November 14, 1808, *JMP-LC.*

58. Cunningham, *Jeffersonian Republicans in Power,* 116, 273–74.

59. "A Farmer, No. VI," *National Intelligencer,* July 13, 1808.

60. *Virginia Argus,* February 16 and March 11, 1808. To John Taylor of Caroline, Monroe later asserted that he "never had any connection" to those who advanced his candidacy for president; and that John Randolph knew nothing about his position on foreign affairs at the time of the latter's break with the Jefferson administration. Monroe to Taylor, September 10, 1810, in *Writings of James Monroe,* ed. Hamilton, 5:133–36. The *Richmond Enquirer* accommodated both sides. Editor Ritchie published an angry letter directed toward those who espoused Randolph's cause. Calling their protest against the caucus vote "vapid" and "spiritless," the column urged the partisans to drop the matter with as much "grace and decency" as they could summon. For its part, Randolph's vanguard denied that it had any responsibility for the development of a schism within the party. It was the Madison group, their leaders said, that had withdrawn from old friends in order to hold a dishonest caucus. Those who were suppressed by that caucus were not about to forget the slight. See *Enquirer,* March 25 and October 17, 1808.

61. Burstein, *Inner Jefferson,* 154–56, 160–61; Ammon, *James Monroe,* 271–77; Brant, 4:428–30.

62. *Virginia Argus,* March 11 and September 23, 1808; *National Intelligencer,* October 21, 1808; Federalist endorsement of Monroe in *Virginia Gazette,* similarly in the *North American and Mercantile Daily Advertiser* [Baltimore], October 21, 1808.

63. "Richard Saunders" in *New-York Evening Post,* June 28, 1808, reprinted from *Republican Crisis* (Albany, N.Y.).

64. Rush to Adams, September 22, 1808, *Letters of Benjamin Rush,* 2:984. Earlier Rush had told Adams that he regarded the embargo as "just," noting that Philadelphians were not greatly hurt by it. By the end of 1808, he would come to feel, as did many other earlier supporters, that the embargo should be lifted.

65. Leonard D. White, *The Jeffersonians: A Study in Administrative History, 1801–1829* (New York, 1961), chap. 24; Theodore J. Crackel, *Mr. Jefferson's Army: Political and Social Reform of the Military Establishment, 1801–1809* (New York, 1987), esp. 178–79, stressing the loyalty of the new army to the partisan Republican agenda. Although the administrative structure was unchanged, this, of course, did not obviate the impact of the partisan press. The *National Intelligencer*, for instance, kept up its extreme language, referring to Federalists as "the enemies of liberty," men of "jaundiced minds," while crediting Jefferson with having preserved peace "amidst convulsions almost without parallel" (issues of May 8 and May 13, 1808).

66. Henry S. Randall, *Life of Thomas Jefferson* (New York, 1858), 1:404–5.

67. Broussard, *Southern Federalists*, 283, 286, 291.

68. On Sheffey, see *Biographical Dictionary of the American Congress, 1774–1949* (Washington, D.C., 1950), 1802–3.

69. Gallatin to Joseph H. Nicholson, December 29, 1808, cited in Brant, 4:473.

CHAPTER THIRTEEN
Road to War, 1809–1812

1. *National Intelligencer*, March 3 and March 6, 1809; Charles Henry Ambler, *Thomas Ritchie: A Study in Virginia Politics* (Richmond, 1913), 49; Margaret Bayard Smith, *The First Forty Years of Washington Society* (New York, 1906), 410. U.S. survey texts, for one, generally highlight the War Hawks' responsibility for the War of 1812, placing Henry Clay at their head and placing President Madison more or less in the background.

2. The full text of the address is in *PJM-PS*, 1:15–18.

3. Madison's letter to a spokesman for the Creek Confederacy in the autumn of 1809 was a boilerplate example of the paternalistic approach of government toward those Indians who complained about encroachment onto their lands. The president assured the Creek leader that agreed-upon borders would not be crossed, then prescribed: "You say you are poor; look at your Father, the President when he talks to you concerning this. Turn your ear to him, and believe what he says. Fence in your Lands, plow as much land as you can, raise corn & Hogs & Cattle. Learn your young Women to card & spin, & let those who are older learn to weave. You will then have food and cloathing and live comfortably. The President advises you to do this. He knows that his red Children can live well if they follow his advice." JM to Hobohoilthle, November 6, 1809, *PJM-PS*, 2:54.

4. Madison would meet with Paul Cuffe, a successful Quaker ship captain and son of a former slave, promising the full support of the federal government for Cuffe's ambitious plan to colonize free blacks in Sierra Leone and to look for ways to increase trade between the United States and West Africa. With Virginia critics such as John Randolph and John Taylor watching his every move, the president was unwilling to risk anything bolder. Madison told Cuffe that he would provide government support "consistent with the Constitution." This language suggests Madison believed slavery protected by the Constitution; he would support colonization without threatening the property or political interests of the slave states. See Cuffe to JM, June 22, 1812, in *JMP-PS*, 4:497–98. See also Elise Lemire, *"Miscegenation": Making Race in America* (Philadel-

phia, 2002); and Bernard Sheehan, *Seeds of Extinction: Jeffersonian Philanthropy and the American Indian* (Chapel Hill, N.C., 1973).

5. Adam Rothman, *Slave Country: American Expansion and the Origins of the Deep South* (Cambridge, Mass., 2005), chap. 3.

6. Smith, *First Forty Years of Washington Society*, 411–12.

7. Martha Jefferson Randolph to TJ, February 17, 1809, *The Family Letters of Thomas Jefferson*, ed. Edwin Morris Betts and James Adam Bear, Jr. (Charlottesville, Va., 1986), 382; *PTJ-RS*, 1:11–13.

8. Robert Allen Rutland, *The Presidency of James Madison* (Lawrence, Kan., 1990), 21.

9. Frances Few diary, cited in Ketcham, 476.

10. Robert Allen Rutland, *James Madison: The Founding Father* (New York, 1987), 179; Smith, *First Forty Years of Washington Society*, 61.

11. *JMB*, 2:1243; account with Joseph Milligan, March 8–10, 1809, *PTJ-RS*, 1:35–37.

12. TJ to JM, April 10, 1809, *RL*, 3:1582.

13. William Seale, *The President's House: A History* (Baltimore, 1986), 119–26.

14. TJ to JM, March 17, 1809; JM to TJ, March 27, 1809, *RL*, 3:1576, 1578; TJ to Elijah Griffiths, May 28, 1809, *PTJ-RS*, 1:236–37.

15. *JMB*, 2:1244–46; Malone, 6:9, 15, 291–92.

16. TJ to JM, March 30, 1809, *RL*, 3:1580.

17. TJ to JM, April 10 and April 27, 1809; JM to TJ, April 24, *RL*, 3:1568, 1583, 1586–87. In alluding to Canada, Jefferson expressed his regret that the British province was not taken during the Revolution.

18. John Chester Miller, *The Wolf by the Ears: Thomas Jefferson and Slavery* (Charlottesville, Va., 1991), 138–41.

19. On House results, see *PJM-PS*, 1:140n.

20. TJ to JM, April 27, 1809, *RL*, 3:1587–88; JM to TJ, May 1, 1809, *RL*, 3:1587; JM to Lafayette, May 1, 1809, *PJM-PS*, 1:150.

21. Blodgett to JM, ca. March 11, 1809, *PJM-PS*, 1:32–34. In June, Aaron Burr's daughter, Theodosia, sent her own tender appeal for clemency to Dolley Madison, who replied warmly but insisted that nothing could be done. See Nancy Isenberg, *Fallen Founder: The Life of Aaron Burr* (New York, 2007), 384–85, 389.

22. Nicholas to JM, ca. March 3, 1809, *PJM-PS*, 1:10–11; TJ to Robert Smith, July 10, 1809, *PTJ-RS*, 1:340; *RL*, 3:1562, 1566; Henry S. Randall, *Life of Thomas Jefferson* (New York, 1858), 3:357n; Malone, 6:30; Ketcham, 475, 481–82.

23. *National Intelligencer*, July 5 and September 6, 1809.

24. Ketcham, 480–81; "Margaret Bayard Smith's Account of a Visit to Monticello," *PTJ-RS*, 1:387; TJ to JM, September 18, 1809, *RL*, 3:1603; TJ to Charles Pinckney, August 29, 1809, *PTJ-RS*, 1:475; *JMB*, 2:1247.

25. TJ to JM, August 17 and September 12, 1809, *RL*, 3:1599–1600, 1602.

26. For a good synthesis, see *RL*, 3:1566–73.

27. Gallatin to JM, July 24, 1809, *PJM-PS*, 1:300. The predictably untrustworthy General James Wilkinson wrote to Madison from New Orleans of a conversation with

the Spanish governor of West Florida, who purportedly wanted the United States to absorb the territory in the wake of Napoleon's takeover of his homeland. On the subject of British designs in Florida, the Spaniard presumed any incursion would backfire because it was destined to belong to the United States. See Wilkinson to JM, May 1, 1809, *PJM-PS,* 1:156.

28. TJ to JM, August 17, 1809, *RL,* 3:1600.

29. JM to TJ, August 23 and November 6, 1809; TJ to JM, August 17 and September 12, 1809, *RL,* 3:1600–1603, 1607; JM to Smith, September 15, 1809, *PJM-PS,* 1:378; Bradford Perkins, *Prologue to War: England and the United States, 1805–1812* (Berkeley, Calif., 1961), 186–87. Perkins concludes that "Canning and all England misunderstood Jeffersonianism and overestimated the amount of condescension America would tolerate." Ibid., 222.

30. See, for example, the *Norfolk Gazette,* issue of April 22, 1810, taking its cue from the *New York Evening Post,* in assessing Federalist turncoat John Quincy Adams as a diplomat: "his master Jefferson or Madison, or who ever is at the head of affairs." The *Norfolk Gazette* published other personal gibes, defining Madison's conduct in office as "passive" (issue of September 24, 1810), and insulting pro-administration editor Thomas Ritchie of the *Richmond Enquirer,* "whose name adds no more weight to paper than the ink used in writing" (February 11, 1811).

31. James H. Broussard, *The Southern Federalists, 1800–1816* (Baton Rouge, La., 1978), 115–16; Donald R. Hickey, *The War of 1812* (Urbana, Ill., 1989), 8–9; Randall, *Life of Thomas Jefferson,* 3:125–30; Malone, 5:497–503. Randall, writing when memories of the War of 1812 were still fairly fresh, described the pressures generally felt by an agricultural and commercial people in "avoidance mode," and a political caste hamstrung by partisan considerations and ill equipped to argue naval policy based purely on tactical expertise; Malone inexplicably states that Jefferson was "less indifferent to the navy" than Madison.

32. *Carolina Gazette,* November 7, 1809; *New Hampshire Gazette,* November 14, 1809.

33. Cullen also reverted to unoriginal attacks on Jefferson's wartime governorship ("more the cautious politician than the soldier") and denied him credit for drawing up the Declaration of Independence. As to the election of 1800, Cullen more trenchantly wrote that after Burr made Jefferson's election possible, "his scared imagination saw in the friend that helped and raised him, the rival also that might depress him." *Memoirs of the Hon. Thomas Jefferson* (New York, 1809), 1:11, 25, 100–101, 2:320–21, 434.

34. *The Death of Washington, with some remarks on Jeffersonian & Madisonian Policy* (New York, ca. 1809). The coarsest criticism of Jefferson centered on his alleged cowardice during the Revolution.

35. JM to the Chairman of the Republican Meeting of Washington County, Maryland, January 31, 1810; to Pinkney, May 23, 1810, *PJM-PS,* 2:215, 348.

36. Macon's Bill no. 1, drafted by Albert Gallatin and introduced in the House by Macon, was a version of the bill that eventually passed. It stirred up argument among Republicans, in addition to opposition from Federalists. It passed the House but died after the influential Senator Samuel Smith chopped it up and House and Senate could not agree on a compromise. Perkins, *Prologue to War,* 239–47; Robert A. Rutland, *Madison's Alternatives: The Jeffersonian Republicans and the Coming of the War of 1812* (Philadel-

phia, 1975), 94–101; Reginald Horsman, *The War of 1812* (New York, 1969), 14–15; Hickey, *War of 1812*, 22–24.

37. Rodney to JM, January 16, 1810, *PJM-PS*, 2:181–86. "I have heard our seafaring men assert that the 'Fair American' & the 'Holker' [two privateers] did more injury to the British commerce in our last war [the Revolutionary] than all our thirteen frigates, the principal part of which, were soon captured." Ibid., 183.

38. George Shackelford, *Jefferson's Adoptive Son: The Life of William Short, 1759–1848* (Lexington, Ky., 1993) 8, 129, 135, 197n; Henry Bartholomew Cox, *The Parisian American: Fulwar Skipwith of Virginia* (Washington, D.C., 1964), chaps. 1, 2, and 5; Harry Ammon, *James Monroe: The Quest for National Identity* (Charlottesville, Va., 1971), 116, 125, 208, 210, 213; JM to TJ, August 13, 1804; TJ to JM, August 18, 1804, *RL*, 2:1334, 1338; Brant, 4:219–20, 363–66; Fulwar Skipwith to TJ, March 8, 1808, *TJP-LC;* Roger G. Kennedy, *Mr. Jefferson's Lost Cause: Land, Farmers, and the Louisiana Purchase* (New York, 2003), 178–92, 295–96n.

39. "Notes on Jefferson's 'Statement' on the Batture at New Orleans"; JM to Albert Gallatin, August 14 and August 22, 1810; to John Graham, August 24, 1810; John Graham to JM, August 20, 1810; John R. Bedford to JM (with August 5 enclosure from Bayou Sara, West Florida), August 26, 1810, *PJM-PS*, 2:475–77, 484, 498, 501–5, 508–10; William B. Hatcher, *Edward Livingston: Jeffersonian Republican and Jacksonian Democrat* (Baton Rouge, La., 1941), 92–98; Stanley Clisby Arthur, *The Story of the West Florida Rebellion* (St. Francisville, La., 1935), 35, 58, 131, 133.

40. Arthur, *Story of West Florida Rebellion*, 95–96, 103–10, 128–29; James A. Padgett, "The West Florida Revolution of 1810, As Told in the Letters of John Rhea, Fulwar Skipwith, Reuben Kemper, and Others," *Louisiana Historical Quarterly* 21 (January 1938): 5–7, 53.

41. Presidential Proclamation, October 27, 1810, *PJM-PS*, 2:595–96. The River Perdido translates from Spanish as "the lost river."

42. James G. Cusick, *The Other War of 1812: The Patriot War and the American Invasion of Spanish East Florida* (Athens, Ga., 2003), 28–37, 56–61, 67–75, 138.

43. *PJM-PS*, 3:xxvii–xxviii; George W. Erving to JM, January 29, 1811, *PJM-PS*, 3:139–41; Frank Lawrence Owsley, Jr., and Gene A. Smith, *Filibusters and Expansionists: Jeffersonian Manifest Destiny, 1800–1821* (Tuscaloosa, Ala., 1997), 66–68; Cusick, *Other War of 1812*, 153.

44. TJ to Eppes, January 5, 1811, *PTJ-RS*, 3:281–82. Fulwar Skipwith's motives, largely financial, were tied to the land of opportunity he knew best. Judging by his extensive activities in France, he would not have been in West Florida had he not figured that he had some land coming to him. During his years abroad, he had failed to get rich, but he never gave up and retained the aims of the Virginians of his class. For insight into the phenomenon of elite-bred Virginians scrambling to be successful, see Jan Lewis, *The Pursuit of Happiness: Family and Values in Jefferson's Virginia* (New York, 1983), chap. 4.

When Mathews took possession of Amelia Island off the coast of Florida in 1812, claiming Madison's approval, Monroe, as secretary of state, found it necessary to revoke his powers and the administration disavowed his actions. There was still some hope, as Georgian William Crawford told Monroe, that a "newly constituted revolutionary government" could be recognized, while keeping the U.S. government's agency hidden, but that prospect quickly faded. Madison wrote Jefferson on the matter: "In E. Florida, Mathews has been playing a tragi-comedy; in the face of common sense, as well as of his instructions." He observed nervously of Mathews: "His extravagences [*sic*] place us in the most distressing dilemma." Clearly, Madison ended up considering Mathews's actions foolhardy and a potential embarrassment to the administration. Crawford to Monroe, April 5, 1812; Mathews to JM, April 16, 1812, *PJM-PS*, 4:291–96, 326–29; JM to TJ, April 24, 1812, *RL*, 3:1694.

45. Madison must have known how questionable his action was. Burr was put on trial not only for treason but for violating a 1794 law against filibustering. Burr and his lawyers had contended that the idea of a filibuster was legally acceptable during a time of war, and that Burr's plan was contingent on the occurrence of a border clash between U.S. troops (led by General Wilkinson) and Spanish forces; as no conflict occurred, Burr abandoned his project. Technically, Fulwar Skipwith and the band of rebels in Baton Rouge should have been prosecuted for violating the same law against filibusters, but they went free.

46. Eppes to JM, December 15, 1809, January 18, 1810, February 18, 1810, and January 31, 1811, *PJM-PS*, 2:135, 189, 224, 3:143; TJ to Eppes, December 7, 1810; Eppes to TJ, December 14, 1810, *PTJ-RS*, 3:244, 256.

47. TJ to Barlow, May 3, 1802, *TJP-LC*; TJ to Barlow, April 16, 1811, *PTJ-RS*, 3:564; Andrew Burstein, *Jefferson's Secrets: Death and Desire at Monticello* (New York, 2005), 214–16; Francis D. Cogliano, *Thomas Jefferson: Reputation and Legacy* (Charlottesville, Va., 2006).

48. JM to TJ, July 17, 1810; TJ to JM, July 26, 1810, *RL*, 3:1640–42; John Wayles Eppes to JM, November 1, 1810, *PJM-PS*, 2:610. The theme of Madison's memory as well as his reluctance to expose himself in partisan readings of the past is addressed at length in the pages of Drew R. McCoy, *The Last of the Fathers: James Madison and the Republican Legacy* (New York, 1989).

49. Ketcham, 481–85; J.C.A. Stagg, *Mr. Madison's War: Politics, Diplomacy, and Warfare in the Early American Republic, 1783–1830* (Princeton, N.J., 1983), 50; Perkins, *Prologue to War*, 267–69; Frank Cassell, *Merchant Congressman in the Young Republic: Samuel Smith of Maryland, 1752–1839* (Madison, Wisc., 1971), 147–53.

50. Ketcham, 487–90; Catherine Allgor, *A Perfect Union: Dolley Madison and the Creation of the American Nation* (New York, 2006), 259–62. While Madison knew that Jefferson fully approved of the administration as it was to be reconstituted, the ex-president tried to maintain civil epistolary relations with Robert Smith by pretending the problem lay beyond the feuding cabinet officers. "No one feels more painfully than I do the separation of friends," Jefferson ventured, shifting blame onto the "Cannibal newspapers" that "harrowed up" the sensibilities of public servants on a daily basis. Smith, declaring himself "one of your old & uniform friends," responded in kind: "I ever will retain a just sense of your dignified, liberal, frank deportment towards me." All this was before Smith's peevish pamphlet, of course, and marked the end of politeness. TJ to Smith, April 30, 1811; Smith to TJ, May 5, 1811, *PTJ-RS*, 3:595, 608; JM to TJ, July 8, 1811, *RL*, 3:1671; Stagg, *Mr. Madison's War*, 71–72; Stagg, "James Madison and the 'Malcontents': The Political Origins of the War of 1812," *William and Mary Quarterly* 33 (October 1976): 574.

51. Andrew Burstein, *The Original Knickerbocker: The Life of Washington Irving* (New York, 2007), 92–93.

52. The malcontents were men with personal as well as political grievances—a few Pennsylvanians along with one prominent, and now disaffected, Virginia Republican: William Branch Giles. The Clintons of New York and Madison's minister to France, John Armstrong, who returned home in the spring of 1811, added to the growing discontent. All called for increased defense expenditures, though none seemed inclined to push through higher taxes to pay for them. See John S. Pancake, "The 'Invisibles': A Chapter in the Opposition to the President," *Journal of Southern History* 21 (February 1955): 28, 33–34; Stagg, *Mr. Madison's War,* 49–59.

53. Eppes to TJ, March 20, 1811; TJ to Eppes, March 24, 1811, *PTJ-RS,* 3:473, 502. Jefferson confirmed Eppes's opinion, noting that John Randolph had "consolidated" with the Federalists—both would be "delighted that Great Britain could conquer & reduce us again under her government."

54. TJ to Duane, March 28, 1811, *PTJ-RS,* 3:506–9.

55. TJ to Duane, April 30, 1811, *PTJ-RS,* 3:593; TJ to JM, May 26, 1811, *RL,* 3:1669. On the divergent characters of Duane, Ritchie, and Samuel Harrison Smith of the *National Intelligencer,* see Jeffrey L. Pasley, *"The Tyranny of Printers": Newspaper Politics in the Early American Republic* (Charlottesville, Va., 2001), 259–62. As Pasley explains, Jefferson long considered Duane a man of extremes whose passions were, in the past, politically useful; Ritchie a man of urbanity and decorum who saw clearly and could be trusted; and Smith completely subservient, a convenient tool of Jefferson's administration.

56. TJ to JM, April 24, 1811; JM to TJ, May 3, 1811, *RL,* 3:1666–68; TJ to Wirt, May 3, 1811, *PTJ-RS,* 3:601–3.

57. JM to TJ, April 1, 1811; TJ to JM, April 7, 1811, *RL,* 3:1662–64; Randall, *Life of Thomas Jefferson,* 3:370–71. Madison's offer to Jefferson of the cabinet position is not contained in any letter, published or unpublished, but was revealed to Randall by "an intimate friend of Mr. Madison, now [1858] living, who heard the fact from his own lips." As for the remark about Randolph, it was not he alone whose frustrations increased with Monroe's entry into the executive branch. Jefferson's personal secretary in the second term, who held the same position at the outset of Madison's administration, wrote from New York to Dolley Madison. He told of cordial, if somewhat mechanical, encounters with the families of both Smith brothers and explained: "The Smiths are said not directly to vent their spleen, but to spur on their relations & friends, many of whom are extremely abusive of the President & Col. Monroe." Thus, Monroe would take the heat, along with Madison. See Coles to Dolley Madison, June 10, 1811, *PJM-PS,* 3:337.

58. Ammon, *James Monroe,* 282–88; Monroe to TJ, April 3, 1811, *PTJ-RS,* 3:528. Ammon carefully untangles the conflicting historiography as to the terms under which Monroe accepted the position from Madison.

59. Perkins, *Prologue to War,* 261–67; Ambler, *Thomas Ritchie,* 55–59.

60. Merrill D. Peterson, *The Great Triumvirate: Webster, Clay, and Calhoun* (New York, 1987), 8–18, quote at 8; Hickey, *War of 1812,* 30; James E. Lewis, Jr., *The American Union and the Problem of Neighborhood* (Chapel Hill, N.C., 1998), 49; James G. Cusick, *The Other War of 1812: The Patriot War and the American Invasion of East Florida* (Athens, Ga., 2003),

24–25; Ronald L. Hatzenbuehler, "The War Hawks and the Question of Congressional Leadership in 1812," *Pacific Historical Review* 45 (February 1976): 19; Ketcham, 508–9.

61. *Alexandria Gazette,* July 10, 1811.

62. Third Annual Message, November 5, 1811, *PJM-PS,* 4:1–5.

63. Gerry to JM, November 17, 1811, *PJM-PS,* 4:23–24.

64. JM to Adams, November 15, 1811, in *PJM-PS,* 4:16–17.

65. Perkins, *Prologue to War,* 282–89; R. David Edmunds, *Tecumseh and the Quest for Indian Leadership* (New York, 1984); Anthony F. C. Wallace, *Jefferson and the Indians: The Tragic Fate of the First Americans* (Cambridge, Mass., 1999), 304–17; Jackson to Harrison, November 28, 1811, *Papers of Andrew Jackson,* ed. Sam B. Smith, et al. (Knoxville, Tenn., 1980–), 2:270; on U.S.-Canada situation: TJ to John Wayles Eppes, September 6, 1811, *PTJ-RS,* 4:133; *PJM-PS,* 3:xxxiii; JM to TJ, February 7, 1812, *RL,* 3:1687. For a good discussion of the relative weight assigned to impressment and western instability as causative factors behind the War of 1812, see Owsley and Smith, *Filibusters and Expansionists,* 83–85.

66. Claiborne to JM, October 8, 1811, *PJM-PS,* 3:479.

67. Hatzenbuehler, "War Hawks and Question of Congressional Leadership in 1812," 17, 19–20; Norman K. Risjord, "1812: Conservatives, War Hawks and the Nation's Honor," *William and Mary Quarterly* 18 (April 1961): 208; Ammon, *James Monroe,* 301.

68. Robert Wright of Maryland made a similar appeal, likening impressment to enslavement and affirming that the army alone could reclaim America's patrimony—its "inheritance purchased by the blood of the fathers of the Revolution." *Annals of Congress,* 12th Cong., 1st sess., 441, 447–51, 456–57, 473; Jennifer Clark, "The War of 1812: American Nationalism and Rhetorical Images of Britain," *War and Society* 12 (May 1994): 10.

69. Joseph Allen to JM, [November] 23, 1811, *PJM-PS,* 4:3, 8, 31–33; *Annals of Congress,* 12th Cong., 1st sess., 473, 497–99; the House plans for raising ten thousand men for the regular army and fifty thousand volunteers had been in Madison's earlier draft for the annual message. Monroe had assured the House Committee on Foreign Affairs that the administration backed even stronger measures; see Stagg, *Mr. Madison's War,* 84. On the significance of winning over conservative southern Republicans and Virginians such as Nelson, see Risjord, "1812: Conservatives, War Hawks and Nation's Honor," 197, 208; and Myron F. Wehje, "Opposition in Virginia to the War of 1812," *Virginia Magazine of History and Biography* 78 (January 1970): 65–86.

70. Stagg, *Mr. Madison's War,* 116.

71. Randall, *Life of Thomas Jefferson,* 3:639–40; TJ to Rush, December 5, 1811, *TJP-LC* and *PTJ-RS,* 5:312–14; Rush to Adams, December 16, 1811; to TJ, December 17, 1811, in *Letters of Benjamin Rush,* ed. L. H. Butterfield (Princeton, N.J., 1951), 2:110–12. Edward Coles was accompanied on the northern excursion by his brother John.

72. Adams to TJ, January 1, 1812; TJ to Adams, January 21, 1812, *The Adams-Jefferson Letters: The Complete Correspondence between Thomas Jefferson and Abigail and John Adams,* ed. Lester J. Cappon (Chapel Hill, N.C., 1959), 290–91.

73. TJ to William Short, October 17, 1812, *PTJ-RS,* 5:400–401; Lucia Stanton, *Free Some Day: The African-American Families of Monticello* (Charlottesville, Va., 2000), 73–82;

JMB, 2:1275; "Non-Congressional Distribution List for Batture Pamphlet," *PTJ-RS,* 4:624–25.

74. *RL,* 3:1620–21; TJ to JM, May 25, 1810, and October 15, 1810, *RL,* 3:1632, 1646–47.

75. TJ to JM, February 19 and March 26, 1812; JM to TJ, April 3, 1812, *RL,* 3:1688–91; Hickey, *War of 1812,* 28.

76. Stagg, *Mr. Madison's War,* 93–99; Hickey, *War of 1812,* 37–39; JM to TJ, March 9, 1812, *RL,* 3:1690.

77. Stagg, *Mr. Madison's War,* 109–15; JM to TJ, June 22, 1812; TJ to JM, June 29, 1812, *RL,* 3:1698–99.

78. JM to Richard Cutts, August 8, 1812, JM to Samuel Spring, September 6, 1812, in *PJM-PS,* 5:128, 280; John Marshall to Harry Heth, March 2, 1812, and *Norfolk Gazette and Publick Ledger,* May 27, 1812, as cited in Wehje, "Opposition in Virginia to War of 1812," 77.

79. Madison's message to Congress, June 1, 1812, *PJM-PS,* 432–39; pro-war speeches by Richard M. Johnson, Peter B. Porter (chairman of the Foreign Affairs Committee), Kentuckian Joseph Desha (also of the Foreign Affairs Committee), *Annals of Congress,* 12th Cong., 1st sess., 415, 459, 488–89.

80. [John Lowell], *Perpetual War, the Policy of Mr. Madison* (Boston, 1812), esp. 15–16, 69–75.

81. Broussard, *Southern Federalists, 1800–1816,* 136–38.

82. TJ to Rush, August 17, 1811, *PTJ-RS,* 4:87–88.

83. Dearborn to TJ, March 10, 1812, *PTJ-RS,* 4:544–45; Carl E. Prince, *New Jersey's Jeffersonian Republicans: The Genesis of an Early American Party Machine, 1789–1817* (Chapel Hill, N.C., 1967), 176–79; JM to TJ, October 14, 1812, *RL,* 3:1705; Stagg, *Mr. Madison's War,* 111; Ketcham, 520.

84. Adams to JM, May 12, 1812, *PJM-PS,* 4:405.

85. JM to TJ, August 17, 1812; TJ to JM, June 29, 1812, *RL,* 3:1698–99, 1702–3; William Pope to JM, July 10, 1812; Monroe to JM, August 4, 1812, *PJM-PS,* 5:4, 114–15; Wehje, "Opposition in Virginia to the War of 1812," 83; Hickey, *War of 1812,* 56–67.

86. Charles Royster, *Light-Horse Harry Lee and the Legacy of the American Revolution* (New York, 1981), 156–85. Madison authorized Monroe to issue a directive (July 7, 1812) from the State Department requesting all British subjects living in the United States to report their names, occupations, and places of residence to U.S. marshals, and to indicate whether they had applied to become naturalized citizens. See *PJM-PS,* 5:42.

87. JM to TJ, August 17, 1812, *RL,* 3:1702–3; Jon Latimer, *1812: War with America* (Cambridge, Mass., 2007), 42–45, 52–57; Hickey, *War of 1812,* 80–88, 283; Stagg, *Mr. Madison's War,* 190–207.

88. Coles to TJ, October 24, 1812, *PTJ-RS,* 5:410–11; JM to TJ, October 14, 1812; TJ to JM, November 6, 1812, *RL,* 3:1705, 1707; Monroe to TJ, August 31, 1812, *TJP-LC;* Milo Quaife, "General William Hull and his Critics," *Ohio Archaeological and Historical Quarterly* 47 (1938): 168–82.

89. Monroe to JM, September 2 and September 4, 1812; Rush to JM, September 4,

1812; JM to William Eustis, September 5, 1812; JM to Monroe, September 5, 1812, *JMP-PS*, 5:252–53, 267–70; Dallas to Rush, September 19, 1812, George M. Dallas Papers, Historical Society of Pennsylvania.

90. Monroe to JM, September 6, 1812; an unidentified correspondent to JM, October 10, 1812, *PJM-PS*, 5:281, 416–17; Hickey, *War of 1812*, 86–90, 93–99; Ketcham, 553–54.

91. JM to TJ, October 14, 1812, *RL*, 3:1706; Burstein, *The Original Knickerbocker*, 96–97; Ketcham, 511–12.

92. Ketcham, 520–21; Peterson, *Great Triumvirate*, 39.

CHAPTER FOURTEEN
Road Out of War, 1813–1816

1. *Federal Republican*, January 18, 1813, reprinting poem in *Connecticut Mirror*, January 1, 1813.

2. C. Edward Skeen, *John Armstrong, Jr., 1758–1843: A Biography* (Syracuse, N.Y., 1981), esp. chap. 7; J.C.A. Stagg, *Mr. Madison's War: Politics, Diplomacy, and Warfare in the Early American Republic, 1783–1830* (Princeton, N.J., 1983), 57–61, 103–4, 240–41, 280–81; Reginald Horsman, *The War of 1812* (New York, 1969), 89; Donald R. Hickey, *The War of 1812* (Urbana, Ill., 1989), 106; Armstrong to JM, May 6, 1810, *PJM-PS*, 2:332–33. Armstrong was accused of speculating in Florida land while negotiating on behalf of the United States for the purchase of the Floridas. Madison and Jefferson discounted all such accusations. The Quaker letter was to Ambrose Spencer, a prominent New York politician and lifelong friend who, though married to DeWitt Clinton's sister, abandoned Clinton around the time Armstrong did.

3. Eustis to JM, December 3, 1812, *JMP-PS*, 5:477; Stagg, *Mr. Madison's War*, 278; Madison's "Review of a Statement Attributed to General John Armstrong" (1814), *JMP-LC*. Despite being abrasive, Armstrong could also flatter, as he did in a letter to Madison in 1812, when he was obviously fishing for the cabinet appointment. He offered "ardent thanks, for that Wisdom and Magnanimity, that have marked all your proceedings, as the Chief Magistrate of this flourishing and Extensive Continent Since yr. Inauguration to yr. Station." Armstrong to JM, October 26, 1812, *PJM-PS*, 5:412.

4. *Annals of Congress*, 12th Cong., 2nd sess., 549, 563, 566, 579; John Randolph to Josiah Quincy, August 30, 1813, in Edmund Quincy, *Life of Josiah Quincy of Massachusetts* (Boston, 1869), 335. When Monroe first proposed taking command of the army in the West, he assumed he could keep his job (allowing Comptroller of the Treasury Richard Rush to act as interim secretary of state); or else become secretary of war while leading the army and finding someone like Jefferson as his replacement at State. See Monroe to JM, September 2, 1812, Richard Rush to JM, September 4, 1812, *PJM-PS*, 5:252–53, 267–68. Monroe's son-in law, George Hay, advised him that he should not command the army and act as secretary of war at the same time. See Stagg, *Mr. Madison's War*, 278–81.

5. Quincy referred to patronage seekers from his region as men who "suck at the money-distilling breasts of the Treasury" and "toads that live upon the vapor of the palace and swallow the spittle of great men at levees." See *Annals of Congress*, 12th Cong., 2nd sess., 550, 580, 600; for Dolley Madison's drawing-room gatherings, see Catherine

Allgor, *Parlor Politics* (Charlottesville, Va., 2000), 60–61, 72, 75–82; David B. Mattern and Holly C. Shulman, *The Selected Letters of Dolley Payne Madison* (Charlottesville, Va., 2003), 95–101.

6. Using phony praise, Hanson slighted Dolley as one "predominantly distinguished throughout the United States for her transcendent virtues, and above all, for her inflexible morality, her exemplary sobriety, and her conjugal fidelity." See "Literary Notice," Georgetown *Federal Republican,* January 15, 1813. The *Federal Republican* reprinted Josiah Quincy's speech on January 22 and 25, 1813. Though Irving Brant noted Hanson's article and Catherine Allgor mentions it (incorrectly placing it in her chapter on the 1808 election), both miss the Corinna allusion. See Brant, 6:135; and Allgor, *A Perfect Union: Dolley Madison and the Creation of the New Nation* (New York, 2006), 133; for Dolley attending Pinkney's courtroom performances, see Margaret Bayard Smith, *The First Forty Years of Washington Society* (New York, 1906), 96–97.

7. On the law aimed at Pinkney, see *Annals of Congress,* 13th Cong., 2nd sess., 766, 2024; Pinkney to JM, January 24, 1814; JM to Pinkney, January 29, 1814, *JMP-LC;* also "Modern Sodom," *Federal Republican,* December 30, 1813. For other attacks on Pinkney and Mrs. Madison, see "The Virtuous Cabinet" and "The Drawing Room," in *Federal Republican,* February 10 and February 19, 1813; the issue of January 29, 1813, criticizes Pinkney, Monroe, and Dolley Madison for her alleged use of federal monies for personal indulgences (i.e., dresses and jewelry). For Pinkney's reputation as a brilliant lawyer, a dandy in appearance, and a man of questionable morals, see Robert Ireland, *The Legal Career of William Pinkney, 1760–1822* (New York, 1976); and Ireland, "William Pinkney: A Revision and Re-Emphasis," *American Journal of Legal History* 14 (July 1970): 235–37.

8. JM to Hamilton, December 31, 1812, *JMP-PS,* 5:334–35; Brant, 6:125–26. Hamilton did not leave quietly. He circulated rumors that Madison had altered his published letter of resignation so it appeared that Hamilton had voluntarily resigned. See "Paul Hamilton," *Concord Gazette,* January 26, 1813; JM to Dearborn, October 7, 1812, *JMP-LC;* Hickey, *War of 1812,* 113, 127–28; Edward K. Eckert, *The Navy in the War of 1812* (Gainesville, Fla., 1973), 16–17, 30–31, 51, 58–59, 71–72, 75–77; Eckert, "William Jones: Mr. Madison's Secretary of the Navy," *Pennsylvania Magazine of History and Biography* 96 (April 1972): 167–82; and Eckert, "Early Reform in the Navy Department," *American Neptune* 33 (1973): 233–38. As an opium trader, see contract with "Young Tom," a buyer in Canton, September 3, 1805; and for Jones's strong opposition to impressment, see Edward Carrington to Jones, October 15, 1805, both in William Jones Papers, Historical Society of Pennsylvania.

9. In his annual address Madison stated: "The enterprising spirit which has characterized our naval force, and its success, both in restraining insults and depredations on our coasts, and in reprisals on our enemy, will not fail to recommend an enlargement of it." *Annals of Congress,* 12th Cong., 2nd sess., 15; William Jones to five of his captains, on U.S. naval inferiority, February 22, 1812, cited in Eckert, *Navy in War of 1812,* 20–21. Brant, 6:39; Gallatin to James W. Nicholson, May 13, 1812, Gallatin Papers, Library of Congress.

10. For Madison's support of the navy during the Revolution, see JM to TJ, April 16, 1781, *RL,* 1:187; Eckert, *Navy in War of 1812,* 24–26; TJ to JM, May 21, 1813; JM to TJ, June 6, 1813; TJ to JM, June 21, 1813, *RL,* 3:1712, 1720–21, 1722–25; Jones to Lloyd

Jones, February 27, 1813, William Jones Papers, Historical Society of Pennsylvania. Editor Hanson's attack on the gunboats is in "Gunboats-Ahoy!," *Federal Republican,* February 19, 1813.

11. Skeen, *John Armstrong,* 127–31; Stagg, *Mr. Madison's War,* 310–11; Eckert, *Navy in War of 1812,* 40–41, 51, 56–58.

12. Gallatin to JM, March 5, 1812; Astor to Gallatin, February 6 and February 14, 1813, Gallatin Papers, Library of Congress; for Madison's earlier view on speculators, see JM to TJ, July 10 and August 8, 1791, in *RL,* 1:698, 708; Stagg, *Mr. Madison's War,* 298–99.

13. *The Centinel* [Salem, N.Y.], February 11, 1813; *Centinel of Freedom* [Newark, N.J.], January 26, 1813; Stagg, *Mr. Madison's War,* 299–301.

14. Madison later speculated that the senators' visit had been an elaborate ruse to corral wavering colleagues to vote to reject. The Senate had first rejected Madison's nomination of Jonathan Russell to serve as minister to Sweden, which was meant as a warning shot to the president. But he persisted in believing he had enough votes to carry Gallatin's appointment. See JM to Gallatin, August 2, 1813, *JMP-LC;* Stagg, *Mr. Madison's War,* 309–311, 313, 316; Ketcham, 559–61; Brant, 6:189–91; Monroe to TJ, June 28, 1813, *TJP-LC;* "Virginius, to James Madison, the President of the United States," *New York Spectator,* July 3, 1813; *Annals of Congress,* 13th Cong., 1st sess., 84–88, 95–96.

15. Horsman, *War of 1812,* 68–69, 74–75.

16. Lord Wellesley's words appeared in American newspapers; see, for example, *Baltimore Patriot,* January 25, 1813; TJ to JM, June 21, 1813, *RL,* 3:1724; Hickey, *War of 1812,* 153–54; William Jones to Alexander J. Dallas, July 19, 1813, Historical Society of Pennsylvania; Brant, 6:206–7; for reports of British atrocities, see "Letter from Col. E. Parker of Westmoreland County, Virginia," in *Richmond Enquirer,* July 16, 1813; and Parke Rouse, Jr., "The British Invasion of Hampton in 1813: The Reminiscences of James Jarvis," *Virginia Magazine of History and Biography* 76 (July 1968): 318–36. The House printed five hundred copies of the report on "British Barbarities" for distribution by members to newspapers as well as to constituents; *Annals of Congress,* 13th Cong., 1st sess., 489–92.

17. Congressman Hanson (editor of the *Federal Republican*) taunted Republicans by asking them why Congress so "studiously shunned an appeal to that unerring test—that touchstone of sincerity and patriotism—*the pocket?*" See *Annals of Congress,* 13th Cong., 1st sess., 355, 370–71, 462; also see Raymond M. Champagne and Thomas J. Reuter, "Jonathan Roberts and the 'War Hawk Congress of 1811–1812,' " *Pennsylvania Magazine of History and Biography* 104 (October 1980): 441, 447.

18. Eppes to TJ, July 21, 1813, *TJP-LC.* Eppes voted against a direct tax (two other Virginians did not cast votes), but he joined the majority in backing the carriage tax, the stamp tax, and the salt tax. His fellow Virginia Republicans seemed more bothered by the salt tax, with nine defections. The Pennsylvania Republicans voted as a solid bloc for the direct, carriage, and salt taxes, with only one Republican missing. There were six missing Pennsylvania votes on the stamp tax. See *Journal of the House,* Library of Congress, 80–81, 88–89; *Annals of Congress,* 13th Cong., 1st sess., 463. Jefferson's other son-in-law, Thomas Mann Randolph, was, the ex-president wrote, "seized with the military

fever." He was appointed a colonel in the U.S. Army and sent north to the Canadian frontier, where he saw little action. He resigned his commission after less than a year and, returning south, took up the defense of Richmond as an officer in the state militia. His eldest son, twenty-one-year-old Thomas Jefferson Randolph, enlisted as a private but remained nearer to home, managing the family's flour mill. See Malone, 6:118–22.

19. TJ to Eppes, June 24, 1813, *TJP-LC;* Herbert E. Sloan, *Principle and Interest: Thomas Jefferson and the Problem of Debt* (Charlottesville, Va., 1995), 205–13; Donald F. Swanson, " 'Bank-Notes Will Be But Oak Leaves': Thomas Jefferson on Paper Money," *Virginia Magazine of History and Biography* 101 (January 1993): 37–52; on Virginia state banks, see Glen Crothers, "Banks and Economic Development in Post-Revolutionary Northern Virginia, 1790–1812," *Business History Review* 73 (Spring 1999): 1–39.

20. Hickey, *War of 1812,* 122–23; Latimer, *1812,* chap. 6; *Argus* quote in Stagg, *Mr. Madison's War,* 320.

21. Hickey, *War of 1812,* chap. 6; Latimer, *1812,* chap. 9; Stagg, *Mr. Madison's War,* 329–47.

22. Monroe to JM, December 23, 1813, *JMP-LC;* Stagg, *Mr. Madison's War,* 366–69, 376.; Eckert, "William Jones: Mr. Madison's Secretary of the Navy," 177.

23. Brant, 6:243–45; Dolley Madison to Hannah Gallatin, January 21, 1814, in *Selected Letters of Dolley Payne Madison,* ed. Mattern and Shulman, 184; Granger to TJ, February 22, 1814; TJ to Granger, March 9, 1814, *TJP-LC;* JM to TJ, February 13, 1814; TJ to JM, March 10, 1814, *RL,* 3:1737–38, 1740–41. Madison knew about Granger's betrayal as early as 1812, when Jonathan Dayton wrote to him that Granger was "a most insidious, artful & decided enemy...who was deeply engaged in plans for changing the administration." Dayton to JM, December 28, 1812, *JMP-PS,* 5:530; Ketcham, 568.

24. Col. John Taylor, *Arator: Being a Series of Agricultural Essays, Agricultural and Political* (Baltimore, 1817), no. 28, "Labour," 82–86. Ignoring the comments on race, Jefferson, a lifelong student of the science of agriculture, dismissed the work in a letter to John Adams: "As you observe, there are some good things, but so involved in quaint, in far-fetched, affected, mystical conceipts [conceits], and flimsy theories, that who can take the trouble of getting at them?" TJ to Adams, January 24, 1814, *The Adams-Jefferson Letters: The Complete Correspondence between Thomas Jefferson and Abigail and John Adams,* ed. Lester J. Cappon (Chapel Hill, N.C., 1959), 421.

25. Taylor, *Arator,* no. 47, "Hogs, continued"; no. 59, "The Pleasures of Agriculture"; and no. 60, "The Rights of Agriculture," 140, 180–84.

26. Tate, *Conservatism and Southern Intellectuals, 1789–1861* (Columbia, Mo., 2005), 58–59, 108–16, 133; Susan Dunn, *Dominion of Memories: Jefferson, Madison, and the Decline of Virginia* (New York, 2007), 38–39; S. Potter to JM, February 13, 1813, *PJM-PS,* 5:650–52.

27. Lynch to TJ, December 25, 1810; TJ to Lynch, January 21, 1811, *PTJ-RS,* 3:267–69, 318–20.

28. "Letters of Edward Coles—Second Instalment: Edward Coles to Thomas Jefferson," *William and Mary Quarterly* 7 (April 1927): 97–98.

29. TJ to Coles, August 25, 1814; Coles to TJ, September 26, 1814, *TJP-LC;* Andrew Burstein, *Jefferson's Secrets: Death and Desire at Monticello* (New York, 2005), 136–38.

30. Paul A. Gilje, *Liberty on the Waterfront: American Maritime Culture in the Age of Revolution* (Philadelphia, 2004), 169–74; Stagg, *Mr. Madison's War,* 370.

31. Hickey, *War of 1812,* chap. 8; Latimer, *1812,* 232–37.

32. Latimer, *1812,* 301–3; JM to TJ, May 10, 1814, *RL,* 3:1742–43.

33. Hickey, *War of 1812,* 195- 202; Stagg, *Mr. Madison's War,* 393–99, 407- 11; Ketcham, 573–74; Brant, 6:271–72; Gerry to JM, July 17, 1814, *JMP-LC.*

34. Hickey, *War of 1812,* 197–98; Horsman, *War of 1812,* 198–200; Latimer, *1812,* 309–15.

35. Latimer, *1812,* 315–20.

36. *Baltimore Patriot,* August 25 and September 2, 1814.

37. *Delaware Gazette* [Wilmington], September 1, 1814.

38. *New Hampshire Sentinel* [Keene], September 3, 1814.

39. Brant, 6:307–8; *National Intelligencer,* August 30, 1814.

40. Latimer, *1812,* 323–24; Ketcham, 581–86; Stagg, *Mr. Madison's War,* 420–23; Skeen, *John Armstrong, Jr.,* 189–90, 199–200. Among the reasons Madison and Monroe had to distrust Armstrong in 1814 was that he blatantly opposed negotiations with London and wished to continue the war regardless of changing circumstances.

41. Jones to Dallas, September 15, 1814, George M. Dallas Papers, Historical Society of Pennsylvania.

42. *Alexandria Gazette,* September 8, 1814; *Boston Spectator,* September 3 and 10, 1814.

43. *Federal Republican,* September 9 and November 29, 1814.

44. Harry Ammon, *James Monroe: The Quest for National Identity* (Charlottesville, Va., 1990), 337.

45. A little over a year before, Jefferson had discussed his views on finance with both Monroe and Jack Eppes, but not with Madison, perhaps for the same reason that Madison had initially withheld from Jefferson his concurrence with Gallatin's recommendation that a new national bank be established. After he finally read one of Jefferson's letters to Monroe (at Jefferson's suggestion), Madison understood what Jefferson wanted: Treasury bills, backed by taxes, to be used as a circulating medium. See JM to TJ, October 10 and October 23, 1814; TJ to JM, September 24 and October 15, 1814, *RL,* 3:1744–51; Stagg, *Mr. Madison's War,* 376–78. It is worth noting that in William Jones's September 15 letter to Alexander Dallas, cited above, Jones observed: "The President is virtuous, able, and patriotic, but finance is out of his reach."

46. What Tompkins told Madison was slightly different from what he really felt: he said he thought he could serve the nation better by remaining in Albany. See Ray W. Irwin, *Daniel D. Tompkins: Governor of New York and Vice President of the United States* (New York, 1968), esp. 186–91; Daniel D. Tompkins, *Free Trade and Sailor's Rights! An Address to the Independent Electors of the State of New York* (Albany, N.Y., 1813); Ammon, *James Monroe,* 336–38.

47. Gallatin to Alexander Dallas, August 20, 1814, George M. Dallas Papers, Historical Society of Pennsylvania.

48. Ketcham, 589–90; Coles to JM, November 23, 1814, *JMP-LC.*

49. Philip S. Klein, ed., "Notes and Documents: Memoirs of a Senator from Pennsylvania: Jonathan Roberts, 1771–1854," *Pennsylvania Magazine of History and Biography* 62 (July 1938): 372.

50. Waterhouse to TJ, February 17, 1813, *PTJ-RS*, 5:640–42.

51. Nicholas to JM, November 11, 1814; JM to Nicholas, November 25, 1814, *JMP-LC*; Burstein, *Jefferson's Secrets*, 71. Jefferson Randolph married Jane Hollins Nicholas in March 1815.

52. Samuel Eliot Morison, *Harrison Gray Otis, 1765–1848: The Urbane Federalist* (Boston, 1969), 327, 336–43; Edmund Quincy, *Life of Josiah Quincy of Massachusetts* (Boston, 1869), 348–49. By the time the Hartford Convention was about to meet, Randolph was expressing a more skeptical attitude. See Stagg, *Mr. Madison's War,* 479.

53. Morison, *Harrison Gray Otis,* 353–82; Quincy, *Life of Josiah Quincy,* 357–58; Stagg, *Mr. Madison's War,* 481–82.

54. Adam Rothman, *Slave Country: American Expansion and the Origins of the Deep South* (Cambridge, Mass., 2005), 145–54, describing the complexities Jackson, Claiborne, and area planters tried to work through in putting slaves and free blacks in a combat zone; Andrew Burstein, *The Passions of Andrew Jackson* (New York, 2003), chap. 4; Stagg, *Mr. Madison's War,* 487–97; Latimer, *1812,* 369–77.

55. *New-York Evening Post,* February 7 and March 22, 1815; Freneau to JM, March 3, 1815, *JMP-LC.*

56. Burstein, *Passions of Andrew Jackson,* 118–19, 122; Joseph T. Hatfield, *William Claiborne: Jeffersonian Centurion in the American Southwest* (Lafayette, La., 1976), 303–4; Jackson to Claiborne, February 5 and February 6, 1815; Alexander Dallas to Jackson, April 12, 1815, *Papers of Andrew Jackson,* ed. Sam B. Smith, Harold D. Moser, et al. (Knoxville, Tenn., 1980–), 3:270–73, 344–46.

57. TJ to JM, March 23, 1815, *RL,* 3:1763–65.

58. Dearborn to TJ, February 27, 1815; TJ to Dearborn, March 17, 1815, *TJP-LC.* The salutation is to "My dear General, friend, & antient colleague."

59. Of those who did not welcome the treaty, British Admiral George Cockburn, who had watched the President's House burn, was filled with lament. He had "Jonathan" nearly caught in a trap, he thought, and wanted only a little more time to finish him off. Along with Admiral Alexander Cochrane, he was poised to strike in Georgia, preparing to enlist ex-slaves and Indians to attack the interior. Amid the blackened buildings of the federal city, Secretary Monroe was ready with a new strategy for the subjugation of Canada but had to shelve his plans. See Latimer, *1812,* 392–94; on Clay, see Merrill D. Peterson, *The Great Triumvirate: Webster, Clay, and Calhoun* (New York, 1987), 45–46.

60. "An Honorable Peace, the Result of a Glorious War," *Providence Patriot,* February 25, 1815, citing an article in the *National Advocate.* On the postwar change in temperament around America, and the renewal of energy and individual enterprise, see Steven Watts, *The Republic Reborn: War and the Making of Liberal America, 1790–1820* (Baltimore, Md., 1987).

61. [Alexander Dallas], *An Exposition of the Causes and Character of the Late War with Great Britain* (Philadelphia, 1815), 70, 73. Just prior to the start of the war, Richard Rush

had written from Washington to Dallas, then in Philadelphia, urging him to compose a pamphlet in support of going to war: "An able, lucid, view of the whole ground of our dispute with Great Britain, with an animated exhortation to crown it, would explode through the nation like Paines common sense, and do as much if not more good . . . I would say—you, Mr. Dallas, can turn off such an exciter in a few days." Rush to Dallas, May 26, 1812, George M. Dallas Papers, Historical Society of Pennsylvania.

62. *An Exposition of the Causes and Character of the Late War with Great Britain,* 69–70, 77–78. In fact, a good many slaves did escape and cross over to the British lines.

63. JM to TJ, March 12, 1815, *RL,* 3:1762–63.

64. TJ to JM, March 23, 1815, *RL,* 3:1763–64.

65. *Alexandria Gazette,* May 3, 1815.

66. Monroe to TJ, April 26, 1815, *TJP-LC;* Monroe to JM, April 30, 1815, *JMP-LC;* Brant, 6:385.

67. John Adams to Richard Rush, January 7, 1814, in J. H. Powell, ed., "Some Unpublished Correspondence of John Adams and Richard Rush, 1811–1816," *Pennsylvania Magazine of History and Biography* 61 (January 1937): 35–36. In defense of his declaration of war, Madison's views on national sovereignty were well captured in his letter to Benjamin Ludlow of New Jersey: "When the U.S. assumed & established their rank among the nations of the Earth, they assumed and established a common Sovereignty on the high seas, as well as an exclusive sovereignty within their territorial limits. The one is as essential as the other, to their Character as an Independent nation." JM to Ludlow, July 25, 1812, *PJM-PS,* 5:82.

68. Madison's recognition of the key role of New England in recruiting was reflected in a letter to Richard Cutts in 1812: "But what are we to do as to the main expedition towards Montreal, under the maneuvering counteractions of Strong & Griswold [two New England governors], and the general chill diffused throughout the region from which the requisite force was to be drawn?" See JM to Cutts, August 8, 1812, *PJM-PS,* 5:127–28; also see Lawrence Dilbert Cress, " 'Cool and Serious Reflection': Federalist Attitudes toward the War of 1812," *Journal of the Early Republic* 7 (Summer 1987): 123–45.

69. Before the war began, Jones, as a sea captain, believed that American ships should resist British attempts at impressment. Ship captains should consider negotiation first, he wrote, but if that failed, they should refuse to hand over the sailors "by firm and cool resistance," followed, if necessary, by "force of arms." See Eckert, "William Jones: Mr. Madison's Secretary of War," 172–73.

70. For Madison's critique of British use of "the merciless savages under their influence," see his "Annual Message to Congress, November 4, 1812," *PJM-PS,* 5:428; for the larger debate over civilized warfare and international law, see Robin F. A. Fabel, "The Laws of War in the 1812 Conflict," *Journal of American Studies* 14 (August 1980): 199–218.

71. Ketcham, 584–85; "Memoirs of a Senator from Pennsylvania," 373.

72. *Catalogue of the Library of Thomas Jefferson,* comp. E. Millicent Sowerby, 5 vols. (Washington, D. C., 1952–59); Malone, 6:171–80.

73. Ketcham, 604; Malone, 6:144–45; James H. Broussard, *The Southern Federalists, 1800–1816* (Baton Rouge, La., 1978), 185–86, and chap. 23; C. Edward Skeen, *1816: America Rising* (Lexington, Ky., 2003), chap. 4. To Virginia state legislator Charles

Yancey, Jefferson voiced his fears with characteristic animation: "Like a dropsical man calling out for water, water, our deluded citizens are clamoring for more banks, more banks." See TJ to Yancey, January 6, 1816, *TJP-LC.*

74. William Plumer, Jr., *Life of William Plumer* (Boston, 1857), 427–28; Skeen, *1816,* chap. 2.

75. Henry Adams, *History of the United States* (New York, 1889–91), vol. 9, chap. 6.

76. Skeen, *1816,* chap. 5. Skeen focuses on how controversial the compensation issue was, both during debate and after passage.

77. *National Intelligencer,* April 3, 1816. Through allies, Crawford declared himself a noncandidate, but this did not stop others, including Federalists, from trying to push him past Monroe. See Skeen, *1816,* 212–17.

78. *Virginia Argus,* May 18, 1816; Ketcham, 606.

79. *Massachusetts Spy,* May 29, 1816; *Alexandria Gazette,* October 28, 1816. The "fawning parasite" charge was originally associated with Monroe's negotiations in England and was leveled at him by a Pennsylvania Republican editor, John Binns of the *Democratic Press,* who was now the "fawning parasite" to Monroe.

80. *Nantucket Gazette,* October 15, 1816.

81. Jeffrey L. Pasley, *"The Tyranny of Printers": Newspaper Politics in the Early American Republic* (Charlottesville, Va., 2001), 273–75, 280–81.

82. Selleck Osborn, *An Oration in Celebration of American Independence* (Windsor, Vt., 1816); also *Vermont Republican,* October 14, 1816; Pasley, *"Tyranny of Printers,"* 281.

83. Ketcham, 606–8; *JMB,* 2:1325.

84. Skeen, *1816,* 230.

85. Indicative of the constitutional complexity he saw, and his willingness to accept conflict, Madison vetoed seven bills during his two terms, the most of any president until the highly confrontational Andrew Jackson. Neither John Adams nor Jefferson used his veto power. See Samuel B. Hoff, "The Legislative Messages of the Madison Administration," in John R. Vile, Wiliam D. Pederson, and Frank J. Williams, eds., *James Madison: Philosopher, Founder, and Statesman* (Athens, Ohio, 2008), 256–58.

86. Leonard D. White, *The Jeffersonians: A Study in Administrative History* (New York, 1951), chap. 31; Skeen, *1816,* chap. 6; TJ to Clinton, April 14, 1817, *TJP-LC;* John Lauritz Larson, *Internal Improvement: National Public Works and the Promise of Popular Government in the United States* (Chapel Hill, N.C., 2001), 66–69, quote at 69.

87. *RL,* 3:1774; Malone, 1:406–7, 2:138; John E. Ferling, *The First of Men: A Life of George Washington* (Knoxville, Tenn., 1988), 321; "Washington's Resignation Speech (Final Draft)," December 23, 1783, Maryland State Archives, Annapolis (online at http://www.msa.md.gov).

CHAPTER FIFTEEN
Madison Lives to Tell the Tale, 1817–1836

1. TJ to Adams, May 27, 1813, *The Adams-Jefferson Letters: The Complete Correspondence between Thomas Jefferson and Abigail and John Adams,* ed. Lester J. Cappon (Chapel Hill, N.C., 1959), 323.

2. JM to TJ, February 15, 1817, *RL,* 3:1783.

3. Ralph L. Ketcham, ed., "An Unpublished Sketch of James Madison by James K. Paulding," *Virginia Magazine of History and Biography* 67 (1959): 435–37; Matthew Mason, *Slavery and Politics in the Early American Republic* (Chapel Hill, N.C., 2006), 82–83. Paulding wrote a sympathetic portrait of the South in 1817, reconciling himself to slavery, and he would write a second book in defense of slavery in the year that Madison died. Paulding would eventually serve as secretary of the navy during the presidency of another Dutch-derived New Yorker, Martin Van Buren. Madison's good-natured style and comfort with Paulding comes through in a chummy note written on behalf of Dolley and himself just after Paulding had gone back to the capital: "We were glad to find that you were not melted on your way to Washington, by the heat, as...we wished you to prolong your asylum [i.e., respite] with us." JM to Paulding, July 23, 1818, *JMP-LC.*

4. Marie Frank, "It Took an Academical Village: Jefferson's Hotels at the University of Virginia," *Magazine of Albemarle History* 59 (2001): 31–68.

5. TJ to Monroe, April 15, 1817, *TJP-LC;* TJ to Adams, May 5, 1817, *Adams-Jefferson Letters,* 513; Andrew Burstein, *Jefferson's Secrets: Death and Desire at Monticello* (New York, 2005), 59–61; Malone, 6:251–57.

6. TJ to Ritchie, December 7, 1818; to Joseph Gales, December 7, 1818, *TJP-LC;* Charles Henry Ambler, *Thomas Ritchie: A Study in Virginia Politics* (Richmond, Va., 1913), 63; Malone, 6:272; *JMB,* 2:1349.

7. JM to Charles Jared Ingersoll, January 4, 1818, *PJM-RS,* 1:198. Ingersoll was a congressman from Pennsylvania during the War of 1812.

8. Lee to JM, August 5, 1824; JM to Lee, August [?] 1824, *JMP-LC;* Burstein, *Jefferson's Secrets,* chap. 8. With Barlow, as soon as Jefferson learned that Marshall was embarking on his history, he spoke for Madison as well when he invoked the first-person plural: "We are rich ourselves in materials, and can open all the public archives to you." Somehow fifteen or twenty years later, no suitable Republican had yet been found to exploit these well-preserved resources.

9. Plumer to JM, July 28, 1818, *JMP-LC.*

10. JM to Richard Cutts, January 16, February 24, and March 14, 1818; Gideon to JM, January 19, February 12, and August 15, 1818; JM to Gideon, January 28, February 20, and August 20, 1818, *PJM-RS,* 1:200, 212–13, 217, 223–26, 237–38, and *JMP-LC; The Federalist,* ed. Jacob E. Cooke (Middletown, Conn., 1961), xiii–xxi.

11. Malone, 6:275–78; Burstein, *Jefferson's Secrets,* 31; *JMB,* 2:1346.

12. Harry Ammon, *James Monroe: The Quest for National Identity* (Charlottesville, Va., 1971), chaps. 20 and 22. There is uncertainty as to when precisely the President's House was popularly called the White House, but it probably postdates the period covered in this book.

13. Burstein, *Passions of Andrew Jackson* (New York, 2003), 125; Jackson to Monroe, March 4, 1817, *Papers of Andrew Jackson,* ed. Sam B. Smith et al. (Knoxville, Tenn., 1980–), 4:93. Jefferson ceremonially toasted Jackson at an affair in Lynchburg, near Poplar Forest, but seems merely to have been cognizant of Jackson's following and unimpressed with his skills beyond the battlefield.

14. Monroe to JM, July 10 and July 20, 1818, *PJM-RS,* 1:301–2, 308; JM to TJ, Febru-

ary 12 and March 6, 1819; TJ to JM, March 3, 1819, *RL,* 3:1806–8; James E. Lewis, Jr., *The American Union and the Problem of Neighborhood, 1783–1829* (Chapel Hill, N.C., 1998), chap. 4; Burstein, *Passions of Andrew Jackson,* 129–37; Ammon, *James Monroe,* chaps. 23 and 24. Ammon takes the position that Monroe never gave Jackson the green light but was opposed to the Florida strategy that the Tennessean pursued because of the risk that it would destabilize U.S. foreign relations with the European powers—especially England. Ironically, it was Crawford, during Jackson's first term as president, who helpfully called Jackson's attention to Calhoun's hypocrisy.

15. Robert Pierce Forbes, *The Missouri Compromise and Its Aftermath: Slavery and the Meaning of America* (Chapel Hill, N.C., 2007), 35–38, 144–46. The widely anticipated end of the Virginia Dynasty may have been one catalyst of the Missouri debate. If not, then it was one derivative of it. Everyone saved face, but no one was truly happy. Illustrative of this disruptive moment, Martin Van Buren was elected U.S. senator from New York. As he took his seat, he made it known that he was a northern man of southern principles, a neo-Jeffersonian. An erstwhile ally of antislavery New Yorker Rufus King in their shared opposition to Governor DeWitt Clinton, Van Buren was supported at home by some outspoken racists. Largely unfazed by the existence of slavery, he was interested in reversing the old order by advancing to the presidency one day with Virginia's help. See ibid., 85–88, 126–29; and Mason, *Slavery and Politics in Early American Republic,* 210–11.

16. Peter S. Onuf, *Jefferson's Empire: The Language of American Nationhood* (Charlottesville, Va., 2000), 110–11; background on Holmes in *Biographical Dictionary of the American Congress, 1774–1949* (Washington, D.C., 1950), 1325.

17. "Mr. Holmes' Letter to the People of Maine," enclosure in Holmes to TJ, April 12, 1820, *TJP-LC.* On Holmes's detractors, see Forbes, *Missouri Compromise and Its Aftermath,* 66–67.

18. Francis D. Cogliano, *Thomas Jefferson: Reputation and Legacy* (Charlottesville, Va., 2006), 204.

19. TJ to Holmes, April 22, 1820, *TJP-LC;* on the fertility of slaves, see Mary Beth Norton, *Liberty's Daughters: The Revolutionary Experience of American Women, 1750–1800* (Boston, 1980), 72–73; also Marie Jenkins Schwartz, *Birthing a Slave: Motherhood and Medicine in the Antebellum South* (Cambridge, Mass., 2006), esp. chap. 3. Jan Lewis and Kenneth A. Lockridge offer evidence that Virginia wives, anxious about the dangers attending childbirth, largely accepted the eventuality, resisting only to the extent of devising ways to space (delay) their pregnancies. The increasingly common description of pregnancy in terms of disease (e.g., as "indisposition") by the early nineteenth century did not result in smaller families. See Lewis and Lockridge, " 'Sally Has Been Sick': Pregnancy and Family Limitation among Virginia Gentry Women, 1780–1830," *Journal of Social History* 22 (Autumn 1988): 5–19.

20. TJ to Holmes, July 8, 1820; Holmes to TJ, June 19, 1820, *TJP-LC.*

21. See Robert J. Allison, " 'From the Covenant of Peace, a Simile of Sorrow': James Madison's American Allegory," *Virginia Magazine of History and Biography* 99 (July 1991): 327–50.

22. Draft in Madison's hand, 1821, *JMP-LC.* In addition to Allison's study, see the analysis of Drew R. McCoy, *The Last of the Fathers: James Madison and the Republican Legacy* (New York, 1989), 274–77. As McCoy observes, we never find out what is done about

Mary's black arm, even as the couple reconcile. "The humanity of the slaves," he notes, "is utterly lost in the allegory."

23. Onuf, *Jefferson's Empire,* 144–46; Roane to Monroe, February 16, 1820, cited in McCoy, *Last of the Fathers,* 273; TJ to Short, April 13, 1820, *TJP-LC.*

24. On Madison's plight, see Ketcham, 629.

25. Charles H. Ambler, *Thomas Ritchie: A Study in Virginia Politics* (Richmond, Va., 1913), 80–83; Jean Edward Smith, *John Marshall: Definer of a Nation* (New York, 1996), 450–53.

26. Roane to JM, April 17, 1821, *JMP-LC;* Smith, *John Marshall,* 456–63; Susan Dunn, *Dominion of Memories: Jefferson, Madison, and the Decline of Virginia* (New York, 2007), 145–48.

27. Roane to JM, April 17, 1821; JM to Roane, May 6 and June 29, 1821, *JMP-LC.* Madison's remarks at this time were consistent with those he made when he answered Roane's complaints about *McCulloch v. Maryland* in 1819. See JM to Roane, September 2, 1819, *JMP-LC.* President Monroe's support of Marshall's decision in *McCullough v. Maryland* angered many Virginians; but his son-in-law's attempts to oppose northern efforts at restriction of slavery in Missouri, presumed to have been undertaken with Monroe's approval, won back support, though Monroe's actual position was not quite as Virginians imagined. See Forbes, *Missouri Compromise and Its Aftermath,* 64–65.

28. TJ to Roane, March 9, 1821, *TJP-LC.*

29. "Autobiography," initially dated January 6, 1821, *TJP-LC.*

30. Ibid.

31. Our interpretation of the relationship between the *Anas* and Autobiography is also that of Cogliano, *Thomas Jefferson,* 54–57.

32. JM to TJ, February 8, 1825, *RL,* 3:1924–25.

33. TJ to JM, August 30, 1823; JM to TJ, September 6, 1823, *RL,* 3:1875–77; Burstein, *Jefferson's Secrets,* 193.

34. JM to TJ, February 8, 1825, *RL,* 3:1925–26.

35. TJ to Gallatin, October 29, 1822, *TJP-LC.*

36. TJ to Lafayette, November 4, 1823, *Letters of Lafayette and Jefferson,* 414–16.

37. JM to Lafayette, November 25, 1820, *JMP-LC.*

38. The rest of Jefferson's commentary on Napoleon was: "a lion in the field only. In civil life a cold-blooded, calculating unprincipled Ursurper [*sic*], without a virtue, no statesman, knowing nothing of commerce, political economy, or civil government, and supplying ignorance by bold presumption." See TJ to John Adams, July 5, 1814, *Adams-Jefferson Letters,* 431; Burstein, *Passions of Andrew Jackson,* 217–28; Merrill D. Peterson, *The Great Triumvirate: Webster, Clay, and Calhoun* (New York, 1987), 129; Ketcham, 642–44.

39. Crawford to JM, April 8, 1824; JM to Crawford, April 13, 1824; JM to Clay, draft letter, April 1824, *PJM-LC;* Ammon, *James Monroe,* 501, 543–47.

40. TJ to Albert Gallatin, October 29, 1822, *TJP-LC.*

41. *Portland Advertiser,* January 12, 1825.

42. For a good rundown of the key personalities in the election and their interactions, see Peterson, *Great Triumvirate,* 116–31. On the first and decisive ballot in the

House runoff, Adams received the votes of thirteen state delegations, Jackson seven, and Crawford four. On the "corrupt bargain" and how it haunted Adams through this presidency, see also Andrew Burstein, *America's Jubilee* (New York, 2001), 146–47, 182–85.

43. JM to TJ, February 17, 1825, *RL,* 3:1927–28. In his exposition of the national debate over federal versus state funding of infrastructure, John L. Larson writes of the "negative rhetoric of watchfulness" that increasingly absorbed southern elites; as sectionalism intensified, distinctions between northern and southern developmental models became more obvious. See Larson, *Internal Improvement: National Public Works and the Promise of Popular Government in the United States* (Chapel Hill, N.C., 2001), chap. 4, quote at 136. North Carolina Republican Nathaniel Macon made Madison's point bluntly: "If Congress can make canals, they can with more propriety emancipate." See Forbes, *Missouri Compromise and Its Aftermath,* 7. On Tucker, see Burstein, *Jefferson's Secrets,* 84–85; Marie Tyler-McGraw, *An African Republic: Black and White Virginians in the Making of Liberia* (Chapel Hill, N.C., 2007), 108–9; and Merrill D. Peterson, *The Jefferson Image in the American Mind* (New York, 1960), 122–27, on Tucker's 1837 biography.

44. JM to TJ, February 17, 1825, *RL,* 3:1927–28.

45. TJ to JM, December 24, 1825, with enclosure, *RL,* 3:1943–46.

46. JM to TJ, December 28, 1825, enclosing letter to Ritchie dated December 18, 1825, *RL,* 3:1947–51; *National Intelligencer,* January 2, 1826, in support of federal improvements. A contributor to the *Richmond Enquirer* at the same time drew distinctions: the Constitution allowed for the establishment of post offices and post roads, but, he complained, "the word 'canal' is not seen in the constitution at all. Yet there are [congressional] committees on roads and canals . . . What was the use of inserting one power in the constitution and excluding another; if Congress can legitimately exercise jurisdiction equally over both?" See *Enquirer,* January 5, 1826.

Federalism, in the constitutional sense, established limits on the states as well as the central government; for Madison, where sovereignty was divided between the general government and the states, "one sovereignty loses what the other gains." The mechanism was in place and had to be allowed to work. If the federal government resolved that it had a right to go ahead with canal legislation, and popular support was broad, Congress would move on it and the Virginians' hands would remain tied. See discussion in McCoy, *Last of the Fathers,* 114–17.

47. JM to Lafayette, November 20, 1820, *JMP-LC.*

48. A. Levasseur, *Lafayette in America in 1824 and 1825, or Journal of a Voyage to the United States* (Philadelphia, 1829), quote at 1:168; see also Burstein, *America's Jubilee,* chap. 1.

49. Levasseur, *Lafayette in America,* 1:212–25.

50. Ibid., 2:245–46.

51. TJ to JM, September 10, 1825, *RL,* 3:1941. On the state of the university in 1825–26, see Frank Edgar Grizzard, "Documentary History of the Construction of the Buildings at the University of Virginia, 1817–1828," Ph.D. diss., University of Virginia, 1996, chaps. 9–11.

52. Malone, 6:425, 465–68; Brant, 6:455; TJ to JM, October 18, 1825, *RL,* 3:1942.

53. TJ to JM, February 17, 1826, *RL,* 3:1964–67. Regarding the obelisk, see Burstein, *Jefferson's Secrets,* 11–12, 281.

54. JM to TJ, February 24, 1826, *RL,* 3:1967–68.

55. TJ to JM, May 3, 1826; JM to TJ, May 6, 1826, *RL,* 3:1970–71.

56. Samuel X. Radbill, "The Autobiographical Ana of Robley Dunglison, M.D.," *Transactions of the American Philosophical Society* 53 (1963); also John M. Dorsey, ed., *The Jefferson-Dunglison Letters* (Charlottesville, Va., 1960), which contains biographical information.

57. George Green Shackelford, *Jefferson's Adoptive Son: The Life of William Short, 1759–1848* (Lexington, Ky., 1993), chap. 14.

58. On Jefferson's personal financial troubles and public positions on matters of economy, see Herbert E. Sloan, *Principle and Interest: Thomas Jefferson and the Problem of Debt* (New York, 1995), esp. 137–39, 218–23; on the slave auction, see Lucia Stanton, *Free Some Day: The African-American Families of Monticello* (Charlottesville, Va., 2000), 141–45.

59. *JMB,* 1:245–46.

60. Burstein, *Jefferson's Secrets,* 274–76.

61. Dunglison to JM, July 1, 1826; Trist to JM, July 4, 1826; JM to Trist, July 6, 1826, *JMP-LC.*

62. Henry S. Randall, *Life of Thomas Jefferson* (New York, 1858), 3:666; Randolph to JM, July 8, 1826; JM to Randolph, July 14, 1826, *JMP-LC;* Ralph Ketcham, *The Madisons of Montpelier: Reflections on the Founding Couple* (Charlottesville, Va., 2009), 130.

63. JM to Lafayette, November [?] 1826, *JMP-LC;* Ketcham, *Madisons of Montpelier,* 95–97.

64. *Memoir, Correspondence, and Miscellanies from the Papers of Thomas Jefferson,* ed. Thomas Jefferson Randolph (Charlottesville, Va., 1829); JM to Thomas Jefferson Randolph, December 22, 1828, and February 28, 1829, *JMP-LC;* Peterson, *Jefferson Image in American Mind,* 29–36. If Randolph proved less than wholly up to the sensitive task of editing his grandfather's papers, Madison cultivated the more discerning Nicholas Trist during this period. One of the favors he did was to introduce Trist to Albert Gallatin, suggesting that the former treasury secretary "ought to discharge his quota of historical debt to truth & posterity." See JM to Gallatin, December 1, 1828; to Trist, December 17, 1828, *JMP-LC.* The letters Randolph opted to include in the four-volume work begin in May 1775, though Jefferson's extant correspondence dates to 1760.

65. *Memoir, Correspondence, and Miscellanies,* ed. Randolph, 4:421–23; JM to Nicholas P. Trist, May 15, 1832, cited in Malone, 6:359.

66. Drew R. McCoy, *The Last of the Fathers: James Madison and the Republican Legacy* (New York, 1989), 124–30, 134. McCoy writes: "Perhaps it was best for Madison that the disconsolate and impetuous Jefferson was no longer around to define the precise terms of his own legacy." Ritchie came to feel that while Jefferson opposed the tariff, he would not have considered it an issue warranting nullification; the Richmond editor was increasingly comfortable with Jackson and Van Buren and disagreed with Calhoun's drift. See Charles Henry Ambler, *Thomas Ritchie: A Study in Virginia Politics* (Richmond, 1913), 141–43.

67. Peterson, *Great Triumvirate*, 159–61, 169; Peterson, *Jefferson Image in American Mind*, 51–59; McCoy, *Last of the Fathers*, 131–56.

68. Herbert Baxter Adams, *The Life and Writings of Jared Sparks* (Boston, 1893), 2:37.

69. *Proceedings and Debates of the Virginia Convention of 1829–30* (Richmond, 1830), 532–33, 537–38. Early in the convention, Monroe (a proponent of colonization) expressed his opposition to a general emancipation. And while defending the institution of slavery as a positive bond between white and black individuals, Randolph predicted, in this case with almost pinpoint accuracy, that the new constitution would not last twenty years before another convention was called. See ibid., 178, 790. Also see Ammon, *James Monroe: The Quest for National Identity*, 563–66; Ketcham, 636–40; Douglas B. Chambers, *Murder at Montpelier: Igbo Africans in Virginia* (Jackson, Miss., 2005), Appendix B.

70. JM to Monroe, April 21, 1831, *JMP-LC*; Ammon, *James Monroe*, 568–72.

71. JM to Paulding, April 1831, draft, in *JMP-LC*.

72. JM to Paulding, June 27, 1831, *JMP-LC*.

73. JM to Thomas Dew, February 23, 1833, *JMP-LC*.

74. Harriet Martineau, *Retrospect of Western Travel* (New York, 1838), 1:190–92.

75. JM to Robert Taylor, July [?] 1835; same letter sent to Hubbard Taylor (of Kentucky), August 15, 1835, in which Madison inserted "occasionally" after "sickly countenance." JM to Jackson, October 11, 1835; to Charles Francis Adams, October 13, 1835; to James Madison Hite (Madison's nephew), November 25, 1835, all in *JMP-LC*.

76. Hugh A. Garland, *The Life of John Randolph of Roanoke* (New York, 1857), 369–71.

77. JM to Woodbury, December 28, 1835; Cranch to JM, February 4, 1836; JM to Cranch, February 9, 1836; to Van Buren, February 12, 1836; to Samuel Southard, February 26, 1836; to Professor Rogers, February 26, 1836, *JMP-LC*. Madison was nominal president of the Washington National Monument Association at the time of his death.

78. Ketcham, *Madisons of Montpelier*, 164–71.

79. Ketcham, 663–71; Brant, 6:509–24; *Richmond Enquirer*, May 27, 1836, citing Fredericksburg source on Dr. Dunglison's visit; Dolley Madison to Lucy Payne Todd, May 9, 1836; JM to Bancroft, April 13, 1836; Tucker to JM, June 17, 1836; JM to Tucker, June 27, 1836, *JMP-LC*.

80. *Register of Debates in Congress*, June 20, 1836 (Washington, D.C.: Gales & Seaton, 1825–37), 1911–12.

81. *National Intelligencer*, July 7, 1826; *Daily National Intelligencer*, July 1, 1836.

82. Allgor, *Perfect Union*, 373–84.

83. Brant, 6:530–31.

CHAPTER SIXTEEN

Thawing Out the Historical Imagination

1. Van Buren to TJ, June 8, July 13, and September 2, 1824; TJ to Van Buren, June 29, 1824, *TJP-LC*. For a good synthesis of Van Buren's courtship of the Old Republicans of the South, see Joseph Hobson Harrison, Jr., "Martin Van Buren and His Southern Supporters," *Journal of Southern History* 22 (November 1956): 438–58.

2. JM to Van Buren, September 20, 1826, March 13, 1827, December 11, 1830, and December 15, 1835, *JMP-LC*. On Van Buren's effort to pursue the Madison and Jefferson line with regard to internal improvements, see *The Autobiography of Martin Van Buren*, ed. John C. Fitzpatrick (Washington, 1920), 317–19. Repeatedly in the autobiography, Van Buren refers to the Jefferson and Madison administrations as seamless and philosophically alike. His Jefferson is fair and principled, and Madison "proverbial for his amiable temper." See ibid., 123.

3. Martin Van Buren, *Inquiry into the Origin and Course of Political Parties in the United States* (New York, 1867), 1–3, 181–86, 267.

4. In his Preface, Randall is effusive in expressing his gratitude to the Jefferson-Randolph family: "They welcomed our undertaking with a prompt and graceful expression of cordial appreciation . . . They furnished us their full recollections and opinions on every class of topics." His other correspondents included Henry Clay, Edward Coles, and Joseph Carrington Cabell. Henry S. Randall, *Life of Thomas Jefferson* (New York, 1858), 1:xi–xii. Epigraph is taken from ibid., 3:312. On Randall's background and his desire to rescue Jefferson's reputation, see Merrill D. Peterson, *The Jefferson Image in the American Mind* (New York, 1960), 149–60.

5. Ketcham, 615–16; Catherine Allgor, *A Perfect Union: Dolley Madison and the Creation of the American Nation* (New York, 2006), 402.

6. Ralph L. Ketcham, ed., "An Unpublished Sketch of James Madison by James K. Paulding," *Virginia Magazine of History and Biography* 67 (1959): 432–37.

7. George Green Shackelford, *Jefferson's Adoptive Son: The Life of William Short, 1759–1848* (Lexington, Ky., 1993), 136. It must be said, however, that Short's opinion of Madison was colored by events. Short held something of a personal grudge after Madison failed to shore up a diplomatic appointment initiated by Jefferson in 1808.

8. In early America, "bilious complaints" connoted a "violent looseness" of the bowels. The most pertinent and widely popular eighteenth-century text containing descriptions, diagnoses, and treatments of ills is William Buchan, *Domestic Medicine* (London, 1785).

9. Another example of an influential text conveying the power of language is Hugh Blair's *Lectures on Rhetoric and Belles Lettres* (1783). Blair was a professor of rhetoric at the University of Edinburgh, and his book went through countless printings between the American Revolution and the American Civil War—a staple text in colleges. Attuned to the need for a thought-filled congressman to convey ideas effectively and affectingly, Madison asked Jefferson to send him a copy of Blair's *Lectures* in 1784—it was one of the first favors his friend did for him. For a good dissection of Madison's language as seen through his note-taking at the convention and his style of argument relative to Hamilton's in *The Federalist*, see Louis C. Schaedler, "James Madison: Literary Craftsman," *William and Mary Quarterly* 3 (October 1946): 515–33.

10. Randall, *Life of Thomas Jefferson*, 1:vi; Peterson, *Jefferson Image in American Mind*, 314–17.

11. Peter S. Onuf, "Making Sense of Jefferson," in Onuf, *The Mind of Thomas Jefferson* (Charlottesville, Va., 2007), 21.

12. The popular author David McCullough undertook a joint study of Jefferson and Adams but opted to do Adams alone after he discovered that he did not particularly

like Jefferson. His decision reminds one of the value in establishing a necessary distance between oneself and the historical subject. In American historiography after 1932, the third president was deftly redrawn as a Roosevelt Democrat. Hamilton, his nemesis, became a herald for big business conservatism. Their rivalry dominated the political narrative in most textbooks, until the all-too-obvious Adams-Jefferson contrast (stout and blunt versus slippery and detached) was thrust upon Americans in the 1990s. When Adams emerged from his long hibernation, founders chic became a popularity contest, mimicking our celebrity-conscious culture, in which voters decide on political candidates based on whether or not they "like" them. Yet Adams's supposed self-deprecation and Jefferson's supposed sneakiness tell us absolutely nothing about their political philosophies. See Peterson, *Jefferson Image in American Mind*, 347–79; Francis D. Cogliano, *Thomas Jefferson* (Charlottesville, Va., 2006).

13. TJ to Taylor, June 4, 1798, *PTJ*, 30:389. The P.S. of this letter reminded the Virginia Republican of Jefferson's particular vulnerability: "It is hardly necessary to caution you to let nothing of mine get before the public. A single sentence got hold of by the Porcupines [i.e., by the likes of William Cobbett] will suffice to abuse & persecute me in their papers for months."

14. John Ferling, *The Ascent of George Washington* (New York, 2009), 231–33, 239.

15. "To the Citizens Who Shall Be Convened This Day in the Fields in the City of New York," April 22, 1796, *PAH*, 20:131–34.

16. Margaret Bayard Smith, *The First Forty Years of Washington Society*, ed. Gaillard Hunt (New York, 1906), 299–300.

17. David Brion Davis, *The Problem of Slavery in the Age of Revolution, 1770–1823* (Ithaca, N.Y., 1975), 92–94, 306–18, quotes at 92, 306–7; Peter Dorsey, "To 'Corroborate Our Own Claims': Public Positioning and the Slavery Metaphor in Revolutionary America," *American Quarterly* 55 (September 2003): 353–86.

18. Douglas Bradburn, *The Citizenship Revolution: Politics and the Creation of the American Union, 1774–1804* (Charlottesville, Va., 2009), chap. 7, esp. 242–43, 253–56.

19. Lafayette to TJ, July 20, 1820, and June 1, 1822, in *The Letters of Lafayette and Jefferson*, ed. Gilbert Chinard (Baltimore, Md., 1929), 398–99, 408–9.

20. Phillip D. Morgan, "Interracial Sex in the Chesapeake and the British Atlantic World," in Jan Ellen Lewis and Peter S. Onuf, eds., *Sally Hemings and Thomas Jefferson: History, Memory, and Civic Culture* (Charlottesville, Va., 1999), 52–84.

21. See John Wood Sweet, *Bodies Politic: Negotiating Race in the American North, 1730–1830* (Baltimore, 2003), 253–54, 260–63. In the early 1780s, while Jefferson was writing *Notes on Virginia*, gradual emancipation programs were in place in Connecticut and Rhode Island, but in those two states the cruel and cynical were still selling indentured black children into slavery in the Carolinas.

22. Ibid., 180–81; Douglas R. Egerton, *Death or Liberty: African Americans and Revolutionary America* (New York, 2009), 231–32; Matthew Mason, *Slavery and Politics in the Early American Republic* (Chapel Hill, N.C., 2006), 210–11.

23. "The Slaves," in *New-York Mirror, and Ladies' Literary Gazette*, February 19, 1825; Douglas R. Egerton, " 'Its Origin Is Not a Little Curious': A New Look at the American Colonization Society," *Journal of the Early Republic* 5 (Winter 1985): 463–80, quote at 469. The standard work on the ACS is P. J. Staudenraus, *The American Colonization Movement,*

1816–1865 (New York, 1961). Recently two compelling reexaminations have been published: Eric Burin, *Slavery and the Peculiar Solution: A History of the American Colonization Society* (Gainesville, Fla., 2005); and with an emphasis on Virginia, Marie Tyler-McGraw, *An African Republic: Black and White Virginians in the Making of Liberia* (Chapel Hill, N.C., 2007).

24. Shackelford, *Jefferson's Adoptive Son,* 176–77. Perhaps it was a lack of imagination that explains Madison's and Jefferson's failure to think that Virginia and the South could free all slaves and hire as wage laborers as many as were willing to remain. To do so, after all, was not to promote a completely integrated society. Legal restrictions would have remained in place to assuage the fears of the most virulent racists. As it was, free blacks did not have ready access to arms. Blacks would have remained a permanent underclass—the very "adjustment" white America made after Reconstruction. But even that was not possible for Madison and Jefferson, who opted instead for colonization of the freed slave. From 1800 on, meanwhile, more and more state legislation was designed to disadvantage, if not punish, free people of color.

25. TJ to JM, April 4, 1800; JM to TJ, April 20, 1800, *RL,* 2:1132–33; Edmund Berkeley, Jr., "Prophet without Honor: Christopher McPherson, Free Person of Color," *Virginia Magazine of History and Biography* 77 (April 1969): 184–85.

26. Drew R. McCoy, *The Last of the Fathers: James Madison and the Republican Legacy* (New York, 1989), 237–38; the author points out Madison's "inadvertent contempt" toward free blacks, dating to the later period of his life, in ibid., 285. See also John Chester Miller, *The Wolf by the Ears: Thomas Jefferson and Slavery* (New York, 1977), 264ff.

27. Egerton, *Death or Liberty,* 247.

28. Clarence E. Walker, *Mongrel Nation: The America Begotten by Thomas Jefferson and Sally Hemings* (Charlottesville, Va., 2009), quote at 60; JM to Coles, September 3, 1819, *JMP-LC.*

29. McCoy, *Last of the Fathers,* 239; TJ to Rush, September 23, 1800, *PTJ,* 32:166–68. In the letter, Jefferson did not capitalize "god." See generally Charles B. Sanford, *The Religious Life of Thomas Jefferson* (Charlottesville, Va., 1984).

30. See in particular Susan Dunn, *Dominion of Memories: Jefferson, Madison, and the Decline of Virginia* (New York, 2007), 123–28.

31. JM to Smith, September 21, 1830, *JMP-LC.* Madison had crossed out "sophistry" and replaced it with "Heretic."

Bibliography

Newspapers and Magazines Consulted
(Originals, Microfilm, or Online)

Alexandria Advertiser; Alexandria Gazette; American Citizen (New York); *American Mercury* (Hartford, Conn.); *American Minerva* (New York); *Baltimore Patriot; Baltimore Telegraph; The Bee* (Stonington, Conn.); *Boston Daily Advertiser; Boston Gazette; Boston Spectator; Carlisle Gazette* (Pa.); *Carolina Gazette* (Charleston, S.C.); *Centinel of Freedom* (Newark, N.J.); *City Gazette* (Charleston, S.C.); *Columbian Herald* (Charleston, S.C.); *Columbian Minerva* (Dedham, Mass.); *Columbian Patriot* (Middlebury, Vt.); *Delaware Gazette; Enquirer* (Richmond); *Federal Galaxy* (Brattleboro, Vt.); *Federal Gazette* (Philadelphia); *Federal Republican* (Baltimore and Georgetown, D.C.); *Federal Republican* (New Bern, N.C.); *Freeman's Journal* (Portsmouth, N.H.); *Gazette of the United States* (Philadelphia); *General Advertiser* (Philadelphia); *Herald of Virginia* (Fincastle); *Hornet* (Fredericktown, Md.); *Independent Gazetteer* (Philadelphia); *Jersey Chronicle* (Mt. Pleasant); *Loudon's Register* (New York); *Massachusetts Spy* (Worcester); *Mirrour* (Concord, N.H.); *Morning Chronicle* (New York); *Nantucket Gazette; National Aegis* (Worcester, Mass.); *National Gazette* (Philadelphia); *National Intelligencer* (Washington, D.C.); *Newburyport Herald* (Mass.); *New-England Palladium; New-Hampshire Gazette; New-Hampshire Sentinel* (Keene); *New-Hampshire Spy* (Portsmouth); *New-Jersey Chronicle* (Mt. Pleasant); *New-Jersey Journal* (Elizabethtown); *New-Jersey Telescope* (Newark); *Newport Mercury* (R.I.); *New-York Evening Post; New-York Gazette; New-York Herald; New-York Journal; Norfolk Gazette* (Va.); *North American* (Baltimore); *Oracle of Dauphin and Harrisburgh Advertiser* (Pa.); *Pennsylvania Gazette; Pennsylvania Mercury; Pennsylvania Packet; Philadelphia Gazette; Political Gazette* (Newburyport, Mass); *Political Intelligencer* (New Brunswick, N.J.); *Port Folio; Portland Advertiser; Republican Advocate* (Fredericktown, Md.); *Republican Farmer* (Bridgeport, Conn.); *The Republican or, Anti-Democrat* (Baltimore); *Republican Star* (Easton, Md.); *Rhode Island Republican; Salem Gazette* (Mass.); *South-Carolina State-Gazette; Stewart Kentucky Herald* (Lexington); *Trenton Federalist; United States Chronicle* (Providence); *Virginia Argus* (Richmond); *Virginia Gazette* (Williamsburg); *Virginia Journal* (Alexandria); *Washington Federalist; Weekly Wanderer* (Randolph, Vt.); *Western Star* (Stockbridge, Mass.).

Pamphlets and Other Eighteenth- and Early Nineteenth-Century Sources

Adams, John Quincy. *An Inaugural Oration Delivered at the Author's Installation as Boylston Professor of Rhetorick and Oratory, at Harvard University.* Boston: Munroe & Francis, 1806.

[Anon.] *An Address to the Independent Citizens of Massachusetts, on the Subject of the Approaching Election, Exhibiting a View of the Leading Measures of the Jefferson and Madison Administrations.* Worcester, Mass.: Isaiah Thomas, 1810.

[Anon.] *The Death of Washington; with Some Remarks on Jeffersonian and Madisonian Policy.* Broadside, place and publisher unknown, ca. 1809.

[Beckley, John]. *Address to the People of the United States with an Epitome and Vindication of the Public Life and Character of Thomas Jefferson.* Richmond, Va.: Meriwether Jones, 1800.

Bishop, Abraham. *Connecticut Republicanism. An Oration on the Extent and Power of Political Delusion.* Albany, N.Y.: John Barber, 1801.

Blyth, Stephen Cleveland. *History of the War between the United States and Tripoli and Other Barbary Powers.* Salem, Mass.: Salem Gazette, 1806.

[Callender, James Thomson]. *The Prospect before Us.* 2 vols. vol. 1: Richmond: M. Jones, S. Pleasants and J. Lyon; vol. 2: Richmond: Pleasants and Field, 1800.

[Carey, James, as "Geoffrey Touchstone"]. *The House of Wisdom in a Bustle.* Philadelphia: Printed for the author, 1798.

[Cobbett, William, as "Peter Porcupine"]. *A Little Plain English, Addressed to the People of the United States on the Treaty Negotiated with His Britannic Majesty.* Philadelphia: Thomas Bradford, 1795.

———. *A New Year's Gift to the Democrats; or, Observations on a Pamphlet, Entitled, "A Vindication of Mr. Randolph's Resignation."* Philadelphia: William Cobbett, 1796.

Cragg, Saunders. *George Clinton Next President, and Our Republican Institutions Rescued from Destruction.* New York: Henry C. Southwick, 1808.

[Cullen, Stephen]. *Memoirs of the Hon. Thomas Jefferson.* 2 vols. New York: n.p., 1809.

[Dallas, Alexander James]. *An Exposition of the Causes and Character of the Late War with Great Britain.* Philadelphia: Thomas S. Manning, 1815.

———. *Features of Mr. Jay's Treaty.* Philadelphia: Mathew Carey, 1795.

———. *Letters from Franklin; on the Conduct of the Executive and the Treaty Negotiated by the Chief Justice of the United States with the Court of Great Britain.* Philadelphia: E. Oswald, 1795.

Davis, John. *Travels of Four Years and a Half in the United States of America; During 1798, 1799, 1801, and 1802.* London: R. Edwards, 1803.

Day, Thomas. *An Oration on Party Spirit, Pronounced before the Connecticut Society of Cincinnati.* Litchfield, Conn.: T. Collier, 1798.

[Dennie, Joseph, as "A Layman"]. *The Claims of Thomas Jefferson to the Presidency, Examined at the Bar of Christianity.* Philadelphia: Asbury Dickins, 1800.

[Fraser, Donald]. *Party-Spirit Exposed, or Remarks on the Times.* New-York: Thomas Kirk, 1799.

Godwin, William. *Enquiry concerning Political Justice and Its Influence on Morals and Happiness.* 2 vols. Philadelphia: Bioren & Madan, 1796.

Levasseur, A[uguste]. *Lafayette in America in 1824 and 1825; or, Journal of a Voyage to the United States.* Philadelphia: Carey & Lea, 1829 (rept., New York: Research Reprints, 1970).

[Lowell, John]. *Perpetual War, the Policy of Mr. Madison.* Boston: Chester Stebbins, 1812.

Martineau, Harriet. *Retrospect of Western Travel.* 2 vols. New York: Harper & Brothers, 1838.

Osborn, Selleck. *An Oration in Celebration of American Independence, Pronounced at Windsor, Vermont, July 4, 1816.* Windsor, Vt.: Jesse Cochran, 1816.

Pendleton, Edmund. *An Address of the Honorable Edmund Pendleton of Virginia to the American Citizens, on the State of Our Country.* Boston: Benjamin Edes, 1799.

Proceedings and Debates of the Virginia Convention of 1829–30. Richmond: Samuel Shepherd & Co., 1830.

Ramsay, David. *The History of the American Revolution.* Edited by Lester H. Cohen. 2 vols. Indianapolis: Liberty Fund, 1990 (1789).

[Randolph, Edmund]. *Germanicus* (1794), Early American Imprints (Evans), no. 27597.

———. *A Vindication of Mr. Randolph's Resignation.* Philadelphia: Samuel H. Smith, 1795.

Ray, William. *Horrors of Slavery; or, the American Tars in Tripoli,* Edited by Hester Blum. Troy, New York, 1808; rept., New Brunswick, N.J.: Rutgers University Press, 2008.

Stiles, Ezra. *The UNITED STATES Elevated to GLORY and HONOUR.* Worcester, Mass.: Isaiah Thomas, 1785.

Taylor, Col. John. *Arator: Being a Series of Agricultural Essays, Agricultural and Political.* Baltimore: J. Robinson, 1817.

[Taylor, John, writing as "Curtius"]. *A Defence of the Measures of the Administration of Thomas Jefferson.* Washington: Samuel H. Smith, 1804.

Tompkins, Daniel D. *Free Trade and Sailor's Rights! An Address to the Independent Electors of the State of New York.* Albany, N.Y.: Office of the *Argus,* 1813.

Wirt, William. *The Life of Patrick Henry.* Hartford, Conn.: Silas Andrus & Son, 1832 [1817].

Wyche, William. *An Examination of the Examiners Examined, Being a Defence of Christianity, Opposed to the Age of Reason.* New-York: Wayland & David, 1795.

———. *Party Spirit: An Oration.* New-York: T & J Swords, 1794.

Published Correspondence and State Papers

The Adams-Jefferson Letters: The Complete Correspondence between Thomas Jefferson and Abigail and John Adams. Edited by Lester J. Cappon. Chapel Hill, N.C.: University of North Carolina Press, 1987 (1959).

Annals of Congress. New York: D. Appleton and Co., 1857.

[Coles, Edward]. "Letters of Edward Coles." *The William and Mary Quarterly* 7 (July 1927): 158–73.

The Documentary History of the Ratification of the Constitution. Edited by Merrill Jensen, John P. Kaminski, et al. 22 vols. to date. Madison: State Historical Society of Wisconsin, 1976–.

The Federalist. Edited by Jacob E. Cooke. Middletown, Conn.: Wesleyan University Press, 1961.

The Letters and Papers of Edmund Pendleton. Edited by David John Mays. 2 vols. Charlottesville: University Press of Virginia, 1967.

Letters from William Cobbett to Edward Thornton, Written in the Years 1797 to 1800. Edited by G.D.H. Cole. London: Oxford University Press, 1937.

Letters of Benjamin Rush. Edited by L. H. Butterfield. 2 vols. Princeton, N.J.: Princeton University Press, 1951.

Letters of Delegates to Congress, 1774–1789. Edited by Paul H. Smith. 26 vols. Washington, D.C.: Library of Congress, 1976–2000.

Memoir, Correspondence, and Miscellanies from the Papers of Thomas Jefferson. Edited by Thomas Jefferson Randolph. 4 vols. Charlottesville, Va.: F. Carr, 1829.

Papers of Andrew Jackson. Edited by Sam B. Smith, Harold D. Moser, et al. 6 vols. to date. Knoxville: University of Tennessee Press, 1980–.

The Papers of Benjamin Franklin. Edited by Leonard W. Labaree et al. 38 vols. to date. New Haven, Conn.: Yale University Press, 1959–.

The Papers of George Mason. Edited by Robert A. Rutland. 3 vols. Chapel Hill: University of North Carolina Press, 1970.

The Papers of William Thornton. Edited by C. M. Harris. 2 vols. Charlottesville: University Press of Virginia, 1995.

Powell, J. H., ed. "Some Unpublished Correspondence of John Adams and Richard Rush, 1811–1816." *Pennsylvania Magazine of History and Biography* 61 (January 1937): 26–53.

The Records of the Federal Constitution of 1787. Edited by Max Farrand. 3 vols. New Haven, Conn.: Yale University Press, 1911.

Revolutionary Virginia: The Road to Independence. Edited by Robert L. Scribner et al. 7 vols. Charlottesville: University Press of Virginia, 1973–81.

Richard Price: Political Writings. Edited by D. O. Thomas. Cambridge, U.K.: Cambridge University Press, 1991.

The Selected Letters of Dolley Payne Madison. Edited by David B. Mattern and Holly C. Shulman. Charlottesville: University of Virginia Press, 2003.

U.S. Office of Naval Records. *Naval Documents Related to the United States Wars with the Barbary Powers.* 5 vols. Washington, D.C.: Government Printing Office, 1939.

William Plumer's Memorandum of Proceedings in the United States Senate, 1803–1807. Edited by Everett Somerville Brown. New York: Macmillan, 1923.

The Works of the Rev. John Witherspoon. 3 vols. Philadelphia: William W. Woodward, 1800.

Writings of James Monroe. Edited by Stanislaus M. Hamilton. 7 vols. New York: G. P. Putnam's Sons, 1898–1903.

Selected Secondary Literature

Ackerman, Bruce. *The Failure of the Founding Fathers: Jefferson, Marshall, and the Rise of Presidential Democracy.* Cambridge, Mass.: Harvard University Press, 2005.

Adair, Douglass. " 'That Politics May Be Reduced to a Science': David Hume, James Madison, and the Tenth *Federalist.*" *Huntington Library Quarterly* 20 (August 1957): 343–60.

Adams, Henry. *John Randolph.* Edited by Robert McColley. Boston: Houghton Mifflin, 1882; rpt. Armonk, N.Y.: M. E. Sharpe, 1996.

———. *History of the United States of America.* 9 vols. New York: Charles Scribner's Sons, 1889–1891.

———. *The Life of Albert Gallatin.* Philadelphia: J. B. Lippincott & Co., 1879.

Adams, Herbert Baxter. *The Life and Writings of Jared Sparks.* 2 vols. Boston: Houghton Mifflin, 1893.

Adams, William Howard. *Gouverneur Morris: An Independent Life.* New Haven, Conn.: Yale University Press, 2003.

———. *The Paris Years of Thomas Jefferson.* New Haven, Conn.: Yale University Press, 1997.

Allen, Gardner W. *Our Navy and the Barbary Corsairs.* Boston: Houghton Mifflin, 1905.

Allgor, Catherine. *Parlor Politics: In Which the Ladies of Washington Help Build a City and Government.* Charlottesville: University Press of Virginia, 2000.

———. *A Perfect Union: Dolley Madison and the Creation of the American Nation.* New York: Henry Holt, 2006.

Allison, Robert J. *The Crescent Obscured: The United States in the Muslim World, 1776–1815.* New York: Oxford University Press, 1995.

———. " 'From the Covenant of Peace, a Simile of Sorrow': James Madison's American Allegory." *Virginia Magazine of History and Biography* 99 (July 1991): 327–50.

Ambler, Charles Henry. *Thomas Ritchie: A Study in Virginia Politics.* Richmond: Bell Book & Stationery, 1913.

Ammon, Harry. *James Monroe: The Quest for National Identity.* New York: McGraw Hill, 1971; rpt. Charlottesville: University Press of Virginia, 1990.

———. "James Monroe and the Election of 1808 in Virginia." *William and Mary Quarterly* 20 (January 1963): 33–56.

Anderson, Fred. *Crucible of War: The Seven Years' War and the Fate of Empire in British North America.* New York: Alfred A. Knopf, 2000.

Arkin, Marc M. "'The Intractable Principle': David Hume, James Madison, Religion, and the Tenth Federalist." *American Journal of Legal History* 39 (April 1995): 148–76.

Arthur, Stanley Clisby. *The Story of the West Florida Rebellion.* St. Francisville, La.: St. Francisville Democrat, 1935.

Bailey, Kenneth. "George Mason, Westerner." *William and Mary Quarterly* 23 (October 1943): 409–17.

———. *The Ohio Company of Virginia and the Westward Movement, 1748–1792.* Glendale, Calif.: Arthur H. Clark Co., 1939.

Bakeless, John. *Background to Glory: The Life of George Rogers Clark.* Philadelphia: J. B. Lippincott, 1957; rpt. Lincoln: University of Nebraska Press, 1992.

Banning, Lance. "James Madison and the Nationalists, 1780–1783." *William and Mary Quarterly* 40 (April 1983): 227–55.

———. *Jefferson and Madison: Three Conversations from the Founding.* Madison, Wisc.: Madison House, 1995.

———. *The Sacred Fire of Liberty: James Madison and the Founding of the American Republic.* Ithaca, N.Y.: Cornell University Press, 1995.

Barker-Benfield, G. J. *The Culture of Sensibility: Sex and Society in Eighteenth-Century Britain.* Chicago: University of Chicago Press, 1992.

Becker, Carl L. *The Declaration of Independence: A Study in the History of Political Ideas.* New York: Alfred A. Knopf, 1922.

Beeman, Richard R. *The Old Dominion and the New Nation, 1788–1801.* Lexington: University of Kentucky Press, 1972.

———. *Patrick Henry: A Biography.* New York: McGraw-Hill, 1974.

———. *Plain, Honest Men: The Making of the American Constitution.* New York: Random House, 2009.

Bemis, Samuel Flagg. *Jay's Treaty: A Study in Commerce and Diplomacy.* New Haven, Conn.: Yale University Press, 1962.

Ben-Atar, Doron, and Barbara B. Oberg, eds. *Federalists Reconsidered.* Charlottesville: University of Virginia Press, 1998.

Blackburn, Robin. "Haiti, Slavery, and the Age of Democratic Revolutions." *William and Mary Quarterly* 63 (October 2006): 643–74.

Bolton, Theodore. "The Life Portraits of James Madison." *William and Mary Quarterly* 8 (January 1951): 25–47.

Bonn, Franklyn George, Jr. "The Idea of Political Party in the Thought of Thomas Jefferson and James Madison." Ph.D. diss., University of Minnesota, 1964.

Bowling, Kenneth R. "The Bank Bill, the Capital City, and President Washington." *Capitol Studies* 1 (Spring 1972): 59–71.

——. "Dinner at Jefferson's: A Note on Jacob E. Cooke's 'The Compromise of 1790.'" *William and Mary Quarterly* 28 (October 1971): 629–48.

——. "'A Tub to the Whale': The Founding Fathers and the Adoption of the Federal Bill of Rights." *Journal of the Early Republic* 8 (Fall 1988): 223–51.

Bradburn, Douglas. *The Citizenship Revolution: Politics and the Creation of the American Union, 1774–1804.* Charlottesville: University of Virginia Press, 2009.

Breslaw, Elaine G. *Dr. Alexander Hamilton and Provincial America.* Baton Rouge: Louisiana State University Press, 2008.

Brewer, Holly. "Entailing Aristocracy in Colonial Virginia: 'Ancient Feudal Restraints' and Revolutionary Reform." *William and Mary Quarterly* 54 (April 1997): 307–46.

Brewin, Mark W. *Celebrating Democracy: The Mass-Mediated Ritual of Election Day.* New York: Peter Lang, 2008.

Broadwater, Jeff. *George Mason: Forgotten Founder.* Chapel Hill: University of North Carolina Press, 2006.

Brooks, George E., Jr. "The Providence African Society's Sierra Leone Emigration Scheme, 1794–1795: Prologue to the African Colonization Movement." *International Journal of African Studies* 7 (1974): 183–202.

Brooks, Robin. "Alexander Hamilton, Melancton Smith, and the Ratification of the Constitution in New York." *William and Mary Quarterly* 24 (July 1967): 340–58.

Broussard, James. *The Southern Federalists, 1800–1816.* Baton Rouge: Louisiana State University Press, 1978.

Brown, Christopher. "Empire Without Slaves: British Concepts of Emancipation in the Age of Revolution." *William and Mary Quarterly* 56 (April 1999): 273–306.

Brown, Everett S. "The Senate Debate on the Breckinridge Bill for the Government of Louisiana, 1804." *American Historical Review* 22 (January 1917): 340–64.

Brown, Roger H. *Redeeming the Republic: Federalists, Taxation, and the Origins of the Constitution.* Baltimore: Johns Hopkins University Press, 1993.

Buchanan, John. *The Road to Guilford Courthouse: The American Revolution in the Carolinas.* New York: John Wiley & Sons, 1997.

Burns, James McGregor, and Susan Dunn. *George Washington.* New York: Times Books, 2004.

Burrows, Edwin G., and Mike Wallace. *Gotham: A History of New York City to 1898.* New York: Oxford University Press, 1999.

Burstein, Andrew. *America's Jubilee: How in 1826 a Generation Remembered Fifty Years of Independence.* New York: Alfred A. Knopf, 2001.

——. *The Inner Jefferson: Portrait of a Grieving Optimist.* Charlottesville: University of Virginia Press, 1995.

———. "Jefferson's Madison versus Jefferson's Monroe." *Presidential Studies Quarterly* 28 (Spring 1998): 394–408.

———. *Jefferson's Secrets: Death and Desire at Monticello.* New York: Basic Books, 2005.

———. *The Original Knickerbocker: The Life of Washington Irving.* New York: Basic Books, 2007.

———. *The Passions of Andrew Jackson.* New York: Alfred A. Knopf, 2003.

———. *Sentimental Democracy: The Evolution of America's Romantic Self-Image.* New York: Hill & Wang, 1999.

Carson, David A. "Jefferson, Congress, and the Question of Leadership in the Tripolitan War." *Virginia Magazine of History and Biography* 94 (October 1986): 409–24.

———. "That Ground Called Quiddism: John Randolph's War with the Jefferson Administration." *American Studies* 20 (April 1986): 71–92.

Cash, Arthur. *John Wilkes: The Scandalous Father of Civil Liberty.* New Haven, Conn.: Yale University Press, 2006.

Cassell, Frank. *Merchant Congressman in the Young Republic: Samuel Smith of Maryland, 1752–1839.* Madison: University of Wisconsin Press, 1971.

Castiglia, Christopher. "Pedagogical Discipline and the Creation of White Citizenship: John Witherspoon, Robert Finley, and the Colonization Society." *Early American Literature* 33 (1998): 192–214.

Catalogue of the Library of Thomas Jefferson. Comp. E. Millicent Sowerby. 5 vols. Washington, D.C.: Library of Congress, 1952–59.

Chambers, Douglas B. *Murder at Montpelier: Igbo Africans in Virginia.* Jackson: University Press of Mississippi, 2005.

Champagne, Raymond M., and Thomas J. Reuter. "Jonathan Roberts and the War Hawk Congress of 1811–1812." *Pennsylvania Magazine of History and Biography* 104 (October 1980): 434–49.

Chaplin, Joyce E. "Slavery and the Principle of Humanity: A Modern Idea in the Early Lower South." *Journal of Social History* 24 (Winter 1990): 299–315.

Clapp, William W. *Joseph Dennie.* Cambridge, Mass.: John Wilson & Son, 1880.

Clarfield, Gerald H. *Timothy Pickering and the American Republic.* Pittsburgh: University of Pittsburgh Press, 1980.

Clark, Jennifer. "The War of 1812: American Nationalism and Rhetorical Images of Britain." *War and Society* 12 (May 1994): 1–26.

Clarkson, Paul S., and R. Samuel Jett. *Luther Martin of Maryland.* Baltimore: Johns Hopkins University Press, 1970.

Cleves, Rachel Hope. *The Reign of Terror in America: Visions of Violence from Anti-Jacobinism to Antislavery.* New York: Cambridge University Press, 2009.

Clifford, John Garry. "A Muddy Middle of the Road: The Politics of Edmund Randolph, 1790–1795." *Virginia Magazine of History and Biography* 80 (July 1972): 286–311.

Coatsworth, John H. "American Trade with European Colonies in the Caribbean and South America, 1790–1812." *William and Mary Quarterly* 24 (April 1967): 243–66.

Cogan, Jacob Katz. "The Reynolds Affair and the Politics of Character." *Journal of the Early Republic* 16 (Autumn 1996): 398–417.

Cogliano, Francis D. *Thomas Jefferson: Reputation and Legacy.* Charlottesville: University of Virginia Press, 2006.

Cohen, I. Bernard. *Science and the Founding Fathers: Science in the Political Thought of Thomas Jefferson, Benjamin Franklin, John Adams, and James Madison.* New York: W. W. Norton, 1995.

Coleman, Aaron N. "'A Second Bounaparty?': A Reexamination of Alexander Hamilton During the Franco-American Crisis, 1796–1801." *Journal of the Early Republic* 28 (Summer 2008): 183–214.

Coleman, Francis X. J. "John Jay on War." *Journal of the History of Ideas* 43 (January–March 1982): 145–51.

Collier, Christopher. *Roger Sherman's Connecticut: Yankee Politics and the American Revolution.* Middletown, Conn.: Wesleyan University Press, 1971.

Commager, Henry Steele. *Jefferson, Nationalism, and the Enlightenment.* New York: George Braziller, 1975.

Conley, Patrick T., and John P. Kaminski, eds. *The Constitution and the States: The Role of the Original Thirteen in the Framing and Adoption of the Federal Constitution.* Madison: University of Wisconsin Press, 1988.

Conway, Moncure Daniel. *Omitted Chapters of History Disclosed in the Life and Papers of Edmund Randolph.* New York: G.P. Putnam's Sons, 1888.

Cooke, Jacob E. "The Compromise of 1790." *William and Mary Quarterly* 27 (October 1970): 524–45.

———. *Tench Coxe and the Early Republic.* Chapel Hill: University of North Carolina Press, 1978.

Cope, Kevin L., ed. *George Washington in and as Culture.* New York: AMS Press, 2001.

Cornell, Saul. *The Other Founders: Anti-Federalism and the Dissenting Tradition in America, 1788–1828.* Chapel Hill: University of North Carolina Press, 1999.

Couch, R. Randall. "William Charles Cole Claiborne: An Historiographical Review." *Louisiana History* 36 (Autumn 1995): 453–65.

Cox, Henry Bartholomew. *The Parisian American: Fulwar Skipwith of Virginia.* Washington, D.C.: Mount Vernon Publishing Co., 1964.

Crackel, Theodore J. *Mr. Jefferson's Army: Political and Social Reform of the Military Establishment, 1801–1809.* New York: New York University Press, 1987.

Cress, Lawrence Dilbert. "'Cool and Serious Reflection': Federalist Attitudes toward the War of 1812." *Journal of the Early Republic* (Summer 1987): 123–45.

Crothers, Glen. "Banks and Economic Development in Post-Revolutionary Northern Virginia, 1790–1812." *Business History Review* 73 (Spring 1999): 1–39.

Crowe, Charles. "The Reverend James Madison in Williamsburg and London, 1768–1771." *West Virginia History* 25 (1964): 270–78.

Cunningham, Noble E., Jr. *The Jeffersonian Republicans: The Formation of Party Organization, 1789–1801*. Chapel Hill: University of North Carolina Press, 1957.

———. *The Jeffersonian Republicans in Power: Party Operations, 1801–1809*. Chapel Hill: University of North Carolina Press, 1963.

———. *The Presidency of James Monroe*. Lawrence: University Press of Kansas, 1996.

Cusick, James G. *The Other War of 1812: The Patriot War and the American Invasion of Spanish East Florida*. Athens: University of Georgia Press, 2003.

Dater, Henry M. "Albert Gallatin, Land Speculator." *Mississippi Valley Historical Review* 26 (June 1939): 21–38.

Davis, David Brion. *The Problem of Slavery in the Age of Revolution, 1770–1823*. Ithaca, N.Y.: Cornell University Press, 1975.

Dawidoff, Robert. *The Education of John Randolph*. New York: W. W. Norton, 1979.

DeConde, Alexander. *Entangling Alliance: Politics and Diplomacy under George Washington*. Durham, N.C.: Duke University Press, 1958.

———. *The Quasi-War: The Politics and Diplomacy of the Undeclared War with France, 1797–1801*. New York: Charles Scribner's Sons, 1966.

Deyle, Steven. "The Irony of Liberty: Origins of the Domestic Slave Trade." *Journal of the Early Republic* 12 (Spring 1992): 37–62.

Dorsey, Peter. "To 'Corroborate Our Own Claims': Public Positioning and the Slavery Metaphor in Revolutionary America." *American Quarterly* (September 2003): 353–86.

Dowling, William C. *Literary Federalism in the Age of Jefferson: Joseph Dennie and the Port Folio, 1801–1812*. Columbia: University of South Carolina Press, 1999.

Downes, Randolph C. "Dunmore's War: An Interpretation." *Mississippi Valley Historical Review* 21 (December 1934): 311–28.

Drayton, Richard. *Nature's Government: Science, Imperial Britain, and the "Improvement" of the World*. New Haven, Conn.: Yale University Press, 2000.

Druckenbrod, Daniel L., and Herman H. Shugart. "Forest History of James Madison's Montpelier Plantation." *Journal of the Torrey Botanical Society* 131 (July–September 2004): 204–19.

DuBois, Laurent. *Avengers of the New World: The Story of the Haitian Revolution*. Cambridge, Mass.: Harvard University Press, 2004.

Dunn, Susan. *Dominion of Memories: Jefferson, Madison, and the Decline of Virginia*. New York: Basic Books, 2007.

———. "Revolutionary Men of Letters and the Pursuit of Radical Change: The Views of Burke, Tocqueville, Adams, Madison, and Jefferson." *William and Mary Quarterly* 53 (October 1996): 729–54.

Eckert, Edward K. "Early Reform in the Navy Department." *American Neptune* 33 (1973): 233-38.

———. *The Navy in the War of 1812*. Gainesville: University of Florida Press, 1973.

———. "William Jones: Mr. Madison's Secretary of the Navy." *Pennsylvania Magazine of History and Biography* 96 (April 1972): 167-82.

Edling, Max M. *A Revolution in Favor of Government: Origins of the U.S. Constitution and the Makings of the American State*. New York: Oxford University Press, 2003.

———. "'So Immense a Power in the Affairs of War': Alexander Hamilton and the Restoration of Public Credit." *William and Mary Quarterly* 64 (April 2007): 287-326.

Egerton, Douglas R. *Death or Liberty: African Americans and Revolutionary America*. New York: Oxford University Press, 2009.

———. *Gabriel's Rebellion: The Virginia Slave Conspiracies of 1800 and 1802*. Chapel Hill: University of North Carolina Press, 1993.

———. "'Its Origin Is Not a Little Curious': A New Look at the American Colonization Society." *Journal of the Early Republic* 5 (Winter 1985): 463-80.

Einhorn, Robin L. "Patrick Henry's Case against the Constitution: The Structural Problem of Slavery." *Journal of the Early Republic* 22 (Winter 2002): 549-73.

Elkins, Stanley, and Eric McKitrick. *The Age of Federalism*. New York: Oxford University Press, 1993.

Ellis, Joseph J. *American Sphinx: The Character of Thomas Jefferson*. New York: Alfred A. Knopf, 1997.

———. *His Excellency: George Washington*. New York: Alfred A. Knopf, 2004.

———. *Passionate Sage: The Character and Legacy of John Adams*. New York: W. W. Norton, 1993.

Elson, James M., comp. *Patrick Henry in His Speeches and Writings and in the Words of His Contemporaries*. Lynchburg, Va.: Warwick House, 2007.

Ernst, Robert. *Rufus King: American Federalist*. Chapel Hill: University of North Carolina Press, 1968.

Estes, Todd. *The Jay Treaty Debate, Public Opinion, and the Evolution of Early American Political Culture*. Amherst: University of Massachusetts Press, 2006.

Fabel, Robin F. A. "The Laws of War in the 1812 Conflict." *Journal of American Studies* 14 (August 1980): 199-218.

Ferling, John E. *Adams vs. Jefferson: The Tumultuous Election of 1800*. New York: Oxford University Press, 2004.

———. *The Ascent of George Washington: The Hidden Political Genius of an American Icon*. New York: Bloomsbury Press, 2009.

———. *The First of Men: A Life of George Washington*. Knoxville: University of Tennessee Press, 1988.

———. *John Adams: A Life.* Knoxville: University of Tennessee Press, 1992.

———. *A Leap in the Dark: The Struggle to Create the American Republic.* New York: Oxford University Press, 2003.

———. *Setting the World Ablaze: Washington, Adams, Jefferson, and the American Revolution.* New York: Oxford University Press, 2000.

Fetter, Frank Whitson. "Who Were the Foreign Mercenaries of the Declaration of Independence?" *Pennsylvania Magazine of History and Biography* 104 (1980): 508–13.

Finkelman, Paul. "James Madison and the Bill of Rights: A Reluctant Paternity." *Supreme Court Review* (1990): 301–47.

———. *Slavery and the Founders: Race and Liberty in the Age of Jefferson.* Armonk, N.Y.: M. E. Sharpe, 1996.

Fiske, John. *The Critical Period in American History, 1783–1789.* Boston: Houghton Mifflin, 1888.

Fliegelman, Jay. *Prodigals and Pilgrims: The American Revolution Against Patriarchal Authority, 1750–1800.* New York: Cambridge University Press, 1984.

Foley, William E. "Lewis and Clark's American Travels: The View from Britain." *Western Historical Quarterly* 34 (Autumn 2003): 301–24.

Foner, Eric. *Tom Paine and Revolutionary America.* 1976; rpt. New York: Oxford University Press, 2005.

Forbes, Robert Pierce. *The Missouri Compromise and Its Aftermath: Slavery and the Meaning of America.* Chapel Hill: University of North Carolina Press, 2007.

Ford, Lacy. "Reconfiguring the Old South: 'Solving' the Problem of Slavery, 1787–1838." *Journal of American History* 95 (June 2008): 95–122.

Frank, Marie. "It Took an Academical Village: Jefferson's Hotels at the University of Virginia." *Magazine of Albemarle History* 59 (2001): 31–68.

Freeman, Douglas Southall. *George Washington: A Biography.* 7 vols. New York: Charles Scribner's Sons, 1948–57.

Freeman, Joanne. *Affairs of Honor: National Politics in the New Republic.* New Haven, Conn.: Yale University Press, 2001.

Frey, Sylvia R. *Water from the Rock: Black Resistance in a Revolutionary Age.* Princeton, N.J.: Princeton University Press, 1991.

Furtwangler, Albert. *American Silhouettes: Rhetorical Identities of the Founders.* New Haven, Conn.: Yale University Press, 1987.

———. *The Authority of Publius: A Reading of the Federalist Papers.* Ithaca, N.Y.: Cornell University Press, 1984.

Gaines, Edwin M. "The Chesapeake Affair: Virginians Mobilize to Defend National Honor." *Virginia Magazine for History and Biography* 64 (April 1956): 131–42.

Gara, Donald J. "Loyal Subjects of the Crown: The Queen's Own Loyal Virginia Regiment and Dunmore's Ethiopian Regiment, 1775-76." *Journal of the Society for Army Historical Research* 83 (2005): 30-42.

Garrigus, John D. *Before Haiti: Race and Citizenship in French Saint-Domingue.* New York: Palgrave Macmillan, 2006.

Gay, Peter. *The Enlightenment: An Interpretation.* 2 vols. New York: W. W. Norton, 1966, 1969.

Geggus, David Patrick. "The British Government and the Saint Domingue Slave Revolt, 1791-1793." *English Historical Review* 96 (April 1981): 285-305.

———, ed. *Impact of the Haitian Revolution in the Atlantic World.* Columbia: University of South Carolina Press, 2001.

———. "Racial Equality, Slavery, and Colonial Secession during the Constituent Assembly." *American Historical Review* 94 (December 1989): 1290-308.

———. *Slavery, War, and Revolution: The British Occupation of Saint Domingue 1793-1798.* Oxford, U.K.: Clarendon Press, 1982.

Gelles, Edith B. *Abigail and John: Portrait of a Marriage.* New York: William Morrow, 2009.

———. *Portia: The World of Abigail Adams.* Bloomington: Indiana University Press, 1992.

Gerber, Scott D. "Roger Sherman and the Bill of Rights." *Polity* 28 (Summer 1996): 521-40.

Ghachem, Malick W. "The Slave's Two Bodies: The Life of an American Legal Fiction." *William and Mary Quarterly* 60 (October 2003): 809-42.

Gibson, Alan. "The Madisonian Madison and the Question of Consistency: The Significance and Challenge of Recent Research." *Review of Politics* 64 (Spring 2002): 311-38.

Gilbert, Felix. *To the Farewell Address: Ideas of Early American Foreign Policy.* Princeton, N.J.: Princeton University Press, 1961.

Gilje, Paul A. *Liberty on the Waterfront: American Maritime Culture in the Age of Revolution.* Philadelphia: University of Pennsylvania Press, 2004.

Girard, Philippe. "Black Talleyrand: Toussaint Louverture's Diplomacy, 1798-1802." *William and Mary Quarterly* 66 (January 2009): 87-124.

———. "The Ugly Duckling: The French Navy and the Saint-Domingue Expedition, 1801-1803." *International Journal of Navy History* 7 (December 2008): 1-25.

Gitlin, Jay. *The Bourgeois Frontier: French Towns, French Traders & American Expansion.* New Haven, Conn.: Yale University Press, 2010.

Gordon-Reed, Annette. *The Hemingses of Monticello.* New York: W. W. Norton, 2008.

———. *Thomas Jefferson and Sally Hemings: An American Controversy.* Charlottesville: University Press of Virginia, 1997.

Gottschalk, Louis. *Lafayette Between the American and the French Revolution, 1783-1789.* Chicago: University of Chicago Press, 1950.

Gould, Eliga H. *The Persistence of Empire: British Political Culture in the Age of the American Revolution.* Chapel Hill: University of North Carolina Press, 2000.

Gould, Eliga H., and Peter S. Onuf, eds. *Empire and Nation: The Revolution in the Atlantic World*. Baltimore: Johns Hopkins University Press, 2005.

Grammer, John M. *Pastoral and Politics in the Old South*. Baton Rouge: Louisiana State University Press, 1996.

Gross, Robert A., ed. *In Debt to Shays: The Bicentennial of an Agrarian Rebellion*. Charlottesville: University of Virginia Press, 1993.

Gutzman, Kevin R. "A Troublesome Legacy: James Madison and the 'Principles of '98.'" *Journal of the Early Republic* 15 (Winter 1995): 569–89.

Hale, Matthew Rainbow. "On Their Tiptoes: Political Time and Newspapers during the Advent of the Radicalized French Revolution, circa 1792–1793." *Journal of the Early Republic* 29 (Summer 2009): 191–218.

Harper, John Lamberton. *American Machiavelli: Alexander Hamilton and the Origins of American Foreign Policy*. Cambridge, U.K.: Cambridge University Press, 2004.

Harrison, Joseph Hobson, Jr. "Martin Van Buren and His Southern Supporters." *Journal of Southern History* 22 (November 1956): 438–58.

Harrison, Richard A. *Princetonians, 1769–1775: A Biographical Dictionary*. Princeton, N.J.: Princeton University Press, 1980.

Hatcher, William B. *Edward Livingston: Jeffersonian Republican and Jacksonian Democrat*. Baton Rouge: Louisiana State University Press, 1941.

Hatfield, Joseph T. *William Claiborne: Jeffersonian Centurion in the American Southwest*. Lafayette: University of Southwestern Louisiana, 1976.

Hatzenbuehler, Ronald L. *"I Tremble for My Country": Thomas Jefferson and the Virginia Gentry*. Gainesville: University Press of Florida, 2006.

——. "The War Hawks and the Question of Congressional Leadership in 1812." *Pacific Historical Review* 45 (February 1976): 1–22.

Hayes, Kevin J. *The Road to Monticello: The Life and Mind of Thomas Jefferson*. New York: Oxford University Press, 2008.

Hellenbrand, Harold. "Not 'To Destroy But to Fulfil': Jefferson, Indians, and Republican Dispensation." *Eighteenth-Century Studies* 18 (Autumn 1985): 523–49.

——. *The Unfinished Revolution: Education and Politics in the Thought of Thomas Jefferson*. Newark: University of Delaware Press, 1990.

Henriques, Peter R. "An Uneven Friendship: The Relationship between George Washington and George Mason." *Virginia Magazine of History and Biography* 97 (April 1989): 185–204.

Henry, William Wirt. *Patrick Henry: Life, Correspondence and Speeches*. 2 vols. New York: Charles Scribner's Sons, 1891.

Hickey, Donald R. "America's Response to the Slave Revolt in Haiti, 1791–1806." *Journal of the Early Republic* 2 (Winter 1982): 361–79.

——. *The War of 1812*. Urbana: University of Illinois Press, 1989.

Hilldrup, Robert Leroy. *The Life and Times of Edmund Pendleton*. Chapel Hill: University of North Carolina Press, 1939.

Hobson, Charles F. "John Marshall, the Mandamus Case, and the Judiciary Crisis, 1801–1803." *George Washington Law Review* 72 (December 2003): 289–308.

——. "The Negative on State Laws: James Madison, the Constitution, and the Crisis of Republican Government." *William and Mary Quarterly* 36 (April 1979): 215–35.

Hodgson, Dennis. "Benjamin Franklin on Population: From Policy to Theory." *Population and Development Review* 17 (December 1991): 639–61.

Holton, Woody. *Forced Founders: Indians, Debtors, Slaves, and the Making of the American Revolution in Virginia*. Chapel Hill: University of North Carolina Press, 1999.

——. *Unruly Americans and the Origins of the Constitution*. New York: Hill & Wang, 2007.

Horn, James, Jan Ellen Lewis, and Peter S. Onuf, eds. *The Revolution of 1800: Democracy, Race, and the New Republic*. Charlottesville: University of Virginia Press, 2002.

Horsman, Reginald. *The Causes of the War of 1812*. Philadelphia: University of Pennsylvania Press, 1962.

——. "The Dimensions of an 'Empire for Liberty': Expansion and Republicanism, 1775–1825." *Journal of the Early Republic* 9 (Spring 1989): 1–20.

——. *The War of 1812*. New York: Alfred A. Knopf, 1969.

Humphrey, Thomas J. "Conflicting Independence: Tenant Farmers and the American Revolution." *Journal of the Early Republic* 28 (Summer 2008): 159–82.

Ireland, Robert M. *The Legal Career of William Pinkney, 1760–1822*. New York: Garland, 1976.

——. "William Pinkney: A Revision and Re-Emphasis." *American Journal of Legal History* 14 (July 1970): 235–46.

Isaac, Rhys. *The Transformation of Virginia, 1740–1790*. Chapel Hill: University of North Carolina Press, 1982.

Isenberg, Nancy. *Fallen Founder: The Life of Aaron Burr*. New York: Viking, 2007.

Jackson, Donald. *Thomas Jefferson and the Stony Mountains: Exploring the West from Monticello*. Urbana: University of Illinois Press, 1981.

Jensen, Merrill. *The Articles of Confederation: An Interpretation of the Social-Constitutional History of the American Revolution, 1774–1781*. Madison, Wisc.: University of Wisconsin Press, 1940.

Johnson, F. Claiborne, Jr. "Federalists, Doubtful, and Antifederalist: A Note on the Virginia Convention of 1788." *Virginia Magazine of History and Biography* 96 (July 1988): 333–44.

Jordan, Daniel P. *Political Leadership in Jefferson's Virginia*. Charlottesville: University Press of Virginia, 1983.

Jordan, Winthrop D. *White Over Black: American Attitudes toward the Negro, 1550–1812*. Chapel Hill: University of North Carolina Press, 1968.

Kaminski, John P. *George Clinton: Yeoman Politician of the New Republic*. Madison, Wisc.: Madison House, 1993.

Kaplan, Catherine O'Donnell. *Men of Letters in the Early Republic: Cultivating Forums of Citizenship*. Chapel Hill: University of North Carolina Press, 2008.

Kaplan, Lawrence S. "Jefferson and the Constitution: The View from Paris, 1786–89." *Diplomatic History* 11 (1987): 321–35.

Kaplan, Sidney. "The 'Domestic Insurrections' of the Declaration of Independence." *Journal of Negro History* 61 (July 1976): 243–55.

Kastor, Peter J. *The Nation's Crucible: The Louisiana Purchase and the Creation of America*. New Haven, Conn.: Yale University Press, 2004.

——. " 'What Are the Advantages of the Acquisition?': Inventing Expansion in the Early American Republic." *American Quarterly* 60 (December 2008): 1003–35.

Keller, William F. *The Nation's Advocate: Henry Marie Brackenridge and Young America*. Pittsburgh: University of Pittsburgh Press, 1956.

Kerber, Linda K. *Federalists in Dissent: Imagery and Ideology in Jeffersonian America*. Ithaca, N.Y.: Cornell University Press, 1970.

Ketcham, Ralph L., ed. "An Unpublished Sketch of James Madison by James K. Paulding." *Virginia Magazine of History and Biography* 67 (1959): 432–37.

Kidd, Thomas S. " 'Is It Worse to Follow Mahomet than the Devil?' Early American Uses of Islam." *Church History* 72 (December 2003): 766–90.

Kitzen, Michael. "Money Bags or Cannon Balls: The Origins of the Tripolitan War." *Journal of the Early Republic* 16 (Winter 1996): 601–24.

Klein, Philip S., ed. "Notes and Documents: Memoirs of a Senator from Pennsylvania: Jonathan Roberts, 1771–1854." *Pennsylvania Magazine of History and Biography* 62 (July 1938): 363–409.

Klubes, Benjamin B. "The First Federal Congress and the First National Bank: A Case Study in Constitutional Interpretation." *Journal of the Early Republic* 10 (Spring 1990): 19–41.

Knudson, Jerry W. *Jefferson and the Press: Crucible of Liberty*. Columbia: University of South Carolina Press, 2006.

Koch, Adrienne. *Jefferson and Madison: The Great Collaboration*. New York: Oxford University Press, 1950.

——. *Madison's "Advice to My Country."* Princeton, N.J.: Princeton University Press, 1966.

——. *The Philosophy of Thomas Jefferson*. New York: Columbia University Press, 1943.

Koch, Adrienne, and Harry Ammon. "The Virginia and Kentucky Resolutions: An Episode in Jefferson's and Madison's Defense of Civil Liberties." *William and Mary Quarterly* 5 (April 1948): 145–76.

Kohn, Richard H. *Eagle and Sword: The Federalists and the Creation of the Military Establishment in America, 1783–1802*. New York: Free Press, 1975.

——. "The Inside History of the Newburgh Conspiracy: America and the Coup d'Etat." *William and Mary Quarterly* 27 (April 1970): 187–220.

Koontz, Louis Knott. *Robert Dinwiddie: His Career in American Colonial Government and Westward Expansion*. Glendale, Calif.: Arthur H. Clark Co., 1941.

Kornfeld, Eve. "Encountering the Other: American Intellectuals and Indians in the 1790s." *William and Mary Quarterly* 52 (April 1995): 287–314.

Kramer, Larry D. "Madison's Audience." *Harvard Law Review* 112 (January 1999): 611–79.

——. "Understanding Marbury v. Madison." *Proceedings of the American Philosophical Society* 148 (March 2004): 14–26.

Kuehl, John W. "Justice, Republican Energy, and the Search for the Middle Ground: James Madison and the Assumption of State Debts." *Virginia Magazine of History and Biography* 103 (July 1995): 321–38.

Kurtz, Stephen G. *The Presidency of John Adams: The Collapse of Federalism, 1795–1800*. Philadelphia: University of Pennsylvania Press, 1957.

Labunski, Richard. *James Madison and the Struggle for the Bill of Rights*. New York: Oxford University Press, 2006.

Lambert, Frank. *The Barbary Wars: American Independence in the Atlantic World*. New York: Hill & Wang, 2005.

Langford, Paul. *Englishness Identified: Manners and Character, 1650–1850*. Oxford: Oxford University Press, 2000.

Larson, John Lauritz. *Internal Improvement: National Public Works and the Promise of Popular Government in the Early United States*. Chapel Hill: University of North Carolina Press, 2001.

Lee, Emery G., III. "Representation, Virtue, and Political Jealousy in the Brutus-Publius Dialogue." *Journal of Politics* 59 (November 1997): 1073–95.

Lehmann, Karl. *Thomas Jefferson, American Humanist*. New York: Macmillan, 1947; rpt. Charlottesville: University Press of Virginia, 1985.

Leibiger, Stuart. *Founding Friendship: George Washington, James Madison, and the Creation of the American Republic*. Charlottesville: University Press of Virginia, 1999.

——. "James Madison and the Amendments to the Constitution, 1787–1789: 'Parchment Barriers.'" *Journal of Southern History* 59 (August 1993): 441–68.

Lemire, Elise. *"Miscegenation": Making Race in America*. Philadelphia: University of Pennsylvania Press, 2002.

Lerner, Ralph. *The Thinking Revolutionary: Principle and Practice in the New Republic*. Ithaca, N.Y.: Cornell University Press, 1979.

Levy, Andrew. *The First Emancipator: The Forgotten Story of Robert Carter, the Founder Who Freed His Slaves*. New York: Random House, 2006.

Lewis, Anthony Marc. "Jefferson and Virginia's Pioneers, 1774–1781." *Mississippi Valley Historical Review* 34 (March 1948): 551–88.

Lewis, Jan. *The Pursuit of Happiness: Family and Values in Jefferson's Virginia.* Cambridge, U.K.: Cambridge University Press, 1983.

Lewis, Jan Ellen, and Peter S. Onuf, eds. *Sally Hemings and Thomas Jefferson: History, Memory, and Civic Culture.* Charlottesville: University of Virginia Press, 1999.

Lillich, Richard B. "The Chase Impeachment." *American Journal of Legal History* 4 (January 1960): 49–72.

List, Karen. "The Role of William Cobbett in Philadelphia Party Press, 1794–1799." *Journalism Monographs* 82 (1993): 1–23.

Livermore, Shaw. *Early American Land Companies: Their Influence on Corporate Development.* New York: Commonwealth Fund, 1939.

Lokke, Carl Ludwig. "Jefferson and the Leclerc Expedition." *American Historical Review* 33 (January 1928): 322–28.

Longmore, Paul K. *The Invention of George Washington.* Berkeley: University of California Press, 1988.

Macleod, Julia H. "Jefferson and the Navy: A Defense." *Huntington Library Quarterly* 8 (February 1945): 153–84.

Magrath, C. Peter. *Yazoo: The Case of Fletcher v. Peck.* New York: W. W. Norton, 1966.

Maier, Pauline. *American Scripture: Making the Declaration of Independence.* New York: Alfred A. Knopf, 1997.

Malone, Dumas. *Thomas Jefferson as Political Leader.* Berkeley: University of California Press, 1963.

Mann, Barbara Alice. *George Washington's War on Native America.* Lincoln: University of Nebraska Press, 2008.

Marston, Jerrilyn Greene. *King and Congress: The Transfer of Political Legitimacy, 1774–1776.* Princeton, N.J.: Princeton University Press, 1987.

Mason, Matthew. *Slavery in the Early Republic.* Chapel Hill: University of North Carolina Press, 2006.

Matthews, Marty. *Forgotten Founder: The Life and Times of Charles Pinckney.* Columbia: University of South Carolina Press, 2004.

Matthews, Richard K. *If Men Were Angels: James Madison and the Heartless Empire of Reason.* Lawrence: University Press of Kansas, 1995.

——. *The Radical Politics of Thomas Jefferson.* Lawrence: University Press of Kansas, 1986.

Matthewson, Tim. "Jefferson and Haiti." *Journal of Southern History* 61 (May 1995): 209–48.

——. "Jefferson and the Nonrecognition of Haiti." *Proceedings of the American Philosophical Society* 140 (March 1996): 22–48.

——. *A Proslavery Foreign Policy: Haitian-American Relations during the Early Republic.* Westport, Conn.: Praeger, 2003.

Mayer, David N. *The Constitutional Thought of Thomas Jefferson.* Charlottesville: University Press of Virginia, 1994.

Mayer, Henry. *A Son of Thunder: Patrick Henry and the American Republic.* New York: Franklin Watts, 1986; rpt. Charlottesville: University Press of Virginia, 1991.

Mays, David John. *Edmund Pendleton, 1721–1803: A Biography.* 2 vols. 1952; rpt. Richmond: Virginia State Library, 1984.

McCants, David A. *Patrick Henry, Orator.* New York: Greenwood Press, 1990.

McConnell, Michael N. *A Country Between: The Upper Ohio Valley and Its Peoples, 1724–1774.* Lincoln: University of Nebraska Press, 1992.

McCormick, Richard P. "The 'Ordinance' of 1784?" *William and Mary Quarterly* 50 (January 1993): 112–22.

McCoy, Drew R. *The Elusive Republic: Political Economy in Jeffersonian America.* New York: W. W. Norton, 1980.

———. "Jefferson and Madison on Malthus: Population Growth in Jeffersonian Political Economy." *Virginia Magazine of History and Biography* 88 (July 1980): 259–76.

———. *The Last of the Fathers: James Madison and the Republican Legacy.* New York: Cambridge University Press, 1989.

McDonald, Forrest. *The Presidency of George Washington.* Lawrence: University Press of Kansas, 1974.

McDonald, Robert M. S. "Thomas Jefferson's Changing Reputation as Author of the Declaration of Independence." *Journal of the Early Republic* 19 (Summer 1999): 169–95.

McDonnell, Michael. *The Politics of War: Race, Class, and Conflict in Revolutionary Virginia.* Chapel Hill: University of North Carolina Press, 2007.

McGaughy, J. Kent. *Richard Henry Lee of Virginia: A Portrait of an American Revolutionary.* Lanham, Md.: Rowman & Littlefield, 2004.

McLaughlin, Jack. *Jefferson and Monticello: The Biography of a Builder.* New York: Henry Holt, 1988.

Meade, Robert Douthat. *Patrick Henry: Patriot in the Making.* Philadelphia: J. B. Lippincott, 1957.

———. *Patrick Henry: Practical Revolutionary.* Philadelphia: J. B. Lippincott, 1969.

Miller, Charles A. *Jefferson and Nature: An Interpretation.* Baltimore: Johns Hopkins University Press, 1988.

Miller, John Chester. *The Wolf by the Ears: Thomas Jefferson and Slavery.* New York: Free Press, 1977; rpt. Charlottesville: University Press of Virginia, 1991.

Miller, Robert J. *Native America, Discovered and Conquered: Thomas Jefferson, Lewis & Clark, and Manifest Destiny.* Westport, Conn.: Praeger, 2006.

Mitchell, Broadus. *Alexander Hamilton: The National Adventure, 1788–1804.* New York: Macmillan, 1962.

Morgan, Edmund. "Safety in Numbers: Madison, Hume, and the Tenth Federalist." *Huntington Library Quarterly* (1986): 95–112.

Morrison, Jeffrey H. *John Witherspoon and the Founding of the American Republic.* Notre Dame, Ind.: Notre Dame University Press, 2005.

Nash, Gary B. *Forging Freedom: The Formation of Philadelphia's Black Community, 1720–1840.* Cambridge, Mass.: Harvard University Press, 1988.

Newman, Simon P. *Parades and the Politics of the Streets.* Philadelphia: University of Pennsylvania Press, 1997.

Nichols, Frederick Doveton, and Ralph E. Griswold. *Thomas Jefferson: Landscape Architect.* Charlottesville: University Press of Virginia, 1978.

Noll, Mark A. *Princeton and the Republic 1768–1822: The Search for the Christian Republic in the Era of Samuel Stanhope Smith.* Princeton, N.J.: Princeton University Press, 1990.

Norton, Mary Beth. "Eighteenth-Century American Women in Peace and War: The Case of Loyalists." *William and Mary Quarterly* 33 (July 1976): 386–409.

O'Connor, John E. *William Paterson: Lawyer and Statesman, 1745–1806.* New Brunswick, N.J.: Rutgers University Press, 1979.

O'Fallon, James M. "Marbury." *Stanford Law Review* 44 (January 1992): 219–60.

Ohline, Howard A. "Republicanism and Slavery: Origins of the Three-Fifths Clause in the United States Constitution." *William and Mary Quarterly* 28 (October 1971): 563–84.

Olson, Alison Gilbert. *Making the Empire Work: London and American Interest Groups, 1690–1790.* Cambridge, Mass.: Harvard University Press, 1992.

Onuf, Peter S., ed. *Jeffersonian Legacies.* Charlottesville: University Press of Virginia, 1993.

———. *Jefferson's Empire: The Language of American Nationhood.* Charlottesville: University Press of Virginia, 2000.

———. *The Mind of Thomas Jefferson.* Charlottesville: University of Virginia Press, 2007.

———. *Origins of the Federal Republic: Jurisdictional Controversies in the United States, 1775–1787.* Philadelphia: University of Pennsylvania Press, 1983.

———. *Statehood and Union: A History of the Northwest Ordinance.* Bloomington: Indiana University Press, 1987.

Ott, Thomas O. *The Haitian Revolution, 1789–1804.* Knoxville: University of Tennessee Press, 1973.

Outram, Quentin. "The Demographic Impact of Early Modern Warfare." *Social Science History* 26 (Summer 2002): 245–72.

Owsley, Frank Lawrence, Jr., and Gene A. Smith. *Filibusters and Expansionists: Jeffersonian Manifest Destiny, 1800–1821.* Tuscaloosa: University of Alabama Press, 1997.

Padgett, James A. "The West Florida Revolution of 1810, As Told in the Letters of John Rhea, Fulwar Skipwith, Reuben Kemper, and Others." *Louisiana Historical Quarterly* 21 (January 1938): 1–129.

Pancake, John S. "The 'Invisibles': A Chapter in the Opposition to the President." *Journal of Southern History* 21 (February 1955): 17–37.

Papenfuse, Eric Robert. "Unleashing the 'Wildness': The Mobilization of Grassroots Antifederalism in Maryland." *Journal of the Early Republic* 16 (Spring 1996): 73–106.

Parkinson, Robert G. "From Indian Killer to Worthy Citizen: The Revolutionary Transformation of Michael Cresap." *William and Mary Quarterly* 63 (January 2006): 97–122.

Parsons, Lynn Hudson. *John Quincy Adams.* Madison, Wisc.: Madison House, 1998.

Parton, James. "Thomas Jefferson a Virginia Lawyer." *Atlantic Monthly* 29 (March 1872): 312–31.

Pasley, Jeffrey. " 'A Journeyman, Either in Law or Politics': John Beckley and the Social Origins of Political Campaigning." *Journal of the Early Republic* 16 (Winter 1996): 531–69.

– —. "The Two National Gazettes: Newspapers and the Embodiment of American Political Parties." *Early American Literature* 35 (2000): 51–86.

– —. *"The Tyranny of Printers": Newspaper Politics in the Early American Republic.* Charlottesville: University Press of Virginia, 2001.

Pedder, Laura Green, ed. *The Letters of Joseph Dennie.* Orono, Me.: University Press, 1936.

Peden, William. "A Book Peddler Invades Monticello." *William and Mary Quarterly* 6 (October 1949): 631–36.

Perkins, Bradford. *Prologue to War: England and the United States, 1805–1812.* Berkeley: University of California Press, 1961.

Peterson, Merrill D. *The Great Triumvirate: Webster, Clay, and Calhoun.* New York: Oxford University Press, 1987.

———. *The Jefferson Image in the American Mind.* New York: Oxford University Press, 1960.

Plumer, William, Jr. *Life of William Plumer.* Boston: Phillips, Sampson & Co., 1857.

Popkin, Jeremy D. *Facing Racial Revolution: Eyewitness Accounts of Haitian Insurrection.* Chicago: University of Chicago Press, 2007.

Prince, Carl E. *New Jersey's Jeffersonian Republicans: The Genesis of an Early Party Machine, 1789–1817.* Chapel Hill: University of North Carolina Press, 1967.

———. "The Passing of the Aristocracy: Jefferson's Removals of the Federalists, 1801–1805." *Journal of American History* 57 (December 1970): 563–75.

Prucha, Francis Paul. *American Indian Policy in the Formative Years.* Cambridge, Mass.: Harvard University Press, 1962.

Rakove, Jack N. "The Great Compromise: Ideas, Interests, and the Politics of Constitution Making." *William and Mary Quarterly* 44 (July 1987): 424–57.

———. *James Madison and the Creation of the American Republic.* New York: HarperCollins, 1990.

———. *Original Meanings: Politics and Ideas in the Making of the Constitution.* New York: Alfred A. Knopf, 1996.

Randolph, Sarah N. *The Domestic Life of Thomas Jefferson*. New York: Harper, 1871; rpt. Charlottesville: University Press of Virginia, 1978.

Reardon, John J. *Edmund Randolph: A Biography*. New York: Macmillan, 1974.

Richards, Leonard L. *Shays's Rebellion: The American Revolution's Final Battle*. Philadelphia: University of Pennsylvania Press, 2002.

Richardson, John. "Atrocity in Mid Eighteenth-Century War Literature." *Eighteenth-Century Life* 33 (Spring 2009): 92–114.

Risjord, Norman K. "1812: Conservatives, War Hawks and the Nation's Honor." *William and Mary Quarterly* 18 (April 1961): 196–210.

———. *The Old Republicans: Southern Conservatism in the Age of Jefferson*. New York: Columbia University Press, 1965.

Robertson, David Brian. *The Constitution and America's Destiny*. Cambridge, U.K.: Cambridge University Press, 2005.

Ronda, James P. "Dreams and Discoveries: Exploring the American West, 1760–1815." *William and Mary Quarterly* 46 (January 1989): 145–62.

———. "'A Knowledge of Different Parts': The Shaping of the Lewis and Clark Expedition." *Montana: The Magazine of Western History* 41 (Autumn 1991): 4–19.

Rothman, Adam. *Slave Country: American Expansion and the Origins of the Deep South*. Cambridge, Mass.: Harvard University Press, 2005.

Rouse, Parke, Jr. "The British Invasion of Hampton in 1813: The Reminiscences of James Jarvis." *Virginia Magazine of History and Biography* 76 (July 1968): 318–36.

Royster, Charles. *Light-Horse Harry Lee and the Legacy of the American Revolution*. New York: Alfred A. Knopf, 1981; rpt. Baton Rouge: Louisiana State University Press, 1994.

———. *A Revolutionary People at War: The Continental Army and American Character, 1775–1783*. Chapel Hill: University of North Carolina Press, 1979.

Rozbicki, Michal J. *The Complete Colonial Gentleman: Cultural Legitimacy in Plantation America*. Charlottesville: University Press of Virginia, 1998.

Rutland, Robert A. *George Mason: Reluctant Statesman*. Baton Rouge: Louisiana State University Press, 1961.

———. *James Madison: The Founding Father*. New York: Macmillan, 1987.

———. *Madison's Alternatives: The Jeffersonian Republicans and the Coming of the War of 1812*. Philadelphia: J. B. Lippincott, 1975.

———. *The Presidency of James Madison*. Lawrence: University Press of Kansas, 1990.

Scanlon, James E. "A Sudden Conceit: Jefferson and the Louisiana Government Bill of 1804." *Louisiana History* 9 (Spring 1968): 139–62.

Schaedler, Louis C. "James Madison: Literary Craftsman." *William and Mary Quarterly* 3 (October 1946): 515–33.

Schoen, Brian. "Calculating the Price of Union: Republican Economic Nationalism and the Origins of Southern Sectionalism, 1790–1828." *Journal of the Early Republic* 23 (Summer 2003): 173–206.

Selby, John E. *The Revolution in Virginia, 1775–1783*. Williamsburg: Colonial Williamsburg Foundation, 1988; rpt. Charlottesville: University of Virginia Press, 2007.

Shackelford, George Green. *Jefferson's Adoptive Son: The Life of William Short, 1759–1848*. Lexington: University Press of Kentucky, 1993.

——. *Thomas Jefferson's Travels in Europe, 1784–1789*. Baltimore: Johns Hopkins University Press, 1995.

Shankman, Andrew. *Crucible of American Democracy: The Struggle to Fuse Egalitarianism and Capitalism in Jeffersonian Pennsylvania*. Lawrence: University Press of Kansas, 2004.

Sharp, James Roger. *American Politics in the Early Republic: The New Nation in Crisis*. New Haven, Conn.: Yale University Press, 1995.

——. "Unraveling the Mystery of Jefferson's Letter of April 27, 1795." *Journal of the Early Republic* 6 (Winter 1986): 411–18.

Shaw, Peter. *The Character of John Adams*. Chapel Hill: University of North Carolina Press, 1976.

Sheehan, Bernard. *Seeds of Extinction: Jeffersonian Philanthropy and the American Indian*. Chapel Hill: University of North Carolina Press, 1973.

Sheehan, Colleen A. "Madison and the French Enlightenment: The Authority of Public Opinion." *William and Mary Quarterly* 59 (October 2002): 925–56.

Sheldon, Garrett Ward, and Daniel L. Dreisbach, eds. *Religion and Political Culture in Jefferson's Virginia*. Lanham, Md.: Rowman & Littlefield, 2000.

Sher, Richard B. *The Enlightenment and the Book*. Chicago: University of Chicago Press, 2006.

Sheridan, Eugene R. "Thomas Jefferson and the Giles Resolutions." *William and Mary Quarterly* 49 (October 1992): 589–608.

Sherwood, H. N. "Early Negro Deportation Projects." *Mississippi Valley Historical Review* 2 (March 1916): 484–508.

Shoemaker, Nancy. *A Strange Likeness: Becoming Red and White in Eighteenth-Century North America*. New York: Oxford University Press, 2004.

Silver, Peter. *Our Savage Neighbors: How Indian War Transformed Early America*. New York: W. W. Norton, 2008.

Skeen, C. Edward. *1816: America Rising*. Lexington: University Press of Kentucky, 2003.

——. *John Armstrong, Jr., 1758–1843: A Biography*. Syracuse, N.Y.: Syracuse University Press, 1981.

Slaughter, Thomas P. *The Whiskey Rebellion: Frontier Epilogue to the American Revolution*. New York: Oxford University Press, 1986.

Sloan, Herbert E. *Principle and Interest: Thomas Jefferson and the Problem of Debt*. New York: Oxford University Press, 1995.

Smith, James Morton. *Freedom's Fetters: The Alien and Sedition Acts and American Civil Liberties.* Ithaca, N.Y.: Cornell University Press, 1956.

———. "The Grass Roots Origins of the Kentucky Resolutions." *William and Mary Quarterly* 27 (April 1970): 221–45.

Smith, Jean Edward. *John Marshall: Definer of a Nation.* New York: Henry Holt, 1996.

Smith, Margaret Bayard. *The First Forty Years of Washington Society.* Edited by Gaillard Hunt. New York: Charles Scribner's Sons, 1906.

Sofka, James R. "The Jeffersonian Idea of National Security: Commerce, the Atlantic Balance of Power, and the Barbary War, 1786–1805." *Diplomatic History* 21 (Fall 1997): 519–44.

Stagg, J.C.A. "James Madison and the 'Malcontents': The Political Origins of the War of 1812." *William and Mary Quarterly* 33 (October 1976): 557–85.

———. *Mr. Madison's War.* Princeton, N.J.: Princeton University Press, 1983.

Stanton, Lucia. *Free Some Day: The African-American Families of Monticello.* Charlottesville, Va.: Thomas Jefferson Foundation, 2000.

Starr, G. A. "Escape from Barbary: A Seventeenth-Century Genre." *Huntington Library Quarterly* 21 (November 1965): 35–52.

Steele, Brian. "Thomas Jefferson's Gender Frontier." *Journal of American History* 95 (June 2008): 17–42.

Swanson, Donald F. " 'Bank-Notes will be but Oak Leaves': Thomas Jefferson on Paper Money." *Virginia Magazine of History and Biography* 101 (January 1993): 37–52.

Sweet, John Wood. *Bodies Politic: Negotiating Race in the American North, 1730–1830.* Baltimore: Johns Hopkins University Press, 2003.

Tachau, Mary K. Bonsteel. "George Washington and the Reputation of Edmund Randolph." *Journal of American History* 73 (June 1986): 15–34.

Tagg, James. *Benjamin Franklin Bache and the Philadelphia Aurora.* Philadelphia: University of Pennsylvania Press, 1991.

Tate, Adam L. *Conservatism and Southern Intellectuals, 1789–1861.* Columbia: University of Missouri Press, 2005.

Tucker, Robert W., and David C. Hendrickson. *Empire of Liberty: The Statecraft of Thomas Jefferson.* New York: Oxford University Press, 1990.

Tyler-McGraw, Marie. *An African Republic: Black and White Virginians in the Making of Liberia.* Chapel Hill: University of North Carolina Press, 2007.

van Alstyne, William W., and John Marshall. "A Critical Guide to Marbury v. Madison." *Duke Law Journal* (February 1969): 1–47.

Van Buren, Martin. *Inquiry into the Origin and Course of Political Parties in the United States.* New York: Hurd & Houghton, 1867.

VanBurkleo, Sandra Frances. " 'Honour, Justice, and Interest': John Jay's Republican

Politics and Statesmanship on the Federal Bench." *Journal of the Early Republic* 4 (Autumn 1984): 239–74.

Van Cleve, George. "Somerset's Case and Its Antecedents in Imperial Perspective." *Law and History Review* 24 (Fall 2006): 601–46.

Van Doren, Carl. *Benjamin Franklin.* New York: Viking Press, 1938.

Vidal, Gore. *Inventing a Nation: Washington, Adams, Jefferson.* New Haven, Conn.: Yale University Press, 2003.

Vile, John R., William D. Pederson, and Frank J. Williams, eds. *James Madison: Philosopher, Founder, and Statesman.* Athens: Ohio University Press, 2008.

Waldstreicher, David. *In the Midst of Perpetual Fetes: The Making of American Nationalism, 1776–1820.* Chapel Hill: University of North Carolina Press, 1997.

———. *Runaway America: Benjamin Franklin, Slavery, and the American Revolution.* New York: Hill & Wang, 2004.

———. *Slavery's Constitution: From Revolution to Ratification.* New York: Hill & Wang, 2009.

Walker, Clarence E. *Mongrel Nation: The America Begotten by Thomas Jefferson and Sally Hemings.* Charlottesville: University of Virginia Press, 2009.

Wallace, Anthony F. C. *Jefferson and the Indians: The Tragic Fate of the First Americans.* Cambridge, Mass.: Harvard University Press, 1999.

Wallenstein, Peter. "Flawed Keepers of the Flame: The Interpreters of George Mason." *Virginia Magazine of History and Biography* 102 (April 1994): 229–60.

Walling, Karl-Friedrich. *Republican Empire: Alexander Hamilton on War and Free Government.* Lawrence: University Press of Kansas, 1999.

Walters, Raymond, Jr. *Albert Gallatin: Jeffersonian Financier and Diplomat.* New York: Macmillan, 1957.

———. *Alexander James Dallas.* Philadelphia: University of Pennsylvania Press, 1943.

Watts, Steven. *The Republic Reborn: War and the Making of Liberal America, 1790–1820.* Baltimore: Johns Hopkins University Press, 1987.

Wehje, Myron F. "Opposition in Virginia to the War of 1812." *Virginia Magazine of History and Biography* 78 (January 1970): 65–86.

Wharton, Anne Hollingsworth. *Salons Colonial and Republican.* Philadelphia: J. B. Lippincott, 1900.

Williams, Patrick G., S. Charles Bolton, and Jeannie M. Whayne. *A Whole Country in Commotion: The Louisiana Purchase and the American Southwest.* Fayetteville: University of Arkansas Press, 2005.

Wills, Garry. *"Negro President": Jefferson and the Slave Power.* Boston: Houghton Mifflin, 2003.

Wilson, Douglas L. "The Evolution of Jefferson's 'Notes on the State of Virginia.'" *Virginia Magazine of History and Biography* 112 (2004): 98–133.

———, ed. *Jefferson's Literary Commonplace Book*. Princeton, N.J.: Princeton University Press, 1989.

Wolf, Eva Sheppard. *Race and Liberty in the New Nation: Emancipation in Virginia from the Revolution to Nat Turner's Rebellion*. Baton Rouge: Louisiana State University Press, 2006.

Wolford, Thorp Lanier. "Democratic-Republican Reaction in Massachusetts to the Embargo of 1807." *The New England Quarterly* 15 (March 1942): 35–61.

Wood, Gordon S. *The Creation of the American Republic, 1776–1787*. Chapel Hill: University of North Carolina, 1969.

———. *The Radicalism of the American Revolution*. New York: Alfred A. Knopf, 1992.

Wyatt, Edward A., IV. "John Thomson, Author of the 'Letters of Curtius,' and a Petersburg Contemporary of George Keith Taylor." *William and Mary Quarterly Historical Magazine* 16 (January 1936): 19–25.

Zagarri, Rosemarie. *The Politics of Size: Representation in the United States, 1776–1850*. Ithaca, N.Y.: Cornell University Press, 1987.

Index

About the Authors

ANDREW BURSTEIN and NANCY ISENBERG are Charles P. Manship Professor of History and professor of history, respectively, at Louisiana State University. Burstein is the author of six other books on early America, including *The Passions of Andrew Jackson* and *Jefferson's Secrets*. Isenberg is the author of *Fallen Founder: The Life of Aaron Burr* and *Sex and Citizenship in Antebellum America*.

About the Type

The text of this book was set in Legacy, a typeface family designed by Ronald Arnholm and issued in digital form by ITC in 1992. Both its serifed and unserifed versions are based on an original type created by the French punchcutter Nicholas Jenson in the late fifteenth century. While Legacy tends to differ from Jenson's original in its proportions, it maintains much of the latter's characteristic modulations in stroke.